FUNDAMENTALS OF
FINANCIAL
PLANNING

Your unique textbook registration number is below. Please register your new textbook at www.money-education.com, for access to the Student Practice Portal, updated errata, Money Tips™, and other valuable resources.

BYAJ0711751Rx

FUNDAMENTALS OF
FINANCIAL
PLANNING

Michael A. Dalton
James F. Dalton
Joseph M. Gillice
Thomas P. Langdon

7th Edition

MONEY EDUCATION
3116 5TH STREET
METAIRIE, LA 70002
888-295-6023

This publication is designed to provide accurate and authoritative information in regard to the subject matter covered. It is sold with the understanding that the publisher, authors, and contributors are not engaged in rendering legal, accounting, tax, financial planning, or other professional services. If legal advice, tax advice, or other professional assistance is required, the services of a competent professional should be sought.

CFP®, CERTIFIED FINANCIAL PLANNER™, and CFP (with flame logo)® are certification marks owned by Certified Financial Planner Board of Standards Inc. These marks are awarded to individuals who successfully complete CFP Board's initial and ongoing certification requirements.

Printed in the U.S.A.

ISBN-13: 978-1-946711-39-7

ABOUT THE AUTHORS

James F. Dalton, MBA, MS, CPA/PFS, CFA®, CFP®

- CEO, Money Education
- Adjunct professor at George Mason University (2014 - 2017)
- Adjunct professor at Georgetown University (2002 - 2014)
- Former Executive Vice President, Assessment Technologies Institute LLC
- Former Senior Vice President, Kaplan Professional
- Former President, Dalton Publications LLC
- Former Senior Manager of KPMG, LLP, concentrating in personal financial planning, investment planning, and litigation consulting
- MBA from Loyola University New Orleans
- Master of Accounting in Taxation from the University of New Orleans
- BS in accounting from Florida State University in Tallahassee, Florida
- Member of the CFP Board of Standards July 1996, Comprehensive CFP® Exam Pass Score Committee
- Member of the AICPA and the Louisiana Society of CPAs
- Member of the Financial Planning Association
- Member of the *Journal of Financial Planning* Editorial Review Board
- Author of *Money Education's Quick Sheets*
- Co-author of *Cases in Financial Planning: Analysis and Presentation* (1st - 4th Editions)
- Co-author of *Retirement Planning and Employee Benefits* (1st - 17th Editions)
- Co-Author of *Fundamentals of Financial Planning* (1st - 7th Editions)
- Contributing Author of *Insurance Planning* (1st - 7th Editions)
- Contributing Author of *Estate Planning* (1st - 12th Editions)
- Author of Kaplan Schweser's Personal Financial Planning Understanding Your Financial Calculator
- Author of Kaplan Schweser's Understanding Your Financial Calculator for the CFA® Exam
- Co-author of BISYS CFA® Study Notes Volumes I and II
- Co-author of Kaplan Schweser's Personal Financial Planning Cases and Applications
- Co-author of the Kaplan Schweser Review for the CFP® Certification Examination, Volumes I–VIII and Kaplan Schweser's Financial Planning Flashcards

Michael A. Dalton, Ph.D., JD, CPA, CLU, ChFC, CFP®

- Former Chair of the Board of Dalton Publications, L.L.C.
- Associate professor of Accounting and Taxation at Loyola University in New Orleans, Louisiana (retired)
- Adjunct professor at George Mason University (2014 - 2017)
- Adjunct professor at Georgetown University (2002 - 2014)
- Former Senior Vice President, Education at BISYS Group
- Ph.D. in Accounting from Georgia State University
- J.D. from Louisiana State University in Baton Rouge, Louisiana
- MBA and BBA in Management and Accounting from Georgia State University
- Former board member of the CFP Board's Board of Examiners, Board of Standards, and Board of Governors
- Former member (and chair) of the CFP Board's Board of Examiners
- Member of the Financial Planning Association
- Member of the *Journal of Financial Planning* Editorial Advisory Board
- Member of the *Journal of Financial Planning* Editorial Review Board
- Member of the LSU Law School Board of Trustees (2000 - 2006)
- Author of *Dalton Review for the CFP® Certification Examination: Volume I – Outlines and Study Guides, Volume II – Problems and Solutions, Volume III - Case Exam Book, Mock Exams A-1 and A-2* (1st - 8th Editions)
- Author of *Retirement Planning and Employee Benefits* (1st - 17th Editions)
- Author of *Estate Planning* (1st - 12th Editions)
- Author of *Fundamentals of Financial Planning* (1st - 7th Editions)
- Author of *Insurance Planning* (1st - 7th Editions)
- Co-author of *Income Tax Planning* (1st - 14th Editions)
- Co-author of *Cases in Financial Planning: Analysis and Presentation* (1st - 4th Editions)
- Co-author of *Dalton CFA® Study Notes Volumes I and II* (1st - 2nd Editions)
- Co-author of *Dalton's Personal Financial Planning Series – Personal Financial Planning Theory and Practice* (1st - 3rd Editions)
- Co-author of *Dalton's Personal Financial Planning Series – Personal Financial Planning Cases and Applications* (1st - 4th Editions)
- Co-author of *Cost Accounting: Traditions and Innovations* published by West Publishing Company
- Co-author of the *ABCs of Managing Your Money* published by National Endowment for Financial Education (NEFE)

ABOUT THE CONTRIBUTING AUTHORS

Sherri Donaldson, CFP®, ChFC®, MSFS, CASL®, CAP®, EA

- Editing Princess for Money Education
- Former Author/Editor/Lead instructor, Keir Educational Resources
- Former Assistant Vice President, Senior Training Specialist, M&T Securities
- Former Associate Financial Consultant, M&T Securities
- Former Financial Sales Specialist, Nationwide Financial
- Former Financial Services Representative, Nationwide Retirement Solutions
- MSFS from The American College Bryn Mawr, PA
- BS in business, concentration in financial services, Pennsylvania State University
- Member of the Financial Planning Association
- Co-Author/Editor of Keir *General Financial Planning Principles* textbook
- Co-Author/Editor of Keir *Risk Management and Insurance Planning* textbook
- Co-Author/Editor of Keir *Introduction to Financial Planning* textbook
- Co-Author/Editor of Keir *Retirement Savings and Income Planning* textbook
- Co-Author/Editor of Keir *Tax Planning* textbook
- Co-Author/Editor of Keir *Estate Planning* textbook
- Co-Author/Editor Keir *Investments Planning* textbook
- Editor Keir *Financial Plan Development* and *Practical Applications for Your Financial Calculator* textbooks
- Co-Author/Editor Keir CFP® exam review books (*Core Knowledge Book 1* and *2*, *Essential Keys* book, *Case Studies* book), practice exams, flashcards, MP3 scripts, Key Concept Infograhics, and Quick Concept videos

Randal R. Cangelosi, JD, MBA

- Practicing litigator throughout Louisiana, in business/commercial law and litigation, products liability litigation, wills and trust litigation, environmental law and litigation, medical malpractice defense, and insurance law and litigation
- Has successfully defended numerous corporations, businesses, and doctors in jury and judge trials
- Juris Doctorate from Loyola University New Orleans
- Masters of Business Administration from Loyola University New Orleans
- BS in Finance from Louisiana State University
- Member of the American & Federal Bar Associations
- Member of the Bar of the State of Louisiana
- Member of the New Orleans and Baton Rouge Bar Associations
- Board Member of La Lupus Foundation
- Board Member of the Baton Rouge Chamber of Commerce
- Former Board Member of the Baton Rouge Area Chapter of the American Red Cross
- Admitted to practice before U.S. District Courts, Western, Eastern & Middle Districts of Louisiana
- Admitted to practice before the Federal 5th Circuit Court of Appeals, the USDC, Southern District of Iowa (Pro Hac Vice), Circuit Court of Wayne County, Mississippi (Pro Hac Vice), Circuit Court of Barbour County, Alabama (Pro Hac Vice), Court of Common Pleas, Darlington County, South Carolina (Pro Hac Vice), Los Angeles County Superior Court, California (Pro Hac Vice), Superior Court of New Jersey: Morris County (Pro Hac Vice), and 17th Judicial Court, Broward County, Florida (Pro Hac Vice)
- Former Chairman of New Orleans Bar Association, Community Service Committee
- Co-author of *Personal Financial Planning: Theory and Practice* (1st - 3rd Editions)
- Co-author of *Professional Ethics for Financial Planners*

ABOUT THE REVIEWERS & CONTRIBUTORS

We owe a special thanks to several key professionals for their significant contribution of time and effort with this text. These reviewers provided meticulous editing, detailed calculation reviews, helpful suggestions for additional content, and other valuable comments, all of which have improved this edition.

Dr. James Coleman has over 15 years teaching experience, including undergraduate, graduate, and Executive MBA programs at Troy University, Mercer University, and Dalton State College. In addition, as Vice President of Market Results, a financial planning training and consulting firm, he has helped hundreds of candidates pass the Certified Financial Planner™ exam over the last decade. Prior to his academic career, Jim spent over a decade in public accounting and corporate management, concluding with the position of Managing Director of Public Relations at Federal Express, where he was responsible for the company's global public and investor relations activities. His degrees include a MS and Ph.D. from University of Alabama as well as BBA in accountancy from University of Mississippi.

Donna Dalton made a significant contribution to this textbook by her thoughtful and meticulous editing throughout the book. She provided many valuable improvements to both the textbook and instructor materials. We are extremely grateful for her contributions. This book would not have been possible without her extraordinary dedication, skill, and knowledge.

Katheleen F. Oakley is the Academic Program Director for classroom and web-based CFP Certification Education programs in the Susanne M. Glasscock, School of Continuing Studies at Rice University. She is co-author of Money Education's Cases in Financial Planning, Analysis and Presentation textbook and instructor manual. Kathy is also former vice president and chief financial planning officer with Kanaly Trust Company (Houston, Texas), the former director of financial planning for the Houston office of Lincoln Financial Advisors, and a former board member of the Pearland Economic Development Corporation. She is a member of the Financial Planning Association. Kathy received her BS in Finance and an MBA from the University of New Orleans.

Randy Martinez is a personal financial planner specializing in personal financial planning, estate, and individual income tax planning. He teaches retirement planning, estate planning, and income tax planning through various CFP® Board-Registered Programs as well as comprehensive reviews for the CFP® certification.

Robin Meyer is a valuable member of our Money Education team. She worked diligently throughout this project by performing numerous reviews and revisions. Robin provided many valuable improvements to both the textbook and instructor materials and this book would not have been possible without her extraordinary dedication, skill, and knowledge. Robin is the joy in our office as she always works tirelessly with a great work ethic and an enormous sense of humor. We are always grateful for her contributions to our products as well as our office happiness.

Dr. Moshe Shmuklarsky has a keen personal interest in the conceptual underpinning and practical knowledge related to business and personal finance as reflected by his Master of Business Administration from the John Hopkins School of Professional Studies and a Certificate in Personal Financial Planning from the Georgetown University. Dr. Shmuklarsky has more than 25 years experience in research and development of drugs and vaccines. Through the application of the Balanced Score Card, Dr. Shmuklarsky has transformed the Department of Clinical Trials at the Walter Reed Army Institute of Research in Washington DC to a center of excellence in clinical research.

Kristi Tafalla is an attorney and personal financial planner specializing in income tax and estate planning. She teaches estate planning, income tax planning and comprehensive case courses through various CFP® Board-Registered Programs as well as comprehensive reviews for the CFP® certification. She is a contributor to Money Education's *Estate Planning* and *Retirement Planning and Employee Benefits*.

Steve Wetzel is the President and founder of a financial planning firm in Pennsylvania. He is both the program director and adjunct professor for the financial planning program at New York University. Mr. Wetzel received his BA in Economics from State University of New York – Stony Brook. He also received his MBA in Finance and International Business from New York University along with his Advanced Professional Certificate in Accounting. Mr. Wetzel is also a CFP® certificant.

Acknowledgments & Special Thanks

We are most appreciative for the tremendous support and encouragement we have received throughout this project. We are extremely grateful to the instructors and program directors of CFP Board-Registered programs who provided valuable comments during the development stages of this text. We are fortunate to have dedicated, careful readers at several institutions who were willing to share their needs, expectations, and time with us.

We have received so much help from so many people, it is possible that we have inadvertently overlooked thanking someone. If so, it is our shortcoming, and we apologize in advance. Please let us know if you are that someone, and we will make it right in our next printing.

PREFACE

Fundamentals of Financial Planning is written for graduate and upperdivision undergraduate level students interested in acquiring an understanding of financial planning from a professional financial planning viewpoint. The text is intended to be used in a Fundamentals course as part of an overall curriculum in financial planning. The text is also intended to serve as a reference for practicing professional financial planners.

This text is designed to meet the educational requirements for a Fundamentals Course in a CFP® Board-Registered Program. Therefore, one of our goals is to assure CFP® Board-Registered Program Directors, instructors, students, and financial planners that we have addressed every relevant topic covered by the CFP® Board Exam Topic List and the most recent model curriculum syllabus for this course. The book will be updated, as needed, to keep current with any changes in the law, exam topic list, or model curriculum.

Special Features

A variety of tools and presentation methods are used throughout this text to assist the reader in the learning process. Some of the features in this text that are designed to enhance your understanding and learning process include:

- **Learning Objectives** – At the beginning of each chapter is a list of learning objectives to help you focus your studying of the material. These learning objectives will provide a preview of the important topics covered in the chapter.

- **Key Concepts** – At the beginning of each subsection are key concepts, or study objectives, each stated as a question. To be successful in this course, you should be able to answer these questions. So as you read, guide your learning by looking for the answers. When you find the answers, highlight or underline them. It is important that you actually highlight/underline and not just make a mental note, as the action of stopping and writing reinforces your learning. Watch for this symbol:

⠿ *Key Concepts*

- **Quick Quizzes** – Following each subsection you will find a Quick Quiz, which checks and reinforces what you read. Circle the answer to each question and then check your answers against the correct answers supplied at the bottom of the quiz. If you missed any questions, flip back to the relevant section and review the material. Watch for this symbol:

☑ *Quick Quiz 1.1*

- **Examples** – Examples are used frequently to illustrate the concepts being discussed and to help the reader understand and apply the concepts presented.

- **Exhibits** – The written text is enhanced and simplified by using exhibits where appropriate to promote learning and application.

- **Cases** – Several chapters contain real world case summaries to help the reader appreciate the application of particular topics being discussed in the chapter.

- **End of Chapter Questions –** Each chapter contains a series of discussion questions and a sample of multiple-choice problems that highlight major topics covered in the chapter. The questions test retention and understanding of important chapter material and can be used for review and classroom discussion. Additional problems are available at money-education.com by accessing the Student Practice Portal.

- **Quick Quiz Explanations –** Each chapter concludes with the answers to the Quick Quizzes contained in that chapter, as well as explanation to the "false" statements in each Quick Quiz.

- **Glossary –** Key terms appear in **boldfaced type** throughout the text to assist in the identification of important concepts and terminology. A compilation of the key terms identified throughout the text is located at the end of the book.

> ## Student Practice Portal
> ### available by registering your textbook at
> ### money-education.com

This book is dedicated to
Donna D. Dalton & Robin D. Meyer
for their incredible ability to make miracles happen
against all odds. They truly went above and beyond
even their own high standards with the publication
of this book. They are the embodiment of Money
Education's spirit and work ethic and we are
honored to have them on our team.

TABLE OF CONTENTS

Chapter 4 | Personal Financial Statements: Preparation and Analysis

Chapter 5 | Risk Management for the Individual Client

Chapter 6 | John and Mary Burke Case and Case Analysis

Chapter 7 | Time Value of Money

Chapter 9 | Investments

Chapter 11 | Retirement Planning Accumulations and Distributions

Chapter 12 | Income Tax Planning

Chapter 13 | Business Entity Selection and Taxation

Chapter 14 | Estate Planning

Chapter 15 | Economics and the External Environment

Chapter 16 | Ethics & Standards of Conduct

Chapter 17 | Planning for Special Circumstances

Chapter 18 | David and Amy Rudolph Case & Case Analysis Part 2

1

INTRODUCTION TO FINANCIAL PLANNING

LEARNING OBJECTIVES

1. Diagram the personal financial planning process as detailed in the CFP Board's *Code of Ethics* and *Standards of Conduct*.*
2. List the contents of a comprehensive financial plan.
3. Describe the establishment and definition of the client relationship including the introductory meeting and engagement letter.
4. Define the activities that are typically part of the scope of an engagement.
5. Describe the client data gathering process including internal and external data.
6. Understand what goes on in the analysis and evaluation of the client's financial status.
7. Understand the development and presentation of financial plan recommendations.
8. Understand the implementation of financial plan recommendations.
9. Understand the monitoring of the plan.
10. Describe the benefits from financial planning.
11. Clearly delineate why clients use a professional financial plan.
12. Have a broad understanding of the practice of financial planning.
13. List and differentiate the various recognized certifications in financial planning.
14. Have a broad view of the employment and job outlook for financial planners and the various means of compensation for financial planning services.
15. Identify the regulatory authorities that impact elements of the financial planning process. (Examples include regulation of accountancy, legal practice, real estate law, insurance regulation, etc.).*
16. Explain the relevant licensing, reporting and compliance issues that may affect the business model used by a financial planning firm.*
17. Discuss the fiduciary standard and its importance to the planner-client relationship.*

Ties to CFP Certification Learning Objectives

INTRODUCTION

This textbook is a valuable resource for financial planning students and practitioners, including those with either limited or substantial experience, and those who are interested in improving their financial planning skills. The broad knowledge base required of a financial planner is covered in an introductory manner throughout this textbook, including the financial planning process from the initial contact with a client to the presentation of the plan itself. Case studies are included in the textbook that cover a range of scenarios from basic to more complex. Varied financial planning approaches are provided to ensure that the financial planner has the appropriate planning methodologies necessary to arrive at logical and substantiated planning recommendations. This textbook should remain an important reference tool for the financial planner seeking knowledge and assistance in the preparation of professional comprehensive personal financial plans.

PERSONAL FINANCIAL PLANNING

Personal financial planning (financial planning) is the process of formulating, implementing, and monitoring financial decisions into an integrated plan that guides an individual or a family to achieve their financial goals.

CFP Board's *Code of Ethics and Standards of Conduct (Code and Standards)* defines financial planning as "a collaborative process that helps maximize a Client's potential for meeting life goals through Financial Advice that integrates relevant elements of the Client's personal and financial circumstances." The CFP Board outlines the **process of financial planning** in seven steps in Section C of the *Standards of Conduct*. These seven steps are highlighted below but discussed in more detail in Chapter 16.

- ***Step 1: Understanding the Client's Personal and Financial Circumstances.*** In this step, the adviser needs to obtain qualitative and quantitative information for the client. The client information must be analyzed to obtain an understanding of the client's personal and financial circumstances. This information will help the adviser and the client with step 2.
- ***Step 2: Identifying and Selecting Goals.*** In this step, the adviser will work with the client to help identify potential goals, especially as it relates to goals that are mutually exclusive. For example, a client may be able to accumulate enough savings for a beach house or a house in the mountains, but not both without delaying retirement for several years. Once the potential goals are discussed and contemplated, the client must select and prioritize the goals with the help of the adviser.
- ***Step 3: Analyzing the Client's Current Course of Action and Potential Alternative Course(s) of Action.*** In this step, the adviser considers the advantages and disadvantages of the client's current financial situation in light of the goals of the client. In addition, alternative courses of action are considered.
- ***Step 4: Developing the Financial Planning Recommendation(s).*** This step is for determining the recommended course(s) of action that will maximize the potential to achieve the goals of the client.
- ***Step 5: Presenting the Financial Planning Recommendation(s).*** In this step, the adviser presents his or her recommendations to the client.
- ***Step 6: Implementing the Financial Planning Recommendation(s).*** The person who is responsible for implementing the plan must be determined. The client or the adviser might have this responsibility depending on the engagement. If the adviser is responsible, then the adviser must identify and analyze actions, products, and services designed to implement the recommendations. The adviser and the client must discuss the basis for actions, products, or service, as well as the timing for implementation. Finally, the adviser must help the client select and implement the actions, products, or services.
- ***Step 7: Monitoring Progress and Updating.*** Financial plans will need to change over time, especially as assumptions underlying the plan change. The responsibility for monitoring the financial plan must be established with the client. If the adviser has responsibility, then he or she must analyze, at appropriate intervals, the progress toward achieving the client's goals. Working with the client, the adviser would then make recommendations to modify the plan as needed and assist with implementing those recommendations.

The following exhibit illustrates this process outlined above.

Exhibit 1.1 | Financial Planning Process[1]

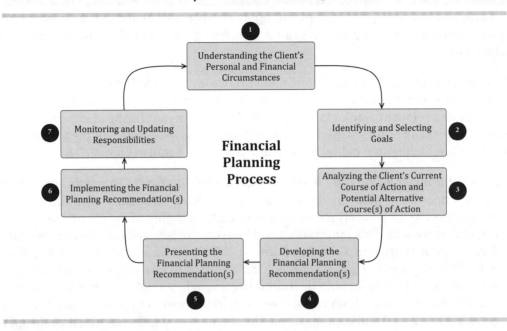

Contents of the Financial Plan

A **financial plan** is a written document that generally sets out a list of recommendations to achieve a set of goals and objectives based on an understanding of a client's current financial and personal situation. A financial plan is the work product and results from the application of several financial planning concepts to a client's current and prospective financial situation. The application of the concepts (listed below) considers the client's financial goals and values (**internal data**) and the external environment (**external data**). The external environment includes current and expected future income, gift and estate taxes, investment returns, inflation and interest rates.

Financial planning concepts applied include:
- an evaluation of the client's risk management portfolio (includes risks retained and risks transferred through the use of insurance contracts)
- financial statement preparation and analysis including cash flow analysis and budgeting
- emergency fund and debt management (short-term goals)
- long-term goal planning including:
  - achieving financial security (retirement planning)
  - education planning for children's or grandchildren's college or private secondary education
  - planning for lump-sum purchases (major expenditures)
  - legacy planning (estate planning)
- income tax planning is integrated throughout all aspects of a financial plan
- the investment planning portfolio is used to fund many of the client's short- and long-term goals

---

1. Abbreviated from the CFP Board's Financial Planning Practice Standards.

In order to apply each of these concepts to a client's current and prospective financial status, the financial planner uses tools such as financial statement preparation and analysis, cash flow analysis, and budgeting. This chapter introduces the preliminary step of establishing the client-planner relationship and the first two steps of the financial planning process: (1) understanding the client's personal and financial circumstances and (2) identifying and selecting goals. The chapter also provides information regarding the financial planning profession. Financial planning approaches are comprehensively reviewed in Chapter 3 (Financial Planning Approaches) and then applied to a case in detail in Chapter 6 (Burke Case). Two additional case studies in Chapters 10 and 18 (Rudolph Case Part 1 and 2) provide additional applications of and insights into the financial planning process.

> ### ☷ *Key Concepts*
>
> 1. Define the steps in the financial planning process.
>
> 2. Explain the difference between internal and external data collected as part of the financial planning process.
>
> 3. Identify financial planning concepts that are applied to a client's financial plan considering the client's profile, financial goals, and values.
>
> 4. Know what the financial planner should attempt to accomplish during the client introductory meeting.

Establish and Define the Client Relationship

Communication with Client

The role of the financial planner is to educate the client, gather relevant information, analyze that information, and assist the client in preparing and implementing a financial plan that will achieve the client's financial goals within the desired time frame.

In order to educate the client and gather relevant information, the financial planner must be able to communicate effectively with the client. The planner must respect the client and establish a relationship of trust. The planner must be empathetic and assess the attitudes and values of the client as well as the client's risk tolerance and views regarding savings, spending, taxation, and financial discipline. Issues such as the importance of work versus leisure time, job security, community service, attitudes regarding children from previous marriages, former spouses, and the client's extended family all are important in understanding and assisting the client to achieve his or her goals.

How does a planner effectively communicate with a client? From the onset, the financial planner should address the client formally (Mr., Mrs., Dr., etc.) using the appropriate salutation. This formality can be relaxed later in the relationship if the client is more comfortable with first names. The planner should actively listen to the client and especially to the verbs the client uses. This often indicates the client's learning style. Use of phrases such as "see what I mean," "imagine that," and any other words that imply that the client is a visual learner suggests that the planner should use examples including charts, graphs, and other visual aids to make the client more comfortable. If the client appears to pay attention to every spoken word or is asking for an explanation of words, the client's learning style is likely that of a verbal learner and graphics may be supplemented with carefully selected words. There is some data that suggest that up to 65 percent of people are visual learners. A generous use of pictures, graphs, and charts is always helpful in the communication process.

As a matter of professional courtesy, the financial planner should respect the client's time. This means being punctual, starting on time, ending on time, and telling the client how long each meeting will last. In order to establish a trusting relationship, the planner can generally share prior experiences. However, the planner must ensure that the client knows that client information is confidential by not identifying details about other clients.

The planner can show empathy by use of nonverbal pacing and showing a genuine interest in the hobbies, activities, vacations, and children of the client. To make communication effective, the financial planner can use restatement, paraphrasing, summarizing, open ended questions, and questions that show interest. These techniques can assure minimal miscommunication allowing the planner to reach the pertinent details.

Introductory Meeting

If there has been little communication before the first meeting, the financial planner should at least provide the client with a list of documents and information that the client needs to bring to the first meeting (e.g., get to know each other, collect some data, answer questions, clarify goals, reduce fears). At the first meeting, the financial planner should assist the client with establishing defined goals and discuss how the client's values fit into those goals. There will also be a general discussion of the client's personal data and family data. Typically the planner will meet with either one, or preferably both spouses to get an overview of the family and extended family (e.g., ages, marital status, children, grandchildren, net worth, income, self employment). From this basic information the planner will make a preliminary assessment of the general risks and goals of the client.

> ### ☷ Key Concepts
>
> 1. List the elements of the financial planning engagement letter.
>
> 2. Describe the purpose of a financial planning client questionnaire.
>
> 3. Summarize the types of necessary quantitative and qualitative data that is collected from the client.
>
> 4. Provide examples of external environment data that a financial planner needs to know in order to properly analyze, evaluate, and make recommendations related to a comprehensive financial plan.

The financial planner and client should mutually agree as to how they will communicate (e.g., email, office telephone, cell phone) and how often they will meet (e.g., 2 hours per week for 10 weeks). The client should be given a time frame over which the plan will be completed (e.g., 3 months). The financial planner should discuss the planning process and fees, provide relevant and required disclosures, and answer questions that the client is likely to have. The planner should effectively manage the client's expectations and have a remedy for instances when the client is dissatisfied. At the end of the introductory meeting the planner should prepare an engagement letter and send it to the client for approval.

Engagement Letter

An **engagement letter** is a legal agreement (a contract) between a professional organization (the planner) and a client that defines their business relationship. The engagement letter should define the parties to the agreement, the specific services to be provided, the duration of the agreement, the methods of communication (email, meetings), and the expected frequency of contact. The letter should also specify the conditions under which the agreement can be terminated.

Elements of an engagement letter:
- define the parties to the agreement
- a description of the mutually agreed upon services (the scope of work)
- the time horizon for the work to be completed
- a description of the fees and costs
- the obligation and responsibilities of each party (planner/client) regarding:
  - defining goals, needs, and objectives
  - gathering data
  - projecting the result of no action
  - formulating alternative possibilities
  - selecting from those alternatives
  - establishing who is expected to implement which elements of the plan (this can be subject to revision at the implementation phase of the process)
  - defining who has monitoring responsibilities
  - delineating services that are not provided, such as legal documents or income, gift, or estate tax return preparation

In addition to the above, there should be a mutual understanding regarding the use of proprietary products and/or other professionals or entities in meeting any of the service obligations in the engagement agreement.

Financial planners, and especially CFP® professionals, should seek to avoid or appropriately manage conflicts of interest. Any conflicts of interest should be disclosed by the planner to the client. Conflicts of interest arise when the interests of one party (the planner) are adverse to the interests of the other party (the client). This situation can occur, for example, when a planner has an economic incentive to recommend one financial product over other financial products. Ideally, these situations are to be avoided, or at the very least continued only with the client's informed consent.

An example of a client engagement letter is provided in **Example 1.2**. While an engagement letter is not required by CFP Board for CFP® professionals providing financial advice or financial planning, the Board does require that certain information and disclosures be provided to clients in one or more documents. CFP Board has provided customizable sample engagement letters which can be used by CFP® professionals at their discretion to fulfill this purpose.[2] Additional information regarding CFP Board's disclosure requirements for CFP® professionals is provided in Chapter 16.

---

2. https://www.cfp.net/ethics/compliance-resources/2020/11/sample-engagement-letters-for-financial-planning-and-financial-advice.

Exhibit 1.2 | Sample Engagement Letter

Sample Engagement Letter

Dear Client:

This letter will confirm the terms of our agreement regarding the financial planning services we will provide for you.

Engagement Objectives

The primary objective of our engagement is to review and analyze your personal financial situation and make recommendations for your financial plan. This review will identify your personal financial goals and objectives, and will include possible strategies to achieve them. Our analysis and recommendations are based on information provided by you that will be relied upon for representations.

Activities

The initial phase involves accumulating and organizing facts about your current financial status, identifying specific goals and objectives, and agreeing upon planning assumptions. This information will be obtained during an initial meeting or conversation with you and/or from the use of a financial planning data questionnaire. We will also review copies of pertinent documents, such as wills, company-provided fringe benefit booklets, prior tax returns, investment account statements, and insurance documents.

After the information has been received, the data will be analyzed and projections will be made. A subsequent meeting will be held to verify the accuracy of the data and will allow you to validate the assumptions used. Alternative courses of action to meet goals and address any issues will be comprehensively discussed.

The projections will then be updated for any required changes and a comprehensive financial planning report containing recommendations in all relevant areas of your financial situation will be presented. We will work with you to finalize the choice of strategies, to set time goals, and to establish responsibilities for your implementation of the plan.

The methods that you choose to follow for the implementation of the financial planning recommendations are at your discretion. You will be responsible for all decisions regarding implementation of the recommendations.

We are available, via a separate engagement, to assist you with implementation of your chosen strategies or to coordinate implementation with other financial professionals of your choosing. As part of this separate engagement, we can answer questions, monitor activities, or make new recommendations regarding your financial matters as circumstances change. In addition, we do not offer legal services such as will or trust preparation; however, we will be happy to refer you to a legal professional.

Your plan should be reviewed with us informally on a semiannual basis and more formally on an annual basis. These update sessions are essential so that adjustments can be made for changes in circumstances, economic conditions, and income, gift, or estate tax law revisions.

Sample Engagement Letter Continued

Fees

The fee for your Comprehensive Financial Plan has been determined by our mutual agreement and is $_____ which is due and payable upon return of this Engagement Letter. Please note that this fee is for the written financial plan alone and the plan shall contain all of our recommendations to you through the date of its delivery.

This agreement and fee does not provide for any product sales that may be offered at no obligation to you. This is a separate service that may be considered a conflict of interest because commissions and/or additional fees may be paid in connection with products purchased. We will inform you if there is any conflict of interest.

If additional conferences and interactions are beyond the scope of the services stated above, our fee for this service is based upon the time necessary to complete the additional agreed upon tasks. The agreed time allocated to accomplish additional tasks will be billed at our rate of $_____ per hour.

We reserve the right to discontinue services if billings are not paid when due.

If at any time you are dissatisfied with our services, you may terminate this agreement. If you do so within three business days of your acceptance, you will receive a full refund. Subsequently, any fees that you have paid to us in advance will be charged for the time and effort that has been devoted, up to that termination time, to prepare your written report and any remaining balance will be refunded.

We anticipate beginning the engagement immediately. If this letter meets with your approval, please sign the enclosed copy in the space provided and return it to us in the enclosed envelope.

We thank you for the opportunity to be of service, and we welcome you as a valued client.

Sincerely,

Financial Planner

I/We agree to the above terms & conditions:

Client Signature: _____   Date: _____

Client Signature: _____   Date: _____

The Scope of the Engagement

A financial planning engagement can be very narrow or fully comprehensive. Activities that are typically part of a comprehensive plan include:

- Preparation and analysis of personal financial statements.
- A review of all risk management policies (including life, health, disability, long-term care, property and liability insurance) and what to do about any uncovered areas of risk.
- An evaluation of short-term financial goals including the emergency fund and debt management.
- The establishment of long-term goals including retirement, education funding, lump-sum (major) expenditures, and legacy planning including documents.
- An evaluation of the current investment portfolio with the objective of creating a new investment approach that helps to achieve the client's goals within the risk tolerance of the client.
- An examination and recommendation regarding any special needs situation of the client (divorce, elderly parent, child with special needs). (See Special Needs chapter.)

Understanding the Client's Personal and Financial Circumstances (Gather Client Data)

The Internal Data Collection Process

The planner must obtain sufficient information (both quantitative and qualitative) from the client in order to assess and analyze the client's financial situation. Quantitative information is measurable and includes the client's age, income, number of children, death benefit of life insurance policies, and much more. Qualitative information is how the client feels about something, or their attitude or belief, including working versus retiring and spending versus saving. The information includes client-provided documents and may be obtained by the planner through the use of questionnaires and/or interviews. See **Exhibit 1.3** for a basic sample of a client questionnaire. The planner will need to explore and evaluate the client's values, attitudes, expectations, and time horizons as they affect client goals, needs, and priorities.

Quantitative information collected must be complete, accurate, verifiable, and free from bias. The information to be collected will include:

- **The family** - list of members, their age, health, education, income, financial competence, and any special situations (e.g., child with special needs, aging parents who are or may become dependents).
- **The insurance portfolio** - collect all insurance policies and a detailed description of any employer-provided or sponsored insurance. Make sure to identify the premiums paid by the client (life, health, disability, long-term care, property including homeowners, flood, auto, boat, etc., and whether the client has a personal or professional liability policy).
- **Banking and investment information** - collect current statements on all bank accounts and investment accounts including qualified plans (IRAs, SEPs, SIMPLEs, 403(b)s, 457s). Obtain from the client detailed information about other investments such as rental or business property, including information such as the valuation, amount of debts, and cash flows.
- **Taxes** - all income, gift and trust tax returns for the last five years if available.
- **Retirement and Employee Benefits** - all retirement information including Social Security statements or benefits (Form SSA 7004 can be used), employer-sponsored retirement plans, and employee benefits (get a copy of the booklets and summary description of plan).
- **Estate Planning** - all wills, durable powers of attorney for health care decisions, all advance medical directives and any trust documents.
- **All personal financial statements** if available including any recently used to obtain debt (balance sheet and income statement) - a list of debts with the original amount, date of inception, interest rate, term of repayment and current balance. Most clients will not have financial statements and either the planner or a CPA will have to prepare them.

The financial planner also needs to collect qualitative information from the client. Qualitative information includes the client's attitude and beliefs regarding:

- Education goals
- Retirement goals
- Employment goals
- Savings goals
- Risk tolerance
- Charitable goals
- General attitude towards spending

The financial planner will request that the client bring all of the above information to the first meeting. Frequently, the client will not have all the quantitative information (such as insurance policies and employee benefits brochures) and rarely do clients have properly prepared personal financial statements. The engagement letter may be modified to include an addendum of missing information needed for later meetings.

Exhibit 1.3 | Sample Financial Planning Questionnaire

Sample of a Financial Planning Client Questionnaire*

General Information:		General Information:	
Client 1 Full Name:		Client 2 Full Name:	
Home Address:		Home Address	
City, State, Zip:		City, State, Zip:	
Home Phone:		Home Phone:	
Work Phone:		Work Phone:	
Mobile Phone:		Mobile Phone:	
Occupation:		Occupation:	
Employer:		Employer:	
Annual Earned Income:		Annual Earned Income:	
Fax:		Fax:	
Email:		Email:	
Social Security #:		Social Security #:	
Birth date:		Birth date:	
Prior Marriage(s):		Prior Marriage(s):	
Family/Dependent Information:		**Family/Dependent Information:**	
Name:		Name:	
Relationship:		Relationship:	
Date of Birth:		Date of Birth:	
Social Security #:		Social Security #:	
Dependent:		Dependent:	
Resides:		Resides:	
Assets:	Ownership: Client 1 or 2	**Assets:**	Ownership: Client 1 or 2
Bank Account:		**Bank Account:**	
Account Number & Type:		Account Number & Type:	
Average Balance:		Average Balance:	
CD – Held:		**CD – Held:**	
Maturity:		Maturity:	
Value:		Value:	
Primary Residence:		**Secondary Residence:**	
Value:		Value:	
Automobile 1:		**Automobile 2:**	
Value:		Value:	
Retirement Accounts:		**Retirement Accounts:**	
Type/Ownership:		Type/Ownership:	
Held by:		Held by:	
Account Number:		Account Number:	
Value:		Value:	
Other Account:		**Other Account:**	
Account Number & Type:		Account Number & Type:	
Value:		Value:	

Sample Financial Planning Questionnaire Continued

Insurance:	Ownership: Client 1 or 2	Insurance:	Ownership: Client 1 or 2
Health/Company:		Health/Company:	
Coverage/Cost:		Coverage/Cost:	
Disability/Company:		Disability/Company:	
Coverage/Cost:		Coverage/Cost:	
Life/Company:		Life/Company:	
Type/Coverage/Cost:		Type/Coverage/Cost:	
Homeowners:		Homeowners:	
Type/Coverage/Cost:		Type/Coverage/Cost:	
Auto:		Auto:	
Type/Coverage/Cost:		Type/Coverage/Cost:	
Umbrella Liability:		Umbrella Liability:	
Type/Coverage/Cost:		Type/Coverage/Cost:	
Professional Liability		Professional Liability:	
Type/Coverage/Cost:		Type/Coverage/Cost:	
Long Term Care:		Long Term Care:	
Type/Coverage/Cost:		Type/Coverage/Cost:	

Liabilities:	Client 1 or 2	Liabilities:	Client 1 or 2
Credit Card:		Credit Card:	
Monthly Pmt. /Balance:		Monthly Pmt. /Balance:	
Residence Loan:		Residence Loan:	
Monthly Pmt. /Balance:		Monthly Pmt. /Balance:	
Auto Loan:		Auto Loan:	
Monthly Pmt. /Balance:		Monthly Pmt. /Balance:	
Other Debt:		Other Debt:	
Monthly Pmt. /Balance:		Monthly Pmt. /Balance:	

Estate Issues:	Client 1 or 2	Estate Issues:	Client 1 or 2
Current Will: Y N		Current Will: Y N	
Living Will: Y N		Living Will: Y N	
Medical Power of Attorney: Y N		Medical Power of Attorney: Y N	
General Power of Attorney: Y N		General Power of Attorney: Y N	

Items that may be needed:
- Prior Year Tax Returns
- Brokerage Account Statements
- Trust account Statements
- Retirement Plan Account Statements
- Loan Documents
- Insurance Policies
- Legal Documents

Current Advisors:
Attorney: _____
Accountant: _____
Insurance Agent: _____
Stockbroker: _____

Comment on advice you are seeking:
_____
_____
_____

The External Data Collection Process

It is important that the planner is cognizant of the current external environmental data including the economic, legal, political, sociological, taxation and technological environment. This general knowledge may be obtained by taking various university courses, attending professional conferences, and reading professional and news related journals.

The financial planner should identify and document the following external information at the inception of the engagement:

- Interest rates
    - the current and prospective outlook including savings rates and mortgage rates
- Housing market - housing is a major asset but markets are local
    - what is the stock of available housing
    - is it a buyer's or seller's market
- Job market
    - what is the unemployment rate
- Investment market
    - current and prospective outlook
- Business cycle
    - peak, contraction, trough, expansion
    - where are we now
- Local insurance costs
    - housing, auto, liability
- Local cost of living
- Expected inflation rate, both short and long term
- Expected rate of increase in the prices of education and medical care
- Legislation that may impact certain industry sectors (e.g., healthcare)
- Current and expected income, gift, and estate tax rates

Identifying and Selecting Goals

Identifying Goals

Prior to moving on to the analysis stage, the planner and client must collaborate to identify and clearly define the client's goals, using reasonable assumptions, and discuss how each goal may impact other goals.

In practice, a client may need help in both clarifying aspirational goals and setting specific objectives. For example, a client may indicate "I want a comfortable retirement." As will be discussed in Chapter 2, the planner will want to explore further to ensure a true understanding of the client's vision of the goal and motives driving the goal. Once the planner fully understands the client's aspirational goal, in order to facilitate the analysis needed to derive a plan that will allow the client to reach that goal, the planner will need to help the client to express a more objectively-stated goal in terms that are specific, measurable, achievable, and realistic. For example, the goal may be quantified as the desire to retire at age 66 with income equal to 80 percent of after-tax pre-retirement income during a 30-year time horizon, inflation-adjusted at three percent per year, from all sources combined. Each goal must then be examined with regard to the client's resources and limitations or constraints.

Selecting Goals

Most clients will have multiple financial planning and life goals at any point in time, and these goals must be prioritized. As resources are finite, clients may be constrained to accept various compromises in their long-term planning. The challenge often is to negotiate the rearrangement of priorities and strategies to optimize the satisfaction of multiple objectives.

Examples of common risks and goals throughout a client's financial life cycle are discussed in Chapter 3. A study of these life cycle goals will reveal a dynamic, rather than constant, set of goals. As clients progress from one life cycle stage to another, initial goals may be achieved and new goals arise. Ultimately, the planner must understand that each client will have her own set of values that determine the goals of greatest importance during each stage of life. Assessing the client's life cycle stage provides a guideline for what the planner may expect, but each client, with the assistance of the planner, will ultimately determine which goals should be explored and developed, revised, or rejected.

Analyzing, Developing, Presenting, Implementing and Monitoring

Analyzing the Client's Current Course of Action and Potential Alternative Courses of Action

Once the planner has collected internal and external data and mutually established the goals, needs, and priorities of the client, the planner will begin the analysis phase. This textbook goes into great detail using many financial planning approaches to analyze, evaluate, and make recommendations to the client. Specifically, Chapter 3 covers additional steps of the financial planning process including the analysis of the client's financial situation and the development and presentation of recommendations.

Developing the Financial Planning Recommendations

While developing and presenting the plan is discussed to some extent in Chapter 3, it is worth mentioning that this phase is one of the most critical steps in the financial planning process. This step comes after the analysis phase. Suggestions made by the financial planner must be based on:
- The scope of the engagement as set forth in the engagement letter
- The goals and objectives of the client
- The information gathered from the client by the planner
- An analysis of the economic environment, including the current and projected tax law environment
- The alternatives available to accomplish the client's goals

These recommendations should also be based on the expertise of the financial planner and may require input from other experts, such as attorneys, accountants, or actuaries.

This step in the process is generally an iterative one. Often, recommendations will be made and discussed with the client with further questions and investigation before an agreement on final plan recommendations can be made. In addition, there will always be alternative solutions that may work for a particular client and it will be part of the process that the alternative solutions are discussed and prioritized before the implementation of the plan.

Example 1.1

Penny, who is a financial planner, advises her client to obtain a disability insurance policy. While a disability policy may be appropriate, there are choices to be made in terms of the elimination period and such choice or choices should be consistent with another choice regarding the emergency fund. Therefore, while the recommendation to cover the risk is sound, there may be alternative solutions in terms of what is ultimately chosen by the client.

The recommendations that are made by the adviser should be based on the criteria listed above and should be made independent of how the adviser is compensated. The adviser should make disclosures about how she is compensated and if there are any conflicts of interest. Disclosures regarding potential conflicts of interest should include sufficient facts to ensure that the client fully understands the conflict and is able to either give their informed consent or to reject them.

Presenting the Financial Planning Recommendations

The planner must then present the final recommendations to the client, along with an explanation of the information and process that was used in selecting the recommendations. As discussed previously, the presentation should be adapted to the client's learning style to ensure that the client is fully engaged in the process and has a clear understanding of the recommendations and whether they are independent or whether a recommendation must be implemented with another recommendation.

In practice, the presentation of the planner's recommendations may involve more than one meeting depending on the complexity of the client's situation and whether the client has the desire to actively review all of the detailed analysis that was utilized in selecting the recommendations or prefers to be provided with a big picture summary.

Throughout the course of presenting the plan, a planner should remain cognizant of the client's body language. Particularly when the plan is both long and complex, clients may reach a point where they simply cannot absorb any additional information. In those circumstances, it is better for the planner to stop and schedule a follow-up meeting to review the rest of the plan. In other cases, the presentation may segue almost seamlessly into the implementation phase.

Implementing the Financial Planning Recommendations

This phase of the financial planning process begins after the client and planner agree on the recommendations and priorities. The client must agree that the recommendations made by the planner are appropriate and will further the achievement of her goals and objectives before implementation can begin.

Implementing the recommendations is the process of taking action on the recommendations. This is the part of the process where change actually occurs. However, there are several steps that may be necessary, including defining the necessary activities for implementation and determining which activities will be performed by the client and which ones will be performed by the planner.

In most cases, part of the implementation process will require the use of and coordination with other professionals. For example, advisers will generally work with attorneys to implement any estate planning or other necessary legal work (e.g., establishment of a family limited partnership). In the case that another professional is necessary as part of the implementation process, the planner or the client will need to coordinate with that professional.

In many cases, implementation will require the selection of financial services products, such as insurance or investment vehicles. Similarly, this may be accomplished directly with the planner or by working with other professionals.

Implementation is critical because without it the plans does not come alive. There are times when a plan will be created and agreed to by the client that does not get implemented. This outcome is unfortunate since the client will be unlikely to accomplish the goals that were the basis for the initial recommendations. However, when clients do follow through with implementation, they are often closer to accomplishing the goals they set out to achieve.

Monitoring Progress and Updating

It is not uncommon to think that once the recommendations are implemented, that is the conclusion of the financial planning process and engagement. However, it is really the beginning of the process. Once the plan is implemented, the planner and the client must monitor the actual results of what was implemented relative to what was expected. For example, if a retirement plan was implemented and was based on specific savings amounts and earnings rates of return, it is important to evaluate periodically to ensure that progress is being made as was expected. If the actual results are different from what was anticipated, then adjustments to the plan may be required.

There are other reasons that require monitoring. For example, to the extent that tax laws change, such changes may positively or negatively impact the financial plan.

The following are some additional situations which typically warrant reviewing the client's financial plan:
- birth of a family member
- death of a family member
- marriage of a family member
- divorce of a family member
- career change
- job loss
- inheritance
- estate and gift tax law changes
- economic recession
- economic recovery

It is important as part of the engagement process to define who will be responsible for monitoring the plan and to define the specifics around monitoring if the planner will be responsible for it, including frequency, depth, and how the results of such monitoring will be communicated.

This process continues until such time as further analysis occurs.

FINANCIAL PLANNING PROFESSION

The Benefits from Financial Planning

The planning process helps to identify risks and to establish and prioritize goals. The process helps to anticipate where financial needs exist (such as, education and retirement needs) and where new risks may arise (for example, long-term care insurance and property and liability insurance on newly acquired major assets).

The plan itself establishes benchmarks (metrics) within a finite time frame where a comparison with actual results creates an early warning system for deviations. It also helps to keep the client focused on achieving the objectives of the plan and provides for more efficient and effective resource utilization. The financial planning process provides the client with choices and alternatives to consider, enhancing the awareness of the opportunity costs of foregone options (see Chapter 15 on Economics for more information on opportunity costs) leading to better decisions. Perhaps the greatest benefit that comes from financial planning is the confidence that with clear direction the client can accomplish their financial goals.

Why Use a Professional Financial Planner

Most clients do not know how to prepare a comprehensive financial plan and do not want to spend the time to learn how. Even where the client may have the knowledge, he typically lacks the confidence to undertake this process and is likely seeking confirmation of his own financial planning decisions.

An expert in financial planning (like any other expert) has probably spent 10,000 or more hours in financial planning over at least 10 years. The education of a competent financial planner generally consists of at least an undergraduate degree (4,000 hours) and additional financial planning related courses (1,000 hours). If the planner is a Certified Financial Planner™, the planner likely has passed a comprehensive exam requiring another 300 - 400 hours of study. A financial planner brings objectivity to an otherwise subjective world. The competent financial planner has knowledge about the following:

> ### :☰ *Key Concepts*
>
> 1. Describe the benefits of a client having a financial plan.
>
> 2. Explain why a client should consider using a professional financial planner.
>
> 3. Summarize the economic forecast for the practice of financial planning.

- mortality risk
- disability risk
- investment returns
- risks associated with various asset classes
- the cost of college education
- the cost of retirement
- the needed savings rate to drive various goals

A client rarely has knowledge of objective factors and instead perceives subjectively that he is fine (e.g., does not need life or disability insurance). One of the most important qualities a professional brings to the client/planner relationship is objectivity.

Finally, the financial planner brings experience from previous engagements with variously situated clients. The client seeks an initial plan that meets his objectives and the trusted, experienced practitioner is more likely to be able to create such a plan.

The Practice of Financial Planning

The position of "financial planner" is largely unregulated. Neither the federal nor the state laws directly regulate the practice of financial planning. There are, however, licenses that must be obtained by those engaging in the sale of insurance products and securities. Financial planning is much broader than the sale of products or securities and is practiced by a wide variety of professionals. In addition to the planners who have earned the certifications listed below, other professionals such as bankers, brokers, accountants, lawyers, and insurance agents practice in the broad field of financial planning.

Recognized Certifications in Financial Planning

In a newly emerging profession such as financial planning, there is an initial lack of regulation. The need for some form of self-regulation and the demand that a financial planner be competent and trustworthy have prompted several independent financial services organizations to introduce certifications and ethical standards. Those who meet the requirements of the certification process and subscribe to specific ethical standards are awarded a professional financial planning designation.

One of the oldest, best-known financial planning certification trademarks is the CERTIFIED FINANCIAL PLANNER™ certification, which has gained global recognition because of its standard setting activities and worldwide presence. The CFP® certification was first introduced in the United States in the early 1970s to meet the needs of consumers. The CFP Board, based in Washington, D.C., owns the CFP® marks within the United States. The CFP® marks are owned outside the United States by the Financial Planning Standards Board, a nonprofit standards-setting body based in Denver, Colorado.

The CFP Board was founded in July 1985 as the International Board of Standards and Practices for Certified Financial Planners, Inc., (IBCFP) by the College for Financial Planning (College) and the Institute of Certified Financial Planners (ICFP). The IBCFP became the Certified Financial Planners Board of Standards Inc. (CFP Board) on February 1, 1994. As a professional regulatory organization acting in the public interest by fostering professional standards in personal financial planning, the CFP Board establishes and enforces education, examination, experience, and ethics requirements for CFP® certificants. The CFP® service mark is promoted world-wide through member associations (such as the Financial Planning Association).

The Chartered Financial Consultant (ChFC®) is another financial planning qualification, conferred by the American College. To date, more than 60,000 individuals have attained this distinction. This designation has also spread to Asia, where designees are found in countries like Singapore, Malaysia, Indonesia, China, and Hong Kong.

In Europe, the European Financial Planner (EFP) designation conferred by the European Financial Planners Association (EFPA) is gaining ground as a financial planning certification mark. The EFPA is the largest professional and educational organization for financial planners and financial advisers in Europe and is the only financial planning association created solely in the interest of European financial planning consumers and practitioners.

Job Satisfaction

A career in financial planning is rewarding and engaging. According to a 2019 survey conducted by the Certified Financial Planner Board of Standards, Inc., 93 percent of CFP® professionals are satisfied with their career choice.[3]

Employment and Job Outlook

As of 2019, the United States Department of Labor reports that personal financial planners hold 263,000 jobs across the country (projected to be 274,600 in 2029).[4] Approximately 19 percent of the reported planners are self-employed and 71 percent work in the finance and insurance industries. With the rising number of baby boomer retirees over the next decade, the occupation is expected to grow by 4 percent (2019 to 2029). As both retirement savings options and the complexity of retirement plans increase, the need for skilled financial planners will grow. Those planners with a college degree, certification, and sales skills will likely be the most successful.

Earnings

Financial planners earn on average $87,850 (2019) annually. This average does not include bonuses or the wages of self-employed practitioners. Financial planners earn compensation in the form of:[5]
- An hourly rate or fee
- A flat fee
- A commission on investment and insurance products sold
- A percentage of the assets managed
- A combination of the above

Personal financial planners can be compensated from their clients for professional financial planning services in a variety of ways. For example, a planner can choose to charge based on an hourly rate or charge a flat fee for a comprehensive plan. The amount of the flat fee may vary based on the complexity of the plan. If the client desires only planning services for a particular issue, the planner can charge a flat fee for the particular module of a plan serviced. Many planners earn the predominant amount of their fees through commissions on the sale of investments and insurance products, having to rely on new client business or updated client plans in order to generate revenue. Others focus on a niche of high wealth clients and charge fees based on the percentage of assets they manage for those clients. In order to build and sustain a financial planning practice, financial planners can offer a variety of fee arrangements to fit the needs of their business and their clients.

Before entering into a relationship with a client, the financial planner should make certain that fee arrangements are in writing and clearly understood by the client. Financial planning is a valuable service, and fee arrangements must be unambiguous in order to manage the client's expectations regarding the cost of the service.

---

3. https://www.cfp.net/knowledge/reports-and-statistics/certificant-surveys/2019-cfp-professionals-survey
4. United States Department of Labor Bureau of Labor Statistics; Occupational Outlook Handbook; www.bls.gov/ooh/Business-and-Financial/Personal-financial-advisors.htm
5. United States Department of Labor Bureau of Labor Statistics; Occupational Outlook Handbook; www.bls.gov/ooh/Business-and-Financial/Personal-financial-advisors.htm

The Business of Financial Planning

Financial planners may work under various business and compensation models depending on the types of planning offered and the demographics and preferences of the clientele or niche market being served. Some planners work with ultra-high net worth individuals or families and provide services such as investment management, real estate management, and tax planning and preparation, and may be compensated based on flat fees, a percentage of assets under management, or another compensation model that specifically meets their needs. Other planners may prefer to work with young clients with minimal wealth to provide services such as debt and student loan management, insurance planning, and budgeting. For those planners, compensation based on flat or hourly fees will provide a better business outcome than a fee based on assets under management. Other planners may fall somewhere in between. Each business and compensation model encompasses its own characteristics, features, limitations, and rules. Practitioners must follow all relevant licensing, reporting, and compliance requirements associated with the business model under which they choose to operate. The model may be insurance only, brokerage only, investment management only, financial planning only, etc.; or it may be any combination of various areas. Those working in business models that are broad in range will be required to report to multiple regulatory agencies, to obtain multiple licenses, and may have separate business entities for each financial planning area.

Regulatory Authorities

Comprehensive financial planning involves addressing a broad range of client needs ranging from recommending appropriate investments to providing advice regarding estate planning documents, and from reducing income taxes to evaluating and recommending insurance policies and retirement plans. Certain aspects of these financial planning services are regulated by various government bodies and organizations, and planners should be careful to remain in compliance in all areas. For example, while the planner may review legal documents, such as trusts, wills, and buy-sell agreements, only a licensed attorney may draft such documents. For the planner to do so would be considered unauthorized practice of law.

As another example, the planner may be asked to prepare income tax returns for a client. If the planner is paid a fee for tax preparation, he or she must apply for a PTIN (Preparer Tax Identification Number) from the IRS and will need to renew the PTIN each year. The IRS offers a voluntary Annual Filing Program to encourage tax preparers to participate in continuing education courses each year, but does not require a competency test or continuing education (unless the preparer falls under a licensed credential requiring them, such as enrolled agents).

following table illustrates some additional planning areas and their regulatory authorities.

Planning Area	Regulatory Authority
Investment advice	Securities and Exchange Commission (SEC) | State securities administrator
Sale of securities	SEC | Financial Industry Regulatory Authority (FINRA) | State securities administrator
Sale of insurance	State insurance commission
Income tax preparation	Internal Revenue Service (IRS)
Legal advice	State Bar Association | American Bar Association (ABA)
Accounting services	State Society of CPAs | American Institute of CPAs (AICPA)
Real estate law	State real estate commission
Banking	Office of the Comptroller of Currency (OCC) | Federal Reserve Board (FED) | Office of Thrift Supervision (OTS)
Adviser to ERISA qualified retirement plans	Department of Labor (DOL) | Internal Revenue Service (IRS)
Municipal securities	Municipal Securities Rulemaking Board (MSRB)

Details regarding some of the most common licensing requirements for financial planners are covered in Chapter 5 (Risk Management) and Chapter 15 (Economics) and details regarding planners who become CFP® professionals are covered in Chapter 16 (Ethics).

Professional Liability Protection for Financial Planners

Financial planners face many liability risks that are similar to liability risks faced by other business owners and professionals and can benefit from various asset protection strategies utilized by other business owners and professionals, such as selecting the appropriate legal form of business entity (covered in Chapter 13). Financial planners, however, also face some unique professional liability risks that other professionals may not face.

The purchase of Errors and Omissions (E&O) insurance will provide the foundation of protection for the planner. Purchasing an E&O policy requires the same care, consideration, and due diligence that the planner exercises when making recommendations to clients. Different types of policies with a wide array of coverages and exclusions are available. Most policies will cover the cost of defense, but may limit the choice of counsel to those attorneys on their approved list. Some policies will have annual limits. The cost of defense, even against claims that have no merit, can be very high. It is also worth asking the insurer about who will make the decision to settle a case covered by the policy. The planner may want to have the final decision whether to defend or settle. In cases where it will be more costly to defend than to settle, the insurer will normally choose to settle, but the planner may disagree and feel that settlement looks like an admission of guilt.

The majority of E&O policies for financial planners are written on a claims-made basis, meaning that the policy provides coverage if the claim is made while the policy is in force. Policies with an extended reporting period will continue to provide coverage even after the planner retires or changes careers.

An E&O policy should cover all of the duties that the planner performs such as providing investment advice, selling insurance, or selling alternative investments. Planners who are fiduciaries of qualified retirement plans may also need to purchase Fiduciary Insurance (also called ERISA liability coverage). It should not be assumed that the E&O policies provide such coverage. A growing number of financial advisers are also seeking cybersecurity coverage, and planners who decide to branch into financial coaching (discussed in Chapter 2) should verify coverage for these types of client interactions as well.

E&O policies provide coverage when a claim is filed against a planner, but a planner should take precautions to prevent such claims. These precautions are good business practice and can reduce the costs of claims. One key to success in defending claims will be documentation of client interaction, including appointments, phone calls, and emails. All recommendations should be stated in the written plan, and the planner should take care to follow up when any recommendations are not implemented. Having an investment policy statement (IPS) for each client will help the planner to defend investment recommendations as having been within the guidelines established by the client. The planner should also take care to protect clients' privacy. Even something as simple as leaving a brokerage account statement on the desk when a planner leaves for lunch could allow anyone entering the planner's office to access client information in violation of confidentiality. Providing written disclosure of all potential conflicts of interest will also help to protect the planner. Planners should take care when handling client instructions, because failure to exercise a client's specific instructions can result in planner liability. Finally, financial planners should avoid giving advice in areas in which they are not competent, not licensed, or not permitted by law. Working with other expert professionals such as CPAs and attorneys should be expected.

The Role of Fiduciaries in Financial Planning

A fiduciary is a person in a position of trust and confidence who is required to act for the benefit and best interests of another person. Financial planners often work with fiduciaries during the planning process, and financial planners are themselves fiduciaries when working in certain capacities with clients.

The planner or adviser has an affirmative duty of utmost good faith and must make full and fair disclosure of all material facts. The fiduciary duty means acting in the client's best interests at all times and placing the client's interests above the interests of the planner or adviser. This fiduciary relationship arises out of the trust and confidence the client places in the financial planner or adviser, particularly that the planner or adviser possesses and will use special skills on behalf of the client.

Types of fiduciary relationships in financial planning include the following:

1. An executor or personal representative of an estate has a duty to act in the best interests of the beneficiaries of the estate.
2. A trustee must act in the best interests of the trust beneficiaries.
3. Guardians are appointed to act in the best interests of the person who is their ward.
4. An agent under a Power of Attorney document is a fiduciary who must act in the best interests of the principal.
5. Advisers to retirement plans have the duty to act in the best interests of the plan participants and beneficiaries.
6. Registered investment advisers are required to provide advice that is in the best interests of the clients.

Fiduciaries are required to manage property under their supervision according to the state laws setting fiduciary standards, but additional powers or duties can be given to a trustee or executor by the trust document or will. For example, a trustee can be authorized to retain a closely held business interest even though state laws concerning prudent investments might require the trustee to sell the interest and reinvest in less risky investments.

Fiduciary Duties

Generally, a fiduciary owes the following duties to beneficiaries:

1. To act for the benefit of beneficiaries in regard to matters within the scope of the fiduciary relationship.
2. To refrain from delegating acts that can be performed by the fiduciary.
3. To make full disclosure of all facts in any transaction with the beneficiary; any transaction must be fair to the beneficiary, or it can be set aside.
4. To refrain from any self-dealing at the expense of the beneficiaries and to remain loyal to beneficiaries.
5. To preserve property and to make it productive.
6. To invest property prudently according to state laws that may consist of a prudent-person rule, legal-list statute, or Uniform Prudent Investor Act.
7. To be impartial toward beneficiaries so as not to favor income beneficiaries over remainder beneficiaries.

Duties of the Executor

The executor or personal representative is appointed by a court to gather the decedent's assets, resolve claims and disputes against the estate, invest assets during the period of administration, prepare an accounting of the estate assets, and make distributions to the beneficiaries according to the will or intestacy laws.

Duties of the Trustee

A trustee is named in a trust document to manage trust assets during the continued existence of the trust. The trustee invests the property, collects income, and makes distributions to the beneficiaries, according to the directions of the trust provisions.

Duties of the Guardian

A guardian is appointed by a court to manage the property of an incompetent person during the period of incompetency. A guardian may be appointed as the guardian of the person or of the property of the person, or ward. A guardian for a minor child is often named in a will, and courts will generally honor a parent's selection of the guardian named in this way. The guardian of property administers these assets and makes payments from the assets for the benefit of the ward. A guardian of the person often provides food, clothing, and shelter for a minor ward.

Duties of the Agent (POA)

A Power of Attorney (POA) is a legal document allowing the principal (the person creating the POA) to name an agent to handle the principal's financial affairs under certain circumstances (a limited POA), or the agent may be granted broad powers to act on behalf of the principal (a general POA). The agent is a fiduciary who must act in the best interest of the principal in fulfilling his or her duties under the POA document. A durable power of attorney (one that survives the incapacity of the principal) is commonly used in planning for incapacity as part of estate planning.

Example 1.2

As part of an estate plan, Mike gives his favorite son, James, a power of attorney that becomes effective upon incapacity. One day, Mike trips while drinking Perrier on his 70-foot yacht, hits his head, and is in a coma. Since Mike is in a coma, he is unable to manage his personal financial affairs. As a result, James will have the power to act on his behalf. Fortunately, Mike wakes from the coma after a two-week period rested and refreshed.

Duties of Fiduciaries Under ERISA

The Employee Retirement Income Security Act (ERISA) established fiduciary responsibility for those who perform any of the following actions when working with qualified retirement plans:

1. exercise discretionary authority or control over the management of qualified retirement plans,
2. exercise any authority or control over the management or disposition of the plan's assets,
3. offer investment advice for a fee or other compensation with respect to plan funds or property, or
4. hold any discretionary authority or responsibility in the plan's administration.

ERISA requires that a fiduciary act "solely in the interest of the participants and beneficiaries" and with the care, skill, prudence and diligence under the circumstances then prevailing that a prudent man acting in a like capacity and familiar with such matters would use in the conduct of an enterprise of a like character and with like aims. Additional details are discussed in chapter 15.

Duties of Registered Investment Advisers

The Investment Advisers Act of 1940 specified the relationship between registered investment advisers and their advisory clients as a fiduciary relationship. The fiduciary standard invokes a duty of loyalty and utmost good faith, creates an obligation to act in the best interest of the client, and requires disclosure of all conflicts of interest.

Some firms operate under a business model that includes both an investment adviser and a broker-dealer (dually registered advisers), and individual advisers who work for the firm may be licensed as both a registered representative of a broker-dealer (with a FINRA Series 6 or Series 7 license), and as an investment adviser representative (with a Series 65 or 66 license). Additional details of regarding these registrations and licenses are provided in Chapter 15.

FINRA Rule 3241

Effective February 15, 2021, FINRA Rule 3241 prohibits "registered persons" (any associated person with a member firm who is registered with the Financial Industry Regulatory Authority (FINRA)) from being named as a beneficiary or as a fiduciary such as executor, trustee, or agent under a power of attorney on behalf of a customer unless written notice is provided to the registered person's member firm and the member firm provides approval for the registered person to act in this capacity. An exception applies when the customer is a member of the registered person's immediate family.[6]

---

6. For the definition of "immediate family member" and other guidelines, see https://www.finra.org/rules-guidance/notices/20-38.

Breach of Fiduciary Duties

A fiduciary who breaches a duty to beneficiaries may be held personally liable for any loss to the beneficiaries. Trustees can be held liable for failing to invest assets in ways that would produce more income for the income beneficiaries. Fiduciaries can also be held liable for self-dealing and for personal use of the assets entrusted to their care and management.

An individual fiduciary can be held liable for failure to exercise the same skill and care that a person of ordinary prudence would exercise in handling his or her own affairs. A professional or corporate trustee will be held to a higher standard because of its expertise.

Some breaches of fiduciary duty are remedied by civil suit and will require the assistance of an attorney. For example, if a client's brother is the executor for their mother's estate and the client suspects that the estate is being mismanaged, the client will need to consult an attorney concerning a suit for damages. If the client's brother is stealing from the estate, then the police and district attorney should be contacted.

Example 1.3

Bernard establishes a trust for the benefit of his son Kevin and names Kevin as the trustee. Instead of investing the trust assets in a diversified portfolio, Kevin decides it is a good idea to invest all of the money in a baseball hitting facility. While the investment might or might not pay off, it is not a prudent investment choice. If the hitting facility is successful, Kevin will likely not be sued. If it is not successful, he will almost definitely be sued, and would be personally liable.

Fiduciary Responsibility of CFP® Professionals

CFP® professionals are held to a fiduciary standard when providing financial advice or financial planning to a client. There is a difference, however, between the fiduciary duties discussed above, which are legally enforceable, and the fiduciary duty required of a CFP® professional. The duties prescribed by CFP Board for CFP® professionals are not grounds for legal liability, but are instead required in the terms of agreement to use the CFP® marks. CFP Board's enforcement of the fiduciary duty ensures that those who use the marks are held to the highest ethical standards. See Chapter 16 for additional details.

DISCUSSION QUESTIONS

SOLUTIONS to the discussion questions can be found exclusively within the chapter. Once you have completed an initial reading of the chapter, go back and highlight the answers to these questions.

1. What is personal financial planning?

2. Define the process of financial planning.

3. What are examples of internal data items collected from the client as part of the "understanding the client's personal and financial circumstances," or data gathering, part of the financial planning process?

4. What are examples of external data items required as part of the "understanding the client's personal and financial circumstances," or data gathering, part of the financial planning process?

5. List some important elements of a financial planning engagement letter.

6. What are some of the benefits a client receives from choosing to use a professional financial planner?

7. What is the job and economic outlook for the financial planning profession?

MULTIPLE-CHOICE PROBLEMS

A sample of multiple choice problems is provided below. Additional multiple choice problems are available at money-education.com by accessing the Student Practice Portal.

1. Raven recently came to your office for her second appointment after receiving your engagement letter. During the meeting you collect several documents from her including her prior year tax returns, estate planning documents, and investment statements and history. You also worked with her on identifying and prioritizing her goals and objectives. Which of the following is the next step in the financial planning process?
    a. Presenting the financial planning recommendations.
    b. Analyzing the client's current course of action and potential alternative courses of action.
    c. Implementing the financial planning recommendations.
    d. Developing the financial planning recommendations.

2. Your client, Jed, engaged you to help him with his financial situation. During the course of your meetings you sold Jed a $1,000,000 life insurance policy. Which part of the financial planning process were you engaged in?
    a. Analyzing the client's current course of action and potential alternative courses of action.
    b. Monitoring progress and updating.
    c. Developing the financial planning recommendations.
    d. Implementing the financial planning recommendations.

3. After meeting with your new client, Nala, you used a Monte Carlo simulation within your financial planning software to project the likelihood of meeting her retirement objective based on his current retirement plan contributions and investment portfolio allocation. Which part of the financial planning process were you engaged in?
    a. Monitoring progress and updating.
    b. Implementing the financial planning recommendations.
    c. Analyzing the client's current course of action and potential alternative courses of action.
    d. Developing the financial planning recommendations.

4. Thalmus, a local CFP® practitioner, recently met with one of his new clients, Merrell. During the course of the meeting Thalmus did the following things:
    1. Thalmus did not meet with Merrell until 10 minutes after the scheduled start time.
    2. In order to establish Merrell's confidence in him, Thalmus told Merrell the names of several well known clients that currently do business with him.
    3. Thalmus asked Merrell several questions regarding Merrell's family situation, hobbies, and activities.

    Which of these actions would be considered inappropriate?
    a. 3 only.
    b. 1 and 2.
    c. 2 and 3.
    d. 1, 2 and 3.

5. Reverend Lola Pak, a prospective client, came to your office for the first time today. Which is the most appropriate way to greet her?
    a. "Welcome to my office."
    b. "Welcome to my office, Ms. Pak."
    c. "Welcome to my office, Reverend Pak."
    d. "Welcome to my office, Lola."

> **Additional multiple choice problems are available at**
> *money-education.com* **by accessing the Student Practice Portal. Access requires**
> **registration of the title using the unique code at the front of the book.**

QUICK QUIZ EXPLANATIONS

Quick Quiz 1.1

1. True.
2. False. Emergency funding is considered a short-term goal, along with debt management. All of the other planning subjects are included in long-term goal planning.
3. True.
4. False. These items are external data information which can be obtained from education and professional reading. Internal data includes the client's pertinent family information, insurance portfolio, banking, investment, tax, retirement, and estate planning information.

2

INTERPERSONAL COMMUNICATION, BEHAVIORAL FINANCE & CLIENT PSYCHOLOGY

LEARNING OBJECTIVES

1. Explain the counseling theories and the schools of thought regarding communications.*
2. Explain the developmental, humanistic, and cognitive-behavioral schools of thought.
3. Identify the elements of communication.*
4. Describe nonverbal behavior or body language.*
5. Differentiate between active listening and passive listening.*
6. Describe reflective listening.*
7. Describe motivational interviewing.*
8. Describe open and closed questions.*
9. Describe ways to clarify or restate a client's statement.
10. Describe client data collection.
11. Explain "joining" and the need for building a trusting relationship with the client.*
12. Describe the concepts and theories behind behavioral finance.*
13. Discuss the assumptions and building blocks of traditional finance.
14. Describe the issues and questions unanswered by traditional finance.
15. Define behavioral finance.*
16. Identify the pyramid of assets and describe its mental accounting layers.
17. Describe what makes investors "normal" instead of "rational."
18. Describe patterns and types of cognitive biases.*
19. Define anchoring, confirmation bias, gambler's fallacy, herding, hindsight bias, overconfidence, overreaction, and prospect theory.*
20. Describe the Disposition Effect.*
21. Describe the adviser's role in monitoring cognitive biases.*
22. Analyze a client's degree of risk tolerance and loss aversion and ensure recommendations are consistent with a client's risk propensity, attitudes, composure (e.g. past behavior during market corrections), capacity, knowledge, and needs.*
23. Explain how a client's psychology, background, preferred learning style and values (socially conscious investor, etc.) impact the financial planning process.*
24. Explain how a client's values, including cultural and religious values and attitudes may impact their goals and the financial planning process.*
25. Describe how a client's psychology, such as their financial comfort zone, socialization, money beliefs, and past financial experiences and behaviors impact their objectives, goals, understanding, decision making and actions.*
26. Demonstrate how a planner can develop a relationship of honesty and trust in client interaction.*
27. Identify a client's motivation for achieving their financial goals.*
28. Explain to the client the consequences of a lack of transparency with spouse or family when making financial decisions.*
29. Identify areas of potential financial conflict between spouse and/or family.*
30. Communicate the importance of agreeing on financial goals and objectives with spouse and/or family.*

*Ties to CFP Certification Learning Objectives

LEARNING OBJECTIVES

31. Identify situations in which money may be used as a means of undue influence, control or abuse in relationships (e.g. power imbalances, financial abuse and financial enabling).*

32. Identify appropriate funds to help clients navigate an unanticipated financial emergency.*

33. Analyze how different types of financial or economic crises impact clients (e.g. market correction or economic decline).*

34. Demonstrate empathy, reliability, and competence to help clients navigate the implications of a crisis.*

Ties to CFP Certification Learning Objectives

INTRODUCTION

This chapter is organized into four main sections. The first section identifies theories and schools of thought for counselors. Knowing these schools of thought can place the adviser in a better position to communicate effectively with the client. The second section addresses communication tools and techniques for financial counselors. The third section discusses and examines the realm of what is referred to as "Behavioral Finance." Traditional or conventional wisdom about finance typically assumed that all investors participating in the market are "rational" machine-like beings. Yet, individuals are different, subject to errors in judgment and are guided or misguided by emotions. To put it simply, people are human. These two realms of financial knowledge will be compared and discussed. The fourth section goes beyond the investment-related concepts of behavioral finance to explore financial psychology and the application of financial therapy in the planning process. Many people like to consider themselves devoid of emotion when it comes to making decisions, especially financial decisions. In reality, emotion drives many decisions in life whether we are conscious of it or not. Emotional issues greatly influence our relationship with money and by extension, work, family members, and more. Ultimately, nearly every decision one makes involving money makes sense to them at the time based on their own life experiences and their psychological makeup. One's childhood, upbringing, and the economic period in which one was raised all impact how a person deals with and manages money.[1]

---

1. Ulrike Malmendier and Stefan Nagel, "Depression Babies: Do Macroeconomic Experiences Affect Risk Taking?*," *The Quarterly Journal of Economics* 126, no. 1 (2011): pp. 373-416, https://doi.org/10.1093/qje/qjq004.

COMMUNICATION WITH CLIENTS FROM A COUNSELING PERSPECTIVE: COUNSELING THEORIES AND SCHOOLS OF THOUGHT

Financial advisers serve to educate their clients on financial matters, identify financial goals or problems, make recommendations and monitor the client's progress. This relationship is that of counselor and client. As will be discussed later in this chapter, there has been a movement in recent times for the financial industry to be more in touch with psychology and sociology due to their effect and persuasiveness in financial matters. Therefore, when dealing with fundamentals of financial planning in the context of communication and counseling, a basic understanding of the different schools of counseling and therapy would benefit the adviser and, ultimately, the client. These counseling theories or schools of thought apply to the *adviser*, and what are the adviser's beliefs, strengths and style. For advisers to be effective, they must first understand from what perspective and school of thought they are most properly situated.

Key Concepts

1. Identify the three general schools of counseling.

2. What is the fundamental belief of the Developmental School of Thought?

3. What is the nature of the relationship between adviser and client in the different Schools of Thought?

A number of theories and models have been developed, investigated and studied so as to account for various aspects of human development and behavior. There are hundreds of models of counseling and therapy and hundreds of different techniques that are linked to these models.[2] Rather than provide an entire course in this area, this chapter provides a general overview of these counseling theories which will assist the later evaluation of communication tools and techniques for the financial planning adviser with clients.[3]

As explained and summarized by Professor MacCluskie, there are three general and noteworthy schools of counseling:

1. Developmental
2. Humanistic
3. Cognitive-Behavioral

These three areas emerged temporally in this same order and sequence in the 20th century.

The specific, numerous theories in each school of thought will not be discussed; however, the common elements of the theories that cluster within each school of thought will be briefly described. These general schools of thought can serve as a guide for the individual counselor's beliefs and style so as to aid the financial counselor in identifying a style that fits himself or herself and in developing and honing in on skills and techniques to make the planner a better counselor. Knowing these schools of thought may also help shape an understanding of client behavior and assist in defining the client's goals during the adviser-client relationship.

---

2. MacCluskie, Acquiring Counseling Skills: Integrating Theory, Multiculturalism, and Self-Awareness, Chapter 7, p. 181-182 (Pearson 2009). Kathryn C. MacCluskie, *Acquiring Counseling Skills: Integrating Theory, Multiculturalism, and Self-Awareness* (Upper Saddle River, NJ: Pearson/Merrill, 2010), 181-182

3. For a detailed look at the various theories and models in the subject of counseling and therapy, see text by MacCluskie.

The "Developmental" School of Thought

The Developmental school of thought, or the "**Developmental Paradigm**" as it will be referred to in this chapter, believes that human development occurs in stages over time. Relationships that are formed early in life become a template for establishing relationships in adulthood. As to emotions, the Developmental Paradigm assumes that all humans develop and progress in a predictable sequence. Disruptions, whether by trauma, incident or otherwise, at a particular stage of that individual's development will result in predictable problems, symptoms, and behavior. Much of the Developmental approach has its origin in and was influenced by Freudian psychoanalytic theory. Counseling in the Developmental Paradigm has an overall aspiration to recount or correct earlier, disrupted development to foster change in the client or the client's behavior. Once the client can resolve those earlier conflicts or disruptions, there is more understanding and self-awareness, thus allowing the client to grow.

For some counselors who follow the Developmental Paradigm, questions could play a larger role in the counseling process than they do for counselors who follow the Humanistic Paradigm (discussed in the next subsection). Questions should be used in moderation for Developmental counselors especially if the counselor is seeking to increase a client's awareness of the developmental tasks or issues associated with a presenting problem. For instance, if a client has had issues in the past with debt accumulation and the adviser has noticed that the client has overspent on personal items to compensate for an event that occurred in that client's earlier stage of life, then the questioning process should be done in moderation.

The "Humanistic" School of Thought

The **Humanistic Paradigm** is dominated by theorists whose models have their origins from a shared philosophical approach. Like the developmental approach, much of the Humanistic approach was influenced by Freudian psychoanalytic theory. For a client to grow, the relationship requires a transparent and genuine counselor. The adviser needs a philosophical stance that humankind is basically good and that people have the inherent capability of self-direction and growth under the right set of circumstances. A Humanistic counselor would define mental health as having congruent and aligned thoughts, feelings, and behavior. Goals in treatment are centered on establishing congruence and acceptance of personal responsibility.

Part of achieving this "congruence" is that treatment emphasizes one's experience of the present moment, freedom of choice, and keeping in touch with oneself. It is therapeutic in and of itself to have an authentic, human relationship between the client and counselor. For example, if an adviser is more comfortable with a close, more friendly relationship with clients (as opposed to a more professional and distant relationship), then the adviser may be more inclined to operate under the Humanistic Paradigm. Indeed, the alliance between the counselor and client is extremely important for Humanistic counselors and is the basis of the treatment or plan of action.

The majority of the Humanistic theories view clients as experts on themselves. Accordingly, counselors who subscribe to the Humanistic Paradigm are disinclined to use questioning with any frequency. When questioning is used, the emphasis is likely to be more weighted on process and feelings rather than details or content. In fact, a humanistic counselor would help clients articulate for themselves what their questions are.

Applying the Humanistic Paradigm to the financial adviser-client relationship, the adviser may consider spending time with the client on discovering what goals will help the client achieve congruence, allow for self-growth, and identify some of the client's feelings about money and tendencies to cognitive biases.

The "Cognitive-Behavioral" School of Thought

In the **Cognitive-Behavioral Paradigm**, humans are beings that are subject to the same learning principles that were established in animal research. The basic principles of classical and operant conditioning are assumed to account for an individual's behavior and understandings throughout their lives. The quintessential example of "classical conditioning" is Ivan Pavlov's initial research conducted on dogs. Meanwhile, B.F. Skinner's related model on "operant conditioning" posited that all behavior is subject to the principles of reinforcement by environmental conditions that reinforce or fail to reinforce a given behavior. Self-talk refers to that ongoing internal conversation one has with oneself that can influence feelings. Self-talk and certain behavior can be reinforced and persist. The counselor's challenge lies in performing a sound evaluation of how reinforcers are maintaining problematic self-talk and behaviors. The counselor is the expert in the Cognitive-Behavioral Paradigm, but the counselor and client have a working alliance where the client must be actively engaged.

For Cognitive-Behavioralists, the questioning process is most prevalent because the counseling process is considerably more directive than it is in either of the other two paradigms. The counselor in the Cognitive-Behavioral Paradigm must identify behavioral excesses and inadequacies, identify their source of reinforcement for these excesses and inadequacies, and try to manipulate these reinforcers to change the client's behavior and thought process. In short, a Cognitive-Behavioral counselor is searching for specific material and information from the client so as to design and implement a counseling intervention or plan that is consistent with Cognitive-Behavioral theory.

If the financial adviser is more attuned to the Cognitive-Behavioral Paradigm, then the adviser may discover goals of the client and may be able to point out, during the relationship, specific areas where the client has succeeded on certain financial issues. The adviser may spend more time on content and positive results that will reinforce the client's belief in the process, in the client's financial behavior, and in the client's trust in the adviser. Cognitive-Behavioral advisers would also want to reinforce positive financial feedback during the plan monitoring stage of the financial planning process which occurs after the recommendation and implementation stages.

Exhibit 2.1 | Comparison of Counseling Paradigms[4]

Theory Group	Nature of Relationship	Emphasis of Treatment (Prominent Themes)	Microskills Most Likely to be Used Frequently
Developmental	• Moderately directive. • Alliance is important. • Provides client a chance to resolve emotional needs not met during earlier development.	• Healthy development. • Focus on past experiences in family of origin and relationship to present difficulties. • Resolution of conflict. • Understanding and self-awareness.	• Active listening. • Client observation. • Paraphrasing. • Feeling reflection. • Supportive challenging. • Reflection of meaning.
Humanistic	• Varies from nondirective (person-centered, existential) to highly directive. • Alliance is extremely important; is the basis of the treatment (person-centered, existential).	• Experiencing present moment. • Accepting personal responsibility. • Emphasis on freedom of choice. • Authenticity, fully in touch with oneself.	• Active listening. • Client observation. • Feeling reflection. • Reflection of meaning. • Supportive challenging.
Cognitive-Behavioral	• Highly directive. • Alliance only important to extent client feels engaged to participate in assignments.	• Identification of behavioral excesses and inadequacies. • Identification of reinforcers. • Manipulation of the reinforcers to change the behavior and thought process.	• Active listening. • Questioning. • Reflection of meaning. • Supportive challenging.

In conclusion, the adviser can better serve the client by understanding what counseling school of thought is most suited to the adviser. Of course, there may be times that the client's style may necessitate a change to a different school of thought or combination of any two or all three. These are decisions that should be made by the adviser using his or her best judgment.

---

4. Id. at p. 156, Table 11.1. This chart was compiled and crafted by Professor MacCluskie in her textbook.

COMMUNICATION TOOLS AND TECHNIQUES FOR FINANCIAL COUNSELORS

Communication is the key factor in the financial adviser-client relationship. The adviser must determine the client's goals and craft a plan designed to reach those goals. The adviser must also educate the client so as to encourage the client to act in a way consistent with the financial plan. Great advice can be given, but if the advice is not followed, then the client's best interests are not served. The adviser must get to know the client in a way that will foster a healthy relationship of trust, so that the correct information is gathered by the adviser and the best advice is followed by the client. While the adviser cannot do some or all of the actual tasks of implementation for the client, having a good relationship with effective communication can be persuasive to and positive for the client.

⋮≡ *Key Concepts*

1. What are the fundamental elements of communication?

2. Identify non-verbal gestures that substitute for or reinforce verbal expressions.

3. Identify situations where the non-verbal communication contradicts the verbal communication.

Financial counselors and advisers must establish and maintain the adviser-client relationship based on their ability to communicate. Proper and practical communication skills and techniques in financial counseling can aid the financial planning adviser. This section of this chapter will identify and discuss effective techniques and skills that will contribute to successful counseling strategies. These techniques and skills are vital to financial advisers' efforts to understand their clients and what their clients' perceptions of their own needs and objectives are.

Elements of Communication

Human communication is comprised of fundamental elements. Societal groups use a system of signs in their communication process. A sign could be a word, object, gesture, tone, quality, image, substance, or other reference according to a code of shared meaning among those who use that sign for communication purposes. While people consciously use language in one way, there are times when the language can be used subliminally or subconsciously. Language can be used to manipulate, conceal or withhold what is really meant or felt by the person speaking. While spoken words are signs used in communication, there are also nonverbal gestures, actions, or other expressions that are not verbal but can substitute or reinforce verbal expressions.

A good example of a purely nonlinguistic but highly expressive system of sign communication is grief. Crying can be a sign of grief, but there are less common instances where it could be a sign of joy. Context is very important with verbal and nonverbal communication. People all experience times when somebody is providing one signal verbally and their body language is providing a different signal. Such communications among people are complex and have a wide range.

While financial advisers obtain a lot of quantitative information from clients, including checkbooks, financial statements, and other documents, the financial adviser should strive to build a rapport with the client, which may help to recognize more of the value or truth of information that clients communicate through verbal, nonverbal, or a combination of these messages.

Nonverbal Behavior or "Body Language"

Nonverbal cues, or body language, can communicate feelings and attitudes from the client to the financial adviser. **Nonverbal behaviors** are mainly provided from the body and the voice. Body position and body movement are important, while voice tone and voice pitch are also telling.[5] When observing nonverbal behavior, the literature stresses that the "observer" should try to notice the ways the body communicates and whether or not the body is in agreement with what is being said. The positioning of the client's body is an early sign for the adviser to observe.

For instance, good posture by the client may indicate positive self-esteem, whereas poor posture may signal a lack of self-esteem. Sitting comfortably can mean that one is relaxed. Leaning slightly forward is a sign of interested involvement. Slouching or slumping may indicate less interest or a lack of trust in the counselor. If arms are uncrossed, the client can be seen as relaxed and open, whereas crossed arms may indicate that the client is defensive, disinterested, or closed-off.

The movements of the client's body could also indicate thoughts or emotions of the client. If the client frequently moves indicating a physical discomfort or perhaps emotional dislike, the counselor should take note of these movements to extrapolate those cues to information that may be learned at a later time. Verbal statements may indicate they are not nervous about something, while at the same time, they may be rocking back and forth or biting their nails. People are prone to say what they think is to be expected, and all the while may not notice that they are actually communicating something quite different through their body language.

Gestures and facial expressions are also very important signs and cues for the listener. Eye contact is an indicator of one being engaged in a conversation where they are peering into the counselor's eyes with interest and openness. There may be times when a client's eyes are shifty and unable to remain on the counselor, and this could indicate distrust, fear, shyness, or even anxiety, something the counselor may wish to explore later on through questions.

As to voice communication, tone and pitch may also indicate feelings of the speaker that at times can be at odds with what is being said. Things can be said softer or louder, which can emphasize or de-emphasize a point. Of course, shouting very loudly could indicate anger or hostility, whereas fear, nervousness, or shyness can be exuded through somebody who speaks very softly. When detecting a change in pitch in one's voice, the listener should observe and try to determine which vocal qualities are natural to a particular client so as to recognize the variations when they occur. These variations can be important clues of strong emotions that may affect the client's motivation, biases, goals, or needs.

---

5. An excellent article in this area of communication was authored by Professor Dale Johnson, entitled "Practical Communications Skills and Techniques in Financial Counseling Part I," The Financial Planner (July 1982), where Professor Johnson highlights the four types of nonverbal signs of meaning: body position, body movement, voice tone and voice pitch.

There can be times that what is being said is opposite to the tone, pitch, or gestures being made or exuded by the speaker. When the indicators cross or are different, this is probably a time when the financial adviser should speak up. It is one thing if all behavior supports what is being said, but when they are at odds or give mixed signals, it is the responsibility of the adviser to ask more questions and to delve into the issues. If there is an incongruent statement with nonverbal behavior, it could be a sign of something else, something that went awry in the prior financial life or personal life of the client, and the planner or adviser ought to seek that out and get to the source of the issue. The adviser should investigate further through questions and learning more information in order to clarify why the adviser perceives one thing and hears another.

Even When Listening, You are a Speaker

Advisers must also be mindful of the verbal and nonverbal cues that they may be communicating to the client. During the relationship, especially in the beginning, there will be times where the client is sizing up the adviser, checking the trust factor, deciding whether to heed the advice, and has other accompanying thoughts. These modes of communication will have their own effects on the client.

In short, one of the main responsibilities of the financial adviser is to extract the goals and desires of the client. This task is accomplished through verbal and nonverbal communication. The adviser must not only listen to the words, but understand clients' conceptions of themselves. The adviser must diligently note the nonverbal cues and the signs being exuded by the client during the counseling sessions and meetings.

Active Listening Versus Passive Listening

The financial adviser's relationship with the client should be one dominated by "active listening" on the part of the adviser, not passive listening.

Passive Listening

Passive listening is listening in the normal or usual conversation or conversational setting to which most people are accustomed at seminars, in class, at social gatherings, or at sermons. Passive listening is invoked when communication rests entirely on another person, and the person receiving the information sits back and listens. The effectiveness of the listening being accomplished by the passive listener is subject to many obstacles, such as interruptions, daydreaming, checks to one's personal handheld device, bathroom or refreshment breaks, and the like. There are numerous obstacles or opportunities to screen out information by the passive listener, depending on the listener's mood or depending on what is going on or where their interests lie. One of the most reported interruptions or disruptions in passive listening is when the listener is thinking about what he or she may say in response to what is being discussed while the listener should instead be listening.

> **≔ Key Concepts**
>
> 1. Define passive listening.
> 2. Define active listening.
> 3. Describe reflective listening.
> 4. Define open and closed questions.
> 5. Explain how thinking of a response can hamper listening.

Active Listening

Active listening, on the other hand, requires the listener's undivided attention. Active listening involves concentration on what the speaker is saying. The listener must put aside irrelevant thoughts. The adviser should not think about "what to say next," but should be listening and observing the speaker's body language. The listening adviser should assume that the data and information conveyed is important, while sorting and sifting various items into categories. To reveal the listener's interest, the listener may nod occasionally, provide follow up comments with brief responses such as "yes," "I understand," or "go on," and smile or use other facial expressions.

The feedback provided during active listening should result in the speaker continuing to speak and provide information. The feedback should not interrupt the speaker. Active listening requires determination and concentration, so that basically everything the speaker says is relevant and interesting.

In short, advisers should strive to be active listeners throughout their sessions with clients. While it is best if the client is engaged in active listening when it comes time for input by the adviser and recommendations to the client, the adviser cannot control the actions of the client; the adviser can control his or her actions, though.

Reflective Listening

Reflective listening is similar to active listening and occurs when the receiver devotes reflective attention to both the content being said and the feelings that are being expressed (or in some cases, that the client is having difficulty expressing or articulating). It is a demonstration of empathy.

In his best-selling book *The 7 Habits of Highly Effective People*, Stephen Covey advises that we seek first to understand, and then to be understood. While most people listen with the intent to reply, reflective listening requires that we listen only with the intent to understand what is being said. There is no judgment or personal reaction on the part of the receiver, and the receiver will check in periodically to clarify that they have understood correctly the facts of what is being said, the client's thoughts and feelings about what is being said, and what the client is seeking.

Example 2.1

Client: I'm so tired of trying to have the conversation with my elderly mom about the need for someone to come to the home to help care for her. She's never been willing to accept help from anyone. I give up. I just don't care anymore.

Financial Adviser: I can certainly understand your feelings of frustration and worry about your mom's safety and quality of life. Let me make sure I understand the situation correctly: you want to make sure your mom can continue to live where she is currently, and you have tried many times to talk to your mom about her health and safety, but she just doesn't seem receptive to having others, perhaps strangers or even friends or family, come into her home to assist her. Do I understand correctly?

Notice in the example above that the adviser did not interject with a story of how she got her own mom to accept help, or pass judgment on the client for wanting to give up on their mom. She kept the focus on the client and on understanding the client's situation and feelings.

Motivational Interviewing

When working with clients toward achieving financial goals, the financial adviser will often experience situations where behavioral changes are necessary in order for clients to achieve financial well-being. **Motivational interviewing (MI)** is a communication technique originally developed to support patients with substance abuse disorders, but which is now used in numerous other applications (e.g., medical care, education, sports, parenting, and financial planning). The focus is on overcoming ambivalence to change by guiding the client to:

1. express the desire and reason a change is needed (their motivation for change),
2. discover their ability to change, and
3. commit to making the change. Ultimately, change will not occur until the client both makes the decision to change and is ready to take action (see **Exhibit 2.4**) later in this chapter).

While financial advisers may have a tendency to lean toward offering advice (e.g., "you must change this pattern of overspending or you will run out of money in retirement"), motivational interviewing avoids doing so and, instead, conveys empathy and acceptance and guides the client to discover their own reasons for making change.

Exhibit 2.2 | Four Key Principles of Motivational Interviewing[6]

Principle	Description
Partnership	MI is a collaborative process.
Evocation	MI draws out the client's priorities, values, and wisdom to explore reasons for change and support success.
Acceptance	The MI practitioner is nonjudgmental, seeks to understand the client's perspectives and experiences, expresses empathy, highlights strengths, and respects a client's right to make informed choices about changing or not changing.
Compassion	The MI practitioner actively promotes and prioritizes clients' welfare and wellbeing in a selfless manner.

Using Open and Closed Questions

During counseling sessions, the use of proper questions is vital for the relationship between the financial adviser and the client to succeed. The focus here is on the form and content of the questions. Questions are an important tool for the adviser.

An **open question** is one that will result in a person answering with a lengthy response, whereas a **closed question** seeks a response that is very specific and commonly involves an answer that can be accomplished with a single word or two. One may be inclined to think that, during a counseling session, open questions are better than closed questions because the client is talking. That may not necessarily be true. In some situations, closed questions are preferable or necessary.

Open questions usually begin with words such as how, what, when, where, who and why. Closed questions often lead with "is, are, do, did, could, would, or have." Sometimes open questions result in a client continuing to talk and providing much material that may or may not be needed. Nonetheless, whether the questions are open or closed, asking questions is vital, and it directs a client into an area to which the adviser needs the counseling session to go or proceed. The adviser must assess the need for an open discussion on a subject, and if so, an open question is needed. However, if the point has been made and only a clarification needed, then a closed question is in order.

---

6. Derived from https://motivationalinterviewing.org/understanding-motivational-interviewing

Open or closed questions may be structured as leading questions in which the question leads the client to a desired or predetermined conclusion or which leads the client's thoughts in a particular direction. For example, the adviser might ask "Don't you think that inflation will increase in the future?" Stated this way, the client is led to the conclusion that inflation should be expected to increase. Likewise, asking a client how she feels about "the benevolent goal of making a contribution to a charity" leads the client to believe he should feel good about doing so, versus simply asking the client how she feels about "making a contribution to a charity." To lead a client's response in a particular direction, an adviser might ask "did you have any issues with investing in stocks in the past," which leads the client to focus on the negative aspects of investing in stocks; or the adviser might ask "what did you find attractive about investing in stocks in the past" to lead the client to focus on the positive aspects of investing in stocks. While leading questions can reveal beneficial information when used appropriately, adviser's must take care to avoid using them in a manner which may viewed as manipulative.

Another form of question which must be used with caution is the "why" question. While "why" questions may help the adviser gain an understanding of the client's motives, the "why" question may be ill-advised because it could have limited benefit for the client. It could place the client in a position of having to justify what was done, and that could put the client in a defensive posture.

Example 2.2

When a client comes in for an initial first session, it is necessary for the counselor to gather information. When establishing an adviser-client relationship, a few pointed well-phrased questions may aid in relationship development more than a lengthy series of questions. Here is an example of an opening:

ADVISER: Thanks for coming in today. Let's start by talking about what brought you here to meet with me.

CLIENT: I found out that I have just inherited a portion of an estate. I am not sure what to do with it.

ADVISER: I can help, but since you just received this information, can you tell me what are some of your goals with this?

Overly open-ended questions are fine to set the client at ease, but they may lead to the client recounting what has happened in his or her life in the recent past. While that may be an intended result, the disadvantage is that overly open-ended questions may take the focus of discussion in a direction that does not really pertain to the tasks at hand.

In the alternative, an adviser can begin a session with a question that immediately focuses the client's attention in a relevant direction.

Example 2.3

ADVISER: At our last meeting, we focused on some things you could do to improve your debt elimination. Were you able to try any of them?

CLIENT: Yes, I tried a few.

ADVISER: Please tell me about that.

Open and closed questions are effective tools for the adviser. They can be used through the adviser-client relationship to improve communication. The adviser must learn which methods and questions to use at appropriate times throughout the planning process to accomplish specific objectives.

Clarifying or Restating a Client's Statement

In the event that a client is trying to communicate a message that is not clear, then the adviser will want to clarify what the client is trying to communicate. It could also be that the client is exuding verbal or nonverbal behavior that is inconsistent with what is being said. If there is an ambiguous meaning, it is best to clarify the statement from the client to insure accuracy or to clear up the ambiguity. Clarifying a client's statement is part of the process of feedback under active listening.

Example 2.4

Frank, a client, indicates that he feels he could obtain a 20% return on some commodities that he frequently trades. When the adviser, Billie Jean, hears this message, she denotes overconfidence from Frank. Billie Jean attempts to understand the statement, but the body language of Frank shows that he is fidgeting, looking at the floor, and biting his nails. This seems inconsistent with overconfidence. This leaves Billie Jean feeling that she should ask an open-ended question to allow Frank to elaborate on the remark.

The follow-up statement from Billie Jean would be something like: "That sounds to me like you are very confident in the commodities market." At that point, Billie Jean can try to understand or clarify the message being conveyed by Frank. Frank's message may not be necessarily overconfidence in the commodities market, but he might be indicating that within a certain area of his portfolio, he is willing to take more risks. This could be a sign that Billie Jean may consider his portfolio in different mental accounting layers and not as a whole. This could lead Billie Jean to assess Frank's overall risk and returns in his portfolio and to check for proper diversification.[7]

This approach is just another way of determining the accuracy of adviser perceptions and getting more information to enhance understanding about the client. By paraphrasing, the adviser may verify or correct an understanding of what the client is communicating. Some of the key tools to use when clarifying client statements include repeating a key word or phrase that was used by the client. Some authors in the literature advocate a direct method to clarify a statement or, at times, suggest a more diplomatic method of asking questions that are pertinent to the statement. When asking relevant questions, the closed questions can help confirm some beliefs that the adviser has understood, whereas open questions may help the counselor obtain more information.

At times, a client will say something that is confusing to the adviser or it will seem to have ambiguous meaning. Where a paraphrase could be helpful, it is just easier and makes more sense to ask a question that clarifies what the client is trying to communicate.

---

7. The mental accounting layers and principles of the Behavioral Portfolio Theory are discussed later in this chapter.

Example 2.5

CLIENT: Well, I was an investor in a joint venture with three other people. Things were not going so well, but we were breaking even. Then, suddenly two of the investors had a blow up. I was mad about the whole thing, and ended up losing $20,000.

ADVISER: Do you mean that the joint venture fell apart because of this blow up?

CLIENT: No, we all decided it was not worth the effort and stress, so we mutually agreed to shut it down and limit our losses.

The adviser must assess the accuracy of his or her perception, and if needed, get more information to enhance his or her understanding. The optimal time for a clarification is *before* leaving a subject matter area during the session.

Proper questions can be effective in accomplishing clarification or checkout. Continuing with the dialogue example above and adding a question could assist in understanding or clarifying what was conveyed by the client.

Example 2.6

Continuing with the dialogue example from above:

CLIENT: Well, I was an investor in a joint venture with three other people. Things were not going so well, but we were breaking even. Then, suddenly two of the investors had a blow up. I was mad about the whole thing, and ended up losing $20,000.

ADVISER: Do you mean that the joint venture fell apart because of this blow up?

CLIENT: No, we all decided it was not worth the effort and stress, so we mutually agreed to shut it down and limit our losses.

ADVISER: So basically, two of the other investors had a disagreement, not about you, and based on the fact of breaking even plus the internal problems, the whole group decided to shut it down and limit losses? Did I understand this correctly?

Quick Quiz 2.3

1. It is better not to make any gestures to the speaker when an adviser is practicing active listening.
   a. True
   b. False

2. Open-ended questions are answerable with lengthy responses.
   a. True
   b. False

3. Active listening, reflective listening, and mirroring are communication tools that help the adviser to join with the client.
   a. True
   b. False

False, True, True.

The adviser must also sharpen the counseling focus as to content and as to process. In the dialogue above, the clarifying questions up to this point have focused on the content of the client's concerns and the details of the story. The questions sharpened the focus on the sequence of events. That same discussion about the client's concerns would go in a completely different direction had the adviser asked questions that emphasized the process rather than the content. Here is an example of how that might unfold:

Example 2.7

Continuing with the same dialogue example:

CLIENT: Well, I was an investor in a joint venture with three other people. Things were not going so well, but we were breaking even. Then, suddenly two of the investors had a blow up. I was mad about the deal, and ended up losing $20,000.

ADVISER: What specifically were you mad about at the time?

CLIENT: I was mad at myself for getting involved in the whole thing. I just did not want to stay in a venture where our chances at making a profit were limited and there was fighting.

ADVISER: It seems like you wanted to rid yourself of a strained situation and limit your losses in terms of money and in terms of stress. I can understand that. Let's discuss what you believe would be a "good situation" in comparison to that one. Could that be helpful?

As seen in the latter part of the dialogue above, the adviser focused on more process questions than content. Either way, the clarifying or "checkout" type of questions aided in the fact gathering process and in learning about the client. For instance, it was learned that the client, Frank, was willing to limit his losses in the form of stress and money. This will help the adviser understand the client's goals and priorities later.

The above dialogue example also illustrates that the emotional underpinnings of many of the client's statements are very important. They not only help to identify priorities, needs, and goals, but as will be discussed later in this chapter, they may shed light on some of the client's leanings, biases, thoughts, and feelings towards money, the market, and other relevant considerations. It is important for the adviser to be mindful of focusing on content and focusing on process when needed. As a result, by repeating or clarifying comments from a client, the financial adviser may be in a better position to understand the goals, priorities, emotions, and needs of the client to know what the client really wants.

Client Data Collection

Collecting the client's data is more than just reviewing bank statements and papers. The adviser needs to learn about who the client is and what are the client's personal and financial goals, needs, and priorities. These goals, needs, and priorities are relevant and, in fact, are likely the very reason the client is consulting the adviser in the first place.

By way of example, the CFP Board's Financial Planning Practice Standards require that the CFP® professional explore the client's values, attitudes, expectations, and time horizons as they affect the client's goals. The process of mutually defining the client's goals is essential in determining what activities may be necessary to proceed with the client engagement. Personal values and attitudes shape the client's goals and objectives, along with the priorities placed on them. Thus, it is very important for the adviser to be able to understand the client's values and attitudes along with the goals and objectives.

Do not be misguided by the word "data." It is not merely the client's net worth that needs to be understood; it is the client's self-worth and goals that need to understood. During the data gathering process, there may be unrealistic goals and objectives that the client may have. If these goals and objectives are unrealistic, then the adviser must explain to the client how or why they are unrealistic.

The information the adviser is gathering is not just numbers, statements, and tax returns. It is also about the beliefs, attitudes, and desires of the client, and includes information about the client's relationships with family members and the dynamics between family members. This type of data gathering is just as important, if not more important, than the gathering of quantitative information and documents.

When getting into personal information and personal goals, sometimes clients may be reluctant to share some information. Asking questions when entering such an area can either diminish the relationship or exacerbate the client's difficulty. For instance, if the adviser notices that the client has omitted some key details in a story or event, the adviser must carefully handle the issue. One way to handle the predicament is through trying a direct question of "What parts have you left out?" While this could be seen as confrontational, using the phrase "left out" provides the client an implied permission to admit to the information that he or she is reluctant to share. However, if the client denies that any information was omitted, the adviser must cease the small confrontation, accept the client's denial, and go on to the next subject matter area.

The quantitative stage of data acquisition is where the adviser receives relevant quantitative information and documents pertaining to the client's financial resources, obligations and personal situation. This is obtained directly from the client or other sources, such as interviews, questionnaires, client records, and other documents. The adviser must communicate to the client a reliance on the completeness and accuracy of the information provided. This information will impact later on conclusions and recommendations.

Appropriate Use of Questionnaires

There is a lot of information that needs to be provided by the client and extracted by the adviser, making questionnaires a valuable and efficient tool for gathering information. Questionnaires provide quick and easy information. They ensure that subject areas are not omitted or forgotten by the adviser. Questionnaires can be very thorough and cover many areas that must be identified during the acquisition of quantitative information from the client. In addition, questionnaires provided by financial planning software programs are typically designed to gather information in the order in which the information is entered into the software program, creating an efficient flow of data entry when using the software. However, especially in the early stages of the relationship including the initial meeting, long questionnaires are considered to be less desirable if the adviser does not know the client well. While getting acquainted and establishing the relationship with the client as a person, the adviser needs to get to know the client and understand the client's goals and desires through interpersonal communication.

If a prospect or new client must bring wills, trusts, tax returns, and other financial statements to the initial meeting, the message sent may be that their belongings or their balance sheet is your main concern, and not the person that the adviser is counseling. The first, or initial, meetings should send a message to the client that the client is important - that the client *is* the subject matter. The relevant question throughout the relationship is how do we make a recommendation and plan for the client in a way that maximizes his or her best interests?

Personal checklists are useful tools to assist with identifying a client's values, life goals, and feelings toward specific financial aspects of the client's life. A short survey or questionnaire is certainly appropriate prior to or during the initial meeting to provide a foundation from which the meeting can progress.

Notably, during the establishment of the financial adviser-client relationship and during the data gathering process, the counseling relationship inherently has an imbalance of power between the client and counselor. Counselors hold power in that they are being sought out for professional services. Financial advisers are in positions of trust and must be cautious not to inadvertently misuse their power and must refrain from wielding a disproportionate amount of the power in interactions with clients. Instead, financial advisers should respect the client's position, hold the client's interest above that of the adviser, and communicate effectively to realize the client's goals.

Developing a Relationship of Trust with the Client

The planning process, including gathering of sensitive information, will proceed more smoothly when the planner has taken steps to build rapport with, and establish trust with, the client. In the mental health field, making a connection with the client and establishing a trusting relationship is referred to as **joining** with the client. Klontz, Kahler, and Klontz assert that establishing a relationship of trust "is as important to a client's financial health as the specifics of an estate plan or the performance of a portfolio."[8]

Communication skills are paramount to building trust. The use of reflective listening emphasizes to the client that the adviser understands what the client is trying to say and affirms for the adviser that they have correctly interpreted the client's message.

Mirroring (a.k.a. matching or pacing) is another communication skill that planners can utilize to help foster trust and create rapport. Mirroring occurs when the planner synchronizes his or her verbal and nonverbal behavior, including body language, gestures, breathing (fast or slow, deep or shallow), and language and voice quality, with those of the client. Mirroring helps to create rapport by signaling affirmation. It tells the client "I like you and agree with who and what you are." Advisers should keep in mind, though, that there is a difference between mirroring and mimicking (imitating).

The financial adviser must reinforce to the client that the client and his or her goals are important to the adviser. Before this can happen, the client must first discover what is truly important to them. An adviser who immediately tries to use technical expertise to fix the client's problems before really getting to know the client is unlikely to be successful in establishing trust. Yes, it is important that the client trust the planner's competency, but ultimately the client must trust that the planner is genuinely interested in her and in helping her achieve financial health. This occurs through active listening and through the use of open-ended questions such as "what is most important to you for us to discuss today?" When the planner engages in active and reflective listening, the client knows that she has been heard and feels valued, allowing the client to explore and set her own agenda.

Equally as important is for the adviser to avoid seeming judgmental and, instead, maintain unconditional positive regard for the client. Clients come from many different backgrounds, cultures, and religions, and have had different life experiences than the adviser, which may cause them to have views that are different from those of the adviser. Unconditional positive regard requires the counselor to value and respect the client regardless of what the client says or does in the course of the financial planning process (an exception applies if the client is suggesting that the adviser assist with something that is illegal or unethical). The effect of such positive regard is to make the client feel appreciated and understood. The caring attitude will also encourage communication and will help to overcome obstacles.

---

8. Brad Klontz, Rick Kahler, and Ted Klontz, *Facilitating Financial Health: Tools for Financial Planners, Coaches, and Therapists*, 2nd ed. (Erlanger, KY: The National Underwriter Company, 2016).

Many clients experience deep emotions (e.g., shame or worship) around money, and the adviser must avoid pointing out to clients what they have done wrong or what they should have done differently. Instead, the planner should make it clear that the planner is able, and has the desire, to help. While clients may be doing something that seems irrational to the planner, somewhere in the client's psyche, whether conscious or not, it makes perfect sense to the client. The client made the appointment to see the adviser, which a positive step toward change, and chastising their past behaviors is counterproductive to facilitating positive changes.

Finally, to establish trust, the financial adviser must demonstrate integrity. Integrity refers to the quality of having strong moral principles and ethics. Establishing a relationship of mutual trust and respect will allow the client and planner the best opportunity to work together to achieve the clients goals.

CONCEPTS AND THEORIES BEHIND BEHAVIORAL FINANCE

Introduction to Behavioral Finance

Before understanding the relatively new area "Behavioral Finance," there must first be an understanding of the more established conventional financial theory, which is known as "Traditional Finance." **Traditional Finance** is also described in the literature as "Modern Portfolio Theory," though some of the concepts of the theory are not necessarily modern and have been subject to much debate and change over recent decades.

Key Concepts

1. Identify the building blocks of Traditional Finance.

2. Explain what Behavioral Finance assumes.

3. Compare what determines returns under Traditional Finance versus Behavioral Finance.

Traditional Finance, or Modern Portfolio Theory, was created and developed during the 1950s and 1960s when a more objective and scientific view of economics and financial markets existed. The development of Traditional Finance provided focus and attention on relevant facts and information about markets, industries, and companies, while having streamlined information that was useful and available for comparison.

More specifically, Traditional Finance extracted information from the markets and made the information narrow, objective, and standardized. This was accomplished with much success through the introduction of scientific method into finance. This was a ground-breaking development, and it helped breathe life into financial market analysis and aided investors and those participating in the market at a time when some may have been intimidated by or felt ignorant of available market information or financial data. The concepts of Traditional Finance and the scientific calculations that developed with it helped synthesize a wealth of information. In an area where there was a vast amount of data, information, and numbers, it aided investors with information akin to a proverbial financial assembly line. To explain this further, the four basic premises of Traditional Finance are discussed.

Assumptions and Building Blocks of Traditional Finance

Traditional Finance is premised on four basic premises:
1. Investors are Rational
2. Markets are Efficient
3. The Mean-Variance Portfolio Theory Governs
4. Returns are Determined by Risk (Beta)

The Rational Investor

Merton Miller and Franco Modigilani (1961) made some significant declarations or assumptions about investors - that they are "rational."[9] The rational investor, it was assumed, preferred more wealth as compared to less wealth. It was also assumed that rational investors were never confused by the manner or form of wealth.

To provide an example of how rational investors are never confused by the form of wealth, a rational investor would be considered to be indifferent or uncaring if a profit is realized by a dividend declared by a company versus if the same profit is realized by selling the stock at a gain. The source of the wealth is not important to the rational investor. The thing that is important to the rational investor is that more value was obtained, or more money was realized or earned.

Efficient Markets

The second assumption in the Traditional Finance framework is that financial markets are considered to be "efficient."[10] This market theory has, at its core, the belief that, at any given time, a stock's share price in the market incorporates and reflects all relevant information about that stock. Stocks are deemed at all times to trade at their fair value on stock exchanges, thus preventing investors from buying undervalued stocks or selling overvalued stocks. In other words, there are no "mispricings" in an efficient market. If there are truly no mispricings, then it is impossible, as the theory goes, to "beat" or "outperform" the market. If it is true that outperforming the overall stock market is impossible, then investors are forced to acquire riskier investments in order to realize higher returns. The activity, inaction, or interaction of all hypothetical rational investors combines into the market as a whole.

When combining all rational investors into the "marketplace," the market is then seen as a "rational market" where stock prices are equal to their intrinsic value. Intrinsic value is the underlying value of a security or stock when considering future cash flows and the riskiness of the security.[11] Intrinsic values, in an efficient market, would therefore be determined by an analysis of reasonable expected cash flows and of the risk associated with those cash flows. According to Traditional Finance proponents, most, if not all, of the other information about the market would be irrelevant or considered to be "noise." Noise aside, if a market is truly efficient in that stock prices are equal to the fundamental or intrinsic value of the stock, then that market cannot be beaten.

Another view, though softer than pure market efficiency, is an "unbeatable" market. An unbeatable market may allow for the generation of excess returns, including times of temporary overvaluation or undervaluation (*i.e.*, mispricings). An overvaluation (*i.e.*, a "bubble") can occur, but such occurrences are rare and seen as anomalies that do not present consistent opportunities for excess returns. Without consistent excess returns, the market is considered "unbeatable," though not truly "efficient."

---

9. Merton H. Miller and Franco Modigliani, "Dividend Policy, Growth, and the Valuation of Shares," *The Journal of Business* 34, no. 4 (1961): pp. 411-433, https://doi.org/10.1086/294442.
10. Eugene F. Fama, "The Behavior of Stock-Market Prices," *The Journal of Business* 38, no. 1 (1965): pp. 34-105, https://doi.org/10.1086/294743.; Eugene F. Fama, "Random Walks in Stock Market Prices," *Financial Analysts Journal* 21, no. 5 (1965): pp. 55-59, https://doi.org/10.2469/faj.v21.n5.55.; Eugene F. Fama, "Efficient Capital Markets: A Review of Theory and Empirical Work," *The Journal of Finance* 25, no. 2 (1970): pp. 383-417, https://doi.org/10.2307/2325486.
11. See Chapter 9 of this textbook, discussing intrinsic value in more detail.

The Mean-Variance Portfolio Theory Governs

The third assumption essential to the realm of Traditional Finance is that investors, as computer-like as they are, follow the Mean-Variance Portfolio Theory faithfully and tailor their portfolios to comply with it constantly. Harry Markowitz is the father of the Mean-Variance Portfolio Theory, as seen in his works in 1952 and 1959, which officially fostered in the process of scientific method into the world of finance.[12] Hypotheses were made, rigorous number crunching and empirical studies would follow, and the scientific assembly line for finance was born. Each question or thought about a company or the economy would invoke a common retort by Traditional Finance proponents, with the retort simply questioning the company's asset price.

Mean-Variance Portfolio Theory spawned the introduction by William Sharpe in 1964 of the Capital Asset Pricing Model ("CAPM") (defined in the next section). Mean-Variance investors choose portfolios by viewing and evaluating mean (averages) and variance. Variance in this sense is the range of expected difference between a projected return and an actual return.

Risk Yields Expected Returns

The fourth and final assumption from Traditional Finance deals squarely with risk. Risk, in this decision-making process, is measured by "Beta." Beta is a concept borrowed from the CAPM. The CAPM calculates the relationship of risk and return for an individual security using Beta (ß) as its measure of risk. The CAPM is derived by combining a risk-free asset with risky assets from an efficient market. The CAPM is the basic theory that links return and risk for all assets. The inputs and results are used to construct the security market line. The difference between the return of the market (r_m) and the risk-free rate of return (r_f) is considered the risk premium $(r_m - r_f)$. The risk premium is the increase in return an investor should be compensated to take on the risk of a market portfolio versus investing in a risk-free asset. The CAPM formula is as follows:[13]

$$r = r_f + Beta\ (r_m - r_f)$$

While leaving the investment specifics for a later chapter, the Beta of a stock is a calculation representing the volatility of an asset in relation to the volatility of the overall market or a given representative index. Stated differently, Beta is the measure of an asset's risk in correlation to the market or to an alternative benchmark.

This inquiry into Beta and risk-return was the main goal of Traditional Finance. It focused on the asset risk in relation to the market.

Issues and Questions Unanswered by Traditional Finance

By introducing Modern Portfolio Theory, Mean-Variance Portfolio Theory, the Capital Asset Pricing Model, and Beta, financial analysts and investors were able to narrow the focus of the financial industry. The framers and proponents of Traditional Finance made many strides, but in this process and evolution, other theorists and observers believed that they ignored many relevant and justified questions and data. For instance, the October 19, 1987 stock market crash, also infamously known as "Black Monday," resulted in a 20 percent decrease in the stock market as a whole. However, no studies or evidence of a 20 percent drop in fundamental values across the nation has ever been uncovered or

---

12. H.M. Markowitz, "Portfolio Selection", *The Journal of Finance* 7, no. 1 (March 1952), pp. 77-91; see also Portfolio Selection: Diversification of Investments, New York (John Wiley & Sons 1959).

13. For a more detailed look at the CAPM and investments, please see discussion in Chapter 9 of this textbook.

proven. As a result, many critics used this event and others to express their concern that markets are not efficient and investors are not rational. These recurring questions and massive shifts in markets provided much empirical data, the very data that was so vital to (and developed by) proponents of Traditional Finance, showing that not all investors are rational, not all markets are efficient, and not all expected returns are tied to risk alone.

Behavioral Finance

A relatively new and evolving area of finance is termed "Behavioral Finance." As will be seen in this chapter, **Behavioral Finance** does not fully reject Traditional Finance's views or methods. Instead, it contains much of the scientific framework and lessons learned from Traditional Finance, amends some of it with basic assumptions based on normal, more human-like behavior, and supplements other aspects of it with notions from psychology and sociology.

Behavioral Finance begins with an assumption - investors are normal people like you, your friends and family, and your neighbors, and some are not like you. Some are smart, but some are not. Some are driven by emotion or by societal beliefs, while some are not so driven. Investors are normal people who make errors and prove that decisions can be made when focused on things that are subjective, not necessarily objective.

In Traditional Finance, the rational investor focused on investments that had average outcomes in an efficient market. Behavioral Finance attempts to understand normal investors and how the action or inaction of these investors reflects collectively in the overall market. The four main premises or assumptions in the area of Behavioral Finance are discussed below.

Investors Are "Normal"

Unlike a rational, number-crunching automaton, proponents of Behavioral Finance theory assume first that investors are "normal," not rational. Normal investors have normal wants and desires, but may commit cognitive errors (through biases or otherwise). Normal investors may be misled by emotions while they are trying to achieve their wants.

The normal investor is considered to be a person with emotions and cognitive biases. However, it is significant to understand that money managers, mutual fund managers, professional traders and others in the market are normal, too. These are people that are subject to the same "normalcy" as all of us.

Markets Are Not Efficient

Behavioral Finance does not suppose that, at every given moment in time, the price of a stock is equal to its fundamental value. Instead, while markets can be difficult to beat, the key concept is that there can be deviations in price from fundamental value so that there are opportunities to buy at a discount or sell at a premium. Conversely, there are times when an investor buys at a premium and sells at a discount. As a result, markets can be tough to beat, but they are not efficient.

Part of the reasoning here is that the market is a collection of normal investors. These are investors who do not know the future, who may be smart or not, who may be informed or not, and who may be lead by emotion or not. For example, if a company's stock is popular and rising, investors take note and frequently join the craze. Sometimes it is profitable; sometimes it is not. Normal investors do not contribute necessarily to efficient markets. This does not mean that markets are "normal" in the same sense as used with investors. It simply illustrates that the market is not truly efficient.

The Behavioral Portfolio Theory Governs

Many proponents of Traditional Finance would consider it a mistake to neglect to look at one's portfolio as a whole. Our next premise, or assumption, in Behavioral Finance involves this relevant question: Would you accept a greater return with less risk if you looked at your portfolio overall instead of looking at your portfolio in layers? A rational investor would certainly choose greater return for less risk. A normal investor may accept a greater risk with less return, but then again, he or she may not. The main problem, however, for normal investors is that they may not even know the risk-return ratios of their portfolio as a whole.

The "Behavioral Portfolio Theory" was introduced by Shefrin and Statman (2000) as a goal-based theory.[14] Under this theory, investors segregate their money into various mental accounting layers. This mental process occurs when people "compartmentalize" certain goals to be accomplished in different categories based on risk. Behavioral Portfolio Theory can be explained by visualizing a pyramid with layers that correspond to certain goals. These goals could include food and shelter, a secure retirement, paying for college education, paying for children's expenses like weddings, or being rich enough to fulfill a lifelong dream or desire.

Investors in the Behavioral Portfolio Theory (hereinafter also referred to as "BPT") hence view their portfolios in distinct mental account layers in a pyramid of assets. This perspective is different from investors under the Mean-Variance Portfolio Theory who view their portfolios as a whole at all times.

As observed by Statman, these mental accounting layers are pigeonholed in the mind of the normal investor to correlate to specific goals. However, they also reflect attitudes or leanings of the investor towards risk from layer to layer.[15]

The following is an example of a pyramid for one who places different assets into different layers, categorized by goals:

Exhibit 2.3 | Risk/Return Relationship

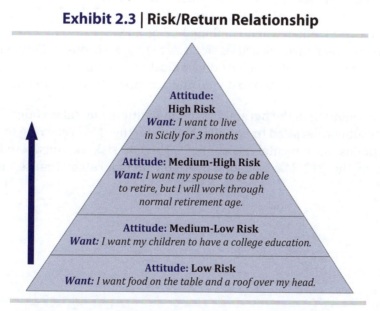

Attitude:
High Risk
Want: I want to live
in Sicily for 3 months

Attitude: **Medium-High Risk**
Want: I want my spouse to be able
to retire, but I will work through
normal retirement age.

Attitude: **Medium-Low Risk**
Want: I want my children to have a college education.

Attitude: **Low Risk**
Want: I want food on the table and a roof over my head.

14. See Shefrin and Statman, "Behavioral Portfolio Theory", Journal of Financial and Quantitative Analysis, Vol. XXXV, No. 2 (June 2000), pp. 127-151.
15. *Ibid*, at pp. 141-142.

Much of the Behavioral Portfolio Theory has its roots dating back to observations by Friedman and Savage (1948), addressing the apparent contradiction of buying lottery tickets and insurance policies. Friedman and Savage studied people who bought lottery tickets and who also purchased insurance policies. They concluded that those who bought lottery tickets were risk-seeking through buying them, but were also averting risk by purchasing insurance. They reasoned that the lottery ticket purchase was to achieve higher social classes, yet the insurance protection safeguarded against dropping into lower social classes. While this could be seen as inconsistent behavior, it can be explained through the process of mental accounting that occurs when one places goals in separate layers with different degrees of risk on the pyramid.

There is one interesting common area between BPT and Modern Portfolio Theory (also referred to as "MPT").[16] Mean-Variance investors choose portfolios by evaluation and decisions based on mean and variance. Behavioral investors, instead, choose portfolios by evaluation and decisions based on expected wealth, desire for security, aspiration levels, and probabilities of aspiration levels.[17] While these show that the two disciplines do not coincide, it does allow for a similar analysis if the investor has only one mental account or one mental layer. Some Behavioral investors may use a framework where there is only one mental account, such as having a desire for food and shelter only.

Such an investor under the BPT is referred to as "BPT-SA," the "SA" referring to a "single account" or just one layer. BPT-SA investors would integrate their portfolios into a single mental account, just as Mean-Variance or MPT investors do by considering covariance.[18] Covariance is the measure of how two securities change or move together when combined or of how the price movements between two securities are related to each other. Covariance is a measure of relative risk.[19] This integration is also called "diversification," the bedrock of Traditional Finance and Modern Portfolio Theory, and one of the most vital and accepted strategies in finance and investing.

The layers of mental accounting in the pyramid result in multiple mental accounts. Behavioral investors with several mental accounts, declared to be "BPT-MA" (with the "MA" referring to "multiple accounts"), segregate their portfolios into mental accounts.[20] Though risk is considered within each layer, behavioral investors in the BPT-MA category overlook or ignore covariance among these differing mental accounts.

> ### ✍ Quick Quiz 2.4
>
> 1. In Traditional Finance, investors are assumed to be rational.
>   a. True
>   b. False
>
> 2. Markets are assumed to be efficient in both Traditional and Behavioral Finance.
>   a. True
>   b. False
>
> 3. Returns are determined by risk (beta) in both Traditional and Behavioral Finance.
>   a. True
>   b. False
>
> True, False, False.

---

16. Ibid, at pp. 138-146.
17. Ibid, at p. 128.
18. Ibid.
19. See discussion of variance and covariance later in Chapter 9 Investments of this textbook.
20. Shefrin and Statman, "Behavioral Portfolio Theory" *supra* note 14, at p. 128.

A popular example with BPT-MA investors is that they may assign risky foreign stocks into one mental account and domestic accounts into another. While they may consider the foreign stocks in emerging or underdeveloped countries to be highly risky, they would in this instance overlook the covariant effect between such foreign and domestic stocks because the pyramid as a whole would not be evaluated in terms of risk and expected return of the portfolio and, hence, would not be viewed as an integrated single account.[21]

Risk Alone Does Not Determine Returns

The fourth and final assumption of Behavioral Finance is that expected returns are not measured by Beta or risk alone. While Traditional Finance has the Capital Asset Pricing Model, Behavioral Finance has the "Behavioral Asset Pricing Model." In its simplest form, the Capital Asset Pricing Model could be expressed in the following equation:

$$\text{Expected Return} = F \text{ (market factor)}$$

However, the Behavioral Asset Pricing Model reaches far beyond the simplicity of an objective risk calculation from the CAPM. The Behavioral Asset Pricing Model determines the expected return of a stock using Beta, book to market ratios, market capitalization ratios, stock "momentum," the investor's likes or dislikes about the stock or company, social responsibility factors, status factors, and more.[22]

In its simplest form, the Behavioral Asset Pricing Model is expressed in the following equation:

$$\text{Expected Return} = F \text{ (market factor, book to market ratio,}$$
$$\text{market capitalization, momentum, affect factor,}$$
$$\text{social responsibility factor, status factor, and more)}^{[23]}$$

The realm of subjective risk is prevalent with the Behavioral Asset Pricing Model. As illustrated by the equation above, there are many more factors that are involved in Behavioral Finance, in contrast to the simpler and more pure pricing models of Traditional Finance. The next section will provide us with a brief look into what makes investors normal in this subjective realm.

What Makes Investors Normal Instead of Rational: Cognitive Biases, Errors and Being Human

What is the difference between a rational investor and a normal one? The answer is that normal investors are prone to making cognitive mistakes due to their beliefs or cognitive biases. Due to the wealth of empirical and theoretical evidence showing that markets are not always "efficient" and investors are not "rational," a large amount of research from the field of psychology and sociology was injected into the financial industry in the last two to three decades.A large number of psychologists and sociologists weighed in on thinking and the decision-making process that was applied to the financial industry. This spurred a lot of literature and studies in Behavioral Finance. With the disciplines of psychology and sociology on one side and the financial industry and planning on the other side, there is a vast amount of information and theories. The following is not an exhaustive list, but a list of the more commonly known biases or heuristics that have been observed or linked to normal investors.

---

21. Ibid.
22. See, Statman, "What is Behavioral Finance?", Behavioral Finance in Investment Management, Handbook of Finance Vol. II, Chap. 9, 2008 Wiley & Sons, Inc., at pp. 5-7)
23. Ibid. at p. 7.

A note on the word "heuristic." A heuristic is a tool used in the minds of people, also known as a "rule of thumb." The heuristic serves to basically shorten the decision-making process for the decision maker, or may make the process easier. However, when things change as they sometimes do, heuristics can lead to biases or can lead to investment decisions that are less than optimal. Some heuristics that are significant in the financial planning industry are the affect heuristic, availability heuristic, and similarity heuristic.

Affect Heuristic

The **affect heuristic** deals with judging something, whether it is good or bad. When stimuli occur, those stimuli cause the mind to have an effective response. This response occurs quickly and, in some cases, automatically and with or without consciousness. For instance, when the word "beautiful" is mentioned, feelings associated with that word are quickly sensed, just as the opposite occurs with the word "hideous." A similar sense of feelings is associated with the word hate versus the word treasure. Relying on these feelings is characterized by the affect heuristic.

Numerous studies have traced the affect heuristic across a variety of research paths. These studies reveal that affect guides judgments and decisions.[24] Studies found evidence that affective emotional reactions appear to drive both perceived benefit and perceived risk.[25] Like houses, cars, watches, and other products, stocks exude "affect." They are considered "good" or "bad," beautiful or ugly. They are liked or disliked. Affect plays an overt role in the pricing of houses, cars, and watches, but according to Traditional Finance, affect plays no

role in the pricing of financial assets. The BAPM outlines how expected returns are high, not only when objective risk is high, but also when subjective risk is high. High subjective risk comes with negative affect. Investors prefer stocks with positive affect, which inflates the prices of those stocks yet depresses their returns."[26] Hence, if an activity was "liked," people tended to judge its risks as being low and its benefits as being high. However, if an activity was "disliked," the judgments were the converse, with high risk and low benefit.[27]

Availability Heuristic

When a decision maker relies upon knowledge that is readily available in his or her memory, the cognitive heuristic known as "availability" is invoked (**availability heuristic**). Rather than examine other alternatives or procedures, pour through research, or investigate further, the decision-makers simply recant knowledge already known to them. Whatever information is available in their memory banks is tapped to reach a decision. This process can lead to decisions based on outdated information, incorrect data, or incomplete information.

In particular, events that bring out emotion, that are vivid in our memory, or that are fairly close in time tend to drive the availability heuristic. One popular example is the fear of flying versus the fear of riding in a car. Many people are fearful of flying based on the belief that it is not as safe as riding in a car. While it is factual that an accident in a plane would likely be more severe than in a car, the incidence of plane

---

24. Brian M. Lucey and Michael Dowling, "The Role of Feelings in Investor Decision-Making," *Journal of Economic Surveys* 19, no. 2 (2005): pp. 211-233, https://doi.org/10.1111/j.0950-0804.2005.00245.x.
25. Meir Statman, Kenneth L. Fisher, and Deniz Anginer, "Affect in a Behavioral Asset-Pricing Model," *Financial Analysts Journal* 64, no. 2 (2008): pp. 20-29, https://doi.org/10.2469/faj.v64n2.8.
26. Ibid, at p. 20.
27. Ibid, at p. 226.

accidents reportedly are extremely small in relation to car accidents. The availability heuristic can also explain, in part, why investors tend to give more weight to the recent or short-term activity of a stock instead of a more prolonged or sustained period of time, as discussed below regarding recency bias.

Similarity Heuristic

The "**similarity**" **heuristic** is used when a decision or judgment is made when a similar situation occurs. The mind of the individual goes back to a similar decision from a prior situation. This happens even though the situation is not exactly the same. The situation could be a prototype or an analogous situation, but is not the exact same situation. In personal relationships, those influenced by a similarity heuristic tend to select and choose to be around people who are similar to us, whether it is a similar age, gender, culture or interest.

An example of the similarity heuristic in investment decision making is investing in October. Some individuals that may have lost value in the stock market in any of the high profile drops in the stock market in October may be inclined to have an emotional reaction to mild news or price changes in the month of October. The investor, if moved to act by the similarity heuristic, would sell a stock based on the similar situation of time (that is the month of October), whereas the situation is very likely much different than an event that occurred years earlier during the month of October.

The Mindset of Losing Versus Taking Losses

When evaluating cognitive biases, heuristics and other decision-making processes that normal people encounter, one begins to understand that the collection of all decisions made by investors is what makes up a marketplace. This is the very essence of Behavioral Finance, and of all the literature and all the studies available, the common theme about normal investors is that there are mental or psychological mistakes that are made by all investors. Investors all make them, although they do not all make all of these mistakes. Some individuals do not look at their portfolio as a whole as they should. Some people have winning stocks and sell them prematurely. Of course, the investor does not know if it is being sold prematurely because this is occurring in real time and is not being done in hindsight.

On the other end, many people keep losing stocks, also known as losers. They keep the losers because their mindset is that, once they sell the losers, it is as if they admit defeat. However, the rational investor knows that when a stock value goes down, even though a sale is not made, the value is lost. Not only is this a distinction between the rational investor and the normal investor, it also shows how a decision is made to refrain from selling a stock out of the fear of actually having to admit that one lost the value in that stock. Some people sell winners so they can talk about it with their friends or others. Some sell the winners for fear of it going back down in value, when in reality investors all know that one should strive to buy low and sell high.

In short, losing value occurs when the stock price drops. Sometimes, the mind does not allow us to realize the loss until it is official, that being when the stock is sold. This leads us to the next area of study by Behavioralists, which studies and observes cognitive biases or other lines of thinking for individuals when making financial decisions.

Patterns and Types of Cognitive Biases

In the financial adviser-client relationship, the adviser should serve as a fiduciary or act in the client's best interests. Further, the client should follow the adviser's recommendations, as the client is the ultimate decision-maker. The challenge lies in delivering good advice that is *accepted* by the client. These recommendations, hence, must pass through the wealth of emotions, biases, and heuristics that the client possesses to deal with the large amount of information that they receive daily, that they receive from friends and colleagues, and that they receive from the adviser.

In behavioral psychology, a comfort zone is a psychological state in which a person functions without anxiety or risk, but behaviors are limited by mental boundaries. In order to step outside the comfort zone, a person must try new behaviors and experience new responses. Psychologists theorize that getting out of the comfort zone raises anxiety, yet increases focus and performance. Anxiety will increase to a point where an optimum performance level is reached, and then higher anxiety will cause performance to decline.

A client may encounter increased anxiety when a planner recommends that the client step outside mental boundaries confining investments and risk taking. The planner may need to help the client overcome the desire to stay in a comfort zone. The planner may especially need to encourage the client to leave the comfort zone in goal setting, providing financial information, making decisions about retirement and death, and taking actions that have been long postponed.

Despite the well-intentioned client, these emotions, biases, and heuristics may come into play. It is therefore beneficial to the adviser (and ultimately beneficial to the client) for the adviser to have a general understanding of the cognitive biases that are prevalent in the realm of financial decision-making.

Of all the information and research, the most commonly reported pattern of cognitive biases contributing to irrational or detrimental financial decision-making is as follows:

Anchoring

Anchoring is defined as attaching or anchoring one's thoughts to a reference point even though there may be no logical relevance or is not pertinent to the issue in question. Anchoring is also known as conservatism or belief perseverance. Anchoring has been reported to be fairly common where decisions are being made in situations that are novel or new to the decision maker.[28]

For example, Kahneman and Tversky (1974) conducted a study where a wheel was spun with the numbers 1 through 100 on it. Study participants were asked if, whether the percentage of U.N. membership accounted for by certain countries was higher or lower than the number on the wheel. Afterwards, the study participants were asked to provide real estimates. It was learned that a seemingly random anchoring value of the number on which the wheel landed had a clear effect on the answer that the participants provided. For example, the average estimate given by participants was 25 percent if the wheel landed on 10, while the average was 45 percent if the wheel landed on 60. The random number resulted in an anchoring effect on the participants' responses even though the number had no correlation to the question.

28. Tversky and Kahneman, "Judgment under Uncertainty: Heuristics and Biases," Science, New Series, Vol. 185, No. 4157. (Sep. 27, 1974): pp. 1124-1131.

When applying this to the world of investments or finance, investors have been found to base decisions on irrelevant figures, data or other statistics. For example, if the stock of a company has fallen considerably in a short period of time, investors may anchor on a recent or even distant high that the stock achieved, believing that the drop in price provides an opportunity to buy the stock at a discount.

In sum, anchoring is the opposite of representativeness or overreaction. Investors are normally slow to notice changes when things are changing gradually. They feel that they are secure and therefore other things are secure. The investor does not react or does not react timely because of the cognitive bias of conservatism or anchoring. Anchoring can lead to a quick answer to a problem that instead required more diligent search and critical analysis.

Confirmation Bias

A commonly used and popular phrase is that "you do not get a second chance at a first impression." This phrase can be borrowed to explain the **confirmation bias**. People tend to filter information and focus on information supporting their opinions. Other information can either be rationalized or ignored. At times, a first impression may lead to a preconceived opinion about something, and this opinion or belief can be hard to shake in the future. This is referred to as confirmation bias where selective thinking dominates.

For example, an investor may have an idea about a stock or may have heard about a stock from another person. When conducting a brief search from one's iPhone or handheld device, a few articles will appear at the bottom. A quick perusal may have various supporting information about the investment dealing with favorable information, but the investor may also gloss over potential problems with the stock or with the company, such as a lawsuit or other problems with the product. Selective thinking may lead to an incomplete picture for the investor.

Recency Bias

Recency bias occurs when too much weight is given to recent observations or stimuli versus long-term historical trends. This may cause a client to erroneously believe that recent trends are likely to repeat themselves over the long term. Conversely, when significant time has passed since the occurrence of an event, recency bias may lead to the belief that it is unlikely to occur again. Recency bias can lead investment clients to desire to take on more risk than is suitable for their goals and time horizon during a long bull market or to panic sell in a down market when they should instead be focused on long-term rather than short-term results. Recency bias is closely related to the availability heuristic discussed previously.

Gambler's Fallacy

In the realm of probabilities, misconceptions can lead to faulty predictions as to occurrences of events. The **gambler's fallacy** is one of the incorrect assumptions from the world of probabilities. The oft-used example from calculus class is 100 coin flips.

When watching successive coin flips, if heads is the result successively, the belief is that the odds of that continuing to happen are slimmer, and therefore it is a better probability of betting on tails. While there would be some support for this logic, the likelihood of heads in a coin flip remains at 50 percent. Because each flip of the coin is a separate action, the probability of the coin flip is no more and no less than 50 percent. In a more strictly gambling sense, if playing roulette in the casino, if one is betting on an odd number versus an even number, the odds of an even number or an odd number coming up on the spin of the wheel is no larger or smaller on the next spin.

Just like with the roulette wheel, investors may sell stock when it has been successful in consecutive trading sessions because they may not believe the stock is going to continue its upward trend. Decisions based on this alone may be less than optimal due to the gambler's fallacy.

Herding

This cognitive bias is explained simply by looking at the word. People tend to follow the masses or the "herd." Individuals that are herding mimic the actions or decisions of a larger group, even though the individual may not have necessarily made the same choice. It is believed that **herding** is based on a person's desire to conform or be accepted by a certain group, while another reason is that if such a large group of people believe something to be correct, then the chances are that the conclusion or the decision they have made is also sound or correct.

While there certainly are numerous examples of when a herd, if large enough in the investment world, begins investing in a certain stock, it may raise the value of the stock by virtue of the demand for it. However, there are numerous examples of where jumping on the proverbial bandwagon has cost many investors. If the stock price is driven up by demand simply because other herders are buying it, the herd actually creates overvaluation that in the long run may mask issues with the underlying fundamentals of the actual investment. In this case, optimism or herding can misprice the value of the stock.

Example 2.8

GameStop was a beloved video game and consumer electronics retail store for kids growing up in the early 2000s. At the end of 2007 GameStop stock was trading at $62.30. In the mid-to late 2000's, however, GameStop's popularity, and sales, declined as online shopping and downloading became more available and popular. GameStop also suffered greatly following the acquisition and subsequent sale at a loss of Spring Mobile which left them with $800 million of debt. By the end of 2018, GameStop stock was trading at $11.96, and by early 2020 it fallen to below $4 per share. Due to an agreement in late 2020 to provide services to Microsoft, the share price began to slowly rise again and was at $17.69 on January 8, 2021. During the month of January 2021, there were no significant changes to the company or its revenue outlook, yet, around January 21, 2021, the share price saw an incredibly steep increase, eventually reaching a high of $483 by January 29, 2021. What happened? traditional finance theories would find this to be an impossible situation since a rational investor would not have changed their decision to buy or not buy if no fundamental changes occurred within the company. Investors, however, are not rational. Some investors who had grown up with GameStop were alarmed by billions of dollars of professional short sales on the very company that held cherished memories for them. A short sale occurs in anticipation of a price decline: the professionals were betting against GameStop. A few posts on widely-followed online trading forums quickly created a short squeeze, driving the price of GameStop up so that the professional would lose. But it didn't stop there. As the price increased and news stories began to appear about what was happening, more and more investors joined the herd, driving the stock price higher and higher at a rapid pace. Within a month, the price had fallen steeply again, to below $41 per share, only to rise again in a subsequent short squeeze fueled by investors following the herd created by the online investing forums.

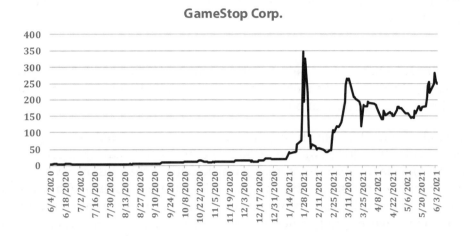

GameStop Corp.

Hindsight Bias

Another potential bias for an investor is what is called **hindsight bias**. People are all too familiar with the test of foresight versus the test of hindsight. Hindsight is looking back after the fact is known. It is human nature to look back upon an adverse event and want to change it retrospectively. Foresight is what one predicts or projects will occur with current information without knowing the future. Psychologists have repeatedly explained that people have an inborn or innate need to find organization in the world by creating explanations that allow us to believe that events are predictable.[29] That is why too many events that have occurred, in hindsight, seem obvious.

For instance, many people lament the fact that, after a sporting event, the outcome of the game was obvious to them. However, before the contest or game, nobody knew what the outcome would be, nor could they accurately predict outcomes to such sporting events. If hindsight bias is present, then the person who is making the investment decision believes that some past event was obvious or predictable. If it is obvious and predictable, then the decision-maker believes that the next problem will be obvious and predictable, and hence can be avoided. Therefore, the hindsight bias may lull the investor into believing they can perform better or more efficiently when armed with this knowledge or bias.

Overconfidence

The **overconfidence bias** usually concerns an investor that listens mostly to himself or herself. Overconfident investors mostly rely on their skills and capabilities to do their own homework or make their own decisions. Many investment portfolios that are not well diversified are in that condition due to a propensity of investors to believe that they can outperform the market based on their beliefs or skills. It has been widely reported in terms of investing that overconfidence is one of the most common biases that can be detrimental to portfolios and the performance of investors over the long haul.

Overconfidence is believed to be a driver of excess trading. Another study put forth evidence that investors with discount brokerage accounts traded too frequently and, in the process, reduced their returns. It was found that higher trading costs were incurred, but more importantly, the stocks that investors bought did not do as well as the ones that they sold. The author concluded that the excess trading was attributed to overconfidence.[30] Numerous researchers have theorized that some investors trade very frequently because they are overconfident.

Overreaction

The key component between a normal investor and a rational investor is that the normal investor has emotion when making decisions in the stock market. One emotion that is common is an **"overreaction"** towards the receipt of news or information.

An interesting study from 1985 involved psychologists' research and investigation into people's tendency to overreact to dramatic news events and whether such behavior affects stock prices.[31] The empirical evidence and data was consistent, as concluded by the authors, with overreaction bias. Interestingly, the results of the study also unearthed information about January returns from prior declared winners and losers, with the portfolios of losers experiencing exceptionally large returns.[32] Yet another study found that overreaction to new information is just as common as under-reaction, leading the author to conclude that overreaction and under-reaction are consistent with market efficiency.[33]

In the world of Traditional Finance, if new information was learned, that information was instantly incorporated into the stock price leading to market efficiency. This theory was partly contradicted in reality because stock market participants overreact to new information. A security's price is then adjusted by an overreaction by a large amount of investors.

People tend to put more emphasis on their recent experience rather than on other factors. Representativeness, or overreaction, is the overweighting of sample information. In other words, when the model is unknown - that is, when the way a very large sample of something looks is unknown - people infer too quickly from too small of a sample. Overweighting sample information leads to overreaction. Investors become worried too quickly or are impressed too quickly based on short, incomplete or very small samples. Investors may remove their money from mutual funds that have recently performed poorly and place their funds into mutual funds that have recently done well. Overreaction has been linked to short-term market momentum for individual stocks when investors move money to stocks that have performed well and away from those that have performed poorly.

Prospect Theory

Kahneman and Tversky presented the **"Prospect Theory"** in 1979.[34] The Prospect Theory provides that people value gains and losses differently and will base their decisions on perceived gains rather than perceived losses. If someone is provided with two equal choices, one being expressed in terms of possible gains and the other in terms of possible losses, people would chose to express in terms of possible gains, even if it means the same economic result.

Kahneman and Tversky conducted a number of studies where participants answered questions about judgments between two monetary decisions involving perspective losses and perspective gains. The

30. Terrance Odean, "Do Investors Trade Too Much?," *American Economic Review* 89, no. 5 (January 1999): pp. 1279-1298, https://doi.org/10.1257/aer.89.5.1279.

31. WERNER F. De BONDT and RICHARD THALER, "Does the Stock Market Overreact?," *The Journal of Finance* 40, no. 3 (1985): pp. 793-808, https://doi.org/10.1111/j.1540-6261.1985.tb05004.x.

32. Ibid, at 793.

33. Fama, "Market Efficiency, Long Term Returns, and Behavioral Finance," Journal of Finance, Vol. 49, No. 3 (September 1998), pp. 283-306.

34. Daniel Kahneman and Amos Tversky, "Prospect Theory: An Analysis of Decision under Risk," *Econometrica* 47, no. 2 (1979): pp. 263-291, https://doi.org/10.2307/1914185.

overwhelming majority of the participants chose stating things in terms of gains rather than losses. The result is, under the Prospect Theory, that people would rather a reasonable level of gains even though they have a chance at earning more, and are willing to engage in risk seeking behavior when they can limit their losses. This means that losses are more heavily weighted than an equal amount of gains. In other words, investors are risk averse when choosing among alternatives that will produce a gain but risk seeking when choosing among alternatives that will produce a loss.

Prospect theory suggests that individuals are faulty in their estimation of probabilities and the associated outcomes. Investors overweight small chance outcomes just to avoid a loss.

In research that contributed to a Nobel Memorial Prize in Economic Sciences, Tversky and Kahneman discuss the impact of framing on decision making.[35] Below is a summary of one of the research studies they conducted on framing. In this questionnaire, they presented a problem with alternative solutions. Students picked between the two alternative solutions.

Problem	Alternatives	152 Total Respondents Choice for A & B
Problem 1: Imagine that the U.S. is preparing for the outbreak of an unusual Asian disease, which is expected to kill 600 people. Two alternative programs to combat the disease have been proposed. Assume that the exact scientific estimate of the consequences of the programs are as follows:	If **Program A** is adopted, 200 people will be saved.	72%
	If **Program B** is adopted, there is 1/3 probability that 600 people will be saved, and 2/3 probability that no people will be saved.	28%

Problem	Alternatives	155 Total Respondents Choice for C & D
Problem 2: Imagine that the U.S. is preparing for the outbreak of an unusual Asian disease, which is expected to kill 600 people. Two alternative programs to combat the disease have been proposed. Assume that the exact scientific estimate of the consequences of the programs are as follows:	If **Program C** is adopted 400 people will die.	22%
	If **Program D** is adopted there is 1/3 probability that nobody will die, and 2/3 probability that 600 people will die.	78%

The outcome of each of the four alternative programs is the same. However, the framing of the alternatives clearly influences the choice by the respondents. In Problem 1, most of the respondents chose the risk-averse program over the riskier option. In Problem 2, most respondents chose the riskier option than the certainty of 400 deaths.

Tversky and Kahneman point out that there is a common pattern about choices. Those that involve gains are often risk-averse, while those involving losses are often risk seeking.

---

35. The Framing of Decisions and the Psychology of Choice, Amos Tversky; Daniel Kahneman, Science, New Series, Vol. 211, No. 4481. (Jan. 30, 1981), pp. 453-458.

The Disposition Effect

With all the above cognitive biases, heuristics, and other mental exercises discussed above, there is another subset of Behavior Finance that should be addressed. Shefrin and Statman (1985) presented the reluctance of an investor to realize a loss in a Behavioral framework.[36] This reluctance stems from a combination of two cognitive biases and an emotion. The cognitive bias was "faulty framing" where normal investors do not mark their stocks to market prices. Investors create mental accounts when they purchase stocks and continue to mark their value to purchase prices even after market prices have changed. They mark stocks to the market only when they sell their stocks and close their mental accounts. Normal investors therefore do not acknowledge the loss in value, referred to as a paper loss, because an open account means that there is still a chance that the stock price will rise, and the stock is not necessarily a loser, but may still turn into a gain. The normal investor does not consider the stock a loser until the stock is sold, at which time the loss is technically realized in the mind of the normal investor. Interfacing with the faulty framing bias is the cognitive bias of hindsight.

Shefrin and Statman explained that hindsight is linked to the emotion of regret, and realization of losses brings on the pain of regret when investors realize in hindsight that they would have been better off had they avoided buying the stock altogether. Hindsight misleads the investor into believing that they could have foreseen the losing stock and avoided the loss which could also lead to overconfidence for subsequent transactions. A defense against regret is to postpone the realization of the loss until later, yet the fact that the stock price dropped is the real moment when the loss occurred, not upon the actual sale.

Another study examined the behavior of individual investors, finding that they realized their profitable stock investments at a much higher rate than their unprofitable ones, except in December. The December sale was obviously explained by motivation for tax purposes.[37]

In summary, the reluctance to realize a loss is a powerful motivator of the normal investor. The **"Disposition Effect"** helps provide some insight into the mind of the normal investor.

Note on Limits to Arbitrage

Behavioral biases among normal investors have an effect on asset prices and returns on investments on a sustained basis only if there are limits to arbitrage that also exist, preventing rational investors from exploiting short-term overvaluation or undervaluation in prices. There is some evidence that suggests limits to arbitrage exist in the failure to eliminate obvious and straightforward "mispricing" situations. For instance, in one paper, Mitchell, Pulvino and Stafford (2002) chronicled 82 instances where the market value of a company was less than the market value of the company's stock in its subsidiary.[38] While this implies there are opportunities for arbitrage that lead to swift correction of the mispricing, these authors also warn of barriers to arbitrage.

36. Hersh Shefrin and Meir Statman, "The Disposition to Sell Winners Too Early and Ride Losers Too Long: Theory and Evidence," *The Journal of Finance* 40, no. 3 (1985): pp. 777-790, https://doi.org/10.1111/j.1540-6261.1985.tb05002.x.

37. Terrance Odean, "Are Investors Reluctant to Realize Their Losses?," *The Journal of Finance* 53, no. 5 (1998): pp. 1775-1798, https://doi.org/10.1111/0022-1082.00072.

38. Hersh M. Shefrin and Meir Statman, "Explaining Investor Preference for Cash Dividends," *Journal of Financial Economics* 13, no. 2 (1984): pp. 253-282, https://doi.org/10.1016/0304-405x(84)90025-4. See also, Hersh Shefrin and Meir Statman, "The Disposition to Sell Winners Too Early and Ride Losers Too Long: Theory and Evidence," *The Journal of Finance* 40, no. 3 (1985): pp. 777-790, https://doi.org/10.1111/j.1540-6261.1985.tb05002.x. These are cites to some of the other evidence cited above. See also, Shefrin and Statman, "Behavioral Capital Asset Pricing Theory," *Journal of Financial and Quantitative Analysis* 29, no. 3 (Sept. 1994): pp. 323-349.

In short, there are many cases and instances where the market value of spun out subsidiaries exceed that of the parent company that retained a majority stock in the spinout, but in these cases, short-selling of the spinout was difficult, expensive or impossible, reducing or eliminating the arbitrage opportunity. The literature also supports other inherent risks in arbitrage, such as trading by uninformed investors that may cause the mispricings to increase before correction, the inability of the arbitrageur to maintain the position in the face of margin calls, and other high implementation calls for arbitrage trades. Therefore, arbitrage in practice is limited by various areas of risk.

Managing Biases

The financial planner is often in a position to help clients change behavior from making irrational or emotionally-driven investment decisions to more rational decisions that align with their risk profile and goals. In some cases, de-biasing is focused on the decision-maker and in some cases it is focused on changing the environment in which the decision is being made.

A client's inclination to follow the crowd by investing in a particular "hot" stock (herding bias) my be managed by revisiting the investment policy statement (discussed in Chapter 9) to see whether the decision to purchase the stock aligns with the parameters set forth in the policy. Alternatively, it may be managed by changing the decision-making environment to one in which the decision-maker is not exposed to other people's influences and choices. Additional information regarding decision making is provided later in this Chapter.

Other types of biases (e.g., confirmation bias and disposition effect) may be overcome by simply educating the client about the bias from a behavior finance perspective. The client and adviser are both susceptible to biases and must be conscientious of making decisions without the influence of these types of biases. In educating the client, the adviser must be careful to avoid coming across as condescending. If the adviser has experienced the impact from, and learned from making the mistake of giving in to, one of these biases in the past, sharing that experience can help build rapport and provide the client with a more meaningful understanding of why it is important not to fall prey to these lines of thinking. Providing regular and timely nonjudgmental feedback when a client's decisions are in disagreement with the stated plan or which will impair the ability to reach their goals may help to guide clients back to the path that is most likely to lead them to success.

Extreme changes in financial markets can elicit extreme emotions. When the market experiences a sudden and significant decline and clients want to immediately sell to "stop the bleeding," a cooling off period (e.g., suggesting they wait a week or two weeks to make that decision) in combination with a review of the investment policy statement may prevent the client from making irrational decisions.

Some biases (e.g., overconfidence bias, herding, etc.) may be mitigated by encouraging the client to serve as his own devil's advocate by asking the client to evaluate whether this still looks like a good investment if the value decreases? For example, when real estate prices inflate quickly, some clients will make the decision to borrow money to flip properties (rapidly resell at an inflated price) or decide to get into the rental business. Asking the client to reflect on whether it would still be a good investment if the property value decreased by ten percent may help the client gain a more rational perspective on whether it is a good investment.

Ensuring that clients understand the risks and potential returns associated with each type of investment can also facilitate better financial decision making. The financial adviser should never assume that a client is knowledgeable regarding the risk characteristics of various investments as these assumptions may be false and counter-productive to helping the client appropriately assess the desirability of a particular investment.

Conclusion About Behavioral Finance

Behavioral Finance involves normal people in various settings, including questions as to why people trade, why they consume more from dividend dollars than from capital funds, why they are eager to invest in hedge funds or why they prefer to invest in socially responsible companies or companies meeting favorable ESG (environmental, social, and governance) criteria.

This chapter points out how cognitive biases, heuristics, and other mental exercises or short-cuts can affect behavior and decisions of investors. As a result, if investors' decisions are subject to their biases, biases also have an effect on stock market pricing. Traditional Finance proponents would explain that bubbles occur when prices are correctly placed and high priced stocks are less risky or have good cash flow prospects. Behavioral Finance proponents would explain that bubbles occur because investor sentiment comes in waves and can drive up a stock price beyond its fundamental value, or if stocks are falling, that fall can lead to a crash because of panic.

Human nature cannot be discounted when trying to understand the market as a whole. Therefore, to have an optimal investment policy and plan for a client, the financial planning practitioner must understand some of the tenets and challenges in Behavioral Finance. While it is hard to make investment decisions without some biases coming into play, understanding and being aware of behavioral biases can aid the investor and financial planning adviser. Everyone makes mistakes including being overconfident, overweighting recent behavior while underrating the long-term view, and refusing to accept a small loss and selling a winning stock prematurely.

If investors and financial planning advisers can understand biases and how they can direct investor behavior, then there is an opportunity for the investor or the financial planning adviser to be mindful of, or to perhaps create an advantage due to, common mistakes made by normal investors. For instance, there may be news that leads numerous investors to overreact. Investors should consider avoiding the over reactive behavior, or perhaps the herding behavior, and consider more long-term goals, or better yet, perform more research or investigation into what the actual problem might be.

✒ *Quick Quiz 2.5*

1. Understanding behavioral biases can aid the financial adviser.
   a. True
   b. False

2. Biases have no effect on stock prices.
   a. True
   b. False

3. Behavioral Finance is pure and concerned only with risk-reward and risk-return.
   a. True
   b. False

4. Behavioral Finance is more subjective than Traditional Finance and does not have a single cohesive theory.
   a. True
   b. False

True, False, False, True.

While many concepts of psychology and sociology enter into the framework in the world of Behavioral Finance, Behavioral Finance does not abandon many of the concepts and use of scientific method from traditional finance. While not abandoning Traditional Finance, advisers who study or educate themselves in Behavioral Finance may be able to improve their clients' outcomes by providing prudent recommendations tailored to the goals of the client in a way that increases the likelihood that the clients will use the recommendations. Traditional Finance is pure and concerned with risk-reward and risk-return.

Behavioral Finance, however, is far more subjective, with consideration to a wide range of cognitive biases and areas of psychology and sociology to consider. Behavioral Finance does not have a cohesive single theory. Behavioral Finance is in its infancy, and a significant amount of research and discovery must occur before there will be a consensus among Behavioral theorists.It is not far fetched to believe that the simplicity of the rational investor or the efficient market hypothesis will never be matched. However, applying Behavioral Finance principles can aid investors and financial advisers to improve the investment process, make effective decisions during the adviser-client relationship, and help advisers reach an optimal plan for planning and investing for the client.

CLIENT PSYCHOLOGY

Introduction

While the previous section focused on behavioral finance and the impact of client heuristics and biases on investment portfolio decisions, often from a cognitive psychology point of view, a wider-ranging study of client psychology is also necessary. The concept of financial psychology can be defined quite broadly and will impact nearly every element of the financial plan and nearly every step in the financial planning process. Financial psychology incorporates a broad spectrum of related disciplines and subspecialties of psychology, which may include, among others, behavioral finance, financial therapy, clinical and cognitive psychology, developmental psychology, and human sciences.[39] Developing an awareness of how a client's psychology impacts their goals and objectives, as well as their ability to follow through on planning recommendations, will better equip the financial planner to go beyond the quantitative aspects of financial advice in a manner that will provide the client the greatest likelihood of achieving their stated goals and objectives, and will serve to enhance the client's financial well-being and sense of financial security.

Key Concepts

1. Define financial well-being.

2. Explain the importance of a planner understanding both the client's and planner's values, attitudes and beliefs.

3. Discuss the significance of multicultural psychology.

The Consumer Financial Protection Bureau (CFPB) defines financial well-being as "a state of being wherein a person can fully meet current and ongoing financial obligations, can feel secure in their financial future, and is able to make choices that allow them to enjoy life."[40] An understanding of client psychology can provide the planner with the skills necessary to assist the client in achieving financial well-being and, beyond that, assist the client in understanding, and altering if necessary, their

---

39. Human sciences is an interdisciplinary field of study which generally incorporates biological, psychological, social, and cultural aspects.

40. CFPB publication *Managing Financial Well-Being: A Guide to Using the CFPB Financial Well-Being Scale*, December 2015. https://www.consumerfinance.gov/data-research/research-reports/financial-well-being-scale.

fundamental beliefs about money that may be holding them back from achieving their dreams. Klontz, Zabek, and Horowttz clarify that the field of "financial psychology draws from behavioral finance and other areas of psychology to help alleviate financial stress and promote healthy financial behaviors. These efforts go beyond cognitive biases and into the realm of the client's idiosyncratic beliefs (e.g., money scripts) and financial behaviors (e.g., resisting financial advice, overspending, financial enabling, financial anxiety, etc.)."[41]

While the study of client psychology and financial therapy contains enough depth to warrant a full degree, or degrees, this chapter is designed to merely provide an overview. As with many of the technical aspects of financial planning (such as tax planning, estate planning, or investments planning), financial professionals should recognize the point at which an expert (e.g., a financial therapist, psychologist, marriage and family therapist, or financial coach) should be called in as part of the planning team to serve the best interests of the client(s).

Financial Therapy

The Financial Therapy Association defines financial therapy as "a process informed by both therapeutic and financial competencies that helps people think, feel, communicate, and behave differently with money to improve overall well-being through evidence-based practices and interventions."[42]

Although the financial planner may rely on a financial therapist for more complex situations, gaining at least an entry-level understanding of the psychology behind unproductive behavior and money-related disorders and learning to employ basic techniques from areas of study such as motivational interviewing and positive psychology (discussed later in this chapter) can enhance the financial planning process and increase the client's progress toward reaching their goals.

Before getting into the details of financial therapy, we will begin our exploration of client psychology by looking at client and planner values, attitudes, and beliefs and their impact on the financial planning process.

Socialization and Client and Planner Values, Attitudes, and Beliefs

The American Psychological Association (APA) Dictionary of Psychology defines **socialization** as "the process by which individuals acquire social skills, beliefs, values, and behaviors necessary to function effectively in society or in a particular group." A client's socialization will often be reflected in the client's goals and will impact the interaction and relationship with the financial planner and the financial planning process. For some clients, anxiety over what others will think or the need for social approval will drive many of the client's behaviors.

Attitudes, values, and biases are often the product of emotions and may be affected by emotional issues. Emotions cannot be dismissed as merely unintelligent, unwise, or illogical. Much work has been done recently by scientists on emotional intelligence and on the reasonableness and wisdom of judgments informed by emotions. Emotions are not simply obstacles to careful financial planning; rather, a client's emotions frequently need to be consulted, and they must be incorporated into the critical step of goal-setting for a financial plan.

---

41. Charles R. Chaffin et al., "Financial Psychology," in *Client Psychology* (Hoboken: Wiley, 2018), pp. 253-266.
42. https://financialtherapyassociation.org.

Budgeting and saving to achieve financial goals can be an emotional issue. Some people find it difficult or impossible to budget, and other people are emotionally committed to saving every penny. People can be accustomed to living a life style that requires expenditure of every dollar earned and will not accept a budget that requires deferral of gratification. Individuals who worked their way through college may find it emotionally disturbing to contemplate saving for a child's college expenses. They may feel that if they did it without family help, then their children can, too.

Many young or middle aged people are emotionally unprepared to think about planning for retirement rather than enjoying the present. In contrast, clients approaching retirement may be fearful of the future and of the prospect of inadequate resources, and these emotions may be powerful drivers to financial planning goals.

Numerous other aspects of financial planning are also impacted by a client' attitudes, values, biases, and perceptions.

Cultural and Religious Values

Multicultural Psychology is defined as "an extension of general psychology that recognizes that multiple aspects of identity influence a person's worldview, including race, ethnicity, language, sexual orientation, gender, age, disability, class status, education, religious or spiritual orientation, and other cultural dimensions, and that both universal and culture-specific phenomena should be taken into consideration when psychologists are helping clients, training students, advocating for social change and justice, and conducting research."[43] Similarly, a multicultural financial planner must exhibit an awareness and consideration of each client's, and the planner's own, worldview.

A client who has come to the United States from another country or who has grown up in a particular ethnic community or with an unconventional home life, for example, may have some attitudes toward personal finances that differ from those of the financial planner. This will be especially true if the planner does not have the same heritage. Even the planner's education and training are likely to create attitudes toward personal finances that differ greatly from attitudes of many clients. A financial planner is in a sense a member of a specific culture and community as a result of having learned the financial planning process and entered the financial planning profession.

While the planning process aspires to be equally applicable to all cultures, some cultures may not be entirely receptive to or have an affinity for traditional financial planning. When encountering a differing worldview, a planner will need to be attentive to attitudes, values, and beliefs that may be very different from the planner's usual experience. Cultural differences may make it more difficult for a planner to establish rapport, to communicate, or to understand client actions. The planner must be careful to avoid imposing his own values on the client and must avoid influencing the client's goals and decisions with his or her own values or beliefs. For example, the planner's culture may place high value on financial independence while the client's culture places greater value on financial interdependence between family members. The planner must be careful in this circumstance to adapt his perceptions to mirror those of the client.

A client's cultural values may greatly influence goal setting, and the planner must be attentive to a client's desires to accomplish both financial and non-financial goals. Instead of accumulating wealth, a client may have a need to benefit the community or to assist charities. Clients may come from a religious

---

43. https://dictionary.apa.org/multicultural-psychology.

tradition that obligates them to make certain financial contributions to their religious organization or to do certain amounts of charitable or missionary work. The client may have goals in connection with religious commitments that impact personal financial goals and that need to be taken into account in the planning process. A planner needs to be sensitive to non-financial goals that may be of equal or greater importance to a client than the financial goals.

Klontz, Britt, and Archuleta articulate that the broad definition of culture "precludes the possibility of any one financial planner understanding every possible cultural influence that exists. However, it is possible to obtain a *general* understanding of the cultural influences relevant to a particular case that then facilitates a deeper understanding of each client's *unique* cultural experiences and beliefs."[44] The key to gaining better empathy with clients of different cultural backgrounds (broadly defined to include not only ethnicity but also the aforementioned gender, sexual orientation, age, class status, spiritual orientation, etc.) is for the planner to continuously engage in self-education and self-awareness.[45]

Ultimately, the planner should be prepared to work with clients with widely-varying values and beliefs which will be influenced by each individual client's worldview. It often helps for the planner to develop a sense of curiosity with regard to client's background, upbringing, and path to where they are today. Most people have an interesting story if one is willing to listen and engage with the client.

Social Consciousness

Financial planning clients will experience varying degrees of **social consciousness** (an awareness of and sense of responsibility for problems or injustices that exist within society). A person's conscience is the moral compass by which they judge situations as right or wrong, and is influenced by cultural, political, economic, and other factors. A person's conscience will guide their actions. Consciousness, on the other hand, refers to awareness. While some clients may be acutely aware of problems or injustices in their society (be socially conscious), others will remain unaware that these situations exist (be socially unconscious). When a client has high degree of social consciousness the financial planning goals and recommendations will likely be reflective of these beliefs.

For example, some investors choose to include in their portfolio only stocks of companies that support the investor's moral and ethical beliefs, or choose to avoid owning the stocks of companies that do not support their moral or ethical beliefs. This type of investing may be in the form of Socially Responsible, Environmental, Social, and Governance (ESG), or Impact investing. An investor may choose to avoid companies that produce or sell addictive substances such as tobacco, alcohol, gambling, or marijuana companies. As an alternative to filtering out certain types of companies, a socially responsible investor may actively seek companies that support the investor's social, moral, or religious beliefs, or companies that invest substantially in their communities. In recent years there has been an increased interest in impact and ESG investing, which focus on the stocks of companies that have a positive measurable social or environmental impact, such as companies that produce sustainable agriculture, renewable energy, and affordable housing.

---

44. Bradley T. Klontz et al., "Seven Steps to Culturally Responsive Financial Therapy," in *Financial Therapy: Theory, Research, and Practice* (Cham: Springer, 2015), p. 88.
45. See Klontz, Britt, and Archuleta, *ibid*, for a 7-step process to aid the planner in becoming more culturally aware.

Well known companies included in the S&P Global 1200 ESG (Environmental, Social, and Governance) Index include:

- Microsoft
- Apple
- Amazon
- Johnson & Johnson
- Exxon Mobile Corp
- Nestle

Impact of Client Background, Risk Tolerance and Loss Aversion, and Preferred Learning Style on Client Goals and the Financial Planning Process

Family situation and familial experiences can influence the goals that a client will set and the resources that will be available for planning. Family background can create certain expectations for an individual in connection with budgeting and saving and in regard to raising and educating children. Financial planners may find married clients struggling with family cultural expectations for education of their children. This clash of expectations can create emotional and marital tensions during financial planning sessions.

Divorce can force clients to change their financial planning completely and may cause some anxiety for clients who have not previously been engaged in managing their finances. Divorced clients may not know whom to trust. A divorced parent with small children may feel the pressures of maintaining a single parent family on a reduced budget. Thus, emotional issues can greatly influence the client's perception of the current financial situation and may present new challenges in the financial planning process.

Families can be a cauldron of emotions even without the disruption of divorce. Parents and children can fight bitterly and for long periods of time. Financial planners may unexpectedly find that they are in the middle of family disputes that give rise to financial planning goals and objectives that make little sense from a traditional family perspective. Estate planning may be affected by second marriages and by the desire of a client to provide for children of a previous marriage. Clients may decide to disinherit children, and financial planners might find the client's goals unfair or illogical from the planner's own perspective. A planner may find it challenging to separate from her own biases and core values to support the client in achieving goals, but must learn to do so in order to empathize and join with the client.

✒️ Quick Quiz 2.6

1. A person's worldview includes race, ethnicity, language, sexual orientation, gender, age, disability, class status, education, religious or spiritual orientation, and other cultural dimensions.
   a. True
   b. False

2. A person's social consciousness is the moral compass by which they judge situations as right or wrong, and is influenced by cultural, political, economic, and other factors.
   a. True
   b. False

3. A client's risk tolerance tends to remain consistent across various areas of planning and static throughout the client's lifetime.
   a. True
   b. False

True, False, False.

Risk Tolerance and Loss Aversion

A financial planner needs to consider a client's risk tolerance in developing a financial plan and in selecting strategies for the client. Unfortunately, determining a client's risk tolerance is not always easy and straightforward.

Risk capacity is a measurement of the amount of risk a client can afford to take on. It may be based on the client's ability to adjust goals, on reliability and sources of income, on the level of emergency funds available, and/or on ability to absorb losses in the investment portfolio without having a detrimental impact on standard of living.

A client's risk propensity, or risk tolerance, doesn't always align with his or her capacity. Risk propensity is the amount of risk a client is actually willing to take on. It is a psychological element based upon the client's comfort level with taking on risk and can be difficult to objectively measure.

Clients may be risk tolerant in one area of their lives but not in another (for example, physical risk-taking versus monetary risk-taking); and they may be risk tolerant in one area of financial planning but not in another (for example, an aggressive investments portfolio but low insurance deductibles). Moreover, over time, a client's risk tolerance can change, and may be different for different goals. A client's attitude toward risk may vary with the type of risk involved, based on who is affected by the outcome (self only versus others), by the client's mental accounting system, by the client's perception of the risk, or numerous other internal and external influences.

Risk appears in all areas of financial planning, but it can be thought of differently in the various areas. For example, in insurance planning, risk is mainly about losses; while in investment planning, risk is defined in terms of variability of returns. Thus, for insurance planning, risk is generally something clients seek to reduce or eliminate; but in investments, risk is something that produces returns and, therefore, may be attractive. In investments, tolerance for risk is often measured on a scale from aggressive to conservative, and people in the middle are described as moderate. Additional details regarding investment risks and measuring investment risk tolerance are discussed in Chapter 9.

A planner may determine risk tolerance by various means. Perhaps the most common approach is for the planner simply to ask the client a series of questions about his or her willingness to take risks. The planner can elicit the client's attitudes toward risk by asking about different kinds of high risk and low risk situations, or the planner may pose various hypothetical situations that require the client to choose among high risk and low risk options. In investments, the planner may ask the client to rank the importance of various characteristics presented by different investments. For example, the client might be asked his or her preference for safety of principal, capital appreciation, dividend or interest income, or income tax advantages.

Questionnaires and quantitative tools have been developed to help with measuring client risk tolerance. While these tools are important, financial planners should not place total reliance on them. Quantitative measurement techniques are not infallible. Generally, quantitative tools should be used but should be combined with qualitative techniques, so a certain amount of professional judgment enters into the assessment process.

Another important source of information about a client's risk tolerance is the client's past financial decisions. **Composure** refers to a client's ability to remain calm and focused when under pressure. An investor's past behaviors during market corrections or other types of financial crises may provide some indication of their ability to maintain composure during periods of high anxiety. Financial planners should recognize, however, that when a client is experiencing a great deal of stress or anxiety, this is likely to hinder their ability to make rational decisions or initiate a change that is necessary to implement the financial plan.

Learning Style

The manner in which a financial planner communicates with clients throughout the planning process may be influenced by the client's learning style. When educating clients on alternative products and strategies, it will be important for the planner to be able to adopt his or her presentation to match the learning style that is most meaningful to the client.

The three major cognitive learning styles are visual, auditory, and kinesthetic (or tactile). When working with client's who have a visual learning style, the planner should make use of pictures, charts, and graphs where possible and appropriate. An auditory learner will understand the plan best by listening to the planner explain each alternative, and may frequently repeat back what the planner has said as a means of both clarifying and remembering what the planner has told them. Kinesthetic learners like things to be hands-on. This client, for example, would prefer to be able to use an online or software calculator to simulate various retirement scenarios more than he or she would appreciate seeing just a graph showing two different comparisons.

When educating client's about risks, financial planners must be able to communicate the risks in a manner that the client is best able to understand. Some clients with low levels of numeracy but who are visual learners will benefit more from a visual depiction than from stated percentages or probabilities.

Example 2.9

Consider the Jefferstone family. Georgette works full time while Louisa has opted to work part time to be able to care for their two young children when they are not in school. They have mutually agreed that it is important to them that Louisa be able to continue part-time work to enable her to be more active with the children and involved in their various activities. The planner is attempting to ensure that they understand the risk associated with the lack of disability insurance on Georgette in light of the fact that her income represents 71% of household income. The planner could present the income breakdown directly from the Statement of Income (discussed in Chapters 3 and 4), as follows:

	Income	Percent of Total Income
Georgette Salary	$110,000	71%
Louisa Salary	$40,000	26%
Dividend Income	$5,000	3%
Total Income	**$155,000**	**100%**

Alternatively, the planner can present the income breakdown using a visual aid such as a pie chart:

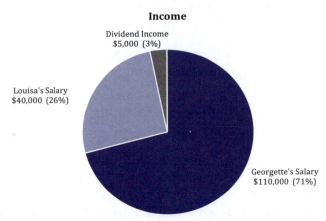

Income

Dividend Income
$5,000 (3%)

Louisa's Salary
$40,000 (26%)

Georgette's Salary
$110,000 (71%)

The visual representation in the pie chart may be more meaningful in allowing Georgette and/or Louisa to conceptualize what 71 percent looks like in relation to their total income, providing them with a better understanding of what is at stake should Georgette become disabled and her income be lost for an extended period of time. When presenting the probability that a female of Georgette's age has a 20% (1 in 5) probability of becoming disabled for a period of 90 days or longer, the planner may invite two staff members into the room (for a total of 5 people) and point out that, if everyone in the room were a female the same age as Georgette, the probability statistics tell us that one of us will be disabled for at least 90 days before reaching age 65. This combination of visual and kinesthetic presentation may be much more meaningful in terms of understanding the risk than simply stating probabilities. Note that the goal is not to create fear so that they buy insurance, it is simply to help visualize the level of risk so that the clients can make an informed decision. They may decide that if Georgette becomes disabled they are willing to forgo the goal of having Louisa at home with the kids in favor of her working full time, but it is a choice that is made with awareness of the risk involved.

PSYCHOLOGICAL BARRIERS TO A SUCCESSFUL FINANCIAL PLANNING ENGAGEMENT

Introduction

Any experienced financial planner can relate stories of times where they created a brilliant plan that would allow their clients to fulfill their stated goals only to be met with resistance and/or failure to implement by the client. What happened? Why would a rational client not follow through? And what could the planner have done differently that might have yielded better engagement and follow-through by the client?

A limited study by Britt, Lawson, and Haselwood suggests the possibility that high levels of physiological stress (as measured by lower skin temperatures at distal skin locations) may indicate that the client has little intent to change, but that clients with lower levels of physiological stress may be more likely to have intent to change.[46] Based on the Prochaska and DiClemente Five Stages of Change model, intent to change is a necessary precursor to taking action to change behavior. Behavioral changes can be difficult, but asking the client to express to the planner the reasons he or she believe change is important to them is a good way to engage and empower the client to begin the change process.

> ### ☷ *Key Concepts*
>
> 1. List and describe the five stages of change.
>
> 2. Discuss how a person's comfort zone impacts their ability to change.
>
> 3. Explain the relevance of money scripts and provide an example of a money script in each of the four broad categories of money beliefs.

Exhibit 2.4 | Five Stages of Change

Stage Number	Stage	Description
1	Pre-Contemplation	No intent to change (may be unaware of or in denial that change is needed)
2	Contemplation	Aware that change is needed and considering making change, but not yet ready to take action
3	Preparation	Gathering information (from a professional) in preparation to make a change
4	Action	Action is taken to implement the plan (changes in behavior, environment, etc.). Bad habits transition to healthier habits
5	Maintenance	Prevention of relapse

A spouse who has been coerced into meeting with the financial planner is likely to be in stage one, while the spouse who encouraged the meeting may be in step two or three. In many cases, the plan will rely on both spouses initiating and maintaining changed behavior in order for the plan to succeed. It is important for spouses to agree upon goals and to both be motivated and committed to working toward achieving the goals. Client motivation is discussed later in this chapter.

---

46. Britt, Sonya L.,Derek R. Lawson, and Camila A. Haselwood. "A Descriptive Analysis of Physiological Stress and Readiness to Change." *Journal of Financial Planning* 29, no. 12(2016): 45-51.

Comfort Zone

As stated previously, a comfort zone is a psychological state in which a person functions without anxiety or risk. In relation to finances, a person's comfort zone is often established by the socioeconomic status in which they grew up. This environment influences how we think about money (e.g., what defines rich or poor) and sets subconscious boundaries around what is acceptable or unacceptable (e.g., use of debt or a mother working outside the home). Breaking through that comfort zone can cause anxiety and stress around the potential of being judged or isolated (no longer belonging in the community that is "home"). Whether it is an aspiration to move into a higher socioeconomic class or the desire or need to learn to live on less, it will require a change in the way the client thinks about money in order to feel comfortable with their new status.

Money Beliefs

Each individual client and each financial planner has, over time, developed a relationship with money. Just as relationships with people can be health or unhealthy, a person's relationship with money can be healthy or unhealthy. A client's perceptions of the purpose of money and how it should be used and managed can have a profound impact, either positive or negative, on the financial planning process and the client's ability to meet their goals. Klontz and Klontz stress that "...chronic self-defeating and self-destructive financial behaviors aren't driven by our rational, thinking minds. The truth is, they stem from psychological forces that lie well outside our conscious awareness, and their roots run deep, deep into our past."[47] Overcoming obstacles presented by a client's money beliefs is possible through the use of financial therapy techniques.

An individual's attitudes, values, and beliefs about money are frequently inherited from parents and other family members.[48] In addition, each client's idiosyncratic background and experiences will inevitably influence their behaviors and values. Although the largest influence usually comes through observation of how parents handle money and make financial decisions, influence may also come from grandparents, aunts, uncles, and peers.[49] These findings are consistent with Albert Bandura's social learning theory, which emphasizes learning through observation and modeling the behavioral and emotional reactions of others.[50] While a child's mental processing of what they hear their parents say about money or how their parents handle money may not be logical from an adult's viewpoint, the beliefs the child developed made sense to the child at that time and are often carried through to adulthood. In addition to what we learn from family and friends, as children we also learned about money and finances from the economic events that occurred during that time, both nationally and locally, as well from the culture that we grew up in. All of these influences travel with us throughout childhood and into adulthood. There is no set pattern that dictates how the belief will manifest as child grows to adulthood. In some cases, the adult will respond by acting in an opposite manner to the beliefs they developed as a child. In other cases, the adult responds by mimicking those beliefs and behaviors, or somewhere in the middle.

---

47. Brad Klontz and Ted Klontz, *Mind over Money: Overcoming the Money Disorders That Threaten Our Financial Health* (New York: Broadway Books, 2009), 2.

48. Bruce Kirkcaldy and Adrian Furnham, "Predictors of Beliefs about Money," *Psychological Reports* 73, no. 3_suppl (1993): pp. 1079-1082, https://doi.org/10.2466/pr0.1993.73.3f.1079.

49. Sonya L. Britt, "The Intergenerational Transference of Money Attitudes and Behaviors," *Journal of Consumer Affairs* 50, no. 3 (March 2016): pp. 539-556, https://doi.org/10.1111/joca.12113.

50. https://www.simplypsychology.org/bandura.html.

While the clients and planners may not consciously recognize that they have deeply ingrained beliefs about money that were developed in their childhood and carried into adulthood, in many cases they do exist and may be an obstacle which is preventing the client from engaging in financially healthy behaviors.

Klontz, Kahler, and Klontz (2016) assert that "money scripts often consist of incomplete, conflicting, partial truths."[51] In other words, these ingrained beliefs may hold some element of truth, but are also in some ways false. The problem occurs when the client behaves and makes decisions as if the money script were entirely true. An examination of these belief patterns can help the client to make sense of their relationship with money, allowing them to overcome an obstacle that may be standing in the way of healthy financial behavior. It is also notable that money scripts are not mutually exclusive. One person can have multiple money scripts. In the exhibit below, money scripts are divided into four broad categories, linking each category to certain observable traits that clients may exhibit and some effects that are often associated with each category, as identified by Klontz, Britt, and Klontz.

---

51. Brad Klontz, Rick Kahler, and Ted Klontz, *Facilitating Financial Health: Tools for Financial Planners, Coaches, and Therapists* (Erlanger, KY: The National Underwriter Company, 2016).

Exhibit 2.5 | Money Scripts®[52]

y	Examples of Money Scripts	Traits	Effect
Money Avoidance	• Rich people get rich by taking advantage of others • Good people should not care about money • I do not deserve a lot of money	• Try not to think about money • Believe they do not deserve money	• Often do not look at financial statements • Likely to suffer from financial denial and/or financial enabling • Unlikely to stick to a budget
Money Worship	• Things would get better if I had more money • Money is power • Its hard to be poor and happy	• Buy things in an effort to create happiness	• Often have lower net worth and carry credit card debt • Likely to suffer from workaholism
Money Status	• I will not buy something unless it is new • Your self-worth equals your net worth • People are only as successful as the amount of money they earn	• Need to keep up the appearance of being successful	• Likely to overspend • Prone to suffer from gambling disorder, financial dependence, and/or financial infidelity
Money Vigilance	• Money should be saved not spent • I would be a nervous wreck if I did not have money saved for an emergency • It is extravagant to spend money on oneself	• Are alert and watchful in matters concerning their finances • May have anxiety about their financial future	• Often results in good financial outcomes • Could result in loss aversion and/or underspending

The first step in overcoming unhealthy money habits developed as a result of the client's money beliefs is to identify the issue and associated money belief. This allows the client to deal with any unaddressed issues that may remain as a result of their childhood experiences with money (if any exist), and then begin the process of learning new ways to think about and manage money.

The Klontz Money Script Inventory-Revised (KMSI-R) is available for use by financial planners to provide insight to the money scripts that may be influencing the client's behaviors and financial well-being.[53] It is important to note that not all clients will fall into one or more of these categories; however, when a client does, understanding the implications can assist the planner in developing the client's plan in the manner that is most likely to have positive results. Identifying the underlying money script allows the planner to initiate conversations with the client to clarify the client's answers to the questions for that script and develop a better understanding of the underlying emotions or beliefs that may be holding the client back from reaching their goals or causing them to make sub-optimal decisions about money.

---

52. Bradley Klontz et al., "Money Beliefs and Financial Behaviors: Development of the Klontz Money Script Inventory," *Journal of Financial Therapy* 2, no. 1 (January 2011), https://doi.org/10.4148/jft.v2i1.451.; and https://www.yourmentalwealthadvisors.com/our-process/your-money-script.

53. Begina, Michelle A., Jessica Hickingbottom, Elaine Lutrull, Megan McCoy, and Bradley Klontz."Identify and Understand Clients' Money Scripts: A Framework for Using the KMSI-R.". *Journal of Financial Planning*, (2018): 46-55.

Some planners may choose to integrate the Money Script Inventory into their data-gathering process, similar to the way a risk tolerance questionnaire may be used for all clients. Other planners may elect to wait until some sort of action, inaction, behavior, or discrepancy alerts the planner that underlying money beliefs may be impeding the client from reaching their goals. Before introducing the Money Script Inventory to the client, the financial planner will need to educate the client about money beliefs, letting the client know that sometimes we have deeply-rooted beliefs about money that we are not even aware or that may have an impact on reaching our goals. Understanding a client's money scripts allows the planner to do a better job of guiding the client, or to refer the client to a trained therapist if warranted. It is also recommended that before incorporating the inventory into use in their practice, the planner complete the inventory as a method of creating self-awareness around the planner's own money beliefs, allowing them to avoid transferring their own money scripts to the client.

Money Disorders and Sources of Money Conflict

As described previously in this chapter, clients will often utilize mental accounting to compartmentalize various funds and accounts with difference sources of income, types of expenditures, or goals. Conflicts often arise when multiple clients, such as spouses, partners, or family members, are faced with the need to agree upon priority of goals or which mental accounts should be used in connection with varying types of expenditures (needs versus wants) or saved toward specified goals. Saving for long-term goals requires a trade-off of current consumption in return for the ability to save, and all parties involved must come to an agreement regarding the appropriate level of sacrifice they are willing to take to achieve their various goals and attain financial well-being.

Key Concepts

1. Describe financial enabling and financial dependence.

2. Identify common sources of money conflict between spouses.

3. Define financial exploitation and discuss its prevalence among older adults.

According to the American Psychological Association's 2014 Stress in America survey, money is among the top sources of stress year-over-year, and, for 31 percent of adults with partners, money is a major source of conflict in their relationship.

Exhibit 2.6 | APA Stress Survey (Top Four Sources of Stress)

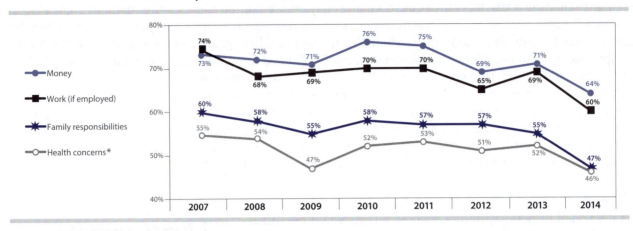

Unfortunately, clients often make financial decisions that are counterproductive to reaching their goals and creating additional money-related stress in their lives. In many cases, these decisions are driven by their biases and perceptions, along with their money beliefs. While an infrequent but occasional slip (e.g., a single bout of overspending) is not necessarily a threat to achieving financial well-being and reaching goals, when patterns of self-destructive behavior persist and cause stress, anxiety, emotional distress and impairment in the client's life, a money disorder may exist.[54]

Money Disorders

Below are some common disorders that may impact a client's relationship with money and, therefore, the likelihood of achieving financial and life goals. While it is important for a financial planner to be able to recognize money disorders, the planner should not attempt to treat them. A professionally trained financial therapist or other similar professional may be called upon to become part of the financial planning team, just as an attorney or CPA may become part of the team to address the areas in which they maintain competency and specialization. When the money disorder coexists with other psychological disorders (e.g., depression), or when a client reveals a serious problem such as addiction, violence or abuse, or suicidal thoughts, a referral should be made to licensed mental health professional or other similar professional (depending on the client's needs).

Money disorders are often rooted in emotion and may be associated with money beliefs (as described previously in this chapter). A financial therapist might employ a technique in which the client is encouraged to identify the deep emotional drivers behind the money disorder, creating an awareness of when emotion is overtaking rational thought. This allows the client to recognize the onset of those emotions and allows rational thought to intervene before the client gives in to the behaviors instigated by these emotions.

54. Brad Klontz and Ted Klontz, *Mind over Money: Overcoming the Money Disorders That Threaten Our Financial Health* (New York: Broadway Books, 2009).

The follow excerpt from *Mind Over Money* describes some questions a client might consider in order to create that awareness:

> Think of a financial situation that ended badly. Let's say it's a shopping trip during which you spent far more than you intended. As much as you'd like to forget the whole thing, sit down and really *think* about it, in detail. How were you feeling when you went to the mall? Did you have certain purchases in mind, or was this an impulse visit? If you were shopping for something specific, how did you find yourself even looking at the other items you bought? Concentrate on remembering your thoughts and emotions at each point. Pretend that you're a detective investigating a crime and trace your actions back to whatever prompted them. When did you lose control of the spending? What were you feeling at that moment?[55]

Klontz and Klontz prescribe that this self-examination be done without self-shame and criticism. It is merely an exercise to create awareness so that the next time these emotions take control of rational thought, the client can recognize what is happening and learn to slow down and take a few deep breaths, allowing rational thought to exert control over the emotional response.

The above is just one example of numerous techniques that a financial therapist may use and all must be employed with care, skill, and diligence. It is important for the financial planner to avoid overstepping her skill set and refer clients to trained financial coaches and therapists as needed. However, the planner must first be able to recognize when the referral is needed. The following are descriptions of some common money disorders that the planner may encounter.

Compulsive Buying Disorder (CBD)
Compulsive buying disorder (CBD) is found worldwide and is characterized by excessive preoccupation with shopping and spending that leads to distress. CBD behavior can be a response to negative feelings and events in one's life. Shopping and buying can provide initial relief with positive feelings that tend to be short lived. This sort of behavior can be detrimental to an attempt at financial discipline and financial independence. CBD can also lead to financial ruin and bankruptcy, often characterized by high credit card debt.

Example 2.10

Ivan and Irene are married and have serious financial difficulties, mostly from credit card and auto debt, which they financed over seven years. Irene's brother Beau is helping them manage the situation. However, on the way home from a meeting with the bankruptcy attorney, Ivan stops at Best Buy and purchases a new 75-inch TV because it is on sale and there is a deal for signing up for Best Buy's credit card. Ivan is clearly unable to manage his spending and does not understand the severity of his financial situation.

Hoarding
Hoarding is a disorder characterized by accumulating and being unable to discard possessions that most people would consider worthless. The accumulation of these types of worthless possessions often creates clutter that negatively impacts living and working spaces. Hoarding disorder can also be associated with money such that one is unwilling to spend money even after becoming successful.

---

55. *ibid*, at p. 46.

Additionally, this behavior may be associated with those who have been raised in poverty, such as those who grew up during the depression. While everyone has rational fears regarding money, the fear of running out of money can become irrational with hoarding behavior, resulting in a client being unable to spend and enjoy their accumulated wealth.

Gambling Disorder

Gambling disorder is a recognized mental health disorder in which persistent and recurring problematic gambling leads to significant impairment and stress. Everyone who has gambled knows the emotional highs and lows of winning and losing a bet. Gambling can be exciting. However, most people who go to a casino also know that in the long run, the house always wins; the odds are stacked in the house's favor.

Workoholism

Workaholism is a compulsive disorder that is often associated with anxiety or depression. Workaholics frequently fear not having enough money and as a result focus on their career at the expense of personal relationships. They often justify their focus on work and avoidance of family and friends.

Financial Enabling/Financial Dependence

Financial dependence is the result of reliance on unearned income from another person to the extent that it creates anxiety around the fear of being cut off from that income. Financial dependence can be detrimental to the individual receiving the income in that it may suppress their motivation and desire to succeed on their own. Financial enabling is the opposite of financial dependence and occurs when one individual provides financial assistance that keeps others dependent. This result may be intentional (money is used as a form of control, resulting in strained relationships) or unintentional. In some cases the financial enabler has high income and assets, but in other cases the enabler is giving away more than they can afford to give, perhaps to the point where they are faced with bankruptcy, due to the inability to say no when asked for financial assistance.

Financial enabling often manifests itself as successful parents financially enabling adult children to the extent that it negatively affects their children's emotional wellbeing. This type of situation is relatively common with wealthy individuals who are successful and continue providing financial support to their adult children, thus depriving them of developing their own financial acumen and responsibility. Other examples of financial enabling include providing support to a sibling or parent who has self-inflicted chronic financial difficulties. Financial enabling can also be seen in many family businesses.

Example 2.11

Karen has two grown sons, Moe and Curley. She had Moe when she was 18 years old and has never been very responsible with money. Moe went to college and, through hard work over the decades, has become fairly successful. Although she has attended numerous financial education seminars and classes through the years, Karen has filed for bankruptcy three times and continues to mismanage her finances. She has no emergency fund and continues to call Moe when there is a financial crisis, such as a need for a new set of tires. Moe continues to enable her poor financial behavior.

Example 2.12

Olivia is a successful financial planner with her own practice and is recognized as a leader in the industry. She hires her two sons, Fitz and Huck, to help run and grow the business. Over a fairly short period of time, she ends up paying her boys several hundred thousand dollars each in salary. However, while Fitz is working fairly hard, he is clearly overpaid for what he is doing. Huck, on the other hand, rarely shows up for work. Olivia is enabling her sons and thus, depriving them of learning how to function in the real world. As she begins to think about retiring, she cannot trust Fitz and Huck to run the financial planning practice and ultimately purchase the business from her nor can she sell the firm to a third-party without the likelihood of the new owner firing at least Huck.

The disorders mentioned above, as well as cognitive errors and emotional biases discussed in behavioral finance, can create friction when establishing financial plans, and especially long-term financial plans such as retirement.

When an adviser is working with a client, it is important for the adviser to identify a client's motivation for achieving their financial goals. It is helpful to understand and identify whether the client is subject to any of these money disorders. Often, financial and lifestyle decisions are motivated by fear of running out of money. This fear can be rational or irrational. Other clients may be motivated by developing a sense of control over their financial situation so that they are no longer dependent on someone else or need to have a job. By clarifying motivations and managing psychological deterrents to appropriate financial management, advisers can often assist clients in devising better financial plans and, ultimately, achieving their life goals.

Common Sources of Money Conflict

It is also important for advisers to understand potential sources of conflict with money when working with clients.

Money is often one of the top sources of conflict both between spouses and among family members. Spouses who have differing philosophies from each other about money often have conflict. For example, if one spouse is a saver (hoarder) and one is a spender (CBD), there will most likely be conflict. The saver will likely resent the spender and vice-versa. Understanding these differences in money beliefs and behaviors prior to marriage is ideal, but having the conversation about money beliefs after marriage can also alleviate and/or resolve some conflicts around money. Some of the more common potential areas of conflict regarding finances between spouses and other family members are discussed below.

Financial Infidelity and Lack of Transparency

Financial infidelity is the act of engaging in significant financial transactions without the knowledge and support of a spouse or partner. While many people engage in financial transactions of some sort without the knowledge of a partner, it becomes problematic when the transactions are significant in amount, such as hiding money, accumulating debt, gambling, or investing in illiquid assets that require the use of debt and leverage. A 2018 research study in which married and cohabitating participants were asked questions about whether they had committed certain acts while in the relationship, 53 percent of participants selected items associated with financial infidelity, although only 27 percent answered yes when asked whether they had kept a financial secret from their partner. This may have occurred because the respondent did not feel that the action rose to the level of infidelity or because they felt that the lie or action was warranted in order to avoid conflict. The most commonly selected behaviors were as follows:[56]

Behavior	Percent of Respondents Answering "Yes"
Hidden purchases	24%
Lied about the price I paid for something	23%
Spent money on the kids without telling my spouse	22%
Said I bought something on sale but paid full price	19%
Pretend a new purchase is an old one	15%
Taken money out of savings without telling my spouse	11%
Opened a credit card without telling my spouse	11%

Marriages, as with other relationships, are predicated on honesty and transparency. Lack of transparency when it comes to financial decisions can be detrimental to marriages and other family relationships.

Example 2.13

Sue and Blue are a married couple saving for a down payment on a new home. Blue buys a new car that is relatively expensive, finances it over seven years, and intentionally deceives Sue about the size of the monthly car payment. This decision and lack of transparency may eventually cause friction between Sue and Blue and is likely to infringe upon their ability to save for a home, a goal that they have mutually agreed upon. These types of financial infidelity over time can lead to resentment, as well as to the erosion of trust.

Saving

Saving is an important process for achieving financial goals. Without savings, many goals would remain unachieved. It is important to understand the objective of the savings and how the savings is achieved, whether through payroll deductions in a 401(k) plan or in a bank savings account. Conflict often occurs when both spouses are not working together toward the same savings goal.

Spending

Spending is required in our society. However, conflict arises when the expenses that one spouse might categorize as frivolous (e.g., boat) or as a luxury item are categorized as necessities by the other spouse.

Priorities

The basic priority of work versus family time often creates conflict if not balanced properly. One spouse may be overly focused on work and providing for the financial needs of the family, while the other spouse may resent the lack of time spent with the family. Those with workaholism often spend the majority of their waking hours focused on their job and not on the family. This focus often creates tension with other family members.

---

56. Michelle Jeanfreau et al., "Financial Infidelity in Couple Relationships," *Journal of Financial Therapy* 9, no. 1 (January 2018), https://doi.org/10.4148/1944-9771.1159.

Requests for Assistance from Family and Friends

Conflicts around money occur not only between spouses, but also between family members, friends, and business associates. Clients with a high level of the personality trait of agreeableness have a tendency to be trusting, sympathetic, altruistic, and cooperative, leaving them susceptible to sacrificing their own financial well-being in favor of succumbing to requests for financial assistance from family members, friends, or charities.[57] These clients may need assistance establishing parameters for separate budget categories for their own well-being versus funds available for assisting others, and mediation may be required if friends and family members object to the newly established barriers to access to the client's funds. Note that a high degree of agreeableness is not necessarily a bad trait, as these individuals tend to be very adaptive and, therefore, tend to experience a high degree of life satisfaction in the retirement phase due to this ability to adapt to life's circumstances. The planner may need to assist these clients in finding balance between their financial well-being and their desire to help others. In the extreme, these types of interactions may reach the level of financial enabling and financial dependence.

The planner must also remain aware of potential cultural values and influences that may be driving the decision to share financial resources among family members. Klontz, Britt, and Archuleta note, for example, that it is common in the Latino culture for financial resources to be shared among family and friends.[58] The financial planner may need to help the client find an appropriate and acceptable balance between exercising this value and maintaining the client's own financial security.

Financial Enmeshment

Parents responsibly teaching minor children about earning, spending, saving, and investing money can result in the child growing up to be a financially healthy adult. However, when parents involve children in adult financial decisions and conflicts at a time when the child is not yet emotionally and cognitively prepared to cope with such decisions and conflicts, **financial enmeshment** occurs.[59] Financial enmeshment can result in impairment of the child's learning system, causing the child to develop unhealthy financial habits.

Example 2.14

Willow, who is now an adult, was 12 years old and the only child of divorced parents who frequently fought about alimony and child support payments. Willow's parents had a habit of putting her into the role of mediator between them, often asking her pass financial messages or requests to the other parent, unmindful of the fact that she was not emotionally or cognitively prepared to deal with such a high level of stress. As a result Willow associates money with anxiety and feelings of insecurity, leading to unhealthy financial behaviors that are preventing her from achieving financial well-being.

Kemnitz, Klontz, and Archuleta (2016) cite evidence that financial enmeshment is significantly correlated with money disorders including hoarding, CBD, gambling disorder, workaholism, financial dependence and financial enabling.[60]

---

57. For additional information regarding personality traits, see Paul T. Costa and Robert R. McCrae, "Normal Personality Assessment in Clinical Practice: The NEO Personality Inventory.," *Psychological Assessment* 4, no. 1 (1992): pp. 5-13, https://doi.org/10.1037/1040-3590.4.1.5.; and Costa, P.T., Jr., and Robert McCrae. *NEO-PI-R: Professional Manual.* Odessa, FL: Psychological Assessment Resources, 1992.
58. Bradley T. Klontz, Sonya L. Britt, and Kristy L. Archuleta, *Financial Therapy: Theory, Research, and Practice* (Cham: Springer, 2015).
59. Randy Kemnitz, Bradley Klontz, and Kristy L Archuleta, "Financial Enmeshment: Untangling the Web," *Journal of Financial Therapy* 6, no. 2 (2016), https://doi.org/10.4148/1944-9771.1085.

Undue Influence, Control, and Abuse

In addition to the above-mentioned financial disorders and money-related conflicts, financial planners may encounter situations in which a client is the victim of finance-related undue influence, control, or abuse.

Couples may agree that it is in the family's best interest for one spouse to stay home and raise children while the other spouse works for income. The spouse that stays home with the children can be at a financial disadvantage if the marriage ends and can be in a situation in which the working spouse withholds financial resources for various reasons. The stay-at-home spouse may feel trapped in a toxic relationship with limited prospects for a job after staying at home for 10 to 20 years.

Another example in which financial influence can appear is within a family business where parents employ children or other family members. It can be difficult to separate the family relationship from the business relationship. For example, a parent might withhold a well-deserved raise or promotion from a child based on a non-business-related perceived transgression.

It is estimated that at least one in ten community-dwelling adults experience some form of abuse (physical, emotional, or financial) every year. It is also acknowledged that that number is likely to be significantly higher due to lack of reporting, with as many as 24 undetected cases for every one that is reported.[61] Seniors are particularly vulnerable to financial exploitation and undue influence due to social isolation and potential cognitive impairments such as dementia. The Older Americans Act defines **financial exploitation** as "The fraudulent or otherwise illegal, unauthorized, or improper act or process of an individual, including a caregiver or fiduciary, that uses the resources of an older individual for monetary or personal benefit, profit, or gain, or that results in depriving an older individual of rightful access to, or use of, benefits, resources, belongings, or assets."[62] Indications that a client may be experiencing financial exploitation include sudden changes in financial account balances or large unexplained withdrawals, abrupt changes to the will or other financial documents, and unpaid bills, among others.

Imbalances in power regarding managing finances or making financial decisions can leave one spouse with a reduced sense of self-worth and lead to conflicts in the marital relationship. Domestic violence is a more serious problem. If the balance of power is so inflated that one spouse is given very little (or no) spending money, if one spouse uses money to limit the other spouse's freedom or interactions with other people or prohibits the spouse from working outside the home, or if one spouse appears to be intimidated by the other, it may be a warning sign of domestic abuse. If domestic violence is suspected, the financial planner should not encourage the couple to talk about their relationship as the abuse may intensify. The planner should consult with a qualified therapist about their concerns and allow the therapist to guide the planners ensuing actions.

Handling everyday financial responsibilities and making financial decisions together can help to create and maintain harmony in the marital relationship, and possibly prevent one spouse becoming subject to undue financial influence, control, or abuse from the other spouse.

---

60. *Ibid*, at p. 4.

61. https://ncea.acl.gov/About-Us/What-We-Do/Research/Statistics-and-Data.aspx.

62. Suspicion of any type of elder abuse (physical, emotional, or financial) should be reported to Adult Protective Services. http://www.napsa-now.org/get-help/help-in-your-area.

Importance of Agreeing on Financial Goals and Objectives with the Spouse and/or Family Members

The above-mentioned sources of tension and conflict regarding financial matters should help to clarify the importance of identifying and agreeing on financial goals with spouses and other family members. Having a clear agreed upon plan for retirement, for example, may help spouses manage conflict when there is tension regarding work as a priority or savings as a means of funding an agreed upon retirement lifestyle. Without an underlying plan, there is little basis for these financial choices, other than "want." Only after the clients (who may be spouses or unmarried individuals in a long-term relationship planning together) agree on their financial goals, and parameters and priorities for current lifestyle adjustments they are willing to make to accomplish the goals, can a financial planner proceed to the analysis required to assist the clients with planning. Agreeing on goals does not mean that one spouse wins and the other loses, it means a compromise is negotiated between them.

Inheritances received upon the death of a family member may be a source of familial conflict due to a lack of communication among family members during the decedent's lifetime. Senior family members may feel uncomfortable discussing their finances and estate plans with their children. However, when parents or grandparents involve their adult children and grandchildren in estate planning decisions, relational stress among surviving family members may be avoided or at least mitigated.

Example 2.15

Hal and Sal are brothers who started a successful business nearly 60 years ago. Hal and Sal are both married and each of them has three children, one who works in the family business and two that have chosen careers in other fields. Several years ago Sal held a family meeting with his spouse and children to discuss his how his estate would be distributed upon his death. As a result of that meeting, each of the stakeholders had the opportunity to express their feelings and desires regarding the family business and other assets. This open dialogue between family members resulted in an estate plan in which Sal left his ownership in the business to the child who works there and life insurance of equal value to each of their other two children. Hal thought that sounded like a good idea, so he did the same, but without first discussing it with his spouse and children.

Hal and Sal died together in a car accident last year while on a business trip. While Sal's family is deeply mourning the loss of their spouse and father, they are firmly united as a family and helping to support one another in every way. Each of them knew exactly what to expect in terms of their inheritance, and had helped to shape the plan into something they all agreed with. Unfortunately, Hal's family has become estranged as a result of the estate plan. The child working in the business feels that it is unfair that his siblings got so much cash while he got none. He feels that they were given the freedom to enjoy their inheritance while he must work for his. One of the siblings who got cash was hoping to have some ownership in the business, although she did not want to work there. Hal's spouse and other child are being pulled into the conflict and are being asked to take sides.

Conflict Resolution

Most of the disorders and conflicts discussed here are serious issues for which the client should be referred to a licensed therapist, mental health professional, psychologist or psychiatrist. When the planner is a licensed therapist, a referral may still be needed due to the ethical concerns surrounding conflicts of interest that may arise due to the dual role of planner and therapist. For these reasons, collaboration between professionals is usually the best alternative.

What, then, can the planner do? Whether working with individuals, couples, or families the planner should always remain nonjudgmental of any of the parties involved. When working with couples or families, the planner should view all parties as equal and active participants in the planning process and be careful not to take sides when conflicts arise. This may sound easy on the surface, but can be very difficult since the planner's own culture, values, beliefs, and biases may align more with one party than with the other(s). It may be even more difficult when couples *want* the planner to take sides. Klontz, Kahler, and Klontz suggest that planners may overcome the risk of over-identifying with one of partners by viewing the clients based on their relationship (coupleship) rather than as the individuals who are in the relationship. To facilitate this and ensure that neither party feels alienated or marginalized, the planner should ensure that all contact and communications include both partners in the relationship.[63]

In some, very uncomfortable, cases, emotional flooding will occur during the meeting with the planner, causing couples to fight with one another. Due to the high level of emotion, the planner will have a difficult time diffusing the situation through reason or logic. The clients need time to overcome the emotion before they will be capable of moving forward. Depending on the level of conflict, the planner may call for a brief time-out by separating clients from each other for twenty or thirty minutes, either physically or by the planner asking them to engage some segregated tasks, such as reading an informational piece on an investment that was proposed earlier in the conversation. The planner should note that he is intentionally changing focus, for example by stating "I can understand both sides, and I believe that we may be at an impasse for now, so let's revisit this issue next time we meet and focus on another element of the plan." Alternatively, the planner may opt to end the meeting and reschedule, or, when the issues and/or intensity of conflict warrant, refer the clients to a financial or family therapist.

---

63. Brad Klontz, Rick Kahler, and Ted Klontz, *Facilitating Financial Health: Tools for Financial Planners, Coaches, and Therapists*, 2nd ed. (Erlanger, KY: The National Underwriter Company, 2016), 181-182.

MOTIVATION AND DECISION MAKING

Identifying the Client's Financial Goals and Motivation for Achieving Those Goals

Understanding the client's motivation for achieving their goals is essential to the financial planner's ability to design the planning experience in a manner that aligns with the client's motivations and goals. In addition to identifying the client's motivation for achieving goals, the financial planner should understand how to create an environment that facilitates the client's motivation to continue working toward those goals, often over a long period of time. In some cases, clients will have difficulty articulating their goals and the motivation for them. To unearth the client's true goals and motivations, the planner may need to ask the client to keep digging further.

≔ *Key Concepts*

1. Explain values-driven financial planning and guided imagery.

2. Describe and compare intrinsic and extrinsic motivation.

3. Describe the three basic psychological needs that determine motivation.

Example 2.16

Planner: It is great to meet you! What is it that brings you in to see me today?

Client: I want to earn more on my investments than I am currently earning.

This initial statement by the client may lead the planner to focus the process, and client meetings, around portfolio management and investment evaluation. Understanding what makes the desire for greater returns important to the client may reveal that the client isn't really interested in the day-to-day management and returns of the portfolio. The conversation continues as follows:

Planner: I may be able to help you with that, but first, can you help me understand what makes earning higher returns on your investment portfolio important to you?

Client: I have some family members who had not saved enough money to support themselves and allow them to enjoy their retirement years, and I don't want to be in that position when I retire.

At this point the planner does not yet know whether the client actually needs to earn higher returns on her portfolio, but to help the client reach her true goal, the planner must continue the process of asking open-ended questions to determine the client's image of what a happy and meaningful retirement is to her. In other words, the planner will need to guide the client from a focus on what she does *not* want retirement to look like to what the client *does* want her retirement to look like.

Planner: Close your eyes and picture yourself in your ideal retirement.

[pauses to allow the client to imagine what life would be like]

Planner: Can you describe for me how you envisioned your ideal life in retirement?

As the relationship continues, the planner in the above example may spend just a few minutes of each annual review meeting discussing investment decisions and markets and more time working with the client on the total process involved in achieving the retirement goal because now the client understands that the true goal is not higher investment returns, the true goal is the client's vision of retirement.

As the example above illustrates, to achieve success from the financial planning engagement the planner may first need to help the client discover and articulate their goals and motivations.

Financial planning is values-driven (or values-based) when the planner seeks to develop a financial plan that serves goals reflecting the client's spiritual, emotional, and personal needs in addition to financial needs. Instead of focusing only on the building of wealth, the planner examines with the client the reasons for building wealth and how it will contribute to the client's well-being and life goals.

In this approach, financial plans are developed to reflect personal priorities and needs. The planner asks questions such as "How would you live your life if you had the money you need?" and "If you only had a few years to live, how would you change your life?" The planner probes the client to find out what he or she really cares about before trying to develop a financial plan. The idea is to bring the financial plan into alignment with the client's vision for his or her life and to have it speak to the larger issue of what the client values.

The use of open-ended questions (or open-ended prompts) and guided imagery can be especially important when practicing values-driven planning.

Exhibit 2.7 | Open-Ended Questions and Guided Imagery Examples

Don't Ask:	Do Ask:
• What is your retirement goal? • Who do you plan to leave your assets to upon your death? • Is this account earmarked for anything? • What are your financial goals?	• Describe your ideal retirement. • Tell me about the legacy you would like to leave when you pass away. This may include legacy goals for family, charities, and your community. • What is it that you hope to accomplish through saving? • If you had all of the time and resources to do anything you wanted, what would you do?

Intrinsic and Extrinsic Motivation

Allowing clients the opportunity to explore and reflect upon their thoughts and feelings, and to picture how their life can change for the better, can motivate the client to take action and change behaviors that may be inhibiting their financial well-being or ability to achieve their goals.

The source of motivation may be intrinsic or extrinsic. **Intrinsic motivation** comes from within and is often associated with satisfaction and enjoyment while **extrinsic motivation** comes from an outside reward (you expect to get something in return) or avoidance of punishment. Those whose motivation is internal tend to have more interest, excitement and confidence, resulting in enhanced performance, persistence, and creativity, and heightened vitality, self-esteem, and general well-being.[64]

---

64. Richard M. Ryan and Edward L. Deci, "Self-Determination Theory and the Facilitation of Intrinsic Motivation, Social Development, and Well-Being.," *American Psychologist* 55, no. 1 (2000): pp. 68-78, https://doi.org/10.1037/0003-066x.55.1.68.

Exhibit 2.8 | Examples of Internal and External Motivation[65]

Examples of Internal Motivation	Examples of External Motivation
• Doing something because you value the activity • Acting based on a sense of personal commitment • Learning something because you are interested in it • Behaving based on a personal commitment to excel	• Doing something because you are bribed to do so • Acting based on external pressure to perform • Learning something because you are punished if you do not • Behaving based on fear of being surveilled

Self-Determination Theory

Self-determination theory (SDT) asserts that there are three main psychological needs that determine motivation: competence, relatedness, and autonomy (see **Exhibit 2.9** below). Satisfaction of these three basic needs yields enhanced self-motivation while obstruction of these needs leads to diminished motivation and well-being.[66] The desire to fulfill these needs is not something that a financial planner can teach a client, or that an educator can teach a student, because they already exist within every person. We all innately want to learn and be creative. We want to have things we know we do well, we want to be connected to others, and we want to be able to make our own decisions and be in control of our own lives.

Exhibit 2.9 | Basic Needs that Determine Motivation

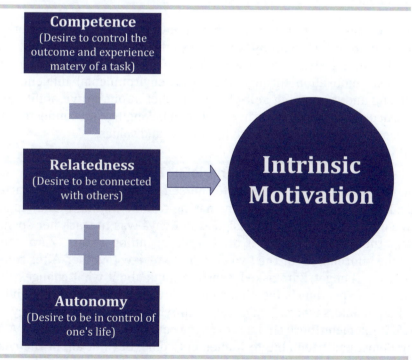

Competence
(Desire to control the outcome and experience matery of a task)

Relatedness
(Desire to be connected with others)

Autonomy
(Desire to be in control of one's life)

Intrinsic Motivation

---

65. Derived from: Ryan and Deci, *Ibid.*
66. *Ibid.*

Cognitive evaluation theory (CET), as presented by Ryan and Deci, is a subtheory of SDT and asserts that social-contextual events such as feedback, communication, and rewards, that are conducive to feelings of competence can enhance intrinsic motivation.[67]

The planner's role in increasing a client's intrinsic motivation is to help the client in the realization of these three basic needs by facilitating an environment in which the client is proactive and engaged in the planning process. The planner may challenge the client with opportunities to complete tasks in the planning process that will help them achieve their goals, and provide the client with positive, non-demeaning, feedback to help create such and environment. For example, assume a client was assigned the implementation tasks of contributing to an IRA and 401(k) plan but at the follow-up meeting had enrolled in the 401(k) but had not established and funded the IRA. Rather than chastise the client for not getting the IRA set up and funded, start by congratulating the client for taking the firsts step by enrolling in the 401(k) and focus on the positive influence that will have on providing their desired lifestyle in retirement. Celebrating a client's, even small, victories are important in supporting self-motivation. Providing the client with opportunities for self-direction in the planning process facilitates the need for autonomy and internal motivation is enhanced when competency stems from self-determined behavior. This can be accomplished by engaging the client in the planning and decision-making process.

Internal motivation, however, will only exist if the activity appeals to the client; otherwise, the principles of CET will not apply. For example, one spouse may be intrinsically motivated to accomplish the tasks required to implement the plan while the other spouse is not. The amotivated spouse is likely attending the planning meetings due to relatedness (the sense of connection the other spouse). Ryan and Deci note that amotivation toward an action may come from not feeling competent to do it or from not expecting it to yield the desired outcome.

Amotivation is a lack of both internal and external motivation. In between amotivation and internal motivation are a continuum of external motivations (gradually moving from fully external to partially external/internal, with varying degrees of each). SDT provides that extrinsic motivation can become self-determined intrinsic motivation through the social environmental influence, by supporting the individual in developing and reinforcing **self-efficacy** (belief in one's own ability to be successful at a given task or in a particular situation), ensuring a sense of belonging and connectedness, and supporting a discovery of how the activity synthesizes with their goals and values.

Example 2.17

Kenya, who has never created a budget for herself in the past, recently started working with Zara, a financial planner. Kenya was having trouble finding money to save for her goals, so one of the first tasks Zara assigned to Kenya was to track her spending for 60 days to help them build a picture of Kenya's spending habits. Zara compiled and categorized the information for the two of them to review together. After completing the review of the past budget, Zara asked Kenya to think about what changes she might be able to make in her spending habits that could free up some money, even if it is only a few dollars, to be put into savings. Kenya came up with a few ideas and they agreed that Kenya would implement those changes over the course of the next month. At the follow-up meeting Kenya had been able to implement some, but not all, of the changes. Zara celebrated those victories with Kenya, reinforcing what Kenya did well, and provided a chart showing how the change from zero dollars saved to the current savings was moving

---

67.*Ibid.*

her toward achieving her goals. Kenya admitted that she was starting to enjoy the process of finding ways to make small changes that can make a difference in her financial well-being. Kenya is motivated to implement the rest of he changes because she feels confident in her ability to do so, and because she knows that the changes were a result of her ideas and her decisions. We can see that she has reached the full extent of internal motivation because she is making changes for the enjoyment and sense of satisfaction she gets from doing so.

Positive Psychology

Researcher, psychologist, and author of the best-selling book *Learned Optimism* Martin Seligman is viewed as the founder of positive psychology. He is the director of the University of Pennsylvania Positive Psychology center, where **positive psychology** is described as "the scientific study of the strengths that enable individuals and communities to thrive. The field is founded on the belief that people want to lead meaningful and fulfilling lives, to cultivate what is best within themselves, and to enhance their experiences of love, work, and play."[68]

> ### ⋮☰ *Key Concepts*
>
> 1. Describe positive psychology.
> 2. Explain choice architecture and "nudges."
> 3. Explain how default options may be used to promote decisions that are in a client's best interest.

Asebedo and Seay apply the concepts of positive psychology to financial planning, and refer to positive financial planning as a move "beyond financial functioning and health to ensure a person's money is maximized as a tool to optimize well-being, such that a flourishing life is possible."[69] Financial functioning is described from a typical financial planner's viewpoint using basic progress measures such as increasing net worth, a good credit score, and consistent savings, while financial flourishing is focused on how money is related to five key elements drawn from well-being theory: positive emotion (happiness), engagement (hobbies and activities), relationships, meaning (purpose in life; belonging to something greater than oneself, such as religious charitable, or special interest groups), and accomplishments, to optimize overall well-being. Based on this concept, the financial planner may help the client explore what types of activities the client enjoys the most (activities that promote positive emotion/create happiness) and work through the budgeting process to allocate more resources to those activities. Alternatively, the planner can help the client find more meaning by encouraging active involvement in religious or charitable organizations that support the client's values.

Optimism is a key component of positive psychology. One example of a positive psychology exercise that may be adapted to financial planning is to re-focus from problems to successes, in other words, to change from a negative outlook to a positive outlook (optimism). This may be reinforced by assigning the client the task of writing down three things that went well (financially) each day, and why they went well. For example, a client attempting to gain control of spending might note that they avoided a non-essential purchase by pausing and thinking about it rather than making the impulse buy. Numerous other exercises from positive psychology can also be successfully applied to financial planning, but are beyond the scope of this textbook.

68. https://ppc.sas.upenn.edu/

69. Asebedo, S., and Martin Seay, "From Functioning to Flourishing: Applying Positive Psychology to Financial Planning." *Journal of Financial Planning* 28, no. 11(2015): 50-58.

Choice Architecture

Choice architecture refers to the structure surrounding the manner in which choices are presented and recognizing that the context in which choices are presented influences the decision maker. A choice architect is someone who designs the environment in which choices are made. Those who select where food is displayed in a cafeteria, for example, are choice architects since the order in which we see the food we are choosing from can impact our selections. Thaler and Sunstein use the term "**nudge**" to describe choice architecture that alters people's behavior in a predictable way without forbidding any options or significantly changing their economic incentives, but stipulate that to be a nudge the intervention must be easy and cheap to avoid. [70] The goal for the financial planner, then, is to design an environment which allows for freedom of choice while facilitating the choices that are in the decision-makers best interests.

When considering the application of choice architecture and nudges to financial planning, planners must be careful to adhere to the old proverb that with great power comes great responsibility. Understanding choice architecture, and that the manner in which the planner structures the presentation of choices, can impact the client's decision-making has important ethical undertones. The planner, as a fiduciary to the client, must always put the client's best interest first and ensure that the use of choice architecture is designed to assist the client in reaching his or her goals and that it is unlikely to cause harm. Nudges are best used only in situations where clients are least likely to make good choices, and where the planner has carefully evaluated the costs and benefits involved.

When financial planners are intentional in how they frame choices, the client benefits from better decision-making capabilities.

Framing

Choice architecture refers to the structure surrounding the manner in which choices are presented and recognizing that the context in which choices are presented influences the decision maker. A choice architect is someone who designs the environment in which choices are made. Framing a glass as half full versus half empty or framing hamburger as 75 percent lean versus 25 percent fat are simple examples of **framing**. Additional examples of the framing effect are discussed under Prospect Theory, earlier in this chapter.

Financial planners presenting various choices to clients must be cognizant of how the choices are framed, as this will impact the client's decisions. Framing around goals can help clients understand the value of their decisions; not just monetary value, but in terms of well-being and reaching their goals. For example, when discussing saving for retirement the discussion can be framed around the amount of

---

70. Cass R. Sunstein and Richard H. Thaler, *Nudge: Improving Decisions About Health, Wealth and Happiness* (New York: Penguin, 2009).

savings (loss of current consumption the client will face) or around the income it can produce in retirement (gain received from the savings program).

Default Options and Number of Options Presented

It is not surprising that when a large number of options are presented or when options become more complex, people struggle to make a decision. Status quo bias occurs when clients have a preference for things to stay the same (often because it feels safe and seems less difficult than making a change) and prevents clients from changing their behaviors to better enable them to reach their goals. Status quo bias often occurs when there is choice overload. Choice overload can be avoided by limiting the number of choices to a more processable amount, or it can be mitigated through the use of default options. A simple example of the use of default options appears when we download new computer programs. We are given the choice to customize which components are installed, but the default option is pre-selected as the one that is optimal for most users.

Studies show that when default options are presented, people tend to not opt out of them. Since choice architecture focuses on creating an environment where clients are nudged in the direction of the choice with the most advantageous outcome while preserving the right to choose, the planner, in some circumstances, may be able to design the presentation of options with a default choice that will create the most desirable outcome. For example, financial planners often work with a businesses to establish a 401(k) retirement plan in which employees can choose whether to save money from their paychecks into the retirement plan. The regulations regarding qualified retirement plans allow for the plan to include a default option whereby upon becoming eligible to participate in the plan the employee is automatically enrolled to contribute a certain percentage of their income. The employee is free to opt out, but that takes effort so many employees will not make the effort to do so, resulting in a larger number of employees enrolled in the plan. This default choice is to their advantage because it allows them to passively make the choice to save for their future.

The U.S. government on occasion also uses choice architecture and default options to encourage outcomes that are advantageous to most Americans. For example, as will be discussed in Chapter 11, retirees reaching the age of 65 who receive Medicare benefits under Part A (with no required premium payments) are automatically enrolled in Part B, but are given the choice to opt out. Since Part B provides medical insurance coverage that is essential for most retirees, this nudges them to make the most advantageous decision while still allowing freedom of choice for those who have coverage elsewhere and do not currently need it from Medicare.

Overcoming Inertia

Clients are faced with thousands of decisions every day, and the mind has only so much capacity to process every option, detail, advantage, and disadvantage of each potential choice. For this reason, heuristics (the mental short-cuts described previously in this chapter) are applied to many of these decisions. Decision fatigue negatively impacts the quality of choices made, and in some cases the client's solution to being overwhelmed by the decision-making process may be to simply do nothing.

Financial planners can mitigate decision fatigue by considering the relevance of the information presented to clients in connection with implementation options being presented, and by limiting the presentation to the most critical elements (additional details can be provided in a supplemental document for the client to review at their leisure if they desire to do so). The planner is tasked with removing the complexity and making choices simple. This is not always easy since the financial planner may enjoy the planning aspects, such as diving into the minutia of the balance sheet and analysis using ratios. The client, on the other hand, may not enjoy those details and may be more interested in simply knowing whether or not they can reach their goal.

Another way the planner can prevent decision fatigue is to break a comprehensive plan down into more palatable segments such that the plan decisions are made and implemented over a period of time. Allowing clients to focus on a smaller number of decisions in the each meeting is likely to yield better decision making and encourage the client to take action. Even the sub-parts of the plan may need to be broken down over a series of meetings.

Clients who are experiencing highly emotional events causing fatigue or distraction are likely to have difficulty making decisions, even when time for doing so is limited. Breaking the meetings down into shorter more focused segments can make a difference in their ability to process and evaluate as necessary for making decisions.

Example 2.18

Lauren, who is 92 year old, recently lost her husband of 70 years and is devastated by the loss. Her will was written more than 20 years ago and left everything to her husband, and if he predeceased her to her sister, Inez. Since then, Inez developed a drug addiction. Lauren does not want all of her assets to go to Inez, who she expects will spend it all on drugs, but she doesn't know how she wants to split her estate among her many nieces, nephews and charities. She realizes that she is 92 years old, so she needs to update her will sooner rather than later, but is overwhelmed by the devastation from losing her husband in conjunction with all of the other decisions that need to be made in settling his estate and evaluating options for her own well-being (having someone come into their home to help take of her versus selling the house and moving to assisted living, etc). The sheer number of decisions are just too much. The financial planner can relieve some of the decision fatigue by meeting with Lauren more frequently, but in shorter more focused segments. Perhaps the first meeting is devoted to the most urgent items in settling her husbands estate. The second meeting may be to simply narrow down the list of people and charities she wants to include in her will. The third meeting may be to determine the amount she wants to leave to those who are most important to her, and so on. This process will require more meetings, but will allow Lauren the greatest opportunity for optimal decision making.

Solution-Focused Therapy and The Miracle Question

Solution-focused therapy (SFT) was developed by Steve de Shazer and Insoo Kim Berg, who describe SFT as a future-focused and goal-directed approach to therapy. While other types of therapy tend to focus on past problems, SFT is focused on the client's hopes for the future. It is based around a process that helps the client recognize their current skills, talents, and strengths that they can use to propel them toward their goals, and in which the therapist (or financial planner) provides reinforcement through compliments and positivity. SFT is a proven therapeutic technique that has been used in diverse fields from health care to criminal justice, to social work and child welfare. SFT assumes that the client has the ability and desire to make changes and empowers them to do so. This is done by encouraging the client to reflect on a similar problem they had in the past and identify how they overcame that problem and what was happening at that time, as opposed to the planner providing advice regarding what the client should do.

Archuleta et. al. outline the assumptions of SFT (as presented by de Shazer) as believing:[71]
1. If it's not broken, don't fix it.
2. If it works, do more of it.
3. If it's not working, do something different.
4. Small steps can lead to big changes.
5. No problems happen all the time; there are always exceptions that can be utilized.

---

71. Bradley T. Klontz et al., "Solution-Focused Financial Therapy," in *Financial Therapy: Theory, Research, and Practice* (Cham: Springer, 2015), pp. 121-141.

Exhibit 2.10 | Key Techniques Associated With SFT[72]

Technique	Description	Purpose
Recognizing and affirming pre-session change	Ask the client about any changes (even small ones) that have occurred since they made the appointment[1]	Helps to increase the client's belief that change can happen
Discussing past attempts	Ask the client to describe past attempts to solve or change the problem (or a similar problem)	Helps the therapist to understand what has or has not worked in the past. Any small things that have worked can be used to help shape solutions
Asking the miracle question	Ask the client to imagine (and describe) what it would be like if a miracle happened overnight that solved all of their problems.	Helps lead to the development of goals
Developing goals	Development of measurable and memorable short-, intermediate-, and long-term goals that are important to the client	Focuses on the future and achievable solutions rather than past or current problems or failures
Asking scaling questions	Ask question based on a scale of 1 to 10 (where are you now and where would you be if the miracle occurred?)[2]	Establishes the relevancy of goals and gauges progress from the client's perspective
Complimenting clients	Compliment progress[3]	Provides encouragement
Taking a curious, unassuming stance as the therapist	Do not judge, but do be curious	Helps how the client that the planner is interested in learning more about the client without being judgmental about what is learned
Developing a collaborative therapeutic relationship	Refrain from taking on the roll of the "expert," instead use a client-centered approach.[4]	Helps the planner adapt to the client's individual situation, building a strong client-planner relationship (referred to as "joining" with the client)

1. This refers to behavioral and cognitive changes that the client may have experienced as a result of making the first appointment.
2. Ask during each meeting and discuss progress or regression. If regression has occurred, do not focus on the regression, focus on the solution (e.g., if the client fell from 4 to 3, ask about what kept them from being 1 or 2, or what would make them 4).
3. If regression has occurred, compliment what kept them from regressing even more. There are no defeats, only experiences that help you learn.
4. Refraining from being the expert means do not just tell a client what to do. The planner should educate the client regarding relevant financial planning matters so that the client has the knowledge and tools to discover the solution that is best for her own values, attitudes, and behaviors.

72. Derived from *Ibid.*

The miracle question (as described in **Exhibit 2.10**) is an important part of SFT, but it is not a stand-alone question. Rather, it leads to additional important follow-up questions that provide a window into how the client would see their life without their current problem(s) and what types of changes the important people in the client's life would see in them. Since the miracle happened while the client was asleep, upon awakening they are unaware that it occurred and the client must think about what things would make them aware that it occurred. In applying the miracle question to financial therapy, Archuleta, et.al. suggest the following follow-up questions:[73]

1. What is the very first thing you notice after you wake up?
2. What would you be doing differently with your money?
3. How will you know that things are improving?
4. How do you discover that things are different?
5. What would your family notice about you that was different?
6. How do other people in your life notice that something was different about you?
7. What other things would be different?

While this discussion may at first feel awkward for the financial planner, it can be a powerful tool for those who are properly trained in its use and who become comfortable with applying it in their practices.

MANAGING AND MITIGATING CRISIS EVENTS WITH SEVERE CONSEQUENCES

Crisis events with severe consequences are difficult to predict, but clients with long-term planning goals are likely to experience one or more of these events at some point during their lives, which can have a significant impact on their lives, psyche, financial situation, and ability to meet their goals.

Studies of low probability, high impact events indicate that people have a tendency to deal with them poorly. whether the event is a natural disaster, war, global pandemic, premature death, living to age 100+, or a market bubble. Many people have a tendency to be overconfident or feel that these things will never be a problem for them, then overreact when such an event does occur, and seek protection from the possibility that the event will occur again. Often, though, within a few years the recency of the event has diminished, and protection no longer seems worth the cost. In cases where psychological biases are causing clients to make irrational and potentially costly decisions, it is up to the financial adviser to serve as the voice of reason and remind clients to continue following sound investment and financial planning principles. These principles include maintaining adequate insurance coverages, maintaining appropriate levels of emergency funds (highly liquid investments), diversifying investment portfolios, and maintaining a long-term outlook.

When faced with fear and/or stress, our brains tend to respond based on emotion rather than logic, often causing us to make irrational and self-defeating decisions. Some may attempt to blame others for these decisions, while others take no action when they should (which may be attributed to denial, or to status quo bias), still others may flee the scene (e.g., sell all stocks when the market corrects). We know that it is difficult to make accurate, rational assessments under stress, so having a plan in place to mitigate the state of crisis can relieve some of that stress. Chapter 17 includes a discussion of how this planning can be effected for crisis situations such as terminal illness, job loss, divorce, and disability.

73.*Ibid*, pp. 121-141.

Depending on the type and severity of the event, the entire planning process (from understanding the new circumstances to goal-setting to monitoring), and all aspects of the plan (from insurance to investments to estate documents) may need to be revisited and revised to adapt to the client's (and/or world's) new norms.

It is important to remember that many crisis events are beyond the client's control and can be emotionally devastating.

Exhibit 2.11 | Stress in America During the 2020 COVID-19 Pandemic (October 2020)[74]

- 78% of adults said the Coronavirus was a significant source of stress in their life.
- When considering the physical and emotional toll of increased stress, nearly half of adults (49%) reported that their behavior was negatively affected.
- A majority of adults (61%) reported experiencing undesired weight changes since the start of the pandemic.
- Gen Z adults (46%) were the most likely generation to say that their mental health has worsened compared with before the pandemic, followed by Xers (33%), Millennials (31%), Boomers (28%) and older adults (9%).
- Nearly 1 in 4 adults (23%) reported drinking more alcohol to cope with their stress during the coronavirus pandemic. This proportion jumps to more than half of adults (52%) who are parents with early elementary school-age children (5-7 years old).

The financial planner will best serve the client by being empathetic to the client's situation, and by demonstrating reliability and competency, including recognizing when the planner has reached the limits of their competency and must refer the client to a mental health professional who may be better able to guide the client through the emotional and psychological aspects of dealing with the crisis.

Emergency Fund Planning

An important area of inquiry for a financial planner, and an essential test of a sound cash flow management plan, is the adequacy of the client's fund to cover major unexpected adverse events (or to take advantage of major unexpected opportunities). As will be discussed in Chapters 3 and 4, many planners recommend an emergency fund equal to three to six months of the client's non-discretionary cash flows. The expenses covered by the emergency fund should include the fixed and variable expenses that the client will have to pay following an emergency. If the client's income is very unstable or their occupational skills have fallen in demand, an emergency fund near the high end of the three to six month range is more appropriate than if the client's income is highly stable or the client is in a high demand job.

Since the emergency fund must be invested in instruments that are very safe and highly liquid (able to be converted to cash quickly without significant loss of value), the assets usually will earn only a modest rate of return, so it is unwise to maintain too large an emergency fund. The client and planner together must determine the appropriate amount. Examples of appropriate instruments in which to invest the emergency fund are cash, checking accounts, money market accounts, money market mutual funds, savings accounts, short-term CDs, and U.S. Treasury bills.

---

74. Findings from the APA October 2020 Report *Stress in America™ 2020: A National Health Mental Health Crisis.*

Example 2.19

Prior to 2020, Logan and Austin had never considered the possibility that a national pandemic would cause them to be out of work for an extended period of time. Fortunately, their financial planner had always encouraged them to have an emergency fund equal to six months of expenses. When the COVID-19 pandemic struck in March of 2020, Logan and Austin were relieved that they did not face the level of financial stress that many of their coworkers were exposed to.

Insurance Planning

As will be discussed in Chapters 3, 4, and 5, a client's risk management plan must consider all potential losses to which the client may be exposed. Insurance is best suited as a form of risk management for risks that are low in frequency but high in severity (can result in high financial loss for the client). This makes insurance an important part of the core foundation of financial planning as it can protect the client from experiencing the full financial impact of the crisis events for which it provides coverage. Examples include life, medical, disability, homeowners, auto, liability, and long-term care insurance. When an event occurs for which clients need to file an insurance claim, the planner can greatly reduce client stress by assisting with the claims process. For example, a recently widowed spouse can be expected to be in the grief period for months or even years. During this time the client may have difficulty keeping up with routine management of finances and may feel overwhelmed by the process of filing a life insurance death benefit claim. An empathetic and competent financial planner can relieve the surviving spouse of the burden of filing the claim by assisting with gathering and filling out claim documents.

Investments Planning

Portfolio diversification can help to reduce the impact of market-related events and economic recessions to a certain extent. Investment managers may also set measurable parameters for unexpected and unusually extreme market volatility that trigger temporary portfolio adjustments or initiate the use of hedging strategies to mitigate the downside effects of these occurrences, while being cautious to avoid overreaction. Communication with clients is critical in that regard. A review of the Investment Policy Statement (discussed in Chapter 9) is often helpful for reminding clients of the long-term goals and objectives for the portfolio.

Estate Planning

Another important part of building a solid financial foundation which may help attenuate a crisis event is to obtain, and keep updated, basic estate planning documents such as a will, power of attorney (for health care and financial decisions), and living will. These documents are discussed in Chapter 14.

CLIENT PSYCHOLOGY AND THE FINANCIAL PLANNING PROCESS

In the preliminary step of establishing the client-planner relationship, Britt, Lawson, and Haselwood propound the idea that the planner can reduce client stress by spending time joining with the client prior to getting into the financial planning conversation.[75] In addition to reducing client stress, joining may help to establish rapport and increase the client's trust in the planner. Britt, et.al. suggest that stress may be reduced by employing some of the following techniques:

- Use scaling questions around a goal that the client has identified (on a scale of 0 to 10, rate where you currently see yourself? Where would you like to be on the scale, and what are you doing already that may help you move up on the scale?)
- At the end of the meeting provide a summary to let the client know that they have been heard.
- When assigning tasks to the client, assign tasks for the planner as well to increase rapport.
- Arrange office furniture to have the feel of a living room, and turn off televisions playing financial news.

As the planning process continues, we have seen how techniques such as motivational interviewing, open-ended questions, and guided imagery can be applied to assist the client with gathering information and setting goals. When analyzing and evaluating the client's current course of action and potential alternative courses of action, the planner may add a new element of analysis: what are the client's money beliefs and in what ways are they likely to contribute to or impede the client's progress toward meeting goals? In developing and presenting recommendations, we have seen how theories from psychology such as choice architecture and framing may impact client decisions. In step six, implementation, we can recognize how stages of change and internal or external motivation may play a role in whether the client follows through with the implementation plan.

But it doesn't end there. In step seven, monitoring, if the client is in the maintenance stage of change, the planner can meet with the client periodically to reinforce what the client is doing correctly and how it is positively impacting the progress toward reaching the goal. The planner can show support and encouragement through the use of affirmative statements that reinforce the positive steps the client has taken.

---

75. Britt, Sonya L.,Derek R. Lawson, and Camila A. Haselwood. "A Descriptive Analysis of Physiological Stress and Readiness to Change." *Journal of Financial Planning* 29, no. 12(2016): 45-51.

CONCLUSION

The majority of education and training in the field of financial planning is focused on gaining competency in the technical aspects of the various areas of planning. One could argue that a large part of technical competence may be replaced with technology (roboadvisors, retirement planning software); however, the planner who is learned in client psychology brings additional value to the planning relationship.

Technical competence in the various areas of financial planning and making the right recommendations to optimize the ability for a client to meet goals does not guarantee success. Emotional, psychological, and relational barriers may prevent the client from agreeing with or acting on the recommendations. These roadblocks and challenges may be difficult for the client to overcome without assistance. An appropriately trained planner can serve as a tour guide through the client's journey, pointing the way and helping client dodge each new boulder that, as in a video game, threatens to propel the client back to a prior level.

The information regarding financial therapy provided in this chapter serves as a broad overview. Financial planners who wish to learn more detail to incorporate therapy into their practice may consider working toward the Financial Therapy Association's Certified Financial Therapist designation,[76] and/or develop relationships with licensed therapists who can be called to join the planning team in a similar manner to the way an attorney or accountant may be invited to become part of the team.[77] Planners who do not wish to pursue a full financial coaching or financial therapy certification may opt instead to develop some related skills by attending coaching workshops (some of which qualify for continuing education credits) from various groups such as the Financial Psychology Institute, the Kinder Institute of Life Planning, or the Sudden Money Institute.

76. https://financialtherapyassociation.org/become-a-financial-therapist.
77. To find a therapist, go to: https://financialtherapyassociation.org/find-a-financial-therapist.

DISCUSSION QUESTIONS

SOLUTIONS to the discussion questions can be found exclusively within the chapter. Once you have completed an initial reading of the chapter, go back and highlight the answers to these questions.

1. Identify and discuss the three general schools of thought for counseling.

2. What are some examples of open questions versus closed questions?

3. Discuss the benefits and drawbacks to the "why" question of a client.

4. What are your options if you sense a client is saying one thing but believes another?

5. Identify and discuss the four basic premises for Traditional Finance.

6. Identify and discuss the four basic premises for Behavioral Finance.

7. Identify and describe some differences between a rational investor and a normal one.

8. Explain the reasoning behind someone buying lottery tickets and insurance at the same time.

9. Discuss the difference between evaluating a portfolio as a whole versus evaluating a portfolio in mental layers.

10. What should you do as a financial adviser if you believe that a client's heuristic is clouding his or her judgment?

11. Discuss the ways in which a client's socialization may impact the planning process.

12. Behavioral change is often a necessary in order for clients to reach their goals. Discuss the importance of intent to change and describe the five stages of change.

13. Discuss the importance of understanding a client's money beliefs.

14. Identify the four broad categories of money beliefs, examples of money scripts within each category, and potential effects of each.

15. Describe some common money disorders that may impact a client's ability to reach their goals and achieve financial well-being.

16. Describe some common money conflicts.

17. Seniors are particularly vulnerable to financial exploitation and undue influence due to social isolation and potential cognitive impairments such as dementia. List some warning signs that a client may be the victim of financial exploitation.

18. Describe values-driven (values-based) financial planning.

19. Discuss the difference between intrinsic and extrinsic motivation, the relevance of Self-Determination Theory (SDT) to the financial planning process, and the planner's role in increasing a client's intrinsic motivation.

20. Describe choice architecture and discuss how framing and default choices impact decision-making.

21. Describe Solution-Focused Therapy (SFT) and its application in the financial planning process.

MULTIPLE-CHOICE PROBLEMS

A sample of multiple choice problems is provided below. Additional multiple choice problems are available at money-education.com by accessing the Student Practice Portal.

1. Which of the following is (are) consistent with the Humanistic Paradigm?
    1. The majority of Humanistic theories view clients as experts on themselves.
    2. The alliance between the counselor and client is extremely important for humanistic counselors and is the basis of the treatment or plan of action.
    3. There needs to be a professional distance between the client and adviser where the adviser should stay close to discussing numbers and data with the client.
        a. 1 only.
        b. 1 and 2.
        c. 1 and 3.
        d. All of the above.

2. Which of the following is NOT a premise in Traditional Finance?
    a. Markets are Efficient.
    b. Investors are Rational.
    c. Markets are Inefficient.
    d. The Mean-Variance Portfolio Theory Governs.

3. Which of the following are important in nonverbal communication and behavior?
    1. Body positioning.
    2. Body movement.
    3. Voice tone.
    4. Voice pitch.
        a. 1 only.
        b. 1 and 2.
        c. 1 and 3.
        d. All of the above.

4. Which of the following investors would apply in the realm of Behavioral Finance?
    a. A rational investor who considers his or her portfolio as a whole at all times.
    b. An investor not moved by emotion or biases.
    c. An investor who at times is subject to emotion or cognitive biases.
    d. An investor guided by risk calculations based on Beta alone.

5. Which of the following choices is false as to open or closed questions?
    a. Open or closed questions are both effective tools for the financial adviser.
    b. An open question starts with the phrase "Isn't it true that ..."
    c. A closed question is narrow and can be answered with a word or two.
    d. A closed question seeks a response that is very specific.

> **Additional multiple choice problems are available at money-education.com by accessing the Student Practice Portal. Access requires registration of the title using the unique code at the front of the book.**

QUICK QUIZ EXPLANATIONS

Quick Quiz 2.1
1. True.
2. False. Self-talk refers to that ongoing internal conversation one has with oneself that can influence feelings.
3. True.

Quick Quiz 2.2
1. True.
2. True.
3. False. Nonverbal communication, including body language, can play an important role in understanding communications, especially when verbal communication is contrary to body language.

Quick Quiz 2.3
1. False. It is better to pay attention and provide supporting facial and/or body gestures (such as nodding in affirmation) when actively listening to encourage the speaker to continue and to convey that the information is important.
2. True.

Quick Quiz 2.4
1. True.
2. False. Markets are assumed to be efficient in Traditional but not Behavioral Finance.
3. False. Returns are determined by risk (beta) in Traditional but not Behavioral Finance.

Quick Quiz 2.5
1. True.
2. False. Normal investors are susceptible to less than optimal decisions due to cognitive biases. When combining the activity and decision of normal investors in the marketplace, biases can have an effect on stock prices.
3. False. Traditional Finance, not Behavioral Finance, is pure and concerned with risk-reward and risk-return.
4. True.

Quick Quiz 2.6
1. True.
2. False. A person's *conscience* is the moral compass by which they judge situations as right or wrong, and is influenced by cultural, political, economic, and other factors. Social consciousness refers to a client's awareness of and sense of responsibility for problems or injustices that exit within society
3. False. Clients may be risk tolerant in one area of financial planning but not in another. Moreover, over time, a client's risk tolerance can change, and may be different for different goals.

QUICK QUIZ EXPLANATIONS

Quick Quiz 2.7

1.   False. Money is often one of the top sources of conflict both between spouses and among family members.
2.   True.
3.   True.

Quick Quiz 2.8

1.   True.
2.   False. When used ethically and appropriately, default options can be advantageous and can help clients overcome choice overload to make decisions that are in their best interest.
3.   True.

3

FINANCIAL PLANNING APPROACHES: ANALYSIS AND RECOMMENDATIONS

LEARNING OBJECTIVES

1. List and describe each of the approaches to financial planning analysis and recommendations.
2. Describe the lifecycle approach and its benefits.
3. Describe the pie chart approach and its benefits.
4. Describe the financial statement and ratio analysis approach.
5. Understand the relationship between time, savings, and withdrawal rates on retirement planning.
6. Understand the exponential nature of the investment assets-to-gross pay benchmark.
7. Describe the two-step, three panel, and metrics approach to financial planning.
8. Analyze the various sources of borrowing available to a client and communicate the advantages and disadvantages of each for meeting a client's financial goal.*
9. Create a debt management plan for a client that minimizes financing costs and maximizes the potential to reach goals.*
10. Explain and compare appropriate financing strategies for purchasing a home.*
11. List each benchmark metric for risk management, short-term savings and investing goals, and long-term savings and investing goals.
12. Communicate the need for liquid assets and emergency funds and recommend strategies for accumulating the appropriate levels of funds.*
13. Calculate savings required to meet financial goals and recommend how to incorporate planned savings into the cash flow plan.*
14. Describe the cash flow approach to analysis.
15. Identify opportunities and challenges related to a client's cash inflows and outflows and make recommendations to assist the client in meeting their current needs and long-term financial goals.*
16. Describe the income tax analysis.
17. Describe and discuss the present value of all goals approach to financial planning analysis.
18. Describe the strategic approach to financial planning analysis.

*Ties to CFP Certification Learning Objectives

INTRODUCTION

Prior to developing and presenting financial plan recommendations to a client, the planner and client should mutually define the client's personal and financial goals, needs, and priorities. The planner must keep the client's values, attitudes, expectations, and time horizons in mind as they affect the goals, needs, and priorities of the client.

Goals and objectives provide a roadmap for the financial planning process. Goals tend to be broad (such as having sufficient assets to retire), while objectives are more narrow, defined, and can effectively be subjected to measurement (e.g., $1,000,000 in investment assets by age 45).

To evaluate the extent to which the client's goals, needs, and priorities can be met by the client's current and future financial resources, the planner must collect and analyze both internal and external data.

REASONABLE ASSUMPTIONS

The planner, in consultation with the client, must establish reasonable assumptions, especially where projections will be used to determine if a goal is likely to be achieved. Some of these assumptions include information about:

- What constitutes an adequate emergency fund (e.g., savings provisions)?
- What is an appropriate emergency fund ratio (the number of months of coverage by cash and cash equivalents of non-discretionary cash flows)?
- What is the total of monthly nondiscretionary cash flows?
- What are appropriate debt ratios? What is an appropriate benchmark for this client? When will the client be out of debt?
- What are the personal, property, and liability risks that this client faces and what are the best ways to cover and manage these risks?
- What retirement benchmarks are to be used, including the retirement age, the percentage of pre-retirement income needed to maintain the retirement lifestyle, the retirement life expectancy, any legacy requirements, inflation rates, income tax rates, and expected investment returns consistent with the client's risk tolerance and actual portfolio asset allocation?
- What estimates will be used to provide for any college education goals - ages of children, education inflation rate, current costs of relevant education?
- What estimates will be used to provide for any lump-sum funding goals - today's cost, the inflation rate, the amount needed to provide an adequate down payment?
- What estimates will be used to provide for legacy goals - defined in dollars (today's), the inflation rate, earnings rate, the expected estate and gift tax rates, exclusions, and exemptions (state and federal)?

THE ANALYSIS

Once the financial planner has established the relationship with the client and has completed the initial financial planning process steps where the required data has been collected and goals have been identified and prioritized, the practitioner can begin analyzing and evaluating the client's situation. Agreed upon assumptions can be taken into consideration, and various financial planning approaches can be applied to arrive at plan recommendations. The concepts discussed in this chapter relate to several steps in the financial planning process, but are largely focused on the first three steps:

1. Understanding the client's personal and financial circumstances,
2. Identifying and selecting goals, and
3. Analyzing the client's current course of action and potential alternative course(s) of action.

Exhibit 3.1 | Financial Planning Process[1]

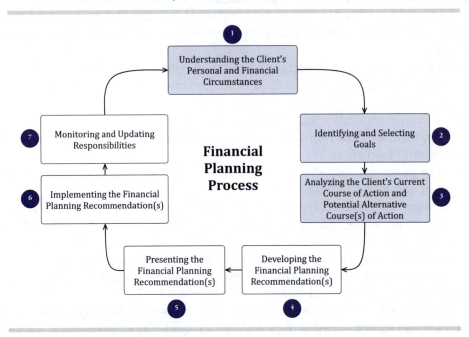

The purpose of the analysis is to identify any weaknesses in the plan and make recommendations that will assist the client in achieving their goals.

THE APPROACHES TO FINANCIAL PLANNING ANALYSIS AND RECOMMENDATIONS

There are a wide array of possible approaches to analyzing, evaluating, and developing recommendations in the financial planning process. Each approach individually is useful and provides the planner and client with a slightly different perspective of the collected data. These approaches are identified and the benefits of each approach are briefly described below with further explanation later in the chapter.

- The **life cycle approach** - Data collection is quick, simple, and relatively nonthreatening to the client. It provides the planner with a brief overview of the client's financial profile permitting the planner to have a relatively focused initial conversation with the client. It is generally used very early in the engagement and is generally high level as opposed to detailed.
- The **pie chart approach** - This approach provides a visual representation of how the client allocates financial resources. It provides a broad perspective on the client's financial status and it is generally used after the collection of internal data and the preparation of financial statements. For example, the balance sheet pie chart illustrates the relative size of liabilities and net worth in comparison to total assets, the relative size of cash/cash equivalents, investment assets to total assets, and personal use assets in comparison to total assets. If a benchmark comparison pie chart from the metrics approach (discussed below) is added, it is often revealing for the client to discover the sources and uses of money and how much is used for debt service.

---

1. Abbreviated from the CFP Board's Financial Planning Practice Standards.

- The **financial statement and ratio analysis approach** - This approach helps to establish a financial snapshot of the client as of today. The ratio analysis provides an opportunity to assess the client's strengths, weaknesses, and deficiencies by comparing the client's ratios to the benchmark metrics. The ratio approach usually follows the pie chart approach and provides the planner with the actual financial ratios with which to compare the benchmarks in the metrics approach.

- The **two-step/three-panel approach** - A step-by-step approach in which the client's actual financial situation is compared against benchmark criteria. This approach is relatively thorough and presents a manageable approach to the client. It stresses the management of risk, seeks to avoid financial dependence, and promotes savings and investing to achieve financial independence.

- The **present value of goals approach** - This approach considers each short-term, intermediate-term, and long-term goal, determines their respective present value, then sums all of these together and treats the sum as an obligation (liability) that can then be reduced by current resources of investment assets, cash, and cash equivalents. The resultant is the net future obligation that will need to be retired over the remaining work life expectancy by savings at the expected rate of investment return using an ordinary annuity. This calculated annuity requirement (in dollars) is then compared to the current annual savings amount after any implemented risk management, other immediate recommendations, and a tax analysis to determine whether the current savings amount is adequate to fund all goals. As part of determining the ability to save, a pre- and post-recommendations tax analysis must be performed to determine whether the client is properly, over- or under-withheld on income taxes.

- The **metrics approach** - This approach uses quantitative benchmarks that provide rules of thumb for a measurement of where a client's financial profile should be. When combined with the two-step/three-panel approach, metrics help establish objectives that are dollar and percentage measurable compared to ratio analysis.

- The **cash flow approach** - This approach takes an income statement approach to recommendations. It uses the three-panel approach and uses a pro forma approach (as if) "to purchase" the suggested recommendations. This approach has the effect of driving down the discretionary cash flow. Next, positive cash flows or the sale of assets are identified and used to finance the recommendations.

- The **strategic approach** - This approach uses a mission, goal, and objective approach considering the internal and external environment and may be used with other approaches.

Key Concepts

1. List assumptions that the financial planner and client need to consider when developing a comprehensive financial plan.

2. Identify the eight approaches to financial planning analysis and recommendations.

3. Describe the types of information the financial planner gathers and analyzes using the life cycle approach.

4. Identify the three phases of the life cycle approach along with each phase's likely risks and goals.

Using any single approach described above is not likely to be adequate to develop a comprehensive financial plan. Employing all of the approaches simultaneously will create some redundancy, but considered together, will probably produce a comprehensive financial plan that is effective for the client. While a beginner planner may want to use all of the approaches, an experienced financial planner will find it sufficient to use a combination of a select few. For example, it is usually essential in any comprehensive plan to use the cash flow approach because it requires the client to prioritize and monetize each recommendation and determine the overall financial impact of each recommendation on ancial statements. Also, the cash flow approach clarifies the current and future resources to be and whether or not they are sufficient to implement all of the recommendations or whether some recommendations will have to be deferred until additional resources are available. Experienced financial planners will combine approaches depending on the preferences of the planner and the needs of the client.

Exhibit 3.2 portrays examples of common financial and risk characteristics, by age group, of individuals with typical financial risks and goals. Financial planners should be familiar with these typical characteristics so that their particular client's financial wants, needs, and goals can be anticipated. This is not to say that everyone will have the same characteristics. Rather, that many people similarly situated will have the same or similar goals and risks.

Exhibit 3.2 | Examples of Common Client Profiles and Their Typical Life Cycle Factors, Financial Risks, and Goals

(These are selected and not intended to be exhaustive)

Life Cycle Factors							
Age	22-30	25-35	25-35	35-45	45-55	55-65	65-75
Marital Status	Single	Married**	Married	Married	Married	Married	Married
Children***	No	No	Yes	Yes	Yes	Yes	Yes
Grandchildren***	No	No	No	No	No	Yes	Yes
Income	$35-$75k	$35-$75k	$45-$100k	$50-$150k	$75-$200k	$100-$200k	$50-$200k
Net Worth	$10-$20k	$10-$20k	$15-$25k	$20-$40k	$50-$100k	$500-$1,200k	$400-$1,500k
Self Employed	No	No	No	No	Yes	Maybe	No
Typical Risks/Insurance Coverage Needs							
Life Insurance	No	Maybe	Yes	Yes	Yes	Yes	No
Disability	Yes	Yes	Yes	Yes	Yes	Yes	No
Health	Yes	Yes	Yes	Yes	Yes	Yes	Yes
Long-Term Care*	No	No	No	No	No	Maybe Yes	Maybe Yes
Property	Yes	Yes	Yes	Yes	Yes	Yes	Yes
Liability	Yes	Yes	Yes	Yes	Yes	Yes	Yes
Typical Goals							
Retirement Security	Yes	Yes	Yes	Yes	Yes	Yes	In Retirement
Education Funding	No	No	Yes	Yes	Yes	No	No
Gifting	No	No	No	No	No	Yes	Yes
Lump-Sum Expenses	Yes	Yes	Yes	Yes	Yes	Yes	No
Legacy	No	No	No	No	No	Maybe	Maybe

* While younger clients will not typically require long-term care insurance, in some circumstances long-term care may be appropriate.

** Married could be married, divorced, or widow(er).

*** Children and grandchildren are always yes, no, or maybe.

THE LIFE CYCLE APPROACH

Using this approach, the planner gathers and analyzes the following information:
- the ages of the client and spouse/partner
- the client's marital status
- the number and ages of children and grandchildren
- the family income by each contributor
- the family net worth
- whether the client is employed, unemployed, self-employed, or retired

The life cycle approach is a broad overview of the client financial profile and is best employed to provide general information with which to focus an initial financial discussion with the client when the financial planner only has partial information. For example, a married couple with small children will probably have a goal to save for the college education of their children. Meanwhile they should be concerned about certain other risks such as their untimely death or disability. The life cycle approach serves as a foundation for a dialog with the client and gives the planner a 60-75 percent perspective of the risks the client is likely to be concerned about, as well as their likely financial goals.

It should be emphasized that there are no absolutes in personal financial planning. Each client is unique. Having said that, many clients fit into similar profiles (see **Exhibit 3.2**). The ages of the spouses may provide an indication as to what phase of life the client is in, as defined below.
- The **asset accumulation phase** usually begins in the early 20s and lasts to mid 50s when discretionary cash flow for investing is low and the debt-to-net worth ratio is high.
- The **conservation (risk management) phase** usually begins in the late 20s and lasts to the early 70s, where cash flow, assets, and net worth have increased and debts have decreased somewhat. In addition, risk management of events like unemployment, disability due to illness or accident, and untimely death become a priority.
- The **distribution (gifting) phase** usually begins in the mid 40s or early 50s and continues to the end of life. It is characterized by the individual having high cash flow, low debt, and high net worth.

Knowing the client's life cycle phase helps the planner to understand the client's likely risks and goals. It is entirely possible for a given client to be in two or even all three of these phases simultaneously. When special circumstances occur, such as the untimely death of a spouse, the conservation phase may even come before the asset accumulation phase.

Exhibit 3.3 | Life Cycles

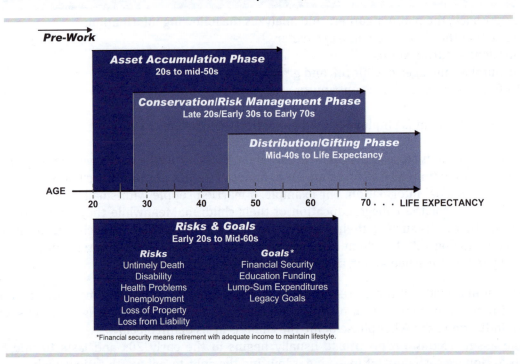

If the client is married, the couple typically files a joint income tax return and relies on both incomes for the payment of family expenses (such as a home mortgage, auto loans, etc.). This financial dependency creates a life insurance and disability insurance need for each spouse. The fact that a client has young children signals a need for both life and disability insurance, regardless of the parent's marital status. Young children may also indicate a client's need, or at least desire, for college education funding. If a client has grandchildren, gifts, tuition payment plans, and other transfers during life (gifts) or at death (bequests) to or for grandchildren may be a consideration. Older clients may also be thinking about estate planning needs.

The planner should conduct a comprehensive review of the complete insurance portfolio for all clients (especially for those in the risk management phase). This review should include an analysis of the need for and the use of life insurance, health insurance, disability insurance, long-term care insurance, property insurance, and liability insurance.

Other client profile characteristics that provide insight into the client's needs include:
- Any client that is simultaneously in the accumulation and conservation phase has financial security (retirement) as a long-term goal.
- Generally, the higher a client's net worth and the greater a client's income, the more interest that client has in income tax minimization.
- If a client is self-employed, it creates opportunities to use employer-sponsored retirement plans to assist that client in accomplishing long-term financial security goals.

Analyzing client data to achieve long-term financial goals takes time. Achieving those financial goals takes persistent savings and good investment returns. Unfortunately, risks that are insured against, such as untimely death, disability, health issues, and loss of property or personal liability, are unexpected events that can occur at any time. An uninsured loss can destroy even the best conceived savings and investment plan. Therefore, clients need to make having an appropriate risk management portfolio their highest priority goal. A great retirement investment plan with a time horizon of 30 years that relies on persistent savings and investment returns can be abruptly derailed if the client becomes disabled before retirement and has no disability insurance benefits.

The life cycle approach provides financial planners with a broad overview of the client's probable risks and likely goals. It is a good place to start, but it lacks the specifics to direct the planner in analyzing internal and external data and in developing a detailed, comprehensive financial plan.

THE PIE CHART APPROACH

A pie chart focuses the client on the relative size of financial variables. People can only spend 100 percent of what they have, and visualizing where the money goes is often a sobering, but helpful exercise. The pie chart approach is an effective analytical and illustrative tool for financial planning clients.

The pie chart approach provides the planner and the client with separate pictorial representations of the balance sheet and the statement of income and expenses. These financial statements are discussed in detail in Chapter 4.

The financial statements are prepared first and then depicted in pie charts. One set of pie charts is for the statement of income and expenses (income statement) and the other set is for the balance sheet (statement of financial position). Note that the statement of income and expenses (income statement) is also referred to as the cash flow statement. For purposes of this textbook, it is not referred to as the cash flow statement because not all cash flows are included in the statement (such as inheritance of cash). The pie chart approach generally uses percentages of the whole, but can use a dollar approach. The percentage approach is usually more effective for comparison purposes.

> ### ≔ *Key Concepts*
>
> 1. Identify the financial planning usefulness of the income statement pie chart.
>
> 2. Understand the questions that the balance sheet pie chart should answer and illustrate.
>
> 3. Identify the reason for creating benchmark pie charts.

Income Statement Pie Chart

The questions that the pie chart approach addresses are:
- What percentage of gross pay is the client paying in taxes (income and Social Security)?
- What percentage of the client's gross pay are they saving?
- What percentage of the client's gross pay goes to protection (insurance)?
- What percentage of the client's gross pay is spent on basic housing costs (principal, interest, tax, and insurance or rent plus insurance)?
- What percentage of the client's gross pay is spent on debt repayments both excluding housing costs and including housing costs?
- What percentage of the client's gross pay is left to live on?

For example, the following sample income statement pie chart reflects total living expenses of 54 percent (housing costs 25% plus other living expenses). This is useful information for the planner to analyze considering a client's other characteristics (e.g., age, gross pay, risks, etc.). To build the pie chart, the planner calculates the client's expenses from the income statement as a proportion of the client's gross pay and portrays them in the income statement pie chart.

Exhibit 3.4 | Income Statement Pie Chart

There are many flexible and creative ways to make a pie chart. One useful way is total income arrayed by percentage of:
- savings
- housing costs
- other debt payments (ODP)
- insurance other than property insurance
- all other living costs (OLC)
- taxes other than property taxes
- net discretionary cash flows (DCF), presuming that they are positive

The pie chart approach has some shortcomings, including that it is difficult to depict negative cash flows in pie charts and it does not lend itself to detailed analysis and recommendation. It is, however, a useful depiction of where the client is at the moment.

Example 3.1

Assume a client has gross pay of $100,000 and expenses as listed in the table below. The data can be reflected in an income statement pie chart, allowing the client to visualize his financial situation as pertains to income and expenses.

Example Income = $100,000

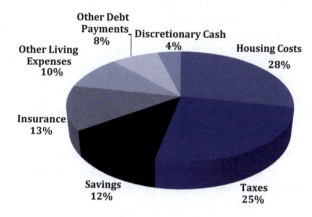

	Amount	Percentage
Gross Income	$100,000	100%
Taxes	$25,000	25%
Savings	$12,000	12%
Insurance	$13,000	13%
Housing Costs	$28,000	28%
Other Debt Payments (ODP)	$8,000	8%
Other Living Costs (OLC)	$10,000	10%
Discretionary Cash Flow (DCF)	$4,000	4%

The data is easy to depict on an income statement pie chart with the percentages that a client is paying for taxes, saving for the future, and paying insurance premiums (25% + 12% + 13% = 50%) to protect the client's assets that have or will be accumulated. That leaves approximately 50 percent of the income for current living expenses, 10-28 percent of which is typically allocated to housing or shelter costs. **Exhibit 3.5** provides targeted example benchmarks for various income statement items.

The pie chart approach assists the planner and client by illustrating if the client is spending too much on debt repayment or too much on housing, either of which may result in undersaving or being underinsured. The financial planner can then present benchmark pie charts that illustrate where a client should be in order to meet typical goals and objectives.

Exhibit 3.5 | Income Statement Targeted Example Benchmarks

	Targeted Example Benchmarks*
Taxes (income and payroll)	15 - 30%
Savings (future asset protection)	10 - 18%
Protection (insurance) (past and future asset protection)	5 - 12%
Living - Present	40 - 60%
Housing (Rent or Mortgage Payment)	≤ 28%
Housing and Other Debt Payments	≤ 36%

These are general and vary widely among individuals.

The pie chart depiction of the income statement provides the planner with an opportunity to discuss with the client their strengths and weaknesses, from a financial point of view. If the benchmark pie chart is agreed to, a step by step plan to get from the current situation to the benchmark can be established.

Balance Sheet Pie Chart

The questions that the balance sheet pie chart approach addresses include, what percentage of total assets are in the form of:

- cash and cash equivalents?
- investment assets?
- personal use assets?
- current liabilities?
- long-term liabilities?
- net worth?

The balance sheet pie chart is portrayed in two pie charts, one for the asset side of the balance sheet and the other for the liabilities and net worth side of the balance sheet. The asset pie chart is broken down into three categories: cash and cash equivalents, investment assets, and personal use assets. **Exhibit 3.6** depicts a sample balance sheet pie chart.

Exhibit 3.6 | Balance Sheet Pie Chart

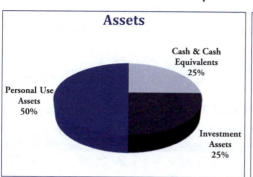

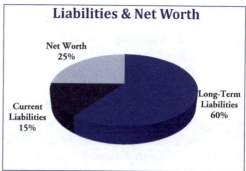

Assume that a client has assets (and liabilities and net worth) totaling $300,000. The balance sheet data can be reflected in the following pie charts.

Exhibit 3.7 | Client Sample Balance Sheet Pie Chart

Assets = 100%		
Cash & Cash Equivalents	$30,000	10%
Investment Assets	$120,000	40%
Personal Use Assets	$150,000	50%
	$300,000	100%

Liabilities & Net Worth = 100%		
Current Liabilities	$75,000	25%
Long-Term Liabilities	$150,000	50%
Net Worth	$75,000	25%
	$300,000	100%

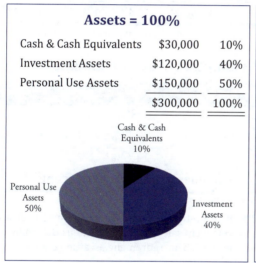

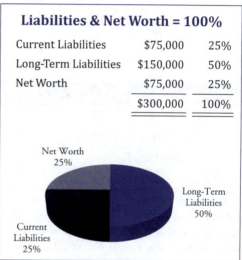

Regardless of the amount of total assets, a portion of assets should be in cash and cash equivalents and a portion should be in investment assets. The percentage needed in cash and cash equivalents is functionally related to the non-discretionary cash outflows on the income statement. The percentage that should be in investment assets is functionally related to the age of the client and the clients' gross pay (see **Exhibit 3.8**).

The liabilities (both short-term and long-term) are then integrated into a separate pie chart opposite the assets, along with the client's net worth. If net worth is negative, the client is technically insolvent and the pie charts for the balance sheet may be unreliable.

The planner should consider the age of the client, the gross pay, and non-discretionary cash flows to develop a benchmark balance sheet pie chart for the client. However, before creating a benchmark pie chart for the example client, we already know that cash and cash equivalents are only 40 percent of current liabilities (10% ÷ 25%) and total debt represents 75 percent of all assets (25% + 50%) with net worth representing only 25 percent of assets (see **Exhibit 3.7**).

Keeping benchmarks in mind, given a client's characteristics, the financial planner can develop balance sheet benchmark pie charts to compare to the client's actual balance sheet pie charts. This creates the opportunity to have a quick and high level discussion of where the client is currently, and where the client should be, based on appropriate benchmarks.

The following exhibit provides typical benchmark goals by age range for a client's balance sheet.

Exhibit 3.8 | An Estimate of Balance Sheet Targeted Benchmarks by Ages

		20s - 30s	40s - 50s	60s - 70s
Assets*	Cash & Cash Equivalents	5 - 20%	5 - 20%	5 - 20%
	Investment Assets	0 - 30%	30 - 60%	60 - 70%
	Personal Use Assets	55 - 90%	25 - 60%	15 - 30%
Liabilities*	Current Liabilities	10 - 20%	10 - 20%	0 - 10%
	Long-Term Liabilities	40 - 72%	16 - 48%	8 - 24%
Net Worth*	Net Worth	8 - 50%	32 - 74%	66 - 82%

* A more detailed description of each category is provided in Chapter 4. These can vary widely among families.

Exhibit 3.9 | Financial Planning Assumptions Used for Exhibit 3.8

Assumptions	
Inflation and Raises	3%
Investment Returns	8.5%
Savings Rate	11.5%*
Retirement Accumulation	18 times pre-retirement income**

*Average Savings Rate = 10-13%; Savings Rate = 11.5% of gross pay.

**Produces an initial wage replacement ratio of 72% of pre-retirement income at retirement at a 4% withdrawal rate (a 4% withdrawal rate is considered a relatively safe withdrawal rate as determined by current research). Wage replacement ratio is the income needed in retirement as a percentage of pre-retirement income.

Pie charts are effective tools for helping the client visualize pictorially and to understand (especially if the client is a visual learner) where their assets are deployed in cash, in investment assets, or for maintaining their current lifestyle (personal use assets) in retirement.

Summary Regarding the Life Cycle and Pie Chart Approaches

The life cycle and pie chart approaches are generally used in the preliminary stages of a financial planning engagement to get a general idea of the financial situation of the client and/or to present, in the case of the pie chart approach, a graphical picture of the current and general benchmark situation. These two approaches are generally not used for detailed financial planning analysis.

THE FINANCIAL STATEMENT AND RATIO ANALYSIS APPROACH

The purpose of calculating and presenting financial ratios is to provide insightful planning information to the user. The financial statement and ratio analysis approach uses financial ratios to help clarify and reveal the true financial situation of a client. The approach uses four types of ratios:

1. **Liquidity ratios:** measure the client's ability to meet short-term obligations.
2. **Debt ratios:** indicate how well the client manages debt.
3. **Ratios for financial security goals:** indicate the progress that the client is making toward achieving long-term financial security goals.
4. **Performance ratios:** indicate the adequacy of returns on investments, given the risks taken by the client.

> ### ≔ *Key Concepts*
>
> 1. Identify the purpose of evaluating liquidity ratios used in the financial statement and ratio analysis approach.
>
> 2. Identify the difference between discretionary and non-discretionary cash flows.

The information covered in this section is an overview and introduction to financial statement and ratio analysis as one method of analyzing, evaluating, and making financial planning recommendations to a client. A more detailed explanation of financial statements and financial statement analysis is provided in Chapter 4. For now, a high level overview of this approach is discussed in this chapter.

Liquidity Ratios

The emergency fund ratio and the current ratio are the two most common financial ratios used to provide meaningful information for measuring the ability to meet short-term obligations. These are essentially coverage ratios.

Emergency Fund Ratio

$$\text{Emergency Fund Ratio} = \frac{\text{Cash \& Cash Equivalents}}{\text{Monthly Non-Discretionary Cash Flows}} = 3 - 6 \text{ Months}$$

The **emergency fund ratio** determines the number of months the client can pay non-discretionary cash flows with current liquidity. The risks covered by an emergency fund are those that arise from loss of employment, injury, or some other unexpected occurrence. The benchmark for coverage is three-to-six months of non-discretionary cash flow coverage. However, this benchmark is highly dependent on the individual client's situation and the job market at the time of the financial emergency. Therefore, the benchmark should be used cautiously and revised accordingly for a particular client and a particular economic climate. For example, a specialty job may require more than six months for a job seeker to replace, especially for an older worker with higher income. On the other hand, a tenured faculty member at a university may be in a low risk situation for being unemployed and would not necessarily need an emergency fund of three months of non-discretionary cash flows. The elimination period of a client's disability policy should also be considered when selecting an emergency fund ratio target.

Definition of Terms

An evaluation of a client's monthly expenses is necessary for the calculation of the emergency fund coverage. Discretionary versus non-discretionary cash flows must be identified to determine the monthly expenses that must be met. **Discretionary cash flows** are those cash flows that can be avoided in the event of loss of income, whereas **non-discretionary cash flows** are generally fixed monthly obligations and expenses that are required to be met regardless of the loss of income. Some monthly cash flows may be discretionary or non-discretionary depending on the client (e.g., church contributions).

Exhibit 3.10 | Discretionary Cash Flows vs. Non-discretionary Cash Flows

Common Non-discretionary Cash Flows	Common Cash Flows that may be either Discretionary or Non-discretionary	Common Discretionary Cash Flows
Mortgage Loan Auto Loan Credit Cards Life Insurance Health Insurance Auto Insurance Homeowners (or Renters) Insurance Tuition and Education Expenses Property Taxes Food Auto Maintenance Utilities Clothing	Charitable Contributions Church Donations Lawn Service Child Care	Entertainment Vacations Satellite or Cable TV

Many costs have both a fixed and variable (controllable) component (e.g., utilities). The financial planner tries to determine how many months of coverage exists for those costs that the client considers to be non-discretionary. Ordinarily, income taxes and payroll taxes are not included in the determination of discretionary versus non-discretionary cash flows because the most likely risk triggering the use of the emergency fund is the loss of employment income. However, the financial planner calculating non-discretionary expenditures should consider whether the client is unemployed and if the client is receiving unemployment benefits (unemployment benefits are subject to federal income tax, but not payroll taxes). In addition, some clients who have lost jobs have an outstanding 401(k) plan (or other qualified plan) loan, which may be treated as a taxable distribution if the loan is not repaid shortly after termination. Unfortunately, some clients who find themselves unemployed, exhaust their qualified plan balance in such a way as to make the distributions subject to both federal and state income tax. The planner should decide whether any of the above should be considered in the determination of non-discretionary expenses.

Current Ratio

$$\text{Current Ratio} = \frac{\text{Cash \& Cash Equivalents}}{\text{Current Liabilities}} \geq 1.00$$

The current ratio provides insight into the client's ability to meet short-term obligations as they come due. Current liabilities represent those liabilities that will be paid within the next year. A larger current ratio implies more liquidity and thus a greater ability to pay current liabilities as they come due. It may appear that there is a liquidity problem when the current ratio is less than one. However, most individuals pay their current liabilities and associated interest out of their current income (statement of income) and not out of their cash and cash equivalents (balance sheet). Therefore, to the extent this is true, a current ratio that is less than one may be adequate.

⋮≡ *Key Concepts*

1. What information is provided by housing ratio 1 and housing ratio 2 and what are the benchmarks for both ratios?

2. How is the savings rate calculated and what are the typical benchmarks for this ratio?

3. Identify the usefulness of the performance ratios.

It also should be noted that the current ratio can be modified by adding the net positive discretionary cash flow to the numerator, which should provide a better measure of liquidity over a period of time. Of course, if net expected discretionary cash flow from the projected income statements is negative, it would have to be subtracted from cash and cash equivalents to provide a clearer picture of liquidity using the current ratio.

Debt Ratios

There are four debt ratios used in the financial statement and ratio analysis approach to help the planner determine how well the client manages debt:
1. housing ratio 1 (basic)
2. housing ratio 2 (broad)
3. debt-to-total assets ratio
4. net worth-to-total assets ratio

Housing Ratio 1 (Basic)

$$\text{Housing Ratio 1} \ = \ \frac{\text{Housing Costs}}{\text{Gross Pay}} \leq 28\%$$

Housing costs include principal payments on the mortgage (or rent), interest, homeowners insurance, property taxes, and association dues, if applicable.

The purpose of housing ratio 1 (HR1) is to calculate the percentage of gross pay that is devoted to basic housing. It does not include utilities, lawn care, maintenance, etc. The benchmark for housing ratio 1 is less than or equal to 28 percent. Generally, a HR1 of 28 percent or less is the initial ratio necessary for a first time home buyer to qualify for a conforming (best) rate mortgage. The conforming rate mortgage generally requires a 20 percent down payment and good credit. Assuming that the mortgage interest rate is fixed and amortized over 15 or 30 years, then as inflation causes salaries and housing values to increase, HR1 should decline gradually.

The HR1 benchmark is used traditionally by mortgage lenders to issue conforming (best) rate mortgages. Note that the ratio should decline to roughly five percent (although not in a state with very high property taxes, such as Texas) at retirement, when the mortgage is assumed to be completely paid off and only taxes, association dues, and insurance expenses continue.

Housing Ratio 2 (Broad)[2]

$$\text{Housing Ratio 2} = \frac{\text{Housing Costs + Other Debt Payments}}{\text{Gross Pay}} \leq 36\%$$

Housing ratio 2 (HR2) combines basic housing costs (HR1) with all other monthly debt payments, including payments for automobile loans, student loans, bank loans, revolving consumer loans, credit card payments, and any other debt payments made on a recurring basis. The HR2 benchmark is less than or equal to 36 percent of gross pay. The planner should be cautious when considering the client's credit card payments for purposes of this ratio. If the client is only making minimum payments on credit cards, the payback period for such debt could be 17 years or longer, depending on the relationship between the interest rate, the minimum payments, and the original balance. In the situation where a client is only making minimum credit card payments, then the planner should calculate a payment using the interest rate on the card that would retire the credit card debt in 36 to 60 months. The planner can then use that payment for this calculation, rather than the minimum payment the client is actually making, so as to avoid underestimating the relevant ratio. Credit card statements are now required to disclose this type of comparison and may save the planner time and effort.

Debt-to-Total Assets Ratio

$$\text{Deb-to-Total Assets Ratio} = \frac{\text{Total Debt}}{\text{Total Assets}} = \text{Benchmark Depends on Client Age}$$

The debt-to-total assets ratio is essentially a leverage ratio. It reflects the portion of assets owned by a client that are financed by creditors. Usually, young people establishing themselves have relatively high debt ratios due to the presence of automobile and student loans. First time home buyers generally have high ratios, even with a 20 percent down payment (implying an 80% mortgage). This ratio, like all other ratios, is best considered over time to monitor the client's progress. This ratio is commonly as high as 80 percent for young people and as low as 10 percent or less for those near retirement age.

Net Worth-to-Total Assets Ratio

$$\text{Net Worth-to-Total Assets Ratio} = \frac{\text{Net Worth}}{\text{Total Assets}} = \text{Benchmark Depends on Client Age}$$

The net worth-to-total assets ratio is the complement of the debt-to-assets ratio described above. The two add up to one (i.e., as debt declines as a percent of total assets, net worth rises). This ratio provides the planner with the percentage of total assets owned or paid for by the client. It is not surprising that this ratio would be 20 percent for young people and up to 90 to 100 percent for retirement age clients. This ratio once again is best observed over time. Note that net worth increases as assets increase in value (home and investments), with additional savings, and with the payoff of obligations (liabilities) over time.

---

2. While the Consumer Financial Protection Bureau (CFPB) allows a debt-to-income (HR 2) ratio of up to 43% to be eligible for a "qualified mortgage," sound financial planning principals require the use of the more conservative 36% ratio maximum. A "qualified mortgage" is defined by the CFPB as one in which certain risky loan features are not permitted and the lender does not charge excessive up front points and fees.

Ratios for Financial Security Goals

Ratios for financial security goals help the financial planner to assess the progress that the client is making toward achieving long-term goals. The two most common ratios used to assess that progress are the savings rate and the investment assets-to-gross pay ratio.

Savings Rate

$$\text{Savings Rate} = \frac{\text{Savings + Employer Match}}{\text{Gross Pay}} = \begin{array}{c}\text{Benchmark Depends on Client Goals} \\ \text{(but at least 10 - 13\%)}\end{array}$$

An appropriate savings rate is critical to achieving long-term goals including retirement, education funding, large lump-sum expenditures (e.g., second home), and legacy plans. The savings rate is calculated by dividing gross savings in dollars, employee elective deferrals into 401(k), 403(b), and 457 plans plus any employer match and any other savings, by gross pay. The savings rate benchmark depends on the number of long-term goals of the client. If the only goal of the client is financial security (retirement) the benchmark savings rate for a young person should be 10 to 13 percent of gross pay. The persistent savings rate needed for a 25-year old with retirement as his only goal should be 10 to 13 percent, excluding Social Security contributions.

If the client has multiple long-term goals, the savings rate must be greater than 10 to 13 percent to achieve those goals. For example, a couple, both age 25, earning $75,000 annually with newborn twins who they plan to send to an in-state college for four years, would need a savings rate of 10 to 13 percent for retirement plus an additional two to three percent for education for a combined savings rate of 12 to 16 percent. The education savings rate is dependent on the type of school their children will attend (in-state / lower costs, private / medium costs, or private / higher costs) and the income level of the client because the savings rate for tuition declines as income increases because tuition is a fixed dollar amount.[3] Note: dividends, interest, capital gains, and other types of portfolio income are not counted or included as part of savings since this type of income is already considered as part of the overall portfolio rate of return, which is used for growth projections. If they were included in both, then they would be double counted. If they were included as part of savings, then the portfolio rate of return would have to be reduced to reflect that treatment.

---

3. This is without regard to need based financial aid or merit based scholarships.

Exhibit 3.11 | Relationship Between Time, Savings, and Withdrawal Rates on Retirement Planning

The following three scenarios help to illustrate the intricate nature of the savings rate on the retirement capital balance, how the savings rate and capital balance impact the withdrawal rate, and the required rate of earnings needed during retirement. The first scenario assumes that the client saves for 40 years, while the second scenario assumes 30 years of savings, and finally, the third scenario assumes 20 years of savings.

Each of the scenarios assumes a **real (inflation-adjusted) rate of return** of 5%, which is generally reasonable over a long period of time. However, increasing or decreasing this rate will have a significant effect on the final result. These scenarios also assume a retirement life expectancy of 30 years, which is very conservative for most of the population.[1]

The first scenario assumes a wage replacement ratio of 80%, which means that retirement income needs are 80% of pre-retirement income. The wage replacement ratio for scenarios 2 and 3 have been reduced from the original 80% to 70% and 60% respectively, to make the models work with a reasonable required **real rate of return** during retirement. Effectively, clients who begin saving later in life are less likely to be able to fund a larger annual withdrawal amount as compared to someone who begins saving at an earlier age. Social Security retirement benefits have purposely been left out of this analysis.

1. Scenarios 1, 2, and 3 assume that savings are made at the end of the year (ordinary annuity) and that withdrawals are made at the beginning of the year (annuity due).

Scenario 1 (40 years of savings, real rate of return 5%, WRR 80%, LE 30 years)					
Annual Savings	**Annual Savings Rate**	**Retirement Capital Balance**	**Annual Needs at Retirement**	**Required Withdrawal Rate**	**Required Real Rate of Return**
$18,000	18%	$2,174,396	$80,000	3.68%	0.70%
$16,000	16%	$1,932,796	$80,000	4.14%	1.57%
$14,000	14%	$1,691,197	$80,000	4.73%	2.62%
$13,000	**13%**	**$1,570,397**	**$80,000**	**5.09%**	**3.24%**
$12,000	**12%**	**$1,449,597**	**$80,000**	**5.52%**	**3.93%**
$11,000	11%	$1,328,798	$80,000	6.02%	4.73%
$10,000	10%	$1,207,998	$80,000	6.62%	5.65%

Income at retirement assumed to be $100,000.

The highlighted section of Scenario 1 illustrates a person, age 25, saving about 12 percent to 13 percent of his income for 40 years and accumulating approximately $1.5 million. The result is that he is able to meet an 80 percent wage replacement ratio with a reasonable required real rate of return (between 3.24 - 3.93%) during retirement. At a 13 percent savings rate, the $80,000 needs at retirement translate to a 5.09 percent withdrawal rate. To maintain this withdrawal throughout retirement, a real return of 3.24 percent would have to be earned. If inflation were three percent, this would equate to an approximate

6.3 percent nominal return, still quite conservative. The calculation of the required real return assumes he has spent all of his capital at the end of the 30-year period.

Scenario 2 (30 years of savings, real rate of return 5%, WRR 70%, LE 30 years)					
Annual Savings	Annual Savings Rate	Retirement Capital Balance	Annual Needs at Retirement	Required Withdrawal Rate	Required Real Rate of Return
$25,000	25%	$1,660,971	$70,000	4.21%	1.71%
$24,000	24%	$1,594,532	$70,000	4.39%	2.02%
$23,000	23%	$1,528,093	$70,000	4.58%	2.36%
$22,000	22%	$1,461,655	$70,000	4.79%	2.72%
$21,000	**21%**	**$1,395,216**	**$70,000**	**5.02%**	**3.11%**
$20,000	**20%**	**$1,328,777**	**$70,000**	**5.27%**	**3.52%**
$19,000	19%	$1,262,338	$70,000	5.55%	3.98%

Income at retirement assumed to be $100,000.

The highlighted section of Scenario 2 illustrates a person, 35 years of age, required to save close to 20 percent of his income to drive a retirement plan with a 70 percent wage replacement ratio. It appears that the 20 percent savings rate is adequate to drive a reasonable withdrawal rate and a reasonable required rate of return of 3.11 to 3.52 percent. Note that this person began saving 10 years later than the one in Scenario 1 and can only sustain an annual retirement annuity of $70,000, which is $10,000 less than the wage replacement ratio in Scenario 1.

Scenario 3 (20 years of savings, real rate of return 5%, WRR 60%, LE 30 years)					
Annual Savings	Annual Savings Rate	Retirement Capital Balance	Annual Needs at Retirement	Required Withdrawal Rate	Required Real Rate of Return
$30,000	**30%**	**$991,979**	**$60,000**	**6.05%**	**4.77%**
$29,000	**29%**	**$958,913**	**$60,000**	**6.26%**	**5.10%**
$28,000	28%	$925,847	$60,000	6.48%	5.44%
$27,000	27%	$892,781	$60,000	6.72%	5.80%
$26,000	26%	$859,715	$60,000	6.98%	6.19%
$25,000	25%	$826,649	$60,000	7.26%	6.60%
$24,000	24%	$793,583	$60,000	7.56%	7.04%

* Income at retirement assumed to be $100,000.

The highlighted section of Scenario 3 illustrates a person, 45 years of age, with only 20 years to save for retirement. In this scenario, 20 years of savings is driving a 30 year withdrawal period. The result of this scenario is that the required savings rate is very high (29-30%) and the wage replacement ratio is significantly less than the results in Scenario 1 or 2 (60% as opposed to 70% or 80%).

The three scenarios clearly illustrate the importance of the timing of savings and the duration of savings. These scenarios were based on a constant real rate of return of five percent during the savings period, however investment returns are not constant or linear in financial markets. Rather, there are ups and downs, and when returns are down, the account balance at retirement (e.g., if negative returns occur for the three years preceding retirement) can be significantly impacted.

Negative portfolio returns can also seriously damage an investment plan if they occur shortly after retirement when there are no additional savings to be added to the plan. In such a case, both withdrawals and negative portfolio returns exacerbate the reduction in the account balance of the retirement fund. This kind of situation increases the probability of running out of money before the end of life (superannuation).

There are a few ways to mitigate the risk of superannuation. Options before retirement include saving more, beginning to save at an earlier age, or delaying retirement. Saving more means saving based on a model such as the capital preservation model or the purchasing power preservation model or working a few extra years to make certain that the capital balance is sufficient to adequately fund retirement. It is important to generate investment returns that provide a sufficient real rate of return. Equities are an important element of any portfolio that is attempting to generate a positive real rate of return. Once in retirement, the primary way to mitigate the risk of superannuation is to maintain a relatively low withdrawal rate and have a balanced investment portfolio that can withstand unexpected fluctuations in investment returns.

Social Security and part-time work in retirement has not been included in the above analysis. Social Security, for average income workers, provides as much as 42 percent of wage replacement, and for higher income workers, provides as low as 26 percent of wage replacement (this assumes a same age non-working spouse who is entitled to a 50 percent benefit of the worker based on the working spouse's earnings history). To adjust these amounts for a single individual, divide the wage replacement percentage for the couple by 150 percent (e.g., 42% ÷ 150% = 28%).

Investment Assets-to-Gross Pay

Saving 10 to 13 percent of gross pay is sufficient to drive the retirement goal only if the client begins saving around age 25. Therefore, it is necessary to calculate a second ratio. The combination of these two ratios provides the planner with a better understanding of the current progress toward achieving the retirement goal. The investment assets-to-gross pay ratio is the second ratio used to assess a retirement plan that persistently has clients saving 10 to 13 percent of gross pay. As used in this textbook, all investment assets are considered, including cash and cash equivalents and education savings. If the client wants to measure retirement assets separately, the planner can redefine the ratio for retirement assets only by leaving out nonretirement savings (e.g., cash and cash equivalents and education savings).

$$\text{Investment Assets-to-Gross Pay} = \frac{(\text{Investment Assets}) + (\text{Cash} + \text{Cash Equivalents})}{\text{Gross Pay}} = \text{Benchmark Depends on Client Age}$$

For this ratio to be effective, the financial planner needs to make sure that all personal use assets are classified correctly (e.g., most homes and various collectibles are not investment assets for this purpose). In the event that a client has multiple goals such as college education for children, lump sum expenditure goals, retirement goals, and legacy goals, the investment assets used in this calculation can be reduced by those that are devoted to goals other than retirement.

The investment assets-to-gross pay benchmark is calculated according to age and is generally reliable for a wide range of income levels (e.g., $40,000 to $400,000 annual income).

Exhibit 3.12 | Investment Assets to Gross Pay Benchmarks to Achieve Retirement Goal

Benchmark for Investment Assets as a Ratio of Gross Pay by Age		
25	0.2:1	A continued savings rate of 10 to 13% of gross pay until retirement age 65 will achieve these ratios if invested in a balanced fund that produces reasonable returns.
30	0.6 - 0.8:1	
35	1.6 - 1.8:1	
45	3 - 4:1	
55	8 - 10:1	
65	16 - 20:1	Inflation and pay raises are included in the analysis.

For example, the exhibit above indicates that a client age 35 should have 1.6 to 1.8 times his annual gross pay in investment assets as savings for retirement. A savings rate of 10 to 13 percent of gross pay will facilitate achieving the financial security (retirement) goal. This table of investment asset ratios is consistent with a four to five percent withdrawal rate at retirement that will mitigate against the risk of superannuation.

A frequent question regarding the above benchmark data table is how a defined benefit plan pension or employer-provided pension plan fits into this analysis. A financial planner has two alternatives to use in addressing the additional retirement funding provided by a defined benefit plan.

1. The first is to calculate the present value of all pension benefits and include that amount on the client's balance sheet under investment assets.
2. The second alternative is to reduce the wage replacement needs amount at retirement for the expected pension income benefit at that time and then recalculate the client's adjusted needs for the amount of savings necessary to drive the new wage replacement ratios (as adjusted by the portion provided by the pension).

In either case, the planner should only include these adjustments when there is reasonable certainty that the client will receive the benefit. The first approach is preferred because it only includes the present value of vested benefits, without making any assumptions about future benefits or whether the client will remain with his current employer until retirement.

Example 3.2

Evonne, age 45, is currently making $78,000 and has been with her employer for 20 years. She is expecting to receive an annual pension of $23,400 at her normal retirement age of 65. The pension formula is 1.5% per year times her final salary of employment.

The present value of the pension today is calculated as follows:

$\quad$ N = 20 (life expectancy at 65 to 85)
$\quad$ i = 4 (the riskless rate if a strong company)
$\quad$ PMT_{AD} = $23,400 (20 years x 1.5% x $78,000)
$\quad$ FV = $0 (a single life annuity)
$\quad$ $PV_{AD@65}$ = $330,734 (from 85 to age 65) (N = 20)[4]
$\quad$ $PV_{@45}$ = $150,943 (from 65 to age 45) (N = 20)

The $330,734 represents the lump-sum amount needed at age 65 to pay Evonne an annuity of $23,400 per year during her retirement assuming an investment return of 4%.[5] The $150,943 represents the lump-sum amount that, if set aside today, will grow to $330,734 at age 65 if invested at 4%. Her salary has intentionally not been adjusted for inflation.

Evonne can add the $150,943 to her balance sheet or reduce her annual needs at retirement by $23,400 at age 65. The balance sheet approach is preferred because most defined benefit pensions are not adjusted for inflation thus making the needs approach more difficult to be precise.

Note, if Evonne remains with the company until age 65 and her salary continues to grow by 3% per year to $140,877, the present value of her pension benefit at age 65 will be $1,194,685, calculated as follows:

N = 20 (life expectancy at 65)
i = 4 (the riskless rate if a strong company)
PMT_{AD} = $84,526 (40 years x 1.5% x $140,877)
FV = $0 (a single life annuity)
PV_{65} = $1,194,685 (at age 65)

---

4. The present value in this step is calculated as an annuity due. The payments are assumed to begin at the beginning of the year.
5. The discount rate of 4% is a relatively low earnings rate. However, it has the effect of a higher present value than using a discount rate of 6% or 7%. At a discount rate of 7%, the PV decreases to approximately $69,000. In other words, the discount rate used represents, in this case, a difference of nearly $80,000 on the client's net worth and any retirement funding ratios.

An important point to consider when evaluating the investment assets-to-gross pay ratio is the context of this ratio within the entire set of ratios. For example, if the client is fairly young, owns a principal residence that is debt free, but has an investment assets-to-gross-pay ratio that is low for his age, this may not be a problem. It may be that a similarly situated person with debt on a principal residence has a higher investment assets-to-gross pay ratio, but a lower savings rate. As long as the client, who is not servicing debt on a residence, has a current and future increasing savings rate, then the investment assets-to-gross pay ratio should grow quickly. Ultimately, the ratio is intended to help track how the client is progressing towards retiring with the necessary funds to sustain the desired lifestyle.

Performance Ratios

Return on Investments, Return on Assets, and Return on Net Worth are the most common performance ratios used to calculate the adequacy of investment returns.

Return on Investments (ROI)

The Return on Investments (ROI) ratio calculates the rate of return on invested assets. The ratio is calculated by taking the ending balance of investments (I_1) minus the sum of the beginning balance of investments (I_0) plus the annual savings (S), divided by the beginning balance of investments.

$$\text{Return on Investments (ROI)} = \frac{I_1 - (I_0 + \text{Savings})}{I_0}$$

This ratio is an appropriate measure of the return on investments made during a year. There is an implicit assumption that savings are made in equal monthly deposits during the year. This calculation produces what is referred to as an arithmetic return (AR), which is appropriate for a one-year period. However, for measuring returns over a long period of time, the arithmetic return is not as accurate as the geometric average, and will generally overstate the return. The geometric average is equivalent to the internal rate of return, while the arithmetic return is a simple average. These concepts are discussed more thoroughly in Chapter 9.

For example, assume that a client had $100 at I_0 and $120 at I_1 and that the client had also saved $1 at the end of each month during the year. The ROI (simple average) is calculated as $120 - ($100 + $12) ÷ $100 = 8%. However, if the ROI was calculated exactly using a **geometric return**, then it would actually be 7.34 percent.

Geometric Return (GR) Calculation

N	= 12 months
PV	= $100
FV	= ($120)
PMT	= $1 per month (12 ÷ 12)
i	= 0.61136 per month x 12 = 7.34% (GR)

The ROI of 7.34 percent is the geometric return. The eight percent return as calculated by the initial formula produces the arithmetic return. In order to calculate the ROI we need two balance sheets. Once again, ROI is best calculated over time and geometric returns are more informationally useful to the financial planner than arithmetic returns.

The ROI benchmark comparison should be made using the same asset class returns as the actual investments. For example, it would be inappropriate to compare a balanced mutual fund (one invested in both equities and fixed income) to the S&P 500 index (an equity index). Instead, the investment (balanced fund) should be compared to a blended index that includes equities and fixed income.

Return on Assets (ROA)

The Return on Assets (ROA) ratio measures total asset returns by calculating the difference between ending assets (A_1) less the sum of beginning assets (A_0) plus any savings (S), divided by beginning assets.

$$\text{Return on Assets} = \frac{A_1 - (A_0 + \text{Savings})}{A_0}$$

This ratio must be used cautiously when the client is adding assets that are leveraged with debt. In the event new assets are added to the balance sheet and they are highly leveraged, the financial planner may consider simply adding the net equity to the year-end assets (A_1) for purpose of calculating ROA.

Return on Net Worth (RONW)

The Return on Net Worth (RONW) ratio further refines the performance set of ratios by calculating the rate of return on net worth. The calculation takes ending net worth (NW_1) less the sum of beginning net worth (NW_0) and savings (S), divided by beginning net worth.

$$\text{Return on Net Worth} = \frac{NW_1 - (NW_0 + \text{Savings})}{NW_0}$$

If the client is adding assets with debt, this ratio should help to clarify the validity of the ROA ratio.

Exhibit 3.13 | Summary of Financial Statement Ratios

Liquidity Ratios			
Ratio	**Formula**	**Measures**	**Benchmark**
Emergency Funds	$\dfrac{\text{Cash \& Cash Equivalents}}{\text{Monthly Non-Discretionary Cash Flows}}$	The number of months of non-discretionary expenses in the form of cash and cash equivalents.	3 - 6 months
Current Ratio	$\dfrac{\text{Cash \& Cash Equivalents}}{\text{Current Liabilities}}$	The number of times a client can satisfy their short-term liabilities.	1.0 - 2.0
Debt Ratios			
Housing Ratio 1 (Basic)	$\dfrac{\text{Housing Costs}}{\text{Gross Pay}}$	The percentage of income spent on housing debt.	$\leq 28\%$
Housing Ratio 2 (Broad)	$\dfrac{\text{Housing Costs + Other Debt Payments}}{\text{Gross Pay}}$	The percentage of income spent on housing and all other recurring debt.	$\leq 36\%$
Debt-to-Total Assets	$\dfrac{\text{Total Debt}}{\text{Total Assets}}$	The percentage of assets being provided by creditors.	As a person ages, this ratio should decline.
Net Worth-to-Total Assets	$\dfrac{\text{Net Worth}}{\text{Total Assets}}$	The percentage of total assets owned or paid for by client.	Depends on age. 20% for young client and 90-100% for retirement age client.
Ratios for Financial Security Goals			
Savings Rate	$\dfrac{\text{Savings + Employer Match}}{\text{Gross Pay}}$	The percentage of income saved towards a retirement goal.	10 – 13% assuming the client starts early, ages 25-35.
Investment Assets-to-Gross Pay	$\dfrac{\text{Investment Assets + Cash \& Cash Equivalents}}{\text{Gross Pay}}$	The progress towards a retirement goal.	Depends on Age 16 to 20 times pre-retirement income at retirement.
Performance Ratios			
Return on Investments	$\dfrac{I_1 - (I_0 + \text{Savings})}{I_0}$	The growth rate of a client's investment assets.	8 – 10%
Return on Assets	$\dfrac{A_1 - (A_0 + \text{Savings})}{A_0}$	A blended growth rate of all assets.	2 – 4%
Return on Net Worth	$\dfrac{NW_1 - (NW_0 + \text{Savings})}{NW_0}$	The growth rate of net worth.	The higher the better. This ratio is likely to become smaller as the client's net worth increases.

Guide for Calculating Financial Ratios

Financial ratios can be created and defined using different criteria according to a particular client's situation. For example, one client's non-discretionary spending (e.g., charitable contributions, church donations, etc.) may be defined by different values as compared to another client's non-discretionary spending.

The following exhibit reflects common financial ratios along with an indication of which financial statements contain the data necessary to calculate each ratio. Some ratios may be calculated using both historical and current financial statements. The same ratios can also be calculated using projected financial statements based on a financial planner's recommendations.

This textbook reflects the reality of various client scenarios and calculates ratios based on current information and projected financial statements. Some ratios can be calculated using only one (current) balance sheet and other ratios (performance ratios) require two balance sheets. The calculated ratios in this textbook are reflective of the particular client's scenario and whether one balance sheet or two balance sheets are available. The financial planner should view a ratio as one part of a mosaic; by itself the ratio does not portray the entire financial picture. Ratios should be viewed individually and then as part of the whole financial "mosaic" to obtain a true understanding of a client's entire financial situation.

Exhibit 3.14 | Financial Statements Needed to Calculate Ratios

Liquidity Ratios			
Ratio	**Formula**	**Balance Sheet**[1]	**Income Statement**
Emergency Funds Ratio[2]	$\dfrac{\text{Cash \& Cash Equivalents}}{\text{Monthly Non-Discretionary Cash Flows}}$	✓	✓
Current Ratio	$\dfrac{\text{Cash \& Cash Equivalents}}{\text{Current Liabilities}}$	✓	

1 Balance sheet ratios may use beginning balance sheet, one year projected, or both.
2 Client must determine non-discretionary payments based on personal values (charitable contributions, church donations, etc.).

Debt Ratios			
Ratio	**Formula**	**Balance Sheet**[3]	**Income Statement**
Housing Ratio 1 (Basic)	$\dfrac{\text{Housing Costs}}{\text{Gross Pay}}$		✓
Housing Ratio 2 (Broad)	$\dfrac{\text{Housing Costs + Other Debt Payments}}{\text{Gross Pay}}$		✓
Debt-to-Total Assets	$\dfrac{\text{Total Debt}}{\text{Total Assets}}$	✓	
Net Worth-to-Total Assets	$\dfrac{\text{Net Worth}}{\text{Total Assets}}$	✓	

3 Balance sheet ratios may use beginning balance sheet, one year projected, or both.

Exhibit 3.15 | Financial Statements Needed to Calculate Ratios (Continued)

Ratios for Financial Security Goals			
Ratio	**Formula**	**Balance Sheet**	**Income Statement**
Savings Rate[4]	$\dfrac{\text{Savings} + \text{Employer Match}}{\text{Gross Pay}}$		✓
Investment Assets-to-Gross Pay[5/6]	$\dfrac{\text{Investment Assets} + \text{Cash \& Cash Equivalents}}{\text{Gross Pay}}$	✓	✓

4 Include any employer matches for retirement funds.
5 Can be separated by goal. If retirement only, use retirement committed investment assets. Education assets and cash and cash equivalents are not included. If calculating total investment assets to gross pay then: All Investment Assets + Cash and Cash Equivalents ÷ Gross Pay.
6 Use all Investment Assets and Cash and Cash Equivalents also in the ratio calculation.

Performance Ratios			
Ratio	**Formula**	**Balance Sheet**	**Income Statement**
Return on Investments - Retirement	$\dfrac{I_1 - (I_0 + \text{Savings})}{I_0}$	✓	✓
Return on Investments - Education	$\dfrac{I_1 - (I_0 + \text{Savings})}{I_0}$	✓	✓
Return on Investments - Total	$\dfrac{I_1 - (I_0 + \text{Savings})}{I_0}$	✓	✓
Return on Assets	$\dfrac{A_1 - (A_0 + \text{Savings})}{A_0}$	✓	✓
Return on Net Worth	$\dfrac{NW_1 - (NW_0 + \text{Savings})}{NW_0}$	✓	✓

HESS CASE EXAMPLE OF APPLYING THE PIE CHART, FINANCIAL STATEMENT, AND RATIO ANALYSIS APPROACH

The purpose of the Hess case is to illustrate how the pie chart approach and the ratio analysis approach may be applied to a client scenario. A more detailed application of these approaches will follow in subsequent chapters.

Jack Hess is a 45-year old marketing manager for a national pharmaceutical company. His annual salary is $73,000. He participates in his company's 401(k) retirement plan and his employer matches three percent of his salary. Jack's wife, Marilyn, is a 43-year old make-up artist with an annual salary of $36,000. There are no company retirement plans available for Marilyn. Jack and Marilyn have been married for 18 years and plan to retire in 20 years. They have a 13-year old daughter, Melba, who is in the 8th grade at a private school in their area. Jack and Marilyn anticipate that Melba will attend a private university with tuition of $21,000 annually in today's dollars. Jack and Marilyn have a moderate level of risk tolerance and rank their financial objectives, by priority, as follows:

1. save for retirement
2. save for private college education for Melba
3. have an adequate insurance portfolio

FINANCIAL STATEMENTS: BALANCE SHEET (12/31/20X1)

Statement of Financial Position Jack and Marilyn Hess Balance Sheet as of 12/31/20X1					
ASSETS[1]			**LIABILITIES AND NET WORTH**		
Current Assets			**Current Liabilities**[2]		
Checking Account	$18,000		Credit Card Balances	$11,000	
Money Market Account	$12,000		**Total Current Liabilities**		**$11,000**
Total Current Assets		**$30,000**			
Investment Assets			**Long-Term Liabilities**[2]		
401(k) Plan	$86,000		Mortgage Balance (Residence)[3]	$145,000	
IRA	$16,000		Auto Loans	$16,000	
CDs	$15,000		**Total Long-Term Liabilities**		**$161,000**
Growth Mutual Fund	$20,000				
Stock Portfolio[4]	$40,000				
Total Investment Assets		**$177,000**	**Total Liabilities**		**$172,000**
Personal Use Assets					
Personal Residence	$155,000				
Personal Property	$57,000		**Total Net Worth**		**$280,000**
Automobiles	$33,000				
Total Personal Use Assets		**$245,000**			
Total Assets		**$452,000**	**Total Liabilities & Net Worth**		**$452,000**

1. Assets are stated at fair market value.
2. Principal balance only.
3. The mortgage is a 30-year note at 8% with an original balance of $145,000. They just purchased the home.
4. Publicly-traded stock.

Financial Statements: Statement of Income and Expenses

Statement of Income and Expenses Mr. and Mrs. Hess Statement of Income and Expenses for 20X1 and Expected (Approximate) For 20X2		
CASH INFLOWS[1]		Totals
Salaries		
Jack's Salary	$73,000	
Marilyn's Salary	$36,000	
Total Cash Inflows		$109,000
CASH OUTFLOWS		
Savings[1]		
Employee - Elective Deferral	$14,600	
Total Savings		$14,600
Ordinary Living Expenses		$26,000
Debt Payments		
Credit Card Payments	$3,300	
Mortgage Loan	$12,768	
Auto Loans	$5,400	
Total Debt Payments		$21,468
Insurance Premiums		
Life Insurance	$1,900	
Health Insurance	$500	
Auto Insurance	$800	
Homeowners Insurance	$1,600	
Total Insurance Premiums		$4,800
Charitable Contributions		$935
Tuition & Education Expenses		$10,000
Entertainment & Vacations		$2,000
Taxes		
Federal Income Tax Withholding	$16,220	
State Income Tax Withholding	$2,869	
Social Security Taxes	$8,339	
Property Tax (Residence)	$2,895	
Total Taxes		$30,323
TOTAL CASH OUTFLOWS		$110,126
NET DISCRETIONARY CASH FLOW		($1,126)

1. Reinvested earnings are not included in gross pay or the savings rate because
   they are included in the overall expected portfolio rate of return.

Financial Statements: Projected Balance Sheet (12/31/20X2)

Statement of Financial Position
Jack and Marilyn Hess
Projected Balance Sheet as of 12/31/20X2

ASSETS[1]			LIABILITIES AND NET WORTH[2]		
Current Assets			**Current Liabilities[3]**		
Checking Account	$16,174		Credit Card Balances	$11,000	
Money Market Account	$12,000		**Total Current Liabilities**		$11,000
Total Current Assets		$28,174			
Investment Assets			**Long-Term Liabilities[2]**		
401(k) Plan	$89,600		Mortgage Balance (Residence)[4]	$143,789	
IRA	$17,000		Auto Loans	$10,600	
CDs	$15,000		**Total Long-Term Liabilities**		$154,389
Growth Mutual Fund	$18,000				
Stock Portfolio[5]	$36,000				
Total Investment Assets		$175,600	**Total Liabilities**		$165,389
Personal Use Assets					
Personal Residence	$160,000				
Personal Property	$57,000		**Total Net Worth**		$285,385
Automobiles	$30,000				
Total Personal Use Assets		$247,000			
Total Assets		$450,774	**Total Liabilities & Net Worth**		$450,774

1. Assets are stated at fair market value.
2. For simplicity purposes, the mortgage debt and the auto debt have not been split into the current portion and the long-term portion. This concept is discussed later in the text.
3. Principal balance only.
4. The mortgage is a 30-year note at 8% with an original balance of $145,000.
5. Publicly-traded stock.

Pie Chart Analysis for Hess Case

From the balance sheet and income statement data, the financial planner can then create pie charts as shown below.

Balance Sheet Data and Pie Charts (12/31/20X1)

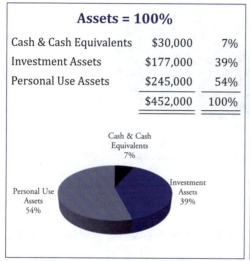

Assets = 100%

Cash & Cash Equivalents	$30,000	7%
Investment Assets	$177,000	39%
Personal Use Assets	$245,000	54%
	$452,000	100%

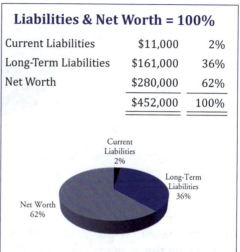

Liabilities & Net Worth = 100%

Current Liabilities	$11,000	2%
Long-Term Liabilities	$161,000	36%
Net Worth	$280,000	62%
	$452,000	100%

Income Statement Data (For Year 20X2)

	Amount	Percentage
Gross Income	$109,000	100%
Taxes	$30,323	27.8%
Savings	$14,600	13.4%
Insurance	$4,800	4.4%
Ordinary Living Expenses	$26,000	23.8%
Other Debt Payments (ODP)	$21,468	19.7%
Charitable, Tuition, Entertainment	$12,935	11.9%
Discretionary Cash Flow (DCF)	($1,126)	(1%)

Income Statement Pie Chart

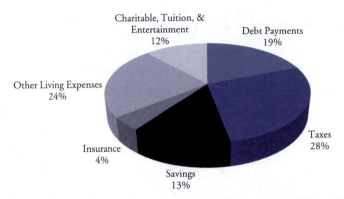

Income = $109,000

Note: Discretionary cash flow is not listed because it is negative $1,126 or -1%.

Financial Ratios for Hess Case

The ratios below are based on the year beginning balance sheet (20X1) except for the performance ratios, that are based on the year-end values (20X2).

Liquidity Ratios

$$\text{Emergency Fund Ratio} = \frac{\$30,000}{(\$66,098 \div 12) = \$5,508.17} = 5.44 \text{ Months Coverage (Good)}$$

$26,000	Ordinary Living Expenses
$21,468	Total Debt Payments
$4,800	Total Insurance Payments
$10,000	Tuition & Education Expenses
$2,895	Residence Property Taxes
$935	Charitable Contributions*
$66,098	Total Non-Discretionary Cash Flows

* Charitable contributions are considered non-discretionary by the client.

$$(20X1) \text{ Current Ratio} = \frac{\$30,000}{\$11,000} = 2.73 \text{ (Good)}$$

$$(20X2) \text{ Current Ratio} = \frac{\$28,174}{\$11,000} = 2.56 \text{ (Good)}$$

Debt Ratios

$$\text{Housing Ratio 1} = \frac{\$12{,}768 + \$1{,}600 + \$2{,}895}{\$109{,}000} = 15.8\% \text{ (Very Good)}$$

$$\text{Housing Ratio 2} = \frac{\$12{,}768 + \$1{,}600 + \$2{,}895 + \$3{,}300 + \$5{,}400}{\$109{,}000} = 23.8\% \text{ (Very Good)}$$

$$\text{Debt-to-Total Assets Ratio} = \frac{\$172{,}000}{\$452{,}000} = 38.1\% \text{ (Good) (20X1)}$$

$$\text{Debt-to-Total Assets Ratio} = \frac{\$165{,}389}{\$450{,}774} = 36.7\% \text{ (Good) (20X2)}$$

$$\text{Net Worth-to-Total Assets Ratio} = \frac{\$280{,}000}{\$452{,}000} = 62\% \text{ (Good) Benchmark Depends on Age (20X1)}$$

$$\text{Net Worth-to-Total Assets Ratio} = \frac{\$285{,}385}{\$450{,}774} = 63\% \text{ (Good) Benchmark Depends on Age (20X2)}$$

Ratios for Financial Security Goals

$$\text{Savings Rate*} = \frac{\$2{,}190 + \$14{,}600}{\$109{,}000} = 15.4\% \text{ (Good) (\$2{,}190 = employer match)}$$

(* Excludes reinvestments)

$$\text{Investment Assets-to-Gross Pay} = \frac{\$177{,}000 + \$30{,}000}{\$109{,}000} = 1.90 \text{ times (Weak)}$$

401(k) Plan Savings	
Employee Elective Deferral	$14,600
Employer Match	$2,190
Total	**$16,790**

Performance Ratios

$$\text{Return on 401(k)} = \frac{\$89{,}600 - (\$86{,}000 + \$16{,}790)}{\$86{,}000} = -15.3\% \text{ (Very Poor)}$$

$$\text{Return on Total Investments} = \frac{\$175{,}600 - (\$177{,}000 + \$14{,}600 + \$2{,}190)}{\$177{,}000} = \frac{-10.3\%}{\text{(Very Poor)}}$$

Overall, the ratio approach suggests the Hess' only have two major weaknesses in the amount of savings to gross pay and return on investments. Additional approaches should be applied to reveal a more comprehensive analysis of the Hess financial position. The additional approaches are covered during the remainder of this chapter.

THE TWO-STEP / THREE-PANEL / METRICS APPROACH

Two-Step Approach

The two-step approach to financial planning recommends covering the risks and saving and investing. The two-step approach considers personal risks as potentially leading to catastrophic losses or dependence on someone else for their financial well being. The two-step approach regards savings and investments as the path to financial security or independence. Dependence on others can be caused by a single catastrophic event that can occur unexpectedly. Financial independence, however, is achieved over a long period of time by saving and investing. In summary, the two-step approach focuses on risk management and appropriate saving and investing.

> ### 🗒 *Key Concepts*
>
> 1. List the two focuses of the two-step approach and the financial categories analyzed by the three-panel approach.
>
> 2. Identify the purpose of the example benchmarks used in the metrics approach.

Three-Panel Approach

The three-panel approach is a slight refinement of the two-step approach. It divides saving and investing into short and long-term objectives. The three-panel approach provides the planner and the client with a methodology for financial planning in order to achieve the goals of covering the risks, saving, and investing. The exhibit below outlines the three-panel methodology.

Exhibit 3.16 | Three-Panel Methodology

Panel 1	Panel 2	Panel 3
Risk Management of Personal, Property, and Liability Risks	*Short-Term Savings and Investments & Debt Management*	*Long-Term Savings and Investments*
Evaluate the need for and quality of personal insurance:	**Evaluate the adequacy of:**	**Evaluate the adequacy of progress toward:**

1. Life Insurance
2. Health Insurance
3. Disability Insurance
4. Long-Term Care Insurance
5. Property Insurance:
  • Homeowner's Insurance
  • Auto Insurance
  • Other Property Insurance
6. Liability Insurance
	1. The emergency fund
	2. The proportion of income spent on housing
	3. The proportion of income spent on debt other than housing debt repayments
		1. The retirement goal
		  • the savings rate
		  • investment assets
		2. The education funding goal
		3. Any large purchase goal
		4. Legacy goals
		  • documents (e.g., wills)
		  • financial

Panel 1 is used to evaluate each of the risks listed and then evaluates the client's actual portfolio of insurance to determine the adequacy of current insurance coverage. The focus is on covering catastrophic risk exposures and not minor risk exposures. Uncovered catastrophic risks can result in financial dependence, while uncovered minor risks do not result in financial dependence.

Panel 2 is used to calculate the emergency fund ratio (which is also available from using the financial statement analysis approach). Next, the planner calculates housing ratio 1 and housing ratio 2 and evaluates the quality of client debt, which is discussed below. The focus is on meeting short-term obligations and evaluating how well the client is managing debt.

Panel 3 focuses on long-term goals. Meeting the financial security goal (ability to maintain the pre-retirement lifestyle throughout retirement) requires persistent savings, adequate investment performance, and investment assets appropriate for the age and gross pay of the client. If the client also expects or wants to provide a college education for children, the savings rate must be increased. If the client also has lump-sum goals (e.g., second home, very expensive trip, boat, airplane) the savings rate should increase at least sufficiently to provide a down payment on the lump-sum asset of 20 percent. Finally, all clients need basic estate planning documents (will, durable power of attorney for health care, advance medical directive). If, in addition to the other goals, the client wants to leave a financial legacy, even more savings is required. A financial legacy means funds or assets that are left to the heirs upon death of the client.

Exhibit 3.17 depicts four scenarios:
1. Client A has no children.
2. Client B has two children and plans to send them to an in-state college.
3. Client C plans to send two children to a good private school and plans to buy a second home at the beach in ten years (current cost $250,000).
4. Client D plans to send the children to an exclusive private school and buy a second home for $350,000 in ten years and leave $1,000,000 in purchasing power to the children at death.

The assumptions for the four scenarios are an eight percent earnings rate, three percent inflation rate, and a wage replacement ratio between 90 percent and 100 percent of pre-retirement income.

Exhibit 3.17 | Savings Rate Necessary for Various Clients / Scenarios

	Client A Single Age 25 (0 children)	Client B Married Age 35 (2 children)	Client C Married Age 40 (2 children)	Client D Married Age 40 (2 children)
Income	$100,000	$100,000	$150,000	$200,000
Retirement Goal Savings Rate (as a % of gross pay)	10 - 13%	10 - 13%	10 - 13%	10 - 13%
Investment Assets	$2,000	$150,000	$365,000	$500,000
Education Goal	0	3%	5%	7%
Lump-Sum Goal	0	0	3%	3.3%
Legacy Goal	0	0	0	6.30%
Overall Savings Rate Needed (as a % of gross pay)	10 - 13%	13 - 16%	18 - 21%	26.6 - 29.6%

The point is not necessarily how much a person needs, but rather whether the retirement goal is being met by: (1) a savings rate of 10 to 13 percent and (2) investment assets of a certain amount that are an appropriate percentage of gross pay depending on the age of the client. If the client has goals other than retirement (education, lump sum, and/or legacy) the overall savings rate will have to be increased to meet those additional goals.

The three-panel approach is comparable to a recipe or a checklist. An advantage of this approach is that it is easy to follow by both the planner and the client. Keep in mind that this methodology does not answer every question in financial planning, nor does it require the analysis of rates of return on investments or evaluate investment risk.

Once the three-panel approach is understood, the financial planner can overlay it with quantitative and qualitative metrics that provide benchmarks to compare to the client's actual financial situation. The result of this analysis will determine deficiencies in the client's risk management portfolio, short-term savings and investing (plus debt management), and long-term savings and investing (to determine if adequate progress is being made towards long-term goals).

Metrics Approach

The metrics approach provides quantitative example benchmarks for the financial planner and client to use as guidance for necessary comprehensive financial goals and objectives. Once the practitioner has analyzed and evaluated the client's actual financial situation, the metrics can be applied to establish financial planning recommendations.

Quick Quiz 3.3

1. The two-step approach considers savings and investments as part of the financial plan leading to financial security (and independence).
   a. True
   b. False

2. The three-panel approach provides a plan for risk management of personal, property, and liability risks, along with both short-term and long-term savings.
   a. True
   b. False

3. The metrics approach provides finite benchmarks for the financial planner to use as a comparison of client actual to client goal.
   a. True
   b. False

True, True, False.

Exhibit 3.18 | Example Benchmarks (Metrics)

Risk Management Data		
	Metric	**Comment / Recommendation**
Life Insurance	12 - 16 times gross pay, if needed.	The amount depends on the needs of surviving dependents.
Health Insurance	Unlimited lifetime benefit.**	Should be guaranteed renewable with reasonable out-of-pocket limits.
Disability Insurance	60 - 70% of gross pay and at least guaranteed renewable.	Covering both sickness and accident and a hybrid or own occupation definition and appropriate elimination period.
Long-Term Care Insurance	If needed, daily or monthly benefits $\geq$ average for appropriate facility.	Benefits inflation adjusted and a benefit period $\geq$ 36 - 60 months.
Homeowners Insurance	$\leq$ full replacement value on both dwelling and contents and coverage for open perils.	
Automobile Insurance	$\leq$ full fair market value for comprehensive and collision.	
Liability Insurance	At least a $1,000,000 personal liability umbrella policy.	Need sufficient underlying homeowners and auto liability to satisfy PLUP issuer.
Short-Term Savings and Investing Goals		
Emergency Fund	Equal to 3 - 6 times the monthly non-discretionary cash outflows.	Should be coordinated with long-term disability insurance elimination period.
Housing	Housing ratio1 should be $\leq$ 28% of gross pay.	Housing ratio 1 should decline to $\leq$ 5% of gross pay at retirement.
Housing and Debt	The total paid for housing costs and other debt payments $\leq$ 36% of gross pay.	Other debt payments include, but are not limited to, credit cards, auto loans, and student loans.
Long-Term Savings and Investment Goals		
Financial Security (Retirement)	Save 10 - 13% of gross pay (include employer match).	Have an appropriate amount of investment assets relative to gross pay for the client's age.
College Education Funding	Save $3,000/$6,000/or $9,000 per child per year for 18 years in a balanced portfolio (60% stocks/40% fixed income).	Savings is dependent on where the child is expected to attend college (in state/mid-private/elite-private).
Lump-Sum Goals	Goals like 2nd home, airplane, or boat require savings of at least 20% of the total price as a down payment.	This additional goal will increase the overall savings rate required to achieve all the goals.
Legacy Goals	Every client under age 50 needs basic documents. Those 50 and over may also need trusts and estate planning.	Basic documents include a will, durable power of attorney for healthcare, advance medical directive (living will), and durable power of attorney for financial matters.

** Historically it was important to make sure that a health care policy has a lifetime limit of at least $1 million. However, under Section 2711 of the Patient Protection and Affordable Care Act, lifetime limits are eliminated and no longer a concern. The financial planning concern was that a patient would have a catastrophic illness that could result in medical bills that totaled $1 million or more.

Risk Tolerance and Asset Allocation

The three-panel approach and the metrics approach are very helpful in providing a framework and benchmarks for the client and planner. However, clients and planners need tools to develop an investment plan. A proper investment plan is a critical element in the pursuit of most financial planning goals, including retirement and education. The investment plan is a bit like the engine in a car – without it, you cannot reach the destination.

In financial planning, calculating savings for retirement or education is sometimes performed without a significant amount of thought and consideration given to a proper expected investment rate of return. However, this "variable" or "input" is an extremely important factor in determining the periodic amount that needs to be saved.

Investing is a challenging component of financial planning as certainty resides only in past and not in future investment performance. However, it is generally accepted that asset allocation is the largest contributor to investment performance over time and the two key components in determining a proper asset allocation are risk tolerance and time horizon.

As part of the investment planning process, the financial planner evaluates the client's goals in terms of both dollar value and time. The client's goals are assessed together with risk tolerance in designing the appropriate investment strategy. The client's risk tolerance is a combination of both the ability and the willingness to accept investment risk. The planner will develop an investment plan considering the client's investment ability (an objective state of being, based on the client's financial profile) and the client's willingness (a subjective state of being) to take on investment risk and to commit dollars over time to reach the investment goals. The ability and willingness of the client to accept risk can be gauged by various factors. For example, the longer the time horizon of a client, the more risk that the client is able to accept in the investment portfolio. The client's ability to accept risk is associated with time horizon, liquidity needs, tax conditions, and unique financial and personal circumstances. The client's willingness to accept risk is associated with the psychological condition of risk tolerance. The risk tolerance questionnaire provides both the planner and the client with a basic understanding of the client's psychological tolerance (willingness) for taking risk.

Financial planners employ tools to assess the client's willingness to accept investment risk, thus helping to determine the client's risk tolerance as part of the investment planning process. The Global Portfolio Allocation Scoring System (PASS) is such a tool.[6] PASS considers both time horizon and risk tolerance in determining an appropriate asset allocation. Step one is to have the client answer the following questions, which have scores ranging from 5 to 1. Once the questions are answered, each of the point values is summed and is used as part of determining the asset allocation.

---

6. Dr. William Droms, CFA, the Powers Professor of Finance in the McDonough School of Business at Georgetown University and a principal with Droms Strauss Advisors, Inc. has granted Money Education permission to use his Global Portfolio Allocation Scoring System (PASS) in this text. More information can be found on Dr. Droms at http://www.droms-strauss.com, as well as the complete article from the Journal of Financial Planning.

Global Portfolio Allocation Scoring System (PASS) for Individual Investors[1]					
	Questions	Strongly Agree	Agree	Neutral	Disagree	Strongly Disagree
1	Earning a high long-term total return that will allow my capital to grow faster than the inflation rate is one of my most important investment objectives.	5	4	3	2	1
2	I would like an investment that provides me with an opportunity to defer taxation of capital gains to future years.	5	4	3	2	1
3	I do not require a high level of current income from my investments.	5	4	3	2	1
4	I am willing to tolerate some sharp down swings in the return on my investments in order to seek a potentially higher return than would normally be expected from more stable investments.	5	4	3	2	1
5	I am willing to risk a short-term loss in return for a potentially higher long-run rate of return.	5	4	3	2	1
6	I am financially able to accept a low level of liquidity in my investment portfolio.	5	4	3	2	1

1. More information can be found on Dr. Droms at http://www.droms-strauss.com, as well as the complete article from the Journal of Financial Planning.

The next step is to determine the time horizon of the investment goal and then to use the PASS score to determine the appropriate asset allocation. The higher the score, the more tolerance for risk the client has shown and the more the portfolio can be aggressively allocated.

	Short-Term Horizon				Intermediate-Term Horizon				Long-Term Horizon			
	RT1	RT2	RT3	RT4	RT1	RT2	RT3	RT4	RT1	RT2	RT3	RT4
	Target	Target	Target	Target	Target	Target	Target	Target	Target	Target	Target	Target
PASS Score	6 - 12	13 - 18	19 - 24	25 - 30	6 - 12	13 - 18	19 - 24	25 - 30	6 - 12	13 - 18	19 - 24	25 - 30
Cash and Money Market Fund	40%	30%	20%	10%	5%	5%	5%	5%	5%	5%	3%	2%
Treasury Bonds/ Bond Funds	40%	30%	30%	20%	60%	35%	20%	10%	30%	20%	12%	0%
Corporate Bonds/ Bond Funds	20%	30%	30%	40%	15%	15%	15%	10%	15%	10%	10%	4%
Subtotal	100%	90%	80%	70%	80%	55%	40%	25%	50%	35%	25%	6%
International Bond Funds	0%	0%	0%	0%	0%	5%	5%	5%	0%	5%	5%	4%
Subtotal	0%	0%	0%	0%	0%	5%	5%	5%	0%	5%	5%	4%
Index Fund	0%	10%	10%	10%	10%	15%	20%	20%	20%	20%	20%	25%
Large Cap Value Funds/Stocks	0%	0%	5%	5%	5%	5%	10%	10%	10%	10%	5%	5%
Large Cap Growth Funds/Stocks	0%	0%	0%	0%	5%	5%	5%	10%	15%	10%	10%	5%
Mid/Small Growth Funds/Stocks	0%	0%	0%	0%	0%	0%	5%	5%	0%	0%	5%	10%
Mid/Small Value Funds/Stocks	0%	0%	0%	5%	0%	5%	5%	5%	0%	5%	5%	10%
Subtotal	0%	10%	15%	20%	20%	30%	45%	50%	45%	45%	45%	55%
International Stock Funds	0%	0%	0%	5%	0%	5%	5%	10%	0%	5%	10%	15%
Subtotal	0%	0%	0%	5%	0%	5%	5%	10%	0%	5%	10%	15%
Real Estate Funds	0%	0%	5%	5%	0%	5%	5%	10%	5%	10%	15%	20%
Subtotal	0%	0%	5%	5%	0%	5%	5%	10%	5%	10%	15%	20%
Total	100%	100%	100%	100%	100%	100%	100%	100%	100%	100%	100%	100%

PASS defines short-term as three years or less, intermediate-term as three to seven years and long-term as more than seven years. With the PASS score and the time horizon, the asset allocation can be determined. There are other models that can be used to assess risk tolerance and determine an appropriate asset allocation. However, Dr. Drom's PASS is a valid model and his article in the Journal of Financial Planning can be used as an additional reference on the subject.

To simplify and to help determine expected return and to consider risk of asset classes, the asset classes above have been condensed into the following asset classes with corresponding expected returns and expected standard deviations:

	Expected Rates of Return	Standard Deviation of Returns
Cash and Money Market Fund	2.5%	2.0%
Treasury Bonds / Bond Fund	4.0%	4.0%
Corporate Bonds / Bond Fund	6.0%	5.0%
International Bond Funds	7.0%	6.0%
Index Funds	9.0%	14.0%
Large Cap Funds / Stocks	10.0%	16.0%
Mid / Small Funds / Stocks	12.0%	18.0%
International Stock Funds	13.0%	22.0%
Real Estate Funds	8.0%	12.0%

These asset classes are used in Money Education's *Cases in Financial Planning: Analysis and Presentation* textbook. In practice, some of these asset classes might be excluded while other asset classes might be included. In addition, expected returns and variability will change over time.

The following chart reflects the condensed asset classes and weightings with the corresponding expected return and estimated standard deviation for each portfolio.[7]

	Short-Term Horizon				Intermediate-Term Horizon				Long-Term Horizon			
	RT1 Target	RT2 Target	RT3 Target	RT4 Target	RT1 Target	RT2 Target	RT3 Target	RT4 Target	RT1 Target	RT2 Target	RT3 Target	RT4 Target
PASS Score	6 - 12	13 - 18	19 - 24	25 - 30	6 - 12	13 - 18	19 - 24	25 - 30	6 - 12	13 - 18	19 - 24	25 - 30
Cash and Money Market Fund	40%	30%	20%	10%	5%	5%	5%	5%	5%	5%	3%	2%
Treasury Bonds/ Bond Funds	40%	30%	30%	20%	60%	35%	20%	10%	30%	20%	12%	0%
Corporate Bonds/ Bond Funds	20%	30%	30%	40%	15%	15%	15%	10%	15%	10%	10%	4%
International Bond Funds	0%	0%	0%	0%	0%	5%	5%	5%	0%	5%	5%	4%
Index Fund	0%	10%	10%	10%	10%	15%	20%	20%	20%	20%	20%	25%
Large Cap Funds/Stocks	0%	0%	5%	5%	10%	10%	15%	20%	25%	20%	15%	10%
Mid/Small Funds/Stocks	0%	0%	0%	5%	0%	5%	10%	10%	0%	5%	10%	20%
International Stock Funds	0%	0%	0%	5%	0%	5%	5%	10%	0%	5%	10%	15%
Real Estate Funds	0%	0%	5%	5%	0%	5%	5%	10%	5%	10%	15%	20%
Total	100%	100%	100%	100%	100%	100%	100%	100%	100%	100%	100%	100%
Expected Return	3.80%	4.65%	5.30%	6.50%	5.33%	6.78%	7.73%	8.58%	6.93%	7.73%	8.51%	9.77%
Expected Standard Deviation (est)	2.79%	3.85%	4.84%	6.40%	5.13%	7.26%	8.73%	10.25%	7.75%	8.94%	10.12%	12.20%

The information in the chart above can be used to support the required returns in a comprehensive case. In practice, this analysis will often be conducted using a software package that incorporates mean variance optimization. However, the above approach is effective for comprehensive cases.

Example 3.3

Misty answers the PASS with the following answers for each of the six questions: strongly agree, agree, agree, neutral, agree, strongly agree. Based on the scoring for each answer, her total score is 25 (5 + 4 + 4 + 3 + 4 + 5). Assuming that she is positioning her portfolio for retirement, a long term goal, then she would be considering the long-term portfolio RT4, with an expected return of approximately 9.77%. She would allocate her portfolio as indicated in the above chart based on the right most column.

THE PRESENT VALUE OF ALL GOALS APPROACH

The present value of all goals approach considers each short, intermediate, and long-term goal. The first step for this approach is to determine the present value of each goal. The next step is to sum these present values together and reduce them by the currently available resources (investment assets and cash and cash equivalents). Finally, the net present value is treated as an obligation to be retired over the remaining work life expectancy at a discount rate equal to the expected portfolio rate of return.

Refer back to Hess Goal (slightly modified for our purposes here). **Note:** New details have been added for example purposes. They now have three goals.

Goal 1: Retire

Assume they want to both retire at Jack's age 65 with an 80 percent wage replacement ratio. Inflation is projected to be three percent, an earnings rate to and through retirement is expected to be 8.0 percent and life expectancy is expected to be 25 years for both spouses (i.e., to 90 and 88 respectively). Assume Social Security will pay $25,000 in today's dollars at age 67 for Jack and $20,000 for Marilyn.

---

7. The standard deviation for each portfolio has been estimated. To calculate it as accurately as possible, a correlation matrix would be required.

Wage Replacement Calculation

Income	$109,000	
WRR%	x 0.80	
Total Needs in Today's Dollars	$87,200	
Jack's Social Security (at age 65)	($21,667)	$25,000 (0.8666)
Marilyn's Social Security	($15,000)	$20,000 (0.75)
Annual Needs in Today's Dollars	$50,533	

Note – Social Security benefits are reduced when payments begin prior to full retirement age. In this case, their full retirement age is age 67 and he is beginning his benefits at age 65, while she is beginning her benefits at age 63. The reduction in benefits is equal to 5/9ths of one percent for each of the first 36 months and 5/12ths of one percent for months beyond the first 36 months.

Retirement Calculation

Step 1		Step 2		Step 3	
N	= 20 (45-65)	PMT_{AD}	= $91,268.21902	$FV_{@65}$	= $1,368,681.23
i	= 3	N	= 25	N	= 20
PV	= $50,533	i	= $((1.08 \div 1.03) - 1) \times 100$	i	= 8
PMT	= 0	FV	= 0	$PV_{@45}$	= $293,648.10
FV	= $91,268.21902	$PV_{@65}$	= $1,368,681.23		

Goal 2: Education for Melba, age 13

Assumptions: Education costs in today's dollars are $21,000 per year for 5 years (added), education inflation is assumed to be 6% per year.

Step 1		Step 2	
N	= 5 years in college	$FV_{@18}$	= $101,182.46
PMT_{AD}	= $21,000 per year	N	= 5 (18 - 13) years to college
i	= $((1.08 \div 1.06) - 1) \times 100$	i	= $((1.08 \div 1.06) - 1) \times 100$
$PV_{@18}$	= $101,182.46	PMT	= 0
FV	= 0	$PV_{@13}$	= $92,154.34

Goal 3: Created for this example.

Assume that the Hess's want to buy a second home for $300,000 in today's dollars 11 years from now and that the price of the home will increase at the inflation rate of 3%.

Step 1		Step 2	
N	= 11 years to goal	FV	= $415,270.16
i	= 3	N	= 11
PV	= $300,000	i	= 8
PMT	= 0	PMT	= 0
FV	= $415,270.16	PV	= $178,102.25

Note: This calculation can also be done in one step using an inflation adjusted discount rate.

The summation of the three goals in present value terms is as follows:

Retirement	$293,648.10
Education	$92,154.34
Second Home	$178,102.25
Total PV of all Goals	$563,904.69

The PV of all goals is reduced by current resources available:

PV of All Goals	$563,904.69	
Current Resources	$207,000.00	(Investment assets and cash at 12/31/20X1)
Short Fall / PV	$356,904.69	
i	8%	(the earnings rate)
N	20	(years to retirement)
FV	0	
PMT_{OA}	$36,351.53	(annual saving needed to fund all goals)

Once the present value of the goals are summed and then reduced by current resources, the remaining present value of goals can be determined and treated hypothetically as a mortgage to be retired at the expected earnings rate. The PV of all goals is determined by discounting the future cash flows at an expected earnings rate. The same earnings rate needs to be used to determine the annual savings requirement. If a different rate is used for determining the annual savings amount compared to the rate used to discount the future expected cash flows, then the calculations are being convoluted and the result is flawed.

This calculation determines how much they need to be saving annually, at year end, to achieve all their goals. That resultant ($36,351.53) can then be compared to their current savings amount to determine its adequacy.

Current Savings Amount	$14,600	Required Annual Savings	$36,351.53
Plus the Employer Match	$2,190	Less Current Savings	$16,790.00
Total Current Savings	$16,790	Necessary Savings Deficit	$19,561.53

They have $19,561.53 deficiency in annual savings in terms of meeting all of their goals ($36,351.53 - $16,790). They should consider some alternatives:
1. Do they have additional discretionary cash flow that they can save? No!
2. Are they over withheld on taxes? The answer to this requires a tax analysis (see below).

Tax Analysis (20X1)

Itemized Deductions[1]		Tax Calculation:		
Mortgage Interest	$11,556	Income	$109,000	
Charitable Contribution	$935	401(k) Deferral	($14,600)	
State Income Tax	$2,869	AGI[2]	$94,400	
Property Tax	$2,895	Standard Deduction[3]	($25,100)	
Total Itemized Deductions	**$18,255**	Taxable Income	$69,300	
		Tax from Schedule	$7,918	2021 Tax Rates
		Child Tax Credit[4]	($2,000)	Melba (13 yr old)
		Tax Liability	$5,918	
		Tax Withheld	($16,220)	
		Over Withheld	**$10,302**	**Refund Due**

1. The mortgage interest is calculated based on 12 months of interest for a 30-year loan of $145,000 at 8%. The other itemized deductions come from the statement of income and expenses.
2. The Taxpayer Certainty and Disaster Tax Relief Act of 2020 allows a temporary above-the-line deduction for up to $600 of charitable contributions by a married couple in 2021; however, for simplicity, we have excluded that deduction in this analysis.
3. MFJ standard deduction is higher than their itemized deductions.
4. For the 2021 tax year only, the American Rescue Plan Act (ARPA) of 2021 increased the child tax credit to $3,000 (for a child over age 5 and under age 18) for married taxpayers filing jointly with adjusted gross income below $150,000. The increase was not included in this analysis due to its limited time of applicability.

It is not uncommon that clients are over-withheld. The problem for many people who are over withheld is that they spend rather than save the refund check. They can increase their 401(k) plan contribution or other savings during the year by changing the withholdings form (W-4).[8]

Below is the revised savings amount based on saving an additional $10,305 (rounded from $10,302), split between their 401(k) plan and a traditional IRA (this amount is calculated without grossing up the over withholding).

Current 401(k) Deferral	$14,600	
Employer Match	$2,190	(3% of $73,000)
Additional 401(k) Deferral	$4,900	(to get to $19,500 maximum employee contribution in 2021)
Traditional IRA Contribution(s)	$5,405	
New Total Annual Savings	$27,095	

While this savings amount is still below the $36,351.53 needed, the wage replacement ratio can also be adjusted to reflect the new savings amount. The wage replacement ratio was originally 80 percent or $87,200 in today's dollars but with the above additional savings, they are currently living on the following:

---

8. If they are over withheld by $10,302, then they can actually save over $12,000 if they defer the savings in a 401(k) plan since the deferral avoids current federal (and possibly state) income tax. This calculation, which is referred to as "grossing up," assumes a 15% combined rate: $10,302 / 0.85 = $12,120.

Gross pay	$109,000	
Less savings	$24,905	($27,095 less employer match of $2,190)
Less Social Security taxes (FICA)	$8,339	
Net	$75,756	(which is a WRR of 70%, not 80%)

While they initially wanted and thought they needed an 80 percent wage replacement ratio, they can actually maintain their lifestyle with a WRR of approximately 70 percent. It is fairly common that a client may have initial desires that exceed what is absolutely necessary to insuring their current standard of living. Through discussions with them, they will likely understand that point.

Consider the following adjustments and alternatives:
1. Delay retirement to normal age retirement of age 67 (2 more years) and reduce the wage replacement ratio from 80% to 72%, which is slightly higher and slightly more conservative than the 70% that was calculated above.
2. Leave all other goals the same as they were.

Impact on calculations:

	$109,000.00	Income
	72%	WRR (assumed)
	$78,480.00	Needs in today's dollars
Social Security Retirement Benefits (Jack)	($25,000.00)	normal age retirement
Social Security Retirement Benefits (Marilyn)	($17,333.33)	2 years early, not 4 (13.33% reduction)
Needs	$36,146.67	Retirement needs in today's dollars

Step 1	Step 2	Step 3
N = 22 years to retirement	PMT_{AD} = $69,260.76	FV = $993,168.10
i = 3 inflation	i = $((1.08 \div 1.03) - 1) \times 100$	i = 8
PV = $36,146.67	N = 23	N = 22
FV = $69,260.76	$PV_{@67}$ = $993,168.10	PV = $182,683.84

The new calculation of the present value of all goals is as follows along with the change in the necessary savings amount required to achieve all goals.

PV of retirement	$182,683.84	
PV of education	$92,154.34	
PV of second house	$178,102.25	
PV	$452,940.43	
Less resources:	$207,000.00	(12/31/20X1)
Short fall PV	$245,940.43	
N	22	(note 2 more years of working)
i	8%	
FV_0	0	
PMT_{OA}	$24,110.05	(new savings amount calculations)

It is clear from the revised calculation of the savings and wage replacement ratio that they can meet all their financial goals simply by delaying retirement by two years and revising their wage replacement needs from 80 percent down to 72 percent. The amount needed to be saved is $24,110.05 and they are currently saving $27,095 (assuming the changes to Form W-4 and the savings to the 401(k) plan and IRA). But what if they do not like this idea? The client can then consider other choices in various combinations.

1. Only pay for four years of college education
2. Reduce the price of the second home to $200,000 from $300,000 or do not buy a second home
3. Use a 72% or 70% wage replacement ratio
4. Delay retirement one year instead of two
5. Perhaps refinance their home
6. Save more and spend less

PRESENTATION OF THE PRESENT VALUE OF ALL GOALS APPROACH

When presenting the present value of all goals approach, it is useful to present values at various times and both the overall savings requirements and specific goal savings requirements. For the discussion of presenting the present value of all goals approach, consider the case of Mr. and Mrs. Brown. The calculations for the Browns are presented below and based on the following assumptions:

- Current age is 42
- Retirement age is 65
- Income of $170,000
- Earnings rate of 8%
- Assume current resources of $200,000
- Inflation rate of 3%
- Education tuition inflation rate of 5%
- The present value of retirement needs is $300,000 (today's dollars)
- The present value of education needs is $195,000 (today's dollars)

They want to pay for education for their three children, whose ages are 2, 4, and 6. They also want to purchase a second home when they retire, which will cost $300,000 in today's dollars.

Exhibit 3.19 | Table 1

Goal	Present Value	Annual Savings Required[1]	Annual Savings Required[2]
# 1 - Retirement	$300,000.00	$28,926.65	$28,926.65
# 2 - Education	$195,000.00	$18,802.32	$23,652.89[3]
# 3 - Second Home	$100,840.00	$9,723.21	$9,723.21
Total	$595,840.00	$57,452.18	N/A
Current Resources[4]	($200,000.00)	($19,284.43)	N/A
Net Needs	$395,840.00	$38,167.75	N/A

1. Savings on an annual ordinary annuity basis over the remaining work life expectancy (23 years)
2. Savings required to the beginning of the draw down.
3. Assume the money is needed in 14 years.
4. Current resources include investment assets and cash and cash equivalents. The annual savings amount is calculated based on the $200,000, 23 years, and an 8% interest rate.

The house is $300,000 in today's dollars. However, when inflated for 23 years at three percent and then discounted over the same period at the earnings rate of eight percent, the present value in terms of required funding is $100,840 in today's dollars.

By presenting the present value in current real dollar terms, the net needs can be hypothetically treated as an obligation (mortgage) to be repaid at the expected rate of return (in this case, 8%) over the work life expectancy (in this case, 23 years). The annual required savings amount of $38,167.75 (22.45%) can then be compared to the current annual actual savings amount to determine whether current savings are adequate to pay for all goals. Presuming annual savings are not adequate, it is relatively easy to see the cost of each goal in terms of annual required savings and consider priorities. For example, in this case, the client might decide the second home is not important or a less expensive one could suffice. The client could decide that one or two more years of working would be preferable to changing other goals. Keep in mind that an additional year of working:
1. increases Social Security benefits up to age 70,
2. increases savings years by one,
3. increases compounding years by one, and
4. decreases consumption by one year. One to two years of delayed retirement can be very significant.

In addition to the Table 1 presentation, it may also be useful to present the values in nominal dollars for each goal at the start of the draw down as in the following table.

Exhibit 3.20 | Table 2

Goal	Present Values	Future Values[1]	Notes
# 1 - Retirement	$300,000.00	$1,761,439.09	Value at the beginning of retirement
# 2 - Education	$195,000.00	$572,752.76	Value at the start of education[2]
# 3 - Second Home	$100,840.00	$592,078.39	Value in 23 years
Income[3]	$170,000.00	$335,509.71	Value in 23 years

1. Assume the value increases at the investment rate of return of 8%.
2. Assume in 14 years.
3. Assume raises are at 3%.

Table 2 data provides a perspective of both the present and future (nominal) dollars required to achieve the financial goals. The current and projected income also provides a relative perspective as between today and the future costs of goals.

In Table 1, it is notable that education (which is sometimes the most important goal) could be fully funded by utilizing all of the current resources. If the goal of the second home were abandoned the required savings rate would decline from 22.45 to 17.01 percent. Table 3 depicts various changes and the impact of each change on the required savings rate.

Exhibit 3.21 | Table 3

Alternatives	Current Savings Rate Required	New Savings Rate Required
# 1 - Abandon 2nd home, fully fund education now with current resources ($200,000), and retire at age 65.	22.45%	17.01%
# 2 - Abandon 2nd home, fully fund education now with current resources ($200,000), and delay retirement 2 years to age 67.*	22.45%	14.38%
# 3 - Fully fund education now with current resources ($200,000), and delay retirement 2 years.**	22.45%	19.43%

* Assumptions for recalculating retirement savings: WRR = 64.421%; life expectancy of age 90, Social Security payments of $50,000 in today's dollars (for simplicity, Social Security payments were not increased as retirement age was extended by 2 years). The required savings amount for retirement is reduced from $28,926.65 to $24,442.47.

**In addition to the assumptions made for recalculating retirement needs, the annual savings requirement for the home must be changed to delay the goal by 2 years. This change causes the present value to be reduced from $100,840 to $91,718.72, resulting in an annual savings amount of $8,592.60.

Ultimately, the questions are "What are the priorities of the client" and "How much (savings percentage or dollars) are they willing to sacrifice to achieve the goals and over what time frame?"

The present value approach assists the planner in understanding the requirements of the goals that the client has specified in present and future dollar terms as well as the corresponding savings required to achieve those goals.

THE CASH FLOW APPROACH

The cash flow approach takes the annual current income statement and adjusts the cash flows by forecasting what they would be after implementing all of the planning recommendations. This approach begins with the discretionary cash flows at the bottom of the income statement and accounts for each of the recommendations in the order of priority. The annual cost of each recommendation is charged against the discretionary cash flows regardless of any negative cash flow impact. This approach separates the recommendations into four impact categories:

1. No cash flow impact.
2. Annual recurring positive (very few) or negative cash flow impact.
3. One-time non-recurring positive (sale of an asset) or negative (pay off debt) cash flow impact.
4. Impact that affects the client in a positive or negative way, but does not affect his cash flow on the income statement (an increase in the employer match in the 401(k) plan as a result of increased employee deferrals or the employer no longer matches thus causing a decrease).

> **:= Key Concepts**
>
> 1. Explain the usefulness of the cash flow approach.
>
> 2. Identify the three focus areas being managed under the cash flow approach.
>
> 3. Define the strategic approach to financial planning.
>
> 4. Understand basic financing for home purchases.

Risk Management

The immediate **risk management recommendations** are usually related to insurance portfolio changes because perils (the cause of a loss) are event driven (e.g., untimely death) and can occur at any time. It takes a long time for an implemented financial plan to provide financial security for a client, with both savings and investing potentially taking 25 to 40 years to be successful. However, a catastrophic loss caused by a peril associated with personal risks (life, health, disability, or long-term care), property loss, or liability can occur suddenly and completely destroy an otherwise well thought out financial plan. As a result, implementing the insurance portfolio recommendations is the first priority. Insurance recommendations may have annual recurring positive, negative, or no cash flow impact. Insurance recommendations involve adding, deleting, changing, or replacing some aspect of the insurance portfolio so as to improve the overall catastrophic protection for the client and maximize premium efficiency. The following provides examples of insurance recommendations impact (or lack of) on cash flows.

Exhibit 3.22 | Insurance Recommendations and Their Impact on Cash Flows

	No Cash Flow Impact
1	• Change name of beneficiary • Assign ownership of policy to another person • Stop driving uninsured vehicle • Clarify the lifetime benefits of an employer-provided health plan
	Positive Annual Cash Flow Impact
2A	• Raise deductibles (e.g., auto, home) • Eliminate duplicate coverage (e.g., disability) • Reduce coverage (e.g., home value declined) • Replace one policy for another (e.g., term life)
	Negative Annual Cash Flow Impact
2B	• Purchase life, health, disability, long-term care, property, or liability insurance • Increasing the amount of current coverage • Lowering deductibles

Insurance recommendations follow the three-panel and metrics approach when a detailed analysis of the insurance portfolio needed for a particular client is conducted. The estimated cash flow impact resulting from changes described in cash flow categories 2A and 2B above can be determined by contacting an insurance agent who sells the product type that is being changed, added, deleted, or replaced (and may also be estimated by a thorough internet search).

For purposes of this chapter and the textbook, assume that the planner has previously investigated the costs and/or savings from changing, adding, deleting, or replacing an insurance policy. Therefore, when the planner implements these recommendations into the cash flow statement, it is an accurate estimate of the cost (e.g., the annual per $1,000 cost of term life insurance for a male age 30 is about 70 cents for a 30-year term policy).

Exhibit 3.23 provides an illustration of risk management recommendations for a client along with the cash flow impact and implementation responsibility.

Exhibit 3.23 | Examples of Risk Management Recommendations

	Recommendation	Annual Recurring Cost <Negative> + Positive*	Non-Recurring Cost	Other	To Be Implemented by Client or Planner
1	Change the beneficiary on life insurance Policy A to wife	None			Client
2	Purchase a $500k 30-year term life insurance policy on husband	<$350.00>			Client
3	Purchase disability insurance for wife 60% of pay, benefits to 65, guaranteed renewable	<$360.00>			Client
4	Change homeowners policy to reflect a decline in value and raise the homeowner's deductible	+$250.00			Client

For the purpose of this textbook, cash flow impacts are estimated.

Debt Management

The next area of recommendations will either involve **debt management** or savings and investing depending on the client's priorities. Since debt management has an impact on savings and investments, debt management will be covered first.

Frequently, people have too much debt, have debt with high interest rates, and/or have debt that is not well managed. The analysis of debt includes calculating housing ratios 1 and 2 and comparing those to the well established benchmarks (metrics) of 28% / 36%. In addition, the financial planner should evaluate the quality and the cost of each client's individual debt. Debt is often categorized as either good, bad, or reasonable.

Good debt tends to have two components: (1) the interest rate is relatively low in comparison to expected inflation and expected investment returns, and (2) the expected debt repayment period is substantially less than the expected economic life of the asset. An example of good debt is a fixed 15-year mortgage on a home with an economic life of the home in excess of 40 years, a house payment that fits within the housing ratios, and an interest rate of five percent (and the lowest rate available) when the client's raise rate is expected to be four percent, inflation is expected to be three percent, and the client's expected investment return is 8.5 percent. Another example of good debt is a student loan used to provide education tied to a profession (e.g., medicine, law, financial planning, accounting, or engineering) for a person with a reasonable work life expectancy. This type of education is essentially an investment that can provide returns well in excess of the capital cost and over a period much longer than the debt repayment period. It remains important that debt is incurred at a reasonable interest rate.

In addition to good debt, there is also **reasonable debt** where the debt repayment period is longer or the returns on the debt are positive, but less certain than for good debt. Examples of reasonable debt include 30-year home mortgages at conforming interest rates and student loans that are for general education.

Bad debt is associated with: (1) high interest rates, or (2) when the economic life of the purchase is exceeded by the associated debt repayment period. An example of bad debt is an automobile loan with a small down payment and a 72-month term where the economic life of the automobile is three to five years. Another example of bad debt involves debt with high interest rates, (which includes most credit cards). Consider the following credit card debt and associated pay off schedule ramifications:

Alternative	Balance	Minimum Payment Due	Term to Pay-Off Balance	Implied Interest Rate	Total Estimated Payments
A	$1,912.78	$39.13	16 years	24%	$7,512.79
B	$1,912.78	$75.04	3 years	24%	$2,701.58
C	$1,912.78	$106.26	1.5 years	0%*	$1,912.78

* The rate is 0% interest because it is a promotional program with 18-months free interest but only if the account is completely paid off by the promotional code expiration date.

Note in the above example that if the client only pays the minimum monthly payment (Alternative A), it will take 16 years and cost $7,512.79 to pay for $1,912.78 of debt.

For Alternative C, note that retailers using promotional rates of zero percent, also use low minimum payments that creates a balloon payment at the end of the promotional term. Retailers expect that most consumers will violate the agreement resulting in them having to pay all of the interest from the original date of purchase.

Exhibit 3.24 | Characteristics of Various Types of Debt

Classification of Debt	Interest Rates	Nature of and Economic Life of Asset Purchased	Repayment Period	Examples
Good Debt	Relatively Low	Typically Long Lived	Substantially less than economic life of asset	• Home purchase with 15-year mortgage • Student loan with vocation • Car loan with repayment period of 3 years or less
Reasonable Debt	Competitive	Typically Long Lived	Less than the economic life of asset	• Home purchase with 30-year mortgage • Student loan for general higher education • Car loan with repayment period of 4-5 years
Bad Debt	High	Short or Long Lived or Consumed Expenditure	Longer than economic life of purchase	• Minimum payments on credit card debt • Car loan with repayment period longer than economic life of car

The following table outlines example debt management recommendations for a client, including the cash flow impact and implementation responsibilities.

Exhibit 3.25 | Debt Management Recommendations

	Recommendations	Annual Recurring Cost <Negative> + Positive	Non-Recurring Cost (Savings)	Other	To Be Implemented by Client or Planner
A	Refinance a home for 15 years at 5% (current loan at 7.5% on $300,000). 3% closing included in mortgage	+ $4,049.73			Client
B	Pay off balance of credit cards (also eliminates recurring payment)	+ $2,150.00	<$9,000> to pay off		Client
C	Pay off furniture loan	+ $1,802.00	<$3,115> to pay off		Client

Home Purchase Financing

Home purchases are generally considered good debt and are generally paid for through a combination of a cash down payment and a mortgage. **Mortgages** are a form of long-term debt, secured by a lien on real estate, such as a home. The purchaser of a home is the mortgagor and typically borrows most of the purchase price from the mortgagee (i.e., the lender, such as a bank). The borrower provides security for the loan by giving a lien or mortgage on the home to the mortgagee. In case of default, the mortgagee is allowed to foreclose on the collateral and sell the home to recover the loan. The cost of a mortgage loan includes the interest rate, loan origination fees, appraisal fees, credit investigation charges, title search costs, and "points," which are simply up-front, lump-sum interest charges.

The planner and client will work together to decide how best to finance the purchase of a home, including the amount of the down payment, the source for closing costs (from other funds or financed into the mortgage), the type of mortgage (fixed or adjustable), and whether points should be paid to reduce the interest rate. Each of these choices will be discussed briefly in this chapter.[9]

Before the client even begins looking at homes to purchase, it is wise to establish the amount of mortgage debt that will fit into the client's budget, also factoring in the added cost of insurance, property taxes, home maintenance, and potentially higher utility bills versus renting. When the client seeks information from a lender regarding the amount of mortgage for which he or she may qualify, the lender will typically use ratios, such as HR1 and HR2 discussed earlier in this chapter as well as in Chapter 4. Nevertheless, just because the client qualifies for a mortgage of a particular amount, does not mean that it fits into his or her budget. Another general rule is that the loan should be no more than 2 times annual gross income, and the purchase price no more than 2½ times gross annual income. These rules of thumb are a helpful starting point, but not a substitute for determining the *actual* amount the client can comfortably afford to borrow.

---

9. More detailed information on housing decisions and mortgage financing can be found at money-education.com.

The Impact of the Down Payment Amount on the Cost of the Loan

One of the decisions required early in the process of buying a home is the amount of down payment the buyer will make. Mortgage loans may be available that allow the client to borrow up to 95 percent of the value of the home but borrowing more than 80 percent of the value will result in additional monthly costs. Lenders will require buyers with less than 20 percent equity in the home to pay for Private Mortgage Insurance (PMI) to protect the lender should the buyer default on payments. The cost of PMI can range from $30 to $90 per month for each $100,000 of debt, depending on the size of the down payment. The PMI premium will continue until the loan-to-value ratio falls below 80 percent, which could be 10 years or longer based on the amortization schedule of the loan payments. When clients believe that the value of the home has appreciated, they may be able to prove that they have reached 80 percent loan-to-value (LTV) by getting a current appraisal. The cost of the appraisal is typically $400 – $600, so if there are still a few years left before the amortization schedule shows 80 percent loan-to-value, it is probably worth paying for the appraisal and requesting that the PMI be removed. It is also worth noting that the PMI can be canceled at the homeowner's request as soon as 80 percent LTV is reached according to the amortization schedule, but may not automatically be canceled until the scheduled payments reduce LTV to below 78 percent, which could mean that the client continues paying the PMI premiums for several months to a year longer than necessary. It is advisable, therefore, for clients and planners to determine when that 80 percent LTV will be reached and to include in the client's action plan a phone call to remove the PMI.

During the first few years of the 30-year loan, the majority of the monthly mortgage payment goes primarily toward interest, with a small portion reducing principal. For example, a 30-year mortgage of $100,000 with a six percent rate will not have a reduction in debt to $90,000 until the 82nd month – almost seven years. The interest over the 82 months totals $39,103 while the principal totals about $10,000.

Closing Costs

Once the amount of down payment has been determined, clients will need to decide how to pay for the closing costs of the loan. These costs generally total between three and five percent of the purchase price of the property (not reduced by the down payment amount). Closing (a.k.a. settlement) costs include expenditures for appraisals, a title search, the filing fee at the courthouse, origination fees, the initial escrow for homeowner insurance and PMI, and the initial escrow for property taxes. When a loan is applied for, a Loan Estimate form (formerly called a HUD-1 Form) will be sent to the applicant. The Loan Estimate lists a breakdown of the settlement costs associated with the loan. Settlement costs can be financed by adding them into the mortgage amount, or they can be paid from another source such as a checking or savings account.

The costs associated with a mortgage may also include the payment of "points." A **point** is one percent of the loan amount. It is an additional prepaid interest charge paid as a lump sum by the borrower at closing in exchange for a lower interest rate on the loan.

Example 3.4

Ashley is offered a 30-year fixed mortgage on a $100,000 loan with a rate of 4.25%, but if she pays 1 point ($1,000), the rate will drop to 4.125%. The monthly payment for the 4.25% loan is $492. The monthly payment if she pays the point is $485. Effectively, Ashley pays $1,000 up front to save $7 per month. It will take 12 years ($1,000/7 = 143 months) to recover the cost of the point. If Ashley is planning to move or refinance before 12 years, it is not worth paying the point.

Another way of evaluating whether points should be paid is to determine the opportunity cost of using the money to pay points versus the next best use of that money. If the money will otherwise sit in a checking account earning no or very little interest for the client, then paying the point from money in the checking account will look more attractive. But if the money will be invested in an account that earns, for example, seven percent per year, the growth on that investment will more than cover the increased interest payment on the mortgage and will be significantly more attractive.

Conventional vs. Adjustable-Rate Mortgage (ARM)

Another decision that must be made when a client is purchasing a home is the type of mortgage loan that will be used. The most common type of mortgage is a conventional mortgage which carries a fixed interest rate for the duration of the loan. An adjustable-rate mortgage (ARM), on the other hand, has an interest rate that changes with changes in the level of interest rates in the economy; however, the rates will change only within limits and only at specified intervals. Adjustable-rate mortgages typically carry lower initial interest than fixed-rate mortgages because of the additional risk the ARM homeowner takes.

Deductibility of Mortgage Interest and Real Estate Taxes

Taxpayers who itemize deductions on Schedule A of Form 1040 are permitted a deduction for qualified mortgage interest.[10] For mortgages entered into on or before December 15, 2017, the mortgage interest on a principal residence and on a second residence is deductible up to a maximum acquisition cost of $1,000,000. For the tax years from 2018 to 2025, the deduction for mortgage interest will be limited to the interest on a mortgage up to $750,00. The deduction for interest on home equity loans is suspended unless the loan is used for improvements to the home. When a pre-December 16, 2017 mortgage is refinanced, interest is still deductible on the loan balance that was outstanding at the time of the refinance up to $1 million for married filing jointly. Private mortgage insurance (PMI) premiums paid or accrued before January 1, 2022 are deductible as qualified mortgage interest, subject to the limitations discussed in this paragraph.[11]

Generally, points paid on the acquisition of a principal residence are deductible in the year paid, even if paid by the seller. Points paid on refinancing a mortgage must be amortized over the life of the loan.

Taxpayers are also permitted to deduct real estate taxes on an unlimited number of properties on Schedule A. For the years 2018 to 2025, the Tax Cuts and Jobs Act limits the deduction for state and local taxes (the "SALT" deduction) to $10,000 ($5,000 for married filing separately).

---

10. TCJA 2017 significantly increased the standard deduction resulting in fewer taxpayers benefiting from itemizing deductions.
11. Taxpayer Certainty and Disaster Tax Relief Act of 2020.

Exhibit 3.26 | Traditional and Reverse Mortgages

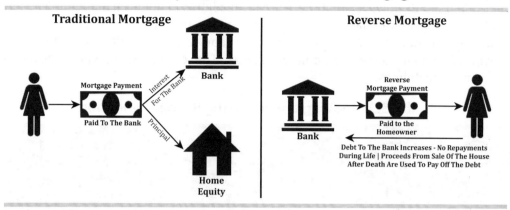

Reverse Mortgage

The **reverse mortgage** technique permits homeowners to use their home equity while still living in the home. With a reverse mortgage, the owner of a home (age 62 or older) that is fully paid for (or that has a substantial amount of equity) receives periodic income from a mortgage lender for a period of years or for life. At the homeowner's death, the lender can sell the home to generate the cash to repay the loan. Any proceeds remaining after paying the loan go to the homeowner's estate. Unlike a home equity loan, a reverse mortgage does not require the owner to make monthly payments on the debt during the owner's lifetime.

In comparing a reverse mortgage to a sale of the home, planners should keep in mind that homeownership does not cause ineligibility for Medicaid (which may be necessary to provide for long-term nursing care for an elderly client). However, a sale during the homeowner's lifetime can cause ineligibility for Medicaid when the homeowner receives cash proceeds. As a result, the homeowner may seek to avoid a sale of the home during his or her lifetime due to the potential impact on Medicaid.

Reverse mortgages that provide an annuity should also be viewed with caution since the annuity income may cause ineligibility for disability benefits under SSI (Supplemental Security Income) or for Medicaid, and because the costs of the reverse mortgage can be high.

Savings and Investing Management

Savings and investing management recommendations may require both an increase in savings and an increase in the emergency fund. Once the planner has calculated the savings rate (savings plus any employer match/gross pay), the rate should equal 10 to 13 percent if the client only has one financial goal, that being financial security. As previously stated, if the client and family have multiple financial goals including retirement, college education, and lump-sum goals (e.g., new house or second home) the savings rate must be increased from the 10 to 13 percent to a savings rate necessary to achieve all of the goals. It is possible that the client can be more tax efficient by saving on a pre-tax rather than post-tax basis. Recall that the 10 to 13 percent savings rate is for a client who is between ages 25 and 35 years old.

The rule of thumb for an emergency fund is three to six months of non-discretionary cash flows. The astute planner understands however, that there are no absolutes in financial planning. The more difficult the labor market and the more unique the worker, the longer the worker may be out of work, which is one of the most significant risks addressed by the emergency fund. The following exhibit contains both savings and investing management recommendations. The cash flow impact is listed along with implementation responsibilities.

Exhibit 3.27 | Saving and Investing Recommendations

	Recommendation	Annual Recurring Cost <Negative> + Positive	Non-Recurring Cost	Other	To Be Implemented by Client or Planner
A	Increase the 401(k) plan employee deferral by $1,000 from $2,000 to $3,000 (note that there is a tax savings of 15% and an increased employer match)	<$1,000> + $150		+ $500 Employer Match	Client
B	Add to the emergency fund to get to 3 months coverage		<$5,000>		Client

Other approach recommendations may include:
- executing estate planning documents (e.g., will, durable power of attorney for health care, advance medical directive)
- managing the withholding of taxes (Form W-4)
- planning for income from part time jobs or changing jobs to earn more
- annuitizing an annuity to create recurring income
- planning to take required minimum distributions from IRAs and qualified plans
- deciding to begin drawing Social Security retirement benefits

These additional recommendations require an analysis of the impact on cash flow and should be implemented in order of priority.

Ultimately, the cash flow approach yields a net recurring cash flow number and a net non-recurring cash flow number. If the cash flow impact is positive, all is well, but if the cash flow impact is negative (as it usually is), then the planner will need to look for the money with which to fund the client's recommendations. There are usually three possible sources of funding that may be available:
- savings from refinancing of a home mortgage
- increased cash flows from adjusting the W-4 (assuming taxes are over withheld)
- cash flows from the sale of assets on the balance sheet

There may also be additional cash flows from raising deductibles on insurance policies. While it is often challenging to implement, there can be savings by reducing expenses. However, reducing expenses is generally challenging.

A lack of funding availability will limit the ability to immediately implement recommendations. However, since the recommendations are already prioritized, the planner can simply cut off implementing recommendations at the point where there is no additional funding remaining and later fund the remainder of the recommendations.

The cash flow approach should include:
- a mortgage refinance calculation, both pre- and post- recommendations
- a current and projected tax analysis pre- and post- recommendations
- a present value analysis of all needs prior to recommendations
- a consideration of alternatives (e.g., delay retirement, include Social Security)

THE STRATEGIC APPROACH

The strategic approach is characterized by a client mission statement (e.g., to achieve financial security), a set of goals, and a set of objectives. Specifically, the planner can construct a plan driven by the client's mission statement. Then, a needs-driven list of client goals is created. From the list of goals, a detailed list of objectives is created that will all together result in the accomplishment of the mission of the client's financial planning. The planner creates a plan by reviewing relevant internal and external data and produces a plan for the long-run (the mission) with both short and intermediate accomplishment of goals and objectives. The plan incorporates capitalizing on a client's strengths (e.g., good salary or savings rate), overcoming a client's weaknesses (e.g., insufficient insurance), taking advantage of external opportunities, and mitigating external threats.

Note that the strategic approach takes into consideration needs versus wants. Needs are defined as those objectives required by law (e.g., auto liability insurance) or essential to make the financial plan successful (e.g., savings). Wants on the other hand are somewhat discretionary (e.g., purchase a new home). Planning using the strategic approach focuses on the needs-driven versus wants-driven priorities that can be successfully implemented following the design of a financial planning mission, goal and objective oriented arrangement.

The typical structure of the strategic approach to financial planning includes:

Mission Statement (An Enduring Long-Term Statement)

- Financial Security – A formal statement of the purpose of the client's financial planning.

Goals (Broadly Conceived Goals)

- Adequate risk management portfolio
- Adequate savings rate for retirement and education
- Adequate emergency fund
- Adequate debt management
- Adequate investment portfolio
- Adequate estate plan

Objectives (Narrow Measurable Objectives)

- **Risk Management** – A risk management objective may include the purchase or increase or decrease in coverage of life, disability, liability, or personal property insurance. In addition, the client may need to sell a liability associated asset that is either uninsured or uninsurable.
- **Debt Management** - Objectives associated with debt management may include reducing or eliminating high interest debt, paying off credit card debt, and reducing housing ratios to appropriate levels (HR1 = $\leq$ 28% and HR2 = $\leq$ 36%).
- **Tax Management and Emergency Fund** - For tax management purposes, the client may need to adjust income tax over withholding as an objective in order to meet other cash-required objectives. The client's emergency fund balance may need to be increased to meet at least a three to six month balance objective.
- **Savings and Investments** - Savings objectives may include creating, adjusting, or increasing amounts associated with retirement, education, or housing funding. Changing the risk of an investment portfolio or either buying or selling existing investments to fit the financial planning mission are possible investment objectives.
- **Estate Plan** - Having estate documents prepared (will, durable power of attorney for financial matters and healthcare, advance medical directive etc.) is an important objective.

Investment Analysis

- Risk tolerance analysis comparison of current implicit rate of return tool with PASS score.
- Investment performance analysis compares current rate of return to the expected rate of return based on the risk tolerance profile applied with the PASS score.

If the planner chooses to start the financial planning process using the strategic approach method, it is likely that this approach will be followed by the use of the cash flow approach and recommendations. This ensures that implementation of the mission, goals, and objectives are feasible.

This chapter has discussed several approaches to analyzing a client's financial planning situation. Each of these approaches has advantages and limitations and most advisers will use a combination of approaches to complete a comprehensive financial plan.

DISCUSSION QUESTIONS

SOLUTIONS to the discussion questions can be found exclusively within the chapter. Once you have completed an initial reading of the chapter, go back and highlight the answers to these questions.

1. List and define the eight approaches to financial planning analysis and recommendations.

2. List the three phases of the life cycle approach.

3. What are some of the questions that an income statement pie chart will answer?

4. What are some of the questions that a balance sheet pie chart will answer?

5. What is an advantage to using the pie chart approach with clients?

6. What are the liquidity ratios used in the financial statement and ratio analysis approach?

7. Discuss the difference between discretionary and non-discretionary cash flows.

8. List the four debt ratios used in the financial statement and ratio analysis approach.

9. Discuss the average savings rate for retirement funding and the average retirement withdrawal rate.

10. List the common performance ratios used in the financial statement and ratio analysis approach.

11. Define the two-step approach to financial planning.

12. What do the three panels of the three panel approach cover?

13. Why is the present value approach easy to understand at the completion of the analysis?

14. Discuss the usefulness of the metrics approach.

15. What is the usefulness of the cash flow approach to financial planning?

16. Define the strategic approach to financial planning.

17. Discuss whether capital gains, dividends, interest and other portfolio income should be part of the savings ratio.

MULTIPLE-CHOICE PROBLEMS

A sample of multiple choice problems is provided below. Additional multiple choice problems are available at money-education.com by accessing the Student Practice Portal.

1. Kiara is 30 years old and single. She is healthy, has no children or pets. Kiara works as a human resources coordinator and earns approximately $40,000 per year. Due to her outstanding student loans, she has a fairly low net worth. She rents an apartment but does own her car outright. All of the following are likely insurance coverage needs, <u>except</u>?
   a. Life Insurance.
   b. Health Insurance.
   c. Disability Insurance.
   d. Liability Insurance.

2. Your new client, Payton, age 35, came into your office today. She provided you with the following information for the year:
   - Income - $100,000
   - Taxes - $18,000
   - Rent - $14,000
   - Living Expenses - $40,000
   - Credit Card Debt - $12,000
   - Savings - $5,000
   - Student Loan Payments - $5,000
   - Car Payment - $6,000

   After receiving this information you created a pie chart to visually depict where her income was spent. Utilizing targeted benchmarks which of the following statements are you most likely to make during you next meeting?
   a. "You are spending too much on housing."
   b. "Your current living expenses are within the normal range."
   c. "Your mortgage and debt payments are within the normal range."
   d. "Your savings is low but still appropriate for your age."

3. Which of the following is true?
   a. Debt ratios measure the ability to meet short-term obligations.
   b. Liquidity ratios indicate how well a client manages debt.
   c. Ratios for financial security determine the progress that the client is making toward achieving short-term financial security goals.
   d. Performance ratios determine the adequacy of returns on investments.

4. Utilizing investment assets to gross pay benchmarks, which of the following individuals is likely on target with their investment assets?
   a. Ross, age 55, earns $150,000 a year and has invested assets of $900,000.
   b. Rachel, age 35, earns $30,000 a year and has invested assets of $15,000.
   c. Monica, age 45, earns $60,000 a year and has invested assets of $150,000.
   d. Joey, age 25, earns $40,000 a year and has invested assets of $9,000.

5. Utilizing the three panel approach, which of the following would be evaluated in Panel 1 - Risk Management?
    a. Emergency Fund.
    b. Education Fund.
    c. Retirement Fund.
    d. Life Insurance.

> **Additional multiple choice problems
> are available at
> money-education.com
> by accessing the
> Student Practice Portal.
> Access requires registration of the title using
> the unique code at the front of the book.**

QUICK QUIZ EXPLANATIONS

Quick Quiz 3.1

1. False. The life cycle approach is a broad view of the client's financial profile and is useful to focus on further financial discussions when the planner only has partial information. The financial statement and ratio analysis approach utilizes the liquidity ratios to analyze the client's financial situation.
2. True.

Quick Quiz 3.2

1. True.
2. True.
3. False. The net worth-to-total asset ratio is a debt ratio that measures the total assets owned or paid for by the client. Another common performance ratio is the return on net worth that measures the change in net worth plus savings over a given period of time.
4. True.

Quick Quiz 3.3

1. True.
2. True.
3. False. While some benchmarks may be finite (housing ratios 1 and 2) other benchmarks will vary based on the client's goals (savings rate to include retirement funding, education funding and/or lump-sum funding) and age (risk tolerance for investment choices).

Quick Quiz 3.4

1. False. The cash flow approach adjusts the cash flows from the income statement (not the balance sheet) for forecasting purposes.
2. True.
3. True.

4

PERSONAL FINANCIAL STATEMENTS: PREPARATION AND ANALYSIS

LEARNING OBJECTIVES

1. Prepare a balance sheet and its components.
2. Differentiate cash and cash equivalents, from investment assets, and personal use assets.
3. Clarify the difference between short- and long-term liabilities.
4. Determine the methodology for evaluating various assets.
5. Determine net worth.
6. List sources of information to properly value assets and liabilities.
7. Prepare a statement of income and expenses.
8. Define a statement of net worth and a statement of cash flows.
9. Construct statements of financial positions and cash-flow statements as applied to clients consistent with sound personal accounting standards.*
10. Evaluate client financial statements using ratios and growth rates and by comparing them to relevant norms.*
11. Describe the fundamental differences between corporate/business accounting practices and those appropriate for personal financial statements.*
12. Describe the value of forecasting and importance of budgeting.
13. Describe the purpose of financial statement analysis including vertical and horizontal analysis.
14. Prepare a ratio analysis including liquidity ratios, debt ratios, ratios for financial security goals, and performance ratios.
15. List appropriate benchmarks for each of the ratios calculated.
16. Discuss the limitations of financial statement analysis including, estimating fair market value, inflation, hard to value assets, illiquidity of certain assets, and uncertain returns.
17. Discuss sensitivity analysis and Monte Carlo analysis.

Ties to CFP Certification Learning Objectives

INTRODUCTION

Personal financial statements are essential for the financial planner to evaluate a client's financial position and to review changes or trends in the client's financial position and financial performance. The planner can use the financial statements to prepare a **financial statement analysis**, which is the process of calculating financial ratios and comparing the actual ratios to industry established benchmarks. Financial statement analysis helps to reveal:

- how well a client is managing debt
- whether the client is saving enough for retirement or education goals
- whether the client's risks are adequately covered
- how well the client is able to meet short-term financial obligations

The process of conducting financial statement analysis permits the financial planner to identify weaknesses in the client's financial position and performance. The planner can then develop an appropriate set of actions to respond to and improve upon those weaknesses.

Clients rarely have well prepared personal financial statements. A financial planner should be prepared to assist the client in the preparation of basic financial statements, including a balance sheet and a statement of income and expenses. This chapter explores the preparation and presentation of a client's financial statements. Financial statement analysis is also covered in this chapter so that the planner is prepared to evaluate the client's financial position and determine trends in the client's financial position and financial performance.

⋮☰ *Key Concepts*

1. Identify the process and purpose of financial statement analysis.

2. Identify the common principal and supplementary financial statements used as part of the financial planning process.

Preparing financial statements is the process of accounting for asset and liability balances, as well as for income and expenses for a client. For personal financial planning purposes, there are two principal financial statements and two supplementary financial statements.

Principal Financial Statements
- The Balance Sheet (A Statement of Financial Position or A Statement of Assets, Liabilities and Net Worth)
- The Income Statement (A Statement of Income and Expenses)[1]

Supplementary Financial Statements
- The Statement of Net Worth
- The Cash Flow Statement

This chapter primarily focuses on the balance sheet and income statement. Although the statements of net worth and cash flow provide useful information, in practice they are rarely prepared for individuals. This chapter also builds on and expands the approaches and analysis discussed in Chapter 3, including the financial statement and ratio analysis, the pie chart approach, and the two-step / three panel approach.

BALANCE SHEET (STATEMENT OF FINANCIAL POSITION)

A **balance sheet**, or as commonly referred to, a statement of financial position, represents the accounting for items the client "owns" (assets) and items that are "owed" (liabilities). The difference between assets and liabilities is the owner's equity (net worth). The balance sheet provides a snapshot of the client's assets, liabilities, and net worth as of a stated date such as at the end of a calendar quarter or at the end of the calendar year. A balance sheet is dated as of a particular date (i.e.,"As of December 31, 20XX"), which represents the value of assets owned, liabilities owed, and resulting net worth at that particular moment in time.

Assets represent anything of economic value that can ultimately be converted into cash. Depending upon the client's intent regarding disposition of an asset, the asset is further classified into one of the following three categories as reflected on the balance sheet:
- Cash and Cash Equivalents (Current Assets)
- Investment Assets
- Personal Use Assets

---

1. In practice, the term "Cash Flow Statement" is sometimes used to describe the Income Statement for an individual client. However, they are different types of documents and serve different purposes. In this textbook the Income Statement and Cash Flow Statement terms will be differentiated according to their accounting purposes, rather than used interchangeably.

Cash and Cash Equivalents

Cash and cash equivalents (current assets) represent assets that are highly liquid, which means they are either cash or can be converted to cash (within the next 12 months) with little to no price concession from the principal amount invested. Cash and cash equivalents represent very safe investments that are unlikely to lose value. An example of a current asset that can be converted to cash within the next 12 months is a certificate of deposit that matures in six months.

Typical assets included in cash and cash equivalents are:
- cash
- checking accounts
- money market accounts
- savings accounts
- certificates of deposit (maturity is $\leq$ 12 months)

Since cash and cash equivalents represent highly liquid, "safe" investments, it is important to the client's financial position and financial performance to maintain sufficient levels of cash and cash equivalents to meet liabilities that are due within the next 12 months. Benchmarks and ratios (discussed later in this chapter) assist the planner in determining whether the client is maintaining sufficient levels of cash and cash equivalents.

Investment Assets

Investment assets include appreciating assets or those assets being held to accomplish one or more financial goals. Typical assets included in this category are:
- retirement accounts (401(k) plans, profit sharing plans, IRAs, annuities)
- brokerage accounts
- education funds
- cash value in a life insurance policy
- business ownership interests
- the vested portion of any pension plan
- rental property
- other: investment partnership interests, oil and gas interests, collections (such as art), etc.

Investment assets are listed on the balance sheet at their current fair market value. As a financial planner, there are important issues to consider when preparing the investment assets section, including ensuring that all investment assets are included (e.g., stock certificates sitting in a safety deposit box) and making sure that the current fair market value of the investment is properly determined.

One of the most difficult investment assets to value is ownership in a privately-held business. Unlike a publicly-traded company, there is no established market value for a privately-held company. The following questions should be considered regarding business valuations:
- **Who prepared the valuation?** If the valuation was prepared by the owner, it may be significantly overstated or understated. Owners often overestimate the value of their own business. Alternatively, a professional valuation expert may have valued the business. However,

it is important to understand the purpose of the valuation and to understand important assumptions of the valuation. Professional valuations are prepared for various reasons (potential sale of part of all of the business, gifting an interest of the business to family members, etc.). In practice, the purpose of the valuation can influence the final valuation of the business. Valuations conducted for purposes of transfer tax reporting (gifting) tend to be lower than valuations conducted for the purposes of selling a business.

- **How current is the valuation?** The valuation may be accurate or it may be understated or overstated if the underlying assumptions no longer apply.
- **Is goodwill associated with the business or with the owner?** Some businesses are critically dependent on the owner and founder of the business and can be negatively impacted upon the owner's departure.
- **Will the business be sold to fund retirement?** It is important to understand how the owner is planning on selling a business and over what time period he expects the proceeds. This information will assist the planner in a conversation about any risks associated with the exit strategy.

For small business owners, a large portion of their net worth is often invested in the business. Financial planners should be very cautious and conservative when valuing business ownership interests on the balance sheet, especially if the proceeds from the sale of the business will be used to fund retirement or other important goals. If the business is valued too high, the client's financial position will be too optimistic, perhaps resulting in a shortfall at retirement. If the business is valued too low, the client's financial resources may be improperly allocated, jeopardizing other financial goals.

Personal Use Assets

Personal use assets are those assets that maintain the client's lifestyle. Examples of assets included in personal use assets are:

- personal residences
- automobiles
- furniture
- clothing
- boats
- jet skis
- vacation homes
- electronics (television, stereo, iPad, etc.)
- collectibles (art, antiques, coins)[2]

The value of personal use assets is usually determined by client estimation as opposed to appraisal. Anytime a financial planner is estimating the value of assets, it is always better to be conservative and not overvalue the assets. Financial statements and financial statement analysis provides insight into the client's financial position, performance, strengths and weaknesses, so accurately valuing assets is an important part of the process.

Although the value of personal use assets will impact net worth, financial planners are more concerned with cash, cash equivalents and investment assets when conducting financial statement analysis. As previously discussed, a properly valued business ownership interest is important, especially if the client

---

2. Collectibles might be categorized as investment assets or personal use assets, depending on the intended purpose of the owner.

is relying on the business to fund retirement or other goals. However, the **exact** economic or fair market value of personal use assets is less important than the exact fair market value of investment assets. Reasonable and conservative estimates are usually adequate when valuing personal use assets, because the client will likely continue to use their personal use assets to maintain their lifestyle through the retirement years. It is important to periodically determine if there are any significant changes in the value of personal use assets, such as the appreciation or depreciation of the primary residence, vacation property, and other high dollar amount items. Also, a question may arise as to whether an item is a personal use asset or an investment asset.

Example 4.1

Holly purchases a $50,000 painting and hangs it on her wall. Is it a personal use asset or an investment asset? The determination is dependent on Holly's intent. Does she intend to leave it on her wall to show her family and friends or does she intend to hold it as an appreciating asset to be sold for a profit? If Holly's intent is to leave the painting on the wall to enjoy, then the painting should be classified as a personal use asset on the balance sheet. If Holly's intent is to hold the painting to advance future profit, then the painting should be classified as an investment asset.

Liabilities

Liabilities represent financial obligations that the client owes to creditors. To satisfy a liability, either a client-owned asset or some other economic benefit must be transferred to the creditor. A liability may be either a legal obligation or moral obligation that resulted from a past transaction. A legal obligation may be a mortgage or a car payment. If a client borrows money from the bank to purchase a house or a car, then there is a legal obligation to repay the loan (a liability). A moral obligation can result from the pledging of a donation to a charity or a not-for-profit entity. A pledge is not necessarily a legal obligation, but if intended to be honored, it does represent a financial liability.

Example 4.2

Ivan is an alumnus of Florida State University and is a football season ticket holder. In April each year, Ivan pledges to contribute $1,000 to the boosters association in return for parking privileges at the football games. Ivan does not have to pay the $1,000 pledge until the end of the year. Ivan has a moral obligation to pay the $1,000, and it should be reflected as a liability on his balance sheet until the $1,000 pledge is paid (assuming he intends to pay the pledge). In some states, pledges to charitable organizations are legally enforceable debts.

Other types of liabilities include unpaid utility bills, credit card bills, insurance premiums that are due and any other debt obligations. Liabilities are valued at their current outstanding balance as of the date of the balance sheet. The current outstanding balance represents the amount owed to the creditor, including amounts for any bills that have been received but not yet paid. Liabilities are categorized according to the timing of when the liability is due or expected to be paid. The categories of liabilities are:

- short-term or current liabilities (expected to be paid within one year)
- long-term liabilities (expected to be paid beyond one year)

Short-Term (Current) Liabilities

Short-term liabilities represent those obligations that are "current" in nature that are due or expected to be paid within the next 12 months (≤ 12 months). Examples of liabilities that are included in short-term or current liabilities are:

- Electric, gas, water, garbage, and sewage bills incurred, but not yet paid
- Principal portion of any debt obligations due within the next 12 months (mortgage and auto loan)
- Unpaid credit card bills
- Outstanding medical expenses
- Insurance premiums due
- Unpaid taxes

When reporting debts such as a mortgage or a car loan, only the principal portion of the loan that is due in the next 12 months is reported as a short-term or current liability. This treatment is the correct accounting methodology, but is rarely used by individuals in preparation of personal financial statements.

Interest expense for the next 12 months is not reported on the balance sheet. If a loan is paid off today, the payoff amount would include the interest expense incurred since the last payment (plus the outstanding principal) because the interest expense is calculated for having a loan outstanding for the previous month. Liabilities only reflect the amount currently owed by the client. Since interest expense for the next 12 months has yet to be incurred, it is not reflected on the balance sheet.

Long-Term Liabilities

Long-term liabilities are financial obligations owed that are due and expected to be paid beyond the next 12 months. Long-term liabilities are usually the result of major financial purchases and resulting obligations that are amortized over multiple years. Examples of liabilities that are included under long-term liabilities are:

- primary residence loans (mortgage)
- vacation home loans (mortgage)
- automobile loans
- student loans
- any other type of loan or promissory note

> ### ✏️ Quick Quiz 4.1
>
> 1. The client's balance sheet represents all income earned less expenses incurred for the period being covered.
>   a. True
>   b. False
>
> 2. Cash and cash equivalents are assets that are highly liquid and are either cash or can be converted to cash within the next 12 months.
>   a. True
>   b. False
>
> 3. Investment assets are those assets that help to maintain the client's lifestyle.
>   a. True
>   b. False
>
> 4. Long-term liabilities represent client financial obligations that are owed to creditors beyond the next 12 months.
>   a. True
>   b. False
>
> False, True, False, True.

When reporting the outstanding balance of a loan, the current portion of the liability should be reported separately from the long-term portion of the liability. This allows the financial planner to make a comparison between current assets and current liabilities and to evaluate the client's liquidity status and ability to meet short-term financial obligations.

Example 4.3

Lisa has a $300,000 mortgage on her house, with a 30-year term at 6% interest. She expects to pay a total of $21,583.82 this upcoming year, including $3,684.04 in principal reduction and $17,899.78 in interest expense (see amortization table below). The loan should be properly categorized as a liability on the balance sheet as follows:

Short-Term Liabilities: Mortgage on Primary Residence = $3,684.04
Long-Term Liabilities: Mortgage on Primary Residence = $296,315.96
Total Liabilities = $300,000.00

Amortization Table for Year 1

Month	Beginning Balance	Interest	Payment	End of Month Balance
1	$300,000.00	$1,500.00	$ (1,798.65)	$299,701.35
2	$299,701.35	$1,498.51	$ (1,798.65)	$299,401.20
3	$299,401.20	$1,497.01	$ (1,798.65)	$299,099.56
4	$299,099.56	$1,495.50	$ (1,798.65)	$298,796.40
5	$298,796.40	$1,493.98	$ (1,798.65)	$298,491.73
6	$298,491.73	$1,492.46	$ (1,798.65)	$298,185.54
7	$298,185.54	$1,490.93	$ (1,798.65)	$297,877.82
8	$297,877.82	$1,489.39	$ (1,798.65)	$297,568.56
9	$297,568.56	$1,487.84	$ (1,798.65)	$297,257.75
10	$297,257.75	$1,486.29	$ (1,798.65)	$296,945.38
11	$296,945.38	$1,484.73	$ (1,798.65)	$296,631.46
12	$296,631.46	$1,483.16	$ (1,798.65)	$296,315.96
Total		$17,899.78	$ (21,583.82)	

Note: Even though Lisa knows how much interest expense she will be paying in the next 12 months ($17,899.78), it is not reported as a liability until the interest expense is incurred. If the interest is paid as incurred, it will not be recorded as a liability but rather simply be reflected in the monthly or annual income statement. She is not legally obligated to pay the interest until it accrues each month. Another way to think about this is to consider that she could pay $300,000 today to retire the debt and thus, avoid the interest next year.

Valuing Assets and Liabilities

As previously stated, it is important that assets reflect their fair market value and that liabilities are stated at their current outstanding principal balance as of the date of the balance sheet.

Net Worth

The **net worth** of the client as reflected on the balance sheet represents the amount of total equity (assets - liabilities = net worth) a client has accumulated as of the date of the balance sheet. When evaluating a client's financial position, net worth is an important consideration because it represents an absolute dollar amount reflective of a client's financial position. A positive net worth may imply the client has done a good job of saving, investing, and managing debt. A negative net worth implies that the client is insolvent and potentially facing bankruptcy.

Unfortunately, there are times when a negative net worth is a reality. The real estate collapse during 2008 and 2009 is an example where real estate values dropped significantly, which resulted in a loss of equity for many people. Many people had homes with a fair market value that was less than the debt on the house, a position that is often referred to as an "upside-down mortgage" or an "underwater mortgage." In some cases, the debt was so much greater than the value of the house that it resulted in a negative net worth.

Exhibit 4.1 illustrates the 20X1 balance sheet for Mr. and Mrs. Zacker that reflects the three types of assets, short-term liabilities, long-term liabilities, and the resulting net worth.

Exhibit 4.1 | Balance Sheet Example

Statement of Financial Position
Mr. and Mrs. Zacker
Balance Sheet as of 12/31/20X1

Assets			Liabilities and Net Worth			
Current Assets			**Current Liabilities**			
JT	Cash & Checking	$5,000	W	Credit Cards	$5,000	
JT	CD Maturing in 6 months	$25,000	H	Auto # 1	$5,000	
JT	Money Market	$50,000	W	Auto # 2	$6,000	
			JT	Personal Residence	$10,000	
Total Current Assets		$80,000	**Total Current Liabilities**			$26,000
Investment Assets			**Long-Term Liabilities**			
H	401(k) Plan	$30,000	H	Auto # 1	$14,000	
W	IRA	$50,000	W	Auto # 2	$17,000	
JT	Brokerage Account	$100,000	JT	Personal Residence	$450,000	
W	Value of Business Interests	$500,000				
W	Education Savings	$75,000	**Total Long-Term Liabilities**			$481,000
Total Invested Assets		$755,000				
			Total Liabilities			$507,000
Personal Use Assets						
JT	Personal Residence	$500,000	**Total Net Worth**			$1,008,000
JT	Furniture, Clothing	$125,000				
H	Auto # 1	$25,000				
W	Auto # 2	$30,000				
Total Personal Use Assets		$680,000				
Total Assets		$1,515,000	**Total Liabilities and Net Worth**			$1,515,000

H = Husband Owns
W = Wife Owns
JT = Jointly owned by husband and wife

The balance sheet formula is: Assets = Liabilities + Net Worth.

Alternatively, the formula can be restated: Assets – Liabilities = Net Worth.

These formulas help us understand how financial transactions impact a client's net worth.

Example 4.4

Josephine buys a house for $400,000. She makes a $50,000 down payment and finances the balance with a mortgage. How is her net worth impacted from this transaction?

	Assets	-	Liabilities	=	Net Worth
Cash and Cash Equivalents	($50,000)				($50,000)
Personal Use Assets	+ $400,000				+ $400,000
Mortgage on New House			$350,000		($350,000)
Net Impact	$350,000	-	$350,000	=	$0

Josephine exchanges one asset ($50,000 cash) for another ($400,000 home) and increases her liabilities ($350,000 mortgage). Therefore, her net worth is not impacted by purchasing the house. However, as time goes by, the increase or decrease in the value of the house will impact her net worth as will the reduction in the principal obligation of the mortgage. The principal reduction is funded mostly by income that would otherwise have increased another asset category on the balance sheet, such as cash or investments.

Example 4.5

One year ago, Elaine purchased a house for $400,000. Today, the house is worth $425,000 and she has reduced her outstanding mortgage principal by $10,000. What is the impact to Elaine's net worth?

	Assets	-	Liabilities	=	Net Worth
Personal Use Assets	+ $25,000				$25,000
Reduction in Outstanding Mortgage Balance			($10,000)		+ $10,000
Net Impact	$25,000	-	($10,000)	=	$35,000

Elaine's net worth increased as a result of the value of her house increasing ($25,000), plus she has paid down her mortgage throughout the year. Since her liabilities have decreased by $10,000, the two actions result in Elaine's net worth increasing by a total of $35,000.

Example 4.6

Luke, his wife, and their five children went on vacation to Disney World for one week. Luke spent $7,000 on the family vacation and paid for it with money in his savings account. What is the impact to his net worth?

	Assets	-	Liabilities	=	Net Worth
Cash and Cash Equivalents	($7,000)				($7,000)
Net Impact	($7,000)	-		=	($7,000)

Luke's net worth has decreased by the $7,000 he spent on the vacation. Although they are certainly priceless, he cannot capture the good times and memories he has from the vacation and report them on his balance sheet.

Sources of Information

In order to properly and accurately prepare personal financial statements, the financial planner needs source documents from the client to properly value assets and liabilities. Source documents include:

- bank statements
- brokerage statements
- loan amortization schedules
- tax returns
- real estate appraisals

> ### ⠿ Key Concepts
>
> 1. Distinguish between sole ownership and tenancy in common.
>
> 2. Distinguish between property owned JTWROS and tenancy by the entirety versus community property.
>
> 3. Identify the importance of footnotes to financial statements.

Account Ownership

As part of the balance sheet presentation, it is important to disclose how an asset or liability is titled (owned). The most common forms of ownership are:

- Sole Ownership
- Tenancy in Common
- Joint Tenancy with Right of Survivorship (JTWROS)
- Tenancy by the Entirety
- Community Property

Below is an explanation of the types of ownership. However, Chapter 14 provides a more thorough discussion of this topic.

Sole ownership is the complete ownership of property by one individual who possesses all ownership rights associated with the property, including the right to use, sell, gift, alienate, convey, or bequeath the property. Typically, a car is owned and titled in the name of one person. When preparing a balance sheet for a husband and wife, (H) is used to designate the asset or liability belongs to the husband only and (W) is used if the asset or liability belongs to the wife only. Alternatively, sole ownership may be delineated using (SP 1) for assets or liabilities belonging to spouse 1 only, and (SP 2) for assets or liabilities belonging to spouse 2 only.

Tenancy in common is an interest in property held by two or more related or unrelated persons. Each owner is referred to as a tenant in common. Tenancy in common is the most common type of joint ownership between nonspouses. Each person holds an undivided, but not necessarily equal, interest in the entire property.

Joint Tenancy with Right of Survivorship (JTWROS) is typically how spouses own joint property. Joint tenancy is an interest in property held by two or more related or unrelated persons called joint tenants. Each person holds an undivided, equal interest in the whole property. A right of survivorship is normally implied with this form of ownership, and at the death of the first joint tenant, the decedent's interest transfers to the other joint tenants outside of the probate process according to state titling law. Probate is the process whereby the probate court retitles assets and gives creditors an opportunity to be heard and stake a claim to any assets to satisfy outstanding debts. Because of this right of survivorship, joint tenancy is often called joint tenancy with right of survivorship.

Tenancy by the entirety is similar to property owned as JTWROS between spouses because property ownership is automatically transferred to the surviving spouse upon death. The two tenants own an undivided interest in the whole asset. However, the ownership cannot be severed without the consent of the other spouse.

Community property is a civil law statutory regime under which married individuals own an equal undivided interest in all property accumulated during their marriage. During marriage, the income of each spouse is considered community property. Property acquired before the marriage and property received by gift or inheritance during the marriage retains its status as separate property. However, if any separate property is commingled with community property, it is often assumed to be community property. The states following the community property regime are Arizona, California, Idaho, Louisiana, Nevada, New Mexico, Texas, Washington, and Wisconsin. Community property does not usually have an automatic right of survivorship feature although some states, including Texas and California, have a survivorship option.

> ### ✒ Quick Quiz 4.2
>
> 1. Community property is an interest in property held by two or more related or unrelated persons.
>   a. True
>   b. False
>
> 2. If property is owned tenancy by the entirety or as community property then probate is avoided.
>   a. True
>   b. False
>
> False, False.

As previously indicated, an important distinction between sole ownership, tenants in common, and sometimes community property versus JTWROS and tenancy by the entirety is that property owned by the former will pass through probate at the death of the owner. Property owned JTWROS and tenancy by the entirety avoids probate and the decedent's interest transfers automatically. Property owned in a revocable trust would be listed on the balance sheet as trust assets.

Footnotes to the Financial Statements

Footnotes are an important source of information regarding the financial statements. Footnotes listed on financial statements can provide information such as how an asset or liability is owned. For example, it may state whether an asset is owned individually or jointly. In addition, footnotes can provide information regarding a client's purchase price of an asset, the date an asset or liability was acquired, how the value of an asset was determined and much more. When reviewing financial statements, it is important that the financial planner always read the footnotes.

STATEMENT OF INCOME AND EXPENSES

A **statement of income and expenses** (income statement) represents all income earned or expected to be earned by the client, less all expenses incurred or expected to be incurred during the time period being covered. The heading of the statement of income and expenses identifies the person or persons that the statement applies to, the type of financial statement, and the time period covered by the statement. To indicate the reporting period, the time period is generally listed as "For the Year Ended 12/31/20X1" or for "January 1, 20X1 – December 31, 20X1." Although financial planners typically prepare and work with annual financial statements, the income statement can also be prepared for a monthly or quarterly period of time.

Income

Examples of recurring **income** accounts earned by the client are:
- Salary
- Interest
- Dividend
- Pension
- Retirement Account Withdrawal
- Business Income
- Alimony Received

Savings Contributions

Along with expenses, recurring **savings contributions** must be reported on the statement of income and expenses. Examples include savings contributions to the following types of accounts:
- 401(k) plan
- 403(b) plan
- 457(b) plan
- IRA (Traditional or Roth)
- Education Savings
- Any other type of savings account contributions

Expenses

Recurring **expenses** represent those items that are paid regularly by the client during the time period being presented. Examples of recurring expenses include:
- Mortgage Principal and Interest
- Utilities
- Taxes
- Insurance
- Telephone
- Water
- Cable or Satellite
- Internet
- Cell Phone

Variable and Fixed Expenses

Expenses can be divided into variable and fixed expenses. **Fixed expenses** remain static for a specific period of time, regardless of changes in spending or income. For example, a homeowner cannot generally change the amount of property taxes. They remain relatively fixed. There is less discretion over fixed expenses in the short term. Examples of fixed expense accounts include:

- Mortgage Payment
- Car Payment
- Boat Payment
- Student Loan Payment
- Property Taxes
- Insurance Premiums
- Federal and State Income Taxes Withheld
- Social Security Payments Withheld

It is important to understand that fixed expenses can change with more extreme changes, such as selling a home or car. Actions, such as these, are sometimes required under extreme circumstances (for example, losing a job without an adequate emergency fund).

Variable expenses are more discretionary than fixed expenses over the short term. A client has more discretion over the amount of variable expenses, which often presents an opportunity for savings if variable expenses are closely monitored and controlled. Examples of variable expense accounts include:

- Entertainment Expenses
- Vacation Expenses
- Travel Expenses
- Charitable Contributions (may or may not be considered variable or discretionary)

Each financial statement provides a different perspective on the financial position of an individual. The statement of income and expenses is a compromise in accounting. Cash transactions that are non-recurring are not included or reported on the statement of income and expenses. Examples of cash transactions that are non-recurring include:

- the sale of stock
- an employer's contribution to a retirement plan
- giving or receiving a gift of cash, or
- an inheritance

In addition, transactions that are non-cash, non-recurring changes in the balance sheet are not reported on the statement of income expenses. Non-cash, non-recurring changes in the balance sheet include gifting (or receiving) stock and gifting (or receiving) personal use assets, and would only be reported in a statement of changes in net worth.

It is precisely because of the lack of perfection in the income statement that a planner should consider the balance sheet and the income statement together. The two documents provide a significantly more complete picture of the client's financial situation than either document alone.

Net Discretionary Cash Flows

Net discretionary cash flow represents the amount of cash flow available after all savings, expenses, and taxes have been paid. The net discretionary cash flow formula is a result of the statement of income and expenses.

The net discretionary cash flow formula from the income statement is:

Income – Savings – Expenses – Taxes = Net Discretionary Cash Flow

Net discretionary cash flow is a critical item when analyzing the statement of income and expenses. Net discretionary cash flow can be positive, negative, or equal to zero. A positive discretionary cash flow indicates that income is greater than savings, taxes, and expenses. This financial situation creates an opportunity for additional savings to accomplish a financial goal, retire debt, or purchase more comprehensive insurance. A negative net discretionary cash flow is one of the most important weaknesses a financial planner must mitigate against. A negative discretionary cash flow indicates that gross income is less than savings, taxes, and expenses. This financial situation requires steps to reduce expenses, taxes, or savings or to increase income. While a client can likely tolerate a negative net discretionary cash flow for a short period of time, ultimately, a negative net discretionary cash flow can lead to financial disaster, including bankruptcy in the most extreme cases.

The following exhibit is the Statement of Income and Expenses for Mr. and Mrs. Zacker, as expected for the complete year 20X2. This statement provides an efficient method of determining where the Zacker's income is being spent or saved during the year.

Exhibit 4.2 | Statement of Income and Expenses Example

Mr. and Mrs. Zacker Statement of Income and Expenses Expected (Approximate) for 20X2		
CASH INFLOWS		Totals
Salary - Husband	$58,000	
Salary - Wife	$100,000	
Total Cash Inflows		**$158,000**
CASH OUTFLOWS		
Savings		
Husband's 401(k) Plan	$5,000	
Wife's 401(k) Plan	$10,000	
IRA Contribution	$5,000	
Education Savings (529 Plan)	$8,000	
Total Savings		**$28,000**
Debt Payments		
Personal Residence (mortgage)	$35,000	
Auto - Husband	$7,000	
Student Loans	$2,500	
Total Debt Payments		**$44,500**
Living Expenses		
Utilities	$3,500	
Gasoline for Autos	$3,000	
Lawn Service	$3,000	
Entertainment	$6,000	
Vacations	$4,000	
Church Donations	$2,000	
Food	$8,000	
Auto Maintenance	$2,500	
Telephone	$3,000	
Clothing	$6,000	
Total Living Expenses		**$41,000**
Insurance Payments		
HO Personal Residence	$4,500	
Auto Premiums	$2,000	
Life Insurance Premiums	$1,000	
Personal Liability Umbrella Premium	$500	
Total Insurance Payments		**$8,000**
Taxes		
Federal Income Taxes Withheld	$15,000	
State Income Taxes Withheld	$4,413	
Social Security Taxes	$12,087	
Property Tax Personal Residence	$4,000	
Total Taxes		**$35,500**
Total Savings, Expenses and Taxes		**$157,000**
NET DISCRETIONARY CASH FLOW		**$1,000**

Sources of Information

Preparing a statement of income and expenses during the initial meetings with a client can be difficult because all sources of information may not yet be available. During the initial or subsequent meetings with a client, the planner should obtain the following documents with which to prepare the statement of income and expenses:

- W-2s (reports income and deferred retirement savings)
- Credit card statements (provides insight to expenses and spending, with year-end statements being especially informative)
- Billing statements (such as utilities, telephone, satellite, internet, water)
- Bank statements (especially those with bill payments)
- Federal and state income tax statements

Frequently, a client will not have all of the above documents and may not have complete records of expenses for an entire year. In these situations, financial planners may need to "back into" expenses over the time period being presented. In other words, if the planner knows the increase (or decrease) in cash, cash equivalents, and savings over the time period being presented, along with the client's income, the planner can calculate the total amount spent on taxes, savings, and expenses over that time period.

Example 4.7

Jan's salary last year was $125,000. According to her bank statements dated 12/31 from the previous two years, her cash and cash equivalents increased by $5,000. Her financial planner can assume that $120,000 ($125,000 - $5,000) was spent by Jan on taxes, savings to retirement plans, education, variable, and fixed expenses. The planner's objective now is to fill in the details of the statement of income and expenses to determine how Jan spent the $120,000 last year.

Projected Income Statements

It is extremely useful to clients that expect a lifestyle change to have the financial planner prepare a projected income statement for the period following the projected lifestyle change (i.e., children go to college or client retires). Projected (pro forma) financial statements of this sort can help identify shortfalls in cash or excess net-discretionary cash flows.

STATEMENT OF NET WORTH

The purpose of the **statement of net worth** is to explain changes in net worth between two balance sheets by reporting financial transactions that are not reported on the income statement or other financial statements. Example of transactions that would appear on the statement of net worth are:

- Giving or receiving property other than cash
- Inheriting property other than cash
- Employer contributions or matches to retirement savings accounts
- Appreciation or depreciation of assets such as a primary residence, investments, auto, jewelry, etc.

The formula for the statement of net worth is:

Beginning balance of net worth (from the January 1st balance sheet)
+ additions (appreciation of assets, receiving a gift or inheritance)
- subtractions (giving gifts other than cash)
= Ending balance of net worth (from the December 31st balance sheet)

Few clients will have a statement of net worth and very few financial planners will actually prepare a statement of net worth for a client. The statement of net worth is a supplementary financial statement that captures and reports transactions that affect net worth that are otherwise not reported on the two principal statements (balance sheet and statement of income and expenses).

CASH FLOW STATEMENT

The purpose of the **cash flow statement** is to explain how cash and cash equivalents were used or generated between the period of two balance sheets. The cash flow statement is a supplementary financial statement of non-recurring transactions not reported on the statement of income and expenses. Recall that the income statement only captures monthly or annually recurring income and expenses. The major sections of the cash flow statement includes how nonrecurring cash transactions were used or generated from investment activities and financing activities.

Exhibit 4.3 | Cash Flow Statement Category Examples

Investing Activities
• Purchase or sale of a personal use asset, such as a car or house for cash (decrease in cash)
• Purchase or sale of an investment asset, such as a mutual fund or stock (increase or decrease)
• Contributing to a retirement or education savings account (decrease in cash)
• Receiving or making gifts of cash (increase or decrease)
• Cash inheritances (increase in cash)

Financing Activities
• Principal reduction of any loans (decrease in cash)
• Taking out any new loans (increase in cash)
• Paying off credit card balances (decrease in cash)

The result of all the transactions on the cash flow statement reflects how cash was used or generated between two balance sheets. Few clients will have a cash flow statement and very few financial planners will actually prepare a cash flow statement.

FORECASTING

After preparing the initial financial statements, the planner will work with the client to overcome any weaknesses and accomplish financial goals. Recommendations may include purchasing additional life insurance, increasing deductibles on insurance policies, contributing more to savings, or retiring debt. The planner should prepare forecasted balance sheets and a statement of income and expenses for several years into the future, such as next year, three years from now, and five years from now. The forecasted financial statements should reflect the following:

- **Implementation of recommendations.** If the planner recommends increasing 401(k) plan savings, the forecasted financial statements should indicate the amount of savings and balance of the 401(k) plan for the next year, the next three years, and the next five years.
- **Inflation adjustment for expenses.** Certain expenses will generally increase over the next five years, such as insurance premiums, utilities, gasoline for autos, groceries, clothing, etc. The financial planner should prepare forecasted statements of income and expenses based on a historical inflation rate that is likely to continue for the next five years. Fixed interest rate debt payments are not impacted by inflation, so no inflation adjustments should be made to fixed rate loans. However, if the client has any variable interest rate loans that are likely to increase over the next five years, adjustments to the forecasted income statement should include increased debt payment for variable rate loans.
- **Inflation adjustment for income.** If the client expects to receive salary increases each year, those salary adjustments should be reflected in the forecasted statement of income and expenses.
- **Other adjustments.** Other adjustments to the forecasted financial statements may include:
  - Whether the client is retiring and experiencing major changes to their income in the next five years. The financial planner should prepare forecasted financial statements to reflect withdrawing retirement assets to generate income. The possibility of the client living on reduced income during retirement should be evaluated and forecasted in financial statements.

- Whether the client is expected to retire debt in the next five years. The financial planner should reflect the retiring of debt on the balance sheet to determine the impact on the balance sheet, net worth, and discretionary cash flow on the statement of income and expenses.
- Whether the client expects to begin paying for college education expenses, and how the tuition payments and living expenses for the child impact the financial statements. The planner should reflect the draw down on any college savings and the increased expenses on the income statement associated with a child living away from home while at college.
- Whether the client expects to borrow money for a car, house, boat, college education, etc. The planner should incorporate the debt into the forecasted balance sheet and statement of income and expenses.

Once the financial planner has prepared forecasted financial statements, the planner can conduct financial statement analysis on the forecasted financial statements which is discussed later in this chapter.

Importance of Budgeting

The purpose in creating a financial budget is to evaluate the client's spending and savings behavior, and to establish a spending and savings plan to assist the client in achieving their financial goals. Typically, clients are resistant to preparing or using a budget because historically they have been unsuccessful at following budgets. Actual expenses turn out to be higher than they anticipated and they often become frustrated by their inability to save or spend as anticipated.

There are three important tips to being successful in preparing and using a budget.

- **Be realistic:** Be realistic with spending behavior. It is easy to overlook credit card expenses for shopping or dining out. Credit cards are an easy way to "blow the budget."
- **Miscellaneous:** Budget a line item expense for miscellaneous expenses and unforeseen expenses. Miscellaneous expenses include gifts at the holidays, car repairs, house repairs, traffic tickets, kid's sporting events, etc. As clients get older, the miscellaneous expense item tends to grow.
- **Practice:** Being successful with a budget takes practice. The more often a client prepares a budget and compares their actual spending to a budget, the better they will become at budgeting. The first few budgets are likely to be unrealistic and not very accurate. Over time, the client will become more comfortable with budgeting and more realistic with their spending, savings, and miscellaneous expenses.

The budgeting process consists of the following steps:
- Establish goals with the client, such as saving for retirement, education, or a lump-sum purchase (a second home, new car, or boat).
- Determine the client's income for a time period, which could be monthly or annually. Income is based on a client's past earnings and expected income for the time period that is being budgeted.
- Determine expenses, both fixed and variable, for the time period of the budget.
- Determine whether the net discretionary cash flow is positive or negative. If net discretionary cash flow is negative, expenses must be reduced or income needs to increase. If net discretionary cash flow is positive, no immediate action is necessary. However, there may be opportunities to further increase discretionary cash flow, which could reduce the time to achieve one or more goals.
- Present expenses as a percentage of income for the time period being presented. At this point, it is necessary to compare expenses as a percentage of income for previous budgets as well. Generally, the expenses as a percentage of income should be level or decreasing over time.

When developing a budget the planner should help their clients create a cash flow plan that follows the presentation of a Statement of Income and Expenses. The budget will identify spending by major categories and line item income and expenses within those categories. The major categories are:
- Income
- Savings
- Debt Payments
- Living Expenses
- Insurance
- Taxes

Income
Income includes all salary, wages, dividends, royalties, interest, and business income.

Savings
Savings include contributions to retirement accounts, education savings accounts, or any other accounts the client deems for a savings goal. As a general rule, clients should save at least 10-13 percent of their gross pay for retirement savings. This amount includes any employer match or contribution. Older clients will have to save a larger percent of their income. If clients have an education goal, clients should include an additional 3-6 percent of savings in their budget.

Debt Payments
Debt payments include a mortgage payment, car payments, student loans, boat loans, etc. Total debt payments should be ≤ 36 percent of gross pay. Housing costs, which is simply a client's mortgage payment, should be ≤ 28 percent of gross pay.

Living Expenses
Clients should budget 50 percent or less of their gross pay for living expenses. Living expenses include all discretionary expenses, plus non-discretionary expenses, and housing costs. Discretionary expenses include entertainment, vacations, clothing, cable television, etc. Non-discretionary expenses are food, utilities, phone, etc.

Example 4.8

Melissa and Mark have the following budget for vacation.

$$\text{Vacations} = \$2,000$$
$$\text{Total Inflows} = \$158,000$$
$$\$2,000/\$158,000 = 1.3\%$$

Therefore, 1.3 percent of their income is spent on vacations.

Insurance

The insurance category includes premiums for life, health, disability, home, auto, long term care, and personal liability. Premiums should be 5-9 percent of gross pay.

Taxes

Clients should budget 20-25 percent of their gross pay for federal, state, and local income taxes, and Social Security.

Presenting the percentage of income being allocated to each line item expense allows the planner and client to evaluate expense trends over time. Over time, with income increasing and controlled spending, expenses as a percentage of income should decrease.

Other alternatives to decrease spending include:

- Focus on 2-3 expenses and reduce them in the short term. Possibly remove a phone land line and just use a cell phone.
- Install a "smart" thermostat to better manage utility expenses.
- Make sure any auto loan is repaid before purchasing a new car.
- Avoid making emotional purchases, instead focus on long term goals.

Initially, an accurate budget is difficult to prepare and unanticipated expenses always seem to occur. Over time, budgeting will become easier and more accurate. As Dr. Dalton says, "Perfection is the enemy of excellence. Budgets don't need to be perfect, it just needs to get better. Eventually, budgeting will be done in a way that can be described as excellent."

Exhibit 4.4 | Budget for Upcoming Year

Mr. and Mrs. Zacker Budget for 20X2			
CASH INFLOWS		% OF INCOME	TARGET
Salary - Husband	$58,000	36.7	
Salary - Wife	$100,000	63.3	
Total Cash Inflows	$158,000	100.0	
CASH OUTFLOWS			
Savings			
Husband's 401(k) Plan	$5,000	3.2	
Wife's 401(k) Plan	$10,000	6.3	
IRA Contribution	$5,000	3.2	
Education Savings (529 Plan)	$8,000	5.1	
Total Savings	$28,000	17.7	13-19% (10-13% for retirement plus 3-6% for education)
Debt Payments			
Personal Residence (mortgage)	$35,000	22.2	Mortgage + HO Ins. + Property Taxes ≤ 28%
Auto - Husband	$7,000	4.4	
Student Loans	$2,500	1.6	
Total Debt Payments	$44,500	28.2	≤36%
Living Expenses			
Utilities	$3,500	2.2	
Gasoline for Autos	$3,000	1.9	
Lawn Service	$3,000	1.9	
Entertainment	$6,000	3.8	
Vacations	$4,000	2.5	
Church Donations	$2,000	1.3	
Food	$8,000	5.1	
Auto Maintenance	$2,500	1.6	
Telephone	$3,000	1.9	
Clothing	$6,000	3.8	
Total Living Expenses	$41,000	25.9	≤ 50% (living expenses plus housing debt = 48.2%)
Insurance Payments			
HO Personal Residence	$4,500	2.8	
Auto Premiums	$2,000	1.3	
Life Insurance Premiums	$1,000	0.6	
Personal Liability Umbrella Premium	$500	0.3	
Total Insurance Payments	$8,000	5.1	5-9%
Taxes			
Federal Income Taxes Withheld	$15,000	9.5	
State Income Taxes Withheld	$4,413	2.8	
Social Security Taxes	$12,087	7.7	
Property Tax Personal Residence	$4,000	2.5	
Total Taxes	$35,500	22.5	8-25%
Total Savings, Expenses and Taxes	$157,000	99.4	
NET DISCRETIONARY CASH FLOW	$1,000	0.6	

FINANCIAL STATEMENT ANALYSIS

Financial statements are designed to assist users in identifying key relationships and trends within the client's financial situation. Financial statement analysis is a critical part of the financial planning process, as the financial planner is measuring a client's progress towards attaining financial goals, assessing the client's ability to meet short-term obligations, and overall debt management. Analyzing a client's course(s) of action is an important part of several steps in the financial planning process.

Financial statement analysis is accomplished by conducting vertical analysis, horizontal analysis, and ratio analysis. Trends will help the planner identify if the client is moving in the right direction and is making adequate progress towards attaining financial goals. It also allows the planner to glean information that the client may not have communicated to the planner that is important to the overall financial plan and to the ability to meet future financial objectives.

≔ *Key Concepts*

1. Identify the purpose of financial statement analysis and the tools used in the comparative financial statement analysis.

2. Identify the purpose of ratio analysis.

Comparative Financial Statement Tools

Vertical analysis and horizontal analysis are two methods of evaluating financial statements over time. The two methods taken together can provide great insight into changes in a person's (or firm's) financial situation. These two methods are discussed below.

Vertical Analysis

Vertical analysis lists each line item on the income statement as a percentage of total income and presents each line item on the statement of financial position (balance sheet) as a percentage of total assets. The restated percentage is known as a common size income statement or balance sheet. Vertical analysis compares each line item using a common size analysis and strips away the absolute dollar size of the line item. The financial planner is then able to compare trends for each percentage over time. Using the Zacker's Statement of Financial Position for 20X1 (**Exhibit 4.1**) and 20X2 (**Exhibit 4.5**), the planner is able to prepare a vertical analysis of their balance sheet (**Exhibit 4.6**).

Exhibit 4.5 | Balance Sheet as of 12/31/20X2

Statement of Financial Position
Mr. and Mrs. Zacker
Balance Sheet as of 12/31/20X2

Assets			Liabilities and Net Worth			
Current Assets			**Current Liabilities**			
JT	Cash & Checking	$5,025	W	Credit Cards	$4,985	
JT	CD Maturing in 6 months	$25,125	H	Auto # 1	$4,985	
JT	Money Market	$51,000	W	Auto # 2	$5,700	
			JT	Personal Residence	$9,700	
Total Current Assets		**$81,150**	**Total Current Liabilities**			**$25,370**
Investment Assets			**Long-Term Liabilities**			
H	401(k) Plan	$30,090	H	Auto # 1	$12,600	
W	IRA	$49,900	W	Auto # 2	$14,450	
JT	Brokerage Account	$106,000	JT	Personal Residence	$438,750	
W	Value of Business Interests	$475,000				
W	Education Savings	$77,250	**Total Long-Term Liabilities**			**$465,800**
Total Invested Assets		**$738,240**				
			Total Liabilities			**$491,170**
Personal Use Assets						
JT	Personal Residence	$505,000	**Total Net Worth**			**$1,007,445**
JT	Furniture, Clothing	$125,025				
H	Auto # 1	$22,500				
W	Auto # 2	$26,700				
Total Personal Use Assets		**$679,225**				
Total Assets		**$1,498,615**	**Total Liabilities and Net Worth**			**$1,498,615**

H = Husband Owns
W = Wife Owns
JT = Jointly owned by husband and wife

Exhibit 4.6 | Balance Sheet Vertical Analysis Example

Mr. and Mrs. Zacker			
Current Assets	**12/31/20X1**	**12/31/20X2**	**Difference**
JT - Cash & Checking	0.33%	0.34%	+0.01%
JT - CD Maturing in 6 months	1.65%	1.68%	+0.03%
JT - Money Market	3.30%	3.40%	+0.10%
Total Current Assets	**5.28%**	**5.42%**	**+0.13%**
Investment Assets			
H - 401(k) Plan	1.98%	2.01%	+0.03%
W – IRA	3.30%	3.33%	+0.03%
JT - Brokerage Account	6.60%	7.07%	+0.47%
W - Value of Business Interests	33.00%	31.70%	-1.31%
W - Education Savings	4.95%	5.15%	+0.20%
Total Invested Assets	**49.83%**	**49.26%**	**-0.57%**
Personal Use Assets			
JT - Personal Residence	33.0%	33.7%	+0.69%
JT - Furniture, Clothing	8.25%	8.34%	+0.09%
H - Auto #1	1.65%	1.50%	-0.15%
W - Auto #2	1.99%	1.78%	-0.20%
Total Personal Use Assets	**44.89%**	**45.32%**	**+0.44%**
Total Assets	**100.00%**	**100.00%**	
Current Liabilities			
W - Credit Cards	0.33%	0.33%	-0.00%
H - Auto #1	0.33%	0.33%	-0.00%
W - Auto #2	0.40%	0.38%	-0.02%
JT - Personal Residence	0.66%	0.65%	-0.01%
Total Current Liabilities	**1.72%**	**1.69%**	**-0.02%**
Long-Term Liabilities			
H - Auto #1	0.92%	0.84%	-0.08%
W - Auto #2	1.12%	0.96%	-0.16%
JT - Personal Residence	29.70%	29.28%	-0.43%
Total Long-Term Liabilities	**31.74%**	**31.08%**	**-0.67%**
Total Liabilities	**33.46%**	**32.77%**	**-0.69%**
Total Net Worth	**66.54%**	**67.23%**	**+0.69%**

Exhibit 4.7 | Statement of Income and Expenses Vertical Analysis Example

Mr. and Mrs. Zacker		
CASH INFLOWS	For 20X2	Totals
Salary-Husband	36.71%	
Salary-Wife	63.29%	
Total Cash Inflows		100%
CASH OUTFLOWS		
Savings		
Husband's 401(k) Plan	3.16%	
Wife's 401(k) Plan	6.33%	
IRA Contribution	3.16%	
Education Savings (529 Plan)	5.06%	
Total Savings		17.71%
Available for Expenses		82.29%
Debt Payments		
Personal Residence (mortgage)	22.15%	
Auto-Husband	4.43%	
Student Loans	1.58%	
Total Debt Payments		28.16%
Living Expenses		
Utilities	2.22%	
Gasoline for Autos	1.90%	
Lawn Service	1.90%	
Entertainment	3.80%	
Vacations	2.53%	
Church Donations	1.27%	
Food	5.06%	
Auto Maintenance	1.58%	
Telephone	1.90%	
Clothing	3.80%	
Total Living Expenses		25.96%
Insurance Payments		
HO Personal Residence	2.85%	
Auto Premiums	1.27%	
Life Insurance Premiums	0.63%	
Personal Liability Umbrella Premium	0.32%	
Total Insurance Payments		5.07%
Taxes		
Federal Income Taxes Withheld	9.49%	
State Income Taxes Withheld	2.80%	
Social Security Taxes	7.70%	
Property Tax Personal Residence	2.53%	
Total Taxes		22.47%
Total Expenses and Taxes		81.66%
NET DISCRETIONARY CASH FLOW		0.63%

The vertical analysis for the Zackers (**Exhibit 4.6** and **Exhibit 4.7**) does not reveal any significant issues on the balance sheet or income statement. However, some important observations include a savings rate of 17.7 percent, debt payments of 28 percent and taxes of 22 percent.

The benefit of vertical analysis is to gain insight into significant changes from one year to another on a common size basis. For example, if the expense category entertainment was two percent one year and 10 percent the next year, as a percent of total income, then that trend would be concerning. The impact of changes can also be seen over time through vertical analysis. For example, if one of the recommendations is to save more, then that should be reflected in the vertical analysis in the year after implementation.

Horizontal Analysis

Horizontal analysis lists each item as a percentage of a base year and creates a trend over time. For example, on the income statement, income may be stated over a six-year period from 20X1 to 20X6, but is reflected as a percentage of 20X1 income. Expenses, taxes and savings are all stated as a percentage of a base year amount.

Example 4.9

Eric earned $100,000 in 20X1 and experienced salary increases each year for the next five years, such that his salary in 20X6 is $128,000.

Horizontal analysis of his income is as follows:

Year	20X1	20X2	20X3	20X4	20X5	20X6
Income	100%	105%	115%	125%	127%	128%

The horizontal analysis of income would indicate that Eric's income has increased each year and his income in 20X6 is 28% more than it was in 20X1. Horizontal analysis will be conducted for each line item on the income statement and balance sheet. This analysis provides the financial planner and client with a trend that identifies potential problems or demonstrates improved financial performance.

Consider an abbreviated horizontal analysis for Eric's income and golf expenses over the past five years.

Year	20X1	20X2	20X3	20X4	20X5	20X6
Income	100%	105%	115%	125%	127%	128%
Golf Expenses	100%	110%	120%	130%	140%	150%

Although Eric's income has increased 28% over the six-year period, his golf expenses have increased 50% over the same time period. In 20X6, his golf expenses were 150% of his golf expenses in 20X1. So, if Eric's golf expenses were $10,000 in 20X1, he paid $15,000 in golf expenses in 20X6. Considering that his income increased by $28,000 on a pre-tax basis, he has spent approximately 18% ($5,000 ÷ $28,000) of his additional income on this one expense item that increased $5,000 since 20X1 Horizontal analysis is able to help identify potentially positive or negative trends over time.

Ratio Analysis

Ratio analysis is the process of calculating key financial ratios for a client, comparing those metrics to industry benchmarks, and then evaluating possible deficiencies. Ratio analysis was introduced in Chapter 3 while discussing the financial statement analysis and the two step / three panel approach to evaluating a client's financial position. This section of Chapter 4 provides a more in-depth discussion of financial statement and ratio analysis. For the purpose of providing a thorough discussion of the benefits and application of ratio analysis, some overlap exists with topics covered in Chapter 3. Ratio analysis provides a historical perspective of the client's financial position and performance because the ratios are calculated based on historical financial statements. Ratio analysis is both an art and a science. The art facet requires the interpretation of the ratios that will form the basis for recommendations to the client. The science element requires the calculation of the financial ratios. When conducting ratio analysis, there is a need for a comparative analysis (benchmarks) to gain perspective about the client's ability to meet short and long-term obligations and goals.

Ratio analysis provides insight to underlying conditions that may not be apparent directly from reviewing the financial statements. This type of analysis expresses the relationship between selected items from the income statement and the balance sheet, and provides additional information for the financial planner to use in building the client's financial plan.

Limitations

Individual ratios generally have limited value without a comparison or a trend analysis. The ratio begins to take on meaning when it is used for comparison purposes over time to identify trends and when combined with information and insight from other ratios.

Ratios become more meaningful when compared to benchmarks. Benchmarks provide a rule of thumb for analyzing client status as it relates to industry standards. Note that the individual circumstances may cause any benchmark to be inappropriate for a given client. It is important that the financial planner recognize circumstances that may cause a benchmark to be inappropriate and to make adjustments accordingly.

The Bowdens case below, is used to demonstrate a financial statement analysis featuring ratios.

☑ Quick Quiz 4.5

1. Vertical analysis is a tool for financial statement analysis using a common size comparison of a statement's line items.
   a. True
   b. False

2. Ratio analysis is the process of calculating financial ratios that are compared to example benchmarks for meaningful interpretation of the client's actual financial status.
   a. True
   b. False

3. The emergency fund ratio measures how many times the client can satisfy their short-term liabilities.
   a. True
   b. False

True, True, False.

FINANCIAL STATEMENT ANALYSIS - THE BOWDENS

Brandon and Jill Bowden

Brandon (age 40) and Jill (age 43) are married with two children, Cole (age 9) and Owen (age 5). Brandon is a vice president with a health care company and Jill manages their family and household. Brandon's salary is $124,000 per year and he contributes three percent of his salary to a 401(k) plan while his employer matches $0.50 for every $1 contributed, up to three percent of his salary.

Bowden's Financial Goals
- Save for retirement
- Save for their children's college education
- Transfer all assets to their children at Brandon and Jill's death

Brandon and Jill Bowden's balance sheets for the beginning of this year and the end of the current year are below.

Exhibit 4.8 | Balance Sheet as of 12/31/20X1

Statement of Financial Position
Brandon and Jill Bowden
Balance Sheet as of 12/31/20X1

ASSETS			LIABILITIES AND NET WORTH			
Current Assets			**Current Liabilities** (current portion of long-term debt)			
JT Cash & Checking	$3,500		W Credit Cards	$20,000		
JT Money Market	$6,650		W Auto # 2	$4,588		
			JT Personal Residence	$3,812		
Total Current Assets		$10,150	**Total Current Liabilities**			$28,400
Investment Assets			**Long -Term Liabilities**			
H 401(k) Plan	$61,800		W Auto # 2	$16,176		
H Education Savings	$11,500		JT Personal Residence	$342,633		
H High Tech Stock[1]	$7,500					
Total Investment Assets		$80,800	**Total Long-Term Liabilities**			$358,809
Personal Use Assets			**Total Liabilities**			$387,209
JT Personal Residence[2]	$390,000					
H Furniture, Clothing	$95,000		**Total Net Worth**			$222,241
H Auto # 1	$9,000					
W Auto # 2[3]	$24,500					
Total Personal Use Assets		$518,500				
Total Assets		$609,450	**Total Liabilities and Net Worth**			$609,450

1. Brandon and Jill intend to use this investment for retirement savings.
2. The house was purchased on 1/1/20X1 for $375,000 with a loan for $350,000 financed over 30 years at 7%.
3. The car was purchased on 1/1/20X1 for $30,000 with $5,000 down, financed over 5 years at 8%.

H = Husband Owns
W = Wife Owns
JT = Jointly owned by husband and wife

Loan Calculation Explanation to Exhibit 4.8

Auto Loan Calculation*			Home Loan Calculation*		
(Present Value) PV	=	$25,000	(Present Value) PV	=	$350,000
(Term) N	=	60	(Term) N	=	360
(Interest Rate) i	=	$\frac{8\%}{12} = 0.667$	(Interest Rate) i	=	$\frac{7\%}{12} = 0.583$
(Future Value) FV	=	0	(Future Value) FV	=	0
(Payment) PMT	=	$506.91	(Payment) PMT	=	$2,328.56
12/31/20X1 Principal Balance	=	$20,764	12/31/20X1 Principal Balance	=	$346,444
12/31/20X2 Principal Balance	=	$16,176 (L-T Liability)	12/31/20X2 Principal Balance	=	$342,632 (L-T Liability)
		$4,588 (Current Liability)			$3,812 (Current Liability)

Ordinary Annuity - use end key

Exhibit 4.9 | Balance Sheet as of 12/31/20X2

Statement of Financial Position
Brandon and Jill Bowden
Balance Sheet as of 12/31/20X2

ASSETS				LIABILITIES AND NET WORTH			
Current Assets				**Current Liabilities**			
JT	Cash & Checking	$3,000		W	Credit Cards	$25,000	
JT	Money Market	$5,000		W	Auto # 2	$4,968	
				JT	Personal Residence	$4,088	
Total Current Assets			$8,000	**Total Current Liabilities**			$34,056
Investment Assets				**Long -Term Liabilities**			
H	401(k) Plan	$75,000		W	Auto # 2	$11,208	
H	Education Savings	$15,000		JT	Personal Residence	$338,544	
H	High Tech Stock[1]	$5,000					
Total Investment Assets			$95,000	**Total Long-Term Liabilities**			$349,752
Personal Use Assets				**Total Liabilities**			$383,808
JT	Personal Residence[2]	$400,000					
H	Furniture, Clothing	$100,000		**Total Net Worth**			$249,192
H	Auto # 1	$8,000					
W	Auto # 2	$22,000					
Total Personal Use Assets			$530,000				
Total Assets			**$633,000**	**Total Liabilities and Net Worth**			**$633,000**

1. Brandon and Jill intend to use this investment for retirement savings.
2. The house was purchased on 1/1/20X1 for $375,000 with a loan for $350,000 financed over 30 years at 7%.
3. The car was purchased on 1/1/20X1 for $30,000 with $5,000 down, financed over 5 years at 8%.

H = Husband Owns
W = Wife Owns
JT = Jointly owned by husband and wife

Loan Calculation Explanation to Exhibit 4.9

Auto Loan Calculation*			Home Loan Calculation*		
(Present Value) PV	=	$25,000	(Present Value) PV	=	$350,000
(Term) N	=	60	(Term) N	=	360
(Interest Rate) i	=	$\frac{8\%}{12}$ = 0.667	(Interest Rate) i	=	$\frac{7\%}{12}$ = 0.583
(Future Value) FV	=	0	(Future Value) FV	=	0
(Payment) PMT	=	$506.91	(Payment) PMT	=	$2,328.56
12/31/20X2 Principal Balance	=	$16,176	12/31/20X2 Principal Balance	=	$342,632
12/31/20X3 Principal Balance	=	$11,208 (L-T Liability)	12/31/20X3 Principal Balance	=	$338,544 (L-T Liability)
		$4,968 (Current Liability)			$4,088 (Current Liability)

Ordinary annuity - use end key.

Exhibit 4.10 | Statement of Income and Expenses

Mr. and Mrs. Bowden Statement of Income and Expenses for 12/31/20X2 and Expected (Approximate) For 12/31/20X3		
CASH INFLOWS		Totals
Brandon's Salary	$124,000	
Total Cash Inflows		**$124,000**
CASH OUTFLOWS		
Savings		
Brandon's 401(k) Plan	$3,720	
Education Savings (529 Plan)	$2,000	
Total Savings		**$5,720**
Debt Payments		
Personal Residence (mortgage)	$27,943	
Jill's Auto	$6,083	
Credit Cards[1]	$7,000	
Total Debt Payments		**$41,026**
Living Expenses		
Utilities	$5,000	
Gasoline for Autos	$4,000	
Lawn Service	$1,500	
Entertainment	$3,000	
Vacations	$2,500	
Church Donations	$1,000	
Food	$6,000	
Auto Maintenance	$1,000	
Telephone	$2,660	
Clothing	$3,000	
Total Living Expenses		**$29,660**
Insurance Payments		
HO Personal Residence	$4,500	
Auto Premiums	$2,000	
Life Insurance Premiums	$1,000	
Total Insurance Payments		**$7,500**
Taxes		
Federal Income Taxes Withheld	$24,800	
State Income Taxes Withheld	$5,475	
Social Security Taxes	$9,145	
Property Tax Personal Residence	$3,500	
Total Taxes		**$42,920**
Total Savings, Expenses and Taxes		**$126,826**
NET DISCRETIONARY CASH FLOW		**($2,826)**

1. The Bowdens make the minimum monthly payments on some of their credit cards.

Categories of Financial Ratios

Financial statement ratios are classified according to the analysis and insight provided by calculating the ratio. Financial statement ratios are broken down into the following categories:

- **Liquidity Ratios** – Measures the amount of cash and cash equivalents relative to short-term liabilities.
- **Debt Ratios** – Measures how well the client is managing their overall debt structure.
- **Ratios for Financial Security Goals** – Measures the client's progress towards achieving long-term financial security goals.
- **Performance Ratios** – Measures the return a client is generating on assets.

The remaining portion of this chapter discusses the ratios within each category, how the ratio is calculated, associated ratio benchmarks, and how to interpret and apply meaning to each ratio.

Liquidity Ratios

Liquidity ratios provide the financial planner insight into the client's ability to meet short-term obligations with current assets. Liquidity ratios include the emergency fund and current ratio.

Emergency Fund Ratio

The **emergency fund ratio** measures the number of months of non-discretionary expenses the client has in the form of cash and cash equivalents or current assets.

The formula for the emergency fund is:

$$\text{Emergency Fund} = \frac{\textbf{Cash and Cash Equivalents}}{\textbf{Monthly Non-discretionary Cash Flows}}$$

Current assets are represented by cash and cash equivalents on the balance sheet.

Non-discretionary cash flows are those expenses that exist even if a job or other income source is lost. Non-discretionary cash flows are typically fixed expenses. Examples of non-discretionary expenses include:

- All debt payments (mortgage, car loan, student loan, boat loan, credit cards)
- Utilities
- Insurance premiums
- Property taxes
- Food

Travel, entertainment, and payroll taxes are examples of expenses that would be minimized or eliminated if a job or other income source was lost.

The benchmark for the emergency fund is three to six months and is important to provide for the following risks:
- Job loss
- Elimination period on a disability policy
- Unexpected expenses

Job Loss

The emergency fund can be used to pay monthly non-discretionary expenses in the event of job loss. Often times, it can take several months or longer to find a job, especially during periods of a recession like the Great Recession experienced during 2008 – 2012 and also during periods of high unemployment.

For families with a single wage earner, the emergency fund ratio should be on the high end of the benchmark, such as five to six months (or higher). For a two wage earner family, the client can be on the low end of the benchmark, such as three months. With a two wage earner family, if one spouse is still working, a three month emergency fund can pay 50 percent of the monthly non-discretionary expenses, while the working spouse can pay the other 50 percent of the monthly non-discretionary expenses. This assumes, of course, that the spouse that is still employed earns enough to pay 50 percent of the monthly non-discretionary expenses. The planner can help guide the client to an appropriate amount of emergency fund based on individual circumstances.

Elimination Period on a Disability Policy

It is important that the emergency fund is able to last at least as long as the elimination period of any disability policy. A disability policy is designed to provide income replacement if the insured is unable to work because of sickness or accident. The elimination period of a disability policy is the amount of time the insured must wait before collecting benefits under the policy. If the elimination period is 180 days, the client must wait six months before collecting benefits under the policy. If the client is unable to work for six months, the emergency fund should cover expenses for at least six months to satisfy the elimination period of the disability policy.

Unexpected Expenses

A comprehensive financial plan should also account for unexpected events. Often, it is the unanticipated risk that can cause the greatest problems. A financial plan that accounts for the unexpected will better position a client to achieve their financial goals. An emergency fund can help mitigate the impact of unexpected expenses. Examples of unexpected expenses that a planner should anticipate include:
- Large deductibles for a homeowners' insurance policy. Many earthquake and flood policies have the insured paying a percentage of the total loss as a deductible.
- Large deductibles for private health insurance. To help reduce the cost of health insurance, some families purchase high deductible health insurance policies ($5,000 or more deductible per person).
- House repairs or additions for dependent family members that may move into the client's home.
- Large auto repairs, household repairs, etc. Many relatively expensive home appliances need to be replaced after 10 to 15 years.

Mitigating Circumstances

Although the emergency fund is important, the planner should keep the emergency fund in perspective when evaluating the client's financial position. Many competing needs may arise, and the client will have limited financial resources to satisfy all of the needs. The financial planner and client must prioritize which competing needs to address first and which needs to postpone until a later time. If the client has access to a home equity line of credit or loan provisions as part of a 401(k) plan or other qualified retirement plan, contributing to the emergency fund may be a lower priority than purchasing health insurance.

Brandon and Jill Bowden's Emergency Fund

The Bowden's monthly non-discretionary expenses (cash outflows) from the Income Statement are:

Property Tax on Personal Residence	$3,500
Debt Payments (Personal residence, auto, credit cards)	$41,026
Utilities	$5,000
Gasoline for Autos	$4,000
Church Donations	$1,000
Food	$6,000
Auto Maintenance	$1,000
Telephone	$2,660
Insurance Premiums	$7,500
	$71,686

$$\text{Emergency Fund } = \frac{\text{Cash and Cash Equivalents}}{\text{Monthly Non-discretionary Cash Flows}}$$

$$\text{Emergency Fund } = \frac{\$10,150}{(\$71,686 \div 12)} = \frac{\$10,150}{\$5,974} = 1.70 \text{ months (20X1)}$$

$$\text{Emergency Fund } = \frac{\$8,000}{(\$71,686 \div 12)} = \frac{\$8,000}{\$5,974} = 1.34 \text{ months (20X2)}$$

The Bowden's have an emergency fund of less than two months. This ratio highlights a weakness that requires planning to overcome in order to have an emergency fund of three to six months. As a one-income family, the Bowden's should have a 6-month emergency fund. However, that would require them to increase their cash and cash equivalents from $8,000 to $35,844 (6 x $5,974 in monthly non-discretionary expenses). Initially a 3-month emergency fund may be the most appropriate recommendation because there may be other sources of emergency funding, such as a home equity line of credit or borrowing provisions from Brandon's 401(k) plan. In addition, it is likely there will be other financial weaknesses the financial planner must help Brandon and Jill overcome, so increasing the emergency fund to three months in the short term will be sufficient. As the financial planner works with Brandon and Jill in the coming years, an evaluation can be made as to when increasing their emergency fund to six months is a more appropriate recommendation.

Current Ratio

The **current ratio** measures how many times the client can satisfy their short-term liabilities with cash and cash equivalents. The current ratio is:

$$\text{Current Ratio} = \frac{\text{Cash \& Cash Equivalents}}{\text{Current Liabilities}}$$

Current assets represent cash and cash equivalents on the balance sheet. Current liabilities represent short-term liabilities on the balance sheet.

For the current ratio, the industry benchmark is 1.0 – 2.0, with the higher the ratio the better. It is also helpful if the financial planner tracks the current ratio over a period of years to determine the trend. If the ratio becomes too large, it could signify that the client needs to reallocate some current assets to more growth oriented investment assets. If the ratio is decreasing, it will likely lead to a lower emergency fund. If the planner addresses the emergency fund first, it will likely lead to an improved current ratio.

Brandon and Jill Bowden's Current Ratio

The current ratio is:

$$\text{Current Ratio} = \frac{\text{Cash \& Cash Equivalents}}{\text{Current Liabilities}} = \frac{\$10,150}{\$28,400} = 0.36 \ (20X1)$$

$$\text{Current Ratio} = \frac{\text{Cash \& Cash Equivalents}}{\text{Current Liabilities}} = \frac{\$8,000}{\$34,056} = 0.23 \ (20X2)$$

The Bowden's have approximately 20 percent (for 20X2) of their current liabilities in the form of current assets. As the Bowden's begin to overcome their emergency fund deficiency, the current ratio will improve at the same time. For example, if the Bowden's increase their emergency fund to three months, they will have $17,922 (3 x $5,974 in monthly non-discretionary expense) in cash and cash equivalents. Assuming their current liabilities do not change, the new current ratio would be 0.53 ($17,922 ÷ $34,056). By increasing the Bowden's emergency fund from 1.34 to 3.0 months, the current ratio would more than double from 0.23 to 0.53.

Debt Ratios

The debt management ratios provide insight into how well the client is managing debt (too much or the right amount) and the quality of that debt.

Housing Ratio1 (Basic)

Housing ratio 1 (HR1) was established by the banking industry to determine if the relationship between the amount of income and the amount of housing debt that a client is carrying is appropriate and affordable. If a borrower meets housing ratio 1, he likely will qualify for a conventional mortgage loan at a favorable rate.

The formula for housing ratio 1 is:

$$\text{Housing Ratio 1} = \frac{\text{Housing Costs}}{\text{Gross Pay}} \leq 28\%$$

Housing Costs = PITI

P = Principal
I = Interest
T = Taxes (property taxes on home)
I = Insurance (home)
Gross Income = Gross pay (before taxes)

Note: The PITI and gross income can be stated on a monthly or annual basis. The PITI and gross income should be stated on the same terms, either both on a monthly basis or both an annual basis.

Brandon and Jill Bowden's Housing Ratio 1
The Bowden's housing costs (PITI) from the Income Statement are:

Principal and Interest on Personal Residence	$27,943
Property Taxes – Personal Residence	$3,500
Insurance HO Personal Residence	$4,500
	$35,943
Total monthly housing costs ($35,943 ÷ 12)	$2,995.25

Their monthly gross pay is:

Total monthly gross pay (Brandon's Salary $124,000 ÷ 12)	$10,333

$$\text{Housing Ratio 1} = \frac{\text{Housing Costs}}{\text{Gross Pay}} \leq 28\%$$

$$\text{Housing Ratio 1} = \frac{\$2,995.25}{\$10,333} = 28.9\%$$

The Bowden's housing ratio 1 is 28.9 percent, which is slightly above the industry benchmark of 28 percent. The difference between their actual ratio and the benchmark represents about $1,224 per year. The actual ratio of 28.9 percent is near the benchmark of 28 percent, so the Bowdens may be able to wait one or two years and allow for Brandon's salary increases to bring the ratio down to the benchmark.

For example, if Brandon receives a five percent raise each year for the next two years, the Bowden's housing ratio 1 would be:

$$\text{Next Year} = \frac{\$2,995.25}{\$10,333 \times 1.05} = 27.6\%$$

$$\text{Next 2 Years} = \frac{\$2,995.25}{\$10,333 \times 1.05 \times 1.05} = 26.3\%$$

This example illustrates how forecasted financial statements provide the financial planner with insight as to how financial ratios will be impacted by salary adjustments, inflation, or the implementation of planning recommendations. Care must be exercised, however, when assuming the ratio will "fix itself" based on future salary adjustments. The client may not receive the salary adjustment, the salary adjustment may or may not be as much as forecasted, or increasing expenses may offset the increased salary. In this example, not only would the financial planner be concerned about Brandon actually receiving the salary adjustment, but would also be concerned that the property taxes or insurance premiums might increase and offset all or part of the increased salary. In this situation, HR1 might remain above 28 percent. It is important to monitor the ratio and consider other alternatives, such as decreasing the insurance premium or refinancing the mortgage.

Housing Ratio 2 (Broad)

Housing ratio 2 (HR2) is also referred to as HR1 plus all other debt. This ratio was established by the banking industry to determine if the total amount of debt that a client is carrying is appropriate for their given level of income. If HR2 is met, the borrower will likely qualify for a conventional loan at a favorable rate.

The formula for HR2 is:

$$\text{Housing Ratio 2} = \frac{\text{Housing Costs + Other Debt Payments}}{\text{Gross Pay}} \leq 36\%$$

Housing Costs = PITI

P = Principal
I = Interest
T = Taxes (property taxes on home)
I = Insurance (home)
Gross Income = Gross pay before taxes

Other debt payments include:
- Car loan payments
- Boat loan payments
- Student loan payments
- Credit cards payments
- Principal and interest on vacation or second homes
- Any other monthly recurring debt

Recurring debt payments do not include utilities, car insurance, property insurance on a second home, or property taxes on a second home.

Note: It is important that PITI, all other debt payments, and gross income are stated on the same terms, either all on a monthly basis or all on an annual basis.

Brandon and Jill Bowden's Housing Ratio 2

The Bowden's housing costs (PITI) and other recurring debt from the Income Statement are:

Principal and Interest on Personal Residence	$27,943
Property Taxes – Personal Residence	$3,500
Insurance HO Personal Residence	$4,500
Jill's Auto	$6,083
Credit Cards	$7,000
	$49,026
Total monthly PITI plus other debt payments ($49,026 ÷ 12)	$4,086

Their monthly gross pay is:

Total monthly gross pay (Brandon's Salary $124,000 ÷ 12)	$10,333

$$\text{Housing Ratio 2} = \frac{\text{Housing Costs + Other Debt Payments}}{\text{Gross Pay}} \leq 36\%$$

$$\text{Housing Ratio 2} = \frac{\$4,086}{10,333} = 39.5\%$$

The Bowden's HR2 of 39.5 percent exceeds the industry benchmark of 36 percent. Since the HR1 of 28.9 percent is so close to the industry benchmark of 28 percent, the primary issue with HR2 is related to all other recurring debt. The financial planner should make recommendations to reduce other debt payments by either using assets on the balance sheet to retire debt or by increasing monthly debt payments. While there may be opportunity to lower the interest rate on the auto loan, the more important debt to reduce is the credit card debt as it almost always carries an exorbitant rate of interest.

Debt-to-Total Assets Ratio

The **debt-to-total assets ratio** indicates the percentage of assets that is owned by creditors. The lower this ratio the better, as it indicates that the assets owned have a low amount of debt owed.

To calculate the debt-to-total assets ratio:

$$\text{Debt-to-Total Assets Ratio} = \frac{\text{Total Debt}}{\text{Total Assets}} = \text{Benchmark Depends on Client Age}$$

Brandon and Jill Bowden's Debt-t- Total Assets Ratio

As of 12/31/20X1:

$$\text{Debt-to-Total Assets Ratio} = \frac{\$387,209}{\$609,450} = 0.6353$$

As of 12/31/20X2:

$$\text{Debt-to-Total Assets Ratio} = \frac{\$383,808}{\$633,000} = 0.6063$$

The total debt-to-total assets ratio has improved for the Bowdens over the past year. The financial planner should continue monitoring the debt-to-total asset ratio trend which should continue decreasing. As HR2 decreases from retiring all other recurring debt, the debt-to-total assets ratio will continue to improve.

Quality of Debt

The quality of debt assessment is based on the relationship between the term of the debt and the useful life of the asset. The quality of debt can be classified into three categories: good, reasonable, and bad debt. Any time the useful life of the asset far exceeds the term of the debt, the debt is considered good debt. Examples of good debt include a 3-year car loan, a 15-year home mortgage, or student loan debt. Chapter 8 discusses the positive correlation between education and earnings. Generally, higher education leads to higher paying jobs. As a result, student debt is generally classified as good debt. However, student debt and education does not always lead to higher paying jobs. It is important for students to consider job opportunities when they are incurring debt for education.

Reasonable debt includes obligations where the useful life of the asset equals the term of the debt. Examples of reasonable debt include a 5-year car loan or a 30-year mortgage. Bad debt implies that the term of the debt far exceeds the useful life of the asset. For example, if a client charges a two-week summer vacation on a credit card, then makes the minimum payments for the next 20 years, the term of the debt far exceeds the two-week useful life of the vacation. When an assessment as to the quality of the debt has been made, the financial planner can develop recommendations for the client to implement (such as retiring bad debt).

> ### Quick Quiz 4.6
>
> 1. The housing ratio 1 industry benchmark is less than or equal to 28 percent.
>   a. True
>   b. False
>
> 2. The savings rate calculation includes reinvestments and the employer match.
>   a. True
>   b. False
>
> 3. The quality of debt assessment is based on the comparison of the term of the debt on an asset and the useful life of the asset.
>   a. True
>   b. False
>
> True, False, True.

When working with a client who has bad debt, such as credit card or consumer debt, the planner should develop a plan to help the client retire the debt as soon as possible. Consider a client with $15,000 in credit card debt incurring interest at a rate of 19 percent. The initial minimum payment may be $500, but as each month passes, the minimum payment will continue to decline. By simply making the minimum payment, it can take between 16 to 20+ years to retire this debt. Instead, the client should at least continue to make a level payment of $500 each month and will be able to retire the debt in less than five years. A better alternative to retiring bad debt includes using assets on the balance sheet to pay down debt. Very few assets will have an expected rate of return that exceeds the rate of interest charged on credit cards. It is the financial planner's responsibility to evaluate the appropriate mix of using assets to pay down debt or retiring the debt within a reasonable amount of time by making monthly payments.

An assessment of the quality of Brandon and Jill's debt reveals that their home is financed for 30 years and the car is financed for five years. The term of the debt on the house and car match the useful life of both assets, so those debt items are considered reasonable debt. However, according to the Statement of Income and Expenses, the Bowden's are making the minimum monthly payment on their credit cards. Credit card debt is clearly bad debt and should be retired as soon as possible.

In the event a financial planner discovers that the client is making minimum payments on credit card debt, it would seem reasonable to recalculate HR2 using a payment more representative of a reasonable term (e.g., 36 months). Credit card minimum payments may require a payback period of 16 to 20+ years. If the credit card debt payment is understated in HR2, the ratio may indicate everything is below the benchmark when really this is a distortion.

For example, three alternatives for paying off a balance of $2,000 on credit cards charging 20 percent interest are:

Alternative	Balance	Monthly Payment	Years	Number of Payments	Total Paid Back
A	$2,000	$34.78	16	192	$6,677.76
B	$2,000	$52.99	5	60	$3,179.26
C	$2,000	$74.32	3	36	$2,675.78

It would seem prudent that if the client were actually paying under alternative A, the planner would recalculate HR2 using the payment under alternative C.

Net Worth-to-Total Assets Ratio

$$\text{Net Worth-to-Total Assets Ratio} = \frac{\text{Net Worth}}{\text{Total Assets}} = \text{Benchmark Depends on Client Age}$$

The **net worth-to-total assets ratio** is the compliment of the debt-to-assets ratio described above. These two should add up to one. This ratio provides the planner with the percentage of total assets owned or paid for by the client. It is not surprising that this would be 20 percent for young people and up to 90 to 100 percent for retirement-age clients. This ratio once again is best observed over time. Note that net worth increases as asset values increase (home and investment), as savings increase, and with the payoff of liabilities.

Brandon and Jill Bowden's Net Worth-to-Total Assets Ratio

$$\text{Net Worth-to-Total Assets Ratio} = \frac{\text{Net Worth}}{\text{Total Assets}} = \frac{\$249,192}{\$633,000} = 39.37\% \ (20X2)$$

While Bowden's net worth-to-total assets ratio of 39.37 percent may appear low, it will improve as their assets increase.

In addition, the ratio can be impacted by the choices of the individual or family. For example, the purchase of a larger house would increase assets and correspondingly liabilities without necessarily changing net worth. This change would decrease the ratio. A smaller house would decrease assets and likely increase the ratio.

Ratios for Financial Security Goals

Ratios for financial security goals provide the planner with insight about the progress (adequate or not) that the client is making towards their long-term goals. For example, ratios can answer questions such as: Is the client earning an appropriate rate of return on retirement investments? Is the client saving an appropriate amount? How much has the client accumulated towards a goal based on age?

Savings Rate

The **savings rate** measures the percentage of income a client is saving towards a retirement goal. If a client begins saving for retirement between ages 25 to 35, there is a need to save about 10 to 13 percent of annual gross income. However, if a client does not begin saving at an early age, then a greater percentage of annual income must be saved to overcome the lost years of contributions and compound earnings.

Age Beginning Regular and Recurring Savings*	Savings (as percent of gross pay) Rate Required to Create Appropriate Capital*
25 - 35	10 - 13%
35 - 45	13 - 20%
45 - 55	20 - 40%**

*Assumes appropriate asset allocation for reasonable-risk investor through accumulation years; also assumes normal raises and an 80 percent wage replacement ratio at Social Security normal retirement age and includes Social Security retirement benefits.

**At age 55 the person will have to delay retirement until age 70.

The formula for the savings rate is:

$$\text{Savings Rate} = \frac{\text{Savings} + \text{Employer Match}}{\text{Gross Pay}} = \text{Benchmark Depends on Client Goals}$$

Note: The savings rate includes any employee and employer contributions.

Example 4.10

Teddy's salary at United Technologies Industries is $100,000 per year. He contributes 8% of his compensation to his 401(k) plan and his employer matches his contributions dollar for dollar, up to 4% of his compensation. His total savings rate is:

$$\text{Savings Rate} = \frac{\text{Employee Contributions} + \text{Employer Contributions}}{\text{Gross Pay}}$$

$$\text{Savings Rate} = \frac{(\$100,000 \times 0.08) + (\$100,000 \times 0.04)}{\$100,000}$$

$$\text{Savings Rate} = \frac{\$8,000 + \$4,000}{\$100,000} = 0.12 \text{ or } 12\%$$

When calculating the savings rate for a married couple, combine both their retirement savings amounts and combine their gross incomes.

Example 4.11

Tom and Gerri are married. Tom has a salary of $45,000 and Gerri has a salary of $75,000. Tom's employer regularly contributes $2,500 to his profit sharing plan. Gerri does not participate in her employer's retirement plan, but contributes $5,000 per year to a Roth IRA. Tom and Gerri's savings rate is:

$$\text{Savings Rate} = \frac{\text{Employee Contributions} + \text{Employer Contributions}}{\text{Gross Pay}}$$

$$\text{Savings Rate} = \frac{(\$2,500 + \$5,000)}{(\$45,000 + \$75,000)}$$

$$\text{Savings Rate} = \frac{\$7,500}{\$120,000} = 0.0625 \text{ or } 6.25\%$$

Brandon and Jill Bowden's Savings Rate

Recall that Brandon contributes three percent of his compensation to his 401(k) plan and that his employer matches $0.50 for each $1 contributed, up to a total employer match of three percent of his compensation.

Brandon's contribution to his 401(k) plan is 0.03 x $124,000 = $3,720
Brandon's employer match is 0.015 x $124,000 = $1,860

Brandon and Jill are also saving for education expenses in a 529 plan.

$$\text{Savings Rate} = \frac{\text{Employee Contributions} + \text{Employer Contribution} + \text{529 Savings}}{\text{Gross Pay}}$$

$$\text{Savings Rate} = \frac{(\$3,720 + \$1,860) + \$2,000 \text{ (education savings)}}{\$124,000}$$

$$\text{Savings Rate} = \frac{\$7,580}{\$124,000} = 0.0611 \text{ or } 6.11\%$$

The Bowden's savings rate of 6.11 percent is well below the industry benchmark of 10 to 13 percent. Recall that the 10 to 13 percent benchmark is to meet a retirement goal only. Their retirement-only savings rate is 4.5 percent [($3,720 + $1,860) ÷ $124,000]. If Brandon increases his 401(k) plan deferral to six percent, his employer will match an additional three percent, bringing Brandon's total savings rate to 10.61 percent (6% + 3% + 1.61% education savings). A 10.61 percent savings rate would be a significant improvement over his current total savings rate of 6.11 percent. The additional savings required by Brandon would only be another three percent of his compensation or $3,720 on a pre-tax basis. On an after tax basis, it would be closer to $3,000. Although the Bowdens have a negative discretionary cash flow of $2,826, this will turn positive once the credit card debt is retired. Once the credit card debt is retired, the Bowdens will have a positive discretionary cash flow of $4,174 ($7,000 - $2,826), which is more than enough to increase Brandon's 401(k) plan deferral by another three percent.

Investment Assets-to-Gross Pay

Investment assets-to-gross pay ratio measures progress towards a client's saving goal, based on the client's age and income. The benchmark (as shown in the following table) is a useful metric because it provides insight as to: (1) whether the client has saved enough towards the retirement goal and (2) how much the client needs in retirement assets to generate a certain level of income at retirement.

Age	Investment Assets as a Ratio to Gross Pay Needed at Varying Ages
25	0.20 : 1
30	0.6 - 0.8 : 1
35	1.6 - 1.8 : 1
45	3 - 4 : 1
55	8 - 10 : 1
65	16 - 20 : 1

The benchmark considers income between $50,000 and $250,000 and inflation at approximately two to three percent. It also considers a balanced investment portfolio of 60/40 (equities to bonds) returning five percent over inflation, a savings rate of 10 to 13 percent of gross pay, and a wage replacement ratio of 80 percent of gross pay.

This ratio can answer the question, "For his age, has the client saved enough towards retirement?"

Example 4.12

Veronica, age 45 with an annual salary of $80,000, has saved $250,000 in her retirement accounts. Veronica should have at least $80,000 x 3 = $240,000 towards her retirement goal. Based on the benchmark, Veronica is on track in terms of accumulated savings for her age.

How much does the client need in retirement assets to generate a certain level of income?

Example 4.13

Archie, age 50, is looking to retire at age 65, with about $100,000 per year in retirement income. Archie should accumulate between $1.6m and $2.0m in retirement savings to generate $100,000 per year in retirement income. This accumulation is based on the 16 to 20 times benchmark at age 65.

Brandon and Jill Bowden's Investment Assets-to-Gross Pay Ratio

The ratio for Brandon (age 40) and Jill (age 43) is based on their age. They should have approximately three times their gross pay in retirement savings using this calculation:

Savings Amount = Salary x Benchmark
Savings Amount = $124,000 x 3
Benchmark Amount of Investment Assets = $372,000

The most current actual retirement savings for the Bowden's is:

Brandon's 401(k) Plan (20X2)	$75,000
High Tech Stock	$5,000
Cash and Cash Equivalents	$8,000
Total	$88,000

$$\text{Actual Ratio} = \frac{\text{Investment Assets} + \text{Cash \& Cash Equivalents}}{\text{Gross Pay}} = \frac{\$88,000}{\$124,000} = 0.71{:}1$$

Their total retirement savings is $88,000, which is well below what is needed based on the benchmark of $372,000. This is a difficult deficiency to overcome in the short term. However, the Bowdens are young enough and have another 20+ years remaining to work and increase their retirement savings. The first step is to increase Brandon's saving ratio from 4.5 percent to nine percent. The financial planner should also recommend the Bowdens consider additional savings opportunities once some of the bad debt is retired. The Bowden's should also evaluate the feasibility of Jill taking on a part-time or full-time job to help overcome the shortfall in savings. Education savings is not included in this calculation as it is targeted exclusively at retirement asset accumulation.

Performance Ratios

Performance ratios provide the planner with information regarding the return the client is earning on assets, net worth, and investments. This section of the chapter provides the appropriate ratios and formulas to calculate these ratios. However, using a financial calculator will provide the most accurate, compounded rate of return (see Chapter 7).

Return on Investments (ROI)

Return on investments (ROI) ratio is a critical performance ratio, as it measures the compounded rate of return on a client's investments. If the client's ROI is too low over a number of years, it may result in the client not having sufficient capital to retire or pay for education.

$$\textbf{Return on Investments} = \frac{I_1 - (I_0 + \text{Savings})}{I_0}$$

I_0	=	Beginning Investments
I_1	=	Ending Investments
S	=	Savings (include employer match)

Beginning investment assets are the investment assets typically from the preceding year balance sheet, and ending investment assets are the investment assets on the balance sheet at the end of the current year. Savings includes any amount contributed to a retirement plan by the employee and employer. In addition, savings includes contributions to an education savings account.

An appropriate benchmark for return on investments depends on the time horizon and risk tolerance of the client. Generally, a client with a long-term time horizon, such as 10 years or more, should have a portfolio more heavily weighted towards equities. A client with a long-term time horizon is expected to have a return on equity of eight to ten percent per year. A client with a shorter time horizon would have a portfolio with a higher weighting of bonds and a return on equity of six to eight percent per year. These concepts will be discussed more in the investments chapter (see Chapter 9).

Brandon and Jill Bowden's Return on Investment Ratio

$$\text{ROI} = \frac{\$95,000 - (\$80,800 + \$5,720 + \$1,860)}{\$80,800} = \frac{\$6,620}{\$80,800} = 0.0819 \text{ or } 8.19\%$$

Based on the age of the Bowdens, a ROI on retirement savings of eight to ten percent is expected, so they are within the ROI benchmark. However, the financial planner should review their High Tech Stock, as their portfolio does not appear to be well diversified and the High Tech Stock lost 33 percent of its value last year.

Return on Assets (ROA)

The **return on assets ratio** provides the planner with insight into the general growth rate of a client's assets.

$$\textbf{Return on Assets} = \frac{A_1 - (A_0 + S)}{A_0}$$

A_0	=	Beginning Assets
A_1	=	Ending Assets
S	=	Savings (include employer match)

Beginning total assets are the total assets typically from the preceding year balance sheet, and ending total assets are the total assets on the balance sheet at the end of the current year.

This measure of return is a blended growth rate of all assets a client owns because it considers returns on low yielding assets like savings and checking accounts, personal residence and auto (an asset declining in value), along with higher returning assets like retirement savings, stocks, and bonds. It is reasonable to expect the return on assets to be low, typically between two to four percent annually. The financial planner should monitor this return over time as it will provide insight into the client's mix of assets (cash and cash equivalents versus investment assets versus personal use assets). If the rate of return on assets begins to trend lower, or below three percent, it may indicate too many low returning assets like personal use assets or cash and cash equivalents.

Brandon and Jill Bowden's Return on Assets

$$\text{Return on Assets} = \frac{\$633,000 - (\$609,450 + \$5,720 + \$1,860)}{\$609,450} = \frac{\$15,970}{\$609,450} = 2.62\%$$

A return on assets of 2.62 percent is somewhat low in comparison to the typical two to four percent annual return expected on total assets. This return includes cash and cash equivalents that earn less than one percent and personal use assets (which include a house that may or may not increase in value), personal autos (that decline in value) and other personal use assets (such as furniture and clothing which do not increase in value each year). The financial planner should review the client's assets and recommend changes to increase the return.

Return on Net Worth (RONW)

The **return on net worth ratio** provides the planner with insight into the average growth rate on net worth.

$$\text{Return on Net Worth} = \frac{NW_1 - (NW_0 + S)}{NW_0}$$

NW_0	=	Beginning Net Worth
NW_1	=	Ending Net Worth
S	=	Savings (include employer match)

Beginning net worth is the total net worth typically from the preceding year balance sheet, and ending net worth is the total net worth on the balance sheet at the end of the current year.

Brandon and Jill Bowden's Rate of Return on Net Worth

$$\text{Return on Net Worth} = \frac{\$249,192 - (\$222,241 + \$5,720 + \$1,860)}{\$222,241} = \frac{\$19,371}{\$222,241} = 0.0872 \text{ or } 8.72\%$$

A return on net worth of 8.71 percent is reasonable. A financial planner should calculate the return on net worth each year and develop a trend over time. The return on net worth is expected to be higher when a client is working, then begin to decline as the client enters retirement (as assets are drawn down to generate income).

Exhibit 4.11 | Bowden Ratio Analysis

Liquidity Ratios				
Ratio	**Formula**		**Comment**	**Benchmark**
Emergency Fund Ratio	$\dfrac{\text{Cash \& Cash Equivalents}}{\text{Monthly Non-Discretionary Cash Flows}}$	$\dfrac{\$8,000}{\$5,974}$ = 1.34 months (20X2)	Weak	3 - 6 months
Current Ratio	$\dfrac{\text{Cash \& Cash Equivalents}}{\text{Current Liabilities}}$	$\dfrac{\$8,000}{\$34,056}$ = 0.23 (20X2)	Low	1.0 - 2.0
Debt Ratios				
Housing Ratio 1 (HR 1)(Basic)	$\dfrac{\text{Housing Costs}}{\text{Gross Pay}}$	$\dfrac{\$2,995.25}{\$10,333}$ = 28.9%	Slightly High	≤ 28%
Housing Ratio 2 (HR 2)(Broad)	$\dfrac{\text{Housing Costs + Other Debt Payments}}{\text{Gross Pay}}$	$\dfrac{\$4,086}{\$10,333}$ = 39.5%	Slightly High	≤ 36%
Debt-to-Total Assets	$\dfrac{\text{Total Debt}}{\text{Total Assets}}$	$\dfrac{\$383,808}{\$633,000}$ = 60.63% (20X2)	High	As a person ages, this ratio should decline.
Net Worth-to-Total Assets	$\dfrac{\text{Net Worth}}{\text{Total Assets}}$	$\dfrac{\$249,192}{\$633,000}$ = 39.37% (20X2)	Low	Depends on age. 20% for young client and 90-100% for retirement age client.
Ratios for Financial Security Goals				
Savings Rate	$\dfrac{\text{Savings + Employer Match}}{\text{Gross Pay}}$	$\dfrac{\$2,000 + \$3,720 + \$1,860}{\$124,000}$ = 6.11%	Low	10 – 13% assuming the client starts early, ages 25-35.
Investment Assets-to-Gross Pay	$\dfrac{\text{Investment Assets + Cash \& Cash Equivalents}}{\text{Gross Pay}}$	$\dfrac{\$88,000}{\$124,000}$ = 0.71:1	Low	Depends upon age. At retirement age – 16:1
Performance Ratios				
Return on Investments	$\dfrac{I_1 - (I_0 + \text{Savings})}{I_0}$	$\dfrac{\$6,620}{\$80,800}$ = 8.19%	Good	8 – 10%
Return on Assets	$\dfrac{A_1 - (A_0 + \text{Savings})}{A_0}$	$\dfrac{\$15,970}{\$609,450}$ = 2.62%	Low	2 – 4%
Return on Net Worth	$\dfrac{NW_1 - (NW_0 + \text{Savings})}{NW_0}$	$\dfrac{\$19,371}{\$222,241}$ = 8.72%	Good	The higher the better. This ratio is likely to become smaller as the client's net worth increases.

Exhibit 4.12 | Summary of Financial Statement Ratios (Generalized)

Liquidity Ratios			
Ratio	**Formula**	**Measures**	**Benchmark**
Emergency Funds	$\dfrac{\text{Cash \& Cash Equivalents}}{\text{Monthly Non-Discretionary Cash Flows}}$	The number of months of non-discretionary expenses in the form of cash and cash equivalents.	3 - 6 months
Current Ratio	$\dfrac{\text{Cash \& Cash Equivalents}}{\text{Current Liabilities}}$	The number of times a client can satisfy their short-term liabilities.	1.0 - 2.0
Debt Ratios			
Housing Ratio1 (Basic)	$\dfrac{\text{Housing Costs}}{\text{Gross Pay}}$	The percentage of income spent on housing debt.	$\leq 28\%$
Housing Ratio 2 (Broad)	$\dfrac{\text{Housing Costs + Other Debt Payments}}{\text{Gross Pay}}$	The percentage of income spent on housing and all other recurring debt.	$\leq 36\%$
Debt-to-Total Assets	$\dfrac{\text{Total Debt}}{\text{Total Assets}}$	The percentage of assets being provided by creditors.	As a person ages, this ratio should decline.
Net Worth-to-Total Assets	$\dfrac{\text{Net Worth}}{\text{Total Assets}}$	The percentage of total assets owned or paid for by client.	Depends on age. 20% for young client and 90-100% for retirement age client.
Ratios for Financial Security Goals			
Savings Rate	$\dfrac{\text{Savings + Employer Match}}{\text{Gross Pay}}$	The percentage of income saved towards a retirement goal.	10 – 13% Assuming the client starts early, ages 25-35.
Investment Assets-to-Gross Pay	$\dfrac{\text{Investment Assets + Cash \& Cash Equivalents}}{\text{Gross Pay}}$	The progress towards a retirement goal.	Depends upon age. At retirement age – 16:1
Performance Ratios			
Return on Investments	$\dfrac{I_1 - (I_0 + \text{Savings})}{I_0}$	The growth rate of a client's investment assets.	8 – 10%
Return on Assets	$\dfrac{A_1 - (A_0 + \text{Savings})}{A_0}$	A blended growth rate of all assets.	2 – 4%
Return on Net Worth	$\dfrac{NW_1 - (NW_0 + \text{Savings})}{NW_0}$	The growth rate of net worth.	The higher the better. This ratio is likely to become smaller as the client's net worth increases.

Limitations of Financial Statement Analysis

Estimating Fair Market Value

When preparing financial statements, the financial planner must estimate the fair market value of certain assets like the primary residence, second homes, boats, cars, and any collectibles. The **fair market value** is generally defined as the price a willing buyer and willing seller would agree to when both have reasonable knowledge of the facts of the transaction and neither is under any compulsion to buy or sell. In addition, if the client owns a small business, it is likely the planner will have to estimate the value of the business as well. Estimating the value of a small business becomes problematic when the client is planning to sell the asset and use the proceeds to fund a goal. The estimate of fair market value must be conservative enough so that the financial goal is not jeopardized because the value was overstated.

Inflation

The impact of inflation makes it very difficult to compare financial statements over multiple years. The financial planner needs to adjust investment returns for inflation to determine a real (after inflation) rate of return. The planner should also adjust income and savings into real (after inflation) dollars. Inflation of even a small rate (e.g., 3%) can have a very serious effect on financial statements over a long period of time (e.g., 10 to 30 years).

Hard to Value Assets

Some assets such as collectibles and private business interests are difficult to value. To the extent the asset is going to fund a financial goal, such as retirement, it is important for the financial planner to use an appraiser to determine an appropriate value of the asset. For example, if a client intends to sell a business ownership interest to fund retirement, the planner wants to make sure the client is going to be able to sell the business interest at the current value. The planner does not want to report the value of the business interest at $1 million on the balance sheet, only to find out years later that the client can only sell the interest for half of the value reported. If the client was including the business interest in the retirement amount calculation and now has a significant shortfall in retirement assets, it is likely to leave the client unable to retire and looking for a new planner.

Liquidity of Certain Assets

Other assets may be difficult to sell, such as a small business or collectible items. If a client is planning to use illiquid assets to fund a financial goal, the client and financial planner must carefully plan the timing of the sale of the asset, as it may not occur exactly as the client intends. For example, if the client is trying to sell a small business to fund retirement at age 62, the client may have to start looking for a buyer five years before the intended retirement date. It may also result in the client having to retire earlier or later than intended.

Uncertain Returns

Many of the benchmarks covered in this chapter assume a certain level of return. Returns are based on historical returns for asset classes such as stocks and bonds. As the markets continue to evolve over time, future returns may be higher or lower than historical returns, which could positively or negatively impact the financial planner's calculations and benchmarks.

Sensitivity Analysis

Financial statements and retirement and education needs that are projected over long periods of time employ many assumptions such as the rate of increase in income, the tax rate, the savings rate, the inflation rate, and the investment return rate. Retirement age and life expectancy are additional assumptions used for retirement projections. Assumptions made for education funding include the cost of education, when the cost will occur, and how many years the student will be in school. With all of these assumptions and variables, the financial planner needs to subject the plan to some sensitivity analysis. This involves slightly rotating the value of the variable toward the risk. For example, what if the client retires one year earlier than expected or inflation is 3.5 percent instead of the assumption used of three percent? Sensitivity analysis can also be used to illustrate to the client how the plan would be impacted if the client decides to pursue one or two years of additional work and savings (delayed retirement).

Conducting Sensitivity Analysis

Sensitivity analysis is the process of changing key variables in planning assumptions, to determine the overall impact of those changes on the plan. When a planner is calculating the amount needed to save towards an education goal, the financial planner must assume an investment rate of return, an inflation rate of return, and future cost of tuition. Sensitivity analysis involves calculating the amount needed to save for education, if the investment rate of return is two, three or more percentage points lower than the original assumption. The planner would also adjust the tuition inflation rate up and then calculate the amount needed to save for education. The planner would then adjust the tuition inflation rate down and recalculate the amount needed to save for education. Sensitivity analysis provides a range of savings required to meet a goal, based upon differing assumptions and the implications of the assumptions changing.

Conducting Monte Carlo Analysis

Monte Carlo analysis is a mathematical simulation to determine the probability of achieving a given outcome. Monte Carlo analysis is useful for financial planners to help measure the probability of certain assumptions being true or false. Suppose a client, age 62, has $1 million in a retirement savings account and wants to know how much can be withdrawn each year for income. If a planner assumes a historical rate of return of eight percent on the investment assets, the planner may suggest $90,000 a year in withdrawals which should last for 30 years. However, if the client experiences negative returns during the first three to four years of retiring, then retirement savings will be depleted in less than ten years. By conducting Monte Carlo analysis, the planner may determine that there is a 20 percent probability of running out of money within ten years of retiring. Then appropriate steps can be taken to adjust the annual withdrawal amount to decrease the probability of running out of money to a more tolerable level.

DISCUSSION QUESTIONS

SOLUTIONS to the discussion questions can be found exclusively within the chapter. Once you have completed an initial reading of the chapter, go back and highlight the answers to these questions.

1. List and define the major categories on the assets side of the balance sheet.

2. List and define the liabilities categories on the balance sheet.

3. Discuss how assets and liability values are reflected on the balance sheet.

4. Define and discuss the net worth category listed on the balance sheet.

5. List documents that a client can provide to the financial planner as sources of information to properly prepare financial statements.

6. List and define the common forms of property ownership.

7. Discuss the difference between income and savings contribution categories listed on the income statement.

8. Define the expense category of the income statement and give examples of variable and fixed expenses.

9. Define net discretionary cash flow.

10. What is the purpose of the statement of net worth?

11. What is the purpose of the cash flow statement?

12. List what should be reflected on forecasted financial statements.

13. What is a financial planner's purpose in creating a client's budget?

14. Define and explain the purpose of financial statement analysis.

15. Define vertical and horizontal analysis as comparative financial statement tools.

16. Define ratio analysis.

17. Define the emergency fund ratio.

18. Define housing ratios 1 and 2.

19. Define the savings rate.

20. Define performance ratios.

MULTIPLE-CHOICE PROBLEMS

A sample of multiple choice problems is provided below. Additional multiple choice problems are available at money-education.com by accessing the Student Practice Portal.

1. Your client, Meg, asked you several questions about her balance sheet. She doesn't understand how the assets, liabilities and net worth are related. Which of the following statements is true?
    a. Net Worth = Assets + Liabilities.
    b. Assets = Net Worth – Liabilities.
    c. Liabilities = Assets – Net Worth.
    d. A balance sheet reflects how the assets, liabilities, and net worth changed over the year.

2. Which of the following statements concerning the valuation of assets on the balance sheet is correct?
    a. Since a financial planner has access to all of the client financials, a privately-held small business is easier to value than a publicly traded company.
    b. Assets should be valued on the balance sheet using replacement cost.
    c. An actuary should be retained to value all personal use assets.
    d. Money market accounts are unlikely to lose value over time.

3. Jay purchased a new home for $100,000. He put $20,000 down and financed the $80,000 balance. What is the impact of this transaction on his net worth?
    a. His net worth increases.
    b. His net worth decreases.
    c. His net worth remains the same.
    d. The net worth will decrease with each mortgage payment made.

4. Which of the following property ownership regimes has a right of survivorship feature?
    a. Sole Ownership.
    b. Tenancy in Common.
    c. Tenancy by the Entirety.
    d. Community Property.

5. Marcus and Theresa are married. Marcus is a police officer and earns $50,000 per year. He contributes 10% of his salary to his retirement plan. His employer also makes a 5% matching contribution. Theresa stays at home with their children and contributes $5,000 to an IRA. What is their total saving rate?
    a. 10.0%.
    b. 20.0%.
    c. 20.5%.
    d. 25.0%.

Additional multiple choice problems are available at *money-education.com* by accessing the Student Practice Portal. Access requires registration of the title using the unique code at the front of the book.

QUICK QUIZ EXPLANATIONS

Quick Quiz 4.1

1. False. This definition is for the statement of income and expenses (income statement). The balance sheet represents the items the client owns (assets), the items that are owed by the client (liabilities), and the difference between the two (net worth).
2. True.
3. False. This definition is for personal use assets. Investment assets are appreciating assets that are being held to accomplish financial goal(s). Investment assets include retirement accounts, brokerage accounts, education funds, etc.
4. True.

Quick Quiz 4.2

1. False. This definition is for tenancy in common property ownership. Community property is for married individuals.
2. False. Community property does not usually avoid probate, but tenancy by the entirety and Joint Tenancy with Right of survivorship both generally avoid probate.

Quick Quiz 4.3

1. False. Assets are listed on the balance sheet, not the income statement.
2. True.
3. True.

Quick Quiz 4.4

1. True.
2. False. This is the definition of an income statement not a cash flow statement. The cash flow statement explains how cash and cash equivalents were used or generated between two balance sheets.
3. True.

Quick Quiz 4.5

1. True.
2. True.
3. False. This is the definition of the current ratio. The emergency fund ratio measures how many months of non-discretionary expenses the client has in cash and cash equivalents.

Quick Quiz 4.6

1. True.
2. False. The savings rate calculation includes savings plus employer match divided by gross pay.
3. True.

5

RISK MANAGEMENT FOR
THE INDIVIDUAL CLIENT

1. Describe and explain the personal risk management process and its steps.
2. Determine and select the best risk management alternatives using the risk management decision chart for individuals.
3. Explain the causes and contributors to losses including perils and hazards.
4. Identify the requisites for an insurable risk.
5. Describe insurance as a legal contract including the elements of a valid contract and the unique characteristics of an insurance contract.
6. Describe insurance on the person including life insurance.
7. Identify the three methods used to determine the amount of life insurance needed and be able to calculate each.
8. Describe the types of life insurance including term and permanent.
9. Describe a health insurance plan and differentiate between an indemnity plan and managed care options.
10. Describe the risk associated with long-term disability and the coverages that long-term disability plans provide.
11. Describe long-term care insurance, activities of daily living, and important features associated with long-term care insurance policies.
12. Describe homeowners and renters insurance policies.
13. Describe automobile insurance policies and which factors affect premium rates.
14. Describe personal liability umbrella insurance policies and the risks that they mitigate against.
15. Describe how insurers use risk pooling to pay for losses incurred by policyholders.*
16. Explain the factors that affect policyholder premiums and recommend strategies for reducing household insurance costs.*
17. Identify and measure liability, automobile, homeowner's, flood, earthquake, health, disability, long-term care, and life risks.*

Ties to CFP Certification Learning Objectives

INTRODUCTION

This chapter introduces the reader to the basics of risk management for an individual and identifies the risks that a typical client faces. A financial plan can then be developed for managing those risks with the ultimate objective being for the client to avoid the consequences of such risks were they to happen. This chapter is a primer and is not designed to take the place of a full semester course in insurance.

The chapter will provide sufficient risk management information for a financial planner to apply this knowledge to relatively simple client risk management scenarios. If the client's risk management situation is complex, the planner needs to have completed at least a full course in insurance and perhaps also needs to consult with an insurance expert.

The Personal Risk Management Process

Personal risk management is a systematic process of identifying, evaluating, and managing pure risk exposures faced by an individual. Pure risk is the chance of a loss or no loss occurring, but with no chance of a gain.

There are several steps in the personal risk management process:
- Determining the objectives of the risk management program.
- Identifying the risks to which the individual is exposed.
- Evaluating the identified risks for the probability of occurrence and severity of the loss.
- Determining the alternatives for managing the risks.
- Selecting the most appropriate alternative for each risk.
- Implementing the risk management plan selected.
- Periodically evaluating and reviewing the risk management program.

Determining the Objectives of the Risk Management Program

The first step in the risk management process is to determine the objectives of the risk management program. If vaguely defined, risk management objectives can conflict with each other and thus be disjointed. Risk management objectives can range from obtaining the most cost-effective protection against risk to continuing income after loss. A client's stated objective may be to insure only those risks that have the potential of catastrophic financial loss and to do so at the minimum premium using as many premium management techniques as are available (e.g., deductibles, co-pays, annual cost comparisons).

> ### ≔ Key Concepts
>
> 1. Identify the seven steps to the personal risk management process.
>
> 2. Identify the difference between personal risks, property risks, and liability risks.
>
> 3. Distinguish between loss frequency and loss severity.

Identifying Risk Exposures

The next step is to identify all possible **pure risk** exposures of the client. Pure risk represents the possibility of loss, but no possibility of gain. The risk exposures for an individual may be subdivided into **personal risks** that may cause the loss of income (untimely death, disability, health issues), or alternatively cause an increase in the cost of living (disability, health issues), **property risks** that may cause the loss of property (automobile, home, or other asset), and **liability risks** that may cause financial loss (injury to another for which the client is determined to be financially responsible).

Evaluating the Identified Risks

Evaluating the potential frequency and severity of losses is the next step in the risk management process. **Loss frequency** is the expected number of losses that will occur within a given period of time. **Loss severity** refers to the potential size or financial damage of a loss. By identifying loss frequency and severity, the planner can prioritize the urgency of dealing with each specific risk and identify the appropriate risk management response(s).

The probability of loss is the chance that a loss will occur. Probability statistics are readily available for many types of loss and are useful when applied to large groups of insureds. However, relying on probability-based predictions for any single individual is not recommended. To the individual, the potential financial severity of the losses, even coupled with a low probability of occurrence, is critical to the risk analysis.

Clients should insure against those **perils** (the proximate or actual cause of a loss, such as fire, liability, or accidental death) that, upon occurrence, could lead to severe financial hardship. We refer to these as catastrophic financial risks. However, catastrophic risks are relative. The loss of a car to a person who depends on it to get to work and has no other money to replace it may be catastrophic, while the loss of a car to a wealthy person may be incidental. Generally, even those persons owning houses without mortgages cannot risk leaving such a substantial asset uninsured.

A general approach to insuring individual risks is as follows:
- For untimely death (earlier in life) - if there are persons other than the insured who depend on the income of the person, that person needs income replacement insurance (life insurance).
- For disability (pre-retirement) - most workers need disability insurance as income replacement insurance at least until they have sufficient assets to no longer need employment. Those who are unemployed will find it difficult to qualify for disability insurance as it is like life insurance (income replacement).
- For healthcare - it is rare that a person can self insure for healthcare. So, in general, everyone needs healthcare coverage.
- For property losses - property owners should insure their property for its replacement cost when available (for some types of property, the maximum coverage available will be for the fair market value of the property, or for the depreciated value of the property). High deductibles should be used as self insurance or loss sharing techniques to manage premiums. Both coverages and costs should be reevaluated annually.
- For liability - most people need a personal liability umbrella policy (PLUP). The minimum coverage is usually $1,000,000 and may be as high as $5,000,000 or more depending on the risks and the financial resources of the person.

Determining and Selecting the Best Risk Management Alternatives

Insurance is not necessary, or even available, for every risk of financial loss that an individual faces. Choosing the appropriate risk management response depends largely on the potential frequency and severity of loss exposures faced. Where more than one tool is deemed appropriate, the costs and benefits of each should be examined to determine which strategy, or combination of strategies, is the most economical and beneficial.

There are four responses to managing risks:
- **Risk avoidance** - Avoiding an activity so that a financial loss cannot be incurred.
- **Risk reduction** - Implementing activities that will result in the reduction of the frequency and/or severity of losses.
- **Risk retention** - The state of being exposed to a risk and personally retaining the potential for loss.
- **Risk transfer** - Transferring or shifting the risk of loss through means such as insurance or a warranty.

It is important to choose the best risk management response for any particular risk. **Exhibit 5.1** is a decision chart to assist the decision maker in selecting the most appropriate risk management tools.

Exhibit 5.1 | Risk Management Decision Chart for Individuals

	Low Frequency of Occurrence	*High Frequency of Occurrence*
High Severity (catastrophic financial loss) (e.g., long-term disability)	Transfer and/or share risk using insurance	Avoid Risk
Low Severity (non-catastrophic financial loss) (e.g., car gets dented in parking lot)	Retain Risk	Retain / Reduce Risk (park away from heavy parking area)

Exposures that are a combination of high frequency and high severity should be avoided. Exposures that are low in frequency but high in potential severity are best handled by insurance coverage. The high-severity losses can leave a client in a dire financial position, yet the low frequency makes sharing the cost of losses with others economically feasible. Examples of high-severity / low-frequency loss exposures include fire damage to a house or a loss due to an automobile collision.

The remaining types of exposures are low in severity. Transferring low-severity losses to an insurer is generally not economically feasible because the insurer has substantial expenses associated with processing small claims. The risk of low-severity losses should generally be retained by the asset owner. When low-severity losses occur with high frequency, their aggregate impact can have financially devastating effects. So, it is recommended that high-frequency, low-severity losses not just be retained but also managed in an effort to reduce the frequency.

Implementing a Risk Management Plan Based on the Selected Alternatives

A risk management plan should reflect the chosen response to each risk scenario. If risk reduction is the appropriate response to a given risk, the proper risk reduction program must be designed and implemented. If a decision is made to retain a risk, the individual should determine whether an emergency fund will be used (pet needs medical care). If the response to a given risk is to transfer the risk by purchasing insurance, an assessment and selection of the appropriate insurer will follow.

Periodically Evaluating and Reviewing the Individual Risk Management Program

The purpose of periodic evaluation and review is twofold. First, the risk management process does not take place independently from external influences. Things change over time, and risk exposures can change as well. The risk management response that was most suitable last year may not be the most prudent this year, and adjustments may need to be made. Second, errors in judgment regarding the selected alternatives may occur, and periodic review allows the planner and client to discover such errors and revise the risk management plan as necessary.

CAUSES OF AND CONTRIBUTORS TO LOSSES

Perils

Too often the concept of risk, or the chance of loss, is confused with the terms peril and hazard. A peril is the proximate or actual cause of a loss. Common perils include accidental death, disability caused by sickness or accident, and property losses caused by fire, windstorm, tornado, earthquake, burglary, and collision.

Insurance policy coverage may be written in either an open-perils or a named-perils format. **Open-perils policies** are called "all-risk" policies, because they cover all risks of loss (perils) that are not specifically excluded from the contract. All-risk proved to be somewhat misleading to the consumer, implying that "all" risks were covered. So, the industry has moved toward the use of the term open-perils to describe this type of coverage. More specifically, an open-perils policy is one in which all perils or causes of loss are covered, unless they are specifically listed under the exclusions section of the policy. A **named-perils policy** provides protection against losses caused by the perils

≡ *Key Concepts*

1. Distinguish between an open-perils policy and a named-perils policy.

2. Identify the three main types of hazards.

3. Identify the four conditions necessary for a risk to be insurable.

that are specifically listed as covered in the policy. Because there is always a chance of loss being caused by an unknown or unlisted peril, an open-perils policy is preferable to a named-perils policy. Consequently, the open-perils policy premium is somewhat higher than a named-perils policy because it provides broader coverage.

Hazards

A **hazard** is a condition that creates or increases the likelihood of a loss occurring. The three main types of hazards are:
- Physical hazard
- Moral hazard
- Morale hazard

Physical Hazard

A **physical hazard** is a tangible condition or circumstance that increases the probability of a peril occurring. Examples of physical hazards include high blood pressure, winding roads, and bad eyesight.

Moral Hazard

A **moral hazard** is a character flaw or level of dishonesty an individual possesses that causes or increases the chance for a loss. In property insurance claims, a good example of a moral hazard is arson. Fraud in auto and health claims is a moral hazard situation that also occurs frequently. Dishonest insureds often justify their claims because the loss is insured. These types of losses result in premium increases for all insureds.

Morale Hazard

A **morale hazard** is indifference to losses based on the existence of insurance. Many people think that because they have insurance there is no need to be concerned about protecting their property. As a direct result of the indifference, the chance of loss is increased. Persons may contend that because they are insured, there is no reason to lock their homes or cars. This should not be confused with a moral hazard, which, for example, would be burning their house down or purposely rear-ending another motor vehicle to collect insurance.

INSURABLE LOSSES

Requisites for an Insurable Risk

Several conditions must exist before a risk is considered insurable:

- A large number of homogeneous (similar) exposure units must exist to help develop statistics for forecasting losses (frequency and severity).
- Insured losses must be accidental from the insured's standpoint. Intentional acts of the insured resulting in a loss are generally not insurable.
- Insured losses must be measurable and determinable.
- The loss must not pose a catastrophic risk for the insurer who has limited reserves.

> ### Key Concepts
>
> 1. Identify the elements of a valid contract.
> 2. Identify some of the unique characteristics of an insurance contract.
> 3. Determine the purpose of life insurance.
> 4. Identify the methods of determining the amount of life insurance needed.
> 5. Distinguish the difference between term life insurance and permanent life insurance.

Insurance is likely unavailable or priced extremely high for risks that are generally not insurable. Risks that are too large cannot be insured due to high premium cost that makes purchasing the insurance impractical. Also, risks that are challenging to measure will be difficult for the insurer to quantify and predict. The insurer in such a circumstance would almost certainly price the premium high in the event a loss occurred that was higher than the insurer was able to anticipate and quantify. A financial planner needs to assist the client in identifying insurable and uninsurable risks as part of the personal risk management process. Then direction can be given for the appropriate alternatives to risk management.

INSURANCE AS A LEGAL CONTRACT

A contract is valid only if the legal system enforces the terms and conditions of the contract. Our legal system has established certain principles upon which insurance contracts are based and interpreted when claims or disputes arise. What constitutes a legally binding contract? The elements of a valid contract are listed below.

Elements of a Valid Contract

- Offer and acceptance (one party makes the offer, the other party accepts, rejects, or counters)
- Legal competency of all parties (generally at least age 18)
- Consideration (usually money or the promise to pay)
- Lawful purpose (the purpose of the contract is not for an unlawful activity)

Insurance as a contract has some unique characteristics, including:

- It is unilateral - Only the insurer is making a promise, therefore it is a unilateral contract.
- It is aleatory - What is paid in by the insured and paid out by the insurer may not be equal amounts.
- It is adhesive - The insured had no opportunity to negotiate terms; thus ambiguities are charged to the insurer.
- It implies utmost good faith - The insurance applicant is truthful in disclosure of pertinent material facts and the insurer discloses critical contract information.
- It is a contract based on the principle of indemnity (insured cannot make a profit from a claim on insurance).
- The insured must have an insurable interest.
- The coverage is conditioned upon the payment of premiums.

As a result of the characteristic of adhesiveness, when interpreting insurance contracts, courts resolve any ambiguity in favor of the insured. This result is equitable since insurance contract language is customarily selected by the insurer and the insured has no opportunity to clarify the language. Therefore, court decisions concerning contract ambiguity will weigh in favor of coverage rather than non coverage.

Insurance companies are regulated by individual states. Local regulation is effective because states know their local and regional markets and the needs of consumers within those markets. States have a direct interest in protecting consumers by making sure insurers remain solvent so that they can meet their contractual obligations of paying claims. In addition, states oversee sales, marketing, policy terms, and conditions of insurance products to ensure consumers are protected when making purchases and filing claims. All insurance products sold in a state must be pre-approved by that state's insurance commissioner. Each state also regulates those who sell, broker, or provide consulting services regarding insurance within the state. Financial planners who wish to provide insurance services must attain the requisite licenses, avoid any ethical or market conduct violations, and complete continuing education as required by the state insurance department.

INSURANCE ON THE PERSON

Insurance on the person includes life insurance, health insurance, disability insurance, and long-term care insurance. In this section we will provide a discussion of whether or not a particular client needs (as opposed to wants) any of these four types of insurance. If the client needs the insurance, the planner should assist the client with: (1) determining the amount of coverage needed, (2) selecting the type of policy that best meets the client's needs, and (3) identifying and selecting key provisions to be included in the policy to ensure adequate coverage at a reasonable price.

Life Insurance

Life insurance at its core is income replacement insurance. If a person dies unexpectedly, what kind of financial hardship results? Would the spouse and/or dependents be left without the income the person has expected to and wanted to provide them? If a person has no dependents, that person typically does not need life insurance to cover this risk, but may choose to maintain at least a minimal amount of coverage to provide for final expenses such as final medical or funeral expenses. Conversely, if there are people who could not afford to lose the income of the person were that person to die, that person should have life insurance. Dependency is the critical issue to life insurance needs and assists in differentiating between a need versus a want. Married couples who are dependent on the income of both spouses to pay a mortgage need life insurance, as do clients with dependent children.

Assuming a person needs life insurance, how much should they have? There are three methods used to determine the amount of life insurance needed. These are:

- The Human Life Value Method
- The Financial Needs Method
- The Capitalization of Earnings Method

The Human Life Value Method

The **human life value (HLV) method** uses projected future earnings as the basis for measuring life insurance needs. The HLV method projects the individual's income throughout his remaining work life expectancy. Then, using a discount rate (usually an inflation-adjusted rate of return using the risk-free rate of return and adjusting for the inflation rate), the present value of the individual's future earnings is determined. Note that cash flows are adjusted downward by amounts that would have otherwise been used for personal consumption and for the payments of taxes on income. The net amount is known as the FSE (family's share of earnings).

> ### ✏ Quick Quiz 5.2
>
> 1. A hazard is a condition that creates or increases the likelihood of a loss occurring.
>   a. True
>   b. False
>
> 2. Moral hazard is the indifference to losses based on the existence of insurance.
>   a. True
>   b. False
>
> 3. The elements of a valid contract include offer and acceptance, legal competency of the parties, legal consideration, and lawful purpose.
>   a. True
>   b. False
>
> True, False, True.

Example 5.1

Fred, who is married and the father of one, is 35 years old and expects to continue to work until age 64. He earns $65,000 per year. Fred expects inflation to be 3% over his working life, and the appropriate risk-free discount rate is 6%. His personal consumption is equal to 20% of his after-tax earnings, and his combined federal and state marginal tax bracket is 25%.

Step 1: Calculate the Family's Share of Earnings (FSE)	
Annual Earnings $65,000	= Annual Taxes = $65,000 x 0.25 = $16,250
Personal Consumption	= (After-tax income x consumption %)
	= [(($65,000 - $16,250) x 0.20)]
	= $9,750
FSE (Family's Share of Earnings)	= Annual Earnings - (annual income taxes + annual personal consumption)
	= $65,000 - ($16,250 + $9,750)
	= $39,000

Step 2: Calculate Work Life Expectancy (WLE)	
WLE	= The expected age at retirement less the current age
	= 64 - 35
WLE	= 29 years

Step 3: Determine Human Life Value (HLV)*	
Future Value (FV)	= 0
Annual PMT$_{OA}$	= $39,000
Interest Rate (i)	= 2.91262 [[(1.06 ÷ 1.03 inflation rate) - 1] x 100]
Term of Years (n)	= 29
Human Life Value (PV)	= $756,642 (Present Value)

* See Chapter 7 for assistance with time value of money calculations.

The $756,642 HLV represents the present value of Fred's life contributions to his family excluding taxes and his consumption. This is the amount of life insurance that he needs using the human life value approach. It would be reduced by any current life insurance that he has to determine his current need.

The Financial Needs Method

The **financial needs method** evaluates the income replacement and lump-sum needs of survivors in the event of an income producer's untimely death. The impact of inflation over time is taken into consideration when using this approach by identifying the timing of the cash flow needs and calculating the present value of each.

A family that loses an income producer is likely to have some or all of the following common financial needs:
- Lump-sum (cash) needs
- Final expenses and debt repayment needs
- Mortgage liquidation or payment fund needs
- Education expense needs
- Emergency expense needs
- Income (cash flow) needs
- Readjustment period needs
- Dependency period needs
- Spousal life income (pre-and post retirement) needs

Lump-Sum (Cash) Needs

The deceased's survivors are expected to maintain a certain lifestyle. Most clients want to make sure that their dependents will not suffer a decrease in standard of living.

Final Expenses and Debt Repayment Needs

After the death of the insured, a fund for final expenses and debts is immediately needed by the survivors to pay for the deceased's out-of-pocket medical expenses prior to death, funeral costs, and other unplanned expenditures. Estate administration expenses, federal estate taxes, state death taxes, inheritance taxes, and income taxes may also be required to be funded from a source outside of the estate of the insured if the estate has insufficient liquid assets.

Mortgage Liquidation or Payment Fund Needs

The family may wish to pay off existing mortgages at the time of the breadwinner's death. This can be an effective way to reduce the future cash flow needs of the surviving family.

Education Expense Needs

If an educational funding plan is not already in place, funds from life insurance may be set aside for college and post-college education. If the survivors choose not to set aside funds, and educational expenses will occur in the future, the expenses should be included in the life income calculation needed by the family.

Emergency Expense Needs

The purpose of this funding is to provide survivors with a cash reserve for unforeseen expenses that may arise as the family makes a transition to life without the deceased.

Readjustment Period Income Needs

The readjustment period typically lasts for one to two years following the death of the breadwinner. During this period, the family is likely to need approximately the same amount of income it received while the deceased was alive. Families will usually have certain non-recurring expenses as they adjust to a new lifestyle. For a family that will experience a decline in its standard of living, this period income allows the family to achieve the necessary readjustment. In addition, with most employers offering only a short period (a few days to a few weeks) of paid time off for bereavement, it may be desirable to provide additional death benefits to allow a working surviving spouse to take some additional unpaid time off to be available at home for emotional support of young children. The readjustment period income should be made available immediately, particularly if the family is not well provided with other liquid resources.

Dependency Period Income Needs

The dependency period is one in which others (the deceased's spouse, children, and, in some cases, parents) would have been dependent of the deceased had she survived. In most cases, income needs are largest during this period. The length of the dependency period is determined by the number of dependents, their ages, and the deceased's contribution to the family's total income needs.

Spousal Life Income Needs

At some point the children will no longer be dependent upon the surviving spouse. However, the surviving spouse may still need to replace a part of the wage earner's income (especially if the surviving spouse was not an income earner). Surviving spouses who re-enter the workforce often find it difficult to find employment that enables them to maintain their prior standard of living. Therefore, it may be advisable to arrange lifetime income for the surviving spouse.

Two income periods should be considered: (1) the blackout period, and (2) the period during which the surviving spouse receives Social Security benefits. The blackout period refers to the period of time beginning when Social Security survivors benefits to a spouse under age 60 are discontinued (usually when the last child reaches age 16) and ending when the spouse begins to receive Social Security retirement or widow(er) benefits at age 60 or later. During the blackout period, income must be provided by employment, insurance, investments, or some other source. Once Social Security benefits resume, the amount of supplemental income may be reduced.

If both spouses earned income prior to the first death, a smaller percentage of total family income must be replaced upon one of the spouses's death. If, however, the sole breadwinner of the family has died, the ability (or desire) of the surviving spouse to secure employment must be considered.

In most cases, the children of the deceased will be entitled to Social Security benefits until they reach age 18. The benefits received by the spouse, as caretaker of the children and on behalf of the children, will decrease the income needs of the family during the dependency period. In addition, if parents were dependents of the deceased, any Social Security survivors benefits received by them as a result of the death of their adult child may also decrease the income needs during the period.

Example 5.2

Assume Fred, age 35, earns $65,000 annually. His spouse, Frederica, age 34, is a homemaker, and they have one child, who just turned age 6. The couple assumes an average annual inflation rate of 3%. Fred and Frederica have set the following goals and assumptions:

Income needed - readjustment period (1 yr.)	$55,250
Income needed - dependency period	$55,250
Income needed - "empty nest" period	$40,000
Income needed - retirement	$36,000
Estate expenses and debts	$15,000
Education fund needed (in today's dollars)	$72,000
Emergency fund needed	$15,000
Investment assets (cash/cash equivalents) current liquid	$200,000
Expected Social Security income while child is under 16	$20,000
Expected Social Security income while child is 17 and 18	$10,000
Expected Social Security income in retirement	$18,000
Frederica's life expectancy	85 years
Frederica expects Social Security benefits to begin	Age 60
Discount rate	6%

Given the previous information, how much life insurance does Fred need?

Step 1: Calculate the family's income (cash flow) needs for each period.

	Readjustment (1 year)	Child's Age (7 - 16)	Child's Age (17 - 18)	Empty Nest/ Blackout Period of Surviving Spouse (Age 46 - 60)	Retirement Period for Surviving Spouse (25 years)
Frederica's Age	34-35	35-45	45-46	46-60	60-85
Fred's (Would Be) Age	36	36-46	46-47	47-61	
Annual Income Needed	$55,250	$55,250	$55,250	$40,000	$36,000
Less: Assumed OASDI (Social Security)	$20,000	$20,000	$10,000	$0	$18,000
Net Annual Income Needed (PMT)	$35,250	$35,250	$45,250	$40,000	$18,000
$i = [(\frac{1.06}{1.03}) - 1] \times 100$	2.9126	2.9126	2.9126	2.9126	2.9126
N = Years Needed	1	10	2	15	25
PV of net annual income needed (use begin mode)	$35,250	$310,832	$89,219	$494,547	$325,730
Discount Period	0	1	11 years	12 years	26 years
Present Value Today	$35,250	**$302,035**	**$65,058**	**$350,417**	**$154,410**

PV of total annual income needed: $907,170 ($35,250 + $302,035 + $65,058 + $350,417 + $154,410)

Step 2: Calculate the family's lump-sum funding needs.

Final expenses and debts	$15,000
Education funding needed (in today's dollars)	$72,000
Emergency fund	$15,000
Total lump-sum funding needs	$102,000

Step 3: Calculate the life insurance death benefit needed.

Total life insurance needed	$1,009,170	($907,170 + $102,000)
Less current life insurance	$0	
Less current liquid assets	($200,000)	
Net death benefit of life insurance needed	$809,170	

The Capitalization of Earnings Method

The **capitalization of earnings method** requires purchase of sufficient life insurance to provide the future need entirely from the investment income without liquidation of the capital. This approach preserves the capital and is calculated using a fraction to determine the life insurance needs. The initial numerator is the client's gross income and the initial denominator is the riskless rate of return (typically the yield on U.S. Treasury Bonds).

Recall the Fred examples (**Example 5.1** and **Example 5.2**):

$$\frac{\text{Income}}{\text{Treasury Bond}} \quad \frac{\$65,000}{0.06} = \$1,083,333 \text{ Life Insurance Needed}$$

This calculation does not initially take into consideration taxes, consumption, or inflation. However, adjustments can be made to the numerator for taxes ($16,250) and for personal consumption ($9,750) and to the denominator for inflation (3%).

$$\frac{\$65,000 - \$16,250 - \$9,750}{[(1.06 \div 1.03) - 1]} = \frac{\$39,000}{0.029126} = \$1,339,000 \text{ Life Insurance Needed}$$

Summary	Life Insurance Needed
Human Life Value Method	$756,642
Financial Needs Method	$809,170
Capitalization Income Method	$1,339,000

Using all three of these methods, we conclude that if life insurance is needed, it should be sufficient if it is approximately 12 - 16 x the client's gross pay ($65,000 x 12 = $780,000 to $65,000 x 16 = $1,040,000). (Note that the average of the three methods is $968,271.)

Types of Life Insurance

There are two general types of life insurance, term and permanent. Permanent is frequently broken down into whole (ordinary life) and universal life. Ordinary life offers a death benefit along with a savings component. Universal life offers more flexibility than ordinary life including the availability of altering the death benefit, savings component, and premium payments. One difference between permanent life insurance and term life insurance is that permanent insurance has a savings and investment component, whereas term insurance does not.

Term life insurance is "pure insurance" and is for a stated temporary period of time (10, 20, 25, 30 years). Term insurance is attractive to consumers because the premiums are significantly lower than the premiums for permanent policies (see **Exhibit 5.2**).

Term life insurance can be annually renewed usually with an increasing premium or it can be level premium for the entire term. A policy that is annually renewed will have increasing premiums to correspond with the increasing risk of mortality as individuals age. Fixed premium term insurance (e.g., 20, 30 years) is attractive because over time it becomes easier to pay the premium assuming the client is receiving pay increases. Initially the premium is higher than an annual renewable term policy because you are paying for not only this year's mortality risk, but also for part of the future mortality risk. Annual renewable term with an increasing premium is attractive initially because of the low initial premium in comparison to level premium term.

Many young people with lower incomes buy term insurance because they can get a death benefit that is sufficiently large for a relatively small premium. The following exhibit compares the annual costs of various term policies and permanent life insurance (universal life).

✎ Quick Quiz 5.3

1. The human life value method of measuring life insurance needs evaluates the income replacement and lump-sum needs of survivors in the event of the insured's death.
   a. True
   b. False

2. The capitalization of earnings method uses the client's gross income divided by the riskless rate of return to arrive at the initial amount of life insurance need.
   a. True
   b. False

3. Term life insurance has both a savings and an investment component.
   a. True
   b. False

False, True, False.

Exhibit 5.2 | Life Insurance Premium Costs Comparison for Term and Universal (per $1,000 of coverage)

Age	Term* (10 year)	Term* (25 year)	Term* (30 year)	Universal Life
25	$0.25	$0.52	$0.60	$2.31
30	$0.25	$0.56	$0.64	$2.92
35	$0.26	$0.65	$0.72	$3.77
40	$0.31	$0.96	$1.04	$4.74
45	$0.51	$1.52	$1.68	$5.99
50	$0.83	N/A	N/A	$7.45
55	$1.40	N/A	N/A	$9.05
60	$2.39	N/A	N/A	$11.74
65	$4.08	N/A	N/A	$15.40

Price is per $1,000 of coverage ($ per 000).
For very healthy non-tobacco using male insured.
* Usually available to terminate at or before age 75.

Health Insurance

A health insurance plan is an arrangement that provides benefits to the insured in the event of sickness or personal injury. Health insurance coverage can include hospitalization coverage, major medical, and indemnity or managed care plan coverage (health maintenance organizations, preferred provider organizations, and point of service plans). Unlimited lifetime benefits are mandated by The Affordable Care Act.

Indemnity Coverage

Indemnity coverage allows the insured to choose health care providers. The insured can go to any doctor, hospital, or other medical provider. Reimbursement is based on services provided and a deductible (an annual amount the insured must pay for services before the insurance provides any coverage) or coinsurance payment (a portion of services billed) may be required of the insured. The policy may have an annual limit to the insured's out-of-pocket expenses where additional covered services beyond the limit are paid in full. Covered services may be restricted and prior authorization may be required for high cost medical services.

A High Deductible Health Plan (HDHP) is a relatively low premium health insurance plan that provides benefits after a high deductible is met. The following exhibit reflects minimum and maximum deductibles for HDHPs.

Exhibit 5.3 | Deductible Limits for HDHPs

	Minimum Deductible		Maximum Deductible and Out of Pocket Expenses	
	2021	2020	2021	2020
Individual	$1,400	$1,400	$7,000	$6,900
Family	$2,800	$2,800	$14,000	$13,800

This type of health plan may be a good option for clients in good health and focused on budgeting expenses.

Managed Care Options

A Health Maintenance Organization (HMO) plan provides access to a network of participating medical providers including physicians, hospitals, and other medical professionals and facilities. The insured selects a network primary care physician who provides medical services and coordinates the insurance care. A HMO plan generally requires less out-of-pocket expenses by the insured and a co-payment for services such as office visits and pharmacy prescriptions is typically required.

A Preferred Provider Organization (PPO) charges on a fee-for-service basis. The medical providers are paid by the insurer on an agreed upon discounted fee schedule. The insured is encouraged to use in-network healthcare providers to maintain lower costs. If the insured chooses an out-of-network medical provider, additional expenses may be incurred.

A Point-of-Service (POS) plan coordinates care through a primary care doctor that makes referrals to other providers who participate in the plan. Referrals by the primary care physician to an out-of-plan provider are typically covered in full. If the insured self-refers to an out-of-network provider, then additional expenses (coinsurance payment) will be incurred.

Patient Protection and Affordable Care Act

The Patient Protection and Affordable Care Act was passed by Congress and then signed into law by the President on March 23, 2010. On June 28, 2012 the Supreme Court rendered a final decision to uphold the health care law. The law, which is thousands of pages long, has been phased in over several years and has made health care coverage more readily available to millions of Americans who would otherwise be uninsured. The law attempts to transform the U.S. health care system, including providing better access, eliminating lifetime medical limits, eliminating the issue of pre-existing conditions, expanding Medicaid access, and imposing penalties on individuals and some businesses for not having health care insurance (although the penalty for individuals was eliminated for tax years after 2018).

Long-Term Disability

The likelihood of long-term disability is far greater than that of untimely death. Actuaries estimate that one in three individuals will suffer a disability that lasts 90 days or more. One of ten persons will be permanently disabled before age 65.

Disability insurance provides replacement income to the insured while the insured is unable to work because of sickness (illness) or injury (accident).

> ### ≔ *Key Concepts*
>
> 1. Determine the purpose of disability insurance.
>
> 2. Identify the various definitions of disability and the associated insurance coverage.

The coverage should include accidental bodily injury and illness. The illness coverage may exclude preexisting conditions (such as colitis).

The critical issues and provisions related to disability insurance include:
- the definition of disability
- coverage for both sickness and accidents
- the amount of benefits per month / year
- the term of benefits
- the elimination period (waiting period during which the insured must self-insure)
- whether or not the policy is noncancelable (the insurer cannot cancel and cannot raise premiums - expensive) or guaranteed renewable (the insurer cannot cancel but can raise premiums if the increase is on everyone in the class or pool)

The range of disability definitions include:

Own Occupation: This disability coverage is determined by whether or not the insured can carry out each and every one of the duties of his employment. If the insured cannot perform each and every one of his usual duties, then he will qualify for disability benefits. This coverage may be either to retirement or may be for a set term of one, two, or five or more years.

Any Occupation: If disability coverage is defined as any occupation, the insured is considered disabled if he cannot work in any occupation for which he is qualified for by education, training, or experience. If the insured can perform the duties of employment that are comparable to the job held prior to the illness or injury, benefits may be discontinued.

Hybrid (sometimes called split definition): Some disability policies, especially group disability policies, offer a definition of disability that contains characteristics from both own occupation and any occupation classifications. For example, a hybrid disability policy may offer own occupation for five years and any occupation after that time period.

Partial Disability: A disability policy may offer coverage for partial disability where the insured can perform either a part of his own occupation or a portion of the previous time in his own occupation. If the insured meets the definition of partial disability, then the insured would receive a proportion of the disability benefit.

Elimination Period: The time between the disability event and the point of which income benefits, under the contract, begin. A common elimination period is 90 days with shorter elimination periods resulting in higher premiums and longer elimination periods resulting in lower premiums. The selection of the length of elimination period must be made with due consideration of the level of emergency funds available to self-insure.

Noncancelable Insurance: A disability policy's noncancelable provision ensures that the insurance will not be canceled and that the premiums will remain fixed for the term of the policy.

Guaranteed Renewable Insurance: A guaranteed renewable feature of a policy obligates the insurer to continue coverage as long as premiums are paid on the policy. While renewal is guaranteed, premiums can increase if they are increased on the entire group.

✎ Quick Quiz 5.4

1. Critical provisions related to disability insurance include the definition of disability, coverage for both sickness and accidents, and whether the policy is noncancelable or guaranteed renewable.
   a. True
   b. False

2. The noncancelable provision of a disability policy ensures that the insurance will not be canceled and that the premiums will remain fixed for the term of the policy.
   a. True
   b. False

3. The guaranteed renewable feature of a disability insurance policy obligates the insurer to continue coverage as long as appropriate premiums are paid on the policy.
   a. True
   b. False

True, True, True.

Exhibit 5.4 | Disability Policy Characteristics

Policy Characteristics	Low Coverage	Medium Coverage	High Coverage
Monthly Benefit	$6,000	$6,000	$6,000
Elimination Period	90 days	90 days	90 days
Benefit Period	5 years	to age 67	to age 67*
Noncancelable	No	No (guaranteed renewable)	Yes
Occupation Specific	No	No	Yes
Partial Benefits (if go back to work part time)	Yes	Yes	Yes
Cost of Living Increases	No	No	Yes

Example policy for 40 year old with annual income of $100,000.
*Or for life if disability occurs before age 50.

Exhibit 5.5 provides sample premiums (by age) for disability policies with low, medium, and high coverage.

Exhibit 5.5 | Disability Policy Monthly Premiums

Age	Low Coverage	Medium Coverage	High Coverage
30	$68	$102	$168
35	$75	$120	$213
40	$100	$137	$263
45	$119	$155	$322
50	$148	$183	$380
55	$195	$218	$411
60	$267	$258	$453

Example individual policy for annual income of $100,000.

Exhibit 5.6 | Long-Term Disability Summary of Issues and Metrics

Issue	Adequate Coverage
Coverage	Both sickness and accident
Term of Benefits	To retirement or for life
Amount of Benefit	60 - 70% of gross pay
Elimination Period	Depends on emergency fund but generally 90 - 180 days
Definition of Disability	Own occupation or hybrid of own (up to 5 years under this definition of coverage), and any occupation for which insured is educated, experienced, or trained for balance
Cancelable	Noncancelable or guaranteed renewable

Long-Term Care Insurance

Long-term care insurance pays benefits when the insured is unable to perform at least two of the activities of daily living (ADL). Those activities typically include: eating, bathing, dressing, toileting, transferring (getting into or out of a bed or chair), and continence. If the insured cannot perform two or more of these activities of daily living or has cognitive impairment, the policy normally pays benefits. Assisting an insured with ADLs is referred to as custodial care (not skilled medical care). Services can be provided in an adult day care center, an assisted living center, or at home.

A client with low income and less than $2,000 in qualifying assets may qualify for Medicaid services for long-term care. Clients who anticipate qualifying for these services might consider not purchasing long-term care insurance. In addition, the client with financial resources to cover long-term care may not want to purchase long-term care insurance. The client who falls in between (cannot afford to self-insure long-term care and does not anticipate qualifying for Medicaid) may want to seriously consider purchasing long-term care insurance.

It is less expensive to purchase long-term care insurance at a younger age (50-60). Purchasing long-term care insurance at a younger age also reduces the likelihood of being rejected for coverage. Some policies have a waiting (elimination) period from when the long-term care is first needed until when the policy begins to pay benefits. The longer the waiting period, the lower the policy premium.

The benefit period can vary from two years to a lifetime. Premiums can be reduced by selecting coverage for three to four years instead of a lifetime. Most policies pay on an expense-incurred basis (reimbursement versus indemnity) up to the policy limits. When purchasing a long-term care policy, an inflation protection provision should be considered to protect the client from the loss of purchasing power of long-term care services. Additional important policy features include:

- Guaranteed renewable - The policy must be renewed by the insurer although the premiums can increase if they are increased for the entire class of policyholders.
- Waiver of premium - No further premiums are due once the insured begins receiving benefits.

HOMEOWNERS AND RENTERS INSURANCE

A home represents a major asset to the client. The frequency of a loss of a home is small, but the severity if it happens is potentially financially catastrophic. The key to homeowners insurance coverage, like any other property insurance, is having the correct risks (perils) covered and having them covered for the proper value (replacement value). **Homeowners insurance coverage** is a package policy covering dwelling, dwelling extensions (garage), personal property, loss of use, medical payments for others, and liability. Standard homeowner policies do not cover flood or earth movement (earthquake, mud slide). In addition, those properties located in an area prone to hurricanes may require a separate policy for wind and hail damage.

Homeowner policies range from covering 18 perils (broad) to open perils (open or "all") and from actual cash value (ACV = replacement cost - depreciation) to replacement value. There may be mixed coverages with open perils and replacement value on the dwelling and broad and actual cash value on personal property. Most homeowners and renters are not knowledgeable about insurance and should generally purchase open perils and replacement value for all property in a homeowners policy. This may require an endorsement for personal property since many homeowners and renters policies only have broad perils covered for personal property and then only for actual cash value.

Key Concepts

1. Identify the insurance coverages in a package homeowners insurance policy.

2. Identify the six parts of a personal automobile policy (PAP).

3. Determine the purpose of a personal liability umbrella policy.

Homeowners policies do not cover everything that can happen. Generally homeowners policies cover damage from fires, tornadoes (wind), trees falling, theft, and loss of use. However, homeowners policies frequently do not cover damage from earth movement (quake, mudslide, sink hole), mold, rising water (flood), sewer backup (without rider), war, nuclear accidents, neglect, dogs, and intentional acts by the insured or family, and some do not cover acts of terrorism.

In addition, valuable collections or items (guns, wine, coins, stamps, cash, jewelry), while perhaps covered, may be limited in value to the amount for which they are covered (e.g., up to $1,000 or some other limit). If the client has such collections, they probably need a policy endorsement (a policy rider which provides additional coverage).

Exhibit 5.7 | Summary of Disasters Covered by Homeowners Policies[1]

Perils	Dwelling & Personal Property Broad HO-2*	Dwelling Special HO-3*	Personal Property			Dwelling & Personal Property Modified Coverage HO-8
			Special HO-3	Renters HO-4	Condo/ Co-op HO-6	
1. Fire or lightning	X	X	X	X	X	X
2. Windstorm or hail	X	X	X	X	X	X
3. Explosion	X	X	X	X	X	X
4. Riot or civil commotion	X	X	X	X	X	X
5. Damage caused by aircraft	X	X	X	X	X	X
6. Damage caused by vehicles	X	X	X	X	X	X
7. Smoke	X	X	X	X	X	X
8. Vandalism or malicious mischief	X	X	X	X	X	X
9. Theft	X	X	X	X	X	X
10. Volcanic eruption	X	X	X	X	X	X
11. Falling object	X	X	X	X	X	
12. Weight of ice, snow or sleet	X	X	X	X	X	
13. Accidental discharge or overflow of water or steam from within a plumbing, heating, air conditioning, or automatic fire-protective sprinkler system, or from a household appliance.	X	X	X	X	X	
14. Sudden and accidental tearing apart, cracking, burning, or bulging of a steam or hot water heating system, an air conditioning or automatic fire-protective system.	X	X	X	X	X	
15. Freezing of a plumbing, heating, air conditioning or automatic, fire-protective sprinkler system, or of a household appliance.	X	X	X	X	X	
16. Sudden and accidental damage from artificially generated electrical current (does not include loss to a tube, transistor or similar electronic component).	X	X	X	X	X	
17. All perils except flood, earthquake, war, nuclear accident, landslide, mudslide, sinkhole and others specified in your policy. Check your policy for a complete list of perils excluded.		X				

* HO-1, HO-2 and HO-3 refer to standard Homeowners Policies.

Note: HO-1 has been discontinued in most states. The 18th peril is not listed and is glass breakage, which is covered by HO-2 (broad form).

---

1. Excerpt from Insurance Information Institute, "What Types of Disasters are Covered?"

AUTOMOBILE INSURANCE

Automobile liability insurance is required in every state. Many people also buy automobile property insurance (comprehensive - theft, and collision - damage from a wreck). The owner of an automobile is concerned about risks associated with the financial loss due to damage to the owned automobile, damage to the property of others, and bodily injury to the insured, family members, and to others.

The **personal automobile policy (PAP)** is a package policy that protects against loss for the three risks mentioned above. The PAP contract is organized into six parts.

- **Part A** - Liability coverage for bodily injury and property damage to others (may be stated in terms of split limits, such as $100,000/$300,000/$50,000 indicating coverage up to $100,000 for bodily injury per person, $300,000 bodily injury per accident, and $50,000 of property damage).
- **Part B** - Medical payments coverage (used to mitigate damage and not necessarily related to fault); may benefit the insured, family members, and/or other occupants of the vehicle.
- **Part C** - Uninsured motorist coverage - covers uninsured and underinsured motorists who cause damage to the insured passengers or the insured's property.
- **Part D** - Coverage for damage to the insured automobile, comprehensive (e.g., theft, tree falling etc.) and collision (striking any inanimate object while moving).
- **Part E** - Duties of the insured (notify insurer, file proof of claim, and cooperate with any investigation).
- **Part F** - General Provisions - Various provisions including that coverage is only valid in the U.S., its territories, and Canada (not Mexico or other foreign countries).

Exclusions

The PAP has exclusions for liability for public livery (the transporting of people or goods for hire), intentional acts, business use of auto, use without permission, for the insured's property, and bodily injury to an employee (except domestic employee).

Exclusions for medical payments include public livery, use without permission, business use, racing, and intentional acts.

Exclusions for uninsured motorist coverage include public livery, regular use of non-owned or nondeclared auto, use without permission, and business use.

Exclusions for damage to the insured's automobile includes public livery, use without permission, racing, intentional acts, business use and, in addition, some items found in the car may not be covered (e.g., radar detectors and electronic equipment not permanently installed).

Rates

Automobile rates vary by zip code, marital status, age, sex, and driving record. In order to manage premiums effectively, the insured should solicit regular quotes (every one to two years) and should raise deductibles.

Exhibit 5.8 | Automobile Insurance Premiums by State (Averages for 2020)

Rank	State	Average Premium	Rank	State	Average Premium
1	Michigan	$2,878	26	Alabama	$1,449
2	Louisiana	$2,389	27	Illinois	$1,434
3	Florida	$2,239	28	Kansas	$1,432
4	Texas	$2,050	29	Washington	$1,426
5	California	$1,968	30	Missouri	$1,411
6	Georgia	$1,936	31	South Dakota	$1,394
7	Washington, D.C.	**$1,928**	32	Nebraska	$1,365
8	Rhode Island	$1,918	33	North Carolina	$1,359
9	South Carolina	$1,759	34	Tennessee	$1,357
10	Delaware	$1,757	35	Alaska	$1,337
11	Colorado	$1,741	36	Oregon	$1,327
12	Montana	$1,693	37	New York	$1,320
13	Connecticut	$1,688	38	Utah	$1,300
14	Wyoming	$1,684	39	Hawaii	$1,295
15	Kentucky	$1,621	40	Vermont	$1,294
16	Arkansas	$1,620	41	Massachusetts	$1,275
17	Mississippi	$1,580	42	Pennsylvania	$1,270
18	Nevada	$1,570	43	Virginia	$1,270
19	New Jersey	$1,558	44	North Dakota	$1,229
20	Arizona	$1,557	45	Indiana	$1,213
	National Average	**$1,517**	46	Iowa	$1,123
21	New Mexico	$1,479	47	Idaho	$1,062
22	Oklahoma	$1,468	48	Wisconsin	$1,049
23	Maryland	$1,467	49	Ohio	$1,034
24	Minnesota	$1,453	50	New Hampshire	$985
25	West Virgina	$1,451	51	Maine	$912

Source: Insure.com; http://www.insure.com/car-insurance/car-insurance-rates.html

It should be noted that personal automobile policies do not cover other types of vehicles (e.g., boats, motorcycles, etc.). In addition, the PAP does not cover business automobiles. Business autos are covered under a Business Auto Policy (BAP).

PERSONAL LIABILITY INSURANCE

Today, lawsuits are common. Juries and judges are awarding larger amounts of money than ever before. Claims arise from incidents at home, while driving an automobile, boat, recreational vehicle, or motorcycle, and from other activities (snow skiing). The question is, are the underlying liability coverages for homeowners policies and automobile insurance packages sufficient to meet the award if a person is judged to be at fault? A Personal liability umbrella coverage provides additional liability coverage beyond what is provided by the homeowner and auto policies.

Some, but not all, personal liability umbrella policies provide for legal defense as well as for paying a claim up to the limit of the policy. However, if the insurer is willing to pay the limit of the policy, then legal defense is not required and the client is on their own. Almost all homeowner policies have inadequate liability coverages. Automobile policies that have limits for bodily injury to others of $100,000 or even $300,000 per person may prove to be inadequate.

This lack of catastrophic liability coverage creates the need for an excess liability policy known as a **personal liability umbrella policy (PLUP)**. A PLUP is usually sold in millions of dollars of coverage (e.g. $1M, $3M, $5M) and provides excess liability coverage and legal defense for liability claims that may arise and that exceed the limits of the underlying homeowners and automobile policies. The PLUP also covers the entire family and fills in the liability gap that exists between the homeowners and automobile policy. The PLUP is relatively inexpensive ($1,000,000 in Louisiana is approximately $300 per year, $4,000,000 in Maryland is approximately $450 per year) and is based on the risk analysis by the underwriter of the insured.

The PLUP is usually sold by the automobile or home insurer and the amount needed is not balance sheet dependent, but rather risk dependent (e.g., what has been the amount of recent awards in a particular state for common, although infrequent, accidental perils).

CONCLUSION

The chapter presents an introduction to the most common types of client risk. Risk management issues are a priority as part of the personal financial plan because catastrophic loss can lead to financial planning failure. A full course in insurance and/or consultation with an insurance expert is recommended for all planners aspiring to competently assist clients with important risk management issues.

DISCUSSION QUESTIONS

SOLUTIONS to the discussion questions can be found exclusively within the chapter. Once you have completed an initial reading of the chapter, go back and highlight the answers to these questions.

1. Describe the personal risk management process.

2. List four responses to managing risk.

3. Define a peril.

4. Define the three main types of hazard.

5. List some of the unique characteristics of an insurance contract.

6. What are three methods used to determine the amount of life insurance needed?

7. Discuss the characteristics of term life insurance.

8. Define the difference between own occupation and any occupation disability definitions and the associated coverage.

9. Discuss the coverage available under a homeowners insurance policy.

10. Define a personal automobile policy (PAP).

11. Discuss why there is a need for personal liability insurance.

12. Differentiate between noncancelable and guaranteed renewable.

MULTIPLE-CHOICE PROBLEMS

A sample of multiple choice problems is provided below. Additional multiple choice problems are available at money-education.com by accessing the Student Practice Portal.

1. Which of the following would <u>not</u> be considered a personal risk?
    a. Becoming disabled due to a car accident.
    b. Injuring a passenger in your vehicle during an auto accident that was your fault.
    c. Dying at age 42 given a normal life expectancy of age 80.
    d. Being diagnosed with a curable form of cancer.

2. You recently met with your client, Leonardo, age 40. Leonardo is widowed and has one dependent child. During your meeting with him you discussed the concept of risk management. Which of the following statements regarding the ways to manage risk is <u>not</u> correct?
    a. The selling of Leonardo's Jet Ski is an example of risk reduction.
    b. Not purchasing life insurance is an example of risk retention.
    c. Purchasing a warranty is an example of risk transfer.
    d. Insurance is not necessary for every risk of financial loss.

3. If a risk has a high frequency of occurrence and a high severity, you should:
    a. Transfer the risk.
    b. Retain the risk.
    c. Reduce the risk.
    d. Avoid the risk.

4. Camila had a very bad year. She wrecked her car in January when she ran a red light (because she could not see properly having left her contacts at home) and crashed into another car completely destroying both cars. The insurance company was very nice to her and she purchased a new car with the insurance proceeds. Camila decided that since she had insurance, it really did not matter if she took proper care of her new car because she could always get a new one. Camila got in the habit of leaving her new car unlocked and it was stolen. After Camila bought another car she decided that she really liked the insurance adjuster and wanted to see him again, so one day she purposefully set her car on fire. In her carelessness, she also caught her hand on fire. Camila was depressed over her circumstances and decided she didn't want to go back to work. She filed a falsified disability claim for the loss of use of her hand (even though she could still use her hand). Which of the following statements is true?
    a. Driving with poor eyesight is not a hazard.
    b. Leaving the car unlocked is a morale hazard.
    c. Burning the car on purpose is a morale hazard.
    d. Filing a false disability claim is a morale hazard.

5. Kayne wants to purchase a life insurance policy on his own life. He is interested in learning about the various approaches to determine the amount needed. Which of the following is **not** true regarding the three most common approaches?

    a. The human life value method estimates the present value of income generated over a person's work life expectancy, after adjusting for the expected consumption of the survivors.

    b. The financial needs method evaluates the income replacement and lump-sum needs of the survivors after the insured dies.

    c. The capitalization of earnings method determines need by dividing the client's gross income by the riskless rate of return.

    d. In practice a financial planner would utilize all three methods and then determine the client's needs based on a combination of factors including affordability.

**Additional multiple choice problems
are available at
money-education.com
by accessing the
Student Practice Portal.
Access requires registration of the title using
the unique code at the front of the book.**

QUICK QUIZ EXPLANATIONS

Quick Quiz 5.1
1. True.
2. True.
3. False. This is the definition for risk reduction. Risk avoidance is avoiding an activity so that a financial loss cannot be incurred.
4. True.

Quick Quiz 5.2
1. True.
2. False. This is the definition of a morale hazard. A moral hazard is a character flaw or level of dishonesty an individual possesses that causes or increases the chance for a loss.
3. True.

Quick Quiz 5.3
1. False. This is the definition of the financial needs method of measuring life insurance need. The human life value method uses projected future earnings as the basis for measuring life insurance needs.
2. True.
3. False. Permanent insurance has both a savings and investment component. Term life insurance has no savings or investment component.

Quick Quiz 5.4
1. True.
2. True.
3. True.

Quick Quiz 5.5
1. True.
2. False. Business use is not an included coverage under a PAP. Exclusions from coverage under a PAP includes liability for public livery, intentional acts, business use of auto, use without permission, for insured's property, and bodily injury to an employee (except domestic employee).
3. True.

6

JOHN AND MARY BURKE
CASE AND CASE ANALYSIS

LEARNING OBJECTIVES

1. Describe an initial meeting, summarize data, and draw conclusions for the life cycle approach.
2. Prepare a comprehensive engagement letter.
3. Gather internal and external data and prepare financial statements.
4. Create the pie chart approach.
5. Prepare financial statement analysis using a ratio analysis approach.
6. Prepare each of the ratios and compare them to the benchmark.
7. Prepare the two-step, three panel, metrics approach with schedules.
8. Prepare the cash flow approach, the tax analysis approach, the strategic approach, and the present value of all goals approach.
9. Identify opportunities and challenges related to a client's cash inflows and outflows and make recommendations to assist the client in meeting their current needs and long-term financial goals.*
10. Make a presentation to the client using current & projected financial statements and ratios.
11. Prepare a closing engagement letter that includes the responsibility for implementation and monitoring.

Ties to CFP Certification Learning Objectives

JOHN AND MARY BURKE CASE

This chapter presents a financial planning case incorporating the introductory information in Chapter 1, the financial planning approaches in Chapter 3, the financial statement analysis in Chapter 4, and the risk management information in Chapter 5 of this textbook. The Burke case analysis is presented in a basic fashion to assist the developing financial planner in understanding the importance of professionally providing the fundamental tasks as well as complicated tasks throughout the comprehensive financial planning process.

Financial Planning Offices of Mitchell and Mitchell
Michael A. Mitchell, CFP®
Robin Delle, Executive Assistant

Dialog of Phone Conversation to 850-555-9876 December 15, 20X1, 10:00 a.m.	
Robin:	Good morning, Mitchell and Mitchell Financial Planners.
Caller:	Is Mr. Michael Mitchell available?
Robin:	He is currently in a meeting. May I have him return your call?
Caller:	Yes, please. This is John Burke. I am calling about financial planning for myself and my wife, Mary. My phone number is 850-555-4321.
Robin:	I can have Mr. Mitchell call you back between 1:00 and 1:30pm. Is that a good time for you?
Mr. Burke:	Yes, thank you. By the way, please tell him I was referred to him by Sally Robbins.
Robin:	I will. Thank you. Goodbye.

	Dialog of Phone Conversation **December 15, 20X1, 1:00 p.m.**
Mike Mitchell:	Hello Mr. Burke (formal, show respect). This is Mike Mitchell returning your call from this morning. I understand you are interested in developing a financial plan for your family. Is that correct (questioning)?
John Burke:	Yes, thank you for returning my call. You come highly recommended from my good friend and mentor, Sally Robbins, who I believe is one of your financial planning clients.
Mike Mitchell:	Well thank you. Yes, Sally has been a client for some time now. I appreciate you letting me know that Sally recommended our services.
John Burke:	You're welcome.
Mike Mitchell:	I expect you want to set up an appointment? How about you and your wife meet with me at 9:00 a.m. on January 4th at my office? Would that work for you? The meeting would last about two hours, giving us time to get to know each other. There is no charge for the initial meeting.
John Burke:	January 4th is fine and I know where your office is located. Do I need to bring anything?
Mike Mitchell:	Well, I would like to send you an email with a list of items to bring. I'll mention them now (internal data collection): your recent bank statements, investment account statements, all insurance policies, five years of tax returns (if you have them), employer benefits brochures, and a set of financial statements (if you have them). No need to write all of this down, I will email you a detailed list. What is your email address?
John Burke:	jburke@hotmail.com
Mike Mitchell:	Ok, great. Please do not worry if you do not have all these things; just bring what you can. The whole process takes time. By the way, would you mind if I asked you a few brief questions to help me form a picture of you and your family (life cycle information)?
John Burke:	No, go ahead.
Mike Mitchell:	Your wife's name is Mary, correct?
John Burke:	Yes.
Mike Mitchell:	How old are each of you?
John Burke:	We are both 30 years old and have been married for three years. I was previously married and have a four year old son, Patrick, but we are estranged. He lives out of state.
Mike Mitchell:	Fine. Do you plan on having additional children in the near future?
John Burke:	Yes, we would like to adopt two newborns in the next few years and are already approved by the adoption agency.
Mike Mitchell:	What is your approximate income and does Mary work?

John Burke:	Mary works as an administrative assistant at an accounting firm making $26,000 per year. I am an assistant marketing manager with Atlanta Gas. My annual income is $36,000 or $3,000 per month. I pay $350 a month to my ex wife for child support.
Mike Mitchell:	Good, I have a good picture now. Do you happen to know what your net worth is? And, do you own your home?
John Burke:	I am guessing our net worth is about $10,000 or so. We are just getting started and we currently rent and are saving to buy a home. We hope you can help us get on the right track.
Mike Mitchell:	That's great. It has been very nice talking with you. Do you have any questions for me at this time?
John Burke:	No, thank you.
Mike Mitchell:	I will send the email to you by tomorrow and I will see you and Mary at my office January 4th at 9:00 a.m. Please do not hesitate to call me if anything comes up during the interim.
John Burke:	Thanks, I am looking forward to meeting you in person. Goodbye.
Mike Mitchell:	Thank you. Goodbye.

Based on the initial telephone communication, here is the relevant information collected:

Summary of Data Collected - Life Cycle Approach	
Ages	John 30, Mary 30
Marital Status	Married Filing Jointly filing status
Children	John has one child, age 4 (living out of state, estranged), they would like two to three within the next five years.
Grandchildren	None
Net Worth	Approximately $10,000
Income	$36,000 John, $26,000 Mary
Self-Employed	No
Other	John pays $350 per month in child support. One of their goals is to save for a home.

Mike Mitchell's Preliminary Conclusions Regarding the Burkes: (using the life cycle approach)

The life cycle data suggests the Burkes are in the accumulation and risk management phases. Therefore, they need a thorough risk management analysis: life needs, health, disability, property, and liability. They also need to save at least 10 - 13 percent of their income for the basic goal of retirement security and probably need a savings rate greater than 10 - 13 percent to accommodate the college education of two to three children.

- Their personal risks are:
    - untimely death
    - health problems
    - disability risks

- They are probably underinsured for catastrophic risks.

- They likely have cars that need the proper liability and property insurance coverage.

- They likely need but do not have a personal liability umbrella policy.

- Their potential goals are:
    - buying a house
    - savings for children's education
    - beginning to save for retirement

- They probably do not have personal financial statements.

- They probably have a wide assortment of debt.

Dear Mr. Burke:

Thank you for calling me. It was a pleasure to talk with you yesterday and I look forward to our meeting on January 4th.

Please bring with you as many of the following items as you can but do not worry if you do not have everything. (You can bring originals and we can copy them or you can bring copies for us to keep.)

Insurance:
- All life insurance policies - the type - the death benefit, the annual premium(s), who pays the premium(s), who owns the policy, the insured, the beneficiary.
- Any Disability policies - who is insured, amount of premium, who pays the premium(s).
- Health insurance policies - who is covered, deductibles, co-pays, etc.
- Automobile insurance policies - who is covered, amount of premium(s).
- Homeowner's policies - what is covered, deductibles, etc.
- Any liability policies - amount of premium(s).
- Any long-term care policies.

Banking and Investments:
- All recent statements for checking and savings accounts.
- All recent statements and year-end statements if available for all brokerage and investment accounts.
- All 401(k) Plan, 403(b) Plan statements.

Tax Returns:
- Five years of Federal income tax returns if you have them.

Wills, Trust:
- All copies of wills, durable powers of attorney for health care, advance medical directives.
- Any trust documents for which you are either grantor or beneficiary if you have them.

Employee Benefits:
- Any employer brochures describing employee fringe benefits that you receive or can receive for both you and Mary.
- Summary plan description for employer-sponsored plans.

Financial Statements:
- Any prepared personal financial statements, balance sheet, and income statement.
- If you do not have financial statements, we can create them for you. Bring a list of assets and debts with interest rates, balances, and terms.
- If you can, prepare an annual or monthly statement of your income and expenses.

Call me if you have any questions. I look forward to seeing you and Mary at 9:00 a.m. on the 4th at my office.

Regards,

Mike Mitchell, CFP®
Partner
Mitchell and Mitchell
850-555-9876

At the first meeting - January 4, 9:00 a.m. - Mike Mitchell Notes

I met with John and Mary Burke and we had a good initial meeting. I described that our services involve comprehensive financial planning. They identified several financial goals. I inquired about additional savings opportunities at their place of employment. I discovered that at this time they have no plans for college education of Patrick (age 4). They did a great job of bringing in their information that I had requested in my email and I will be putting that together in a case file. While they did not have financial statements prepared, they were able to list for me their assets and liabilities. I told them that in the case file I would send them, there would be financial statements that we prepared, a prepared pie chart graphic, and some ratios for their review. I mentioned that if we were missing any data we would contact John by email.

I informed them that for this engagement we would bill $3,000 for the initial plan. Any additional services are billed per diem at the rate of $200 per hour for myself and $125 per hour for any assistant time. John informed me that his father would be paying for the comprehensive financial plan. I also explained that it would take us about twelve weeks to complete the process if we met once a week for about an hour. We discussed implementation and they indicated that where they could, they would handle the implementation.

We set the next meeting for January 18th to allow time for us to build the case file and prepare the financial statements.

Engagement Letter

Financial Planning Offices of Mitchell and Mitchell

January 4, 20X2

John and Mary Burke
1420 Elm Street
Pensacola, FL 32501

RE: Financial Planning Engagement Letter

Dear Mr. and Mrs. Burke:

This letter will confirm the terms of our recent conversation regarding the financial planning services we will provide for you. The primary objective of our engagement is to prepare a review of your personal financial situation. This review will identify your personal financial goals and objectives, and will include possible strategies to achieve them. Our analysis and recommendations are based on information provided by you that will be relied upon.

The initial phase involves accumulating and organizing facts about your current financial status, identifying specific goals and objectives, and agreeing upon planning assumptions. After your financial information has been received, the data will be analyzed and projections will be made. Subsequent meetings will be held to verify the accuracy of the data and will allow you to validate the assumptions used. Alternative courses of action to meet goals and alleviate any issues will be comprehensively discussed. We will meet over a period of approximately twelve weeks (based on weekly meetings).

The methods that you choose to follow for the implementation of the financial planning recommendations are at your discretion. As you have indicated, you will be responsible for all decisions regarding implementation of the recommendations.

The fee for your comprehensive financial plan has been determined by our mutual agreement and is $3,000 which is due and payable upon return of this Engagement Letter and will be paid by John Burke's father. Please note that this fee is for the written financial plan alone and the plan shall contain all of our recommendations to you through the date of its delivery. In addition, please be advised that this fee does not include preparation of any legal documents or tax returns.

We anticipate beginning the engagement immediately. If this letter meets with your approval, please sign the enclosed copy in the space provided and return it to us. You are free to terminate this agreement at any time and we will bill you for the portion of work that is complete.

We thank you for the opportunity to be of service, and we welcome you as a valued client.

Sincerely,
Michael A. Mitchell, CFP®

I/We agree to the above terms & conditions:

Client Signature: _____   Date: _____
                         John Burke

Client Signature: _____   Date: _____
                         Mary Burke

> ### Mike Mitchell's Email to John Burke
> ### January 11, 20X2
>
> Dear John and Mary:
>
> I am sending you our complete case file of internal and external data collected along with:
> - Income Statement for the year 20X2
> - Statement of Financial Position as of 1/01/20X2
> - Pie chart of your current Income Statement along with a benchmark pie chart
> - Pie chart of your current Statement of Financial Position along with a benchmark pie chart
>
> Please review these for accuracy and we can discuss them at our next meeting on the 18th.
>
> Regards,
>
> Mike Mitchell, CFP®
> Partner
> Mitchell and Mitchell
> 850-555-9876

PERSONAL BACKGROUND AND INFORMATION COLLECTED

The Family

John Burke, age 30, is an assistant manager in the marketing department of Florida Gas. His annual salary is $36,000. His wife, Mary, is an administrative assistant with an accounting firm. Mary is also 30 years old and has an annual salary of $26,000.

John and Mary have been married for three years and have no children from their marriage. They hope to have two to three children in the next five years. However, John has one child, Patrick (age 4), from a former marriage. Patrick lives with his mother, Kathy, out of state and as a result, John has not seen Patrick for three years.

John pays $350 per month in child support to Kathy for Patrick until he reaches age 18. John also pays for a term life insurance policy on himself for Kathy (beneficiary) as a result of the divorce. The contingent beneficiary on the policy is Patrick. Patrick's education is fully funded by a 529 Plan established by Kathy's father.

EXTERNAL INFORMATION

Economic Information

- Inflation is expected to be 3.0% annually.
- The Burkes' salaries should increase 4.0% for the next five to ten years.
- There is no state income tax.
- It is expected that there will be a slow growth economy; stocks are expected to return an average of 9.0% annually.

Bank Lending Rates

- 15-year mortgage rate is 5.0%.
- 30-year mortgage rate is 5.5%.
- Secured personal loan rate is 8.0%.
- Credit card rates are 18%.
- Prime rate is 3.0%.

Expected Investment Returns

- Their expected rate of return is 8.5%.

	Return	Standard Deviation
Cash and Money Market Fund	2.5%	2.5%
Guaranteed Income Fund	2.5%	2.5%
Treasury Bonds/ Bond Funds	4.0%	4.0%
Corporate Bonds/ Bond Funds	6.0%	5.0%
Municipal Bonds/ Bond Funds	5.0%	4.0%
International Bond Funds	7.0%	6.0%
Index Fund	9.0%	14.0%
Large Cap Funds/Stocks	10.0%	16.0%
Mid/Small Funds/Stocks	12.0%	18.0%
International Stock Funds	13.0%	22.0%
Real Estate Funds	8.0%	12.0%

INTERNAL INFORMATION

Insurance Information

Life Insurance

	Policy A*	Policy B	Policy C
Insured	John	John	Mary
Face Amount	$500,000	$50,000	$26,000
Type	Term	Group Term	Group Term
Cash Value	$0	$0	$0
Annual Premium	$600	$178	$50
Who pays premium	John	Employer	Employer
Beneficiary	Kathy then Patrick	Kathy	John
Policy Owner	Kathy	John	Mary
Settlement options clause selected	None	None	None

*John is required, as a result of the divorce, to maintain a term life insurance policy (Policy A) of $500,000.
The premiums are $50 per month.*

Health Insurance

John and Mary are both covered under John's employer health plan. The policy is an indemnity plan with a $300 deductible per person per year and an 80/20 major medical coinsurance clause with a family annual stop loss (out-of-pocket maximum) of $2,000. Patrick's health insurance is provided by his mother.

Long-Term Disability Insurance

- John is covered by an "own occupation" policy with premiums paid by his employer. The benefits equal 60 percent of his gross pay after an elimination period of 90 days. The policy covers both sickness and accidents and is guaranteed renewable. The term of benefits is to age 66.
- Mary is not covered by disability insurance.

Long-Term Care Insurance

- Neither John nor Mary have long-term care insurance.

Renters Insurance

- The Burkes have an HO4 renters policy (a Contents Broad Form policy that covers contents and liability) without endorsements. The annual premium is $600.
- Content coverage is $25,000 and liability coverage is $100,000.

Automobile Insurance

- Both their car and truck are covered.

- They do not have any separate insurance on John's motor scooter.

Type	PAP
Bodily Injury	$50,000/$100,000
Property Damage	$10,000
Medical Payments	$5,000 per person
Physical Damage	Actual Cash Value
Uninsured Motorist	$25,000/$50,000
Comprehensive Deductible	$200
Collision Deductible	$500
Premium (annual)	$3,600

Personal Liability Insurance
- Neither John nor Mary have PLUP coverage.

Investment Information

John owns 1,000 shares of Crossroads Inc. stock that was inherited by him. Its current value is $8,000 and it pays a dividend of 34 cents per share for a total of $340 per year, which is not included in the income statement because it is reinvested. John also owns 100 shares of Gladwell, Inc. stock that was received by him as a gift. The adjusted taxable basis is $4,000 and the fair market value is $4,000. Both the Gladwell and Crossroads stocks are large cap stocks.

Five years ago, John invested in a balanced mutual fund that was initially started with $8,000 he received as a gift. He has reinvested all dividends and capital gains each year. The gains and dividends together reported on their tax returns and reinvested from the balanced mutual fund were as follows:

	Dividends & Interest	Capital Gains	Total
5 Years Ago	$160	$140	$300
4 Years Ago	$170	$580	$750
3 Years Ago	$180	$1,020	$1,200
2 Years Ago	$190	$600	$790
Last Year	$200	$760	$960

The 401(k) plan portfolio is invested in a balanced mutual fund expected to earn 8.5%. Their overall expected investment rate of return is 8.5%.

Risk Tolerance Questionnaire

Global Portfolio Allocation Scoring System (PASS) for Individual Investors[1]

Questions	Strongly Agree	Agree	Neutral	Disagree	Strongly Disagree
1. Earning a high long-term total return that will allow my capital to grow faster than the inflation rate is one of my most important investment objectives.	J	M			
2. I would like an investment that provides me with an opportunity to defer taxation of capital gains to future years.		M	J		
3. I do not require a high level of current income from my investments.		J, M			
4. I am willing to tolerate some sharp down swings in the return on my investments in order to seek a potentially higher return than would normally be expected from more stable investments.	J	M			
5. I am willing to risk a short-term loss in return for a potentially higher long-run rate of return.		J	M		
6. I am financially able to accept a low level of liquidity in my investment portfolio.		J	M		

J = John, M = Mary

---

1. Global Portfolio Allocation Scoring System (PASS) for Individual Investors - developed by Dr. William Droms (Georgetown University) and Steven N. Strauss, (DromsStrauss Advisors Inc.) - model used with permission.

Financial Statements

Statement of Financial Position 1/1/20X2

<table>
<tr><td colspan="6" align="center">Statement of Financial Position
John and Mary Burke
Balance Sheet as of 1/1/20X2</td></tr>
<tr><td colspan="3" align="center">Assets[1]</td><td colspan="3" align="center">Liabilities and Net Worth</td></tr>
<tr><td colspan="3">CURRENT ASSETS</td><td colspan="3">CURRENT LIABILITIES[2]</td></tr>
<tr><td>JT</td><td>Checking Account</td><td>$3,000</td><td>H</td><td>Credit Card Balance Visa</td><td>$336</td></tr>
<tr><td>JT</td><td>Savings Account</td><td>$0</td><td>W</td><td>Credit Card Balance MC</td><td>$187</td></tr>
<tr><td colspan="2">Total Current Assets</td><td>$3,000</td><td>W</td><td>Auto Loan - Mary</td><td>$3,192</td></tr>
<tr><td colspan="2">Investment Assets</td><td></td><td>H</td><td>Student Loan - John</td><td>$3,813</td></tr>
<tr><td>H</td><td>Crossroads Inc.
(1,000 Shares)[3]</td><td>$8,000</td><td colspan="2">Total Current Liabilities</td><td>$7,528</td></tr>
<tr><td>H</td><td>Gladwell Inc. (100 Shares)</td><td>$4,000</td><td></td><td></td><td></td></tr>
<tr><td>H</td><td>Balanced Mutual Fund</td><td>$12,000</td><td colspan="2">Long-Term Liabilities2</td><td></td></tr>
<tr><td>H</td><td>401(k) Plan Account Balance</td><td>$4,320</td><td>H</td><td>Credit Card Balance Visa</td><td>$8,664</td></tr>
<tr><td colspan="2">Total Investment Assets</td><td>$28,320</td><td>W</td><td>Credit Card Balance MC</td><td>$4,813</td></tr>
<tr><td></td><td></td><td></td><td>W</td><td>Auto Loan - Mary</td><td>$6,856</td></tr>
<tr><td colspan="2">Personal Use Assets</td><td></td><td>H</td><td>Student Loan - John[4]</td><td>$50,485</td></tr>
<tr><td>W</td><td>Auto - Mary</td><td>$18,500</td><td colspan="2">Total Long-Term Liabilities</td><td>$70,818</td></tr>
<tr><td>H</td><td>Truck - John</td><td>$12,000</td><td></td><td></td><td></td></tr>
<tr><td>H</td><td>Motor scooter - John</td><td>$2,000</td><td colspan="2">Total Liabilities</td><td>$78,346</td></tr>
<tr><td>JT</td><td>Personal Property & Furniture</td><td>$25,000</td><td colspan="2">Total Net Worth</td><td>$10,475</td></tr>
<tr><td colspan="2">Total Personal Use Assets</td><td>$57,500</td><td></td><td></td><td></td></tr>
<tr><td colspan="2" align="center">Total Assets</td><td>$88,820</td><td colspan="2">TOTAL LIABILITIES & NET WORTH</td><td>$88,820</td></tr>
</table>

1. Assets are stated at fair market value. Numbers may be rounded
2. Liabilities are stated at principal only as of January 1, 20X2 (prior to January payments). The current portion of long-term debt is included in current liabilities.
3. Crossroads Inc.'s current dividend is $0.34 per year per share and is reinvested.
4. The interest rate on the student loan is 7.3842% for a 10-year term on a consolidation loan John just made.

JT = Joint Tenancy
H = Husband
W = Wife

Statement of Income and Expenses

Statement of Income and Expenses Mr. and Mrs. Burke Statement of Income and Expenses for Past Year and Expected (Approximate) For 20X2		
CASH INFLOWS		**Totals**
Salaries		
John's Salary	$36,000	
Mary's Salary	$26,000	
Variable Annuity Income	$1,300 *	
Total Cash Inflows		$63,300
CASH OUTFLOWS		
Savings		
Savings - House down payment	$2,500	
401(k) Plan Contribution	$1,080	
Total Savings		$3,580
Fixed Outflows		
Child Support	$4,200 ND	
Life Insurance Payment (Term)	$600 ND	
Rent	$8,400 ND	
HO 4 Renters Insurance	$600 ND	
Utilities	$720 ND	
Telephone	$360 ND	
Auto payment P&I	$3,600 ND	
Auto Insurance	$3,600 ND	
Gas, Oil, Maintenance for Auto	$2,400 ND	
Student Loan Payments	$7,695 ND	
Credit Card Payments	$3,000 ND	
Total Fixed Outflows		$35,175
Variable Outflows		
Taxes - John FICA	$2,754	
Taxes - Mary FICA	$1,989	
Taxes - Federal Tax Withheld	$12,660	
Food	$3,600 ND	
Clothing	$1,000 ND	
Vacations	$1,500	
Total Variable Outflows		$23,503
Total Cash Outflows		$62,258
NET DISCRETIONARY CASH FLOWS		$1,042

ND = Non-Discretionary

* The $1,300 is income from an inherited variable annuity with a remaining term of 5 years.

Income Tax Information

The filing status of the Burkes for federal income tax is married filing jointly. Patrick is claimed as a dependent on Kathy's tax return as part of John and Kathy's divorce agreement. There is no state income tax.

Retirement Information

John currently contributes three percent of his salary to his 401(k) plan. The employer matches each $1 contributed with $0.50 up to a total employer contribution of three percent. Mary has a 401(k) plan that provides a match of 25 percent of her contributions up to six percent. Mary has never contributed to her 401(k) plan.

Gifts, Estates, Trusts, and Will Information

- John has a will leaving all of his probate estate to Patrick. He did not change the will after his marriage to Mary.
- Mary does not have a will.
- The Burkes live in a common law property state.

INFORMATION REGARDING ASSETS AND LIABILITIES

Automobile

The automobile was purchased January 1, 20X0 for $19,993 with 20 percent down and 80 percent financed over 60 months with payments of $300 per month.

Financial Goals

- Increase savings.
- Debt reduction.
- Save enough for a down payment on a home of 20 percent of $180,000 in today's dollars for purchase in three years. Property taxes are expected to be one percent of the value of home. Homeowners insurance (HO3 endorsed - a Special Form Homeowner's policy that covers a wide variety of perils) will be one percent of the value of the home.
- For education, they plan to spend $20,000 per year for four years for each of the two children at the child's age 18. The expected education inflation rate is five percent. Assume they have twins two years from now for the calculation of education funding.
- For retirement, they want to plan for 100% ($62,000) wage replacement at age 65, without any consideration of Social Security. If they cannot achieve that they will consider a compromise between delaying retirement and lowering the wage replacement ratio as long as the wage replacement is no less than 75% and the delayed retirement is no later than age 67. They expect to live to age 95.
- Have a good risk management portfolio and assume a rate of return of 8.5%.
- Develop a comprehensive financial plan.

CASE ANALYSIS

Based on the initial telephone communication, here is the relevant information collected.

Summary of Data Collected - Life Cycle Approach	
Ages	John 30, Mary 30
Marital Status	Married Filing Jointly filing status
Children	John has one child, age 4 (living out of state, estranged), they would like two to three additional children within the next five years.
Grandchildren	None
Net Worth	Approximately $10,000
Income	$36,000 John, $26,000 Mary
Self-Employed	No
Other	John pays $350 per month in child support. One of their goals is to save for a home.

Mike Mitchell's Preliminary Conclusions Regarding the Burkes: (using the life cycle approach)

The life cycle data suggests the Burkes are in the accumulation and risk management phases. Therefore, they need a thorough risk management analysis: life needs, health, disability, property and liability. They also need to save at least 10 - 13 percent of their income for the basic goal of retirement security and probably need a savings rate greater than 10 - 13 percent to accommodate the college education of two to three children.

- They are probably underinsured for catastrophic risks, such as untimely death, disability, and perhaps health, property, and liability.
- They likely have cars that need proper liability and property insurance coverage.
- They likely need but do not have a personal liability umbrella policy.
- Their potential goals are:
  - buying a house
  - saving for children's education
  - saving for retirement
- They probably do not have competent and complete personal financial statements.
- They probably have a wide assortment of debt.

Applying Financial Planning Approaches

The Burke client relationship has now been established, the internal and external data has been collected, and the goals have been identified. Next, the financial planner is ready to analyze and evaluate the client's financial status. The following approaches will be applied in order to form client recommendations.

- Pie Chart Approach
- Financial Statement Analysis-Ratio Analysis Approach
- The Two-Step / Three-Panel / Metrics Approach
- The Present Value of All Goals Approach
- The Cash Flow Approach
- Strategic Approach

Each approach is applied to the Burke case for practical application purposes so that the financial planner can learn how to identify weaknesses in the financial situation. In addition, the practitioner can also learn how to use the varied approaches together to analyze and evaluate the client's financial circumstances to arrive at the best recommendations for the client.

PIE CHART APPROACH

Introduction

The pie chart approach to analysis provides the financial planner and the client with a visual representation of the balance sheet and the income statement. The financial statements are prepared first and then they are depicted in pie charts. The pie charts provide a fairly high level view, rather than a detailed analysis, and are only used as a starting point for discussions with the client. They do, however, provide the planner with sufficient insight to the client's financial profile to have that high level conversation. Below each pie chart are the planner's observations, which affords the opportunity for a more in-depth discussion with the clients on each observation point.

Data for Pie Chart Approach - Balance Sheet 1/1/20X2

Burke Balance Sheet

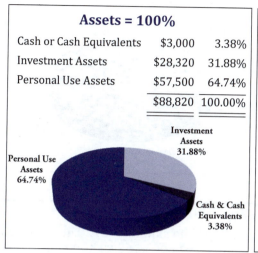

Assets = 100%		
Cash or Cash Equivalents	$3,000	3.38%
Investment Assets	$28,320	31.88%
Personal Use Assets	$57,500	64.74%
	$88,820	100.00%

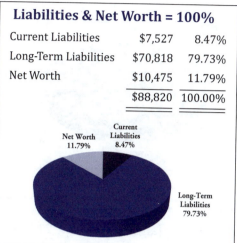

Liabilities & Net Worth = 100%		
Current Liabilities	$7,527	8.47%
Long-Term Liabilities	$70,818	79.73%
Net Worth	$10,475	11.79%
	$88,820	100.00%

Benchmark Balance Sheet

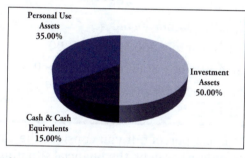

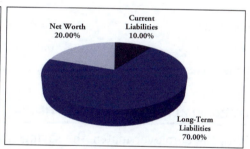

Note: The balance sheet benchmarks are never exact, but it is clear that the Burkes should have a greater amount of money in an emergency fund and more investment assets for their current age. It is also clear that relative to the benchmarks, debt is high.

Observations

The balance sheet pie chart indicates the following:

- Cash and cash equivalents are low (3.38%), therefore the emergency fund and current ratios are also probably low.
- The net worth is low relative to the client's age.
- Investment assets are low relative to gross pay.

These deficiencies can be overcome in a relatively short period of time by increasing the savings rate, reducing debt, and managing interest rates on debt.

Data for Pie Chart Approach - Income Statement 1/1/20X2

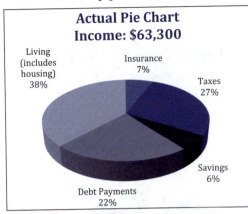

Actual Pie Chart
Income: $63,300

Living (includes housing) 38%
Insurance 7%
Taxes 27%
Savings 6%
Debt Payments 22%

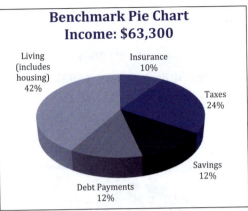

Benchmark Pie Chart
Income: $63,300

Living (includes housing) 42%
Insurance 10%
Taxes 24%
Savings 12%
Debt Payments 12%

INCOME	100.00%	**$63,300**
Living Expenses (all other)	21.77%	$4,200 child support + $720 utilities + $360 phone + $2,400 gas + $3,600 food + $1,000 clothes + $1,500 vacation = $13,780
Debt Payments	22.58%	$3,600 auto + $7,695 student loan+ $3,000 credit cards = $14,295
Savings Rate	5.66%	$3,580 (employee only)
Insurance	6.64%	$3,600 auto + $600 life = $4,200
Housing Costs	14.22%	$8,400 rent + $600 HO4 ins. = $9,000
Taxes	27.49%	$2,754 + $1,989 + $12,660 = $17,403
Discretionary Cash Flows	**1.64%**	**$1,042**

Notes: (1) With the employer match, the savings rate is 6.5 percent. If you consider the child support ($350 per month) and life insurance payment ($50 per month) as debt, the financial situation is weaker. (2) Keep in mind that benchmarks are averages for a group and may not apply exactly to a client's personal financial situation. (3) The pie chart provides a broad overview while the table provides a more detailed view by separating the housing costs and discretionary cash flows from the living expenses.

Observations

The initial observations are that the expenditures for debt repayments are high (22.58%) and the savings rate (5.66%) is low. In addition, the expenditure percentage for insurance looks to be low relative to the benchmark. Each of these issues will require investigation and resolution. While it is not uncommon to have percentages like these, the Burkes are more likely to meet their goals by reducing debt, increasing savings, and making sure they are adequately protected by insurance.

The overall savings rate with the employer 401(k) plan match is 6.5 percent and can easily be increased by John increasing his elective deferral to receive the maximum match from his employer. An additional $1,080 elective deferral would generate an additional match of $540 and would change the savings rate to 9.1 percent.

Financial Statement Analysis - Ratio Analysis Approach

Introduction

The liquidity ratios provide insight into the client's ability to pay short-term obligations and fund an emergency. The housing ratios and total debt to asset ratios help the financial planner to assess the client's ability to manage debt. The savings rate provides the planner with a good perspective of whether the client is committed financially to all of his goals, which includes saving for retirement and other goals. In addition, the investment assets to gross pay ratios help the planner to determine the progress of the client in achieving the goal of financial security based on the client's age and income. Lastly, the performance ratios indicate how well the investment assets have performed to benchmarks. The ratios should be compared to appropriate benchmarks to be meaningful.

Burkes' Ratio Analysis

Liquidity Ratios				
Ratio	**Formula**		**Comment**	**Benchmark**
Emergency Fund Ratio*	$\dfrac{\text{Cash \& Cash Equivalents}}{\text{Monthly Non-Discretionary Cash Flows}}$	$\dfrac{\$3,000}{\$3,315}$ = 91% < 1 month	Very Weak	3 - 6:1
Current Ratio	$\dfrac{\text{Cash \& Cash Equivalents}}{\text{Current Liabilities}}$	$\dfrac{\$3,000}{7,528}$ = 40%	Very Weak	1 - 2
Debt Ratios				
Housing Ratio 1 (HR 1)	$\dfrac{\text{Housing Costs}}{\text{Gross Pay}}$	$\dfrac{\$9,000}{\$63,300}$ = 14.22%	Strong	$\leq 28\%$
Housing Ratio 2 (HR 2)	$\dfrac{\text{Housing Costs + Other Debt Payments}}{\text{Gross Pay}}$	$\dfrac{\$23,295}{\$63,300}$ = 36.80%	Weak	$\leq 36\%$
Debt-to-Total Assets	$\dfrac{\text{Total Debt}}{\text{Total Assets}}$	$\dfrac{\$78,346}{\$88,820}$ = 88.21%	Weak	Age Dependent
Net Worth-to-Total Assets	$\dfrac{\text{Net Worth}}{\text{Total Assets}}$	$\dfrac{\$10,475}{\$88,820}$ = 11.79%	Weak	Age Dependent
Ratios for Financial Security Goals				
Savings Rate	$\dfrac{\text{Savings + Employer Match}}{\text{Gross Pay}}$	$\dfrac{\$3,580 + \$540}{\$63,300}$ = 6.5%	Weak	Goal Driven At Least 10-13%
Investment Assets-to-Gross Pay	$\dfrac{\text{Investment Assets + Cash \& Cash Equivalents}}{\text{Gross Pay}}$	$\dfrac{\$28,320 + \$3,000}{\$63,300}$ = 0.49:1	Very Weak	1:1 Age Dependent
Performance Ratios				
Return on Investments =	$\dfrac{I_1 - (I_0 + \text{Savings})}{I_0}$	Unavailable (Need beginning and ending balance sheet)	N/A	
Return on Assets =	$\dfrac{A_1 - (A_0 + \text{Savings})}{A_0}$	Unavailable (Need beginning and ending balance sheet)	N/A	
Return on Net Worth =	$\dfrac{NW_1 - (NW_0 + \text{Savings})}{NW_0}$	Unavailable (Need beginning and ending balance sheet)	N/A	

*Although $63,300 is used as the denominator, $62,000 could also be used without significantly changing the ratio.

Comments on Calculated Ratios

Many of the Burkes' ratios are currently low, but can be substantially improved over the next few years.

The Burkes are just getting started in their married life and while many of their ratios are weak today, they have a long work life expectancy. They will want to build an emergency fund, increase savings, and pay off their credit card debt. They may even want to delay the purchase of a home if the rent they are paying will be substantially less than the net after tax amount of the mortgage they will be paying. This decision will depend on market rates of rent, cost of houses, interest rates for mortgages, and marginal tax rates, presuming mortgage interest remains an itemized deduction for income tax purposes. This analysis should be made in the three to five year period ahead.

THE TWO-STEP / THREE-PANEL / METRICS APPROACH

Introduction

The two-step approach (cover the risks, save, and invest), looks at personal risks as potentially leading to catastrophic financial results and dependence on someone else for well being. Savings and investments are the road to financial security or independence in the long run. Generally, dependence can be caused by an event that can occur at any moment, whereas financial independence is earned over a long period of time.

A modification to the two-step approach is the three-panel approach, which provides the planner and the client with a methodology for planning. Step 1 is to evaluate each of the insurance risks and then evaluate the client's actual portfolio of insurance to determine the adequacy of the current coverage. Step 2 is to calculate the emergency fund ratio and housing ratios (or take them from the financial statement analysis approach). Step 3 focuses on the long-term savings and investments in order to meet the financial security goal (retirement with adequate income to maintain the pre-retirement lifestyle) and requires persistent savings, adequate investment performance, and a benchmark of investment assets appropriate for the age and gross pay of the client. Step 3 also considers education goals, lump-sum goals, and legacy goals. The goal of the three-panel / metrics approach is to identify specific recommendations for the client to improve the overall financial plan.

Risk Management Data

	Actual	Metric	Comment / Recommendation
Personal Insurance:			
Life Insurance[1,2]	$50,000 + $26,000	$360k - $576k $260k - $416k	They are significantly underinsured for life insurance.
Health Insurance	Indemnity 80 /20 Stop Loss $2,000 Lifetime Benefit Unlimited	Same	Okay
Disability Insurance	John - 60% of Gross Pay/ Guaranteed Renewable / 90-day Elimination/ Own Occupation Mary - None	John is fine. Mary needs disability insurance.	Mary needs disability insurance.
Long-Term Care Insurance	None	None at this time	Okay
Property and Liability Insurance:			
Homeowners Insurance	HO4 without endorsements	HO4 with endorsements	Add endorsements for open perils and replacement value.
Automobile Insurance[3]	$50,000/$100,000/$10,000	$100k/$300k/ $50k	Upgrade the liability per the requirements of PLUP carrier and re-quote the premium. Should be in $2,000 - $2,500 range.
Motor Scooter Insurance	None	$\leq$ FMV + Liability	Stop driving, add insurance, or sell motor scooter.
Liability Insurance	None	Need $1M PLUP coverage.	Add PLUP coverage of $1M.

[1] Note that the owner of the $500,000 term policy is John's ex-wife, Kathy, and that is why it is not included here.

[2] They need to change Policy B beneficiary to Mary from Kathy at no cost.

[3] Note that they requested auto quotes, but due to their driving records, the premium was not lowered.

Short-Term Savings and Investments

	Actual	Metric	Comment / Recommendation
Emergency Fund	0.91 month	3 - 6 months	Deficient
Housing Ratio 1 (HR1)*	14.22%	$\leq$ 28%	Excellent
Housing Ratio 2 (HR2)	36.80%	$\leq$ 36%	Fair - need to improve metric for home purchase.

*Although the Burkes do not own a home, the financial planner should evaluate their housing ratios using their rent and renter's insurance in the calculation.

Debt Management Data

	Balance	Interest Rate	Payment	Balance of Term	Comment / Recommendation
Credit Cards	$14,000	18% /yr.	$250 / month	124 months	Pay off if possible.
Auto	$10,047	4.75% /yr.	$300 / month	36 months	Pay as agreed.
Student Loans	$54,298	7.3842%/ yr.	$7,695 / year	10 years	Pay as agreed.

Long-Term Goals

	Actual	Metric	Comment / Recommendation
Overall Savings Rate	6.5%	At least 10 - 13%	Too Low to Meet Goals / Increase
Investment Assets / Gross Pay	0.49:1	1:1	Too Low for Age / Increase Over Time

Home Purchase Analysis - Schedule A

Home Down Payment Calculation

The purpose of this calculation is to determine the funds required to meet a 20 percent down-payment for the Burkes' home purchase goal.

PV	=	$180,000 (current price of home)
N	=	3 (periods until expected purchase)
i	=	3% inflation
PMT	=	0
FV	=	$196,690.86 (future value of house) x 20% = $39,338 down payment required

Mortgage on Home

The purpose of the following computations is to determine the projected debt ratios should the Burkes purchase a home.

PV ($196,690.86 x 0.80)	=	$157,352.69 (loan amount)
N (term in months)	=	360 months
i (interest rate)	=	5.5 ÷ 12
FV (balance in 30 yrs)	=	0
PMT_{OA} (monthly payment)	=	$893.43 (principal and interest)

	Monthly	Annually
Principal and Interest	$893.43	$10,721
Property Taxes	$163.92	$1,967
HO Insurance	$163.92	$1,967
Total House Payment	$1,221.27	$14,655

Projections for the Home Purchase (in three years)

- Projected income = $62,000 \times (1.04)^3 = \$69,742$ in three years.
- Therefore, HR1 = 21.01% [Excellent ($14,655 ÷ $69,742)].
- As adjusted HR2 = 32% [Okay, qualifies ($14,655 + $7,695 ÷ $69,742)].
- The car and credit cards are paid off and the student loan is the only debt remaining.

Savings Schedule - Schedule B

The following schedule projects the savings requirement and debt retirement needed to meet the Burkes' 3-year goals.

Objective	Cash Needed	Comment / Recommendation
Save for home down payment	$39,338	Will need to save $12,117 at 8.5% per year for three years.
Pay off auto	$10,047	Will be paid off in three years with current payments of $3,600 per year.
Pay off credit cards	$14,000	Will be paid off immediately by using the proceeds from the sale of assets.
Total Cash Needed	**$63,385**	**Cash required in the next three years.**

Payment Schedule - Schedule C

Knowing the debt retirement issues shown in Schedule B, the practitioner can plan for debt reduction on a monthly basis. Note that for comparison purposes, if the Burkes pay $250 per month on their credit card balance, they would remain with a $5,000 balance (plus interest) in three years.

Scheduled Payments	Annual Payment	Current Balance	Balance 3 Years Future	Payments
Auto Loan	$3,600	$10,047	$0	$300 / month
Credit Cards*	$3,000	$14,000	$5,000 + interest	$250 / month

* Note that the credit cards, however, will be paid off now with the sale of the assets.

Auto Interest - Schedule D

Automobile Interest Rate Calculation		Calculation		
Purchase Price	$19,993.00			
20% Down	- 3,998.60	FV	=	0
Balance	$15,994.40	PV	=	$15,994.00
Payment	$300	PMT	=	($300)
Term	60	N	=	60 months
Therefore i = annual rate	**4.75%**	**i**	**=**	**0.3957 x 12 = 4.75%**

Comments on Three-Panel / Metrics Approach Analysis

The Burkes need life insurance because they are dependent on each other's income to support their current lifestyle and they have told the financial planner that they want to have two to three children fairly soon.

Their health insurance is adequate although they are dependent on their employer for coverage. They would be covered under COBRA for 18 to 36 months if John was terminated. They could also be covered under the Affordable Care Act.

The Burkes need disability insurance on Mary because it provides for income replacement.

The homeowners (renters) policy can be improved by endorsing the personal property coverage for all risks and for replacement value. The standard HO4 policy has coverage for 18 perils (not all) and actual cash value (not replacement value).

The Burkes should also purchase a personal liability insurance policy. The PLUP issuer will likely require that they increase their auto insurance liability coverages to $100k/$300k/$50k. They need to annually shop the automobile insurance premium because it is high due to their recent driving records.

The emergency fund needs to be increased. The Burkes currently cover about one month (0.91) of non-discretionary cash flow with their cash and cash equivalents. They would be in financial difficulty if one or both of them lost their jobs.

The Burkes' housing ratio 1 is excellent at 14.22 percent, but the back ratio of 36.80 percent indicates they have too much debt. They will need to improve this ratio significantly before buying a home.

The Burkes need to pay off the credit cards and pay off the automobile loan within the 36 months remaining. Schedule D above reflects the calculation of the rate of interest on the auto loan (4.75%).

The Burkes' overall savings rate, including the employer match, is only 6.5 percent of gross pay. It needs to be 10 to 13 percent of gross pay just to drive the financial security goal. If the Burkes are going to have a home purchase goal and college education goal for two to three children, they are going to need to increase the savings rate to 10 to 13 percent for retirement, save an average of 19 percent for the home purchase down payment (see Schedules A and B), and four to five percent per child for college education (total 33 to 39% (See Schedule B)). This is an important task and they might consider delaying the home purchase until such time as they have saved the 20 percent down payment. They need to increase the 401(k) plan deferrals to maximize employer matches.

Schedule C illustrates that the client will have the auto paid off in three years and can at that time add the $3,600 per year to their savings rate.

The three-panel / metrics approach dictates that the recommendations are prioritized (see the cash flow approach) and that there is an estimate of the impact of each on the income statement and balance sheet (see projected financial statements later in this chapter). In the case of the Burkes, the financial planner is able to improve the insurance portfolio, increase savings and increase the employer match to the maximum in the 401(k) plan, and pay off the credit cards. The credit card debt reduction is accomplished by selling the individual stocks and the motor scooter. The individual stocks were not diversified and the scooter was not insured. The complete rearrangement provides the Burkes with a much better financial plan.

The financial planner should note that the client will need to address the large student loan balance and it will take time to save for the home they expect to purchase, especially if they have two to three children relatively soon. The Burkes have been advised that they need to get their wills and other estate planning documents in order and they expect to complete them soon.

It is important for the financial planner to take note of where they can usually find the resources to pay for the recommendations. The places we find resources are:
- Refinancing a home mortgage at a lower rate.
- Reducing our withholding of income tax.
- The sale of assets from the balance sheet (usually from an inappropriate or no longer desired investment or personal use asset).
- Changing lifestyle (this is the last place we look because it requires behavioral change, such as cutting vacations).

Sometimes there simply are not sufficient financial resources to solve all the problems immediately. That is why, in the cash flow approach, recommendations are listed in order of priority. In the event there are insufficient financial resources, the financial planner and client simply solve the problems that they can today and use future resources as they become available. Whatever financial weaknesses the client has generally took some time to develop, and may also take some time to resolve.

Risk Tolerance and Asset Allocation

The following chart depicts the scoring system for the PASS risk tolerance questionnaire. Based on the Burkes' answers, their PASS[2] score is 23.5, which corresponds to the RT3 target.

Global Portfolio Allocation Scoring System (PASS) for Individual Investors						
Questions	Strongly Agree	Agree	Neutral	Disagree	Strongly Disagree	John & Mary
1. Earning a high long-term total return that will allow my capital to grow faster than the inflation rate is one of my most important investment objectives.	5	4	3	2	1	4.5
2. I would like an investment that provides me with an opportunity to defer taxation of capital gains to future years.	5	4	3	2	1	3.5
3. I do not require a high level of current income from my investments.	5	4	3	2	1	4
4. I am willing to tolerate some sharp down swings in the return on my investments in order to seek a potentially higher return than would normally be expected from more stable investments.	5	4	3	2	1	4.5
5. I am willing to risk a short-term loss in return for a potentially higher long-run rate of return.	5	4	3	2	1	3.5
6. I am financially able to accept a low level of liquidity in my investment portfolio.	5	4	3	2	1	3.5

23.5

2. Global Portfolio Allocation Scoring System (PASS) for Individual Investors - developed by Dr. William Droms (Georgetown University) and Steven N. Strauss, (DromsStrauss Advisors Inc.) - model used with permission.

Below are the recommended portfolios based on the time horizon and answers to the risk tolerance questionnaire.

	Short-Term Horizon				Intermediate-Term Horizon				Long-Term Horizon			
	RT1	RT2	RT3	RT4	RT1	RT2	RT3	RT4	RT1	RT2	RT3	RT4
	Target	Target	Target	Target	Target	Target	Target	Target	Target	Target	Target	Target
PASS Score	6 - 12	13 - 18	19 - 24	25 - 30	6 - 12	13 - 18	19 - 24	25 - 30	6 - 12	13 - 18	19 - 24	25 - 30
Cash and Money Market Fund	40%	30%	20%	10%	5%	5%	5%	5%	5%	5%	3%	2%
Treasury Bonds/ Bond Funds	40%	30%	30%	20%	60%	35%	20%	10%	30%	20%	12%	0%
Corporate Bonds/ Bond Funds	20%	30%	30%	40%	15%	15%	15%	10%	15%	10%	10%	4%
Subtotal	**100%**	**90%**	**80%**	**70%**	**80%**	**55%**	**40%**	**25%**	**50%**	**35%**	**25%**	**6%**
International Bond Funds	0%	0%	0%	0%	0%	5%	5%	5%	0%	5%	5%	4%
Subtotal	**0%**	**0%**	**0%**	**0%**	**0%**	**5%**	**5%**	**5%**	**0%**	**5%**	**5%**	**4%**
Index Fund	0%	10%	10%	10%	10%	15%	20%	20%	20%	20%	20%	25%
Large Cap Value Funds/Stocks	0%	0%	5%	5%	5%	5%	10%	10%	10%	10%	5%	5%
Large Cap Growth Funds/Stocks	0%	0%	0%	0%	5%	5%	5%	10%	15%	10%	10%	5%
Mid/Small Growth Funds/Stocks	0%	0%	0%	0%	0%	0%	5%	5%	0%	0%	5%	10%
Mid/Small Value Funds/Stocks	0%	0%	0%	5%	0%	5%	5%	5%	0%	5%	5%	10%
Subtotal	**0%**	**10%**	**15%**	**20%**	**20%**	**30%**	**45%**	**50%**	**45%**	**45%**	**45%**	**55%**
International Stock Funds	0%	0%	0%	5%	0%	5%	5%	10%	0%	5%	10%	15%
Subtotal	**0%**	**0%**	**0%**	**5%**	**0%**	**5%**	**5%**	**10%**	**0%**	**5%**	**10%**	**15%**
Real Estate Funds	0%	0%	5%	5%	0%	5%	5%	10%	5%	10%	15%	20%
Subtotal	**0%**	**0%**	**5%**	**5%**	**0%**	**5%**	**5%**	**10%**	**5%**	**10%**	**15%**	**20%**
Total	**100%**	**100%**	**100%**	**100%**	**100%**	**100%**	**100%**	**100%**	**100%**	**100%**	**100%**	**100%**

This information and the risk and return information are used to determine and estimate the expected return for the current portfolio versus the recommended PASS[3] portfolio.

	Current Porfolio (Dollars)	Current Portfolio Percentage	PASS Recommended Portfolio	Difference	Expected Rates of Return	Current Expected Return	PASS Expected Return
Cash and Money Market Fund	$3,000	9.6%	3%	6.6%	2.5%	$75	$23
Treasury Bonds/ Bond Funds	$0	0.0%	12%	-12.0%	4.0%	$0	$150
Corporate Bonds/ Bond Funds	$8,160	26.1%	10%	16.1%	6.0%	$490	$188
International Bond Funds	$0	0.0%	5%	-5.0%	7.0%	$0	$110
Index Fund	$8,160	26.1%	20%	6.1%	9.0%	$734	$564
Large Cap Funds/Stocks	$12,000	38.3%	15%	23.3%	10.0%	$1,200	$470
Mid/Small Funds/Stocks	$0	0.0%	10%	-10.0%	12.0%	$0	$376
International Stock Funds	$0	0.0%	10%	-10.0%	13.0%	$0	$407
Real Estate Funds	$0	0.0%	15%	-15.0%	8.0%	$0	$376
	$31,320	100.0%				$2,499	$2,664
					Expected Return	7.98%	8.51%

As indicated above, the expected return slightly increases over the current portfolio and the return is consistent with the required return in the case. In addition, the portfolio should be better positioned to reflect the risk tolerance of the Burkes.

---

3. Global Portfolio Allocation Scoring System (PASS) for Individual Investors - developed by Dr. William Droms (Georgetown University) and Steven N. Strauss, (DromsStrauss Advisors Inc.) - model used with permission.

The Present Value of all Goals Approach

Goals:

1. Retirement - $62,000 in today's dollars, 3% inflation, at 65 to 95 without consideration of Social Security.
2. Education of 2 children - $20,000 per year in today's dollars, starting in 20 years. Inflation is expected to be 5%. The children will attend college for 4 years each. They do not plan to pay for Patrick.
3. Home down payment - $36,000 down payment three years from now.

Calculation of Retirement Needs in PV Terms

N	= 35	PMT_{AD}	= $174,459.47	FV	= $2,718,862.76
i	= 3	N	= 30	N	= 35
PV	= $62,000	i	= (1.085 ÷ 1.03 - 1) x 100	i	= 8.5
FV	= $174,459.47	$PV_{@65}$	$2,718,862.76	PV_{Today}	= $156,439.51

Calculation of Education Needs in PV Terms

PMT_{AD}	= $20,000	FV	= $152,423.22 (for 2 children)
i	= (1.085 ÷ 1.05 - 1) x 100	N	= 20 (children born 2 years from now)
N	= 4	i	= (1.085 ÷ 1.05 - 1) x 100
$PV_{@18}$	= $76,211.60757	PV_{Today}	= $79,112.00

Calculation of Home Down Payment in PV Terms

N	= 3	FV	= $39,338.17
i	= 3	i	= 8.5
PV	= $36,000	N	= 3
FV	= $39,338.17	PV	= $30,798.17

Summary of the Present Value of All Goals

Retirement	$156,439.51	
Education	$79,112.00	
Home Down Payment	$30,798.17	
Total	$266,349.68	
Current Resources	$31,320.00	(this is before using $14,000 to pay off credit cards)
Net PV of Goals	$235,029.68	
N	35	(to retirement)
i	8.5%	(portfolio rate)
PMT_{OA}	$21,197.17	(annual savings needed)
Current Savings	- $4,120.00	(includes employer match)
Tax Analysis Savings	- $8,920.00	(See Schedule D in the Presentation section below; before recommendations)
Shortfall	**$8,157.17**	

The Burkes still have a shortfall for their annual savings. However, by adding the additional 401(k) deferrals along with the estimated tax savings from the deferrals (see cash flow approach), they will reduce the shortfall.

The Burke's want to plan for a 100 percent wage replacement ratio (WRR). However, a more realistic WRR is closer to 70 percent to 75 percent. Consider the following estimate:

	After Recommendations
Income	$62,000
Less:	
Retirement Savings (Adjusted*) [$1,080 + $1,080 + $1,560]	$3,720
Discretionary Cash Flow (Adjusted) [$8,397 - $8,920]	- $523
Tax Analysis Savings (Adjusted)	$8,920
FICA	$4,743
Income Needs	**$45,140**

*See Cash Flow Approach below for recommended adjustments to retirement savings.

The income needs is close to $45,000, which equates to 72.45 percent of their current income. This calculation does not take into considerations other adjustments that might lower the income needs even further. Based on this analysis, the Burkes could use 75 percent as a WRR, which would reduce the PV of retirement needs by more than $39,000. The annual savings needed could be reduced by $3,527.30.[4] The remaining shortfall, after considering the modified WRR and the increase in 401(k) savings, can likely be made up with raises over the 35 years prior to retirement.

---

4. This reduction can be calculated by redoing the calculation above (Summary of Present Value of All Goals) after reducing the retirement needs by 25% to reflect a 75% WRR.

THE CASH FLOW APPROACH

The cash flow approach essentially adjusts the cash flows on the income statement to what they would be after implementing all of the recommendations that the planner has suggested. It starts with the discretionary cash flows at the bottom of the income statement and accounts for the recommendations in the order of priority by charging the cost of the expense against the discretionary cash flows, regardless of any negative cash flow impact. The analysis is prepared carefully to differentiate between recurring cash flows and non-recurring cash flows.

Burke Cash Flow Approach with Recommendations

	Income Statement Recurring Cash Flows	Statement of Financial Position Non-Recurring Cash Flows	Comments/Explanations
Beginning Cash Flow (Income Statement)	**$1,042**		From the original income statement
Recommendations:			
Risk management:			
Term life insurance for John	($375)		Buy $500,000 term.
Term life insurance for Mary	($250)		Buy $500,000 term.
Disability insurance for Mary	($600)		Buy disability.
Homeowners insurance	($100)		Endorse.
Automobile insurance	($400)		Upgrade.
Motor scooter	$0	$2,000	Sell motor scooter.
Personal liability umbrella	($200)		$1,000,000 PLUP
Prepare proper estate documents		($1,000)	
Debt management:			
Pay off credit cards		($14,000)	Reduces expenditures by $3,000/yr.
Savings from credit card payoffs	$3,000		Pay off credit cards with proceeds from asset sale.
Increase John's 401(k) plan deferrals*	($1,080)		3% additional
Begin Mary's 401(k) plan deferrals*	($1,560)		6% of salary
Savings from Change in W-4**	$8,920		Includes $317 tax savings from increase in 401(k) deferrals.
Ending cash flow after implementation	$8,397		This is the positive recurring cash flow to add to savings. This will initially go to the emergency fund.
Sell assets to pay credit card (Crossroads and Gladwell stock)		$12,000	Sold stocks, etc. to pay off credit cards.
TOTAL of Changes in Cash Flows	**$8,397**	**($1,000)**	

Note that the numbers in parenthesis are expenditures.

* The Burkes had to choose between increasing savings to the 401(k) plan and paying down on the student loans. They expect John will get a substantial raise in 4-5 years and choose to save rather than pay the student loans even though they were at 7.3842% interest. There also is a possibility that their parents will help with the student loans.

** See Tax Analysis.

Assets Sold to Pay Off Credit Cards - Schedule A

Assets Sold to Pay Off Credit Cards	
Motor scooter	$2,000
Crossroads Inc.	$8,000
Gladwell Inc.	$4,000
TOTAL	**$14,000**

STRATEGIC APPROACH

Introduction

The strategic approach encompasses establishing a mission statement, a set of goals, and a set of objectives. The planner analyzes the mission, goals, and objectives given both internal client data and relevant external data and creates a plan for the long-run accomplishment of the mission with the short and intermediate accomplishment of objectives and goals.

Mission Statement (An Enduring Long-Term Statement)

- Financial security (maintaining lifestyle without the need for current employment).

Goals (Broadly Conceived Goals)

- Adequate risk management portfolio.
- Adequate savings rate for retirement and education.
- Adequate emergency fund.
- Adequate debt management.
- Adequate investment portfolio.
- Adequate estate plan.

Objectives (Narrow Measurable Objectives)

Risk Management

- Immediately buy term life insurance on both John and Mary at $500,000 each.
- Purchase disability insurance on Mary at 60% to 70% of gross pay with a 90 day elimination period.
- Add endorsement for HO4 to all risk / replacement value.
- Upgrade liability on automobile insurance to meet PLUP carrier requirements.
- Sell motor scooter.
- Add PLUP of $1,000,000.

Debt Management

- Pay off credit cards ($14,000).
- Keep credit card purchases to $1,000 per year.

Tax Management and Emergency Fund

- Use the adjusted cash flow of $8,397 to build an emergency fund. (See Cash Flow Approach, and Schedule D - Tax Analysis on the following pages.)

Savings and Investments

- Increase John's 401(k) plan deferral to $2,160 (increasing the employer match to $1,080).
- Have Mary defer $1,560 to her 401(k) plan (employer match is $1,560 x 0.25 = $390).
- Move all 401(k) plan investments to a balanced portfolio.

Estate Plan

Have estate planning documents prepared (will, durable power of attorney for healthcare, advance medical directive) within the second year (expected cost = $1,000).

Comments on Strategic Approach

The strategic approach takes into consideration needs versus wants. Needs are defined as necessary by law (e.g., auto liability insurance) or required to make the plan work (e.g., savings). Wants on the other hand are somewhat discretionary (e.g., home purchase, vacation).

Even if the planner started with the strategic approach, the financial planning method would probably follow with the cash flow approach and recommendations to be assured that the implementation is feasible.

PRESENTATION TO JOHN AND MARY BURKE PROJECTED FINANCIAL STATEMENTS AND RATIOS

The next step for the financial planner is to project financial statements at least one year out to be able to present to the client where they will be in a year if they follow and implement the recommendations. This is one way to help clients get and stay motivated while implementing the plan. In order to project both the balance sheet and the income statement and to prepare pro forma (projected) ratios, the planner will need to prepare schedules of savings and earnings. For the Burkes, the planner has prepared Schedules A - E and the projected financial statements.

Schedule A - Analysis of John's 401(k) Plan

	Beginning Balance January 1	Employee Deferrals	Employer Match	Earning Rate 8.5%*	Ending Balance December 31
20X2	$4,320	$2,160	$1,080	$505	$8,065
20X3	$8,065	$2,246	$1,123	$830	$12,264
20X4	$12,264	$2,336	$1,168	$1,191	$16,959
20X5	$16,959	$2,429	$1,215	$1,596	$22,199

* Earnings are for 1/2 year on new deposits. Rounded.

Schedule B - Analysis of Mary's 401(k) Plan

	Beginning Balance January 1	Employee Deferrals	Employer Match	Earning Rate 8.5%	Ending Balance December 31
20X2	$0	$1,560	$390	$83	$2,033
20X3	$2,033	$1,622	$406	$259	$4,320
20X4	$4,320	$1,687	$422	$456	$6,885
20X5	$6,885	$1,755	$439	$678	$9,757

* Earnings on the balanced mutual fund is 8.5% for 1/2 year on new deposits. Rounded to nearest $1.

Schedule C - Combined Savings Rate After Recommendations (including tax overwithheld)

	Savings
House Savings	$2,500
John's 401(k) Plan Deferral	$2,160
Employer 401(k) Plan Match	$1,080
Mary's 401(k) Plan Deferral	$1,560
Employer 401(k) Plan Match	$390
Cash from Cash Flow Analysis	$8,397
	$16,087 ÷ $63,300 = 25% current savings rate (rounded)

* The reinvestment of investment income is not included in the calculation of the savings rate because it is included in the overall portfolio rate.

Schedule D - Income Tax Analysis

The Burkes current (without changes) average income tax rate is approximately 6.4 percent and their marginal income tax rate is 12 percent. The Burkes are significantly overwithheld and should invest this amount annually in the emergency fund or a retirement account by changing the income tax withholding form (W-4).

Abbreviated Tax Analysis

	20X2 Before Recommendations	20X2 After Recommendations
Gross Income	$63,300	$63,300
401(k) Deferral - John	($1,080)	($2,160)
401(k) Deferral - Mary		($1,560)
Adjusted Gross Income (AGI)	$62,220	$59,580
Personal & Dependency Exemptions**	$0	$0
Standard Deduction*	$25,100	$25,100
Taxable Income	$37,120	$34,480
Tax Liability (estimated)*	$4,056	$3,740
Child Tax Credit***	$0	$0
Withholding	$12,660	$12,660
Over Withheld Refund Expected	$8,604	$8,920
Average Tax Rate	6.4%	6.0%

* Using 2021 standard deductions and tax rates.
** Eliminated from TCJA 2017.
*** No children currently.

Projected Statement of Financial Position

Statement of Financial Position Mr. and Mrs. Burke Projected Balance Sheet End of 20X2				
Assets[1]			**Liabilities and Net Worth**	
CURRENT ASSETS			**CURRENT LIABILITIES**[2]	
Cash and Cash Equivalents[4]	$10,397		Credit Card Balance	$0
Crossroads Inc. (1,000 Shares)	$0		Auto Loan - Mary	$3,347
Gladwell Inc. (100 Shares)	$0		Student Loan[3] - John	$4,104
Total Current Assets		$10,397	**Total Current Liabilities**	$7,451
Investment Assets			**Long-Term Liabilities**[2]	
Crossroads Inc. (1,000 Shares)	$0		Auto Loan - Mary	$3,509
Gladwell Inc. (100 Shares)	$0		Student Loan[3] - John	$46,381
House Down Payment[5]	$2,500			
Balance Mutual Fund	$13,020		**Total Long-Term Liabilities**	$49,890
John's 401(k) Plan	$8,065			
Mary's 401(k) Plan	$2,033			
Total Investment Assets		$25,618		
Personal Use Assets			**Total Liabilities**	$57,341
Auto - Mary	$18,500			
Truck - John	$12,000		**Total Net Worth**	$34,174
Motor scooter - John	$0			
Personal Property & Furniture	$25,000			
Total Personal Use Assets		$55,500		
Total Assets		$91,515	**Total Liabilities & Net Worth**	$91,515

1. Assets are stated at fair market value.
2. Liabilities are stated at principal only as of December 31, 20X2 before January payments.
3. The interest rate on the student loan is 7.3842% for 10 years on a consolidation loan.
4. Beginning cash of $3,000 plus $8,397 less $1,000. See Burke cash flow approach.
5. See Statement of Income.

Schedule E - Reconciliation of Year-End Net Worth

Change in Projected Net Worth January 1, 20X2 - December 31, 20X2	
Beginning Net Worth	$10,475
Home Savings Growth	$2,500
Emergency Fund Growth	$0
Debt Reduction (student loan)	$3,813
Debt Reduction (automobile loan)	$3,191
Growth of John's Mutual Fund	$1,020
Growth of John's 401(k) Plan	$3,745
Growth of Mary's 401(k) Plan	$2,033
Cash from Cash Flow Analysis*	$7,397
Total Ending Net Worth	**$34,174**

* Net of $1,000 for estate documents

Projected Statement of Income and Expenses

Statement of Income and Expenses Mr. and Mrs. Burke Statement of Income and Expenses for Past Year and Expected (Approximate) For 20X3			
CASH INFLOWS			
Salaries***			
John's Salary	$37,440		
Mary's Salary	$27,040		
Variable Annuity Income	$2,067		
Total Cash Inflows			$66,547
CASH OUTFLOWS			
Savings			
Savings - House down payment	$2,500		
401(k) Plan Contribution - John***	$2,246		
401(k) Plan Contribution - Mary***	$1,622		
Total Savings			$6,368
Fixed Outflows			
Child Support/Court Rqd. Insurance	$4,800	ND	
Rent	$8,400	ND	
HO 4 Renters Insurance*	$718	ND	
Utilities*	$742	ND	
Telephone	$360	ND	
Auto payment P&I	$3,600	ND	
Auto Insurance	$4,000	ND	
Gas, Oil, Maintenance for Auto*	$2,472	ND	
Student Loan Payments	$7,695	ND	
Insurance (Life, Disability, PLUP)	$1,425	ND	
Fee for Estates Documents	$1,000		
Credit Card Payments**	$1,000	ND	
Total Fixed Outflows			$36,212
Variable Outflows			
Taxes - John and Mary FICA	$4,933		
Taxes - Federal Tax Withheld	$3,740		
Food*	$3,708	ND	
Clothing	$1,000	ND	
Vacations	$1,500		
Total Variable Outflows			$14,881
Total Cash Outflows			$57,461
NET DISCRETIONARY CASH FLOWS (AVAILABLE FOR SAVINGS)			$9,086

*Subject to 3% inflation.

**They continue to incur $1,000 yearly in credit card debt for incidentals.

*** Subject to 4% increases.

SELECTED RATIOS

Schedule F - Current and Projected Ratios

Current and Projected Ratios		
	January 1, 20X2	December 31, 20X2
1 Current Ratio	0.40 to 1	1.40 to 1
2 Emergency Fund Ratio	0.91 to 1	3.13 to 1
3 HR 1	14.22%	13.70%
4 HR 2	36.80%	32.18%
5 Net Worth / Total Assets	11.79%	37.34%
6 Savings Rate	6.51%	11.87%
7 Investment Assets / Gross Pay	0.49 to 1	0.54 to 1

Ratio	Formula	January 1, 20X2	December 31, 20X2
Current Ratio	$\dfrac{\text{Cash \&Cash Equivalents}}{\text{Current Liabilities}}$	$\dfrac{\$3,000}{\$7,528}= 0.40{:}1$	$\dfrac{\$10,397}{\$7,451}= 1.40{:}1$
Emergency Fund Ratio	$\dfrac{\text{Cash \&Cash Equivalents}}{\text{Monthly Non-Discretionary Cash Flows}}$	$\dfrac{\$3,000}{\$3,315}= 0.91$	$\dfrac{\$10,397}{\$3,327}= 3.13$
Housing Ratio 1 (HR1)	$\dfrac{\text{Housing Costs}}{\text{Gross Pay}}$	$\dfrac{\$9,000}{\$63,300}= 14.22\%$	$\dfrac{\$9,118}{\$66,547}= 13.70\%$
Housing Ratio 2 (HR2)	$\dfrac{\text{Housing Costs + Other Debt Payments}}{\text{Gross Pay}}$	$\dfrac{\$23,295}{\$63,300}= 36.80\%$	$\dfrac{\$21,413}{\$66,547}= 32.18\%$
Net Worth-to-Total Assets	$\dfrac{\text{Net Worth}}{\text{Total Assets}}$	$\dfrac{\$10,475}{\$88,820}= 11.79\%$	$\dfrac{\$34,174}{\$91,515}= 37.34\%$
Savings Rate	$\dfrac{\text{Savings + Employer Match}}{\text{Gross Pay}}$	$\dfrac{\$4,120}{\$63,300}= 6.51\%$	$\dfrac{\$7,897}{\$66,547}= 11.87\%$
Investment Assets-to-Gross Pay	$\dfrac{\text{Investmest Assets + Cash \& Cash Equivalents}}{\text{Gross Pay}}$	$\dfrac{\$31,320}{\$63,300}= 0.49{:}1$	$\dfrac{\$36,015}{\$66,547}= 0.54{:}1$

SUMMARY

Assuming the Burkes follow and implement all of the recommendations, they will have significantly increased their emergency fund ratio, reduced both housing ratios 1 and 2, almost tripled their net worth, and increased their savings rate from 6.5 percent to 11.87 percent at the end of the first year. These are remarkable results to accomplish in one year. If the Burkes continue on the plan, they will meet their financial goals as they come due.

Closing Engagement Letter

Financial Planning Offices of Mitchell and Mitchell

April 18, 20X2

John and Mary Burke
1420 Elm Street
Pensacola, FL 32501

RE: Financial Plan

Dear Mr. and Mrs. Burke:

This letter will confirm the completion of our services related to your current financial plan. At this time, we have delivered your financial plan based on your goals and objectives. The financial plan was reviewed in detail with you at our April 11, 20X2 meeting. As previously indicated, our analysis and recommendations are based on information provided by you that were relied upon.

In addition, the methods that you choose to follow for the implementation of the financial planning recommendations are at your discretion. As you have indicated, you will be totally responsible for all decisions regarding implementation of the recommendations. The financial plan presented provides the following recommendations for your implementation:

Financial Planning Category	Specific Planning Area	Recommendation
Risk Management		
	Life Insurance	Both John and Mary need additional life insurance ($500,000 each) to protect each other and to protect any future children.
	Disability Insurance	Mary needs disability insurance in the event of loss of income due to disability.
	Homeowner's/Renters Insurance	There is a need to increase coverage on the renter's policy by endorsing the personal property coverage for all risks and for replacement value.
	Personal Liability Insurance	There is a need to purchase personal liability insurance. This may require the need to increase automobile liability coverage.
*Debt Management		
	Credit Cards, Auto and Student Loans	The credit cards need to be paid off immediately and the auto and student loans need to be paid as agreed. Note that the parents may assist with student loan debt.

**Savings Management		
	Emergency Fund	The emergency fund will be increased to reach a 3–6-month balance, rather than the current 0.91-month balance from savings from tax analysis.
	Retirement Savings	Currently the overall savings rate is 6.5% of gross pay (including employer match). For the retirement savings goal, the savings rate needs to be increased to 10-13%. John needs to increase his 401(k) plan deferral for maximum employer match and Mary needs to begin contributing to her 401(k) plan.
	Home Purchase Savings	The savings rate needs to reach 19% of gross pay for the home purchase 20% down payment ($39,338 needed in three years). Note that the parents may contribute towards down payment.
	College Savings for Children	The savings rate for college education for children should be 4-5% of gross pay per child.
Investment Management		
	Retirement Plans	All 401(k) plan investments need to be placed in a balanced portfolio.
Estate Planning Management		
	Estate Planning Documents	Have estate documents (will, durable power of attorney for healthcare, advance medical directive, etc.) prepared within two years.

*Note that the credit card debt can be paid off by funds acquired from the sale of the motor scooter and the sale of Crossroads and Gladwell stock.
**The savings rate can be increased after the automobile is paid off.

We thank you for the opportunity to be of service. Please contact us with any questions you may have regarding your current financial plan. We look forward to continuing a long-term relationship with you as your financial situation requires additional planning services.

Sincerely,

Michael A. Mitchell, CFP®

7

TIME VALUE OF MONEY

LEARNING OBJECTIVES

1. Describe and prepare a timeline of the cash flows associated with time value money.
2. List the time value of money variables.
3. Calculate the present value and future value of a lump sum.
4. Differentiate between an ordinary annuity and an annuity due.
5. Calculate the present value and future value of an ordinary annuity and an annuity due.
6. Solve a time value of money problem for i, PV, N, PMT, or FV.
7. Solve time value of money problems using uneven cash flows.
8. Describe and calculate NPV and IRR.
9. Explain and calculate the inflation adjusted rate of return.
10. Calculate serial payments.
11. Prepare an amortization schedule.
12. Apply time value of money concepts to financing and mortgages.
13. Calculate present value and future value of single amounts, annuities, annuities due, uneven cash flows and serial payments.*
14. Calculate amortization payments and annual savings required to meet a goal.*
15. Calculate NPV and IRR and be able to apply the techniques to financial planning problems.*

Ties to CFP Certification Learning Objectives

INTRODUCTION

Time Value of Money (TVM) is a mathematical concept that determines the value of money, at a point or over a period of time, at a given rate of interest. There is an expression that "a dollar received today is worth more than a dollar received tomorrow." Most people would choose money today if offered the option between receiving it today or one year later. For example, if a person has $100 today, it could be invested and earn a rate of return that would increase the $100 to something more than that in one year. Money received in the future forgoes the potential earnings from today to the time the funds are received.

Time value of money concepts begin with two key values, the present value and the future value. The **present value** is the value today of one or more future cash flows discounted to today at an appropriate interest rate. The **future value** is the value at some point in the future of a present amount or amounts after earning a rate of return for a period of time.

Time value of money concepts allow questions to be answered, such as how much $100 earning three percent is worth in one year. TVM also allows a financial planner and the client to answer other quantitative questions, such as:

- If I invest a certain sum of money into my IRA each year beginning now, and assuming a fixed interest rate and identified time period, how much will I have at the end of the period?
- If my goal is to pay for my children's college education, how much do I need to save each year beginning today or at some time in the future?
- If I borrow money to buy a house or car, how much is my monthly payment?
- If I want to retire debt early, how much in additional principal payments would be required?
- Should I purchase a piece of equipment for my business or rent it?
- What is my annual rate of return on an investment?

Throughout this chapter, the tools and skills necessary to answer these questions and more are provided. The chapter begins with an approach to solve time value of money calculations using a financial calculator. The appendix to this chapter, located online at money-education.com, provides other methods of solving time value of money calculations, such as mathematical formulas, factor tables, and accumulation schedules. Today, most financial planners use a financial calculator, but these other methods are helpful to illustrate the actual mathematical calculations and concepts behind the time value of money calculations. Note that additional TVM calculations for education funding and retirement funding are found in Chapters 8 and 11, respectively.

Exhibit 7.1 illustrates the value of annual savings and compound earnings. To accumulate $1 million, an individual would have to save annual amounts at various interest rates for a certain number of years. The chart indicates the years it would take given a specific annual savings and a specific interest rate. For example, a 20-year-old saving $4,000 annually at four percent would take 61.14 years (until the age of 82) to generate a total future value of $1 million. However, a 25-year-old saving $6,000 in her IRA earning 10 percent per year would accumulate $1 million in 30.13 years (before she was 60 years old). What's even more interesting is that the 25-year-old would have sacrificed $180,000 to accumulate $1 million. The difference of $820,000 is from investment returns. This objective is attainable, but requires sacrifice, time, and discipline.

Exhibit 7.1 | Years to Become a Millionaire

Annual Savings	Annual Rate of Return								
	4%	5%	6%	7%	8%	9%	10%	11%	12%
$ 4,000	61.14	53.34	47.58	43.12	39.56	36.63	34.18	32.10	30.30
$ 6,000	51.93	45.78	41.15	37.53	34.60	32.17	30.13	28.38	26.86
$ 10,000	41.04	36.72	33.40	30.73	28.55	26.72	25.16	23.81	22.63
$ 15,000	33.13	30.05	27.62	25.64	23.98	22.58	21.37	20.32	19.39
$ 20,000	28.01	25.68	23.79	22.23	20.91	19.78	18.80	17.94	17.17

For all time value of money calculations in this chapter, keystrokes are provided for the HP 10BII/ HP10BII+ and HP 12C financial calculators. This chapter assumes a basic working knowledge of a financial calculator such as how to add, subtract, multiply, divide, powers, roots and string calculations. Refer to the calculator manual for operation instructions, especially for the HP 12C, that uses reverse polish notation where every operator ([+], [-], [x], [÷]) follows all of its operands.

APPROACH FOR SOLVING TIME VALUE OF MONEY CALCULATIONS

Solving time value of money calculations requires both an understanding of time value of money concepts and the knowledge and skill to properly operate a financial calculator. To avoid common keystroke and data entry errors, it is important to establish a disciplined approach to working TVM calculations. One such approach is the following four-step method:
1. Start with a timeline of cash flows.
2. Write down the TVM variables.
3. Clear all registers in the financial calculator.
4. Populate the TVM variables in the calculator.

As you work through the examples in this chapter, be sure to practice the four-step approach. For those that are experienced and confident with a financial calculator, you may decide to only use steps 3 and 4. For those less experienced with a financial calculator and time value of money concepts, steps 1 through 4 should be used with all of the problems.

Step One: Start with a Timeline

A timeline is a useful tool that illustrates the amount, timing, and direction (inflows versus outflows) of cash flows for a TVM calculation. A timeline graphically depicts all TVM variables, which helps easily identify present value, future value, an interest rate, and the number of periods. The example below demonstrates the setup of a timeline.

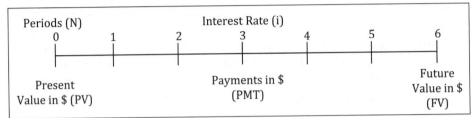

Present Value (PV): Represents the value of the cash flow today in dollars.

Payments (PMT): Represents any recurring payments, such as an income stream or debt repayment.

Future Value (FV): Represents the dollar value at some point in the future, of a current deposit(s), earning a rate of return over a period of time.

Periods (N): Represents the number of periods of compounding, which may be annual, semi-annual, quarterly, monthly, or daily. In the above timeline there are six periods.

Interest Rate (i): Represents the rate being earned on an investment or interest paid on a loan.

When drawing a timeline, it is important to identify the direction of the cash flow such as whether the cash flow is an inflow or outflow. To determine the direction of a cash flow, consider whether the cash flow is being received or is being paid. When an amount is being received, the direction of the cash flow is positive. When an amount is being paid or invested, the direction of the cash flow is negative. A cash inflow is a positive amount on the timeline. A cash outflow is a negative amount on the timeline. This textbook uses < > to represent outflows on the timeline.

Examples of cash inflows, which are positive amounts:
- A client is receiving annuity payments each month during retirement.
- A client takes out a loan to purchase a house (the loan amount received is a positive amount).
- The lump-sum amount that is accumulated after a period of savings.
- Any type of income received during retirement, inheritance, or distribution of savings.

Examples of cash outflows, which are negative amounts:
- A client makes tuition payments.
- Any type of periodic savings or a lump-sum amount contributed / deposited to a savings account.
- Periodic repayment of any type of debt.
- The purchase of a piece of equipment or investment.

Values are entered as positive amounts in the financial calculator when they are cash inflows (see examples above). Values that represent cash outflows (examples above) are entered as negative numbers (note that answers will calculate as a negative amount when the facts indicate the calculation is being solved for a cash outflow). To change the sign between a positive and negative value being entered into a financial calculator, use one of the following keys:

10BII Keystrokes	12C Keystrokes
[+/-]	[CHS]

Step Two: Write Down the TVM Variables

Write down the time value of money input variables before entering them into a financial calculator. When writing down the variables, always write them down in the same order as they appear on the financial calculator, from left to right (N, i, PV, PMT, and FV).

The variables on the financial calculator correlate to the timeline drawn in step #1. Listed below are the letters on the financial calculator and an explanation of how they relate to the timeline.

N: Represents the **N**umber of "Periods" or the term. Periods or term can be stated as the number of years, quarters, months or days.

I/YR (HP 10BII) or i (HP 12C): Represents the **i**nterest rate or discount rate. The interest rate is typically stated on an annual, semi-annual, quarterly or monthly basis.

PV: Represents the "**P**resent **V**alue" on the timeline. The present value is the value of an amount, as of today or at time period zero on the timeline.

PMT: Represents "**P**ayments" on the timeline, which can be debt payments, savings contributions, income payments received, or any other type of periodic cash flow. The PMT register is only used for even cash flows or cash flows of an equal amount.

FV: Represents "**F**uture **V**alue" on the timeline. The future value is the value of an amount at some point in the future, at some interest rate, for some period of time.

Step Three: Clear all Registers in the Financial Calculator

Before starting any calculation of a time value of money problem, it is critical to completely clear the financial calculator. If the calculator is not cleared, it is possible to calculate a wrong answer based on a previously inputted value that remains in the memory or financial registers of the calculator.

10BII Keystrokes	12C Keystrokes
[ORANGE] [C ALL]	[f] [CLX]

Step Four: Populate the TVM Variables in the Calculator

Always populate the input values in the financial calculator in the same order as they are written down in step #2 (N, i, PV, PMT, and FV). By entering the values in the same order as written down, you are less likely to skip or forget to enter a value. To enter a value, simply press the number and then the TVM register on the financial calculator. To solve for a TVM register once all the values are populated, press the TVM register (e.g., i, N, PV, etc.) that is being solved (see [FV] in **Example 7.1**).

Example 7.1

How much is $100 deposited today, worth in one year, if it earns 5% interest?

10BII Keystrokes	12C Keystrokes
1 [N]	1 [n]
5 [I/YR]	5 [i]
100 [+/-] [PV]	100 [CHS] [PV]
0 [PMT]	0 [PMT]
[FV]	[FV]
Answer: 105.00	**Answer: 105.00**

TIME VALUE OF MONEY CONCEPTS

Present Value of $1

The **present value of a future amount** of $1 is the current value today of that $1. The future amount is discounted over time using a discount rate (an interest rate that reflects the individual's risk or opportunity cost that could be earned on a similar project or investment) to arrive at the present value. The present value of $1 is used when calculating how much should be deposited today to meet a financial goal in the future.

☷ *Key Concepts*

1. Distinguish between present value and future value of a lump-sum deposit and that of an annuity.

2. Distinguish between an ordinary annuity and an annuity due.

Example 7.2

Axel requires $25,000 in 5 years as a down payment for a house. Assume Axel can earn a 6 percent rate of return, compounded annually. How much must Axel deposit today to have the $25,000 in 5 years?

10BII Keystrokes	12C Keystrokes
5 [N] 6 [I/YR] 0 [PMT] 25,000 [FV] [PV]	5 [n] 6 [i] 0 [PMT] 25,000 [FV] [PV]
Answer: <18,681.45>	**Answer: <18,681.45>**

Future Value of $1

The future value of $1 is the value of a present lump-sum deposit after earning interest over a period of time. The future value of $1 is used when determining a future amount based on today's lump-sum deposit that will be earning interest (e.g., a certificate of deposit).

The interest that an investment earns can be simple or compound interest. When using simple interest, the interest rate is only applied to the original investment. Compound interest involves earning interest on the original balance, plus interest on any previously accumulated interest. Throughout this chapter, and in most time value of money calculations made by a financial planner, compound interest is used.

Example 7.3

Yoshe deposits $30,000 into an account earning 4% interest, compounded annually. How much will her account balance be in 3 years?

10BII Keystrokes	12C Keystrokes
3 [N] 4 [I/YR] 30,000[+/-] [PV] 0 [PMT] [FV]	3 [n] 4 [i] 30,000[CHS] [PV] 0 [PMT] [FV]
Answer: 33,745.92	**Answer: 33,745.92**

Periods of Compounding Other than Annual

Annual compounding assumes that the interest earned is calculated and applied to the beginning of the year balance, only once each year, at the end of the year. If interest is compounded semi-annually, quarterly, monthly or daily, there are more than one period of compounding per year as the following chart illustrates.

Compounding	Periods of Compounding Per Year
Annual	1 time
Semi-Annual	2 times
Quarterly	4 times
Monthly	12 times

In **Example 7.3**, Yoshe earned four percent interest per year, compounded annually for three years. What would her account balance be if the interest were compounded semi-annually, quarterly, or monthly? For this type of calculation, the period and interest rate must all be stated in the same terms. The following chart summarizes the impact to the period and interest rate, based upon the periods of compounding per year. Note that the more periods of compounding, the larger the final balance, as summarized in **Exhibit 7.2**.

Exhibit 7.2 | Periods of Compounding Impact to Term and Interest Rate

Compounding	Periods of Compounding Per Year	Impact to Period (N)	Impact to Interest Rate (i)
Annual	1x	None	None
Semi-Annual	2x	Years x 2	Rate ÷ 2
Quarterly	4x	Years x 4	Rate ÷ 4
Monthly	12x	Years x 12	Rate ÷ 12

Example 7.4

Yoshe deposits $30,000 in an account earning 4% interest, compounded *semi-annually*. How much will her account balance be in 3 years?

10BII Keystrokes	12C Keystrokes
3 x 2 = [N]	3 [ENTER] 2 [x] [n]
4 ÷ 2 = [I/YR]	4 [ENTER] 2 [÷] [i]
30,000[+/-] [PV]	30,000[CHS] [PV]
0 [PMT]	0 [PMT]
[FV]	[FV]
Answer: 33,784.87	**Answer: 33,784.87**

Notice that for a semi-annual problem, there are two periods of compounding each year. The number of years is multiplied by two and the interest rate is divided by two. Also, notice that the greater the frequency of compounding the higher the future value.

Example 7.5

Yoshe deposits $30,000 in an account earning 4% interest, compounded *quarterly*. How much will her account balance be in 3 years?

10BII Keystrokes	12C Keystrokes
3 x 4 = [N]	3 [ENTER] 4 [x] [n]
4 ÷ 4 = [I/YR]	4 [ENTER] 4 [÷] [i]
30,000[+/-] [PV]	30,000[CHS] [PV]
0 [PMT]	0 [PMT]
[FV]	[FV]
Answer: 33,804.75	**Answer: 33,804.75** ✓

n = 3×4
i = 4÷4
PV = -30k
PMT = 0
FV

Notice that for a quarterly compounding problem, there are four periods of compounding each year. The number of years is multiplied by four and the interest rate is divided by four.

Example 7.6

Yoshe deposits $30,000 in an account earning 4% interest, compounded *monthly*. How much will her account balance be in 3 years?

10BII Keystrokes	12C Keystrokes
3 x 12 = [N]	3 [ENTER] 12 [x] [n]
4 ÷ 12 = [I/YR]	4 [ENTER] 12 [÷] [i]
30,000[+/-] [PV]	30,000[CHS] [PV]
0 [PMT]	0 [PMT]
[FV]	[FV]
Answer: 33,818.16	**Answer: 33,818.16** ✓

n = 3×12
i = 4÷12

Notice that for a monthly compounding problem, since there are 12 periods of compounding each year, the number of years is multiplied by 12 and the interest rate is divided by 12.

Exhibit 7.3 | Compounding Summary

Account balance after investing $30,000 for 3 years at 4% interest			
Annual Compounding	Semi-Annual Compounding	Quarterly Compounding	Monthly Compounding
$33,745.92	$33,784.87	$33,804.75	$33,818.16

The more often the periods of compounding, the larger the future account balance because the interest rate is being compounded (or calculated on previous interest earnings) more frequently. This results in interest on previous interest earnings. Financial calculators are able to accommodate periods of compounding other than one year. For example, the HP 10BII can be set to semi-annual periods of compounding by pressing 2 [ORANGE] [P/YR], which would avoid having to manually adjust the number of periods and interest rate. However, the problem with this approach is that it is easy to forget that a financial calculator is set to something other than annual periods of compounding. Throughout this chapter, assume that the calculator is always set to one period of compounding per year. Any adjustments to the periods of compounding will be made manually by making the appropriate adjustment to the number of periods, interest rate and/or payments.

For any HP 10BII calculators, be sure to set default compounding periods to one for the remainder of this chapter. The HP 10BII is set by default to 12 periods of compounding. To change the calculator to 1 period of compounding per year:

10BII Keystrokes	12C Keystrokes
1 [ORANGE] [P/YR]	Not applicable as the HP 12C is set to one period of compounding per year.

Annuities

Ordinary Annuity vs. Annuity Due

An **annuity** is a recurring cash flow, of an equal amount that occurs at periodic (but regular) intervals. Annuities are reflected on a financial calculator as a PMT (payment). An **ordinary annuity** occurs when the timing of the first payment is at the end of a period. The period may be the end of a week, month, quarter, or the end of a year. An **annuity due** occurs when the timing of the first payment is at the beginning of the period. The period may be the beginning of a week, month, quarter, or year.

Examples of an ordinary annuity:
- Most debtor payments (car loans, student loans, or mortgages)
- Many savings contributions to an IRA or 401(k) if regular and recurring and made at month, quarter, or year end

Examples of an annuity due:
- Rents (usually paid in advance)
- Tuition payments (usually paid at the beginning of the term in advance)
- Retirement income (usually paid at the beginning of the month or year in advance)

The mathematical difference between an ordinary annuity and an annuity due is captured on a timeline by reflecting whether the first payment occurs at time period zero or at time period one. For an annuity due, the first payment occurs at time period zero. For an ordinary annuity, the first payment occurs at time period one.

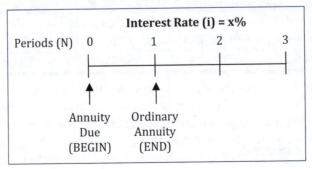

Example 7.7

Kenny deposits $100 into a savings account, at the end of each year, for three years, earning 5% annually. What is the account value in three years?

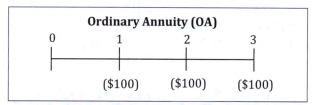

Handwritten notes:
END
AMT 100
I = 5
FV
N 3

Example 7.8

Kenny deposits $100 into a savings account, at the beginning of each year, for three years, earning 5% annually. What is the account value in three years?

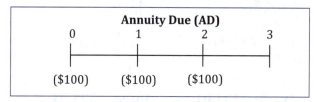

Once the timing of the cash flows has been illustrated on a timeline, the financial planner needs to identify the timing of the annuity as part of the keystrokes for the financial calculator. For an annuity due, the financial calculator should be in "BEGIN" mode, to signify the timing of the first payment is at the beginning of the period. Both the 10BII and 12C will display "BEGIN" when the calculator is in BEGIN mode. For an ordinary annuity, the calculator should be in "END" mode. When the 10BII and 12C are in END mode, the BEGIN is no longer displayed. The calculators do not display END when in end mode. If the financial calculator is in END mode, the following keystrokes will set the calculator to BEGIN mode:

10BII Keystrokes	12C Keystrokes
[ORANGE] [BEG/END]	[g] [BEG]

If the financial calculator is in BEGIN mode, the following keystrokes will set the calculator to END mode:

10BII Keystrokes	12C Keystrokes
[ORANGE] [BEG/END]	[g] [END]

Calculation for Example 7.7 (Ordinary Annuity)

10BII Keystrokes	12C Keystrokes
3 [N]	3 [n]
5 [I/YR]	5 [i]
0 [PV]	0 [PV]
100 [+/-] [PMT]	100 [CHS] [PMT]
[FV]	[FV]
Answer: 315.25	**Answer: 315.25** ✓

Calculation for Example 7.8 (Annuity Due)

10BII Keystrokes	12C Keystrokes
[ORANGE] [BEG/END]	[g] [BEG]
3 [N]	3 [n]
5 [I/YR]	5 [i]
0 [PV]	0 [PV]
100 [+/-] [PMT]	100 [CHS] [PMT]
[FV]	[FV]
Answer: 331.01	**Answer: 331.01** ✓

Notice that the difference in the future values between the annuity due ($331.01) and the ordinary annuity ($315.25) is simply the difference between the first (period 0) payment for the annuity due and the last (period 3) payment for the ordinary annuity compounded by five percent (e.g., $15.76). Also, the future value of an annuity due will always be greater than the future value of an ordinary annuity by exactly the interest earned on the first payment of the annuity due over the total term. Another way to look at the problem is to see that the annuity due has one more period of compounding. Therefore, $315.25 x (1.05) = $331.01.

Present Value of an Ordinary Annuity of $1 (Even Cash Flows)

The **present value of an ordinary annuity of $1** is today's value of an even cash flow stream received or paid over time. The present value of an ordinary annuity assumes that the first annuity payment is made at the end of a period. Examples of questions that may be answered using the present value of an ordinary annuity may include:

- If a client needs x dollars at the end of each year while in retirement, how much should be deposited today?
- Given the amount of debt repayment, how much was originally borrowed?
- How much would a client be willing to pay today for an annuity or income stream that begins at the end of the year?

✒ Quick Quiz 7.2

1. The present value of a future amount is the value of a present lump-sum deposit after earning interest over a period of time.
   a. True
   b. False

2. An annuity due occurs when the timing of the payment is at the end of a period (e.g., end of month, end of quarter, end of year).
   a. True
   b. False

False, False.

Example 7.9

William wants to withdraw $12,000 at the end of each year (ordinary annuity) from a savings account for the next 5 years. How much must he deposit today, if the account earns 6%, compounded annually? (Note: The calculator is set to end mode for this question.)

10BII Keystrokes	12C Keystrokes
5 [N]	5 [n]
6 [I/YR]	6 [i]
12,000 [PMT]	12,000 [PMT]
0 [FV]	0 [FV]
[PV]	[PV]
Answer: <50,548.37>	Answer: <50,548.37>

[handwritten notes: -12K PMT / 5 N / PV? / i =6]

Present Value of an Annuity Due of $1 (Even Cash Flows)

The difference between the present value of an ordinary annuity and **present value of an annuity due of $1**, is the timing of the first payment. For the ordinary annuity, the timing of the first payment is at the end of the period, whereas for an annuity due the timing of the first payment is at the beginning of a time period (today) representing today's value of that even cash flow stream. On a timeline, the first payment occurs at time period zero (now).

Example 7.10

William wants to withdraw $12,000 at the beginning of each year from a savings account for the next 5 years, to pay for his college tuition. How much must he deposit today, if the account earns 6%, compounded annually?

10BII Keystrokes	12C Keystrokes
[ORANGE][BEG/END]	[g][BEG]
5 [N]	5 [n]
6 [I/YR]	6 [i]
12,000 [PMT]	12,000 [PMT]
0 [FV]	0 [FV]
[PV]	[PV]
Answer: <53,581.27>	Answer: <53,581.27>

[handwritten notes: BEG / N 5 / PMT -12K / PV / i =6%]

Notice that if William waits until the end of the year to make his first withdrawal, he would deposit $3,032.90 ($53,581.27 - $50,548.37) less than if he makes the first withdrawal at the beginning of the year. By waiting until the end of the year to make his first withdrawal, he is able to take advantage of compounding interest on his entire deposit of $50,548.37. Whereas, if William takes a withdrawal immediately, he is only earning interest on his deposit, less the initial withdrawal or $41,581.27 ($53,581.27 - $12,000).

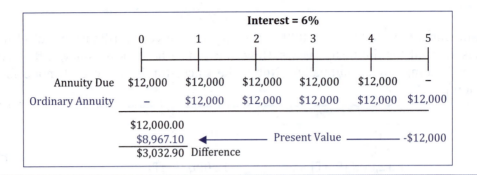

As previously stated, the present value of an annuity due will always be greater than the present value of an ordinary annuity. The difference is the last payment made under the ordinary annuity discounted to time period zero at the given interest rate as compared to the first payment made under the annuity due. In **Example 7.10**, the $12,000 at time period five is worth $8,967.10 at time period zero. ($12,000 - $8,967.10 = $3,032.90).

Future Value of an Ordinary Annuity of $1 (Even Cash Flows)

The **future value of an ordinary annuity of $1** is the value of equal periodic payments or deposits, at some point in the future. The future value of an ordinary annuity assumes that deposits are made at the end of a period or end of a year. This calculation is useful to determine the value of saving contributions over time, earning a constant compounded rate of return.

Example 7.11

Lisa deposits $2,500 into an account at the end of each year. If she earns 6% compounded annually, how much will the account be worth in 7 years? (Note that the calculator should be set to END mode).

10BII Keystrokes	12C Keystrokes
7 [N]	7 [n]
6 [I/YR]	6 [i]
0 [PV]	0 [PV]
2,500 [+/-] [PMT]	2,500 [CHS] [PMT]
[FV]	[FV]
Answer: 20,984.59	Answer: 20,984.59

handwritten: n 7, i 6, PV 0, PMT -2.5K, FV ✓

Future Value of an Annuity Due of $1 (Even Cash Flows)

The **future value of an annuity due of $1** is the future value of equal periodic deposits, made at the beginning of the period. This calculation is useful to determine the value of savings contributions at some point in the future for payments made at the beginning of each period, assuming a compounded rate of return.

Example 7.12

Lisa deposits $2,500 into an account at the beginning of each year. If she earns 6% compounded annually, how much will the account be worth in 7 years? (Note that the calculator should be set to BEGIN mode)

Beg

10BII Keystrokes	12C Keystrokes
[ORANGE] [BEG/END] 7 [N] 6 [I/YR] 0 [PV] 2,500 [+/-] [PMT] [FV]	[g][BEG] 7 [n] 6 [i] 0 [PV] 2,500 [CHS] [PMT] [FV]
Answer: 22,243.67	Answer: 22,243.67 ✓

Remember that the present value of an annuity due will always be greater than the present value of an ordinary annuity because of the timing of the first withdrawal and compounded interest. Likewise, the future value of an annuity due will also always be greater than the future value of an ordinary annuity because of the additional periods of compounding. To equate the two examples above, multiply the ordinary annuity by (1 + i) or (1.06) to get the value of the annuity due. Thus, $20,984.59 x 1.06 = $22,243.67.

Future Value of an Ordinary Annuity vs Annuity Due Comparison

The future value of an annuity can be separated into individual future value calculations for each cash flow. For example, the future value of a series of deposits made over a number of years can be determined by calculating the future value of each individual deposit.

Future Value of an Ordinary Annuity of $1

In **Example 7.11**, Lisa deposits $2,500 at the end of each year for seven years, earning six percent compounded annually. The future value of her account can be determined by calculating the future value of each $2,500 deposit. Her first deposit, for example, has six periods of compounding with a future value of $3,546.30. Whereas, her last deposit of $2,500 at the end of the seventh year has zero periods of compounding, resulting in a future value is $2,500.

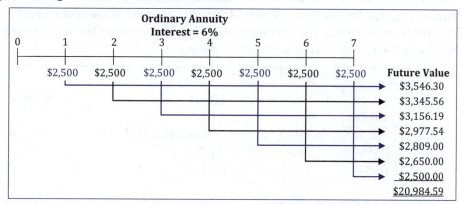

Future Value of an Annuity Due of $1

The difference in the future value between an ordinary annuity (OA) of $1 and an annuity due (AD) of $1 is attributed to additional periods of compounding for the first annuity due deposit. For example, consider **Example 7.12** where Lisa deposits $2,500 at the beginning of each year for seven years, earning six percent compounded annually. Again, the future value of her account can be determined by calculating the future value of each $2,500 deposit. Lisa's first deposit has seven periods of compounding, therefore the future value of the first deposit is $3,759.08. Whereas, her last deposit of $2,500 at the beginning of the sixth year only has one period of compounding and a future value of $2,650.

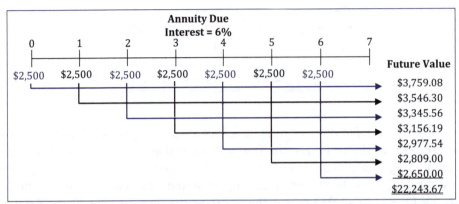

Note that the additional earnings of $1,259.08 ($22,243.67 - $20,984.59) under the annuity due calculation are attributable to the additional compounding of the first deposit under the annuity due $3,759.08 in comparison to the last (7th) deposit under the ordinary annuity $2,500 ($3,759.08 - $2,500.00 = $1,259.08).

Ordinary Annuity Payments from a Lump-Sum Deposit

The **ordinary annuity payments from a lump-sum deposit** are the payments that can be generated at the end of each period, based on a lump-sum amount deposited today. This calculation is useful in determining an:

- Amount of payment required to repay a loan
- Amount of income payments that can be generated from a lump-sum amount

---

Example 7.13

Kenzie has an investment account with a balance of $200,000. She intends to make withdrawals each year for the next 10 years from this account. If the investment account earns 7%, compounded annually, how much can Kenzie receive at the end of each year? (Note that the calculator should be set to END mode.)

10BII Keystrokes	12C Keystrokes
10 [N]	10 [n]
7 [I/YR]	7 [i]
200,000 [+/-] [PV]	200,000 [CHS] [PV]
0 [FV]	0 [FV]
[PMT]	[PMT]
Answer: 28,475.50	Answer: 28,475.50

Annuity Due Payments from a Lump-Sum Deposit

The **annuity due payments from a lump-sum deposit** are the payments that can be generated at the beginning of each period, based on a lump-sum amount deposited today. This calculation is useful in determining:

- Amount of retirement income payments that can be generated from a lump-sum amount
- Amount of periodic income payments that can be generated from a lump-sum amount

Example 7.14

Leroy won $3,000,000 in the Florida lottery. He intends to receive income payments at the beginning of each year, for the next 12 years. Assuming the proceeds are invested with a 3% annual return, how much can Leroy receive at the beginning of each year? (Note that the calculator should be set to BEGIN mode).

[handwritten: BEG, 3m PV, ? PMT, n 12, i 3, 0 FV]

10BII Keystrokes	12C Keystrokes
[ORANGE][BEG/END] 12 [N] 3 [I/YR] 3,000,000 [+/-] [PV] 0 [FV] [PMT]	[g] [BEG] 12 [n] 3 [i] 3,000,000[CHS][PV] 0 [FV] [PMT]
Answer: 292,608.02	**Answer: 292,608.02** ✓

Solving for Term (N)

Term calculations provide the amount of time required to accomplish a financial goal. This calculation is useful in determining an:

- Amount of time required to attain an account balance given a certain rate of return
- Amount of time to retire a debt

Example 7.15

Ivan has $25,000 invested in a mutual fund that earns 9% per year. Ivan wants to know how long it will take for his investment to double?

[handwritten: 9 i, -25K PV, 50K FV]

10BII Keystrokes	12C Keystrokes
9 [I/YR] 25,000 [+/-] [PV] 50,000 [FV] 0 [PMT] [N]	9 [i] 25,000 [CHS] [PV] 50,000 [FV] 0 [PMT] [n]
Answer: 8.0432	**Answer: 9.0** ✓

Notice that the HP 10BII calculates the time for Ivan to double his investment as 8.04 years, whereas the HP 12C calculates 9 years. A limitation of the 12C is that it rounds up to integers (whole numbers) when calculating periods or term. To verify which answer is correct, we can use both 8.04 and 9.0 to determine which term results in the closest amount to $50,000.

Using 9 as the number of years to double Ivan's investment. If the registers have not been cleared, simply press FV.

10BII Keystrokes	12C Keystrokes
9 [N]	9 [n]
9 [I/YR]	9 [i]
25,000 [+/-] [PV]	25,000 [CHS] [PV]
0 [PMT]	0 [PMT]
[FV]	[FV]
Answer: 54,297.33	**Answer: 54,297.33**

Using 8.0432 as the number to double Ivan's investment:

10BII Keystrokes	12C Keystrokes
8.0432 [N]	8.0432 [n]
9 [I/YR]	9 [i]
25,000 [+/-] [PV]	25,000 [CHS] [PV]
0 [PMT]	0 [PMT]
[FV]	[FV]
Answer: 49,999.86	**Answer: 50,007.74**

Using 8.0432 results in the closest future value of Ivan doubling his money from $25,000 to $50,000 (earning 9% per year, compounded annually). If using the HP 12C, be mindful of the integer rounding when calculating term, and note that it always rounds up, regardless of whether the decimal is higher or lower than 0.50.

Common Errors

Note that in **Example 7.15**, the PV was a cash outflow entered as a negative number, while the FV was a cash inflow entered as a positive number. This represents the fact that Ivan must forego current consumption of the $25,000 in order to invest it for the future when he will receive $50,000. When dealing with lump sum amounts to solve for the number of periods or the interest rate, either PV or FV must be a positive number (inflow) and the other must be a negative number (outflow) since you cannot receive something in the future without giving something up today (or vice versa). If both PV and FV are entered as positive numbers the following error messages will appear on the calculator display:

10BII Keystrokes	12C Keystrokes
No Solution	Error 5

Solving for Interest Rate (i)

Interest rate calculations provide the financial planner and client with the interest rate that is required to attain a certain goal and also may be used to calculate the interest rate being charged on a debt obligation.

Example 7.16

Tyrese borrowed $25,000 to buy a new car. His payment is $600 per month, at month end, and he is making equal monthly payments for the next four years. What is the implicit interest rate on this loan?

10BII Keystrokes	12C Keystrokes
4 x 12 = [N]	4 [ENTER] 12 [x] [n]
25,000 [PV]	25,000 [PV]
600 [+/-] [PMT]	600 [CHS] [PMT]
0 [FV]	0 [FV]
[i]	[i]
Answer: 0.5930 per month, so multiply by 12 to state the interest rate on an annual basis 7.1158 (0.5930 x 12).	**Answer: 0.5930** per month, so multiply by 12 to state the interest rate on an annual basis 7.1158 (0.5930 x 12).

(handwritten notes: PMT -600, PV 25K, n 4x12, i .5930 ÷ 12, FV 0)

Uneven Cash Flows

So far, the discussions regarding annuity payments have focused on even dollar amounts, recurring at periodic equal intervals. When an investment or project has periodic cash flows that are not even dollar amounts or not at even intervals, the calculation is referred to as an **uneven cash flow** calculation.

During the discussion of the next two topics (Net Present Value and Internal Rate of Return) it will be necessary to use the uneven cash flow keys on a financial calculator.

For the HP 10BII, the following keys are used for uneven cash flow problems:
- **CF_j**: Represents the periodic cash flows. The "j" represents each period of cash flows.
- **N_j**: Represents the number of consecutive times the periodic cash flow is an equal amount going in the same direction (inflow or outflow). This key allows you to reduce the number of keystrokes in the calculation by entering the number of consecutive times a periodic cash flow occurs.

For the HP 12C, the following keys are used for uneven cash flow problems:
- **CF_0**: Represents the cash flow amount at time period zero.
- **CF_j**: Represents the periodic cash flows after time period zero. The "j" represents each period of cash flows beyond zero.
- **N_j**: Represents the number of consecutive times the periodic cash flow is an equal amount going in the same direction (inflow or outflow).

The following example demonstrates how to use the CF_j and Nj buttons.

Example 7.17

Sheryl makes the following investments into her savings account:

Year 0 – 4: $200 (a total of 5 deposits)
Year 5 – 10: $300 (a total of 6 deposits)
Year 11 – 15: $400 (a total of 5 deposits)

Note that there is no answer to this cash flow scenario. It is only meant to illustrate how to use the [N_j] key to populate multiple periods of even cash flows.

The keystrokes using CF_j, the N_j shortcut is:

10BII Keystrokes	12C Keystrokes
200 [+/-] [CF_j]	200 [CHS] [g] [CF_0]
200 [+/-] [CF_j] *	200 [CHS] [g] [CF_j] **
4 [ORANGE] [N_j]	4 [g] [N_j]
300 [+/-] [CF_j]	300 [CHS] [g] [CF_j]
6 [ORANGE] [N_j]	6 [g] [N_j]
400 [+/-] [CF_j]	400 [CHS] [g] [CF_j]
5 [ORANGE] [N_j]	5 [g] [N_j]

* The HP10 BII does not permit the use of the Nj shortcut at this point. You must enter the cash flow at time period zero and time period one separately. However, the is not the case for the 10BII+ calculator.

** The HP12C permits the use of the Nj shortcut at this point. You do not have to enter the cash flow at time period zero and time period one, separately.

Net Present Value

Net Present Value (NPV) is used in capital budgeting by managers and investors to evaluate investment alternatives. NPV measures the excess or shortfall of cash flows based on the discounted present value of the future cash flows, less the initial cost of the investment. NPV uses the investor's required rate of return as the discount rate. NPV assumes that the cash flows generated from the project are reinvested at the required rate of return or discount rate. The formula for NPV is:

NPV = Present Value of the Future Cash Flows – Cost of the Investment

OR

NPV = PV of CF – Cost (initial outlay)

A positive NPV indicates that the project or investment is generating cash flows in excess of what is required based on the required rate of return. A negative NPV means that the project or investment is not generating cash flows sufficient enough to meet the required rate of return. An NPV equal to zero indicates that the investment is generating a stream of cash flows with a rate of return equal to the required rate of return.

Example 7.18

David purchased a new printer for his book publishing company. The printer was purchased for $10,000 and is expected to generate the following cash flows for the next four years at the end of each year:

Year 1: $3,000
Year 2: $4,000
Year 3: $2,500
Year 4: $1,000

Assume the printer can be sold for $2,000 at the end of year 4 and David's required rate of return is 8%. What is the net present value and should he purchase the printer?

10BII Keystrokes	12C Keystrokes
10,000 [+/-] [CF$_j$]	10,000 [CHS] [g] [CF$_0$]
3,000 [CF$_j$]	3,000 [g] [CF$_j$]
4,000 [CF$_j$]	4,000 [g] [CF$_j$]
2,500 [CF$_j$]	2,500 [g] [CF$_j$]
1,000 + 2,000 =[CF$_j$]	1,000 [Enter] 2,000 [+] [g] [CF$_j$]
8 [I/YR]	8 [i]
[ORANGE] [NPV]	[f] [NPV]
Answer: 396.80	Answer: 396.80

Since the NPV is greater than zero, David should consider purchasing the printer. The value of $396.80 represents the difference between the present value of the future cash flows discounted at the required rate of return less the initial investment.

Recall the NPV formula, which is:

NPV = Present Value of the Future Cash Flows – Cost of the Investment

---

Example 7.19

What is the present value of the future cash flows from this new printer David is considering?

NPV = PV of CF – Cost of Investment
$396.80 = PV of CF – $10,000
$10,000 + $396.80 = PV of CF
$10,396.80 = PV of CF

The calculation can be proved as follows:

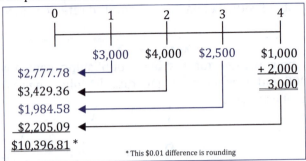

Year	Cash Flow	Discounted Present Value
Year 1	$3,000	$2,777.78
Year 2	$4,000	$3,429.36
Year 3	$2,500	$1,984.58
Year 4	$1,000 + $2,000 = $3,000	$2,205.09
Total Discounted Present Value of Cash Flow Stream		**$10,396.81**

When entering cash flows it is important to net any cash flows occurring in the same time period since the calculation involves discounting back to a PV based on the number of periods, as illustrated in the timeline in **Example 7.19**. If the $1,000 and $2,000 in period four were entered separately, the first entry would be discounted over four years and the calculator would assume the second entry occurred in period five and it would be discounted over five years. Since both occur in period four, they must be netted and entered as a single cash flow.

Example 7.20

Daisy anticipates making the following tuition payments for her son, Bo, who is starting his first year of college today.

Year	Tuition Payment
Year 1	$10,000
Year 2	$10,000
Year 3	$15,000
Year 4	$15,000

How much must Daisy have in a college savings account to make the tuition payments above, if she can earn 5%, each year, on her investments?

10BII Keystrokes	12C Keystrokes
10,000 [+/-] [CF$_j$]	10,000 [CHS] [g] [CF$_0$]
10,000 [+/-] [CF$_j$] *	10,000 [CHS] [g] [CF$_j$] **
15,000 [+/-] [CF$_j$]	15,000 [CHS] [g] [CF$_j$]
2 [ORANGE] [N$_j$]	2 [g] [N$_j$]
5 [I/YR]	5 [i]
[ORANGE] [NPV]	[f] [NPV]
Answer: <46,086.82>	**Answer: <46,086.82>**

The HP10 BII does not permit the use of the Nj shortcut at this point. You must enter the cash flow at time period zero and time period one separately. However, the is not the case for the 10BII+ calculator.

** *The HP12C permits the use of the Nj shortcut at this point. You do not have to enter the cash flow at time period zero and time period one, separately.*

Internal Rate of Return (IRR)

The **Internal Rate of Return (IRR)** is the compound rate of return that equates the cash inflows to the cash outflows. IRR allows for the comparison of projects or investments with differing costs and cash flows. An investment is considered acceptable when the IRR equals or exceeds the client's required rate of return. Alternatively, an investment should be rejected if the IRR is less than the client's required rate of return.

IRR is that discount rate that will cause the sum of the discounted present value of all the future cash flows to equal the cost of the investment. An important assumption about the internal rate of return is that it assumes that cash flows are reinvested at the internal rate of return.

Example 7.21

David purchased a new printer for his book publishing company. The printer was purchased for $10,000 and is expected to generate the following cash flows for the next four years:

Year 1: $3,000
Year 2: $4,000
Year 3: $2,500
Year 4: $1,000

Assume the printer can be sold for $2,000 at the end of year 4 and David's required rate of return is 8 percent. What is David's internal rate of return if he purchases the printer?

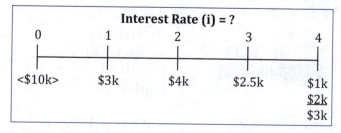

10BII Keystrokes	12C Keystrokes
10,000 [+/-] [CF$_j$]	10,000 [CHS] [g] [CF$_0$]
3,000 [CF$_j$]	3,000 [g] [CF$_j$]
4,000 [CF$_j$]	4,000 [g] [CF$_j$]
2,500 [CF$_j$]	2,500 [g] [CF$_j$]
1,000 + 2,000 = [[CF$_j$]	1,000 [ENTER] 2,000
[ORANGE] [IRR/YR]	[+] [g] [CF$_j$]
	[f] [IRR]
Answer: 9.81%	Answer: 9.81%

The NPV for this problem, calculated using the required rate of return of 8%, is positive, meaning David is earning a return greater than his required rate of return. His required rate of return was 8%, but the actual internal rate of return on this investment would be 9.81%.

As previously mentioned, the internal rate of return calculation can be used to measure the compounded rate of return, when considering uneven cash flows.

Example 7.22

Three years ago, Tawny purchased a stock for $75. Over the past three years, the stock has paid the following dividends.

Year 1: $2.25
Year 2: $2.50
Year 3: $2.75

At the end of the third year, the stock was selling for $85. What was Tawny's compounded rate of return (IRR)?

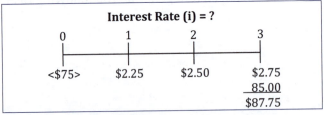

10BII Keystrokes	12C Keystrokes
75 [+/-] [CF$_j$]	75 [CHS] [g] [CF$_0$]
2.25 [CF$_j$]	2.25 [g] [CF$_j$]
2.50 [CF$_j$]	2.50 [g] [CF$_j$]
2.75 + 85 = [[CF$_j$]	2.75[ENTER]85
[ORANGE] [IRR/YR]	[+][g][CF$_j$]
	[f][IRR]
Answer: 7.45%	Answer: 7.45%

Inflation Adjusted Rate of Return

An **inflation adjusted rate of return** adjusts the nominal rate of return into a real (after inflation) rate of return. **Nominal interest rates** are the actual rate of return earned on an investment. Real rates of return are adjusted for inflation's impact. The formula for the real rate of return is:

$$\text{Real Rate of Return} = \frac{(1 + R_n)}{(1 + i)} - 1 \times 100$$

Where:
Rn = nominal rate of return or investment rate of return
i = inflation rate

Example 7.23

Assume $5 is invested for one year earning 6% and the inflation rate during that one year is 3%. What is the inflation adjusted rate of return?

Return: $5 x 1.06 = $5.30
Inflation: $5 x 1.03 = $5.15
Difference: $5.30 - $5.15 = $0.15
The return above and beyond the impact of inflation is:
$0.15 ÷ $5.15 = 0.0291 or 2.91%

Using the real rate of return formula:
Real Rate of Return = [(1 + Rn) ÷ (1 + i) – 1] x 100
Real Rate of Return = [(1.06) ÷ (1.03) – 1] x 100
Real Rate of Return = [1.0291 – 1] x 100
Real Rate of Return = 0.0291 x 100
Real Rate of Return = 2.91%*

(caution: rounding 2.9126214 to 2.91 will cause a slight error)

The inflation adjusted rate of return should be used when there is an account balance growing at one rate of return and simultaneously an expense is growing at a different rate of return. In addition, it is used when there is an investment return at one rate and inflation (loss of purchasing power) at another rate. An inflation adjusted rate of return should be used in an education funding situation where there is a lump-sum amount growing at an investment rate of return and tuition expense is growing at a tuition inflation rate.

Example 7.24

Fred and Wilma are planning for their son's education. Tuition currently costs $15,000 per year and is paid in advance (annuity due) and they expect their son to attend college for 4 years, beginning today. They expect their investments to earn 7.5% per year and for tuition inflation to be 5% each year. How much must Fred and Wilma invest today, to meet their goal?

10BII Keystrokes	12C Keystrokes
[ORANGE] [BEG/END] 4 [N] 1.075 ÷ 1.05 - 1 x 100 = [I/YR]* 15,000 [+/-] [PMT] 0 [FV] [PV]	[g] [BEG] 4 [n] 1.075 [ENTER] 1.05 [÷] 1 [-] 100 [x] [i]* 15,000 [CHS] [PMT] 0 [FV] [PV]
Answer: 57,939.24	**Answer: 57,939.24**

The inflation adjusted [i] = 2.3809524 unrounded.

The 10BII+ calculators have a setting for algebraic or chain calculations. To toggle between the two settings, press [Blue][On]. When calculating an inflation adjusted rate of return, set the calculator to "chain." The default setting is "chain."

In the above example, the reason that the current cost of tuition ($15,000) is used as the payment to solve for the present value is that because of the inflation adjusted discount rate, all of the factors in the calculation are in current dollars. The inflation adjusted discount rate takes into consideration the rate of earnings as well as the rate of inflation.

An inflation adjusted rate of return can be also used for retirement funding where there is a lump-sum amount earning an investment return and the income being generated by the lump sum is adjusted for inflation each year. If a client wants income throughout retirement equivalent to "today's dollars," an inflation adjusted rate of return must be used.

Example 7.25

Barney and Betty are planning to retire today. They would like to receive $25,000 per year in today's dollars, at the beginning of each year, for the next 25 years. Barney and Betty expect their investments to earn 8% per year and inflation to be 2% each year. How much must Barney and Betty have today, to meet their goal?

10BII Keystrokes	12C Keystrokes
[ORANGE] [BEG/END] 25 [N] 1.08 ÷ 1.02 - 1 x 100 = [I/YR]* 25,000 [PMT] 0 [FV] [PV]	[g] [BEG] 25 [n] 1.08 [ENTER] 1.02 [÷] 1 [-] 100 [x] [i]* 25,000 [PMT] 0 [FV] [PV]
Answer: <342,198.97>	**Answer: <342,198.97>**

* The inflation adjusted [i] = 5.8823529 unrounded.

In the above retirement needs example, the current retirement needs ($25,000) are used as the payment to solve for the present value. Once again, problems that use an inflation adjusted discount rate are generally working with today's dollars.

Serial Payments

Serial payments are different from annuity payments in that annuity payments are an equal dollar amount throughout the payment period. **Serial payments** are adjusted upward periodically throughout the payment period at a constant rate, usually in order to adjust for inflation's impact. Each serial payment will increase, to maintain the real dollar purchasing power of the investment.

$$\left(\frac{1.08}{1.025}\right) - 1 \times 100$$

Example 7.26

Omar wants to purchase a boat in 4 years, which costs $50,000 in today's dollars. He can earn 8% on his investments and expects inflation to be 2.5% per year. What serial payment should Omar make at the end of the first, second, third, and fourth year to be able to purchase the boat in four years?

10BII Keystrokes	12C Keystrokes
4 [N] 1.08 ÷ 1.025 - 1 x 100 = [I/YR] 0 [PV] 50,000 [FV] [PMT] = <11,537.69> x 1.025 = <11,826.13>* **Answers:** End of First Year: <11,826.13> x 1.025 = End of Second Year: <12,121.79> x 1.025 = End of Third Year: <12,424.83> x 1.025 = End of Fourth Year: <12,735.45>	4 [n] 1.08 [ENTER] 1.025 [÷] 1 [-] 100 [x] [i] 0 [PV] 50,000 [FV] [PMT] = 11,537.69 1.025 [x] = 11,826.13* **Answers:** End of First Year: <11,826.13> 1.025 [x] = End of Second Year: <12,121.79> 1.025 [x] = End of Third Year: <12,424.83> 1.025 [x] = End of Fourth Year: <12,735.45>

* Note: The calculated first payment for a serial payment is determined using the same keystrokes as an ordinary annuity, but the calculated payment is then increased by the inflation rate to determine the first serial payment to be made at the end of year one.

Serial payment calculations make use of the concept of inflation adjusted discount rates. As a result, the current cost or present value of what is being funding can be used as the future value in the calculation. In the above example, the current cost of the boat is used as the input for future value. $50,000 is not actually the future value. However, using the inflation adjusted discount rate allows us to use the $50,000 as the future value because all of the inputs are in terms of today's dollars. The following exhibit illustrates:

- The price of the boat ($50,000) is being inflated at 2.5% per year, which results in a future value of $55,190.64. That amount will be the actual cost of the boat in four years.
- The present value of the future cost is discounted at 8%. This value equals $40,566.77, which represents the amount of money that would be needed today, that, if invested to earn 8%, would grow to equal exactly $55,190.64.

Exhibit 7.4 | Omar's Boat Cost

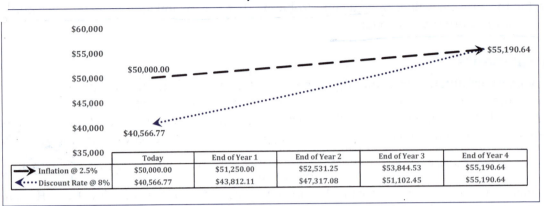

	Today	End of Year 1	End of Year 2	End of Year 3	End of Year 4
Inflation @ 2.5%	$50,000.00	$51,250.00	$52,531.25	$53,844.53	$55,190.64
Discount Rate @ 8%	$40,566.77	$43,812.11	$47,317.08	$51,102.45	$55,190.64

In the example above, the serial payment was calculated by using the PV of $50,000 as the future value and calculating the payment, as an ordinary annuity. The resulting payment equals $11,537.69. Because the problem is using the inflation adjusted discount rate, it must be increased by one period's worth of inflation to determine the payment at the end of the year. Although ordinary annuities occur at the end of the period, this payment must still be adjusted because all of the numbers are in today's dollars and the first payment occurs one year from today.

This type of problem could also be solved by solving for the PV of $40,566.77 and then using the inflation adjusted discount rate to determine the payment. The result will be the same value of $11,537.69, which must be multiplied by 1.025 to determine the first year's serial payment, as depicted in the following exhibit.

Exhibit 7.5 | Omar's Boat Cost 2

10BII Keystrokes	12C Keystrokes
4 [N] 1.08 ÷ 1.025 - 1 x 100 = [I/YR] 0 [FV] 40,566.77 [PV] [PMT] = 11,537.69 x 1.025 = 11,826.13*	4 [n] 1.08 [ENTER] 1.025 [÷] 1 [-] 100 [x] [i] 0 [FV] 40,566.77 [PV] [PMT] = 11,537.69 1.025 [x] = 11,826.13*
Answers End of First Year: <11,826.13> x 1.025 = End of Second Year: <12,121.79> x 1.025 = End of Third Year: <12,424.83> x 1.025 = End of Fourth Year: <12,735.45>	**Answers** End of First Year: <11,826.13> 1.025 [x] = End of Second Year: <12,121.79> 1.025 [x] = End of Third Year: <12,424.83> 1.025 [x] = End of Fourth Year: <12,735.45>

Note: The calculated first payment for a serial payment is determined using the same keystrokes as an ordinary annuity, but the calculated payment is then increased by the inflation rate to determine the first serial payment to be made at the end of year one.

Effectively, $50,000 as a future value and $40,566.77 as a present value are the same, assuming the inflation adjusted discount rate in the problem. The exhibit below is a proof that the savings amounts found in **Example 7.26** accumulate to the needed future value.

Exhibit 7.6 | Omar's Boat Proof of Cash Flows

Accumulation Schedule (Proof)

Period	Beginning of Year Account Balance	Earnings @ 8%	Year-End Deposit (Pmt)	End of Year Account Balance
0	$0.00	$0.00	$11,826.13	$11,826.13
1	$11,826.13	$946.09	$12,121.79	$24,894.01
2	$24,894.01	$1,991.52	$12,424.83	$39,310.36
3	$39,310.36	$3,144.83	$12,735.45	$55,190.64

Future Value of Deposits (Proof):

Interest Rate = 8%					
Time Period	0	1	2	3	4
Payment 1		$11,826.13			$14,897.52
Payment 2			$12,121.79		$14,138.85
Payment 3				$12,424.83	$13,418.82
Payment 4					$12,735.45
				Future Value =	$55,190.64

Retirement and education savings amounts are often calculated as an annual savings amount that remains the same over the savings term. In other words, the same amount, in terms of dollars, is saved each year. However, wages generally increase annually, often in relation to the cost of living. Serial payments, which might increase each year, can be used to better match savings amounts to rising wages over time. The result of using a serial payment is that the beginning payments will be less than a straight annuity and the later payments will be greater than a straight annuity.

Example 7.27

Charming Charlie loves to plan in advance. He recently started dating Channel, who he is certain is the woman he wants to spend the rest of his life with. Charlie doesn't like to rush into things so he anticipates that he will wait ten years to ask her to marry him. He wants to make the engagement a big, romantic, event with a six-month trip around the world. He would like to save enough to pay for a trip that would cost $100,000 in today's dollars. He believes that the cost of the trip should increase by 4% per year. His current compensation is $160,000 and he expects raises of 4% per year. He can save 5% of his salary each year and he believes his investment return will be 10%. The amount he would need to save the first year is as follows:

10BII Keystrokes	12C Keystrokes
10 [N] 1.1 ÷ 1.04 - 1 x 100 = [I/YR] 0 [PV] 100,000 [FV] [PMT] = <7,669.41> x 1.04 = <7,976.18> **Answers** End of First Year: <7,976.18>	10 [n] 1.1 [ENTER] 1.04 [÷] 1 [-] 100 [x] [i] 0 [PV] 100,000 [FV] [PMT] = (7,669.41) 1.04 [x] = 7,976.18 **Answers** End of First Year: <7,976.18>

* Note: The calculated first payment for a serial payment is determined using the same keystrokes as an ordinary annuity, but the calculated payment is then increased by the inflation rate to determine the first serial payment to be made at the end of year one.

The chart below illustrates the future needs of the trip ($148,024.43) as well as the expected savings balance over the ten years and the annual savings amounts. In addition, the savings as a percent of salary remains the same at 4.985% each year.

Year	End of Year Value of Trip / Payment	Salary	BOY Balance	Earnings	Annual Savings	EOY Balance
1	$104,000.00	$166,400.00	$ -	$ -	**$7,976.18**	$7,976.18
2	$108,160.00	$173,056.00	$7,976.18	$797.62	$8,295.23	$17,069.03
3	$112,486.40	$179,978.24	$17,069.03	$1,706.90	$8,627.04	$27,402.98
4	$116,985.86	$187,177.37	$27,402.98	$2,740.30	$8,972.12	$39,115.40
5	$121,665.29	$194,664.46	$39,115.40	$3,911.54	$9,331.01	$52,357.94
6	$126,531.90	$202,451.04	$52,357.94	$5,235.79	$9,704.25	$67,297.98
7	$131,593.18	$210,549.08	$67,297.98	$6,729.80	$10,092.42	$84,120.20
8	$36,856.91	$218,971.05	$84,120.20	$8,412.02	$10,496.11	$103,028.33
9	$142,331.18	$227,729.89	$103,028.33	$10,302.83	$10,915.96	$124,247.12
10	$148,024.43	$236,839.09	$124,247.12	$12,424.71	$11,352.60	$148,024.43

Debt Repayments

Time value of money concepts can be used to calculate the monthly, quarterly, or annual payment necessary to retire a debt obligation. Debt repayment calculations can be used for any type of debt including student loans, credit cards, mortgages, or car loans. In addition to the payment required to retire the debt, the financial planner can determine the amount of interest and principal paid over a period of time.

Remember, most debt repayments are ordinary annuities (they are made in arrears), so repayment calculations are in END mode. Even though most mortgage payments are made at the beginning of the month, the repayment is still an ordinary annuity (because each payment includes a portion of principal repayment and interest expense incurred from the loan being outstanding for the previous month).

Example 7.28

Malcolm and Raven bought a house for $400,000 on August 1. They made a down payment of 20% and financed the balance over 15 years at 5% annual interest. What is their monthly mortgage payment and when do they make it? Note that they make the first payment one month in arrears.

10BII Keystrokes	12C Keystrokes
15 x 12 = [N]	15 [ENTER] 12 [x] [n]
5 ÷ 12 = [I/YR]	5 [ENTER] 12 [÷] [i]
400,000 x 0.80 = [PV]	400,000 [ENTER]
0 [FV]	0.80 [x] [PV]
[PMT]	0 [FV]
	[PMT]
Answer: <2,530.54>	**Answer: <2,530.54>**

Their first payment is due on September 1. How much interest will they pay in the first calendar year (4 payments)?

10BII Keystrokes	12C Keystrokes
1 [INPUT] 4	4 [f] [AMORT]
[ORANGE][AMORT][=] 4,818.84-principal	
[=]	
Answer: <5,303.32>	**Answer: <5,303.32>**

Note: They will make four payments during the current calendar year (September, October, November, and December). Therefore, the loan must be amortized for four months.

Their first payment is due on September 1. How much principal will they repay in the first calendar year?

10BII Keystrokes	12C Keystrokes
See above	[X≥Y]
([=] 4,818.84-principal)	
Answer: <4,818.84>	**Answer: <4,818.84>**

Their first payment is due on September 1. What is the outstanding principal balance on their loan at calendar year end?

10BII Keystrokes	12C Keystrokes
[=]	[RCL]
	[PV]
Answer: 315,181.16	**Answer: 315,181.16**

Amortization Schedule

An **amortization schedule** illustrates the repayment of debt over time. Each debt payment consists of both interest expense and principal repayment. The further into the repayment of a debt, the bigger the portion of the payment that is applied to the outstanding principal. The following yearly amortization schedule illustrates the repayment of Malcolm and Raven's 15 year mortgage from the previous example; but assumes the loan was taken out January 1 and the first payment was made January 31.

Inputs:	
Amount Borrowed	$320,000
Interest Rate	5%
Term	15

Year	Beginning Balance	Payment	Principal Amount	Interest Amount	Ending Balance
1	$320,000	($30,366.48)	($14,700.32)	($15,666.15)	$305,299.68
2	$305,300	($30,366.48)	($15,452.42)	($14,914.06)	$289,847.26
3	$289,847	($30,366.48)	($16,243.00)	($14,123.48)	$273,604.27
4	$273,604	($30,366.48)	($17,074.02)	($13,292.46)	$256,530.25
5	$256,530	($30,366.48)	($17,947.56)	($12,418.92)	$238,582.70
6	$238,583	($30,366.48)	($18,865.79)	($11,500.69)	$219,716.91
7	$219,717	($30,366.48)	($19,831.00)	($10,535.48)	$199,885.92
8	$199,886	($30,366.48)	($20,845.59)	($9,520.89)	$179,040.33
9	$179,040	($30,366.48)	($21,912.09)	($8,454.39)	$157,128.24
10	$157,128	($30,366.48)	($23,033.16)	($7,333.32)	$134,095.09
11	$134,095	($30,366.48)	($24,211.58)	($6,154.90)	$109,883.51
12	$109,884	($30,366.48)	($25,450.29)	($4,916.19)	$84,433.23
13	$84,433	($30,366.48)	($26,752.37)	($3,614.11)	$57,680.86
14	$57,681	($30,366.48)	($28,121.07)	($2,245.41)	$29,559.80
15	$29,560	($30,366.48)	($29,559.80)	($806.68)	$0.00

Note: The amortization table could have easily been prepared on a monthly rather than yearly basis.

Note: According to the amortization schedule, the ending balance of the mortgage after the first year is $305,299.68 which is different than the $315,181.16 originally calculated (**Example 7.28**) due to the original loan only being amortized for four months. In the amortization schedule above, the loan was amortized for a full 12 months for each year.

OTHER PRACTICAL APPLICATIONS

The time value of money principles covered in this chapter can also be applied to everyday decisions that clients face. Some other questions that can be answered using time value of money include:

1. Should a client take the cash rebate or zero percent financing on a new car?
2. Should a client pay points to reduce their mortgage payment when purchasing a new home?
3. Should a lottery winner receive a lump-sum payment or annuity over 20 years?
4. Should a client make additional periodic payments to pay off a mortgage early?
5. Should a client buy or lease a car or a house?

> ### ✅ *Key Concepts*
>
> 1. Evaluate the benefit of a cash rebate or zero percent financing.
> 2. Determine whether the payment of points is beneficial.
> 3. Calculate the breakeven rate that equates a lump-sum option and an annuity option for a lottery winner.
> 4. Understand how various techniques can help reduce the overall interest paid on a mortgage.
> 5. Consider the advantages and disadvantages of leasing versus buying certain assets.

Cash Rebate or Zero Percent Financing

When a client is considering a car purchase or other expensive item that requires financing, special terms may be offered. The seller may offer a cash rebate or zero percent financing and the client must determine which offer is the most financially beneficial. Time value of money skills can be applied to answer this question.

Example 7.29

Jan is considering purchasing a new car for $40,000. The dealer is offering two options on the purchase:

- Option 1: Receive a $5,000 rebate on the price of the car and finance the balance over 5 years at 4% interest, or
- Option 2: Finance the vehicle for 6 years at 0% interest, but no rebate.

If Jan elects option #1, her payment would be:

10BII Keystrokes	12C Keystrokes
5 x 12 = [N] 4 ÷ 12 = [I/YR] 40,000 – 5,000 = [PV] 0 [FV] [PMT]	5 [ENTER] 12 [x] [n] 4 [ENTER] 12 [÷] [i] 40,000[ENTER] 5,000 [-] [PV] 0 [FV] [PMT]
Answer: <644.58>	**Answer: <644.58>**

The HP 12C can automatically accommodate monthly compounding by pressing the number of years [g] [N], which will multiply the number of years by 12 and populate the number of months into the [n] register. The 12C will also account for monthly interest by pressing the annual interest [g] [i], which will divide the annual interest rate by 12 and populate the [i] register.

Her total cost under option #1 is $38,675 ($644 x 60 months).

If Jan elects option #2, her payment would be:

10BII Keystrokes	12C Keystrokes
6 x 12 = [N] 0 [I/YR] 40,000 [PV] 0 [FV] [PMT]	6 [g] [n] 0 [i] 40,000 [PV] 0 [FV] [PMT]
Answer: <555.56>	**Answer: <555.56>**

Her total cost under option #2 would be $40,000 ($555.56 x 72 months).

Based on the total cost (purchase price – rebate + interest expense), Jan would be better off by electing option #1 and selecting the rebate, as she would save $1,325 ($40,000 - $38,675) over the repayment period.

Payment of Points on a Mortgage

Another type of financing decision a client may consider is whether or not to pay points on a mortgage to reduce the interest rate. Points are a percentage of the amount being borrowed that is paid by the borrower to the lender. The higher the points paid, the lower the interest rate on the loan. The decision to pay (or not pay) points is primarily a function of the time of ownership of the property, so the borrower can recoup the points paid through savings on a lower interest rate (interest expense). Time value of money concepts can be applied to determine the appropriate amount of points to pay or not pay when borrowing to purchase a house.

Example 7.30

Sylvia is considering purchasing a new home for $500,000. She intends to put 20% down and finance $400,000, but is unsure which financing option to select. Sylvia is considering the following financing options:

- Option 1: Fixed rate mortgage over 30 years at 5.5% interest, zero points
- Option 2: Fixed rate mortgage over 30 years at 5% interest, plus two discount points

How long would her financial planner recommend that she live in the house to justify option #2?

First, determine how much paying the points will cost Sylvia. Paying two discount points will cost her $8,000 ($400,000 x 0.02).

Second, determine the monthly mortgage payment under each financing option.

Option #1

10BII Keystrokes	12C Keystrokes
30 x 12 = [N]	30 [g] [n]
5.5 ÷ 12 = [I/YR]	5.5 [g] [i]
400,000 [PV]	400,000 [PV]
0 [FV]	0 [FV]
[PMT]	[PMT]
Answer: <2,271.16>	**Answer: <2,271.16>**

Option #2

10BII Keystrokes	12C Keystrokes
30 x 12 = [N]	30 [g] [n]
5 ÷ 12 = [I/YR]	5 [g] [i]
400,000 [PV]	400,000 [PV]
0 [FV]	0 [FV]
[PMT]	[PMT]
Answer: <2,147.29>	**Answer: <2,147.29>**

Third, determine the cost savings and amount of time required to payback the $8,000 paid in discount points.

Option #1 Payment: $2,271.16

Option #2 Payment: $2,147.29

Savings Per Monthly Payment: $123.87 ($2,271.16 - $2,147.29)

$8,000 ÷ $123.87 = 64.6 months or 5.4 years (64.6 ÷ 12)

Therefore, if Sylvia intends to live in the new house for more than 5.4 years, she would be better off with option #2 and paying the discount points now.

Note: If the $8,000 is included on the mortgage, the payment would be comparable at $2,190.23 (savings of $80.93 per month). The ownership period to recoup the $8,000 would then be: $8,000 ÷ $80.93 = 98.9 months or 8.2 years.

Lottery Winnings - Lump Sum or Annuity

Should a client (or financial planner) be so fortunate as to win a lump-sum amount from a lottery, a decision must be made whether to take a lump-sum distribution or an annual annuity. Typically, the annual annuity will begin immediately and is therefore an annuity due. Along with many other considerations, the lottery winner should decide whether an almost risk-free rate of return can be earned that is greater than what is implied in an annuity payout. If a risk-free rate of return can be earned that is greater than what is being implied in an annuity payout, the lottery winner should take the lump-sum amount. If the lottery winner is unable to earn a risk-free return greater than what is implied in the annuity, then the annuity should be considered. Ultimately, the decision will be based on many factors including the winner's expected earnings rate.

Example 7.31

Big Money Bob won $50 million in the New York lottery. He can elect to receive a single lump-sum payout of $22 million after taxes or receive an annual annuity of $1,500,000 after tax, which begins immediately and lasts for 20 years. What rate of return would he need to earn to make the lump-sum payout, equivalent to the annuity payment? Should Bob take the lump-sum payment or the annuity?

What rate of return would he need to earn to make the lump-sum payout equivalent to the annuity payment?

10BII Keystrokes	*12C Keystrokes*
[ORANGE] [BEG/END] 20 [N] 22,000,000 [+/-] [PV] 1,500,000 [PMT] 0 [FV] [I/YR]	[g] [BEG] 20 [n] 22,000,000 [CHS] [PV] 1,500,000 [PMT] 0 [FV] [i]
Answer: 3.54%	**Answer: 3.54%**

Should Bob take the lump-sum payment or the annuity?

If Bob can invest the lump-sum payout and earn a return greater than 3.54% risk-free (without risk) he should take the lump-sum payout. If Bob is uncertain if he can earn a riskless 3.54%, he should consider electing the annuity payment. This example is only intended to illustrate how time value of money may be used in the decision making process. There are other considerations such as current financial needs and the ability to manage assets that must be considered.

Mortgage Reduction Techniques

Over the life of a standard 30-year mortgage, the home owner will often pay as much or more in interest payments as principal payments. The breakeven interest rate is about 5.3 percent. However, even with interest rates of less than 5.3 percent, the home owner will pay a substantial amount of interest. There are many techniques to pay off a mortgage in less than 360 months by paying additional principal payments every month or every year. Four options are discussed below.

Double the monthly payment - This technique calls for increasing the monthly mortgage payment by 100 percent or doubling it. The increased payment will go entirely towards paying down the principal owed, which can significantly reduce the number of months of required mortgage payments. The higher the interest rate, the more months will be reduced with this technique.

Mortgage payment plus 10% - This technique calls for paying an extra 10 percent of the mortgage payment. Naturally, the increase could be more or less than 10 percent. Even at a 10 percent increase, the term of the mortgage will be noticeably reduced. For example, if a mortgage payment was $600 per month then the owner would pay $660 per month.

Extra payment each year - This technique calls for making an additional mortgage payment at the end of each year. This additional payment would go directly to paying off principal.

Extra $100 every month - This technique calls for paying an extra $100 every month that goes to pay down the mortgage debt. This amount could be an extra $20 or an extra $1,000. Any additional payments will result in less total interest over the life of the loan and will shorten the loan.

Example 7.32

Ollie purchases a house with a 30-year mortgage of $100,000 at a 6% interest rate. His payment is calculated to be $599.55 per month. If he pays off his mortgage on schedule, he will pay back a total of $215,838, of which $115,838 is interest. The chart below depicts several alternative payment structures that save interest and result in a shorter mortgage term.

Technique	Standard Payment	Double the Monthly Payment	Increase Monthly Payment by 10%	Increase Monthly Payment by 20%	Extra Payment at the End of Each Year	Extra $100 (0.1%) Every Payment
Total Payments	$215,838	$129,714	$187,690	$171,274	$192,197	$175,236
Total Interest Saved	N/A	$86,124	$28,149	$44,564	$23,641	$40,602
Month Mortgage Paid Off	360	108	285	238	297	252

The example above illustrates that even small increases to a monthly payment can have a dramatic effect on the overall interest paid on the mortgage. Just paying $100 (0.1 percent (or 10 basis points) of the loan amount) extra per month reduces total interest over $40,000 or by about 19 percent.

Buy vs. Lease/Rent

For some financial goals, the client may have the option to rent or lease rather than purchase the asset using debt or savings. When this option is available, the first factor to consider is the length of time the client plans to use the asset. How long will the client keep the car, furniture, computer, or home? If the time frame is short term, it often makes sense to lease or rent rather than purchase. The length of time, however, is not the only factor that should be considered.

In a lease, the lessor owns the item, and the lessee pays rent for the use of it. A closed-end lease entails a known, fixed cost. At the end of the lease period, no further money is owed by the lessee. An open-end lease, on the other hand, has a lower periodic lease payment but may require an additional payment by the lessee at the end of the lease period. The additional payment may be due to the lessee not keeping the asset in good condition, so the actual value at the end is less than was projected at the start of the lease.

Leasing a Vehicle

There are several reasons for clients choosing to lease rather than purchase a vehicle. Some people find that they can get a higher value vehicle for fewer dollars per month under a lease; some people like to trade in their vehicle for a new one frequently; and some people enjoy the maintenance convenience of leasing a new car that is covered under warranty.

A lease is not the best choice for clients who will put a lot of miles on a car. Most leases will impose additional charges when a renter exceeds an annual mileage limit, so leases are better for clients who will only be driving 12,000 to 15,000 miles per year. Clients should also make an assessment of the amount of wear and tear that is likely to occur since the leased vehicle must be returned in excellent condition or an extra fee will be applied. The actual cost of the lease will vary based on how good the client's credit score is.

While leasing may allow the client to get a higher priced car at lower cost per month, the client is not necessarily saving money. If the client will need a car for many years, buying the car and keeping it longer than the lease term of three or four years may be less costly.

A planner should help a client make a comparison of the total costs of each option. This comparison should factor in the down payment required for leasing versus buying because many leases require an up-front, lump-sum payment, which is nonrefundable, called a "capitalized cost reduction" payment. The comparison should also show the monthly payment amount, the residual value of the vehicle (which will be zero for leasing since at the end of the lease term the lessee does not own the vehicle), plus any additional fees and maintenance costs.

Buying a Home Versus Renting

In addition to the number of years expected to be in the home, the choice between buying and leasing a home requires consideration of all the cash outflows and inflows associated with each option and how those cash flows may change over the planning period.

- Outflows from leasing a home include the security deposit, rent payments, some insurance costs, and utilities costs.
- Outflows from owning a home include the down payment, closing costs, principal and interest payments, property taxes, all insurance costs, utilities costs, and maintenance expenses.
- Inflows from leasing a home include the return of the security deposit and possibly earnings on savings if the lease payment is low.
- Inflows from owning a home include tax savings due to deductibility of interest, points, and property taxes, possibly some rental income, and capital gains (less any taxes) on sale of the house.

Exhibit 7.7 | Issues to Consider in Deciding to Buy or Lease Assets

- Is the asset likely to go up in value? If so, buying is preferable.

- Are there income tax advantages to one or the other? All else being equal, choose the option with the favorable tax treatment.

- Is the item likely to become obsolete soon? If so, leasing is probably preferable.

- Is the individual likely to add improvements to the asset at his or her own expense? If so, purchasing may be the way to go.

CONCLUSION

The important time value of money concepts, including ordinary annuity and annuity due, are necessary subjects for the financial planner to master in order to properly understand and assist clients with goal-oriented recommendations. Common financial planning needs such as retiring debt, financing decisions, and goal attainment (i.e., retirement and education funding) require time value of money knowledge to properly serve clients. Financial planners must immerse themselves in this subject matter to effectively and successfully practice in their chosen profession.

DISCUSSION QUESTIONS

SOLUTIONS to the discussion questions can be found exclusively within the chapter. Once you have completed an initial reading of the chapter, go back and highlight the answers to these questions.

1. Define time value of money.

2. Discuss the difference between the present value and the future value of money.

3. List and define the four steps to solving time value of money calculations.

4. Define the present value of a future amount.

5. Define the future value of a lump-sum amount.

6. Discuss the difference between ordinary annuity and annuity due.

7. Define present value of an ordinary annuity.

8. Define the present value of an annuity due.

9. Define the future value of an ordinary annuity.

10. Define the future value of an annuity due.

11. Distinguish between an ordinary annuity payment with a lump-sum deposit versus an annuity due payment with a lump-sum deposit.

12. Define Net present Value (NPV).

13. Define Internal Rate of Return (IRR).

14. Define an inflation adjusted rate of return.

15. Define a serial payment.

16. Define what an amortization schedule illustrates.

17. List applications other than education, retirement funding, mortgages, and loans for TVM.

> **Additional multiple choice problems are available at *money-education.com* by accessing the Student Practice Portal. Access requires registration of the title using the unique code at the front of the book.**

MULTIPLE-CHOICE PROBLEMS

A sample of multiple choice problems is provided below. Additional multiple choice problems are available at money-education.com by accessing the Student Practice Portal.

1. Raj and his wife, Shirley, recently opened an investment account with the intention of saving enough to purchase a house. Their goal is to have $45,000 for a down payment in 5 years. Their account will guarantee them a return of 8% compounded annually. How much do they need to put into the account right now to reach their goal?
   a. $30,626.24.
   b. $39,546.09.
   c. $46,778.96.
   d. $51,214.75.

2. Dee's grandfather set up a savings account for her with a $25,000 gift when she was first born. The account accumulated interest annually at a rate of 6% per year and no other deposits were made to the account. Dee is 21 years old today. To date, how much has accumulated in Dee's account?
   a. $79,231.88.
   b. $84,989.09.
   c. $98,656.75.
   d. $101,378.92.

3. Alberto saved enough tip money from working at the casino to place $125,500 in an investment account generating 9.25% compounded monthly. He wants to collect a monthly income of $1,350, at the beginning of each month, for as long as the money lasts. Approximately, how many months will Alberto have this income coming to him?
   a. 139.
   b. 145.
   c. 152.
   d. 162.

4. Liam bought a piece of equipment for $10,000. He paid $3,000 for upgrades during year 1 and the equipment generates $2,000 in cash flow for year 1. In year 2 the equipment generated $3,000 and in year 3 it generated $4,000, but Liam sells it for $6,000 and pays a $500 commission. What is his IRR?
   a. 3.4%.
   b. 3.9%.
   c. 4.4%.
   d. 4.9%.

5. Cher buys a house for $500,000, putting 20% down. Her loan is for 30 years at 6% and she includes closing costs of 3% into her mortgage. How much is her monthly payment (rounded to whole dollars)?
   a. $2,457.
   b. $2,470.
   c. $2,754.
   d. $2,785.

8

EDUCATION AND EDUCATION FUNDING

1. Understand the current cost of higher education, as well as the historical trend in higher education inflation.
2. Identify the various types of financial aid and the expected family contribution amount.
3. Describe qualified tuition plans including prepaid tuition plans and college savings plans.
4. Identify the role of U.S. government savings bonds in higher education funding.
5. Describe the tax implications for education expenses and student loan interest deduction.
6. Describe the American opportunity tax credit and the lifetime learning credit.
7. Calculate education funding needs using the uneven cash flow method, the traditional method, the account balance method, and the hybrid approach.
8. Calculate the dollar amount needed to meet the education goals of the client.*
9. Review and describe the likelihood and types of qualifying financial aid generally available.*
10. Evaluate the client's qualifications for various types of financial aid as part of an education plan.*
11. Compare and contrast the tax implications and other features for the primary account types or strategies used for saving for higher education expenses.*
12. Recommend appropriate education savings vehicles given tax implications, dollar amount of savings needed, and the client's preferences and situation.*

Ties to CFP Certification Learning Objectives

INTRODUCTION

Besides wanting a healthy, happy baby, one of the most common desires of a parent is for their child to grow up, attend college and be successful. While not historically the case, paying for children's college education is now one of the top goals for many families. As a result, education planning and funding represents an important area of expertise financial planners should develop. Planners should be able to answer client questions regarding:

- How much does college cost?
- How much is tuition expected to increase in the future?
- Besides tuition, what other costs are associated with a college education?
- What types of financial aid are available and where is information regarding financial aid found?
- What tax advantaged plans, income tax deductions, and tax credits are available for education funding?
- What are the repayment options for federal student loans, and which option is the best for a student to select based on their particular circumstances upon graduation?

Current Education Costs

According to the U.S. Department of Education's National Center for Education Statistics, undergraduate enrollment in postsecondary degree granting institutions increased from 13.2 million in 2000 to 16.8 million undergraduates in 2018.[1] However, projections do not reflect a significant increase in enrollments over the next decade.

---

1. https://nces.ed.gov/programs/coe/indicator_cha.asp

One of the reasons parents want their children to attend college is the higher average compensation associated with an undergraduate or graduate degree in comparison with the compensation accompanying a high school diploma. Consider the two exhibits below. The first one reflects the relationship between years of education and annual earnings. The second exhibit below depicts the unemployment rate and median income based on educational achievement.[2]

Exhibit 8.1 | Years of Education and Annual Earnings

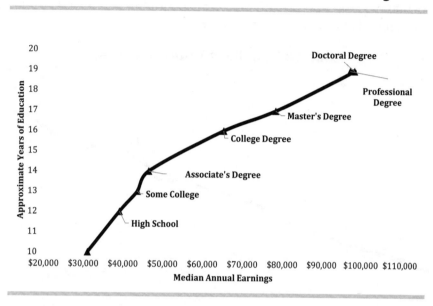

Exhibit 8.2 | Unemployment Rates and Earnings by Educational Attainment

Unemployment rates and earnings by educational attainment, 2019

Educational Attainment	Unemployment Rate (%)	Median Usual Weekly Earnings ($)	Median Usual Annual Earnings	Approx. Years of Education	Δ Earnings / Year of Education After High School
Professional degree	1.6%	1,861	$96,772	19	$8,283
Doctoral degree	1.1%	1,883	$97,916	19	$8,446
Master's degree	2.0%	1,497	$77,844	17	$7,810
Bachelor's degree	2.2%	1,248	$64,896	16	$6,526
Associate's degree	2.7%	887	$46,124	14	$3,666
Some college, no degree	3.3%	833	$43,316	13	$4,524
High school diploma	3.7%	746	$38,792	12	
Less than a high school diploma	5.4%	592	$30,784	10	

Note: Data are for persons age 25 and over. Earnings are for full-time wage and salary workers.
Source: Current Population Survey, U.S. Department of Labor, U.S. Bureau of Labor Statistics

---

2. Bureau of Labor Statistics, Employment Projections, September 2020.

Higher levels of education are associated with lower unemployment and higher annual salaries. The median earnings for a person with a bachelor's degree are 67 percent higher than for a person with a high school diploma. Over 40 years, that difference can amount to more than $1 million based on the current earnings rates. The average earnings for a master's degree are nearly twice that of a high school diploma.

The cost of college tuition has increased significantly over the last few decades, with current tuition averaging over $35,000 per year at a private four-year institution and over $10,000 for a public four-year institution. The exhibit below illustrates this trend.

Exhibit 8.3 | College Tuition and Fees

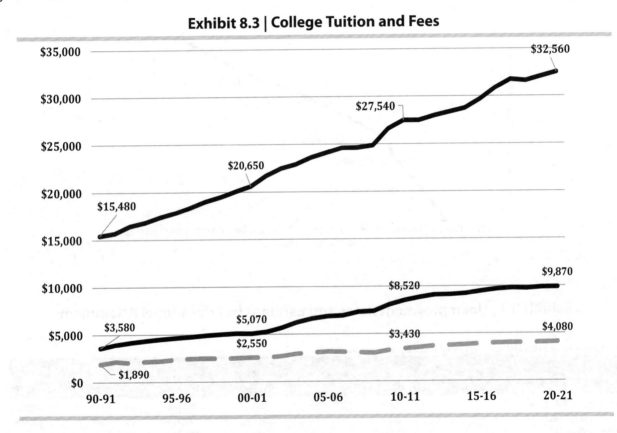

Room and board costs are typically $10,000 or more per year. In addition, out-of-state tuition at public universities is often 100 percent to 150 percent of the in-state tuition.

Other Costs Besides Tuition

Tuition and fees discussed above do not include living expenses associated with attending college, such as room and board, transportation, insurance, internet access, etc. The total cost of attending college is significantly greater than just tuition and fees. According to the College Board's *Trends in College Pricing 2020*, tuition and fees account for 68 percent of the total cost of attending a private four-year college, and 39 percent of the total cost for in-state public universities. Although the other costs besides tuition are similar to what one would experience as part of every day life without going to college, the issue is that if a student is attending college full-time, instead of working, how does the student pay for the other costs? There's an opportunity cost associated with going to college, rather than working to provide income to pay for ordinary living expenses. It is not uncommon for the total cost of education to be twice tuition and fees.

Key Concepts

1. Identify all costs associated with funding a college education and the impact of tuition inflation on education funding.

2. Identify the financial aid process and describe the three formulas used to determine the EFC.

Tuition and fees are expensive, but only represent between 39 percent and 68 percent of the total cost for college. The exhibit below breaks down the costs for students living on campus at public four-year colleges, both in-state and out-of-state, as well as for private four-year schools.

Exhibit 8.4 | Student Budget

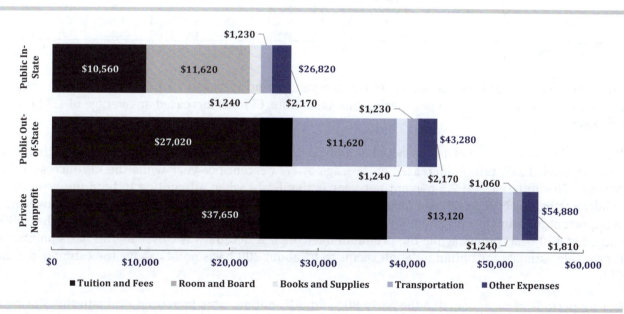

As reflected in the chart above, universities charge a premium for out-of-state students to attend. The cost for tuition and fees for out-of-state students is often twice that for in-state students. It should be noted that good high school grades and good scores on one of the standardized tests (ACT or SAT) can dramatically reduce the cost of college and increase the options for college.

Future Tuition Costs

A financial planner should be able to forecast the future cost of tuition and other costs. Such forecasting requires an understanding of the historical tuition inflation rate and inflation rate for other costs besides tuition.

Historically, the cost of tuition increased at a higher rate of inflation than the general consumer price index (CPI). As a result, the CPI rate could not be used when planning for education costs over a 10 - 20-year period. The following exhibit depicts the cost of college (both private and public in-state) from the 10-11 academic year to the 20-21 academic year.[3]

Exhibit 8.5 | Trend in College Prices

	Tuition and Fees in 2020 Dollars				Tuition and Fees and Room and Board in 2020 Dollars					
Academic Year	Private Nonprofit Four-Year	One-Year % Change	Public Four-Year	One-Year % Change	Private Nonprofit Four-Year	One-Year % Change	Public Four-Year	One-Year % Change	Year	CPI
10-11	$ 31,820		$ 9,070		$ 43,340		$ 19,230		2010	1.6%
11-12	$ 31,970	0.5%	$ 9,500	4.7%	$ 43,550	0.5%	$ 19,680	2.3%	2011	3.2%
12-13	$ 32,790	2.6%	$ 9,780	2.9%	$ 44,620	2.5%	$ 20,150	2.4%	2012	2.1%
13-14	$ 33,420	1.9%	$ 9,860	0.8%	$ 45,430	1.8%	$ 20,390	1.2%	2013	1.5%
14-15	$ 34,020	1.8%	$ 9,950	0.9%	$ 46,170	1.6%	$ 20,590	1.0%	2014	1.6%
15-16	$ 35,110	3.2%	$ 10,240	2.9%	$ 47,640	3.2%	$ 21,250	3.2%	2015	0.1%
16-17	$ 36,070	2.7%	$ 10,410	1.7%	$ 48,830	2.5%	$ 21,700	2.1%	2016	1.3%
17-18	$ 36,740	1.9%	$ 10,560	1.4%	$ 49,750	1.9%	$ 22,010	1.4%	2017	2.1%
18-19	$ 36,680	-0.2%	$ 10,500	-0.6%	$ 49,650	-0.2%	$ 22,000	0.0%	2018	2.4%
19-20	$ 37,240	1.5%	$ 10,540	0.4%	$ 50,360	1.4%	$ 22,170	0.8%	2019	1.8%
20-21	$ 37,650	1.1%	$ 10,560	0.2%	$ 50,770	0.8%	$ 22,180	0.0%	2020	1.2%
Ten year average		1.7%		1.5%		1.6%		1.4%		1.7%

The average annual tuition increases over this ten-year period averaged 1.7 percent for private colleges and 1.5 percent for public colleges. During this same time, CPI has increased an average of 1.7 percent per year.

Historically, tuition inflation has been higher and has exceeded CPI by a large spread. Consider that from 1970 through 1999, tuition increased an average of 7.7 percent per year while the CPI increased 5.2 percent. This difference of 2.5 percent per year is significant when attempting to fund future costs of children attending college. CPI and tuition inflation have been much lower in the last decade. However, it is important to estimate a premium for tuition inflation over that of CPI. The premium during the 1980s exceeded 400 basis points, while the premium over the last decade was closer to 150 basis points.[4] A reasonable estimate for tuition inflation seems to be about 200 basis points above the estimate for the CPI.

During periods of recession, like the early 80s and 90s, tuition rates increased dramatically. During a recession, the unemployment rate increases, causing state tax revenues to decrease. State governments often react by reducing their budget, potentially impacting the state funding of higher education. In these situations, state universities often increase tuition. Periods of tuition inflation of eight percent or higher occur during the worst of economic times with high unemployment, so it can significantly impact families that have not saved enough for the cost of college education. Those families are likely to turn to

---

3. College tuition inflation rates are based on the average rate of tuition increases at public universities (both in-state and out-of-state tuition), private and not-for-profit universities. Source: trends.collegeboard.org.
4. 100 basis points represents 1%.

financial aid to bridge the gap between funds available for education and the higher cost of attending college. Fortunately, there are alternatives to relying on financial aid. Alternatives include tax-deferred savings (typically used by families that have children ten or more years away from college), tax deductions, and tax credits, which are discussed later in the chapter.

Financial Aid

Financial aid represents an important tool for families that are inadequately prepared to pay for their children's college education. Most financial aid is administered by the U.S. Department of Education, (states and universities offer aid as well), and consists of grants, loans for students and parents, and work-study programs. According to the U.S. Department of Education, 86 percent of all full-time undergraduate students received some type of financial aid (federal or state), in 2017 – 2018.[5]

Where to Find Information about Financial Aid

Information about financial aid is available online, at high schools, and college campuses. The U.S. Department of Education offers information about financial aid offered by the federal government, as well as providing a list of all state higher education agency websites.[6] The state higher education agency websites provide information about financial aid available by state.[7] The Consumer Financial Protection Bureau website provides information and tools to assist with comparisons of financial aid offers and evaluation of student loan repayment options.[8]

In addition to online resources, many high schools and all college campuses have a financial aid office and financial aid counselors. Students and parents should contact their high school and prospective universities to schedule a time to meet with a financial aid counselor. The counselors can provide details on financial aid that is available, as well as qualification requirements and deadlines for applying.

FINANCIAL AID PROCESS

The financial aid process is initiated by completing the **Free Application for Federal Student Aid (FAFSA)**. This form is used to determine a student's eligibility for all types of financial aid, including grants, work-study, and loans. The FAFSA is used to determine the Expected Family Contribution amount (EFC).[9] The EFC is calculated based on the information provided in the FAFSA, as a family's income and assets are applied to a Federal Methodology, which determines the family's financial strength and how much it can contribute towards education costs. The Federal Methodology determines the EFC using one of three methods:

1. Regular Formula: Income and Assets
2. Simplified Method
3. Automatically Assessed Formula

---

5. https://nces.ed.gov/fastfacts/display.asp?id=31.
6. https://studentaid.gov/understand-aid/types.
7. www2.ed.gov (under "State Contracts" under "About Us").
8. consumerfinance.gov/paying-for-college.
9. https://studentaid.gov/h/apply-for-aid.

Regular Formula: Income and Assets

The regular formula considers a family's income and assets. This method is the formula that is used for most families. The federal methodology considers the following:

- Income
- Assets
- Dependency status
- Household size
- Number of children in college
- Cost of supporting the family

The EFC is based on a formula that considers both the parent's and the student's income and assets. The parent's expected contribution from their annual income is calculated by first reducing their income by their taxes and basic living expenses. Contributions based on assets owned by parents are expected to be 12 percent of discretionary assets (determined without regard to retirement assets, home equity, annuities, cash value of life insurance, and an asset protection allowance). The value used for assets is the "net worth," which is the fair market value less any debt associated with the asset. Income and assets are then totaled and a percentage is counted towards the EFC. The maximum percentage that applies is 47 percent, resulting in a net maximum of 5.64 percent (47% x 12%) of parent assets expected to be utilized for college expenses. A student's expected contribution is calculated as 50 percent of income, as reduced by an income protection allowance, plus 20 percent of their net worth.

The EFC is a combination of the parent's expected contribution plus the student's contribution.

Simplified Method

The simplified method does not consider the family's assets. In order to qualify for the simplified formula for the 2021-2022 award year, both of the following must be met:

1. The parents are either not required to file a federal income tax return, or filed a 2019 Form 1040 but did not file a Schedule 1;[10] or anyone included in the parents' household size received benefits during 2019 or 2020 from a designated means-tested federal benefit program (includes Medicaid, SSI, SNAP, free or reduced price school lunch program, TANF, and WIC); or the student's parent is a dislocated worker.
2. The total adjusted gross income of the parents is less than $50,000.

In order to qualify for the simplified formula for the 2021-2022 award year, when the student is not claimed as a dependent, both of the following must be true:

1. Student (and spouse, if married) filed a 2019 Form 1040 but did not file a Schedule 1, or was not required to file a federal income tax return; or anyone included in the student's household size received benefits during 2019 or 2020 from a designated means-tested federal benefit program (includes Medicaid, SSI, SNAP, free or reduced price school lunch program, TANF, and WIC); or the student or student's spouse is a dislocated worker.
2. Student's (and spouse, if married) adjusted gross income is less than $50,000.

10. A few exceptions apply to filing Schedule 1. For details see: https://ifap.ed.gov/efc-formula-guide/2122EFCFormulaGuide.

Automatically Assessed Formula

The automatically assessed formula simply calculates the EFC at zero, which allows for the maximum amount of student aid. In order to qualify for this method for the 2021-2022 award year:[11]

- Student or parents filed a 2019 Form 1040, but did not file a Schedule 1, or were not required to file a federal income tax return; or anyone included in the student's or parents' household size received benefits during 2019 or 2020 from a designated means-tested federal benefit program (includes Medicaid, SSI, SNAP, free or reduced price school lunch program, TANF, and WIC); or the student or parent is a dislocated worker.
- Student or parents' adjusted gross income is $27,000 or less.

Once the EFC is determined by using one of the three Federal Methodologies, the EFC is subtracted from the cost of attendance at a university, which can include living expenses. The formula is:

$$
\begin{array}{l}
\text{Cost of Attendance} \\
\underline{- \text{ Expected Family Contribution (EFC)}} \\
= \text{Financial Need}
\end{array}
$$

Once the FAFSA is completed, students can then request that the information contained in the FAFSA be provided to universities. Families can access a copy of a Student Aid Report by logging in to their account at fafsa.gov, which will contain information provided on the FASFA, including the EFC.

Universities will prepare a financial aid package, which helps students satisfy their financial need. Financial aid may consist of grants (money that doesn't have to be repaid), loans, and work-study programs (where the student can work on or off campus to help pay for education expenses). After determining a student's financial need, a university may not be able to offer an aid package that provides 100 percent of education expenses.

Example 8.1

Marshall and Lily have a daughter, Robyn, who is applying to Northwest State University. The total cost of attendance is $20,000 per year and their EFC is $5,000 per year. The financial aid office has put together an aid package covering $12,000 per year. The gap of $3,000 ($20,000 - $5,000 - $12,000) must be covered by other possible resources such as student or parent education loan(s).

The FAFSA is available for filing on October 1st of the prior year. Students are able to file the FAFSA for the 2021–2022 academic year on October 1, 2020. When the FAFSA is filed in October, income is reported from a year earlier. This is referred to as the "prior-prior year" income because it is the income from two years before the college semester start date on the FAFSA. Students filing the FAFSA for 2021–2022 will use their 2019 income information (the most recent tax return filed prior to filling out the FAFSA; two years before the start of the 2021-2022 school year). Assets, however, are reported as of the FAFSA filing date.

A dependent student of separated or divorced parents will report the income and assets of the custodial parent on the FAFSA, including the income and assets of a step-parent if the custodial parent has remarried as of the date the FAFSA is filed. The custodial parent is the parent the student lived with the

---

11.Independent students with no dependents other than a spouse are not eligible for an automatic zero EFC.

most during the twelve months preceding the filing of the FAFSA, and is not necessarily the parent who claims the student as a dependent on their tax return.[12]

The FAFSA Simplification Act of 2020

The FAFSA Simplification Act of 2020 makes numerous changes to the FAFSA beginning on July 1, 2023, for the 2023-2024 award year. The first date to file a FAFSA under the new rules will be October 1, 2022.

Under these new rules, the expected family contribution (EFC) will be replaced by the student aid index (SAI). The amount of need for any student for financial assistance will be equal to the cost of attendance, minus the student aid index for the student, minus other financial assistance.

**New Formula for 2023-2024
Award Year**

Cost of Attendance
- Student Aid Index (SAI)
- Other Financial Assistance
= Financial Need

The cost of attendance is determined by the institution and includes tuition and fees, and an allowance for books, course materials, supplies and equipment, transportation, and miscellaneous personal expenses, along with an allowance for living expenses such as food and housing. Special definitions of cost of attendance will apply to students attending only by correspondence and students who are incarcerated.

The Act prescribes a somewhat simplified method for determining the student aid index, versus the current calculation of the expected family contribution. The simplified FAFSA will ask fewer questions than the pre-October 1, 2022 FAFSA (for the 2023-2024 award year), and applicants who do not file a tax return or who are recipients of specified means-tested benefits will only be required to answer demographic and benefit-related questions. Other applicants will answer the same basic questions along with asset-related questions, and will have income information transferred directly from the IRS.

The updated FAFSA will include an authorization for information from the FAFSA to be shared with education institutions, as well as the State Higher Education Agency and designated scholarship organizations. The Act grants discretionary authority for financial aid administrators to, on a case-by-case basis, make adjustments to the cost of attendance, the values of the data used to calculate the student aid index, the values of the data used to calculate the Federal Pell award, or the dependency status of the student. Dependency status changes are limited to applicants with unusual circumstances, as defined in the Act, and are based on the individual student rather than a group of students.

In addition to the FAFSA changes, the Act extends financial aid eligibility, including Pell Grants, to incarcerated students enrolled in a qualified prison education program.

Additional Information To Assist With College Selection

The information from the FAFSA is used by educational institution to design a financial aid package (the combination of grants, loans, and other types aid, discussed later in this chapter) for the student. The financial aid package offered by each college to which the student has applied can vary and will have a

---

12.https://studentaid.gov/apply-for-aid/fafsa/filling-out/parent-info.

large impact on the level of debt that the student will be burdened with upon graduation. This will likely be a primary factor in terms of school selection. Other considerations, such as whether the student's chosen field of study is likely to result in a career providing an income that will allow the student to make the required loan payments while maintaining a desirable quality of life and the percent of graduates who find work in their field of study are also important factors. To assist student evaluation of potential colleges and programs of study, the U.S. Department of Education provides a comparison tool on their College Scorecard website.[13] Available information includes the percentage of students in the field of study who receive loans, the median total debt upon graduation, the typical monthly loan payment, and the percentage of borrowers who, two years after graduation, are making progress paying down their student loans, as well as the percentage who have paid their loans in full, who have loans in deferment (discussed later in this chapter), who are not making progress on paying their loans, and those who are delinquent in repayment.

TYPES OF FINANCIAL AID

Grants

Grants are money provided to students for postsecondary education that does not require repayment. Grants are typically awarded based on financial need. The federal government only awards grants for undergraduate studies. The following grants are discussed in this chapter:

- Federal Pell Grant
- Teacher Education Assistance for College and Higher Education (TEACH) Grant
- Federal Supplemental Educational Opportunity (FSEOG) Grant

Federal Pell Grant

A **Federal Pell Grant** is need-based financial aid for students who have not earned an undergraduate degree or a professional degree. One of the nice features of a Pell Grant is that it does not have to be repaid.

> ### Key Concepts
>
> 1. Define a college grant.
> 2. Identify different types of education grants and the qualifications required for each grant.

Pell Grants are based on an academic year, from July 1st to June 30th. The amount of a Pell Grant awarded to a student is dependent upon the family's EFC, cost of attendance, and whether the student is attending full-time or part-time. The maximum Pell Grant award for the 2021-22 award year (July 1, 2021 to June 30, 2022) is $6,495 and is paid directly to the school or the student. Students have a choice of: 1) allocating their Pell Grant toward tuition, fees, and course materials, which allows the grant to be tax-free, but reduces the expenses that qualify for the American Opportunity Tax Credit (AOTC; discussed later in this chapter); or 2) allocating the Pell Grant to living expenses, causing that portion of the grant to be taxable income to the student, but allowing tuition and fees to remain qualified expenses for the AOTC.[14] Effective July 1, 2012 a student may not receive the Pell Grant for more than 12 semesters. As a benefit to military families, the maximum Pell Grant amount is awarded to students whose parent or guardian died as a result of military duty in Iraq or Afghanistan after September 11, 2001 (if the student was under 24 years old at the time of the parent or guardian's death). Similarly, the

---

13. https://collegescorecard.ed.gov.
14. For details regarding the analysis of this decision see www.treasury.gov/resource-center/tax-policy/Documents/Report-Pell-AOTC-Interaction-2014.pdf

maximum Pell Grant may be awarded to a student whose parent was a public safety officer and died as a result of active service in the line of duty.

Teacher Education Assistance for College and Higher Education (TEACH) Grant

The **Teacher Education Assistance for College and Higher Education (TEACH) Grant** provides up to $4,000 per year for students who intend to teach in a public or private elementary, middle, or high school, or an educational service agency, that serves a community of low-income families.[15] If a student fails to meet the teaching requirements, the grant is converted to a Federal Direct Unsubsidized Stafford Loan, which must be repaid by the student. Recipients of the TEACH grant have a six-month grace period after the grant is converted to a Stafford Loan before repayment must begin. If a TEACH grant is converted to a Stafford Loan, interest accrues from the first date the funds were disbursed.

In order to be eligible for the TEACH grant, applicants must meet the following criteria:

- Complete a FAFSA.
- Be a U.S. citizen or eligible non-citizen.
- Be enrolled in an undergraduate, post-baccalaureate or graduate program at a university that participates in the TEACH Grant program.
- Be enrolled or plan to complete courses that prepare a student for a career in teaching.
- Score above the 75th percentile on college admission testing or maintain a Grade Point Average (GPA) greater than or equal to 3.25.
- Sign a TEACH Grant Agreement to Serve each year the grant is received.

For each TEACH Grant eligible program for which TEACH Grant funds are received, the student must serve as a full-time teacher for a total of at least four academic years within eight calendar years after completing or withdrawing from the academic program for which the TEACH Grant was received.

Federal Supplemental Educational Opportunity Grant (FSEOG Grant)

The **Federal Supplemental Educational Opportunity Grant (FSEOG)** is awarded to students with exceptional financial need. Pell Grant recipients with the lowest EFC are considered first for a FSEOG. Students awarded the FSEOG can receive between $100 to $4,000 per year.

Coronavirus-Related Rules for Grants and Subsidized Loans

As a result of the COVID-19 pandemic in 2020, the Coronavirus Aid, Relief, and Economic Security Act (CARES Act) of 2020 provided for FSEO Emergency Grants up to the maximum Pell grant amount to assist undergraduate or graduate students with unexpected expenses due to a qualifying emergency. A qualifying emergency is a Coronavirus-related public health emergency declared by the Secretary of

---

15. Federal sequestration requires TEACH grants disbursed on October 1, 2020 and before October 1, 2021 to be reduced by 5.7% of the amount awarded. Note: The reduction for the 2021-2022 year was not yet available as of the time of printing.

Health and Human services, an event related to Coronavirus which the President has declared a major disaster or emergency, or a national emergency related to Coronavirus declared by the President. Emergency financial aid grants received under the CARES Act are not included in the gross income of the recipient and do not reduce the amount of qualified education expenses for purposes of the American Opportunity Tax Credit or Lifetime Learning Tax Credit (discussed later in this chapter).[16]

The COVID-19 pandemic caused a major disruption to higher eduction in the spring of 2020. In order to avoid penalizing students who needed to drop out of school due to the pandemic, the CARES Act provides that Pell Grant and Subsidized Stafford Loan limits (discussed below) will not count the term if the student dropped out as a result of COVID-19. In addition, students are not required to repay the loan or return the grant if it is a result of a qualifying emergency as described above.

In addition, under the CARES Act, teachers who completed only a partial year of teaching as a result of the COVID-19 pandemic will receive credit for teaching the full year for purposes of fulfilling their obligations under the TEACH Grant and will receive credit for a full year toward Teacher Loan Forgiveness eligibility.

Campus-Based Aid

Campus-based aid is administered directly by the financial aid office of the university. The three types of campus-based aid are Federal Supplementary Educational Opportunity Grant, Federal Work-Study and Federal Perkins Loan Program. Schools may offer some or all three campus-based aid programs. Unlike the Federal Pell Grant, which provides funding to all students who qualify, campus-based aid may or may not be available if a student qualifies. Once the school has allocated their campus-based aid, no further aid can be allocated from that program for the year. Students should apply early for financial aid, as the campus-based aid may not always be available.

Financial Aid - Loans

The U.S. Department of Education and many colleges and universities offer low interest rate loans for students and parents. Unlike grants, most loans are not based on financial need but are part of an overall financial aid package offered to students. Some loans are based on financial need, such as the Federal Perkins Loan and Subsidized Stafford Loans, which are discussed below.

Stafford Loans

Stafford Loans are student loans administered by the U.S. Department of Education. Prior to July 1, 2010, there were two types of Stafford Loans: the Federal Family Education Loan (FFEL) and Direct Stafford Loan. However, as part of The Student Aid and Fiscal Responsibility Act, passed on March 30, 2010, the federal government has eliminated the FFEL program. Education loans are now only issued by the U.S Department of Education as part of the Direct Loan program. With the Direct Loan program, the funds are provided by the federal government, whereas under the FFEL, the funds were provided by a bank or other lender. As part of The Student Aid and Fiscal Responsibility Act, students with low incomes and large loan

> ### ☷ Key Concepts
>
> 1. Identify the types of student and parent loans available for college funding.
>
> 2. Define the repayment terms available for government funded loans.
>
> 3. Identify the consequences of defaulting on student loans.

---

16. COVID-Related Tax Relief Act (COVIDTRA) of 2020, Sec. 277.

balances are only required to repay up to 10 percent of their income each year. Previously, the law permitted up to 15 percent of a borrower's income to repay student loans. In addition, The Student Aid and Fiscal Responsibility Act forgives loans after 20 years of repayment, whereas prior to the Act, borrowers were eligible for loan forgiveness after 25 years of repayment.

A student may qualify for subsidized or unsubsidized Direct Loans. Qualification for a subsidized loan is based on a student's financial need. For a subsidized loan, the federal government pays interest on the loan while the borrower is attending school and during the six-month grace period after graduation before repayment begins. Unsubsidized loans are not needs-based, and the borrower is responsible for interest from the time the funds are disbursed. Students may pay the interest expense as it is incurred or allow the interest to be added to the loan's outstanding principal.

The following are maximum limits on the amount that can be borrowed by a dependent student under the Stafford Loan program for a full academic year:
- First year students: $5,500 but no more than $3,500 of this amount can be in subsidized loans.
- Second year students: $6,500 but no more than $4,500 of this amount can be in subsidized loans.
- Beyond the second year: $7,500 but no more than $5,500 of this amount can be in subsidized loans.

For undergraduate students who are independents (not claimed as a dependent on parent's tax return) and for dependent students whose parents did not qualify for a Parent Loan for Undergraduate Students (PLUS) Loan, the following are maximum limits on the amount that can be borrowed under the Stafford Loan program in a full academic year:
- First year students: $9,500 but no more than $3,500 of this amount can be in subsidized loans.
- Second year students: $10,500 but no more than $4,500 of this amount can be in subsidized loans.
- Beyond the second year: $12,500 but no more than $5,500 of this amount can be in subsidized loans.

For graduate or professional degree students, the following are maximum limits on the amount that can be borrowed under the Stafford Loan program in a full academic year:
- Each Year: $20,500 in unsubsidized loans.
- Graduate students are no longer eligible for subsidized Stafford loans.

The maximum amount of Stafford Loan debt a student can graduate with from graduate school is $138,500, which also includes amounts borrowed for undergraduate studies. Some health profession programs will allow students to borrow up to $224,000. No more than $65,500 out of the $138,500 can be in subsidized loans.

Stafford Loan funds are paid directly to the school, which applies the loan proceeds to tuition, fees, room, and board. Any remaining amounts will be paid directly to the student. Funds are paid through the school in at least two installments.

Students pay two fees associated with Stafford Loans. The first fee is an origination fee that ranges from 1.0-1.5 percent of the loan amount (depending on when the funds are disbursed), which is used to offset the cost of administering the loan. The second fee is an annual interest rate. The interest rate for unsubsidized Stafford Loans varies depending on when the funds are disbursed. For loans disbursed 7/1/20-6/30/21 the interest rate for undergraduate Stafford Loans is 2.75 percent. For graduate or professional Stafford Loans, the interest rate is 4.3 percent. Interest rates for Stafford Loans can be found at the U.S. Department of Education's Federal Student Aid website.[17]

The interest rate only applies to loans disbursed during the time periods shown below. It does not apply to any previously disbursed loans and it does not apply to unsubsidized Stafford Loans.

The following is a summary of the interest rate schedule for Direct Subsidized Stafford Loans:

Funds Disbursed	Interest Rate
July 1, 2010 – June 30, 2011	4.5%
July 1, 2011 – June 30, 2012	3.4%
July 1, 2012 – June 30, 2013	3.4%
July 1, 2013 – June 30, 2014	3.86%
July 1, 2014 – June 30, 2015	4.66%
July 1, 2015 – June 30, 2016	4.29%
July 1, 2016 – June 30, 2017	3.76%
July 1, 2017 – June 30, 2018	4.45%
July 1, 2018 – June 30, 2019	5.05%
July 1, 2019 - June, 30, 2020	4.53%
July 1, 2020 - June 30, 2021	2.75%

For borrowers on active military duty, the interest rate on Direct Stafford Loans obtained prior to active duty service is capped at six percent during periods of active duty.

Borrowers must begin repaying a Stafford Loan after a six-month grace period that begins after graduation, leaving school, or dropping below half-time status. For subsidized Stafford Loans, the borrower is not responsible for interest payments during the grace period. However, for unsubsidized Stafford Loans, the borrower still incurs interest charges, during the grace period, that will need to be repaid.

Students generally have 10 to 25 years to repay a Stafford Loan. There are seven repayment methods for a Stafford Loan, which include:
1. Standard Repayment
2. Extended Repayment
3. Graduated Repayment
4. Income Based Repayment
5. Income Contingent Repayment
6. Pay As You Earn Repayment
7. Revised Pay As You Earn Repayment

---

17. https://studentaid.gov/understand-aid/types/loans/interest-rates. Note: The interest rates for loans disbursed 7/1/21-6/30/22 will be released in June 2021.

Standard Repayment

A standard repayment schedule will amortize the loan for up to a 10-year time period, with minimum monthly payments of at least $50. The standard repayment schedule has the borrower repaying the loan in the shortest amount of time. The shorter repayment schedule allows the borrower to pay the least amount of interest on the loan, as compared to the other repayment schedules.

Extended Repayment

The extended repayment schedule allows borrowers with more than $30,000 outstanding in either FFEL Stafford Loans or Direct Stafford Loans, to repay the loans over a period of time not to exceed 25 years. Since the repayment period under an Extended Repayment schedule is up to 15 years longer than the Standard Repayment schedule, borrowers can expect to pay significantly more in interest using the Extended Repayment plan.

Example 8.2

Dominic has $40,000 in Direct Stafford Loans and is considering the Standard Repayment over 10 years or Extended Repayment over 25 years. The summary below compares the difference in payments and interest between the two repayment plans.

	Standard	Extended
Term	10 years	25 years
Amount of Loan	$40,000	$40,000
Interest Rate	6.8%	6.8%
Monthly Payment	$460.32	$277.63
Total Interest Paid Over Life of Loan	$15,238	$43,289

Although the Extended Repayment schedule will result in a lower monthly payment, the borrower will pay three times the amount of interest, in comparison to the Standard Repayment schedule. Borrowers should consider their cash flow and ability to make monthly payments. During a borrower's initial working years after graduating, they may not be able to afford the higher payments. However, as the borrower's earnings increase, the payment amount should be increased, in order to retire the debt in a reasonable amount of time.

Graduated Repayment

The graduated repayment schedule allows borrowers to repay a Stafford Loan for up to 10 years. Borrowers are able to initially make low payments, but the payments will increase every two years. This feature allows borrowers to increase their loan payments as their income increases. Under the graduated repayment schedule, no monthly loan payment will be more than three times the lowest monthly loan payment.

Income Based Repayment

The Income Based Repayment (IBR) schedule caps the monthly payment based on the borrower's income and family size. To qualify for the IBR schedule, the amount of payment calculated using the IBR method must be less than the monthly payment under the standard repayment schedule over a 10-year term.

The following loans are available to use the IBR schedule:
- Stafford loans (FFEL or direct)
- PLUS loans made to graduate or professional students (PLUS loans made to parents are not eligible)
- Consolidation student loans

Other benefits of the IBR schedule include:
- The monthly payment will be 10 percent of discretionary income (15 percent for borrowers with a loan balance prior to July 1, 2014) and cannot be more than required under the standard 10-year repayment plan.
- For subsidized loans, if the repayment amount calculated under the IBR schedule is less than the monthly interest that is due, the federal government will pay the remaining interest for up to three consecutive years from the date loan payments commence. Beyond the third year, any interest deficiencies will be added to the outstanding balance of the loan.
- If a borrower has been paying under the IBR schedule for 20 years (25 years for borrowers with a loan balance prior to July 1, 2014), still has a balance due, and meets certain other requirements, the balance due will be canceled.
- If a borrower is making payments under the IBR schedule for 10 years, has Direct Stafford Loans, and has been working in public service for a qualifying employer for 10 years, the remaining balance due can be canceled. If a borrower has FFEL Stafford Loans, it is possible to convert the loans to a Direct Stafford Loan to take advantage of the 10 Year Public Service Loan Forgiveness Program. The borrower will still have to meet the 10-year payment requirement on a Direct Stafford Loan. Any outstanding loan amount forgiven may be subject to income taxation.

Income Contingent Repayment

The income contingent repayment (ICR) schedule is for Direct Stafford Loans, Direct Graduate PLUS Loans, Direct Consolidation Loans, and FFEL Consolidation Loans only. Parent Direct or FFEL PLUS Loan borrowers are not eligible for the ICR repayment schedule unless the loans are consolidated to a Direct or FFEL Consolidation Loan (PLUS Loans are discussed later in this chapter). The amount of payment under the ICR schedule is the lesser of:
- The amount required under a 12-year repayment schedule times an income percentage factor that varies based on annual income.
- 20 percent of the borrower's monthly discretionary income.

If the payments calculated under the ICR schedule are insufficient to pay the monthly interest expenses, the unpaid portion is capitalized, or added to the outstanding principal, once per year. If after 25 years, the loan has not been repaid, the outstanding balance will be canceled.

Pay As You Earn (PAYE) Repayment Plan

The Pay As You Earn (PAYE) repayment schedule is available if the borrower has a high debt-to-income ratio, and will cap the monthly payment based on the borrower's income and family size.

The following loans are available to use the PAYE schedule:
- Direct Stafford loans
- Direct PLUS loans made to graduate or professional students (PLUS loans made to parents are not eligible)
- Direct and FFEL Consolidation loans (consolidated PLUS loans made to parents are not eligible)

Other benefits of the PAYE schedule include:
- The monthly payment will be 10 percent of discretionary income and cannot be more than required under the standard 10-year repayment plan.
- For subsidized loans, if the repayment amount calculated under the PAYE schedule is less than the monthly interest that is due, the federal government will pay the remaining interest for up to three consecutive years from the date loan payments commence. Beyond the third year, any interest deficiencies will be added to the outstanding balance of the loan.
- If a borrower has been paying under the PAYE schedule for 20 years, still has a balance due, and meets certain other requirements, the balance due will be canceled.
- If a borrower is making payments under the PAYE schedule for 10 years, has Direct Stafford Loans, and has been working in public service for a qualifying employer for 10 years, the remaining balance due can be canceled. Any outstanding loan amount forgiven may be subject to income taxation.

Revised Pay As You Earn (REPAYE) Repayment Plan
The Revised Pay As You Earn (REPAYE) repayment schedule will cap the monthly payment based on the borrower's income and family size.

The following loans are available to use the REPAYE schedule:
- Direct Stafford loans
- Direct PLUS loans made to graduate or professional students (PLUS loans made to parents are not eligible)
- Direct and FFEL Consolidation loans (consolidated PLUS loans made to parents are not eligible)

Other benefits of the REPAYE schedule include:
- The monthly payment will be 10 percent of discretionary income.
- For subsidized loans, if the repayment amount calculated under the REPAYE schedule is less than the monthly interest that is due, the federal government will pay the remaining interest for up to three consecutive years from the date loan payments commence, and will pay half of the remaining interest beyond the three-year period.
- For unsubsidized loans, if the repayment amount calculated under the REPAYE schedule is less than the monthly interest that is due, the federal government will pay half of the remaining interest that is due, for all periods.
- If a borrower has been paying undergraduate loan payments under the REPAYE schedule for 20 years (25 years if any loans are graduate or professional loans), still has a balance due, and meets certain other requirements, the balance due will be canceled.
- If a borrower is making payments under the REPAYE schedule for 10 years, has Direct Stafford Loans, and has been working in public service for a qualifying employer for 10 years, the remaining balance due can be canceled. Any outstanding loan amount forgiven may be subject to income taxation.

For IBR and PAYE, discretionary income is the amount of income exceeding 150 percent of the poverty guideline for the borrower's family. For ICR, discretionary income is the amount of income exceeding 100 percent of the poverty guideline for the borrower's family.

Example 8.3

Khabib recently graduated from college and is considering the Pay as You Earn Repayment Plan. Khabib is single and will have a starting salary and AGI of $25,000. His student loan balance is $26,946. The federal poverty guideline for a single individual in his state is $12,880. Khabib's payment is calculated as follows:

150% of federal poverty guideline (1.5 x $12,880) = $19,320
Khabib's adjusted gross income = $25,000
Discretionary income ($25,000 - $19,320) = $5,680
10% of discretionary income (0.10 x $5,680) = $568
Monthly amount ($568/12) = $47.33

Income Sensitive Repayment

The income sensitive repayment schedule is for FFEL Stafford Loans only. This repayment schedule will vary, based on the borrower's income. As the borrower's income increases (or decreases), the repayment amount will increase (or decrease). The repayment period for an Income Sensitive Repayment Schedule is up to 10 years.

Deferment and Forbearance

If a borrower becomes unable to repay a student loan, it is possible to request a deferment or forbearance. During this time, payments are suspended but may or may not incur interest expense. For a subsidized Stafford Loan, the borrower will not be responsible for interest payments during the forbearance period. However, for unsubsidized Stafford Loans, the borrower is still responsible for interest charges during the forbearance period.

Automatic Forbearance in 2020 Due to COVID-19

As a result of the COVID-19 pandemic, the CARES Act of 2020 provided for an automatic suspension (administrative forbearance) of payments on student loans owned by the Department of Education (including defaulted and non-defaulted direct loans, FFEL loans, and federal Perkins loans) from March 13, 2020 through September 30, 2020 with no interest charged during the time of suspension. The suspension and waiver of interest were extended on August 8, 2020 by President Trump through December 31, 2020, and further extended by President Biden through September 2021. During the period of suspension, suspended payments are treated as if regularly scheduled payments have made for purposes of credit reporting and for purposes of any student loan forgiveness.

Federal Perkins Loan Program

The **Federal Perkins Loan** program is for undergraduate and graduate students with exceptional financial need. The Perkins Loan is a low interest rate loan (5%), which is offered through a university's financial aid office. The university serves as the lender and the federal government provides the funds. No new Perkins loans are available after September 30, 2017.

Repayment on the Federal Perkins Loan begins after a nine-month grace period. The grace period begins once the student graduates, leaves school, or drops below half-time status.

Parent PLUS Loans

PLUS Loans are for parents to borrow to help pay for a dependent's undergraduate education expenses. The dependent student must be attending at least half-time, in an eligible school, and in an eligible program. PLUS Loans are not based on need, have no debt-to-income ratio limitations, and require only that the parents do not have any adverse credit history. PLUS Loans are appropriate for parents that have not saved enough for the child's education, their child is close in age to attending college, and the parents have sufficient cash flow to repay the loans.

PLUS Loans are available as a Direct PLUS Loan from the U.S. Department of Education. The amount of a PLUS Loan a parent may borrow is the cost of attendance less any other financial aid awards. The school determines the amount of PLUS Loan the borrower is eligible to receive. Loan funds are disbursed in at least two equal payments. The funds are sent to the school and are used to pay tuition, fees, room and board. Any remaining funds are paid directly to the parents or can be held by the school for future education expenses.

For Direct Plus Loans disbursed July 1, 2020-June 30, 2021, the interest rate is 5.30 percent. The interest rate is fixed for the life of the loan. Prior to July 1, 2006, the interest rate was variable. Interest on PLUS Loans begins as soon as the first disbursement is paid. There are no subsidized PLUS Loans and repayment begins either 60 days after the loan is fully disbursed or may be postponed until six months after the dependent student ceases to be enrolled on at least a half-time basis. The parents can elect either repayment method.

In addition to the interest expense, PLUS Loans also charge a fee of about 4.3 percent for funds disbursed in 2019 and 2020 of the amount borrowed.

Similar to a Stafford Loan, PLUS Loans are eligible for deferment or forbearance. While the loan is in forbearance, it continues to accrue interest that can be paid immediately or added to the outstanding principal of the loan.

PLUS Loans for Graduate and Professional Degree Students

PLUS Loans for Graduate and Professional Degree Students (or **Graduate PLUS Loans**) are for students seeking graduate and professional degrees. A Graduate PLUS Loan is based on the student's credit history, although a parent may endorse (agree to make the loan payments if the student is unable) the loan if the student has an adverse credit history. Graduate PLUS loans are not based on financial need. In order to receive a Graduate PLUS Loan, students must have applied for the maximum Stafford Loan amount available for graduate students. The amount of Graduate PLUS Loans available is based on the cost of attendance, less other financial aid.

Grace Period for Repayment of Student Loans

After graduating, leaving school, or falling below half-time status, borrowers have a grace period before repayment begins. The grace period depends on the type of loan, as described below.

Loan	Grace Period
PLUS Loans	60 Days after Final Disbursement*
Stafford Loans (Direct and FFEL)	Six Months
Federal Perkins Loans	Nine Months

* For a Parent PLUS Loan borrower, where the funds are disbursed on or after July 1, 2008, the borrower can elect to defer payment for six months after the student is no longer enrolled at least half-time. For a Graduate PLUS Loan, repayment is automatically deferred for six months after the borrower is no longer enrolled at least a half-time.

Consolidation Loans

Consolidation loans take all of a student's outstanding loans and consolidate them into one payment. The interest rate for a consolidation loan is based on a weighted average of the interest rates of the loans being consolidated. There is no application fee to consolidate federal student loans into a Direct Consolidation Loan.

The following loans are eligible for consolidation:[18]

- Subsidized and unsubsidized Direct and FFEL Stafford Loans
- Federal Perkins Loans
- Parent PLUS Loans
- Graduate PLUS Loans

To be eligible for consolidation, loans must be in the grace period or be in repayment. Graduates who are repaying loans under an income-driven repayment plan offering forgiveness after a stipulated number of payments or who have made qualifying payments for Public Service Loan Forgiveness will lose credit for payments previously made when those loans are consolidated. For that reason, those loans should generally not be included in the consolidation loan.

Repayment of a consolidation loan begins within 60 days of the funds being disbursed and the repayment period is from 10 to 30 years. Borrowers should keep in mind that although the consolidation loan payment may be less than the original payments, if the repayment period is being extended to 30 years, the total cost of repayment can be significantly more under a consolidation loan because of the total interest expense. As with all debt, every effort should be made to retire the debt within a reasonable amount of time.

Exhibit 8.6 | Summary of Repayment Options NOT Based on Income

	Standard Repayment	Graduated Repayment	Extended Repayment
Available For	FFEL and Direct Stafford loans, FFEL and direct PLUS loans, FFEL and Direct Consolidation loans	FFEL and Direct Stafford loans, FFEL and direct PLUS loans, FFEL and Direct Consolidation loans	FFEL and Direct Stafford loans, FFEL and direct PLUS loans, FFEL and Direct Consolidation loans; with more than $30,000 of debt outstanding
Payment Amount	Fixed	Starts off lower but increases every two years	May be fixed or graduated; lower that Standard or Graduated repayment plans
Term	Up to 10 years (30 for consolidation loans)	Up to 10 years (30 for consolidation loans)	Up to 25 years
Other Notes	Results in least amount of interest paid		

18. For a complete list of eligible loans see https://studentaid.gov/manage-loans/consolidation.

Exhibit 8.7 | Summary of Repayment Options Based on Income

	Revised Pay as You Earn (REPAYE) Repayment	Pay As You Earn (PAYE) Repayment	Income-Based Repayment (IBR)	Income-Contingent Repayment (ICR)
Available For	Direct Stafford loans, Direct PLUS loans made to students (PLUS loans made to parents do not qualify), and Direct Consolidation loans (excluding PLUS loans to parents); FFEL Stafford and PLUS loans to students if consolidated (unconsolidated FFEL loans and PLUS loans to parents do not qualify).	Direct Stafford loans, Direct PLUS loans made to students (PLUS loans made to parents do not qualify), and Direct Consolidation loans (excluding PLUS loans to parents); FFEL Stafford and PLUS loans to students if consolidated (unconsolidated FFEL loans and PLUS loans to parents do not qualify); borrower has high debt relative to income.	Direct Stafford loans, Direct PLUS loans made to students (PLUS loans made to parents do not qualify), and Direct Consolidation loans (excluding PLUS loans to parents); FFEL Stafford and PLUS loans to students; borrower has high debt relative to income.	Direct Stafford loans, Direct PLUS loans made to students, and Direct Consolidation loans (including consolidated PLUS loans to parents); FFEL Stafford and PLUS loans (including PLUS loans to parents) if consolidated.
Payment Amount	10% of discretionary income (recalculated each year).	10% of discretionary income (recalculated each year); never more than 10-year Standard payment amount.	10% or 15% of discretionary income (recalculated each year); never more than 10-year Standard payment amount.	Recalculated each year; Lesser of: 1) 20% of discretionary income, or 2) amount that would be paid on a repayment plan with a fixed payment over 12 years, adjusted according to income.
Does the Payment Calculation Count Spouse's Income	Yes, regardless of whether file taxes jointly or separately (individual income used if separated from spouse).	Yes, if file a joint tax return; married filing separately uses only the borrower's income.	Yes, if file a joint tax return; married filing separately uses only the borrower's income.	Yes, if file a joint tax return; married filing separately uses only the borrower's income.
Term	20 or 25 years	20 years	20 or 25 years	25 years
Outstanding Balance Forgiven at End of Term	Yes (may be taxable)	Yes (may be taxable)	Yes (may be taxable)	Yes (may be taxable)
Can Payment Be Higher Than the Payment Under the Standard Plan	Yes	No	No	Yes

	Revised Pay as You Earn (REPAYE) Repayment	*Pay As You Earn (PAYE) Repayment*	*Income-Based Repayment (IBR)*	*Income-Contingent Repayment (ICR)*
May be Favorable for Those Seeking Public Service Loan Forgiveness*	Yes	Yes	Yes	Yes
Does the Government Pay Remaining Interest if Calculated Payment is Less Than Accrued Interest	Yes. Subsidized loans - government pays interest above the payment amount during first three years of repayment, plus half of the interest above the payment amount beyond three years. Unsubsidized loans - government pays half of the interest above the payment amount for all periods.	Yes. Subsidized loans - government pays interest above the payment amount during first three years of repayment.	Yes. Subsidized loans - government pays interest above the payment amount during first three years of repayment.	No
Other Notes				Parent borrowers are eligible if they consolidate parent PLUS loans into a Direct Consolidation loan.

* Requires 120 qualifying monthly payments while working full-time for a qualifying employer, such as a government or nonprofit organization or full-time service as a volunteer for AmeriCorps or Peace Corps. Additional details may be found at: https://studentaid.gov/manage-loans/forgiveness-cancellation/public-service

Selecting the Repayment Option

The repayment option that is best will vary depending on a client's circumstances, plans for the future, and attitude toward debt, as well as on the current economic environment, among other factors. For example, if the interest rate on the student loans is low, rather than paying more on the loans to pay them off faster, it may be advantageous to keep the payment as low as possible and allocate the additional funds to other goals. On the other hand, even with low interest rates, some clients may be particularly uncomfortable with debt and will have the desire to pay it off as quickly as possible. Clients can find additional information on selecting a repayment plan for their student loans at: https://studentaid.gov/h/manage-loans.

Loan service providers may offer a discount on the interest rate for payments that are set up as a direct debit from the checking account each month. While the interest rate reduction may seem to be a small amount, it can result in thousands of dollars of savings over the life of the loan. In addition, the direct debit results in payments that are always made on time, which helps to increase the borrower's credit score. For these reasons, it is advisable to always take advantage of the opportunity to set up payments via direct debit.

While a detailed discussion of unique education financing options and loan terms for service members is beyond the scope of this textbook, it is worth noting that when planners are working with clients who serve, or have served, in the military, additional benefits may be available and all options should be explored.

Consequences of Defaulting on Student Loans

For many families, student loans represent the only way to pay for a college education. Among 2019 college graduates, 69 percent of students took out student loans.[19] Today, there are about 43 million students who have outstanding federal student loan balances.[20]

Total student loan debt in the U.S. has risen steadily from $481 billion in 2006, to over $1.5 trillion dollars in 2019. The average amount of student loan debt, per borrower, was $16,700 in 2004 and has risen to $33,654 in 2019.[21] Balances of student loan debt is greater than both auto loans and credit card debt. Student loan debt is now the largest form of consumer debt outside of mortgages.

The sheer magnitude of student loan debt presents a major threat to the financial security of student borrowers. Approximately one-third of all student debt is owed by individuals age 30 and under. This same age group consistently experiences the highest unemployment rates in the country. When considering the high unemployment rate and amount of student loan debt in the under 30 age group, it's understandable why many of these young people are forced to move back in with their parents after graduating, are unable to purchase their own homes, and are forced to delay starting their own families.

A Department of Education study on cohort default rates indicates that 10.1 percent of student loan borrowers who entered repayment between October 1, 2015 and September 30, 2016 had defaulted prior to September 30, 2018 (a decrease from 10.8 percent for the prior year's cohort).[22] Students who do not complete their degrees struggle the most when it comes to repaying their student loans. Students who do not complete their degree have a higher default rate than students who complete their degree.

Student loan debt is one of the exceptions in bankruptcy and is typically not a dischargeable debt. While it is possible for student loan debt to be discharged under an undue hardship exception, these exceptions are not often granted and the student loan payments must continue to be made.

Cosigners

Neither Perkins nor Stafford loans require a cosigner. Private student loans often require a parent to co-sign for the loan. From the lender's perspective, a loan to a student is a high risk because students likely have no assets, no credit history and a very uncertain future income stream. When parents or grandparents co-sign a loan, they become responsible for repaying the loan if the student falls behind on their payments. If a child becomes delinquent on a student loan, the lender may initiate collection efforts against the cosigner. If the loan is past due, late fees, additional interest, penalties, and collection costs will be added to the outstanding balance, which will ultimately negatively impact both the child and co-signer's credit report. To collect the outstanding student loan, the co-signer's wages may be garnished and/or state or federal income tax refunds may be withheld. In addition, a co-signer's Social Security benefit may be reduced to repay an outstanding student loan if such loan is owed to the federal government.

More than 114,000 retirees have their Social Security benefit reduced due to outstanding student loans. This represents a major risk to a retiree's income during retirement because up to 15 percent of a Social Security benefit may be withheld, although benefits of $750 or less are generally not reduced.[23]

---

19. https://studentloanhero.com/student-loan-debt-statistics/
20. https://studentaid.gov/data-center/student/portfolio.
21. https://www.credible.com/blog/statistics/average-student-loan-debt-statistics/
22. https://www.ed.gov/news/press-releases/national-federal-student-loan-cohort-default-rate-continues-decline.
23. https://www.gao.gov/products/GAO-17-45

Considering that 45 percent of people age 48 to 64 do not save enough for basic needs during retirement, a reduction in Social Security benefits for student loan repayment can significantly delay retirement or even impact the ability to pay for necessary medication and medical care.[24]

Defaulting on student loans can have severe and long-term financial consequences for the borrower and co-signer. Families should try all possible alternatives to reduce the amount borrowed for education such as savings, grants, work-study, living at home after graduating for a period of time, and taking advantage of one of the income-driven repayment schedules which permits payments over 20 to 25 years and limits the amount of repayment to 10 to 20 percent of discretionary income.

Financial Aid - Federal Work-Study

Federal Work-Study (FWS) are jobs on campus or off campus for undergraduate or graduate students to help students pay for their education expenses. To be eligible, students must complete the FAFSA and have financial need. Universities will pay students in the FWS an hourly rate, not less than the minimum wage. The amount of earnings in an FWS program cannot exceed the amount of a total FWS award, as described in the student's financial aid package. Income earned through FWS does not count as student income on the FAFSA and, therefore, does not reduce future financial aid.

Exhibit 8.8 | Financial Aid Comparison

	GRANTS		LOANS			
	Pell Grants	Supplemental Educational Opportunity Grants	Perkins Loans (no new loans after 2017)	Subsidized Stafford Loans	Unsubsidized Stafford Loans	PLUS Loans
Needs to be repaid	No	No	Yes	Yes	Yes	Yes
Available to full-time students	Yes	Yes	Yes	Yes	Yes	Yes
Available to half-time students	Yes	No	Yes	Yes	Yes	Yes
Available for undergrad students	Yes	Yes	Yes	Yes	Yes	Yes - to the parent
Available for graduate students	No	No	Yes	No	Yes	Yes - to the student
Payments deferred while in school	N/A	N/A	Yes + 9 mo. after	Yes + 6 mo. after	Yes + 6 mo. after	Yes + 6 mo. after
Interest subsidized while in school	N/A	N/A	Yes, No interest charged	Yes	No	No
Based on Need	Yes	Yes	Yes	Yes	No	No

---

24. Employee Benefit Research Institute

Tax Deferred Savings, Deductions, Credits or Other Education Planning Benefits

This chapter's discussion so far has focused on paying for a college education with loans, grants, and work-study provided by financial aid. For families that are planning for a college education goal that is 10 or more years away, there are other opportunities besides financial aid. Congress has passed laws establishing savings accounts that allow families to save towards an education goal and permit the account to grow on a tax-deferred basis. If the funds are used for qualified education expenses, then any distributions from the savings accounts are tax-free.

The types of tax-deferred savings vehicles permitted by Congress are:
- Qualified Tuition Plans (Includes Prepaid Tuition and College Savings Plans)
- Coverdell Education Savings Accounts
- U.S. Government Savings Bonds

Although each of the savings vehicles have different characteristics, features, and rules, they all share the same basic principal of excluding any appreciation and earnings from taxable income, as long as the funds are used for qualified education expenses. The Internal Revenue Service's Publication 970 provides information on education funding.

Qualified Tuition Plans

Qualified tuition plans or Savings Plans, allow families to save for education expenses on a tax-deferred basis. Section 529 of the Internal Revenue Code authorized states and educational institutions to adopt qualified tuition plans, either as a prepaid tuition plan or a college savings plan.

Prepaid Tuition

States may sponsor a **prepaid tuition plan** that will allow a parent to purchase college credits today and use those credits when the child attends college. States typically require parents to reside in the state where they are purchasing prepaid tuition credits and then use those credits to attend a college that is part of the state university system. Prepaid tuition plans are designed to only pay the cost of tuition, not room and board. When the credits in a prepaid tuition plan are used to attend college, there are no income tax consequences to the parents for the difference between the amount paid for the college credits and the current cost of the college credits.

A popular misconception about prepaid tuition is that credits are purchased at "today's cost." In fact, many states will charge a premium over the current cost per credit hour when parents purchase prepaid tuition credits. Currently, only 10 states still offer prepaid tuition plans to new investors. Those states are: Florida, Maryland, Massachusetts, Michigan, Mississippi, Nevada, Pennsylvania, Texas, Virginia, and Washington. Many states have been forced to close their prepaid tuition plans due to education costs increasing faster than anticipated and poor investment returns.

Another type of prepaid tuition plan is the Private College 529 Plan, which allows parents to purchase prepaid tuition credits to nearly 300 private universities across the country. Parents purchase prepaid tuition credits that can be used to attend universities such as Stanford, Notre Dame, Emory and MIT. Parents can use the credits purchased to attend any of the nearly 300 private universities that participate in the program. Students must still meet entrance requirements, which are separate and independent of the prepaid tuition plan. There is no preferential acceptance to private universities because the parents participate in a Private College 529 Plan.

The disadvantages to prepaid tuition are that universities in the home state may not offer a curriculum that appeals to the student or the student may be offered a scholarship to attend a university out of their home state. If parents decide to cancel the prepaid tuition plan or not use the tuition credits, the rules vary by state, but generally parents will receive what they paid for the tuition credit, less some administrative expenses. Some states will return any earnings on the investments.

Planners should advise clients to carefully research their states' prepaid tuition plans before investing. Many plans are facing difficulty as the investment returns have not outpaced or maintained tuition inflation rates. Some states are facing significant shortfalls in the amount of assets in the prepaid tuition plans, which are not keeping up with the cost of tuition at the universities in the state and the tuition credit hours promised are exceeding the assets of the plan. As a result, many states have closed their prepaid tuition plans or have frozen the plans to prevent future purchases. However, most states offer a guarantee that the state will make up any shortfall between plan assets and the cost of tuition.

Prepaid tuition credits are considered assets of the parent for financial aid purposes. As previously discussed, a smaller percentage of a parent's income and assets are deemed available for education than the child's. Anytime an asset is treated as an asset of the parent, it results in more favorable treatment when determining the amount of financial aid the family qualifies to receive.

College Savings Plan

College Savings Plans (or 529 Savings Plans) allow for college saving on a tax-deferred basis with attendance at any eligible education institution. According to the IRS, "An eligible education institution is any college, university, vocational school, or other postsecondary educational institution eligible to participate in a student aid program administered by the U.S. Department of Education." Distributions from a College Savings Plan are federal and state income tax-free, as long as they are used to pay for qualified education expenses. Qualified education expenses include: tuition and fees, books, supplies, and equipment. Qualified education expenses also include room and board for students enrolled at least half-time and cannot exceed the greater of:

- Allowance for room and board as part of the cost of attendance provided by the school as part of the financial aid process.
- The actual amount charged if the student resides in housing owned or operated by the university.

The American Recovery and Reinvestment Act of 2009 expanded qualified education expenses to include computer technology or equipment. Computer technology and equipment includes any computer and related peripheral equipment, such as a printer, internet access, and software used for educational purposes. The Tax Cuts and Jobs Act of 2017 expanded the definition of qualified expenses to allow distributions of up to $10,000 per year per beneficiary to pay tuition at elementary or secondary public or private schools. The Setting Every Community Up for Retirement Enhancement (SECURE) Act of 2019 further expanded qualified distributions to include fees, books, supplies, and

Key Concepts

1. Distinguish between a prepaid tuition plan and a college savings plan.

2. Identify the levels and types of education expenses that can be funded using distributions from a Coverdell education savings account.

3. Identify the criteria required for an individual to receive the income exclusion benefit associated with U.S Government Series EE and I bonds.

equipment required for an apprenticeship program registered and certified with the Secretary of Labor under Section 1 of the National Apprenticeship Act, and distributions of up to $10,000 (lifetime maximum) for qualified student loan repayments (including those for siblings), effective for distributions made after December 31, 2018.

A federal income tax deduction is not permitted for contributions to a College Savings Plan. However, states that have a state income tax will generally offer a state income tax deduction for those residents that contribute to their state's College Savings Plan.

There are no phase-outs (income limitations) on who can contribute to a College Savings Plan and a Savings Plan can be opened benefiting anyone (e.g., family member, friend, neighbor, or the owner of the plan). The owner of the Savings Plan can at any time change the beneficiary to another beneficiary who is a family member of the original beneficiary. However, when the 529 Savings Plan was funded from a Uniform Gift to Minors (UGMA) or Uniform Transfer to Minors (UTMA) account, the beneficiary may only be changed with the consent of the original beneficiary at age of majority. This is because gifts to UGMA/UTMA accounts are irrevocable gifts to the minor beneficiary. When a beneficiary is changed, there are no gift tax consequences as long as the new beneficiary is a family member assigned to the same generation as the original beneficiary. A family member includes the following beneficiaries:

- Son, daughter, stepchild, foster child, adopted child, or their descendants
- Brother, sister, stepbrother, or stepsister
- Stepfather or stepmother
- Son or daughter of a brother or sister
- Brother or sister of father or mother
- Son-in-law, daughter-in-law, and first cousin
- Father, mother, or ancestor of either

Exhibit 8.9 | Lineal Descendants

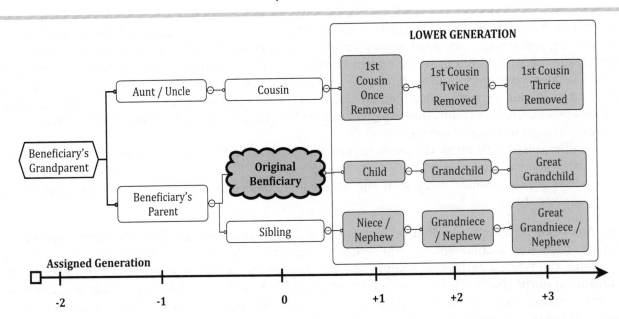

A transfer which occurs by reason of a change in the designated beneficiary, or a rollover of credits or account balances from the account of one beneficiary to the account of another beneficiary, will be treated as a taxable gift by the old beneficiary to the new beneficiary if the new beneficiary is assigned to a lower generation than the old beneficiary, as defined in IRC Section 2651, regardless of whether the new beneficiary is a member of the family of the old beneficiary. The transfer will be subject to the generation-skipping transfer tax if the new beneficiary is assigned to a generation that is two or more levels lower than the generation assignment of the old beneficiary.[25]

Example 8.4

In Year 1, Bob makes a contribution to a College Savings Plan on behalf of Bob's child, Beth. In Year 4, Bob directs that a distribution from the account for the benefit of Beth be made to an account for the benefit of Bob's grandchild, Dylan. The rollover distribution is treated as a taxable gift by Beth to Dylan, because, under section 2651, Dylan is assigned to a generation below the generation assignment of Beth.

Contributors to a Savings Plan are permitted to open a Savings Plan in any state. The funds in that Savings Plan can be used to pay for qualified education expenses at any eligible institution regardless of whether the institution is in the same state as the Savings Plan or not.

Example 8.5

Naomi lives in Georgia and contributes to New York's Savings Plan for the benefit of her daughter, Wynonna. Wynonna decides to attend the University of Southern California (USC). Naomi is permitted to use the funds in her New York Savings Plan to pay qualified tuition expenses for Wynonna to attend USC.

Example 8.6

Barbie lives in California and contributes to California's Savings Plan for the benefit of her son, Ken. Ken decides to attend Massachusetts Institute of Technology (MIT). Barbie is permitted to use the funds in her California Savings Plan to pay qualified education expenses for Ken to attend MIT.

Contributions to a Savings Plan are limited to the amount necessary to provide for the qualified education expenses of the beneficiary. Individual states will impose contribution limits per beneficiary, based on the most expensive university in a state, allowing contribution limits of $250,000 - $500,000 in most state plans. A student may be the beneficiary of multiple Savings Plans.

A contributor can contribute up to the annual gift tax exclusion amount ($15,000 in 2021) and not incur any gift tax liability. Spouses can elect gift splitting and give two times the annual gift tax exclusion amount or $30,000 ($15,000 x 2 for 2021) in one year, per beneficiary, and not incur gift tax liability. In addition to the annual exclusion, each person has an $11,700,000 (2021) lifetime applicable gift tax exclusion.

---

25. Treas. Reg. 1.529-5(3).

College Savings Plans permit a contributor to contribute up to five times the annual gift tax exclusion amount or $75,000 (5 x $15,000) as a lump sum, in one year. The $75,000 gift tax exclusion is for one beneficiary and the contributor will not incur gift tax liability if the contributor elects to treat the gift as an annual exclusion gift, for that year of the gift, and for each of the next four years. A married couple can elect gift splitting and contribute a lump-sum amount of $150,000 (5 x $15,000 x 2) in one year, per beneficiary and not incur gift tax liability. The IRS will recognize 1/5 of the contribution as being contributed each year, even though the lump-sum amount was contributed in one year. This strategy is often referred to as "front loading" the Section 529 plan.

Example 8.7

Josiah opens a Savings Plan for his favorite nephew, Matthew. In 2021, Josiah can contribute a maximum amount of $75,000 (5 x $15,000 for 2021) into a Savings Plan for Matthew and not incur gift tax consequences since the IRS will only count 1/5 of the total contribution as being contributed each year, so long as Josiah files a gift tax return to elect to treat the contribution ratably over the 5 year period beginning with the year of the gift.

Example 8.8

Darnell and Nia decide to open a Savings Plan for their favorite grandson, Marcus. In 2021, Darnell and Nia can contribute a maximum amount of $150,000 in one year to Marcus' Savings Plan and not incur gift tax consequences.

When an amount that, when distributed equally over five years, is less than the full annual exclusion, or when the annual exclusion amount increases, additional gifts can be made to bring the total contribution up to the annual exclusion amount each year.

Example 8.9

Flo makes a contribution of $60,000 to a 529 Savings Plan for her favorite nephew Tommy in 2020 and elects to treat the gift as made ratably over the five year period. Assume the annual gift tax exclusion in 2020, 2021, and 2022 is $15,000 and that the annual exclusion in 2023 and 2024 is $16,000. The 2020 gift is treated as $12,000 contributed each year for five years. In 2020, 2021, and 2022, Flo can make an additional gift to Tommy (including an additional contribution to the 529 plan for 2021 and 2022) of $3,000 each year, and in 2023 and 2024 she can make an additional gift to Tommy of $4,000 each year.

Note that if the donor makes a gift of $75,000 in 2021 (and chooses front-loading to avoid gift taxes), and then dies before the full 5 years have passed, a portion of the gift will be brought back into the donor's gross estate for federal estate tax purposes.

Example 8.10

Aurora opens a Section 529 Savings Plan for her niece, Belle, contributing $75,000 in 2021 and filing a gift tax return on which she elects to treat the gift as made ratably over a 5-year period. If Aurora dies in 2023, she will have only lived long enough to make annual exclusion gifts for 3 years (2021, 2022, and 2023); therefore, $30,000 (2 years of annual exclusion gifts) will be brought into her estate for estate tax purposes.

Distributions of contributions are always income tax-free and penalty free. Accumulated earnings withdrawn for purposes other than qualified education expenses are taxable and carry a 10 percent penalty tax. Nonqualified distributions are treated as a pro rata distribution of contributions and earnings. Previously, the distributions were required to be aggregated if the same owner and beneficiary maintained multiple 529 plan accounts, but now the earnings portion of a distribution is computed separately for each 529 plan account. If tuition is paid from a 529 plan distribution and then is refunded, the refund is treated as a qualified expense if the amount that is refunded is re-contributed to a 529 account within 60 days. Exceptions to the 10 percent penalty rule are listed below.

If the distribution is due to: • Death of the beneficiary • Disability of the beneficiary
If the distribution is included in income because the beneficiary received: • Tax-free scholarship • Veterans' educational assistance • Employer-provided educational assistance • Any other nontaxable (tax-free) payments (other than gifts or inheritances) received as educational assistance
If the beneficiary is attending a U.S. military academy, and the distribution is not in excess of the cost of attendance
If the distribution is included in income only because the qualified education expenses were taken into account in determining the American Opportunity or Lifetime Learning Credits (discussed later in this chapter)

Example 8.11

Simone, an accomplished high school gymnast, received an athletic scholarship worth $35,000 per year from Stanford University to compete on the gymnastics team. Simone's parents may take a distribution from her Savings Plan for $35,000 to use for other, non-qualified, expenses. They will include the earnings on the $35,000 distribution in ordinary income, but there is no 10% penalty on the earnings because the distribution is taken as a result of the beneficiary's athletic scholarship.

Example 8.12

Simone forgoes her scholarship to Stanford and instead uses her gymnastic skills to join the circus as part of the flying trapeze show. Simone's parents are less than thrilled with her decision and decide to withdraw all of the funds in her Savings Plan and purchase a boat to sail around the world. The earnings associated with the withdrawal will be included as ordinary income for Simone's parents and subject to a 10% penalty.

Investment options for Savings Plans typically include mutual funds and annuities and most Savings Plans offer age banded investments that become more conservative as the beneficiary becomes closer to age 18. The contributor or beneficiary is permitted to change the investment selection up to twice per year.

Savings Plans offer a unique advantage for grandparents looking for ways to provide for the grandchildren's college education. Funds in a Savings Plan are not included in the grandparent's gross estate when calculating any estate tax due. As discussed previously, the grandparent's contribution may be recognized as a series of annual exclusion gifts over a five year period. If during that five year period the grandparents die, any remaining years (excluding the year of death) are brought back into the gross estate.

Grandparents still retain control over the asset and have the flexibility to change the beneficiary or remove the funds from the Savings Plan. If the 529 plan is owned by a third party, such as a grandparent or a non-custodial divorced parent, the assets are not reported on the FAFSA, but qualified distributions are treated as untaxed income to the child on the FAFSA for the following year. This income for a child has a greater negative impact on financial aid than assets of the parent, so ownership by third parties should generally be avoided, or distributions limited to the final two years of postsecondary education when the income will no longer impact an upcoming FAFSA (due to prior-prior year income reporting).

Assets in a College Savings Plan owned by the parent or by the student who is a dependent of the parent are considered assets of the parent for financial aid purposes. Remember, a smaller percentage of a parent's income and assets are deemed available for education than the child's. Anytime an asset is treated as an asset of the parent, it results in more favorable treatment when determining the amount of financial aid the family qualifies to receive.

State savings plans often provide additional benefits other than the benefits discussed above. These benefits might include state income tax deductions for contributions or return enhancements. To encourage residents to save for college education, states may provide a state income tax deduction on contributions to a savings plan. Generally, the deduction is limited to a certain amount per beneficiary or donor. For example, deposits made to a Louisiana savings plan account can be excluded from taxable income reported on the account owner's Louisiana income tax return, up to $2,400 per year per beneficiary for single account owners and up to $4,800 per year per beneficiary for account owners filing a joint return. Louisiana also permits unused exclusions to be carried forward to subsequent tax years. In addition to a tax deduction, the Louisiana savings plan provides "Earnings Enhancements," which are effectively an additional contribution to the plan that increases the plan value and grows over time based on the plan account investment choices.

> ## ☑️ Quick Quiz 8.4
>
> 1. Prepaid tuition plans allow a parent to purchase college credits today for availability when the child attends college.
>   a. True
>   b. False
>
> 2. Distributions for qualified education expenses from a College Savings Plan are federal and state income tax-free when the student is attending any eligible educational institution.
>   a. True
>   b. False
>
> 3. The American Recovery and Reinvestment Act of 2009 expanded qualified education expenses to include books, supplies, and equipment.
>   a. True
>   b. False
>
> True, True, False.

In addition to benefits discussed above, states often provide scholarships for state residents to attend state schools. These scholarships are often merit based and require academic achievement while in college to maintain the scholarships.

Coverdell Education Savings Account

A **Coverdell Education Savings Account (ESA)** is a tax deferred trust or custodial account established to pay for qualified higher education or qualified elementary / secondary school expenses.

For a Coverdell ESA, qualified higher education expenses include tuition, fees, books, room, board, and computer related expenses. Qualified elementary and secondary expenses include tuition, fees, books, supplies, equipment, tutoring, computer related expenses, and special needs services for special needs beneficiaries. Qualified elementary and secondary expenses also include room and board, uniforms and transportation if required or provided by the institution.

Distributions from a Coverdell ESA used for qualified education expenses are tax-free, as long as the distribution does not exceed the qualified education expenses, reduced by any financial assistance.

Example 8.13

Rudy receives a $15,000 per year scholarship to attend Notre Dame. The cost of attending Notre Dame is $35,000 per year. Rudy may take a tax-free distribution from his Coverdell ESA, up to $20,000 ($35,000 - $15,000).

Any distributions in excess of qualified education expenses or distributions not used for qualified education expenses will cause the earnings to be taxable as ordinary income and to be subject to a 10 percent penalty.

Although a distribution is included in income, it may not be subject to a 10 percent penalty. Following is a list of the exceptions to the 10 percent penalty rule.

If the distribution is due to: • Death of the beneficiary   • Disability of the beneficiary
If the distribution is included in income because the beneficiary received: • Tax-free scholarship   • Veterans' educational assistance   • Employer-provided educational assistance   • Any other nontaxable (tax-free) payments (other than gifts or inheritances) received as educational assistance
If the beneficiary is attending a U.S. military academy, and the distribution is not in excess of the cost of attendance
If the distribution is included in income only because the qualified education expenses were taken into account in determining the American Opportunity or Lifetime Learning Credits (discussed later in this chapter)

When the Coverdell ESA is established the beneficiary must be under age 18 or qualify as a special needs beneficiary. Contributions to a Coverdell ESA are limited to $2,000 per beneficiary per year and are not deductible for federal or state income taxes. Although a beneficiary can have multiple Coverdell ESAs, the total annual contribution to all Coverdell accounts cannot exceed $2,000 per beneficiary. Contributions to Coverdell accounts must be in cash and contributions are not permitted once the beneficiary attains age 18 unless the beneficiary has special educational needs.

The phase-out for contributing to a Coverdell ESA is based on the taxpayer's Modified Adjusted Gross Income (MAGI). For most taxpayers, MAGI is the same as adjusted gross income (AGI). The phase-out limits for a Coverdell ESA are:

- Single: $95,000 - $110,000
- Married Filing Jointly: $190,000 - $220,000

Assets from one Coverdell can be rolled over to another Coverdell, however, there is a limit of one rollover of funds that are distributed then contributed into another ESA as a rollover (within 60 days) per year. There is no limit on the number of trustee-to-trustee transfers during the year. While an ESA cannot be directly rolled over to a Section 529 Savings Plan, a contribution to a Section 529 plan is a qualified expense for an ESA. A distribution must be made from the ESA and the contribution made to the 529 plan for the same beneficiary (or a member of the beneficiary's family) in the same tax year. The beneficiary designation for a Coverdell can also be changed and not subject to income tax as long as the new beneficiary is a member of the original beneficiary's family and is under the age of 30. Funds in a Coverdell ESA must be distributed within 30 days of the beneficiary attaining age 30.

A Coverdell ESA owned by the parent or by the student who is a dependent of the parent is treated as an asset of the parent for financial aid purposes.

U.S. Government Savings Bonds

U.S. Government Series EE (issued after 1989) and Series I bonds can be redeemed to pay for qualified education expenses with the interest earned on the bonds excluded from taxable income. For purposes of excluding interest income using U.S. Government savings bonds, qualified education expenses only include tuition and fees. Expenses for room and board are not permitted.

In order to receive the income exclusion benefit, the bond must be purchased in the name of the parent (or parents), the bonds must be issued when the owner is at least 24 years old, and the bonds must be redeemed in the year that qualified education expenses are incurred. The qualified education expenses must be for the taxpayer, the taxpayer's spouse, or dependents of the taxpayer. If a parent is using the bonds for a child's education, they cannot be registered in the name of the child. The child can be listed as a beneficiary on the bond, but the child cannot be a co-owner.

There are also MAGI based income limitations determining who can benefit from the interest income exclusion for Series EE and I bonds.

The income limitations (as of 2021) are:
- Single: $83,200 - $98,200
- Married Filing Jointly: $124,800 - $154,800

If a taxpayer's MAGI in the year in which the bonds are redeemed is less than the threshold, then the taxpayer is eligible to exclude the interest income. If a taxpayer's MAGI is greater than the threshold limit then interest income is not excludable for a series EE or I bond. If the taxpayer's MAGI is between the lower and upper phaseout limit, the taxpayer will be permitted to exclude a portion of the interest from taxable income.

In addition to the ability to exclude the interest earned on a Series EE or I bonds in the year qualified education expenses are incurred, owners of these bonds may convert the bonds into a College Savings Plan (529 Plan) or Coverdell Education Savings Account. Since only cash may be contributed to a Savings Plan or Coverdell account, the bonds must first be redeemed, and then invested in the Savings Plan or Coverdell ESA.

Series EE and I bonds are deemed assets of the owner of the bond for financial aid purposes. So, if the parents own the bonds, then the bonds are deemed owned by the parents for financial aid purposes.

TAX IMPLICATIONS

Tax Deductions for Education Expenses

Congress permits taxpayers to deduct certain education-related expenses for income tax purposes. While not as valuable as tax credits, deductions reduce taxable income, whereas tax credits are a dollar for dollar reduction in tax owed.

Deductions that are taken before calculating adjusted gross income are valuable because the taxpayer does not have to itemize deductions on their tax return to take advantage of some specific deductions. The student loan interest deduction is a deduction before adjusted gross income.

Student Loan Interest Deduction

Generally, the interest expense on most personal loans is not tax deductible, with few exceptions, including mortgage interest on a primary residence. The tax law does allow taxpayers that pay interest related to a student loan to deduct up to $2,500 of interest expense per year. Taxpayers do not have to itemize their deductions to receive the student loan interest deduction because the deduction is taken before adjusted gross income (also known as an adjustment for AGI).

Key Concepts

1. Identify the criteria required to receive the student loan interest deduction.

2. Distinguish between the American Opportunity Tax Credit and the Lifetime Learning Credit.

3. Distinguish between scholarships and fellowships.

4. Identify the income tax consequences associated with education funding from IRA distributions.

Taxpayers with income in excess of the phase-out thresholds are not eligible to deduct student loan interest expense. The phase-outs (as of 2021) are based on MAGI:
- Single: $70,000 - $85,000
- Married Filing Jointly: $140,000 - $170,000

To qualify for the student loan interest deduction, the student loan proceeds must have been used to pay for qualified education expenses. Qualified education expenses include tuition and fees, books, supplies, equipment, and other necessary expenses such as transportation, room and board. The qualified education expenses must have been paid by the taxpayer, the taxpayer's spouse, or a dependent of the taxpayer.

As part of the student loan interest deduction, not only is the interest expense on a student loan deductible, but so are loan origination fees, credit card interest expenses, and any capitalized interest expenses. Loan origination fees are financial institution charges associated with issuing a loan. The origination fee is included on a pro-rata basis over the repayment period as a student loan interest expense deduction.

Example 8.14

Yvette receives a $4,000 student loan used for qualified education expenses. Her lender charges an origination fee of 3% or $120. Yvette repays the loan over a 10-year period, therefore she is entitled to deduct $12 ($120 ÷ 10) per year for the origination fee. In addition to the origination fee deduction, Yvette can deduct the interest expense paid on the loan as part of the student loan interest deduction.

Credit card interest is deductible as part of the student loan interest deduction if the credit card charges incurred were solely for qualified education expenses. If the taxpayer is carrying a large credit card balance, it may be difficult to determine the portion of the outstanding balance that is only associated with qualified education expenses. In addition, because of high interest rates on credit cards, the $2,500 student loan interest expense limit will be attained with only $10,000 - $15,000 in credit card debt.

Capitalized interest is the interest expense that is added to the outstanding balance of a loan, while the taxpayer is enrolled at least half-time. Remember, with unsubsidized Stafford Loans, the borrower can either pay the interest expenses as incurred or capitalize the interest expense.

Loan Forgiveness

Usually, any discharge of indebtedness or forgiveness of debt is considered income for federal and state income tax purposes unless a specific exception applies under Internal Revenue Code Section 108. Therefore, if someone borrowed $1,000 and the loan is subsequently forgiven, it would generally be treated as taxable income. There is an exception under IRC 108 for specific student loans.

Generally, student loan forgiveness is excluded from income if the forgiveness is contingent upon the student working for a specific number of years in certain professions.[26] Public service loan forgiveness, teacher loan forgiveness, law school loan repayment assistance programs, and the National Health Service Corps Loan Repayment Program are not taxable. Loan discharges for closed schools, false certification, unpaid refunds, and death and disability are considered taxable income. The forgiveness of the remaining balance under the various income-driven repayment plans after 20 to 25 years is considered taxable income.

The American Rescue Plan Act (ARPA) of 2021 created an exclusion from income for discharges of certain student loans occurring after December 31, 2020 and before January 1, 2026. Qualifying loans

---

26. IRC Section 108(f).

are those provided expressly for post-secondary education expenses if the loan was made, insured, or guaranteed by the federal government or a state or local government, or by an eligible educational institution. Private education loans and certain loans from specified charitable or tax-exempt organizations also qualify for the exclusion from income. Discharge of loans made by educational institutions or private lenders do not qualify, however, if the discharge is based on services performed for the educational institution or private lender.

Tax Credits for Education-Related Expenses

The federal tax law permits two types of tax credits for education related expenses. The two types of tax credits are:
- The American Opportunity Tax Credit (formerly the Hope Scholarship Credit)
- Lifetime Learning Credit

Credits are more valuable to taxpayers than income tax deductions, as credits are a dollar for dollar reduction in any federal income taxes owed.

The American Opportunity Tax Credit (Formerly the Hope Scholarship Credit)

The **American Opportunity Tax Credit (AOTC)** was created by the American Recovery and Reinvestment Act of 2009 and amended by the Tax Relief, Unemployment Insurance Reauthorization, and Job Creation Act of 2010. The new legislation increased the amount of the tax credit and provided other benefits beyond that of it's predecessor, the Hope Credit.

The AOTC provides a tax credit of up to $2,500 per student per year for the first four years of qualified education expenses for postsecondary education. To qualify, students must be in their first four years of college and enrolled on at least a half-time basis. The credit is not available if, at any time, the student was convicted of a state or federal felony drug offense. The tax credit is calculated as follows:
- 100% x the first $2,000 of qualified education expenses, plus
- 25% x the second $2,000 of qualified education expenses.

Since the AOTC is "per student," a family that has multiple children in the first four years of college may qualify for multiple American Opportunity Tax Credits in one year.

Example 8.15
Felix has two children, Dean and Jessie, who are attending the University of Oregon. Felix pays qualified education expenses of $6,000 for Dean and $3,000 for Jessie. Felix is entitled to an AOTC of $2,500 for Dean [(100% x $2,000) + (25% x $2,000)] and $2,250 for Jessie [(100% x $2,000) + (25% x $1,000)] for a total tax credit of $4,750.

Qualified education expenses include tuition and fees (including student activity fees) as long as those fees are paid directly to the university. Qualified education expenses also include books, supplies, and equipment, but they do not have to be purchased directly from the university.

To qualify for the AOTC the taxpayer must pay qualified education expenses for the taxpayer, the taxpayer's spouse, or dependent of the taxpayer. In addition, taxpayers with income in excess of the phase-out thresholds are not eligible for the AOTC. The 2021 phase-outs are based on MAGI:
- Single: $80,000 - $90,000
- Married Filing Jointly: $160,000 - $180,000

Taxpayers can receive up to 40 percent of the American Opportunity Tax Credit as a refundable credit. Refundable tax credits are treated as a tax payment. This means that rather than being limited to reducing the tax owed to zero (as is the limit for most tax credits), up to 40 percent of the AOTC credit can be received as a refund that is larger than the amount of money the taxpayer actually paid in during the year. However, no portion of the credit is refundable if the taxpayer claiming the credit is a child subject to the kiddie tax (discussed later in this chapter).

Lifetime Learning Credit

The **Lifetime Learning Credit** provides a tax credit of up to $2,000 (2021) per family for an unlimited number of years of qualified education expenses. The qualified education expenses must be related to a postsecondary degree program or to acquire or improve job skills. The tax credit is calculated as follows:

20% x qualified education expenses (up to $10,000)

Example 8.16

Patrick and Jill are married and both have an undergraduate degree. Patrick goes back to school for a certificate in financial planning while Jill goes back to school to earn her master's degree in nursing. Patrick incurs $5,000 of qualified education expenses and Jill incurs $15,000 of qualified education expenses. Patrick and Jill can take a total Lifetime Learning Credit of $2,000 (($5,000 + $15,000) x 20% limited to $2,000 maximum credit) in the current year. Next year, if Patrick and Jill incur the same amount of qualified education expenses, they can take another $2,000 Lifetime Learning Credit.

Qualified education expenses include tuition and fees, student activity fees, books, supplies, and equipment as long as those fees are paid directly to an eligible education institution. An eligible education institution is any accredited public, nonprofit and private profit-making postsecondary institution eligible to participate in a student aid program administered by the U.S. Department of Education.

To qualify for the Lifetime Learning Credit the taxpayer must pay qualified education expenses for the taxpayer, the taxpayer's spouse, or a dependent of the taxpayer. In addition, taxpayers with income in excess of the phase-out thresholds are not eligible for the Lifetime Learning Credit. The 2021 phase-outs are based on MAGI:[27]

- Single: $80,000 - $90,000
- Married Filing Jointly: $160,000 - $180,000

An important difference between the AOTC and the Lifetime Learning Tax Credit is that AOTC qualified education expenses include related expenses of books, supplies, and equipment, regardless of whether the expenses are paid directly to the university. The Lifetime Learning Credit requires related educational expenses such as activity fees, course books, supplies, and equipment be paid directly to the university in order for these expenses to be included in the credit.

---

27. Prior to January 1, 2021, the Lifetime Learning credit phase-out thresholds were lower (scheduled to be $59,000 - $69,000 Single, $119,000 - $139,000 MFJ in 2021). In addition, an above-the line deduction for qualified tuition and related expenses was available on a year-by-by year basis (as extended by Congress). The Taxpayer Certainty and Disaster Tax Relief Act of 2020 permanently repealed the above-the-line deduction and permanently increased the phase-outs of the Lifetime Learning Credit, bringing the LLC phase-outs into alignment with those of the AOTC, for tax years beginning after December 31, 2020.

There are many similarities between the AOTC and Lifetime Learning Credits such as the timing of when qualified expenses count toward an education tax credit calculation, adjustments to qualified education expenses, no double dipping on benefits, and nonqualified education expenses.

Timing of When Qualified Expenses Count Toward the Tax Credit Calculation

When calculating qualified education expenses for the AOTC and Lifetime Learning Credits, the taxpayer may include expenses paid in December, related to attending the university during the first three months of the following year. This includes whether the taxpayer uses cash from their checking account or funds from a loan.

Example 8.17

Robin paid $15,000 winter tuition for her daughter Reese on December 15th, for classes that begin January 24th. Robin paid $2,000 from her checking account and used $13,000 from a PLUS Loan to pay the remaining $13,000. Robin is permitted to use the $2,000 paid from her checking account and $2,000 of the $13,000 from the PLUS Loan when calculating the AOTC or Lifetime Learning Credit.

Most taxpayers are cash basis taxpayers, meaning that they pay tax on income in the year the income is received and deduct expenses in the year in which they are paid. This timing may be significant in consideration of the tax credits when tuition is paid for the spring semester of college. The tuition bill will typically arrive in December of the prior year. For example, if the semester begins January 9, 2022, the tuition bill will be sent in December of 2021. If tuition is paid in 2021, the Form 1098-T will show that payment for 2021, even though the bill was not due until 2022. If no other tuition payments are made in 2022 (for example, because the spring semester was the final semester prior to graduation), then a tax credit will not be available for 2022.

A taxpayer or dependent student must receive a Form 1098-T as a condition to being entitled to one of the education credits. Higher education institutions must provide a Form 1098-T (Tuition Statement) to the IRS and to the student, indicating the amount paid by or billed to the student for qualified tuition and related expenses for the tax year. However, a Form 1098-T may not reflect the total amount of qualified expenses. For example, course materials may have been purchased from a vendor other than the educational institution. If that is the case, then the total amount of qualifying expenses for the AOTC will be higher than what is reported on the Form 1098-T, and the taxpayer will still be able to count these expenses, as long as they are able to substantiate them as qualified expenses.

Adjustments to Qualified Education Expenses

If the student receives any tax-free education assistance, the amount of qualified education expenses is reduced by that amount before calculating the AOTC or Lifetime Learning Credit. Examples of tax-free education support include:

- Pell Grants
- Tax-Free Scholarships
- Employer-Provided Education Assistance
- Tax-Free Distribution from a Savings Plan or Coverdell ESA

Emergency financial aid grants received under the CARES Act of 2020, however, do not reduce the amount of qualified education expenses for purposes of the American Opportunity Tax Credit or Lifetime Learning Tax Credit.[28]

A gift or inheritance used for qualified education expenses does not reduce the amount of expenses considered when calculating the AOTC or Lifetime Learning Credit.

Example 8.18

Dorothy's daughter, Sophia, is attending Arizona State University and receives a Pell Grant in the amount of $4,000. Qualified tuition expenses for Sophia to attend Arizona State are $7,000 per year. Dorothy may only use $3,000 ($7,000 - $4,000) of the qualified education expenses to calculate the AOTC or Lifetime Learning Credit.

Example 8.19

Estelle's son, Stanley, is attending Duke University and incurs $35,000 of qualified tuition expenses. Estelle takes a distribution from Stanley's 529 Savings Plan in the amount of $33,000. Estelle may only use $2,000 ($35,000 - $33,000) of the qualified education expenses to calculate the AOTC or Lifetime Learning Credit. If Estelle otherwise qualifies for the AOTC, she would receive a greater benefit from paying $4,000 of the tuition expense from funds outside of the 529 Savings Plan and taking a qualified distribution from the Savings Plan in the amount of $31,000. This will allow her to receive the full $2,500 AOTC.

As discussed previously, students have a choice of allocating a Pell Grant or scholarship toward tuition, fees, and course materials or allocating a Pell Grant or scholarship to living expenses, causing that portion of the grant to be taxable income to the student, but allowing tuition and fees to remain qualified expenses for the AOTC.

No Double Dipping on Benefits

There are coordination of benefit rules when using multiple tax-deferred savings, tax deductions and tax credits to pay for higher education expenses. The general rule is that a taxpayer is not allowed to receive a double benefit for the same expenses. The following specific rules apply:

- The taxpayer cannot claim both the AOTC and the Lifetime Learning Credits for the same child in the same year.
- The taxpayer cannot claim both the AOTC and the Lifetime Learning Credits for the same qualified education expenses.
- The taxpayer cannot use the same expenses used for a tax-free distribution from a Qualified Tuition Plan (529 Savings Plan) or Coverdell ESA and use those expenses to calculate an AOTC or Lifetime Learning Credit.
- The taxpayer cannot claim an AOTC or Lifetime Learning Credit if the taxpayer received tax-free education assistance, such as a scholarship, grant, or employer-provided education assistance (unless the student elects to treat the Pell grant or scholarship as taxable income paying for living expenses, as noted previously).
- The taxpayer cannot take a tax-free distribution from both a Section 529 Savings Plan and an ESA, or from a 529 plan or ESA along with a tax-free redemption of Series EE or I bonds for the same expenses.

28.COVIDTRA 2020, Sec. 277.

It is permissible, however, to receive multiple tax benefits in the same year for the same student for different expenses. The definition of qualified expenses for 529 Savings Plans and ESAs is more extensive than for the tax credits and Series EE or I bond redemption, which may allow for the use of multiple tax advantages for different expenses.

Example 8.20

Brian's son, Stewie, is in his freshman year of college. Brian is single and his AGI is $65,000 this year. Brian has saved $7,000 in an ESA, $40,000 in a Section 529 Savings Plan, and $8,000 in Series EE bonds for Stewie's education. Tuition and fees are $10,000 and room and board are $12,000 for the year. Brian pays $4,000 of the tuition from his checking account, allowing him to qualify for the AOTC of $2,500. Since Brian's AGI is below the phaseout range, he may also redeem tax-free up to $6,000 ($10,000 tuition less $4,000 for tuition utilized by the AOTC) of Series EE bonds. Brian can then take a tax-free distribution of $7,000 from the ESA and $5,000 from the 529 Savings Plan to pay the room and board expenses. Since each distribution is for different expenses, no tax benefits are lost.

Nonqualified Education Expenses

The AOTC and the Lifetime Learning Credits do not allow certain education related expenses to be counted as qualified education expenses. Examples of expenses that are not qualified education expenses for the AOTC and Lifetime Learning Credits are:

- Room and Board
- Insurance
- Student Health Fees
- Transportation Expenses

The above expenses are not qualified expenses for the AOTC and Lifetime Learning Credit, even if the fees are a condition of enrollment and are paid directly to the education institution.

Exhibit 8.10 | Summary of Education Related Tax Credits

	American Opportunity	Lifetime Learning
Calculation	100% x 1st $2,000 + 25% of 2nd $2,000	20% x up to $10,000
Maximum Amount	$2,500	$2,000
Phase-Out (2021)	Single: $80 - $90k MFJ: $160 - $180k	Single: $80 - $90k MFJ: $160 - $180k
Qualified Education Expenses include textbook and equipment	Yes - Does not have to be paid directly to the university	Yes - Only if paid directly to the university
Qualified Education Expenses include room and board	No	No

OTHER SOURCES OF EDUCATION FUNDING

This section discusses some of the tax advantages and disadvantages of using scholarships, fellowships, IRA distributions, and custodial accounts to pay for post-secondary education expenses. A planner should understand all of the tax consequences of each of these education related benefits.

Scholarships and Fellowships

Scholarships are a grant of financial assistance made available to students to assist with the payment of education-related expenses. Scholarships are available for academic or athletic achievement. Many private organizations will also fund scholarships based on various fields of study, religious affiliations, or military service. Scholarships can be provided to undergraduate or graduate students.

Information on various scholarships and organizations awarding scholarships can be found on the Federal Student Aid website, which is an office of the U.S. Department of Education.[29] There is also a research tool for scholarships available on U.S. Department of Labor website.[30]

Fellowships are typically paid to students for work, such as teaching while studying for a Master's degree or conducting research while working towards a Doctorate of Philosophy degree (Ph.D.). Fellowships can also be provided to an M.D. working on a specialty field of medicine. Fellowships can last from a few weeks to a few years, depending on the depth and level of work involved.

A scholarship or fellowship is tax-free to the recipient if the recipient is:
- A candidate for a degree at an eligible education institution, and
- The recipient uses the proceeds to pay for qualified education expenses.

The recipient is considered a candidate for a degree if:
- The recipient is attending a primary or secondary school or is pursuing a degree at a college or university, or
- The recipient is attending an accredited education institution (that is authorized to provide full credit towards a bachelor's degree or higher, or provides training for students for gainful employment in a recognized occupation).

An eligible education institution is one that maintains a regular faculty and curriculum, and normally has an enrolled student body at a place where education activities are conducted.

Qualified education expenses for the purpose of tax-free scholarships and fellowships include tuition and fees, course related expenses such as books, supplies, and equipment that are required by the eligible education institution.

A scholarship or fellowship may be taxable if the scholarship or fellowship is used for:
- Expenses that do not qualify
- Payments for services
- Scholarship prizes

29.https://studentaid.ed.gov
30.https://www.careeronestop.org/toolkit/training/find-scholarships.aspx

Expenses That Do Not Qualify

Expenses that do not qualify as qualified education expenses for the purpose of tax-free scholarships include:

- Room and Board
- Transportation Expenses
- Equipment and Other Fees not Required for Attendance

The above expenses are not qualified expenses for the tax-free scholarships and fellowships, even if the fees are a condition of enrollment and are paid directly to the education institution. Scholarships and fellowships used to pay the above expenses will lose their tax-free status and the recipient must include that portion of the scholarship or fellowship in taxable income.

Payment for Services

If a scholarship or fellowship is intended to compensate the recipient for past, present or future services, such as teaching or research, then the scholarship or fellowship is included in taxable income.

Example 8.21

Felipe receives a fellowship to attend Duke University's medical school in the amount of $80,000 per year. As a condition of the fellowship, Felipe must serve one year on staff at Duke University's Hospital upon his graduation from medical school. Since the fellowship requires one year of work in the future, the fellowship represents a payment for services and must be included in Felipe's income in the year he receives the fellowship.

Scholarship Prizes

Generally, scholarships won as a result of a competition and awarded as a prize are included in taxable income unless the scholarship meets the following requirements:

The recipient is:

- A candidate for a degree at an eligible education institution, and
- The recipient uses the proceeds to pay for qualified education expenses.

The recipient is considered a candidate for a degree if:

- The recipient is attending a primary or secondary school or is pursuing a degree at a college or university, or
- The recipient is attending an accredited education institution.

IRA Distributions

Distributions from an IRA are another source of funds to pay for college education. However, these distributions have tax implications that need to be considered. In addition, the planner should work with the client to determine if taking distributions from an IRA will adversely impact retirement goals.

With distributions from IRAs, taxpayers need to be concerned with whether the distribution is subject to income tax and whether it is subject to a penalty. Distributions from a traditional IRA are generally included in taxable income and may be subject to an early withdrawal penalty if the distribution is made prior to the attainment of age 59½. However, there is an exception to the penalty if the distribution from the IRA is used to pay for higher education expenses.[31] Therefore, distributions from an IRA can be used for college funding, but will generally be treated as taxable income.

There are also tax implications to using distributions from Roth IRAs as a source of funds for college funding. Roth IRAs are generally funded with after-tax contributions or conversions from traditional IRAs.

The tax characteristics of funds held in a Roth IRA take one of three forms:

1. Contributions
2. Conversions
3. Earnings

Contributions to a Roth IRA consist of after-tax dollars for which no tax deduction is taken at the time of the contribution. Contributions to a Roth IRA represent the owner's basis in the IRA and can be withdrawn, without tax consequences at any time.

Conversions represent pre-tax dollars, typically in a Traditional IRA, that were converted to a Roth IRA. The account owner recognized income on the amount converted and the conversion became after-tax dollars since income was recognized and income taxes were paid on the converted amount. Conversions represent the owner's basis in the IRA and can be withdrawn, without tax consequences at any time. However, conversions withdrawn within five years of the date of conversion may be subject to a 10 percent penalty.

Earnings represent the growth from investing contributions and conversions. Distributions of earnings may be tax-free, if the distribution is a qualified distribution.

A qualified distribution from a Roth IRA must meet the following two requirements:

1. The distribution must occur at least five years after the Roth IRA owner established and funded the Roth IRA, and
2. At least one of the following requirements must be met:
   - The Roth IRA holder must be at least age 59½ when the distribution occurs
   - The Roth IRA owner becomes disabled
   - Death of the Roth IRA owner
   - Distributed assets limited to $10,000 are used towards the purchase or rebuilding of a first home for the Roth IRA holder or a qualified family member.

If the distribution is a qualified distribution, there is no tax or penalty associated with the distribution. If the distribution is not a qualified distribution, then any amount distributed in excess of the contributions and conversions will be treated as taxable income, but will not be subject to the 10 percent

---

31. This exception does not apply to distributions from qualified plans.

penalty if the funds are used for qualified higher education expenses. Qualified higher education expenses include tuition, fees, books, supplies, and equipment at an eligible educational institution for the taxpayer, the taxpayer's spouse, the taxpayer's child, or the taxpayer's grandchild. An eligible educational institution is any college, university, vocational school, or other postsecondary educational institution eligible to participate in the student aid programs administered by the U.S. Department of Education.

While the funds inside the Roth IRA are not countable assets for financial aid calculation purposes, the distributions are reported as untaxed income on the FAFSA and may impact the need-based financial aid offered for the academic year that begins two years after the year of the distribution (based on prior-prior year income reporting on the FAFSA). For this reason, saving for college in a Section 529 Savings Plan is more advantageous than saving in a Roth IRA with the intent to distribute contribution amounts to pay for college expenses. As mentioned above, it is important to keep in mind that using assets in an IRA to fund education expenses may impact the attainment of a client's retirement goal. It may be more appropriate to borrow for education expenses, as you cannot borrow to finance a retirement goal.

Uniform Gift to Minors Act (UGMA) & Uniform Transfer to Minors Act (UTMA) Custodial Accounts

The **Uniform Gift to Minors Act (UGMA)** allows minors to own cash or securities. The **Uniform Transfer to Minors Act (UTMA)** allows minors to own cash, securities, and real estate. The UGMA / UTMA accounts are governed by state law that requires the custodian of the account, usually a parent or grandparent, to manage the account for the benefit of the minor child. When the child reaches age of majority (18 or 21 depending on the state), the child can access the account without permission of the custodian.

> ### ✍️ *Quick Quiz 8.7*
>
> 1. Traditional IRA distributions by an individual prior to age 59½ made for qualified education expenses are subject to a 10% tax penalty.
>   a. True
>   b. False
>
> 2. An UGMA account allows a minor to own cash or securities and an UTMA account allows minors to own cash, securities, and real estate.
>   a. True
>   b. False
>
> 3. An employer-provided education assistance program only reimburses employees for education expenses directly related to the employee's current job duties.
>   a. True
>   b. False
>
> False, True, False.

UGMA and UTMA accounts were popular education savings accounts prior to the passage of Section 529 (Prepaid Tuition and Savings Plans). However, there are two primary disadvantages to using UGMA / UTMA accounts to fund a college education.

The first disadvantage is that once a child reaches the age of majority, he can use the assets in an UGMA / UTMA for something other than a college education. The account custodian, or parent, will be unable to control the asset to ensure the funds are used for a college education.

The second disadvantage is that the earnings in the UGMA / UTMA may cause a "kiddie tax" issue. The kiddie tax rules state that if unearned income is above a certain threshold ($2,200 in 2021), then the additional unearned income is taxed at the parents' tax rate, which is likely to be higher than the child's rate. Unearned income is any income that is not derived from working, which includes interest, dividends, and realized capital gains.

To be subject to the kiddie tax rules, one of the following conditions must be present:
- Children under the age of 19, or
- Full time students under the age of 24.[32]

Example 8.22

Huey, age 8, has an UGMA account that earned $2,500 in interest in 2021. Since Huey is under age 19 and has unearned income in excess of $2,200, he is subject to the kiddie tax rules. The first $2,200 will be taxed at Huey's tax rate, $300 will be taxed at his parents' tax rate.

Example 8.23

Dewey, age 19, has unearned income of $3,000 in his UGMA account in 2021. Dewey signed a contract to play professional hockey out of high school and is not attending college. Since Dewey is older than 18 years old and is not a full time student, he is not subject to the kiddie tax. The entire $3,000 will be taxed at Dewey's tax rate.

Example 8.24

Louie, age 21, is attending college full time. He has unearned income of $1,500 in his UGMA account in 2021. Although Louie is a full time student under the age of 24, his unearned income is below $2,200 (2021) therefore he is not subject to the kiddie tax. The entire $1,500 of unearned income will be taxed at Louie's tax rate.

The UGMA/UTMA custodian can control the amount of income by investing the UGMA/UTMA funds in securities such as growth stocks which produce very little, if any, income until sold, or by investing in municipal bonds which produce tax-free income.

Employer-Provided Education Assistance

An **employer-provided education assistance program** is a program established by an employer to reimburse employees for education expenses. The education expenses may or may not be directly related to the employee's current job duties; it depends on the employer's policy. Reimbursement of education expenses by an employer, up to $5,250 (2021) per year, is not taxable to the employee. Any education expenses reimbursed above $5,250 are included in income for the employee.

To qualify for the tax-free reimbursement of education expenses, the employer's education assistance program must be in writing, and the reimbursement must be for tuition, fees, books, supplies, and equipment.[33]

---

32. IRC Section 152(C)(3).
33. Payments from the employer-provided education assistance program used to repay eligible student loans of the employee after March 27, 2020 and before January 1, 2026 are also tax free (under the CARES Act through December 31, 2020, and extended under the Taxpayer Certainty and Disaster Tax Relief Act of 2020 through December 31, 2025). These payments are subject to the $5,250 maximum.

Life Insurance

In some cases, cash value life insurance may be used as a savings vehicle for college funding. If there is a dual need for a death benefit and a savings element, life insurance may be a suitable choice. For example, if the parents are just starting to save for college and they want to ensure that whether they live or die the cost of college will be funded, the death benefit can provide the needed funds if the parent dies before the full amount has been saved.

Life insurance cash values are not countable assets in the federal financial aid formula, so a significant amount of accumulation can occur without impact on financial aid. Universal life insurance policies are popular because they can be over-funded in the early years, then premium payments can be skipped while the child is in college, allowing those funds to be used to pay for additional college expenses. Variable universal policies may be utilized if the child is young and there is a desire to invest in subaccounts that offer stock and bond investments rather than a fixed interest rate.

Withdrawals from the cash value in a universal life insurance policy are taxed on a FIFO (first-in-first-out) basis, so tax-free withdrawals can be made up to the cost basis of the policy (approximately equal to the premiums paid). Once all of the basis has been distributed, additional withdrawals will be taxed as ordinary income; however, rather than continuing to take withdrawals, loans can be taken against the remaining cash value on a tax-free basis. Loans from cash value life insurance policies have the advantage of low interest rates and no required repayment schedule. The trade-off for not repaying the loan, though, is that the death benefit is reduced by the amount of the loan if the insured dies before the loan is repaid.

Private Student Loans

Private student loans (loans that are not funded or subsidized by the federal government) may be available to students who need funding beyond Stafford loans. Most private student loans will require that the parents be guarantors or cosigners of the loans, although some allow for the parent/guarantor to be removed after a set number of payments (typically 24 - 36 months) have been made on time. The terms of private student loans will vary from lender-to-lender, so a careful review of the terms of the various available private loans is essential. Private student loans are generally used only after all government-funded loans have been exhausted because the private loans have several disadvantages in comparison to federal student loans, as outlined in the exhibit below.

Exhibit 8.11 | Federal versus Private Student Loans

	Federal Student Loans	Private Student Loans
Who is the lender?	The federal government	Banks, credit unions, credit card companies, etc.
Who sets the terms of the loan?	The federal government	The lender
Is a guarantor or cosigner required?	No guarantor or cosigner required on loans to students	Will typically require a guarantor or cosigner
Does interest accrue while the student is in school?	The federal government may subsidize interest payments on some loans (e.g., Subsidized Stafford Loans) while the student is in school	Interest accrues while the student is in school (no subsidized interest payments)
Is the interest rate fixed or variable?	Fixed interest rate	Variable interest rate (may increase based on market conditions)
Will the student's or cosigner's credit score impact the interest rate?	Interest rate is not based on credit score	Rate offered is based on credit score and other factors
Are payments required while the student is enrolled in school at least half-time?	No payments required while the student is in school at least half-time	Payments may be required while the student is in school

Home Equity Loans

Home equity loans and home equity lines of credit (HELOC) are popular for funding education due to their highly competitive interest rates, but the tax deduction that was previously available for interest on the first $100,000 of home equity debt is no longer available. To qualify, the parents must meet the debt-to-income ratio requirements of the lender. The disadvantage of using a home equity loan is that the payments on the debt must start immediately and the home is used as collateral for the debt, so if financial circumstances change later and the clients are not able to make payments, the home may be at risk.

401(k) Loans

A 401(k), 403(b), or 457 retirement plan may allow for loans up to the lesser of $50,000 or 50 percent of the vested account balance. These loans must be repaid (with interest) to the plan in five years, usually by payroll deduction. The loan does not affect need-based financial aid because it is not treated as income, and there are no debt-to-income ratio requirements to qualify for the loan. The borrowed funds are not taxable, and there is no 10 percent penalty; however, if separation of service from the employer occurs before the loan is fully repaid, the entire loan balance must be immediately repaid or will be treated as a distribution subject to tax plus a 10 percent penalty if under age 59½. There is no 10 percent penalty exception for distributions from a qualified plan used to pay for higher education expenses.

COORDINATING COLLEGE SAVINGS WITH FINANCIAL AID

When a child enrolls in college, any assets held in the child's name will be considered 20 percent available by the financial aid needs analysis formula. On the other hand, the parents' discretionary assets are assessed at a maximum rate of 5.64 percent. Retirement assets, home equity, annuities, and cash value of life insurance are excluded. In addition, a portion of the parent assets are sheltered from consideration by an asset protection allowance. The allowance is based upon the age of the older of the parents. For example, if the oldest parent is age 40, then $5,500 of assets are protected for the 2021-2022 academic year (increased from $4,900 for the 2020-2021 year); if the oldest parent is age 50, then $7,000 of assets are protected (increased from $6,300 for 2020-2021). The asset protection allowance steadily decreased over the past several years, from a high of $25,100 for a 40-year-old oldest parent and $31,800 for a 50-year-old oldest parent in 2015-2016 to a low of $4,900 and $6,300 respectively in 2020-2021, but has increased slightly for 2021-2022.

In most cases the family is better off using a savings vehicle that financial aid considers a parent asset instead of one that is considered a child asset. Income is a much bigger factor than assets in determining financial aid.

The list below specifies some of the consequences of funding selections on financial aid:
- Qualified plan balances, IRA balances, and cash value of life insurance are not countable assets in the financial aid formula.
- The annual pre-tax contributions to IRAs and 401(k)s are counted as income for the year.
- Income reported on the FAFSA is for the prior-prior year; therefore, the first year of income that is reported on the FAFSA will be the year the student starts his or her junior year of high school. In other words, the base year of income that is reported on the FAFSA is two years before the high school graduation year. For example, income for 2019 will be used on the FAFSA for 2021-2022. If assets held in a taxable brokerage account are to be sold to pay for college, parents can reduce the amount of income reported on the FAFSA by selling in the year the student begins his or her sophomore year of high school, 2018 for students starting college in the fall of 2021. (See Exhibit 8.13)
- Since student assets have a greater impact on financial aid, assets in the student's name (e.g., UGMA and UTMA accounts) should be spent first; preferably before the first FAFSA is filed. Since UGMA/UTMA funds can used for any purpose that benefits the child, and assets are reported as of the FAFSA filing date, these funds can be used in the fall of the student's senior year of high school to purchase items the student will need at college that are not qualified expenses for other types of savings vehicles (e.g. furniture for an apartment, bed sheets and towels, travel to visit colleges, etc.).
- 529 Savings Plans, including UGMA and UTMA- owned 529 plans, are considered assets of the parent in the financial aid formula.
- Qualified distributions from a 529 Savings Plan owned by the parent or the child are not treated as income on the FAFSA if the child is a dependent of the parent. If the 529 Savings Plan is owned by a third party, such as a grandparent or a non-custodial divorced parent, the assets do not show up on the FAFSA, but qualified distributions are treated as untaxed income to the child on the FAFSA for the academic year beginning two years after the year of the distribution (based on prior-prior year income reporting). This income for a child has a greater negative impact on financial aid than assets of the parent, so ownership by third parties should generally be avoided or distributions limited to the final two years of college when the distributions will no longer impact financial aid.

- When a trust has been established to provide for the education of the student as the beneficiary, the trust assets are typically included as student assets on the FAFSA, and distributions to the student/beneficiary are treated as student income.

Exhibit 8.12 | Capital Gains and FAFSA

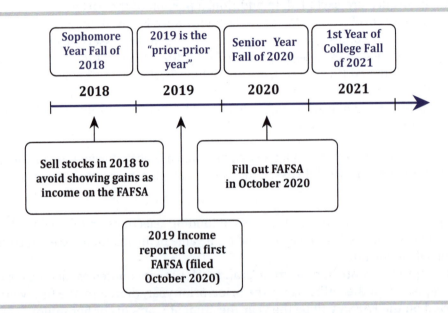

Exhibit 8.13 | Impact of Funding Choices on Financial Aid

	Countable Asset?	Countable Income?
Qualified plan balances, IRA balances, cash value in life insurance	No	N/A
Annual pre-tax contributions to IRAs and 401(k)s	No	Yes
UGMA/UTMA with student as beneficiary	Account balance is student asset HIGH NEGATIVE IMPACT	Yes - income is student income HIGH NEGATIVE IMPACT
529 savings plan when student is a dependent of the parent; owned by student or parent	Account balance is parent asset (even if it is an UGMA/UTMA 529)	No (if qualified distributions)
529 savings plan owned by a third party (e.g., grandparent)	No	Yes - distribution is student income HIGH NEGATIVE IMPACT
Education Savings Account (ESA) when student is a dependent of the parent; owned by student or parent	Account balance is parent asset	No (if qualified distribution)
Education Savings Account (ESA) owned by a third party (e.g., grandparent)	No	Yes - distribution is student income HIGH NEGATIVE IMPACT

Exhibit 8.14 | Typical Education Funding Techniques

High-Income Families	Middle and Low-Income Families
Section 529 Plans UGMA/UTMA PLUS Loans Unsubsidized Stafford Loans Scholarships	Section 529 Plans UGMA/UTMA Coverdell ESA Series EE Bonds American Opportunity Tax Credit Lifetime Learning Credit Interest Deduction on Higher Education Loans Subsidized Stafford Loans PLUS Loans Grants Scholarships

EDUCATION FUNDING NEEDS ANALYSIS

By using our time value of money skills, we are able to determine the lump sum required to fund a college education or annual savings required to attain a lump sum to pay for college. **Education funding needs analysis** represents a coalescing of many of the concepts covered in Chapter 7 and are some of the more challenging time value of money calculations. There are four primary methods for solving an education funding calculation, which are:

1. Uneven Cash Flow Method
2. Traditional Method
3. Account Balance Method
4. Hybrid Approach

> ### Key Concepts
>
> 1. Identify the steps of the uneven cash flow method used for education funding.
>
> 2. Identify the four methods used to calculate education funding.

College education funding calculations can be made by various methods. The planner can use real, rather than nominal dollars or vice versa. The financial planner can use an annuity due concept coupled with either a real or nominal dollar calculation or an ordinary annuity concept. Some additional college education funding alternatives include:

- Fully fund the plan today, as a grandparent might by using a 529 Plan.
- Fund the plan from date of birth to the start date of college.
- Fund the plan from date of birth through the expected college years (or some other fixed period).
- Fund the savings in an ordinary annuity funding plan on a monthly or yearly basis.
- Fund the savings in an annuity due funding plan on a monthly, yearly, or serial payment basis.

All of these possible variations make education funding calculations seem quite different whereas they are relatively similar. The traditional method uses real dollars and an annuity due funding plan to determine the present value of the education today. The account balance method uses nominal dollars initially and then an annuity due concept. The hybrid approach uses an ordinary annuity concept. Refer to Chapter 7 for information and examples related to the hybrid approach and establishing timelines for time value of money calculations.

Uneven Cash Flow Method

The uneven cash flow method is a good approach for education funding calculations because it consists of only two steps and it works for any type of education funding situation. Other methods may not work if a client continues saving while the child is attending college and will only work if the client stops saving when the child starts going to college.

The uneven cash flow method has two steps:
1. Determine the net present value of the cash flow stream in today's dollars. This step will determine the lump-sum amount needed today, to fund the college education goal. During this step, be sure to use an inflation adjusted rate of return.
2. Determine the annual savings required to fund the education goal. During this step, be sure to determine how long the client intends to save and whether the savings payments are at the beginning or end of the year.

Saving Until the Child Reaches College Age

In this example, we will determine the amount required to save each year, assuming the client saves until the child reaches college age.

Example 8.25

Jan wants to plan for her daughter's education. Her daughter, Rachel was born today and will go to college at age 18 for five years. Tuition is currently $15,000 per year, in today's dollars. Jan anticipates tuition inflation of 7% and believes she can earn an 11% return on her investments. How much must Jan save at the end of each year, if she wants to make her last payment at the beginning of her daughter's first year of college?

Step #1: Determine the NPV at time period zero of the cash flows. Recall that this step determines the amount that could be deposited today, to satisfy the education funding need.

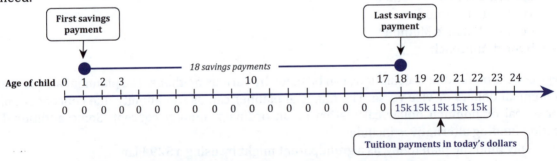

10BII Keystrokes	12C Keystrokes
0 [CFj]	0 [g] [CF0]
0 [CFj]	0 [g] [CFj]
17 [ORANGE] [Nj]	17 [g] [Nj]
15,000 [+/-] [CFj]	15,000 [CHS] [g] [CFj]
5 [ORANGE] [Nj]	5 [g] [Nj]
1.11 ÷ 1.07 - 1 x 100 = [I/YR]	1.11 [ENTER] 1.07 [÷] 1[−] 100 x
[ORANGE] [NPV]	[i]
	[f] [NPV]
Answer: < 36,046.41>	**Answer: <36,046.41>**

Step #2: Determine the annual savings required to meet the education goal. Note: During this step it is important to determine two items: (1) How long does the client intend to save and (2) When will the savings payments be made? In this problem, Jan's daughter was born today and Jan intends to save until the beginning of her daughter's first year of college or 18 years of savings. Jan also intends to "save at the end of each year" which indicates that this is an ordinary annuity problem (END mode).

10BII Keystrokes	*12C Keystrokes*
18 [N]	18 [n]
11 [I/YR]	11 [i]
36,046.41 [PV]	36,046.41 [PV]
0 [FV]	0 [FV]
[PMT]	[PMT]
Answer: <4,680.37>	**Answer: <4,680.37>**

Therefore, Jan must save $4,680.37 each year, at the end of each year, for the next 18 years to satisfy her education goal.

Saving Until the Child's Last Year of College

In this section, we will assume that the client is going to save until the child's last year of college. Note how this funding approach impacts the annual savings required.

Example 8.26

Assume that Jan decides to save until the beginning of her daughter's last year of college, how much would Jan have to save at the end of each year to meet her goal? Recall the other facts are: tuition is currently $15,000 per year, tuition inflation is 7%, Jan's investment return is expected to be 11%, and her daughter will go to college at age 18 for five years.

Step #1: Determine the NPV at time period zero of the cash flows. This step in the problem does not change from the previous example.

10BII Keystrokes	*12C Keystrokes*
0 [CFj]	0 [g] [CF0]
0 [CFj]	0 [g] [CFj]
17 [ORANGE] [Nj]	17 [g] [Nj]
15,000 [+/-] [CFj]	15,000 [CHS] [g] [CFj]
5 [ORANGE] [Nj]	5 [g] [Nj]
1.11 ÷ 1.07 - 1 x 100 = [I/YR]	1.11 [ENTER] 1.07 [÷] 1[–] 100 x [i]
[ORANGE] [NPV]	[f] [NPV]
Answer: <36,046.41>	**Answer: <36,046.41>**

Step #2: Determine the annual savings required to meet the education goal. Recall we must determine two items: (1) How long does the client intend to save and (2) When will the savings payments be made? In this problem, Jan's daughter was born today and Jan intends to save until the beginning of her daughter's **last** year of college or 22 years of savings. Jan also intends to "save at the end of each year" which indicates that this is an ordinary annuity problem (END mode).

10BII Keystrokes	*12C Keystrokes*
22 [N]	22 [n]
11 [I/YR]	11 [i]
36,046.41 [PV]	36,046.41 [PV]
0 [FV]	0 [FV]
[PMT]	[PMT]
Answer: <4,408.95>	**Answer: <4,408.95>**

Example 8.27

Instead of Jan making her savings payments at the end of each year, lets assume she makes her savings payments at the beginning of each year. So, if Jan decides to save until the beginning of her daughter's last year of college, how much would Jan have to save at the beginning of each year to meet her goal? Recall the other facts are: Tuition is currently $15,000 per year, tuition inflation is 7%, Jan's investment return is expected to be 11%, and her daughter will go to college at age 18 for five years.

Step #1: Determine the NPV at time period zero of the cash flows. There are no changes to this step of the calculation.

10BII Keystrokes	**12C Keystrokes**
0 [CFj]	0 [g] [CF0]
0 [CFj]	0 [g] [CFj]
17 [ORANGE] [Nj]	17 [g] [Nj]
15,000 [+/-] [CFj]	15,000 [CHS] [g] [CFj]
5 [ORANGE] [Nj]	5 [g] [Nj]
1.11 , 1.07 - 1 x 100 = [I/YR]	1.11 [ENTER] 1.07 [÷] 1[−] 100 x [i]
[ORANGE] [NPV]	[f] [NPV]
Answer: <36,046.41>	**Answer: <36,046.41>**

Step #2: Determine the annual savings required to meet the education goal. We must determine: (1) How long does the client intend to save and (2) When will the savings payments be made? In this problem, Jan's daughter was born today and Jan intends to save at the beginning of the year and until the beginning of her daughter's **last** year of college. Since Jan is going to start saving today, that represents the first savings payment, such that when her daughter is 22, Jan will be making her 23rd savings payment. Jan intends to "save at the beginning of each year" which indicates that this is an annuity due problem (BEGIN mode).

10BII Keystrokes	**12C Keystrokes**
[ORANGE] [BEG/END]	[g] [BEG]
23 [N]	23 [n]
11 [I/YR]	11 [i]
36,046.41 [PV]	36,046.41 [PV]
0 [FV]	0 [FV]
[PMT]	[PMT]
Answer: 3,928.45	**Answer: 3,928.45**

Multiple Children

The best approach to use in calculating education funding for multiple children is using the uneven cash flow method. This method allows the planner to combine multiple cash flows during the same time periods.

Example 8.28

Joe has two children, Sydney age 5 and William age 2, that he wants to provide for their education funding. Currently, tuition is $10,000 per year and tuition inflation is 6%. Joe expects to earn 10% on his investments and he expects the children to start college at age 18 and go to college for 4 years. Joe wants his last savings payment to be made when the oldest child starts college. How much must Joe save at the end of each year?

Step #1: Determine the NPV at time period zero of the cash flows. Recall that this step determines the amount that could be deposited today, to satisfy the education funding need.

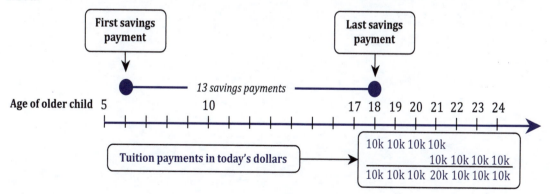

10BII Keystrokes	12C Keystrokes
0 [CFj]	0 [g] [CF0]
0 [CFj]	0 [g] [CFj]
12 [ORANGE] [Nj]	12 [g] [Nj]
10,000 [+/-] [CFj]	10,000 [CHS] [g] [CFj]
3 [ORANGE] [Nj]	3 [g] [Nj]
20,000 [+/-] [CFj]	20,000 [CHS] [g] [CFj]
10,000 [+/-] [CFj]	10,000 [CHS] [g] [CFj]
3 [ORANGE] [Nj]	3 [g] [Nj]
1.10 ÷ 1.06 - 1 x 100 = [I/YR]	1.10 [ENTER] 1.06 [÷] 1 [–] 100 x [i]
[ORANGE] [NPV]	[f] [NPV]
Answer: <44,334.65>	Answer: <44,334.65>

Step #2: Determine the annual savings required to meet the education goal. Note: During this step it is important to determine two criteria: (1) How long does the client intend to save and (2) When will the savings payments be made? In this problem, Joe's oldest child is 5 and he intends to save until she starts college, which is in 13 years. He also indicates that he wants to "save at the end of each year" which indicates that this is an ordinary annuity problem (END mode).

10BII Keystrokes	12C Keystrokes
13 [N]	13 [n]
10 [I/YR]	10 [i]
44,334.65 [PV]	44,334.65 [PV]
0 [FV]	0 [FV]
[PMT]	[PMT]
Answer: <6,241.37>	Answer: <6,241.37>

Traditional Method

The traditional method of education funding uses real dollars and the annuity due funding plan to calculate the present value of the cost of education.

Example 8.29

Continuing with **Example 8.25** where Jan is interested in funding the college education of her daughter, Rachel, the traditional method is applied.

Step 1: Determine the present value at age 18 using real dollars.

10BII Keystrokes	*12C Keystrokes*
[ORANGE] [BEG/END] 5 [N] 1.11 [÷] 1.07 – 1 x 100 = [I/YR] 15,000 [PMT]$_{AD}$ 0 [FV] [PV]	[g] [BEG] 5 [n] 1.11 [ENTER] 1.07 [÷] 1 [-] 100 [x] [i] 15,000 [PMT]$_{AD}$ 0 [FV] [PV]
Answer: <69,785.90>	**Answer: <69,785.90>**

Step 2: Determine the present value at age zero using real dollars.

10BII Keystrokes	*12C Keystrokes*
18 [N] 1.11 [÷] 1.07 – 1 x 100 = [I/YR] 0 [PMT] 69,785.90 [FV] [PV]	18 [n] 1.11 [ENTER] 1.07 [÷] 1 [-] 100 [x] [i] 0 [PMT] 69,785.90 [FV] [PV]
Answer: <36,046.41>	**Answer: <36,046.41>**

Step 3: Treat the present value calculated above as an opportunity for grandparent(s) to fully fund a 529 Plan (at a cost of $36,046.41). Alternatively, determine the amount the parents will have to save by treating the present value as a mortgage to be paid off by Rachel's age 18 as an ordinary annuity or annuity due at the earnings rate (in this example, 11%).

10BII Keystrokes	*12C Keystrokes*
[ORANGE] [BEG/END] 18[N] 11 [I/YR] 0 [FV] 36,046.41 [PV] [PMT]$_{OA}$	[g] [END] 18 [n] 11 [i] 0 [FV] 36,046.41 [PV] [PMT]$_{OA}$
Answer: <4,680.37>*	**Answer: <4,680.37>***

* Annual payment amount.

Summary of Savings Options

A financial planner should be able to present a client with alternative strategies to save for college education, such that the best strategy is implemented. Options to lower the amount of annual savings required include continuing to save while the child is in college and making savings payments at the beginning of each year. The primary consideration for the client when determining which funding strategy to use is the amount of current income available for education savings.

	Saving Until Age 18	Saving Through College (Age 22)	Saving Through College (Age 22) and Saving at the Beginning of each Year
Annual Savings	$4,680.37	$4,408.95	$3,928.45
Total Savings Contributions	$84,246.66	$96,996.90	$90,354.35

Traditional Method and Serial Payments

As indicated, the traditional method of education fund uses real dollars and the annuity due funding plan to calculate the present value of the cost of education.

Example 8.30

Benjamin and Betty Shelton would like to save for their son, Blake's, college education. They expect Blake, who was born today, to attend a private college for 4 years starting at age 18. Current tuition at the college of their choice is $20,000 per year. Tuition inflation rate is expected to be 7 percent, while CPI is expected to be 3 percent. The Sheltons expect to earn twelve percent after-tax return on their investments. How much should they deposit in a lump-sum amount into a college fund today to fully fund the education?

10BII Keystrokes	12C Keystrokes
[ORANGE] [BEG/END] 4 [N] 1.12 ÷ 1.07 - 1 x 100 = [I/YR] 20,000 [PMT] 0 [FV] [PV] Answer: <74,800.51> 18 [N] 4.6729 [I/YR] 0 [PMT] 74,800.51 [FV] [PV] Answer: <32,876.69>	[g] [BEG] 4 [n] 1.12 [ENTER] 1.07 [÷] 1[−] 100 x [i] 20,000 [PMT] 0 [FV] [PV] Answer: <74,800.51> 18 [n] 4.6729 [i] 0 [PMT] 74,800.51 [FV] [PV] Answer: <32,876.69>

Example 8.31

Assume the same Shelton education funding situation except instead of a lump sum invested today, the Sheltons would like to invest annually in equal payments at the <u>end</u> of each year (ordinary annuity). What should their annual investment be assuming the last investment is made when Blake is 18 years old?

10BII Keystrokes	12C Keystrokes
18 [N]	18 [n]
12 [I/YR]	12 [i]
0 [FV]	0 [FV]
32,876.69 [PV]	32,876.69 [PV]
[PMT]$_{OA}$	[PMT]$_{OA}$
Answer: <4,534.92>	Answer: <4,534.92>

Example 8.32

Assume the same Shelton education funding situation except they would like to invest annually in equal payments at the <u>beginning</u> of each year (annuity due). What should their annual investment be assuming the last investment is made when Blake is 18 years old?

10BII Keystrokes	12C Keystrokes
[ORANGE] [BEG/END]	[g] [BEG]
19 [N]	19 [n]
12 [I/YR]	12 [i]
0 [FV]	0 [FV]
32,876.69 [PV]	32,876.69 [PV]
[PMT]$_{AD}$	[PMT]$_{AD}$
Answer: <3,985.21>	Answer: <3,985.21>

Serial Payments

Example 8.33

Assume the same Shelton education funding situation except that instead of a lump sum invested today, the Sheltons would like to make serial saving payments at the end of each year until Blake is 18 years old. What would be their first and second payments (with a tuition inflation rate of 7 percent?

10BII Keystrokes	12C Keystrokes
18 [N]	18 [n]
4.6729 [I/YR]	4.6729 [i]
74,800.51 [FV]	74,800.51 [FV]
0 [PV]	0 [PV]
[PMT]$_{OA}$	[PMT]$_{OA}$
Answer: <2,741.05>	Answer: <2,741.05>

$PMT_0 = 2,741.05$
$PMT_1 = 2,741.05 \times 1.07 = 2,932.93$
$PMT_2 = 2,932.93 \times 1.07 = 3,138.23$

The first payment is equal to payment at time zero ($2,741.05) increased by inflation for one year. All subsequent payments are increased by the rate of inflation over the prior period's payment.

Account Balance Method

The account balance method is a three-step approach that determines the lump-sum amount needed when the child starts college and how much must be saved to attain that lump-sum amount. Note that the method assumes parents will stop saving when the child starts college and begins withdrawals.

Example 8.34

Harold and Maude Clark's son, Seth, was born today. They anticipate that Seth will begin college at age 18. College education expenses are $25,000 per year in today's dollars and are expected to increase at an annual rate of six percent. The Clarks can earn an after-tax annual return of 11 percent. How much should the Clarks deposit at the end of each year to pay for Seth's education. The last deposit will be made when Seth reaches his 18th birthday.

Step #1: Calculate the future value cost of one year of Seth's education in 18 years (based on today's cost of $25,000-in nominal dollars).

10BII Keystrokes	12C Keystrokes
18 [N]	18 [n]
6 [I/YR]	6 [i]
25,000 [PV]	25,000 [PV]
0 [PMT]	0 [PMT]
[FV]	[FV]
Answer: <71,358.48>	**Answer: <71,358.48>**

Step #2: Calculate the amount of education funding needed at Seth's age 18.

10BII Keystrokes	12C Keystrokes
[ORANGE] [BEG/END]	[g] [BEG]
4 [N]	4 [n]
1.11 ÷ 1.06 - 1 x 100 = [I/YR]	1.11 [ENTER] 1.06 [÷] 1[−] 100 x [i]
0 [FV]	0 [FV]
71,358.48 [PMT]$_{AD}$	71,358.48 [PMT]$_{AD}$
[PV]	[PV]
Answer: <266,720.48>	**Answer: <266,720.48>**

Step #3: Calculate how much in annual savings is necessary to reach the age 18 savings goal.

10BII Keystrokes	12C Keystrokes
18 [N]	18 [n]
11 [I/YR]	11 [i]
266,720.48 [FV]	266,720.48 [FV]
0 [PV]	0 [PV]
[PMT]$_{OA}$	[PMT]$_{OA}$
Answer: <5,292.50>	**Answer: <5,292.50>**

Comparison of the Account Balance Method to the Traditional Method

The example below illustrates the use of the traditional method to calculate the annual savings for Seth. The annual savings is the same using both methods. However, the approaches are different.

Example 8.35

Step #1: Calculate the present value of the cost of Seth's education in real dollars at his age 18.

10BII Keystrokes	12C Keystrokes
[ORANGE] [BEG/END]	[g] [BEG]
4 [N]	4 [n]
1.11 ÷ 1.06 - 1 x 100 = [I/YR]	1.11 [ENTER] 1.06 [÷] 1[−] 100 x [i]
0 [FV]	0 [FV]
25,000[PMT]$_{AD}$	25,000 [PMT]$_{AD}$
[PV]	[PV]
Answer: <93,443.86> (in real dollars)	**Answer: <93,443.86>** (in real dollars)

Step #2: Calculate the present value today of the cost of funding Seth's education at 18.

10BII Keystrokes	12C Keystrokes
18 [N]	18 [n]
1.11 ÷ 1.06 - 1 x 100 = [I/YR]	1.11 [ENTER] 1.06 [÷] 1 [−] 100 x [i]
93,443.86 [FV]	93,443.86 [FV]
0 [PMT]$_{OA}$	0 [PMT]$_{OA}$
[PV]	[PV]
Answer: <40,760.80>	**Answer: <40,760.80>**

Step #3: Calculate how much in annual savings is necessary to reach the age 18 savings goal.

10BII Keystrokes	12C Keystrokes
18 [N]	18 [n]
11 [I/YR]	11 [i]
0 [FV]	0 [FV]
40,760.80 [PV]	40,760.80 [PV]
[PMT]$_{OA}$	[PMT]$_{OA}$
Answer: <5,292.50>	**Answer: <5,292.50>**

Hybrid Approach

The hybrid approach combines the concepts of the uneven cash flow and account balance methods.

Example 8.36

Jen and Neal are planning to save for their daughter Averey's college education. Averey was born today and will attend college for 4 years, starting at age 18. Tuition currently costs $20,000 per year and tuition inflation is expected to be 6%. They believe they can earn 9% on their investments. How much must Jen and Neal save at the end of each year using the hybrid approach?

Step #1: Determine the present market value of the tuition payments at age 17.

10BII Keystrokes	12C Keystrokes
4 [N]	4 [n]
1.09 ÷ 1.06 - 1 x 100 = [I/YR]	1.09 [ENTER] 1.06 [÷] 1[–] 100 x [i]
20,000 [PMT]	20,000 [PMT]
0 [FV]	0 [FV]
[PV]	[PV]
Answer: <74,644.84>	**Answer: <74,644.84>**

Step #2: Determine the present value of the lump sum calculated from Step #1, at time period zero.

10BII Keystrokes	12C Keystrokes
17 [N]	17 [n]
1.09 ÷ 1.06 - 1 x 100 = [I/YR]	1.09 [ENTER] 1.06 [÷] 1[–] 100 x [i]
0 [PMT]	0 [PMT]
74,644.84 [FV]	74,644.84 [FV]
[PV]	[PV]
Answer: <46,446.08>	**Answer: <46,446.08>**

Step #3: Determine the annual savings required to fund the college tuition.

10BII Keystrokes	12C Keystrokes
18 [N] 9 [I/YR] 46,446.08 [PV] 0 [FV] [PMT] **Answer: <5,304.71>**	18 [n] 9 [i] 46,446.08 [PV] 0 [FV] [PMT] **Answer: <5,304.71>**

The hybrid approach is the least often used method because the ordinary annuity concept can be confusing to the first-time learner. Note that with the same facts, all methods lead to the same answer.

Exhibit 8.15 | Summary of Education Funding Methods

Method	Real or Nominal Dollars	Number of Steps to Present Value	Total Steps to Annual Funding	Annuity Method of Calculation*
Uneven Cash Flow	Real	1	2	Annuity Due
Traditional	Real	2	3	Annuity Due
Account Balance	Nominal/Real	2 steps to Future Value (at college age 18)	3 Total	Annuity Due
Hybrid	Real	2 steps to Present Value	3	Ordinary Annuity

The use of the annuity due calculation generally means that present value is calculated using 18 periods. The use of ordinary annuity calculation (hybrid approach) uses 17 periods.

CONCLUSION

For many families, paying for their children's college education is one of their largest financial goals, next to retiring and paying off debt. It is the responsibility of the financial planner to help the client prioritize how to allocate their cash flow and savings. Paying off a mortgage, fully funding a retirement, and saving an adequate amount for education may not be possible for some families. The planner should advise the client as to all of the education funding options, including financial aid (grants, loans, and work-study) and scholarships. The planner should also advise the family regarding tax-deferred savings, tax deductions, and tax credits.

With the average cost of tuition ranging from $10,000 for a public state university and up to $35,000 + for a private university, it is important for the financial planner to also consider other cost factors besides tuition when determining the total cost of attendance, (such as room and board, insurance, travel, entertainment etc.). The total cost of attending college is likely to be an additional 50 to 75 percent of the cost of tuition. Tax deferred savings is an ideal way to save for education funding for clients with the means to save for a college education and a time horizon greater than 10 years. The longer the time horizon until the child enters college, the more beneficial tax deferred savings becomes. As the education funding needs analysis section of this chapter demonstrated, the longer the time horizon (savings period), the less the family must save each year. The planner should present alternative saving strategies to the client to determine which strategy is most likely to be implemented (based on the amount of income available for education funding).

For clients that do not have the means to save for college education or do not have a sufficient time horizon to take advantage of tax deferred savings, the financial planner must advise the family as to the various types of financial aid, such as grants and loans. It is also important that the planner advise the client as to the tax consequences of grants, loans, scholarships and possible tax deductions and credits related to education. With changing tax laws, education planning can be a challenging area for planners that is also very rewarding when helping a family achieve education funding goals for their children.

DISCUSSION QUESTIONS

SOLUTIONS to the discussion questions can be found exclusively within the chapter. Once you have completed an initial reading of the chapter, go back and highlight the answers to these questions.

1. List and define the three methods used to determine the Expected Family Contribution (EFC) for financial aid.

2. Distinguish the difference between an educational grant and an educational loan.

3. List the repayment options for a Stafford Loan.

4. What are the two types of PLUS Loans?

5. What are the consequences for defaulting on student loans?

6. Define the two types of qualified tuition plans.

7. Define a Coverdell Education Savings Account (ESA).

8. Discuss a tax advantage to the student loan interest deduction.

9. Distinguish between the American Opportunity Tax Credit and the Lifetime Learning Credit.

10. Discuss tax deductions / tax credits restrictions as pertains to education expenses.

11. Discuss the differences between scholarships and fellowships.

12. Explain the disadvantages to using UGMA / UTMA accounts to fund a college education.

13. Discuss the features of a nontaxable employer-provided education assistance program.

14. List and briefly describe the four primary methods for calculating the amount needed for education funding.

MULTIPLE-CHOICE PROBLEMS

A sample of multiple choice problems is provided below. Additional multiple choice problems are available at money-education.com by accessing the Student Practice Portal.

1. Which of the following statements concerning educational tax credits and savings opportunities is correct?
    a. The Lifetime Learning Credit is equal to 10% of qualified educational expenses up to a certain limit.
    b. The American Opportunity Tax Credit (AOTC) is only available for the first 3 years of postsecondary education.
    c. A parent who claims a child as a dependent is entitled to take the AOTC credit for the educational expenses of the child.
    d. The contribution limit for Coverdell Education Savings Accounts is applied per year per donor.

2. Mitch and Nina have AGI of $125,000 and have not planned for their children's education. Their children are ages 17 and 18 and the parents anticipate paying $20,000 per year, per child for education expenses. Which of the following is the most appropriate recommendation to pay for the children's education?
    a. 529 Savings Plan.
    b. PLUS Loan.
    c. Pell Grant.
    d. Coverdell ESA.

3. The following type of financial aid is awarded to students with a low EFC, and funds are guaranteed to be available if a student qualifies:
    a. Pell Grant.
    b. Plus Loan.
    c. Work-Study.
    d. Stafford Loan.

4. What is one of the primary differences between a Coverdell ESA and a 529 Savings Plan?
    a. A Coverdell has contribution limits far below those of 529 Savings Plans.
    b. A Coverdell does not have a phase-out limit for those making contributions.
    c. A 529 Savings Plan has a phaseout limit for those making contributions.
    d. A Coverdell allows 5-year proration of contributions.

5. What is the present value of all college education for 5 children ages 0, 1, 1, 3, and 5 if the cost of education is today's dollars is $17,000 per year, education inflation is 5%, and the parents expected portfolio rate of return is 8.5%? The children are expected to be in college 4 years and they will each start at age 18.
    a. $88,775.02.
    b. $148,958.22.
    c. $192,007.89.
    d. $203,085.22.

> **Additional multiple choice problems are available at**
> *money-education.com* **by accessing the Student Practice Portal. Access requires registration of the title using the unique code at the front of the book.**

QUICK QUIZ EXPLANATIONS

Quick Quiz 8.1

1. True.
2. False. The financial aid process is initiated by completing the Free Application for Federal Student Aid (FAFSA). The Student Aid Report is available after the completion of the FAFSA and contains the EFC.

Quick Quiz 8.2

1. True.
2. True.
3. False. The grant for students pursuing a career in teaching who agree to teach at least four years in a community that serves low-income families is the TEACH grant. The FSEOG is awarded to students with exceptional financial need (those with the lowest EFC).

Quick Quiz 8.3

1. False. For an unsubsidized Stafford Loan, the borrower is responsible for interest from the time the funds are disbursed. However, the student may pay the interest expense as incurred or may choose to allow the interest to be added to the loan's outstanding principal. Interest is paid by the federal government on subsidized loans while the borrower is in school and during the six-month grace period before repayment begins.
2. True.
3. False. PLUS Loans are not based on financial need.
4. True.

Quick Quiz 8.4

1. True.
2. True.
3. False. The Act expanded education expenses to include computer technology or equipment (computer and related peripheral equipment) used for educational purposes.

Quick Quiz 8.5

1. True.
2. False. Qualified education expenses do not include room and board when using redeemed Series EE and I bonds funds.

QUICK QUIZ EXPLANATIONS

Quick Quiz 8.6
1. True.
2. False. This is the definition for the Lifetime Learning Credit. The American Opportunity Tax Credit provides a tax credit of up to $2,500 (2021) per student for the first four years of qualified education expenses.
3. False. This is the definition for a Fellowship. Scholarships are made available to students to assist with the payment of education related expenses and are for academic or athletic achievement.

Quick Quiz 8.7
1. False. IRA distributions made prior to age 59½ are typically made subject to a 10% tax penalty, which is waived when used for qualified education expenses.
2. True.
3. False. The education expenses may or may not be directly related to the employee's current job duties depending on the employer's policy.

Quick Quiz 8.8
1. False. The uneven cash flow method is the best approach to use when saving continues through the years of college attendance.
2. True.
3. False. The hybrid approach used for education funding calculation combines the concepts of the uneven cash flow and account balance methods.

9

INVESTMENTS

LEARNING OBJECTIVES

1. Understand risk tolerance and how it is measured.
2. Understand historical returns and the relationship between equities, bonds, and Treasury securities.
3. Describe the investment planning process.
4. Describe the components of an investment policy statement.
5. Describe and calculate the various measurements of investment returns.
6. Identify the various types of investment risk and how they are measured.
7. Be able to calculate standard deviation and describe beta and semi-variance.
8. Be able to identify the risk-adjusted performance measures including Sharpe, Treynor, and Jensen.
9. Describe modern portfolio theory, the efficient frontier, and the capital asset pricing model.
10. Define portfolio statistics including correlation coefficient, the coefficient of determination, and portfolio risk for a two asset portfolio.
11. Describe alternative investments such as equity, debt, real estate, and derivatives.
12. Identify the methods of valuing an equity security.
13. Identify the risks to investing in bonds, real estate, and derivatives.
14. Describe investment companies, unit investment trusts, exchange traded funds, open-ended investment companies, closed-ended investment companies, and various types of mutual funds.
15. Understand asset allocation and investment analysis for an individual client.
16. Differentiate between investment knowledge that is proper to use in the evaluation of securities and insider information.*

*Ties to CFP Certification Learning Objectives

INTRODUCTION

Investing is the process whereby capital resources are allocated and committed by investors with the expectation of earning future positive economic returns. The overall investment return expected is primarily a function of, and usually dependent upon, the riskiness of the investment. Investment returns can be in the form of current income (interest or dividends) and/or capital appreciation. This chapter discusses the relationship between risk and return and provides the financial planner with the means to measure both risk and return for the individual client/investor. Investment alternatives are then reviewed, as well as the importance of asset allocation and investment performance analysis.

Financial planners employ tools to assess the client's ability and willingness to accept investment risk, thus determining the client's risk tolerance as part of the investment planning process. An **investment policy statement** is a written document, agreed upon by the client and the adviser, which specifically identifies the investment goals of the clients and the strategies and parameters, such as risk tolerance, time horizon, asset allocation, and acceptable investment vehicles, that will be employed to reach such goals. The investment goals are stated in dollar terms and also in terms of time. To achieve the investment goals, the client should be expected to invest at a risk level consistent with an assessment of his risk tolerance. The risk tolerance assessment can be used to build an investment portfolio that has the desired expected returns that will help to achieve the client's goals. All of these factors are included in the investment planning process and are expressed in an investment policy statement (discussed later in this chapter).

INVESTMENT PLANNING

As part of the investment planning process, the financial planner evaluates the client's goals in terms of both dollar value and time. The client's goals are assessed together with risk tolerance in designing the appropriate investment strategy. The client's risk tolerance is a combination of an ability and willingness to accept investment risk. The planner will develop an investment plan considering the client's investment ability (an objective state of being, based on the client's financial profile) and willingness (a subjective state of being) to take on investment risk and to commit dollars over time to reach the investment goals. The risk tolerance questionnaire provides both the planner and the client with a clear understanding of the client's tolerance for taking risk.

Key Concepts

1. Identify the purpose of a risk tolerance questionnaire.

2. Determine how the ability and willingness of the client to accept risk is gauged.

3. Identify the four steps of the investment planning process.

4. Identify the components of an investment policy statement.

Risk Tolerance - Capacity (Ability to Handle Risk)

Ability to take on investment risk is a function of objective measures (the client's financial profile) such as the investment goals, the time horizon for each goal, the need for liquidity, the client's tax situation, and the unique circumstances facing the investor, such as a high ability to save, high salary, or low living expenses relative to income. Basically, the more a person can save, the longer the time horizon for the investment goals, and the less current the need for liquidity, the greater the investor's ability to take on risk. However, ability does not mean willingness, which is psychological in nature.

Risk Tolerance Questionnaire (Willingness to Take on Risk)

A **risk tolerance questionnaire** evaluates an investor's willingness to take on risk by inquiring about risk issues, usually by asking questions or evaluating statements, such as:

- In a volatile stock market that is expected to be down 20 percent, what percentage of your portfolio are you willing to lose?
- Rank your understanding of the stock market.
- Rank your comfort level with investing in the stock market.
- By what percentage do you want your stock portfolio to increase during an up market?

These questions and statements can help the planner determine whether the client is psychologically risk averse or risk tolerant. A risk averse investor is more conservative and requires significantly more return in order to consider investing in a higher risk investment. A risk tolerant investor is more willing to accept risk for a small increase in return than a risk averse investor.

Other questions the financial planner should ask to further evaluate risk tolerance include the investment time horizon of the investor, as follows:

- At what point in time does the investor expect to require the use of the invested capital?
- How much does the investor have in an emergency fund and how long will the funds last?
- What are the investor's short-term, intermediate term, and long-term goals?

Exhibit 9.1 | Sample Risk Tolerance Questionnaire (Abbreviated)

Risk Tolerance Questionnaire

How much do you have in cash reserves to cover non-discretionary cash flows?
1. Less than two months.
2. Two to three months.
3. Three to five months.
4. Six months or more.

How long is it until you need the money from your investment for your goal?
1. Five years or less.
2. Six to ten years.
3. Ten to fifteen years.
4. Greater than fifteen years.

If the stock market is down 20% or more for the year, how much of your investment are you willing to lose?
1. None.
2. 5% or less.
3. 10% or less.
4. It does not matter as long as the investments are appropriate for my objective.

Which statement best describes your investment experience?
1. None.
2. I have little background in purchasing stocks, some mutual funds.
3. I am comfortable with purchasing mutual funds, bonds, and stocks.
4. I have extensive investment experience with mutual funds, bonds, stocks, and derivates.

If the stock market is up 20% for the year, how much do you expect your investments to return?
1. Less than ½ of the market, however preserving capital is my primary goal.
2. Half of the market but protecting against potential losses by a riskier portfolio is not preferred.
3. 15-20% by accepting a sufficient amount of risk.
4. More than 20% by investing in an investment portfolio more risky than the market.

Total Score:_____ (Add the point value next to each response)

Point Ranges:
16 - 20: Aggressive
11 - 15: Moderately Aggressive
6 - 10: Moderate
1 - 5: Conservative

Recommended Portfolios:
Aggressive: 80% Equities / 20% Bonds
Moderately Aggressive: 65% Equities / 35% Bonds
Moderate: 50% Equities / 50% Bonds
Conservative: 20% Equities / 80% Bonds

Note: See the Approaches chapter for a discussion of the Global Portfolio Allocation Scoring System (PASS) for Individual Investors - developed by Dr. William Droms (Georgetown University) and Steven N. Strauss, (DromsStrauss Advisors Inc.). PASS will be used in the Rudolph Part 1 case.

The ability and willingness of the client to accept risk can be gauged by various factors. For example, the longer the time horizon of a client, the more risk that the client is able to accept in the investment portfolio. The client's **ability** to accept risk is associated with time horizon, liquidity needs, tax conditions, and unique circumstances. The client's **willingness** to accept risk is associated with the psychological condition of risk tolerance.

The charts below identify various potential risk tolerance levels. For example, if the client's ability to take on investment risk is higher than the client's willingness, then the financial planner needs to educate the client accordingly.

	Ability	*Willingness*
Low		✓
Medium	✓	
High	✓	

If the client's ability to take on investment risk is lower then the client's willingness, then the financial planner needs to educate until the client has a clearer understanding of his objective financial ability.

	Ability	*Willingness*
Low	✓	
Medium		✓
High		✓

Typically, only when the client's willingness and ability to take risk are equal does the financial planner proceed to develop an investment strategy. However, if willingness remains less than ability after the client is fully informed, then the planner will have to use the willingness measure to develop an investment strategy. The reverse is not true.

Once the client's risk tolerance is understood, it can be translated into a risk measurement (conservative, moderate, or aggressive) that is then used to guide investment choices.

The more risk the client is able and willing to accept, the greater the allocation of the investment portfolio to equities (stocks), which have greater volatility than bonds. Volatility is measured by standard deviation, which measures the total risk for an investment portfolio. If the client's portfolio is appropriately diversified, the financial planner can use beta for risk measurement, otherwise standard deviation should be used. Semivariance is an additional measure of risk that only takes into consideration downside volatility. The chart below illustrates the historical risk (as measured by standard deviation) and return relationship between equities, bonds, and Treasury bills (short-term U.S. government debt issues).

Exhibit 9.2 | Historical Returns, Inflation-Adjusted Returns, and Standard Deviation of Asset Classes[1]

Asset Class	Historical Returns	Inflation-Adjusted Returns	Standard Deviation	Real Return After-Tax and Inflation
Small-Capitalization Stocks	12.0%	9.0%	32.0%	6.6%
Large-Capitalization Stocks	10.0%	7.0%	20.0%	5.0%
Long-Term Government Bonds	5.5%	2.5%	10.0%	0.9%
U.S. T-Bills	3.5%	0.5%	3.0%	(0.50%)
Consumer Price Index (CPI)	3.0%	N/A	N/A	N/A

Expected Return

Expected return is generally the compound annual rate of return expected for an investment or investment portfolio. The return an investor expects from an investment is primarily a function of the riskiness of the investment(s). If an investor is investing in a risk-free asset, like a short-term U.S. Treasury bill, then both the expected rate of return and the required rate of return are likely to be relatively low. If an investor takes on substantially more risk by investing in a small startup company, the investor will require a higher expected rate of return. There are various methods of calculating actual return, which are discussed later in this chapter.

The Investment Planning Process

The **investment planning process** is a series of steps the financial planner and client follow to build an investment portfolio, which is designed to achieve the client's investment goals. The investment planning process consists of the following four steps:

1. The client and planner create a written investment policy statement (with risk tolerance having been derived from the risk tolerance questionnaire and financial profile), which serves as a guide to the client's investment strategy. The written investment policy statement assists the client by helping to ensure realistic return expectations consistent with acceptable risk and enforces discipline in the investment process.
2. The planner examines the external environment focusing on the expected short-term and intermediate term economic, political, social, legal, and tax conditions.
3. The planner and client select an investment portfolio consistent with the investment policy statement.
4. Periodic monitoring, updating, and evaluating of investment performance by the planner is required, as well as revisiting those conditions described in step 2 above.

Investment Policy Statement

An investment policy statement is a written document, agreed upon by the client and the adviser, which specifically identifies the investment goals of the clients and the strategies and parameters, such as risk tolerance, time horizon, asset allocation, and acceptable investment vehicles, that will be employed to reach such goals. The statement guides the financial planner and client regarding appropriate investment choices and serves as a benchmark to measure performance.

---

1. Approximations from 1926-2017. Assumes an equity tax rate of 20% and bond tax rate of 30%.

The investment policy statement should begin with a broad set of goal(s) such as:

- Capital appreciation for retirement
- Capital appreciation for the education goal
- Generate income to fund retirement
- Capital appreciation and preservation for a down payment on a house

The client's objectives expressed in terms of both risk and expected return should also be included in the investment policy statement. A client's return objective can be expressed either as a broad measure (capital appreciation, capital preservation, or current income) or as an absolute or relative percentage return (i.e., 8% or a spread of 4% over inflation). The returns on various asset classes for various years are presented later in this chapter.

The investment policy statement should also include a section that establishes the conditions under which the investment portfolio will be rebalanced. Rebalancing will generally be necessary when the overall riskiness of the portfolio attains a level that is inappropriate for the investor or the amount allocated to a particular asset class is inappropriate because of gains or losses in that particular asset class. By establishing a predetermined rebalancing threshold and policy, the adviser and client have a plan with which to manage the investment portfolio.

An additional section of the investment policy statement covering constraints to the investment policy should be included. The financial planner should be aware of the types of constraints that may impact the selection of investments. Constraints generally include:

- Liquidity needs (i.e., for a retiree)
- Investment time horizon
- Tax issues (taxable versus tax-deferred account)
- Social
- Legal
- Regulatory issues
- Unique circumstances to the client (i.e., dependent parent(s), high net worth client, children with special needs, etc.)

> ### 📝 Quick Quiz 9.1
>
> 1. A risk tolerance questionnaire identifies an investor's investment goals and guides the investor regarding appropriate investment choices.
>   a. True
>   b. False
>
> 2. The expected return is a function of the riskiness of an investment and is the rate of return expected for an asset or investment portfolio.
>   a. True
>   b. False
>
> 3. The investment planning process includes creating an investment policy statement, examines the external environment, involves selecting a portfolio consistent with the investment policy statement, and includes the periodic monitoring, updating and evaluating of investment performance.
>   a. True
>   b. False
>
> False, True, True.

The following exhibit depicts a simplified version of an investment policy statement that covers the criteria necessary to manage a client's investment portfolio selection.

Exhibit 9.3 | Sample Investment Policy Statement

Investment Policy Statement
Client: Michael
Age: 42 (divorced)

Goals:
- Save for retirement
- Retirement Goal: 80% of pre-retirement income at age 67
- Provide college education funding for four children (Jordan age 6, Colin age 4, Cate age 2 & Caroline age 1)
- Education Goal: Provide each child with $30,000 in today's dollars for college at their age 18

Returns and Inflation
- Expected Return: 8.5% annually or 5.5% real returns
- Expected Inflation: 3% annually
- Expected Education Inflation: 5% annually

Risks and Inflation
- Risk Tolerance: Moderately aggressive
- Risk Measure: Standard deviation for overall portfolio of 12%

Rebalance
- When the overall portfolio standard deviation is outside the range of 12% +/- 2%

Constraints
- Time Horizon Retirement: 25 years
- Time Horizon Education: 12-18 years
- Liquidity Needs: none for 12 years.
- Tax Rate: 35% marginal federal and no state income tax
- Regulatory Issues: none
- Unique: Income of $250,000 annually, lives modestly, saves 18-20% of current income, pays modest child support.

The next section of this chapter focuses on several methods of measuring investment returns, which allows a financial planner to assist clients in comparing investment performance among and between various investments.

MEASURING INVESTMENT RETURNS

The following methods of calculating actual and expected return are discussed in this section of the chapter:

- The Holding Period Return (HPR)
- The Arithmetic (Average) Return (AR)
- The Geometric Return (GR)
- Effective Annual Rate (EAR)
- The Weighted Average Return (WAR) and/or Weighted Average Expected Return
- The Internal Rate of Return (IRR)
- Dollar Weighted and Time Weighted Returns

The Holding Period Return (HPR)

The **holding period return** represents the total return for an investment or portfolio over the period of time the investment or portfolio was held. The holding period return is not a compound rate of return because there is no consideration for the time period over which the investment was made. While the calculation is straightforward, it is primarily useful when the holding period is one year. If comparing the holding period return between investments, it is important that the holding periods are the same for the two investments, so as to make a fair comparison of performance. Note that holding period return is not an annual return.

$$HPR = \frac{\text{Selling Price - Purchase Price +/- Cash Flows}}{\text{Purchase Price}}$$

Key Concepts

1. Identify the seven ways to measure actual investment returns.

2. Identify which measurements of actual investment returns take compounding into consideration and which ones do not.

3. Determine the difference between systematic risk and unsystematic risk.

4. Determine the different measurements of investment risks.

Example 9.1

Carson purchases a stock at $100 per share, receives $5 of dividends per share, and later sells the stock at $125. His holding period return is:

$$HPR = \frac{\text{Selling Price - Purchase Price +/- Cash Flows}}{\text{Purchase Price}}$$

$$HPR = \frac{\$125 - \$100 + \$5}{100}$$

HPR = 30%

While a 30% return sounds great, it does not speak to the time period over which it was earned. If the investment was held for 10 years, the return would only average 3% annually.

The following formula is an alternative method of calculating the holding period return when provided with periodic returns, instead of cash flows.

$$\text{HPR} = [(1 + r_1) \times (1 + r_2) \times ...(1 + r_n)] - 1$$

Where:
r_n = % return for period n
n = number of periods

Example 9.2

Assume Carson earns the following monthly returns:

January	0.019 = 1.9%
February	0.023 = 2.3%
March	-0.015 = (1.5%)
April	0.017 = 1.7%
May	0.0275 = 2.75%
June	0.036 = 3.6%

The six-month holding period return is equal to:

HPR = $[(1 + 0.019) \times (1 + 0.023) \times (1 + -0.015) \times (1 + 0.017) \times (1 + 0.0275) \times (1 + 0.036)] - 1$

HPR = $[(1.019) \times (1.023) \times (0.985) \times (1.017) \times (1.0275) \times (1.036)] - 1$

HPR = $[1.1116] - 1$

HPR = $0.1116 = 11.16\%$

The Arithmetic (Average) Return (AR) or Arithmetic Mean

The **arithmetic or average return** is also known as the simple average return or arithmetic mean. The arithmetic return does not take compounding into consideration, because it is a simple average return. It is the sum of all returns, divided by the number of periods:

$$\text{AR} = \frac{\sum_{i=1}^{n} r_i}{n} \quad \text{or} \quad \text{AM} = \frac{a_1 + a_2 + a_3 + ... + a_n}{n}$$

Where:
r_i = return for period i
a_n = return for period n
n = number of periods

Example 9.3

Rachael has owned a stock for three years, with the following returns:
Year 1: 12%
Year 2: 5%
Year 3: <2%>
The arithmetic return is:

$$\frac{12 + 5 + (2)}{3} = 5\%$$

While the arithmetic return is useful, it also has limitations. Since it does not take compounding into consideration, the AR can provide misleading results, especially with volatile returns.

Example 9.4

Aiden purchases a stock for $100 per share. At the end of the first year, the stock is worth $200 per share, representing a 100% return. At the end of the second year, the stock has declined to $100, representing a 50% loss.

The average return is calculated as:

$$\frac{100\% + (50\%)}{2} = 25\%$$

The average return is calculated as 25%. However, the actual return cannot possibly be 25% when the value of the stock at the end of the second year is the same as the value when it was purchased. Clearly, the actual return is 0%. Since the arithmetic return does not take compounding into consideration, the result is misleading. To overcome this limitation, the geometric return is preferred.

The Geometric Return (GR)

The **geometric return** is a time-weighted compounded rate of return. In other words, the geometric return takes compounding into consideration. The formula for the geometric return is:

$$GR = \sqrt[n]{(1 + r_1)(1 + r_2)\dots(1 + r_n)} - 1$$

Where:
  r_n = % return for period n
  n = number of periods

Example 9.5

Bennett purchases a stock for $100 per share. At the end of the first year, the stock is worth $200 per share, representing a 100% return. At the end of the second year, the stock has declined to $100, representing a 50% loss.

The geometric return is calculated as follows:

$$\sqrt{(1 + 100\%)(1 - 50\%)} - 1$$

Answer: 0%

Notice that the geometric return calculates the actual return of 0% because it takes into consideration compounding. It is a more precise calculation than the arithmetic return discussed above.

Example 9.6

Caitlynn has owned a stock for three years, with the following returns:

Year 1: 12%

Year 2: 5%

Year 3: <2%>

$$\sqrt[3]{(1.12)(1.05)(0.98)} - 1$$

Answer: 4.8442%

Note: this answer is equivalent to the internal rate of return (IRR). You should also quickly be able to calculate the arithmetic return, which is equal to 5%. The geometric mean will generally be less than or equal to the arithmetic mean.

Effective Annual Rate (EAR)

The **effective annual rate** is an investment's annual rate of return when compounding occurs more than once per year. This formula below takes into consideration the compounding of earnings.

$$EAR = \left(1 + \frac{i}{n}\right)^n - 1$$

Where:

i = stated annual interest rate

n = number of compounding periods

Example 9.7

Assume Tonya invests $100 and earns 10%, compounded quarterly. What is the effective annual rate of 10% compounded quarterly? Also, what is her investment worth at the end of the year?

The effective annual rate of 10% compounded quarterly is:

$$EAR = \left(1 + \frac{0.10}{4}\right)^4 - 1$$

$$EAR = (1 + 0.025)^4 - 1$$

$$EAR = (1.025)^4 - 1$$

$$EAR = 1.1038 - 1 = 0.1038 = 10.38\%$$

Her investment at the end of the year is worth $110.38:

This value can be determined by multiplying the beginning investment amount of $100 by the effective annual rate of 10.38% (calculated above). Alternatively, it can be found by compounding a return of 2.5% for four periods and multiplying the result by the beginning investment of $100: [$100 x $(1.025)^4$].

The Weighted Average (Expected) Return (WAR)

The **weighted average return** is based on the dollar amount or percentage of a portfolio invested in each asset or security. Investments with a larger allocation or weighting will contribute more to the overall return of the portfolio whereas investments with a smaller allocation or weighting will contribute less to the overall return of the portfolio.

Example 9.8

Aretha owns the following securities in her portfolio. What is the weighted average expected return of the portfolio?

Security	Fair Market Value	Expected Return
A	$10,000	10%
B	$15,000	8%
C	$25,000	6%

Security	Fair Market Value	Total Portfolio Value	% of Portfolio	Expected Return	Weighted Return
A	$10,000	$50,000	20%	x 10%	0.020
B	$15,000	$50,000	30%	x 8%	0.024
C	$25,000	$50,000	50%	x 6%	0.030
Weighted Average Expected Return					0.074 or 7.4%

The Internal Rate of Return (IRR)

The **Internal Rate of Return (IRR)** is the compounded annual rate of return for investments of differing cash inflows and cash outflows. The internal rate of return assumes that any periodic payments are reinvested at the internal rate of return. If an investor reinvests the income at a lower rate than the IRR, then the investor's actual IRR will be lower than originally calculated.

Example 9.9

Three years ago, Murphy purchased a stock for $20. Over the past three years, the stock has paid the following dividends, which Murphy has reinvested.

Year 1: $1.00
Year 2: $1.25
Year 3: $1.50

What is Murphy's compounded rate of return (IRR) if he sells the stock investment for $24 at the end of three years?

10BII Keystrokes	12C Keystrokes
20 [+/-] [CFj] 1.00 [CFj] 1.25 [CFj] 1.50 [+] 24 [=] [CFj] [ORANGE] [IRR/YR]	20 [CHS] [g] [CF0] 1.00 [g] [CFj] 1.25 [g] [CFj] 1.50 [ENTER] 24 [+] [g] [CFj] [f] [IRR]
Answer: 12.08%	**Answer: 12.08%**

Dollar-Weighted and Time-Weighted Returns

The dollar and time-weighted returns are internal rates of return or compounded rate of return measures. A dollar-weighted return is the IRR based on the investor's actual cash flows, while the time-weighted return is the IRR based on the security's cash flow.

Example 9.10

Arturo purchases 1 share of XO stock for $75. One year later the stock pays a dividend of $5, and Arturo purchases an additional share for $90. Arturo sells both shares of the stock one year later for $100 per share. What is Arturo's dollar-weighted and time-weighted return?

Dollar-Weighted Return

Period	Cash Flow	
0	($75)	
1	($85)	$5 dividend - $90 share purchase
2	$200	2 shares sold at $100 each

10BII Keystrokes	12C Keystrokes
75 [+/-][CFj] 85 [+/-][CFj] 200[CFj] [ORANGE] [IRR/YR]	75 [CHS] [g] [CF0] 85 [CHS] [g] [CFj] 200 [g] [CFj] [f] [IRR]
Answer: 16.19%	**Answer: 16.19%**

Time-Weighted Return

Period	Cash Flow	
0	($75)	Beginning Investment
1	$5	$5 dividend
2	$100	Ending share price

10BII Keystrokes	**12C Keystrokes**
75 [+/-][CFj] 5[CFj] 100[CFj] [ORANGE][IRR/YR]	75 [CHS] [g] [CF0] 5 [g] [CFj] 100 [g] [CFj] [f] [IRR]
Answer: 18.85%	**Answer: 18.85%**

An investor is always concerned with dollar-weighted returns because dollar-weighted returns take into consideration exactly when the shares were purchased (at what price), any subsequent cash flows (such as dividends), and when (and at what price) the shares were sold. Mutual funds always report time-weighted returns because they are concerned about the price of the fund at the beginning of a period, the end of a period, and any distributions made during the period. Depending on the cash flows of the investor, he may experience similar or vastly different rates of return compared to the investment's time-weighted return.

INVESTMENT RISKS

Risk is the uncertainty associated with investment returns. More specifically, risk is the possibility that actual returns will be different from what is expected. There is a direct relationship between risk and an investor's expected return. As risk increases, so does the investor's expected rate of return. The risk premium is the amount of return above the risk-free rate of return that an investor will require to invest in a risky asset. The risk-free rate is generally considered to be the U.S. Treasury rate. The risk premium is determined by the amount of risk associated with an investment. This next section of the chapter discusses the components of risk, the measurement of risk, and how to maximize an investor's return for any given level of risk.

Types of Investment Risks

Investments can be subject to many different risks. These risks are generally grouped into two categories: systematic risks and unsystematic risks. While unsystematic risks can be reduced or eliminated through diversification, systematic risks cannot be eliminated.

Systematic Risks

Systematic risk represents the risk that is inherent in the "system" and cannot be eliminated through diversification. The system represents U.S. market risk. Regardless of how many stocks and industries are combined into a portfolio, the portfolio will still be subject to at least one systematic risk. Examples of systematic risk are:
- Purchasing Power Risk
- Reinvestment Rate Risk
- Interest Rate Risk
- Market Risk
- Exchange Rate Risk

Purchasing Power Risk

Purchasing power risk is the risk that inflation will cause prices to increase and a dollar today will not be able to purchase the same amount of goods and services tomorrow. Investments that provide a fixed return, such as a bond paying a fixed interest rate, will be subject to more purchasing power risk than those investments that tend to change in value as prices change, such as commodities.

Reinvestment Rate Risk

Reinvestment rate risk is the risk that an investor will not be able to reinvest income received from current investments at the same rate of return as the current investment return. Investments that pay current income, such as a bond paying interest or a stock paying a dividend, are subject to reinvestment rate risk. Investments that do not pay current income, such as a non-dividend paying stock or a zero-coupon bond are not immediately subject to reinvestment rate risk.[2] Once an investment is sold, the investor is subject to reinvestment rate risk.

Interest Rate Risk

Interest rate risk is the risk that changes in interest rates will inversely impact both equities (stocks) and fixed income securities (bonds). Generally, as interest rates increase (decrease), the price of equities and bonds decreases (increases). Changes in interest rates impact the cost of borrowing for companies, the discount rate or required rate of return for investors when valuing securities and the overall attractiveness of alternative investments.

Market Risk

Market risk is the risk that in the short term, the daily fluctuations of the market tend to bring all securities in the same direction. Many securities are highly correlated with the market. The old expression, "during high tide all boats rise, during low tide all boats fall" holds true for the market and security prices. When the market increases, most equities will also increase in price. When the market declines, most equities will decrease in price.

Exchange Rate Risk

Exchange rate risk is the risk that international investments and domestic companies that import or export goods are subject to changes in the relationship between the price of a dollar and foreign currencies. Changes in foreign currency rates can adversely effect the value of foreign investments or of domestic investments with substantial foreign operations.

Unsystematic Risks

Unsystematic risk represents the risk that can be diversified away by combining multiple stocks (or securities or portfolios) from multiple industries into one portfolio. Unsystematic risks are unique to one firm, industry, or country and can be reduced and perhaps eliminated by building a diversified portfolio. Examples of unsystematic risk are:

- Accounting Risk
- Business Risk
- Country Risk
- Default Risk
- Executive Risk
- Financial Risk
- Government / Regulation Risk

---

2. The term "coupon" refers to the periodic interest payment paid to the bondholder. Zero-coupon bonds do not pay periodic interest.

Accounting Risk

As the valuation of companies is based on the free cash flow available to shareholders, accurate accounting statements is a fundamental requirement for a stock market. Without proper accounting, investors have no way to measure that which gives value to what they are buying. Accounting risk is the risk that financial statements do not accurately reflect the financial condition of a business, due to fraud or error.

Business Risk

Business risk is the inherent risk of conducting business within a particular industry. Different industries have different risks that make their industry unique. Microsoft is primarily in the software development industry and it faces the risk of copyright infringement and illegal copying and distribution of it's software. Those risks are significantly different than Exxon Mobile, which is subject to commodity pricing risk and regulatory risk. Business risk is associated with the asset side of the balance sheet.

Country Risk

Country risk is the risk of political and economic stability or instability for a country that a company faces when doing business in that particular country. Starting and operating a business in the U.S. has significantly different country risk than starting and operating a business in Iraq, Venezuela, or North Korea.

Default Risk

Default risk is the risk that a company or government may not be able to repay its debt obligations. Debt may include bonds issued by a company or municipality. U.S. Government securities (such as T-bills and Ginnie Maes) are free of default risk since they are backed by the full faith and credit of the Federal government, and the U.S. government has never defaulted on its debt obligations. Default or credit risk is on the liability side of the balance sheet.

Executive Risk

Executive risk is the risk of moral character of the executives running the company. The extent to which executives break laws, regulations, or ethical standards that may negatively impact a company and investment returns. Executives may also manage a business to generate short-term returns at the expense of long-term gains. The short-term gains may mask the risks to the long-term success of the company.

> ### ✏️ Quick Quiz 9.2
>
> 1. The holding period return represents the time period an investment return is measured.
>   a. True
>   b. False
>
> 2. The geometric return is known as the simple average return.
>   a. True
>   b. False
>
> 3. Purchasing power risk is a type of unsystematic risk and is the risk that inflation will cause prices to increase.
>   a. True
>   b. False
>
> True, False, False.

Financial Risk

Financial risk is the amount of leverage the company is using in its capital structure. Leverage is a measure of the amount of debt a company uses to capitalize the business. Capital structure may consist of a combination of both debt and equity. The more debt a company takes on, the more leverage it is using and the more financial risk that is present. Some companies have zero debt in their capital structure, so there is no financial risk. However, the airline and cable industries use high degrees of leverage because of the large initial and continuing capital investment required. Historically, both the airline and cable industries are subject to significant financial risk. Financial risk is on the liability side of the balance sheet.

Government/Regulation Risk

Government or regulation risk is the potential risk that a country may pass a law or regulation that negatively impacts a particular industry. In 2003, Japan stopped importing beef from the U.S. due to a mad cow disease breakout in the U.S. At the time, Japan was the top international importer of beef from the U.S. The impact of Japan's decision on the U.S. beef industry is an example of government or regulation risk.

One of the goals in building a portfolio is to combine stocks from a broad range of industries, which will eliminate diversifiable risk and reduce the overall variability of returns within the portfolio. As carefully selected securities are added to a portfolio, the total riskiness of the portfolio, as measured by standard deviation, is reduced. On average, a portfolio with approximately 20 carefully selected securities will result in a diversified portfolio.

Exhibit 9.4 | Total Risk

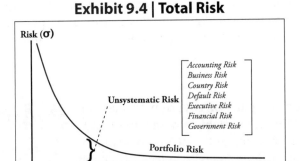

Exhibit 9.4 illustrates how unsystematic risk is reduced and may be eliminated in a well-diversified portfolio, such that the only relevant risk is systematic risk. As more securities from multiple industries are combined within a portfolio, both unsystematic risk and total risk in the portfolio will be reduced.

Measuring Investment Risks

Investment risk is broadly defined as the uncertainty surrounding returns. Risk can be measured using both Beta (β) and Standard Deviation (σ). Beta is used to measure the risk for a well-diversified investment portfolio, while standard deviation is used to measure the total risk of any investment portfolio regardless of whether the portfolio is well diversified.

Beta

Beta is a common measure of risk that is derived from regression analysis when comparing the returns for a particular security or portfolio to market benchmark returns. Beta is a measure of systematic risk and provides a comparison of the volatility of a security or portfolio to the market benchmark. The market is predefined as having a beta of 1.0. Portfolios that have a beta greater than 1.0 are more volatile than the market, whereas portfolios with a beta less than 1.0 are less volatile than the market. A portfolio with a beta of 1.50 is 50 percent more volatile than the market. A beta that is negative means that the security or portfolio generally moves the opposite direction of the market. The discussion of the capital asset pricing model later in the chapter illustrates how beta can be used to determine the expected return for an investment or portfolio.

Since beta only measures systematic risk, it is a good measure of risk only when the portfolio is well diversified. Diversified portfolios have little or no unsystematic risk and, therefore, the majority of diversified portfolio returns are a result of systematic risk or market risk. However, if a portfolio is not well diversified (much of the return is due to unsystematic risk) then beta does not capture all of the relevant risk. If beta does not capture all of the relevant risk, then beta is not an appropriate measure of total risk and the planner should use standard deviation as the appropriate risk measure.

The beta of a stock can be found on Yahoo finance (finance.yahoo.com) under the key statistics for a company. The beta of a mutual fund can be found on Morningstar (morningstar.com) under fund risk.

Standard Deviation

Standard deviation (represented by the Greek letter sigma σ) measures the total risk of an investment. The larger the standard deviation, the more risky the asset. Standard deviation also measures the amount of variation around a historical average or mean return. A small standard deviation indicates that the annual returns are close to the average return, while a large standard deviation indicates a large variation around the average return and therefore, more uncertainty. Standard deviation is calculated using the following formula:

$$\sigma_r = \sqrt{\frac{\sum\limits_{t=1}^{n}(r_t - \bar{r})^2}{n}}$$

Where:

σ_r = standard deviation (population)

n = number of periods

r_t = actual return for period t

$\bar{r}$ = average return

If all the data points are known, the standard deviation of a population formula (σ_r) will calculate the standard deviation. If, however, only a set of data or sample from a population is used, the standard deviation of a sample size (S_r) can be used.

$$S_r = \sqrt{\frac{\sum\limits_{t=1}^{n}(r_t - \bar{r})^2}{n-1}}$$

Where:

S_r = standard deviation (sample)

n = number of periods

r_t = actual return for period t

$\bar{r}$ = average return

Example 9.11

For example, the returns for a portfolio over the last three years are as follows:

Year 1   8%

Year 2   10%

Year 3   12%

The average return is ten percent $[(0.08 + 0.10 + 0.12) \div 3]$ and the standard deviation is two percent.

$$S_r = \sqrt{\frac{(8\% - 10\%)^2 + (10\% - 10\%)^2 + (12\% - 10\%)^2}{3 - 1}}$$

$$S_r = \sqrt{\frac{4\% + 0\% + 4\%}{2}}$$

$$S_r = 2$$

Alternatively, a financial calculator can be used to calculate the standard deviation.

Example 9.12

Given the annual returns below, which investment is more risky (using standard deviation as the risk measure)?

	Investment A	Investment B
Year 1	10%	21%
Year 2	13%	19%
Year 3	7%	23%

Keystrokes for Investment A:

10BII Keystrokes	12C Keystrokes
10 [Σ+] 13 [Σ+] 7 [Σ+] [ORANGE] [Sx,Sy]	10 [Σ+] 13[Σ+] 7 [Σ+] [g] [s]
Answer: 3 or 3%	**Answer: 3 or 3%**

Keystrokes for Investment B:

10BII Keystrokes	12C Keystrokes
21[Σ+] 19 [Σ+] 23 [Σ+] [ORANGE] [Sx,Sy]	21 [Σ+] 19[Σ+] 23 [Σ+] [g] [s]
Answer: 2 or 2%	**Answer: 2 or 2%**

Therefore, investment A is more risky than investment B because the standard deviation for A is greater than the standard deviation of B. It is important to note that the key strokes above are calculating the standard deviation based on a sample of returns as opposed to the population of returns.

Normal distributions are frequently used in science and other fields to describe the distribution of occurrences or outcomes from a specific event. It turns out that investment returns are often distributed in the shape of a normal distribution, allowing us to make estimates about potential investment outcomes.

A **normal distribution** describes how investment returns are dispersed around the average return. A normal distribution results in a bell shaped curve, as depicted in the following graph.

Exhibit 9.5 | Normal Distribution Curve

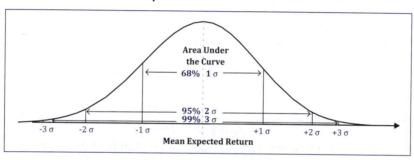

A normal distribution will have the following distribution expectations.

Standard Deviation	Probability of Returns
+/- 1	68%
+/- 2	95%
+/- 3	99%

The two charts above illustrate that for a normal distribution, 68 percent of outcomes will fall within one standard deviation from the mean return, approximately 95 percent of outcomes will fall within two standard deviations from the mean and that approximately 99 percent of all outcomes will fall within three standard deviations from the mean. The mean return is calculated as a simple average and the standard deviation is calculated as described above.

Consider the example from above with returns of 8%, 10%, and 12%. The mean of this distribution is 10% and it has a standard deviation of 2%. Therefore, the range from the mean minus one standard deviation to the mean plus one standard deviation should contain 68% of all outcomes. This range is from 8% (10% - 2%) to 12% (10% + 2%). It follows that 95% of outcomes will fall between 6% and 14% by moving out two standard deviations from the mean and 99% of outcomes will fall between 4% and 16% by moving out three standard deviations from the mean.

The normal distribution relationship allows the adviser to predict probabilities of returns (outcomes), which can assist in determining the likelihood of reaching specific goals of a client and understanding the likelihood of receiving negative returns.

Example 9.13

Mutual fund SCG has an average return of 12% and a standard deviation of 12%. What is the probability that the fund will return less than 0% in a given year?

At +/- 1 standard deviation from the average, 68% of the area under the curve is covered. By taking the 68% and dividing by 2, the area between 0 to 12% is 34%. Add 34% to the probability that the returns are greater than 12% (note that this is 50% of the area under the curve) equals 84% of the area under the curve. By subtracting 84% from 100% = 16% (the probability that the fund returns less than 0%).

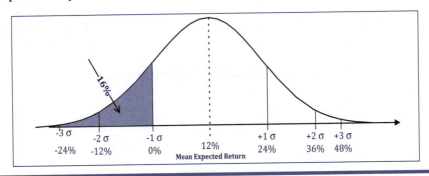

Example 9.14

Mutual fund HLG has an average return of 10% and a standard deviation of 5%. What is the probability that the fund will return less than 0%?

At +/- 2 standard deviations from the average, 95% of the time the fund will have a return between 0 - 20%, therefore 5% (100% - 95%) of the time the return will be greater than 20% or less than 0%. The probability of a return less than 0% is one half of that or 2.5% (5% ÷ 2).

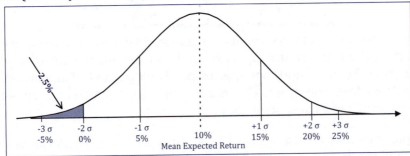

Example 9.15

Mutual fund WJG has an average return of 9% and a standard deviation of 3%. What is the probability that the fund will return less than 0%?

At +/- 3 standard deviations from the average, 99% of the time the fund will have a return between 0-18%, therefore 1% (100% - 99%) of the time the return will be greater than 18% or less than 0%. The probability of a return less than 0% is 0.5% (1% ÷ 2).

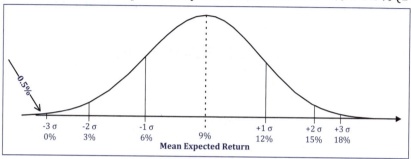

Semivariance

Investors certainly complain about volatility below their average return, but usually not above their average return. While standard deviation measures volatility or variation around the average return, both above and below the average, **semivariance** measures the possibility of returns below the average. Therefore, semivariance is a measure of downside risk. For investors seeking to minimize their downside risk, managing semivariance will reduce the probability of a large loss in their portfolio.

Risk-Adjusted Return Measures

When evaluating the return performance for any security or portfolio, calculating the actual total return is insufficient for a proper analysis. The actual return does not take into consideration the riskiness of the investment. It is important for the financial adviser and client to ask, "did I receive an appropriate amount of return, given the riskiness of the investment?" The most common **risk-adjusted performance measures** are Sharpe, Treynor and Jensen's Alpha, which can be used to measure the performance of any type of investment including stocks, bonds, mutual funds, and portfolios. These risk-adjusted performance measures are used when evaluating mutual funds and other securities and are discussed later in this chapter.

MODERN PORTFOLIO THEORY

Modern Portfolio Theory was developed by Harry Markowitz, who concluded that investors will seek to maximize their expected returns, for any given level of risk. Effectively, it is a methodology for developing and constructing portfolios. Harry Markowitz found that different combinations of securities produced portfolios with varying returns and volatilities. He realized that he could create portfolios with specific expected returns at varying levels of risk or portfolios with varying returns at a specific level of risk. By identifying the portfolios with the highest return per unit of risk, he created the **efficient frontier**.

Exhibit 9.6 | Efficient Frontier

Compare various portfolios from above based on their risk-return relationship:

- **Portfolio A vs. Portfolio C:** Investors prefer Portfolio A because it provides the same amount of returns as Portfolio C, but with less risk.
- **Portfolio B vs. Portfolio C:** Investors prefer Portfolio B because it provides a higher return than Portfolio C, for the same amount of risk.
- **Portfolio B vs. Portfolio E:** Investors prefer Portfolio B because it provides a higher return and less risk than Portfolio E.

Results of the Efficient Frontier

Portfolios A and B lie on the efficient frontier, therefore portfolios A, B and all portfolios that lie on the efficient frontier represent the highest return achievable for any given level of risk. Any portfolio that lies below the efficient frontier (such as Portfolios C and E) is **inefficient** because there is another portfolio that provides a higher level of return, for that same level of risk. Since the efficient frontier represents the most efficient portfolios in terms of the risk-return relationship, no portfolios can lie above the efficient frontier. Therefore, Portfolio D does not exist and is unattainable. The efficient frontier represents portfolios of 100 percent of risky assets.

> ### ☷ *Key Concepts*
>
> 1. Determine what the Efficient Frontier represents.
>
> 2. Identify what the Capital Asset Pricing Model calculates.
>
> 3. Determine the difference between the Security Market Line and the Capital Market Line.
>
> 4. Determine the methods used to measure correlation of securities and portfolios relative to other securities or the market.

The **Capital Asset Pricing Model (CAPM)** calculates the relationship of risk and return for an individual security using beta (β) as its measure of risk. CAPM is derived by combining a risk-free asset, with risky assets from the original efficient frontier. The result is a new efficient frontier.

Exhibit 9.7 | Efficient Frontier

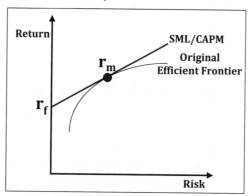

The tangent point of the old efficient frontier and the new efficient frontier is a **market portfolio** and represents 100 percent risky assets. The basic theory that links return and risk for all assets is the capital asset pricing model (CAPM). The CAPM formula is often referred to as the Security Market Line (SML) equation because its inputs and results are used to construct the SML. The difference between the return of the market (r_m) and the risk-free rate of return (r_f) is considered the **risk premium** ($r_m - r_f$). The risk premium is the increase in return an investor should be compensated to take on the risk of a market portfolio versus investing in a risk-free asset. The CAPM formula is:

$$r = r_f + \beta(r_m - r_f)$$

Where:

r   = required or expected rate of return
r_f = risk-free rate of return
β = beta (a measure of the systematic risk associated with a particular portfolio)
r_m = return of the market
$r_m - r_f$ = risk premium

Example 9.16

If mutual fund XYZ has a beta of 1.5, the total return of the market is 10% and the risk-free rate of return is 3%, what is the expected return for mutual fund XYZ?

$r = r_f + \beta(r_m - r_f)$
$r = 0.03 + 1.5(0.10 - 0.03)$
$r = 0.03 + 1.5(0.07)$
$r = 0.135$ or 13.5%

The relationship between risk and return as defined by the CAPM (when graphically plotted) results in the **Security Market Line (SML)**. Both the CAPM and SML assume an investor will earn a rate of return at least equal to the risk-free rate of return. The SML may be used to determine an expected return for individual securities.

Exhibit 9.8 | Security Market Line

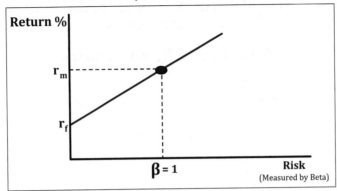

The SML suggests a linear relationship between risk and return. For each unit of nondiversifiable risk, as measured by beta, the SML results in an expected return. The SML represents the risk-return relationship for an individual security.

Capital Market Line

The **Capital Market Line (CML)** is the macro aspect of the Capital Asset Pricing Model (CAPM). It specifies the relationship between risk and return in all possible portfolios. The CML is not used to evaluate the performance of a single security. The formula for the CML is:

$$r_p = r_f + \sigma_p \left(\frac{r_m - r_f}{\sigma_m} \right)$$

Where:

r_p = required portfolio rate of return
r_f = risk-free rate of return
r_m = return on the market
σ_m = standard deviation of the market
σ_p = standard deviation of the portfolio

Exhibit 9.9 | Capital Market Line

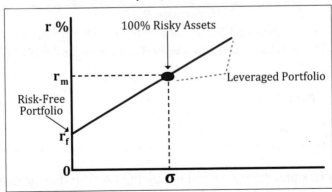

The CML graph suggests that in order to receive a higher level of returns, an investor must take on additional risk. Clients are often enticed into the latest and greatest mutual fund that had the best returns for the previous year. It is important for the adviser to caution the investor to consider the amount of return, relative to the amount of risk. Risk-adjusted returns are discussed later in this chapter.

Portfolio (MPT) Statistics

As previously discussed, diversification is achieved by combining stocks from multiple industries and various types of securities, such as stocks and bonds. In this section, portfolio statistics that determine the amount of diversification achieved are discussed. To develop a diversified portfolio, the financial planner must understand the relationship between asset classes and how the returns for securities change relative to each other.

Correlation Coefficient

Correlation coefficient measures the movement of one security relative to that of another security. Correlation ranges from +1 to -1 and provides the investor with insight as to the strength and direction two assets move relative to each other. A correlation of +1 suggests that two assets are perfectly positively correlated. A correlation of 0 suggests that assets are completely uncorrelated or there is no relationship between the price change of the two securities. A correlation of -1 suggests a perfectly negative correlation. For example, if the correlation between Stock A and Stock B is -1, then it is expected that Stock B will decrease by 10 percent when Stock A increases by 10 percent.

The following exhibit illustrates two variables (A & B) plotted against each other with correlations ranging from +1 to -1.

Exhibit 9.10 | Correlation Examples

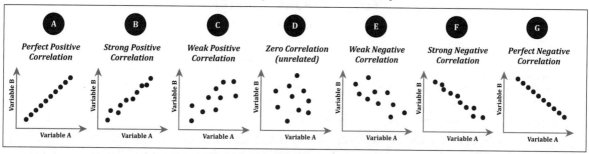

Example 9.17

Bryson uses electricity to cool his house in the summer. As the temperature outside increases, so does his consumption of electricity. Bryson's consumption of electricity is positively correlated to the temperature outside. As one goes up, so does the other.

Bryson uses gas to heat his house in the winter. As the temperature outside decreases, his consumption of gas increases. His consumption of gas is negatively correlated to the temperature outsides. As the temperature outside goes down, his consumption of gas increases.

Bryson is attempting to determine the correlation between his consumption of electricity, relative to the distance he commutes to work. Since there is no correlation between his consumption of electricity and the distance he commutes to work, they are uncorrelated. Keep in mind that correlation and causation are not the same.

Correlation is measured using the Greek symbol rho or R and plays an important role in determining the overall volatility of a portfolio. The benefit of diversification occurs when securities with correlations of less than one are added to a portfolio. Correlation is a key concept in the Efficient Frontier and in building efficient portfolios. Anytime correlation is less than one, the overall volatility of the portfolio is reduced. This concept will be discussed in more detail at the end of the *Portfolio Risk* section of this chapter.

Covariance

Covariance is the measure of how two securities or portfolios change or move together when combined. In other words, how the price movements between two securities are related to each other. Covariance is a measure of relative risk. If the correlation coefficient is known, covariance can be calculated as follows:

$$\mathbf{COV_{AB}} = (\sigma_A)(\sigma_B)(R_{AB})$$

Where:

σ_A = Standard deviation of Security A
σ_B = Standard deviation of Security B
R_{AB} = Correlation between Security A and B

Example 9.18

If the standard deviation for asset A and asset B are 30% and 12%, respectively, and the correlation coefficient between assets A and B is 0.18, what is the covariance?

$$COV_{AB} = (0.30)(0.12)(0.18)$$
$$COV_{AB} = 0.0065$$

Since COV_{AB} is positive, when asset A has a positive return, asset B will also have a positive return.

Coefficient of Determination (R-squared OR R^2)

The **coefficient of determination** (R-squared or R^2) is a measure of how much return for a security or a portfolio is attributable to changes in the market. R-squared ranges from 0 to 100 percent and the closer to 100 percent that the R-squared is for a security, the more that the return for that security is a result of the market. If R-squared is 1.00 for a mutual fund, then 100 percent of return for that fund is a result of the market. For example, for an S&P 500 index fund, the R-squared should be 100 percent. If the R-squared for some other fund is 0.50, then only 50 percent of the return is attributable to changes in the market. To calculate R-squared, simply square the correlation coefficient.

Example 9.19

If mutual fund JMG has a correlation coefficient of 0.90, then its R-squared is 0.81 (0.90 x 0.90), which means 81% of fund JMG's return is a result of market changes.

R-squared also provides the investor with insight into the diversification of a portfolio, because the higher the R-squared, the higher percentage of return that is the result of the market (systematic risk) and the less from unsystematic risk. R-squared also tells the investor whether Beta is an appropriate measure of risk or not. If R-squared is greater than 0.70, then the portfolio is fairly well diversified and beta is a reasonably appropriate measure of risk. If R-squared is less than 0.70, then the portfolio is not well diversified and beta is not an appropriate measure of risk and standard deviation should be used to measure total risk.

Example 9.20

Mutual fund JMG has a 10-year geometric return of 15%, with a standard deviation of 20%. JMG has a beta of 1.5 with a correlation of 0.80 to the S&P 500 (which is the market). What percent of the JMG return is a result of market returns to the S&P 500?

The correlation coefficient is 0.80, therefore R-squared is 0.64 (0.80 x 0.80), which means that 64% of the return for mutual fund JMG is a result of the S&P 500 (the market).

R-squared can also be used to determine the appropriate benchmark with which to measure performance. The higher the R-squared, the more of the security's return is explained by that market, and the better the market serves as a benchmark for performance comparisons.

Example 9.21

William is considering which of the two indexes below to compare the performance of mutual fund SCG against.

	Index 1	Index 2
Beta	0.60	0.95
Standard Deviation	8%	12%
R-Squared	0.60	0.89

Based on R-squared, Index 2 explains 89% of the returns for mutual fund SCG. Therefore William should use Index 2 as the benchmark for SCG.

Portfolio Risk (Two Asset Portfolio)

The risk of a portfolio can be measured through determination of the interactivity of the standard deviation and covariance of securities in the portfolio. This process also utilizes the weight of both securities involved, the standard deviations of the respective securities and the correlation coefficient of the two securities. To determine the standard deviation of a two asset portfolio, the following formula is used:

$$\sigma_p = \sqrt{(w_A)^2(\sigma_A)^2 + (w_B)^2(\sigma_B)^2 + (2)(w_A)(w_B)(COV_{AB})}$$

Where:

w_A = weight of Asset A
σ_A = the standard deviation of Asset A
w_B = weight of Asset B
σ_B = the standard deviation of Asset B
COV_{AB} = covariance formula $[COV_{AB} = (\sigma_A)(\sigma_B)(R_{AB})]$

Example 9.22

Sydney has a portfolio with the following two investments:

	Amount	Standard Deviation	Weighting
Stock # 1	$60,000	15%	60%
Stock # 2	$40,000	8%	40%

What is the standard deviation of the portfolio if the correlation is 1, 0 and -1, respectively?

If correlation is 1:

$$\sigma_p = \sqrt{(0.60)^2(0.15)^2 + (0.40)^2(0.08)^2 + (2)(0.60)(0.40)(0.15)(0.08)(1)}$$

$$\sigma_p = \sqrt{0.00810 + 0.00102 + 0.00576}$$

$$\sigma_p = 12.198\%$$

If correlation is 0:

$$\sigma_p = \sqrt{(0.60)^2(0.15)^2 + (0.40)^2(0.08)^2 + (2)(0.60)(0.40)(0.15)(0.08)(0)}$$

$$\sigma_p = \sqrt{0.00810 + 0.00102}$$

$$\sigma_p = 9.55\%$$

If correlation is -1:

$$\sigma_p = \sqrt{(0.60)^2(0.15)^2 + (0.40)^2(0.08)^2 + (2)(0.60)(0.40)(0.15)(0.08)(-1)}$$

$$\sigma_p = \sqrt{0.00810 + 0.00102 - 0.00576}$$

$$\sigma_p = 5.797\%$$

Summary Chart	
R	σ_p
R =1	12.198%
R = 0	9.55%
R = -1	5.797%

Notice that as the correlation coefficient decreases, the portfolio becomes less volatile (and less risky), as measured by standard deviation. Diversification benefits begin when correlation is something less than 1. As soon as assets do not move in the same exact direction and strength (correlation is less than 1), the standard deviation of the portfolio is reduced. The greatest diversification benefits occur when the correlation is equal to negative 1.

From a practical application perspective, not many portfolios only have two assets. Portfolios have many securities and even though the above formula could be extended to accommodate a multi-asset portfolio, it would be mathematically cumbersome without the aid of computer software. Instead, tools are available to professionals, such as Morningstar Principia, that will calculate the standard deviation, beta, and other characteristics of a multi-asset portfolio.

INVESTMENT ALTERNATIVES

The primary goal when building an investment portfolio is to construct a well-diversified portfolio that provides the greatest return, for the level of risk that the investor is willing to accept. Each investment security has its own unique risk and return characteristics. The next section of this chapter discusses investment alternatives, advantages, disadvantages, and risk and return relationships. The following four investment alternatives are discussed in this section of the chapter:

1. Equity Securities
2. Debt Securities
3. Real Estate and Tangible Investments
4. Derivative Securities

> **Key Concepts**
>
> 1. Identify the three methods used to value stock.
> 2. Identify the different types of bonds and the bond pricing relationships.
> 3. Determine various types of real estate investment assets.
> 4. Identify the different types of derivatives.

Equity Securities

Equity represents ownership in a business or property. The most common form of equity is common stock. Shareholders of common stock are entitled to a pro rata share of the profits generated and distributed by a company. Common shareholders' claims on company assets and earnings are subordinate to the company's creditors. Return on equity is provided by capital appreciation and from return of profits in the form of dividend income.

The advantages of equity investments are:
- The historical and expected returns are higher with equity than with debt.
- Equities are easy to invest in, either directly by purchasing shares through a broker or investing indirectly through a mutual fund.
- Stocks listed on major exchanges are marketable and current prices are easily obtained.

The disadvantages of equity investments are:
- Equity returns are significantly more volatile than returns for fixed income securities.
- It is difficult to consistently select equities that earn their expected return and outperform the market.
- Most equities do not pay significant dividends, which may result in little or no current income.

Stock Valuation

Part of the investment process is to determine the intrinsic value of an equity security. **Intrinsic value** is the underlying value of a security, considering both the future cash flows and the riskiness of the security. Stock valuation is unique to each investor, as each investor's required rate of return will differ from others, based on the riskiness of a security. Although there are multiple valuation models, theories and methods, the purpose of this section is to introduce two basic stock valuation tools and how to apply these tools. The stock valuation methods include the dividend valuation models (zero growth dividend model and constant growth dividend model) and the price-to-earning relative valuation model (PE approach).

The dividend valuation models consider the future cash flows that will be generated by the security. The dividend valuation models discount the future cash flows, based on the investor's required rate of return, to obtain a present value.

The PE approach is a relative valuation model that estimates the intrinsic value of the security based on the company's future earnings and how much investors are willing to pay for each dollar of earnings.

Zero Growth Dividend Model
The **zero growth dividend model** assumes that a security pays annual income in the form of a dividend, each and every year, and the amount of the dividend does not change. This model values a security based on the stock's capitalized amount of the annual dividends. The zero growth dividend model formula is:

$$V = \frac{D}{r}$$

Where:
- V = intrinsic value of a stock
- D = annual dividends
- r = required rate of return

Example 9.23
Robin is considering purchasing a stock that pays an annual dividend of $2.52. The stock is expected to continue paying $2.52 and is currently trading at $20 per share. Robin has a required rate of return of 12%, should she purchase the stock?

$$V = \frac{D}{r}$$

$$V = \frac{\$2.52}{0.12}$$

$$V = \$21.00$$

Since Robin believes the stock is worth $21, and the stock is currently trading at $20, she should consider purchasing the stock.

Example 9.24

If Robin's required rate of return is 15%, how much would she be willing to pay for the stock?

$$V = \frac{D}{r}$$

$$V = \frac{\$2.52}{0.15}$$

$$V = \$16.80$$

Example 9.25

If Robin's required rate of return is 9%, how much would she be willing to pay for the stock?

$$V = \frac{D}{r}$$

$$V = \frac{\$2.52}{0.09}$$

$$V = \$28.00$$

Required Rate of Return	Implicit Intrinsic Value	Relationship	If Stock Price is $20, Robin Should...
9%	$28.00	As the required rate of return decreases, the intrinsic value increases.	Buy Now
12%	$21.00	Robin's original required rate of return.	Buy Now
15%	$16.80	As the required rate of return increases, the intrinsic value decreases.	Sell

Constant Growth Dividend Discount Model

The **constant growth dividend discount model** values a company's stock by discounting the future stream of cash flows (dividends). This model assumes that dividends will grow indefinitely at a constant growth rate (g). The constant growth dividend model is most appropriate to value mature companies, with steady and predictable growth rates in earnings and dividends. The constant growth dividend formula is:

$$V = \frac{D_1}{(r-g)}$$

Where:

- V = intrinsic value of a stock
- D_1 = next period's dividends
- r = required rate of return
- g = dividend growth rate

The constant growth dividend model uses the "next period's dividend" when determining the intrinsic value. Next period's dividend is a function of this periods dividend multiplied by (1 + dividend growth rate).

Example 9.26

A stock recently paid a dividend of $3.00. The market price of the stock is $50 and the dividend growth rate is 3%. If an investor's required rate of return is 9%, what is the intrinsic value of this stock?

$$V = \frac{D_1}{(r-g)}$$

$$V = \frac{(\$3.00 \times 1.03)}{(0.09 - 0.03)}$$

$$V = \frac{\$3.09}{0.06}$$

$$V = \$51.50$$

This model also captures the relationship between dividends and required return. As the dividend (or dividend growth rate) increases or the required rate of return decreases, the intrinsic value of the security will increase. Alternatively, as the dividend decreases, or the required rate of return increases, the intrinsic value of the security will decrease.

Example 9.27

Continuing with the above example where the stock recently paid a dividend of $3.00, the dividend growth rate is 3% and the investor's required rate of return is 9%. The chart below demonstrates the relationship between the dividend and the intrinsic value of the stock. As the dividend decreases, the intrinsic value also decreases. As the dividend increases, the intrinsic value also increases for a given required rate of return.

Assumed Dividend	Required Rate of Return	Dividend Growth Rate	Intrinsic Value
$2.00	9%	3%	$34.33
$3.00	9%	3%	$51.50
$4.00	9%	3%	$68.67

The chart below demonstrates the relationship between the required rate of return and the intrinsic value of the stock. As the required rate of return decreases, the intrinsic value of the stock increases. As the required rate of return increases, the intrinsic value decreases.

Assumed Dividend	Required Rate of Return	Dividend Growth Rate	Intrinsic Value
$3.00	8%	3%	$61.80
$3.00	9%	3%	$51.50
$3.00	10%	3%	$44.14

PE Approach

The **price earnings (PE) approach** to valuing equity securities is a relative valuation model based on earnings that places a premium on the amount investors are willing to pay for each dollar of earnings. The PE ratio is a measure of the relationship between a stock's price and its earnings. PE ratios are useful to value the stock of a company that pays no dividends. The relationship of price to earnings is known as the PE multiplier, and is used to determine the price of a stock. The formula for the PE approach is:

$$PE = \frac{\text{Price per Share}}{\text{Earnings per Share}}$$

OR

$$\text{Price per Share} = PE \times \text{Earnings per Share}$$

Example 9.28

Phyllis' Home Furnishings recently reported earnings per share of $3.50. The stock has a fair market value of $59.50 per share. The PE ratio is 17 ($59.50 ÷ $3.50). If earnings next year are expected to be $4.00 per share and the stock trades at its current PE ratio of 17, the stock should be worth $68 (17 x $4.00) per share.

Debt Securities

Debt represents the lending of funds in exchange for periodic interest payments and the repayment of the principal debt obligation. **Bonds** are a debt instrument where the bond issuer makes a promise to make periodic coupon payments (interest) and repayment of the par value (principal) at maturity.

Bonds can assist an investor in accomplishing a variety of investment goals. If an investor is income oriented, bonds are appropriate since they provide periodic income. If the investor's goal is capital appreciation, bonds may provide capital gains depending on changes in interest rates and credit spreads. Bond values and prices are inversely related to changes in interest rates. As interest rates increase, bond prices will decrease. As interest rates decrease, bond prices will increase.

Bonds provide diversification benefits to a stock portfolio by reducing the overall volatility in such a portfolio because the correlation between bonds and equities is relatively low. Bonds are only slightly correlated to stocks. However, the correlation will fluctuate based on the time period for which it is being calculated. Correlations often increase during period of economic crisis.

Bonds are generally less risky than equities because of interest payments and collateral (many bonds have specific assets as collateral) and they have priority as to claims before equity holders in bankruptcy.

The disadvantages of bonds are:
- Bonds generally provide lower rates of return than equities.
- Bond prices are inversely related to changes in interest rates. As interest rates increase, bond prices decrease.

Types of Bonds

There are three primary issuers of bonds, the U.S. government, municipalities (state and local governments) and corporations. The U.S. government issues bonds to finance the national debt and to fund deficit spending. The three primary types of bonds issued by the U.S. government are:

- Treasury Bills - have maturities of 12 months or less
- Treasury Notes - have maturities between 2 - 10 years
- Treasury Bonds - have maturities greater than 10 years

Interest earned on **U.S. government bonds** is excluded from state and local income taxes, but is included for federal income taxes. Bonds issued by the U.S. government are considered default risk free because they are backed by the full faith and credit of the U.S government.

Municipal Bonds

Municipal bonds are issued to fund projects and spending for state or local governments. The three primary types of municipal bonds are general obligation bonds, revenue bonds, and private activity bonds.

General obligation bonds are backed by the taxing authority that issued the bonds. The bonds are repaid through taxes that are collected by the municipality. General obligation bonds are considered the least risky of the various types of municipal bonds.

Revenue bonds are issued to raise capital to fund a particular revenue-generating project. The revenue generated by the project will be used to repay the bond issuance. For example, revenue bonds can be used to fund construction of a highway and the revenue from tolls can be used to retire the debt.

A **private activity bond** is issued to finance a joint project between the private sector and a municipality. Private activity bonds are often issued to fund the building of professional sports stadiums.

Interest income earned on a municipal bond is tax-free at the federal level and may be exempt from income tax at the state level. States do not generally tax interest from municipal bonds issued by that state but may tax interest income from municipal bonds issued by other states. Therefore, purchasing a bond issued by your state of residence will likely result in tax-free interest income.

Corporate Bonds

Corporate bonds are issued by firms to raise capital to fund ongoing operations, retire debt, fund capital projects or acquisitions. Corporate bonds have default risk because the company is backing the bonds with a promise to repay the bondholder. Corporate bonds can be backed by an asset of the company, such as equipment, financial securities, or a pool of loans. Income received from corporate bonds is taxable both at the federal and state level.

Zero-Coupon Bonds

Zero-coupon bonds are bonds that are sold at a discount to par value and do not make periodic interest payments. Instead, the bonds increase in value each year, so that at maturity the bonds are worth their par value. Zero-coupon bonds with a maturity in excess of one year create a "phantom income" issue where the increase in value of the bond each year is recognized as taxable income, even though no actual cash is received. [3]

Risks to Investing in Bonds

Like any financial security there are risks to investing in bonds. Some of the most important risks to consider when investing in bonds are:

- Interest rate risk
- Reinvestment rate risk
- Purchasing power risk
- Default risk
- Call risk

Interest Rate Risk

Interest rate risk is the risk that changes in interest rates will cause changes in the price of a bond. Interest rate changes are inversely related to bond price changes. As interest rates increase, bond prices will decrease. As interest rates decrease, bond prices increase. Some bonds are more sensitive to changes in interest rates than others. This means that some bonds will experience larger percentage price changes than other bonds, given the same change in interest rates. The longer the term to maturity and the lower the coupon rate, the more sensitive the bond is to changes in interest rates. The following graph depicts the relationship between bond prices, term, and interest rates presuming a six percent coupon paying $30 semi-annually.

Exhibit 9.11 | Bond Pricing Relationships

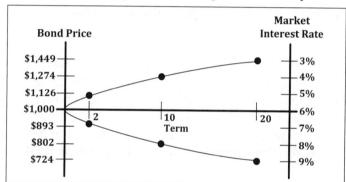

Exhibit 9.12 | Bond Pricing at Various Interest Rates (20-Year Term)

3%	6%	9%
N = 40 (20 x 2)	N = 40 (20 x 2)	N = 40 (20 x 2)
i = 1.5 (3 ÷ 2)	i = 3 (6 ÷ 2)	i = 4.5 (9 ÷ 2)
PMT = 30	PMT = 30	PMT = 30
FV = 1,000	FV = 1,000	FV = 1,000
PV = $1,449	PV = $1,000	PV = $724

Assume that a bond is paying a six percent coupon and market interest rates decrease or increase. What happens to the price of the bond? Notice, the longer the term of the bond, the bigger the price change of the bond when interest rates change.

---

3. These types of bonds are referred to as OID (original issue discount) bonds. OID is a form of interest, which equals the excess of a debt instrument's stated redemption price at maturity over its issue price (acquisition price for a stripped bond or coupon). Zero-coupon bonds and debt instruments that pay no stated interest until maturity are examples of debt instruments that have OID.

The concept regarding bond sensitivity to changes in interest rates is explained by a concept called duration, which is beyond the scope of this textbook. However, duration is an effective measure of a bond's sensitivity to changes in interest rates with the higher the number indicating a higher sensitivity.

Reinvestment Rate Risk

Reinvestment rate risk is the risk that an investor may not be able to reinvest the proceeds (interest and principal) from a bond at the same rate of return as was invested previously. As interest rates decrease, an investor will have a more difficult time reinvesting at the same rate of return as before, without taking on additional risk. The effect of reinvestment rate risk is that the actual IRR (or yield to maturity) for the bond investment will be less than initially expected.

Purchasing Power Risk

Purchasing power risk is the risk that inflation will erode the investor's purchasing power. For example, one dollar today will likely not be able to purchase the same amount of goods and services one year from now. An investor that purchases a ten year term bond will receive a coupon payment every six months for ten years and the par value of the bond at maturity. As inflation causes prices to increase, the coupon payments have less purchasing power and the par value of the bond will not purchase the same amount of goods and services ten years from now that it would today. Fixed income investments that are used to mitigate the risk of purchasing power loss are bonds that make adjustments for inflation. Two examples include U.S. Treasury issued I bonds, which adjust the interest rate for inflation and TIPS (Treasury Inflation Protected Securities), which adjust the par value for inflation.

Default Risk

Default risk is the risk that the bond issuer will be unable to timely repay the interest or principal of the bonds. Rating agencies such as Moody's and Standard & Poor's rate company's bond issuance on the likelihood of the company being able to repay both principal and interest. Companies that receive the highest credit ratings have the least amount of default risk, therefore they tend to pay the lowest yields. Bonds that receive the lowest credit ratings have the highest amount of default risk, therefore they are required to pay the highest yields to compensate investors for the higher default risk.

Call Risk

Call risk is the risk that a bond will be retired early by the issuing company. Bonds that have a call feature entitle the issuer to retire the bond before maturity by paying a call price, an amount generally above the par value to compensate investors for the bond being called. Many bond investors have the objective of generating income, so having the bond called early forces the bondholder to find another bond, of similar risk, paying the same rate of return (an example of reinvestment risk). Often, companies will retire bonds because the interest rate on the bond is higher than the current prevailing interest rates or the company wants to simply retire the debt or refinance the debt at a lower rate of interest.

Application of Bonds in a Portfolio

When structuring an investment portfolio, the primary objective of the client will determine the total percentage of the portfolio allocated to bonds. If the primary objective is growth and diversification, (assuming a long-term time horizon and appropriate risk tolerance), only 20 - 40 percent of the portfolio would likely be invested in bonds. However, if the investor's primary goal is income and diversification, then a larger weighting towards bonds, perhaps in excess of 40 percent, is expected.

An important consideration when investing in bonds is the type of bond and the type of taxability of the account that will hold the bonds. For example, a municipal bond that is "double tax-free" is ideally held in a taxable account. There is no additional tax benefit to holding a municipal bond in an account that is tax-deferred such as an IRA or 401(k) plan. Bonds that create taxable events, such as corporate bonds or zero-coupon bonds are ideally held in a tax-deferred account. Remember, corporate bonds pay taxable interest income each year and zero-coupon bonds create "phantom income," so tax deferred accounts, such as IRAs and 401(k) plans are ideal for holding those types of bonds.

Real Estate and Tangible Investments

Real estate represents an asset class that is often overlooked in an investment portfolio. Real estate may be an important component in an investment portfolio because of the low correlation between real estate and equities/bonds. Generally, real estate performs well during periods of high inflation whereas equities and bonds generally decrease in value as interest rates rise to mitigate the impact of inflation. Investors not only invest in real estate for the diversification benefits but also to generate income. Purchasing commercial or residential real estate that is expected to generate rental income may assist an income-oriented investor to attain their investment goals.

Real estate investment trusts (REITs) are a type of mutual fund that pools investor contributions to purchase real estate or make construction or mortgage loans. There are three general types of REITs:

1. **Equity REITs** buy, operate, and sell real estate in the hopes of earning a return in the form of capital appreciation for the property they own.
2. **Mortgage REITs** issue construction and mortgage loans. The mortgage REIT's investment return is in the form of interest on the loans.
3. **Hybrid REITs** invest in a combination of the ownership of real estate and issuing loans. A hybrid REIT's return is a combination of capital appreciation and income.

Derivative Securities

Derivatives are financial securities that derive their value from some underlying asset. Examples of derivatives include options, warrants, and futures. **Options** include both calls and puts. **Calls** give the holder the right to buy the underlying security at a certain price by a certain date. **Puts** give the holder the right to sell the underlying security at a certain price by a certain date. A **warrant** is a long-term option that gives the holder the right to buy a certain number of shares of stocks in a particular company by a certain date. A **futures contract** is a commitment to make or take the delivery of an amount of a certain item at a specified date at an agreed upon price. The underlying asset for options may be a stock, currency, Treasury security, or an index. The underlying asset for warrants are stocks. The underlying asset for futures contracts are commodities and financial securities. A commodity may be corn, wheat, cotton, gold, or oil. A financial security may be a currency, Treasury security, or stock index.

> ### ☑ Quick Quiz 9.5
>
> 1. The zero growth dividend model assumes that a security pays annual income or a dividend, each and every year, and the amount of the dividend does not change.
>   a. True
>   b. False
>
> 2. Risks associated with bond investment include interest rate, reinvestment rate, purchasing power, default, and call risks.
>   a. True
>   b. False
>
> 3. Mortgage REITs issue construction and mortgage loans with return being in the form of interest on the loans.
>   a. True
>   b. False
>
> 4. Calls give the holder the right to sell the underlying security at a certain price by a certain date.
>   a. True
>   b. False
>
> True, True, True, False.

Call options are contracts between buyers and sellers. The seller of an option receives a premium and the buyer pays the premium. Under the terms of the derivatives contract the buyer and seller agree to trade the underlying asset, at a pre-determined price known as the strike price, and the contract is good until a certain date (the expiration date).

Derivatives can be extremely complex and risky, depending on the trading strategy. The actual trading mechanics, strategies, and valuation of options is beyond the scope of this textbook.

INVESTMENT COMPANIES

Investment companies are financial services companies that sell shares to the public and use the proceeds to buy portfolios of securities. Mutual funds are one type of investment company in which investors buy shares in a fund and own a pro rata portion of the investment portfolio, entitling them to a share of capital gains, interest and dividend income. Other types of investment companies include unit investment trusts and exchange-traded funds. Investment companies are generally nontaxable entities because income flows through from the investment company to the investor. Therefore, investors will report their pro rata portion of dividends, capital gains, and interest on their income tax returns. This income is reported by the investment company on Form 1099.

Investment companies are regulated by the Securities and Exchange Commission and directly by the Investment Company Act of 1940.[4] This act requires investment companies to disclose to shareholders the investment company's objective, financial condition, structure, and operations. The Investment Company Act of 1940 does not provide the SEC with the authority to make judgments regarding investment decisions or merits of investments held by the investment company.

The most common types of investment companies are:
- Unit Investment Trusts
- Exchange Traded Funds
- Open-End Investment Companies
- Closed-End Investment Companies

Unit Investment Trusts

A **unit investment trust (UIT)** is an investment company that passively manages a portfolio of either bonds or stocks, known as a bond or equity UIT. Typically, municipal bonds are the most popular form of a unit investment trust where investors purchase shares in the UIT, and income generated from the bonds is distributed to shareholders. For an equity UIT, the investor's motivation is typically profit from capital appreciation of the stocks held by the trust.

When a UIT is established, the trust establishes a termination date. Once the termination date is reached, all assets are liquidated and the proceeds are returned to the shareholders. In the case of a bond UIT, the termination date is the maturity date of the bonds. Once the bonds mature, the principal proceeds are

Key Concepts

1. Identify the different types and characteristics of investment companies.

2. Determine the difference between open-end investment companies and closed-end investment companies.

3. Differentiate the types of investments made by a mutual fund based on its investment objective.

---

4. http://www.sec.gov/about/laws.shtml

repaid to the shareholders. Since UIT's are passively managed, no additional securities are purchased or sold once the trust is established. Essentially, investors in a UIT know exactly what securities will be held throughout the life of the UIT. A list of those securities is provided in the prospectus of the UIT.[5]

Shares of a UIT are traded at Net Asset Value (NAV). Typically, a sponsor of a UIT will offer shares during a one time offering. Any subsequent trading of the UIT is between the investor and sponsor. If an investor decides to redeem shares in a UIT, the UIT will redeem those shares at net asset value. The primary advantages to a UIT are the diversification offered by holding many bonds in the trust and the periodic income payments. The primary disadvantage is the loss in purchasing power for UIT's that are held for a long period of time. As income payments from the UIT remain constant, inflation will erode the investor's purchasing power.

$$\text{Net Asset Value} = \frac{\text{Market Value of Investments Held} - \text{Liabilities}}{\text{Shares Outstanding}}$$

Exchange Traded Funds

Exchange traded funds (ETF's) are another form of an investment company that typically have very low expense ratios. An ETF invests in securities that are included in a particular index. The ETF attempts to mimic the performance of an index by simply buying shares of the stocks in that index, in the same proportion that the stocks are included in the index. For example, QQQ represents the NASDAQ 100, SPIDERS or SPDR represents the S&P 500, Diamonds or DIA represents the Dow Jones Industrial Average. In 1993, the American Stock Exchange developed and launched the first ETF, which was the Standard and Poor's Depositor Receipts (SPDR), which tracked the performance of the S&P 500. There are now over 2,000 ETFs with assets exceeding $4.3 trillion in the United States as of the end of 2019.[6]

The majority of ETFs are passively managed, similar to a UIT, such that active security analysis and selection is not needed or conducted. ETF's trade on exchanges and are bought and sold through a broker at or near NAV. Occasionally an ETF is required to rebalance its portfolio when new stocks are added or removed from an index.

Advantages of an ETF

ETFs offer individual investors several advantages over traditional mutual funds including: intraday trading, the opportunity to purchase on margin (with borrowed money), tax efficiency, instant diversification, and low cost.

Intraday Trading

ETFs are similar to mutual funds in that a share represents a pro rata ownership percentage of a basket of underlying securities. However, ETFs can be bought and sold throughout the day, without any timing restrictions. ETFs can also be purchased on margin and can be sold short.[7] In addition, investors can buy and sell at predetermined prices, unlike mutual funds which are priced at the end of the trading day.

---

5. A fund's prospectus is a disclosure document which provides pertinent information to the fund's investors, including the fund's goals and strategies for investing, principal risks associated with investing in the fund, and fund fees and expenses.
6. Investment Company Institute (www.ici.org).
7. A short sale occurs when the investor borrows shares to sell currently, in anticipation of a price decline, then purchases the shares at a lower price to return them to the lender, keeping the difference between the sale price and purchase price (less transaction costs) as profit.

Tax Efficient Holdings

Another advantage to ETFs is that they are tax efficient because they have very low turnover of the assets within the portfolio. Since ETFs own the stocks that comprise an index and the assets within an index change infrequently, this results in low turnover. The only time an index ETF liquidates a position is when the index changes. Anytime an actively managed mutual fund sells an investment at a gain, either capital gains or ordinary income is passed along to the shareholders. Since the majority of ETFs are passively managed, which does not involve active buying and selling of securities, any underlying assets that appreciate in value are simply reflected in the ETF's per share price. Once an investor decides to sell the ETF, tax consequences will follow, but the timing is up to the investor.

Diversification

Immediate diversification is another benefit of an ETF because the investor is really purchasing a basket of securities that represent the market. Owning a basket of stocks mitigates the risk of one particular stock performing poorly, which may be offset by other stocks performing well. Building a diversified portfolio (reducing risk as measured by standard deviation), is a key component to meeting long-term goals through proper asset allocation.

Low Cost Investment

ETFs have very low expenses associated with managing the fund because they are passively managed. For example, the Vanguard S&P 500 index fund has an expense ratio of 0.14 percent (14 basis points), whereas many ETFs have an expense ratio of 0.10 percent (10 basis points) or less.[8] Since ETFs are purchased through a broker there may be commissions associated with a purchase, although many brokers offer commission-free ETF trades.

Open-End Investment Companies

An **open-end investment company**, also referred to as a mutual fund, is an investment company that buys and sells shares to investors directly. This type of investment company has increased dramatically in popularity over the last 40 years. In 1940 there were only 40 mutual funds, and by 1980, that number had grown to slightly over 500. Today, there are nearly 8,000 mutual funds, managing over $20 trillion dollars in assets. As more individuals take personal responsibility for their retirement and education goals, the role of mutual funds and percent of individuals participating in funds has increased dramatically. Currently, 46 percent of all U.S. households own a mutual fund, compared to less than six percent in 1980 and 23 percent of household financial assets are held in investment companies.[9]

One of the primary reasons for the increase in the number of mutual funds has been less reliance on defined benefit plans or pension plans offered by corporations and more reliance on self-funded retirement plans such as 401(k) plans or IRAs. Mutual funds offer investors the opportunity to take advantage of the tax deferred nature of these plans, while investing in well-diversified portfolios, managed by professional money managers.

In addition to more individuals relying on their own personal savings and investments for retirement, there has been a cultural shift in the attitude towards who is paying for their children's college education. In the 1950 - 70 time period, parents (and children) did not have an expectation that parents would pay for their children's college education. Many students relied on loans, grants, personal savings,

---

8. Some classes of Vanguard's S&P 500 fund have lower fees than 14 basis points.
9. https://www.ici.org/pdf/2020_factbook.pdf.

and worked through college. Over the last 20 to 30 years, there has been a shift in attitude among parents (and children) towards parents assuming the responsibility of paying for their children's education. With long-term planning and using mutual funds as the primary savings vehicle over a child's first 18 years, parents are able to plan for one of the largest expenditures in their lifetime. Mutual funds have been the investment vehicle of choice for many parents, combined with plans that offer a tax deferred or even tax-free benefit if funds are used for qualified education expenses.

Advantages of Mutual Funds

Mutual funds offer individual investors many advantages including diversification, professional management, better returns than those obtained by the average investor, low minimum investment requirements, and many convenient services.

Diversification

Mutual funds offer investors an easy and economical method of diversifying a portfolio. Many mutual funds have 100 or more securities in their portfolio, offering an investor instant diversification with a relatively low initial investment. For example, consider an investor with $5,000 to invest who wants to build a diversified portfolio. The investor would have difficulty purchasing shares of all the companies that comprise the S&P 500. With such a small initial investment, it is virtually impossible to build a portfolio of stocks to match the performance of the S&P 500. However, with as little as $1,000 an investor can purchase a mutual fund that owns 100 or more stocks in its portfolio and the investor is immediately diversified. Alternatively, the investor can purchase shares in an index mutual fund, which matches the performance of select indexes.

Professional Management

With the busy lifestyles many working individuals and families maintain, it is often difficult to find the time or interest to research investment opportunities, analyze current positions, and make well-timed investment decisions. Professional mutual fund managers have teams of analysts researching hundreds and thousands of companies on a daily basis to determine the most attractive investments given the fund's objectives. In addition, mutual fund managers and their teams of analysts have investment selection experience, which is helpful when making asset selections, given current and anticipated economic conditions.

Higher Returns than the Average Investor

Historically, individual investors underperform the broader market indices. According to Dalbar's 2017 Quantitative Analysis of Investor Behavior study, the 20-year average equity fund investor's return was 4.79 percent, while the S&P 500 returned 7.68 percent.[10] Reasons for the individual investor's poor performance include selling during market declines, not continuing periodic investments during market declines, and poor asset allocation. The study goes on to state that much of the lack of investment performance is attributable to psychological factors, which are behavioral finance related.

Fund managers are better able to maintain a disciplined approach to investing, whereas the average investor tends to make emotion-based decisions rather than relying on well-researched facts. Individual investors also have a tendency to buy when the market is high and sell when it is low leading to significantly lower than average returns.

---

10. 2017 Quantitative Analysis of Investor Behavior, Dalbar Inc.

Low Minimum Investment Requirements

Many mutual funds have minimum initial investments anywhere between $1,000 to $2,500 or more to open an account. Many mutual funds will waive the initial investment requirement if an investor enrolls in a periodic monthly investment plan. Consider that most bonds are priced in denominations of $1,000 and many stocks are priced at $20 to $100 or more, therefore, it can be difficult for an individual investor to build a diversified portfolio with a modest initial investment. Mutual funds allow for all investors to have access to professionally managed, well-diversified portfolios, regardless of their initial investment. The low initial threshold for investing in equity and bond securities via mutual funds opens these markets up to many investors who otherwise would not have the means to invest in these securities.

Other Services

Many fund families provide convenient services for investors. Services such as conversions from one fund to another, within the same family, but with a different objective. Other services include systematic withdrawal plans for retirees or investors with income needs that allow the investor to receive periodic payments from the mutual fund on a monthly or quarterly basis. In addition, fund families also provide wire transfer services, periodic investment plans, record keeping, and automatic reinvestment of interest and dividends.

Disadvantages to Mutual Funds

While mutual funds offer many advantages to investors, mutual funds have unique disadvantages as well. Disadvantages include poor performance relative to a benchmark, liquidity constraints, expenses, and built in capital gains.

Performance

Most mutual funds do not outperform their appropriate investment benchmarks. Only a small percentage of mutual funds outperform the appropriate index over time. One explanation for this underperformance is that mutual funds have expenses that must be incurred for the operation of the fund. In addition, funds must maintain cash reserves to meet redemptions, which undermines the fund's ability to be fully invested and only generate money market type returns for cash reserves.

Despite underperformance by fund managers, investment companies provide competitive returns compared to what most individual investors would be able to achieve investing on their own. Given sub-benchmark returns, many investors are opting for index funds, which provide returns that are superior to most fund managers and have extremely low fees.

Liquidity

While liquidity is a primary advantage of mutual funds, it can also be a disadvantage. To accommodate cash flowing in and out of a fund on a regular basis, funds must maintain significant cash reserves that are uninvested. This results in a fund not being fully invested and having lower rates of return than what could be achieved if the fund was fully invested. Maintaining cash reserves to meet redemptions is one of the obstacles that prevents mutual funds from consistently beating their benchmark. One of the ways funds attempt to overcome the need for maintaining cash reserves is through leverage using futures contracts. Futures contracts essentially allow the fund to control a large amount of the underlying index with a small investment. If the index increases in value, so will the value of the futures contract. Alternatively, if the index decreases in value, the futures contract will also lose value.

Fees, Loads, and Expenses

Investors should be conscious of fees, loads, and expenses of mutual funds. While all funds will have operating and management expenses, some funds have fairly high sales charges. The higher the fund costs, the more difficult it will be to outperform the appropriate benchmark and the lower the overall return to the investor. Once again, many individuals are opting for index funds to achieve market performance combined with low operating fees.

Built in Capital Gains

Mutual fund portfolios often have highly appreciated security positions from investments that have been held for years. This appreciation is essentially a built in capital gain that need to be distributed to the shareholders. Once the security is sold, the capital gains will be allocated to each shareholder, typically at year end. If an investor is unfortunate enough to purchase a mutual fund late in the year and did not participate in the appreciation the fund experienced over the previous year, the investor may be paying capital gains taxes on capital gains that were never realized. Investors should be careful about purchasing mutual funds with significant amounts of unrealized capital gains, especially near the end the year. Built-in-gains is one of the reasons mutual fund investors will postpone making a large fund purchase in November or December, instead opting to make the purchase the following year in January or February. Investors do not want to be hit with large capital gains at year end, when they did not participate in the funds appreciation. However, if the investor does receive an interest and capital gains distribution and the funds are reinvested, the cost of the new shares will increase the investor's tax basis in the mutual fund.

Closed-End Investment Companies

Closed-end investment companies are another type of investment company that trade on stock market exchanges. Closed-end funds do not generally issue additional shares after their initial offering. Shares of a closed-end fund will trade on an organized exchange, such as the New York Stock Exchange or Nasdaq Stock Exchange, which means shares are generally not redeemable by a fund family. Instead, shares are traded between investors, with the assistance of a broker.

Shares of a closed-end fund generally trade at a discount or premium to net asset value, depending upon the demand for the fund shares. Since a closed-end fund does not issue additional shares after the initial public offering, a closed-end fund generally has a fixed capitalization. An open-end fund has unlimited capitalization because the fund family will issue additional shares as investors buy more shares. Since closed-end funds have a fixed capitalization and shares are not redeemed by the fund family, the fund manager has greater flexibility regarding investments and does not have to maintain significant amounts of cash to meet redemptions. This characteristic allows the manager to be fully invested resulting in the opportunity to earn higher returns than those returns generated when holding cash.

Types of Mutual Funds

Equity Funds

Equity mutual funds typically invest in equity securities, but may have different overall objectives. Typical objectives include large, mid, or small cap growth, large, mid, or small cap value stocks, balanced funds and growth and income. Investor's objectives when investing in equity mutual funds may be capital appreciation or income through ownership of preferred or common stock with high dividend payments. Equity mutual funds have consistently provided investors with higher rates of return than fixed-income funds, however equity funds are more volatile. Equity funds are appropriate for investors with a long-term time horizon and who prefer to minimize tax consequences. Tax consequences associated with equity funds are typically capital gains (assuming a turnover of 12 months or greater), whereas fixed income funds typically generate ordinary income, which is taxed at a higher tax rate than capital gains.

Fixed Income Funds

Fixed income or bond funds typically invest in bonds of various maturities. A fixed income fund's primary objective is to create income for its shareholders and protect principal, which is appropriate for many retirees and investors looking to diversify their portfolio.

Fixed income mutual funds are well diversified, but there are still inherent risks associated with these funds. The two primary risks are interest rate risk and reinvestment rate risk. Since fixed income mutual funds invest primarily in bonds, their value is sensitive to changes in interest rates. During the early 2000's when the market experienced declining interest rates, fixed income mutual funds performed well because as interest rates decreased, the bonds held by these funds increased in value.

Growth Funds

Growth mutual funds typically invest in large and mid-cap stocks, where price appreciation is the primary objective. Growth funds invest in growth stocks that can be characterized as stocks that are more risky, have high PE ratios, and have little to no dividends. Growth funds are considered more aggressive than most other funds and are appropriate for investors that have a high risk tolerance.

Aggressive Growth Funds

Aggressive growth funds typically invest in small cap stocks, where price appreciation is the primary objective. Aggressive growth funds are more risky than growth funds because of the volatility associated with small cap, growth stocks. Typically, small cap, growth stocks have little to no earnings, rapid sales growth, high PE ratios, and no dividends. Aggressive growth funds are appropriate for investors with a very high risk tolerance.

Value Funds

Value funds typically invest in securities that are deemed to be out of favor or extremely under-valued. Value funds, invest in value stocks that are characterized by lower PE ratios and higher dividend yields. Value funds are less volatile than growth funds and are preferred by more conservative investors because of the low volatility. During the early 2000's, when many growth stocks performed poorly because of concern over valuation and earnings, value funds significantly outperformed growth funds.

Balanced Funds

Balanced funds typically invest in both fixed income securities and equity securities. The objective of a balanced fund is to provide both income from fixed income securities and growth from equity securities. Anywhere between 25 to 50 percent of a balanced fund can be invested in fixed income securities. Balanced funds are less volatile than growth or value funds.

Income Funds

Income funds typically invest in corporate and government bonds. The primary objective is generating income, rather than capital appreciation. Considering that most bonds are in denominations of $1,000, income funds provide investors (even with small initial investments), the opportunity to participate in the fixed income market. In addition, income funds offer investors diversification because of the low correlation between equity and bond funds. Finally, income funds are more conservative and less risky than equity funds.

Growth and Income Funds

Similar to a balanced fund, **growth and income funds** invest in both equities and fixed income securities. However, a much larger percentage of the fund is allocated to equities in a growth and income fund. In fact, a growth and income fund can have up to 90 percent of its capital invested in equities. Growth and income funds are more risky than a balanced fund, but less risky than a growth or aggressive growth fund. A growth and income fund is appropriate for investors with a moderate to high risk tolerance.

Sector Funds

A **sector fund** restricts investments to a particular segment of the market. For example, there are technology, healthcare, telecommunications, financial, and pharmaceutical sector funds, just to name a few. Sector funds concentrate their holdings to firms that operate within a particular industry. Sector funds are more risky than most mutual funds because they are not diversified across industries. Sector funds do not eliminate the industry or business risk associated with a particular segment of the market. Sector funds are appropriate for investors who are speculating that a segment of the market may outperform other segments of the market.

Specialty Funds

Socially Responsible funds restrict their investments to firms that are good corporate citizens and do not operate in industries such as alcohol, gambling, or tobacco. Green Funds are mutual funds that only invest in companies that are environmentally friendly. Historically, returns for socially responsible funds have under-performed the market.

In contrast to socially responsible funds, there are funds that invest only in "sin stocks." Sin stocks include the alcohol, tobacco, and gambling stocks. These funds tend to outperform socially responsible funds and can be considered defensive stocks during periods of a recession.

Money Market Mutual Funds

Money market mutual funds provide investors with access to short-term, high quality, large denomination investments. Money market mutual funds invest in short-term government securities, certificates of deposit, commercial paper and bankers acceptances. Commercial paper are in denominations of $100,000, which are beyond the access of many individual investors. Money market mutual funds typically maintain a net asset value of $1.00 and provide investors with a slightly higher rate of return than most checking or savings accounts.

Index Funds

An **index fund** purchases a basket of stocks to match or replicate the performance of a particular market index. While index funds replicating the S&P 500 are the most well-known, there are index funds, both in the form of mutual funds and ETFs, for most indexes.

Index funds take the approach, "if you can't beat 'em, join 'em." Over the long term it is difficult to outperform the market. Even professional money managers have a difficult time beating the market, especially after considering expenses. Actively managed funds have three distinct disadvantages versus index funds. Those disadvantages are:

1. Maintaining cash reserves
2. Higher expense ratios
3. Turnover costs

Actively managed funds maintain cash reserves to meet redemptions and to take advantage of investment opportunities.

Index funds simply use cash to meet redemptions, all excess cash is used to purchase an appropriate weighting of each stock within an index. Derivatives are used to leverage the remaining cash, so that the index does not materially underperform the market due to cash on hand. Actively managed funds also have a higher expense ratio to compensate the fund managers and staff for market research and security selection. Within an index fund, expenses are significantly lower, since there is no active asset selection process. Index funds typically have expense ratios under 20 basis points (0.20%), whereas actively managed funds can have expense ratios around 100 basis points (1.0%). Finally, actively managed funds turnover their holdings as often as once or more per year. The buying and selling of securities creates transaction costs that diminish returns. When considering the disadvantages of actively traded mutual funds, it is easy to understand why index funds tend to outperform actively managed funds.

Small, Mid, and Large Cap Funds

Small, mid, and large cap funds may have an objective regarding the size of a firm's market capitalization before making an investment. Capitalization of a firm is determined by multiplying the stock price by the number of shares outstanding. Below is a breakdown of the categories of companies for market size:

- Small -cap - Less than or equal to $2 billion
- Mid-cap - Between $2 and $10 billion
- Large-cap - Greater than $10 billion[11]

Capitalization is an important consideration, especially when matching an investor's risk tolerance to an appropriate mutual fund. Small-cap stocks and mutual funds that focus on small-cap stocks are more volatile than large cap stocks or funds that invest in large caps. Small-cap stocks tend to be more volatile because they are more likely to experience large percentage increases or decreases in revenue or earnings. Comparatively, it is easier for the regional coffee house chain to double revenues and earnings relative to a company like Starbucks.

---

11. Mega-cap stocks have market values in excess of $200 billion, such as Apple, Microsoft, Amazon, and Google.

International Funds

International funds invest in securities and firms that are outside of the U.S. domestic market. International funds provide investors with the opportunity to diversify some U.S. market risk. International funds provide diversification benefits because of the low correlation between the U.S. and foreign markets. With improved technology and reliance on imports and exports, U.S. markets are more highly correlated with foreign markets than they were 15 to 20 years ago. As a result, this correlation translates into less diversification benefits than seen in the past.

International funds present unique risks to investors. Foreign firms may not have the same financial reporting requirements as in the U.S., therefore it can be difficult to properly value foreign firms. In addition, investors in international mutual funds are subject to exchange rate risk. Even though the mutual fund trades in U.S. dollars, the investments held by the mutual fund, may be denominated in foreign currencies.

Global Funds

The major difference between international and **global funds** is that global funds not only invest in foreign securities and markets, but also in U.S. domestic securities. As with international investing, there are unique risks such as laws regarding financial reporting and tariffs, which may be significantly different than laws in the U.S.

PERFORMANCE MEASURES

With nearly 8,000 mutual funds to choose from, how does an individual investor or investment adviser select an appropriate fund? The most important starting point is determining the investor's goals and objectives. Other considerations are the investor's risk tolerance and time horizon, and their impact on an appropriate asset allocation. The next step is to evaluate securities and/or mutual funds to determine whether or not the security and/or mutual fund fits into the investor's established goals and objectives on the investment policy statement.

Key Concepts

1. Identify the four different types of risk-adjusted performance measures.

2. Determine the difference between an absolute risk-adjusted performance measurement and a relative risk-adjusted performance indicator.

3. Determine how an investor's asset allocation can be determined.

When evaluating a mutual fund, many individual investors consider the five-year average return of the fund and overall expenses. Some investors may think the higher the five-year return, the better. While this may be a good starting point, financial advisers understand that evaluating a fund based on its five-year historical return does not complete the story. Fund managers may have taken on additional risk, which resulted in a higher five-year average return than other funds, but may not have adequately compensated investors for all the risk taken. Mutual funds as well as other investments should be evaluated on a risk-adjusted return basis. Those funds with the highest risk-adjusted returns provide investors with the highest amount of return, for a given level of risk.

In addition to evaluating a fund's risk-adjusted return, advisers use databases of mutual fund information, such as Morningstar, to evaluate a fund's performance and narrow the universe of mutual funds down to a few that meet the client's goals and objectives. These databases contain a substantial amount of data regarding mutual funds and allow the user to build criteria regarding the riskiness of the fund, the expenses, manager tenure, historical performance, asset turnover, minimum initial investments, investment objective, and more criteria. By inputting the investment criteria, the software will generate of list of appropriate funds to be considered. For individual investors who do not have access to Morningstar, much of the same information can be found in a funds prospectus or by visiting a website such as Morningstar.com.

The primary determining factor when evaluating the performance of a mutual fund or of any investment is the investment return calculated on a risk-adjusted basis. There are four risk-adjusted performance measures to consider, Jensen's Alpha, Sharpe, Treynor, and the Information Ratio.

Jensen's Alpha

Jensen's Alpha is an absolute risk-adjusted performance measure. The term absolute indicates that Jensen's Alpha is an independent (versus relative) measure of the fund manager's performance compared to the expected returns based on the risk of the portfolio. A positive Alpha indicates the fund manager exceeded expectations, while a negative alpha indicates the fund manager did not produce enough return, given the level of risk undertaken. The formula for Jensen's alpha is:

$$\alpha_p = r_p - [r_f + \beta_p(r_m - r_f)]$$

Where:
r_p = actual return of the portfolio
r_f = risk-free rate of return
r_m = expected return of the market
α_p = alpha, the difference between the actual return
generated by the fund and the expected return
β_p = beta of the portfolio

Alternatively, alpha can be expressed as follows:

Alpha = actual return - expected return
Expected Return = CAPM formula $[r_f + \beta_p(r_m - r_f)]$

Alpha is the difference between the actual return generated by the fund and the expected return, given the level of riskiness of the fund, as measured by beta. Expected return is calculated using the Capital Asset Pricing Model formula. The higher the alpha the better, meaning the more return generated for a given level of risk. However, Jensen uses beta as its risk measure so if the portfolio is not well diversified, the calculated alpha may be misleading. The determination of a well-diversified portfolio is an R-squared greater than or equal to 0.70.

Example 9.29

Holly's mutual fund has a beta of 1.20 and generated an 11% return, while the S&P 500 generated a 10% return. R-squared is 0.85. The risk-free rate of return is 3%. What is Jensen's alpha and did the fund manager exceed expectations?

Alpha = Actual Return - Expected Return
Alpha = 0.11 - [0.03 + 1.2(0.10 - 0.03)]
Alpha = 0.11 - 0.114
Alpha = - 0.004

Holly's mutual fund has a negative alpha. Her fund slightly underperformed the market on a risk adjusted basis. Notice if the investor only compared the actual return of 11% relative to the S&P 500 return of 10%, the investor may incorrectly infer that the fund outperformed the market. It is critical for a mutual fund investor to evaluate a fund's performance on a risk-adjusted basis.

Sharpe Ratio

The **Sharpe ratio** is a relative risk-adjusted performance indicator, meaning the ratio by itself does not provide any insight. A Sharpe ratio for one fund needs to be compared to the Sharpe ratio for another fund to take on meaning. The fund with the highest Sharpe ratio provides the investor with the highest return for the risk taken. The formula for Sharpe is:

$$S_p = \frac{r_p - r_f}{\sigma_p}$$

Where:
r_p = actual return of the portfolio
r_f = risk-free rate of return
σ_p = standard deviation of the portfolio

This formula provides the investor with the incremental return above the risk-free rate of return. Sharpe ratio is also a measure of the amount of incremental return, for each unit of risk. After calculating the Sharpe ratio for a set of funds or portfolios, the investor ranks the Sharpe ratios from highest to lowest. The fund with the highest Sharpe ratio will provide the investor with the best risk-adjusted performance (the most return, per unit of risk). Notice that Sharpe uses standard deviation as its risk measure.

Example 9.30

Cheyenne wants to know which of the following mutual funds provided her with the best risk-adjusted return. Using the Sharpe ratio, which fund provided the highest return, per unit of risk, if the risk-free rate of return was 3% and the S&P 500 returned 12%?

	Total Return	Beta	Standard Deviation	R-Squared	Sharpe
Fund A	10%	0.75	4%	0.50	1.75
Fund B	15%	1.00	8%	0.68	1.50

Fund A

$$S_p = \frac{r_p - r_f}{\sigma_p} = \frac{0.10 - 0.03}{0.04} = 1.75$$

Fund B

$$S_p = \frac{r_p - r_f}{\sigma_p} = \frac{0.15 - 0.03}{0.08} = 1.50$$

Sharpe Ranking:
Fund A = 1.75

Fund B = 1.50

Fund A has a higher risk-adjusted rate of return, even though its actual return is less than Fund B. In other words, Fund A provided Cheyenne with 1.75% incremental return above the risk-free rate of return, for each unit of risk, as measured by standard deviation. Notice that the 1.75 is a relative measure and has no absolute meaning.

Treynor Ratio

The **Treynor ratio**, like Sharpe, is also a relative risk-adjusted performance indicator. A Treynor ratio for one fund requires comparison to the Treynor ratio for another fund. The fund with the highest Treynor ratio provides the investor with the highest return for risk undertaken. The formula for Treynor is:

$$T_p = \frac{r_p - r_f}{\beta_p}$$

Where:
r_p = actual return of the portfolio
r_f = risk-free rate of return
β_p = beta of the portfolio

Example 9.31

Bianca is evaluating two mutual funds. She is interested in determining which fund offers the highest risk adjusted return, based on its Treynor measure. Which of the two below would you recommend?

	Total Return	Beta	Standard Deviation	R-Squared	Treynor
Fund C	10%	0.75	4%	0.80	0.093
Fund D	20%	1.25	12%	0.89	0.136

Fund C

$$T_p = \frac{r_p - r_f}{\beta_p} = \frac{0.10 - 0.03}{0.75} = 0.093$$

Fund D

$$T_p = \frac{r_p - r_f}{\beta_p} = \frac{0.20 - 0.03}{1.25} = 0.136$$

Treynor Ranking:
Fund D = 0.136
Fund C = 0.093

Fund D provided a higher risk-adjusted return than Fund C. Fund D provided 0.136% return for each unit of risk. Keep in mind that Treynor is a relative measure as is Sharpe, while Jensen is an absolute measure.

When to Use Alpha, Sharpe, and Treynor

R-squared helps to determine which risk-adjusted performance measure should be used. R-squared measures how well diversified a portfolio is and how much return is due to the market. The higher the R-squared, the more well diversified the portfolio, and the more reliable beta is as a measure of total risk. If $R^2 \geq 0.70$, then the portfolio is considered well diversified and beta is an appropriate measure of total risk. Once R-squared falls below 0.70, the portfolio is considered undiversified, meaning beta is not a reliable measure of total risk.

If beta is an appropriate measure of total risk ($R^2 \geq 0.70$), then Treynor and Alpha can be used since both use beta in their calculations. If beta is not an appropriate measure of total risk (R-squared < 0.70) then standard deviation is the appropriate measure of total risk and Sharpe should be used as the risk-adjusted performance measure.

Information Ratio (IR)

The **information ratio** measures the excess return above a benchmark, such as the S&P 500, per unit of risk. This formula is similar to the Sharpe ratio, however the Sharpe ratio measures the excess return above the risk-free rate of return and the information ratio measures the excess return above a benchmark. The formula for the information ratio is:

$$IR = \frac{(r_p - r_b)}{\sigma_A}$$

Where:

r_p = actual return of the portfolio
r_b = return of the benchmark
σ_A = standard deviation of the active return (tracking error)

The information ratio provides investors with insight regarding the fund manager's excess returns above the benchmark. A high information ratio can be the result of high actual returns, a low return for the benchmark, or a low standard deviation.

Example 9.32

Consider the following:
- Mutual Fund ABC had a return of 15% and a standard deviation of 12%.
- Mutual Fund XYZ had a return of 10% and a standard deviation 5%.
- The benchmark index has returns of 5%.

Mutual Fund ABC's IR

$$IR = \frac{(r_p - r_b)}{\sigma_A} = \frac{0.15 - 0.05}{0.12} = 0.83$$

Mutual Fund XYZ's IR

$$IR = \frac{(r_p - r_b)}{\sigma_A} = \frac{0.10 - 0.05}{0.05} = 1.00$$

Mutual Fund XYZ experienced lower returns than Mutual Fund ABC, but has a higher information ratio. A higher information ratio indicates that Mutual Fund XYZ's manager provided higher risk-adjusted returns more efficiently by taking on less risk.

ASSET ALLOCATION

Asset allocation is the process of dividing a portfolio into various asset classes. The chart below illustrates the appropriate riskiness or volatility of a portfolio (for a retirement goal) as measured by standard deviation. The investor's risk tolerance (ability and willingness) determines whether the client is a conservative, moderate, or aggressive investor. The following three exhibits illustrate possible expected standard deviations and expected returns based on combinations of equities and fixed income securities. These are meant to be illustrative of the concepts discussed in this chapter.

Exhibit 9.13 | Standard Deviation Expressed in %

Age:	25-30	31-35	36-40	41-45	46-50	51-55	56-60	61-65	66-70	71+
Conservative	10%	9.6%	9.1%	8.7%	8.2%	7.8%	7.3%	6.9%	6.4%	6%
Moderate	12%	11.4%	10.9%	10.3%	9.8%	9.2%	8.7%	8.1%	7.6%	7%
Aggressive	14%	13.3%	12.7%	12%	11.3%	10.7%	10%	9.3%	8.7%	8%

Based on the investor's time horizon and risk tolerance (as measured above by standard deviation), an allocation between equities and bonds can be recommended, as follows (% allocated to equities / % allocated to bonds):

Exhibit 9.14 | Equities % / Bond %

Age:	25-30	31-35	36-40	41-45	46-50	51-55	56-60	61-65	66-70	71+
Conservative	50/50	47/53	43/57	40/60	37/63	33/67	30/70	27/73	23/77	20/80
Moderate	65/35	61/39	57/43	53/47	48/52	44/66	40/60	36/64	32/68	28/73
Aggressive	80/20	75/25	70/30	65/35	60/40	55/45	50/50	45/55	40/60	35/65

When considering the riskiness of a portfolio, as measured by standard deviation, and the allocation between equities and bonds based on the time horizon, we can then determine an expected rate of return. The expected rate of return in **Exhibit 9.15** is based on historical equity returns of 10.4 percent and corporate bond returns of 5.6 percent. Keep in mind that these are long-range historical returns and future returns may or may not be close to historical returns.

Exhibit 9.15 | Expected Returns

Age:	25-30	31-35	36-40	41-45	46-50	51-55	56-60	61-65	66-70	71+
Conservative	8.0%	7.8%	7.7%	7.5%	7.4%	7.2%	7.0%	6.9%	6.7%	6.6%
Moderate	8.7%	8.5%	8.3%	8.1%	7.9%	7.7%	7.5%	7.3%	7.1%	6.9%
Aggressive	9.4%	9.2%	9.0%	8.7%	8.5%	8.2%	8.0%	7.8%	7.5%	7.3%

The expected returns should be consistent with the required rate of return to attain the goals identified in the investment policy statement. If the expected returns are lower than the required return, the investor may have to take additional risk or make adjustments such as increasing the amount of savings toward a goal, or delaying the time horizon to take advantage of additional savings and compounding of earnings

INVESTMENT ANALYSIS FOR AN INDIVIDUAL CLIENT

During the data gathering phase of the financial planning process, the client is likely to provide a number of investment statements including brokerage accounts, savings accounts, mutual funds, education savings accounts, and retirement savings plans (IRAs, 401(k) plans, etc). The financial planner must analyze and evaluate the investments of a client to determine if the asset allocation is appropriate, if the riskiness of the portfolio is appropriate, and what changes need to be made to the portfolio. The process of analyzing investments includes:

1. Develop an investment policy statement.
2. Calculate characteristics of the portfolio including historical annual return, beta, standard deviation, and expected return.
3. Evaluate whether the portfolio is consistent with the investment policy statement. The evaluation should consider each category of the investment policy statement, such as:
   - Is the current portfolio appropriate given the goals of the client?
   - Are the investments appropriate give the time horizon for the client?
   - Based on the expected return in the investment policy statement, is the allocation of the portfolio such that the expected return is attainable?
   - Is the riskiness (beta or standard deviation) of the portfolio appropriate based on the client's risk tolerance as assessed by a risk tolerance questionnaire?
   - Based on constraints in the investment policy statement, are any of the current investments violating or contradictory to the constraints?
   - Are the types of securities held in taxable versus nontaxable accounts appropriate?
4. Make recommendations to rebalance and realign the investment portfolio such that it is consistent with the investment policy statement.

The investment analysis for an individual client is one of the most important components to developing a comprehensive financial plan. Investment analysis can occur simultaneously when applying any of the approaches described earlier in the textbook, such as financial statement analysis, the cash flow approach, metrics approach, or pie chart approach.

DISCUSSION QUESTIONS

SOLUTIONS to the discussion questions can be found exclusively within the chapter. Once you have completed an initial reading of the chapter, go back and highlight the answers to these questions.

1. Discuss important issues covered by a risk tolerance questionnaire.

2. Discuss a client's ability and willingness to accept risk associated with personal investment.

3. Define the steps involved in the investment planning process.

4. Discuss the purpose of an investment policy statement.

5. List the different ways to measure actual investment returns.

6. Define risk that is associated with investment choices.

7. What is the difference between systematic and unsystematic risk and how are they measured?

8. What is used to measure investment risk?

9. What is modern portfolio theory and the efficient frontier?

10. Explain the difference between the Capital Market Line and the Security Market Line.

11. Differentiate between correlation coefficient, covariance, and coefficient of determination.

1. Discuss the three types of measuring models used in this chapter to value equity securities.

12. Discuss how bonds can assist an investor to accomplish a variety of investment goals.

13. List the types of risks inherent to investing in bonds.

14. Discuss why an investor may choose to invest in real estate.

15. Summarize the common types of derivatives discussed in this chapter?

16. Define an investment company and list types of investment companies.

17. List the different types of mutual funds.

18. What are the risk-adjusted performance measures?

19. Define asset allocation.

MULTIPLE-CHOICE PROBLEMS

A sample of multiple choice problems is provided below. Additional multiple choice problems are available at money-education.com by accessing the Student Practice Portal.

1. Sylvia has a two assets in her portfolio, asset A and asset B. Asset A has a standard deviation of 40% and asset B has a standard deviation of 20%. Fifty percent of her portfolio is invested in asset A and 50% is invested in asset B. The correlation for asset A and asset B is 0.90. What is the standard deviation of her portfolio?
    a. Greater than 30%.
    b. Less than 30%.
    c. Equal to 30%.
    d. Not enough information to determine.

2. Municipal bonds that are backed by the income from specific projects are known as:
    a. Income bonds.
    b. Revenue bonds.
    c. General obligation bonds.
    d. Debenture bonds.

3. Elvin's investment portfolio consists of several types of stocks, bonds, and money market instruments. The portfolio has an overall standard deviation of 12%, a beta of 1.06, and a total return for the year of 11%. Elvin is considering adding one of two alternative investments to his portfolio. Stock A has a standard deviation of 13%, a beta of 0.87, and a correlation coefficient with the portfolio of 0.6. Stock B has a standard deviation of 11%, a beta of 0.97, and a correlation coefficient of 0.95. Which stock should Elvin consider adding to his portfolio, and why?
    a. Stock A because it has a lower correlation coefficient.
    b. Stock A because it has a lower beta than that of the portfolio.
    c. Stock B because it has a lower standard deviation than that of the portfolio.
    d. Stock B because it has a higher correlation coefficient.

4. Given a mean of 13% and a standard deviation of 9%, what is the range for 99% of all possible results?
    a. 1 standard deviation: 4% to 22%.
    b. 2 standard deviations: -5% to 31%.
    c. 3 standard deviations: -14% to 40%.
    d. None of the above.

5. Which of the following returns do mutual funds use when reporting a five-year historical return?
    a. Time-Weighted Return.
    b. Dollar-Weighted Return.
    c. Arithmetic Mean.
    d. Holding Period Return.

> **Additional multiple choice problems are available at money-education.com by accessing the Student Practice Portal. Access requires registration of the title using the unique code at the front of the book.**

QUICK QUIZ EXPLANATIONS

Quick Quiz 9.1
1. False. A risk tolerance questionnaire evaluates a client's willingness to take risk by addressing risk issues (e.g., understanding of stock market, comfort level with investing in stock market etc.). An investment policy statement identifies an investor's investment goals and guides the investor regarding appropriate investment choices.
2. True.
3. True.

Quick Quiz 9.2
1. True.
2. False. The simple average return is the arithmetic or average return. The geometric return is a compound rate of return equal to the IRR.
3. False. Purchasing power risk is a type of systematic risk.

Quick Quiz 9.3
1. False. Standard deviation measures the total risk of an investment. Beta is a measure of systematic risk.
2. True.

Quick Quiz 9.4
1. False. The Efficient Frontier compares various portfolios based on their risk-return relationship.
2. True.
3. True.
4. False. The risk of a portfolio can be measured through determination of the interactivity of standard deviation and the covariance of securities in the portfolio.

Quick Quiz 9.5
1. True.
2. True.
3. True.
4. False. Puts give the holder the right to sell the underlying security at a certain price by a certain date. Calls give the holder the right to buy the underlying security at a certain price by a certain date.

Quick Quiz 9.6
1. False. An open-end investment company is an investment company where investors purchase their shares from and sell them back to the mutual fund itself. A closed-end investment company trades on stock market exchanges.
2. False. Balance funds typically invest in both fixed income securities and equity securities.

Quick Quiz 9.7
1. True.
2. True.

10

DAVID AND AMY
RUDOLPH CASE & CASE
ANALYSIS PART 1

LEARNING OBJECTIVES

1. Describe an initial meeting and summarize data and draw conclusions for the life cycle approach.
2. Prepare a comprehensive engagement letter.
3. Gather internal and external data and prepare financial statements.
4. Create the pie chart approach.
5. Prepare financial statement analysis using a ratio analysis approach.
6. Prepare each of the ratios and compare them to the benchmark.
7. Prepare the two-step, three panel, metrics approach with schedules.
8. Prepare the cash flow approach and the strategic approach.
9. Identify opportunities and challenges related to a client's cash inflows and outflows and make recommendations to assist the client in meeting their current needs and long-term financial goals.*
10. Make a presentation to the client using current and projected financial statements and ratios.
11. Prepare a closing engagement letter that includes the responsibility for implementation and monitoring.

Ties to CFP Certification Learning Objectives

DAVID & AMY RUDOLPH CASE - INTERNAL DATA

The Family (January 1, 20X2)

David Rudolph (age 51, born on December 4th) is the owner of an office furniture company, DR Office Furniture Inc., (DRI) and is married to Amy Rudolph (age 35, born on February 14th) who is a self-employed real estate broker. David's salary is $275,000. The clients' net worth is $4.3 million; of which $3.325 million is the value of his business, DRI.

This marriage is both David and Amy's second marriage. David has a 30-year-old son, Trevor, from his first marriage. Trevor is married and has one child, Trevor Jr. (age 2). Amy has a child from her former marriage, Madelyn (age 14, born on March 31st), who lives with Amy's former husband, George (age 35, born on October 23rd), who is her legal guardian. David and Amy have a child on their own, Danny (age 1). Amy was divorced from George two years ago and, unfortunately, they have a very contentious relationship.

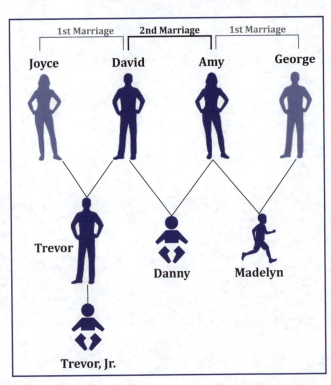

Amy is self-employed and has Schedule C net income of $150,000 per year before self-employment tax or any deduction for any qualified or tax advantaged retirement plan.

Personal and Financial Objectives

1. They want to provide for Danny and Madelyn's education.
2. They want to retire debt free when David reaches age 62 (when they both plan to retire).
3. They need adequate retirement income.
4. They want to have adequate risk management coverage.
5. David is primarily concerned with providing income to Amy for the duration of her life and secondarily, leaving the remainder of his estate to their child, Danny.

Summary of Initial Data Collected - Life Cycle Approach

Using the approaches learned earlier in the textbook, the financial planner will initially prepare the life cycle characteristics approach. This approach seeks to efficiently establish which phase or phases of the life cycle the client is in and to then deduce from that assessment the likely client goals and risks of the client. The life cycle approach, while easy and efficient, lacks sufficient detail to permit the financial planner to prepare a complete financial plan.

Based on the initial client communication, the information collected is as follows:

Summary of Data Collected - Life Cycle Approach	
Ages	• David (age 51) • Amy (age 35)
Marital Status	• Married (likely MFJ income tax filing status)
Children & Grandchildren	• Trevor (age 30) - From David's previous marriage with one child Trevor Jr. (age 2) • Madelyn (age 14) - From Amy's previous marriage, lives with George (former husband) • Danny - Child of David and Amy (age 1)
Net Worth	• Approximately $4.3 million (Dependent on DRI valuation)
Income	• Amy $150,000 self-employed (Schedule C) - proprietorship • David owner of DRI / employee $275,000
Self-Employed	• Amy is self-employed with no employees • David is owner / employee of a C corporation (DRI) with 31 employees

Preliminary Conclusions Regarding the Rudolphs (Life Cycle Approach)

Using the information from the life cycle approach, the financial planner can get an indication of the Rudolph family's risks and probable goals. Notice that David (age 51) and Amy (age 35) are in their middle years, suggesting that they are in both the asset accumulation and conservation (risk management) phases. They have children and a grandchild, suggesting a need for education funding for their child and a possible interest in setting up a 529 Savings Plan for the grandchild. Having a young child clearly establishes the need for both life and disability insurance for income replacement (both parents). David and Amy probably file joint federal and state income tax returns. Amy's Schedule C income creates the opportunity to establish a Keogh (self-employed) retirement plan (could be a SEP, SIMPLE, or qualified plan such as a 401(k) plan or profit sharing plan). The net worth of $4.3 million suggests the need for estate planning, possibly beyond just the basic estate planning documentation.

What a financial planner does not know about the Rudolphs using the life cycle approach is the quality of the relationship between the parties (which could seriously affect the planning), what specific insurance coverages they have, what their ratios are (e.g., savings rate), or what their detailed financial statements look like. We can, however, deduce that they are probably interested in retirement planning, a comprehensive review of their risk management, investments, estate planning portfolios, and education funding. DRI is their largest asset so there are valuation, disposition, and lack of diversification (concentration of wealth) issues. The Rudolphs may or may not have conflicting goals relating to retirement and the management and interaction with children and grandchildren.

RUDOLPH CASE FILE - ADDITIONAL DATA
External Information

Economic Information
- General inflation is expected to average 2.5% annually for the foreseeable future.
- Education inflation is expected to be 6% annually.
- Real GDP has been 2.75% and is expected to continue to be 2.75% for the next several years.
- It is expected that the S&P 500 will return approximately 9% this year and for the foreseeable future.
- T-bills are considered the appropriate proxy for the risk-free rate of return and are currently earning 3.5%.

Bank Lending Rates
- 15-year conforming mortgage is 4.75%.
- 30-year conforming mortgage is 5.0%.
- Any closing costs associated with mortgage refinance are an additional 3% of the amount mortgaged.
- The secured personal loan rate is 8.0%.
- Credit card rates are 18%.

Exhibit 10.1 | Economic Outlook - Investments

	Return	Standard Deviation
Small Company Stocks	12%	18%
Large Company Stocks (Actively Managed)	10%	16%
S&P 500	9%	14%
Corporate Bonds	6%	5%
Long-term Treasury Bonds	6%	4%
T-bills	3.5%	2%

Additional Internal Information

Insurance Information

Life Insurance

Policy 1	
Insured	David Rudolph
Face Amount	$2,500,000
Type	Term Policy / 30 Year Level Term
Cash Value	$0
Annual Premium	$10,000
Beneficiary	David Rudolph
Owner	David Rudolph

Policy 2	
Insured	David Rudolph
Face Amount	2x Salary=$550,000
Type	Group Term - Employer Provided
Cash Value	$0
Annual Premium	$700
Beneficiary	David Rudolph
Owner	David Rudolph

Policy 3	
Insured	Amy Rudolph
Face Amount	$250,000
Type	Term Policy	Ten Year Level Term
Cash Value	$0
Annual Premium	$500
Beneficiary	Madelyn
Owner	Amy Rudolph

Health Insurance

David currently has an indemnity group health and major medical hospitalization plan through his company. Amy, David, and Danny are currently covered by his health insurance plan. DRI pays the entire premium for the health insurance policy. Madelyn is covered under both David and George's health insurance plans. David's plan has the following characteristics:

- $500 per individual deductible
- $1,000 total family deductible
- 80% coinsurance clause for major medical
- $3,000 annual family maximum out-of-pocket limit

Long-Term Disability Insurance

Long-Term Disability Policy - David	
Type	Own Occupation / Guaranteed Renewable
Insured	David
Guaranteed Renewable	Yes
Benefit	60% of Gross Pay
Premium Paid By	Employer
Residual Benefits Clause	Yes
Elimination Period	90 Days
Annual Premium	$2,000

Amy is not covered by a long-term disability insurance policy.

Long-Term Care Insurance

Neither David nor Amy have long-term care insurance.

Property and Liability Insurance

Homeowners Insurance

Personal Residence	
Type	HO3 without endorsements
Dwelling	$1,500,000
Other Structures	$150,000
Personal Property	$500,000
Personal Liability	$100,000
Medical Payments	$10,000
Deductible	$1,000
Coinsurance %	80 / 20
Annual Premium	$4,200

Lake House	
Type	HO3 without endorsements
Dwelling	$200,000
Other Structures	$20,000
Personal Property	$100,000
Personal Liability	$100,000
Medical Payments	$10,000
Deductible	$1,000
Coinsurance %	80 / 20
Annual Premium	$3,500

There is no flood insurance on the personal residence or the lake house.

Auto Insurance

	Auto #1 David's Car	Auto # 2 Amy's Car
Type	Personal Automobile Policy (PAP)	Personal Automobile Policy (PAP)
Liability (Bodily Injury)	$100,000/$300,000/$50,000	$100,000/$300,000/$50,000
Medical Payments	$10,000	$10,000
Uninsured Motorist	$100,000/$300,000	$100,000/$300,000
Collision Deductible	$1,000	$500
Comprehensive Deductible	$500	$250
Annual Premium	$900	$1,200

Boat Insurance

There is no boat insurance (property or liability).

Liability Insurance

There is no personal liability umbrella policy (PLUP).

Exhibit 10.2 | Financial Statements: Statement of Financial Position (Beginning of Year)

Statement of Financial Position
David and Amy Rudolph
Balance Sheet as of 1/1/20X1

Assets[1]			Liabilities and Net Worth		
Current Assets			**Current Liabilities[2]**		
JT Cash & Checking	$20,000		W Credit Cards	$15,000	
JT Money Market	$250,000		**Total Current Liabilities**		$15,000
Total Current Assets		$270,000			
Investment Assets			**Long-Term Liabilities[2]**		
H DR Office Furniture, Inc[3]	$3,325,000		JT Principal Residence	$1,185,264	
H Brokerage Account	$410,000		H Lake House	$153,434	
H Education Accounts[4](529)	$46,000		H Boat	$78,734	
H 401(k) Plan	$32,000		**Total Long-Term Liabilities**		$1,417,432
W Traditional IRA	$11,000				
W Roth IRA	$16,000				
Total Investment Assets		$3,840,000	**Total Liabilities**		$1,432,432
Personal Use Assets					
JT Principal Residence	$1,300,000				
H Lake House	$450,000				
JT Furniture, Clothing	$100,000		**Total Net Worth**		$4,642,568
H Car # 1	$25,000				
W Car # 2	$35,000				
H Boat	$55,000				
Total Personal Use Assets		$1,965,000			
Total Assets		$6,075,000	**Total Liabilities & Net Worth**		$6,075,000

1. Assets are stated at fair market value.
2. Liabilities are stated at principal only as of January 1, 20X1 before January payments.
3. This value represents David's 75% interest and the value is based on his estimate.
4. Section 529 Savings Plans for Madelyn (current balance $25,760) and Danny (current balance $20,240). David currently saves $3,000 per year into each of these accounts ($6,000 total). See portfolio.

Title Designations:
H = Husband (Sole Owner)
W = Wife (Sole Owner)
JT = Joint Tenancy with Survivorship Rights

Exhibit 10.3 | Financial Statements: Statement of Financial Position (End of Year)

Statement of Financial Position David and Amy Rudolph Balance Sheet as of 12/31/20X1 (and 1/1/20X2)				
Assets[1]			**Liabilities and Net Worth**	
Current Assets			**Current Liabilities[2]**	
JT Cash & Checking	$25,000		W Credit Cards	$15,000
JT Money Market	$270,000		**Total Current Liabilities**	$15,000
Total Current Assets[5]		$295,000		
Investment Assets			**Long-Term Liabilities[2]**	
H DR Office Furniture, Inc[3]	$3,325,000		JT Principal Residence	$1,169,619
H Brokerage Account	$500,000		H Lake House	$148,038
H Education Accounts[4](529)	$46,000		H Boat	$70,276
H 401(k) Plan	$50,000		**Total Long-Term Liabilities**	$1,387,933
W Traditional IRA	$15,000			
W Roth IRA	$20,000			
Total Investment Assets		$3,956,000	**Total Liabilities**	$1,402,933
Personal Use Assets				
JT Principal Residence	$800,000			
H Lake House	$450,000			
JT Furniture, Clothing	$100,000		**Total Net Worth**	$4,313,067
H Car # 1	$25,000			
W Car # 2	$35,000			
H Boat	$55,000			
Total Personal Use Assets		$1,465,000		
Total Assets		$5,716,000	**Total Liabilities & Net Worth**	$5,716,000

1. Assets are stated at fair market value.
2. Liabilities are stated at principal only as of December 31, 20X1 before January 20X2 payments.
3. This value represents David's 75% interest and the value is based on his estimate.
4. Section 529 Savings Plans for Madelyn (current balance $25,760) and Danny (current balance $20,240). David currently saves $3,000 per year into each of these accounts ($6,000 total) See portfolio.
5. David received an inheritance of $25,000 from his great uncle Cameron.

Title Designations:
H = Husband (Sole Owner)
W = Wife (Sole Owner)
JT = Joint Tenancy with Survivorship Rights

Exhibit 10.4 | Financial Statements: Income Statement

Statement of Income and Expenses
David and Amy Rudolph
Statement of Income and Expenses for Past Year (20X1) and
Expected (Approximate) For This Year (20X2)

		Totals
Cash Inflows		
David's Salary	$275,000	
Amy's Self-Employment Income	$150,000	
Total Cash Inflows		$425,000
Cash Outflows		
Savings		
Money Market	$0	
401(k) Plan	$23,000	
Education (529 plans)	$6,000	
Total Savings		$29,000
Taxes		
Federal Income Taxes Withheld & Estimated Payments	$63,800	
State Income Taxes Withheld	$16,491	
David's Social Security Taxes	$13,516	
Amy's Social Security Taxes & Estimated Payments	$21,195	
Property Tax Principal Residence	$8,000 ND	
Property Tax Vacation Home	$4,000 ND	
Total Taxes		$127,002
Debt Payments (Principal & Interest)		
Principal Residence	$86,335 ND	
Lake House	$15,967 ND	
Boat	$15,201 ND	
Credit Cards	$15,000 ND	
Total Debt Payments		$132,503
Living Expenses		
Utilities Principal Residence	$5,000 ND	
Lake House Expenses (net of rental income of $5,000)	$15,000 ND	
Gasoline for Autos	$5,000 ND	
Lawn Service	$2,000 ND	
Entertainment	$15,000	
Vacations	$25,000	
Church Donations	$10,000 ND	
Clothing	$18,000 ND	
Auto Maintenance	$2,000 ND	
Satellite TV	$1,800 ND	
Food	$8,000 ND	
Miscellaneous	$10,000 ND	
Total Living Expenses		$116,800
Insurance Payments		
HO Insurance Principal Residence	$4,200 ND	
HO Insurance Lake House	$3,500 ND	
Auto Premiums	$2,100 ND	
Life Insurance #1	$10,000 ND	
Life Insurance #3	$500 ND	
Total Insurance Payments		$20,300
Total Cash Outflows		$425,605
Net Discretionary Cash Flows		($605)

ND = Non-Discretionary cash flow per mutual understanding between financial planner and client.

Investment Information

As part of a financial planning engagement, David and Amy fill out a risk tolerance questionnaire. Their answers to the questions in the Global Portfolio Allocation Scoring System (PASS) are as follows:

Global Portfolio Allocation Scoring System (PASS) for Individual Investors						
Questions	Strongly Agree	Agree	Neutral	Disagree	Strongly Disagree	David & Amy
1. Earning a high long-term total return that will allow my capital to grow faster than the inflation rate is one of my most important investment objectives.		D	A			3.5
2. I would like an investment that provides me with an opportunity to defer taxation of capital gains to future years.		D	A			3.5
3. I do not require a high level of current income from my investments.		D, A				4
4. I am willing to tolerate some sharp down swings in the return on my investments in order to seek a potentially higher return than would normally be expected from more stable investments.		D	A			3.5
5. I am willing to risk a short-term loss in return for a potentially higher long-run rate of return.			D, A			3
6. I am financially able to accept a low level of liquidity in my investment portfolio.		D, A				4
						21.5

Global Portfolio Allocation Scoring System (PASS) for Individual Investors – developed by Dr. William Droms (Georgetown University) and Steven N. Strauss, (DromsStrauss Advisors Inc.) – model used with permission.

Based on the scoring of 5 for "Strongly Agree" and decreasing by 1 for each column to the right with 1 point for "Strongly Disagree," the Rudolphs' score is 21.5. This score equates to the RT3 Target portfolio.

Exhibit 10.5 | PASS for Individual Investors

	Short-Term Horizon				Intermediate-Term Horizon				Long-Term Horizon			
	RT1 Target	RT2 Target	RT3 Target	RT4 Target	RT1 Target	RT2 Target	RT3 Target	RT4 Target	RT1 Target	RT2 Target	RT3 Target	RT4 Target
PASS Score	6 - 12	13 - 18	19 - 24	25 - 30	6 - 12	13 - 18	19 - 24	25 - 30	6 - 12	13 - 18	19 - 24	25 - 30
Cash and Money Market Fund	40%	30%	20%	10%	5%	5%	5%	5%	5%	5%	3%	2%
Treasury Bonds/ Bond Funds	40%	30%	30%	20%	60%	35%	20%	10%	30%	20%	12%	0%
Corporate Bonds/ Bond Funds	20%	30%	30%	40%	15%	15%	15%	10%	15%	10%	10%	4%
Subtotal	100%	90%	80%	70%	80%	55%	40%	25%	50%	35%	25%	6%
International Bond Funds	0%	0%	0%	0%	0%	5%	5%	5%	0%	5%	5%	4%
Subtotal	0%	0%	0%	0%	0%	5%	5%	5%	0%	5%	5%	4%
Index Fund	0%	10%	10%	10%	10%	15%	20%	20%	20%	20%	20%	25%
Large Cap Value Funds/Stocks	0%	0%	5%	5%	5%	5%	10%	10%	10%	10%	5%	5%
Large Cap Growth Funds/Stocks	0%	0%	0%	0%	5%	5%	5%	10%	15%	10%	10%	5%
Mid/Small Growth Funds/Stocks	0%	0%	0%	0%	0%	0%	5%	5%	0%	0%	5%	10%
Mid/Small Value Funds/Stocks	0%	0%	0%	5%	0%	5%	5%	5%	0%	5%	5%	10%
Subtotal	0%	10%	15%	20%	20%	30%	45%	50%	45%	45%	45%	55%
International Stock Funds	0%		0%	5%	0%	5%	5%	10%	0%	5%	10%	15%
Subtotal	0%	0%	0%	5%	0%	5%	5%	10%	0%	5%	10%	15%
Real Estate Funds	0%		5%	5%	0%	5%	5%	10%	5%	10%	15%	20%
Subtotal	0%	0%	5%	5%	0%	5%	5%	10%	5%	10%	15%	20%
Total	100%	100%	100%	100%	100%	100%	100%	100%	100%	100%	100%	100%

Global Portfolio Allocation Scoring System (PASS) for Individual Investors – developed by Dr. William Droms (Georgetown University) and Steven N. Strauss, (DromsStrauss Advisors Inc.) – model used with permission.

The above asset allocation and the following expected returns (see the approaches chapter) can be used to determine an expected return.

Exhibit 10.6 | Asset Class Expected Return and Standard Deviation

	Expected Rates of Return	Standard Deviation of Returns
Cash and Money Market Fund	2.5%	2.0%
Treasury Bonds / Bond Fund	4.0%	4.0%
Corporate Bonds / Bond Fund	6.0%	5.0%
International Bond Funds	7.0%	6.0%
Index Funds	9.0%	14.0%
Large Cap Funds / Stocks	10.0%	16.0%
Mid / Small Funds / Stocks	12.0%	18.0%
International Stock Funds	13.0%	22.0%
Real Estate Funds	8.0%	12.0%

The following exhibit depicts the PASS allocation multiplied by the expected rates of return for each asset class, which results in an overall expected return of 8.51 percent. However, to be on the conservative side and since they scored on the lower side of the RT3 Target, the Rudolphs have requested that an eight percent (8%) required rate of return be used as part of the analysis.

Exhibit 10.7 | Calculation of Expected Portfolio Return

	PASS Recommended Portfolio	Expected Rates of Return	PASS Expected Return
Cash and Money Market Fund	3%	2.5%	0.075%
Treasury Bonds/ Bond Funds	12%	4.0%	0.480%
Corporate Bonds/ Bond Funds	10%	6.0%	0.600%
International Bond Funds	5%	7.0%	0.350%
Index Fund	20%	9.0%	1.800%
Large Cap Funds/Stocks	15%	10.0%	1.500%
Mid/Small Funds/Stocks	10%	12.0%	1.200%
International Stock Funds	10%	13.0%	1.300%
Real Estate Funds	15%	8.0%	1.200%
		Expected Return	8.51%

Other Investment Information

- David expects to be able to sell his interest at retirement in DRI to fund his retirement.
- Their emergency fund is primarily invested in a taxable money market account earning 0.75 percent.

Description of Investment Assets

DR Office Furniture, Inc.

When valuing his business, David's accountant advised him to use a multiple of revenue approach. David's accountant suggested using a multiple of 2.5 x revenue. David estimated the value of the business on revenues for 20X1.

Brokerage Account

The brokerage account consists of the mutual funds described below. Any interest and dividends earned on the investments is reflected in the account balance and is not counted or separately stated on the income statement.

Exhibit 10.8 | Investment Portfolio - Mutual Funds as of 12/31/20X1

Mutual Funds									
Name	Shares	Cost per Share	NAV	Beta	R^2 to S&P 500	Yield	One Year Return	Standard Deviation	Total FMV
A	2,526	$50	$75	1.1	0.76	0.9%	6%	0.16	$189,450
B	1,468	$25	$20	0.98	0.95	1.2%*	12%	0.15	$29,360
C	2,570	$22	$87	1.24	0.88	0.5%	14%	0.14	$223,590
D	1,200	$45	$48	0.78	0.5	1.4%	4%	0.13	$57,600
								Totals	$500,000

* The dividend for mutual fund B is expected to grow at 3% per year.

David is considering replacing Mutual Fund A with Mutual Fund Z. Both mutual funds have a similar investment objective.

Mutual Fund									
Name	Shares	Cost per Share	NAV	Beta	R^2 to S&P 500	Yield	One Year Return	Standard Deviation	Total FMV
Z	-	-	$89	1.35	0.89	0.75%	7.5%	0.17	-

Education and Education Accounts (529)

The contributions to these accounts are invested in a diversified portfolio of mutual funds based on each beneficiary's age. David selected an overall investment strategy that resulted in "moderate risk" investments. The current annual cost of education in today's dollars is $20,000 with an expected inflation rate of six percent. The Rudolphs currently plan to pay for four years each for Madelyn and Danny.

DRI 401(k) Plan with Roth Account Option

David is uncertain about which retirement plan mutual funds to allocate his contributions to, so he decided to keep 100 percent of the account balance in cash. David made his first contribution to this account two years ago.

Traditional IRA

The Traditional IRA is invested in a series of zero coupon bonds. The investment returns in this account over the past five years have been:

Year	Returns
1	6.50%
2	4.75%
3	- 3.25%
4	- 2.5%
5	5.25%

David is uncertain what his compounded investment rate of return has been and whether the investments are appropriate for his goals.

Roth IRA

The Roth IRA is currently invested in a tax-free municipal bond mutual fund, earning 1.75 percent per year. The income is reinvested and not reflected on the income statement.

Income Tax and Social Security Tax Information

The Rudolphs are in the higher marginal income tax brackets for federal income tax purposes and their state income tax rate is four percent. Capital gains are taxed up to 20 percent at the federal level and four percent at the state level.

David's Social Security Tax Withholding		
Social Security Retirement and HI	$142,800 x 0.0765 =	$10,924.20
HI above wage base	($275,000 - $142,800) x 0.0145 =	$1,916.90
Surtax (0.009)*	($275,000 - $200,000) x 0.009 =	$675.00
	Total	$13,516.10

Amy's income tax withholding and Social Security are estimated.
* For employer withholding purposes, $200,000 is used even though the limit for MFJ filer is $250,000.

Retirement Information[1]

David has a safe harbor 401(k) plan through his company (DRI). He contributes part of his salary each year, plus a catch-up contribution. His total contribution, including the catch-up, each year is $23,000. David has not elected Roth contributions, therefore, his contributions are made pretax. His company matches dollar for dollar on the first three percent of salary and then $0.50 on the dollar on the next two percent of salary to a maximum contribution of four percent of his covered compensation.[2] David also has an integrated profit sharing plan through his company (DRI). The company adds the amount necessary to the profit sharing plan to fund an overall defined contribution amount of $57,500, including David's $23,000 deferral (with catch-up) and the company match. Amy is self-employed and does not currently have a retirement plan.

---

1. Note: He could have contributed a higher amount to the 401(k) for 20X1 but chose to only contribute a total of $23,000.
2. The DRI 401(k) plan limits plan compensation to a maximum of $245,000 for matching and profit sharing contributions.

The Rudolphs define adequate retirement income as approximately 80 percent of pre-retirement income or an adjusted percent to maintain their lifestyle. They both plan to live until age 95 after retiring at age 62 but only want to consider his age in retirement capital needs projections. He is expecting to receive $20,000 at normal age retirement (age 67) in Social Security benefits but will only receive $14,000 in today's dollars at age 62. Any Social Security that Amy would receive is to be disregarded, for retirement purposes, because of her age.

Estate Information

David has not arranged for any estate planning. Amy has a will leaving all of her assets outright to her daughter, Madelyn. Other than Amy's will, she has not arranged for any other estate planning.

Other Information Regarding Assets and Liabilities

Personal Residence

The Rudolphs purchased their personal residence for $1,500,000 two years ago (they have made exactly 24 payments as of January 1, 20X2). Their mortgage payment is $7,195 per month. They borrowed $1,200,000 over 30 years at six percent. They were considering refinancing the house but decided not to refinance when the appraised value dropped to $800,000 due to market conditions. They pay their homeowners insurance premiums and property taxes separately from their mortgage. Their property taxes are $8,000 yearly.

Lake House

The lake house was formerly David's personal residence for the last 15 years (he has made exactly 180 payments as of January 1, 20X2). He purchased the lake house for $250,000, by putting down 20 percent and borrowing the rest at seven percent for 30 years. His current payment is $15,967 per year. The lake house is rented for 14 days a year to one of David's key customers for $5,000. The $5,000 is used against expenses as reflected on the income statement. The property taxes are $4,000 per year and homeowners insurance is $3,500 per year. Both taxes and insurance are paid separately.

Boat

The Rudolphs purchased their boat for $125,000 four years ago (they have made exactly 48 payments as of January 1, 20X2). It is a 54' Hatterus with twin inboard motors. Their boat payment is $1,267 per month. They borrowed $100,000 over 10 years at nine percent on a signature loan to finance the purchase of the boat. The Rudolphs do not have a separate property or liability insurance policy on the boat.

DR Office Furniture, Inc. (DRI)

David started working at DR Office Furniture, Inc. over 20 years ago when he inherited the business from his father. Today, it is one of the largest office furniture companies in the southeast. Over the years, David has sold 25 percent of the equity in his company to his top employees. The value of the business is expected to grow at three percent each year. Paul Carter, Brian Conner, and Sally Walker (the top employees) have agreed to buy the business in 11 years. David insists that this sale will provide an adequate capital balance upon which to retire. DR Office Furniture, Inc. has traditionally offered employees health insurance, group term life insurance, a 401(k) plan with a Roth component and an integrated profit sharing plan. The profit sharing plan's eligibility requirement is age 21 and one year of service.

PIE CHART APPROACH

Introduction

The pie chart approach to financial planning (as discussed in detail in Chapter 3) provides a visual representation of both the client's balance sheet and the income statement. The Rudolphs' pie chart analysis of the income statement is shown below.

Data for Pie Chart Approach - Income Statement

Exhibit 10.9 | David and Amy Rudolph 1/1/20X2

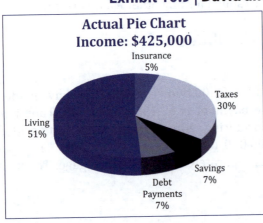

Actual Pie Chart
Income: $425,000

Insurance 5%
Taxes 30%
Savings 7%
Debt Payments 7%
Living 51%

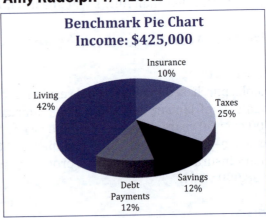

Benchmark Pie Chart
Income: $425,000

Insurance 10%
Taxes 25%
Savings 12%
Debt Payments 12%
Living 42%

Notes:
- Debt payments excludes both mortgages. The mortgages are included in living expenses.
- The savings percentage does not include the employer contributions to the 401(k) plan and the integrated profit sharing plan.
- Living expenses = $116,800 + $86,335 + $15,967
- The table below provides a more detailed view than the pie chart by separating out the housing costs (principal & interest, taxes, and insurance) for the principal residence and the lake house.

Income	100%	$425,000
Other Living Expenses	27.48%	The balance of living expenses - $116,800
Other Debt Payments*	7.11%	($15,201 + $15,000)
Savings Rate	6.82%	($23,000 + $6,000)
Insurance**	2.97%	($2,100 + $10,000 + $500)
Housing Costs** (Personal Residence Only)	23.18%	($86,335 + $8,000 + $4,200)
Housing Costs** (Lake House)	5.52%	($15,967 + $3,500 + $4,000)
Taxes**	27.06%	($63,800 + $16,491 + $13,516 + $21,195)
Discretionary Cash Flows	(0.14%)	- $605

* Other debt payments excludes both mortgages.

** Property taxes and insurance on residences is included with housing costs.

Observations

Although the overall savings rate of 6.82 percent appears to be low, it increases to 14.9 percent (which is excellent) when calculated (later in the case) including the employer contributions.

The Rudolphs are spending 28.7 percent of their overall income on the principal residence and lake house, not including utilities and other expenses. Vacations are listed at $25,000. These two expenses (housing and vacations) combined suggest that perhaps the Rudolphs should consider vacationing at the lake house and paying off or refinancing the seven percent mortgage.

Unfortunately, the Rudolphs are underwater (negative equity) in the principal residence, but mortgage rates are one percent less than when they first bought the house. If they paid down the mortgage to $640,000 (80% loan to value) and then refinanced, they would have a monthly payment of approximately $3,538.73 instead of $7,195.00. To refinance the house, it would require $529,619 of cash, which does not look promising.

Because of the decline in the value of the principal residence, the Rudolphs should definitely challenge the property tax assessment, which could reduce their property taxes to as little as $4,000 and increase their discretionary cash flows by the $4,000 savings.

Data for Pie Chart Approach - Balance Sheet

David and Amy Rudolph 12/31/20X1
Rudolph Balance Sheet

Assets = 100%		Liabilities & Net Worth = 100%	
Cash or Cash Equivalents	$295,000	Current Liabilities	$15,000
Investment Assets	$3,956,000	Long-Term Liabilities	$1,387,933
Personal Use Assets	$1,465,000	Net Worth	$4,313,067
	$5,716,000		$5,716,000

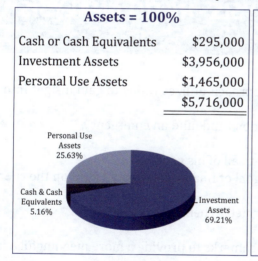

Benchmark Balance Sheet

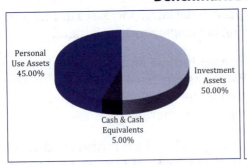

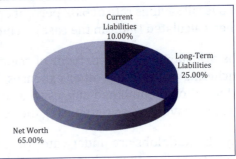

Observations

The Rudolphs' balance sheet appears to be in excellent condition with five percent cash and cash equivalents. The most significant issue on the balance sheet is the valuation of DRI. The footnote to their balance sheet indicates that the DRI value is based on David's estimate. The company value represents 77 percent of their net worth and 84 percent of their investment assets. To justify a valuation of this magnitude, the net after-tax cash flows need to be approximately $500,000 per year, discounted for 25 years at 15 percent. It is probably wise to have the buyer employees begin to buy sooner rather than later. It is also a good idea to obtain an expert to value the business. David continues to own 75 percent of the business and could continue to control the business with 50.1 percent ownership and perhaps even less. The objective is to reduce the risk of a large concentration in wealth.

FINANCIAL STATEMENT ANALYSIS - RATIO ANALYSIS APPROACH

Introduction

The financial statement analysis - ratio analysis approach utilizes ratios to gain insight into the client's financial situation. The approach assesses:

1. the client's ability to pay short-term obligations and fund an emergency,
2. the client's ability to manage debt,
3. whether the client is committed financially to all of his goals,
4. the progress of the client in achieving the goal of financial security based on the client's age and income, and
5. how well the investment assets have performed to benchmarks.

The ratios should be compared to appropriate benchmarks to provide a more meaningful analysis.

Exhibit 10.10 | Ratio Analysis

Liquidity Ratios Based on 20X2 Financial Statements				
Ratio	**Formula**		**Comment**	**Benchmark**
Emergency Fund Ratio*	$\dfrac{\text{Cash \& Cash Equivalents}}{\text{Monthly Non-Discretionary Cash Flows}}$	$\dfrac{\$295,000}{\$20,134} = 14.65$	Very Strong	3 - 6:1
Current Ratio	$\dfrac{\text{Cash \& Cash Equivalents}}{\text{Current Liabilities}}$	$\dfrac{\$295,000}{\$15,000} = 19.7:1$	Very Strong	0.5:1

Monthly non-discretionary cash flows = $20,134 as indicated on Statement of Income and Expenses by ND ($241,603 / 12).

Debt Ratios Based on 20X1 Financial Statements				
Housing Ratio 1 (HR 1) (Includes both homes.)	$\dfrac{\text{Housing Costs}}{\text{Gross Pay}}$	$\dfrac{\$122,002}{\$425,000} = 28.7\%$	High	$\leq 28\%$
Housing Ratio 2 (HR 2) (Includes both homes.)	$\dfrac{\text{Housing Costs + Other Debt Payments}}{\text{Gross Pay}}$	$\dfrac{\$152,203}{\$425,000} = 35.8\%$	High	$\leq 36\%$
Debt-to-Total Assets	$\dfrac{\text{Total Debt}}{\text{Total Assets}}$	$\dfrac{\$1,402,933}{\$5,716,000} = 24.54\%$	Very Strong	Age Dependent
Net Worth-to-Total Assets	$\dfrac{\text{Net Worth}}{\text{Total Assets}}$	$\dfrac{\$4,313,067}{\$5,716,000} = 75.46\%$	Very Strong	Age Dependent

Ratios for Financial Security Goals Based on 20X1 Financial Statements				
Savings Rate (Overall)	$\dfrac{\text{Savings + Employer Match}}{\text{Gross Pay}}$	$\dfrac{\$63,500}{\$425,000} = 14.94\%$	Very Strong	Goal Driven At Least 10-13%
Savings Rate (Retirement)	$\dfrac{\text{Employee Contributions + Employer Contributions}}{\text{Gross Pay}}$	$\dfrac{\$57,500}{\$425,000} = 13.53\%$	Very Strong	10 - 13%
Investment Assets-to-Gross Pay (Does not include education savings.)	$\dfrac{\text{Investment Assets + Cash \& Cash Equivalents}}{\text{Gross Pay}}$	$\dfrac{\$3,910,000 + \$295,000}{\$425,000} = 9.9:1$	Very Strong	Approx. 4:1 at Age 50

Performance Ratios Based on 20X1 and 20X2 Financial Statements				
Return on Investments =	$\dfrac{I_1 - (I_0 + \text{Savings})}{I_0}$	= 1.37% (See calculation below)	Poor	8-10%
Return on Assets =	$\dfrac{A_1 - (A_0 + \text{Savings})}{A_0}$	= -6.96% (See calculation below)	Very Poor**	2-4%
Return on Net Worth =	$\dfrac{NW_1 - (NW_0 + \text{Savings})}{NW_0}$	= -8.47% (See calculation below)	Very Poor**	The higher the better. This ratio is likely to become smaller as the client's net worth increases.

*** The substantial decrease in the value of the Rudolph's principal residence has resulted in a negative return on total assets and a negative return on net worth.*

Liquidity Ratios Based on 20X2 Financial Statements		
Performance Ratios Calculations*		
Return on Investments = (Excludes cash and cash equivalents)	$$\frac{\$3,956,000 - (\$3,840,000 + \$29,000 + \$34,500)}{\$3,840,000} = 1.37\%$$	
Return on Assets =	$$\frac{\$5,716,000 - (\$6,075,000 + \$29,000 + \$34,500)}{\$6,075,000} = -6.96\%$$	
Return on Net Worth =	$$\frac{\$4,313,067 - (\$4,642,568 + \$29,000 + \$34,500)}{\$4,642,568} = -8.47\%$$	
*** $34,500 of savings is derived from the employer match of 4% of $245,000 (compensation limit for the DRI Plan) which equals $9,800 plus $24,700 from the profit sharing plan. (See Schedule C Part 2.)		

Observations

The short-term liquidity and ability to pay ratios are excellent. The two housing ratios are high. However, both ratios consider the Rudolphs owning two homes. The other debt ratios are appropriate. The Rudolphs' overall savings rate is excellent at 14.94 percent as is their retirement savings rate of 13.53 percent and the investment assets-to-gross pay ratio at 9.9:1 for his age.

Once again, the issue is the reliability and certainty of the valuation of DRI. David says DRI grows in value at an annual rate of three percent This value should be demonstrated by net after-tax cash flows growing year over year by at least three percent.

The investment performance ratios are poor, but are somewhat skewed because of no change in the balance sheet value of DRI and the decline in the value of the principal residence. The performance ratios need to be compared to market returns for the year. However, investment returns are best measured over a longer time period (five years) and then compared to market benchmarks.

The performance ratios suggest the financial planner should take a much closer look at the investment portfolios and the valuation of DRI. The decline in the value of the principal residence has less consequences if the Rudolphs intend to remain living in the house for the long term.

THE TWO-STEP/THREE-PANEL/METRICS APPROACH

Introduction

The next approach used is the two-step approach (manage the risks and save and invest) modified to be applied as the three-panel approach, with metrics added. First the Rudolphs' risk management portfolio is evaluated, followed by their short-term emergency fund, housing ratios, and debt management. Finally, the Rudolphs' long-term goals are analyzed.

Risk Management Data - Schedule A

	Actual	*Metric*	*Comments / Recommendations*
Life Insurance:			
Policy 1 - David	$2,500,000	$2,750,000	Adequate coverage Ownership issue for estate tax Change beneficiary
Policy 2 - David	$550,000		Group Term - okay Change beneficiary
Policy 3 - Amy	$250,000	$1,500,000	Depends on risk tolerance and priorities Change owner Consider trust for Madelyn
Health Insurance	Yes	Adequate	Adequate coverage DRI provided
Disability Insurance			
David	60% Gross Pay / Guaranteed Renewable	60 - 70%	Adequate coverage DRI provided - Taxable
Amy	None		Consider adding disability insurance
Long-Term Care Insurance	None	36-60 months of savings	Examine merits of adding - This is a low priority
Property & Liability Insurance			
Personal Residence	$1,500,000	≤ FMV	Reduce coverage to FMV* Endorse HO3
Lake House	$200,000	≤ FMV	Consider raising coverage to FMV Endorse HO3
Automobile # 1 and # 2	100 / 300	100 / 300	Adequate coverage Consider raising deductibles
Boat	None	≤ FMV	At minimum, need liability insurance
Liability Insurance	None	$1 - 4 million	Need PLUP = $1 - $4 million

* Recommendation assumes replacement cost is equal to FMV and that the mortgage loan terms allow for coverage to be reduced below the balance of the mortgage.

Observations

Determining whether Amy's life insurance is adequate will require additional conversations with the client to arrive at a conclusion. The fact that David is the owner of his life insurance policies will cause inclusion in his gross estate at his death.[3] During the estate planning phase of the engagement, the financial planner should explore other (trust) ownership options. In any event, he should change the beneficiary to Amy.

Amy needs disability insurance to protect her stream of income.

The Rudolphs need to reduce the homeowners insurance coverage on the residence, increase it on the lake house, and endorse the personal property for all risk and replacement value. A separate property and liability policy on the boat is needed.

The Rudolphs also need to add a personal liability umbrella policy of coverage ranging from $1,000,000 to $4,000,000 to protect against personal law suits. They need to be sure to notify the PLUP provider about the boat and both homes.

Short-Term Savings and Investments - Schedule B

	Actual	Metric	Comments
Emergency Fund	14.65 x	3 - 6 month	More than adequate.
Housing Ratio:			
1 - Principal Residence	23.2%	≤ 28%	
2 - Principal Residence	30.3%	≤ 36%	
1 - Lake House	5.52%	≤ 28%	
1 - Combined	28.7%	≤ 28%	These are high for their ages but do not exceed the metric.
2 - Combined	35.8%	≤ 36%	
Evaluation of Debt			The principal residence is underwater and this will have to be resolved to be able to refinance. Mortgage rates are low enough to refinance and thus improve housing ratios 1 & 2. However on principal residence there is a loan-to-value issue.

---

3. David's current estate is below the federal estate tax exemption; however, many states use exemption amounts much lower than the federal amount, so the value of the gross estate must be managed appropriately.

Observations

The Rudolphs' emergency fund is substantial at 14.65 times monthly non-discretionary cash flows. They are right up against the maximum metric for both HR1 and HR2 when the two properties are combined. The client may want to pay off all credit card and boat debt, and possibly the lake house debt. In order to refinance the principal residence, the Rudolphs would have to pay the mortgage down to $640,000 to meet the 80 percent loan to value requirements of most lenders. This option seems unlikely.

Informational Inputs		
Non-Discretionary Cash Flows	$20,134 per month $241,603 annually	Income Statement
Cash and Cash Equivalents	$295,000	Balance Sheet
Principal Residence (PR)	P&I & T&I = $98,535	Income Statement
Lake House (LH)	P&I & T&I = $23,467	Income Statement
Other Debt Payments (Boat)	$15,201	Income Statement
Credit Card Payments	$15,000	Income Statement
Gross Pay	$425,000	Income Statement

Long-Term Savings and Investments - Schedule C

To achieve financial security (retirement) requires persistent savings of 10 to 13 percent of gross pay and investment assets that are appropriate for the age of the client and the gross pay. Many clients have multiple goals such as retirement, education funding, lump-sum expenditures, and legacy aspirations. The more goals a client has the greater the need for an increased savings rate.

Schedule C - Part 1

	Actual	Metric	Comments
Retirement Security Goal			
Overall Savings Rate	14.94%	At least 10% - 13% of gross pay	Excellent
Retirement Savings Rate	13.53%	10% - 13% of gross pay	The total savings rate is consistent with the retirement goal.
Investment Assets as% of Gross Pay	9.9 x	8 x	They currently exceed the necessary investment assets for retirement (for their age). Education assets are excluded. Valuation of DRI is critical.
Educational Funding	$6,000 per year	$6,000 per year	Adequate
Lump-Sum Goals	None	None	Okay
Estate Planning	None	Documents	Critical estate planning documents and planning needed.

Schedule C - Part 2

Informational Inputs * **	
Savings:	
• 401(k) Plan Deferral + Catch-up	$23,000
• 401(k) Plan Match ($245,000 x 4%)	$9,800
• Profit Sharing Plan	$24,700
Total Retirement	**$57,500**
Education Savings	$6,000
Total Savings	**$63,500**
Salary (gross pay)	$425,000
Investment Assets less Education Assets =	$3,910,000

* Income Statement plus 401(k) plan match plus profit sharing plan.
** Essentially no estate planning completed.

Observations

The Rudolphs have an excellent savings rate of 14.94 percent ($57,500 + $6,000) ÷ $425,000) overall and have investment assets equal to 9.9 x their gross pay which, using David's age (51), the benchmark or metric is 8x. The most significant issue is the value of the business. DRI makes up 84 percent of the investment assets. There is a serious issue regarding valuation and concern over whether the employees will be willing and able to buy the business in eleven years, at David's retirement. This issue is central to the overall plan and alternatives will have to be developed.

THE CASH FLOW APPROACH

The cash flow approach adjusts the cash flows on the income statement as projected after implementing all of the financial planner's recommendations. The approach starts with the discretionary cash flows at the bottom of the income statement and accounts for the recommendations in the order of priority by charging the cost of the expense against the discretionary cash flows regardless of any negative cash flow impact. The analysis is prepared carefully to differentiate between recurring cash flows and non-recurring cash flows.

Cash Flow Approach with Recommendations - Schedule D

	Income Statement Recurring Impact	Balance Statement Non-Recurring Impact	Comments/Explanations
Rudolph Cash Flow Approach with Recommendations			
Beginning Cash Flow (Income Statement)	**($605)**		
Recommendations:			
Risk Management:			
• Term Life Insurance for Amy	($750)		$1,000,000 for 20 years
• Disability Insurance for Amy	($3,000)		60% Gross Pay / Guaranteed Renewable 90 day to 65
• Long-Term Care			Do nothing now
• Homeowners - principal residence and lake house	($400)		Endorse personal property to open perils / replacement value. Lower dwelling value on principal residence. Raise dwelling value on lake house.
• Boat Property and Liability Insurance	($800)		Cover both property and liability.
• Personal Liability Insurance $2M	($400)		Advise PLUP carrier of boat.
Debt Management:			
• Pay off credit cards	+ $10,000	($15,000)	Recurring annual $5,000 expenditure
• Pay off boat loan	+ $15,201	($70,276)	
• Refinance Lake House Mortgage	+ $1,735		New loan balance $152,479
Retirement Savings:			
• Amy's 401(k) Plan Roth	($17,500)		401(k) plan individual
• Tax savings on 401(k) plan	0		Average 20% tax rate (Roth = 0)*
Estate Planning:			
• Documents for David and Amy		($1,000)	Will,** Durable Power of Attorney, Advance Medical Directive; need to begin estate planning process.
TOTALS	**+ $3,481**	**($86,276)**	Creates positive annual cash flow (reflected in income statement), reduces cash and cash equivalents by $86,276 thus negatively impacting the emergency fund ratio.

( ) indicates a negative impact on cash flow and + indicates a positive impact on cash flow.

* Assume Amy will use the Roth account and therefore will make after-tax contributions. Note that she could have contributed a higher amount but they chose to limit contributions to the amounts stated.

** David's will naming Amy and Danny as heirs.

Debt Management - Schedule E

Debt Management			
	Old Information (Loan)	New Loan	Comments
Refinance Lake House			
• Loan	$200,000	$152,479.14	($148,038 + 3%)
• Term	360 months	180 months	
• Interest Rate	7%	4.75%	
• Payment per month	($1,330.60)	($1,186.03)	Saves $144.57 per month Saves $1,734.84 annually
Alternative:			
• Pay Off Lake House	($148,038)		Saves $15,967 annually
• Pay Off the Boat	($70,276)		Saves $15,201 annually
• Pay Off Credit Cards	($15,000)		Saves $15,000 annually[1]
• Total Debt Pay Off	($233,314)		Saves $46,168 annually

1. In reality, they will continue to incur $5,000 annually for a savings of $10,000 per year.

Observations

The Rudolphs have debt that is expensive, such as the boat (10%) and the lake house (7%). The financial planning recommendations are to pay off the debt on the boat and credit cards, and to refinance the lake house over 15 years at 4.75 percent to coincide with the retirement objective. These actions would increase the discretionary cash flows by $3,481 per year (Schedule D). They could alternatively payoff the boat, lake house, and credit cards increasing their cash flows annually by another $15,967, giving them net discretionary cash flows (even after Amy's 401(k) plan contribution) of $15,967 + $3,481 = $19,448. The problem is that it would take $233,314 from cash and cash equivalents to pay off the debt.

STRATEGIC APPROACH

Mission Statement

- Financial Security (the ability to maintain one's lifestyle without employment income)

Goals

- Adequate risk management portfolio
- Adequate savings rate for retirement and education
- Adequate emergency fund
- Adequate debt management
- Adequate investment portfolio
- Adequate estate plan

Personal and Financial Objectives of the Rudolphs

1. They want to provide for Danny and Madelyn's education.
2. They want to retire debt free when David reaches age 62 (when they plan to retire).
3. They need adequate retirement income.
4. They want to have adequate risk management coverage.
5. David is concerned about providing income for Amy and leaving the remainder of his estate to their child, Danny.
6. The Rudolphs want to have an appropriate investment portfolio.

Personal and Financial Objectives Recommended by the Financial Planner

Risk Management

*   Consider changing the ownership and beneficiary for David's life insurance policy #1 to Amy with contingent beneficiary as Danny.
*   Purchase individual disability policy on Amy.
*   Endorse the principal residence and lake house homeowners policies for open perils and replacement value.
*   Purchase a personal liability umbrella policy (PLUP) $1 - $4 million.

Budgeting

*   Refinance the lake house or pay it off.
*   Request a reassessment of the property taxes on their principal residence because of the decline in value.

Retirement

*   Amy should establish a retirement plan: SEP, SIMPLE, 401(k) plan, or profit sharing plan.
*   DRI makes up 84 percent of investment assets and the sale to employees at David's retirement is questionable. David should sell off at least a portion of this asset as soon as possible.
*   David insists that retirement income is covered with DRI. The financial planner recommends, and David agrees, to a valuation and then a capital needs analysis within the next year.

Tax

*   An appropriate retirement plan for Amy could shelter income tax and reduce payroll taxes.

Entity

*   Amy should change her business entity status from sole proprietorship to an S Corporation or LLC.

Estate Plan

*   Have estate documents prepared (will, durable power of attorney for health care, advance medical directive).

Debt Management

*   David and Amy are not yet able to meet their goal of being debt free at David's age 62 because of the 30-year mortgage on the principal residence and the 15-year mortgage on the lake house.

Investments

*   David is very disappointed in his current investment performance except for his business.

PRESENTATION TO DAVID AND AMY RUDOLPH - FINANCIAL STATEMENTS AND RATIOS POST RECOMMENDATIONS

New Emergency Fund Ratio

Old emergency fund monthly non-discretionary expenses	$20,134.00
Increases in risk management costs $\frac{\$5,350}{12}$	$445.83
Decreases in debt management $\frac{\$26,936}{12}$	($2,244.67)
401(k) plan contribution does not affect non-discretionary cash flows	0
New non-discretionary cash flows	**$18,335.16**
New cash & cash equivalent $295,000 - $86,276 non-recurring expenditures	$208,724.00
New emergency fund ratio $\frac{\$208,724.00}{\$18,335.16}$ **(excellent)**	**11.38 Months**

New Savings Rate (EE = employee, ER = employer)

David	401(k) Plan (EE) Deferral	$23,000	(including Over 50 Catch-Up)
	ER Match	$9,800	
	Profit Sharing (ER)	$24,700	
	David Total	**$57,500**	(See Retirement Information)
	Education	$6,000	
Amy	401(k) Plan (EE) Deferral	$17,500	
	Combined Total	**$81,000**	
	New Savings Rate:	$\frac{\$81,000}{\$425,000}$	= 19.06% Excellent

Housing Ratios

New Housing Ratio - Combined HR 1 (after refinance of lake house)

Principal - P & I	$86,335.00
Principal - HO	$4,200.00
Lake House - P & I	$14,232.36 ($1,186.03 x 12)
Lake House - HO	$3,500.00
Endorsements	$400.00
Principal - Property Tax	$8,000.00 *A reassessment is to be requested.
Lake House - Property Tax	$4,000.00
	$120,667.36

$$\frac{\$120,667.36}{\$425,000} = 28.39\% \text{ (slightly exceeds 28\%)}$$

New Housing Ratio - Combined HR 2

$$\$120,667.36 + \$5,000^* = \frac{\$125,667.36}{\$425,000} = 29.57\% \text{ (good)}$$

* credit card recurring payment

Investment Analysis

Following the investment analysis process, the financial planner should develop an investment policy statement and then analyze the portfolio performance against the investment policy statement.

The Rudolphs' investment policy statement is as follows:

Rudolphs' Investment Policy Statement January 1, 20X2	
Retirement Goals	• Generate adequate retirement income. • Retire debt free.
Education Goals	• Provide for Danny and Madelyn's education.
Return Requirements	• They require an 8% return on their overall portfolio.
Risk Tolerance	• They have a moderate risk tolerance.
Time Horizon	• Retirement for David is 11 years away. • Retirement for Amy is 11 years away. • Education for Danny is 17 years away. • Education for Madelyn is 4 years away.
Constraints	• They have liquidity issues with a majority of their net worth being in a small business that they are planning to sell and then use the proceeds for retirement. • They have a very short time horizon to fund Madelyn's education, which is only four years away.

Investment Portfolio Analysis

The analysis of an investment portfolio is accomplished by comparing the objectives in the investment policy statement to the actual performance of the investment portfolio. The Rudolphs' investments are compared to their investment policy statement for an analysis of their progress towards accomplishing their goals.

Overall Investment Growth

The Rudolphs' investment assets grew from $3,840,000 (1/1/20X1) to $3,956,000 (1/1/20X2). The Rudolphs made investment contributions of $63,500 ($29,000 plus $34,500 from the employer, as indicated on Schedule C - Part 2), which means they only earned an annual return of 1.37 percent. This overall rate of return is too low given their time horizon and risk tolerance. One likely issue is the valuation of DRI which has not increased. There are other issues that are contributing, to a lesser extent, to the low annual return such as the Roth IRA return of 1.75 percent and David's 401(k) plan entirely invested in cash.

Recommendations:
- Obtain an updated valuation on DRI.
- Reallocate the investments in the Roth IRA and David's 401(k) plan to be more consistent with the investment goals.

Education Goal Investment Growth

The total balance in the 529 Savings Plans was $46,000 at the beginning of 20X1 and ended the year (12/31/20X1) at $46,000. However, the Rudolphs contributed $6,000 to the funds during 20X1. Therefore the accounts declined 13 percent for the year.

With a 529 Savings Plan, the investment options may be limited based on the age of the children and their time horizon until they enter college. Some 529 Savings Plans have the option of an aggressive allocation or moderate allocation based on the child's age. In the Rudolphs' case, there is not enough information to determine the riskiness of the investments held. However, since some 529 Savings Plans become more conservative as the beneficiary approaches age 18, it is likely that the Rudolphs' education investments are appropriate. The client and planner agree to investigate.

Recommendations:
- The financial planner should review the investment options for the 529 Savings Plan to determine if the funds are appropriately allocated between aggressive and moderate risk investments.

Risk Tolerance
- They have a moderate risk tolerance.

Time Horizons
- Retirement for David is 11 years away.
- Retirement for Amy is 11 years away.
- Education for Danny is 17 years away.
- Education for Madelyn is 4 years away.

Although the financial planner was not provided with the riskiness of each investment, certain conclusions can be drawn based on the investments held.

DRI

The Rudolphs have significant single-asset risk because 77 percent of their net worth is based on the value of DRI. Although David's top three employees have agreed to purchase the business, there is some risk that the employees will be unable or unwilling to buy the remainder of DRI at the time projected. There are still other risks that must be discussed with the client, such as:

- *Business Risk* - what are the inherent risks of doing business in the office furniture industry?
- *Executive Risk* - what if something happens to any of the key employees, will the others still be able to purchase the business?
- *Financial Risk* - how do the key employees intend to finance the purchase of the business and will David receive a lump sum or annuity payout?
- *Valuation Risk* - does the revenue multiple of 2.5x represent an appropriate value for the business? The business valuation may be dated, so we should consider an updated valuation based on net after-tax cash flows.

These are all important questions regarding the financial security of the Rudolphs. Their goal is to reduce the risk and diversify their investment portfolio. Throughout the monitoring phase of the financial planning process, the financial planner should continue to work with the Rudolphs to eliminate the single-asset risk.

Investment Portfolio of Mutual Funds (Brokerage Account)

The brokerage account consisting of mutual funds has a standard deviation of 15 percent, which appears to be reasonable for their time horizon and risk tolerance. However, when considering the client's investment in DRI and the brokerage account together, the brokerage account may create a diversification issue with too heavy a weighting on equities. The Rudolphs only have the Traditional IRA of $15,000 and Roth IRA of $20,000 invested in fixed income investments. The Rudolphs need 30 to 40 percent of their investment assets allocated to fixed income investments because of the correlation between equities and fixed income investments and the diversification benefits from proper asset allocation.

401(k) Plan with Roth Account Option

The allocation to cash in this portfolio is too conservative. The financial planner needs to work with David to select an appropriate allocation between equities and fixed income investments in this account. His current allocation is 100 percent cash, which is not appropriate given his time horizon and risk tolerance. Additional information is required from David's plan administrator regarding available investment options.

Traditional IRA

The traditional IRA holds a series of zero coupon bonds. Zero coupon bonds generate "phantom income" or income that is taxed, but not actually received until the bond is sold. Holding zero coupon bonds in a tax deferred account is appropriate to avoid the phantom income issue. However, the financial planner needs to gather more information regarding the types of bonds, the term of the bonds and credit rating of the bonds to make an evaluation regarding the riskiness of these bonds. The planner also needs to review the expected returns.

Roth IRA

Investments that are expected to experience significant capital appreciation are most appropriate for a Roth IRA. Since municipal bonds generate income that is free from federal income taxes, and possibly state income taxes as well, municipal bonds are best held in a taxable account not in a Roth.

Overall Recommendations Regarding Retirement Assets:

- The asset allocation is too heavily weighted towards equities and not enough to fixed income investments because of DRI. It is likely that the standard deviation of the portfolio is significantly higher than 15 percent when considering the riskiness of DRI. Adding bonds to the portfolio will help reduce the overall riskiness of the investment portfolio.
- Since the Rudolphs are 11 years away from selling DRI, they should consider annual valuations and develop a plan to begin selling part of the business to the key employees so they can build a more diversified portfolio and reduce some of their risk.

Other Investment Observations

- A small percentage of the Rudolphs' investment assets are in tax-deferred retirement savings accounts. David and Amy are only 11 years away from retirement, but we should consider taking advantage of tax-deferred savings for both of them during this period.
- David is considering replacing Mutual Fund A in his portfolio with Mutual Fund Z. Mutual Fund Z is showing a higher one-year return than Mutual Fund A. However, the funds should be evaluated on a risk adjusted basis. Since the r-squared for both mutual funds is greater than 0.70, we can rely on Beta as a reasonable measure of total risk and we can use the Treynor ratio to determine which fund returned the higher risk adjusted rate of return. The calculation is as follows:

Treynor Ratio	$\dfrac{\text{Actual Return} - \text{Risk Free Rate}}{\text{Beta}}$
Mutual Fund A	$\dfrac{6\% - 3.5\%}{1.1} = 2.27\%$
Mutual Fund Z	$\dfrac{7.5\% - 3.5\%}{1.35} = 2.96\%$

Mutual Fund Z provides a higher risk adjusted rate of return than Mutual Fund A. Replacing Mutual Fund A with Mutual Fund Z may be an appropriate recommendation.

- David is uncertain regarding their compounded rate of return on the retirement bonds, so the financial planner should use the geometric mean to determine the compounded rate of return. The calculation is as follows:

$$\text{Geometric Mean} = \sqrt[5]{(1.065)(1.0475)(0.9675)(0.9750)(1.0525)} - 1 \times 100 = 2.06\%$$

*This is a fairly low compounded rate of return for bond investments, which would be expected to be in the five to six percent range. The financial planner needs to evaluate the type of bonds, the credit quality and possibly replace the current zero coupon bonds.

Exhibit 10.11 | Post Recommendation Balance Sheet - Abbreviated - Schedule F

Assets		Liabilities and Net Worth	
Current Assets		**Current Liabilities**	
Cash & Cash Equivalents	$208,724	Credit Cards	$0
Invested Assets	$3,956,000	**Long-Term Liabilities***	$1,322,098
Personal Use Assets	$1,465,000	**Net Worth**	$4,307,626
Total Assets	**$5,629,724**	**Total Liabilities & Net Worth**	**$5,629,724**

Long-term liabilities include the principal residence and the lake house.

Change in Net Worth - Reconciliation

$4,313,067	Before Recommendations
$4,307,626	After Recommendations
$5,441	Net Reduction
$4,441	Lake House closing costs 3% ($148,038 x 0.03)
$1,000	Paid for basic estate planning documents ($1,000)

RETIREMENT GOAL

The retirement goal initially was 80 percent of income in today's dollars at age 62 (11 years from now) and using David's life expectancy to age 95 (33 years). The inflation rate is assumed to be 2.5 percent and the portfolio earnings rate is assumed to be eight percent.

Calculation of Retirement Needs at Year 1 of Retirement:

N   = 11

i   = 2.5

PV = $326,000
       (($425,000 x 0.80 = $340,000); ($340,000 less Social Security of $14,000 = $326,000))

PMT = 0

FV = $427,740.25

Calculation of Capital Needs at Retirement (Annuity Approach):

$$
\begin{array}{lll}
\text{N} & = & 33 \\
\text{i} & = & [((1.08 \div 1.025) -1) \text{ x } 100] \\
\text{FV} & = & 0 \\
\text{PMT}_{AD} & = & \$427,740.25 \\
\text{PV}_{@62} & = & \$6,902,528.41
\end{array}
$$

Calculation of Capital Needs in Present Value Terms:

$$
\begin{array}{lll}
\text{N} & = & 11 \\
\text{i} & = & 8 \\
\text{FV} & = & \$6,902,528.41 \\
\text{PMT} & = & 0 \\
\text{PV}_{@51} & = & \$2,960,376.12
\end{array}
$$

It is clear that even without additional savings, the Rudolphs have sufficient assets to retire but the valuation of assets is heavily dependent on the valuation of DRI.

Adjusted Wage Replacement Ratio:
The Rudolphs are likely to need a wage replacement ratio that is less than their original estimate of 80 percent to maintain their lifestyle and therefore they have an adequate savings plan depending on the business valuation.

EDUCATION GOAL

The education goal for Madelyn and Danny, as stated, is four years of college beginning at age 18. The current cost is $20,000, the expected education inflation is six percent, and the expected earnings rate is eight percent.

Calculation of 4 Years of College in Today's Dollars:

$$
\begin{array}{lll}
\text{N} & = & 4 \\
\text{i} & = & [((1.08 \div 1.06) -1) \text{ x } 100] \\
\text{PMT}_{AD} & = & \$20,000 \\
\text{PV}_{@18} & = & \$77,805.09 \\
\text{FV} & = & 0
\end{array}
$$

Calculation for Madelyn Age 14:

$$
\begin{array}{lll}
\text{N} & = & 4 \\
\text{i} & = & [((1.08 \div 1.06) -1) \text{ x } 100] \\
\text{FV} & = & \$77,805.09 \\
\text{PV} & = & \$72,199.87
\end{array}
$$

Calculation for Danny Age 1:

N = 17

i = [(1.08 ÷ 1.06) -1) x 100]

FV = $77,805.09

PV = $56,624.43

Summary of Education Costs in Present Value Terms:

Madelyn	$72,199.87
Danny	$56,624.43
Total	**$128,824.30**

Again, the Rudolphs have sufficient assets to pay for the education goal.

SUMMARY

When the Rudolphs came to the financial planner they had the following strengths and weaknesses:

Strengths

1. Income $425,000 annually
2. Savings rate of 14.94%
3. Net Worth of $4.3 million
4. Investment assets of $3.956 million
5. Adequate life insurance on David
6. Adequate health insurance
7. Adequate disability insurance on David
8. Excess homeowners insurance on residence
9. Adequate automobile insurance, although deductibles were too low
10. Excellent ratios, except investment performance ratios

Weaknesses

1. Low net discretionary cash flows (negative $605)
2. Questionable life insurance on Amy
3. Inadequate disability insurance on Amy
4. No long-term care insurance on David or Amy
5. Inadequate property insurance on lake house
6. No property and liability insurance on the boat
7. No personal liability umbrella policy
8. Poor investment returns
9. No estate planning documents
10. Negative equity on the client's principal residence
11. The interest rates for the debt on the boat and the lake house are too high
12. Property taxes on the personal residence are too high

Recommendations - Implemented

The financial planner solved the clients' weaknesses as follows:

- They added disability insurance on Amy.
- They added a personal liability insurance policy (PLUP).
- The financial planner is continuing to work on the investment returns and is encouraging the clients to consider life insurance on Amy and long-term care for both David and Amy.
- The valuation of DRI is critical to the retirement plan and David should have a complete valuation prepared by an independent and qualified appraiser within a couple of months.
- The boat loan is paid off and the lake house is refinanced at a lower rate over 15 years.
- The revised annual net discretionary cash flows are $3,481 (from negative $605).
- The estate documents were prepared.

Unmet Goals

The retirement income goal of 80 percent of pre-retirement income is dependent on the appraisal of DRI.

The goal to be debt free at David's age 62 (retirement) is questionable given the mortgage on the principal residence.

Investment returns remain an issue that will require periodic monitoring and reevaluation.

11

RETIREMENT PLANNING ACCUMULATIONS AND DISTRIBUTIONS

INTRODUCTION

With nearly 35 percent of Americans having less than $25,000 in savings (excluding the value of their primary home and any defined benefit plans) and practically one in five with savings of less than $1,000, it is easy to make the case that most Americans are not financially prepared for retirement.[1] Financially prepared at retirement means that a person has:

1. Sufficient asset accumulation at retirement,
2. An appropriate investment plan, and
3. A plan for taking distributions from savings.

There are multiple factors to each of the three aspects of financial preparedness. This chapter examines the factors affecting retirement planning, the calculation of retirement needs, and methods of distributing assets during retirement.

FACTORS AFFECTING RETIREMENT PLANNING

Individuals face many decisions regarding retirement planning. In particular, they must decide what retirement means to them. Does retirement mean withdrawing from the workforce when financially able, or does it mean changes in lifestyle and family situations? For most, it is a momentous lifestyle change resulting from a significant shift in how they spend their time, money, and energy.

Individuals planning for retirement need to understand several basic factors that impact how much money is needed to fund retirement and how much money can be accumulated by the start of retirement. This chapter discusses the primary factors affecting retirement planning.

---

1. The 2020 Retirement Confidence Survey, EBRI, April 23, 2020.

The factors discussed in this chapter are:

- the remaining work life expectancy (RWLE)
- the savings amount and rate
- the wage replacement ratio (WRR)
- inflation expectations
- and other qualitative factors

- the annual income needed (needs) during retirement
- the retirement life expectancy (RLE)
- the sources of retirement income
- investment returns

A retirement plan must produce sufficient resources and income streams at retirement to ensure that a comfortable pre-retirement lifestyle is maintained throughout the retirement period. A discussion of each factor, its associated risks, and the calculations essential to retirement planning (capital needs analysis) is presented below.

Exhibit 11.1| Factors Affecting Retirement Planning

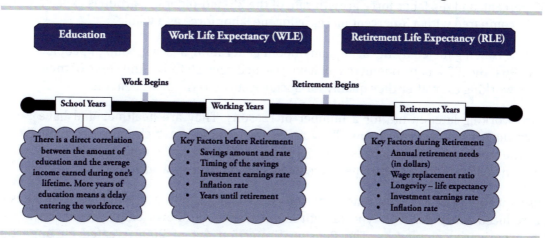

Remaining Work Life Expectancy (RWLE)

Work life expectancy (WLE) is the period of time a person is expected to be in the work force. This time period may be as long as 30 to 40 years and is essential in retirement planning because it is the period during which one saves and accumulates funds to use during retirement. Increasing or decreasing the work life expectancy impacts the time period over which individuals can save for retirement. The United States has seen a substantial decline in the overall WLE in the last several decades primarily due to individuals pursuing advanced education (undergraduate and graduate degrees), which delays their entry into the workforce, and those taking early retirement, which hastens their exit from the workforce.

Normal retirement has historically occurred at age 65 primarily because Social Security designated it as such and other employer provided retirement plans followed suit. The age at which recipients of Social Security can begin receiving benefits is age 62, but they must wait until Full Retirement Age to receive their full benefits under the system. Until recently, the average retirement age in the United States had steadily decreased since the 1970s due to a variety of factors including early retirement options from employer plans, early retirement under Social Security, and to some extent, positive investment performance during the 1980s and 1990s, which increased retirees' wealth.

However, Bureau of Labor (BLS) data show that the trend of earlier retirement is reversing and the age at which people are retiring has risen over the last several years. For example, in 2020, 22.3 percent of men aged 65 or older were employed, compared with 16.3 percent in 1990 and 17.5 percent in 2000. Among women 65 or older, 14.5 percent were working in 2020, compared with 8.6 percent in 1990 and 9.4 percent in 2000.[2]

Although they make up a smaller number of workers overall, the 65- to 74-year-old and 75-and-older age groups are projected to have faster rates of labor force growth annually than any other age groups. Over the entire 2014-24 decade, the labor force growth rate of the 65- to 74-year-old age group is expected to be about 55 percent, and the labor force growth rate of the 75-and-older age group is expected to be about 86 percent, compared with a 5-percent increase for the labor force as a whole.

This increase is being fueled by the aging baby-boom generation, a large group of people born between 1946 and 1964. By 2024, baby boomers will have reached ages 60 to 78. And some of them are expected to continue working even after they qualify for Social Security retirement benefits.

People are working later in life for a number of reasons. They are healthier and have a longer life expectancy than previous generations. They are better educated, which increases their likelihood of staying in the labor force. And changes to Social Security benefits and employee retirement plans, along with the need to save more for retirement, create incentives to keep working.

There also appears to be a recent trend of partial retirement, whereby an employee continues working but at a reduced schedule. This type of retirement transition allows employers to reduce cost but maintain experienced employees. The Pension Protection Act of 2006 created an opportunity for employees to begin receiving pension benefits while remaining employed after the attainment of age 62, and the Bipartisan American Miners Act of 2019 further expanded this opportunity by reducing the minimum age from 62 to 59½.

The trends discussed above are illustrated in **Exhibit 11.2**.

---

2. U.S. Department of Labor, Bureau of Labor Statistics.

Exhibit 11.2 | Labor Force Participation for Workers 65 and Older

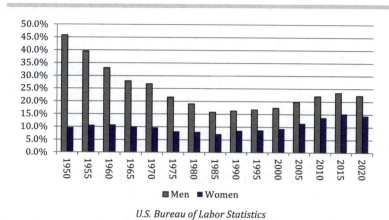

U.S. Bureau of Labor Statistics

Exhibit 11.2 illustrates that retirement age steadily declined over the last six decades, but is now increasing. According to research done by the Center for Retirement Research, based on US Census data, the average retirement age for men increased from age 62 to age 64 over the last 20 years. In addition, they found that the average age of retirement for women is age 62.[3] It is important for advisers to understand this information because it can provide them with a benchmark to use when calculating retirement needs. Thus, the adviser needs to talk with the client to determine the age the client is planning to retire.

The **remaining work life expectancy (RWLE)** is the work period that remains at a given point in time prior to retirement. For example, someone who is 30 years old and expects to retire at age 65 has a RWLE of 35 years. The RWLE is critical as it represents the remaining number of years over which savings can occur for the purpose of funding retirement.

Retirement Life Expectancy (RLE)

Retirement life expectancy (RLE) represents the total amount of time expected during retirement. This period begins at retirement and extends until death. Many retirees live as long as 20 to 40 years in retirement. However, this longevity has not always been the case. The average life expectancy for a newborn child in 1900 was 47 years[4], and many individuals worked as long as they were able. During this time, the country was more agrarian and families lived together. As family members aged, they were cared for by the younger members of the family. There was not an official "retirement period." The concept of retirement, as we know it today, did not exist. **Exhibit 11.3** presents data depicting the increase in life expectancy at birth from 1900 to 2018, and **Exhibit 11.4** depicts the increase in life expectancy at age 65.[5]

> **Quick Quiz 11.1**
>
> 1. Approximately 80% of men work past age 65.
>   a. True
>   b. False
>
> 2. The RLE is the time period beginning at retirement and ending at death.
>   a. True
>   b. False
>
> 3. As the RLE increases because of early retirement, there is generally both an increased need of funds to finance the RLE and a shortened WLE in which to save and accumulate assets.
>   a. True
>   b. False
>
> False, True, True.

---

3. What is the Average Retirement Age?, Alicia H. Munnell, Center for Retirement Research at Boston College, August 2011.
4. It should be noted that the life expectancy in 1900 is biased due to a high infant death rate at the time.

Population trends provide the adviser with a good understanding of how long a person might live in retirement. Women born in 2018 are expected to live on average 81.2 years, while men born in 2018 are expected to live on average 76.2 years. The average woman retiring in 2018 at age 65 has an average life expectancy of 20.7 years. Similarly, a man retiring in 2018 at age 65 has an average life expectancy of 18.1 years. The problem with this information is that average life expectancy is just that - an average. Fifty percent of women age 65 in 2018 are expected to live longer than 20.7 years and 50 percent of men age 65 in 2018 are expected to live longer than 18.1 years. In addition, the older an individual gets, the more likely they are to live beyond their average life expectancy as determined at birth or at age 65. Proper planning is needed because if the retired individual lives longer than he or she planned for, there is a risk of running out of money. This risk is known as superannuation.

Exhibit 11.3 | Life Expectancy at Birth

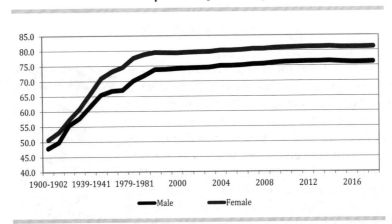

Source: Centers for Disease Control, NCHS, Mortality in the United States, 2018 (www.cdc.gov)

Exhibit 11.4 | Life Expectancy at Age 65

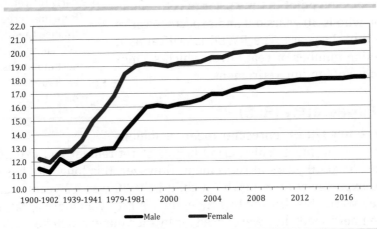

Source: Centers for Disease Control, NCHS, Mortality in the United States, 2018 (www.cdc.gov)

---

5. U.S. Department of Health & Human Services, CDC *NCHS, Mortality in the United States, 2018.*"

The Relationship Between The WLE and The RLE

The WLE and the RLE together make up a person's remaining life expectancy post education. Because this remaining period is effectively fixed, any change in one factor inversely impacts the other factor. If a person wants to increase their time during retirement, then that correspondingly shortens the WLE. A shortened WLE means less time to save and accumulate funds to satisfy a longer RLE. A person who is unable to save enough during their WLE to retire at a desired age, such as age 62, needs to consider delaying retirement, which is equivalent to increasing the WLE and decreasing the RLE. **Exhibit 11.5** visually depicts this relationship.

Exhibit 11.5 | The Relationship Between WLE and RLE

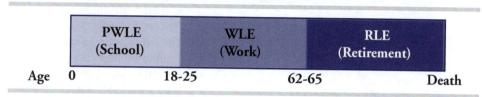

The prework life expectancy (PWLE) occurs prior to fully entering the work force and generally extends to some point between ages 18 and 25. The point at which the PWLE ends generally depends on the amount of education the person is undertaking. Some individuals may begin full time employment after high school graduation, while others may have four years of college education combined with years in post graduate study.

The WLE represents the time a person is working, saving, and accumulating wealth for retirement. This period begins once a person finishes their education, and it continues until retirement.

The RLE typically begins between age 62 and 65 and continues for the remainder of a person's life. As discussed earlier, the average life expectancy of someone who reaches the age of 65 is around 20 years. However, the RLE could last significantly longer, depending on the health of the person. Because life expectancy is unknown, retirement plans must be sufficiently flexible to allow for people who outlive the averages to not outlive their retirement income and savings.

Savings and Investment Issues

Retirees generally have multiple sources of income to pay for expenses during retirement. These sources generally include Social Security benefits, pension income, personal savings, and/or income from continued work during retirement. Most retirees cannot maintain their pre-retirement lifestyles on Social Security alone. Most need personal savings to sustain a relatively consistent standard of living during retirement. These sources of income are discussed in greater detail later in this chapter.

Personal savings is a critical element of most people's retirement funding plan and their ability to maintain their standard of living from their working years into their retirement years. The amount of personal savings a person has at retirement is dependent upon the following factors:
- The savings amount and the savings rate
- The timing of the savings and the period over which the savings grows
- The investment returns earned on the savings

In general, a person who begins saving between 10 percent and 13 percent of their income at or near age 25 will have sufficient funds accumulated at retirement, if the savings are invested in such a way as to earn a reasonable investment rate of return. Consider **Exhibit 11.6**, which illustrates a person saving 12 percent of their income from age 25 to age 65 earning eight percent, while inflation equals three percent. In this case, the savings accumulation takes care of their needs throughout retirement without the need for Social Security.

Exhibit 11.6 | Savings Balance from Age 25 to Age 100

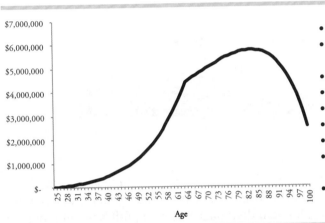

- Beginning age is 25
- Beginning salary is $100,000, which will increase at the rate of inflation
- Retirement begins at age 65
- Life expectancy is age 100
- Annual savings rate is 12%
- Earnings rate is 8%
- Inflation rate is 3%
- Distributions begin at age 65 based on a wage replacement ratio of 80%
- No Social Security benefits are included in the analysis

Regrettably, most individuals who are in their mid-twenties are unaware that funding for retirement is an important consideration, even though retirement may be forty years away. In addition, most people do not have a very good grasp of investment concepts and the total returns that are available through compounded annual returns.

The Savings Amount

The required amount of savings to fully or partially fund retirement is dependent on when a person begins to save for retirement. As mentioned, a person who begins to save 12 percent of their income at age 25 will accumulate an adequate amount of funds for retirement. Beginning to save early allows for compound investment returns that help savings grow significantly. However, when people delay saving for retirement, the amount of savings must be increased to overcome the lost contributions as well as the investment returns from lost years of annual compounding. **Exhibit 11.7** illustrates the percentage of income individuals must save if they begin saving at different ages.

> ### ≔ *Key Concepts*
>
> 1. What savings and investment concepts are important to retirement planning?
>
> 2. Why is it important to begin to save early for retirement?
>
> 3. Why is it important to understand investment decisions and their consequences in retirement planning?
>
> 4. How is inflation relevant to retirement planning?

Exhibit 11.7 | Required Savings Rate for Retirement
(Assume $0 of Accumulated Savings at the Beginning Age)

Age Regular Savings Begins*	Required Savings Rate*
25 - 35	10 - 13%
35 - 45	13 - 20%
45 - 55	20 - 40%**

*Assumes reasonable rate of return, normal raises, 80% wage replacement ratio, and Social Security benefits.

** At age 55, the person will realistically have to delay retirement until age 70.

Many people find it hard to begin any type of savings plan, let alone one that must continue for decades to be successful. Savings requires sacrificing current consumption for the purpose of higher future consumption. As **Exhibit 11.7** illustrates, the problem with delaying saving for retirement is that the rate that must be saved increases significantly over time. Saving 12 percent or even 15 percent at age 25 is generally easier than attempting to save 30 percent at age 50.

Exhibit 11.8 illustrates the required annual savings percentage necessary based on the time until retirement and the rate of return earned on invested assets.[6] Notice that if the RWLE is shortened from 40 years to 30 years and the portfolio continues to earn eight percent, the contribution increases from 12 percent to 22 percent. This example helps illustrate the importance of beginning a savings program early.

Exhibit 11.8 | Required Annual Savings Percentage[7]

Based on Exhibit 11.6 Assumptions		Number of Years Until Retirement						
		40	35	30	25	20	15	10
Rate of Return	4%	29%	34%	40%	50%	64%	87%	134%
	5%	23%	28%	35%	44%	58%	81%	128%
	6%	19%	24%	30%	39%	53%	76%	123%
	7%	15%	19%	25%	34%	48%	70%	117%
	8%	12%	16%	22%	30%	43%	66%	112%
	9%	9%	13%	18%	26%	39%	61%	107%
	10%	7%	11%	15%	23%	35%	57%	102%
	11%	6%	9%	13%	20%	31%	52%	98%
	12%	4%	7%	11%	17%	28%	49%	93%

6. **Exhibit 11.6** used future dollars whereas **Exhibit 11.8** uses today's dollars. The inflation rate remains at 3 percent, so the real rate of earnings at 8 percent is 4.8544 percent. The target future value is $1,399,103, which is the future value (in today's dollars) based on the same assumptions as **Exhibit 11.6**.

7. **Exhibit 11.8** uses the same assumptions as **Exhibit 11.6**. This result is the same as in **Exhibit 11.6**. Note also that as the time until retirement decreases, the required savings percentage increases significantly. Remember that this example includes zero savings at the beginning of the problem (PV = $0.00).

As an alternative to **Exhibit 11.7**, consider **Exhibit 11.9**, which assumes that each person is saving 10 to 13 percent of gross pay, including any employer retirement plan contribution. Assuming that the person saves 10 to 13 percent and also has an investment account balance equal to what they need at each age, they are making adequate progress toward the goal of financial security at retirement. If the person does not have the appropriate investment assets or has a lower savings rate than 10-13 percent, the shortfall will eventually emerge. Therefore, both investment assets on the balance sheet and the savings rate are relevant to achieving the desired capital balance for retirement.

Exhibit 11.9 | Benchmark for Investment Assets as a Percentage of Gross Pay

Age	Investment Assets as a Ratio to Gross Pay Needed at Varying Ages
25	0.20 : 1
30	0.6 - 0.8 : 1
35	1.6 - 1.8 : 1
45	3 - 4 : 1
55	8 - 10 : 1
65	16 - 20 : 1

The benchmarks as calculated consider incomes between $50,000 and $350,000, inflation at approximately two to three percent, a balanced investment portfolio of 60 / 40 equities to bonds returning five percent over inflation, a savings rate of 10 to 13 percent of gross pay, and a wage replacement ratio of 80 percent of gross pay. To the extent that any of these assumptions are incorrect for a particular person, the results may be misleading and require a specific personal calculation. These benchmarks are only a beginning.

Note that **Exhibit 11.9** illustrates that a person planning to retire at age 65 will need investment assets approximately 16 to 20 times the pre-retirement gross pay. A person at age 55 who plans to retire at 65 will need investment assets equal to eight times their current gross pay and will need to continue to save 10 to 13 percent of gross pay, including any employer contributions, and will need to earn an adequate investment rate of return on the retirement assets to achieve adequate retirement funding. More precise calculations are addressed throughout this chapter. While this schedule is only a benchmark, it works well for incomes between $50,000 and $350,000, inflation at two to three percent, and a balanced portfolio earning about five percent over inflation.

Exhibit 11.9 also illustrates that a tremendous amount of retirement asset accumulation occurs toward the end of the working years (ages 55 to 65). This increase is attributable to the compounding that occurs during the last ten years of work life expectancy based on the accumulation at age 55. Assuming that returns during this ten-year period are average, the accumulated assets should be what was expected. However, if the last ten years underperform from an investment return perspective, the investor may have to delay retirement or reduce spending during retirement.

Example 11.1

Assume Carrie, age 45, comes to you and is currently earning $100,000 per year. She has $350,000 (3.5 times her annual earnings) of investment assets (cash, mutual funds, retirement funds, etc.), not including personal use assets (equity in personal residence) and is saving $10,000 of her gross pay (10%). Carrie is concerned about making adequate progress towards her retirement goals. Assuming that Carrie is invested in an appropriate investment portfolio, she appears to be making adequate progress towards retirement if that is her only goal. Note that she will have to save more if she expects to live well beyond average life expectancy. Assume she can earn 8% with inflation of 3%. If she continues to spend as expected, she will run out of money at age 89. However, average expenditures for retirees tend to decline during retirement.

Step 1: Determine Future Income at Age 65

Current Earnings - PV	$100,000
Inflation - I	3%
WLE - N	20 years
Future Earnings - FV	$180,611

Step 2: Determine Needs at Retirement

WRR	80%
Retirement Payment	$144,489 ($180,611 x 80%)

Step 3: Project Savings at Retirement

Current Assets - PV	$350,000
Annual Savings - PMT	$10,000
Earnings Rate - I	8%
Work Life Expectancy - N	20 years
Assets at Retirement - FV	$2,088,955

Step 4: Determine Period of Time Funds will Last

Asset at Retirement - PV	($2,088,955)
Annual Inflation Adjusted Annuity Payment - PMT_{AD}	$144,489
Inflation Adjusted Earnings Rate - I	4.85437 ((1.08/1.03)-1) x 100
Funds at End - FV	$0
Years in Retirement that Funds will Last (Approximate)	24 Years

*Note that savings amount will increase each year with raises.

Savings Rate

The **U.S. personal savings rate** identifies the average savings amount in the U.S. The savings rate is interpreted as personal saving as a percentage of disposable personal income. The personal savings rate has declined significantly since the 1970s. In fact, the personal savings rate fell from a high of 13.5 percent in 1973 to 3.1 percent in 2005, increased to 8.8 percent in 2012 and was at 7.5 percent in 2019. **Exhibit 11.10** illustrates the historical trends.[8] The growth in personal expenditures may be the cause

8. https://fred.stlouisfed.org/series/PSAVERT#.

of the drop in savings over the past few decades and suggests that individuals are not saving enough for retirement. This low savings rate is extremely concerning. Recall that in order to meet just the retirement goal, a savings rate of 10 to 13 percent of gross pay over a long period is necessary. Unfortunately, most people are not well prepared for retirement, in terms of savings amount, savings rate, or accumulated savings.

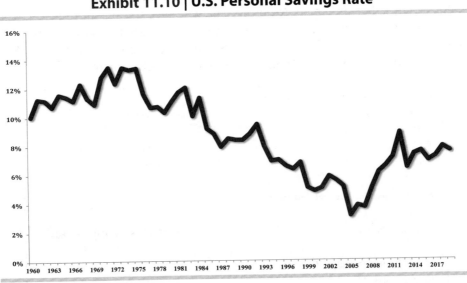

Exhibit 11.10 | U.S. Personal Savings Rate

Timing of Savings

The timing of savings is also critical as it dictates the number of years over which savings can earn investment returns and grow. More compounding periods for savings to grow results in less total savings needed over the WLE. When individuals delay savings, the potential earnings that would have been achieved through compounding during those periods is lost. Consider **Example 11.2** which illustrates the power of compound returns.

Example 11.2

Peter saves $5,000 each year on his birthday, from age 35 through age 65, for a total of 30 payments. He invests the funds so that he earns an 8% rate of return over the 30 years. His friend, Lori, began saving the same amount on her birthday at age 25. She saved $5,000 each year from age 25 through age 34. She also earned an 8% rate of return on her investments. Surprisingly, Lori has a larger savings balance at age 65 than Peter. **Exhibit 11.11** summarizes their accumulated savings.

Exhibit 11.11 | Time/Savings Example (Lori and Peter Example)

	Lori	*Peter*
Total Invested	$50,000 (10 years)	$150,000 (30 Years)
Balance at age 65	$728,867	$566,416
Earnings Rate	8%	8%
Investment Return Multiple	14.58x	3.78x

While Peter invested three times as much as Lori, Lori has 29 percent more than Peter at age 65. **Exhibit 11.12** graphically illustrates the power of saving early and compounding.

Exhibit 11.12 | Lori and Peter Investment and Accumulation

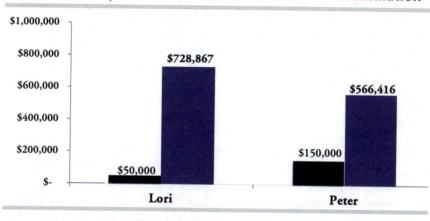

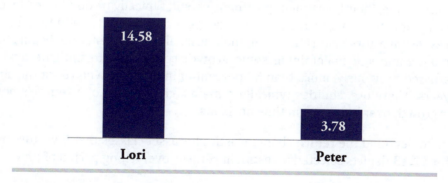

The second chart in **Exhibit 11.12** illustrates the final balance for Lori and Peter as a multiple of their respective savings totals. Lori accumulates 14.58 times what she saved, while Peter only accumulated 3.78 times what he saved. Essentially, by saving early, Lori is able to consume $100,000 more than Peter before retirement and accumulate more than Peter at retirement.

Investment Considerations

A successful retirement plan is dependent on a successful investment plan. A retirement plan is dependent on savings over time, but it is also dependent on the earnings and growth of those funds during the asset accumulation phase and throughout retirement. In **Exhibit 11.6**, with the 25-year old saving 12 percent of his income for 40 years earning 8 percent, approximately 80 percent of the accumulated balance at retirement is derived from investment earnings, while 20 percent is from savings.

An investment plan must take into consideration the risk tolerance of the investor as well as the time horizon of the goal. Consideration must be given to historical and expected returns for the various asset classes, diversification, and the types of assets included in tax-deferred accounts versus taxable accounts. All of these factors go into constructing a portfolio to achieve specific goals, such as retirement planning.

The risk tolerance of an investor is essentially the willingness and ability to accept risk for potential returns. As indicated below, assets with larger returns typically have larger risks or larger variations in returns (standard deviation). Risk tolerance is typically assessed through questionnaires, an understanding of the investor's experience with risky assets and with the time horizon of the investment goal. If both the willingness and the ability to accept risk are high, the risk tolerance is high. If both the willingness and the ability are low, then the risk tolerance is low. If, however, there is a mismatch between ability and willingness (one high and the other low), then it suggests that the investor may need additional education.

The **suitability** of an investment or portfolio is greatly impacted by the time horizon of an investment goal. Longer-term goals can generally tolerate higher amounts of risk than shorter-term goals. Investments for the accomplishment of short-term goals should generally consist of relatively safe or stable assets, such as short-term debt instruments. Investments for the accomplishment of long-term goals can consist of assets that generate higher returns, but have a tendency to fluctuate more sharply when markets or the economy changes.

When investors are young, their investment portfolios should typically be dominated by common stocks because, due to long time horizons, young investors can generally afford the additional risk (fluctuation) of common stocks. As investors near retirement, their asset allocation generally begins to shift so that it becomes less risky while still maintaining some growth component to mitigate against the risk of inflation. As discussed previously, more than 50 percent of individuals who reach the age of 65 live for more than 20 years. Therefore, equities typically remain a critical part of a retiree's portfolio because they provide for growth over longer-term time horizons.

It is important to understand the return characteristics for asset classes that investors may include in a portfolio. **Exhibit 11.13** depicts selected investment returns over a long period of time.

Exhibit 11.13 | Historical Returns, Inflation-Adjusted Returns, and Standard Deviation of Asset Classes[9]

Asset Class	Historical Returns	Inflation-Adjusted Returns	Standard Deviation	Real Return After-Tax and Inflation
Small-Capitalization Stocks	12.0%	9.0%	32.0%	6.6%
Large-Capitalization Stocks	10.0%	7.0%	20.0%	5.0%
Long-Term Government Bonds	5.5%	2.5%	10.0%	0.9%
U.S. T-Bills	3.5%	0.5%	3.0%	(0.50%)
Consumer Price Index (CPI)	3.0%	N/A	N/A	N/A

Exhibit 11.13 illustrates that equities provide the best opportunity to have positive real returns, after taking into consideration taxes and inflation. Equities are generally an important element of a portfolio during asset accumulation as well as during retirement. Equities are important during retirement as it may last 20 to 40 years.

The risk tolerance and time horizon of the investor, as well as the expected risk and returns from various investment choices are considered in constructing an asset allocation and portfolio. The asset allocation is responsible for the majority of variation in returns within the portfolio and is a critical element in retirement planning.

Appropriate Assets for Tax Advantaged and Taxable Accounts

In addition to the asset allocation decision, investors should consider the appropriateness of assets for the different types of investment accounts. Income earned in a taxable account, such as a brokerage or bank account, is subject to current taxation, whereas income earned in a tax-deferred account, such as an IRA or 401(k) plan, is not subject to current taxation. Because there is a significant difference in the tax rates of capital gains and dividends compared to interest income from fixed income securities, such as bonds, it is logical to hold fixed income assets in tax-deferred accounts. This decision results in all fixed income securities residing in tax-deferred accounts. However, investors must also consider liquidity needs that are better met through fixed income investments and more easily accessed in taxable accounts. Therefore, there must be a balance between tax efficiency or tax optimization and the liquidity needs of the investor.

An investor must also consider limitations on the types of securities that can be held in various retirement accounts.[10] Investors managing assets held in IRAs and qualified plans should also be aware of the rules relating to unrelated business taxable income, discussed below.

---

9. Approximations from 1926-2017. Assumes an equity tax rate of 20% and bond tax rate of 30%.

10. These limitations are beyond the scope of this textbook, but are discussed in Money Education's Retirement Planning and Employee Benefits textbook.

Unrelated Business Taxable Income

Unrelated business taxable income (UBTI) is a term used to describe income earned by a tax-exempt entity that is subject to taxation. The tax on unrelated business income applies to most organizations exempt from tax under §501(a). These organizations include charitable, religious, scientific, and other corporations described in §501(c), as well as employees' trusts forming part of pension, profit-sharing, and stock bonus plans described in §401(a). In addition, the following are subject to the tax on unrelated business taxable income:

1. Traditional IRAs
2. Roth IRAs
3. Simplified Employee Pensions (SEP-IRAs)
4. Savings Incentive Match Plans for Employees (SIMPLE IRAs)
5. State and municipal colleges and universities
6. Qualified state tuition programs
7. Medical savings accounts (MSAs)
8. Coverdell savings accounts

Because of the UBTI rules, IRAs and qualified plans, in addition to the other entities listed, are impacted if UBTI is earned within the entity. The impact is that the entity has to pay income tax on the UBTI and file Form 990-T if UBTI exceeds $1,000. The purpose of these rules is to prevent a tax-exempt entity from unfairly competing against tax paying businesses. This concept is reflected in the following excerpt from Treas. Reg. §1.513-1.

> "The primary objective of adoption of the unrelated business income tax was to eliminate a source of unfair competition by placing the unrelated business activities of certain exempt organizations upon the same tax basis as the nonexempt business endeavors with which they compete."

The term "unrelated business taxable income" generally means the gross income derived from any unrelated trade or business regularly carried on by an exempt organization, less the deductions directly connected with carrying on the trade or business. Previously, if an organization regularly carried on two or more unrelated business activities, its unrelated business taxable income was the total of gross income from all such activities less the total allowable deductions attributable to all the activities. However, for tax years beginning after December 31, 2017, the Tax Cuts and Jobs Act of 2017 requires that the UBTI from each unrelated trade or business be calculated separately, such that losses from one business can no longer offset income from another.

Generally, an unrelated trade or business includes one that meets the following three requirements:

1. It is a trade or business,
2. It is regularly carried on, and
3. It is not substantially related to furthering the exempt purpose of the organization.

Example 11.3

BU, an exempt scientific organization, enjoys an excellent reputation in the field of biological research. It exploits this reputation regularly by selling endorsements of various items of laboratory equipment to manufacturers. The endorsing of laboratory equipment does not contribute importantly to the accomplishment of any purpose for which the tax exemption is granted to BU. Accordingly, the income derived from the sale of endorsements is gross income from unrelated trade or business (UBTI).

Generally, income in the form of dividends, interest, payments with respect to securities loans, and annuities are excluded in computing unrelated business taxable income. In addition, royalties and rental income are generally not included in determining UBTI. However, investment income that is generally excluded from UBTI must be included to the extent it is derived from debt-financed property. The amount of income included is generally proportionate to the debt on the property.

Typically, a qualified plan, or an IRA, is subject to the UBTI rules if it:

- Operates a trade or business,
- Owns an interest in a pass through organization, such as a partnership or S corporation, that is operating a trade or business,
- Owns an interest in a master limited partnership, or
- Uses debt to generate portfolio income, as in the case of margin debt.

Example 11.4

Jamar's IRA owns an interest in Sushi & Saki LLC, a restaurant. The LLC is taxed as a partnership. Because the LLC interest is held in an IRA, the IRA's share of income from the LLC is subject to UBTI tax.

Inflation

Inflation represents a general increase in the price of goods and a corresponding decrease in the purchasing power of money. Inflation is an important factor for retirement planning because inflation erodes the purchasing power of money throughout a person's life, but especially during the retirement years. Because retirement can last 20 to 40 years, the erosion of purchasing power resulting from inflation can be substantial. **Exhibit 11.14** illustrates the decline in purchasing power of $100,000 over a 40-year period.

Exhibit 11.14 | Impact of Inflation: Purchasing Power Lost Over 40 Years

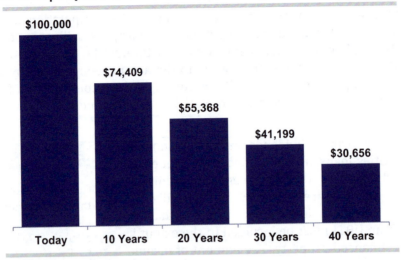

Example 11.5

Parker is 65 years old and spends $300 per month on groceries. If inflation is 3 percent, he can expect to spend over $540 when he is 85 years old for the same groceries. While an annual 3 percent increase is hardly noticeable in the short term, it amounts to an 80 percent increase over the 20 years.

As illustrated, in year 10 the $100,000 has lost 26 percent of its purchasing power. After 10 years, one can only buy $74,409 worth of items using $100,000 of today's dollars. More disturbing is the fact that in year 20, the same person would only be able to purchase $55,368 worth of assets for that same $100,000. Imagine a person with a fixed income who is expected to have a carefree retirement in 20 years with the same $100,000 income they have today.

The exhibit below provides an additional perspective of inflation over long periods of time. It depicts how many times greater the cost of an item was in 2013 compared to the price 100 years earlier.[11] 2013 marked the 100th anniversary for the Consumer Price Index. As depicted in the exhibit below, cheese was 26.27 times more expensive in 2013 compared to 1913.

Inflation over many years is a significant obstacle to overcome for retirees attempting to manage their finances and is an important factor to consider in retirement planning.

11.Stephen Reed,"One hundred years of price change: the Consumer Price Index and the American inflation experience," Monthly Labor Review, U.S. Bureau of Labor Statistics, April 2014.

Exhibit 11.15 | Impact of Inflation Over 100 Years

Number of Times Larger 2013 Price is over 1913 Price

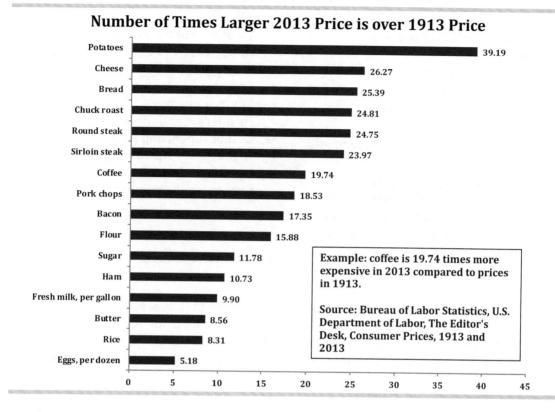

Potatoes	39.19
Cheese	26.27
Bread	25.39
Chuck roast	24.81
Round steak	24.75
Sirloin steak	23.97
Coffee	19.74
Pork chops	18.53
Bacon	17.35
Flour	15.88
Sugar	11.78
Ham	10.73
Fresh milk, per gallon	9.90
Butter	8.56
Rice	8.31
Eggs, per dozen	5.18

Example: coffee is 19.74 times more expensive in 2013 compared to prices in 1913.

Source: Bureau of Labor Statistics, U.S. Department of Labor, The Editor's Desk, Consumer Prices, 1913 and 2013

Retirement Needs Analysis

Retirement needs analysis is the process of determining how much money a person needs to accumulate to be financially independent during retirement. One of the first steps is to determine the expenses a person will have when they retire. Most people prefer to maintain their pre-retirement standard of living during retirement. Therefore, the expenses they have when they are working will likely be similar to the expenses they have during retirement. However, there are some expenses that will increase during retirement, such as vacations and medical care, and expenses that will decrease during retirement, such as work related expenses, FICA expenses, and annual savings. **Exhibit 11.16** lists expenses that may increase or decrease during retirement.

Key Concepts

1. List the common factors that increase and decrease retirement income needs.

2. What is the wage replacement ratio?

3. Identify the two alternative methods for calculating the wage replacement ratio.

4. How is the WRR calculated utilizing the two applicable methods?

Exhibit 11.16 | Expenses that May Increase or Decrease During Retirement

Decreasing Expenses	Increasing Expenses
• Savings is no longer necessary at retirement • FICA payments are eliminated • Mortgage payments may end • Lower income means lower income taxes • Automobile costs are lower due to less driving • Work related expenses (clothes, coffees, lunches, etc.) are eliminated • Cost of insurance (life insurance may no longer be needed, limits might be reduced on property insurance)	• Vacation and travel costs • Hobby costs (race car driving, golf, etc.) • Costs for a second home • Lifestyle changes • Health care and medical costs • Cost of supporting adult children • Higher costs due to inflation (property tax, groceries, etc.) • Gifts to family members

Pre-Tax or After-Tax Planning for Retirement

Planning for retirement can be done on a pre-tax basis or an after-tax basis. Many people find it easier to plan on a pre-tax or gross income basis, out of which income taxes are paid. However, CPAs, accountants, and those who emphasize after-tax cash flows may plan on an after-tax basis. Either way works. In this text, the pre-tax approach is generally used because it is easier for most people to understand.

Wage Replacement Ratio (WRR)

Retirement needs analysis is the process of determining how much money a person needs to accumulate at the beginning of retirement to be financially independent during retirement. Part of this process is determining how much money will be spent in retirement on an annual basis. The amount of money needed in retirement as a percentage of income earned prior to retirement is called the **wage replacement ratio (WRR)**. It is calculated by dividing the retirement expenses by the pre-retirement income.

$$\text{WRR} = \frac{\text{Expenses in Retirement}}{\text{Pre-retirement Income}}$$

Generally, most individuals need less income during retirement compared to what they need while working. The reason for this decrease is that many expenses are eliminated. However, other expenses may increase during retirement. A WRR of 70 percent to 80 percent is often cited as an appropriate range for many people. While this range may work for many people, it is far from a uniform range that all people can rely on for a reasonable wage replacement ratio. Consider the following examples.

Example 11.6

Shondra makes $100,000 per year and is about to retire. She has the following expenses that will be eliminated when she retires:

- House payment (annual) - $30,000 (the mortgage will be paid off when she retires)
- Savings into her 401(k) plan - $24,000
- Commuting costs to work - $5,000 (includes tolls, gas, parking, etc.)
- Work clothes per year - $2,000
- Lunches & coffees at work - $2,000
- FICA payments - $7,650

The total of these expenses that will be eliminated equals $70,650. Assume that she has other expenses that might increase, such as travel, which increases her expenses from $29,350 to $40,000. If that were the case, Shondra's wage replacement ratio needed equals 40% ($40,000 divided by $100,000), which is dramatically different than the commonly cited 70% to 80% WRR.

Example 11.7

Rob makes $120,000 per year and is about to retire. He is the hotel manager for the Boston Zenith Hotel. Zenith Hotels is an international chain of luxury hotels based in the U.S. and Europe. As part of his compensation, he has the following benefits:

- He lives in the hotel with his family - he has never owned a home nor does he have homeowners insurance.
- He eats in the hotel with his family or eats at local hotels, both of which are paid for as part of his compensation.
- He has access to a vehicle when he needs it - he does not own a car nor does he have car insurance.
- He stays at Zenith properties when he vacations with his family.

Rob expects that when he retires, he will have to replace many of the benefits that he has received as part of his compensation. Here is a list of a few items on an annual basis:

- Housing costs - $35,000 (utilities, insurance, cable, etc.)
- Auto expenses - $15,000
- Vacation expenses - $10,000
- Food - $10,000

He has other expenses that will decrease, such as:

- Savings into his 401(k) plan - $20,000
- Work clothes per year - $2,000
- FICA payments - $9,180

If Rob adds the additional retirement costs to his compensation and subtracts the costs that will decrease, he ends up with retirement expenses needed of $158,820, which is 32.35% higher than his current salary and represents a WRR of 132%. Fortunately for Rob, he is able to save a great deal more during employment than most employees as a result of his employment perks.

Determining the WRR for a person is an individualized process in which specific expenses are considered for inclusion in the calculation. There are two frequently used methods to determine the WRR. The first, which was illustrated above, is called the top-down approach. The second approach is called the bottom-up approach or budgeting approach.

Top-Down Approach

The top-down approach begins with 100 percent of pre-retirement income and adjusts the percentage up or down depending on expenses that may be eliminated or added. This approach, which was illustrated in the two previous examples, is less precise than the bottom-up approach, but is generally quicker to calculate. The top-down approach is more appropriate for planning for people who are young and for those not close enough to retirement to worry about great precision.

Example 11.8

Marleen is 55 years old and makes $100,000 per year. She saves $12,350 per year and pays FICA expense of $7,650. She wants to assume that any other expense reductions will be offset by increased retirement expenditures, such as health care and vacations. Based on these assumptions, her WRR equals 80%.

$100,000	=	100.00%	of salary in % terms
(12,350)	=	(12.35%)	less: current savings in % terms
(7,650)	=	(7.65%)	less: payroll taxes in % terms (not paid in retirement)
$80,000	=	80.00%	wage replacement ratio in % terms

Marleen lives off about 80% of her pre-retirement income. Therefore, she will need about $80,000 in income during retirement. The remaining 20% or $20,000 is currently spent on retirement savings and FICA taxes.

Bottom-Up (Budgeting) Approach

The bottom-up approach to determining the WRR is also referred to as the budgeting approach because it determines total expenses in the same manner that is used to build a budget. This approach is more rigorous than the top-down approach, but is also more precise as it requires examining each category of expense to determine whether it will increase, decrease or remain the same during retirement. As a result, this approach is generally used by people who are very near retirement and can anticipate the expenses and changes that will occur once they retire. Keep in mind that some expenses will remain fixed, such as life insurance premiums and fixed mortgage payments, some will increase by inflation, and some will change differently.

Example 11.9

Assume Anna and Bart have the same amount of income and the same expenses and both are about to retire. They both want to determine their appropriate WRR. Anna's house and car will be paid off before retirement, while Bart will continue to have to make mortgage payments and car loan payments in retirement. They both have other expenses that will decrease by the same amount. Below is the bottom-up approach to calculating each WRR.

	Anna & Bart	Anna	Bart
	Current Budget	**Retirement Budget**	**Retirement Budget**
Income	$120,000	***	***
Expenses:			
Income Taxes (28%)	$33,600*	$33,600	$33,600
Social Security Taxes (FICA)	2,500	0	0
Health Insurance	2,000	2,000	2,000
Auto Insurance	1,200	1,200	1,200
Food (at home or away from home)	5,400	5,400	5,400
Utilities/Phone	6,000	6,000	6,000
Mortgage	18,000**	0	18,000
Auto Payment	6,000	0	6,000
Entertainment	6,000	6,000	6,000
Clothing	4,000	2,500	2,500
Auto Maintenance	1,000	750	750
Church Support	2,400	2,400	2,400
Retirement Savings	12,000	0	0
Other	19,900	17,850	17,850
Total Expenses (Needs)	**$120,000**	**$77,700**	**$101,700**
Wage Replacement Ratio (WRR)		**64.75%**	**84.75%**

*Assume for this example that Anna and Bart's income tax liability remains the same during retirement.
**Note that the mortgage of both is 15% of current income before retirement, but 0% for Anna and 18% of needs for Bart after retirement.
*** The current budget at retirement will be equal to the needs.

Spending By Age

Annual expenditures generally change as people age. Typically, people spend more as they move into middle age and then expenditures decrease. In retirement, expenses also decrease as individuals get older and approach life expectancy. Therefore, the WRR that is calculated for the beginning of retirement is likely to be higher than a WRR necessary in the later part of life.

While the amount of spending changes over a person's lifetime, as indicated in **Exhibit 11.17**, most of the categories of spending remain the same. In fact, many of the expenditures remain relatively constant on a percentage basis from younger to older ages. Consider the chart below from 2019.

Exhibit 11.17 | Average Annual Expenditures by Income and Age

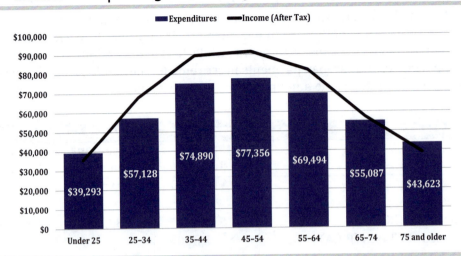

Bureau of Labor Statistics: Consumer Expenditure Survey 2019

Exhibit 11.18 | Consumer Spending by Age (In Percentages)

Spending Category	Under 25 years	25-34 years	35-44 years	45-54 years	55-64 years	65 and older
Total	100%	100%	100%	100%	100%	100%
Housing	32.4	35.9	33.0	30.9	30.5	34.8
Transportation	21.1	18.0	18.3	17.3	16.4	14.9
Personal insurance and pensions	8.5	12.7	12.8	13.4	13.2	5.7
Food at home	7.0	6.7	7.3	7.3	7.3	8.1
Healthcare	3.8	5.5	6.4	6.9	8.6	13.6
Food away from home	7.9	6.2	5.7	5.7	5.0	5.0
Entertainment	3.5	4.2	4.9	5.0	5.7	4.7
Cash contributions	1.1	1.5	2.9	2.7	3.4	5.1
Apparel and services	3.6	3.3	3.3	3.1	2.6	2.6
Education	7.6	2.1	1.6	3.5	2.6	0.7
Miscellaneous	0.8	1.2	1.3	1.4	1.7	1.6
Personal care products and services	1.2	1.1	1.2	1.3	1.2	1.4
Alcoholic beverages	0.8	0.9	0.7	0.9	1.0	1.0
Tobacco products and smoking supplies	0.5	0.6	0.5	0.5	0.6	0.4
Reading	0.1	0.1	0.1	0.1	0.1	0.3

Note: The seven categories highlighted represent between 84% and 90% of total spending.
Source: BLS Consumer Expenditure Survey 2019

Naturally, some expenses vary on a percentage basis, such as healthcare and education. Healthcare increases as a percentage with age. Education tends to decrease as a percentage with age. However, housing tends to remain between 30 percent and 36 percent of total spending. Transportation tends to remain between 15 percent and 21 percent. Insurance and pension expenses start low, increase during mid-life, and taper off during retirement.

The determination of the appropriate WRR is a very useful process as it identifies the amount of money needed in retirement and forms the basis for determining the amount of money that must be accumulated by the time retirement occurs. While spending may decrease during retirement, most of the calculations presented in this text assume a level WRR. This assumption provides a certain built-in level of conservatism when it comes to the calculations.

Sources of Retirement Income

Most retirees rely on a combination of funds to finance retirement, including Social Security, employer-sponsored retirement plans, income from personal retirement plans (IRAs), income from personal savings, and in some cases, income from part-time employment (earnings). These sources of funds are intended to complement each other to provide adequate retirement income. **Exhibit 11.19** illustrates the percent of income for the average retiree from 1962 to 2015 from each of these sources.

Exhibit 11.19 | Retirement Income Sources for the Elderly

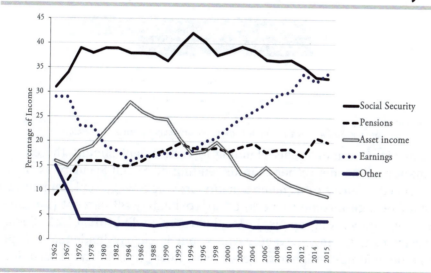

Source: Social Security Administration: Fast Facts & Figures About Social Security, 2017

Notice in the previous exhibit that the average retiree receives more than 30 percent of retirement income from Social Security. Social Security may provide a lower wage worker with a wage replacement ratio of 60 plus percent. However, Social Security only provides a wage replacement ratio of 18 to 27 percent for a worker with income of $200,000 (see **Exhibit 11.21**). Therefore, such a worker will need to look to other sources of funds to make up the amount of short-fall in wage replacement to maintain the worker's desired lifestyle.

Social Security

For most individuals, Social Security is the foundation of retirement income. Social Security provides benefits to nearly 90 percent of retirees. However, Social Security was never designed or intended to provide retirement benefits that would equate to a 100 percent WRR. It was signed into law in 1935 and was designed as a safety net for the "old-age" population. As **Exhibit 11.20** illustrates, Social Security is the major source of income for retired individuals and makes up more than 90 percent of income for a significant percentage of the retired population.

Exhibit 11.20 | Percentage of Retired Individuals Receiving Social Security Benefits by Relative Importance to Total Retirement Income

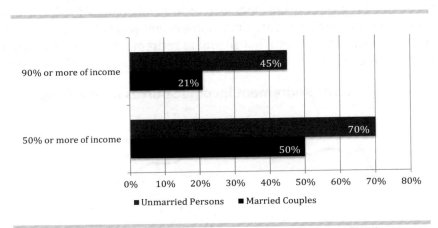

Source: Social Security Administration, Social Security Basic Facts (2020)

Most middle to higher income individuals planning for retirement should, therefore, consider Social Security as a foundation of income rather than depending on Social Security as their main source of retirement income. Social Security retirement benefits provide a wage replacement ratio ranging from less than 20 percent (for high-income earners) to approximately 80 percent (for low-income earners who have a same age, nonworking spouse). As illustrated in **Exhibit 11.21**, Social Security is an adequate wage replacement for lower wage earners, but is clearly inadequate to provide sufficient replacement income for middle-to-higher-wage earners. Keep in mind that Social Security was never meant to be the only source of income upon retirement. President Franklin D. Roosevelt implied this reality in his statement while signing the Social Security Act on August 14, 1935:

> "We can never insure one hundred percent of the population against one hundred percent of the hazards and vicissitudes of life, but we have tried to frame a law which will give some measure of protection to the average citizen and to his family against the loss of a job and against poverty-ridden old age."

Exhibit 11.21 | Wage Replacement Percentage for Social Security

Earnings	Worker WRR*	Worker with Same Age, Nonworking Spouse Total WRR	Comment
$15,000	78%	117%	Low Income
$20,000	67%	100%	(WRR Good)
$25,000	60%	90%	
$30,000	55%	83%	
$35,000	52%	78%	Middle Income
$50,000	46%	69%	(WRR Adequate)
$75,000	41%	61%	
$100,000	34%	51%	High Income
$200,000	19%	28%	(WRR Poor)

*Estimated based on single person at normal retirement age (2021).
At same age, nonworking spouse can expect to receive 50 percent of the benefits of the covered worker.

Employer-Sponsored Retirement Plans

Most people in the United States have access to an employer sponsored retirement plan. These plans, which may be sponsored by private companies, public companies, or governmental entities, may be in the form of a defined contribution plan or a defined benefit plan. Today, there are significantly more defined contribution plans than defined benefit plans. Employees who participate in these plans can save part of their compensation on a pre-tax basis over many years. These savings can accumulate for decades and help provide a substantial amount of income during retirement.

Personal Assets and Savings

Personal assets and savings is another important source of retirement funds and the one that is almost completely influenced by the individual. This is a more difficult way to accumulate savings for retirement because savings may have to accumulate in a taxable account instead of a tax deferred account. While there are some tax deferred alternatives, such as traditional and Roth IRAs, there are limitations regarding how much can be contributed to these accounts. However, personal savings can be a significant source of retirement income.

✒ Quick Quiz 11.4

1. Retirees generally rely on Social Security, private pension plans, and personal savings to fund their retirement incomes.
   a. True
   b. False

2. Social Security is an adequate wage replacement for most individuals.
   a. True
   b. False

3. Personal savings is the source of retirement income most influenced by the individual.
   a. True
   b. False

True, False, True.

There is a noticeable difference between retirees who have income from personal assets and those who do not. According to the Social Security Administration, 66 percent of those with income from personal assets have retirement income in the highest category ($30,000 or more), while only 25 percent of those without income from personal assets are in the highest category. It is in most people's best interest to accumulate wealth for retirement.

Exhibit 11.22 | Income of Retirees with and without Income from Personal Assets

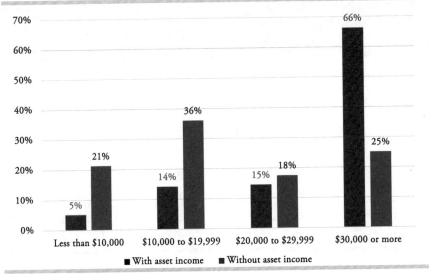

Source: Social Security Administration: Income of the Aged Chartbook 2014

The section below discusses the calculation of retirement needs, as well as the determination of required personal savings.

RETIREMENT FUNDING (CAPITAL NEEDS ANALYSIS)

Retirement funding (also known as retirement needs analysis or **capital needs analysis**) is the process of determining how much money a person needs to accumulate to be financially independent during retirement. Being financially independent means being able to maintain the pre-retirement lifestyle during retirement and manage the adverse effects of inflation.

The process of calculating the needed capital balance at retirement requires making assumptions about variables that cannot be known, such as future rates of return or life expectancy. These assumptions are discussed below, along with four methods of calculating retirement needs. These four methods are not the only methods for determining retirement needs and are relatively straight forward. Today's financial planning software certainly allows for more complicated assumptions. However, these four methods provide the foundation for estimating the needed capital at retirement.

Key Concepts

1. What is capital needs analysis and why is it important in retirement planning?

2. What are the four most common methods for analyzing capital needs?

3. How do each of these methods differ?

4. What assumptions must be made in capital needs analysis?

Accurate Assumptions

Retirement funding requires projecting savings amounts, spending patterns, investment returns, and inflation over extremely long periods of time. As a result, small changes in these assumptions can create large variations in retirement funding and annual savings requirements.

WRR - The wage replacement ratio should be calculated using the top-down approach for those who are more than a few years away from retirement. The bottom-up approach should be used when retirement is expected to take place within a few years and realistic retirement expenses can be estimated on a line item basis. It is important to consider the types of lifestyle changes that may take place in retirement and the cost considerations for those activities.

Life expectancy - While no one can predict with certainty how long any individual will live, life expectancy is an important variable to forecast. Life insurance companies, the Society of Actuaries, and the IRS have mortality tables that provide estimates of the average life expectancies for men and women. The life expectancy for men and women who attain the age of 65 are provided earlier in this chapter. However, it is generally far better to consider family longevity when estimating life expectancy.

Example 11.10

Roman is trying to prepare a retirement funding calculation. He is unsure about his life expectancy. Roman is healthy with no diseases or health concerns. He runs and swims regularly and maintains a healthy weight and good diet. Three of his grandparents lived into their 90s and his grandmother on his mother's side is still alive at age 99 and might live to age 110. Even though the average life expectancy for men is less than 80 years at birth, Roman should consider estimating a life expectancy of at least mid-90s, based on his family history. He might even consider a life expectancy of 100 for his retirement planning.

Earnings rate and inflation - Predicting rates of return and inflation is challenging over both short periods and long periods of time. Access to historical rates of return and inflation is widely available to professionals as well as non-professionals. While there is no indication that average historical returns or average inflation will necessarily continue, they do provide a basis for estimating these variables for the future.

The earnings rate used in retirement needs analysis should take into consideration the expected return of an individual's portfolio, based on the portfolio's asset allocation. More aggressive portfolios tend to have higher expected rates of return, while more conservative portfolios tend to have lower expected rates of return. Inflation should be estimated based on historical trends. It is wise to be somewhat conservative for both these variables, as the retirement calculation model is very sensitive to these inputs. The difference between the expected earnings rate and the expected inflation rate should also be considered and compared to historical real rates of return. If the difference between the two rates is significantly higher than historical real rates of return, then it is an indication that either the estimate for inflation is too low or the estimate for the expected return is too high.

Because these assumptions may not be precise, it is important to revisit a retirement needs analysis regularly to determine whether adequate progress is being made towards the retirement goal. In addition, it is important to periodically assess whether there are changes to the underlying assumptions that should be incorporated into the retirement analysis. A retirement needs calculation should not be performed only once and considered to be fixed in terms of required savings and/or needs analysis. Retirement planning is more of a dynamic process that extends over a person's work life expectancy and into retirement. In addition, retirement planning, or capital needs analysis, may incorporate a variety of assumptions about how much money is left or to be left at life expectancy. The section below discusses the most basic method of determining retirement needs, known as the annuity method, as well as three more conservative variations of capital needs analysis.

Annuity Method (4-Step Approach)

The **annuity method** is the simplest way to determine retirement needs, and is based on the **pure annuity concept**. The annuity method assumes the individual saves for a period of time, begins taking distributions at retirement, and then dies with a zero accumulation balance on the projected life expectancy date. Because the annuity method assumes that all funds will be consumed at the point of life expectancy, it does not provide any room for error if a person lives beyond life expectancy, nor does it generally provide for an estate for heirs. However, the annuity method is the basic method for capital needs analysis.

The annuity method can be calculated using one of two methods, the traditional 4-step approach or the uneven cash flow approach. Both methods work well for this type of calculation, as they are both methods of time value of money. However, the uneven cash flow method has a few limitations in comparison to the 4-step approach. The 4-step approach is designed to determine the amount of money that must be accumulated at retirement and the amount of money that needs to be saved each year up until retirement. The 4-step approach is outlined below:

Step 1: Determine the funding amount in today's dollars.
This step is designed to determine the amount of money in today's dollars that a person will need when they retire. At the most basic level, it adjusts the needs first by the wage replacement ratio and then reduces that resultant by the expected Social Security payments in today's dollars. The WRR reflects the change in needs during retirement in comparison to current earnings. Social Security payments are an income stream in retirement that does not need to be funded through personal savings. This approach assumes that the Social Security payments will increase because of the annual cost of living adjustment (COLA) at the same rate as inflation. While that assumption may not be exact, it is a reasonable assumption that simplifies the calculation.

Step 2: Inflate the needs from Step 1 to the beginning of retirement.
This step determines the needs in future dollars for the first year of retirement. It is determined by inflating the amount from Step 1 at the rate of inflation for the number of years until retirement. The amount that is needed in any subsequent year is increased by the rate of inflation from one year to the next.

Step 3: Determine the funding needs at retirement age.

This step calculates the amount of money that needs to be accumulated at retirement age, which is found by discounting the annuity from Step 2 for the number of years during retirement. The annual needs must be discounted at the earnings rate, while also being increased by the rate of inflation. To accommodate the simultaneous discounting and inflating of the annual needs, the inflation adjusted discount rate is used. The result of this step is the sum that should be accumulated at the time retirement begins. This calculation assumes the annuity stream during retirement is an annuity due because once retirement begins, funds are immediately needed.

Step 4: Determine the required annual savings amount.

This step calculates the amount of money needed to be saved each year to accumulate the funds determined in Step 3. The value from Step 3 is used as the future value (FV), while any funds set aside for retirement are the input for present value (PV) in the calculation. The earnings rate is used as the input for "i."

To determine the amount to save during the work life expectancy, discount the capital needed at retirement using the savings rate, being mindful as to whether the client is expected to save annually or more frequently and whether the client is expected to save under an annuity due or an ordinary annuity scheme.

Example 11.11 illustrates the use of the 4-step method. This example will also be used for the other retirement needs calculations in the chapter.

Example 11.11

Jordan, age 42, currently earns $70,000. Her wage replacement ratio is 80 percent. She expects that inflation will average 3 percent for her entire life expectancy. She expects to earn 9.5 percent on her investments and retire at age 62, possibly living to age 90. Her Social Security retirement benefit in today's dollars adjusted for early retirement is $15,000 per year.

1. Calculate Jordan's capital needed at retirement at age 62 and the amount Jordan must save at the end of each year, assuming she has no current savings accumulated for retirement.

Step 1: Determine the funding amount in today's dollars.		
	$70,000	Salary
	X 80%	WRR
=	$56,000	Total needs in today's dollars
	- 15,000	Less Social Security in today's dollars
=	$41,000	Annual amount needed in today's dollars
Step 2: Inflate the needs from Step 1 to the beginning of retirement.		
PV	=	41,000 (Step 1) Retirement needs in today's dollars
N	=	20 (62 - 42) Work Life Expectancy
i	=	3 (inflation)
PMT	=	0
FV	=	74,050.56 (to Step 3) First year needs for retirement

Step 3: Determine the funding needs at retirement age (use begin key).		
PMT_{AD}	=	74,050.56 (from Step 2) this is also an annuity due
N	=	28 (90 – 62) Retirement Life Expectancy (use begin key)
i	=	6.3107 [(1 + earnings rate) ÷ (1 + inflation rate)] – 1 x 100 [(1.095 ÷ 1.03) – 1] x 100
FV	=	0 (Annuity model is 0 at life expectancy)
$PV_{AD@62}$	=	1,022,625.85 (to Step 4 - amount needed at age 62)[1]
Step 4: Determine the required annual savings amount.		
$FV_{@62}$	=	$1,022,625.85 (from Step 3)
N	=	20
i	=	9.5
PV	=	0
PMT_{OA}	=	18,894.75 (annual savings)

1. $961,922 is the result of not using the begin key. This is not correct. To correct this error, change the setting on the calculator to "begin" or annuity due.

Note: The math in this example assumes unrounded numbers are used throughout the calculation. If the calculator is cleared at each step and a rounded number for i is used, the results will be slightly lower.

2. Calculate the amount she must save at the end of each year, assuming she presently has $50,000 in retirement savings.

$FV_{@62}$	=	$1,022,625.85
N	=	20
i	=	9.5
PV	=	($50,000)
PMT_{OA}	=	$13,220.91 (annual savings)

Exhibit 11.23 | Asset Accumulation and Distribution (Using Data from Example 11.11)

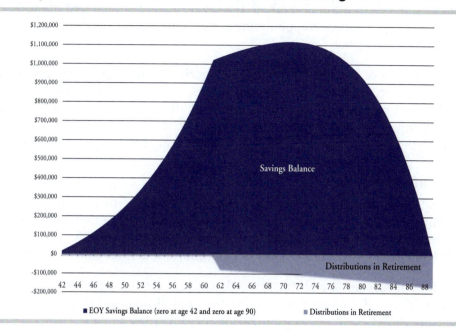

Uneven Cash Flow Method of Retirement Funding

This basic retirement needs calculation can also be performed using the uneven cash flow keys on a financial calculator. For this method, zeros are entered for each period up to the retirement age. Then, the needs in today's dollars (Step 1) are entered as the cash flow for the periods during retirement. The inflation adjusted discount rate is used to account for earnings and inflation over the entire period (WLE and RLE). Once these inputs are entered, net present value (NPV) is then calculated. The NPV equals the amount of funds necessary to pay for all of the retirement needs in today's dollars, based on the assumptions used. Consider the example of Jordan above. The time line below illustrates the cash flows and describes the calculations.[12]

Exhibit 11.24 | Uneven Cash Flow Method

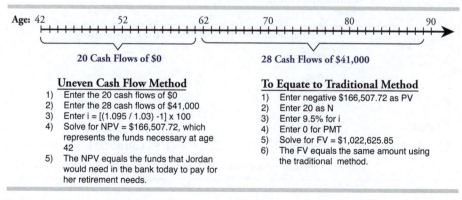

---

12. The uneven cash flow is effective for simple retirement needs calculations. It will not work when the earnings rate during retirement is different than the earnings rate during the accumulations phase.

Once the NPV is calculated, it can be used to determine the periodic funding amount. This amount is the same as calculated using the traditional method. However, mixing annual and monthly compounding causes the numbers to vary. If annual compounding is used throughout the two approaches, then there should be minimal difference, if any.

To mitigate against the risk of the assumptions being overly optimistic, changes can be made, such as adjusting the inflation rate upward, the earnings rate downwards, or making use of a capital preservation model, a purchasing power preservation model, or a capitalization of earnings model rather than a simple annuity model to determine capital needs. These three additional models help to overcome the risks of the pure annuity model (primarily the risk of running out of money).

Capital Preservation Model

The annuity method for retirement planning is the most basic type of retirement needs analysis. It results in exhausting all assets at the point of life expectancy, presuming that all assumptions occur as expected. Due to the nature of the assumptions of this model, a person who lives beyond their assumed life expectancy will be effectively destitute. They will have no assets from which to pay bills.

There are alternative approaches to retirement needs analysis that incorporate a level of conservatism into the calculations. Three of the other models are the **capital preservation model**, the **purchasing power preservation model**, and the **capitalization of earnings model**. These models provide a cushion in the event someone lives beyond their anticipated life expectancy. The capital preservation model assumes that the accumulated fund balance necessary under the annuity model is preserved until life expectancy. In other words, the balance that a retiree had at retirement under the annuity method is also expected at life expectancy. This approach necessarily requires that additional funds are accumulated by retirement so that the original needs are maintained until life expectancy. This additional calculation step is illustrated in **Example 11.12**.

Example 11.12

Recall that the amount needed for Jordan at age 62 calculated from **Example 11.11** was $1,022,625.85. If that amount is discounted at the expected earnings rate of 9.5 percent, then the result equals the additional amount of capital necessary to leave an estate of exactly $1,022,625.84 at life expectancy.

$FV_{@90}$	=	$1,022,625.85 (amount at life expectancy)
N	=	28
i	=	9.5
PMT	=	0
$PV_{@62}$	=	$80,560.37
$1,103,186.21	=	$80,560.37 + $1,022,625.85 (rounded)
		(amount needed for capital preservation model at retirement)

The capital preservation model requires Jordan to accumulate an additional $80,560 more at retirement than under the annuity model. However, it reduces her risk of **superannuation**, which is the risk that she outlives her available savings. This model requires a greater accumulation and therefore requires a larger annual savings amount.

The following chart compares the required annual savings under the capital preservation model with that of the annuity model for this example.

	Capital Preservation Model		Annuity Model		The Difference	
	Beginning Balance of Zero Savings	Beginning Balance of $50,000	Beginning Balance of Zero Savings	Beginning Balance of $50,000	Beginning Balance of Zero Savings	Beginning Balance of $50,000
FV$_{@62}$	1,103,186.21	1,103,186.21	1,022,625.85	1,022,625.85		
N	20	20	20	20		
i	9.5	9.5	9.5	9.5		
PV	0	- $50,000	0	- $50,000		
PMT$_{OA}$	20,383.24	14,709.40	18,894.75	13,220.91	1,488.49	1,488.49

The capital preservation model requires additional savings of approximately $1,500 per year, but mitigates against many of the risks in the traditional annuity approach.

Purchasing Power Preservation Model

The second model that mitigates superannuation is the **purchasing power preservation model**. The purchasing power model is even more conservative than the capital preservation model and assumes that the purchasing power of the accumulated fund balance necessary under the annuity model is preserved until life expectancy. This approach necessarily requires that additional funds are accumulated by retirement so that the purchasing power of the original needs are maintained until life expectancy. The required balance and the annual savings under this model are greater than what is required under the annuity model or the capital preservation model.

Example 11.13

Again recall **Example 11.11**. The capital balance of $1,022,625.85 is used as the future value, and then the entire calculation made in the original capital preservation model is repeated. By doing this, the $1,022,625.85 is simultaneously inflated at the rate of inflation and discounted at the earnings rate.

FV	=	$1,022,625.85
N	=	28
i	=	6.3107 [(1.095 ÷ 1.03) – 1] x 100
PMT$_{AD}$	=	$74,050.56 (amount needed the first year of retirement)
PV$_{@62}$	=	$1,206,942.14 (if i is not rounded, it will be $3 more)
		capital needed for purchasing power preservation model

The purchasing power preservation model requires Jordan to accumulate an additional $184,316 more at retirement than the annuity model. However, it reduces her risk of superannuation even more than the capital preservation model. This model requires a greater accumulation and therefore requires a larger annual savings amount. The chart below compares the required annual savings under the annuity model with the required savings under the purchasing power preservation model.

	Purchasing Power Model		Annuity Model	
	Beginning Balance of Zero Savings	Beginning Balance of $50,000	Beginning Balance of Zero Savings	Beginning Balance of $50,000
$FV_{@62}$	1,206,942.14	1,206,942.14	1,022,625.85	1,022,625.85
N	20	20	20	20
i	9.5	9.5	9.5	9.5
PV	0	- 50,000	0	- 50,000
PMT_{OA}	22,300.30	16,626.47	18,894.75	13,220.91

The purchasing power preservation model requires that Jordan save approximately $3,400 (18%) more each year compared with the annuity method. While this difference may or may not be significant to Jordan, the accumulation of assets and the risk mitigation are both significant.

Capitalization of Earnings Model

The third, and most conservative, model that mitigates superannuation is the capitalization of earnings model. The capitalization of earnings model is designed to produce a perpetual income stream. In the purchasing power preservation model illustrated in **Example 11.13** the desired income can continue to age 118, at which point the full account will have been liquidated. Since a capitalization of earnings calculation is based on the concept that the investments will produce sufficient income to support the desired withdrawal each year, the principal amount remains intact and withdrawals can continue through multiple generations. This, of course, requires an even higher level of savings.

The capitalization of earnings calculation is widely used to value investments that produce a perpetual income by simply dividing the annual income produced by the investment by the appropriate discount rate (expected rate of return). For example, if a preferred stock pays a dividend of $5 per year and the investor's required (or expected) return is 12 percent, the investor would be willing to pay $41.66. This investment of $41.66 earning 12 percent would produce income of $5 per year for an infinite number of years. This simple formula assumes that income earned throughout the year is distributed at the end of each year. For the purposes of the retirement needs analysis calculation, a few adjustments must be made. First, rather than dividing by the investment return, we must divide by the real return so that the annual income will increase with the rate of inflation. Second, the resulting need must be adjusted to account for beginning of year withdrawals, either by multiplying by the sum of 1 + the real return, or by adding an amount equal to the first year's payment.

Example 11.14

Recall in **Example 11.11** that Jordan's first year of retirement income needed at age 62 is $74,050.56.

If Jordan needed $74,050.56 as a flat dollar amount (not adjusted for inflation) at the end of each year, a simple capitalization of earnings calculation of $74,050.56 ÷ 0.095 = $779,479.58 would suffice. However, since Jordan needs her retirement income at the beginning of each year and needs the dollar amount to increase each year, adjustments must be made as follows:

$$\frac{\$74,050.56}{(1.095 \div 1.03) - 1} = \$1,173,416.56$$

Step 2: Adjust for beginning of year payments.

$$\$1,173,416.56 \ \times \ \frac{(1.095)}{(1.03)} = \$1,247,467.12$$

Note that the same result for Step 2 can be realized by adding the first-year income ($74,050.56) to the results of Step 1.[13]

If the assumptions for investment earnings and inflation remain constant, Jordan will have an income stream that can continue indefinitely, isolating her from the risk of superannuation.

The chart below compares the required annual savings under the annuity model with the required savings under the capitalization of earnings model.

Exhibit 11.25 | Capitalization of Earnings Model Comparison

	Capitalization of Earnings Model		Annuity Model	
	Beginning Balance of Zero Savings	Beginning Balance of $50,000	Beginning Balance of Zero Savings	Beginning Balance of $50,000
$FV_{@62}$	1,247,467.12	1,247,467.12	1,022,625.85	1,022,625.85
N	20	20	20	20
i	9.5	9.5	9.5	9.5
PV	0	-50,000	0	-50,000
PMT_{OA}	23,049.07	17,375.24	18,894.75	13,220.91

13. A common application of the capitalization of earnings concept is found in the constant growth dividend discount model used to value common stocks, V = D1/(r-g), where v is the current intrinsic value of the stock, D1 is the dividend (the income stream produced by the stock) one year from today, r is the required rate of return, and g is the growth rate of the dividend. Using this formula to calculate Jordan's capital needs at retirement, V = (74,050.56 x 1.03) ÷ (0.095 - 0.03) = $1,173,416.56. This amount must then be multiplied by the sum of 1 + the real return to adjust for beginning of year payments. $1,173,416.56 x (1.095 ÷ 1.03) = $1,247,467.12.

The capitalization of earnings model requires that Jordan save approximately $4,155 (22%) more each year compared with the annuity method. If Jordan has the wherewithal to accomplish this level of savings, and investment returns and inflation are as projected (or more favorable), her investments will produce an income stream that neither she nor her heirs will outlive

The exhibit below summarizes the required capital amount at retirement as well as the annual required savings amounts for each of the four models discussed.

Exhibit 11.26 | Capital Needs Analysis Comparison for Jordan Example[14]

	Annuity Model	Capital Preservation Model	Purchasing Power Preservation Model	Capitalization of Earnings Model
Capital needed at retirement	$1,022,625.85	$1,103,186.21	$1,206,942.14	$1,247,467.12
Annual savings with no initial balance	$18,894.75	$20,383.24	$22,300.30	$23,049.07
Annual savings with $50,000 initial balance	$13,220.91	$14,709.40	$16,626.47	$17,375.24

The Serial Payment Approach

The four models discussed so far are very similar except for the amount of money that remains at life expectancy. Each of these models assumes a level amount of annual savings over the remaining work life expectancy. Because each of the models assumes level funding, the savings amount over time should become a smaller percentage of annual income, as most people's income increases during their later working years. However, another method of funding the necessary retirement accumulation is to increase the savings amount each year, which often correlates to typical salary increases over a career. The increase from one year to another can be equal to inflation or can equal any other reasonable assumption. This type of approach is referred to as a serial payment.

Example 11.15

Consider the prior example with Jordan. The amount of money she needed to accumulate at retirement under the annuity method equals $1,022,625.85. That does not change with the serial payment approach. However, solving for the annual savings amount involves a few different calculations. The first adjustment is to convert the future retirement needs into today's dollars. The second adjustment is to determine the annual payment in today's dollars based on the annual increase in the savings amount. For this

---

14. Although we concentrate on the Annuity Model, Capital Preservation Model, and Purchasing Power Model in this textbook, the capital needed at retirement can also be calculated based on complex actuarial assumptions. In order to verify our results in the Jordan example, we sought the advice of an actuary who used a different approach (but one that we verified was competent), which assumed no particular start balance. He calculated the capital needed at retirement to be approximately $1,245,000. We do not present the details of this calculation due to the complexity of the assumptions and calculations. Suffice it to say that the capital needed is $1,200,000 to $1,250,000 regardless of the assumptions. If you are looking for a rule of thumb, it costs 10% more for the Capital Preservation Model and 20% more for the Purchasing Power Preservation Model as long as you have similar factors (e.g., 28 years and 3% inflation), but there is no substitution for exact calculations.

example, assume that Jordan would like to increase her annual savings amount by 8% each year.

Present value of retirement needs:

FV	=	$1,022,625.85
N	=	20
i	=	9.50%
PMT	=	$0.00
PV	=	($166,507.72)

The $166,507.72 represents the amount of money needed today to fully fund the retirement needs for Jordan based on the annuity model.[15] The calculation below converts this amount into an annual savings amount.

PV	=	($166,507.72)
N	=	20
i	=	1.3889% [(1.095 ÷ 1.08) – 1] x 100
FV	=	$0.00
PMT_{OA}	=	$9,592.47 (in today's dollars)

The first payment at the end of year one equals $10,359.87, which represents an 8% increase over the PMT in today's dollars. The payment at the end of the second year, as well as each future years, will increase by 8% per year from the previous year.

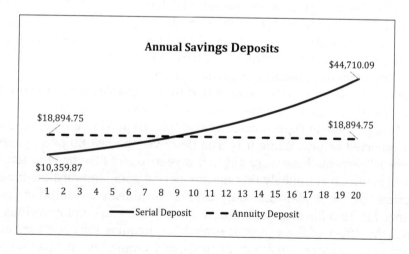

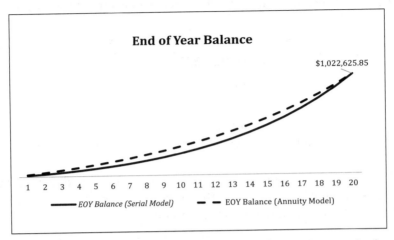

The charts graphically illustrate that the accumulation at retirement is the same for the annuity and serial payment approaches, but the annual funding for the serial payment starts lower than the annuity approach and then increases over the 20-year period. This funding method can be used with any of the three models discussed above.

Range Estimates, Sensitivity Analysis, Simulations, and Monte Carlo Analysis

As one might expect, small changes in assumptions regarding earnings, inflation, life expectancy, and retirement funding needs can have a dramatic impact on a retirement plan. One of the problems with traditional capital needs analysis is that advisers use deterministic estimates (i.e., the estimate is predetermined as opposed to a probability estimate) for each of the variables (needs, inflation, portfolio returns, life expectancies, etc.). While point estimates help the adviser

⧉ Key Concepts

1. Explain how sensitivity analysis is used.

2. What is a Monte Carlo Analysis?

create a plan for the client, it is unrealistic to think that these variables are really predictable to an exact deterministic point (given). Instead they may and will likely vary. Generally, point estimates used in deterministic models are the mean expectancy. For example, 10 percent on large capitalization common stocks is the mean expected return. While it is true that over the last 80 or so years large-cap stocks' average returns were 10 percent, there were only a few years out of 80 when the actual return was close to the mean expected return. It is unlikely that for any period going forward the investment return will replicate the historical return. A plan that only uses deterministic assumptions is likely to produce results that may range far from the original forecast. The adviser can employ various techniques to help begin to understand the effect of the range of probable outcomes for each variable in a plan. These techniques include range estimates, sensitivity analysis, and simulations such as Monte Carlo Analysis.

Range Estimates
Using range estimates allows the adviser to project the outcome using a range of assumptions (e.g., 2.5% to 3.5% inflation) for a variable as opposed to a single mean expectation (three percent inflation). A range estimate approach produces multiple outcomes that allow us to gain insight into the impact of a change in one variable or changes in a set of variables. Range estimate assumptions are usually conducted around the mean estimate, both lower and higher than the mean point estimates. If an adviser wanted to rotate the assumed coefficient of the variable toward the risk of an adverse outcome

(e.g., an investor who is more concerned with down side losses than upside potential returns may use semivariance analysis or alternatively, the number of months returns that were less than T-bill returns), then the technique to employ is sensitivity analysis rather than range estimating.

Sensitivity Analysis

Small deviations in one variable may significantly impact the entire plan. **Sensitivity analysis** consists of rotating each variable assumption toward the undesirable side of the risk to determine the impact of a small change in that variable on not achieving the overall plan.

For example:

1. One additional year of employment often makes a retirement plan work because there is one more year of savings, one more year of earnings accumulation, and one less year of consumption. The opposite is also true; one less year of work could make an otherwise achievable plan unworkable.

2. Small changes in the spread between the earnings rate and the inflation rate can have a significant impact on a plan, both positively and negatively.

3. A small increase in inflation can have a significant negative impact on an otherwise achievable retirement funding plan.

Understanding the importance of each individual variable and the risk involved if there is a change from the assumed number to a more conservative number allows the adviser to use sensitivity analysis to build a set of slightly worse case scenarios and then determine the impact of these more conservative assumptions on the overall plan.

Example 11.16

Recall the assumptions given in the Jordan annuity calculation (**Example 11.11**). The left columns below identify the given variables while the right columns below identify alternative variables that could be used.

Deterministic *Example 11.11 Selected Assumptions*		*Sensitivity Analysis* *Conservative Assumptions*
N	20 years to retirement	• Try 19 years
i	3% inflation	• Try 3.5% inflation
PV	$41,000 current needs	• Try $42,000 needs
PMT	$0	
FV	$74,050.56 future needs	

Deterministic *Example 11.11 Selected Assumptions*		*Sensitivity Analysis* *Conservative Assumptions*
N	28 years in retirement	• Use 30 years in retirement instead of 28
i	$[(1.095 \div 1.03) - 1] \times 100 = 6.3$	• Use a real rate of 5.75 instead of 6.3
PMT_{AD}	$74,050.56 future needs	• Use $80,745 as future needs rather than $74,050.56
$PV_{@62}$	$1,022,625.84 needed at retirement	
FV	$0	

Notice that slightly more conservative assumptions were used for the sensitivity analysis than were used in the original example in order to determine the robustness, or alternatively the sensitivity, of the previously calculated solution. If the retirement plan was recalculated using all of the sensitivity analysis assumptions previously identified, Jordan would need $200,000 more at retirement than originally expected, an increase of 20% just for the annuity model.

Annuity Model *Solution with Conservative Assumptions* *Using Sensitivity Analysis*	
N	19 years to retirement (instead of 20)
i	3.5 inflation (instead of 3.0)
PV	$42,000 current needs (instead of $41,000)
PMT	$0
FV	$80,745 future needs (instead of $74,050.56)
N	30 years in retirement (instead of 28)
i	5.75 real rate of return (instead of 6.3)
PMT_{AD}	$80,745 real payment (future dollars)
$PV_{@62}$	$1,207,472 (compared to $1,022,625) needed at age 62
FV	$0

Approximately $160,000 of the $184,847 change was caused by one variable, the inflation assumption being 3.5% instead of 3%.

Approximate Cause of Change		Explanation
1. Inflation 3.0 to 3.5	$158,916	• Inflations drives up future needs and drives down real return.
2. Change years 20 to 19	$15,857	• A shorter work life expectancy drives future needs higher, but over a shorter term.
3. Change years 28 to 30	$25,902	• A longer retirement period makes more annuity payments.
Total	$200,676	• The reconciliation is not exact because of the changes in terms and rates and the interaction of the variables.
Actual Change	$184,847	

Simulations and Monte Carlo Analysis

There is uncertainty associated with any retirement funding projection. The assumptions can be analyzed using the latest retirement planning software packages that incorporate simulations, such as Monte Carlo Analysis (MCA). As illustrated below, most retirement projections are based on fixed (deterministic) assumptions. While useful during retirement planning, deterministic projections do not account for variations. A **Monte Carlo Analysis** is a mathematical tool that illustrates the unpredictability of the "real" world and its effects on an individual's retirement plan. MCA uses a random number generator for inputs into a software package that will provide an output with specific probabilities of outcomes. MCA provides insight into the most likely outcome, but also provides other possible outcomes. It allows for a variety of alternative assumptions, such as changes in investment rates of return, the variability of inflation, adjustments to life expectancy, and many other market-condition scenarios. Such a method is invaluable to the adviser, as it allows the adviser to observe a large number of projections illustrating a potential range of future outcomes based on changing variables. Various software programs are available that allow the adviser to run simulations projecting various scenarios, thereby increasing the probability that the individual's retirement plan will be successful.

A simulation calculates multiple scenarios of a model by repeatedly sampling values from probability distributions for uncertain variables. Traditional range estimates calculate outcomes on a best case, expected case, and worst case basis. Sensitivity analysis allows the model user to manipulate variables usually one at a time or one set of variables at a time. Simulations allow for an unlimited (or very large) number of simultaneous ranging of variables, possibly leading to more insight into the problem and into the impact of interacting variables.

Because retirement is frequently 20 to 30 years or longer and there are many historical patterns of investment returns for selected 20 to 30 year periods, the adviser simply does not know what the market conditions will be when the client retires, nor does the adviser know what pattern of market returns will follow a particular retirement date. Monte Carlo Analysis helps the adviser to understand the possibilities and probabilities. However, Monte Carlo Analysis cannot predict particular events. An excellent discussion of the problems with Monte Carlo Analysis was written in the Journal of Financial Planning by David Rawrocki (November 2001, Article 12) and is summarized in **Exhibit 11.27**.

📝 Quick Quiz 11.6

1. Sensitivity analysis eliminates the risk of retirement planning.
   a. True
   b. False

2. Monte Carlo analysis predicts particular events.
   a. True
   b. False

3. Simulations allow for an unlimited number of simultaneous ranging variables.
   a. True
   b. False

False, False, True.

Exhibit 11.27 | Selected Problems with Monte Carlo Analysis

- Assumes normal distributions, serial independence, and linear relationships for investment returns (none of which are true).
- Stock returns are not normally distributed - kurtosis is higher than expected. (Stock returns are actually **leptokurtic**, meaning that they do not have a normal distribution.)
- Means and standard deviations for stock returns vary over time rather than remaining static.
- Many Monte Carlo Analyses ignore income tax consequences.

Monte Carlo Analysis is a valuable tool and an interesting exercise. However, as with any analytical tool, it should not be used in a vacuum. It is useful to provide insight, but it should not take the place of professional judgment. As with most financial planning, retirement planning is a process that includes regular monitoring and adjustments to the plan as needed. Clients should visit their advisers regularly (at least annually) to modify and update their retirement plans to adjust for changes in the preselected variables so that their retirement objectives can be met.

Alternatives to Compensate for Projected Cash-Flow Shortfalls

Sometimes a retirement projection simply works. Occasionally, a person's assets are significantly greater than their needs, and they may actually need encouragement to spend some of their money, or they may need assistance transferring it to loved ones or donating it to charity. These situations are generally easier to deal with than those involving unrealistic expectations and shortfalls.

Situations can be challenging when the required annual savings amount is unrealistically high or the expressed needs of a client greatly exceed the assets available. In these situations, the plan simply does not work. There are several alternatives to consider, some of which have already been discussed briefly in this chapter. However, many of these alternatives are closely linked to the variables that are quite sensitive in the capital needs analysis model. These include the amount of retirement needs, the amount of the required savings, the length of the WLE, the length of the RLE, the earnings rate, and the rate of inflation. With that in mind, the plan may work if one or more of the following adjustments can occur:

1. The annual or monthly retirement needs are reduced
2. The annual or monthly savings amount is increased
3. Expected investment earnings are increased
4. Expected inflation is reduced
5. The WLE is increased
6. The RLE is decreased

Obviously, there are implications and limitations to each of the possibilities listed above. However, a combination of these adjustments may help to resolve the budget shortfall. For example, a solution might entail refining the needs a bit more precisely, resulting in a decrease in what is actually needed combined with working a few additional years and increasing the portfolio risk slightly, assuming of course that the portfolio is not already heavily weighted toward equities. This solution reduces needs, increases the years of savings, decreases the years of needs, and increases the expected return from the portfolio.

Caution should be taken when adjusting the expected investment returns and inflation. The expected investment return should be based on reasonable expectations about the returns from risky assets and should generally be an output from an asset allocation model that incorporates the investor's risk tolerance and time horizon. Capital needs analysis models are extremely sensitive to changes in expected return and inflation and care should be taken when adjusting these input variables.

Example 11.17

BJ is 45 years old and plans on retiring at age 65 and living until age 95. Assume that he currently earns $100,000 and his wage replacement ratio is 70 percent and Social Security will provide $20,000 (in today's dollars) in retirement benefits. Also assume that he expects inflation to be 3 percent and expects that he can earn 6 percent on his investments.

Scenario 1: Step 1 of this problem is to determine the needs to be funded in today's dollars. His current income adjusted for the WRR and Social Security result in a funding need of $50,000 ($100,000 x 70% - $20,000) in today's dollars. Step 2 inflates this need until retirement. Based on inflation and when he is retiring, he will need $90,306 his first year of retirement. Step 3 determines the balance he needs in his investment accounts at retirement, which is $1,842,331. Finally, Step 4 calculates the required annual savings of $50,083. The annual funding is problematic because it is 50 percent of his income.

As would likely be the case, assume that Scenario 1 does not work for BJ. Scenarios 2, 3, 4, and 5 illustrate how changing the assumptions impact the annual funding requirements:

Scenario 2: Requires BJ to work an additional three years. This adjustment increases his accumulation period by three years and decreases his distribution period by three years.

Scenario 3: Requires a greater investment return from his portfolio increasing the return during his savings years from 6 percent to 9 percent. It does not change the return during retirement.

Scenario 4: Combines Scenarios 2 and 3.

Scenario 5: Combines Scenarios 2 and 3 and requires that he sell an asset, such as land or a boat, for $75,000 and uses the proceeds as the initial funding for his retirement plan.

		Scenario 1 (original projection)	Scenario 2 (work 3 more years)	Scenario 3 (increase investment return)	Scenario 4 (Scenarios 2 & 3 combined)	Scenario 5 (Scenario 4 & sale of asset)
Step 2: Inflate funds to retirement age	PV	($50,000)	($50,000)	($50,000)	($50,000)	($50,000)
	N	20	23	20	23	23
	i	3.00%	3.00%	3.00%	3.00%	3.00%
	PMT	0	0	0	0	0
	FV	$90,305.56	$98,679.33	$90,305.56	$98,679.33	$98,679.33
Step 3: PV of retirement annuity	PMT	$90,305.56	$98,679.33	$90,305.56	$98,679.33	$98,679.33
	N	30	27	30	27	27
	i	2.9126%	2.9126%	2.9126%	2.9126%	2.9126%
	FV	0	0	0	0	0
	PV	($1,842,330.85)	($1,880,625.32)	($1,842,330.85)	($1,880,625.32)	($1,880,625.32)
Step 4: Annual funding amount	FV	$1,842,330.85	$1,880,625.32	$1,842,330.85	$1,880,625.32	$1,880,625.32
	N	20	23	20	23	23
	i	6.00%	6.00%	9.00%	9.00%	9.00%
	PV	$0.00	$0.00	$0.00	$0.00	($75,000.00)
	PMT	($50,082.95)	($40,016.86)	($36,011.07)	($27,046.93)	($19,218.29)
Savings as a % of income		50%	40%	36%	27%	19.2%

The impact of these changes is that his annual savings requirement decreases from $50,083 in Scenario 1 to $19,218 in Scenario 5, which is certainly more reasonable based on his income. These changes may or may not be acceptable to BJ, nor are they necessarily all the choices or the best choices. However, they illustrate how a plan can be adjusted to more realistically achieve the level of funding desired. One obvious choice that was not included was to decrease the annual needs, which would result in a lower savings requirement. Another alternative is to maintain the same 9 percent investment assumption throughout his life. This adjustment combined with Scenario 5 results in an annual savings required amount of $12,363.45.

There are numerous other ways one might adjust a plan to help with its viability. Other considerations include potential inheritances that would offset future costs or reduced spending needs toward the later part of retirement, which is consistent with the spending patterns of many retirees (see **Exhibit 11.17** and **Exhibit 11.18**). Part time work may also be a possibility for those who are in good health. Finally, paying off mortgage debt (which often represents 30-35 percent of a budget) prior to retirement can significantly reduce required expenses during retirement. The examples above are not an exhaustive list. Instead, they should be considered as a starting point for situations in which a retirement plan initially does not work. Investors generally have to make a choice of sacrificing today, working longer, or sacrificing during retirement when there are projected shortfalls.

IMPLICATIONS OF CAPITAL NEEDS ANALYSIS

Once the question of how much money will be needed at retirement is determined, consideration must be given to how that goal will be achieved. Individuals have several sources of funding for retirement, including personal savings, retirement plans from work, Social Security, and working while in retirement. Personal savings can be accomplished through banks and brokerage accounts. However, these accounts are not "tax-advantaged," meaning that income earned on accumulated assets are subject to current taxation. It is generally accepted that in most cases, deferral of taxation is beneficial to the taxpayer. Taxpayers with earned income may be able to fund individual retirement accounts (IRAs) with pre-tax dollars up to $6,000 ($7,000 for those age 50 or over) for 2021. IRAs are beneficial because they defer taxation until retirement. However, the IRA contribution limit is relatively small compared to what may need to be saved on an annual basis.

The other method to save on a pre-tax basis is through employer-sponsored retirement plans that permit employee salary deferrals, such as 401(k) plans, 403(b) plans, SARSEPs, 457 plans and SIMPLEs, which each permit employees to defer significantly more than can be contributed to an IRA.

Social Security benefits act as a base source of retirement funding and the amount received is influenced by the number of years that are worked as well as the amount of earnings.

OTHER CONSIDERATIONS

Most of this chapter has focused on factors that impact retirement needs and retirement funding. It is important to realize that retirees also face qualitative factors as they make the transition from the work force to retirement. In addition, risks can impede the best retirement plan. These two issues are briefly discussed below.

For many, work provides a sense of purpose and helps maintain mental wellness. When individuals retire, it is helpful to fill the void of work with activities that provide the person with a sense of purpose and help maintain cognitive functions. Ego and self-esteem are often tied to a person's occupation. However, work is not the only source of ego. Many people are successful at maintaining their self-esteem in retirement by becoming more involved with family, hobbies, charities, or through fulfilling long-term dreams or goals.

Example 11.18

Eric and Erica worked in private equity for the last twenty years and are retiring at age 60. They have amassed a sufficient amount of wealth to buy their retirement home in Punta Gorda, Florida. They plan on keeping their condominium in New York City and residing there part of the year to spend time with their grandchildren. During the winters, they plan on living in their retirement home on the water. Both Eric and Erica are volunteers with several charities. They are effectively managing their transition from a high pressure work environment to a meaningful retirement.

While **Example 11.18** illustrates a couple who is effectively transitioning to retirement, they do so while maintaining their primary home and support system. For many people, retiring to a new city or country is a lifelong dream. These types of decisions should be carefully planned. By moving away from the community they have lived in, retirees give up their support systems, which can often be undervalued until they are no longer available. In addition, relationships with physicians, professionals, and the like must be established. Relocating may necessitate travel to spend time with children, grandchildren, and other family members. Relocating can be a wonderful experience during retirement. However, it should be carefully considered.

In addition to factors that affect retirement planning, consideration must be given to the risks that can undermine a retirement plan. These risks include the factors discussed in the chapter, such as savings amounts and earnings rates. However, these risks also include untimely death, disability, and liability or creditor issues. These are examples of why a sufficient focus must be placed on risk management concerns.

MANAGING RETIREMENT DISTRIBUTIONS

One of the biggest challenges for retirees is determining how to manage their wealth once they retire. How much can they spend every year or week? How long will their money last? The risk of running out of money is referred to as superannuation, which is one of the primary concerns for most retirees. This issue is of paramount concern more today than in the past due to the decreased pensions and the increased number of defined contribution account type plans (e.g., 401(k) plan).

When defined benefit plans were prevalent, the risk of superannuation was pooled together among the plan participants. The defined benefit plan was responsible for paying a pension for as long as the retired participants lived. Naturally, some retirees would live longer than others and some would not live very long. Actuaries could mathematically estimate the average life expectancy of the pool of employees and determine the funding necessary to meet those needs. However, the pooling of risk ceased as defined benefit plans were replaced with defined contribution plans. No longer is the risk of outliving resources mitigated with shared risk. Now, retirees are responsible for the funds they have accumulated and must determine how to make those funds last throughout their retirement. While self-reliance is generally a great attribute, the reality is that many, if not most, retirees are ill-equipped to manage their portfolios themselves and will need the assistance of financial advisers. This responsibility can be daunting to retirees.

While managing one's assets in retirement has its challenges, there are ways to mitigate against superannuation. The simple answer is to shift the risk instead of retaining the risk. This risk shifting can be accomplished with annuities. Annuitized income is equivalent to the stream of income that was paid from defined benefit plans.

The simple fact is that annuities reduce the risk of superannuation. Whether from corporate or government pensions, insurance companies, or Social Security, annuities provide a base of cash flow that allows retirees to meet a certain percentage of necessities. There is published research that indicates a positive correlation between annuitized income and happiness. That correlation is not an endorsement for all annuities. Instead, it is a reflection of the risk averse nature of many investors and retirees and the simple fact that annuities reduce one aspect of risk. Those retirees who are extremely risk averse should have a larger portion of their assets annuitized compared to retirees who are less risk averse. While annuities have advantages, they also have disadvantages that investors must consider.

One of these disadvantages of purchasing an annuity or choosing an annuity is that the funds used for the annuity are no longer available for unexpected emergencies or unexpected desires. In addition, if the retiree does not live to at least his or her life expectancy, then the purchase of the annuity reduced the assets that would have been available to transfer to heirs. Annuities are by no means a panacea. However, they are a prodigious solution that can be partially implemented without much difficulty.

Assuming that a retiree is going to retain the risk or some of the risk, many different approaches can reduce the risks of outliving retirement accumulation. Two of the more common approaches are:

1. *4 Percent Per Year Approach:* Limit withdrawals from the capital accumulation to four percent per year.
2. *Multiple Portfolio Approach (Bucket Approach):* Divide capital into unequal tranches with each tranche representing five years of retirement. Invest the funds for each tranche in varying asset classes expected to produce inflation adjusted returns of about five to six percent per year.

4 Percent of Capital Balance Approach

Conceptually, this approach is relatively simple to understand and implement. It provides for distributions equal to four percent of the capital balance each year and generally has a very high success rate, especially when the assets are invested in a balanced portfolio, such as one with 60 percent equities and 40 percent fixed income. Such a portfolio should generally provide a good balance between income, growth, and downside protection.

However, one scenario that is a risk for retirees is when the retirement portfolio is subjected to several years of relatively large losses combined with distributions of four percent or more of the portfolio. In this scenario, the portfolio balance may decline so fast that it is irreparably impacted, without the retirees dramatically changing their lifestyles or going back to work.

It should be noted that some advisers and clients might choose to use a 3.5 percent model or a 4.5 percent model. Adjustments such as these provide more confidence or less confidence in the funds lasting through the retirement time period.

A four percent level of withdrawal initially indicates an account balance that is 25 times the income needed and implies a needed earnings rate of only 1.310 percent to pay out at a four percent rate for 30 years, assuming no inflation and annuity due payments. A four percent inflation adjusted withdrawal rate (assume inflation is three percent) would require an earnings rate of 4.349 percent annually for 30 years.

	Required Earnings Rate		
Withdrawal Rate	**Fixed Payment Required Earnings Rate**	**Inflation Adjusted Required Earnings Rate**	**Portfolio Allocation**
3%	-0.711%	2.268%	Very Conservative
4%	1.310%	4.349%	Conservative
5%	3.079%	6.171%	Moderate Conservative
6%	4.696%	7.837%	Moderate
7%	6.218%	9.405%	Moderate Aggressive
8%	7.678%	10.908%	Aggressive

As mentioned above and implicit in the chart above, the investment of the retirement assets is critical to successfully managing the risk of superannuation. The four percent withdrawal rate is an appropriate approach that generally achieves the objectives of clients as long as the beginning retirement portfolio is large enough.

Multiple Portfolio Approach (Bucket Approach)

This approach divides assets into six five-year tranches and funds each tranche with sufficient money and the correct investment choices to provide retirement income for that period. The schedule below is an example that indicates the percent of capital necessary in each tranche, the expected investment return required for that tranche, and the type of asset class necessary to sustain this return.

Years	% of Capital	Rate of Return Required	Investments
1-5	28%	2%	Money Markets
6-10	26%	4%	Treasuries
11-15	20%	6%	Corporate Bonds
16-20	13%	8%	Balanced Fund
21-25	7%	10%	Large Cap & International Stock
26-30	6%	12%	Small Cap & International Stock

This approach is expected to produce a real overall return between five percent and six percent. The goal of this approach is to replenish the first five-year increment (the immediate income) every five years. It should be noted that this method is not a significant deviation from historical methods of managing assets. In fact, the overall portfolio allocation is similar to that of a moderately allocated portfolio. This model is a different way of accounting for the funds and retirement needs. It should also be noted that the investor and adviser might choose to change the percent of capital percentages as well as the number of tranches. For example, seven five-year tranches might be used in lieu of six. This approach helps the client focus on current needs, which are funded by the most stable types of investments, while longer term investments are invested to provide for growth and future needs.

These two approaches are effective for developing retirement income distribution strategies for clients. It is important to keep in mind that not all models work with all clients, and clients often have unique goals or needs that must be accounted for specifically.

DISCUSSION QUESTIONS

SOLUTIONS to the discussion questions can be found exclusively within the chapter. Once you have completed an initial reading of the chapter, go back and highlight the answers to these questions.

1. List the major factors affecting retirement planning.

2. Define work life expectancy.

3. Define retirement life expectancy.

4. What is the median retirement age for individuals in the U.S.?

5. Explain the work life expectancy/retirement life expectancy dilemma.

6. List the major savings and investment concepts that are important to retirement planning.

7. Explain the importance of beginning a retirement savings plan early.

8. Explain the importance of understanding investment decisions and their consequences in retirement planning.

9. How is inflation relevant to a retirement plan?

10. Why do an individual's needs increase or decrease during retirement?

11. List some of the common factors that increase an individual's retirement income needs.

12. List some of the common factors that decrease an individual's retirement income needs.

13. Define the wage replacement ratio.

14. What is the most common estimate range (in percentage terms) for the wage replacement ratio?

15. Describe why a person may or may not need the same wage replacement percentage dollar amount or purchasing power amount throughout their entire retirement period.

16. List the two alternative methods for calculating an individual's wage replacement ratio.

17. How is the WRR calculated utilizing the top-down approach?

18. How is the WRR calculated utilizing the budgeting approach?

19. List the three most common sources of an individual's retirement income.

20. Explain how Social Security affects an individual's retirement income.

21. Describe the importance of personal savings to an individual's retirement income needs.

22. List some of the qualitative considerations that are important in retirement planning.

23. List some of the common factors that negatively affect retirement planning.

24. Explain capital needs analysis and its importance to retirement planning.

25. List the four most common methods for analyzing an individual's capital needs.

26. Identify the main assumptions necessary for capital needs analysis.

27. Describe how Monte Carlo Analysis can be used in retirement planning.

28. Explain how the annuity model calculates retirement needs.

29. What assumption does the capital preservation model make to mitigate the risk of an individual outliving their retirement savings?

30. Why is sensitivity analysis important to retirement planning?

MULTIPLE CHOICE PROBLEMS

A sample of multiple choice problems is provided below. Additional multiple choice problems are available at money-education.com by accessing the Student Practice Portal.

1. Which of the following expenditures will most likely increase during retirement?
    a. Clothing costs.
    b. Travel.
    c. FICA.
    d. Savings.

2. Gemma, a 35-year-old client who earns $45,000 a year, pays 7.65% of her gross pay in Social Security payroll taxes, and saves 8% of her annual gross income. Assume that Gemma wants to maintain her exact pre-retirement lifestyle. Calculate Gemma's wage replacement ratio using the top-down approach (round to the nearest %) and using pre-tax dollars.
    a. 70%.
    b. 80%.
    c. 84%.
    d. 90%.

3. Clay would like to determine his financial needs during retirement. All of the following are expenditures he might eliminate in his retirement needs calculation except:
    a. The $200 per month he spends on drying cleaning for his work suits.
    b. The $1,500 mortgage payment he makes that is scheduled to end five years into retirement.
    c. The FICA taxes he pays each year.
    d. The $2,000 per month he puts into savings.

4. Scarlett has the following expenditures during the current year:

Expense	Amount
1. Health Care	$800
2. Savings	$4,000
3. Travel	$500
4. Gifts to Grandchildren	$1,000

    Which of these expenditures would you expect to decrease during Scarlett's retirement?
    a. 2 only.
    b. 1 and 3.
    c. 2 and 4.
    d. 1, 2, 3, and 4.

5. Niles and Daphne are near retirement. They have a joint life expectancy of 25 years in retirement. Daphne anticipates their annual income in retirement will need to increase each year at the rate of inflation, which they assume is 4%. Based on the assumption that their first year retirement need, beginning on the first day of retirement, for annual income will be $85,000, of which they have $37,500 available from other sources, and an annual after-tax rate of return of 6.5%, calculate the total amount that needs to be in place when Niles and Daphne begin their retirement.

    a. $743,590.43.
    b. $859,906.74.
    c. $892,478.21.
    d. $906,131.31.

> **Additional multiple choice problems**
> **are available at**
> **money-education.com**
> **by accessing the**
> **Student Practice Portal.**
> **Access requires registration of the title using**
> **the unique code at the front of the book.**

QUICK QUIZ EXPLANATIONS

Quick Quiz 11.1

1. False. The average age men retire is age 64. Labor force participation for men over age 65 is under 30 percent.
2. True.
3. True.

Quick Quiz 11.2

1. False. Given that a savings rate of 10% to 13% of gross pay over a long period of time is necessary to meet the retirement goal, the savings rate in the U.S. is insufficient for retirement planning.
2. False. Common stocks provide the best hedge against inflation. The real economic returns for fixed-income securities are low and are not a good hedge against inflation.
3. True.

Quick Quiz 11.3

1. True.
2. True.

Quick Quiz 11.4

1. True.
2. False. Social Security is not a sufficient source of income replacement during retirement for most income levels. Social Security provides 100% of income to only 20% of individuals aged 65 or older receiving Social Security benefits.
3. True.

Quick Quiz 11.5

1. True.
2. True.
3. True.

Quick Quiz 11.6

1. False. While sensitivity analysis does not eliminate all risk associated with retirement planning, it does allow the adviser to build a slightly worse case scenario and to determine the impact of more conservative assumptions on the overall plan.
2. False. Monte Carlo Analysis does not predict particular events. Rather, it provides insight into the most likely outcome while also providing other possible outcomes, both good and bad.
3. True.

12

INCOME TAX PLANNING

LEARNING OBJECTIVES

1. Describe the three tax systems.
2. Describe the three types of income.
3. Describe the three types of tax accounting.
4. Describe three key tax principles.
5. Identify the sources of tax law.
6. Describe the interest and penalties for noncompliance.
7. Identify the preparer penalties.
8. Summarize the failure to pay, failure to file, accuracy related, and fraud penalties.
9. Compare and contrast the fundamental components of the income tax system including filing forms, filing status, income, exemptions, exclusions, deductions, adjustments, credits, and tax rates.*
10. Describe the tax formula for individual taxpayers.
11. Determine what is included and excluded in gross income.
12. List deductions for adjusted gross income.
13. List itemized deductions.
14. Determine which type of deduction is better above or below the line.
15. Understand what is adjusted gross income.
16. Determine the standard deduction and additional standard deduction for varying filing statuses.
17. Determine who qualifies as a dependent.
18. Determine the appropriate tax filing status.
19. Identify various tax credits.
20. Compare tax credits to deductions.
21. Understand basis and how it is determined and the various adjustments to basis.
22. Understand capital gain holding periods and tax rates.
23. Describe the sale of a personal residence and its tax exemption.

*Ties to CFP Certification Learning Objectives

INCOME TAXES AND THE IRS

The Three Tax Systems

In the United States, there are three separate and distinct tax systems that are relevant to financial planning: (1) the income tax system, (2) the estate and gift tax system, and (3) the generation-skipping transfer tax system. While many individuals assume that the Internal Revenue Code is one set of rules that all work together, this is not the case. There are three tax systems, and those systems do not always fit together perfectly. It is important for tax professionals and financial planners to understand which tax system they are dealing with when engaging in a transaction. It is possible, for example, for one single transaction to be treated as a gift for income tax purposes and as a sale for estate and gift tax purposes. The tax consequences for income tax purposes and for estate/gift tax purposes will, therefore, differ. This chapter covers fundamental income tax rules.

Three Types of Income

In the U.S. income tax system, there are three types of income: (1) active (ordinary) income, (2) portfolio income, and (3) passive income. Every bit of income earned by a taxpayer must be classified into one of these three categories.

Active income is income derived from labor and income connected with the active conduct of a trade or business. Portfolio income is income derived from investments, such as interest, dividends, and capital gains. Passive income is income derived from dealings in real estate and from the conduct of a trade or business in which the taxpayer does not materially participate.

Categorization of income is important for two reasons: (1) different tax consequences apply to each type of income; and (2) the "bucket rule" limits a taxpayer's ability to write off losses in one income bucket against the gains in that same bucket.

Active income (and loss) is subject to ordinary income tax rates, which are the highest tax rates in our system. Some types of portfolio income are subject to favorable income tax rates, such as the 15 percent rate (or 20 percent rate) that applies to long-term capital gains and qualified dividends. Passive income is subject to a host of anti-abuse rules, and therefore constitutes a separate category of income.

> **:≡ *Key Concepts***
>
> 1. Identify the three primary sources of tax law.
>
> 2. Describe the legal basis for the modern income tax.
>
> 3. Identify how statutory tax law is established.
>
> 4. Identify the sources of administrative tax law.

The "bucket rule" limits losses in one bucket to gains in the same bucket. For example, if a taxpayer incurred $5,000 in investment gains and $20,000 in investment losses, $5,000 of the loss could offset the investment gain but could not, under the bucket rule, be used to offset other types of income (such as ordinary or passive income). As in all other areas of tax law, there are exceptions to this rule. In the case of portfolio losses, up to $3,000 of net losses in the portfolio bucket can be used to offset either active or passive income.

Three Types of Tax Accounting

For income to be reported properly, taxpayers must follow some method to account for income. There are three methods of accounting that are used for federal income tax purposes: (1) the cash method, (2) the accrual method, and (3) the hybrid method.

The cash method of accounting is the method used by most individuals and small businesses. Under the cash method, income is taxed when it is received, and allowable deductions are claimed when they are paid. Understanding the cash method is particularly important for financial planners, who are typically providing financial advice and planning to individuals and small businesses.

The accrual method of accounting is the method frequently used by larger businesses. Under the accrual method of accounting, income is taxed when it is earned (whether or not it has been received), and deductions are claimed when they are incurred (whether or not they have been paid).

Any method of accounting other than the cash method or accrual method that is approved by the IRS is referred to, collectively, as the hybrid method. The hybrid method is used by some businesses to better reflect their economic income on their income tax returns.

Three Key Tax Principles

Three key tax principles underlie personal income taxation. They are: (1) the doctrine of constructive receipt, (2) the economic benefit doctrine, and (3) the doctrine of the fruit and the tree (assignment of income doctrine).

While most individuals account for their income using the cash method, certain circumstances may arise that will subject income that has not yet been received to current taxation. The **doctrine of constructive receipt** states that if income is permanently set aside in an account for the benefit of a taxpayer, or if a taxpayer is given the choice to receive income now or defer it to the future, that income will be taxed to the taxpayer currently even if he does not receive it until sometime in the future. For example, consider interest that is earned on a three-year certificate of deposit. Even though a taxpayer does not receive the interest until the certificate of deposit matures, he is taxed on the earned interest currently, since the interest earnings are permanently set aside in an account for the taxpayer's benefit.

The doctrine of constructive receipt (income that is permanently set aside in an account for the taxpayer's benefit) is a special exception to the cash-basis method of income tax accounting. The doctrine states that even if you have not actually received the income, if you have constructively received it, then it is income. For example, if a taxpayer goes to his mailbox on December 31st and sees a check made out to that taxpayer for work he performed, immediately closes the mailbox, and comes back to get the check on January 1st, the income is reported as of December 31st. In fact, the doctrine of constructive receipt is at the cornerstone of retirement planning, and constructive receipt must be avoided if a taxpayer wishes to defer income and taxes into the future to fund his or her retirement.

Income received by a taxpayer, in any form, is subject to income tax. The **economic benefit doctrine** simply states that if a taxpayer receives an economic benefit as income, the value of that benefit will be subject to tax. For example, if a taxpayer is provided group term life insurance by an employer, the value of that group term insurance is subject to income tax, since it is an economic benefit received in return for labor. Congress has, however, for public policy reasons, exempted part of the value of group term life insurance from income tax, but excess amounts are taxable under the economic benefit doctrine.

The third key principal of income taxation is that income is taxed to either: (1) the person who earns it, or (2) the person who owns the asset that produced the income. This principle is referred to as the assignment of income doctrine or the **doctrine of the fruit and the tree**. He who owns the tree pays income tax on the fruit that the tree produces. This doctrine is really an anti-abuse provision. It is designed to prevent taxpayers from assigning income to a family member in a lower income tax bracket while retaining the asset that produces the income.

Sources of Tax Law

There are three primary sources of tax law: statutory sources, administrative sources, and judicial sources. These sources of law reflect the structure of our political system.

Before we elaborate on the direct sources of tax law, however, it is important to understand the origin of our income tax system. As originally adopted, the U.S. Constitution did not give the federal government the ability to collect a tax on income. At the founding of our nation, there was a great deal of suspicion surrounding the new, federal, centralized government, and the states did not want the power of the federal government to get out of hand. Consequently, they imposed limitations on the federal government's ability to impose taxes. As time went on, however, and as the federal government began to assume a more active governance role, a source of revenue was needed to fund the cost of these activities. While Congress had enacted an income tax on several previous occasions, these taxes were either temporary, or were declared unconstitutional by the Supreme Court. With the obvious need for revenue, and the Supreme Court's decree that a federal income tax was unconstitutional, it became clear that a constitutional amendment would be needed to grant the Congress the power to lay and collect taxes on income.

On February 25, 1913, the 16th Amendment to the U.S. Constitution was adopted. This short amendment stated, "The Congress shall have power to lay and collect taxes on income, from whatever source derived, without apportionment among the several States, and without regard to any census or enumeration."

The Constitution, through enactment of the 16th Amendment, became the foundation of income tax law in the United States. Two clauses of the 16th Amendment are particularly important in developing an understanding of our income tax system: (1) the "power to lay and collect taxes on income," and (2) the clause "from whatever source derived."

The term "income" is not as easily interpreted as it may first seem. Generally, any accretion to an individual's wealth is income, and is therefore subject to taxation. However, when certain proposals seem to have gone too far, limitations on the definition of income have been imposed by various branches of the government. Exemptions and exclusions also allow some accretions to wealth to avoid income taxes altogether.

As the second important clause from the 16th Amendment indicates, a U.S. citizen is subject to income tax on income "from whatever source derived." In other words, the worldwide income of U.S. citizens from any source is subject to taxation by the U.S.

Exhibit 12.1 | Tax Triads

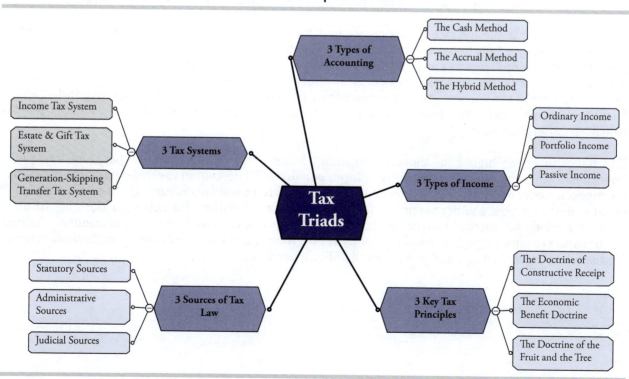

Exhibit 12.2 | Sources of Tax Law

Source	Authority	Law
Statutory	Congressionally derived law through legislative power provided by the 16th Amendment to the U.S. Constitution.	Internal Revenue Code of 1986, as amended.
Administrative	• **Treasury Department:** Executive authority of law enforcement delegated to the Treasury Department. • **Internal Revenue Service:** Tax collection authority delegated by the Treasury Department to the Internal Revenue Service.	• **Treasury Regulations:** a. Proposed Regulations b. Temporary Regulations c. Final Regulations • **IRS Determinations:** a. Revenue Rulings b. Private Letter Rulings c. Determination Letters d. Revenue Procedures
Judicial	Judicial authority to determine if tax laws enacted by Congress and enforced by the President are constitutional. Also, decides whether a regulation or IRS position follows the intent of Congress.	**Case Law:** Usually a case or controversy between a taxpayer and the IRS resulting in case law expressed in the opinion of a court.

Interest and Penalties for Noncompliance

Taxpayers who choose not to comply with the filing requirements are subject to a series of penalties, including the failure to file penalty, the failure to pay penalty, and the accuracy related penalty.

If a taxpayer fails to file his income tax return on time, the **failure to file penalty** under Section 6651 applies. If a taxpayer fails to pay the tax due on the due date, Section 6651 also imposes a **failure to pay penalty**. Section 6662 imposes an **accuracy-related penalty** on taxpayers who file incorrect returns as a result of: (1) a failure to make a good faith effort to comply with the tax law, (2) a substantial understatement of tax liability (generally more than 10 percent of the correct tax liability and at least a $5,000 deficiency), (3) a substantial valuation understatement, or (4) a substantial estate or gift tax valuation understatement.

The stakes are even higher for those who commit fraud while failing to file or pay, and those who intentionally understate their tax liability. A fraud penalty of 75 percent of the underpayment of tax may be imposed under Section 6663. If a frivolous or incomplete income tax return has been filed, a $5,000 penalty may be imposed under Section 6702 regardless of tax liability. Intentional actions constituting fraud, or a willful failure to file or pay the tax liability that is due can rise to the level of criminal offenses. For obvious reasons, taxpayers should properly report their income and deductions on their tax returns, file them in a timely fashion, and pay the tax liability when due.

Exhibit 12.3 | Failure to File

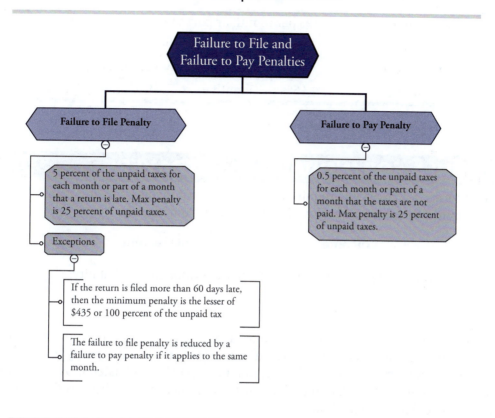

Preparer Penalties

In addition to tax penalties that may be assessed on taxpayers, tax preparers may also be subject to penalties. IRC Section 6694(a) states that if a tax preparer takes an unrealistic position on a tax return and the preparer knew or reasonably should have known of the position, then the penalty is the greater of $1,000 or 50 percent of the income derived by the preparer for preparing the return. If the understatement was due to willful or reckless conduct, the penalty is the greater of $5,000 or 50 percent of income derived by the preparer for the return.

Other penalties may also be assessed, including penalties for failure to sign a return prepared by the tax preparer (IRC Section 6695(b)), failure to provide a copy of the tax return to the taxpayer (IRC Section 6695(a), failure to keep a copy of the return (IRC Section 6695(d)) and a client list, and failure to comply with due diligence requirements when claiming the earned income credit (IRC Section 6695(g)).

Exhibit 12.4 | Summary of Penalties

Failure to File	5% per month or part thereof to 25% maximum
Failure to Pay	0.5% per month or part thereof to 25% maximum
Accuracy Related	20% of underpayment to 30%*
Fraud	15% per month up to 75% of underpayment

*40% if due to substantial valuation misstatement, substantial overstatement of pension liabilities, or substantial estate or gift tax valuation understatement.

TAX FORMULA FOR INDIVIDUAL TAXPAYERS

In very general terms, a taxpayer is required to pay a federal income tax on taxable income. **Taxable income** is determined by subtracting allowable deductions from income:

Income – Deductions = Taxable Income

Taxable income is multiplied by the income tax rate to determine the tax liability:

Taxable Income x Tax Rate = Tax Liability

There is a more extensive tax formula for individual taxpayers than the simple tax calculation presented above. The more complete formula includes exclusions from income, different types of deductions, and tax credits. In addition, there are intermediate calculations (such as adjusted gross income) that can be important considerations in tax planning. Each of these items will be discussed in this chapter and throughout the remainder of the textbook.

Income Broadly Defined	**$xx,xxx**
Less: Exclusions	(x,xxx)
Gross Income	**$xx,xxx**
Less: Deductions for Adjusted Gross Income (*above-the-line deductions*)	(x,xxx)
Adjusted Gross Income ("The Line")	**$xx,xxx**
Less: Deductions from Adjusted Gross Income (*below-the-line deductions*) Greater of Standard or Itemized Deductions, and the Qualified Business Income Deduction	(xx,xxx)
Taxable Income	**$xx,xxx**
Tax on Taxable Income	**$x,xxx**
Less: Credit for Taxes Withheld	(x,xxx)
Less: Credit for Estimated Tax Payments	(x,xxx)
Less: Other Tax Credits	(x,xxx)
Tax Due or (Refund Due)	**$xxx**

Individuals report their income, deductions, exemptions, and other information required for the calculation of the federal tax liability on Form 1040. Form 1040SR is a simplified version of the Form 1040, and may be utilized by taxpayers age 65 and older who do not have complicated tax situations. Forms 1040 and 1040SR are accompanied by various Schedules which provide additional details to the information reported on the Form 1040 or 1040SR.

☰ *Key Concepts*

1. Explain the basic tax formula.
2. Define income.
3. Identify items excluded from gross income.
4. Identify items included in gross income.

Income

Income, broadly defined, means the gross amount of money and the fair market value of property, services, or other accretion to wealth received, but it does not include borrowed money or a return of invested dollars (sometimes referred to as return of capital or return of adjusted taxable basis).

Gross Income

Gross income includes all income items that must be reported on the federal income tax return and that are subject to the federal income tax. It includes all income as broadly defined, less exclusions. Some of the most common gross income items are listed in **Exhibit 12.5**.

Exhibit 12.5 | Items Included in Gross Income

• Gains from the sale of assets	• Compensation (salaries and wages, etc.)
• Distributions from retirement plans	• Interest income
• Rental income	• Dividend income
• Unemployment compensation benefits	• Alimony received (divorced before 2019)
• Royalty income	• Gross income from self-employment

Exclusions

Exclusions are income items that are not subject to income tax. Each exclusion must be specifically authorized by Congress and set forth in the Internal Revenue Code (IRC) or must be determined by the courts to be outside the definition of income as it is used in the 16th Amendment to the U.S. Constitution. Most exclusions from gross income are allowed by IRC Sections 101 through 150. Some of the more common exclusions permitted by the Code are listed in **Exhibit 12.6**.

Exhibit 12.6 | Partial List of Exclusions

• Interest income from municipal bonds	• Cash or property received by gift
• Alimony received (divorced after 2018)	• Deferral contributions to certain retirement plans
• Child support payments received	• Gain on the sale of a principal residence
• Cash or property received by inheritance	• Scholarship or fellowship
• Qualifying distributions from a Roth IRA during retirement	• Life insurance proceeds received because of the death of the insured
• Specified employee fringe benefits	

Deductions

Deductions are subtracted from gross income in arriving at taxable income. For individual taxpayers, deductions are divided into two categories: Deductions *for* (before) adjusted gross income and deductions *from* (after) adjusted gross income. Deductions for adjusted gross income are called **above-the-line deductions**, and deductions from adjusted gross income are called **below-the-line deductions**, itemized deductions, or Schedule A deductions. A small sample of deductions for adjusted gross income (above-the-line deductions) is listed in **Exhibit 12.7**.

Exhibit 12.7 | Partial List of Deductions for Adjusted Gross Income

- Alimony paid (divorced before 2019)
- Contributions to traditional IRAs
- Educator expenses (up to $250)
- Interest paid on student loans (up to $2,500)
- Business expenses
- Rental or royalty income expenses
- Losses from the sale of business property
- Moving expenses (active duty military only)

Note that the "line," for income tax purposes, is adjusted gross income (AGI). AGI sets many of the phase-outs and thresholds that will have to be met to take advantage of certain deductions and tax planning tools. Understanding where deductions are taken in the tax formula, therefore, is important when considering tax planning alternatives for clients.

When considering income tax deductions and their planning implications for clients, it is helpful to recall the income tax formula.

	Gross Income
-	Exclusions
-	Adjustments (Above-the-line deductions)
=	**Adjusted Gross Income (AGI)**
-	The greater of the Standard Deduction or Itemized Deductions (Below-the-line deductions)
-	Qualified Business Income Deduction (Below-the-line deduction)
=	**Taxable Income**

Exhibit 12.8 | Form 1040 Adjustments Section

10	Educator expenses	10
11	Certain business expenses of reservists, performing artists, and fee-basis government officials. Attach Form 2106	11
12	Health savings account deduction. Attach Form 8889	12
13	Moving expenses for members of the Armed Forces. Attach Form 3903	13
14	Deductible part of self-employment tax. Attach Schedule SE	14
15	Self-employed SEP, SIMPLE, and qualified plans	15
16	Self-employed health insurance deduction	16
17	Penalty on early withdrawal of savings	17
18a	Alimony paid	18a
b	Recipient's SSN . . . . ▶ ___|_|___	
c	Date of original divorce or separation agreement (see instructions) ▶ _____	
19	IRA deduction	19
20	Student loan interest deduction	20
21	Tuition and fees deduction. Attach Form 8917	21
22	Add lines 10 through 21. These are your **adjustments to income.** Enter here and on Form 1040, 1040-SR, or 1040-NR, line 10a	22

Deductions for AGI (Above-the-Line)

Adjustments, or above-the-line deductions, reduce a taxpayer's adjusted gross income (AGI). Most above-the-line deductions relate to expenses for business and production of income activities (from investment activities) by taxpayers, but there are some deductions permitted for individual taxpayers as well (such as IRA deductions, student loan interest, and educator expenses, to name a few). Above-the-line deductions are listed in IRC Section 62, and they can be claimed by the taxpayer even if the taxpayer does not itemize deductions.

Whenever expenses are associated with a business activity, they are above-the-line deductions. Only the net income of the business (gross receipts from the business less expenses incurred in producing that income) is included in the taxpayer's gross income for the year. For example, if a taxpayer operates a sole proprietorship, the financial results will be reported on Schedule C of the taxpayer's individual tax return. If, instead of operating a business, a taxpayer engages in rental real estate activities, the gross receipts from the rental activity less expenses associated with the rental activity will be reported on Schedule E of the income tax return, and only the net income from the activity will be reported in the taxpayer's gross income for the year. Schedules C and E are essentially income statements for the business and production of income activities, detailing the gross receipts and expenditures incurred in the activity. Since business related and production of income related expenses directly reduce gross income, they are effectively treated as above-the-line deductions.

All other above-the-line deductions are found in the adjustments section on Schedule 1 of Form 1040.

Itemized Deductions (Below-the-Line)

When most taxpayers think of deductions, they usually think of itemized deductions. Itemized, or below-the-line, deductions are deductions that are allowed for personal expenses and losses that are not typically associated with the conduct of a business or with production of income activities. While there are fewer itemized deductions (there are only six categories of itemized deductions) than above-the line deductions, itemized deductions are sometimes more important when planning for individual clients.

Taxpayers may take the greater of their itemized deductions or the standard deduction in determining taxable income. In order to achieve a tax benefit, the taxpayer will need his total itemized deductions to be greater than the standard deduction.

Exhibit 12.9 | Partial List of Itemized Deductions

• Miscellaneous expenses	• Medical and dental expenses in excess of 7.5% of AGI
• Charitable contributions	• State and local income taxes*
• Home mortgage interest	• Real property taxes on home*
• Investment interest expense	• Property taxes based on the value of a car*
• Certain investment expenses	• Casualty losses from a Federally declared disaster

The deduction for state and local income and property taxes is limited to a combined maximum of $10,000 (TCJA 2017).

Example 12.1

Corbin (age 52) and Maria (age 50) have no dependents. During this year, they paid $7,000 in state income taxes, $10,000 in charitable contributions, $8,000 in home mortgage interest, and $2,000 in property taxes on their home. The total of their itemized deductions is $27,000, which exceeds their standard deduction. Therefore, they should itemize deductions rather than use the standard deduction.

In three situations, a taxpayer is not allowed to use the standard deduction and *must* itemize deductions:

1. A married individual who files a separate return (married filing separately filing status) cannot use a standard deduction if that person's spouse itemizes deductions.
2. A nonresident alien and a dual-status alien are not allowed to use a standard deduction.
3. An individual who files a tax return for less than 12 months because of a change in annual accounting period is not allowed to use a standard deduction (not common for individual taxpayers).

Which Type of Deduction is Better – Above or Below-the-Line Deductions?

Due to the limitations imposed on itemized deductions (including various **floors** and **ceilings**, as well as **phase-outs**), above-the-line deductions are usually considered to be more favorable to the taxpayer on a dollar-for-dollar basis.

Adjusted Gross Income (AGI)

Adjusted gross income (AGI) is gross income reduced by above-the-line deductions. When determining whether deductions are taken above-the-line (for AGI) or below-the-line (from AGI), "the line" is AGI. Adjusted gross income is also used to determine limitations on several below-the-line deductions, on several income tax credits (discussed later in this chapter), and on a few other items on the tax return. Adjusted gross income is a concept that applies to individual tax returns; it does not apply to corporate or other entity tax returns.

⠿ *Key Concepts*

1. Define adjusted gross income.
2. Identify the difference between the standard deduction and itemized deductions.
3. Identify when a taxpayer is not permitted to use the standard deduction.

Deductions from Adjusted Gross Income

Deductions from adjusted gross income (below-the-line deductions) are those deductions that are subtracted from AGI. They consist of the greater of the standard deduction or certain allowable itemized deductions and the deduction for **qualified business income**.

Standard Deduction

An individual taxpayer is allowed to deduct the greater of the standard deduction or allowable itemized deductions. Prior to 2018, approximately 70 percent of individual taxpayers used the standard deduction. The number of taxpayers using the standard deduction increased to over 87 percent beginning in 2018 due to the higher standard deduction amounts implemented by the Tax Cuts and Jobs Act. The **standard deduction** is a standard amount used to offset AGI that is specified by Congress. The standard deduction is adjusted for inflation on an annual basis. The total standard deduction includes a basic standard deduction plus additional standard deduction amounts for taxpayers age 65 or older and for taxpayers who are blind. The basic standard deduction amounts depend on the taxpayer's filing status (discussed below). The standard deduction amounts for nondependents are listed in **Exhibit 12.10**. The standard deduction for a dependent is different and is discussed below.

Exhibit 12.10 | Standard Deduction

Filing Status	2021
Married Filing Jointly	$25,100
Married Filing Separately	$12,550
Surviving Spouse	$25,100
Head of Household	$18,800
Single	$12,550

Additional Standard Deduction - Aged or Blind

An additional standard deduction is allowed for a taxpayer or spouse (not for a dependent) who is 65 years of age or older or blind. The age of the taxpayer is determined as of the end of the year. It is therefore possible for an unmarried taxpayer to receive one or two additional standard deductions and for a married couple to receive up to four additional standard deductions. The amounts allowed for each additional standard deduction are adjusted for inflation and depend upon the filing status of the taxpayer. The additional standard deduction amounts are listed in **Exhibit 12.11**.

Exhibit 12.11 | Additional Standard Deduction

Filing Status	2021
Married Filing Jointly	$1,350
Married Filing Separately	$1,350
Surviving Spouse	$1,350
Head of Household	$1,700
Single	$1,700

Additional Standard Deduction - Qualified Disaster-Related Casualty Losses[1]

The Taxpayer Certainty and Disaster Tax Relief Act of 2020 created an additional standard deduction for net qualified personal casualty losses related to a presidentially declared disaster, subject to a $500 per disaster floor. Previously, personal casualty losses resulting from a qualified disaster were only deductible as an itemized deduction subject to a $100 per disaster floor, and only the loss in excess of ten percent of AGI was deductible.

---

1. A qualified disaster loss is a casualty or theft loss of personal-use property attributable to a major disaster declared by the President under Section 401 of the Stafford Act.

Calculation of the Standard Deduction for a Dependent

An individual who can be claimed as a dependent by someone else cannot use the regular basic standard deduction, as discussed above. The basic standard deduction for someone who can be claimed as a dependent by another taxpayer is determined using a three-step process:

- The minimum basic standard deduction is $1,100 for 2021.
- If larger, the basic standard deduction is equal to the earned income (wages, salary, self-employment income, or taxable scholarships or fellowships) of the taxpayer plus $350 for 2021.
- The maximum basic standard deduction is equal to the normal basic standard deduction for the taxpayer's filing status. Any additional standard deductions for age or blindness are added to the basic standard deduction.

Claiming Dependents

A taxpayer may claim certain other individuals as **dependents** on her tax return. Doing so allows the taxpayer to deduct eligible expenses of the dependent and claim tax credits tied to the dependent. An individual may be claimed as a dependent on only one tax return. Normally, the child of a taxpayer qualifies as the taxpayer's dependent if the child is under age 19 (24 if a full-time student), although in some cases the taxpayer's own child may not qualify as a dependent. A relative of the taxpayer (such as a parent or adult child) may qualify as a dependent if the taxpayer provides more than 50% of the relative's support and the relative's income is below a modest threshold amount.

Tax on Taxable Income

The income tax on taxable income is determined by applying certain tax rates to taxable income. The tax rates currently range from 10 percent to 37 percent. The amount of taxable income subject to tax at each rate (each tax bracket) depends on the filing status of the taxpayer.

Although the tax can be determined by directly applying the tax rates from the tax rate schedules to taxable income, taxpayers are required to determine the tax using tax tables provided by the Internal Revenue Service, if possible. These tax tables, published by the Internal Revenue Service in the instructions for individual income tax returns, show small ranges of taxable income and the amount of tax for taxable income within each range.

Exhibit 12.12 | Tax Rate Schedules

2021 Unmarried Individuals

If taxable income is over--	But not over--	The tax is:
$0	$9,950	10% of taxable income
$9,950	$40,525	$995 plus 12% of the amount over $9,950
$40,525	$86,375	$4,664 plus 22% of the amount over $40,525
$86,375	$164,925	$14,751 plus 24% of the amount over $86,375
$164,925	$209,425	$33,603 plus 32% of the amount over $164,925
$209,425	$523,600	$47,843 plus 35% of the amount over $209,425
$523,600	no limit	$157,804.25 plus 37% of the amount over $523,600

2021 Married Filing Jointly or Surviving Spouse

If taxable income is over--	But not over--	The tax is:
$0	$19,900	10% of taxable income
$19,900	$81,050	$1,990 plus 12% of the amount over $19,900
$81,050	$172,750	$9,328 plus 22% of the amount over $81,050
$172,750	$329,850	$29,502 plus 24% of the amount over $172,750
$329,850	$418,850	$67,206 plus 32% of the amount over $329,850
$418,850	$628,300	$95,686 plus 35% of the amount over $418,850
$628,300	no limit	$168,993.50 plus 37% of the amount over $628,300

2021 Head of Household

If taxable income is over--	But not over--	The tax is:
$0	$14,200	10% of taxable income
$14,200	$54,200	$1,420 plus 12% of the amount over $14,200
$54,200	$86,350	$6,220 plus 22% of the amount over $54,200
$86,350	$164,900	$13,293 plus 24% of the amount over $86,350
$164,900	$209,400	$32,145 plus 32% of the amount over $164,900
$209,400	$523,600	$46,385 plus 35% of the amount over $209,400
$523,600	no limit	$156,355 plus 37% of the amount over $523,600

2021 Married Filing Separately

If taxable income is over--	But not over--	The tax is:
$0	$9,950	10% of taxable income
$9,950	$40,525	$995 plus 12% of the amount over $9,950
$40,525	$86,375	$4,664 plus 22% of the amount over $40,525
$86,375	$164,925	$14,751 plus 24% of the amount over $86,375
$164,925	$209,425	$33,603 plus 32% of the amount over $164,925
$209,425	$314,150	$47,843 plus 35% of the amount over $209,425
$314,150	no limit	$84,496.75 plus 37% of the amount over $314,150

2021 Estates and Trusts

If taxable income is over--	But not over--	The tax is:
$0	$2,650	10% of taxable income
$2,650	$9,550	$265 plus 24% of the amount over $2,650
$9,550	$13,050	$1,921 plus 35% of the amount over $9,550
Over $13,050	no limit	$3,146 plus 37% of the amount over $13,050

Filing Status

The filing status of a taxpayer is used to determine the amount of the taxpayer's standard deduction, the tax rate schedule (or tax table) to be used, and the eligibility of the taxpayer to use various tax benefits. A list of filing statuses is presented in **Exhibit 12.13**.

Exhibit 12.13 | Filing Status for Individuals

Married Filing Jointly

Married Filing Separately

Surviving Spouse

Head of Household
(Including an Abandoned Spouse)

Single

Marital Status

The determination of whether a taxpayer is married is normally made as of the close (the last day) of the tax year. However, if a taxpayer's spouse dies during the year, the marital status of the taxpayer is determined on the date of the spouse's death. A married person normally has two filing status options: married filing jointly or married filing separately.

If a person is not married, then he or she may qualify for the surviving spouse, head of household, or single filing status. A very rare situation is discussed below which may allow a married person to file as a single taxpayer. A taxpayer who is legally separated from his spouse under a decree of divorce or of separate maintenance is not considered to be married for federal income tax purposes.

Married Filing Jointly

Married taxpayers are allowed to choose either married filing jointly or **married filing separately filing status**. Most married taxpayers use the **married filing jointly filing status**. This filing status allows a married couple to combine their gross income and deductions. If they do not itemize deductions, the basic standard deduction when filing jointly is double the size of the basic standard deduction for a married taxpayer filing separately. Each tax bracket (the 12 percent tax bracket, for example) for joint filers is twice as broad as for a married taxpayer filing separately, subjecting twice as much income to the lower rates. In addition, a married couple is required to file jointly in order to be eligible for certain benefits such as the American Opportunity Tax Credit (AOTC) for qualified education expenses, discussed in Chapter 8.

Married Filing Separately

A married taxpayer can elect to file separately for any reason. This may be necessary if the spouses are separated at the end of the year, or if the taxpayer is not sure that his spouse is accurately reporting income. It may also be used for tax minimization purposes, by permitting one spouse to deduct more of his unusually large medical expenses for the tax year.

For a taxpayer whose spouse dies during the year, a joint return can be filed. The joint return will include the income and deductions of the taxpayer for the full year and the income and deductions of the spouse for the part of the year that the spouse lived. If the surviving taxpayer remarries before the end of the year, she will be able to file a joint return with the new spouse but not with the deceased spouse. In this situation, the final income tax return for the deceased spouse must use the married filing separately filing status.

Abandoned Spouse

There is one situation in which a legally married taxpayer will be allowed to use a filing status (head of household) generally reserved for unmarried taxpayers. As discussed below, the head of household status is more favorable than filing as married filing separately and when an individual cannot locate his spouse, and does not want to file a tax return with him, it may be available. To be eligible to file as an abandoned spouse (and therefore use the head of household filing status), the taxpayer must meet *all* of the following requirements:

- Must be married.
- Must file a separate tax return from the spouse.
- Must maintain as his/her home a household which for more than one-half of the taxable year is the principal place of abode of a child who can be claimed as a dependent.
- Must furnish over one-half of the cost of maintaining the household.
- The spouse must not be a member of the household during the last six months of the tax year.

Unmarried Taxpayers

A taxpayer who is not married on the final day of the tax year may be able to file as surviving spouse, head of household, or single. The tax benefits for the surviving spouse filing status are most favorable, those for head of household are next, and those for the single filing status are the least favorable.

Surviving Spouse

The **surviving spouse filing status** affords the same basic standard deduction and tax rates as the married filing jointly filing status. However, eligibility for this filing status is not something that most people desire. To be eligible, the spouse of the taxpayer must have died within the two preceding tax years of the taxpayer. Specifically, a taxpayer must meet all of the following requirements to qualify:

- The taxpayer's spouse must have died during either of the two preceding tax years.
- The taxpayer must maintain (pay more than half the cost of) a household as his home which is also the principal place of residence of a dependent child (son, stepson, daughter, or stepdaughter).
- The taxpayer has not remarried.
- The taxpayer and spouse were eligible to file a joint return for the spouse's year of death.

It should be noted that the filing status called surviving spouse in the Internal Revenue Code and Treasury Regulations is referred to as the qualifying widow(er) filing status in IRS publications. Surviving spouse and qualifying widow(er) are alternate names for the same filing status.

Head of Household

The **head of household filing status** provides a basic standard deduction and tax bracket sizes that are less favorable to the taxpayer than those for the surviving spouse, but more favorable than those for the single filing status. Head of household filing status can be used by an unmarried taxpayer who is not a surviving spouse. The taxpayer must maintain (pay more than half the cost of) a household as his home, which is also the principal place of residence for more than half the year for:

- a qualifying child of the taxpayer who is claimed as a dependent (discussed previously in this chapter) of the taxpayer,
- an unmarried qualifying child who lives with the taxpayer but is not a dependent of the taxpayer (e.g., a taxpayer's child or grandchild who lives in the taxpayer's household but is claimed as the dependent of another person), or
- a qualifying relative (discussed previously in this chapter) who is: (1) claimed as a dependent of the taxpayer, and (2) actually related to the taxpayer.

If a married child of the taxpayer lives with the taxpayer but cannot be claimed as a dependent of the taxpayer either because the child: (1) files a joint return (married filing jointly) with her spouse, or (2) fails to meet a citizenship or residency test, the taxpayer is not allowed to use the head of household filing status.

Special Rule for the Father or Mother of the Taxpayer

In order to use the head of household filing status, a qualifying child or a qualifying relative must normally live with the taxpayer. However, a taxpayer may also qualify for the head of household status by maintaining a separate household for the father or mother of the taxpayer who qualifies as the taxpayer's dependent.

Single

The **single filing status** must be used by an unmarried taxpayer who is not eligible to use the surviving spouse nor head of household filing status. It provides the least desirable basic standard deduction and tax brackets for an unmarried taxpayer.

Payment of Taxes Through Withholdings

Although income taxes could (in theory) all be paid at the time the tax return is filed, Congress has decided that federal income taxes should be withheld by an employer from the employee's wages or salary and sent to the government during the year. This not only provides the government with revenues throughout the year, but it also taxes the employee when the employee has the wherewithal (the cash) to pay. This withholding is merely a prepayment of income tax. Therefore, the employee is allowed to subtract any federal income taxes withheld during the year from the tax on taxable income when a tax return is filed.

FICA

The Federal Insurance Contributions Act (FICA) provides for old-age, survivors, disability, and hospital insurance. This coverage is financed by Social Security and Medicare taxes. Employers are required to withhold Social Security and Medicare tax from an employee's wages with the employer paying a matching amount of tax. The Social Security tax has a wage base limit of $142,800 for 2021. Employers are required to contribute 6.2 percent of each employee's income up to the Social Security wage base for 2021. The required Medicare tax is collected from an employee at a rate of 1.45 percent of their salary or wages, with a matching tax of 1.45 percent collected from the employer (2.9% total). The Medicare tax is not subject to a wage base limit.[2]

Employers who are required to withhold income tax and FICA tax must file a federal return each quarter on Form 941. This form must be filed by the last day of the month that follows the end of the previous quarter.

FUTA

The Federal Unemployment Tax Act (FUTA) exists in concert with state unemployment systems to pay unemployment compensation to employees who have become unemployed. This tax is paid by the employer only and is taxed at a rate of 6.0 percent (historically) on the first $7,000 that an employer pays in each employee's wages (note: the state wage base may be different). FUTA tax is reported annually on federal Form 940. A credit is allowed for unemployment taxes paid to states.

Self-Employment Tax

A self-employed individual pays income tax, as well as self-employment FICA taxes of 15.3 percent (12.4% for Social Security and 2.9% for Medicare), on his earnings up to the wage base of $142,800 (2021) and 2.9 percent beyond the wage base for Medicare. However, the self-employed worker is not required to pay FUTA tax on himself. In addition, a self-employed person can take a FICA deduction for adjusted gross income on his own tax return, in the amount of one-half of his total FICA taxes paid.

Tax Credits

A **tax credit** is an amount that is subtracted from calculated tax. Tax credits can reduce the tax on taxable income to zero, and some tax credits can also generate a tax refund in excess of tax pre-payment. Tax credits come in two forms; nonrefundable or refundable. Nonrefundable credits may only apply to the current year or, in some cases, they may be carried back to an earlier year, carried forward to future years, or both. Refundable tax credits can be used to reduce or eliminate the current year's tax, but can also generate a refund.

---

2. Beginning in 2013, the Additional Medicare Tax (IRC §1401(b)(2) and §3101(b)(2)), which is part of the Affordable Care Act, of 0.9 percent (above the 1.45% or 2.9%) applies to individuals' wages, other compensation, and self-employment income over certain thresholds. The additional Medicare tax of 0.9 percent applies to earned income over $200,000 for individuals and to earned income over $250,000 for couples filing jointly.

Nonrefundable Tax Credits

Nonrefundable tax credits can reduce the tax on taxable income to zero, but they cannot generate a tax refund, an excess withholding, estimated payments, amounts applied from prior years tax refunds to this year's tax liability, and excess Social Security tax contributions. Nonrefundable tax credits include:

- Foreign Tax Credit
- Credit for Child and Dependent Care (refundable in 2021 only (American Rescue Plan Act (ARPA) of 2021))
- Credit for the Elderly or Disabled
- Education Credits: Lifetime Learning and part or all of the American Opportunity Tax Credit
- Retirement Savings Contributions Credit
- Child Tax Credit (up to $1,400 refundable in all years except 2021; fully refundable in 2021 (American Rescue Plan Act (ARPA) of 2021))
- Other Dependent Credit
- Residential Energy Efficient Property Credit
- Nonbusiness Alternative Motor Vehicle Credit
- Nonbusiness Alternative Fuel Vehicle Refueling Property Credit
- General Business Credit

Example 12.2

Monica's tax on taxable income is $600. She is eligible for a nonrefundable tax credit of $700. Monica is allowed to use the credit to reduce her tax to $0 for the year, but she is not allowed to use the remaining $100 of the credit to generate a refund.

Carryback or Carryforward of a Credit

If a nonrefundable credit exceeds the tax on taxable income for a tax year, the excess credit is normally lost. With certain credits, however, the excess can be carried back and/or carried forward to be offset against the tax on taxable income for the years to which the excess credit is carried.

Refundable Tax Credits

Refundable tax credits can be used not only to reduce or eliminate the current year's tax, but also to generate a tax refund in excess of tax pre-payment.

Tax on Taxable Income – Refundable Credits = Tax Due (or Refund Due)

For federal income tax purposes, nonrefundable credits are used before refundable credits. A more complete presentation of the use of tax credits is presented by the following formula:

Tax on Taxable Income – Nonrefundable Credits – Refundable Credits = Tax Due (or Refund Due)

Example 12.3

The tax calculated on the taxable income of Johnny and Jennifer Johnson is $3,000. They are eligible to claim a $1,000 nonrefundable credit and a refundable credit of $2,800. They can claim a tax refund of $800 ($3,000 - $1,000 - $2,800) even if they had no withholding or other tax prepayments for the year.

Exhibit 12.14 | Refundable Tax Credits

Item	IRC Section	IRS Publication	Reported on Form
American Opportunity Tax Credit (formerly the Hope Scholarship Credit)	25A	970	8863/1040
Earned Income Credit	32	17/596	Sched. EIC
Credit for Tax on Undistributed Capital Gain From: A Mutual Fund A Real Estate Investment Trust (REIT)	852(b)(3)(D)(ii) 857(b)(3)(D)(ii)	17/564/550 17/550	2439 2439
Health Coverage Tax Credit	35	17/502	8885
Credit for Excise Taxes on Gasoline and Special Fuels	34	510	4136

Tax Credits vs. Tax Deductions

The benefit received by a taxpayer from a tax credit is not dependent on the taxpayer's **marginal tax rate** (tax bracket). A tax credit of $1,000 provides the same $1,000 tax reduction for a taxpayer in the 12 percent tax bracket or the 37 percent tax bracket. On the other hand, the tax reduction received by a taxpayer for a tax deduction is entirely dependent on the marginal tax rate of the taxpayer. A tax deduction of $1,000 generates a tax reduction of $120 ($1,000 x 0.12) for a taxpayer in the 12 percent bracket and a tax reduction of $370 ($1,000 x 0.37) for a taxpayer in the 37 percent tax bracket.

Tax Credit Requirements

In order to claim a tax credit, a taxpayer must normally do the following:

- Meet eligibility requirements.
- Determine the amount of the credit by multiplying a base by an applicable rate(s).
- Apply any specified limitations to the credit.
- Subtract the allowable credits from the tax in the proper sequence
- Carryback or carryforward any amounts disallowed for the current tax year, if permitted.

Quick Quiz 12.4

1. Only children under age 19 may be claimed as dependents on a taxpayer's return.
   a. True
   b. False

2. Nonrefundable tax credits can reduce the tax on taxable income to zero and can generate a tax refund.
   a. True
   b. False

3. For federal income tax purposes, nonrefundable credits are used before refundable credits.
   a. True
   b. False

False, False, True

INTRODUCTION TO BASIS

Basis represents capital (or after-tax income) that a taxpayer uses to purchase an investment. Taxpayers keep track of the capital that was used to purchase the investment, or basis, so that the capital can be recovered without the imposition of a second income tax.

Uses of Basis

Basis is the income tax system's method of keeping track of capital in an investment, and is used in several different ways. First, basis is used to determine gain or loss on an investment when it is sold. An investor would subtract his or her basis from the sales proceeds of the investment to determine the taxable gain or loss. Second, basis is used to determine depreciation deductions that an investor can take on an investment. Third, basis is used to determine the amount an investor has "at risk" which limits loss deductions for income tax purposes under the at risk and passive activity loss rules.

> ### ☰ *Key Concepts*
>
> 1. Define the purpose of basis.
> 2. Identify the uses of basis.
> 3. Define the cost basis of an asset.
> 4. Identify items that increase basis.
> 5. Identify items that decrease basis.

Determining Basis

Cost Basis

Cost basis is the initial basis an investor acquires in an asset by using capital to purchase an investment. As explained above, it represents the amount of after-tax dollars that the investor has dedicated to purchasing an investment. For most investments, the initial basis in an investment is the cost basis.

The amount paid for an asset includes not only its purchase price, but also any amounts paid for sales tax, freight, installation and testing of the asset, and any other costs necessary to acquire the asset and get it into operations. All of the items below are included in the cost basis of the asset.

Items Included in Basis
Purchase Price
Sales Tax
Freight
Installation and Testing Costs
"All costs to get the asset into operations"

Example 12.4

If Clive acquired construction equipment, his basis in the property is determined by his method of acquisition.

Acquisition Method	Affect on Basis
Purchase	Clive's basis is the price he paid for the equipment, plus other costs associated with making the equipment operational.
Gift	Clive's basis is the donor's basis plus a portion of any gift tax the donor has paid.
Inheritance	Clive's basis is the equipment's fair market value at the decedent's date of death (or alternative valuation date for federal estate tax purposes).

Adjustments to Basis

Once an asset is acquired and it's initial cost basis is established, that basis may be adjusted over the holding period of the asset, resulting in an adjusted basis for income tax purposes.

Increases in Basis

The first and most frequently encountered adjustment to basis is an upward adjustment to cost basis for additions to the investment. If additional capital is added to the investment, the cost basis must be increased to reflect this so that upon sale, the investor receives all of his or her capital back income tax-free. Examples of capital infusions that increase a taxpayer's basis in an investment include subsequent investments in the same vehicle, additions to the investment, or changes to the investment.

Decreases in Basis

If an individual's basis in an investment increases when capital is added to the investment, the opposite will happen when capital is removed from an investment. When capital is removed from an investment, a basis reduction must occur because the taxpayer has received a refund of some of his or her capital. Capital can be taken out of an investment in several ways. Two of the most common methods of removing capital from an investment are: (1) distributions from business entities that have pass-through tax treatment (such as partnerships, LLCs, and S corporations), and (2) claiming depreciation deductions.

Realization and Recognition

Unlike ordinary income, which is subject to income tax when earned, gains on capital assets are subject to tax only when there has been both a **realization event** (implying that the asset has been sold or exchanged) and a **recognition event** for federal income tax purposes. Recognition occurs when a realized gain is required to be included on a taxpayer's income tax return. Generally, all realized gains are recognized (that is, all realized gains are subject to current taxation) unless a provision can be found in the Code that either exempts the gain from taxation, or defers the gain to a future tax period.

CAPITAL GAIN HOLDING PERIODS AND TAX RATES

Holding Periods

The **holding period** for an asset can be either short-term or long-term.

If a taxpayer holds an asset for a year or less, the taxpayer has a short-term holding period for that asset. If the holding period is more than one year, it is said to be a long-term holding period.

Exhibit 12.15 | Holding Period Summary

Capital Gain/Loss	Holding Period
Long-Term Capital Gain/Loss	> 1 Year
Short-Term Capital Gain/Loss	≤ 1 Year

Property Acquired by Inheritance

There are a few special rules concerning holding periods that are worth noting. First, whenever property is received from a decedent's estate, it is deemed to have a long-term holding period, regardless of when the asset was acquired by the decedent. An easy way to remember this rule is to recall that "death is long-term."

Gifted Property

The second special rule concerning holding periods applies to gifted property. When gifted property has a fair market value in excess of the donor's basis in the property on the date of the gift, the donee's holding period will tack on to the donor's holding period. In other words, the donee's holding period begins on the date the donor acquired the property.

Capital Gains Tax Rates

The capital gains tax rate that applies to a particular transaction is a function of the holding period of the asset.

Short-term gains and losses are subject to tax at the taxpayer's ordinary marginal income tax rate. There is no tax benefit afforded to assets held for a short-term holding period.

If the asset sold was held for a long-term holding period, the gain or loss will be subject to long-term capital gains tax rates, which are lower than the taxpayer's ordinary marginal income tax rate. Generally speaking, if the transaction results in a gain, this is a good result since the taxpayer will pay less tax on the gain. If the transaction results in a loss, however, the taxpayer will receive less of a tax benefit. As discussed in our review of asset categorization, capital gains are good, but capital losses are bad for the taxpayer.

The maximum long-term capital gains tax rate is 20 percent; however, most taxpayers will have a long-term capital gains rate of 15 percent. To ensure that all taxpayers would receive a tax break for long-term capital gains, Congress eliminated the long-term capital gains tax rate for lower income taxpayers.

The breakpoints between the long-term gains tax rates in 2021 are based on taxable income as follows:

Tax Rate	Married Filing Jointly Taxable Income	Single Taxable Income
0%	$0 - $80,800	$0 - $40,400
15%	$80,801 - $501,600	$40,401 - $445,850
20%	Over $501,600	Over $445,850

SALE OF PERSONAL RESIDENCE (SECTION 121)

Perhaps the most widely used exclusion occurs when an individual sells his or her principal residence. IRC Section 121 excludes up to $500,000 of the gain from the sale of a principal residence from income tax if certain requirements are met.

The amount of the available exclusion will depend on the filing status of the individual who claims the exemption. For married couples filing jointly, up to $500,000 of the gain is excluded from income tax. All other individuals may exclude up to $250,000 of the gain from income tax. Any gain on the sale of a principal residence in excess of this amount is subject to income tax, typically long-term capital gains.

Qualifications

To qualify for the exclusion of gain under IRC Section 121, two requirements must be met. First, the taxpayer must have owned and used the home as his principal residence for two out of the last five years (the ownership and use test). Ownership implies that the taxpayer holds title to the home outright, or the home is owned by a grantor trust (see Ltr. Rul. 199912026). If the home is owned by a partnership, family limited partnership, or irrevocable trust, the taxpayer is not deemed to own the home for purposes of claiming the Section 121 exclusion (see Ltr. Rul. 200029046 and Ltr. Rul. 200104005). Second, to claim the exemption, the taxpayer must not have excluded gain on the sale of a principal residence within the last two years. An individual will qualify for this exclusion as often as the individual can meet these two requirements.

Married couples who wish to claim up to the $500,000 exclusion must meet conditions in addition to the two requirements set forth above. For the $500,000 exclusion to apply for a married couple, they must file a joint tax return for the year (filing status must be married filing jointly), and both spouses must have used the residence for two out of the previous five years as a principal residence (referred to as the use test). Only one of the spouses must have owned the residence for two out of the previous five years (the ownership test). Furthermore, if either spouse claimed the Section 121 exclusion within the previous two years, the gain cannot be excluded from income taxation.

If, however, a couple is getting divorced and are filing separate returns, and a principal residence is sold, both spouses can exclude up to $250,000 of gain from the sale if the ownership and use tests are otherwise met.

Proration of the Exclusion

If a principal residence is sold before the two-year ownership and use test is met, or if the exclusion was used during the last two years, it may be possible to qualify for a reduced exclusion. A reduced exclusion will be available when the sale of the principal residence is caused by: (1) a change of employment, (2) a change of health, or (3) an unforeseen circumstance. When one of these exceptions apply, the amount of the exclusion is determined by dividing the number of months the taxpayer used the home as a principal residence, or the number of months since the exclusion was used last, by 24 (the number of months in a two year period), and multiplying that result by the otherwise applicable exclusion. The formula for calculating the partial exclusion may be expressed as:

$$\frac{\text{\# of months of use (or last exclusion)}}{24} \times \text{Applicable Exclusion (\$250,000 or \$500,000)}$$

DISCUSSION QUESTIONS

SOLUTIONS to the discussion questions can be found exclusively within the chapter. Once you have completed an initial reading of the chapter, go back and highlight the answers to these questions.

1.   What are the three primary sources of tax law?

2.   What is the legal basis for today's income tax?

3.   What are the statutory sources of tax law?

4.   What are the administrative sources of tax law?

5.   How is income defined?

6.   What are exclusions and where do they come from?

7.   Define gross income.

8.   List some examples of items that would be included in gross income.

9.   What are the two types of deductions?

10. What is adjusted gross income and what is its significance?

11. Under what circumstances may a taxpayer be entitled to an additional standard deduction?

12. What are the different filing statuses available to taxpayers?

13. Compare and contrast nonrefundable and refundable tax credits.

14. Why is a tax credit generally more beneficial than a tax deduction of the same amount?

15. What is basis and what is the purpose of basis?

16. Describe three uses of basis.

17. What is cost basis?

18. Name several items that increase basis.

19. Name several items that decrease basis.

20. What is the amount realized?

21. What is the difference between a short-term and long-term holding period?

22. How is the holding period determined for property received from a decedent's estate?

23. What is the difference between the tax rate for short-term capital gains and long-term capital gains?

MULTIPLE-CHOICE PROBLEMS

A sample of multiple choice problems is provided below. Additional multiple choice problems are available at money-education.com by accessing the Student Practice Portal.

1. Zoey filed her tax return on April 15. At that time, she owed $800 on a total tax liability of $10,000 and she submitted a check for $800 with her tax return. Which of the following penalties will apply to Zoey?
    a. Failure to file.
    b. Failure to pay.
    c. Both failure to file and failure to pay.
    d. None of the above.

2. Dwight, a consultant, uses the cash method of accounting for his business. Dwight recently provided consulting services to his best customer, Roman. When should Dwight recognize income from this service?
    a. When Roman writes a check, made out to Dwight.
    b. When Dwight deposits Roman's check.
    c. When Roman gives the check to Dwight.
    d. When Roman receives an invoice from Dwight for the service.

3. Which of the following is not an itemized deduction from adjusted gross income?
    a. Alimony paid (divorced prior to 2019).
    b. Medical expenses in excess of 10% of AGI.
    c. Charitable contributions.
    d. Home mortgage interest.

4. On September 20 of Year 1, Sean purchased 1,000 shares of Austin Enterprises, Inc. common stock for $25,000. He sold the shares for $35,000 on September 20 of Year 2. Which of the following statements correctly identifies the tax consequences of this transaction?
    a. Sean will recognize a $10,000 ordinary gain on the sale.
    b. Sean will recognize a $10,000 short-term capital gain on the sale.
    c. Sean will recognize a $10,000 long-term capital gain on the sale.
    d. Sean will not be required to recognize the gain on the transaction.

5. Jason has three capital transactions for the current year:
    - Short-term capital loss of $5,000
    - Short-term capital gain of $3,000
    - Long-term capital loss of $2,000

    What is the net effect on Jason's taxes if he is in the 32% tax bracket?
    a. $1,280 tax reduction.
    b. $960 tax reduction.
    c. $800 tax reduction.
    d. $450 tax reduction.

> **Additional multiple choice problems are available at**
> *money-education.com* **by accessing the Student Practice Portal. Access requires registration of the title using the unique code at the front of the book.**

QUICK QUIZ EXPLANATIONS

Quick Quiz 12.1
1. False. The three top sources of tax law includes statutory, administrative (Treasury Department and Internal Revenue Service), and judicial.
2. True.
3. True.

Quick Quiz 12.2
1. False. The basic tax formula is Income - Deductions = Taxable Income.
2. False. Income, broadly defined, means the gross amount received, but it does not include borrowed money or a return of invested dollars.
3. True.
4. True.

Quick Quiz 12.3
1. False. Adjusted gross income is gross income reduced by above-the-line deductions.
2. True.
3. False. Nonresident aliens and dual-status aliens are not allowed to use a standard deduction and must itemize deductions.

Quick Quiz 12.4
1. False. The child of a taxpayer typically qualifies as a dependent if the child is under age 19, or under age 24 if a full-time student. In addition, a relative of the taxpayer may qualify as a dependent if a support test and income test are met.
2. False. Nonrefundable tax credits cannot generate a tax refund.
3. True.

Quick Quiz 12.5
1. False. The purpose of basis is to keep track of after-tax dollars an individual invests so that upon the sale of the investment, income is not taxed twice.
2. True.

13

BUSINESS ENTITY SELECTION AND TAXATION

INTRODUCTION

One of the most important decisions new business owners make is the selection of the entity type to be used for conducting the business activities of the enterprise.

The most common legal forms of business (entity types) used in the United States are the sole proprietorship, general and limited partnerships, including limited liability partnerships (LLPs) and family limited partnerships (FLPs), the limited liability company (LLC), the regular C corporation, and the S corporation.

The selection process includes consideration of the following factors:

1. Ease and cost of formation
2. Complexity of management and governance
3. How transferability and dissolution are achieved
4. Liability protection for owners' personal assets
5. Reporting requirements and taxation

Ease and Cost of Formation

Proprietorships and general partnerships are less complex, inexpensive, and easy to form, while the other entity types are more complex and expensive to form. Entities are almost always formed under state law. Therefore, the state dictates the requirements for legal formation and the formalities that must be followed to maintain the entity's status.

Complexity of Management and Governance

Proprietorships are the least complex in terms of management and governance. In addition, the administrative requirements and formalities dictated by state law are the least burdensome for sole proprietorships. Proprietorships and general partnerships do not typically require an initial filing registration with the state and have fewer state-imposed annual filing requirements. Furthermore, proprietorships and general partnerships have fewer state-imposed operational requirements that must be met to assure continuation of the entity's status and the benefits that the status brings.

Transferability and Dissolution

Transferability of an ownership interest is easiest with a proprietorship and becomes increasingly more difficult as we move along a spectrum of business entities to the C corporation. Partnerships, limited partnerships, LLPs, FLPs, LLCs, S corporations, and smaller C corporations generally have limited or restricted transferability rights. Unlike other business forms, proprietorships can be dissolved at the election of the owner and do not require any formal steps for dissolution.

Liability Protection for Owners' Personal Assets

Some business forms offer liability protection for investors. If liability protection is available, the investors in such business ventures or entities will not have their personal assets exposed to business (entity) debts or obligations. This protection, which may be the most important factor in entity choice, is not available to proprietorships or general partnerships, nor to general partners of a limited partnership and only to a limited extent for limited liability partnerships (LLP). We refer to this protection as limited liability.

There are situations in which an entity that has limited liability protection for its owners under state law can lose that protection. The state requires that for such protection to continue, the entity must alert the public to its status in a clear and identifiable manner so as to put business creditors on notice that the entity has such protection. Entities do this through markings on business correspondence such as invoices, letterhead, business cards, and through markings on vehicles (with the name and LLC or Inc. designated), which signals the limited liability status to the public. The entities receiving such protection usually are required to maintain a reasonable amount of liability insurance to protect the public (e.g., vehicle and general liability insurance) and are required to be vigilant in meeting any annual formalities to maintain the state-granted entity status.

General Liability Issues

Relying on the entity as the primary source of liability protection is dependent on it maintaining a clear and consistent identity of the entity as a corporation, limited partnership, or limited liability company. Failure to maintain that identity in contracts and correspondence could result in a court "**piercing the veil**" of liability protection, which may result in personal liability for the owner(s). Piercing the veil means disregarding the status of the entity that gives the owners limited liability protection. A secondary source of protection is liability insurance, which must be sufficient in amount and sufficiently comprehensive in risk coverage, to cover the reasonable anticipated claims of creditors.

To avoid piercing the veil, the entity should keep its books and records separate from the personal books and records of the owners, segregate activities of business from personal affairs, follow corporate formalities such as meeting requirements and filings, and address all content in contracts and correspondence from the view point of the business entity (rather than the individual owners').

Reporting Requirements and Taxation

States individually require annual filings and other types of compliance reporting. All entities that have employees have payroll reporting at both the state and federal level. All entities that have retail sales have sales tax returns to prepare in states that impose sales taxes.

There are few, if any, other state reporting requirements for proprietorships and general partnerships. However, for all other types of entities there will be annual reporting requirements that are state-imposed to maintain the entity's protected status.

For federal income tax purposes, the income of a proprietorship or a single-member LLC is reported on the Schedule C of the individual owner's Form 1040. For all other types of entities, an entity-level tax return is filed. A partnership files Form 1065, an S corporation files Form 1120S, and a C corporation files Form 1120. All of the returns other than the C corporation return are informational returns because there is no tax at the entity level. The income and losses of such entities "flow through" to the individual owners. Each owner's share of the entity's income or loss is reported to the owner on a Schedule K-1.

The C corporation is a separate entity for taxation and its income is taxed at the entity level. However, it does have the advantage of being able to accumulate profits at the corporate level without the owners having to pay income taxes on those profits until they are distributed to the owners by the corporation.

Choosing the appropriate entity type requires an understanding of each type of the entity, its advantages and disadvantages, competing considerations including each of the factors identified and discussed above, and business loss considerations.

In general, the most important factors in entity selection are ease of formation, liability protection, and the manner of taxation. However, serious thought should be given to all of the factors to make the right choice for the nature of the business and the objectives of the owners.

It is also important to periodically review the choice of legal form (entity) to determine whether changes in circumstances may suggest a change in entity type.

> ### ✍ Quick Quiz 13.1
>
> 1. Not all entities are separate legal entities for the purposes of taxation.
>   a. True
>   b. False
>
> 2. "Piercing the veil" may occur if business owners fail to keep their personal records with their business records.
>   a. True
>   b. False
>
> True, False.

SOLE PROPRIETORSHIPS

Sole proprietorships are business ventures owned and operated by a single individual. A sole proprietorship arises when an individual engages in a business for profit. A sole proprietorship can operate under the name of the owner or it can conduct business under a trade or fictitious name such as "The Corner Pocket." No filings are required with the Secretary of State and no annual filing fees are required. There is no transfer of assets to the entity because the entity is considered a legal extension of the proprietor.

Formation

Formation is easy and inexpensive, although the proprietorship may be required to obtain a local business license. In addition, if the proprietorship will be collecting sales taxes, it must register with the state or local taxing authority. Operation is easy in that all decisions are made by the proprietor. Any trade names or assets are owned by the individual proprietor.

Interest, Disposal of Interest, and Dissolution

A proprietor has a 100 percent interest in the proprietorship assets and income. It is relatively easy to sell assets of a proprietorship, but it does require finding a buyer. Dissolution is achieved by simply discontinuing business operations and paying creditors or by the death of the proprietor.

Capital

Capital for a proprietorship is limited to the resources of the proprietor including the proprietor's ability to borrow.

Liability

One of the major disadvantages of a sole proprietorship is the potential legal liability. The sole proprietor is personally legally liable for the debts and torts of his sole proprietorship business. There is no separate legal entity under which limited liability protection for personal assets may be claimed.

Management/Operations

The proprietor has the day-to-day management and decision-making responsibilities, including the hiring and firing of employees. There is no guarantee of continuity beyond the proprietor.

> ### ☰ *Key Concepts*
>
> 1. Describe the formation and operation of a sole proprietorship.
> 2. Describe the liability issues associated with a sole proprietorship.
> 3. Explain how a sole proprietorship can raise capital.
> 4. Explain the tax attributes of a sole proprietorship.

Income Taxation and Payroll (Social Security) Taxes

The cost of tax compliance is low because the proprietor simply adds a Schedule C to his Form 1040 (**Exhibit 13.1**) and generally does not even obtain a separate federal taxpayer tax identification number (unless the proprietor hires employees, in which case an Employer Identification Number (EIN) must be obtained). Rather, the proprietor conducts business under his own Social Security number. There is no ability to allocate income to other taxpayers since there is only one owner. A sole proprietor does not have to pay unemployment taxes on himself, but he must pay unemployment taxes for his employees. However, the proprietor does pay self-employment tax (up to 15.3 percent) on his own earnings (**Exhibit 13.2**) and one-half of Social Security taxes for his employees.

Taking Deductions

The proprietor can deduct all ordinary and necessary business expenses from gross income. The business deductions are in Part II of Schedule C, lines 8-27 (**Exhibit 13.1**). The net profit or loss from line 31 of Schedule C is then carried over to line 3 of Schedule 1 of Form 1040 (identified by the arrow in **Exhibit 13.1** and the first arrow in **Exhibit 13.3**). The proprietor may also make deductible contributions to a qualified or other retirement plan, but these contributions are reported on his Form 1040 as a deduction for AGI on line 15 of Schedule 1 of Form 1040 (identified by the second arrow in **Exhibit 13.3**).

Employer Deduction for Retirement Plans

The proprietor can usually deduct, subject to certain limitations, contributions made to a qualified plan for employees, including those made for the proprietor. The contributions (and the attributable earnings and gains) are generally not taxed to the employee until distributed by the plan. The deduction limit for contributions to a qualified plan depends on the type of plan.

The deduction for contributions to a defined contribution plan cannot exceed 25 percent of the compensation paid or accrued during the year to eligible employees participating in the plan. The proprietor must reduce this limit in figuring the deduction for contributions made to his own account. The maximum compensation that can be taken into account when calculating plan funding for each employee is the covered compensation limit, $290,000 for 2021.

The deduction for contributions to a defined benefit plan is based on actuarial assumptions and computations. Consequently, an actuary must calculate the appropriate amount of mandatory funding.

In the case of an employer who maintains both a defined benefit plan and a defined contribution plan, the funding limit set forth is combined. The maximum deductible amount is the greater of:
- 25 percent of the aggregate covered compensation of employees
- The required minimum funding standard of the defined benefit plan

This limit does not apply if the contributions to the defined contribution plan consist entirely of employee elective deferrals (elective contributions to the plan by employees). In other words, employee elective deferrals do not count against the plan limit.

Exhibit 13.1 | Form 1040 Schedule C

SCHEDULE C
(Form 1040)

Department of the Treasury
Internal Revenue Service (99)

Profit or Loss From Business
(Sole Proprietorship)

▶ Go to *www.irs.gov/ScheduleC* for instructions and the latest information.
▶ **Attach to Form 1040, 1040-SR, 1040-NR, or 1041; partnerships generally must file Form 1065.**

OMB No. 1545-0074

2020

Attachment
Sequence No. **09**

Name of proprietor

Social security number (SSN)

A Principal business or profession, including product or service (see instructions)	**B** Enter code from instructions ▶
C Business name. If no separate business name, leave blank.	**D** Employer ID number (EIN) (see instr.)

E Business address (including suite or room no.) ▶
City, town or post office, state, and ZIP code

F Accounting method: **(1)** ☐ Cash **(2)** ☐ Accrual **(3)** ☐ Other (specify) ▶

G Did you "materially participate" in the operation of this business during 2020? If "No," see instructions for limit on losses ☐ Yes ☐ No

H If you started or acquired this business during 2020, check here ▶ ☐

I Did you make any payments in 2020 that would require you to file Form(s) 1099? See instructions ☐ Yes ☐ No

J If "Yes," did you or will you file required Form(s) 1099? ☐ Yes ☐ No

Part I Income

1	Gross receipts or sales. See instructions for line 1 and check the box if this income was reported to you on Form W-2 and the "Statutory employee" box on that form was checked ▶ ☐	**1**
2	Returns and allowances	**2**
3	Subtract line 2 from line 1	**3**
4	Cost of goods sold (from line 42)	**4**
5	**Gross profit.** Subtract line 4 from line 3	**5**
6	Other income, including federal and state gasoline or fuel tax credit or refund (see instructions)	**6**
7	**Gross income.** Add lines 5 and 6 ▶	**7**

Part II Expenses. Enter expenses for business use of your home **only** on line 30.

8	Advertising	**8**	**18**	Office expense (see instructions)	**18**
9	Car and truck expenses (see instructions)	**9**	**19**	Pension and profit-sharing plans	**19**
10	Commissions and fees	**10**	**20**	Rent or lease (see instructions):	
11	Contract labor (see instructions)	**11**	**a**	Vehicles, machinery, and equipment	**20a**
12	Depletion	**12**	**b**	Other business property	**20b**
13	Depreciation and section 179 expense deduction (not included in Part III) (see instructions)	**13**	**21**	Repairs and maintenance	**21**
			22	Supplies (not included in Part III)	**22**
			23	Taxes and licenses	**23**
			24	Travel and meals:	
14	Employee benefit programs (other than on line 19)	**14**	**a**	Travel	**24a**
15	Insurance (other than health)	**15**	**b**	Deductible meals (see instructions)	**24b**
16	Interest (see instructions):		**25**	Utilities	**25**
a	Mortgage (paid to banks, etc.)	**16a**	**26**	Wages (less employment credits)	**26**
b	Other	**16b**	**27a**	Other expenses (from line 48)	**27a**
17	Legal and professional services	**17**	**b**	Reserved for future use	**27b**

28	**Total expenses** before expenses for business use of home. Add lines 8 through 27a ▶	**28**
29	Tentative profit or (loss). Subtract line 28 from line 7	**29**
30	Expenses for business use of your home. Do not report these expenses elsewhere. Attach Form 8829 unless using the simplified method. See instructions. **Simplified method filers only:** Enter the total square footage of (a) your home: _____ and (b) the part of your home used for business: _____. Use the Simplified Method Worksheet in the instructions to figure the amount to enter on line 30	**30**
31	**Net profit or (loss).** Subtract line 30 from line 29.	

- If a profit, enter on both **Schedule 1 (Form 1040), line 3,** and on **Schedule SE, line 2.** (If you checked the box on line 1, see instructions). Estates and trusts, enter on **Form 1041, line 3.**
- If a loss, you **must** go to line 32.

31

32 If you have a loss, check the box that describes your investment in this activity. See instructions.

- If you checked 32a, enter the loss on both **Schedule 1 (Form 1040), line 3,** and on **Schedule SE, line 2.** (If you checked the box on line 1, see the line 31 instructions). Estates and trusts, enter on **Form 1041, line 3.**
- If you checked 32b, you **must** attach **Form 6198.** Your loss may be limited.

32a ☐ All investment is at risk.
32b ☐ Some investment is not at risk.

For Paperwork Reduction Act Notice, see the separate instructions.　　Cat. No. 11334P　　Schedule C (Form 1040) 2020

Exhibit 13.2 | Form 1040 Schedule SE

SCHEDULE SE
(Form 1040)

Department of the Treasury
Internal Revenue Service (99)

Self-Employment Tax

▶ Go to *www.irs.gov/ScheduleSE* for instructions and the latest information.
▶ **Attach to Form 1040, 1040-SR, or 1040-NR.**

OMB No. 1545-0074

20**20**

Attachment
Sequence No. **17**

Name of person with self-employment income (as shown on Form 1040, 1040-SR, or 1040-NR)

Social security number of person
with **self-employment** income ▶

Part I	**Self-Employment Tax**

Note: If your only income subject to self-employment tax is **church employee income,** see instructions for how to report your income and the definition of church employee income.

A   If you are a minister, member of a religious order, or Christian Science practitioner **and** you filed Form 4361, but you had $400 or more of **other** net earnings from self-employment, check here and continue with Part I . . . . ▶ ☐

Skip lines 1a and 1b if you use the farm optional method in Part II. See instructions.

1a	Net farm profit or (loss) from Schedule F, line 34, and farm partnerships, Schedule K-1 (Form 1065), box 14, code A . .	**1a**	
b	If you received social security retirement or disability benefits, enter the amount of Conservation Reserve Program payments included on Schedule F, line 4b, or listed on Schedule K-1 (Form 1065), box 20, code AH	**1b**	( )

Skip line 2 if you use the nonfarm optional method in Part II. See instructions.

2	Net profit or (loss) from Schedule C, line 31; and Schedule K-1 (Form 1065), box 14, code A (other than farming). See instructions for other income to report or if you are a minister or member of a religious order	**2**	
3	Combine lines 1a, 1b, and 2	**3**	
4a	If line 3 is more than zero, multiply line 3 by 92.35% (0.9235). Otherwise, enter amount from line 3 .	**4a**	
	Note: If line 4a is less than $400 due to Conservation Reserve Program payments on line 1b, see instructions.		
b	If you elect one or both of the optional methods, enter the total of lines 15 and 17 here .	**4b**	
c	Combine lines 4a and 4b. If less than $400, **stop;** you don't owe self-employment tax. **Exception:** If less than $400 and you had **church employee income,** enter -0- and continue . . . . ▶	**4c**	
5a	Enter your **church employee income** from Form W-2. See instructions for definition of church employee income	**5a**	
b	Multiply line 5a by 92.35% (0.9235). If less than $100, enter -0-	**5b**	
6	Add lines 4c and 5b	**6**	
7	Maximum amount of combined wages and self-employment earnings subject to social security tax or the 6.2% portion of the 7.65% railroad retirement (tier 1) tax for 2020	**7**	137,700
8a	Total social security wages and tips (total of boxes 3 and 7 on Form(s) W-2) and railroad retirement (tier 1) compensation. If $137,700 or more, skip lines 8b through 10, and go to line 11	**8a**	
b	Unreported tips subject to social security tax from Form 4137, line 10 . . .	**8b**	
c	Wages subject to social security tax from Form 8919, line 10	**8c**	
d	Add lines 8a, 8b, and 8c	**8d**	
9	Subtract line 8d from line 7. If zero or less, enter -0- here and on line 10 and go to line 11 . . . ▶	**9**	
10	Multiply the **smaller** of line 6 or line 9 by 12.4% (0.124)	**10**	
11	Multiply line 6 by 2.9% (0.029)	**11**	
12	**Self-employment tax.** Add lines 10 and 11. Enter here and on **Schedule 2 (Form 1040), line 4** . .	**12**	
13	**Deduction for one-half of self-employment tax.** Multiply line 12 by 50% (0.50). Enter here and on **Schedule 1 (Form 1040), line 14**	**13**	

Part II	**Optional Methods To Figure Net Earnings** (see instructions)

Farm Optional Method. You may use this method **only** if **(a)** your gross farm income[1] wasn't more than $8,460, **or (b)** your net farm profits[2] were less than $6,107.

14	Maximum income for optional methods	**14**	5,640
15	Enter the **smaller** of: two-thirds ($2/3$) of gross farm income[1] (not less than zero) **or** $5,640. Also, include this amount on line 4b above	**15**	

Nonfarm Optional Method. You may use this method **only** if **(a)** your net nonfarm profits[3] were less than $6,107 and also less than 72.189% of your gross nonfarm income,[4] **and (b)** you had net earnings from self-employment of at least $400 in 2 of the prior 3 years. **Caution:** You may use this method no more than five times.

16	Subtract line 15 from line 14	**16**	
17	Enter the **smaller** of: two-thirds ($2/3$) of gross nonfarm income[4] (not less than zero) **or** the amount on line 16. Also, include this amount on line 4b above	**17**	

[1] From Sch. F, line 9; and Sch. K-1 (Form 1065), box 14, code B.
[2] From Sch. F, line 34; and Sch. K-1 (Form 1065), box 14, code A—minus the amount you would have entered on line 1b had you not used the optional method.
[3] From Sch. C, line 31; and Sch. K-1 (Form 1065), box 14, code A.
[4] From Sch. C, line 7; and Sch. K-1 (Form 1065), box 14, code C.

For Paperwork Reduction Act Notice, see your tax return instructions.   Cat. No. 11358Z   **Schedule SE (Form 1040) 2020**

Exhibit 13.3 | Form 1040 Schedule 1

SCHEDULE 1 (Form 1040) Department of the Treasury Internal Revenue Service	**Additional Income and Adjustments to Income** ▶ Attach to Form 1040, 1040-SR, or 1040-NR. ▶ Go to *www.irs.gov/Form1040* for instructions and the latest information.	OMB No. 1545-0074 20**20** Attachment Sequence No. **01**

Name(s) shown on Form 1040, 1040-SR, or 1040-NR	Your social security number

Part I Additional Income

1	Taxable refunds, credits, or offsets of state and local income taxes	**1**	
2a	Alimony received	**2a**	
b	Date of original divorce or separation agreement (see instructions) ▶ _____		
3	Business income or (loss). Attach Schedule C	**3**	◀
4	Other gains or (losses). Attach Form 4797	**4**	
5	Rental real estate, royalties, partnerships, S corporations, trusts, etc. Attach Schedule E	**5**	
6	Farm income or (loss). Attach Schedule F	**6**	
7	Unemployment compensation	**7**	
8	Other income. List type and amount ▶ _____	**8**	
9	Combine lines 1 through 8. Enter here and on Form 1040, 1040-SR, or 1040-NR, line 8	**9**	

Part II Adjustments to Income

10	Educator expenses	**10**	
11	Certain business expenses of reservists, performing artists, and fee-basis government officials. Attach Form 2106	**11**	
12	Health savings account deduction. Attach Form 8889	**12**	
13	Moving expenses for members of the Armed Forces. Attach Form 3903	**13**	
14	Deductible part of self-employment tax. Attach Schedule SE	**14**	
15	Self-employed SEP, SIMPLE, and qualified plans	**15**	◀
16	Self-employed health insurance deduction	**16**	
17	Penalty on early withdrawal of savings	**17**	
18a	Alimony paid	**18a**	
b	Recipient's SSN . . . . ▶		
c	Date of original divorce or separation agreement (see instructions) ▶ _____		
19	IRA deduction	**19**	
20	Student loan interest deduction	**20**	
21	Tuition and fees deduction. Attach Form 8917	**21**	
22	Add lines 10 through 21. These are your **adjustments to income.** Enter here and on Form 1040, 1040-SR, or 1040-NR, line 10a	**22**	

For Paperwork Reduction Act Notice, see your tax return instructions.   Cat. No. 71479F   Schedule 1 (Form 1040) 2020

Deduction Limit for Self-Employed Individuals (Keogh Plans)

Sole proprietors who file a Schedule C, partners of a partnership, and members of an LLC are generally treated as self-employed individuals for tax purposes. In contrast, owners of C corporations or S corporations may also be employees of those entities. While self-employed individuals may adopt almost any qualified plan, they cannot normally choose a stock bonus plan or an employee stock ownership plan (ESOP) because there is no stock involved with sole proprietorships, partnerships, or LLCs. A qualified retirement plan selected by a self-employed individual is referred to as a **Keogh plan**. A Keogh plan is simply a qualified plan for a self-employed person usually structured as a profit sharing plan, a money purchase pension plan (MPPP), or a combination of both (note that self-employed individuals may also be able to establish a 401(k) plan). An important characteristic of a Keogh plan is the reduced contribution that can be made on behalf of the self-employed individual. The employees of a firm that maintains a Keogh plan will generally be treated in the same manner as if the plan were not a Keogh plan. Employees will generally receive a benefit based on their W-2 income. The reason for the distinction is that self-employed individuals do not receive a W-2 form and will instead file a Schedule C or receive a K-1 which details the owner's earnings.

There is a special computation needed to calculate the maximum contribution and tax deduction for a Keogh plan on behalf of a self-employed individual. Since self-employed individuals do not have W-2s, the IRC uses the term "earned income" to denote the amount of compensation that is earned by the self-employed individual.

Earned income is defined as net earnings from self-employment less one-half of self-employment tax less the deduction for contributions to the qualified plan on behalf of the self-employed person. Through this process, the IRC attempts to treat self-employed individuals as if they were corporations instead of self-employed individuals. An employer and an employee each pays one-half of the employee's Social Security taxes; however, in the case of self-employed individuals, they are required to pay both halves. If the company was a corporation, then it would deduct one half of the self employment taxes paid on behalf of the individual in arriving at net income. Therefore, earned income for self-employed individuals is the self-employment income reduced by one-half of self-employment tax. Similarly, a corporation would deduct the contribution made to a qualified retirement plan in arriving at net income. Therefore, calculating earned income for a self-employed individual also requires a reduction for the amount of the contribution to the Keogh plan.

The two primary parts of the Social Security system are OASDI (Old Age Survivor Disability Insurance) and Medicare. Both employers and employees contribute to the system through FICA payments that generally consists of 6.2 percent for OASDI and 1.45 percent for Medicare. The OASDI portion of 6.2 percent applies to income up to the Social Security wage base ($142,800 for 2021) while the Medicare portion applies to all income with no limit. The net effect for a self-employed individual is a tax of 15.3 percent on income up to the Social Security wage base, plus 2.9 percent on income above the wage base.

The deduction for the self-employed person's own plan contribution and his net earnings are interrelated. For this reason, the self-employed person must determine the deduction for his own contributions by using simultaneous equations or a circular calculation or by using the simpler method described below that adjusts the plan contribution rate for the self-employed person.

To calculate the self-employed individual's 2021 contribution to the Keogh plan, utilize the following formulas:

1. Calculate the self-employed individual's contribution rate:

$$\frac{\text{Self-Employed}}{\text{Contribution Rate}} = \left(\frac{\text{Contribution Rate to Other Participants}}{1 + \text{Contribution Rate to Other Participants}} \right)$$

2. Calculate Self-Employment Tax:

Net Self-Employment Income

Times: 92.35%

Net Earnings subject to Self Employment Tax

Times: 15.3% up to \$142,800 + 2.9% over \$142,800

Equals: Self-Employment Tax

3. Calculate the self-employed individual's contribution:

Net Self-Employment Income

Less: ½ of Self-Employment Taxes

Equals: Adjusted Net Self-Employment Income (Earned Income)

Times: Self-Employed Contribution Rate

Equals: Self-Employed Individual's Qualified Plan Contribution

---

Example 13.1

Alex has Schedule C net income of \$200,000 and wants to know the maximum amount he can contribute to a Keogh profit sharing plan. In this instance Alex can contribute \$37,694 to the plan. The contribution is calculated as follows:

1. Calculate the self-employed individual's contribution rate:

$$\text{Self-Employed Contribution Rate} = \left(\frac{25\%}{1 + 25\%} \right)$$

Self-Employed Contribution Rate = 20%

2. Calculate Self-Employment Tax:

2021

$200,000	Net Self-Employment Income
x 0.9235	Times: 92.35%
$184,700	Net Earnings subject to Self-Employment Tax
x 15.3%/2.9%	Times: 15.3% up to $142,800 + 2.9% over $142,800
$23,063	Equals: Self-Employment Tax ($21,848 + $1,215) *Rounded

3. Calculate the self-employed individual's contribution:

2021

$200,000	Net Self-Employment Income
$11,532	Less: ½ of Self-Employment Taxes (50% x $23,063)
$188,468	Equals: Adjusted Net Self-Employment Income
x 0.20	Times: Self-Employed Contribution Rate
$37,694	Equals: Self-Employed Individual's Qualified Plan Contribution

Check figure:

2021

$$\frac{\$37,694}{\$188,468 - \$37,694} = 25\%$$

When solving the Keogh contribution calculation, it is important to understand that while 25 percent of compensation is the limit for deductible employee contributions, the self-employed individual maximum contribution is 25 percent of the self-employed individual's earned income. The 25 percent of earned income effectively translates to 20 percent of net self-employed income less one-half of self-employment tax.

Example 13.2

In the previous example, Alex's earned income is calculated as follows:

2021

$200,000	Schedule C net income
- $11,532	Less: ½ self-employment taxes
- $37,694	Less: Keogh contribution
$150,774	Earned income
x 0.25	Times: 25% to determine Keogh contribution
$37,694	Total Keogh contribution

Notice that the maximum Keogh contribution for each year is exactly 25% of the earned income.

Example 13.3

Cargile Co., a sole proprietorship, employs B, C, D, and E as well as the sole proprietor, A, who files a Schedule C 1040 for his business.

	Compensation	Contributions
A*	$150,000	See note below
B	$100,000	$15,000
C	$80,000	$12,000
D	$50,000	$7,500
E	$20,000	$3,000

*A's compensation is Schedule C net income

Cargile maintains a Keogh profit sharing plan with a 15% contribution to each employee (not the owner). In spite of the fact that each employee receives exactly 15%, A is limited to receiving 13.04% (0.15/1.15) of $150,000 less one-half of the self-employment taxes due on his earnings.

$150,000	Schedule C net income
$10,000	Less: ½ self-employment taxes ($20,000 assumed for ease of calculation)
$140,000	Self-employment income
x 0.1304	Contribution rate (0.15/1.15)
$18,260.87	Contribution on behalf of A *

*Rounding was not utilized when applying the contribution rate.

The special calculation is required because Schedule C net income must be reduced by both the self-employed person's qualified plan contribution and one-half of his self-employment tax before the reduced contribution rate is applied. For all of the other employees, their contribution is calculated based upon 15% of their compensation.

Exhibit 13.4 | A Summary of Advantages and Disadvantages of Sole Proprietorships

Advantages
• Easy to form
• Simple to operate
• Easy to sell business assets
• Few administrative burdens
• Income is generally passed through to the owner on Schedule C of Form 1040

Disadvantages
• Generally have limited sources of capital
• Unlimited liability
• No guarantee of continuity beyond the proprietor
• Business income is subject to self-employment tax

GENERAL PARTNERSHIPS

Partnerships are joint business ventures among two or more persons or entities. The parties are co-owners under their names or under a trade or fictitious name. A partnership is automatically created when two or more individuals conduct business for a profit. There are different types of partnerships and we will examine each type, including general partnerships and limited partnerships. Typically, **general partnerships** are not required to be registered with the Secretary of State in the state of formation, but limited partnerships are required to register.

Formation

Although partnerships are easy to form, state law will govern the relative rights and obligations of the partners (including equal sharing of profits and losses regardless of contributions of property or effort), unless there is a contrary agreement among the partners. Ownership of a general partnership may be in the form of partnership units, shares, or percentages.

Interest, Disposal of Interest, and Dissolution

A partner's interest in a partnership is frequently referred to as his partnership percentage interest. The partners usually have voting power in proportion to their ownership interest. Thus, majority voting rules generally apply.

It is generally difficult to dispose of a partnership interest because any buyer will not only have to evaluate the business, but also the other partners. In addition, partnership agreements often require the approval of non-selling partners before a partner's share can be sold to an outside party.

Partnership dissolution is either voluntary or judicial (ordered by a court). Partners usually vote for voluntary dissolution and, if affirmed, pay creditors and then distribute remaining assets to partners in accordance with either the partnership agreement or in proportion to their individual partnership interests. Judicial dissolution may be necessary when the partners cannot agree on how to conduct the business or whether to dissolve the entity. This situation is most likely to arise when partnership votes are required to be unanimous.

> ### ☰ Key Concepts
>
> 1. Discuss the formation and operation of a general partnership.
>
> 2. Explain why disposing of a general partnership interest may be difficult.
>
> 3. Describe the sources of liability for a general partnership.
>
> 4. Explain the tax attributes of a general partnership.

Capital

The amount of capital contributed usually determines the ownership interest of a partner in a partnership. However, sometimes partners allocate ownership interest differently from capital contributed. Such a situation could occur when one partner brings ideas and talent and the other brings money. Whenever partners are deviating from ownership based on capital contributed, there should be a written partnership agreement that clarifies partnership interests and each partner's distributive share of partnership profits and losses. If a partnership wants to divide profits and/or losses in a proportion that does not equal partnership interest, it will be considered a special allocation. There must be a sound business purpose for a special allocation and partners are well advised to seek the counsel of an attorney or CPA.

Liability

The co-owner partners share the risks and rewards of the business. Each partner is jointly and severally liable for partnership obligations. Like a sole proprietorship, a partner's personal assets can be seized to satisfy partnership obligations.

A principal disadvantage of the general partnership arrangement is that all general partners in a partnership are subject to joint and several liability for the debts and obligations of the partnership. These liabilities can arise from

1. Negligence and acts of employees
2. Negligence of other partners
3. Commercial liabilities (e.g., loans) to the partnership
4. Commercial obligations to other trade creditors

Management/Operations

Partnerships are generally managed equally by all partners. It is possible to name a "**managing partner**" to have responsibilities for some specific task or day-to-day operations. Partnerships can even appoint presidents and vice presidents as officers. If so, these should be spelled out in the written partnership agreement. Partnerships are not required to have annual meetings of partners, but rather have a relatively relaxed set of rules regarding formalities.

Employees of general partnerships are eligible to receive a wide variety of tax-free fringe benefits provided by the employer such as health care. This is not so for partners since partners are not considered to be employees for most employee fringe benefit purposes. However, partners can participate in company-sponsored retirement plans, but they have the same limitations as proprietors in terms of calculations (see discussion under proprietorships).

Income Taxation and Payroll (Social Security) Taxation

Partnerships are not subject to entity level taxation. Partnerships file a Form 1065 (See **Exhibit 13.6**), including Schedule K (**Exhibit 13.7**), which is the summary of all distributive items to individual partners. Income and losses are then "passed through" to the individual partners in proportion to their partnership interests on Form 1065 Schedule K-1 (see **Exhibit 13.8**) regardless of whether the income is distributed to partners in the form of cash. However, partnership taxation may be complex because of the tax rules related to basis. All partnership business net income is subject to self-employment tax up to 15.3 percent. Partnerships are legal entities and thus are required to obtain a Federal Employer Identification Number (FEIN). The year-end for tax purposes is usually the calendar year-end.

Partnerships can deduct all "ordinary and necessary" business expenses from their income. Partners can deduct partnership losses against other ordinary income to the extent of their investment (the amount they have at risk). However, passive

> ### ✎ Quick Quiz 13.3
>
> 1. General partnerships are governed by federal law.
>   a. True
>   b. False
>
> 2. The owners of a general partnership have limited liability from the debts and obligations of the partnership.
>   a. True
>   b. False
>
> 3. General partnerships are pass-through entities for tax purposes.
>   a. True
>   b. False
>
> ———————————
> False, False, True.

partners (those not actively involved in the enterprise) may not be able to deduct losses due to passive activity rules even if they are at-risk. Limited partners may not be subject to self-employment tax.

Partners' Basis in a Partnership

When a partnership is formed by partners contributing assets to the partnership in return for an interest in it, the transfer is generally tax-free to the partners. This is true even if the assets which the partners contribute have market values greater than the contributing partners' basis. The partners then have basis in the partnership shares equal to their basis in the property contributed. Thus, any gain realized on the contribution of appreciated property to the partnership is reflected in the lower bases of the partners' interests and will be deferred until the partnership interest is sold.

If the partners contribute assets which are subject to liabilities to the partnership, the transfer is still tax-deferred. A partner's basis in his or her partnership interest is equal to the basis the partner had in the property contributed, less the share of the liability assumed by new partners.

Example 13.4

Sophia contributes a building with a $120,000 value and a basis of $80,000, subject to a mortgage of $40,000, to an equal partnership with JoJo. Sophia will not recognize gain on the transaction, and her basis in the partnership interest is the $80,000 basis from the building less the $20,000 (half) of the mortgage assumed by JoJo.

If a partner contributes services to a partnership in return for a partnership interest, the market value of the services is taxable to the partner as compensation (ordinary) income. However, the partner's basis in the partnership interest is increased by this ordinary income.

Increases and Decreases of Basis

A partner's basis is increased by all items of income allocated to the partner and by any subsequent contributions. Basis is reduced by items of loss allocated to a partner, by any distributions of money or property to a partner, and by charitable contributions allocated to a partner. A partner's basis is increased by the partner's share of the partnership's liabilities. Changes in the liabilities of the partnership will affect the partner's basis.[1] Partnerships report the partner's tax basis capital account in Part II of Schedule K-1

A partner cannot have basis reduced below zero. Any distributions that exceed a partner's basis will be treated as capital gain to the partner. Any losses that exceed a partner's basis will not be deductible until the business entity creates income in future years or capital contributions are made which increase the partner's basis sufficiently to absorb the losses.

---

1. A partner's at-risk basis increases for the partner's share of recourse debt and for the partner's share of qualified nonrecourse debt. Qualified nonrecourse debt is debt that is used by the taxpayer in the activity of holding real property, is secured by the real property, and is borrowed from a person or entity who is actively and regularly engaged in the business of lending money. See IRC Sec. 465(b).

Example 13.5

Elwood and his brother, Jake, decide to form a partnership to open a deli. Elwood will contribute property with a basis of $50,000 and fair market value of $75,000 in exchange for his interest in the partnership. Jake will contribute $112,500 of cash in exchange for his interest in the partnership. Elwood owns 40% of the partnership and all income and expenses are allocated to each partner based on the partner's percentage of ownership. Elwood's original basis in his partnership interest is $50,000.

In the first year of operation, the partnership income is $30,000. Elwood receives a Schedule K-1 showing his $12,000 share of the partnership income ($30,000 x 40% = $12,000). The partnership made a $10,000 distribution to Elwood in the same year. Elwood's basis is increased by the partnership income allocated to him, but is decreased by the distribution made to him. His basis at the end of the first year is $52,000 ($50,000 + $12,000 - $10,000 = $52,000).

During the following year, the partnership takes out a loan for $22,500. At the end of the year, the partnership shows a loss of $8,000 and Elwood receives a Schedule K-1 indicating his share of the loss is $3,200. Elwood's basis in the partnership interest is increased by $9,000 ($22,500 x 40%) due to the loan, but is decreased by the $3,200 loss. His basis at the end of the second year is $57,800 ($52,000 + $9,000 - $3,200 = $57,800).

Exhibit 13.5 | A Summary of Advantages and Disadvantages of Partnerships

Advantages

- More sources of initial capital than proprietorships
- Usually have more management resources available than proprietorships
- Have fewer administrative burdens than corporations
- Income and losses are generally passed through to the partners for tax purposes

Disadvantages

- Transfer of interests is more difficult than for proprietorships
- Unlimited liability - each partner is liable for partnership debts and obligations
- Partnership income tax and basis adjustment rules can be complex
- Business net income is subject to self-employment tax
- Partners are entitled to few tax-free fringe benefits that are generally available to employees

Exhibit 13.6 | Form 1065

Form **1065**		**U.S. Return of Partnership Income**		OMB No. 1545-0123

Department of the Treasury
Internal Revenue Service

For calendar year 2020, or tax year beginning _____ , 2020, ending _____ , 20____ .

20 20

▶ Go to *www.irs.gov/Form1065* for instructions and the latest information.

A Principal business activity	Name of partnership	**D** Employer identification number
B Principal product or service	**Type or Print**	Number, street, and room or suite no. If a P.O. box, see instructions.	**E** Date business started
C Business code number		City or town, state or province, country, and ZIP or foreign postal code	**F** Total assets (see instructions) $

G Check applicable boxes: **(1)** ☐ Initial return **(2)** ☐ Final return **(3)** ☐ Name change **(4)** ☐ Address change **(5)** ☐ Amended return

H Check accounting method: **(1)** ☐ Cash **(2)** ☐ Accrual **(3)** ☐ Other (specify) ▶ _____

I Number of Schedules K-1. Attach one for each person who was a partner at any time during the tax year ▶ _____ ▶ ☐

J Check if Schedules C and M-3 are attached . . . . ▶ ☐

K Check if partnership: **(1)** ☐ Aggregated activities for section 465 at-risk purposes **(2)** ☐ Grouped activities for section 469 passive activity purposes

Caution: Include **only** trade or business income and expenses on lines 1a through 22 below. See instructions for more information.

Income (see instructions for limitations)

1a	Gross receipts or sales	1a	
b	Returns and allowances	1b	
c	Balance. Subtract line 1b from line 1a	1c	
2	Cost of goods sold (attach Form 1125-A)	2	
3	Gross profit. Subtract line 2 from line 1c	3	
4	Ordinary income (loss) from other partnerships, estates, and trusts (attach statement)	4	
5	Net farm profit (loss) (attach Schedule F (Form 1040))	5	
6	Net gain (loss) from Form 4797, Part II, line 17 (attach Form 4797)	6	
7	Other income (loss) (attach statement)	7	
8	**Total income (loss).** Combine lines 3 through 7	8	

Deductions (see instructions for limitations)

9	Salaries and wages (other than to partners) (less employment credits)	9	
10	Guaranteed payments to partners	10	
11	Repairs and maintenance	11	
12	Bad debts	12	
13	Rent	13	
14	Taxes and licenses	14	
15	Interest (see instructions)	15	
16a	Depreciation (if required, attach Form 4562)	16a	
b	Less depreciation reported on Form 1125-A and elsewhere on return .	16b	
		16c	
17	Depletion **(Do not deduct oil and gas depletion.)**	17	
18	Retirement plans, etc.	18	
19	Employee benefit programs	19	
20	Other deductions (attach statement)	20	
21	**Total deductions.** Add the amounts shown in the far right column for lines 9 through 20 . . .	21	
22	**Ordinary business income (loss).** Subtract line 21 from line 8	22	

Tax and Payment

23	Interest due under the look-back method—completed long-term contracts (attach Form 8697) .	23	
24	Interest due under the look-back method—income forecast method (attach Form 8866) . . .	24	
25	BBA AAR imputed underpayment (see instructions)	25	
26	Other taxes (see instructions)	26	
27	**Total balance due.** Add lines 23 through 26	27	
28	Payment (see instructions)	28	
29	**Amount owed.** If line 28 is smaller than line 27, enter amount owed . . .	29	
30	**Overpayment.** If line 28 is larger than line 27, enter overpayment . . .	30	

Sign Here

Under penalties of perjury, I declare that I have examined this return, including accompanying schedules and statements, and to the best of my knowledge and belief, it is true, correct, and complete. Declaration of preparer (other than partner or limited liability company member) is based on all information of which preparer has any knowledge.

▶ _____
Signature of partner or limited liability company member

▶ _____ Date

May the IRS discuss this return with the preparer shown below? See instructions. ☐ Yes ☐ No

Paid Preparer Use Only

Print/Type preparer's name	Preparer's signature	Date	Check ☐ if self-employed	PTIN
Firm's name ▶			Firm's EIN ▶	
Firm's address ▶			Phone no.	

For Paperwork Reduction Act Notice, see separate instructions.　　Cat. No. 11390Z　　Form **1065** (2020)

Exhibit 13.7 | Form 1065 Schedule K

Schedule K	Partners' Distributive Share Items		Total amount
Income (Loss)	**1** Ordinary business income (loss) (page 1, line 22)	**1**	
	2 Net rental real estate income (loss) (attach Form 8825)	**2**	
	3a Other gross rental income (loss) **3a**		
	b Expenses from other rental activities (attach statement) **3b**		
	c Other net rental income (loss). Subtract line 3b from line 3a	**3c**	
	4 Guaranteed payments: **a** Services **4a** **b** Capital **4b**		
	c Total. Add lines 4a and 4b	**4c**	
	5 Interest income	**5**	
	6 Dividends and dividend equivalents: **a** Ordinary dividends	**6a**	
	b Qualified dividends **6b** **c** Dividend equivalents **6c**		
	7 Royalties	**7**	
	8 Net short-term capital gain (loss) (attach Schedule D (Form 1065)) . . .	**8**	
	9a Net long-term capital gain (loss) (attach Schedule D (Form 1065)) . . .	**9a**	
	b Collectibles (28%) gain (loss) **9b**		
	c Unrecaptured section 1250 gain (attach statement) . . . **9c**		
	10 Net section 1231 gain (loss) (attach Form 4797)	**10**	
	11 Other income (loss) (see instructions) Type ▶	**11**	
Deductions	**12** Section 179 deduction (attach Form 4562)	**12**	
	13a Contributions	**13a**	
	b Investment interest expense	**13b**	
	c Section 59(e)(2) expenditures: **(1)** Type ▶ _____ **(2)** Amount ▶	**13c(2)**	
	d Other deductions (see instructions) Type ▶	**13d**	
Self-Employ-ment	**14a** Net earnings (loss) from self-employment	**14a**	
	b Gross farming or fishing income	**14b**	
	c Gross nonfarm income	**14c**	
Credits	**15a** Low-income housing credit (section 42(j)(5))	**15a**	
	b Low-income housing credit (other)	**15b**	
	c Qualified rehabilitation expenditures (rental real estate) (attach Form 3468, if applicable) . .	**15c**	
	d Other rental real estate credits (see instructions) Type ▶ _____	**15d**	
	e Other rental credits (see instructions) Type ▶ _____	**15e**	
	f Other credits (see instructions) Type ▶	**15f**	
Foreign Transactions	**16a** Name of country or U.S. possession ▶ _____		
	b Gross income from all sources	**16b**	
	c Gross income sourced at partner level	**16c**	
	Foreign gross income sourced at partnership level		
	d Reserved for future use ▶ **e** Foreign branch category . . . . . ▶	**16e**	
	f Passive category ▶ _____ **g** General category ▶ _____ **h** Other (attach statement) ▶	**16h**	
	Deductions allocated and apportioned at partner level		
	i Interest expense ▶ _____ **j** Other . . . . ▶	**16j**	
	Deductions allocated and apportioned at partnership level to foreign source income		
	k Reserved for future use ▶ **l** Foreign branch category . . . . . ▶	**16l**	
	m Passive category ▶ _____ **n** General category ▶ _____ **o** Other (attach statement) ▶	**16o**	
	p Total foreign taxes (check one): ▶ Paid ☐ Accrued ☐ . . . . ▶	**16p**	
	q Reduction in taxes available for credit (attach statement)	**16q**	
	r Other foreign tax information (attach statement)		
Alternative Minimum Tax (AMT) Items	**17a** Post-1986 depreciation adjustment	**17a**	
	b Adjusted gain or loss	**17b**	
	c Depletion (other than oil and gas)	**17c**	
	d Oil, gas, and geothermal properties—gross income	**17d**	
	e Oil, gas, and geothermal properties—deductions	**17e**	
	f Other AMT items (attach statement)	**17f**	
Other Information	**18a** Tax-exempt interest income	**18a**	
	b Other tax-exempt income	**18b**	
	c Nondeductible expenses	**18c**	
	19a Distributions of cash and marketable securities	**19a**	
	b Distributions of other property	**19b**	
	20a Investment income	**20a**	
	b Investment expenses	**20b**	
	c Other items and amounts (attach statement)		

Form **1065** (2020)

Exhibit 13.8 | Form 1065 Schedule K-1

651119

☐ Final K-1   ☐ Amended K-1   OMB No. 1545-0123

Schedule K-1
(Form 1065)
Department of the Treasury
Internal Revenue Service

20**20**

For calendar year 2020, or tax year

beginning ___/___/ 2020   ending ___/___/___

Partner's Share of Income, Deductions, Credits, etc.   ▶ See separate instructions.

Part III	Partner's Share of Current Year Income, Deductions, Credits, and Other Items

Part I — Information About the Partnership

A Partnership's employer identification number

B Partnership's name, address, city, state, and ZIP code

C IRS Center where partnership filed return ▶

D ☐ Check if this is a publicly traded partnership (PTP)

Part II — Information About the Partner

E Partner's SSN or TIN (Do not use TIN of a disregarded entity. See instructions.)

F Name, address, city, state, and ZIP code for partner entered in E. See instructions.

G ☐ General partner or LLC member-manager   ☐ Limited partner or other LLC member

H1 ☐ Domestic partner   ☐ Foreign partner

H2 ☐ If the partner is a disregarded entity (DE), enter the partner's:
TIN _____ Name _____

I1 What type of entity is this partner? _____

I2 If this partner is a retirement plan (IRA/SEP/Keogh/etc.), check here ☐

J Partner's share of profit, loss, and capital (see instructions):

	Beginning	Ending
Profit	_____%	_____%
Loss	_____%	_____%
Capital	_____%	_____%

Check if decrease is due to sale or exchange of partnership interest . . ☐

K Partner's share of liabilities:

	Beginning	Ending
Nonrecourse . . .	$_____	$_____
Qualified nonrecourse financing . . .	$_____	$_____
Recourse . . .	$_____	$_____

☐ Check this box if Item K includes liability amounts from lower tier partnerships.

L   **Partner's Capital Account Analysis**

Beginning capital account . . .	$_____
Capital contributed during the year . .	$_____
Current year net income (loss) . . .	$_____
Other increase (decrease) (attach explanation)	$_____
Withdrawals & distributions . . .	$(_____)
Ending capital account	$_____

M Did the partner contribute property with a built-in gain or loss?
☐ Yes ☐ No   If "Yes," attach statement. See instructions.

N Partner's Share of Net Unrecognized Section 704(c) Gain or (Loss)
Beginning . . . . $_____
Ending . . . . $_____

For IRS Use Only

Part III — Partner's Share of Current Year Income, Deductions, Credits, and Other Items

1	Ordinary business income (loss)		15	Credits
2	Net rental real estate income (loss)			
3	Other net rental income (loss)		16	Foreign transactions
4a	Guaranteed payments for services			
4b	Guaranteed payments for capital			
4c	Total guaranteed payments			
5	Interest income			
6a	Ordinary dividends			
6b	Qualified dividends			
6c	Dividend equivalents		17	Alternative minimum tax (AMT) items
7	Royalties			
8	Net short-term capital gain (loss)			
9a	Net long-term capital gain (loss)		18	Tax-exempt income and nondeductible expenses
9b	Collectibles (28%) gain (loss)			
9c	Unrecaptured section 1250 gain			
10	Net section 1231 gain (loss)			
11	Other income (loss)		19	Distributions
12	Section 179 deduction		20	Other information
13	Other deductions			
14	Self-employment earnings (loss)			

21 ☐ More than one activity for at-risk purposes*

22 ☐ More than one activity for passive activity purposes*

*See attached statement for additional information.

For Paperwork Reduction Act Notice, see Instructions for Form 1065.   www.irs.gov/Form1065   Cat. No. 11394R   Schedule K-1 (Form 1065) 2020

LIMITED PARTNERSHIPS (LP)

Limited partnerships are associations of two or more persons as co-owners to carry on a business for profit except that one or more of the partners have limited participation in the management of the venture and thus limited risk exposure. If the limited partners participate in the management of the enterprise, they become general partners for liability purposes. In the normal limited partnership, there is at least one general partner. Because limited partners are passive investors in the enterprise, their liability is normally limited to the amount of their investment. A limited partner's personal assets cannot normally be seized to satisfy partnership obligations.

> ### ≔ *Key Concepts*
>
> 1. Describe the ways in which a limited partnership is different from a general partnership.
>
> 2. Explain the advantages and disadvantages of a limited partnership.

Formation

Limited partnerships are generally required to file a partnership agreement or any other required documentation with the domiciliary state to establish the limited partnership. Those states that require initial filings also require annual filings to maintain the entity status. The written partnership agreement specifies which partners are limited partners and which partners are general partners.

Interest, Disposal of Interest, and Dissolution

The dissolution and transfer of an interest in a limited partnership is essentially the same as for a general partnership. Although the limited liability feature might attract more buyers, the inability for limited partners to have a say in the day-to-day operations of the company is likely to make the transfer of a limited partnership share very difficult.

Capital

It is easier to raise capital in a limited partnership than in a general partnership because of the availability of the liability shield for the non-managing limited partners. However, the limited liability may negatively affect the partnership's ability to obtain outside financing. Third party lenders may desire personal guarantees from the partners (which would partially defeat the benefits associated with the limited liability feature).

> ### ✏ *Quick Quiz 13.4*
>
> 1. Limited partnerships are generally required to register with the state.
>   a. True
>   b. False
>
> 2. Limited partnerships offer limited liability for all partners.
>   a. True
>   b. False
>
> True, False.

Liability

Liability for limited partners is limited as long as they refrain from participating in the management of the enterprise. The general partners, who are responsible for the day-to-day operations in a limited partnership, have unlimited liability for enterprise debts and obligations.

Management/Operations

A limited partnership is somewhat of a hybrid entity. The general partners run the business and are exposed to personal liability. The limited partners must avoid making management decisions to protect their limited liability status.

Income Taxation and Payroll (Social Security) Taxes

Limited partners are not usually subject to self-employment tax since they are passive investors who do not participate in management. The general partners in a limited partnership have self-employment income. As with the general partnership, the entity files a Form 1065 and issues Schedule K-1s to both its general and limited partners.

Exhibit 13.9 | A Summary of Advantages and Disadvantages of Limited Partnerships

Advantages
• Favorable pass-through partnership taxation status
• Flexibility in structuring ownership interests
• Limited partners are not personally liable for the debts and obligations of the limited partnership as long as they do not engage in management

Disadvantages
• Must file with the state to register
• In most states, general partners are liable for debts and other obligations of the limited partnership
• Losses for limited partners are generally passive losses (subject to special tax rules limiting deductibility)

LIMITED LIABILITY PARTNERSHIPS (LLP)

A **limited liability partnership (LLP)** is a hybrid entity that provides partial liability protection to its members and may be taxed as either a corporation or partnership. LLPs are similar to LLCs, but may not offer complete liability protection. The limited liability partnership is generally one comprised of licensed professionals such as accountants, attorneys, and doctors who practice together. The partners may enjoy liability protection from the acts of their other partners, but each partner remains personally liable for his own acts with respect to malpractice.

> ### ≔ *Key Concepts*
>
> 1. Explain who can form a limited liability partnership.
>
> 2. Explain the ways in which an LLP differs from a general partnership.

Formation

Limited liability partnerships are generally required to file with the domiciliary state to establish the limited liability partnership. Those states that require initial filings also require annual filings to maintain the entity status.

Interest, Disposal of Interest, and Dissolution

The dissolution and transfer of an interest in a limited partnership is essentially the same as for a general partnership. If the LLP is comprised of licensed professionals, however, transfer of an interest will usually be more difficult because such interest may only be transferred to another similarly licensed professional.

Capital

The amount of capital contributed usually determines the ownership interest in a partnership. However, sometimes partners allocate ownership interest differently from capital contributed. Such a situation could occur when one partner brings ideas and talent and the other brings money. Whenever partners are deviating from ownership based on capital contributed, there should be a written partnership agreement that clarifies partnership interests and each partner's distributive share of the profits and losses. If a partnership divides profits and/or losses in a proportion that does not reflect partnership interests, the arrangement is considered to be a special allocation. There must be a sound business purpose for special allocations and partners are well advised to seek the counsel of an attorney or CPA.

> ### ✍ Quick Quiz 13.5
>
> 1. Limited liability partnerships are generally owned by licensed professionals.
>   a. True
>   b. False
>
> 2. The transferability of an interest in an LLP is the same as for any other type of partnership.
>   a. True
>   b. False
>
> True, False.

Liability

A principal disadvantage of the general partnership arrangement is that all general partners in a partnership are subject to joint and several liability for the debts and obligations of the partnership. These liabilities can arise from:
1. liability for the negligence and acts of employees
2. negligence of other partners
3. commercial liabilities (e.g., loans) to the partnership
4. commercial obligations to other trade creditors

However, general partners of an LLP can insulate themselves from liabilities arising from the acts of other partners. General partners of an LLP will not be personally liable for the debts and obligations arising from errors, omissions, negligence, incompetence, or acts committed by another partner or representative of the partnership who is not under the supervision or direction of the first partner. It is important to note that general partners remain personally liable for commercial and trade obligations. If the partners wish to insulate themselves from these obligations, they should consider an LLC and once formed, they should not personally guarantee commercial obligations.

Management/Operations

The management of an LLP is generally the same as for any general partnership. Note that unlike a limited partnership, the LLP confers limited liability status on all partners, not just limited partners.

Income Taxation and Payroll (Social Security) Taxes

For federal income tax purposes, the entity may elect to file as a corporation or as a partnership. This choice is known as "**checking the box**." Choosing to be taxed as a C corporation allows owners to take advantage of tax-free fringe benefits which may be provided by C corporations. Operating as a partnership has the disadvantages of subjecting income to employment taxes and limited fringe benefits for owners. If the entity files as a partnership it will file Form 1065. If it files as a corporation, it will file either the Form 1120S (if it elects S corporation status) or Form 1120 (if it files as a C corporation).

Exhibit 13.10 | A Summary of Advantages and Disadvantages of Limited Liability Partnerships

Advantages
• Favorable pass-through partnership taxation status available
• Flexibility in structuring ownership interests
• Partners can insulate themselves from the acts of other partners

Disadvantages
• Required to file with the state to register
• Unlimited liability for own acts of malpractice

FAMILY LIMITED PARTNERSHIPS (FLP)

A **family limited partnership** (FLP) is a special type of limited partnership created under state law with the primary purpose of transferring assets to younger generations using annual exclusions and valuation discounts for minority interests and lack of marketability.

Formation

Usually, one or more family members transfer highly appreciated property that is expected to continue to appreciate to a limited partnership in return for a general partnership interest and limited partnership interests. It is common that the general partnership interest is one percent and the limited partnership interests represent 99 percent of the value. In a limited partnership, the general partner has unlimited liability and the sole management rights of the partnership, while the limited partners are passive interest holders with limited liability and no management rights.

≔ *Key Concepts*

1. Describe how the tax attributes of an FLP can be useful in other areas of financial planning.

2. Explain the advantages of using an FLP to protect family assets.

Exhibit 13.11 | Family Limited Partnership

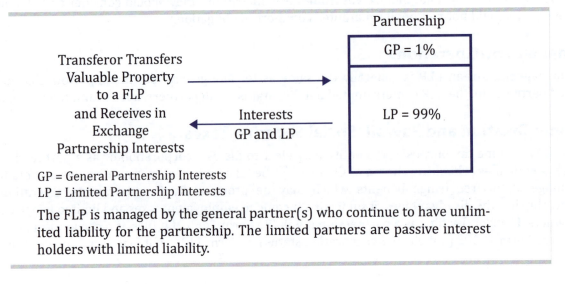

Transferor Transfers Valuable Property to a FLP and Receives in Exchange Partnership Interests

Interests GP and LP

Partnership
GP = 1%
LP = 99%

GP = General Partnership Interests
LP = Limited Partnership Interests

The FLP is managed by the general partner(s) who continue to have unlimited liability for the partnership. The limited partners are passive interest holders with limited liability.

Interest, Disposal of Interest, and Dissolution

Upon creation of the partnership (FLP), there are neither income nor gift tax consequences because the entity created (the limited partnership and all of its interests, both general and limited) is owned by the same person, or persons, who owned it before the transfer.

Once the FLP is created, the owner of the general and limited partnership interests values the limited partnership interests. Since there are usually transferability restrictions on the limited partnership interests (lack of marketability), and since the limited partners have little control of the management of the partnership (lack of control), limited partnership interests are usually valued at a substantial discount from their fair market values. It is not uncommon for the discount of such interests to range between 20 and 40 percent for the purpose of calculating gift taxes payable by the transferor. The original transferor (grantor) then begins an annual gifting program utilizing the discounts, the gift tax annual exclusions, and gift-splitting (where applicable) to transfer limited partnership interests to younger generation family members at reduced transfer costs.

Example 13.6

Charles, age 52, is married to Debbie, and they have three children and nine grandchildren. The three children are happily married and Charles and Debbie think of their children's spouses as their own children. Charles transfers a 100% interest in a business with a fair market value of $3,200,000 to a family limited partnership. Charles, in return, receives a general partnership interest of one percent and 158.4 units of limited partnership interests representing 99 percent, at $20,000 (($3,200,000 x 99%) / 158.4) per unit. Charles then transfers two limited partnership units to each child, the spouse of each child, and each grandchild using a 25 percent discount, the annual exclusion ($15,000 for 2021), and the gift-splitting election.

FMV Per Unit	$20,000
x 2 Units Per Family Member = Value Per Donee	$40,000
x 15 Donees = Total Value Transferred	$600,000
Gift Value Per Unit (with 25% Discount to FMV)	$15,000
x 2 Units Per Family Member = Total Gift Value Per Donee	$30,000
x 15 Donees = Total Value for Gift Tax Purposes	$450,000

In this scenario, Charles does not pay any gift tax due to the annual gift tax exclusion. It will take six years with this level of gifting for Charles to transfer his entire limited partnership interest to his children, their spouses, and his grandchildren without paying any gift taxes.

Capital

One of the unique features of the FLP, and perhaps its most important non-tax benefit, is that the original owner/transferor can maintain control of the property transferred to the limited partnership by only retaining a small general partnership interest. If the FLP is funded with a business interest, the general partner could remain president of the business, direct the company's strategic plan, receive reasonable compensation and fringe benefits, hire and fire employees, receive executive perks, and generally control the limited partners' interests. As with all limited partnerships, the limited partners have no control over any of these enumerated management decisions.

The FLP is often undertaken as a series of transfers, including an initial nontaxable contribution of property to the partnership followed by annual exclusion gifts of limited partnership interests. While a general partner has control over partnership affairs, an individual who transfers his property to an FLP needs to be financially secure without the transferred property, both from a net worth and cash flow perspective.

Liability

The use of the FLP structure can also help protect family assets. By placing the assets in the FLP and only making gifts of limited partnership interests to heirs, judgments or liens entered against a donee (limited partner) will not jeopardize the assets of the partnership. A donee's creditor would not be able to force the donee to liquidate his interest, since the donee does not have the right to force the liquidation of a limited partnership interest.

Transferring limited partnership interests to children and children's spouses can also help protect assets from divorce claims. If the child and his spouse divorce, even if the divorced spouse received a limited partnership interest, he or she could not force distributions from the partnership, participate in management, require his or her interest to be redeemed, or force a liquidation of the partnership.

Taxation

The creation of family limited partnerships and the use of discounts to transfer value at a lower gift tax cost has been regularly contested by the IRS. However, in several cases, the courts have ruled in favor of the taxpayer and upheld discounts on the valuation of limited partnership interests in the range of 10 percent to 40 percent, as long as the FLP was operated like a separate business. The IRS has won, and the valuation discounts have not been allowed, in cases where the family withdrew money from the business at leisure, shared checking accounts with the business, had the FLP pay medical or other ordinary living expenses for the family, and when other non-business transactions were prevalent within the FLP.

The estate planning benefits of the FLP are lost and expenses are increased (as the result of legal fees) when the IRS successfully contests the use of the FLP arrangement. To mitigate against this risk and to ensure the use of the favorable discounts, the FLP should possess economic substance by having its own checking accounts, tax identification number, payroll (including payment of reasonable compensation to the general partner if he is managing the business), and should not allow family members to withdraw funds at will, nor should the FLP pay for personal expenses of its owners.

A FLP is taxed as a partnership and the entity files a Form 1065 and issues Schedule K-1s to both general and limited partners. The general partner may be a corporation or an individual. The treatment of payroll taxes will be determined by whether the general partner is an individual or a corporation. The limited partners are passive and not subject to employment tax.

Exhibit 13.12 | Advantages and Disadvantages of Family Limited Partnerships

Advantages
• Control retained by senior family member
• Valuation discounts are available for minority interests
• Annual exclusion gifts are generally used to transfer interests to family members
• Some creditor protection
• Restrictions can be placed on transferability of limited partnership interests of junior family members
• FLP is commonly used as an estate planning strategy
Disadvantages
• Attorney setup fees and costs
• Periodic valuation costs
• Operational requirements
• Potential IRS challenges regarding valuations and discounts

LIMITED LIABILITY COMPANIES (LLC)

Limited Liability Companies are separate legal entities formed by one or more individuals by meeting state statutory requirements necessary for the formation of an LLC. These are one of the most common and, therefore, most important entities for small businesses and investments.

Formation

LLCs are formed in much the same way as corporations. They are chartered entities registered with the Secretary of State in the state of organization. The charter document is called **Articles of Organization** and the state requires the entity to have a resident agent. In addition, the state will require annual filings.

Interest, Disposal of Interest, and Dissolution

Usually, owners' contributions determine the ownership percentage of an LLC. However, sometimes the organization will want to divide the ownership interests in an amount differently than the initial contributions. They can do this in a variety of ways, including revaluing assets or issuing units for some obligation.

Disposal or transferability of interests may be difficult and may be restricted to transferring only to named parties. Such restrictions are clarified in the operating agreement.

> ### ≔ *Key Concepts*
>
> 1. Discuss the formation and operation of an LLC.
> 2. Discuss the liability protection offered by an LLC.
> 3. Explain the tax attributes of an LLC.

Capital

Capital is easier to raise in an LLC than in a proprietorship. Ease of raising capital in an LLC is similar to the ease of raising capital in a partnership.

Capital Structure

There is no limitation on the number of members or the types of members in an LLC. Members may include foreign (nonresident aliens) individuals, estates, trusts, corporations, etc. LLCs may allocate items of income and gains in any manner agreed to by the members in the operating agreement and can also create different classes of ownership interests which have different rights.

Liability

The most important feature of an LLC is that the LLC's individual owners are protected from personal liability for the LLC's debts and obligations unless they personally guarantee such obligations.

The liability protection is not absolute. Piercing the veil and alter ego concepts give courts the power to disregard the LLC liability protection in extraordinary cases of owner/manager abuse or failure to maintain a clear and continuing identity.

Management/Operations

An LLC usually is managed by virtue of an **operating agreement**. The operating agreement is similar to corporate bylaws and may be amended from time to time. The agreement specifies how and who will manage the LLC, how interests may be transferred, etc. Operating agreements are not filed with the state. Operating agreements sometimes specify simple majority rules for some decisions and super majority rules for other decisions (e.g., 2/3 or 3/4 to take on debt in excess of certain amounts) and unanimous votes for special situations (e.g., changing the operating agreement). Caution should be used with requirements for unanimous agreement provisions because they essentially give a minority owner (member) a veto power over all other members.

Note that an LLC is not legally required to have an operating agreement. If an LLC does not have an operating agreement, it will (by default) be governed by the state laws regarding LLCs. Although this might be sufficient for some LLCs, it is generally best to have a written operating agreement signed by all members that specifies the rules and regulations pertinent to the governing of the LLC.

Income Taxation and Payroll (Social Security) Taxes

An LLC which has a single member/owner is typically a disregarded entity for federal income tax purposes. In this case, the owner files a Schedule C of Form 1040 for the LLC, the same as for a proprietorship. Such an LLC owner has the same issues as proprietors with respect to self-employment tax, unemployment compensation, and fringe benefits. Alternatively, a single member LLC may elect for federal income tax purposes to be taxed as an S corporation (Form 1120S with Schedule K-1), or a C corporation (Form 1120 with W-2 income to the owner).

An LLC with two or more members can elect to be taxed for federal income tax purposes as a partnership (Form 1065 with Schedule K-1s), an S corporation (Form 1120S with Schedule K-1s), or a C corporation (Form 1120 with W-2 income to the owners).

> ### 📝 Quick Quiz 13.7
>
> 1. There is no limitation on the number of members of a LLC.
>   a. True
>   b. False
>
> 2. A written operating agreement is an important element of the management of a LLC.
>   a. True
>   b. False
>
> True, True.

Taxation of Income

The LLC is not taxed at the entity level if it is taxed as a partnership. As a pass-through entity, an LLC's income is taxed to members at their personal rates. LLC losses are deductible on personal income tax returns to the extent of basis and may be limited by the passive activity rules. A unique characteristic of LLCs is that no gain or loss is recognized upon the distribution of appreciated property from an LLC to an LLC member. Gain will only be recognized to the extent that cash received exceeds the members adjusted basis.

Fringe Benefits

LLCs are usually taxed as partnerships. Therefore, members are not generally allowed to exclude from gross income the value of fringe benefits paid on their behalf by the LLC.

Employment Tax on Income

LLCs are usually taxed as partnerships. Income earned by the LLC members is normally subject to self-employment tax on the tax returns of individual members. There are exceptions: (1) for LLC income derived from rental real estate, and (2) for LLC members who are not the managing member and are the equivalent of limited partners.

Once elected, the tax status (partnership, S corporation, or C corporation) will dictate the handling of self-employment tax and fringe benefits.

Exhibit 13.13 | A Summary of Advantages and Disadvantages of LLCs

Advantages
• Members have limited liability.
• Number of members is unlimited but a single member LLC is typically a disregarded entity for tax purposes (File Form 1040 Schedule C).
• Members may be individuals, corporations, trusts, other LLCs, and other entities.
• Income is passed through to the members, usually on Schedule K-1.
• Double taxation affecting most C corporations is avoided if partnership tax status is elected.
• Members can participate in managing the LLC.
• Distributions to members do not have to be directly proportional to the members' ownership interests as they do for S corporations.
• Can have multiple classes of ownership.
• Entity may elect to be taxed as a partnership, an S corporation, or a C corporation.

Disadvantages
• May have limited life (often by termination on the death or bankruptcy of a member).
• Transfer of interests is difficult and sometimes limited by operating agreement.
• Some industries or professions may not be permitted to use LLC status.
• Laws vary from state to state regarding LLCs.
• Laws are relatively new for LLCs; therefore, precedent from prior court cases are limited.
• For tax purposes, the complex partnership rules generally apply.
• Members not meeting exceptions are subject to self-employment tax on all earned income if partnership status is elected.

C CORPORATIONS

Corporations are chartered legal entities formed by one or more individuals by meeting state statutory requirements necessary for the formation of a corporation. There are two types of corporations: the C corporation and the S corporation. For tax purposes, S corporations are simply C corporations with a special tax election and will be discussed in the next section.

Formation

Corporations can only be created by filing a charter document with the state of incorporation (called **articles of incorporation**). The articles of incorporation generally require a corporation to disclose its name, number of shares, and the purpose of the corporation. The corporation's purpose may be broad (e.g., to engage in any lawful activity) or specific (e.g., to sell textbooks). In addition, the corporation will be required to name a registered agent located in the state of incorporation.

Interest, Disposal of Interest, and Dissolution

Ownership interests in a corporation are held by a shareholder and are evidenced by shares of stock certificates. Shares may be easy to transfer if there is a market, but certain small corporations restrict the transfer of shares through a shareholder agreement. The shares of stock issued by the corporation may be all one class or several classes. Different classes of stock generally have different values and/or voting rights.

Capital

Corporations can raise capital more easily than a proprietorship or partnership. The limited liability status appeals to outside non-employee owner/investors.

Liability

Liability in corporations is limited to the invested capital. Individual shareholders of the corporation have limited liability, presuming the corporation behaves in such a way as to clearly and consistently maintain its identity and complies with state-mandated requirements.

Management/Operations

Corporations are managed by one or more officers appointed by the board of directors. The board of directors is the governing body of a corporation. The board of directors appoints various officers to run the corporation (usually includes president, chief financial officer, secretary, treasurer). The board of directors acts, or should act, in a very formal way and is required under the corporate charter to meet and follow certain formalities. Observing corporate formalities, and maintaining good standing with the Secretary of State in the state of incorporation, is an ongoing requirement.

Income Taxation and Payroll (Social Security) Taxes

A corporation is taxed as a C corporation unless S corporation status is elected. C corporations must file Form 1120 (**Exhibit 13.16**) and pay taxes on their own income on a calendar or fiscal year basis. The owner/employees of both C corporations and S corporations are treated as employees for payroll tax purposes. Therefore, the entity withholds 7.65 percent of the employee's pay for Social Security taxes and matches such withholding for Social Security taxes. The owner/employee's compensation is not considered to be self-employment income.

Distributions of cash and other assets to a shareholder/employee in his capacity as a shareholder rather than as an employee are considered to be dividends. A C corporation is not allowed to take a tax deduction for dividends distributed to shareholders, but shareholders must include the dividends in gross income. Therefore, the income of a C corporation can be taxed two times, once at the corporation level and a second time at the shareholder level when dividends are distributed. In a closely-held corporation, careful tax planning can minimize or even eliminate this double taxation.

When noncash distributions of appreciated property are made to shareholder/employees, the gain must be recognized at the corporate level as though the property had been sold and the cash proceeds distributed. For a C corporation, this gain must be recognized at the corporation level. For an S corporation, the gain is passed through to shareholders and taxed on their individual income tax returns based on their ownership interests in the S corporation. Unlike this corporation treatment, appreciated assets can be distributed by an LLC or by any entity taxed as a partnership without any gain recognition at the time of the distribution.

> ### Quick Quiz 13.8
>
> 1. A corporation's purpose must be narrowly defined in the articles of incorporation.
>   a. True
>   b. False
>
> 2. In-kind distributions of appreciated assets by a C corporation are treated as a deemed sale by the corporation.
>   a. True
>   b. False
>
> False, True.

Exhibit 13.14 | Tax Formula for C Corporation

Total Income (From Whatever Source Derived)	$XX,XXX
Less: Exclusions From Gross Income	(X,XXX)
Gross Income	$XX,XXX
Less: Deductions	(X,XXX)
Taxable Income	$XX,XXX

Prior to the Tax Cuts and Jobs Act (TCJA 2017), C corporations paid graduated federal income-tax rates of 15 percent, 25 percent, 34 percent, and 35 percent.

For tax years beginning after December 31, 2017, TCJA 2017 establishes a flat 21 percent corporate rate.

Exhibit 13.15 | Advantages and Disadvantages of C Corporations

Advantages
• Relative ease of raising capital • Limited liability of shareholders • Unlimited life of entity • Ease of transfer of ownership interests • Generally more management resources • Shareholder/employees may receive the full array of employer-provided tax-free fringe benefits

Disadvantages
• Potential for double taxation due to entity level taxation • Administrative burdens (e.g., filings) • More difficult to form, and dissolution can cause taxable gains • Borrowing may be difficult without stockholder personal guarantees, which negates part of the advantage of limited liability • Requires a registered agent • Requires a federal tax ID number

Exhibit 13.16 | Form 1120

Form 1120
Department of the Treasury
Internal Revenue Service

U.S. Corporation Income Tax Return

For calendar year 2020 or tax year beginning _____, 2020, ending _____, 20 _____

▶ Go to *www.irs.gov/Form1120* for instructions and the latest information.

OMB No. 1545-0123

2020

A Check if:

1a Consolidated return (attach Form 851) ☐
 b Life/nonlife consoli-dated return . ☐
2 Personal holding co. (attach Sch. PH) . ☐
3 Personal service corp. (see instructions) . ☐
4 Schedule M-3 attached ☐

TYPE OR PRINT

Name

Number, street, and room or suite no. If a P.O. box, see instructions.

City or town, state or province, country, and ZIP or foreign postal code

B Employer identification number

C Date incorporated

D Total assets (see instructions)
$

E Check if: **(1)** ☐ Initial return **(2)** ☐ Final return **(3)** ☐ Name change **(4)** ☐ Address change

Income	1a	Gross receipts or sales	1a	
	b	Returns and allowances	1b	
	c	Balance. Subtract line 1b from line 1a	1c	
	2	Cost of goods sold (attach Form 1125-A)	2	
	3	Gross profit. Subtract line 2 from line 1c	3	
	4	Dividends and inclusions (Schedule C, line 23)	4	
	5	Interest	5	
	6	Gross rents	6	
	7	Gross royalties	7	
	8	Capital gain net income (attach Schedule D (Form 1120))	8	
	9	Net gain or (loss) from Form 4797, Part II, line 17 (attach Form 4797) .	9	
	10	Other income (see instructions—attach statement)	10	
	11	**Total income.** Add lines 3 through 10 . . . . ▶	11	
Deductions (See instructions for limitations on deductions.)	12	Compensation of officers (see instructions—attach Form 1125-E) . . ▶	12	
	13	Salaries and wages (less employment credits)	13	
	14	Repairs and maintenance	14	
	15	Bad debts	15	
	16	Rents	16	
	17	Taxes and licenses	17	
	18	Interest (see instructions)	18	
	19	Charitable contributions	19	
	20	Depreciation from Form 4562 not claimed on Form 1125-A or elsewhere on return (attach Form 4562) . .	20	
	21	Depletion	21	
	22	Advertising	22	
	23	Pension, profit-sharing, etc., plans	23	
	24	Employee benefit programs	24	
	25	Reserved for future use	25	
	26	Other deductions (attach statement)	26	
	27	**Total deductions.** Add lines 12 through 26 . . . . . . ▶	27	
	28	Taxable income before net operating loss deduction and special deductions. Subtract line 27 from line 11. .	28	
	29a	Net operating loss deduction (see instructions) 29a		
	b	Special deductions (Schedule C, line 24) 29b		
	c	Add lines 29a and 29b	29c	
Tax, Refundable Credits, and Payments	30	**Taxable income.** Subtract line 29c from line 28. See instructions	30	
	31	Total tax (Schedule J, Part I, line 11)	31	
	32	2020 net 965 tax liability paid (Schedule J, Part II, line 12) . .	32	
	33	Total payments, credits, and section 965 net tax liability (Schedule J, Part III, line 23)	33	
	34	Estimated tax penalty. See instructions. Check if Form 2220 is attached . . . . ▶ ☐	34	
	35	**Amount owed.** If line 33 is smaller than the total of lines 31, 32, and 34, enter amount owed	35	
	36	**Overpayment.** If line 33 is larger than the total of lines 31, 32, and 34, enter amount overpaid	36	
	37	Enter amount from line 36 you want: **Credited to 2021 estimated tax** ▶ _____ Refunded ▶	37	

Sign Here

Under penalties of perjury, I declare that I have examined this return, including accompanying schedules and statements, and to the best of my knowledge and belief, it is true, correct, and complete. Declaration of preparer (other than taxpayer) is based on all information of which preparer has any knowledge.

▶ _____ _____ ▶ _____
Signature of officer   Date   Title

May the IRS discuss this return with the preparer shown below? See instructions. ☐ Yes ☐ No

Paid Preparer Use Only

Print/Type preparer's name	Preparer's signature	Date	Check ☐ if self-employed	PTIN
Firm's name ▶			Firm's EIN ▶	
Firm's address ▶			Phone no.	

For Paperwork Reduction Act Notice, see separate instructions.

Cat. No. 11450Q

Form **1120** (2020)

S CORPORATIONS

An **S corporation** is normally created under state law by first forming a C corporation and then filing an "S" election with the IRS. The incorporation is normally the same as for a C corporation. There are, however, significant ways in which an S corporation differs from a C corporation.

Interest, Disposal of Interest, and Dissolution

Like a C corporation, the ownership interests in an S corporation are held by shareholders and are evidenced by shares of stock. Transferability of shares may be restricted by shareholders agreement.

Capital

It is easier to raise capital in an S corporation than in a proprietorship or partnership because of the limited liability protection but the limited number of allowable shareholders may have a negative affect on the ability to raise capital. The IRC does, however, allows close family members to be treated as a single shareholder.

> ### ≔ *Key Concepts*
>
> 1. Explain how an S corporation differs from a C corporation.
>
> 2. Discuss the advantages and disadvantages of an S corporation.

Liability

An S corporation offers the same limited liability protection as a C corporation or an LLC.

Management/Operations

Corporations are managed by one or more officers appointed by the board of directors. The board of directors is the governing body of a corporation. The board of directors appoints various officers to run the corporation. The board of directors acts (or should act) in a very formal way and is required under the corporate charter to meet and follow certain formalities. Observing corporate formalities and maintaining good standing with the Secretary of State in the state of incorporation is an ongoing requirement.

The number of shareholders of an S corporation is limited to 100 and the S corporation can only have one class of stock. LLCs, partnerships, and other corporations are prohibited from becoming S corporation shareholders. Additionally, non-resident aliens and most trusts may not be S corporation shareholders.

Income Taxation and Payroll (Social Security) Taxes

The income of an S corporation is passed through to shareholders and is not taxed at the corporation level. Therefore, an S corporation provides many of the benefits of a corporation without any double taxation of income earned by the corporation.

The owner/employees of S corporations are employees for payroll tax purposes. Therefore, the entity withholds 7.65 percent of the employees' pay for Social Security taxes and matches such withholding for Social Security taxes. The owner/employee compensation is not considered self-employment income. Additional distributions to shareholders beyond reasonable compensation are treated as dividends not subject to payroll tax.

Since the income of an S corporation is taxed to the shareholders for the year in which it is earned, dividend distributions to shareholders are normally not subject to income tax at the time they are distributed. Stated differently, S corporation dividends normally represent the distribution of income that has previously been taxed to the shareholder.

As indicated in the C corporation discussion, in-kind distributions of appreciated assets will be treated as a deemed sale; thus, such distributions will generate a capital gain in the case of an S corporation to all shareholders in proportion to their ownership even if the asset was only distributed to one shareholder.

Generally, S corporations file Form 1120S (**Exhibit 13.18**) on a calendar year basis and provide each shareholder with a Form 1120S Schedule K-1 (**Exhibit 13.19**).

S Corporation Owners' Basis

The S corporation owner's initial basis is generally the amount of cash paid for the shares or value of property contributed to the corporation. In a manner similar to partnership basis adjustments, the stock basis of an S corporation owner will be adjusted each year based on the flow-through of income or loss, as well as distributions. Income and additional capital contributions increase basis while losses, deduction items, charitable contributions, and distributions decrease basis. Unlike partnership basis, an S corporation shareholder's basis will increase for amounts the shareholder loans to the corporation, but not for a guarantee of a loan made to the corporation by a third party. Additional rules regarding adjustments to S corporation stock basis can be rather complex, and are beyond the scope of this textbook.

> ### ☑ Quick Quiz 13.9
>
> 1. The number of S corporation shareholders is limited to 100.
>   a. True
>   b. False
>
> 2. All payments from an S corporation to an S corporation shareholder will be treated as income subject to payroll taxes.
>   a. True
>   b. False
>
> True, False.

Exhibit 13.17 | Advantages and Disadvantages of S Corporations

Advantages
• Income is passed through to the shareholders for federal income tax purposes
• Income is taxed at the individual level which may be a lower tax rate than the applicable corporate rate
• Shareholders have limited liability
• Distributions from S corporations are exempt from the payroll tax system, assuming the corporation provides adequate compensation to those shareholders who are employees of the corporation

Disadvantages
• Limited to 100 shareholders
• Only one class of stock is permitted
• Cannot have corporate, partnership, certain trust, or nonresident alien shareholders
• Shareholder employees owning more than two percent of the company must pay taxes on a range of employee fringe benefits that would be tax-free to a shareholder/employee of a C corporation
• The tax rate of the individual shareholder may be higher than the corporate tax rate
• Borrowing may be difficult without stockholder personal guarantees, which negates part of the advantage of limited liability

Exhibit 13.18 | Form 1120S

Form **1120-S**	**U.S. Income Tax Return for an S Corporation**	OMB No. 1545-0123
Department of the Treasury Internal Revenue Service	▶ Do not file this form unless the corporation has filed or is attaching Form 2553 to elect to be an S corporation. ▶ Go to *www.irs.gov/Form1120S* for instructions and the latest information.	20**20**

For calendar year 2020 or tax year beginning _____, 2020, ending _____, 20____

A S election effective date	**Name**	**D** Employer identification number
B Business activity code number (see instructions)	TYPE OR PRINT Number, street, and room or suite no. If a P.O. box, see instructions.	**E** Date incorporated
C Check if Sch. M-3 attached ☐	City or town, state or province, country, and ZIP or foreign postal code	**F** Total assets (see instructions) $

G Is the corporation electing to be an S corporation beginning with this tax year? ☐ Yes ☐ No   If "Yes," attach Form 2553 if not already filed

H Check if: **(1)** ☐ Final return   **(2)** ☐ Name change   **(3)** ☐ Address change   **(4)** ☐ Amended return   **(5)** ☐ S election termination or revocation

I Enter the number of shareholders who were shareholders during any part of the tax year . . . . ▶ _____

J Check if corporation: **(1)** ☐ Aggregated activities for section 465 at-risk purposes   **(2)** ☐ Grouped activities for section 469 passive activity purposes

Caution: Include **only** trade or business income and expenses on lines 1a through 21. See the instructions for more information.

Income	**1a** Gross receipts or sales	1a	
	b Returns and allowances	1b	
	c Balance. Subtract line 1b from line 1a	1c	
	2 Cost of goods sold (attach Form 1125-A)	2	
	3 Gross profit. Subtract line 2 from line 1c	3	
	4 Net gain (loss) from Form 4797, line 17 (attach Form 4797)	4	
	5 Other income (loss) (see instructions—attach statement)	5	
	6 **Total income (loss).** Add lines 3 through 5 . . . . ▶	6	
Deductions (see instructions for limitations)	**7** Compensation of officers (see instructions—attach Form 1125-E)	7	
	8 Salaries and wages (less employment credits)	8	
	9 Repairs and maintenance	9	
	10 Bad debts	10	
	11 Rents	11	
	12 Taxes and licenses	12	
	13 Interest (see instructions)	13	
	14 Depreciation not claimed on Form 1125-A or elsewhere on return (attach Form 4562)	14	
	15 Depletion **(Do not deduct oil and gas depletion.)**	15	
	16 Advertising	16	
	17 Pension, profit-sharing, etc., plans	17	
	18 Employee benefit programs	18	
	19 Other deductions (attach statement)	19	
	20 **Total deductions.** Add lines 7 through 19 . . . . ▶	20	
	21 **Ordinary business income (loss).** Subtract line 20 from line 6	21	
Tax and Payments	**22a** Excess net passive income or LIFO recapture tax (see instructions) . . .	22a	
	b Tax from Schedule D (Form 1120-S)	22b	
	c Add lines 22a and 22b (see instructions for additional taxes)		22c
	23a 2020 estimated tax payments and 2019 overpayment credited to 2020 . .	23a	
	b Tax deposited with Form 7004	23b	
	c Credit for federal tax paid on fuels (attach Form 4136)	23c	
	d Reserved for future use	23d	
	e Add lines 23a through 23d		23e
	24 Estimated tax penalty (see instructions). Check if Form 2220 is attached . . . . . ▶ ☐		24
	25 **Amount owed.** If line 23e is smaller than the total of lines 22c and 24, enter amount owed . .		25
	26 **Overpayment.** If line 23e is larger than the total of lines 22c and 24, enter amount overpaid . .		26
	27 Enter amount from line 26: **Credited to 2021 estimated tax ▶** **Refunded ▶**		27

Sign Here	Under penalties of perjury, I declare that I have examined this return, including accompanying schedules and statements, and to the best of my knowledge and belief, it is true, correct, and complete. Declaration of preparer (other than taxpayer) is based on all information of which preparer has any knowledge. ▶ _____ ▶ _____ Signature of officer Date Title	May the IRS discuss this return with the preparer shown below? See instructions. ☐ Yes ☐ No

Paid Preparer Use Only	Print/Type preparer's name	Preparer's signature	Date	Check ☐ if self-employed	PTIN
	Firm's name ▶			Firm's EIN ▶	
	Firm's address ▶			Phone no.	

For Paperwork Reduction Act Notice, see separate instructions.   Cat. No. 11510H   Form **1120-S** (2020)

Exhibit 13.19 | Form 1120S Schedule K-1

671120

☐ Final K-1	☐ Amended K-1

OMB No. 1545-0123

Schedule K-1
(Form 1120-S)
Department of the Treasury
Internal Revenue Service

2020

For calendar year 2020, or tax year

beginning ___ / ___ / 2020   ending ___ / ___ / ___

Shareholder's Share of Income, Deductions, Credits, etc.

▶ See separate instructions.

Part I	**Information About the Corporation**

A Corporation's employer identification number

B Corporation's name, address, city, state, and ZIP code

C IRS Center where corporation filed return

Part II	**Information About the Shareholder**

D Shareholder's identifying number

E Shareholder's name, address, city, state, and ZIP code

F Current year allocation percentage .   .   . _____ %

G Shareholder's number of shares
    Beginning of tax year . . . . . . _____
    End of tax year . . . . _____

H Loans from shareholder
    Beginning of tax year . . . . . $ _____
    End of tax year . . . . $ _____

For IRS Use Only

Part III	**Shareholder's Share of Current Year Income, Deductions, Credits, and Other Items**	
1 Ordinary business income (loss)	**13** Credits	
2 Net rental real estate income (loss)		
3 Other net rental income (loss)		
4 Interest income		
5a Ordinary dividends		
5b Qualified dividends	**14** Foreign transactions	
6 Royalties		
7 Net short-term capital gain (loss)		
8a Net long-term capital gain (loss)		
8b Collectibles (28%) gain (loss)		
8c Unrecaptured section 1250 gain		
9 Net section 1231 gain (loss)		
10 Other income (loss)	**15** Alternative minimum tax (AMT) items	
11 Section 179 deduction	**16** Items affecting shareholder basis	
12 Other deductions		
	17 Other information	
18 ☐ More than one activity for at-risk purposes*		
19 ☐ More than one activity for passive activity purposes*		

* See attached statement for additional information.

For Paperwork Reduction Act Notice, see the Instructions for Form 1120-S.   www.irs.gov/Form1120S   Cat. No. 11520D   **Schedule K-1 (Form 1120-S) 2020**

Comparison of S Corporations and LLCs

Many business owners know that they want limited liability and a flow-through tax entity, but cannot distinguish between an S corporation and a LLC (taxed as a partnership). Below is a side-by-side comparison of these two very important entity types.

Exhibit 13.20 | Comparison of S Corporations and LLCs (Taxed as a Partnership)

	S Corporation	LLC / Partnership
Double taxation	No	No
Pass through tax losses	Yes	Yes
Availability of preferred return for certain investors (1 class of stock in S)	No	Yes
Partnerships, corporations, and trusts can be entity owners	No	Yes
Foreign investors	No	Yes
Distribute in-kind appreciated assets to owners without gain recognition	No	Yes
Ability to transfer interest to trust for estate planning	No	Yes
Low filing fees	Yes (Generally)	No
Self-employment tax on all income for owner/ employees	No	Yes (Generally)
Limited number of owners	Yes (100)	No
Owner's basis for deductibility of losses includes pro-rata share of loans to entity by third parties	No	Yes
The law is well settled pertaining to the entity	Yes	No
Filing date with extensions	September 15th	September 15th

Exhibit 13.21 | Entity Comparison

	Proprietorship	General Partnership	Limited Partnership	LLP	FLP	LLC	S Corp.	C Corp.
Cost to create (money & time)	Low	Medium	Medium-High	High	High	High	High	High
Personal liability of investors for enterprise debt	Yes	Yes	No (if limited partner)	Yes	Yes	No	No	No
Annual state filing requirement	No	Generally Not	Yes	Yes	Yes	Yes	Yes	Yes
Maximum owners	One	Unlimited	Unlimited	Unlimited	Unlimited	Unlimited	100	Unlimited
Owners are known as	Owner	Partner	Partner or Limited Partner	Partner or Limited Partner	Partner or Limited Partner	Member	Shareholder	Shareholder
Tax filing alternatives	Schedule C 1040	Form 1065 K-1 flows to Schedule E of Form 1040	Form 1065 K-1 flows to Schedule E of Form 1040	May file as corporation or partnership	Form 1065 K-1 flows to Schedule E of Form 1040	If one member, entity is disregarded and owner files Schedule C of Form 1040. If two or more members, choice of Form 1065 (Partnership), Form 1120-S (S Corporation), or Form 1120 (C Corporation)	Form 1120S K-1 to shareholders	Form 1120
Federal Tax ID required	No	Yes	Yes	Yes	Yes	No, if one member Yes, if two or more members	Yes	Yes
Taxation concept	Individual	Flow Through	Flow Through	Flow Through	Flow Through	Flow Through	Flow Through	Entity
Owners income	Self Employment	Self employment but limited partners/members are not subject to Soc. Sec. tax unless they perform personal services for the entity	Self employment but limited partners/members are not subject to Soc. Sec. tax unless they perform personal services for the entity	Self employment but limited partners/members are not subject to Soc. Sec. tax unless they perform personal services for the entity	Self employment but limited partners/members are not subject to Soc. Sec. tax unless they perform personal services for the entity	Depends on filing choice, but limited partners/members are not subject to Soc. Sec. tax unless they perform personal services for the entity	W-2 and ordinary income. Excess profits distributed are not subject to Soc. Sec. tax	W-2 and dividend income

THE QUALIFIED BUSINESS INCOME (QBI, OR SEC. 199A) DEDUCTION

Introduction

One of the primary objectives of the Tax Cuts and Jobs Act (TCJA 2017) was to lower tax rates on businesses. For the years leading up to its enactment, many businesses were discontinuing operations in the United States and moving those operations overseas due to tax and cost considerations. Many businesses also engaged in corporate inversions, which were designed to remove the business entity itself outside of the U.S. to avoid high taxes on corporate income. In the years before 2018, U.S. Corporate tax rates, especially when combined with the taxes imposed on dividend distributions from corporations to their shareholders, were among the highest in the world.

TCJA 2017 achieved its objective of reducing tax burdens on corporations by lowering the corporate tax rate from a marginal rate structure with rates as high as 35 percent to a flat 21 percent tax rate. Many members of Congress were concerned about the potential disparity this would cause between corporate and pass-through business entities which would have been subjected to tax on business income at personal tax rates (up to 37%), and sought to make sure that pass-through business entities enjoyed similar tax rates to corporations. The result was the Qualified Business Income (QBI, or Sec. 199A) deduction, which permits sole proprietors and owners of pass-through business entities (as described previously) up to a 20 percent deduction on qualified business income. The QBI deduction does not lower adjusted gross income (AGI), which means it is not an above-the-line deduction, and can be taken regardless of whether a taxpayer itemizes deductions. By enacting the QBI deduction, TCJA created a new form of below-the-line deduction - a below the line deduction that can be taken in addition to the greater of the taxpayer's itemized or standard deduction.

While an exhaustive review of the QBI deduction is beyond the scope of this text, a basic understanding of its application is important for financial professionals.

Qualified Business Income

Sec. 199A defines **qualified business income (QBI)** as the net amount of qualified items of income, gain, deduction, and loss with respect to any trade or business (sole proprietorships, partnerships, limited partnerships, limited liability companies, limited liability partnerships, and S corporations) within the United States that is included or allowed to be included in determining taxable income for the year.

Since the purpose of the new deduction was to lower the tax rate on business income, certain types of income are excluded from the definition of QBI, including:
- Capital gains and losses
- Dividends
- Interest not allocable to a trade or business
- Commodities transactions
- Reasonable compensation for S corporation owners
- Guaranteed payments to partners for services rendered

Special rules concerning the determination of QBI also clarify that guaranteed payments for the use of capital, net operating losses, and income associated with a trade or business performing services as an employee are not attributable to the trade or business for the purposes of calculating the deduction.

The QBI Deduction General Rule

For a taxpayer owning an interest in only one pass-through business entity, the QBI deduction equals the lesser of (1) 20 percent of the qualified business income of the taxpayer, or (2) 20 percent of the taxpayer's adjusted taxable income. The taxpayer's adjusted taxable income equals taxable income from all sources (after taking above-the-line deductions - excluding the deductions related to the business for self-employment tax, self-employed health insurance premiums, and self-employed retirement plan contributions, and taking either the standard or itemized deductions), including the spouse's income if married filing jointly, reduced by net capital gains.

For example, if the taxpayer's share of qualified business income from a partnership is $90,000, and the taxpayer's total adjusted taxable income from all sources (after taking above-the-line deductions not related to the business, and either the standard or itemized deduction, but before taking the 20 percent deduction for QBI) is $70,000, the deduction is the lesser of: (1) 20% x $90,000, or (2) 20% x 70,000; which limits the deduction to $14,000. On the other hand, if the taxpayer's share of qualified business income from a partnership is $90,000, and the taxpayer's total adjusted taxable income from all sources (after taking above-the-line deductions not relating to the business and either the standard or itemized deduction, but before taking the 20 percent deduction for QBI) is $110,000, the deduction is the lesser of: (1) 20% x $90,000, or (2) 20% x 110,000; which limits the deduction to $18,000.

The QBI deduction is phased down for taxpayers with taxable income above specified levels, and, in some cases, for businesses that are classified as specified service trades or businesses (SSTBs).

Specified Service Trades and Businesses (SSTBs)

Specified Service Trades and Businesses (SSTBs), sometimes referred to as "out of favor" service businesses, will be subject to a phase-down of the QBI deduction once the taxable income of the business owner reaches certain amounts.

The Code specifies that trades or business involving performance of services in the fields of health, law, accounting, actuarial services, consulting, performing arts, athletics, financial services, investing, investment management, trading or dealing in securities (including partnership interests and commodities) and any trade or business where the principal asset of the business is the reputation or skill of one or more of its owners are SSTBs.

Specifically excluded from the definition of SSTBs are businesses that provide engineering and architectural services.

Deduction Phase-Down and Transition

Taxpayers who qualify to claim the QBI deduction are subject to either a phase-down or transition of the deduction amount depending upon their taxable income from all sources (without regard to the Sec. 199A deduction, but including the spouse's income if MFJ). There are two taxable income tiers which will determine the amount of the deduction: The threshold amount, and the phaseout amount.

Exhibit 13.22 | QBI Threshold & Phaseout Amounts (2021)

Filing Status	Threshold Amount	Phaseout Amount
MFJ	$329,800	$429,800
All Others	$164,900	$214,900

All taxpayers with taxable income below the threshold amount are eligible to claim a QBI deduction for business income regardless of whether or not that income was derived from a SSTB. Once the taxpayer's income exceeds the threshold amount, the deduction is phased-down until the taxpayer's taxable income reaches the phaseout amount. Once taxable income reaches the phaseout amount, income from SSTBs no longer qualifies for the QBI deduction, and income from businesses which are not SSTBs are subject to an alternate calculation that takes into consideration the wages paid by the business and the business' unadjusted basis in its depreciable property to determine the amount of the deduction.

Planning Applications

While detailed calculations of the QBI (or Sec. 199A) deduction are beyond the scope of this text, financial professionals should be aware of the threshold and phaseout amounts that qualify or deny a taxpayer this deduction. Generally speaking, all taxpayers with taxable income less than $329,800 (MFJ) or $164,900 (all other filing statuses) in 2021 will qualify for the QBI (Sec, 199A) below-the-line deduction. The deduction begins to phase out above these amounts, and is completely phased out above the Phaseout thresholds discussed above for SSTBs. Taxpayers who have income close to the threshold and phase-in amounts may wish to engage in tax planning to make sure they can qualify for this deduction.

Tax Analysis: C Corporation versus Pass-Through Entity with QBI Deduction

The net result of the QBI deduction is to reduce the tax rate on qualified business income by 20 percent. For example, for a taxpayer in the highest marginal bracket (37% in 2021), the tax on the deductible amount of qualified business income is effectively reduced to 29.60% (37% x (1 - 0.20) = 29.60%).

Even though corporate earnings are subject to double taxation, there is still some potential for income tax reduction as a result of incorporating a business. Taxpayers in the higher marginal income tax brackets may want to incorporate a profitable business as a C corporation to take advantage of the lower tax rate of 21 percent on corporate taxable income.

By creating a separate tax entity, the owners can take advantage of the lower tax rate, as well as the special tax breaks available to corporations. The tax savings can be retained and reinvested in the company for growth. If the company is sold later, the gains will be taxed at the same favorable capital gains rates that apply to dividends, or may qualify for exclusion under Section 1202.

When flow-through entities retain earnings, those earnings are still taxed to the owners even when no distribution is made. When a C corporation retains earnings, however, those earnings are taxed only to the entity, relieving the owners of paying tax on that retained income. For this reason, a profitable business that retains earnings for growth is a good candidate for incorporation as a C corporation.

If earnings are expected to be distributed, the comparison becomes complicated by the Section 199A qualified business income deduction. The earnings of sole proprietorships, partnerships, and S corporations are taxed directly to the participating individual or individuals at their marginal tax rate, which may be as high as 37 percent (a net rate of 29.6% on the business income if the pass-through income is fully eligible for the Sec. 199A qualified business income deduction). C corporation income is taxed at a flat 21 percent, although the double taxation when distributed must also be considered if it is likely that distributions will be made. If dividends are distributed to an owner in the highest marginal tax bracket, the combined corporate tax, dividend rate, and 3.8 percent Medicare tax will be 39.80 percent [0.21 + ((1-0.21)(0.238))]. An analysis of an individual's situation will be required in order to determine the most favorable tax treatment, as well as to evaluate other features of the various entities. If losses are expected, the flow-through entities will generally be more advantageous because the business losses can offset an owner's income from other sources.

PROTECTING OWNERS FROM EACH OTHER

As the old saying goes "there is risk in the future." The choice of entity provides certain advantages and disadvantages to the partner, member, or shareholder. However, there are certain recurring situations where a little forethought could have prevented a bad result. Some of these situations are unexpected events like death or disability of an owner, divorce, bankruptcy, retirement, or a voluntary or involuntary disassociation with the entity.

Each individual owner faces the above risks. In entities where there are multiple owners, a written shareholder agreement, partnership agreement, or operating agreement addressing the listed issues and any others that are of concern should be considered.

Protecting Minority Shareholders/Members

A minority shareholder or member who is also an employee should have two different types of protection from termination by having an employment agreement (rather than being an employee at will) and should also have a shareholder agreement with a buyout provision in the event of termination.

Elements of Shareholder/Partnership Agreements

For each risk there should be a method provided for valuing the entity and funding the departing owner's interest. For example:

- For the first five years, a voluntary departing owner gets nothing.
- After five years, a voluntary departing owner is entitled to his proportional share. The company shall be valued at 1.5 times the average revenues for the three previous years.
- If an owner is terminated for cause, the company shall be valued at 50 percent of the average annual revenue for the last three years.

It is not enough to identify the risk and calculate the valuation; a funding method must also be provided. While cross purchase or entity life insurance may work for untimely death, life insurance does not work for voluntary termination. A payout over time that will not burden the remaining owners and entity may be a solution. Whatever the solution, it needs to be clearly articulated in the shareholder agreement, the operating agreement, or the partnership agreement.

Issues Regarding Additional Capital Required

In the situation where multiple owners have made a certain initial investment into a business enterprise, there is always the chance that additional capital will be needed. What happens if one of the investors refuses to pay his proportional share of such new capital? Can the partners or shareholders compel the unwilling owner to pay? At the outset of an entity the initial owners should prepare an analysis of the risks of needing additional capital (e.g., debt service is certain). If additional capital is likely or even possibly needed, the joint owners should prepare for it. One option is to have all owners put up a negotiable letter of credit for a reasonable period of time to assure cash calls will be met. Additionally, a provision should be put in the partnership agreement, shareholder agreement, or operating agreement to the effect that any owner who defaults on a cash call obligation automatically forfeits his original investment and such default makes the letter of credit immediately due and payable.

DISCUSSION QUESTIONS

SOLUTIONS to the discussion questions can be found exclusively within the chapter. Once you have completed an initial reading of the chapter, go back and highlight the answers to these questions.

1. What are the different types of legal entities from which a business owner can conduct business?

2. How is a general partnership taxed?

3. What are the differences between a a general and a limited partnership?

4. How do different types of business entities differ from each other with regard to the personal liability of owners for business obligations?

5. How is a C corporation taxed?

6. What type of business entity should be chosen if the owners expect losses in the first few years and the owners want limited personal liability?

7. How is a limited liability company taxed if it has one or more owners?

8. Compare an S corporation to a limited liability company.

9. How can an entity avoid having a court "pierce the veil?"

10. Why is it often difficult to dispose of an interest in a partnership?

11. What is the principal disadvantage of the general partnership arrangement?

12. How does the limited partnership arrangement affect an entity's ability to raise capital?

13. Define "checking the box."

14. How is a family limited partnership usually formed?

15. What are the risks associated with the taxation of an FLP?

16. What is an operating agreement and why is it important to have this document?

17. What are some of the advantages of a corporation?

18. What are some of the disadvantages of an S corporation?

19. Describe the purpose and general calculation of the Qualified Business Income deduction.

MULTIPLE CHOICE PROBLEMS

A sample of multiple choice problems is provided below. Additional multiple choice problems are available at money-education.com by accessing the Student Practice Portal.

1. An architect performed services for Edith and Archie and, in lieu of her normal fee, accepted a 10 percent interest in a partnership with a fair market value of $10,000. How much income from this arrangement should the architect report on her income tax return?
    a. The architect does not have any currently taxable income.
    b. The architect has realized $10,000 in capital gains.
    c. The architect must recognize $10,000 in compensation income.
    d. The architect has realized $10,000 in compensation income, but does not have to recognize it until she sells her interest in the partnership.

2. Which of the following statements is/are true?
    1. Partnerships offer limited liability protection to partners.
    2. LLCs offer limited liability protection to members.

    a. 1 only.
    b. 2 only.
    c. Both 1 and 2.
    d. Neither 1 nor 2.

3. Which entity does <u>not</u> have all of the following characteristics?
    1. Limited liability.
    2. Ability to distribute in-kind appreciated assets to owners without gain recognition.
    3. Can have foreign investors.

    a. LLC.
    b. S corporation.
    c. Limited partnership.
    d. LLP.

4. Which entity will meet the following requirements?
    1. Disregarded entity.
    2. Limited liability.
    3. Self-employment tax on all income.

    a. Partnership.
    b. Single-member LLC.
    c. S corporation.
    d. Proprietorship.

5. Which of the following can file as a corporation or partnership?
    a. LLC and LLP.
    b. LLC only.
    c. LLP only.
    d. LLC and S corporation.

> **Additional multiple choice problems are available at**
> ***money-education.com* by accessing the Student Practice Portal. Access requires registration of the title using the unique code at the front of the book.**

QUICK QUIZ EXPLANATIONS

Quick Quiz 13.1
1. True.
2. False. To avoid piercing the veil, the entity should keep books and records separate from the personal books and records of the owners, segregate activities of business from personal affairs, follow corporate formalities such as meeting requirements and filings, and address all content in contracts and correspondence from the viewpoint of the business entity (rather than the viewpoint of the owners).

Quick Quiz 13.2
1. False. A proprietorship may be required to obtain a local business license or register with the state or local taxing authority if it will be collecting sales tax.
2. True.
3. True.

Quick Quiz 13.3
1. False. General partnerships are governed by the laws of the state in which they are formed.
2. False. A principal disadvantage of the general partnership arrangement is that all general partners in a partnership are jointly and severally liable for the debts and obligations of the partnership.
3. True.

Quick Quiz 13.4
1. True.
2. False. Limited partnerships offer limited liability for the limited partners. The general partners run the business and are exposed for personal liability.

Quick Quiz 13.5
1. True.
2. False. If the LLP is comprised of only licensed professionals, transfer of an interest will usually be more difficult because such interest may only be transferred to another similarly licensed professional.

Quick Quiz 13.6
1. False. Only a general partner can manage a family limited partnership.
2. False. Upon creation of the partnership (FLP), there are neither income nor gift tax consequences because the entity created (the limited partnership and all of its interests, both general and limited) is owned by the same person, or persons, who owned it before the transfer.

QUICK QUIZ EXPLANATIONS

Quick Quiz 13.7
1. True.
2. True.

Quick Quiz 13.8
1. False. The corporation's purpose may be broad (e.g., to engage in any lawful activity) or specific (e.g., to sell textbooks).
2. True.

Quick Quiz 13.9
1. True.
2. False. Additional distributions to shareholders beyond reasonable compensation are treated as dividends not subject to payroll tax. In-kind distributions of appreciated assets will be treated as a deemed sale; thus, such distributions will generate a capital gain in the case of an S corporation to all shareholders in proportion to their ownership even if the asset was only distributed to one shareholder.

14
ESTATE PLANNING

LEARNING OBJECTIVES

1. Define estate planning.
2. List and discuss the goals, objectives, and risks of estate planning.
3. Describe the estate planning process.
4. Identify the basic documents included in an estate plan including wills, side letters, powers of attorney and appointment, and directives regarding healthcare.
5. Clearly differentiate between limited and general powers.
6. Compare and contrast the most common types of titling property (sole ownership, joint tenancy with rights of survivorship, tenants in common, tenants by the entirety, and community property.*
7. Describe the probate process, its advantages, disadvantages, and costs.*
8. Understand the difference between testate and intestate succession.
9. Identify the common duties of an executor and/or administrator.
10. Describe the use of trusts in estate planning.
11. Describe the federal estate and gift tax system.
12. Describe the characteristics of a gift, the valuation of gifts, and exclusions and exemptions associated with gifts.
13. Discuss a basic understanding of the estate tax system.

Ties to CFP Certification Learning Objectives

INTRODUCTION

Many philosophers and great thinkers have contemplated the inevitability of death and taxes. Benjamin Franklin is known for his famous saying that "in this world nothing is certain but death and taxes." Despite Mr. Franklin's words of wisdom, there is often uncertainty when it comes to both death and taxes. While no one likes to plan for death, the fact remains that no one lives forever. Unless we prepare for our deaths, there is uncertainty as to where our assets and liabilities will end up when we die. The best way to eliminate some of that uncertainty is through a properly prepared estate plan that incorporates planning for the accumulation, protection, and disposition of wealth.

Estate planning is complex. Among other things, it is about planning for risks, including the risks of untimely death, ill health, artificially sustaining life, inability to manage property, immaturity of heirs, and application of state intestacy rules that may be totally inconsistent with a person's end of life transfer wishes. In large measure, estate planning is about the transfer of property, either during life or at death, the methods of effecting those transfers, and the risks associated with those transfers. It is also about the process of growing old, or not, and the planning for financial consequences of each possible outcome, as well as providing the greatest assistance (financial and otherwise) for loved ones left behind.

If we knew exactly what we would face in the future, we would arrange our financial affairs, prepare our families and loved ones, get our financial records in order, identify who is to receive what property, advise our relatives what to do if we are unable to make our own decisions, select someone to make critical healthcare decisions for us, confide in someone about our funeral and burial wishes, select someone to care for our children, provide for our children's education, and provide for our spouse. We would evaluate whether we could, in good conscience, leave money or property outright to particular heirs or whether we need to have someone else protect them from themselves and others.

Estate Planning Defined

Estate planning may be broadly defined as the process of accumulation, management, conservation, and transfer of wealth considering legal, tax, and personal objectives. Estate planning is financial planning in anticipation of a client's inevitable death. The goal of estate planning is the effective and efficient transfer of assets. An **effective transfer** occurs when a person's assets are transferred to the person or institution intended by that person. An **efficient transfer** occurs when transfer costs are minimized consistent with the greatest assurance of effectiveness. Some estate planning experts define estate planning more narrowly to include only conservation and transfer, ignoring the accumulation factor in the broader definition above.

≔ Key Concepts

1. What is estate planning?
2. Explain the differences between an efficient and effective transfer.
3. What are the common goals of estate planning?

GOALS, OBJECTIVES, AND RISKS OF ESTATE PLANNING

Common goals and objectives of estate planning include:

- Transferring (distributing) property to particular persons or entities consistent with client wishes.
- Minimizing taxes (income, gift, estate, state inheritance, and generation-skipping transfer taxes).
- Minimizing transaction costs associated with the transfer (costs of documents, lawyers, accountants, and the probate process, which is the legal process of changing title to the decedent's assets from the decedent to the heirs and legatees). Note: An **heir** is a person who inherits under state law, whereas a **legatee** is a person named in a will. Within this chapter the term "heir" will be used to include both heirs and legatees.
- Maximizing the transfer of assets to heirs; providing for guardianship.
- Providing the estate of the decedent with sufficient liquidity to pay for costs that commonly arise upon or around one's death, such as taxes, funeral expenses, and final medical costs.

Exhibit 14.1 | Estate Planning Goals and Objectives

- Fulfill client's property transfer wishes
- Minimize transfer taxes
- Minimize transfer costs
- Maximize net assets to heirs
- Provide for guardianship
- Provide needed liquidity at death
- Fulfill client's healthcare decisions

Everyone needs a basic estate plan to address health care issues, property management, and the ultimate transfer of property according to their wishes. Typically, the most important estate planning objective is to assure that the decedent's property is transferred to the person, persons, or entities consistent with the decedent's wishes.

The risks associated with failing to plan for an estate transfer include the transfer of property contrary to the client's wishes, insufficient financial provision for the client's family, and the emergence of liquidity problems at the time of death. Any one of these risks could be catastrophic for the decedent's heirs and family.

Exhibit 14.2 | Risks in Failing to Plan an Estate

- Client's property transfer wishes go unfulfilled.
- Transfer taxes are excessive.
- Transfer costs are excessive.
- Client's family not properly provided for financially.
- Insufficient liquidity to cover client's debts, taxes, and costs at death.

THE ESTATE PLANNING PROCESS

The Seven Basic Steps

There are seven basic steps in the estate planning process:

1. Gather and analyze the information necessary to understand the client's personal and financial circumstances, including the client's current financial statements and existing estate planning documents.
2. Identify and select the client's transfer objectives, including family and charitable objectives.
3. Analyze the client's current estate plan and potential alternative courses of action.
4. Develop a comprehensive plan of transfers consistent with all information and objectives.
5. Present the estate planning recommendations.
6. Implement the estate planning recommendations.
7. Review the estate plan periodically and update the plan when necessary (especially for changes in family situations).

The first two steps will be discussed in this chapter and the remaining steps generally follow the financial planning process covered earlier in the text.

Establish the Client/Planner Relationship

Preliminary to the seven-step estate planning process, the relationship between the client and planner must be established and defined. The client / planner relationship may arise in several different ways, but clients are often reluctant to seek out a planner to plan their estate. This reluctance may stem from several causes including concern about the expense associated with estate planning, the belief that estate planning is only for the extremely wealthy, or the desire to avoid the inevitability of the client's own mortality. Therefore, the opportunity to discuss the issue of estate planning generally arises when the planner is meeting with the client for financial planning matters other than estate planning.

Key Concepts

1. Identify the risks associated with failing to plan for estate transfer.

2. Identify the seven basic steps of the estate planning process.

3. What is usually the most important estate planning client objective?

The estate planning engagement is the same as any other financial planning engagement. The planner should meet with the client, detail the services to be provided, and the expectations of both the client and the planner. The financial planner should then send an engagement letter to the client detailing the information discussed in the meeting.

Collecting Client Information and Defining Transfer Objectives

Collecting a client's information is essential to gain a complete financial and family picture of the client and to assist the client in identifying their financial risks. Information about prospective heirs and legatees needs to be collected to properly arrange for any transfer the client wants to make.

To begin the estate planning process, the planner should collect:
- Current financial statements (Statement of Financial Position, Income Statement).
- A detailed list of assets and liabilities, including, for each asset, the fair market value, adjusted basis, expected growth rate, how title is being held, and the date acquired.
- Family information - information about parents and children, including the age and health of each family member.
- Copies of medical, disability, and long-term care insurance policies.
- Copies of all current life insurance policies identifying the owner of each policy, the named insured, and the designated beneficiaries.
- Copies of annuity contracts.
- Copies of wills and trusts.
- Identification of powers of attorney and general powers of appointment.
- Copies of all previously filed income tax, gift tax, and estate tax returns.
- Identification of assets previously transferred to loved ones.

After collecting the client and family information, the client's transfer objectives must be determined. Usually the client's most important objective is to transfer his assets as he wishes (an effective transfer). Next, the client generally wishes to maximize the net transfers to his heirs while minimizing the reduction in his or her estate due to taxes and transfer costs. **Exhibit 14.3** provides a list of common transfer objectives.

Exhibit 14.3 | Common Transfer Objectives

1. Transfer property as desired and minimize estate and transfer taxes to maximize the assets received by heirs.
2. Avoid the probate process.
3. Use lifetime transfers – gifts.
4. Meet liquidity needs at death.
5. Plan for children.
6. Plan for the incapacity of the transferor.
7. Provide for the needs of the transferor's surviving spouse.
8. Fulfill the transferor's charitable intentions.

BASIC DOCUMENTS INCLUDED IN AN ESTATE PLAN

Effective estate planning usually requires the execution of some basic estate planning documents. These documents effectuate the transfer of property at the death of the testator, grant powers to others for both property and health care decisions, and direct doctors and hospitals on matters concerning the artificial sustenance of life. The basic documents that are used in estate planning include:

- wills
- side letters of instruction
- powers of attorney for property
- durable powers of attorney for health care
- living wills or advance medical directives
- do not resuscitate orders

Wills

A **will** is an essential part of any estate plan. A will is a legal document that gives the **testator** (will-maker) the opportunity to control the distribution of his property at death and thus avoid his state's intestacy laws (the distribution scheme provided by each state for those individuals that die without a valid will). A will may be amended or revoked by the testator at any time prior to his death provided that the testator is competent. In addition, the provisions of a will are not invoked until the death of the testator. Any assets that do not automatically transfer upon the testator's death under state contract laws, state property titling law, or state trust law (such as retirement benefits with a designated beneficiary, jointly owned property, and life insurance policies) will become part of the probate estate, which is normally distributed according to the will. The will is the voice of the decedent directing how probate assets should be administered and distributed through the probate process.

Types of Wills

In most states, the only requirements necessary to execute a valid will are that the will:

1. must be in writing
2. must be signed at its logical end by the testator

The three basic forms of wills are statutory, holographic, and nuncupative. While most wills are statutory wills (professionally drafted by an attorney), some states continue to recognize the other two types of wills.

- **Statutory wills** are drawn by an attorney, and comply with the statutes for wills of the domiciliary state (the state in which the testator has made their home, is registered to vote, files their state income taxes, etc.). Statutory wills are generally witnessed and attested. Statutory wills must be typed or be in writing, be signed by the testator (generally in front of witnesses), and be signed by the witnesses. Typically, a statutory will includes a self-proving affidavit which aids in the institution of probate proceedings when the testator dies.

- **Holographic wills** are handwritten (not typed) by the testator and include the material provisions of a will. The holographic will must be dated and signed by the testator, but most states do not require a witness. Holographic wills are valid in most states.
- **Nuncupative wills** are oral, dying declarations made before a sufficient number of witnesses. In some states, nuncupative wills may only be effective to pass personal property, not real property, and the dollar amount transferred by this method may be limited. The use of nuncupative wills is restrictive and is not valid in most states. In states where such wills are permitted, the witnesses must generally submit an affidavit declaring the testator's final wishes.

Side Instruction Letter

Another separate document from the will, the **side instruction letter**, or personal instruction letter, details the testator's wishes regarding the disposition of specific tangible possessions (such as household goods), as well as funeral and burial wishes. The side instruction letter exists separately from the will, to avoid cluttering the will with small details that may create conflicts among heirs and is not binding in the probate process. In many states, burial is required before probate can begin, and the side letter of instruction gives specific instructions to the heirs. This letter, which is given to the executor, may contain information regarding the location of important personal documents, safe deposit boxes, outstanding loans, and other personal and financial information that the executor will use to administer the decedent's estate. While the letter has no legal standing, the executor will generally carry out the wishes of the decedent.

> ### 🗐 *Key Concepts*
>
> 1. What is a power of attorney?
> 2. Identify and discuss the parties to a power of attorney.
> 3. What is a durable power of attorney for health care and why are they used?
> 4. What is a living will and why are they used?
> 5. What is a DNR and why are they used?

Powers of Attorney and Powers of Appointment

Power of Attorney

People frequently need a trusted person to make decisions or sign papers for them regarding their property or health. A **power of attorney** is a legal document that authorizes a trusted person to act on one's behalf. It grants a right to one person, the **attorney-in-fact** (sometimes called the power holder or agent), to act in the place of the other person, the **principal** (the grantor of the power). Generally, any person who is legally capable to act for himself may act as an attorney-in-fact for another. The principal must have reached the age of majority, defined in most states as 18 years old, and be legally competent in order to grant the power. All powers are revocable by the principal and all powers granted cease at the principal's death.

General Power of Attorney

The broadest power a person can give another is a general power of attorney. The person who is given the power of attorney will be able to act in the principal's place as though he is the principal. Essentially the general power of attorney gives the agent the power to do anything that the principal could do. The general power of attorney may be revoked by the principal by giving notice, usually with a revocation form, to the agent and is automatically revoked at the principal's death.

Limited Power of Attorney

A limited power of attorney, also referred to as a special power of attorney, gives the agent very specific, detailed powers. The power granted in a limited power of attorney may be extremely narrow, only authorizing the agent to act on a specific matter. For example, if the principal were purchasing a new home and was unable to attend the actual closing because he was out of the country, he can give a power of attorney to someone else specifically authorizing them to sign his name at the act of sale. Other uses for a limited power of attorney include situations where a principal gives an agent the authority to act on his behalf to pay his bills, or handle a specific business transaction.

Exhibit 14.4 | Graphical Depiction of Powers of Attorney

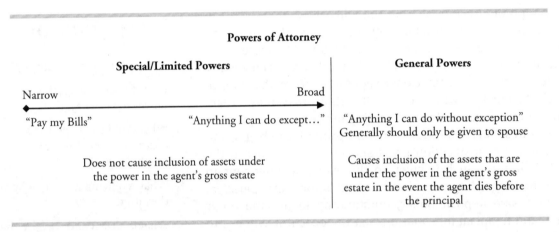

Power of Appointment

A power of appointment is sometimes included in a power of attorney. A **power of appointment** is a power to appoint the assets of one person to another and may be either general or limited.

General Power of Appointment

A general power of appointment allows the holder of the power the opportunity to appoint the property, subject to the power, to himself, his creditors, his estate, or his estate's creditors. If the agent dies before the principal and is holding a general power of appointment over assets of the principal, the agent's gross estate will include the fair market value of the principal's assets over which the agent held the power of appointment regardless of whether the power has been invoked. Therefore, a general power of appointment should be granted sparingly and with forethought.

Limited Power of Appointment

Like a general power of appointment, a limited power of appointment is the power to affect the beneficial enjoyment of property. Unlike a general power of appointment, a limited power of appointment is limited in some way. One of the ways in which a power of appointment can be limited is by the application of an ascertainable standard. According to the Internal Revenue Code, a power is limited by such a standard if the extent of the holder's duty to exercise and not to exercise the power is reasonably measurable in terms of his needs for health, education, maintenance, or support (or any combination of them). If a power of appointment is limited by an ascertainable standard, then the property subject to the power will not be includible in the gross estate of the power holder. Furthermore, the use of an ascertainable standard allows the principal to give the power holder the ability to appoint assets to himself without creating a general power of appointment.

Example 14.1

Jack gives Diane the power to appoint the $1,000,000 in his bank account to herself or her mother. Jack has given Diane a general power of appointment. If Diane dies while holding the power of appointment, the $1,000,000 bank account will be included in her gross estate.

Example 14.2

Jack gives Diane the power to appoint the $1,000,000 in his bank account to herself or to her mother, but only for educational expenses. Even though Diane can appoint the assets to herself (which would usually create a general power of appointment), she has a limited power of appointment because she is limited by the fact that the assets can only be used for educational expenses. Therefore, if Diane dies while holding the power, the value of Jack's bank account will not be included in her gross estate.

Exhibit 14.5 | Graphical Depiction of Powers of Appointment

Powers of Appointment

Limited Power

General Power

Narrow   Broad

"Property may be appointed to our children Doug and Betty"

Ascertainable Standard

"Property may be appointed to the power holder (agent) for health, education, maintenance, or support"

"Property may be appointed to anyone except the power holder (agent), the holder's estate, the holder's creditors, or the creditors of the holder's estate"

A general power of appointment exists if the property may be appointed to any one of the following: 1) the holder (agent), 2) the holder's estate, 3) the holder's creditors, or 4) the creditors of the holder's estate. The ability to appoint the property to oneself essentially gives the holder (agent) complete control over the property (e.g., may appoint to self then gift or bequeath to anyone they choose).

> Does not cause inclusion of the assets under the power in the holder's (agent's) gross estate

> Causes inclusion of the assets under the power in the holder's (agent's) gross estate in the event the holder dies before the grantor (principal)

Exhibit 14.6 | Power of Attorney vs. Power of Appointment

Power of Attorney	Power of Appointment
• A stand alone document that allows an agent to act for the principal and may include the power to appoint assets	• A power, usually included in a trust or power of attorney, allowing the power holder to direct assets to another
• Power to act	• Power to transfer assets
• Ends at the death of the principal	• May survive the death of the grantor
• May be general or limited	• May be general or limited
• May be revoked at any time by the principal	• May be revoked by the principal during life or at death (via last will and testament)

Directives Regarding Health Care

Directives regarding health care are probably the most controversial and difficult documents to discuss with your client. Individuals tend to have strong feelings regarding their health care and the ability of others to make health care decisions for them. This section discusses some of the alternative documents available in most states.

Durable Power of Attorney for Health Care

A **durable power of attorney for health care**, also called a medical power of attorney or health care proxy, is a legal document that appoints an agent (someone with authority to act on behalf of another) to make health care decisions on behalf of a principal who is unable to make those decisions for him/herself. Unlike the living will, which states the person's wishes regarding the sustainment of life, the durable power of attorney for health care puts health care decision making in the hands of a third person.

The durable power of attorney for health care may provide direction in terminal and nonterminal situations, such as disclosure of medical records, blood transfusions, cardiac resuscitation, organ transplants, and selection of medical support staff, but generally does not provide the right to end life-sustaining treatment. (Note that in some states a power of attorney for health care may provide the right to withhold or end life-sustaining treatment.) The durable power of attorney for health care eliminates the necessity of petitioning a local court to appoint a guardian to make health care decisions for a person who is incapacitated or disabled.

Living Wills/Advance Medical Directives

A **living will**, also known as an **advance medical directive** or in some states, a Natural Death Declaration or Instruction Directive, is not a will at all, but rather a legal document expressing an individual's last wishes regarding sustainment of life under specific circumstances. The living will establishes the medical situations and circumstances in which the individual no longer desires life-sustaining treatment in the event he is no longer capable of making those decisions. The document only covers a narrow range of situations, and is usually limited to decisions concerning administering artificial life support treatments when there is no reasonable expectation of recovery from extreme physical or mental disability. Almost every state has legislation in place that disregards the living will if the patient is pregnant.

The purpose of the living will is to allow individuals who are terminally ill to die on their own terms, or as it has been coined, "die with dignity." Many states have adopted Natural Death Acts stating that the withholding or discontinuance of any extraordinary means of keeping a patient alive, or the withholding or discontinuance of artificial nutrition and hydration, shall not be considered the cause of death for any civil or criminal purpose, nor shall it be considered unprofessional conduct, thus allowing terminal individuals the right to choose the healthcare provided to them.

The living will is also used to avoid the expense of sustaining life artificially and thus to preserve assets for the decedent's heirs. The living will is prepared in advance of an illness to: (1) explicitly state the client's wishes, and (2) avoid the necessity for heirs to seek court approval for life-sustaining or termination decisions. The document, though authorized in all states, must meet the specific requirements of the individual's state statute. If the document is not drafted by a competent attorney, problems may arise with vagueness or ambiguities in drafting. Some states have developed a computerized registry of those who have filed living wills so if a person is alive solely because of life-sustaining treatments, the institution providing care can determine if the document exists, and thus comply with the wishes of the registrants. In addition, privately administered national registries have also increased in popularity in the wake of the highly publicized case of Terri Schiavo in 2005.[1] Schiavo's case highlights the importance of having a living will regardless of age or current health.

Do Not Resuscitate Order (DNRs)

Individuals may also have a document called a "**DNR**" which stands for **Do Not Resuscitate**. These documents declare the principals wish to avoid having cardiopulmonary resuscitation (CPR) performed in the event their heart stops beating. This is not generally prepared as part of an overall estate plan unless the individual is already terminally ill. These types of orders are generally prepared once an individual has already been admitted to the hospital and is near death, and are commonly used by patients with advanced cancer or kidney damage, or patients suffering from significant ailments relating to old age.

DNRs are generally executed on a form provided by the state and may be filed with the patient's medical records. Some states also provide statewide registries allowing these documents to be placed on file for easy access. Some states provide medical bracelets to patients with DNRs that have been sent home to spend their remaining days. The bracelet notifies emergency personnel of the individual's wish to decline CPR.

It is crucial to understand that DNRs only apply to CPR and do not apply to any other medical treatment. DNRs are not sufficient to avoid other life sustaining treatment. As the application of DNRs vary by state, a thorough understanding of the individual state law is imperative when working with DNRs.

---

1. The Terri Schiavo case was a 15-year struggle involving whether to extend life support after being diagnosed by multiple physicians as being in a persistent vegetative state. Her husband wanted to remove Terri's feeding tube, while her parents fiercely contested this action. Terri suffered cardiac arrest in 1990, cutting off oxygen to her brain and was kept alive until March 2005. This case illustrates the importance of having a living will.

TYPES OF PROPERTY INTEREST

Ownership and Transfer of Property

In our legal system, all property interests are classified into one of three categories: (1) real property, (2) tangible personal property, or (3) intangible personal property. **Real property** (realty) includes land and anything permanently attached to the land (such as buildings, trees, and items permanently affixed to buildings, called fixtures). **Tangible personal property** consists of all property that is not realty (not affixed to the land and generally movable) and that has physical substance. **Intangible personal property** is property that is not real property and is without physical substance (such as stocks, bonds, patents, and copyrights). Some types of property require a state title as proof of ownership. Examples of titled property include real estate, automobiles (assuming the state has a motor vehicle title law), stocks, bonds, bank accounts, and retirement accounts. Other property, such as household goods, may not have a specific title. State law determines the forms of ownership interest available as well as the ways in which property interests can be transferred from one person to another during lifetime or at death.

Sole Ownership - Fee Simple

Sole ownership is the complete ownership of property by one individual who possesses the property fee simple, meaning all ownership rights associated with the property, including the right to use, sell, gift, alienate, convey, or bequeath the property. The key characteristic of **fee simple** ownership is that the owner has the unfettered right to transfer his ownership interest in the property during lifetime (gift, sale) or at death by a will. Fee simple ownership is the most common way to own property interests today both by a sole owner and by joint owners. It consists of the maximum rights that an owner can have.

The ability to use, consume, or dispose of one's property in the form of fee simple is often referred to as fee simple absolute. The entire fair market value of the property interest is included in the owner's gross estate for federal estate tax purposes. When a person dies owning property in sole ownership, that property is passed to the decedent's heirs (or whomever else the decedent specifies) through the probate process by virtue of the will or, where no will exists, by virtue of the state's intestacy laws. If, however, real property is located in a state that is not the **residence domiciliary** (decedent's state of residence) of the decedent, it will be subject to **ancillary probate** (probate in a state where the owner is not domiciled) in the state of situs.

When someone owns property in sole ownership, they can mortgage that property and use it in any way they desire. Of course, jurisdictional restrictions may place reasonable limits on the use of property. For example, if someone owns land in the middle of an urban area, certain zoning laws may prohibit the owner from using the land to hunt, conduct outdoor concerts, or engage in other types of activities that could endanger others or interfere with the rights other people have to the quiet enjoyment of their own property.

Exhibit 14.7 | Sole Ownership (Fee Simple) Summary

Number of Owners	Only 1
Right to Transfer	Freely
Automatic Survivorship Feature	No, transfers at death via will or intestacy laws
Included in the Gross Estate[1]	Yes, 100%
Included in the Probate Estate[2]	Yes, 100%

1. The "gross estate" is used to determine the value of property that will be subject to federal estate taxes.
2. The "probate estate" consists of property that is transferred as directed in the will or by state intestacy law, and must be retitled.

Tenancy in Common (TIC)

Tenancy in common is an interest in property held by two or more related or unrelated persons. Each owner is referred to as a tenant in common. Tenancy in common is the most common type of joint ownership between nonspouses. Each person holds an undivided, but not necessarily equal, interest in the entire property. Each co-owner does not own a designated portion of the property, instead he owns an interest in the entire property.

For example, if Jim and Bill own a two story home together, Jim does not own the top floor and Bill does not own the bottom floor. Instead, they each own a percentage of the entire house, and both are entitled to use the entire property.

Exhibit 14.8 | Tenancy in Common Ownership Summary

Number of Owners	2 or more
Right to Transfer	Freely without the consent of other co-tenants
Automatic Survivorship Feature	No, transfers at death via will or intestacy laws
Included in the Gross Estate	Usually the FMV of ownership percentage
Included in the Probate Estate	Yes, fair market value of interest
Partitionable	Yes, with or without consent of joint owner

Joint Tenancy with Right of Survivorship (JTWROS)

Joint tenancy is an interest in property held by two or more related or unrelated persons called joint tenants. Each person holds an undivided, equal interest in the whole property. Each joint tenant shares equally in the income and expenses of the property in proportion to his interest.

A right of survivorship is normally implied with this form of ownership, and at the death of the first joint tenant, the decedent's interest transfers to the other joint tenants outside of the probate process according to state titling law. Because of this right of survivorship, joint tenancy is often called joint tenancy with right of survivorship (JTWROS).

Exhibit 14.9 | Joint Tenancy with Right of Survivorship Ownership Summary

Number of Owners	2 or more
Right to Transfer	Freely without consent
Automatic Survivorship Feature	Yes, transfers at death to other owners
Included in the Gross Estate	Yes, FMV times the % contributed
Included in the Probate Estate	No
Partitionable	Yes, with or without consent of joint owner

Tenancy by the Entirety (TE)

Tenancy by the entirety is very similar to joint tenancy between spouses. To understand this form of ownership it is important to remember the following four key components:

1. Tenancy by the entirety applies to joint ownership only between married couples.
2. Neither tenant is able to sever their interest without the consent of the other tenant (spouse).
3. Property ownership interest is automatically transferred to the surviving spouse upon death.
4. It may involve the ownership interest of either real or personal property.

In most respects, tenancy by the entirety is simply a JTWROS that can only occur between spouses. Tenancy by the entirety exists throughout the length of the marriage and terminates upon divorce or death. Upon divorce, the tenancy by the entirety form of ownership ceases to exist, thus transforming the ownership interests of both parties to some form of joint ownership, usually tenants in common.

In most states, neither tenant (spouse) is able to sever their interest in property titled tenancy by the entirety without the consent of the other tenant (spouse). If either spouse wishes to transfer their share of interest in the property to a third party (through sale or gift), both parties must join (or consent) in a mutual transfer of the property. This stipulation helps to prevent any termination of the other spouse's right of survivorship by transfer of property to a third party. In such cases, the interest in the property between the remaining tenant (spouse) and the new third party owner becomes a joint tenancy or tenancy in common. Spouses may choose to convert their tenancy by the entirety ownership into a tenancy in common or a joint tenancy. The form of property ownership is simply changed without triggering any gift tax consequences.

Exhibit 14.10 | Tenancy by the Entirety Ownership Summary

Number of Owners	2 - spouses only
Right to Transfer	Need consent of other spouse
Automatic Survivorship Feature	Yes, transfers at death to other spouse
Included in the Gross Estate	Yes, always 50% of FMV
Included in the Probate Estate	No
Partitionable	Not without consent of spouse / joint owner

Community Property and Separate Property in Community Regimes

Community property is a civil law originating statutory regime under which married individuals own an equal undivided interest in all property accumulated during their marriage. During marriage, the income of each spouse is considered community property. Property acquired before the marriage and property received by gift or inheritance during the marriage retains its status as separate property. However, if any separate property is commingled with community property, it is often assumed to be community property. The states following the community property regime are Arizona, California, Idaho, Louisiana, Nevada, New Mexico, Texas, Washington, and Wisconsin. In addition, Alaska allows residents and nonresidents to enter into community property agreements permitting in-state property to be treated as community property. Community property regimes may vary slightly from state to state; thus, a thorough understanding of a client's state laws is needed for proper planning.

Exhibit 14.11 | Community-Property States

Community property does not usually have an automatic right of survivorship feature although some states, including Texas and California, have a survivorship option. When the first spouse dies, one half of the value of the property will pass through the probate process for retitling per the direction of the decedent's will or the state intestacy law. Each spouse's one-half interest will also be included in their own federal gross estate.

THE PROBATE PROCESS DEFINED

When a person dies, there are many things the survivors must do. Relatives and friends must be notified, funeral and burial arrangements must be made, and the survivors must begin to rebuild their lives without the decedent. After facing the emotional distress that naturally occurs upon the death of a loved one, the survivors must evaluate their financial security and the process of transferring the decedent's assets from the decedent's estate to the heirs. Surviving heirs need a method to obtain clear legal title to property inherited from the decedent. The **probate process** is the legal process through which the decedent's assets that are not automatically transferred to their

> ### Key Concepts
>
> 1. Define the probate process.
> 2. List the elements of a gift.
> 3. How much can an individual transfer, gift tax-free, each year?
> 4. What is the lifetime gift tax applicable exclusion amount?

heirs by contract law, titling law, or trust law, are retitled in the name of the heirs. The probate process can be defined as the legal proceeding that serves to prove the validity of an existing will, supervise the orderly distribution of a decedent's assets to the heirs, assure heirs that they receive clear title, and protect creditors by insuring that valid debts of the estate are paid prior to distribution of assets to heirs.

Testate vs. Intestate Succession

The preparation of the will is often considered the first step in an overall estate plan, since it expresses some or all of the decedent's transfer wishes regarding property. In theory, every person who dies has an estate plan. If the decedent did not establish his own estate plan by executing a will, the state in which he is domiciled has created one for him under the state intestacy laws. The state intestacy laws specify to whom assets will be transferred for a person who does not validly transfer assets by will, contract law, state titling law, or trust law.

A person who dies with a valid will is said to die testate, whereas a person who dies without a valid will is said to die intestate. A person named in a will to receive property is referred to as a legatee, while a person who receives property under the state intestacy laws is called an heir. In addition, the term devisee is used to refer to a person who inherits real property under the will. Historically, the term heir was reserved only for those individuals who received property under the intestacy laws, but the term is now used more widely to include heirs, legatees and devisees and may refer to any individual who inherits property from the decedent, even under a will. A planner should understand these distinctions since there are legal differences in some states, but realize that clients and non-professionals may not always use the technical terminology appropriately.

Advantages of Probate

Transferring assets through the probate process has several advantages over transferring assets outside of probate. The central advantage to the probate process is the protection of the individuals involved in the probate process. The advantaged parties include the decedent, the decedent's legatees and creditors. The following is a discussion of the more common advantages of the probate process.

Exhibit 14.12 | Advantages of Probate (Summary)

1. Implements disposition objectives of testator.
2. Provides for an orderly administration of assets.
3. Provides clean title to heirs or legatees.
4. Increases the chance that parties of interest have notice of proceedings and, therefore, a right to be heard.
5. Protects creditors by insuring that debts of the decedent are paid.

Disadvantages of the Probate Process

The probate process also has certain disadvantages. While the advantages of probate center around protecting individuals, the disadvantages center around the losses individuals may face. The losses include time (delays), money (costs), and privacy (publicity).

Exhibit 14.13 | Disadvantages of Probate (Summary)

1. Can be complex and excruciatingly slow - Delays
2. Can result in substantial monetary costs - Costs
3. The process is open to public scrutiny - Publicity

Property Passing Through Probate

Property passing through probate includes property that can be disposed of by a will, such as sole ownership property, the decedent's share of property held as tenancy in common, and the decedent's share of community property.

Property Passing Outside of the Probate Process

Property that passes outside of the probate process includes property that passes by state contract law, state property titling law, and state trust law. All of these transfers reduce the probate estate and therefore reduce probate transaction costs, reduce the time it takes for property to pass through probate, and may improve liquidity for the named heirs and legatees.

Exhibit 14.14 | Common Duties of Executor and/or Administrator

When the Decedent Dies Testate (with a will)	When the Decedent Dies Intestate (without a will)
The Executor: • Locates and proves the will • Locates witnesses to the will • Receives letters testamentary from court	The Administrator: • Petitions court for his or her own appointment • Receives letters of administration • Posts the required bond
Duties of the Executor or Administrator	
• Locates and assembles all of the decedent's property • Safeguards, manages, and invests property • Advertises in legal newspapers that the person has died and that creditors and other interested parties are on notice of the death and opening of probate • Locates and communicates with potential beneficiaries of the decedent • Pays the expenses of the decedent • Pays the debts of the decedent • Files both federal and state income, fiduciary, gift tax, and estate tax returns (such as Forms 1040, 1041, 709, and 706 for federal tax purposes) and makes any required tax payments • Distributes remaining assets to beneficiaries according to the will or to the laws of intestacy • Closes the estate formally or informally	

TRUST PROPERTY

Trusts are used in estate planning to provide for the management of assets and flexibility in the operation of the plan. Most trusts, other than charitable trusts, provide great flexibility by allowing the trustee to make decisions based on criteria set forth in the trust document by the grantor. This flexibility can be particularly important when the trust arrangement will last for an extended period of time. The basic structure of a trust is depicted by the following exhibit.

Exhibit 14.15 | Basic Trust Structure

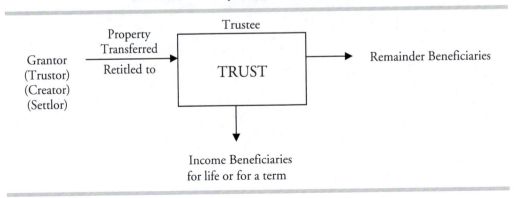

A **trust** is a structure that vests legal title to assets in one party, the trustee, who manages those assets for the benefit of others, the beneficiaries of the trust. The beneficiaries hold the beneficial, or equitable, interest in the trust. By dividing the ownership rights into two parts (legal and equitable), a trust can be a useful tool in managing both the property and the tax consequences attached to the transfer of property.

⋮☰ *Key Concepts*

1. Identify the parties to a trust.
2. Identify at least three reasons to use a trust.

To form a trust, a grantor of a trust transfers (retitles) money or other property to the trustee. The money or property transferred is referred to as the trust principal, corpus, res, or fund. The trust principal will be managed by the trustee to accomplish the grantor's objectives as expressed in the detailed provisions of the trust document.

Parties

The three parties to a trust agreement are the grantor, the trustee, and the beneficiaries. The **grantor** is the person who creates and initially funds the trust. The **trustee** is the individual or entity responsible for managing the trust assets and carrying out the directions of the grantor that are formally expressed in the trust instrument. The **beneficiary** is the person (or persons) who holds the beneficial title to the trust assets. While the beneficiary's name does not appear on the deed to the trust assets, the trustee must manage the assets in the best interests of the beneficiary and is upheld to a fiduciary standard.

Why Use a Trust?

Management

In addition to using a trust to avoid probate, a principal reason for establishing a trust is to provide for the management of the trust property. Not everyone is adept at managing assets. A person not experienced in handling wealth may squander it or invest imprudently. A trust can be used to provide professional management of assets for individuals who are not suited, by training or experience, to manage assets for themselves.

Example 14.3

Charlotte thinks of herself as the world's foremost expert in the fields of financial planning and money management. Her husband and children have relied on her to manage all of the family finances. Instead of leaving her property outright to her family when she dies, Charlotte can transfer the property into a trust, name professional money managers as trustees, and they will manage the money for her husband and children based on the investment guidelines intended in the trust documents.

Creditor Protection

When asked, most individuals would say they would rather receive an outright transfer of money than a transfer in trust. This statement is often based on the belief that with an outright transfer, they will have complete control over the assets and can use the assets in a way that will maximize their utility. If, however, an outright transfer of assets is made, creditors of the recipient (judgment creditors or otherwise) will have access to those funds to satisfy outstanding obligations.

If property is placed in a trust with appropriate spendthrift protection provisions instead of being transferred outright, the creditors of the beneficiary will not be able to access the funds in the trust to satisfy outstanding creditor claims. A spendthrift clause, coupled with a provision that allows the trustee to make distributions solely on a discretionary basis, is a very strong and effective asset protection tool. The **spendthrift clause** simply states that the beneficiary may not anticipate distributions from the trust, and may not assign, pledge, hypothecate, or otherwise promise to give distributions from the trust to anyone and, if such a promise is made, it is void and may not be enforced against the trust. Most states enforce spendthrift clauses, since the property in trust never belonged to the beneficiary and the beneficiary cannot be sure that he will ever receive discretionary distributions from the trustee. In some states, claims for spousal or child support can be obtained from a trust despite the presence of a spendthrift clause.

Example 14.4

Dory, a registered nurse, always wanted her children to enter the medical profession. None of her children became physicians, but her grandson, Marlin, decided to go to medical school. Understanding the malpractice dilemma faced by physicians, Dory decided she wanted to protect any property that would pass during her lifetime, or at her death, to Marlin from Marlin's creditors. She created a trust that named Marlin as the discretionary income beneficiary for life and upon Marlin's death, would distribute the trust corpus to Marlin's children in equal shares, per stirpes. The trust included a spendthrift clause. If a malpractice claim is filed against Marlin, the assets in the trust will not be available to satisfy those claims. If the trust purchases assets for Marlin's use instead of making distributions to Marlin, those assets will also be protected. Note that if Dory had not used a trust, any assets that she transferred to Marlin directly would be subject to malpractice claims.

FEDERAL ESTATE AND GIFT TAXES

The federal government uses a linked set of taxes on estates, gifts, and generation-skipping transfers to tax transfers of wealth from one generation to the next and to limit the extent to which wealth can be given away during life to avoid taxation at death. Federal taxes on transfers of wealth at death have been enacted in various forms since 1797, initially to raise revenue during crisis or war, and have been modified periodically over time.[1] The United States has collected revenues from the current form of the tax, an estate tax, since 1916. A gift tax, first introduced in 1924, prevents wealthy individuals from avoiding the estate tax by transferring wealth while they are alive.

---

1. Congressional Budget Office May 2019 supplement to Update and Budget Projections 2019 - 2029.

Federal transfer taxes have historically made up a relatively small share of total federal revenues, accounting for one percent to two percent of total revenues in most of the past 60 years. The Congressional Budget Office (CBO) projects that, under current law, federal revenues from estate and gift taxes will be $265 billion, or less than 0.1 percent of total revenues, over the 2020–2029 period.

THE GIFT TAX SYSTEM

Historical Background and Purpose

The **gift tax** is an excise tax on the right to transfer assets gratuitously to another person during life. Like the federal estate tax, the gift tax exists as a method of raising revenue for the federal government and functions as a method of social reallocation of wealth by taxing wealth transferred from one generation to subsequent generations. The gift tax is paid from the taxpayer's wealth to the federal government and thus is reallocated to other members of society through social programs and other expenditures of the federal government.

Introduction to Gifts

While the gift tax system is replete with rules, exceptions, and exemptions, the overall scheme of gift taxation can be understood by asking four basic questions:
1. Disregarding all other factors, is the transfer a taxable gift?
2. Is the gift nontaxable because of an available exemption, exclusion, or due to legislative grace?
3. If the gift is taxable, what is the tax due and how is it reported?
4. Is the gift appropriate considering the objectives and goals of donor and donee?

Characteristics of a Gift

The first step in the gift tax system is to determine if a transfer is a gift. This section covers the elements and types of gifts.

Parties

There are two parties involved in a gift transfer. The **donor** is the person who makes the gift. The **donee** is the person who receives the gift.

Definition of a Gift

A **gift** is a voluntary transfer, for less than full consideration, of property from one person (a donor) to another person or entity (a donee).

Elements of a Gift

In general, the elements of a gift are:
1. The donor must have the intent to make a voluntary transfer.
2. The donor must be competent to make the gift.
3. The donee must be capable of receiving the gift.
4. The donee must take delivery.
5. The donor must actually part with dominion and control over the gifted property.

Valuation of a Gift

The value of a gift for gift tax purposes is equal to the fair market value of the gifted property on the date of the gift. For real estate and closely-held businesses, an appraisal is usually necessary to determine the fair market value of the property. Publicly-traded securities are valued at the average of the high and low trading price for the day.

Exclusions and Exemptions

Once a transfer is determined to be a gift, the donor should determine whether an exclusion or exemption applies making the transfer a nontaxable transfer.

The Annual Exclusion

All individuals may gift transfer-tax-free, up to $15,000 for 2021 per donee per year to a related or unrelated party, under an exemption known as the **annual exclusion**. The annual exclusion is an effective wealth transfer tool that can be used to reduce a person's taxable estate over several or many years. It can be used to transfer many types of property, including interests in real property, trusts, and family limited partnerships. To qualify for the annual exclusion, the gift must be of a present interest, allowing the donee an unrestricted right to the immediate use of the property. A beneficiary who receives income from a trust has a present interest in the income, but a beneficiary entitled only to the remainder of a trust at some point in the future has a future interest that does not qualify for the gift tax annual exclusion.

There is a special annual exclusion for non-citizen spouses equal to $159,000 (as indexed) for 2021. In addition to the annual exclusion, each person has a $11,700,000 lifetime applicable gift tax exclusion (2021). The $11,700,000 exclusion can be used to transfer wealth during life or upon death. Transfers during life that are taxable gifts are reported to the IRS on Form 709.

ESTATE TAX

When a citizen of the United States dies, his estate may be subject to the estate tax if it is sizable enough. As mentioned above, the lifetime exemption is currently $11,700,000 (2021). Therefore, an individual is permitted to transfer up to $11,700,000 during life and death without incurring transfer tax. Transfers above the $11,700,000 level will incur a transfer tax, whether during life or at death.

The **estate tax** is imposed when the sum of the decedent's taxable estate and lifetime gifts exceeds the $11,700,000 level. The decedent's taxable estate is the difference between the gross estate (all property owned by the decedent at death) and various deductions. Lifetime gifts are added to the taxable estate in the determination of the estate tax.

The estate tax applies to both citizens and residents of the United States and to nonresidents of the United States. For U.S. citizens and residents, estate tax is imposed on worldwide assets. Non-U.S. citizens and non-U.S. residents only pay estate tax on assets located within the United States.

Generation-skipping transfer tax (GSTT) is an additional transfer tax that is imposed on transfers that skip a generation. The purpose of this tax is to prevent a transfer from the first generation to the third generation allowing for transfer tax to be avoided at the second generation.

As with gift tax and estate tax, there is a lifetime GST exemption of $11,700,000 (2021) that allows a taxpayer to transfer up to $11,700,000 to a third or fourth generation person without incurring the additional transfer tax. In addition, the annual exclusion also applies to generation-skipping transfers. Therefore, a gifting strategy can be implemented to transfer wealth to "skip persons" using the annual exclusion and thereby avoiding both gift tax and GST tax.

A "skip person" is either a natural person assigned to a generation that is two or more generations below the generation assignment of the transferor, or a trust, if all the interests in the trust are held by skip persons.[1]

GSTT is imposed at a flat rate equal to the highest federal estate tax rate, currently 40 percent and is added to the value of a gift in determining the gift tax calculation.

Example 14.5

Will wants to transfer $11,700,000 in 2021 to Jada, who is Will's great granddaughter. Will has already used his lifetime GST exemption and already transferred the annual exclusion amount to Jada earlier in the year, Will would have to pay $11,232,000 calculated as follows:

GST tax = $11,700,000 x 40% = $4,680,000 [$11,700,000+ $4,680,000 = $16,380,000]

Gift tax = $16,380,000 x 40% = $6,552,000 (GSTT adds to the gift. Will is assumed to be at the top rate for gift tax.)

Total transfer tax = $11,232,000 (GST tax plus gift tax)

Properly leveraging one's GST lifetime exemption can result is large transfers to lower generations while avoiding a significant amount of transfer tax.

---

1. IRC Section 2613.

ESTATE PLANNING LIMITS

Update for Estate, Gifts, and GST Tax

- There was no estate or generation-skipping transfer (GST) tax for 2010. There is an $11,700,000 exemption for 2021.
- The gift, estate, and GST tax rate is 40%.
- The annual gift tax exclusion is $15,000 per donee, per donor for 2021.
- The lifetime gift exemption is $11,700,000 for 2021.
- The credit equivalency for the gift exemption is $4,625,800 for 2021.[1]

Exhibit 14.16 | Gift and Estate Tax Rate Schedule

If the amount with respect to which the tentative tax to be computed is	The tentative gift/Estate tax is:
Not over $10,000	18% of such amount
Over $10,000 but not over $20,000	$1,800, plus 20% of the excess over $10,000
Over $20,000 but not over $40,000	$3,800, plus 22% of the excess over $20,000
Over $40,000 but not over $60,000	$8,200 plus 24% of the excess over $40,000
Over $60,000 but not over $80,000	$13,000 plus 26% of the excess over $60,000
Over $80,000 but not over $100,000	$18,200 plus 28% of the excess over $80,000
Over $100,000 but not over $150,000	$23,800 plus 30% of the excess over $100,000
Over $150,000 but not over $250,000	$38,800 plus 32% of the excess over $150,000
Over $250,000 but not over $500,000	$70,800 plus 34% of the excess over $250,000
Over $500,000 but not over $750,000	$155,800 plus 37% of the excess over $500,000
Over $750,000 but not over $1,000,000	$248,300 plus 39% of the excess over $750,000
Over $1,000,000	$345,800 plus 40% of the excess over $1,000,000

---

1. Credit equivalency: $345,800 + 40% x ($11,700,000 - $1,000,000) = $4,625,800.

DISCUSSION QUESTIONS

SOLUTIONS to the discussion questions can be found exclusively within the chapter. Once you have completed an initial reading of the chapter, go back and highlight the answers to these questions.

1. Define estate planning.
2. What is an effective transfer?
3. What is an efficient transfer?
4. List three common goals of estate planning.
5. Discuss some of the risks associated with failing to plan for estate transfer.
6. List the seven basic steps of the estate planning process.
7. What is usually the most important client objective?
8. List the basic documents used in estate planning.
9. Briefly define the types of wills.
10. What is a living will?
11. What is a power of attorney?
12. Identify and discuss the parties to a power of attorney.
13. List and define the three major types of property.
14. List at least three types of property ownership.
15. Define sole ownership (fee simple property ownership).
16. Define tenancy in common.
17. Define joint tenancy.
18. Define right of survivorship.
19. Can a joint tenancy be partitioned?
20. Define community property.
21. Which states recognize community property?
22. Describe the probate process.
23. Describe at least three advantages and three disadvantages of the probate process.
24. Why are trusts used in estate planning?
25. What is a trust?
26. List the common parties of a trust.
27. What is a spendthrift clause and why is it included in a trust?
28. List the elements of a gift.

MULTIPLE-CHOICE PROBLEMS

A sample of multiple choice problems is provided below. Additional multiple choice problems are available at money-education.com by accessing the Student Practice Portal.

1. Which of the following is included in the definition of estate planning?
   1. Asset management.
   2. Accumulation of wealth.
   3. Asset preservation.
      a. 1 only.
      b. 1 and 2.
      c. 2 and 3.
      d. 1, 2, and 3.

2. Which of the following does not need estate planning?
      a. Ross, age 30, married with two minor children, and a net worth of $375,000.
      b. Rachel, age 35, never been married, one son with a severe disability.
      c. Monica, age 45, single, has a net worth of $450,000 and two dogs.
      d. All of the above need estate planning.

3. Which type of will is handwritten and does not generally require a witness?
      a. Holographic.
      b. Oral.
      c. Nuncupative.
      d. Statutory.

4. Maxine is terminally ill. Her doctors gave her twenty-four months to live thirty-six months ago. Maxine has decided that she does not want to be placed on life support. Which document will direct Maxine's doctors to refrain from putting her on life support?
      a. Living will.
      b. Power of attorney.
      c. Durable power of attorney.
      d. General power of appointment.

5. Which of the following are advantages of allowing property to pass through the probate process?
   1. Assets do not need to be retitled if they pass though probate.
   2. There are limitations on creditors' time to make claims against the estate.
   3. There is stricter supervision of the disposition and management of assets.
   4. The probate process is private.
      a. 1 and 2.
      b. 2 and 3.
      c. 3 and 4.
      d. 1, 2 and 3.

> **Additional multiple choice problems are available at *money-education.com* by accessing the Student Practice Portal. Access requires registration of the title using the unique code at the front of the book.**

QUICK QUIZ EXPLANATIONS

Quick Quiz 14.1

1. False. To result in an effective transfer of assets, estate planning must first consider the goals and objectives of the client. Given the overriding goals of the client, his or her affairs should be arranged to minimize estate taxes and other transfer costs.
2. True.

Quick Quiz 14.2

1. False. A durable power of attorney for health care does not typically direct the termination of life-sustaining treatment, although this is allowed in some states.
2. False. A living will is concerned with the provision or withholding of life-sustaining treatment. It does not direct the transfer of property during life.

Quick Quiz 14.3

1. False. Automobiles and stocks are examples of tangible and intangible personal property. Land is real property.
2. False. Property owned tenancy in common can be transferred without consent of the other owner(s).
3. True.

Quick Quiz 14.4

1. False. A tenancy by the entirety is essentially a joint tenancy with right of survivorship between spouses that cannot be severed without the consent of both spouses.
2. True.

Quick Quiz 14.5

1. True.
2. False. One of the classic reasons for using a trust is to protect assets from the claims of the beneficiaries' creditors.
3. False. A spendthrift clause provides asset protection by legally restricting a beneficiary's ability to anticipate distributions from the trust. A properly constructed spendthrift clause will prevent creditors from being able to access trust assets unless they are distributed to the beneficiary.

15

ECONOMICS AND THE EXTERNAL ENVIRONMENT

LEARNING OBJECTIVES

1. Describe the external environment and its makeup.
2. Define macroeconomics and define gross national product, gross domestic product, inflation, interest rates, and unemployment.
3. Describe the business cycle and summarize the key economic variables.
4. Identify the three types of economic indicators that describe the current and future economy and business cycle.
5. Explain monetary and fiscal policy and the role of the Federal Reserve including its goals and tools.
6. Explain microeconomics, demand and supply, and shifting demand and supply curves.
7. Explain price elasticity of demand and the factors that impact elasticity.
8. Explain opportunity costs and diminishing returns.
9. Explain the external legal environment including bankruptcy laws and other consumer protection laws.
10. Explain investor protection laws including SIPC, the Securities Act of 1933, the Securities Exchange Act of 1934, the Investment Company Act of 1940, and the Investment Advisers Act of 1940.
11. Explain the role of FINRA and the Sarbanes-Oxley Act of 2002.
12. Identify worker protection laws and explain the impact of ERISA, workman's compensation, unemployment benefits, and OSHA.
13. Compare the secondary market institutions and their regulators for each security (stock, bond, ETFs, real estate, commodities and options exchanges) and of primary market institutions (investment banking firms, mutual funds and hedge funds).*
14. Apply the following economic concepts and measures in making financial planning recommendations: (1) Supply and demand, (2) National Income Accounts (including GDP), (3) Business cycles (unemployment, recession, fiscal and monetary policy), (4) Interest rates (including its term structure and the yield curve) and inflation, and (5) Exchange rates.*
15. Describe and distinguish between the elements of agency, suitability, fiduciary responsibility and the duties of agents to their principals including clients and their employers and the duties of fiduciaries to their clients and employers.*
16. Demonstrate a comprehensive understanding of investment adviser regulation and financial planning aspects of the ERISA.*

Ties to CFP Certification Learning Objectives

INTRODUCTION

Economics is the social science that studies individual and firm behavior and the interrelationship between consumer choices and government decisions that result in the production, distribution, and consumption of wealth. The study of economics is divided into the study of microeconomic and macroeconomic factors. Microeconomics focuses on the decisions of individuals and firms, such as those that affect supply and demand and the resulting pricing of products and services. Macroeconomics is centered on the entire or broader economy and uses measurements such as the Gross Domestic Product, inflation, unemployment, and investment in order to determine the performance of the overall economy. Individuals and firms then use the information derived from studying economic performance in order to make choices. Government uses the economic information to legislate issues such as consumer protection and to make monetary and fiscal decisions in an attempt to positively influence economic results. This chapter covers microeconomic and macroeconomic topics that are important for the financial planner to understand in order to properly guide client recommendations based on current and projected economic data.

External forces such as the economic, political, technological, sociological, and legal environments impact client choices. While all external economic forces are relevant, this chapter covers external economic and legal factors (bringing an equalizing of bargaining power between government, industry, and the individual) including consumer protection, investor protection, and worker protection laws. **Exhibit 15.1** portrays some external environmental factors and the impact those factors can have on client finances and decisions. For example, economics impacts the client's cost of borrowing, the rate of taxation, the price of goods and services, overall economic activity, and investment returns.

Clients look to their financial planner for professional, competent, and objective advice related to a wide array of topics including current and future economic conditions and clients' rights as consumers, investors, and workers. By having a thorough understanding of current economic conditions and government policies, the planner is better able to forecast future economic conditions and perhaps potential investment returns. After developing an economic forecast, the planner can position the client to achieve appropriate investment returns and mitigate investment risks.

Exhibit 15.1 | External Environment

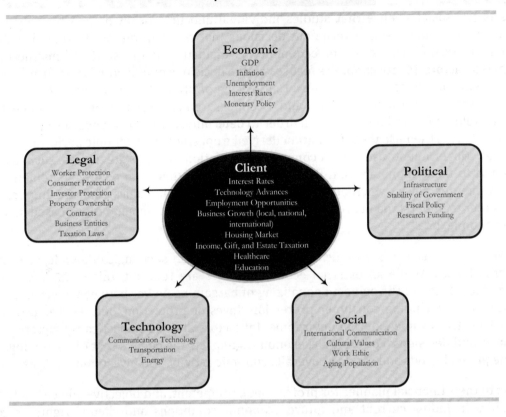

As previously stated, the study of economics can be divided into macroeconomics and microeconomics. **Macroeconomics** is the study of large economic factors that are reflective of the entire economy such as gross domestic product (GDP), the unemployment rate, and the inflation rate. GDP measures the total economic output for a country. The unemployment rate measures the percentage of workers that are unable to find work. The inflation rate measures the rate at which prices are increasing. **Microeconomics** is the study of factors that impact small or individual economies, such as supply and demand for a product. All of these macro and micro economic variables are discussed in this chapter.

> ### ⠿ *Key Concepts*
>
> 1. Distinguish between microeconomic and macroeconomic factors.
>
> 2. Identify the difference between GNP and GDP.
>
> 3. Distinguish between inflation, disinflation, and deflation.

MACROECONOMICS
Economic Output

Gross National Product
Gross National Product (GNP) measures the total final output by the citizens of a country, whether produced domestically or in a foreign country. GNP does not include the output of foreigners in a country.

Gross Domestic Product
Gross Domestic Product (GDP) represents the total final output of a country, by its citizens and foreigners in the country, over a period of time. GDP is typically measured on a quarterly and annual basis. Although comparing GDP between two countries is difficult, GDP is useful for measuring the growth or contraction in the output of a country over time. Historically, the GDP rate has been a three percent real increase.

Example 15.1
A Russian national hockey player that plays professional hockey in the U.S. would be included in the U.S. GDP, but not in the U.S. GNP.

Example 15.2
A U.S. businessman who owns a manufacturing company in China would be included in U.S. GNP, but not U.S. GDP.

GDP is calculated by the Bureau of Economic Analysis, which is part of the U.S. Department of Commerce. A positive GDP is generally a sign that the economy is expanding, a negative GDP is a sign that the economy is contracting. The following exhibit is a compilation of the United States GDP from 1930 - 2019. The graph reflects the negative GDP of the Great Depression (1930's) as well as the subsequent recovery of output. Other periods of positive and negative output reflect the associated economic stability or instability, including the negative output associated with the period (2007 - 2009) referred to as the Great Recession.

Nominal GDP measures the value of goods and services in current prices. The disadvantage of nominal GDP is that if the price of goods and services increases, nominal GDP will increase even though there was not an increase in the amount of goods and services produced. If the quantity of goods and services produced remains constant but the price increases, nominal GDP may be misleading because it reflects inflation rather than a quantitative increase in goods and services.

Real GDP measures the value of goods and services at a base year price. Real GDP only changes when the quantity of goods and services produced changes, not when prices change. Real GDP is a better measure of economic output than nominal GDP since prices are held constant when calculating real GDP. A recession is characterized by a decline in real GDP for at least six months (two quarters).

Exhibit 15.2 | Gross Domestic Product (1930 - 2019)

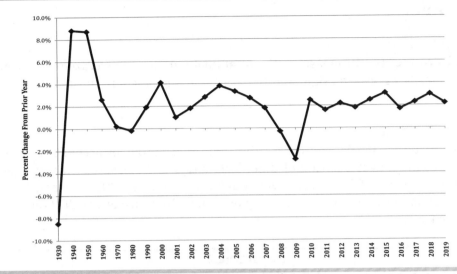

Source: Bureau of Economic Analysis

The **GDP deflator** measures the current price of goods and services (nominal GDP) relative to a base year (real GDP). The formula for the GDP deflator is:

$$\text{GDP Deflator} = \frac{\text{Nominal GDP}}{\text{Real GDP}}$$

Alternatively, we could take $\frac{\text{Nominal GDP}}{\text{GDP Deflator}}$ to determine the real GDP, therefore stating the nominal GDP in real terms. The GDP deflator could also be thought of as a measure of price increases or decreases.

Inflation

Inflation represents an increase in the general level of prices of goods and services representing the economy as a whole over a period of time and without a corresponding increase in productivity. The biggest risks inflation presents are the loss of purchasing power and price instability. Individuals on fixed incomes are impacted the most by a loss of purchasing power, such as a retiree on a fixed pension while income remains constant, the cost of goods and services increase.

Inflation causes a decline in the real value of money, as consumers holding cash are priced out of goods and services because prices for those items increase. A primary cause of inflation is when the money supply increases faster than the growth in real GDP. The Federal Reserve is responsible for controlling the money supply to keep inflation at reasonable levels, typically targeted at two to three percent per year.

⠿ Key Concepts

1. Identify measures of inflation.

2. What is an interest rate and what influences increases or decreases in the rate?

3. Identify how unemployment is measured and the different types of unemployment.

4. Explain what the business cycle represents and the phases of the business cycle.

5. Identify the three types of economic indicators.

A financial planner must be aware of the current and future conditions of the economy, including the status of inflation, in order to make proper financial planning recommendations to the client. Inflation's erosion of purchasing power can impact the client's successful implementation of a financial plan. For example, purchases of personal use assets may be negatively impacted due to inflation driving up prices and the cost of borrowing. The planner may choose to recommend that investments are made in stocks in order to hedge inflationary pressure. The planner who understands the impact of inflation and the mechanics of economics will remain informed of inflationary pressures and important government reaction, such as the Federal Reserve raising short-term interest rates in order to decrease the money supply (slowing down inflation). This knowledge will result in better client recommendations and more successful implementation of financial plans.

Disinflation is a slowdown in the rate of inflation or a slowdown in the rate of price increase of goods and services. Inflation is continuing, but at a declining rate.

Deflation is a decrease in overall price levels of goods and services. As a result of deflation, there is a transfer of wealth from borrowers (like homeowners) to holders of cash. During periods of deflation, the real value of money increases as the dollars consumers hold are able to buy more goods and services as prices, such as homes, continue to decrease. A deflationary spiral is likely to lead to lower GDP because consumers prefer to hold their money, while waiting for lower prices.

Measures of Inflation

The **Consumer Price Index (CPI)** measures the overall price levels for a basket of goods and services consumers purchase. According to the Bureau of Labor Statistics, items included in the CPI are:[1]

- Food and Beverages: cereal, milk, coffee, snacks, etc.
- Housing: rent, mortgage, etc.
- Apparel: items of clothing.
- Transportation: new vehicles, airline fares, gasoline, insurance.
- Medical Care: prescription drugs, physician services, eye care, etc.
- Recreation: televisions, toys, pets and pet products, sports equipment, etc.
- Education and Communication: college tuition, postage, telephone services, computer software and accessories, etc.
- Other Goods and Services: tobacco and smoking products, haircuts and other personal expenses, etc.

The CPI is a measure of prices at the retail level relative to the price levels of the same basket of goods and services in some base year. The **Producer Price Index (PPI)** measures the inflation rate for raw materials used in the manufacturing process. The PPI is an important measure of inflation, since inflation in the manufacturing process will likely lead to inflation at the retail level.

Although the CPI and GDP deflator measure price changes, there are major differences between these two measures. The GDP deflator measures price changes for all goods and services, whereas the CPI measures changes for a fixed basket of goods and services at the retail level only. Another difference is that the GDP deflator only measures the price of goods and services produced domestically. The CPI measures changes in prices of goods manufactured overseas and sold in the U.S., such as cars produced overseas and sold in the U.S. A final difference between the GDP deflator and CPI is that the CPI measures

---

1. https://www.bls.gov/cpi/questions-and-answers.htm#Question_10

the price changes of a fixed basket of goods and services, whereas the GDP deflator will change over time as the economic output of a country changes.

The CPI is the most widely quoted and relied upon measure of inflation. Social Security benefit increases are tied to the CPI through Cost Of Living Adjustments (COLA) so that retirees receiving Social Security income will not lose purchasing power during their retirement or benefit years.

The inflation rate is calculated as follows:

$$\text{Inflation Rate } = \frac{P_1 - P_0}{P_0}$$

Where:

P_1 = Current prices
P_0 = Prices during a prior period

The inflation rate, as measured by the CPI and calculated by the U.S. Bureau of Labor and Statistics for the last ten years reported is:

Year	Annual CPI	Year	Annual CPI
2019	1.8%	2014	1.6%
2018	2.4%	2013	1.6%
2017	2.1%	2012	2.1%
2016	1.3%	2011	3.2%
2015	0.1%	2010	1.6%

Source: www.bls.gov/cpi/

Example 15.3

Assume a widget costs $100 in 2009. If the widget increased in price in accordance with the CPI, it would cost $119.26 at the end of 2019.[2]

Interest Rates

An **interest rate** is the price that a borrower pays to borrow money. The interest rate is an important factor in decision making by individuals and firms. Individuals make purchasing decisions, such as a home or automobile purchase, that consider the cost of financing as a key factor. Firms make business decisions regarding investment projects where the borrowing interest rate must be exceeded by the yield or return on the project.

The nominal interest rate represents the real rate of return plus an adjustment for anticipated future inflation. When lenders loan funds, the real rate of return represents their income. The real rate of interest is the nominal interest rate less inflation. If the lending interest rate were equal to inflation, there would be no income derived from the loan, so lenders need to lend at the nominal interest rate to earn revenue.

---

2. Calculated using a geometric mean return, as described in chapter 9, for the average annual rate of inflation over the 10-year period.

Interest rates are influenced by the demand for and the supply of loanable funds. When the supply of money increases, there is the tendency to temporarily hold more money than necessary. When the excess money is no longer held, interest rates fall and consumers make purchases because the cost of borrowing (the interest rate) has decreased. In addition, interest rates can be influenced by fiscal and monetary policy. If monetary policy is to tighten the supply of money resulting in upward pressure on interest rates, then purchases would likely fall. The fiscal and monetary policy can also include easing the supply of money in order to stimulate the economy, in which case, downward pressure on interest rates would occur and purchases would rise.

Financial planners need to be aware of economic forecasts of anticipated inflation and corresponding expected changes in interest rates, because this will affect many financial plans. If there is an anticipated rise in inflation, then client purchases or refinancing should be considered earlier rather than later as the cost of borrowing (the interest rate) is currently priced more favorably. If anticipated inflation is expected to fall, then purchases should be delayed to take advantage of the future lower price of borrowing.

Unemployment

The measurement of unemployment is important because aggregate supply and aggregate demand (discussed under the microeconomics section of this chapter) are affected when unemployment increases as output decreases and GNP falls below its potential. On a more personal level, high unemployment can lead to depressed personal income and economic distress for individuals and families.

In order to understand what the measurement of unemployment means, the criteria used to measure unemployment is essential. **Unemployed** refers to those individuals 16 years of age and older who are not working and are making an effort to seek employment. The government measurement of unemployment does not include those individuals who are underemployed (overqualified for a job such as a PhD waiting tables) or those who are discouraged and have discontinued their job search. Some unemployment is consistent with economic efficiency, but prolonged high rates of unemployment are an indication of economic instability. Economists have divided unemployment into three categories as follows:

> **Quick Quiz 15.1**
>
> 1. Microeconomics is the study of economic factors that impact the economy as a whole including GDP, unemployment, and inflation.
>   a. True
>   b. False
>
> 2. Inflation results in a transfer of wealth from borrowers to holders of cash.
>   a. True
>   b. False
>
> 3. CPI measures the overall price levels for a basket of goods and services that consumers purchase.
>   a. True
>   b. False
>
> False, False, True.

- **Frictional unemployment** occurs when people are voluntarily unemployed because they are seeking other job opportunities and they haven't found the desired employment yet.
- **Structural unemployment** occurs when there is inequality between the supply of adequately skilled workers and the demand for workers.
- **Cyclical unemployment** occurs when there is an overall downturn in business activity and fewer goods are being produced causing a decrease in the demand for labor (related to changes in the business cycle).

Given that some unemployment is normal, **full employment** is defined as the rate of employment that exists when there is efficiency in the labor market. Full employment can include both frictional and structural unemployment when there is efficiency in the labor market that results in approximately 95 percent employment of the labor force. Conversely, note that high cyclical unemployment is an indication of problematic unemployment economy-wide and can reflect overall economic inefficiencies. Very low unemployment (e.g., 2-3 percent) can also be problematic leading to inflationary issues. Therefore, economic policy is to sustain a **natural rate of unemployment**, being the lowest unemployment rate where labor and product markets are in balance. At the natural rate of unemployment both price and wage inflation is stable.

The following exhibit is a representation of the annual unemployment rate from 1970 – 2019, and the monthly rate in April and September 2020.[3] Recessionary periods are identifiable and associated with periods of high unemployment. The COVID-19 pandemic resulted in a sudden spike in the unemployment rate in April 2020. As of September 2020, the rate had begun to decline from the April high, but remained higher than the post-recession/pre-pandemic lows of the previous five years.

Exhibit 15.3 | Unemployment from 1970 - September 2020 (In Percentages)

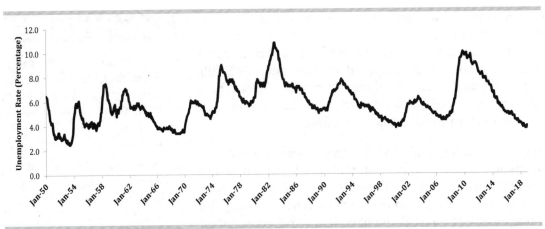

Source: http://www.bls.gov/web/empsit/cpseea01.htm

Business Cycle

Both firms and consumers make financial decisions to maximize their utility, based on constraints. The primary constraint for both firms and consumers is limited financial resources. **Utility** is the benefit firms and consumers receive when allocating or spending financial resources. Firms are constrained by the capacity of their workforce, products they offer, and the level of competition. Firms maximize their utility by making decisions on how to best use their resources to maximize profits. Consumers and households maximize their utility by making decisions on employment, spending for today, and saving for tomorrow. Consumers are constantly evaluating how to allocate their limited resource of funds to meet the necessities of life and planning for financial goals of tomorrow. Consumers evaluate how to allocate their scarce resource of funds based on the cost and benefits derived from making decisions to spend today or save for tomorrow. One of the decisions many families face is whether to have both parents work outside of the home. Opportunity cost represents the cost of the highest valued alternative that is forgone. For families that decide one parent will not work outside of the house, the opportunity

3. Bureau of Labor Statistics: Annual average unemployment rate, civilian labor force 16 years and over (percent).

cost is the income that is forgone. These families value the benefit of having a parent at home as exceeding the cost of the forgone income.

Consumer spending, which accounts for approximately two-thirds of GDP, is a key economic variable that drives the U.S. economy and the business cycle. The **business cycle** measures economic activity, or GDP, over time. As consumer spending increases, firms hire more employees and produce more goods and services. When consumer spending slows, firms stop hiring or reduce their workforce and produce less goods and services. These fluctuations in consumer spending and output by firms are reflected in the business cycle.

The business cycle shown in **Exhibit 15.4** is characterized by the following phases:
- Expansion
- Peak
- Contraction or Recession
- Trough

Exhibit 15.4 | Business Cycle

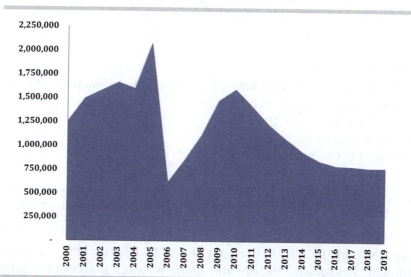

A contraction in the business cycle is characterized by a slow down in consumer spending, which leads to lower output by firms. As the output of firms decreases, GDP decreases and the unemployment rate increases, as firms reduce staff to offset the lower demand for their products and services. As GDP decreases, inflation begins to decrease, as consumers are demanding fewer goods and services, which may lead to lower prices. In an effort to stimulate economic activity, the Federal Reserve will ease monetary policy, by increasing the money supply and lowering interest rates to reduce the cost of borrowing and encourage consumers to begin spending again.

As GDP reaches its lowest levels and unemployment reaches its highest point, the business cycle is entering the trough phase. Generally, the trough phase represents lower GDP, lower inflation, lower interest rates, and higher unemployment.

Exhibit 15.5 | Summary of Business Cycle and Key Economic Variables

	Expansion	*Peak*	*Contraction*	*Trough*
GDP	Increasing	High	Decreasing	Low
Inflation	Increasing	High	Decreasing	Low
Interest Rates	Increasing	High	Decreasing	Low
Unemployment	Decreasing	Low	Increasing	High

Once the financial planner has an idea of where current economic conditions are in the business cycle and the direction of key economic variables, the planner is in a good position to forecast where the economy may be in the next three to six months. Investment returns are highly correlated to the business cycle and GDP. During periods of expansion, increasing GDP, and low unemployment, consumers have more money to spend. Consumer spending drives corporate earnings and corporate earnings drive equity prices and investment returns. The planner can position a client's investments to take advantage of the likely increasing equity prices and positive investment returns. As the economy is approaching or at the peak, the planner may forecast an upcoming contraction, leading to lower GDP, lower consumer spending, lower interest rates, and higher unemployment. During periods of a contraction, corporate earnings decrease, leading to lower equity prices and potentially negative equity returns. However, as interest rates decrease, bond prices will increase which presents an opportunity for the planner to position the client's investments to take advantage of increasing bond prices.

Economic Indicators

There are three types of **economic indicators** that describe the current and future economy and business cycle. The three types of economic indicators are:[4]
- Index of Leading Economic Indicators
- Index of Lagging Economic Indicators
- Index of Coincident Economic Indicators

All three types of indicators incorporate key economic data that is used by economists to predict future economic activity or confirm current assessments of the economy and business cycle.

The Index of Leading Economic Indicators

The index of leading economic indicators is comprised of 10 data points that are relied on to predict changes in the economy. Economists believe the index of leading economic indicators can predict changes to the economy six to nine months before the change actually occurs. The index consists of the following indicators:
- Average weekly hours, manufacturing
- Average weekly initial claims for unemployment insurance
- Manufacturers' new orders, consumer goods and materials
- ISM® Index of New Orders (supplier deliveries, imports, production, inventories, new orders)
- Manufacturers' new orders, non-defense capital goods
- Building permits, new private housing units
- Stock prices, 500 common stocks
- Leading Credit Index™ (credit conditions, including yield curve data)
- Interest rate spread, 10-year Treasury bonds less federal funds
- Average consumer expectations for business conditions

---

4. The composite indexes of leading, coincident, and lagging indicators produced by The Conference Board (www.conference-board.org).

The Index of Lagging Economic Indicators

The index of lagging economic indicators summarizes past performance. The index of lagging economic indicators does not predict future trends in the economy, instead it validates current assessments of the economy. The index consists of the following indicators:

- Average duration of unemployment
- Inventories to sales ratio, manufacturing and trade
- Labor cost per unit of output, manufacturing
- Average prime rate
- Commercial and industrial loans
- Consumer installment credit to personal income ratio
- Consumer price index for services

The Index of Coincident Indicators

The index of coincident indicators is comprised of economic variables that change along with the business cycle. The index of coincident indicators reflects where the economy is in the business cycle. The index consists of the following indicators:

- Number of employees on non-agricultural payrolls (payroll employment)
- Index of Industrial Production or industrial output
- Level of manufacturing and trade sales which measures total spending in real dollars
- Personal income measured in real dollars, excluding transfer payments (Social Security)

Monetary Policy

Monetary policy represents the intended influence on the money supply and interest rates by the central bank of a country. In the United States, the central bank is the Federal Reserve. The Federal Reserve system is composed of the Board of Governors and twelve regional Federal Reserve Banks. Monetary policy is established by:

- The Chairman of the Federal Reserve and the Board of Governors, who are appointed by the President of the United States and confirmed by the U.S. Senate.
- The Federal Open Market Committee (FOMC), which is comprised of members of the Board of Governors, the president of the Federal Reserve Bank of New York, and four presidents of other Federal Reserve Banks serving on a rotating basis.

> ### ⋮☰ *Key Concepts*
>
> 1. What is monetary policy?
>
> 2. Identify and define the four tools that are used to implement monetary policy.
>
> 3. Distinguish between fiscal policy and monetary policy.
>
> 4. Identify the two tools that the government can use to implement fiscal policy.

The FOMC meets eight times a year to set monetary policy and make decisions regarding how monetary policy will be implemented.

The Federal Reserve has three primary goals:

- Maintain price levels
- Maintain long-term economic growth
- Maintain full employment

The Federal Reserve accomplishes its goals by influencing money supply and interest rates. If GDP is slowing and unemployment is increasing the Federal Reserve may want to stimulate or expand the economy. In an effort to expand the economy, it may ease monetary policy. The Federal Reserve will take steps to increase the money supply, which will put downward pressure on interest rates. Interest rates represent the cost of borrowing money, so when the money supply is abundant, the cost to borrow will be low and encourage consumers to borrow money to buy houses and cars. Alternatively, if the Federal Reserve believes the economy is growing too quickly and inflation is showing signs of increasing or is actually increasing, the Federal Reserve may **tighten** monetary policy. It will then take steps to decrease the supply of money and ultimately increase short-term interest rates, in an effort to slow down consumer spending. A financial planner that is knowledgeable regarding the business cycle (**Exhibit 15.4**) can analyze the actions of the Federal Reserve to anticipate the expected direction of the economy and assist the client with informed decisions accordingly.

The Federal Reserve has four tools that it uses to implement monetary policy. The four tools are:
- Reserve Requirement
- Discount Rate / Federal Funds Rate
- Open Market Operations
- Excess Reserve Deposits

Reserve Requirement

The Federal Reserve requires that banks maintain a certain percentage of their deposits on hand, in the form of cash known as their **reserve requirement**. A simplified bank's balance sheet might appear as follows:

Assets	Liabilities
Loans	Deposits
Cash	

Banks receive deposits that are applied to checking accounts, savings accounts, money market accounts, and Certificates of Deposit. Those deposits actually represent liabilities since the bank owes those funds to its depositors. A bank creates an asset when it uses deposits to lend funds to businesses and consumers for commercial or personal purposes. A bank also maintains a percentage of deposits as available cash for future loans or to meet the reserve requirement. Historically, the reserve requirement for banks (as set by the Federal Reserve), was effectively 10 percent.[5] For every $10 in deposits, a bank could lend $9 and keep $1 in cash to meet the reserve requirement. However, in response to the COVID-19 pandemic, the Federal Reserve Board reduced reserve requirements to zero percent, eliminating the

☑ Quick Quiz 15.2

1. An expansion phase in the business cycle is characterized by an increase in consumer spending resulting in higher output by firms.
   a. True
   b. False

2. The index of leading economic indicators summarizes past performance.
   a. True
   b. False

3. Monetary policy represents the government's position on whether to expand or contract the economy by using taxation and government spending.
   a. True
   b. False

True, False, False.

5. In the past, reserve requirements for banks were tiered, based on net transaction accounts. As of January 16, 2020, banks with less than $16.9 million in accounts were not required to maintain a minimum reserve level. The reserve requirement for banks over $16.9 million up to $127.5 million was 3 percent. Banks with over $127.5 million were required to maintain a 10 percent reserve.

reserve requirement for all depository institutions, as of March 26, 2020. The Board announced that it has no plans to re-impose reserve requirements, but retains the right to do so in the future if warranted by a change in economic conditions.[6]

Banks create money by taking a liability in the form of a deposit and then lending that money to a business or consumer. Bank business models are impacted by the unique risk of being in the business of lending money in order to make a profit. However, during the peak of the business cycle they are lending money to businesses, consumers, and investors who are making purchases when prices and values are at their peak. The reserve requirement is influential in controlling how much leverage and risk banks can undertake. Since banks are able to lend 100 percent of every deposit that they receive, they may undertake significant financial risk during periods of peak prices.

The Federal Reserve can increase or decrease the reserve requirement, which will have a direct impact on the money supply and ultimately influence interest rates. If the Federal Reserve's monetary policy is to tighten the money supply, it can increase the reserve requirement which causes banks to maintain more deposits in the form of cash and have less funds available for loans. Since there are fewer funds available for loans, the money supply will decrease and interest rates will increase.

Alternatively, if the Federal Reserve's monetary policy is to ease the money supply, it will decrease the reserve requirement, as occurred in March 2020 when the reserve requirement was reduced to zero. Banks will maintain fewer deposits in the form of cash and will increase the funds available for loans. Since there are more funds available for loans, the money supply will increase and interest rates will decrease.

Exhibit 15.6 | Summary Chart

Monetary Policy	Reserve Requirement	Money Supply	Interest Rates
Tighten	Increase	Decrease	Increase
Ease	Decrease	Increase	Decrease

Discount Rate

The **discount rate** is the interest rate that the Federal Reserve charges financial institutions for short-term loans. Loan borrowing from the Federal Reserve institutions go to the discount window, which is the term used from when financial institutions would send a representative to the Federal Reserve's bank window to borrow funds. Borrowing is now accomplished electronically, but the term discount window is still used.

The Federal Reserve sets the discount rate and the rate is increased or decreased based on the Federal Reserve's monetary policy. The discount rate represents the overnight borrowing rate that banks are charged for funds used to meet their reserve requirement or other liquidity issues. The discount rate is typically 100 basis points (or 1%) higher than the rate banks charge each other to borrow.

When the Federal Reserve tightens monetary policy, the discount rate increases. If the Fed eases monetary policy, they are going to decrease the discount rate.

---

6. https://www.frbservices.org/resources/central-bank/faq/reserve-account-admin-app.html.

The bank to bank lending rate is the **federal funds rate** (also known as the overnight rate). It is important to be able to differentiate between the discount rate and federal funds rate. The supply and demand of funds is an important consideration when federal funds rates are negotiated between banks. In years where the reserve requirement is greater than zero, if a number of banks have reserve deficiencies and a few banks have excess reserves, the federal funds rate is likely to increase, since the demand for funds is higher than the supply. If a number of banks have excess reserves and a few banks have reserve deficiencies, the federal funds rate is likely to decrease. Since the discount rate is usually higher than the federal funds rate, the Federal Reserve has historically been known as the bank of last resort. However, as a result of the COVID-19 pandemic, on March 16, 2020 the Federal Reserve implemented a strategy to improve liquidity and stability in the banking system by reducing the targeted spread between the discount rate and the federal funds rate to 0 - 0.25%, thereby encouraging active use of the discount window.

Prior to the credit crisis of 2007 to 2009, the discount rate was an overnight interest rate and the funds had to be repaid the next day. Since many banks were facing insolvency (CITI, Bank of America, etc.) during this time period, the terms of the discount rate were temporarily extended for up to 90 days. The discount window returned to primarily overnight lending following the credit crisis, but the repayment term was again extended to 90 days, beginning on March 16, 2020, as a result of the COVID-19 pandemic.

The Federal Open Market Committee (FOMC) sets the discount rate and also a target for the federal funds rate. The Federal Reserve does not directly control the federal funds rate, because banks negotiate the federal funds rate between themselves. However, the Federal Reserve's target rate is typically very close to the actual rate.

Open Market Operations

Through the Federal Reserve's open market operations, it can directly influence the money supply and interest rates. **Open market operations** is the process by which the Federal Reserve will buy or sell U.S. Treasury securities such as T-bills, notes, and bonds. This process is done electronically with the Federal Reserve crediting or debiting financial institution's transactions. Only about 10 percent of the country's money supply is in the form of bank notes or cash; the rest is maintained electronically.

If the Federal Reserve's monetary policy is to tighten, then it will sell U.S. Treasury securities and reduce the deposits held by banks at the Federal Reserve. When deposits are decreased, the money supply decreases and interest rates are likely to increase.

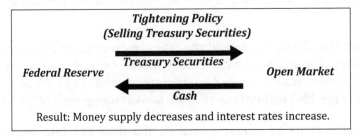

If the Federal Reserve's monetary policy is to ease, then it will buy U.S. Treasury securities and increase the deposits held by banks at the Federal Reserve. When deposits increase, the money supply is increasing and interest rates are likely to decrease.

Result: Money supply increases and interest rates decrease.

Excess Reserves

As previously discussed, banks must maintain a minimum level of cash reserves (based on the amount of their deposits), which is determined by the reserve requirement. The cash reserves are on deposit with the Federal Reserve. **Excess reserves** represent the amount of cash or deposits with the Federal Reserve in excess of the minimum amount required. Prior to 2008, it was disadvantageous for financial institutions to keep cash in excess of their reserve requirement on deposit with the Federal Reserve because there was no return on that capital. Institutions were more inclined to keep reserve deposits at minimum levels and instead took risks by lending the excess reserves to generate higher returns.

The Financial Services Regulatory Relief Act of 2006 established that on October 1, 2011, the Federal Reserve could begin paying interest on cash balances financial institutions have on deposit at the Federal Reserve. The Economic Stabilization Act of 2008 changed the effective date from October 1, 2011 to October 1, 2008. The impact of the Federal Reserve paying interest on deposits is that financial institutions have an incentive to keep excess reserves on deposit with the Federal Reserve. The Federal Reserve now has the ability to increase or decrease the interest rate paid on excess reserves to help control the money supply.

If the Federal Reserve's policy is to slow down or contract the economy, it will increase the interest rate paid on excess reserves. This creates an incentive for institutions to keep cash on deposit with the Federal Reserve, as opposed to making risky loans.

If the Federal Reserve's policy is to stimulate or expand the economy, it will decrease the interest rate paid on excess reserves. This creates an incentive for financial institutions to lend money and grow the money supply.

As a result of the Federal Reserve's move to zero percent required reserves in March 2020, all bank reserves are currently excess reserves.

Fiscal Policy

Fiscal policy is exerted by Congress as a means of expanding or contracting the economy. Congress uses taxes and government spending to implement fiscal policy. Congress has the same three goals the Federal Reserve has, which are to:

- Maintain price levels
- Maintain long-term economic growth
- Maintain full employment

Fiscal policy is an attempt to either stimulate or reduce aggregate demand within a country. Fiscal policy is implemented using three tools: taxes, spending, and deficit management.

Taxes

When taxes decrease, consumers will have more income to spend on products and services. As consumers demand more products and services, consumer spending will increase causing aggregate demand to increase. Congress is likely to decrease taxes when fiscal policy is to expand the economy. Alternatively, when taxes increase, consumers will have less income to spend on products and services. As consumers demand fewer products and services, consumer spending will decrease, causing aggregate demand to decrease or slow down. Congress is likely to increase taxes when fiscal policy is to contract the economy.

Fiscal Policy Tax Impact	
Taxes	**Fiscal Policy**
Decrease	Expand
Increase	Contract

Spending

Spending by the federal government can directly impact aggregate demand. As the federal government spends funds on building more roads, hiring law enforcement, and strengthening national defense, the spending may result in a positive impact on unemployment.

A disadvantage of spending to implement fiscal policy occurs when the U.S. government borrows money, which increases the federal deficit. Deficit spending is exaggerated during periods of decreasing or negative GDP because tax revenues are lower and the federal government is spending more to help stimulate the economy. The only way to finance deficit spending is to print more money (which can have serious inflation implications) or to borrow more money. As the federal government borrows more money, it has a crowding out effect where business and consumers are either unable to borrow or they are forced to borrow at higher interest rates. An implication of deficit spending is that it may ultimately lead to lower aggregate demand since businesses and consumers are interest rate sensitive when borrowing. As the cost of borrowing increases, businesses and consumers are less likely to borrow, which can lead to slower economic growth and have the opposite consequences than what was intended by the spending policy.

An expansion is characterized by an increase in consumer spending, which leads to higher output by firms. As the output increases, GDP increases and the unemployment rate decreases, as firms are hiring more employees to meet the demand for the firm's products. If GDP continues to increase, inflation in the form of higher prices for goods and services begins to increase. Higher prices are the result of consumer spending and high demand for a limited supply of products and services. Because the government is also committed to price stability, it will use contractionary fiscal policy to restrain inflation.

Deficit Management

Deficit spending is a financial circumstance that is avoided by most consumers, individuals, and firms alike, because spending beyond available cash (increasing debt) can be problematic and lead to insolvency. However, the concept of deficit spending and the resulting management and decision making associated with this type of spending must be examined based on need. For example, if a fiscal policy of deficit spending is chosen in an unstable economy, such as a deep recession or depression, the deficit increase can be worth the risk. However, if deficit spending is related to overspending or failure to follow a budget, then the risks associated with deficit spending are not reasonable. In the latter case, fiscal policy should include a cut in spending (including a reduction in expenses, if necessary) to meet budget constraints.

MICROECONOMICS

Demand

Demand represents the quantity consumers are willing to purchase of a good or service, at a particular price. The quantity consumers are willing to demand is known as the quantity demanded and is inversely related to price, so as price increases, quantity demand decreases. As price decreases, quantity demand will increase. The **aggregate demand curve** is a graphical representation of the quantity of goods and services consumers are willing to buy at any given price level.

Exhibit 15.7 | The Demand Curve

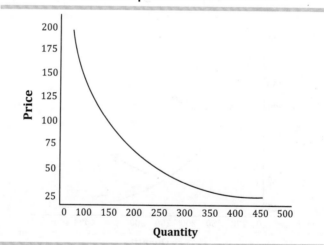

It is important to differentiate between shifts in the demand curve and movements along the demand curve. Anytime something other than price changes, the demand curve will shift, either up and to the right or down and to the left. The easiest way to determine when the demand curve is going to shift, is based on changes to the amount of money in the consumer's pocket. If consumers have more money in their pocket to spend, the demand curve will shift up and to the right. If consumers have less money to spend, the demand curve will shift down and to the left.

The examples below are events that cause the demand curve to shift up and to the right, which means consumers are willing to demand more of a good or service, at a higher price:
- Increase in disposable income
- Decrease in tax rates
- Decrease in unemployment rate
- Decrease in savings rate
- Increase in price of a substitute product
- Decrease in price of a complement product

Exhibit 15.8 | Shifting Demand Curve

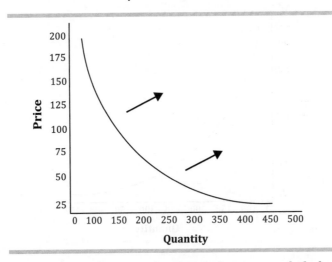

The examples below are events that will cause the demand curve to shift down and to the left, which means consumers are willing to demand less of a good or service, at a lower price:
- Decrease in disposable income
- Increase in tax rate
- Increase in unemployment rate
- Increase in savings rate
- Decrease in price of a substitute product
- Increase in price of a complement product

Exhibit 15.9 | Shifting Demand Curve

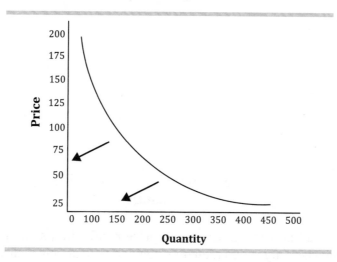

Substitutes and Complements

Substitutes are products that serve a similar purpose, whereas **complements** are products that are consumed jointly. For substitutes and complements, when the price of one product changes, it will impact the quantity demand for both the original product and the substitute or complement product.

Example 15.4

If the price of movie tickets increases, the quantity demanded for movie tickets is likely to decrease. However, if digital movie rentals are a substitute product, as the price of movie tickets increase, the demand for digital movie rentals is likely to increase.

Example 15.5

If flashlights and batteries are complements, then if flashlights are on sale, it is likely to increase the demand for batteries.

Price Elasticity of Demand

As discussed, consumer demand will change with price. As price decreases, the quantity demanded will increase. The question is, how much will demand increase, based on changes in price? This question is answered by looking at the price elasticity of demand. For some products, such as gasoline, changes in price will result in a relatively small change in the quantity demanded within a given range of prices. For other products, such as luxury goods, a small change in price may lead to a relatively large change in the quantity demanded.

The elasticity of demand is measured by the following formula:

$$\text{Elasticity} = \frac{\text{Percentage Change in Quantity Demanded}}{\text{Percentage Change in Price}}$$

Demand is elastic if a small percentage change in price, results in a large percentage change in the quantity demanded. Anytime elasticity is greater than 1, demand is considered to be elastic.

Exhibit 15.10 | Elastic Demand (Luxury Cars)

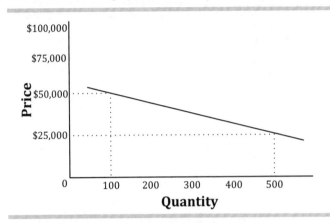

Demand is inelastic if a small percentage change in price results in a small percentage change in the quantity demanded. When elasticity is less than one, demand is relatively inelastic.

Exhibit 15.11 | Inelastic Demand (Gasoline)

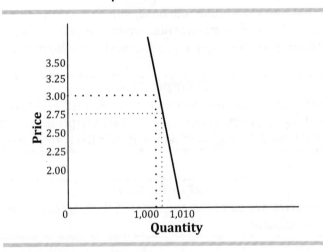

If a one percent change in price leads to a one percent change in quantity demanded, then elasticity is one, which is defined as unit elasticity. If demand is perfectly inelastic, regardless of what happens to price, the quantity demanded will not change. If demand is perfectly elastic, given a small price change, consumers will demand an unlimited amount of the good or service.

Factors that Impact Elasticity

The elasticity of demand is impacted by three primary factors. The first factor is whether there are substitute products. If there are substitute products, then a small price increase for one product will lead to lower demand and increase the demand for the substitute product. Substitute products lead to elastic demand.

Example 15.6

If the price of steak increases and consumers substitute chicken instead of steak, the demand for steak will decrease.

The second factor that impacts elasticity is consumer's income. If prices increase and consumer's income remains constant, then consumer's are going to demand less of the good or service. Whether the demand is elastic or inelastic will depend on the percentage change in the quantity demanded. The third factor that impacts elasticity is time. If consumers don't have a substitute product in the short-term, demand is likely to be inelastic. However, over time as consumers find substitute products, demand will become more elastic.

Supply

Supply represents the quantity firms are willing to produce and sell of a good or service, at a particular price. The quantity firms are willing to supply is known as the quantity supplied and is directly related to price, such that as price increases, quantity supplied increases. As price decreases, quantity supplied will decrease. The **aggregate supply curve** is a graphical representation between quantity supplied and price.

Exhibit 15.12 | The Supply Curve

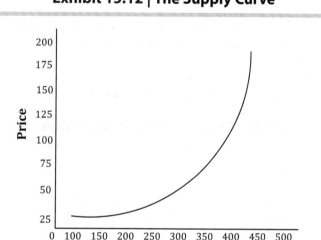

As it was with the demand curve, it is also important to differentiate between shifts in the supply curve and movements along the supply curve. Anytime something other than price changes, the supply curve will shift, either up and to the left or down and to the right. A change in price is movement along the supply curve, impacting the quantity supplied.

The examples below are situations that cause the supply curve to shift up and to the left, which means firms are supplying less of a good or service, at a higher price:
- Decreased competition
- Outdated technologies
- Increased price of an input used in the manufacturing process

Exhibit 15.13 | The Supply Curve Shifting

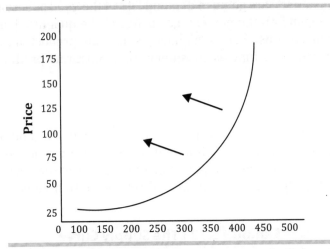

The examples below are situations that cause the supply curve to shift down and to the right, which means firms are willing to supply more of a good or service, at a lower price:

- Increased competition
- Improved technology to increase efficiency
- Decreased price of an input used in the manufacturing process

Exhibit 15.14 | Shift in Supply Curve

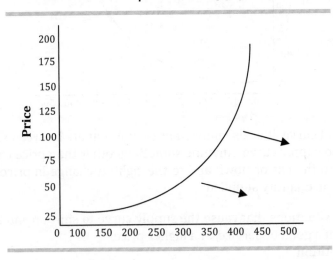

Equilibrium

It is not every day that financial planners work with the concepts of supply and demand. However, it is important to understand these concepts since they help to explain or anticipate how changes in unemployment, taxes, savings, and competition can impact the overall economy as well as the price of goods and services.

When combining supply and demand curves on one graph, the intersection of the supply and demand curve is the equilibrium price. The **equilibrium price** represents the price at which the quantity demanded equals the quantity supplied.

The following is a graph reflecting the money supply, the demand for funds, and the cost for those funds as measured by interest rates (price).

Exhibit 15.15 | Equilibrium Graph

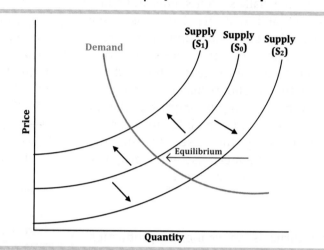

As the money supply shifts up (decreases) from S_0 to S_1, a new equilibrium price will be established, which is higher price (interest rates). As a result, businesses and consumers will demand less money at the higher interest rates. As the money supply shifts down (increases) from S_0 to S_2, businesses and consumers will demand more money as the money supply increases and a new equilibrium price is established, which is lower price (interest rates).

Opportunity Costs and Diminishing Returns

Opportunity Costs

Opportunity cost represents the value of the best foregone alternative. What is the significance of opportunity cost to the financial planner? The planner will evaluate the client's financial opportunities together with personal goals and objectives to make recommendations that require a review of alternative choices. A recommendation may be to pay off a high balance, high interest rate credit card by selling a client's favorite recreational vehicle (e.g., a boat). However, the client may find such value in the recreational vehicle that he is not willing to lose the opportunity of that enjoyment. So instead, the client might choose another opportunity, like delaying the purchase of a home (as the best alternative that is foregone) in order to keep the boat and use the savings from the home purchase to pay off the credit card debt. Therefore, it is important for the planner to appreciate that a client's opportunity cost is subjective and should be considered when making financial planning recommendations.

Another important aspect of opportunity cost is considering what a resource could earn using its best alternative use. A financial planner can evaluate the client's use of assets to determine a better alternative asset use leading to an improved financial status.

Example 15.7

Sally is a financial planner. Sally's clients, Luis and Mary, own several acres of land that are being used for infrequent family camping trips. Luis and Mary hire a vendor for maintenance of the acreage. Sally recommends that Luis and Mary lease the land for agricultural crop growth. The clients may have to forego the use of the property for camping trips, but this in turn, will eliminate the need for the maintenance vendor and will earn revenue from the asset. Leasing the property may be the better financial use of the property depending on the client's utility preferences.

Diminishing Returns

The law of diminishing returns is an economic production concept that states, as more and more additional units of a variable input are applied to a fixed input, output will eventually increase by smaller and smaller amounts. For example, a person who has consumed five chocolate bars is unlikely to have the same utility for the last bar consumed as a person who eats his first chocolate bar. The financial planner should have an understanding of this economic concept because it is common sense and applicable to business decisions where resource decisions are made and an evaluation of return on investment occurs. As part of analyzing a client's financial profile, the planner may need to assess the assets available and recommend where an increase in variable inputs should be applied and at what point is there a diminishing return on those inputs.

Example 15.8

Continuing with Sally's clients, Luis and Mary, from above. Mary, who has a degree in horticulture, decides that she can manage the crop growth on their land. Mary successfully grows and harvests the crops for a couple of years and refines her method of production by applying more and more fertilizer to increase the harvest output. Eventually, Mary's cost of more and more fertilizer is producing less and less amounts of crop since the land (fixed input) will not support any further production. Mary is experiencing the law of diminishing returns.

THE EXTERNAL LEGAL ENVIRONMENT

A financial planner should have an understanding of consumer protection laws, investor protections laws, and worker protection laws. Consumer protection laws are designed to protect the rights of individual consumers while promoting competition and fair business practices. Investor protection laws are designed to promote investor confidence in security markets and protect investors from fraudulent or inappropriate investments. Worker protection laws protect the rights of workers, ensure fair treatment by current employers, provide unemployment and worker insurance benefits, and require safe and healthy working conditions.

⋮≣ *Key Concepts*

1. Identify the difference between Chapter 7, Chapter 11, and Chapter 13 bankruptcies.

2. What is the purpose and mission of the FTC?

3. Identify important consumer protection laws and their purpose.

4. What are the three goals of the FDIC?

5. Identify the rules regarding FDIC insurance as pertains to account ownership and the amount of insurance coverage.

Consumer Protection

Bankruptcy Laws

The Bankruptcy Reform Act of 1978 defines the law governing all federal bankruptcy cases in the U.S. Over the years, the Act of 1978 has been amended and additional acts have been passed to refine and address current day issues. The bankruptcy laws generally favor the rehabilitation of the debtor rather than punishing the debtor. There are no debtor jails and the bankruptcy process generally does not have criminal consequences. The bankruptcy laws provide the debtor with an opportunity to reorganize, adjust, and repay their debts. The bankruptcy laws are designed to protect both the debtor and creditors. Bankruptcy proceedings allow creditors an opportunity to be heard and to potentially lay claim to nonexempt assets of the debtor.

There are three primary chapters to the bankruptcy law that most individuals and businesses will use when filing for bankruptcy.[7] The three primary chapters are:
- Chapter 7 – For wage earners to discharge debts by liquidation
- Chapter 11 – For companies to reorganize and adjust debts
- Chapter 13 – For wage earners to repay a portion of debts with income over the future 36 to 60 months

Chapter 7 Bankruptcy

Chapter 7 bankruptcy allows individuals or businesses to obtain protection from creditors. Under Chapter 7, assets are liquidated to repay all or a portion of the debts. A Chapter 7 bankruptcy can be voluntary or involuntary. Voluntary bankruptcy is when the debtor files a bankruptcy petition with the courts. Involuntary bankruptcy is when the creditors file the petition for bankruptcy and force the debtor into bankruptcy.

To initiate bankruptcy protection, a debtor must file a bankruptcy petition with the federal bankruptcy court in the appropriate federal judicial district. Once the petition is filed, the court notifies creditors and all collection calls, lawsuits, and wage garnishments must stop. Typically within 40 days of filing the bankruptcy petition, the U.S. Trustee or bankruptcy administrator will hold a creditor's meeting with the debtor and creditors. During this meeting, assets are disclosed that may be available to satisfy creditor's claims.

---

7. www.uscourts.gov/services-forms/bankruptcy/bankruptcy-basics

As a result of the Bankruptcy Abuse Prevention and Consumer Protection Act (BAPCPA) of 2005, a "means test" is applied by the bankruptcy court to determine if the debtor's income is above or below the average income for their state. If the debtor's income is below the average income, the debtor is permitted to file bankruptcy under Chapter 7 but may file under Chapter 13. If the debtor's income is above the average income, the debtor is typically not permitted to file under Chapter 7 and must file under Chapter 13.

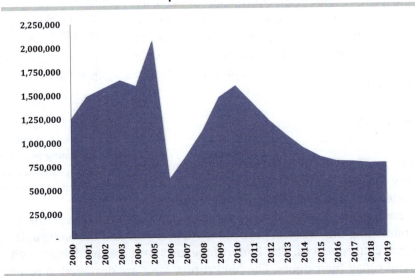

Exhibit 15.16 | Total Bankruptcy Filings

Source: http://www.uscourts.gov/report-name/bankruptcy-filings

The BAPCPA also requires that before filing for bankruptcy, a debtor must attend a credit counseling program. Once a debtor has filed for bankruptcy, the debtor must attend a personal financial management course before their debts are discharged.

As part of the bankruptcy proceedings under Chapter 7, the court will liquidate nonexempt assets to repay creditors. This may include losing a secured asset, such as a primary residence. This is known as "relief through liquidation."

Some assets and property are exempt from the bankruptcy court and creditors, such as:[8]
- Federal law limits the homestead exemption to $170,350 of equity if the home was purchased within 40 months of filing for bankruptcy. However, if the debtor has resided in the state for longer than 40 months, the state's laws prevail. In states like Florida, a debtor has an unlimited homestead exemption, so they can keep their house on the beach. In Georgia, a debtor is only allowed $21,500 of home equity ($43,000 if married).
- Traditional and Roth IRAs up to $1,362,800 (as indexed in 2019; indexed every three years).
- Rollover IRAs for an unlimited amount.
- Qualified retirement plans, certain types of deferred compensation, and certain tax–deferred annuities.
- Some personal property including one car, one television, etc.
- Education funds contributed to a qualified tuition plan, although there are limits based on the timing and amounts of the contributions.

8. https://www.thebankruptcysite.org/exemptions/federal.html

The federal bankruptcy law allows a debtor to list their exempt property by following either the federal or their state's bankruptcy law. A debtor may elect either their state or the federal property exemption amounts. Usually, states have more favorable asset exemption amounts and debtors elect to follow their state laws, unless the federal law takes precedence, like the homestead exemption amount.

The bankruptcy court will liquidate assets and use those proceeds to repay creditors. Certain debts are not discharged in bankruptcy, and include:

- Most student loans
- Property liens
- Three years of back taxes
- Child support
- Alimony
- Debts obtained through fraud

Another important law revision as a result of BAPCPA is that a debtor must wait eight years before filing again under Chapter 7 bankruptcy. Prior to BAPCPA, the law required a six year waiting period before filing again under Chapter 7.

Note that Chapter 7 bankruptcy is designed to liquidate assets to repay creditors. The debtor may be able to keep a house or an automobile, but will still have a mortgage or automobile loan payment.

Chapter 11 Bankruptcy

Chapter 11 bankruptcy is known as "reorganization bankruptcy" for corporations, sole proprietorships, and partnerships. A Chapter 11 bankruptcy can be voluntary or involuntary.

Under Chapter 11, the debtor is a "debtor in possession" of assets of the company. The debtor in possession is responsible for managing the assets of the company and acting as a fiduciary, which places the interest of the company ahead of the individual.

Companies that file under Chapter 11 are required to file a reorganization plan with the courts, which must be approved by the creditors and bankruptcy court. The plan is deemed to be accepted by all creditors, if the plan is accepted by creditors that hold at least two-thirds of the debt and more than one-half the number of claims in the class of creditors. A reorganization plan outlines how the company will restructure contracts, which assets will be liquidated, and to what extent creditors will be repaid. All contracts, debts, and obligations will be discharged once the reorganization plan is approved by the creditors and the court. The company must adhere to any payment schedules agreed to in the reorganization plan.

Example 15.9

General Motors (GM) filed for Chapter 11 bankruptcy on June 1, 2009 and emerged as a new company on July 6, 2009. Under terms of the bankruptcy reorganization GM, the U.S. Government, United Auto Workers Union, and debt holders agreed to the following terms:

- The company created a new entity with all remaining assets of the original GM company. The new entity was 61% owned by the U.S. Government, 17% owned by the United Auto Workers Pension Fund, 12% owned by the Canadian government, and 10% owned by bondholders of the original GM.
- Much of the debt was forgiven or restructured. GM's debt went from $94 billion to $17 billion under the new entity.
- Many debtholders were forced to accept equity in the new entity in exchange for giving up their debt position.

The result of GM's Chapter 11 bankruptcy was a new company without the burden of significant debt, liabilities, and poor performing product lines.

Chapter 13 Bankruptcy

Chapter 13 bankruptcy, also known as a "wage earners plan," is for individuals or self-employed workers who want to keep their assets and payoff a portion of their debts over time. Corporations and partnerships are not eligible to file Chapter 13.

The BAPCPA requires that before filing for a Chapter 13 bankruptcy, a debtor must attend a credit counseling program. Once a debtor has filed for bankruptcy, the debtor must attend a personal financial management course before their debts are discharged. Similar to Chapter 7, once the debtor files a bankruptcy petition, the court notifies creditors and all collection calls, lawsuits, and wage garnishments must stop.

If a debtor's income is greater than the mean average for their state, the debtor's "applicable commitment period" to repay all or a portion of their debts (at least as much under the plan as the creditor would receive if the debtor's assets were liquidated under Chapter 7) is five years. If the debtor's income is less than the mean average for their state, the debtor's "applicable commitment period" to repay all or a portion of their debts (at least as much under the plan as the creditor would receive if the debtor's assets were liquidated under Chapter 7) is three years. Repayment under a Chapter 13 bankruptcy is made by the debtor to the trustee. The trustee is responsible for allocating the payment to the creditors, according to the terms of the repayment plan.

Generally, any secured creditors are repaid in full. Any unsecured creditors will likely receive less than the full amount owed. If the debtor fails to make payments to the trustee as agreed, the court will dismiss the Chapter 13 bankruptcy filing or force a Chapter 7 liquidation bankruptcy.

Certain debts are not discharged in Chapter 13 (similar to Chapter 7). Those debts that are not discharged include:

- Most student loans
- Property liens
- Three years of back taxes
- Child support
- Alimony
- Debts obtained through fraud

There are differences between Chapter 13 and Chapter 7 which may make Chapter 13 more attractive. Note that some debts are dischargeable in Chapter 13, but not in Chapter 7 (a discussion of this topic is beyond the scope of this textbook).

Other Consumer Protection Laws and Agencies

Federal Trade Commission (FTC)

The **Federal Trade Commission (FTC)** was created in 1914 and its purpose was to prevent unfair methods of competition in commerce as part of the battle to "bust the trusts."[9] Since then, many consumer protection laws have been passed by Congress, which the FTC is responsible for enforcing. The overriding mission of the FTC is to protect the consumer and prevent unfair, anti-competitive business practices. The FTC works for the consumer to prevent fraudulent, deceptive, and unfair business practices in the marketplace and to provide information to help consumers identify, prevent, and avoid them. Several major consumer protection laws are discussed below.

Fair Packaging and Labeling Act

The purpose of the **Fair Packaging and Labeling Act (FPLA)** is to help consumers compare the value of products and to prevent unfair or deceptive packaging and labeling of many household items. This Act requires manufacturers to disclose the manufacturer's name, address, and contents of the package. The act also prevents deceptive packaging with regards to ingredients, labeling, and misleading presentation of package sizes. This act does not regulate food, drugs, or cosmetics.

Equal Credit Opportunity Act

The **Equal Credit Opportunity Act** prohibits discrimination, when evaluating a decision to grant consumer credit. Denying credit as a result of any of the following **would** constitute discrimination under this Act:

- On the basis of race, color, religion, national origin, sex, marital status, age or receipt of public assistance.
- The consumer's income derives from any public assistance program.
- The consumer exercised a right that is due to him under this Act.

The following actions by a creditor **would not** constitute discrimination:

- For the creditor to ask about the consumer's marital status, as long as the information is used to determine the creditor's recourse if the debt is not satisfied and the information is not used to determine credit-worthiness.
- For the creditor to ask for the consumer's age or, if their income is from public assistance if the creditor is ascertaining the probability of the consumer maintaining their current income level.

---

9. www.ftc.gov/ftc/about.shtm

If an applicant is denied credit (adverse action), this Act requires that the creditor provide the applicant with reasons why the decision was made to deny extending credit.

A good credit history of responsibly managing the amount of your debt and making timely payments will lead to good credit and increase the likelihood of future credit being extended.

Credit history is used to determine an individual's credit score. The most popular method of determining a credit score is the Fair Isaac Credit Organization (FICO) method. A FICO score is used to evaluate the creditworthiness of a borrower. The three major credit reporting agencies Equifax, Experian, and TransUnion track an individual's credit history, amount of credit available, amount of credit used, timeliness of payments, credit inquiries, and more to determine a credit or FICO score. Although there are other formulas used to derive a credit score, the FICO score is the most widely used credit scoring methodology. A FICO score will range from 300 – 850. The higher the credit score, the more likely a borrower is to qualify for credit, at the lowest interest rates available. The national average FICO score was 706 in 2019.

Based on the key factors evaluated in the credit report, the best ways to increase a FICO score are to:[10]
- Pay all bills on time (payment history is 35% of the score)
- Avoid having payments go into collections
- Keep outstanding balances low on revolving credit accounts (amount of debt/utilization is 30% of the score)
- Don't close old unused credit cards (length of credit history is 15% of the score)
- Do rate shopping within a short period of time (hard inquiries of the same type, such as from several mortgage companies, within a 14- to 45-day period are treated as a single inquiry)
- Be aware of the types of debt on your report, for example, credit card, installment loan, or mortgage loan (type of credit is 10% of the score)

Fair Credit Reporting Act

The **Fair Credit Reporting Act** protects consumer's information collected by the major credit bureaus (Equifax, TransUnion, and Experian). The information contained in a credit report can only be provided to a person who has a specific purpose that is detailed in the Act, such as a potential employer considering making a job offer, a creditor considering extending credit, or an insurance company evaluating an insurance application. Companies that report information to the credit bureaus have a legal duty to investigate any disputed items in a credit report. Credit reporting agencies must correct or remove inaccurate or unverified information within 30 days of being notified. Anyone who relies on information contained in a credit report must notify the consumer of negative items on the credit report that may have led to being denied a job offer, credit, or insurance. Anyone relying on the information in a credit report must notify the consumer of the credit bureau that supplied the information, so the consumer can take the appropriate steps to remedy the negative item. Negative items cannot be reported beyond seven years and bankruptcies cannot be reported beyond 10 years.

The Fair Credit Reporting Act entitles consumers to one free credit report each year from each of the major credit reporting bureaus.[11] In response to many websites promoting "free credit reports" but requiring consumers to enroll in credit monitoring programs, starting April 2, 2010 any websites or advertisements that promote free credit reports must include the following disclosure:

10.https://ficoscore.com/education/#ManagingRespobsibly
11.http://AnnualCreditReport.com

Some web sites have circumvented the above rule by charging $1 for the reports, which, when paid, automatically subscribes the card holder to a credit monitoring service for which the card holder will be billed monthly. Consumers should instead access their free, no obligation, credit reports directly from AnnualCreditReport.com.

Fair Debt Collection Practices Act

The **Fair Debt Collection Practices Act** prevents third-party debt collectors from using deceptive or abusive methods to collect debts. Examples of deceptive or abusive tactics prevented by this Act include:

- Debt collectors cannot threaten legal action if there is no intention to bring legal action.
- Debt collectors cannot disclose the debt to employers, co-workers, other family members, or anyone else, in an attempt to embarrass the debtor. In addition, the debt collector may not contact the debtor at their place of employment, if they know that the debtor's employer prohibits the contact.
- The collectors cannot contact the debtor at unusual hours or make repeated, harassing telephone calls. Appropriate times to contact the debtor are from 8:00 a.m. – 9:00 p.m. Debt collectors are not allowed to contact debtors outside of those hours.
- Debt collectors cannot threaten to use violence as a means of collecting the debt.
- If the debtor informs the collector that they have retained an attorney and the collector should contact the attorney, the debt collector can no longer contact the debtor and must contact the attorney.

Truth in Lending Act

The **Truth in Lending Act** was written to protect consumers so that they fully understand the terms of a loan. Regulation Z of the Truth in Lending Act outlines the specific requirements of lenders. For example, this Act requires creditors to disclose all finance charges and the costs of credit in writing. Lenders must state the interest rate using the annual percentage rate. This Act also requires that debtors be provided with a "three-day right of recession" for loans that are secured by the debtor's primary residence. The Act also regulates how creditors may advertise loan and financing costs.

Fair Credit Billing Act

This Act amended the Truth in Lending Act. The **Fair Credit Billing Act** requires timely, written verification to a consumer disputing a billing error. The creditor must provide a written acknowledgment of the consumer dispute within 30 days of being notified. This Act also requires that creditors promptly credit consumer's accounts to reflect payment.

Examples of billing errors that are covered under this Act include:

- Charges posted with a wrong date or dollar amount.
- Charges for goods or services that were never received.
- Failure of the creditor to credit payment to the consumer's account.
- Failure of the creditor to send the bill to the correct address, if the consumer has notified the creditor of the correct address, in writing, with at least 20 days notice prior to the end of a billing period.

12. http://www.ftc.gov/opa/2010/02/facta.shtm

Consumers must take the following steps to dispute a billing error:

1. Notify the creditor, in writing, within 60 days of receiving the bill, about the disputed item.
2. The creditor must notify the consumer of receiving the dispute, in writing, within 30 days of receiving the notification.
3. The creditor has 90 days to resolve the billing dispute, after receiving notification from the consumer.

During the time period that the error is being investigated, the creditor may not take any legal action to collect the disputed amount and cannot impose finance or penalty related charges. While an item is being disputed, the creditor cannot report the unpaid amount to a credit reporting agency and negatively impact a consumer's credit score. The Act also stipulates that credit card holders are only responsible for the lesser of the charges incurred or $50 for lost or stolen credit cards.

The Fair Credit Billing Act applies to credit cards and revolving charge accounts that are typically issued by big chain stores. This Act does not apply to loans a consumer repays over a period of time or on a fixed repayment schedule, such as automobile payments or installment type payment plans.

Bankruptcy Abuse Prevention and Consumer Protection Act (BAPCPA) of 2005

The **BAPCPA of 2005** amends the Truth in Lending Act in various respects, including requiring certain creditors to disclose on the front of billing statements a minimum monthly payment warning for consumers and a toll-free telephone number, established and maintained by the Commission, for consumers seeking information on the time required to repay specific credit balances.

Credit Card Accountability, Responsibility and Disclosure (CARD) Act of 2009

The **CARD Act of 2009** prevents credit card companies (and banks) from charging hidden fees and extraordinary interest rates as well as promoting easy to understand statements.

The CARD Act of 2009 addressed the following issues:

- **Prevent certain rate increase practices** - Credit card companies can no longer increase interest rates on a credit card at any time for any reason, or no reason at all. Prior to the CARD Act a credit card company would raise their interest rate if a consumer missed payments on another card. Alternatively, credit card companies would offer extremely low introductory rates to entice balance transfers, only to later raise the rate. Credit card companies would follow a "universal default" policy, such that if a cardholder would default on one credit card, other credit card companies would raise the interest rate. Credit card companies can no longer penalize cardholders for defaults or missed payments on other credit cards. Credit card companies cannot retroactively increase a promotional interest rate, unless the cardholder is at least 60 days late on their payments. In addition, promotional interest rates must last at least six months and low interest rates for purchases on a new credit card must last at least one year.

- **Prevent hidden fees and confusing payment due dates** - Credit card companies can no longer charge for over the limit fees, without consent from the cardholder. In the past, credit card companies would allow a cardholder to go over their credit limit, but charge an over the limit fee. In addition, credit card companies must provide at least 21 days from the date the bill is mailed until the payment is due. Credit card companies may not randomly change the billing due date, or require payments due on a weekend or holiday.

- **Easy to understand disclosures** - All language regarding the terms and conditions of a credit card must be in plain, easy to understand language, and no more fine print. Credit terms must be disclosed before an account is opened. On the monthly statements, credit card companies must disclose how long and how much it will cost to pay off the current balance if only the minimum payment is made. Credit card companies must display the total cost if the balance is paid off in 36 months. Credit card companies must now give 45 days notice regarding any changes that will negatively impact the cardholders. Credit card companies must also give cardholders the option of canceling the card, rather than accepting the changes.

- **Protection for young adults** - Credit card companies are not permitted to issue a credit card to anyone under the age of 21, without a co-signer.

- **Requires that payment in excess of the minimum payment amount be applied in favor of the cardholder** - Any payment above the minimum required payment amount must be applied first to the balance with the highest interest rate.

Example 15.10

Jasper has the following balances on his credit card:

	Rate	Balance
Cash Advance	21%	$3,500
Purchases	14%	$900
Balance Transfer	0%	$5,000

The minimum payment for this billing cycle is $140. If the Jasper pays $400, the credit card company can allocate the $140 minimum payment in any manner of its choosing (most likely applying it to the balance with the lowest rate, which would reduce the 0% balance transfer balance to $4,860). The extra $260 must be applied to the balance with the highest rate, which is the cash advance. This will reduce the cash advance balance to $3,240, and the purchases balance will remain unchanged.

Federal Deposit Insurance Corporation (FDIC)

The **Federal Deposit Insurance Corporation (FDIC)** was formed in 1933, as a result of the bank failures that occurred in the 1920's and 1930's. The three goals of the FDIC are to:
- Insure deposits
- Manage receiverships
- Supervise financial institutions for financial stability and consumer protection

In 2008, the FDIC insurance amount for insured deposits was increased from $100,000 to $250,000, as a result of the turmoil experienced in the financial markets in 2008 and 2009. As part of the Dodd-Frank Wall Street Reform and Consumer Protection Act, the increase from $100,000 to $250,000 was made permanent.

FDIC insurance only applies to deposit accounts. Deposit accounts include: checking accounts, savings accounts, money market deposit accounts, and certificates of deposit. FDIC insurance does not apply to stocks, bonds, mutual funds, money market mutual funds, insurance products, or annuities. In addition, FDIC insurance does not apply to deposits that are only payable outside the United States.

The FDIC is funded entirely through premiums charged to banks, to insure their deposits, known as deposit insurance. The FDIC insures up to $250,000 per depositor, per legal account ownership, per financial institution. Legal account ownership includes five distinct categories for non-business account owners, which are: Individual, Joint, Revocable Testamentary (for example revocable trust or Pay On Death), Irrevocable Trust, and Retirement accounts. It is possible for a person to have $250,000 of coverage in an individual, joint, testamentary, and retirement account at one financial institution and have a total of $1,000,000 or more of FDIC coverage. While irrevocable trusts are insured up to $250,000 per trust, revocable testamentary accounts, such as revocable trusts, payable-on-death accounts or Totten trusts, provide coverage of up to $250,000 per owner per beneficiary. For example, a husband and wife can set up a revocable trust naming their three children as beneficiaries, and the FDIC will insure up to $1,500,000 (coverage of $250,000 x 3 children = $750,000 for the husband, and another $250,000 x 3 children = $750,000 for the wife).[13]

13. https://www.fdic.gov/deposit/covered/categories.html

Example 15.11

Homer and Marge are married and have one child, Bart. They have the following accounts at First Bank of Springfield.

Account Title	Account Ownership Category	Owner(s)	Account Balance	Amount Insured Homer	Amount Insured Marge	Amount Insured Bart	Not Insured
CD 1	Individual Account	Homer	$75,000	$75,000 (Individual)			
Savings	Joint Account	Homer and Marge	$150,000	$75,000 (Joint)	$75,000 (Joint)		
IRA (CD's)	Retirement Account	Homer	$300,000	$250,000 (Retirement)			$50,000 (Retirement)
Checking A	Joint Account	Homer and Marge	$50,000	$25,000 (Joint)	$25,000 (Joint)		
CD 2	Joint Account	Homer, Marge, and Bart	$600,000	$150,000 (Joint)	$150,000 (Joint)	$200,000 (Joint)	$100,000 ($50,000 for Homer and $50,000 for Marge's Joint)
UGMA	Custodian	For Bart, Marge is Custodian	$100,000			$100,000 (Individual)	
Checking B	Individual Account	Bart	$10,000			$10,000 (Individual)	
Revocable Trust	Testamentary	Marge owner, Bart beneficiary	$300,000		$250,000 (Testamentary)		$50,000
Single Totals				$75,000		$110,000	
Joint Totals				$250,000	$250,000	$200,000	
Testamentary Totals					$250,000		
Retirement Totals				$250,000			
Amount Uninsured							$200,000

Since the FDIC limits apply per bank, Marge and Homer could obtain FDIC coverage on the $200,000 that is currently not covered by moving those balances to a different bank.

Summary of Example

Individual Account Ownership

All accounts titled as an individual account by the same person are combined and insured, up to $250,000. The individual account ownerships in the example are Homer's CD for $75,000 and Bart's checking account for $10,000. Both individual accounts are fully insured for FDIC purposes.

Joint Account Ownership

The entire balance for accounts titled as joint account ownership are divided evenly by the number of persons on the account. So, if there are two owners on a joint account, the balance is divided 50/50 between the two account owners. If there are three owners on a joint account, the account balance is divided evenly - one-third for each owner. The joint account ownership in the example are Homer and Marge's savings account of $150,000, which is allocated $75,000 to Homer's joint account and $75,000 to Marge's joint account. Checking account A for $50,000 is also a joint account, which is allocated $25,000 to Homer's joint account and $25,000 to Marge's joint account. CD 2 for $600,000 is a joint account and is allocated $200,000 to Homer, $200,000 to Marge and $200,000 to Bart. However, when combining the savings account, plus the checking account A, plus the CD 2, Homer and Marge are each $50,000 over the FDIC limit.

Revocable Trust Account Ownership

The amount of FDIC insurance coverage of revocable trust accounts is determined by the amount of the trust's deposits belonging to each owner for each beneficiary. For the above example, Marge has a trust with a value of $300,000 and only one beneficiary; therefore, only $250,000 of the $300,000 is insured for FDIC purposes.

Investor Protection

Securities Investor Protection Corporation (SIPC)

The **Securities Investor Protection Corporation (SIPC)** was formed in 1970 as a statutorily created nonprofit membership corporation funded by its member securities broker-dealers, with the goal of returning cash and securities to investors, in the event a brokerage firm becomes insolvent. SIPC covers cash, stocks, bonds, and investment company shares (mutual funds). The SIPC does not cover annuity contracts, gold, silver, or futures contracts. The SIPC is not intended to protect investors from poor investment selection or losses arising from bad investments.

The SIPC provides coverage if a broker-dealer becomes insolvent or if there is unauthorized trading in an investor's account. The brokerage customer is not required to be a U.S. citizen or to reside in the U.S.; if the brokerage firm is a member of SIPC, coverage is provided.

> ### ≔ Key Concepts
>
> 1. Identify the purpose of the SIPC.
>
> 2. Distinguish between the Securities Act of 1933 and the Securities Exchange Act of 1934.
>
> 3. What is an investment adviser and what rules must an investment adviser adhere to?
>
> 4. What is FINRA?
>
> 5. Identify the purpose of the enactment of the Sarbanes-Oxley Act.

Example 15.12

Hans is a citizen of Germany who resides in Italy. Hans' friend Emily is a U.S. citizen who resides in Australia. Both Hans and Emily have opened brokerage accounts with a SIPC-member brokerage firm in New York City. If the broker-dealer becomes insolvent, both Hans and Emily are protected, up to the SIPC limits.

When a broker-dealer becomes insolvent, the SIPC will step in and return the investor's cash and securities, up to $500,000 in securities. The $500,000 limit includes up to $250,000 in cash. Money market mutual funds held within a brokerage account are securities and are covered under the $500,000 limit. When a brokerage customer has multiple accounts, SIPC coverage applies based on each "separate capacity." Separate capacities include:[14]

- individual accounts,
- joint accounts (joint accounts with different co-owners are covered separately),
- corporate accounts,
- trust accounts,
- traditional IRAs,
- Roth IRAs,
- accounts held by estate executors, and
- custodial accounts for minors.

Example 15.13

Jessie has securities worth $100,000 and cash of $350,000 in his brokerage account. If the brokerage firm becomes insolvent, Jessie's securities worth $100,000 would be returned to him but only $250,000 of his $350,000 in cash would be covered.

Example 15.14

Honus has two individual accounts at Big Brokerage Firm (BBF), a SIPC-member firm. Honus' wife Bessie has an individual account and a Roth IRA at BBF. Honus and Bessie also have a joint account at BBF. Should BBF become insolvent, Honus' two individual accounts combined are covered up to $500,000; Bessie's individual account is covered up to $500,000; Bessie's Roth IRA is covered up to $500,000; and the joint account is covered up to $500,000.

Example 15.15

Milton has 10,000 shares of ABC stock trading at $30 per share, plus $75,000 of cash. SIPC provides coverage of the securities for $300,000 (10,000 shares x $30) and his cash of $75,000.

In the event that Milton's broker-dealer becomes insolvent, the SIPC will either replace the securities or give Milton a check for the amount of his account, up to the $500,000 limit. There is some risk that a broker-dealer could become insolvent when Milton's stock is trading at $30 per share and the broker-dealer is shut down. It may take a few months before the SIPC is appointed as a trustee and the stock price could fall to $20 per share.

14. https://www.sipc.org/for-investors/investors-with-multiple-accounts.

The SIPC could return the shares to Milton or give him a check for his 10,000 shares at $20 per share. Alternatively, if the stock price increased to $40 per share before the SIPC was appointed as a trustee, then Milton would receive the 10,000 shares or a check for $475,000 ($400,000 in securities + $75,000 in cash). The market risk associated with the stock price increasing or decreasing before the SIPC is appointed trustee is not covered by the SIPC.

Securities Act of 1933

The **Securities Act of 1933** requires that any new security be registered with the Securities and Exchange Commission (SEC) by filing a registration statement with the SEC. Since this Act regulates new securities, it regulates the primary market. This Act requires disclosure of financial and other significant information regarding new securities and prohibits deceit, misrepresentations, and fraud in the sale of new securities.

Registering a security includes the filing of a registration statement and financial statements with the SEC. The registration process discloses information such as a description of the company, the security and information about management. This Act also requires a prospectus that contains information in the registration statement, and is provided to prospective investors. This information allows investors to make well-informed investment decisions. After filing registration statements with the SEC, there is a 20-day cooling off period. During this cooling off period, the security's issuer may distribute a red herring prospectus. A red herring prospectus does not include the price of the security or the amount of the security being sold. Once the registration with the SEC is complete, the security can be bought and sold.

Certain securities are exempt from being registered with the SEC. These are some examples of securities that are exempt from the registration requirements:
- Securities of a municipal, state, or federal government.
- Intrastate offerings where the investors and issuers are residents of the same state where the issuer performs most activities.
- Commercial paper with a maturity of 270 days or less.
- Securities issued by a bank, savings institution, common carrier, or farmers' cooperative and subject to other regulatory legislation.
- Stock dividends, stock splits, and securities issued in connection with corporate reorganizations.
- Insurance, endowment, and annuity contracts.

Regulation A is a process for small businesses to sell shares through an initial public offering. Regulation A requires a less stringent registration process for small issues, less than $75,000,000 during a 12 month period.[15] Tier 1 offerings up to $20 million follow more relaxed rules while Tier 2 offerings up to $75 million have additional rules and reporting requirements. Tier 2 offerings may be sold to accredited investors (as defined below) without limitation; however, non-accredited investors in Tier 2 offerings are subject to limitations on the amount of the investment.

15.Increased from $5 million to $50 million in 2015 as a result of the Jumpstart Our Business Startups (JOBS) Act. Increased to $75 million in 2021 under SEC Release 33-10844, effective March 15, 2021.

Regulation D provides three exemptions to registration for small issues, such as:

- **Rule 504:** Securities of up to $10,000,000 in a 12 month period to investors who receive restricted securities, that may not be resold without registration or meeting an exemption.[16] Companies may sell non-restricted securities if:
  - The company registers the offering exclusively in one or more states that require a publicly filed registration statement and delivery of a substantive disclosure document to investors.
  - A company registers and sells the offering in a state that requires registration and disclosure delivery and also sells in a state without those requirements, so long as the company delivers the disclosure documents required by the state where the company registered the offering to all purchasers (including those in the state that has no such requirements).
  - The company sells exclusively according to state law exemptions that permit general solicitation and advertising, so long as the company sells only to "accredited investors." An accredited investor is:[17]
    - A person who has an individual net worth, or joint net worth with the person's spouse (or spousal equivalent)[18], that exceeds $1million (excluding the value of the primary residence) at the time of the purchase.
    - A person with income exceeding $200,000 in each of the two most recent years or joint income with a spouse (or spousal equivalent) exceeding $300,000 for those years and a reasonable expectation of the same income level in the current year.
    - A bank, insurance company, registered investment company, business development company, small business investment company, or rural business investment company.
    - A charitable organization, corporation, partnership, or limited liability company with assets exceeding $5 million.
    - A director, executive officer, or general partner of the company selling the securities.[19]
    - An individual who holds a FINRA Series 7 (General Securities Representative) license, Series 65 (Investment Advisor Representative) license, or Series 82 (Private Securities Offering Representative) license.[20]
    - With respect to investment in a private fund, a natural person who is a "knowledgeable employee" of the fund.[21]
    - SEC- and state- registered investment advisors.
    - A family office (and the family clients of such family offices) with at least $5 million in assets under management.
    - Other entities, including Indian tribes, government bodies and entities organized under the laws of foreign countries, owning investments in excess of $5 million, that were not formed for the specific purpose of acquiring the securities being offered.

---

16. Increased from $5 million to $10 million in 2021 under SEC Release 33-10844, effective March 15, 2021. (
17. As updated in SEC release 33-10824, effective December 8, 2020.
18. A spousal equivalent is defined as a cohabitant occupying a relationship generally equivalent to that of a spouse.
19. Includes managers of LLCs, who serve in a capacity similar to directors of a corporation.
20. The individual must maintain the license in good standing to retain status as an accredited investor. The SEC reserves the right to add additional licenses or designations to this list in the future.
21. A "knowledgeable employee" is defined in Rule 3c-5(a)(4) of the Investment Company Act and includes individuals such as an executive officer, director, trustee, general partner, or advisory board member of the private fund, as well as employees who oversee the fund's investments.

- **Rule 506:** Sales of any amount of securities to accredited investors or up to 35 other purchasers that have a sufficient knowledge and experience in financial and business matters to make them capable of evaluating the merits and risks of the prospective investment. The shares must be restricted and investors cannot freely trade the securities in the secondary markets.

Securities Exchange Act of 1934

The **Securities Exchange Act of 1934** created the Securities and Exchange Commission (SEC) and provides the SEC with the authority to regulate the secondary market. The secondary market includes the subsequent trading of securities, after their initial public offering. The SEC has the power to regulate brokerage firms, stock market exchanges [(New York Stock Exchange, National Association of Securities Dealers Automated Quotations (NASDAQ))] and self regulatory organizations, such as the Financial Industry Regulatory Authority (FINRA).

This Act requires companies with more than 500 shareholders and $10 million in assets to file and disclose financial statements with the SEC. The reporting requirements include quarterly financial statements (10Q) and audited annual financial statements (10k).

This Act requires that information such as shareholder proxy materials soliciting shareholder votes be filed with the SEC prior to distribution to shareholders. The SEC ensures compliance with disclosure requirements. This Act also requires the disclosure by anyone attempting to purchase more than five percent of a company's securities.

This Act prohibits insider trading, which is the trading of a security while in the possession of material non-public information. Basically, if you have information that is not public, you cannot trade on that information. This Act also prohibits price manipulation of a security and making misleading statements about a security. An investment adviser may be liable for an investor's losses under this Act if all of the following conditions are met:
1. There was a material misstatement or omission.
2. The person intended to deceive the investor.
3. The client relied on the misrepresentation and incurred a loss as a result.

Regulation T under this Act provides the Federal Reserve with the authority to set the margin trading requirements. The Federal Reserve has set the minimum initial margin to 50 percent, which requires investors who borrow from the broker to enter a securities transaction to contribute at least 50 percent equity and borrow up to 50 percent of the transaction total.

Investment Company Act of 1940

The **Investment Company Act of 1940** set standards to regulate investment companies such as open-end, closed-end, and unit investment trusts. Investment companies are more broadly thought of as mutual funds, which pool investor resources and purchase securities in anticipation of earning a return for the investors.

This Act requires investment companies to register with the SEC. The Act also requires that investment companies disclose the financial statements, investments, costs, objectives, and management of the investment company. These disclosures must be made when the security is initially sold and on an ongoing basis.

Investment Advisers Act of 1940

The **Investment Advisers Act of 1940** requires investment advisers to register with their state or the SEC. Under this Act, an investment adviser is anyone who "receives compensation, engages in the business of advising others, either directly or through publications or writings, as to the value of securities or as to the advisability of investing in, purchasing, or selling securities, or who, for compensation and as part of a regular business, issues or promulgates analyses or reports concerning securities."

The Act can be broken down into a three-pronged test to determine who is an investment adviser. The three-pronged test is:

1. Does the person provide **advice or analysis** regarding securities? Advice or analysis can be as simple as recommending that a client invest in some index mutual funds and providing the client with a list of index funds for the client to choose. Advice does not constitute discussing the current economy or business cycle with a client.

2. Does the person hold themselves out as "**in the business?**" Investment advice regarding securities does not need to be the adviser's primary business. For example, an accounting firm that primarily offers tax preparation and audit services with a small financial planning division that provides investment advice would meet the "in the business" requirement.

3. Does the person receive **compensation** for their advice? Compensation can be in the form of commissions, flat rate, or a fee for a financial plan where investment advice is a part of the overall plan and services provided by the planner.

An adviser who meets all three of the three-pronged test must register as a Registered Investment Adviser (RIA) with their state or the SEC, unless the adviser meets an exception. Investment advisers with assets in excess of $110,000,000 are required to register with the SEC. Advisers with assets below $100,000,000 are required to register with their state. If an adviser manages between $100 and $110 million of client funds, he or she may elect to register with the SEC or with his or her state.

SEC Release IA-770 and IA-1092

In 1981, in response to requests for clarification by financial planners, the SEC issued Release #IA-770 to interpret the Investment Advisers Act as it relates to the advice typically given by financial planners. In the release, the SEC considered whether merely general recommendations of securities instead of other investment possibilities, such as stamps, coins, or commodities, would make the financial planner an investment adviser. The SEC determined that advice or recommendations even general in nature would render a financial planner an investment adviser under the Act, if the recommendations were performed as part of a business and compensation was received for services. Under Release #770, the compensation received by the adviser need not be paid directly by the persons receiving investment advice. Compensation is interpreted broadly and includes any commission or other economic benefit from the sale of securities. A later release, IA-1092 in 1987, reaffirmed the content of IA-770 and made it clear that all investment advisers, not just those subject to registration with the SEC, are subject to the anti-fraud provisions of the 1940 Act. IA-1092 also imposed on investment advisers a fiduciary responsibility to their clients.

Exclusions and Exemptions from Registration

The Act provides **exclusions** from the definition of an investment adviser. Even if an adviser meets the three-pronged test, but meets one of the exclusions, they are not considered an investment adviser under the Act, do not have to register, and are generally not regulated by the Act. The following are **exclusions** from the definition of:

1. A bank, or any bank holding company as defined in the Bank Holding Company Act of 1956, which is not an investment company.
2. Any lawyer, accountant, engineer, or teacher whose performance of such services is solely incidental to the practice of his profession.
3. Any broker or dealer whose performance of such services is solely incidental to the conduct of his business as a broker or dealer and who receives no special compensation.
4. The publisher of any bona fide newspaper, news magazine, or financial publication of general and regular circulation.
5. Any person whose advice, analyses, or reports relate to no securities other than securities which are direct obligations of or obligations guaranteed as to principal or interest by the United States.

The Act provides for **exemptions** from registration as an investment adviser, however they are still considered investment advisers and are subject to the anti-fraud provisions of the Act. The following are **exemptions** from registering as an investment adviser:

- A foreign adviser without a U.S. office or other place of business that manages less than $25 million of client assets or has fewer than 15 U.S. clients and does not hold itself out to the public as an investment adviser in the U.S.
- An adviser whose only clients are insurance companies.
- An adviser whose clients are all residents of the state in which the adviser maintains his, her, or its principal office and place of business and who only gives advice regarding securities that are not listed on any exchange and/or does not have unlisted trading privileges on any national securities exchange.
- An adviser whose only clients are venture capital funds.
- An adviser whose only clients are private funds and the adviser has less than $150 million in assets under management in the U.S.

Once an adviser is deemed an investment adviser, they have certain duties under the Investment Advisers Act of 1940. Some of the duties include:

- Register as an Investment Adviser
- No Fraudulent Activities
- Disclosure to Prospective and Current Clients (Brochure Rule)
- Prohibits the Assignment of Advisory Contracts
- Proper Use of the Term "Registered Investment Adviser"
- Books and Records to be Maintained

Registering as an Investment Adviser

To file as an investment adviser with the SEC or state, Form ADV must generally be filed electronically through the IARD website. There are three parts to Form ADV:[22]

- Part 1 contains information about the adviser's business and disciplinary history within the last ten years.
- Part 2 includes information on an adviser's services, fees, investment strategies, education and background, disciplinary actions, and conflicts of interest.
- Part 3 is a Client Relationship Summary (CRS) designed to provide retail customers with information to assist them with the decision-making process regarding the establishment or termination of an investment advisory relationship and/or engaging a particular firm or financial professional. Additional details are discussed later in this chapter under the Regulation Best Interest and Form CRS section.

To withdraw registration as an investment adviser with the SEC, Form ADV-W must be filed.

No Fraudulent Activities

The Act prohibits fraud by the investment adviser, either directly or indirectly, by:

- Employing any device, scheme, or artifice to defraud any client or prospective client.
- Engaging in any transaction, practice, or course of business which operates as fraud or deceit upon any client or prospective client.
- Acting as principal for his own account, knowingly to sell any security to or purchase any security from a client, or acting as broker for a person other than such client, knowingly to effect any sale or purchase of any security for the account of such client, without disclosing to such client in writing before the completion of such transaction the capacity in which he is acting and obtaining the consent of the client to such transaction.
- Engaging in any act, practice, or course of business which is fraudulent, deceptive, or manipulative.

Disclosure to Prospective and Current Clients (Brochure Rule)

This Act requires a registered investment adviser to provide clients with a written disclosure prior to entering an advisory contract. The requirement is for registered investment advisers to disclose their education background, services provided, fees, business practices and any legal or disciplinary action, within the last 10 years, taken against the adviser. This disclosure requirement is known as the "brochure rule." The registered investment adviser must provide the written disclosure before or at the time of the signing of an investment advisory contract. SEC Release IA-3060 requires that the brochure be written in plain English describing the adviser's business, conflicts of interest, disciplinary history, and other important information that would help clients make an informed decision about whether to hire or retain the adviser. Part 2A of Form ADV contains 18 disclosure items that must be included in the adviser's brochure. Part 2B of Form ADV provides supplemental information about supervised persons who may provide advisory services to the client. The information contained in Part 2B must be included as a supplement to the brochure for each supervised person of the adviser who provides investment advice or interacts with the client.

In addition, the brochure or Form ADV Part 2 must be provided to all clients annually, without charge.

---

22. Part 3 was added in 2020 as a result of the adoption of the SEC's Regulation BI and Form CRS Relationship Summary, as discussed below.

Prohibits the Assignment of Advisory Contracts

Investment advisers who sell their business are prohibited from assigning current investment contracts to the new owner. An investment adviser owes clients the care of a fiduciary, which is the highest professional level of responsibility. The duty of a fiduciary cannot be assigned without the written consent of a client. For a planner that is selling their investment advisory business, they must obtain a written consent from each client in order to transfer that client's contract to the new business owner.

Proper Use of the Term "Registered Investment Adviser"

Advisers who are registered under the Investment Advisers Act of 1940 are Registered Investment Advisers (RIAs). The term Registered Investment Adviser must be spelled out and the adviser is not permitted to use the letters "RIA" after their name, as it may lead clients to believe RIA is a professional designation or credential that required a unique education and/or experience background. Use of the letters RIA may also create unjustified expectations on behalf of the client.

Books and Records to be Maintained

A registered investment adviser is required to maintain accurate and current financial statements, ledgers, journals, copies of instructions from clients regarding purchases and sales of securities, advertisements, reports, or other investment advisory services sent to more than 10 persons. The registered investment adviser is generally required to keep records for at least 5 years, even if they leave the business for another career. State laws may be more restrictive and require longer periods of record retention.

Enforcement

If any of the rules and regulations of the Investment Advisers Act are not followed, the SEC has the authority to investigate, to compel submission of books and records, and to levy fines for failure to cooperate. The SEC may also suspend or revoke an adviser's registration or seek to enjoin activities in violation of the Act. Furthermore, the SEC may refer a case to the Justice Department for criminal prosecution that can result in fines up to $10,000, imprisonment up to five years, or both.

Financial Industry Regulatory Authority (FINRA)

The **Financial Industry Regulatory Authority (FINRA)** is a self-regulatory organization for all security firms doing business in the United States. FINRA was created in July 2007 by the merging of the National Association of Security Dealers (NASD) and the enforcement functions of the New York Stock Exchange. Any individual who sells securities must register with FINRA under the sponsorship of a broker-dealer. Representatives of broker-dealers and investment advisers register with their state and the Financial Industry Regulatory Authority (FINRA) by filing Form U4. Essentially this form is disclosing background information about representatives and investment advisers with the industry's self-regulatory organization, which is FINRA. In addition to filing Form U4, an individual must pass the appropriate securities licensing exam(s). To withdraw registration, Form U5 is filed.

Some of the security licensing exams are listed below.
- **Series 3** – Permits an individual to sell futures contracts.
- **Series 6** – Permits an individual to sell investment company products such as a mutual fund or unit investment trust and variable life and variable annuities. Note: A person must also have a state insurance license to sell insurance products. Individuals holding a Series 6 license are not permitted to sell corporate or municipal securities.

- **Series 7** – General Securities Registered Representative – Permits an individual to sell stocks, bonds, government and municipal bonds, options, REITS and investment company products. It does not permit the selling of futures. This is the most comprehensive and most common of the registered representative exams.
- **Series 24** – General Securities Principal - qualifies individuals required to register as general securities principals in order to manage or supervise the member's investment banking or securities business for corporate securities, direct participation programs, and investment company products/variable contracts.
- **Series 26** - Investment Company Products/Variable Contracts Limited Principal - This examination qualifies an individual who will function as a principal for the solicitation, purchase, and/or sale of redeemable securities of companies registered pursuant to the Investment Company Act of 1940; securities of closed-end companies registered pursuant to the Investment Company Act of 1940 during the period of original distribution only; and variable contracts and insurance premium funding programs and other contracts issued by an insurance company.
- **Series 63** – Uniform Securities Agent State Law Exam – Most states require an individual to pass the Series 63 exam before being registered with the state. The Series 63 exam tests primarily state laws and regulations, often referred to as blue sky laws. Blue sky laws prohibit fraud by requiring securities and advisers to be registered with the state. The name blue sky laws is a phrase used to describe an investor being sold a highly speculative investment or nothing more than the big blue sky.
- **Series 65** – Uniform Investment Adviser Law Exam – This license is required for an individual to register as an Investment Advisor Representative (IAR) with the state. Most states do not require the Series 65 exam if an individual already passed the Series 7 and Series 66 exams.
- **Series 66** – Uniform Combined State Law Exam - This exam combines the Series 63 and 65 exams into one exam. Passing this exam qualifies for registering as an Investment Adviser Representative (IAR) with all 50 states.

Beginning in 2018, FINRA implemented a new structure to securities exams that eliminates a student's need to restudy the same information for multiple exams. To accomplish this objective, a new exam called the Securities Industry Essentials (SIE) exam was created to test on the common content, and became the initial exam for securities licensing. The SIE exam does not require sponsorship from a broker-dealer. The Series 6 and Series 7 exams (as well as a few other less common exams) have been restructured as specialized knowledge exams that are taken after the prerequisite SIE exam, and still require sponsorship from a broker-dealer.

> ✒️ **Quick Quiz 15.7**
>
> 1. The SIPC is a statutorily created nonprofit membership corporation funded by its member securities broker-dealers, with the goal of returning cash and securities to investors, in the event a brokerage firm becomes insolvent.
>   a. True
>   b. False
>
> 2. The Securities Exchange Act of 1934 requires that any new security be registered with the SEC by filing a registration statement.
>   a. True
>   b. False
>
> 3. FINRA is a self-regulatory organization for all security firms doing business in the United States and requires any person who sells securities to register with the organization.
>   a. True
>   b. False
>
> True, False, True.

Sarbanes-Oxley Act of 2002

The **Sarbanes-Oxley Act of 2002** was passed in response to accounting scandals at firms like Enron and Tyco that ultimately caused those company's stocks to collapse resulting in billions of dollars of losses for investors. The legislation established new or enhanced standards for all U.S. public company boards, management, and public accounting firms. This Act addressed the issues that led to the accounting scandals through the following actions:

- Established the Public Company Accounting Oversight Board, to provide independent oversight of public accounting firms providing audit services.
- Established standards for external auditor independence and to limit conflicts of interest. It also established new auditor approval requirements, audit partner rotation every five years, and auditor reporting requirements. It restricts auditing companies from providing non-audit services, such as consulting services, for the same clients.
- Mandates that senior executives take individual responsibility for the accuracy and completeness of corporate financial reports. It requires that, typically the CEO and CFO personally certify the integrity of the financial statements.
- Requires internal controls for assuring the accuracy of financial reports and disclosures, and mandates both audits and reports on those controls. It also requires timely reporting of material changes in financial condition and specific enhanced reviews by the SEC or its agents of corporate reports.
- Defines the codes of conduct for securities analysts and requires disclosure of knowable conflicts of interest.
- Describes specific criminal penalties for manipulation, destruction or alteration of financial records, or other interference with investigations, while providing certain protections for whistle-blowers.
- Increased the criminal penalties associated with white-collar crimes and conspiracies.

Regulation Full Disclosure (FD)

Regulation Full Disclosure (or Regulation FD) was implemented in October 2000 by the SEC to level the playing field between investment analysts and the general public. Prior to Regulation FD, companies would disclose important information about the performance of a company behind closed doors to the investment community, which consisted of mutual fund managers and stock analysts. Regulation FD requires companies to disclose all material information simultaneously to both the investment community and individual investors. Firms comply with Regulation FD by disclosing material information during earnings conference calls and press releases.

Dodd-Frank Wall Street Reform and Consumer Protection Act

The Dodd-Frank Wall Street Reform and Consumer Protection Act, also known as "Dodd-Frank" was signed into law on July 21, 2010 as a result of the Great Recession. The Great Recession was a worldwide economic downturn that started in December 2007 and peaked in September 2008. Many economic conditions contributed to the Great Recession. Some of the most important conditions included risky lending practices by banks, sub-prime mortgage defaults, and mortgage-backed securities that received high credit ratings, but ultimately resulted in default, high unemployment, and sovereign debt concerns in Europe. The Dodd-Frank Act was passed to prevent a collapse of major financial institutions, promote transparency, and to protect consumers from abusive financial services practices.

The Dodd-Frank Act consists of sixteen major sections addressing everything from debit card transaction fee limits to preventing firms that are "too big to fail," and much more. Some the more relevant parts for financial panning include FDIC limits and ordering a study to potentially require broker-dealers to abide by a fiduciary duty of care.

The Dodd-Frank Act permanently increased FDIC insurance for interest bearing accounts from $100,000 to $250,000. Prior to Dodd-Frank, the FDIC limit was temporarily increased from $100,000 to $250,000 in response to the Great Recession, to avoid a run on the banks where customers would attempt to withdraw all their deposits at a bank. Banks only maintain 10 percent of deposits in the form of cash, so banks would be unable to meet all withdrawal requests from their depositors if the withdrawal requests occurred over a very short period of time. Raising the FDIC limit was intended to provide reassurances in our banking system that all deposits are safe.

SEC Regulation Best Interest (Regulation BI) and Form CRS Relationship Summary

The Dodd-Frank Act also gave the SEC the authority to require broker-dealers to abide by a fiduciary standard duty of care, rather than the long-standing suitability standard applied to broker-dealers. This objective was accomplished in 2019 when the SEC adopted a new rule-making package including **Regulation Best Interest** (Regulation BI) and the Form CRS Relationship Summary.

Prior to Regulation BI, broker-dealers were required only to determine if an investment was suitable for a client before making an investment recommendation. To fulfill the suitability standard of care, a broker-dealer would require a client to complete a risk tolerance questionnaire. The suitability standard simply requires that an investment is appropriate given an investor's risk tolerance and time horizon, without regard to the overall impact to a client's investment portfolio and other investments. The suitability standard does not require that the interests of the client come first, and does not require disclosure of conflicts of interest. This standard is not as beneficial for the client because the adviser can recommend products that may not be the best available as long as they are suitable. The adviser can recommend products that provide greater compensation to the adviser when products paying less compensation would be more beneficial to the client.

A fiduciary duty of care is required by Registered Investment Advisers (RIAs) and CFP® professionals which requires both to put their client's interest ahead of their own and to always act in the best interest of the client. A fiduciary duty of care requires the adviser to consider the overall impact to a client's investment portfolio before recommending an investment and generally applies on an ongoing basis. While the SEC has specifically avoided referring to Regulation BI as a "fiduciary" duty to avoid confusion with other fiduciary definitions, such as those for Registered Investment Advisers (RIAs), Regulation BI does draw from key fiduciary principles.

Broker-dealers were required on June 30, 2020 to begin compliance with Regulation Best Interest (BI), which requires that broker-dealers (and their representatives) "act in the best interest of the retail customer at the time the recommendation is made, without placing the financial or other interest of the broker-dealer ahead of the interest of the retail customer." This includes recommendations to roll over or transfer assets from a qualified retirement plan account to an IRA, and recommendations to take distributions from a retirement plan. When a broker-dealer has agreed to provide account monitoring services, recommendations to buy, sell or hold (even when the recommendation to hold is implicit) are also governed by Regulation BI. Regulation BI does not apply to services that are distinct from making these types of recommendations; for example, when executing an unsolicited transaction for a retail customer.

Regulation BI includes the general obligation to act in the customer's best interest and avoid placing the broker-dealer's or representative's interests ahead of the customer's interest. In addition, broker-dealers are charged with upholding several other obligations, including:

- **Disclosure Obligation:** The broker-dealer must provide to the customer, before or at the time of the recommendation, prescribed disclosures of material facts about the relationship (the capacity in which the broker is acting, fees, type and scope of services, conflicts of interest, etc.).
- **Care Obligation:** A broker-dealer must exercise reasonable diligence, care and skill when making a recommendation to a retail customer, including understanding potential risks, rewards, and costs associated with the recommendation to ensure that the recommendation is in the retail customer's best interest, in light of the customer's investment profile, at the time the recommendation is made.
- **Conflict of Interest Obligation:** The broker-dealer must establish, maintain, and enforce written policies and procedures reasonably designed to identify and disclose or eliminate conflicts of interest.
- **Compliance Obligation:** The broker-dealer must establish, maintain and enforce policies and procedures reasonably designed to achieve compliance with Regulation BI as a whole.

Broker-dealers using the term "adviser" or "advisor" in their titles are presumed by the SEC to be in violation of the disclosure obligation of Regulation BI if they are not also registered investment advisers.[23]

The SEC's Form CRS Relationship Summary requirements apply to both broker-dealers and registered investment advisers. Effective June 30, 2020, investment advisers and broker-dealers are required to deliver a two- to four-page relationship summary, written in plain English, to retail investors at the beginning of their relationship. The relationship summary document follows a standardized question-and-answer format in a prescribed order to allow for ease of comparison by retail investors and must include a link to a page on the SEC's investor education website, Investor.gov/CRS, which offers educational information about broker-dealers and investment advisers. Form CRS includes information about services, fees and costs, conflicts of interest, legal standard of conduct, financial professionals' compensation, disciplinary history, and how to obtain additional information (for example a hyperlink to a detailed fee schedule or to an investment adviser's Form ADV Part 2 Brochure), along with a list of "conversation starters" that retail customers can use to initiate dialogue with their financial professional about their circumstances. For registered investment advisers, the Form CRS is incorporated in the Form ADV as Part 3.

The implementation of Regulation BI and Form CRS affords greater transparency to retail investors in selecting the type of investment relationship that best meets their needs, while preserving the fiduciary (or best interest) duty of the investment professional in all cases.

---

23. https://www.sec.gov/tm/faq-regulation-best-interest#disclosure.

Investment Adviser Representative vs. Registered Representative of a Broker-Dealer					
	License Required	*Relationship with Clients*	*Investors Pay for Services via*	*Permitted to Use the Terms "Adviser" or "Advisor"*	*Standard of Care*
Registered representative of a broker-dealer	Series 6 or 7	Matches buyers and sellers of securities (places trades and sells investment products)	Commission paid on purchase or sale of securities	Only when also a registered investment adviser representative	Prior to June 30, 2020 Suitability Beginning June 30, 2020 "Best Interest" fiduciary (Regulation BI)
Registered investment adviser representative	Series 65 or 66	Provides investment advice to clients for a fee	Fees for advice (typically a percentage of assets under management or fixed fee)	Yes	Fiduciary (Investment Advisers Act of 1940)

Worker Protection

ERISA

The **Employee Retirement Income Security Act (ERISA)** of 1974 was designed to protect employee retirement savings accounts from creditors and from plan sponsors. Some of the ERISA protection benefits include:

- Anti-alienation protection over all assets within a qualified retirement plan. This anti-alienation protection prohibits any action that may cause the plan assets to be assigned, garnished, levied, or subject to bankruptcy proceedings while the assets remain in the qualified retirement plan.
- Laws, rules, and enforcement provisions to protect employees from abuse and misuse of the qualified plan by employers as plan sponsors.

Example 15.16

O.J. Simpson was found guilty in civil court for the wrongful death of Ronald Goldman and Nicole Simpson. The judgment against O.J. Simpson was for $33.5 million, however because of ERISA protection, his NFL pension and qualified retirement plans cannot be used to satisfy the judgment. Those funds are exempt assets under both federal and Florida law.

Through ERISA, fiduciary responsibility was established and made applicable to (1) those who exercise discretionary authority or control over the management of a retirement plan, (2) those who exercise any authority or control over the management or disposition of retirement plan assets, (3) those who offer investment advice for a fee or other compensation with respect to plan funds or property, and (4) those who have any discretionary authority or responsibility in a retirement plan's administration.[24]

---

24. ERISA Sec. 3(21)

ERISA requires that a fiduciary act "solely in the interest of the participants and beneficiaries." An ERISA fiduciary must use the care, skill, prudence and diligence that a prudent man acting in a like capacity and familiar with such matters would use in the conduct of an enterprise of a like character and with like aims. In addition, a fiduciary under ERISA must diversify the investments of the retirement plan in order to minimize the risk of large losses unless under the circumstances it is clearly prudent not to do so. A fiduciary must strictly follow the terms of the plan document when making decisions. Fiduciaries must also ensure that fees and expenses paid out of retirement plan assets are reasonable. Participants in a participant-directed plan must be provided with information regarding the plan fees and expenses on a regular and periodic basis and fiduciaries are required to use standard methodologies when calculating and disclosing expense and return information.

☷ *Key Concepts*

1. Identify some ERISA protections.

2. Identify the benefits available under Workers' Compensation.

3. What are unemployment benefits and what are conditions associated with receiving benefits?

4. Identify the purpose of OSHA.

Financial planners who work with clients to establish qualified retirement plans, who provide investment advice for qualified plans, or who administer qualified retirement plans should be aware of these fiduciary responsibilities and diligently uphold all ERISA rules.

Workers' Compensation

Workers' compensation is designed to protect employees if they are injured while at work. Workers' compensation will provide income replacement if the employee is unable to work. It will also provide medical expense coverage if the employee is injured while at work and it can provide a death benefit to an employee's beneficiary. Workers' compensation is an absolute form of liability, which simply means that regardless of why or how the employee is injured, they can collect workers' compensation benefits. So, regardless if an employee's injury is the result of the employer or employee's negligence, they will still collect workers' compensation benefits. Benefits received under workers' compensation are not subject to income tax.

Example 15.17

Oliver works at a winery and is responsible for putting corks in wine bottles. Oliver has a history of drinking a few glasses of wine during his lunch break. Although it is against company policy to drink while on the job and even though his boss has repeatedly reprimanded him, he continues to drink wine at lunch. On St. Patrick's Day, Oliver celebrated by drinking two bottles of his favorite wine at lunch. After lunch and feeling quite inebriated, he still went back to work. Unfortunately, he was in no condition to be corking wine bottles and accidentally used his finger as a cork. He was rushed to the hospital but lost his finger. Even though Oliver's injury was his fault because he drank too much wine at lunch which is against company policy, he is still entitled to workers' compensation benefits.

Example 15.18

Cynthia, who works in HR, was not very good at using the paper shredder. One day, Cynthia was talking on her cell phone while shredding some documents at work. Unfortunately for Cynthia, she wasn't paying attention and her finger became stuck in the paper shredder and she had to be rushed to the emergency room. Even though Cynthia wasn't paying attention and caused her own injury, workers' compensation will still provide her with benefits.

Unemployment Benefits

Unemployment benefits are designed to provide an unemployed worker with income for a period of time. Unemployment compensation is a program offered jointly by the state and federal governments through unemployment insurance premiums paid by employers. Both the state and federal government have an unemployment tax paid by employers. As a condition of receiving unemployment benefits, the worker must be unemployed and also actively seeking work. Unemployment benefits are taxable income to the recipient.[25] Unemployment benefits do not apply to part-time workers, seasonal workers, or self-employed individuals. To collect unemployment benefits, the worker must be unemployed through no fault of their own, usually as the result of layoffs.

Occupational Safety and Health Administration

OSHA (Occupational Safety and Health Administration) was created by Congress under the Occupational Safety and Health Act of 1970 to promote safe and healthy working conditions for workers by providing training, outreach, education, and assistance. The program covers private employers and employees and is administered federally or by a federally approved state-run organization. OSHA establishes rules for employers to follow to protect their employees from hazards. There are differing standards for the worksites of various industries including construction, maritime, and general industry. For example, rules are established to limit hazardous chemical exposure for protection of workers. OSHA also requires employers to keep records of workplace injuries and illnesses.

If a worker believes an employer is not following OSHA standards or if there is a serious hazard at the worksite, the worker can file a complaint with OSHA (confidentiality is provided upon request). The law gives worker protection such that a worker cannot be fired, demoted, transferred, or discriminated against for filing a complaint or otherwise using their OSHA rights.

CONCLUSION

While a financial planner may find studying economics is less interesting than studying other financial planning topics, the rudiments of this topic must be understood. The planner needs to be able to competently assist clients with making choices potentially involving scarce resources. Financial planning decisions are affected by the business cycle, interest rates, inflation, supply and demand, as well as the concept of opportunity cost which are the basis for making informed client recommendations. Knowledge regarding the external legal environment is also important because laws that protect the consumer, investor, and worker will likely at some point involve a client's financial situation. Currently, changes in product and technology affect economies so quickly that an understanding of economic concepts and relationships is vital for the capable and successful financial planner.

---

25. The American Rescue Plan Act (ARPA) of 2021 allows taxpayers with adjusted gross income below $150,000 to exclude from income up to $10,200 of unemployment compensation received during 2020.

DISCUSSION QUESTIONS

SOLUTIONS to the discussion questions can be found exclusively within the chapter. Once you have completed an initial reading of the chapter, go back and highlight the answers to these questions.

1. Discuss why a financial planner must understand economic concepts and the direction of the current economy.

2. Discuss the economic measurements associated with the Gross Domestic Product (GDP).

3. What is inflation and how is it measured?

4. Describe the phases of the business cycle.

5. Define the three indexes of economic indicators.

6. What are the goals of the Federal Reserve's monetary policy and how are those goals implemented?

7. Discuss how fiscal policy is implemented.

8. Discuss the factors and relationships associated with measuring demand.

9. Discuss the factors and relationship associated with measuring supply.

10. List and discuss the three types of bankruptcy filings.

11. What is the purpose of the Federal Trade Commission (FTC)?

12. List and describe some major consumer protection laws.

13. What is the function of the Federal Deposit Insurance Corporation (FDIC)?

14. List and describe some major investor protection laws.

15. List and describe some major worker protection laws.

MULTIPLE-CHOICE PROBLEMS

A sample of multiple choice problems is provided below. Additional multiple choice problems are available at money-education.com by accessing the Student Practice Portal.

1. During a period of recession /contraction, which of the following would be true?
    1. The supply of goods and services would be decreasing.
    2. Interest rates would be decreasing.
    3. Unemployment would be increasing.
    4. Inflation would be decreasing.
        a. 1 and 2.
        b. 1 and 3.
        c. 1, 2 and 4.
        d. 1, 2, 3, and 4.

2. Phyllis had three credit cards stolen. Before she realized they were stolen, the following amounts were already fraudulently charged:

American Express	$2,000
VISA	$500
MasterCard	$40

    How much is Phyllis' expected liability for the fraudulent charges?
        a. $50.
        b. $140.
        c. $150.
        d. $2,400.

3. Due to a shortage in supply, the price of corn increases suddenly, causing a decrease in the demand for corn and an increase in the demand for carrots. Which term best describes the relationship between corn and carrots?
        a. Substitute.
        b. Complement.
        c. Equilibrium.
        d. Elastic.

4. Movement along the demand curve represents a change in quantity demanded. Which of the following is the likely cause of a change in quantity demanded?
        a. Increased savings rate.
        b. Decrease tax rate.
        c. Price change.
        d. More suppliers.

5. If the Federal Reserve wants to increase interest rates, which of the following actions might it take (assume the reserve requirement is not currently at zero percent)?
    a. Buy government securities.
    b. Sell government securities.
    c. Decrease the reserve requirement.
    d. Decrease federal government spending.

> **Additional multiple choice problems**
> **are available at**
> **money-education.com**
> **by accessing the**
> **Student Practice Portal.**
> **Access requires registration of the title using**
> **the unique code at the front of the book.**

QUICK QUIZ EXPLANATIONS

Quick Quiz 15.1
1. False. This is the definition of macroeconomics. Microeconomics is the study of factors that impact small or individual economies, such as supply and demand for a product.
2. False. This is a result of deflation, which is a decrease in the overall price levels of goods and services.
3. True.

Quick Quiz 15.2
1. True.
2. False. This is the definition of the index of lagging economic indicators. The index of leading economic indicators predicts changes in the economy.
3. False. This is the definition of fiscal policy. Monetary policy is the intended influence on the money supply and interest rates by the central bank of a country.

Quick Quiz 15.3
1. True.
2. True.

Quick Quiz 15.4
1. False. This is the definition of supply. Demand represents the quantity consumers are willing to purchase of a good or service, at a particular price.
2. True.
3. True.
4. False. A change in price will cause a movement along the supply curve impacting the quantity supplied whereas a shift in the supply curve is cause by other factors such as decreased competition or outdated technologies.

Quick Quiz 15.5
1. False. This is the definition of Chapter 7 bankruptcy. Chapter 11 bankruptcy is known as "reorganization bankruptcy" for corporations, sole proprietorships, and partnerships.
2. True.
3. True.

Quick Quiz 15.6
4. True.
5. False. The insured amount is $250,000.

Quick Quiz 15.7
1. True.
2. False. This is the purpose of the Securities Act of 1933. The Securities Exchange Act of 1934 created the SEC and gives authority to the SEC to regulate the secondary market.
3. True.

16

ETHICS & STANDARDS OF CONDUCT

1. Describe the *Standards of Conduct*.
2. Identify and describe each of the principles in the *Code of Ethics*.
3. Identify the six sections to the *Standards of Conduct*.
4. Discuss the fiduciary requirements for CFP® professionals.
5. Understand the term "financial planning" and when the practice standards apply.
6. Clearly differentiate the disclosure obligations and whether they may be made orally or must be in writing for different types of client engagements.
7. Identify activities within each of the seven steps of the Financial Planning Process.
8. Describe the various disciplinary rules and procedures paying particular attention to the categories of sanction.
9. Describe the fitness standards for candidates and Professionals Eligible for Reinstatement.
10. Discuss the issues and outcome of the various anonymous case histories.
11. Recognize unethical practices in the financial planning profession based on CFP Board *Standards of Professional Conduct*.*

Ties to CFP Certification Learning Objectives

INTRODUCTION

The **Certified Financial Planner Board of Standards, Inc. ("CFP Board")** is a non-profit organization whose mission is to benefit the public by granting the CFP® certification and upholding it as the recognized standard of excellence for competent and ethical personal financial planning. CFP Board maintains professional standards necessary for competency and ethics in the financial planning profession for those professionals who have been granted the right to use the CFP® certification marks. CFP Board has exclusive authority to determine who may use their markings, including CFP®, CERTIFIED FINANCIAL PLANNER™, and CFP® certification (hereinafter "CFP®") in the United States. Considering that CFP Board has this exclusive authority, CFP Board conditions permission, and grants to such individuals the right to use these marks on their agreement to abide by certain terms and conditions specified by CFP Board. CFP Board also enforces the requirements, including ethics, for CFP® professionals[1] and Professionals Eligible for Reinstatement (PERs; those who are not currently certified, but have been certified in the past and are eligible to reinstate their certification without the need to pass the current CFP®exam), through, among other things, a series of professional and ethical standards designed to protect the public and advance professionalism in the financial planning industry.

CFP Board's *Code of Ethics* and *Standards of Conduct ("Code and Standards")* reflects the commitment that all CFP® professionals make to high standards of competency and ethics. CFP Board's *Code and Standards* benefits and protects the public, provides standards for delivering financial planning, and advances financial planning as a distinct and valuable profession. Compliance with the *Code and Standards* is a requirement of CFP® certification that is critical to the integrity of the CFP® marks. Violations of the *Code and Standards* may subject a CFP® professional to discipline.

---

1. May also be called a CFP® practitioner or CFP® certificant.

The first *Code of Ethics* was introduced in 1985 and has evolved through numerous revisions over the past three decades. The most recent update became effective October 1, 2019 after a three-year review process.

The ***Pre-2019 Standards of Professional Conduct*** were comprised of three categories:

1. *Code of Ethics and Professional Responsibility* ("Code of Ethics")
2. *Rules of Conduct*
3. *Financial Planning Practice Standards* ("**Practice Standards**")

The *Standards of Professional Conduct* were enforced through the procedures outlined in the *Disciplinary Rules and Procedures* ("**Disciplinary Rules**") and *Appeal Rules and Procedures*. In addition, a set of *Fitness Standards* which applied to candidates for CFP® certification as well as to former CFP® professionals eligible for reinstatement (PERs), was established to ensure that the candidate or PER's previous conduct would not reflect poorly on the CFP® marks.

The *Rules of Conduct* and the *Financial Planning Practice Standards* are now contained in the *Standards of Conduct* and the *Disciplinary Rules and Procedures* and *Appeal Rules and Procedures* are now contained in the *Procedural Rules*.

Exhibit 16.1 | Current Standards of Professional Conduct

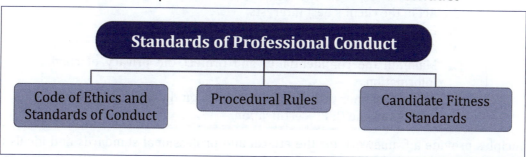

The *Code and Standards* form part of the certification process and create terms and conditions imposed upon CFP® professionals on a continuing basis beyond initial certification.

CFP Board has placed the highest ethical and professional standards upon CFP® professionals. The interrelated and organized set of rules and guidelines encourages sound practices and standards and creates a mechanism to penalize those who do not meet the high professional and ethical standards of conduct.

By doing so, CFP Board has created a streamlined and objective set of standards on par with those applicable to doctors, attorneys, and certified public accountants. The profession benefits from setting high standards and legitimizing its services and process. Ultimately, the public is the primary beneficiary from the establishment and enforcement of the ethics, conduct, practices, procedures, and standards. This chapter will evaluate each of the sections of CFP Board's *Code and Standards* and review the *Procedural Rules*.

CODE OF ETHICS

The fundamental starting point is CFP Board's *Code of Ethics*. The *Code of Ethics* is organized into six overriding principles that espouse general statements regarding ethical and professional ideals that CFP® professionals are expected to enact into their professional activities. The *Code of Ethics* provides mandatory principles that are grounded in basic tenets of integrity and professionalism to which all in this profession should aspire, or examples of how CFP® professionals should act.

The previous *Code of Ethics* consisted of seven principles - Integrity, Objectivity, Competence, Fairness, Confidentiality, Professionalism, and Diligence. While the new code no longer uses the term "principle," we will continue to use it to describe the required actions within the new *Code of Ethics* and *Standards of Conduct*.

Exhibit 16.2 contains the actual *Code of Ethics*, word-for-word, as promulgated by CFP Board:[2]

Exhibit 16.2 | Code of Ethics

A CFP® professional must:
1. Act with honesty, integrity, competence, and diligence.
2. Act in the client's best interests.
3. Exercise due care.
4. Avoid or disclose and manage conflicts of interest.
5. Maintain the confidentiality and protect the privacy of client information.
6. Act in a manner that reflects positively on the financial planning profession and CFP® certification.

These principles provide a framework for the ethical and professional standards and ideals for CFP® professionals. **Integrity** brings out honesty and candor in the provision of professional services.

Competence requires that CFP® professionals must obtain and maintain an adequate level of knowledge and skill, along with the ability to recognize those times when one's knowledge is limited such that consultation with, or referral to, other professionals is appropriate.

Diligence requires that the CFP® professional provide professional services and respond to client inquiries in a prompt and thorough manner.

Due care requires engaging in conduct that a reasonable and prudent individual would exercise under the same or similar circumstances. Acting with prudence is a core element of the duty of care required of CFP® professionals.

---

2. See CFP Board's *Code and Standard* Booklet page 2.

Professionalism requires behaving with dignity, courtesy, and respect to clients, fellow professionals, and others in business-related activities. Upholding professionalism and adhering to a strong ethical code reflect positively on the CFP® professional, the profession of financial planning, and the CFP® certification.

CFP® professionals must be fair and reasonable in all professional relationships. It is here where disclosure of conflicts of interest is paramount. **Confidentiality** is a key component in any relationship where clients place personal information or assets in trust of another. The professional must safeguard that information, which, in turn, will build the relationship of trust and confidence between the client and the CFP® professional.

The *Code of Ethics* demonstrates CFP Board's commitment to ensuring that all CFP® professionals achieve and maintain a high level of standards of competency and ethics, which, in turn, benefits and protects the public, provides standards for delivering financial planning, and advances financial planning as a distinct and valuable profession.

STANDARDS OF CONDUCT

The *Standards of Conduct* are not designed to be a foundation of legal liability to third parties. Rather, the *Standards of Conduct* establish expected high standards and also describe the level of professionalism required. The *Standards of Conduct* govern all those who have the right to use the CFP® marks, whether or not those marks are actually used. CFP Board cannot enumerate in the *Standards of Conduct* every area of service that may be provided by financial planning professionals, and the *Standards of Conduct* may not apply to every specific activity. It is up to the CFP® professional to determine the CFP® professional's demonstration of the completed required action. Similar to the *Code of Ethics*, the *Standards of Conduct* yield a broad set of principles that can be used as an overarching guide to the conduct expected of the CFP® professional, with the *Standards* themselves outlining additional detailed guidance and expectations as discussed throughout the remainder of the chapter.

> ### ☷ *Key Concepts*
>
> 1. Identify the six different categories of the *Standards of Conduct*.
>
> 2. Identify the fifteen Duties Owed to Clients.
>
> 3. Determine when a CFP® professional is held to the duty of a fiduciary.

Exhibit 16.3 | Principles that Guide the CFP® Professional in Client Engagements

Code of Ethics	Standards of Conduct	
	Fiduciary Duty	**Duties to Clients**
Honesty		
Integrity	Loyalty	Integrity
Competence	Care	Competence
Due Care	Prudence	Diligence
Confidentiality		Objectivity
Professionalism		Confidentiality

The *Standards of Conduct* are divided into six categories, as identified in the following exhibit.

Exhibit 16.4 | Standards of Conduct

A. Duties Owed to Clients
B. Financial Planning and Application of the Practice Standards for the Financial Planning Process
C. Practice Standards for the Financial Planning Process
D. Duties Owed to Firms and Subordinates
E. Duties Owed to CFP Board
F. Prohibition on Circumvention

Within the following pages, each section of the *Standards of Conduct* will be provided, word-for-word, with additional details and examples provided. Within the *Standards of Conduct*, certain terms and phrases have specific definitions, as provided in **Exhibit 16.5.**

Exhibit 16.5 | CFP Board Code and Standards - Glossary
Effective October 1, 2019

CFP® Professional's Firm(s). Any entity on behalf of which a CFP® professional provides Professional Services to a Client, and that has the authority to exercise control over the CFP® professional's activities, including the CFP® professional's employer, broker-dealer, registered investment adviser, insurance company, and insurance agency.

Client. Any person, including a natural person, business organization, or legal entity, to whom the CFP® professional provides or agrees to provide Professional Services pursuant to an Engagement.

Conflict of Interest. (a) When a CFP® professional's interests (including the interests of the CFP® Professional's Firm) are adverse to the CFP® professional's duties to a Client, or (b) When a CFP® professional has duties to one Client that are adverse to another Client.

Control. The power, directly or indirectly, to direct the management or policies of the entity at the relevant time, through ownership, by contract, or otherwise.

Control Person. A person who has Control.

Engagement. An oral or written agreement, arrangement, or understanding.

Family. Grandparent, parent, stepparent, father-in-law/mother-in-law, uncle/aunt, spouse, former spouse, spousal equivalent, domestic partner, brother/sister, step-sibling, brother-in-law/sister-in-law, cousin, son/daughter, stepchild, son-in-law/daughter-in-law, nephew/niece, grandchild, and any other person the CFP® professional, directly or indirectly, supports financially to a material extent.

*** continued ***

Financial Advice.

a. A communication that, based on its content, context, and presentation, would reasonably be viewed as a recommendation that the Client take or refrain from taking a particular course of action with respect to:

1. The development or implementation of a financial plan;
2. The value of or the advisability of investing in, purchasing, holding, gifting, or selling Financial Assets;
3. Investment policies or strategies, portfolio composition, the management of Financial Assets, or other financial matters;
4. The selection and retention of other persons to provide financial or Professional Services to the Client; or

b. The exercise of discretionary authority over the Financial Assets of a Client.

The determination of whether Financial Advice has been provided is an objective rather than subjective inquiry. The more individually tailored the communication is to the Client, the more likely the communication will be viewed as Financial Advice. The provision of services or the furnishing or making available of marketing materials, general financial education materials, or general financial communications that a reasonable CFP® professional would not view as Financial Advice, does not constitute Financial Advice.

Financial Assets. Securities, insurance products, real estate, bank instruments, commodities contracts, derivative contracts, collectibles, or other financial products.

Financial Planning. A collaborative process that helps maximize a Client's potential for meeting life goals through Financial Advice that integrates relevant elements of the Client's personal and financial circumstances.

Material. Information is material when a reasonable Client or prospective Client would consider the information important in making a decision.

Professional Services. Financial Advice and related activities and services that are offered or provided, including, but not limited to, Financial Planning, legal, accounting, or business planning services.

Related Party. A person or business entity (including a trust) whose receipt of Sales-Related Compensation a reasonable CFP® professional would view as benefiting the CFP® professional or the CFP® Professional's Firm, including, for example, as a result of the CFP® professional's ownership stake in the business entity. There is a rebuttable presumption that a Related Party includes:

a. **Family Members.** A member of the CFP® Professional's Family and any business entity that the Family or members of the Family Control; and

b. **Business Entities.** A business entity that the CFP® professional or the CFP® Professional's Firm Controls, or that is Controlled by or is under common Control with, the CFP® Professional's Firm.

Scope of Engagement. The Professional Services to be provided pursuant to an Engagement.

Section A: Duties Owed to Clients

Section A of the *Standards of Conduct* (provided in **Exhibit 16.6**) expressly and succinctly lays out fifteen duties owed to clients.

Exhibit 16.6 | CFP Board Code and Standards - Section A

Section A
Duties Owed to Clients

1. **Fiduciary Duty**
   At all times when providing Financial Advice to a Client, a CFP® professional must act as a fiduciary, and therefore, act in the best interests of the Client. The following duties must be fulfilled:

   a. **Duty of Loyalty.** A CFP® professional must:
      i. Place the interests of the Client above the interests of the CFP® professional and the CFP® Professional's Firm;
      ii. Avoid Conflicts of Interest, or fully disclose Material Conflicts of Interest to the Client, obtain the Client's informed consent, and properly manage the conflict; and
      iii. Act without regard to the financial or other interests of the CFP® professional, the CFP® Professional's Firm, or any individual or entity other than the Client, which means that a CFP® professional acting under a Conflict of Interest continues to have a duty to act in the best interests of the Client and place the Client's interests above the CFP® professional's.

   b. **Duty of Care.** A CFP® professional must act with the care, skill, prudence, and diligence that a prudent professional would exercise in light of the Client's goals, risk tolerance, objectives, and financial and personal circumstances.

   c. **Duty to Follow Client Instructions.** A CFP® professional must comply with all objectives, policies, restrictions, and other terms of the Engagement and all reasonable and lawful directions of the Client.

2. **Integrity**
   a. A CFP® professional must perform Professional Services with integrity. Integrity demands honesty and candor, which may not be subordinated to personal gain or advantage. Allowance may be made for innocent error and legitimate differences of opinion, but integrity cannot co-exist with deceit or subordination of principle.

   b. A CFP® professional may not, directly or indirectly, in the conduct of Professional Services:
      i. Employ any device, scheme, or artifice to defraud;
      ii. Make any untrue statement of a material fact or omit to state a material fact necessary in order to make the statements made, in the light of the circumstances under which they were made, not misleading; or
      iii. Engage in any act, practice, or course of business which operates or would operate as a fraud or deceit upon any person.

3. **Competence**
   A CFP® professional must provide Professional Services with competence, which means with relevant knowledge and skill to apply that knowledge. When the CFP® professional is not sufficiently competent in a particular area to provide the Professional Services required under the Engagement, the CFP® professional must gain competence, obtain the assistance of a competent professional, limit or terminate the Engagement, and/or refer the Client to a competent professional. The CFP® professional shall describe to the Client any requested Professional Services that the CFP® professional will not be providing.

*** continued ***

4. **Diligence**

   A CFP® professional must provide Professional Services, including responding to reasonable Client inquiries, in a timely and thorough manner.

5. **Disclose and Manage Conflicts of Interest**

   a. **Disclose Conflicts.** When providing Financial Advice, a CFP® professional must make full disclosure of all Material Conflicts of Interest with the CFP® professional's Client that could affect the professional relationship. This obligation requires the CFP® professional to provide the Client with sufficiently specific facts so that a reasonable Client would be able to understand the CFP® professional's Material Conflicts of Interest and the business practices that give rise to the conflicts, and give informed consent to such conflicts or reject them. A sincere belief by a CFP® professional with a Material Conflict of Interest that he or she is acting in the best interests of the Client is insufficient to excuse failure to make full disclosure.

      i. A CFP® professional must make full disclosure and obtain the consent of the Client before providing any Financial Advice regarding which the CFP® professional has a Material Conflict of Interest.

      ii. In determining whether the disclosure about a Material Conflict of Interest provided to the Client was sufficient to infer that a Client has consented to a Material Conflict of Interest, CFP Board will evaluate whether a reasonable Client receiving the disclosure would have understood the conflict and how it could affect the advice the Client will receive from the CFP® professional. The greater the potential harm the conflict presents to the Client, and the more significantly a business practice that gives rise to the conflict departs from commonly accepted practices among CFP® professionals, the less likely it is that CFP Board will infer informed consent absent clear evidence of informed consent. Ambiguity in the disclosure provided to the Client will be interpreted in favor of the Client.

      iii. Evidence of oral disclosure of a conflict will be given such weight as CFP Board in its judgment deems appropriate. Written consent to a conflict is not required.

   b. **Manage Conflicts.** A CFP® professional must adopt and follow business practices reasonably designed to prevent Material Conflicts of Interest from compromising the CFP® professional's ability to act in the Client's best interests.

6. **Sound and Objective Professional Judgment**

   A CFP® professional must exercise professional judgment on behalf of the Client that is not subordinated to the interest of the CFP® professional or others. A CFP® professional may not solicit or accept any gift, gratuity, entertainment, non-cash compensation, or other consideration that reasonably could be expected to compromise the CFP® professional's objectivity.

7. **Professionalism**

   A CFP® professional must treat Clients, prospective Clients, fellow professionals, and others with dignity, courtesy, and respect.

8. **Comply with the Law**

   a. A CFP® professional must comply with the laws, rules, and regulations governing Professional Services.

   b. A CFP® professional may not intentionally or recklessly participate or assist in another person's violation of these Standards or the laws, rules, or regulations governing Professional Services.

*** continued ***

9. Confidentiality and Privacy

a. A CFP® professional must keep confidential and may not disclose any non-public personal information about any prospective, current, or former Client ("client"), except that the CFP® professional may disclose information:

  i. For ordinary business purposes:

   a) With the client's consent, so long as the client has not withdrawn the consent;

   b) To a CFP® Professional's Firm or other persons with whom the CFP® professional is providing services to or for the client, when necessary to perform those services;

   c) As necessary to provide information to the CFP® professional's attorneys, accountants, and auditors; and

   d) To a person acting in a representative capacity on behalf of the client;

  ii. For legal and enforcement purposes:

   a) To law enforcement authorities concerning suspected unlawful activities, to the extent permitted by the law;

   b) As required to comply with federal, state, or local law;

   c) As required to comply with a properly authorized civil, criminal, or regulatory investigation or examination, or subpoena or summons, by a governmental authority;

   d) As necessary to defend against allegations of wrongdoing made by a governmental authority;

   e) As necessary to present a civil claim against, or defend against a civil claim raised by, a client;

   f) As required to comply with a request from CFP Board concerning an investigation or adjudication; and

   g) As necessary to provide information to professional organizations that are assessing the CFP® professional's compliance with professional standards.

b. A CFP® professional may not use any non-public personal information about a client for his or her direct or indirect personal benefit, whether or not it causes detriment to the client, unless the client consents.

c. A CFP® professional, either directly or through the CFP® Professional's Firm, must take reasonable steps to protect the security of non-public personal information about any client, including the security of information stored physically or electronically, from unauthorized access that could result in harm or inconvenience to the client.

d. A CFP® professional, either directly or through the CFP® Professional's Firm, must adopt and implement policies regarding the protection, handling, and sharing of a client's non-public personal information and must provide a client with written notice of those policies at the time of the Engagement and thereafter not less than annually (at least once in any 12-month period) unless (i) the CFP® professional's policies have not changed since the last notice sent to a client; and (ii) the CFP® professional does not disclose non-public personal information other than as permitted without a client's consent.

e. A CFP® professional shall be deemed to comply with this Section if the CFP® Professional's Firm is subject to, and the CFP® professional complies with, Regulation S-P under the federal securities laws or substantially equivalent federal or state laws or rules.

*** continued ***

10. **Provide Information to a Client**
   a. **When Providing Financial Advice.** When providing or agreeing to provide Financial Advice that does not require Financial Planning in accordance with the Practice Standards, a CFP® professional must provide the following information to the Client, prior to or at the time of the Engagement, and document that the information has been provided to the Client:
   i. A description of the services and products to be provided;
   ii. How the Client pays for the products and services, and a description of the additional types of costs that the Client may incur, including product management fees, surrender charges, and sales loads;
   iii. How the CFP® professional, the CFP® Professional's Firm, and any Related Party are compensated for providing the products and services;
   iv. The existence of any public discipline or bankruptcy, and the location(s), if any, of the webpages of all relevant public websites of any governmental authority, self-regulatory organization, or professional organization that sets forth the CFP® professional's public disciplinary history or any personal bankruptcy or business bankruptcy where the CFP® professional was a Control Person;
   v. The information required under Section A.5.a. (Conflict of Interest Disclosure);
   vi. The information required under Section A.9.d. (Written Notice Regarding Non-Public Personal Information);
   vii. The information required under Section A.13.a.ii. (Disclosure of Economic Benefit for Referral or Engagement of Additional Persons); and
   viii. Any other information about the CFP® professional or the CFP® Professional's Firm that is Material to a Client's decision to engage or continue to engage the CFP® professional or the CFP® Professional's Firm.
   b. **When Providing Financial Planning.** When providing or required to provide Financial Planning in accordance with the Practice Standards, a CFP® professional must provide the following information to the Client, prior to or at the time of the Engagement, in one or more written documents:
   i. The information required to be provided in Sections A.10.a.i.-iv. and vi. -viii.; and
   ii. The terms of the Engagement between the Client and the CFP® professional or the CFP® Professional's Firm, including the Scope of Engagement and any limitations, the period(s) during which the services will be provided, and the Client's responsibilities. A CFP® professional is responsible for implementing, monitoring, and updating the Financial Planning recommendation(s) unless specifically excluded from the Scope of Engagement.
   c. **Updating Information.** A CFP® professional has an ongoing obligation to provide to the Client any information that is a Material change or update to the information required to be provided to the Client. Material changes and updates to public disciplinary history or bankruptcy information must be disclosed to the Client within ninety (90) days, together with the location(s) of the relevant webpages.

11. **Duties when Communicating with a Client**
   A CFP® professional must provide a Client with accurate information, in accordance with the Engagement, and in response to reasonable Client requests, in a manner and format that a Client reasonably may be expected to understand.

*** continued ***

12. Duties when Representing Compensation Method

A CFP® professional may not make false or misleading representations regarding the CFP® professional's or the CFP® Professional's Firm's method(s) of compensation.

a. **Specific Representations**

   i. **Fee-Only.** A CFP® professional may represent his or her or the CFP® Professional's Firm's compensation method as "fee-only" only if:

     a) The CFP® professional and the CFP® Professional's Firm receive no Sales-Related Compensation; and

     b) Related Parties receive no Sales-Related Compensation in connection with any Professional Services the CFP® professional or the CFP® Professional's Firm provides to Clients.

   ii. **Fee-Based.** CFP Board uses the term "fee and commission" to describe the compensation method of those who receive both fees and Sales-Related Compensation. A CFP® professional who represents that his or her or the CFP® Professional's Firm's compensation method is "fee-based" or any other similar term that is not fee-only:

     a) May not use the term in a manner that suggests the CFP® professional or the CFP® Professional's Firm is fee-only; and

     b) Must clearly state that either the CFP® professional or the CFP® Professional's Firm earns fees and commissions, or that the CFP® professional or the CFP® Professional's Firm are not fee-only.

b. **Sales-Related Compensation.**

Sales-Related Compensation is more than a de minimis economic benefit, including any bonus or portion of compensation, resulting from a Client purchasing or selling Financial Assets, from a Client holding Financial Assets for purposes other than receiving Financial Advice, or from the referral of a Client to any person or entity other than the CFP® Professional's Firm. Sales-Related Compensation includes, for example, commissions, trailing commissions, 12b-1 fees, spreads, transaction fees, revenue sharing, referral or solicitor fees, or similar consideration. Sales-Related Compensation does not include:

   i. Soft dollars (any research or other benefits received in connection with Client brokerage that qualifies for the "safe harbor" of Section 28(e) of the Securities Exchange Act of 1934);

   ii. Reasonable and customary fees for custodial or similar administrative services if the fee or amount of the fee is not determined based on the amount or value of Client transactions;

   iii. Non-monetary benefits provided by another service provider, including a custodian, that benefit the CFP® professional's Clients by improving the CFP® professional's delivery of Professional Services, and that are not determined based on the amount or value of Client transactions;

   iv. Reasonable and customary fees for Professional Services, other than for solicitations and referrals, the CFP® professional or CFP® Professional's Firm provides to a Client that are collected and distributed by another service provider, including under a Turnkey Asset Management Platform; or

   v. A fee the Related Party solicitor receives for soliciting clients for the CFP® professional or the CFP® Professional's Firm.

c. **Related Party.** A person or business entity (including a trust) whose receipt of Sales-Related Compensation a reasonable CFP® professional would view as directly or indirectly benefiting the CFP® professional or the CFP® Professional's Firm, including, for example, as a result of the CFP® professional's ownership stake in the business entity. There is a rebuttable presumption that a Related Party includes:

   i. Family Members. A member of the CFP® professional's Family and any business entity that the Family or members of the Family Control; and

   ii. Business Entities. A business entity that the CFP® professional or the CFP® Professional's Firm Controls, or that is Controlled by or is under common Control with, the CFP® Professional's Firm.

*** continued ***

d. **In Connection with any Professional Services.** Sales-Related Compensation received by a Related Party is "in connection with any Professional Services" if it results, directly or indirectly, from Client transactions referred or facilitated by the CFP® professional or the CFP® Professional's Firm.

e. **Safe Harbor for Related Parties.** Sales-Related Compensation received by a Related Party is not "in connection with any Professional Services" if the CFP® professional or the CFP® Professional's Firm adopts and implements policies and procedures reasonably designed to prevent the CFP® professional or the CFP® Professional's Firm from recommending that any Client purchase Financial Assets from or through, or refer any Clients to, the Related Party.

f. **Misrepresentations by a CFP® Professional's Firm.** A CFP® professional who Controls the CFP® Professional's Firm may not allow the CFP® Professional's Firm to make a representation of compensation method that would be false or misleading if made by the CFP® professional. A CFP® professional who does not Control the CFP® Professional's Firm must correct a CFP® Professional's Firm's misrepresentations of compensation method by accurately representing the CFP® professional's compensation method to the CFP® professional's Clients.

13. **Duties When Recommending, Engaging, and Working with Additional Persons**
   a. When engaging or recommending the selection or retention of additional persons to provide financial or Professional Services for a Client, a CFP® professional must:
      i. Have a reasonable basis for the recommendation or Engagement based on the person's reputation, experience, and qualifications;
      ii. Disclose to the Client, at the time of the recommendation or prior to the Engagement, any arrangement by which someone who is not the Client will compensate or provide some other material economic benefit to the CFP® professional, the CFP® Professional's Firm, or a Related Party for the recommendation or Engagement; and
      iii. When engaging a person to provide services for a Client, exercise reasonable care to protect the Client's interests.
   b. When working with another financial or Professional Services provider on behalf of a Client, a CFP® professional must:
      i. Communicate with the other provider about the scope of their respective services and the allocation of responsibility between them; and
      ii. Inform the Client in a timely manner if the CFP® professional has a reasonable belief that the other provider's services were not performed in accordance with the scope of services to be provided and the allocation of responsibilities.

14. **Duties when Selecting, Using and Recommending Technology**
   a. A CFP® professional must exercise reasonable care and judgment when selecting, using, or recommending any software, digital advice tool, or other technology while providing Professional Services to a Client.
   b. A CFP® professional must have a reasonable level of understanding of the assumptions and outcomes of the technology employed.
   c. A CFP® professional must have a reasonable basis for believing that the technology produces reliable, objective, and appropriate outcomes.

15. **Refrain from Borrowing or Lending Money and Commingling Financial Assets**
   a. A CFP® professional may not, directly or indirectly, borrow money from or lend money to a Client unless:
      i. The Client is a member of the CFP® professional's Family; or
      ii. The lender is a business organization or legal entity in the business of lending money.
   b. A CFP® professional may not commingle a Client's Financial Assets with the Financial Assets of the CFP® professional or the CFP® Professional's Firm.

*** END ***

Fiduciary Duty

In Section A.1 of the *Standards of Conduct*, CFP Board requires the duty of a **fiduciary** for a CFP® professional who is "providing Financial Advice to a Client." The definitions of "Financial Advice" and "**Client**" are central to understanding when the fiduciary duty applies.

Example 16.1

Josephine is a CFP® professional and is attending a backyard barbecue at a friend's home when an acquaintance asks her about real estate investments. Josephine provides the individual with some general information about real estate investments, both direct ownership and through the purchase of Real Estate Investment Trusts (REITs). Is Josephine held to a fiduciary duty regarding the conversation at the barbecue?

A fiduciary duty is required when a CFP® professional provides Financial Advice to a Client. A look at the definitions of "Client" (any person to whom the CFP® professional provides or agrees to provide Professional Services pursuant to an Engagement), and "Financial Advice" (a communication that, based on its content, context, and presentation would be reasonably viewed as a recommendation that the client take or refrain from taking a particular course of action, or the exercise of discretionary authority over the client's financial assets) will reveal that the individual with whom Josephine is conversing is not a client, and that Josephine is not providing financial advice to a client. Therefore, Josephine is not held to a fiduciary duty.[3]

Conflicts of Interest

In Section A.5 of the *Standards of Conduct*, CFP Board has provided guidelines for dealing with **conflicts of interest**. When an actual or potential conflict of interest arises, the CFP® professional must:

1. Disclose the conflict,
2. Obtain the client's informed consent, and
3. Manage the conflict in the client's favor.

"Managing the conflict in the client's favor" makes clear that the fiduciary duty is not eliminated by the mere act of disclosing a conflict of interest.

---

3. For additional details regarding when a CFP® professional is providing Financial Advice to a Client see Exhibit 16.9 below and CFP Board's *Frequently Asked Questions*, *Code of Ethics* and *Standards of Conduct*, question A.1.3. https://www.cfp.net/-/media/files/cfp-board/standards-and-ethics/compliance-resources/cfp-board-code-and-standards-faq.pdf?la=en&hash=1F8C6E24F3A93533CACA16231CC8B8B6

While the disclosure may be made orally or in writing when providing Financial Advice or **Financial Planning**, if made orally, the CFP® professional must document the fact that the information was provided. CFP Board suggests, as a best practice, that CFP® professionals provide the disclosure in writing.

Example 16.2

Kane is a CFP® professional and is faced with a potential conflict of interest during his work for a client. Kane asks you if the *Code and Standards* are invoked when actual or potential conflicts of interest arise? What is the most vital action to take when a conflict of interest arises?

The *Code and Standards* expressly discuss conflicts of interest and address some aspects of conflicts of interest. While some conflicts are unavoidable or only perceived, the vital action that must be taken on the CFP® professional's behalf is to avoid or disclose and manage any actual or perceived conflicts of interest to the client.

A conflict of interest often occurs when a professional's personal interests conflict with their professional duty to their client. The *Standards of Conduct* specifically require a general disclosure of compensation types such as **fee-only**, **commission** only (referred to broadly as **sales-related compensation** in the *Code and Standards*), or **commission and fee**. Throughout the process of providing financial planning services the CFP® professional should recognize and disclose to the client specific situations which appear to be a conflict of interest or result in a conflict of interest due to the manner in which the CFP® professional is compensated.[4]

Example 16.3

Orion is a recent college graduate with a degree in finance. He started his first full-time job a few months ago and is excited to begin investing toward future goals. Orion currently has no emergency fund or disability insurance, and he has $2,000 of credit card debt at 14% interest and $38,000 of student loan debt at 4% interest. Orion's aunt generously gave him a $15,000 gift last month. He hired Juliet, a CFP® professional who is a fee-only planner compensated via a 1% fee on assets under management, to assist him with decisions regarding the best use of the $15,000 gift. Juliet has identified the following five alternatives for Orion: (1) deposit the $15,000 into a savings account at the bank to establish an emergency fund, (2) use the $15,000 to pay off the credit card debt and a portion of the student loan debt, (3) invest the $15,000 in a portfolio managed by Juliet to build funds for Orion's goals, (4) contribute to his company's 401(k), or (5) a combination of the other options. Juliet must disclose to Orion the conflict of interest presented by the alternatives. If Juliet recommends option 1, 2, or 4 she does not get paid. If she recommends option 5 her compensation will be lower than if she recommends option 3.

---

4. CFP Board's "CFP Board's Code of Ethics and Standards of Conduct: Implications for "Fee-Only" CFP® Professionals" document.

Example 16.4

Assume the same facts as in **Example 16.3**, except that Juliet is compensated via commissions on the sale of securities or insurance, that option 3 is to purchase mutual funds, and that a sixth option, purchasing a disability policy, is also presented. Again, Juliet's compensation method presents a conflict of interest which must be disclosed to Orion since she will receive no compensation with options 1, 2, or 4 and her compensation will be impacted by the amount of commission paid on the mutual funds or disability policy.

Example 16.5

Assume the same facts as in **Example 16.4**, except that Juliet is compensated via an hourly fee. Juliet still has a conflict of interest in that the amount of time required to locate an appropriate disability policy or research appropriate mutual funds may be greater than the time required to simply advise Orion to save the money in a savings account or 401(k) or to pay off debt. In addition, Juliet could spend time providing projections to illustrate Orion's anticipated financial situation in the future under each of the alternatives, which will increase her fee.

Note that the existence of a conflict does not mean that it is improper for Juliet, in the examples above, to recommend the alternatives that provide her with compensation. In fact, if those are the alternatives that are in the best interest of Orion, she is expected to make those recommendations. CFP® professionals must, however, remain acutely aware of these types of compensation-related conflicts of interest, which may require additional disclosure and management.

Disclosures

In Section A of the *Standards of Conduct*, CFP Board requires that certain information and disclosures be provided to the client. Whether the information is provided to the client in writing, or whether it may be made orally, depends upon whether the CFP® professional is providing Financial Advice that does not require Financial Planning according to the Practice Standards, or whether the CFP® professional is providing Financial Advice that does require Financial Planning according to the Practice Standards.[5] This distinction is discussed in the following section.

> ### ☰ *Key Concepts*
>
> 1. Identify the three steps a CFP® professional must take when a conflict of interest arises.
>
> 2. Identify which disclosures must be made orally or in writing.
>
> 3. Determine whether an investment adviser's Form ADV brochure meets CFP Board's disclosure requirements.

---

5. See also CFP Boards *Financial Advice Engagements Compliance Checklist* and *Financial Planning Engagements Compliance Checklist* documents. https://www.cfp.net/ethics/compliance-resources?limit=10&pg=1&q=&type=7966afbe700a42398e0fccdf3c92f552

Exhibit 16.7 | Disclosures Made Orally or in Writing[6]

Disclosure	Financial Advice	Financial Planning
Privacy Policy	In Writing	In Writing
Conflicts of Interest	Oral (documented) or in Writing*	Oral (documented) or in Writing*
Services and Products	Oral or in Writing	In Writing
How Client Pays	Oral or in Writing	In Writing
How the CFP® Professional is Compensated	Oral or in Writing	In Writing
Public Discipline and Bankruptcy	Oral or in Writing	In Writing
Referral Compensation	Oral or in Writing	In Writing
Other Material Information	Oral or in Writing	In Writing
Terms of Engagement	N/A	In Writing
Implementation Responsibilities	N/A	In Writing
Monitoring and Updating Responsibilities	N/A	In Writing

*CFP® Professionals who are registered representatives of a broker-dealer or investment adviser representatives must also comply with the SEC's Regulation BI (see Chapter 15, and the section comparing Regulation BI to the Code and Standards later in this chapter), which requires that conflicts of interest be disclosed in writing.

Financial planning encompasses advice regarding virtually all aspects of a client's financial situation, from budgeting and managing debt, to investment advice and tax planning. CFP® professionals offering investment advice to clients must be properly licensed under the Investment Advisers Act of 1940 and are required to provide clients with a disclosure brochure which includes information from the adviser's Form ADV, as described in Chapter 15. While the disclosures provided in the brochure may appear to be comprehensive, a brochure that contains only the information required under the brochure rule will not be sufficient to satisfy the Duty to Provide Information to a Client under Standard A.10 of the *Standards of Conduct*. A CFP® professional may, however, choose to include the additional requirements under Standard A.10 in their Form ADV brochure so as to comply with both the Investment Advisers Act and CFP Board's *Standards of Conduct* in a single disclosure document provided to the client.

> ### ≔ *Key Concepts*
>
> 1. Define financial planning.
> 2. Determine the circumstances under which a CFP® professional must comply with the Practice Standards.
> 3. List the alternatives available to a CFP® professional who otherwise must comply with the Practice Standards when a client does not agree to engage the CFP® professional to provide financial planning.

Section B: Financial Planning and Application of the Practice Standards

Financial planning is a process that CFP® professionals use to help clients achieve their financial and life goals in an efficient manner, focusing not just on the individual components but on how each area of the client's financial plan impacts each of the other areas of planning. When a CFP® professional uses the seven-step financial planning process (discussed in Section C of the *Code and Standards*) in connection with an engagement involving multiple financial planning subject areas, both the duty of care and disclosure requirements are more prominent. Section B of the *Code and Standards* provides additional guidance for CFP® professionals and is reproduced word-for-word in **Exhibit 16.8**.

6. See CFP Board's *Roadmap to the Code of Ethics* and *Standards of Conduct* booklet for additional details.

Exhibit 16.8 | CFP Board Code and Standards - Section B

Section B
Financial Planning & Application of the Practice Standards for the Financial Planning Process

1. **Financial Planning Definition**

   Financial Planning is a collaborative process that helps maximize a Client's potential for meeting life goals through Financial Advice that integrates relevant elements of the Client's personal and financial circumstances.

2. **Examples of Relevant Elements of the Client's Personal and Financial Circumstances**

   Relevant elements of personal and financial circumstances vary from Client to Client, and may include the Client's need for or desire to: develop goals, manage assets and liabilities, manage cash flow, identify and manage risks, identify and manage the financial effect of health considerations, provide for educational needs, achieve financial security, preserve or increase wealth, identify tax considerations, prepare for retirement, pursue philanthropic interests, and address estate and legacy matters.

3. **Application of Practice Standards**

   The Practice Standards set forth the Financial Planning process. A CFP® professional must comply with the Practice Standards when:

   a. The CFP® professional agrees to provide or provides (i) Financial Planning; or (ii) Financial Advice that requires integration of relevant elements of the Client's personal and/or financial circumstances in order to act in the Client's best interests ("Financial Advice that Requires Financial Planning"); or

   b. The Client has a reasonable basis to believe the CFP® professional will provide or has provided Financial Planning.

4. **Integration Factors**

   Among the factors that CFP Board will weigh in determining whether a CFP® professional has agreed to provide or provided Financial Advice that Requires Financial Planning are:

   a. The number of relevant elements of the Client's personal and financial circumstances that the Financial Advice may affect;

   b. The portion and amount of the Client's Financial Assets that the Financial Advice may affect;

   c. The length of time the Client's personal and financial circumstances may be affected by the Financial Advice;

   d. The effect on the Client's overall exposure to risk if the Client implements the Financial Advice; and

   e. The barriers to modifying the actions taken to implement the Financial Advice.

5. **CFP Board Evaluation**

   In a disciplinary proceeding in which a CFP® professional denies CFP Board's allegation that the CFP® professional was required to comply with the Practice Standards, the CFP® professional must demonstrate that compliance with the Practice Standards was not required

6. **No Client Agreement to Engage for Financial Planning**

   If a CFP® professional otherwise must comply with the Practice Standards, but the Client does not agree to engage the CFP® professional to provide Financial Planning, the CFP® professional must either:

   a. Not enter into the Engagement;

   b. Limit the Scope of Engagement to services that do not require application of the Practice Standards, and describe to the Client the services the Client requests that the CFP® professional will not be performing;

   c. Provide the requested services after informing the Client how Financial Planning would benefit the Client and how the decision not to engage the CFP® professional to provide Financial Planning may limit the CFP® professional's Financial Advice, in which case the CFP® professional is not required to comply with the Practice Standards; or

   d. Terminate the Engagement.

The fiduciary duty applies when financial advice is provided to a client. **Exhibit 16.9** below provides a list of types of advice and activities that are likely to be considered financial advice and those that are not likely to be financial advice.

Exhibit 16.9 | Types of Activities Likely to be Considered Financial Advice

Activities That May Be Considered Financial Advice	*Activities That May NOT Be Considered Financial Advice*
• Developing a financial plan for a client • Recommending that the client refrain from investing in certain types of financial assets • Recommending a portfolio allocation for the client • Recommending the client gift financial assets • Recommending investment strategies for the client • Selecting or retaining other professionals to provide services to the client • Exercising discretionary authority over the client's brokerage account or other financial assets	• Acting as an order-taker for brokerage services • Providing general education materials • Distributing marketing materials that would generally not be viewed as financial advice by a CFP® professional

*Note that in the above list if the communication is tailored directly to the client, it is likely to be viewed as financial advice.

Once it has been determined that the planner is providing financial advice, the next step is to determine whether the financial advice is a financial planning engagement that requires the application of the Practice Standards. The relationship is a financial planning engagement if any of the following are true:

1. The CFP® professional has agreed to provide financial planning, or
2. The client has reasonable basis to believe that the CFP® professional will provide (or has provided) financial planning, or
3. The financial advice requires integration of relevant elements of the client's personal or financial circumstances in order to act in the client's best interest. Integration factors include the number of elements affected by the advice, the portion of the client's financial assets affected by the advice, the length of time the client's circumstances may be affected by the advice, and barriers to modifying the actions taken to implement the financial advice.

Merely collecting information as required by FINRA's "Know Your Customer" rule does not constitute financial planning.

Example 16.6

Trace is a CFP® professional and has recommended his client invest 40% of his portfolio in a hedge fund. Once invested, the client may be limited to liquidating his position only upon approval by the fund managers. In the past, the fund managers have not been generous in approving such requests within the first seven years after the investment is made.

Due to the length of time, the risk involved with investing in a hedge fund, the high percentage of the portfolio impacted by the recommendation, and the barriers to modification of the recommended investment, Trace falls under number 3 above, and is, therefore, in a financial planning engagement that requires compliance with the Practice Standards. Notice that this is a single recommendation and is for a single product, but is still considered financial planning. There is no requirement that multiple recommendations be made, that multiple products be involved, or that multiple financial planning areas be considered for an engagement to meet the guidelines requiring compliance with the Practice Standards.

Now that the application of the Practice Standards has been established, we will analyze the Practice Standards for the Financial Planning Process.

Section C: Practice Standards for the Financial Planning Process

CFP Board established a Board of Practice Standards in 1995. The Board of Practice Standards was composed exclusively of CFP® practitioners who were commissioned to draft Standards of Practice for financial planning. Ultimately, the Board of Practice Standards drafted and revised the Practice Standards by considering input from CFP® professionals, consumers, regulators, and other organizations, resulting in CFP Board adopting the Revised Standards in 2005. The Practice Standards became effective as of July 1, 2008, with amendments in March and July 2009. The Practice Standards were again revised as part the new *Code and Standards*, and became effective in October 2019.

The Practice Standards were not designed to be a basis for legal liability to third parties. Rather, the Practice Standards sought to establish the level of professional practice expected of those engaged in financial planning. Regardless of the person's title, job position, type of employment, or method of compensation, the Practice Standards are mandatory when the CFP® professional provides financial planning (actual or based on client's perception) or financial advice that requires integration of relevant elements of the client's personal or financial circumstances in order to act in the client's best interest, as discussed previously.

Key Concepts

1. Identify the description of the Practice Standards.
2. Identify the seven steps of the financial planning process outlined in the Practice Standards.

The Practice Standards now delineate seven elements of the financial planning process (see **Exhibit 16.10**) that comprise the best practices of CFP® professionals.

Exhibit 16.10 | Financial Planning Process

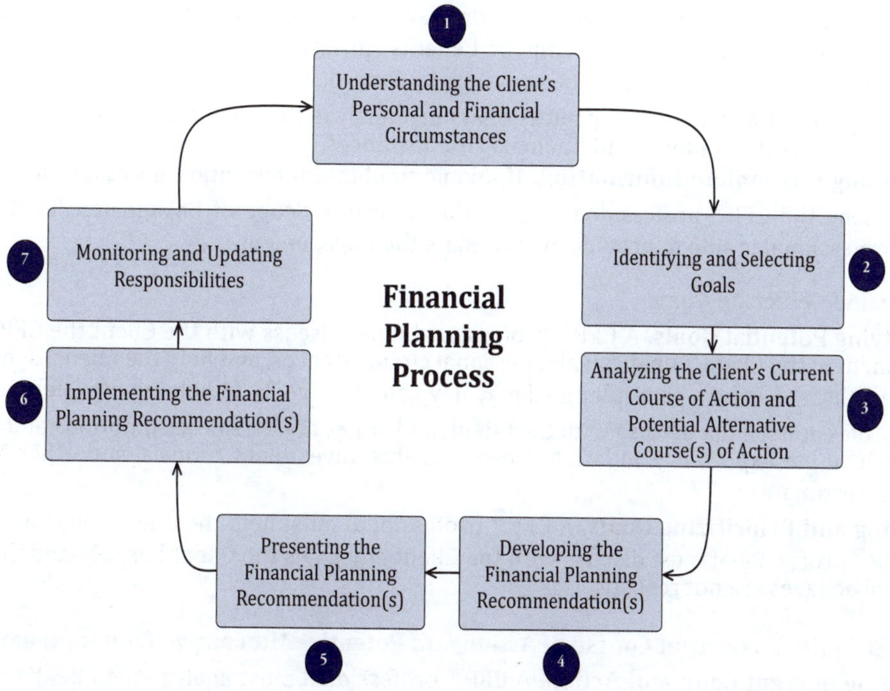

The Practice Standards are substantially updated and re-organized by the 2019 revisions. They provide more detailed requirements for the financial planning process, which has expanded from a six-step to a seven-step process. The Practice Standards for the Financial Planning Process are located in Section C of the *Code and Standards*, and are reprinted in **Exhibit 16.11**.

Exhibit 16.11 | CFP Board Code and Standards - Section C

Section C
Practice Standards for the Financial Planning Process

In complying with the Practice Standards, a CFP® professional must act prudently in documenting information, as the facts and circumstances require, taking into account the significance of the information, the need to preserve the information in writing, the obligation to act in the Client's best interests, and the CFP® Professional's Firm's policies and procedures.

1. **Understanding the Client's Personal and Financial Circumstances**
   a. **Obtaining Qualitative and Quantitative Information.** A CFP® professional must describe to the Client the qualitative and quantitative information concerning the Client's personal and financial circumstances needed to fulfill the Scope of Engagement and collaborate with the Client to obtain the information.
      i. Examples of qualitative or subjective information include the Client's health, life expectancy, family circumstances, values, attitudes, expectations, earnings potential, risk tolerance, goals, needs, priorities, and current course of action.
      ii. Examples of quantitative or objective information include the Client's age, dependents, other professional advisers, income, expenses, cash flow, savings, assets, liabilities, available resources, liquidity, taxes, employee benefits, government benefits, insurance coverage, estate plans, education and retirement accounts and benefits, and capacity for risk.
   b. **Analyzing Information.** A CFP® professional must analyze the qualitative and quantitative information to assess the Client's personal and financial circumstances.
   c. **Addressing Incomplete Information.** If unable to obtain information necessary to fulfill the scope of Engagement, the CFP® professional must either limit the Scope of Engagement to those services the CFP® professional is able to provide or terminate the Engagement.

2. **Identifying and Selecting Goals**
   a. **Identifying Potential Goals.** A CFP® professional must discuss with the Client the CFP® professional's assessment of the Client's financial and personal circumstances, and help the Client identify goals, noting the effect that selecting a particular goal may have on other goals. In helping the Client identify goals, the CFP® professional must discuss with the Client, and apply, reasonable assumptions and estimates. These may include life expectancy, inflation rates, tax rates, investment returns, and other Material assumptions and estimates.
   b. **Selecting and Prioritizing Goals.** A CFP® professional must help the Client select and prioritize goals. The CFP® professional must discuss with the Client any goals the Client has selected that the CFP® professional believes are not realistic.

3. **Analyzing the Client's Current Course of Action and Potential Alternative Course(s) of Action**
   a. **Analyzing Current Course of Action.** A CFP® professional must analyze the Client's current course of action, including the material advantages and disadvantages of the current course and whether the cur-rent course maximizes the potential for meeting the Client's goals.
   b. **Analyzing Potential Alternative Courses of Action.** Where appropriate, a CFP® professional must consider and analyze one or more potential alternative courses of action, including their material advantages and disadvantages of each alternative, whether each alternative helps maximize the potential for meeting the Client's goals, and how each alternative integrates the relevant elements of the Client's personal and financial circumstances.

*** continued ***

4. **Developing the Financial Planning Recommendation(s)**

From the potential courses of action, a CFP® professional must select one or more recommendations designed to maximize the potential for meeting the Client's goals. The recommendation may be to continue the Client's current course of action. For each recommendation selected, the CFP® professional must consider the following information:

a. The assumptions and estimates used to develop the recommendation;

b. The basis for making the recommendation, including how the recommendation is designed to maximize the potential to meet the Client's goals, the anticipated material effects of the recommendation on the Client's financial and personal circumstances, and how the recommendation integrates relevant elements of the Client's personal and financial circumstances;

c. The timing and priority of the recommendation; and

d. Whether the recommendation is independent or must be implemented with another recommendation.

5. **Presenting the Financial Planning Recommendation(s)**

A CFP® professional must present to the Client the selected recommendations and the information that was required to be considered when developing the recommendation(s).

6. **Implementing the Financial Planning Recommendation(s)**

a. **Addressing Implementation Responsibilities.** A CFP® professional must establish with the Client whether the CFP® professional has implementation responsibilities. When the CFP® professional has implementation responsibilities, the CFP® professional must communicate to the Client the recommendation(s) being implemented and the responsibilities of the CFP® professional, the Client, and any third-party with respect to implementation.

b. **Identifying, Analyzing, and Selecting Actions, Products, and Services.** A CFP® professional who has implementation responsibilities must identify and analyze actions, products, and services designed to implement the recommendations. The CFP® professional must consider the basis for each selection, which must include:

i. How the action, product, or service is designed to implement the CFP® professional's recommendation; and

ii. The advantages and disadvantages of the action, product, or service relative to reasonably available alternatives.

c. **Recommending Actions, Products, and Services for Implementation.** A CFP® professional who has implementation responsibilities must recommend one or more actions, products and services to the Client. The CFP® professional must discuss with the Client the basis for selecting an action, product, or service, the timing and priority of implementing the action, product, or service, and disclose and manage any Material Conflicts of Interest concerning the action, product or service.

d. **Selecting and Implementing Actions, Products, or Services.** A CFP® professional who has implementation responsibilities must help the Client select and implement the actions, products, or services. The CFP® professional must discuss with the Client any Client selection that deviates from the actions, products, and services the CFP® professional recommended.

7. **Monitoring Progress and Updating**

a. **Monitoring and Updating Responsibilities.** A CFP® professional must establish with the Client whether the CFP® professional has monitoring and updating responsibilities. When the CFP® professional has responsibilities for monitoring and updating, the CFP® professional must communicate to the Client:

i. Which actions, products, and services are and are not subject to the CFP® professional's monitoring responsibility;

ii. How and when the CFP® professional will monitor the actions, products, and services;

*** continued ***

iii. The Client's responsibility to inform the CFP® professional of any Material changes to the Client's qualitative and quantitative information;

iv. The CFP® professional's responsibility to update the Financial Planning recommendations; and

v. How and when the CFP® professional will update the Financial Planning recommendations.

b. **Monitoring the Client's Progress.** A CFP® professional who has monitoring responsibilities must analyze, at appropriate intervals, the progress toward achieving the Client's goals. The CFP® professional must review with the Client the results of the CFP® professional's analysis.

c. **Obtaining Current Qualitative and Quantitative Information.** A CFP® professional who has monitoring responsibility must collaborate with the Client in an attempt to obtain current qualitative and quantitative information concerning the Client's personal and financial circumstances.

d. **Updating Goals, Recommendations, or Implementation Decisions.** Where a CFP® professional has updating responsibility, and circumstances warrant changes to the Client's goals, recommendations, or selections of actions, products or services, the CFP® professional must update as appropriate in accordance with these *Practice Standards*.

*** END ***

The Practice Standards were developed and promulgated to benefit clients serviced by CFP® professionals. The purpose of the Practice Standards is to advance professionalism in financial planning, enhance the value of the CFP® professional, and assure that CFP® professionals follow established norms of practice. This monumental effort was 20-plus years in the making, but financial planning practitioners are left with an informative and detailed roadmap for a sound, organized financial planning process.

Summary as to Practice Standards

The following exhibit summarizes how the Practice Standards are incorporated into the financial planning process:

Exhibit 16.12 | Practice Standards Summary

Step	Task within Step
1. Understanding the Client's Personal and Financial Circumstances	• Obtain qualitative and quantitative information. • Analyze information. • Address incomplete information.
2. Identifying and Selecting Goals	• Identify potential goals. • Select and prioritize goals.
3. Analyzing the Client's Current Course of Action and Potential Alternative Course(s) of Action	• Analyze the material advantages and disadvantages of the Client's current course of action. • Consider and analyze potential alternative courses of action.
4. Developing the Financial Planning Recommendation(s)	• Select recommendations designed to maximize the potential for meeting the Client's goals. • Consider the assumptions and estimates used.
5. Presenting the Financial Planning Recommendation(s)	• Present to the Client the selected recommendations and information required to be considered when developing the recommendations.
6. Implementing the Financial Planning Recommendation(s)	• Address implementation responsibilities. • Identify, analyze and select actions, products and services. • Recommend actions, products and services for implementation. • Select and implement actions, products, or services.
7. Monitoring Progress and Updating	• Monitor and update responsibilities. • Monitor the Client's progress. • Obtain current qualitative and quantitative information. • Update goals, recommendations, or implementation decisions.

Example 16.7

Willie, a client, asks Nelson (a CFP® professional) to draft a financial plan for him. Willie generally explains his financial situation and his goals and objectives over the telephone to Nelson. Nelson requests quantitative information and documents, but before receiving the quantitative information and documents, Nelson provides Willie with a thorough and detailed financial plan that matches Willie's goals, expectations and timeline. Willie is satisfied. Has Nelson complied with the Practice Standards?

Answer: No. The CFP® professional must obtain sufficient quantitative information and documents from the client relative to the scope of the engagement prior to any recommendations being made or implemented.

Section D: Duties Owed to Firms and Subordinates

Section D of the *Standards of Conduct* relates to duties owed by the CFP® professional to firms and to subordinates.

Exhibit 16.13 | CFP Board Code and Standards - Section D

Section D Duties Owed to Firms and Subordinates
1. **Use Reasonable Care When Supervising** A CFP® professional must exercise reasonable care when supervising persons acting under the CFP® professional's direction, including employees and other persons over whom the CFP® professional has responsibility, with a view toward preventing violations of applicable laws, rules, regulations, and these Standards.
2. **Comply with Lawful Objectives of CFP® Professional's Firm** A CFP® professional: a. Will be subject to discipline by CFP Board for violating policies and procedures of the CFP® professional's Firm that do not conflict with these Standards. b. Will not be subject to discipline by CFP Board for violating policies and procedures of the CFP® professional's Firm that conflict with these Standards.
3. **Provide Notice of Public Discipline** A CFP® professional must promptly advise the CFP® Professional's Firm, in writing, of any public discipline imposed by CFP Board.

Note that the requirement to report public discipline by CFP Board in Section D.3 does not apply merely to suspensions or revocations; rather, it applies to any public discipline by CFP Board.

Example 16.8

Owen, who is a CFP® professional, owns his own firm, ABC Advisers (ABC). Jake, who is not a CFP® professional, is an employee of ABC and has worked for the firm for several years. ABC has a policy that employees are not permitted to be designated as beneficiaries for ABC clients. Could Owen be subject to disciplinary action if Jake was found to be a beneficiary on several ABC client accounts? The answer is yes, as Owen has a duty to supervise Jake's activities.

Working As A Member Of A Team

Through additional Compliance Resources available on CFP Board's website, the Board has addressed the duties of a CFP® Professional when working as part of a team at the CFP® professional's firm.[7] If a situation arises in which the CFP® professional has actual knowledge that another member of the team has not provided professional services in the client's best interest, the fiduciary duty requires that the CFP® professional take reasonable steps to help ensure that the services are in the client's best interest. If the CFP® professional does not have responsibility to supervise the other team member, the CFP® professional should first determine whether the firm has established policies and procedures which can be followed to communicate these concerns with appropriate personnel. In the absence of existing

---

7. https://www.cfp.net/ethics/compliance-resources/2020/07/the-fiduciary-duty-to-take-reasonable-steps-when-providing-professional-services

policies and procedures, the CFP® professional should first inform the other team member that the CFP® professional believes the services provided were not in the client's best interest and the reason for that belief, and allow the team member an opportunity to demonstrate why the services were in the client's best interest or to take action to ensure that the services provided are in the best interest of the client. If the team member cannot demonstrate why the services were in the best interest of the client and refuses to take action to correct the situation, the CFP® professional should inform his supervisor (or another appropriate person within the firm) about his or her concerns.

Section E: Duties Owed to CFP Board

Section E of the *Standards of Conduct* relates to duties owed by the CFP® professional to CFP Board. CFP® professionals may not engage in conduct that reflects adversely on their integrity or fitness as a CFP® professional, upon the CFP® marks, or upon the profession.

Exhibit 16.14 | CFP Board Code and Standards - Section E

Section E
Duties Owed to CFP Board

1. Definitions

The following definitions apply:

a. **Felony.** A felony offense, or for jurisdictions that do not differentiate between a felony and a misdemeanor, an offense punishable by a sentence of at least one-year imprisonment or a fine of at least $1,000.

b. **Relevant Misdemeanor.** A criminal offense, that is not a Felony, for conduct involving fraud, theft, misrepresentation, other dishonest conduct, crimes of moral turpitude, violence, or a second (or more) alcohol and/or drug-related offense.

c. **Regulatory Investigation.** An investigation initiated by a federal, state, local, or foreign governmental agency, self-regulatory organization, or other regulatory authority. A regulatory investigation does not include preliminary or routine regulatory inquiries or requests for information, deficiency letters, "blue sheet" requests or other trading questionnaires, or examinations.

d. **Regulatory Action.** An action initiated by a federal, state, local, or foreign government agency, self-regulatory organization, or other regulatory authority.

e. **Civil Action.** A lawsuit or arbitration.

f. **Finding.** A finding includes an adverse final action and a consent decree in which the finding is neither admitted nor denied, but does not include a deficiency letter, examination report, memorandum or understanding, or other similar information resolution of a matter.

g. **Minor Rule Violation.** A violation of a self-regulatory organization rule designated as a minor rule violation under a plan approved by the U.S. Securities and Exchange Commission. A rule violation may be designated as "minor" under a plan if the sanction imposed consists of a fine of $2,500 or less, and if the sanctioned person does not contest the fine.

*** continued ***

2. Refrain from Adverse Conduct

A CFP® professional may not engage in conduct that reflects adversely on his or her integrity or fitness as a CFP® professional, upon the CFP® marks, or upon the profession. Such conduct includes, but is not limited to, conduct that results in:

a. A Felony or Relevant Misdemeanor conviction, or admission into a program that defers or withholds the entry of a judgment of conviction for a Felony or Relevant Misdemeanor;

b. A Finding in a Regulatory Action or Civil Action that the CFP® professional engaged in fraud, theft, misrepresentation, or other dishonest conduct;

c. A personal bankruptcy or business bankruptcy filing or adjudication where the CFP® professional was a Control Person of the business, unless the CFP® professional can rebut the presumption that the bankruptcy demonstrates an inability to manage responsibly the CFP® professional's or business's financial affairs;

d. A federal tax lien on property owned by the CFP® professional, unless the CFP® professional can rebut the presumption that the federal tax lien demonstrates an inability to manage responsibly the CFP® professional's financial affairs; or

e. A non-federal tax lien, judgment lien, or civil judgment that has not been satisfied within a reasonable amount of time unless the CFP® professional can rebut the presumption that the non-federal tax lien, judgment lien, or civil judgment demonstrates an inability to manage responsibly the CFP® professional's financial affairs.

3. Reporting

A CFP® professional must provide written notice to CFP Board within 30 calendar days after the CFP® professional, or an entity over which the CFP® professional was a Control Person, has:

a. Been charged with, convicted of, or admitted into a program that defers or withholds the entry of a judgment or conviction for, a Felony or Relevant Misdemeanor;

b. Been named as a subject of, or whose conduct is mentioned adversely in, a Regulatory Investigation or Regulatory Action alleging failure to comply with the laws, rules, or regulations governing Professional Services;

c. Had conduct mentioned adversely in a Finding in a Regulatory Action involving failure to comply with the laws, rules, or regulations governing Professional Services (except a Regulatory Action involving a Minor Rule Violation in a Regulatory Action brought by a self- regulatory organization);

d. Had conduct mentioned adversely in a Civil Action alleging failure to comply with the laws, rules, or regulations governing Professional Services;

e. Become aware of an adverse arbitration award or civil judgment, or a settlement agreement, in a Civil Action alleging failure to comply with the laws, rules, or regulations governing Professional Services, where the conduct of the CFP® professional, or an entity over which the CFP® professional was a Control Person, was mentioned adversely, other than a settlement for an amount less than $15,000;

f. Had conduct mentioned adversely in a Civil Action alleging fraud, theft, misrepresentation, or other dishonest conduct;

g. Been the subject of a Finding of fraud, theft, misrepresentation, or other dishonest conduct in a Regulatory Action or Civil Action;

h. Become aware of an adverse arbitration award or civil judgment, or a settlement agreement in a Civil Action alleging fraud, theft, misrepresentation, or other dishonest conduct, where the conduct of the CFP® professional, or an entity over which the CFP® professional was a Control Person, was mentioned adversely;

i. Had a professional license, certification, or membership suspended, revoked, or materially restricted because of a violation of rules or standards of conduct;

*** continued ***

Reporting (continued)

   j.   Been terminated for cause from employment or permitted to resign in lieu of termination when the cause of the termination or resignation involved allegations of dishonesty, unethical conduct, or compliance failures;

   k.   Been named as the subject of, or been identified as the broker/adviser of record in, any written, customer-initiated complaint that alleged the CFP® professional was involved in:

      i.   Forgery, theft, misappropriation, or conversion of Financial Assets;

      ii.   Sales practice violations and contained a claim for compensation of $5,000 or more; or

      iii.   Sales practice violations and settled for an amount of $15,000 or more.

   l.   Filed for or been the subject of a personal bankruptcy or business bankruptcy where the CFP® professional was a Control Person;

   m.   Received notice of a federal tax lien on property owned by the CFP® professional; or

   n.   Failed to satisfy a non-federal tax lien, judgment lien, or civil judgment within one year of its date of entry, unless payment arrangements have been agreed upon by all parties.

4. **Provide Narrative Statement**

The written notice must include a narrative statement that accurately and completely describes the Material facts and the outcome or status of the reportable matter.

5. **Cooperation**

A CFP® professional may not make false or misleading representations to CFP Board or obstruct CFP Board in the performance of its duties. A CFP® professional must satisfy the cooperation requirements set forth in CFP Board's Procedural Rules, including by cooperating fully with CFP Board's requests, investigations, disciplinary proceedings, and disciplinary decisions.

6. **Compliance with Terms and Conditions of Certification and License**

A CFP® professional must comply with the *Terms and Conditions of Certification and License*.

*** END ***

Section E.3 provides a robust list of situations that require reporting to CFP Board within 30 calendar days. It is worth noting that the transgressions that require reporting are not limited to those which are directly related to the CFP® professional's financial planning practice, and that reporting is required in some cases where the CFP® professional has merely been accused or mentioned but has not been convicted or found guilty of the wrongdoing or crime. For example, under Section E.3.f, if the CFP® professional owns rental properties and is named in a civil suit alleging misrepresentation regarding the rental properties, the allegation must be reported to CFP Board even though it does not relate to the CFP® professional's financial planning practice. It appears that the intention is for CFP Board to be notified upon the initial accusation (e.g., been charged with a crime in E.3.a; been named a subject of a regulatory investigation in E.3.b; been mentioned in a civil action in E.3.d and E.3.f; or been named as the subject of a complaint in E.3.k) as well as when a decision has been determined (e.g., been convicted of a crime in E.3.a; had conduct mentioned adversely in a finding in a regulatory investigation in E.3.c; or been the subject of a finding in E.3.g).

Example 16.9

Jayden is a CFP® professional who enjoys going out for a drink with friends now and then. Unfortunately, Jayden recently made the mistake of driving herself home after one too many drinks and was charged with a misdemeanor DUI. Does Jayden need to report the charge to CFP Board, and if so, within what time frame?

Section E.1.b. defines a Relevant Misdemeanor as a criminal offense that is not a felony, for conduct involving fraud, theft, misrepresentation, other dishonest conduct, crimes of moral turpitude, violence, or a second (or more) alcohol and/or drug-related offense. Section E.3.a. requires written notice to CFP Board within 30 calendar days after the CFP® professional has been charged with, convicted of, or admitted into a program that defers or withholds the entry of a judgment or conviction for, a Felony or Relevant Misdemeanor. Section E.4 requires that the written notice include a narrative statement that accurately and completely describes the Material Facts and outcome of the reportable matter.

Because this was Jayden's first alcohol-related misdemeanor offense, she does not need to report to CFP Board. If Jayden receives a second alcohol-related charge, she must report to CFP Board, in writing, within 30 calendar days. Note: Under the previous *Standards of Professional Conduct* and *Disciplinary Rules and Procedure* (prior to October 2019), reporting was not required unless the CFP® professional was *convicted* of a crime, including DUI; however, under the current *Code and Standards*, reporting is required when the CFP® professional is merely *charged with* a felony crime or Relevant Misdemeanor (including a second (or more) DUI). Reporting is also required upon conviction.

Ultimately, the CFP® professional must provide written notice to CFP Board within 30 calendar days of both the initiation and conclusion of the reportable matter, including a narrative statement describing the material facts and outcome or status of the matter. Additionally, the reportable matter must be disclosed on the Ethics Declaration when renewing certification each year.[8] It is important to understand that reporting does not always result in an investigation or in a violation of the *Code and Standards*, however, failure to report is always a violation of the *Code and Standards*.

It is also important to note that, while the reportable events outlined in Section E.3 closely resemble the disclosure requirements on Form U4 (as discussed in Chapter 15), some types of conduct that are not reportable on the U4 must still be reported to CFP Board, and reporting on the U4 is not a substitute for reporting directly to CFP Board.[9]

---

8. CFP Board's *Duty to Report Information to CFP Board and Duty to Cooperate with CFP Board Investigations* document.
9. "CFP Board's Code of Ethics and Standards of Conduct: Implications for "Fee-Only" CFP® Professionals" document.

Proper Use of the CFP® Marks

Under Section E.6, a CFP® professional must comply with the *Terms and Conditions of Certification and License*. These terms and conditions include proper use of the CFP® marks, which are described in **Exhibit 16.15**. Those who are in the process of completing the requirements to become a CFP® professional are not permitted to use the CFP® marks; however, under the terms of the *Pathway to CFP® Certification Agreement*, individuals who have completed a CFP Board registered education program may present themselves as a **"Candidate for CFP® Certification"** for a period of up to five years following completion of the education program while fulfilling the remaining exam and experience requirements. Those who publicly present themselves as a Candidate for CFP® Certification must comply with, and are bound by, the *Code and Standards*.

Exhibit 16.15 | How to Use the CFP® Marks

Please refer to the following guidelines for proper use of the CFP® certification marks. When used, the trademarks must be displayed under strict use and reproduction guidelines, or their value as trademarks could be lost.

CFP®

- Always use capital letters.
- Never use periods.
- Always use the ® symbol.
- Always use with one of CFP Board's approved nouns ("**certificant**," "professional," "practitioner," "certification," "mark" or "exam") unless directly following the name of the individual certified by CFP Board.
- Always associate with the individual(s) certified by CFP Board.
- The CFP® mark must not be used as a parenthetical abbreviation for the CERTIFIED FINANCIAL PLANNER™ mark, and vice versa.
- Certificants are strictly prohibited from using the CFP® mark and CERTIFIED FINANCIAL PLANNER™ in domain names/URLs and email addresses.

CERTIFIED FINANCIAL PLANNER™

- Always use capital letters or small cap font.
- Always use the ™ symbol.
- Always use with one of CFP Board's approved nouns ("certificant," "professional," "practitioner," "certification," "mark" or "exam") unless directly following the name of the individual certified by CFP Board.
- Always associate with the individual(s) certified by CFP Board.

CFP
CERTIFIED FINANCIAL PLANNER®

- Always reproduce the plaque design from original artwork (available on CFP Board's website).
- Never alter or modify the plaque design.
- Always associate with the individual(s) certified by CFP Board.
- Maintain a minimum size of 0.5 inches in print or 50 px on screen.
- Always maintain clear space around the mark to maintain legibility.

https://www.cfp.net/career-and-growth/market-yourself/how-to-use-the-cfp-marks

Continuing Education

The *Terms and Conditions of Certification and License* require that the CFP® professional satisfy continuing education requirements. CFP® professionals are required to complete 30 credit hours of continuing education accepted by CFP Board every two years. Of the 30 hours, two hours must be by completion of a CFP Board-approved Ethics course.

Section F: Prohibition on Circumvention

A CFP® professional may not do indirectly, or through or by another person or entity, any act or thing that the *Code and Standards* prohibit the CFP® professional from doing directly.

This last Standard of Conduct is included to make sure that CFP® professionals live up to the spirit, as well as the actual rules, of the *Code of Ethics* and the *Standards of Conduct*. CFP Board does not want someone to be able to claim that their actions were permitted because they were not explicitly enumerated in the *Code of Ethics* or the *Standards of Conduct*.

Summary of Standards of Conduct

As a certifying and standards-setting body, CFP Board has made it clear that violations of the *Standards of Conduct* may subject CFP® professionals to discipline. **Exhibit 16.16** provides a synopsis of CFP® professionals' various duties and responsibilities found in CFP Board's *Standards of Conduct* to clients, employers and CFP Board.

Exhibit 16.16 | CFP® Professional Duties and Responsibilities

Duties Owed To Clients
1) Fiduciary Duty
2) Integrity
3) Competence
4) Diligence
5) Disclose and Manage Conflicts of Interest
6) Sound and Objective Professional Judgement
7) Professionalism
8) Comply with the Law
9) Confidentiality and Privacy
10) Provide Information to a Client
11) Duties when Communicating with a Client
12) Duties when Representing Compensation Method
13) Duties when Recommending, Engaging, and Working with Additional Persons
14) Duties when Selecting, Using, and Recommending Technology
15) Refrain from Borrowing or Lending Money and Commingling Financial Assets

Duties Owed To Employers
1) Use Reasonable Care when Supervising
2) Comply with Lawful Objectives of CFP® Professional's Firm
3) Provide Notice of Public Discipline

Duties Owed To CFP Board
1) Refrain from Adverse Conduct
2) Reporting
3) Provide a Narrative Statement
4) Cooperation
5) Compliance with *Terms and Conditions of Certification and Trademark License*

Comparison of the SEC's Regulation BI and CFP Board's Code and Standards

As part of their financial planning practice, many CFP® professionals provide investment advice and/or engage in securities transactions on behalf of clients. These activities require proper licensing and adherence to federal and state securities laws as discussed in Chapters 1 and 15. Just as CFP® Professionals are held to a fiduciary duty of care by the *Code of Ethics and Standards of Conduct*, investment adviser representatives are held to a fiduciary duty of care by the Investment Advisers Act of 1940. CFP Board's fiduciary standard outlines a duty of loyalty, duty of care, and duty to follow client instructions, as described previously. The SEC's interpretation of the fiduciary duty under the Investment Advisers Act of 1940 includes a duty of care, which includes a duty to provide advice that is in the best interest of the client, the duty to seek the best execution, and the duty to provide advice and monitoring over the course of the relationship, and also includes a duty of loyalty.[10] In requiring a fiduciary duty of investment advisers, Congress had the intent to "eliminate, or at least expose, all conflicts of interest which might incline an investment adviser - consciously or unconsciously - to render advice which is not disinterested."[11] While not an exact match, the fiduciary duty of a CFP® professional and the fiduciary duty of an investment adviser are closely aligned, and require that the CFP® professional or investment adviser act in the client's best interest at all times and disclose any potential conflicts of interest. In addition, these fiduciary duties apply to the entire relationship between the CFP® professional or adviser and the client, regardless of whether the client is a retail household, business, or other entity. As outlined in Exhibit 16.16 and discussed in Chapter 15 of this text, the best interest standard required of broker-dealers applies only at the time of the recommendation, and only when working with a retail customer, making it more narrow in scope.

Investment adviser representatives and registered representatives of broker-dealers must follow the rules set forth in the SEC's Regulation Best Interest (Regulation BI) and Form CRS Relationship Summary, as outlined in Chapter 15. **Exhibit 16.17** provides a summary comparison of Regulation BI versus CFP Board's Code and Standards. (Note: some requirements of Reg. BI have yet to be fully interpreted and clarified by the SEC.) It is important to note that, while investment advisers must follow the rules set forth in Regulation BI and Form CRS, the fiduciary obligation of an investment adviser is not diminished by Reg. BI; rather, the investment adviser is still held to the standard of care imposed by the Investment Advisers Act of 1940, as described above.

---

10. SEC Release No. IA-5248; effective July 12, 2019.
11. SEC v. Capital Gains Research Bureau, Inc., 375 U.S. 180, 194 (1963) ("SEC v. Capital Gains").

Exhibit 16.17 | Summary Comparison of SEC's Regulation BI Versus CFP Board's *Code of Ethics and Standards of Conduct*

	SEC's Regulation BI	CFP Board's Code and Standards
Fiduciary Duty	No	Yes
Best Interest Standard	Yes	Yes
Best Interest Standard applies	At the time of the recommendation, when working with retail customers (natural persons or their legal representatives)	At all times, when working with a client (includes natural persons as well as some business organizations and legal entities to whom the CFP® professional agrees to provide professional services pursuant to an engagement)
Duty of Care	Requires care, skill, and diligence (note: the SEC has stated that they believe prudence is implied by these requirements)	Requires care, skill, diligence, and prudence
Duty of Loyalty	Yes (recommendations must made without placing the interests of the broker-dealer ahead of the interest of the retail client)	Yes (the CFP® professional must place the interest of the client above the interests of the CFP® professional or his or her firm, and must act without regard to the interests of anyone but the client)
Conflicts of Interest	Broker-dealer required to establish policies and procedures designed to mitigate conflicts of interest (based on whether they are reasonably designed to reduce the incentive for the associated person to make a recommendation that places the associated person's or firm's interest ahead of the retail customer)	Disclose, obtain informed consent, and manage all conflicts of interest; and adopt and follow business practices designed to prevent conflicts from compromising the ability to act in the client's best interest*
Conflict of Interest Disclosures	Written	Oral or Written
Covered Recommendations	Recommendations involving securities transactions and investment strategies involving securities (including recommendations as to account types, as well as rollovers from one account type to another) made to a retail customer (as defined above) primarily for personal, family, or household purposes	Recommendations regarding all financial assets (includes securities, insurance products, real estate, bank instruments, commodities, derivatives, collectibles, and other financial products) made to a client (as defined above)

Source: CFP Board's Comparing CFP Board's Code of Ethics and Standards of Conduct to the SEC's Regulation Best Interest document.

*A case study regarding managing conflicts of interest involving proprietary products can be reviewed at https://www.cfp.net/ethics/compliance-resources/2019/11/the-duty-to-disclose-and-manage-material-conflicts-of-interest-involving-proprietary-products

PROCEDURAL RULES

The *Procedural Rules* provide detailed procedures followed by CFP Board in enforcing the *Code of Ethics* and *Standards of Conduct*. The *Procedural Rules* clearly set out the process whereby CFP® professionals and candidates for CFP® certification are given notice of potential violations. The process is intended to be fair and allow opportunities for CFP® professionals to be heard by a panel of other professionals. To promote and maintain the integrity of the marks for the benefit of clients and potential clients of CFP® professionals, CFP Board has the power to enforce the provisions of the *Code of Ethics* and *Standards of Conduct*. Those who violate these regulations are subject to discipline or sanctions.

The Procedural Rules are lengthy and are organized into 17 sections entitled "Articles." For a full text of the *Procedural Rules*, go to https://www.cfp.net/ethics/enforcement. The *Procedural Rules* are designed to provide a fair and reasonable process for CFP® professionals and candidates for CFP® certification against whom allegations of violations of the *Code of Ethics* and *Standards of Conduct* are brought. The term "**Respondent**" is used to refer to any person who has agreed to CFP Board's *Terms and Conditions of Certification and Trademark License* (CFP® professionals) or *Pathway to CFP® Certification Agreement* (candidates for CFP® certification). **CFP Board Counsel** (including CFP Board staff operating at the direction of CFP Board Counsel) has the authority to investigate and file a complaint against a Respondent for alleged violations of the *Code and Standards* or the *Pathway to CFP® Certification Agreement*.

> ## ≔ *Key Concepts*
>
> 1. Identify the purpose of the *Procedural Rules*.
>
> 2. Describe the categories of sanction for CFP® professionals and for candidates for CFP® certification.
>
> 3. Describe the three categories of adverse conduct under the *Fitness Standards for Candidates for CFP® Certification and Former CFP® Professionals Seeking Reinstatement*.
>
> 4. Outline the sanction guidelines for single bankruptcies and for multiple bankruptcies.
>
> 5. Explain the consequences of being in Default.

Investigation

CFP Board may learn about matters that may reveal misconduct via:
- complaints submitted to CFP Board,
- self-disclosure by CFP® professionals, or
- CFP Board background checks.

CFP Board, through its Counsel, reviews allegations to determine if further investigation is warranted.[12] If CFP Board Counsel determines that an investigation is warranted, the CFP® professional is provided with a written Notice of Investigation containing the general nature of the allegations. The CFP® professional has 30 calendar days from the date of the Notice of Investigation to file a written acknowledgment of receipt of the Notice of Investigation. If no timely acknowledgment is received, a second notice is issued. Failure to respond within an additional 30 calendar days may be deemed a **Default** under which CFP Board Counsel may, depending on the seriousness, scope, and harmfulness of the allegations deliver any of the following:[13]
- an administrative order of suspension of the respondent's certification for one year and one day (applies to current CFP® professionals),

---

12. *Procedural Rules*, Article 1.1.
13. *Procedural Rules*, Articles 1.1, 4.1, and 4.2.

- an administrative order of temporary bar that bars the respondent from seeking certification for one year and one day (applies to candidates for certification),
- an administrative order of revocation that revokes the respondent's certification (applies to current CFP® professionals), or
- an administrative order of permanent bar that permanently bars the respondent from certification (applies to candidates for certification).

Requests for Documents and Information

CFP Board Counsel may include with the Notice of Investigation, or may send later, requests for the respondent to provide documents, answer questions, and/or either admit or deny the truth of the matters asserted. The respondent must deliver the requested information within 30 calendar days from the initial request and within 14 calendar days from any subsequent request. Failure to timely respond results in the issuance of a notice of failure to cooperate, which constitutes grounds for sanction and may also give rise to an adverse inference that presumes the respondent would have provided the requested information if it was not unfavorable to the respondent.[14]

Upon reviewing the submitted information, CFP Board Counsel determines if there is probable cause to believe grounds for sanction exists and shall either:[15]
- dismiss the allegations as not warranted,
- dismiss the allegations with a letter of dismissal indicating that the respondent may have violated the *Code and Standards* or the *Pathway Agreement*, but that the conduct does not warrant referral to the Disciplinary and Ethics Commission (DEC) for a sanction,
- present a settlement offer to the DEC, or
- begin processing a complaint against the CFP® professional.[16]

The **Disciplinary and Ethic Commission (DEC)** is responsible for reviewing and taking appropriate action with respect to alleged violation of the *Code of Ethics* and *Standards of Conduct* and conduct reviewed pursuant to the *Fitness Standards for Candidates and Professionals Eligible for Reinstatement* (discussed below).[17]

If probable cause exists, a formal complaint against the respondent and a notice of hearing is provided. The complaint must contain the allegations of misconduct with the potential *Code of Ethics* or *Standards of Conduct* violations, providing the respondent with thirty calendar days from receipt of the complaint to file an answer. If no answer is received, the respondent is in Default, and the CFP® professional's right to use the CFP® marks may be administratively suspended or revoked.[18]

---

14. *Procedural Rules*, Article 1.3.
15. There is no formal definition of probable cause in CFP Board's *Procedural Rules*. Generally, "probable cause" in this context could be defined as information sufficient to warrant a reasonable person's belief that Respondent has committed the alleged violation. Probable cause is commonly believed to require more than a reasonable suspicion, but less that what is required for a criminal conviction.
16. *Procedural Rules*, Article 1.4.
17. See https://www.cfp.net/about-cfp-board/councils-and-commissions/disciplinary-and-ethics-commission.
18. *Procedural Rules*, Articles 4.1 and 4.2.

Exhibit 16.18 | Summary of the Investigative Process

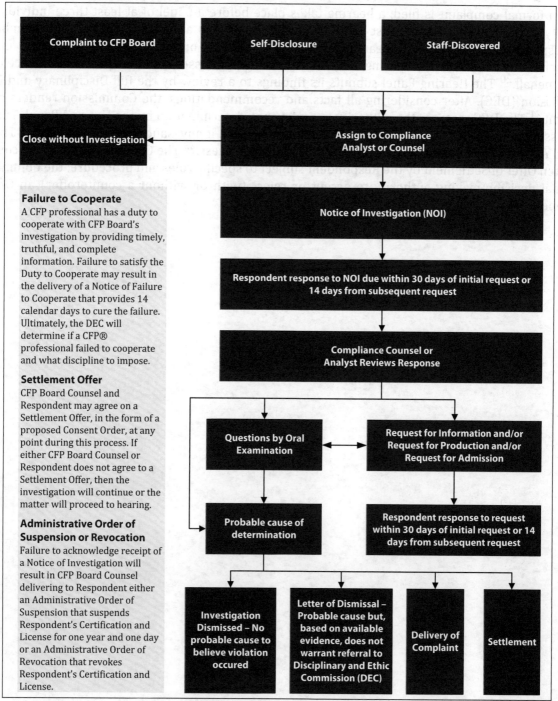

Complaint to CFP Board — **Self-Disclosure** — **Staff-Discovered**

Close without Investigation ← **Assign to Compliance Analyst or Counsel**

Notice of Investigation (NOI)

Respondent response to NOI due within 30 days of initial request or 14 days from subsequent request

Compliance Counsel or Analyst Reviews Response

Questions by Oral Examination ↔ **Request for Information and/or Request for Production and/or Request for Admission**

Probable cause of determination — **Respondent response to request within 30 days of initial request or 14 days from subsequent request**

Investigation Dismissed – No probable cause to believe violation occured

Letter of Dismissal – Probable cause but, based on available evidence, does not warrant referral to Disciplinary and Ethic Commission (DEC)

Delivery of Complaint

Settlement

Failure to Cooperate

A CFP professional has a duty to cooperate with CFP Board's investigation by providing timely, truthful, and complete information. Failure to satisfy the Duty to Cooperate may result in the delivery of a Notice of Failure to Cooperate that provides 14 calendar days to cure the failure. Ultimately, the DEC will determine if a CFP® professional failed to cooperate and what discipline to impose.

Settlement Offer

CFP Board Counsel and Respondent may agree on a Settlement Offer, in the form of a proposed Consent Order, at any point during this process. If either CFP Board Counsel or Respondent does not agree to a Settlement Offer, then the investigation will continue or the matter will proceed to hearing.

Administrative Order of Suspension or Revocation

Failure to acknowledge receipt of a Notice of Investigation will result in CFP Board Counsel delivering to Respondent either an Administrative Order of Suspension that suspends Respondent's Certification and License for one year and one day or an Administrative Order of Revocation that revokes Respondent's Certification and License.

Source: CFP Board's Enforcement Process document, effective June 30, 2020

*Note: The above CFP Board summary states that the time to acknowledge a second Notice of Investigation is 14 days; however, Procedural Rules Article 1.1 identifies this time frame as 30 calendar days. Clarification was requested from CFP Board, and the correct time frame confirmed as **30 days** to respond to a second Notice of Investigation.*

Hearing Process

When a formal complaint is filed, a hearing takes place before a panel of at least three individuals. A majority of the **Hearing Panel** must be CFP® professionals, and a majority must be DEC members.[19] The respondent is entitled to appear in person, by telephone, or by video conference, and may be represented by counsel at the hearing, may cross-examine witnesses, and may present evidence on his or her behalf.[20] The Hearing Panel submits its findings to a review by the full Disciplinary and Ethics Commission (DEC). After considering all facts and recommendations, the Commission renders a final decision.[21] The DEC reserves the authority to review any determination by the Hearing Panel. The DEC must issue a final order of its findings to the respondent and, if any, sanctions are imposed.[22] There is also an Appeals Committee that provides for an appellate process.[23] The Commission may also consider a written Offer of Settlement by the Respondent subject to specific rules and procedure; the Commission has final decision-making authority to accept or reject (with or without a counteroffer) an Offer of Settlement.[24]

---

19. Procedural Rules, Article 10.5.
20. *Procedural Rules*, Articles 10.1 and 10.3.
21. *Procedural Rules*, Articles 10.8, 12.2, and 12.3.
22. *Procedural Rules*, Article 12.3.
23. *Procedural Rules*, Article 15. (Note: CFP Board changed the name of the Appeals Committee to the Code and Standards Enforcement Committee as of October 1, 2020.)
24. *Procedural Rules*, Article 8.

Exhibit 16.19 | Summary of the Hearing Process

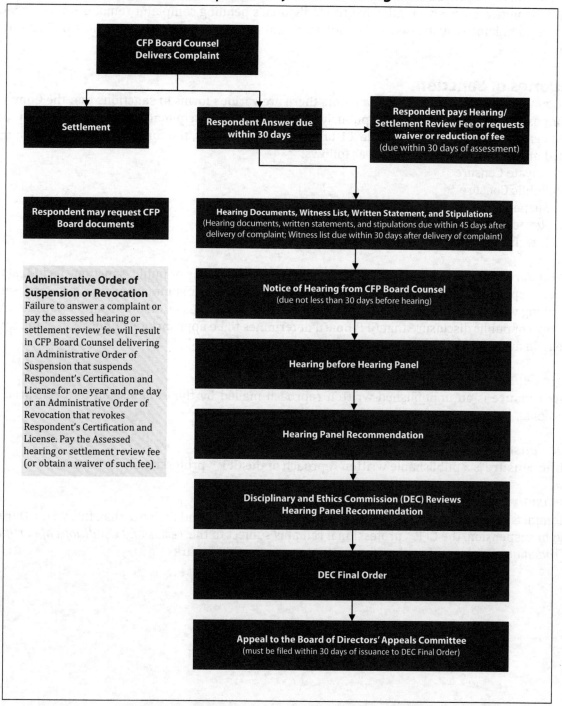

Source: CFP Board's Enforcement Process document, effective June 30, 2020.

When a complaint against a Respondent was filed with CFP Board by an individual, CFP Board Counsel will provide notice every six months that the individual's pending complaint remains under review, and when the complaint is dismissed or adjudicated, notice that a public sanction has or has not been issued.[25]

Categories of Sanction

If the Commission finds grounds for sanction, there are various forms of sanctions that the Commission may impose. The Commission may publicly disseminate all disciplinary actions, except for private written censure. As provided in Article 11 of the *Procedural Rules*, the forms of sanction which may be imposed upon CFP® professionals are as follows:[26]

- Private Censure
- Public Censure
- Suspension
- Revocation
- Interim Suspension

The *Procedural Rules* provide that CFP Board will publish all forms of public sanction (including public censure, suspension, interim suspension, and revocation) with a summary of the facts and sanction order, along with the name of the CFP® professional, in a press release, on CFP Board's website, and any other form of public disclosure that CFP Board determines to be appropriate. Publication of the sanction will remain available to the public on CFP Board's website.[27]

Private Censure

Private censure is an unpublished written reproach mailed by the Commission to a censured CFP® professional.

Public Censure

A **public censure** is a publishable written reproach of the CFP® professional's behavior.

Suspension

The Commission may order **suspension** for no less than 90 days and no more than five years. During the period of suspension, the CFP® professional remains subject to the *Terms and Conditions of Certification and Trademark License*, although not permitted to use the CFP® marks.[28]

---

25. *Procedural Rules*, Article 17.9.
26. Additional forms of sanction may be applied to candidates for CFP® certification and former CFP® professionals seeking reinstatement whose certification has not been suspended, as discussed in the Fitness Standards section below.
27. *Procedural Rules*, Article 17.7.
28. The *Terms and Conditions of Certification and Trademark License* govern the CFP® professional's use of the CFP® marks in the U.S. (the marks cannot be used outside of the U.S.), including proper usage of the marks as outlined in Exhibit 16.14.

Revocation

As for **revocation**, the Commission may order permanent revocation of a CFP® professional's right to use the marks.

After a suspension or revocation, a respondent must provide CFP Board evidence that the respondent has ceased using the marks within 45 calendar days of receiving the suspension or revocation order.[29]

During the hearings that take place under the *Procedural Rules*, rules of procedure and evidence applicable in a court of law are not required.[30] Proof of misconduct must be established to a standard of a preponderance of the evidence, which is more commonly known as a standard of more probable than not, or more likely than not.

Interim Suspension

The *Procedural Rules* also provide for more abrupt and precise action by CFP Board. Certain conduct by CFP® professionals may cause CFP Board to issue an **Interim Suspension** of the right to use the CFP® marks during the pendency of an investigation.[31]

- CFP Board Counsel may issue Motion for Interim Suspension Order requiring the respondent to respond within 14 calendar days. If a CFP® professional's conduct poses an immediate threat to the public, and the gravity of the conduct significantly impinges upon the stature and reputation of the marks, the Hearing Panel must grant the Motion and issue an interim suspension order.
- An automatic interim suspension may immediately be issued without a hearing when CFP Board Counsel receives evidence of a conviction or a professional discipline for any of the following conduct:[32,33]
  - Misdemeanor conviction or felony conviction for fraud, theft, misrepresentation, violence, or crimes of moral turpitude;
  - Respondent is the subject of a civil finding that Respondent engaged in fraud, theft, misrepresentation, violence, or a crime of moral turpitude;
  - Respondent is the subject of professional discipline that resulted in a revocation, bar, or equivalent sanction;[34]
  - Voluntary termination or surrender of a financial professional license or registration while Respondent is the subject of a regulatory investigation; or
  - Consents to the entry of an interim suspension.

---

29. *Procedural Rules*, Article 11.3.
30. *Procedural Rules*, Article 1.2.
31. *Procedural Rules*, Article 2.
32. While "automatic interim suspension" implies that the suspension will always occur, the use of the term "may" within this provision provides CFP Board with some discretion in issuing the automatic interim suspension, to account for situations where the interim suspension is not necessary or premature, including instances where there may be an appeal or where CFP Board is close to reaching a final resolution.
33. "Professional Discipline" is defined in the *Procedural Rules*, Article 7.2.
34. The term "equivalent sanction" is used to account for variations in the manner in which regulatory bodies impose sanctions. It refers to the most severe sanction imposed and is typically permanent.

Sanction Guidelines

CFP Board's *Sanction Guidelines* document (as revised June 30, 2020) provides guidance on sanctions that may apply to particular violations of the *Code and Standards*.[35]

Example 16.10

Iris, Lily, and Dahlia are all CFP® professionals. Iris has been disciplined by her employer for a violation of employer policies regarding contacting clients via text messaging. Lily erroneously reported CE credit which did not qualify for CFP CE and, therefore, did not complete the required number of hours prior to her renewal deadline. Dahlia was so excited about receiving a preliminary pass upon completion of the CFP® exam that she immediately began using the CFP® marks even though she had not completed the remaining requirements for certification and been issued an email from CFP Board authorizing use of the marks.

Iris has an employer policy violation, Lily has a continuing education violation, and Dahlia has a marks usage violation, The most likely sanction for Iris, Lily, and Dahlia is private censure.

Example 16.11

Will, Carlton, Hillary, Ashley, and Jazz are all CFP® professionals. When Will needed extra money to pay for his divorce this year, one of his best clients offered to lend him the money and Will took her up on the offer. Carlton failed to disclose a conflict of interest when he recommended a proprietary mutual fund to a client. Hillary was convicted of her second DUI in the last six years and was sentenced to probation but was not sentenced to serve time in prison. Ashley was disciplined by FINRA for a minor rule violation due to an unintentional error. Jazz filed for personal bankruptcy last year after his DJ business (a sole proprietorship) failed. Jazz had no other personal or business bankruptcies at any time.

Will is in violation of the *Code and Standards* for borrowing money from a client. Carlton is in violation for failing to disclose a relevant conflict of interest. Hillary is in violation due to the conviction within the last ten years of a felony or Relevant Misdemeanor (a second or more DUI is a Relevant Misdemeanor)[36] without time served in jail (note: a sentence involving jail time is treated more seriously). Ashley is in violation due to the securities law violation (note: intentional securities law violations are treated more seriously than unintentional violations). Jazz is in violation due to a single personal or business bankruptcy. The most likely sanction for Will, Carlton, Hillary, Ashley, and Jazz is public censure.

---

35. The *Sanctions Guidelines* serve as guidance only and are not binding on the DEC or the Code and Standards Enforcement Committee (Note: prior to October 1, 2020 this committee was called the Appeals Committee and is referenced as such within the *Procedural Rules* document). https://www.cfp.net/ethics/enforcement/sanction-guidelines
36. See *Code and Standards* Section E.1.b for the definition of a Relevant Misdemeanor.

Example 16.12

Robin, Cardinal, Jay, Wren, and Sparrow are all CFP® professionals. Robin made a recommendation to a client that resulted in a greater payout to her rather than another alternative that would have been more favorable to the client. Cardinal, with the consent of multiple clients, commingled client funds with his own funds. Jay forgot to have a client applying for insurance sign the application. When Jay contacted the client, the client told Jay to sign it for him and Jay followed those instructions, forging the client's signature on the application. Six years ago, Wren was arrested and convicted for inciting a riot in a neighboring state (a felony). Wren was sentenced to one year imprisonment. Sparrow's state insurance license was suspended for a period of 90 days due to a violation of state insurance laws.

Robin is in violation of the *Code and Standards* due to a breach of fiduciary duty. Cardinal is in violation due to commingling client funds with funds of the CFP® professional or the CFP® professional's firm (note: under the pre-2019 *Standards of Professional Conduct*, commingling was permitted with client consent; however, under the new *Code and Standards*. the ban on commingling is absolute).[37] Jay is in violation due to forgery (note: although the *Code and Standards* includes a duty to follow a client's reasonable and lawful instructions, forgery is unlawful; therefore Jay should not have followed the client's instructions). Wren is in violation as a result of a conviction within the last 10 years of a felony involving a jail sentence. Sparrow is in violation as a result of professional discipline involving a suspension of more than thirty days. The most likely sanction for Robin, Cardinal, Jay, Wren, and Sparrow is suspension.

Example 16.13

Dorothy, Sophia, and Rose are all CFP® professionals. Dorothy filed personal bankruptcy twelve years ago when her spending got out of control following a divorce. Last week, Snarky Tee Shirt Emporium, a business over which Dorothy maintained control, filed for bankruptcy as a result of Dorothy's mismanagement of the business. Sophia has recently been convicted of fraud due to her involvement in a ponzi scheme. Rose recently had her CPA license revoked as a result of filing a fraudulent tax return on behalf of a client.

Dorothy is in violation of the *Code and Standards* due to having two or more personal or business bankruptcies. Sophia is in violation due to her involvement in a ponzi scheme. Rose is in violation due to revocation of a professional license (e.g., FINRA, insurance, accountant, investment adviser). The most likely sanction for Dorothy, Sophia, and Rose is revocation.

37. CFP Board's *Commentary to the Code of Ethics and Standards of Conduct; March 2018, as Revised in November 2018* document. https://www.cfp.net/ethics/compliance-resources/2018/11/commentary-on-new-code-of-ethics-and-standards-of-conduct

Exhibit 16.20 | Sanction Examples

Type of Sanction	Definition	Examples of Violations That May Result in This Type of Sanction*
Private Censure	An unpublished written reproach	Continuing education violation, diligence violation, employer policies violation, misuse of CFP® marks
Public Censure	A written reproach published in a press release and on CFP Board's website	One personal or business bankruptcy, borrowing from a client, conflict of interest violation, conviction within the last 10 years of a felony or any Relevant Misdemeanor (see Code and Standards section E.1.b) involving probation only, securities law violation (note: intentional acts are treated more seriously)
Suspension	A period in which Respondent remains subject to the Terms and Conditions of Certification and Trademark License but is prohibited from using the CFP® certification marks	Breach of fiduciary duty, commingling, forgery, conviction within the last 10 years of a felony or any Relevant Misdemeanor (see Code and Standards Section E.1.b) involving a jail sentence, suitability violations, professional discipline involving a suspension of more than 30 days
Interim Suspension	A suspension issued prior to a final order	Conduct posing an immediate threat to the public (see text section regarding interim suspensions and automatic interim suspensions)
Revocation	A termination of Respondent's Certification and Trademark License.	Two or more personal or business bankruptcies, ponzi scheme, revocation of a financial professional license (e.g., FINRA, insurance, accountant, or investment adviser)

Source for examples: CFP Board's Sanction Guidelines document, as revised June 30, 2020; Interim Suspensions, Procedural Rules, Article 2. Sanction definitions: Procedural Rules, Article 11.

*The Sanction Guidelines provide guidance on the sanction that might apply to particular violations. They are not binding on the DEC or Appeals Committee ; they serve as guidance only. (Note: CFP Board changed the name of the Appeals Committee to the Code and Standards Enforcement Committee as of October 1, 2020)

Cooperation With Investigation

There is one very common theme throughout the Anonymous Case Histories (summaries of disciplinary actions taken in the past, discussed in detail later in this chapter). That theme is failing to cooperate with CFP Board or its disciplinary process may result in severe penalties or discipline (a "default," as discussed previously, which may result in an administrative suspension or revocation). Cooperation with the process is paramount. Stated another way, cooperating does not necessarily mean that one has to admit to the allegations; instead, it means that the respondent must timely respond within the time frames and procedures outlined in the *Procedural Rules*. To ensure that respondents receive documents and notifications from CFP Board, Article 16.1 requires that any changes to a respondent's mailing address or email address be updated with CFP Board within 30 calendar days.

Default Example

Failure to respond to a second Notice of Investigation is a default and is likely to result in the revocation of a certificant's license to use the CFP® marks.

Example 16.14

In an Anonymous Case History, CFP Board permanently revoked Respondent's right to use the CFP® marks after Respondent failed to respond to a complaint initiated by CFP Board. CFP Board investigated Respondent's company and asserted that the company's use of a mark was confusing to the public and diluted the CFP® certification marks[38]. The Respondent did not comply with the procedure outlined in the Disciplinary Rules (the rules in effect at that time) by failing to respond to CFP Board's Complaint. As a result, the allegations in the complaint were deemed admitted, and an order of revocation was issued.

Exhibit 16.21 | Procedural Rules Key Days

Description	Number of Days	Consequences of Missed Deadline
Response to Notice of Investigation	Within 30 calendar days	A second notice is sent
Response to second Notice of Investigation (issued if the Board does not receive a response to the first notice within the allotted time frame)	Within 30 calendar days	Default
Response to Request for Documents	Within 30 calendar days	A second request is sent
Response to second Request for Documents (issued if the Board does not receive a response to the first request within the allotted time frame)	Within 14 calendar days	Notice of failure to cooperate, which constitutes grounds for sanction (and may result in an adverse inference that presumes the respondent would have provided the information if it were not unfavorable to him or her)
Response to Motion for Interim Suspension	Within 14 calendar days	*
Suspension of use of marks	May last for 90 day to 5 years	N/A
Revocation of use of marks	Permanent	N/A
Evidence provided to CFP Board that certificant receiving suspension or revocation order has stopped using the marks	Within 45 calendar days	*
Notify CFP Board of change of mailing address or email address	Within 30 calendar days	*

The consequences of missing these deadlines are not specifically stated in the Procedural Rules.

---

38. See discussion later in this chapter entitled "Anonymous Case Histories" for a more complete discussion of CFP Board's reporting of actual disciplinary cases.

Sanction Guidelines for Bankruptcies

Prior to July 1, 2012, personal or business bankruptcies were presumed to be a result of the candidate or CFP® professional's inability to manage responsibly the candidate or CFP® professional's financial affairs unless the respondent could demonstrate otherwise. Beginning July 1, 2012, CFP Board ceased investigating and adjudicating single bankruptcy-only cases. Instead, all bankruptcies were disclosed on the CFP® professional's public profile displayed on CFP Board's website for 10 years, and their names were included once in a press release issued periodically by the Board.

Under the current *Code and Standards* and *Procedural Rules*, effective October 1, 2019, a single personal bankruptcy or any business bankruptcy where the CFP® professional was a control person is grounds for sanction and public censure unless the CFP® professional can rebut the presumption that it demonstrates an inability to responsibly manage the CFP® professional's financial affairs.[39] For single bankruptcies, a streamlined adjudication process is utilized under which the CFP® professional may:

1. accept public censure without incurring a hearing fee, or
2. pay a hearing fee and follow an expedited adjudication procedure.

Multiple bankruptcies will follow the normal adjudication process outlined in the *Procedural Rules*.

When the CFP® professional is able to make the showing that the bankruptcy is not a result of inability to manage financial affairs, the CFP® professional will not be subject to discipline, and CFP Board will not issue a press release announcing the bankruptcy. However, in all cases, bankruptcies must be reported to CFP Board within 30 calendar days and must be disclosed to clients within 90 days. Client disclosures must include the location(s) of all relevant public websites of any governmental authority, self-regulatory organization, or professional organization that sets forth the bankruptcy.[40]

Example 16.15

Waylon, a CFP® professional, recently filed for bankruptcy protection after his spouse developed a medical condition requiring 24-hour custodial care, frequent travel to another state for medical treatment, and high out-of-pocket costs for medical expenses not covered by insurance. Since this is his first bankruptcy and he believes that it reflects a severely challenging life situation rather than his inability to manage financial affairs, he has decided to pay the hearing fee and proceed through the expedited adjudication procedure in an effort to avoid the publicity of a public censure under which the bankruptcy will be published in a press release and on CFP Board's website. Regardless of the outcome of the adjudication process, Waylon understands that he will be required to disclose the bankruptcy to clients within 90 days, including the location of relevant public websites of any governmental authority that sets forth the bankruptcy.

---

39. The business need not be related to the CFP® professional's practice as a financial planner, the bankruptcy of any type of business over which the CFP® professional was a control person is treated as a bankruptcy of the CFP® professional.
40. CFP Board's *Notice Regarding Bankruptcy Standard and Procedures* document; *Procedural Rules*, Articles 3.3 and 3.4; and CFP Board's *Frequently Asked Questions, Code of Ethics* and *Standards of Conduct*; question 24

Example 16.16

Be Nimble corporation, a C corporation over which Jack, a CFP® professional, was a control person, recently filed for bankruptcy. Neither Jack nor any other business over which he was a control person has filed for any other bankruptcy in the past. Jack decides to avoid the adjudication process and accept the public censure since he does not believe it will negatively impact his financial planning business and he realizes that he must disclose the bankruptcy to all clients within 90 days, including the location of relevant public websites of any governmental authority that sets forth the bankruptcy, regardless of whether of not the public censure is imposed.

Example 16.17

Miranda, a CFP® professional, has had a run of bad luck in her life. Fifteen years ago she started a lawn care business, a corporation in which she was the only owner and employee. Unfortunately, two years later business became extremely slow due to a major economic recession and the business filed for bankruptcy. At that point Miranda decided to pursue a business in financial planning, but the long hours she put in building her financial planning business and studying for the CFP® exam while simultaneously running an unrelated start-up web-based company over the next several years took a toll on her marriage and her spouse filed for divorce shortly after Miranda received her CFP® certification. As a result of the divorce, Miranda has recently filed for personal bankruptcy. Since this is Miranda's second or more bankruptcy, she must notify CFP Board within 30 days and will follow the normal adjudication procedure for a violation of the *Code and Standards*. Miranda must also disclose the bankruptcy to clients within 90 days, including the location of relevant public websites of any governmental authority that sets forth the bankruptcy.

Exhibit 16.22 | Bankruptcy Standard and Procedures Summary*

A bankruptcy is grounds for sanction and public censure unless the CFP® professional can rebut the presumption that the bankruptcy demonstrates inability to manage responsibly the CFP® professional's or business's financial affairs.

Number of Bankruptcies	Report To	Adjudication
One	• CFP Board within 30 calendar days • Clients within 90 days (must include notice of the existence of the bankruptcy and location(s) of the webpages of all relevant public websites of any governmental authority, self-regulatory organization, or professional organization	Choose: 1. Accept a public censure without incurring a hearing fee, or 2. Pay a hearing fee and follow a streamlined adjudication procedure
Two	Same as above	Follows normal disciplinary procedure for adjudicating complaints

*Includes personal bankruptcy and/or business bankruptcy where the CFP® professional was a control person.

FITNESS STANDARDS FOR CANDIDATES AND PROFESSIONALS ELIGIBLE FOR REINSTATEMENT (PER)

CFP Board has established standards for candidates for CFP® certification and **Professionals Eligible for Reinstatement** (those who are not currently certified, but have been certified in the past and are eligible to reinstate their certification without the need to pass the current CFP® exam). The *Fitness Standards for Candidates for CFP® Certification and Former CFP® Professionals Seeking Reinstatement* (hereinafter also referred to as "**Fitness Standards**"), ensure specific character and fitness standards as to an individual's conduct before certification. These rules allow candidates an opportunity to determine in advance of taking the CFP® exam whether prior conduct will bar or delay their certification.

Categories of Adverse Conduct

The Fitness Standards identify three categories of adverse conduct which may impact a candidate or PER's eligibility to become certified:
1. Conduct that is unacceptable,
2. Conduct that is presumed to be unacceptable, and
3. Other conduct that may reflect adversely upon the individual's integrity or fitness, the profession, or the CFP® marks.

Conduct That is Unacceptable

Conduct that is on the "unacceptable" list will permanently bar the individual from becoming certified. Various types of felony convictions or revocation of financial or professional licenses will "always bar an individual from becoming certified." CFP Board's list of unacceptable conduct that will always bar an individual from becoming certified is as follows:
1. Felony conviction for theft, embezzlement or other financially-based crimes;
2. Felony conviction for tax fraud or other tax-related crimes;
3. Revocation of a financial professional license (e.g., FINRA, accountant, investment adviser), unless revocation was administrative in nature (such as the result of the individual knowingly letting the license expire by not paying the required fees);
4. Felony conviction for any degree of murder or of rape; or
5. Felony conviction for any other violent crime within the last five years.

The above list is also referred to as the "**always bar list**."

Conduct That is Presumed to Be Unacceptable

CFP Board also provides a specific list of conduct that is presumed to be unacceptable and will bar an individual from becoming certified unless that individual petitions the DEC for a fitness determination and the Commission grants the petition or allows the individual to reapply at a later date. The list of presumed unacceptable conduct (also referred to as the "**presumptive bar list**") requiring a petition from the individual is:
1. Two or more personal or business bankruptcies;
2. Revocation or suspension of a non-financial professional license (e.g., real estate, attorney), unless the revocation is administrative in nature (such as the result of the individual knowingly not renewing the license by not paying the required fees);
3. Suspension of a financial professional license unless the suspension is administrative in nature;
4. Felony conviction for nonviolent crimes, including perjury, within the last five years; or
5. Felony conviction for violent crimes (other than murder or rape) that occurred more than five years ago.

Other Adverse Conduct

When reviewing candidates or Professionals Eligible for Reinstatement for CFP® certification, CFP Board also considers customer complaints, arbitrations and other civil proceedings, felony convictions for non-violent crimes that occurred more than five years ago, misdemeanor convictions and employer investigations and terminations.

CFP Board and the Commission will continue to review matters that result in the delay or denial of certification but do not result in an automatic bar (unless one of the always bar list items provides a time frame, as with felony convictions for any violent crime other than any degree of murder or rape, within the last five years). One method by which CFP Board learns of a candidate's or Professionals Eligible for Reinstatement's fitness is through the disclosure of matters on the ethics portion of the initial certification application, also known as the declaration page. Adverse conduct may also be discovered via a background check performed by CFP Board.[41]

Petitions for Fitness Determination

CFP Board provides the candidate or Professionals Eligible for Reinstatement who has a violation on the presumptive bar or other adverse conduct list with an opportunity to petition the DEC for reconsideration by filing a Petition for Fitness Determination request. In determining whether a candidate's or Professionals Eligible for Reinstatement's conduct will bar certification, CFP Board has outlined the following factors as relevant to determining fitness for certification:[42]

- The extent to which the relevant conduct reflects adversely on the profession or CFP® certification marks;
- Whether and how the respondent has taken actions designed to prevent the relevant conduct from reoccurring in the future;
- Whether and how the respondent has integrated the *Code and Standards* in Respondent's practice;
- Whether Respondent has submitted positive letters of reference from current clients, supervisors, colleagues, or other professionals concerning the relevant conduct or the respondent's character; and
- Any other factors the DEC determines are relevant.

The Commission may either: (1) grant the petition after determining the conduct does not reflect adversely on the individual's fitness as a candidate or Professionals Eligible for Reinstatement for CFP® certification or upon the profession or upon the CFP® certification marks, and certification should be permitted; (2) deny the petition after determining the conduct reflects adversely on the individual's fitness as a candidate or Professionals Eligible for Reinstatement for CFP® certification or upon the profession or the CFP® certification marks, whereby certification is permanently barred; or (3) deny the petition and issue a temporary bar, allowing the individual to reapply for CFP® certification after a specified period of time.[43] The *Procedural Rules* allow for an appeals process under Article 15.

---

41. Prior to registering for the CFP® exam, candidates must accept the *Pathway to the CFP® Certification Agreement*, which authorizes CFP Board to conduct a background review including criminal history, regulatory history, public records, and interviews with third parties.
42. *Procedural Rules*, Article 5.2.
43. *Procedural Rules*, Article 13.

Exhibit 16.23 | Fitness Standards Summary

	Conduct Which Is Unacceptable	Conduct Which Is Presumed Unacceptable	Conduct Which Reflects Adversely Upon the Individual's Integrity or Fitness, the Profession, or the CFP® Marks
Result	Permanent bar	Barred from certification unless petition the DEC and the DEC grants the petition or permits the individual to reapply at a later date	Barred from certification unless petition the DEC and the DEC grants the petition or permits the individual to reapply at a later date
Conduct Falling Within This Category	• Felony conviction for theft, embezzlement, or other financially-based crimes • Felony conviction for tax fraud or other tax-related crimes • Revocation of a financial professional license (unless administrative) • Felony conviction for any degree of murder or rape • Felony conviction for any other violent crime within the last five years	• Two or more personal bankruptcies • Revocation or suspension of a non-financial license (unless administrative) • Suspension of a financial professional license (unless administrative) • Felony conviction for non-violent crimes within the last five years • Felony conviction for violent crimes other than murder or rape that occurred more than five years ago	• Customer complaints • Arbitrations and other civil proceedings • Felony convictions for non-violent crimes that occurred more than five years ago • Misdemeanor convictions • Employer investigations and terminations

Exhibit 16.24 | Sanction Term and Required Action Summary (Procedural Rules, Article 11)

Respondent Type	Governed By	Type of Sanction[1,2]	Term	Required Actions
CFP® Certificant	Terms and Conditions of Certification and Trademark License; Code and Standards; Procedural Rules	Private censure	N/A	N/A
		Public censure	Remains on CFP Board's website	Respondent must advise their firm of the sanction and advise all clients of the sanction and location of disciplinary history on CFP Board's web site within 45 days
		Interim suspension (during pendency of proceedings)	No longer than 5 years; remains on CFP Board's website[3]	Same as public censure, PLUS cease use of the CFP® marks and remove all marks from internet sites and tangible materials (must deliver evidence of compliance to CFP Board within 45 days)
		Suspension	Minimum 90 calendar days; maximum 5 years; remains on CFP Board's website	Same as interim suspension
		Revocation	Permanent; remains on CFP Board's website	Same as interim suspension
Candidate for CFP® certification & former CFP® professionals seeking reinstatement whose certification has not been suspended	Pathway to CFP® Certification Agreement (candidates) or Terms and Conditions of Certification and Trademark License (PERs); Fitness Standards; Code and Standards; Procedural Rules	Private censure	N/A	N/A
		Public censure	Published and remains on CFP Board's website	Respondent must advise their firm of the sanction and advise all clients of the sanction and location of disciplinary history on CFP Board's web site within 45 days
		Temporary bar	Published and remains on CFP Board's website	Same as public censure
		Permanent bar	Permanent; Published and remains on CFP Board's website	Same as public censure

1. The DEC may also order remedial education or work.
2. For a single bankruptcy, CFP Board counsel may order an interim suspension, administrative suspension, administrative revocation, or public censure.
3. If an order is issued to vacate an interim suspension (e.g., if the criminal conviction, civil liability, or professional discipline is vacated or reversed), respondent may request that CFP Board remove the publication of the interim suspension and/or request that CFP Board publish in a press release and on CFP Board's website the fact that CFP Board vacated the interim suspension order and some or all of the facts relevant to the order to vacate the interim suspension (Article 2.3).

Note: Reinstatement is not automatic when a suspension period ends. The respondent must file a petition for reinstatement. Failure to do so within 5 years of the first date of the suspension will result in permanent relinquishment of the CFP® certification, with no opportunity for reinstatement (Articles 11.5 and 14.1).

ANONYMOUS CASE HISTORIES

As part of its multi-prong effort to improve ethics and standards in the financial planning profession, CFP Board publishes a review of misconduct cases processed by CFP Board and the Disciplinary and Ethics Commission. These are referred to as "**anonymous case histories**," which provide a summary of the relevant events in certain cases of misconduct, accompanied by an explanation of any discipline penalty, action by CFP Board, and other information. The intent behind publication of these anonymous case histories is, among other things, to provide an understanding for those using the CFP® marks as to what types of allegations are made and what form of discipline is administered.

Failing to cooperate with CFP Board or its disciplinary process will result in severe penalties or discipline. The Respondent must timely respond according to the procedures outlined in the *Procedural Rules*. Specifically, Article 4.1 provides that if Respondent does not timely respond to a formal complaint, then the respondent is in default (as discussed previously), and the CFP® professional's right to use the CFP® marks may be administratively suspended or revoked.

The following are summaries of actual anonymous case histories provided by CFP Board.

Anonymous Case History # 30358[44] - [Misrepresentation of Source of Email]

Respondent's client wished to move funds from Company 1 to Company 2 (where Respondent was employed) to be managed by Respondent. Company 1 had loaned the client $20 million with the securities in the account as collateral and, therefore, required that the loan be repaid prior to transferring the securities. Respondent arranged a loan with Company 2, using the securities as collateral, which was used to repay the loan to Company 1 and the securities were transferred in-kind. However, a problem occurred in transferring a portion of the securities in the account and they were bounced back to Company 1. Company 2 warned Respondent and client that the securities received would be sold off to pay off the loan if the remaining securities were not transferred. Respondent contacted Company 1 and their representative explained that there was an issue with the wire instructions but refused to put the correct instructions in an email for Respondent to provide to Company 2. Respondent drafted an email with the instructions on how to resolve the issue with the wire instructions and signed it with the name of the representative from Company 1, and forwarded it to the credit analyst at company 2 as if it had originated from the representative at Company 1. Company 2 terminated Respondent's employment as a result of the misrepresented source of the email. As a result of the Form U5 submission, FINRA opened an investigation and issued a Cautionary Action Letter regarding a violation of FINRA Rule 2010, just and equitable principles of trade, and FINRA Rule 451 1(a), preserving books and records. The Respondent and the DEC entered into a settlement agreement in which the Respondent consented to the findings of fact and grounds for discipline.

> ### Quick Quiz 16.4
>
> 1. When the Commission finds grounds for discipline of a CFP® professional, the forms of discipline available include private censure, public censure, suspension, revocation, and interim suspension.
>   a. True
>   b. False
>
> 2. The CFP Board publishes a review of misconduct cases processed by CFP Board and the Commission.
>   a. True
>   b. False
>
> True, True.

44. This case number refers to the case number assigned to the case by CFP Board on its website. https://www.cfp.net/ethics/enforcement/anonymous-case-history. Full details regarding each case may be reviewed by searching for the case number using the search tool provided.

While this decision involved the former *Code of Ethics*, the decision noted violation of *Rules of Conduct* Rules 4.3 (a certificant shall be in compliance with applicable regulatory requirements governing professional services provided to the client) and 5.1 (a certificant who is an employee/agent shall perform professional services with dedication o the lawful objectives of the employer/principal and in accordance with CFP Board's *Code of Ethics*). The circumstances provided grounds for a sanction under the then-current Sanction Guidelines for a violation of employer policy.

<u>Commission's Decision</u>: Settlement - Private Censure

Anonymous Case History # 29131 - [Suitability Violation]

Respondent, a Candidate for CFP® Certification, had been the subject of a customer complaint alleging that he sold the clients unsuitable investments when he recommended that they place 100% of their retirement assets in a variable annuity, knowing that spouse 1 had been diagnosed with stage 4 cancer and the couple planned to spend time traveling to various locations around the world while spouse 1 was still able to do so. Respondent's firm agreed to a settlement to terminate the annuity contracts without surrender changes. The cost to the firm was approximately $42,000. The DEC found that Respondent sold his clients unsuitable investments that were not in the client's best interest. In doing so, Respondent engaged in conduct that may reflect adversely on the profession or on the CFP® certification marks. The Petition for Consideration (as it was called under the prior *Disciplinary Rules* and *Fitness Standards*; now called a Petition for Fitness Determination) was denied, with the ability to reapply for CFP® certification after 6 months, provided that at the time of reapplication Respondent has completed, in addition to his normal continuing education requirements, four hours of remedial education in each of three areas: general principles of financial planning, insurance planning, and retirement planning.

<u>Commission's Decision</u>: Temporary Bar

Anonymous Case History # 30309 - [Revocation of FINRA License]

Respondent, a financial adviser with Company, was a junior producer working with Senior producer. Respondent and Senior Producer had a practice of moving commissions from one production number to the other. The partnership began to fray and Respondent and Senior Producer began to disagree with how commissions were allocated. Company began investigating the allocation of commissions, and Respondent resigned. In connection with Respondent's resignation, FINRA requested Respondent's testimony. Respondent, through his counsel, informed FINRA that he would not appear for testimony, which is a violation of FINRA Rules 8210 and 2010. Respondent entered into a Letter of Acceptance, Waiver and Consent (AWC) with FINRA, in which he consented to a bar from working with any FINRA member in any capacity. Respondent failed to notify CFP Board in writing within 30 days (as required by the then-current *Standards of Conduct* and *Disciplinary Rules*) of FINRA's professional discipline.

The DEC determined that Respondent violated (based on the *Standards of Professional Conduct* and *Disciplinary Rules* in effect at the time) *Rules of Conduct* Rule 4.3 (a certificant shall comply with applicable regulatory requirements governing professional services provided to the client) and Rule 6.5 (a certificant shall not engage in conduct which reflects adversely on his or her integrity or fitness as a certificant, upon the CFP® marks, or upon the profession). Articles 13.1 and 13.4 of the Disciplinary Rules provide that professional discipline (suspension, bar, or revocation) by a governmental or industry self-regulatory authority will serve as conclusive proof of the basis for discipline. In addition, Article 13.2 requires a CFP® professional who is the subject of professional discipline must notify CFP

Board within 30 calendar days. Respondent failed to provide notification within the required time frame; an omission that violates Article 13.2.

Commission's Decision: Permanent Revocation

Anonymous Case History # 30894 - [Termination from Employment for Cause]

Respondent was a registered representative at Company. Another registered representative resigned and Company reassigned a number of that representative's accounts to Respondent. Three of these clients held variable annuities issued by Insurance Company. When Respondent tried to log into the accounts with Insurance Company to gain information regarding their accounts, she discovered that she had not yet been listed as the agent of record and could not access their full account information. Rather than notify Company and ask them to correct the oversight, Respondent filled out a change of agent of record form, signing the client's names in the shareholder signature box, and submitted it directly to Insurance Company. Respondent notified Company that she had submitted the forms and signed the clients names without receiving permission from the clients to do so. As a result her employment with Company was terminated. FINRA investigated the termination and issued a Cautionary Action Letter to Respondent. The DEC and Respondent entered into a Settlement Agreement in which Respondent consented to the findings of fact and grounds for discipline, and the DEC issued a Public **Letter of Admonition**.

In coming to its decision to enter the Settlement Agreement, the Commission considered the following mitigating factors: (1) Respondent took responsibility for her actions, (2) Respondent was remorseful, (3) Respondent did not have any direct financial gain, (4) there was no client harm, (5) the client's signature was not necessary on the form, and (6) this was a one-time occurrence.

Commission's Decision: Settlement - Public Letter of Admonition

Anonymous Case History # 23408 - [Ethics Violation on Ethics CE Course]

Respondent allowed a trainee to complete portions of his required CFP Board continuing education credits. As a result, Respondent received a 10-day FINRA suspension and $5,000 fine, and entered into a Stipulation and Consent Agreement with the state securities regulator for violation of state securities laws, as a result of the same act, under which he agreed to a 10-day suspension and $5,000 fine. Respondent did not report the suspensions to CFP Board. Respondent was terminated by his employer for directing the trainee to complete a portion of his CFP Board continuing education credits. The DEC found that Respondent: (1) engaged in conduct involving dishonesty, fraud, deceit, and misrepresentation, (2) failed to exercise reasonable and prudent professional judgment in providing professional services, (3) failed to perform professional services with dedication to the lawful objectives of his employer, (4) failed to perform professional services in accordance with applicable laws, rules, and regulations of governmental agencies, (5) failed to perform services in accordance with the rules, regulations, and policies of CFP Board, and (6) engaged in conduct that reflects adversely on his integrity and fitness as a CFP® professional, upon the marks, and upon the profession. The DEC considered as an aggravating factor that the course Respondent allowed the trainee to complete on his behalf was a CFP Board ethics course.

Commission's Decision: Settlement - Suspension

Anonymous Case History # 22586 - [Conduct Reflecting Adversely on the Profession]

In August 2008, Respondent, a candidate for CFP® certification, disclosed on his initial Certification Application form that while in college in 1979, he was charged and convicted with misdemeanor theft when he failed to pay for a meal he consumed at a restaurant. The DEC found that Respondent engaged in conduct that reflects adversely on the integrity or fitness of a CFP® certificant, upon the marks, and upon the profession. The DEC dismissed the case and issued a caution to Respondent stressing the importance of conducting himself in a manner which reflects positively on the financial planning profession. The DEC considered the following mitigating factors: (1) Respondent had no previous incidences of misconduct, (2) Respondent acknowledged his actions were wrong, and (3) the offense was a misdemeanor which occurred nearly 30 years prior to the application, when Respondent was in college.

Commission's Decision: Dismissed with Caution

Anonymous Case History # 14547 - [Tax Fraud]

In August 2004, Respondent, a CFP® certificant, was subject to an IRS investigation regarding a scheme to market and sell sham foreign and domestic trusts. Respondent was alleged to have committed seven acts, including assisting clients in hiding income, assisting clients in claiming false deductions on trust tax returns, and assisting clients in obstructing IRS audits. Respondent was indicted on federal tax fraud charges and, in May 2008, Respondent was convicted of 12 counts of tax fraud conspiracy felonies. CFP Board's Disciplinary and Ethics Commission ordered an interim suspension pendency a full hearing on the grounds that Respondent posed an immediate threat to the public and that the gravity of the nature of Respondent's conduct impinged upon the stature and reputation of the CFP® marks. Ultimately, Respondent's right to use the marks was revoked.

Commission's Decision: Interim Suspension; Revocation

Anonymous Case History # 31074 - [DUI]

In June 2018 Respondent notified CFP Board that he had plead guilty to a felony DUI charge and was sentenced in May 2018. Respondent had three prior misdemeanor DUI charges in the state and the state's criminal code provided that after three prior misdemeanor DUI convictions, a DUI becomes a class 4 felony. In accordance with CFP Board's *Standards of Professional Conduct* and *Disciplinary Rules and Procedures* applicable at the time (prior to October 2019), an automatic interim suspension was issued without hearing, based on a conviction for any felony. Ultimately, the Commission and Respondent entered into a settlement agreement under which the Commission issued a suspension of one year and one day, as provided in the then-current *Disciplinary Rules*. Aggravating factors included that Respondent had multiple infractions (three prior DUIs), fled the scene of the accident, made false statements to the police, and tried to blame a friend for driving his car.

Commission's Decision: Automatic Interim Suspension; Settlement - Suspension

Anonymous Case History # 28173 - [Revocation of Life Insurance License]

In 2009 Respondent's state insurance license was restricted due to a misdemeanor domestic violence conviction. The terms of the restriction required Respondent to obey all laws and regulations of the state. In 2011 Respondent had a second misdemeanor domestic violence conviction. Respondent first stated, incorrectly, that neither the state's department of insurance nor CFP Board required reporting of a misdemeanor conviction. Respondent then stated that he thought he had taken care of his reporting requirements. The state's department of insurance requires reporting within thirty days. In July 2012, the state insurance department issued a revocation of Respondent's restricted license. Respondent's attorney filed a petition for reconsideration with the state insurance department, presenting numerous arguments for why Respondent' license should not be revoked. The petition was denied and his insurance license was revoked. Respondent stated that it was his understanding that after one year he could reapply for a state insurance license, and that he intended to follow that route rather than appeal. After one year, his insurance license had, in fact, been reinstated.

The DEC determined that Respondent engaged in conduct that reflects adversely on his integrity and fitness, on the CFP® marks, and on the profession. Based on the *Disciplinary Rules and Procedures* in effect at that time, the commission issued a suspension for one year and one day. The commission cited as mitigating factors that Respondent's file contained no customer complaints and stood as testimony to his ability to meet client needs with integrity, and that Respondent was remorseful and despondent over the conduct at issue. He understood the severity of his actions and had taken steps to eliminate the potential for reoccurrence by completing activities outlined by other authorities.

<u>Commission's Decision</u>: Suspension

SUMMARY

CFP Board requires CFP® Professionals to maintain professional standards and ethics in the financial planning profession. CFP Board has accomplished this through an interrelated series of professional and ethical standards designed to protect the public and advance professionalism in the financial planning industry. These standards are all connected through the *Code of Ethics, Standards of Conduct*, and *Procedural Rules*.

The CFP Board has placed the highest ethical and professional standards upon CFP® Professionals. The profession as a whole benefits from these standards. More importantly, the public benefits from these procedures and standards. However, these rules should be a mere formality, as all CFP® professionals should act and aspire to act towards actual and prospective clients, the public, the profession, and employers as described throughout the *Code and Standards*.

DISCUSSION QUESTIONS

SOLUTIONS to the discussion questions can be found exclusively within the chapter. Once you have completed an initial reading of the chapter, go back and highlight the answers to these questions.

1. What is the function of the Certified Financial Planner Board of Standards, Inc. (CFP Board)?

2. What is CFP Board's mission?

3. What is the *Code of Ethics*?

4. Discuss the *Standards of Conduct* and the six sections within the Standards.

5. Define the CFP® professional's fiduciary requirement.

6. Define and describe the Financial Planning Practice Standards.

7. Discuss what are the *Procedural Rules*.

8. Discuss the investigative process under the *Procedural Rules*.

9. Discuss the hearing process and forms of discipline under the *Procedural Rules*.

10. Define the forms of discipline by the Commission.

11. Summarize the sanction guidelines for single and multiple bankruptcies and the CFP® professional's reporting responsibilities regarding bankruptcies.

12. Define the Candidate Fitness Standards and the "always bar list."

13. Discuss the purpose of the publication of anonymous case histories.

MULTIPLE-CHOICE PROBLEMS

A sample of multiple choice problems is provided below. Additional multiple choice problems are available at money-education.com by accessing the Student Practice Portal.

1. CFP Board is a certification and standard-setting organization that:
    a. Establishes and enforces education requirements for CFP® professionals.
    b. Establishes and enforces examination requirements for CFP® professionals.
    c. Establishes and enforces ethics requirements for CFP® professionals.
    d. All of the above.

2. Which of the following is not in the *Code of Ethics*?
    a. Frugality.
    b. Integrity.
    c. Competence.
    d. Avoid or disclose and manage conflicts of interest.

3. Which of the following are true with respect to the Practice Standards?
    1. Each Practice Standard makes up one of seven steps in the financial planning process.
    2. Includes monitoring responsibilities after a financial plan is implemented.
    3. The scope of the engagement does not have to be in writing when providing financial advice that does not require financial planning.
    a. 3 only.
    b. 1 and 3.
    c. 1, 2, and 3.
    d. None of the above.

4. Dierk is a client and seems to be suffering from dementia and wants to remove his children from his will and give all of his wealth to Bentley, a neighbor who periodically visits Dierk and delivers him groceries. What should the CFP® professional do?
    a. He should contact Dierk's children to let them know.
    b. He should do what Dierk asks.
    c. He should contact the doctor to confirm if he is suffering from dementia or not.
    d. He should contact Dierk's lawyer.

5. What is the client's responsibility during the financial planning process?
    a. To interpret all the information that is gathered.
    b. To provide the professional with all requested information.
    c. To pay their fees.
    d. To implement the financial plan.

> **Additional multiple choice problems are available at**
> ***money-education.com* by accessing the Student Practice Portal. Access requires registration of the title using the unique code at the front of the book.**

QUICK QUIZ EXPLANATIONS

Quick Quiz 16.1
1. True.
2. True.

Quick Quiz 16.2
1. False. Section A of the *Standards of Conduct* are organized into 15 different subsections which establish expected high standards and describe the level of professionalism required when working with clients.
2. True.
3. True.

Quick Quiz 16.3
1. False. The Practice Standards are not designed to be a basis for legal liability to third parties.
2. False. Defining the scope of engagement is not in the Practice Standards. It is a preliminary step taken prior to beginning the financial planning process.
3. True.

Quick Quiz 16.4
1. True.
2. True.

17

PLANNING FOR SPECIAL CIRCUMSTANCES

LEARNING OBJECTIVES

1. Identify at least six situations that call for special financial planning needs.
2. Understand some of the emotional and all of the financial issues associated with a dependent with special needs.
3. Describe the typical governmental benefits for dependents with special needs including the special education programs and Social Security benefits.*
4. List and explain other public benefits that are or may be provided by state and local governments.*
5. List some examples of not for profit organizations that are funded by states for the support of dependents with special needs.*
6. Describe the steps that a caregiver should take in planning for a dependent with special needs.
7. Describe special-needs trusts and their elements and the benefits that they can provide.*
8. Describe a third-party special needs trust (SNT).*
9. Describe a special-needs trust under 42 U.S.C. Section 1396p (d)(4)(A).*
10. Describe a pooled trust created under 42 U.S.C. Section 1396p(d)(4)(C).*
11. Describe the funding of ABLE accounts and the expenses for which they may be used.*
12. List and describe the content of a letter of intent.
13. Describe the need for financial planning necessary for divorcing couples.
14. Discuss the need for gathering information that is complete and reliable prior to entering into any divorce agreement.
15. List the common mistakes with regard to financial planning that divorcing spouses make.
16. List the financial planning issues that arise in planning for terminal illness.
17. List the financial planning recommendations for terminal illness planning.
18. Discuss the issue of financial planning for the non-traditional household.
19. Describe civil unions and registered partners.
20. Identify the major issues in planning for the death of a partner in a non-traditional household.
21. Describe each of the ways that property owned by a decedent passes to heirs or legatees.
22. Discuss the issue of job loss or job change with regard to financial planning.
23. Identify the factors that weigh on financial planning decisions with regard to job loss or job change.*
24. Discuss the issues related to financial planning for a financial windfall.
25. List and discuss the financial planning recommendations for a windfall recipient.
26. Identify the impact of divorce and/or remarriage on an estate plan including asset titling and distribution, changes in beneficiary status, and selection of heirs.*
27. Recommend strategies that can be implemented to help ensure the appropriate management and transfer of assets to a same-sex, non-traditional and/or non-married partners.*

Ties to CFP Certification Learning Objectives

INTRODUCTION

Many clients consider themselves inimitable and having unique financial circumstances and often they do. Financial planners are trained to approach clients from the perspective of every client being unique and the planning for clients should be individually tailored. However, with hundreds of millions of people in America and millions more around the world, the simple fact is that many people have common goals - retirement, education funding for children, and mitigation of catastrophic risks. These common goals and similar life cycle positioning allows for bucketing or grouping of people into specific profiles. Earlier in Chapter 3 seven different, but frequently seen client profiles, were identified. Using the life cycle approach, the usual risks and goals for each profile were identified. While it is useful to realize that many families fit into one of these seven profiles, it is also true that these seven profiles do not represent all families or persons, nor all of their different financial situations.

Key Concepts

1. Identify the common client profiles and their typical financial risks and goals

2. Identify the statistics regarding the frequency and types of special needs situations.

3. List the types of issues that related to a special needs situation.

4. Understand the key steps and tasks that a caregiver should perform regarding an individual with special needs.

This chapter presents special financial planning situations that are less common then the seven profiles presented in Chapter 3, but that occur frequently enough in our society that a well-educated and well-trained financial planner should be able to assist such a client with the financial planning needs associated with these unique circumstances.

The special circumstances covered in this chapter include planning for the family that has a dependent with special needs, planning for divorce, planning for terminal illness, planning for non-traditional households, planning for job loss and job change, and planning for monetary windfalls. These are clearly not the only special needs situations, but rather represent a large percentage of special needs situations. There are common threads through many of these situations, including emotional as well as financial needs.

Special Financial Planning Situations
Planning for Dependents with Special Needs
Planning for Divorce
Planning for Terminal Illness
Planning for the Non-Traditional Household
Planning for Job Loss or Job Change
Planning for Monetary Windfalls

In each of these special financial planning situations, the financial planning issues may not be as immediately important as the emotional issues. Nonetheless, they need to be addressed sooner or later. A client with such needs should identify and begin to address the emotional issues related to the particular situation prior to attempting to solve the financial issues. Regardless of the planning situation, the financial planning issues will include planning for cash flows, perhaps legal issues or documents, perhaps government benefits (e.g. Social Security, unemployment, or other), and family support issues.

Exhibit 17.1 | 7 Common Client Profiles and Their Typical Financial Risks and Goals

Life Cycle Factors							
Age	22-30	25-35	25-35	35-45	45-55	55-65	65-75
Marital Status	Single	Married	Married	Married	Married	Married	Married
Children	No	No	Yes	Yes	Yes	Yes	Yes
Grandchildren	No	No	No	No	No	Yes	Yes
Income	$35-$75k	$35-$75k	$45-$100k	$50-$150k	$75-$200k	$100-$200k	$50-$200k
Net Worth	$10-$20k	$10-$20k	$15-$25k	$20-$40k	$50-$100k	$500-$1,200k	$400-$1,500k
Self Employed	No	No	No	No	Yes	Maybe	No
Typical Risks/Insurance Coverage Needs							
Life Insurance	No	Maybe	Yes	Yes	Yes	Yes	No
Disability	Yes	Yes	Yes	Yes	Yes	Yes	No
Health	Yes	Yes	Yes	Yes	Yes	Yes	Yes
Long-Term Care*	No	No	No	No	No	Maybe Yes	Maybe Yes
Property	Yes	Yes	Yes	Yes	Yes	Yes	Yes
Liability	Yes	Yes	Yes	Yes	Yes	Yes	Yes
Typical Goals							
Retirement Security	Yes	Yes	Yes	Yes	Yes	Yes	In Retirement
Education Funding	No	No	Yes	Yes	Yes	No	No
Gifting	No	No	No	No	No	Yes	Yes
Lump-Sum Expenses	Yes	Yes	Yes	Yes	Yes	Yes	No
Legacy	No	No	No	No	No	Maybe	Maybe

* While younger clients will not typically require long-term care insurance, in some circumstances, long-term care may be appropriate.

Financial Planning in Relation to Special Circumstances

The special situations discussed in this chapter require the financial planner to evaluate changes that may be necessary in all areas of the client's financial plan. For each special situation or unique change in a client's circumstances, the planner will need to address the six core areas of financial planning:

1. **Fundamentals:** What changes will occur or be necessary regarding the client's cash flow situation, assets, and liabilities? Have new goals surfaced or do prior goals need to be redefined in light of the new circumstances? Has priority of goals changed in light of the new circumstances?
2. **Insurance and Risk Management:** What additional protection might be needed? Are there any current policies in place that will no longer be needed? Do beneficiary designations need to be changed?
3. **Investments:** Has risk tolerance or risk capacity changed? Is there a need to reallocate investment accounts to produce more income or seek greater tax efficiency? Is the current asset allocation appropriate in light of newly defined goals?
4. **Income Taxation:** What impact does the special circumstance have on income taxation and what changes should be made to ensure tax efficiency?

5. **Retirement Plan:** How does the change in circumstances affect the overall retirement plan and assumptions? Will decisions need to be made regarding existing qualified plans and other retirement assets?

6. **Estate Plan:** Which estate planning documents will need to be redrafted? Are there additional estate planning documents needed in light of the new situation? Do beneficiary designations need to be changed? How does the new situation affect the efficiency of transfers in the estate plan? How should assets be titled in light of the new situation?

PLANNING FOR A DEPENDENT WITH SPECIAL NEEDS

Many families have one or more dependents with special needs. A **dependent with special needs** could be an infant, adolescent, or adult. The dependent could have a wide range of challenges from very mild physical, emotional, or psychological, to a situation where around the clock care is required. Consider that:

- One out of nine children (11%) under the age of 18 in the U.S. receives special education services.
- Two out of seven families (29%) reported having at least one family member with a disability.
- One of every 26 (4%) families reported raising children with a disability.
- One of every three families (33%) with a female head of household and no husband present reported members with a disability.
- An estimated 2.8 million families in the U.S. are raising at least one child aged 5 - 17 with a disability.[1]

Clients who have dependents with special needs will require some unique planning. A holistic approach means the financial planner must understand that parents of children with special needs may be overwhelmed by the prospect of caring and providing for their child. It will be important for the planner to show empathy and understanding and to break the planning process into achievable, logical steps. The planner must keep in mind that planning for a dependent with special needs also requires the same elements as planning for a traditional family. In other words, just because the individual with special needs requires additional planning, the family isn't relieved of the planning required by other families. They will still have goals like buying a home, saving for retirement, and planning the estate.

Whether the individual with special needs is a child born with a disability or an adult suffering a debilitating disease later in life, the process must start with a vision for the future. This goal-setting is similar to what is done with traditional planning clients, but must also take into account the concerns of the individual with special needs.

In step one of the traditional planning process, a planner gathers information regarding available resources. For special needs families, the planner will provide information on the usual resources, such as net worth, income sources, earnings, and expenses, but significant research may be needed to identify additional social and government benefit resources. Such benefits may include SSI, Medicaid, vocational rehabilitation, and subsidized housing.[2]

---

1. U.S. Census Bureau Report "Disability and American Families: 2000."
2. Supplemental Security Income (SSI) is a Federal income supplement program funded by general tax revenues (not Social Security taxes). It is designed to help aged, blind and disabled people, who have little or no income. SSI provides cash to meet basic needs for food, clothing and shelter.

Planning for the future of an individual with special needs requires knowledge of federal and state laws; federal, state, and local benefits; legal documents; and legal arrangements (not to mention a lot of love and care). There are both financial and quality of life issues to consider.

Of immediate concern to the parent / guardian is how:

- to provide a good quality of life for the child or dependent
- to preserve government benefit eligibility for the child or dependent
- to provide lifetime care for the child or dependent as needed
- to have appropriate health insurance for the dependent
- to have sufficient resources to supplement government benefits to enhance quality of life for that dependent

For each stage during the life of a dependent with special needs, from birth to adult, parents or guardians will need comprehensive advice and strategies to address each of the following issues:

- ***financial issues*** - from budgeting to investments
- ***legal issues*** - estate planning, guardianship, and other arrangements such as trusts
- ***government benefits*** - identifying, obtaining, and preserving government benefits
- ***family and support factors*** - family values, careers, siblings, extended family, and community resources
- ***emotional factors*** - dealing with positive and negative emotions of the dependent, siblings, and parents

Special Needs Planning in Relation to Major Financial Planning Areas

A look at each of the major financial planning areas will reveal some unique concerns for special needs families:

1. **Fundamentals:** In addition to normal budget items, the family will also have supplemental expenses for the individual with special needs. One of the key foundations for a special needs family will be to maintain eligibility for Social Security and SSI.

2. **Insurance and Risk Management:** Insurance planning will include not only protecting the family against premature death or disability of the parent, but also providing for the supplemental lifetime needs of the child with special needs. Life insurance should be purchased on both the wage-earner parent and the parent who may be at home caring for the individual with special needs. While the caregiver may not be earning an income, the cost to replace the care and support they provide may be quite large. In calculating the death benefit need, the planner must also consider the need to provide for, not one, but two generations. The planner must also be cognizant of the type of life insurance selected to fund this need. While term insurance is less costly, it provides temporary coverage and should not be used to cover the special needs, which require permanent protection. It is likely that a combination of term and permanent insurance

will be used since the family will still have some of the traditional temporary needs for life insurance protection in combination with the permanent special needs. It is likely that the permanent protection will be purchased in a special needs trust (discussed below), and it is important that the individual with special needs not be named as the direct beneficiary of the insurance policy. Other family members should also be advised that the individual with special needs should not be directly named as a beneficiary. Unfortunately, even a well-meaning relative naming the individual with special needs as beneficiary of a small death benefit could cause the child with special needs to suffer the loss or suspension of the government benefits that are the core foundation of the financial plan.

3. **Investments:** While investment planning for a traditional family may focus largely on risk and return, investment planning for a special needs family will also focus on trust administration and investment management. Since one of the main goals is always to protect eligibility for government benefits, distributions from special needs trusts (discussed later in this chapter) must be managed very carefully by a trustee who is knowledgeable and competent in these matters. Custodial accounts such as Uniform Gift to Minors Accounts (UGMA) and Section 529 Qualified Tuition Plans for the child with special needs should generally be avoided since these assets may disqualify the child from receiving government disability benefits, although Section 529A ABLE accounts (discussed below) may be utilized to a limited extent. As a general rule, the individual with special needs should have no more than $2,000 of assets in his or her name.

4. **Income Taxation:** Families who itemize deductions on their income tax return are eligible to deduct medical expenses in excess of a 7.5 percent floor (7.5% of the Adjusted Gross Income calculated on their income tax return). Special needs families will often have significant medical expenses and will need to be made aware of the types of expenditures that are deductible as medical expenses. For example, IRS Publication 502 lists the following deductible expenses:
   - Medical expenses include the costs of buying, training, and maintaining a guide dog or other service animal to assist a person with visual impairment or who is hearing disabled or a person with other physical disabilities. This deduction generally includes costs, such as food, grooming, and veterinary care, incurred in maintaining the health and vitality of the service animal so that it may perform its duties.
   - Medical expenses can include fees paid on a doctor's recommendation for a child's tutoring by a teacher specially trained and qualified to work with children who have learning disabilities caused by mental or physical impairments.
   - Medical expenses can also include the cost (tuition, meals, and lodging) of attending a school that furnishes special education to help a child to overcome learning disabilities. Attendance at the school must be recommended by a doctor, and overcoming the learning disabilities must be a principal reason for attending the school. In addition, any ordinary education received must be incidental to the special education provided. Revenue Ruling 78-340 provides additional guidance regarding this medical expense deduction.
   - Expenses paid for admission and transportation to a medical conference concerning the chronic illness of the dependent with special needs are another deductible medical expense. The majority of time spent at the conference must be spent attending sessions for medical information, but the expenses for meals and lodging while attending the conference are not deductible.
   - Deductible medical expenses may include amounts paid for special equipment installed in a home, or for improvements, if their main purpose is medical care. The cost of improvements

that increase the value of the home are partially deductible, based on the extent to which the cost does not increase the value. If there is no increase in value, the full cost is deductible. The following improvements typically do not increase the value of the home, making the cost fully deductible:

- Constructing entrance or exit ramps for the home
- Widening doorways at entrances or exits to the home
- Widening or otherwise modifying hallways and interior doorways
- Installing railings, support bars, or other modifications to bathrooms
- Lowering or modifying kitchen cabinets and equipment
- Moving or modifying electrical outlets and fixtures
- Installing porch lifts and other forms of lifts (however, elevators generally add value)
- Modifying fire alarms, smoke detectors, and other warning systems
- Modifying stairways
- Modifying hardware on doors
- Modifying areas in front of entrance and exit doorways
- Grading the ground to provide access to the residence

Note that only reasonable costs to accommodate the home to a disabled condition are considered medical care. Additional costs for personal motives, such as for architectural or aesthetic reasons, are not medical expenses.

The income tax rules discussed are quite complicated, so it is likely the financial planner will need to work closely with the client's CPA or other tax adviser.

5. **Retirement Planning:** Parents of a child with special needs must continue to plan for their own retirement, just as parents in traditional families do. The potential for increased expenses and the likelihood that one parent may stay home to care for the child with special needs may make it more challenging to save, but it is important for the parents to make planning for their retirement a priority.

6. **Estate Planning:** While a will is a core part of estate planning for traditional families, the need for a valid will is even greater for a special needs family. Parents dying intestate (without a will) will have their estates distributed according to intestate laws in which all children are generally treated equally. An intestate distribution to a child with special needs could cause that child to lose access to government benefits for a period of time. Careful consideration must also be given to naming the guardian of the person (who is responsible for the care and well-being of the individual with special needs) and the guardian of the property (who manages the property for the benefit of the individual with special needs). The two guardians need not be the same person or entity. The guardian named to care for the individual with special needs should be both willing and capable of caring for the special needs. A planner should advise the parents not to assume that a brother or sister of a child with special needs will take on that responsibility. Before naming their children as guardians, parents should have a conversation with them to ensure that they are comfortable with that role. Parents of the child with special needs should also be advised to create a letter of intent (discussed in detail below) that explains everything a new caregiver should know about the individual with special needs. This information will make the transition between caregivers easier for everyone involved.

Typical Federal, State, and Other Benefits

The federal government does not provide adequate funding for every need of a dependent with special needs. Thus, the need to plan for the financial future of the dependent is critical.

Key Current Programs at the Federal and State Level:
Federal
- **Special Education Programs** - supported by Individuals with Disability Education Improvement Act 2004.
- **Social Security Benefits** - including disability, SSI, and Medicaid. Social Security has a booklet on its website that provides helpful information for these situations, entitled, *Benefits For Children With Disabilities SSA Publication No. 05-10026, January 2021, ICN 455360.*
- **Benefits for Disabled Veterans** - The Department of Veterans Affairs offers programs for disabled veterans.
- The following websites provide great information for special needs families, and provide links to other national organizations that may provide assistance to those with special needs situations:
  - www.usa.gov/disability-programs
  - www.specialneedsalliance.org

State and Local
- **Other Public Benefits** - state and local services may include:
  - Residential services
  - Transportation services
  - Respite Care Services
  - Family Support Services
  - Day Program Services
  - Employment Services

There are many state based and local based organizations that provide assistance and information for these situations. There are also parent and caregiver groups that can be easily located through social media or an internet based search.

Non-Profit Organizations

Each state has support services, which may vary from state to state. Eligibility for benefits must be determined and the amount and type of benefits provided must be determined. Some examples of non-profit support organizations are:
- The Arc
- United Health Care Children's Foundation
- National Autism Association
- Easter Seals

The above references can help the client and planner evaluate the types and amounts of resources that may be available to assist the individual with special needs. The analysis stage of planning will identify gaps between resources and goals and will seek to identify strategies that may be used to fill those gaps. The planner may also be called upon to help coordinate implementation of the various strategies identified, taking care that any strategies commonly used to achieve traditional planning goals do not impede the availability of government resources to help fund the special needs goals.

Planners working with special needs families also need to be particularly mindful to monitor the plan, because social and government benefits are likely to change at various ages. For example, different benefits may be available for a child of school age versus a child beyond school age. Since there is often a drop or change in government benefits beyond school age, some families will pool resources to purchase a home for a long-term residence that can be staffed to allow the individuals with special needs a certain amount of independence that can continue even beyond their parents' deaths.

What Should a Caregiver Do

Caregivers will be responsible for completing numerous tasks on an ongoing basis, which may initially feel overwhelming. Having a checklist to organize and prioritize those tasks can provide the caregiver with a clear path to success. An example of a Caregiver Checklist is provided below. Additional items may be added to customize the list to the individual circumstances of the special needs family.

Exhibit 17.2 | Caregiver Checklist

✔	Research and fully understand the diagnosis and potential changes to expect throughout the lifetime of the individual with special needs.
✔	Understand resources and accommodations that are available for the education of the dependent with special needs.
✔	Have a vision and plan for how the dependent will live after the initial caregiver is no longer able to serve as caregiver.
✔	Prepare a letter of intent (see **Exhibit 17.4** for content).
✔	Identify and name a guardian, and possibly a trustee for the dependent. This guardian may have general or limited powers. The caregiver / guardian must specify the types of powers for the trustee.
✔	Prepare a will. The caregiver should be certain not to leave assets directly to a dependent with special needs. Rather, assets for dependents with special needs should be directed to a special needs trust that preserves potential government benefits.
✔	Ensure that the individual with special needs acquires and maintains adequate health insurance.
✔	Appoint a health care proxy to make medical decisions for the dependent with special needs if the primary caregiver is unable to do so. Ensure that the person named as the health care proxy is continually aware of the dependent's medical conditions and treatments, including a list of current medications, doses, and times administered.
✔	Understand resources and accommodations that are available for the education of the dependent with special needs.
✔	Have a complete and documented understanding of Social Security disability (SSDI), Supplemental Social Security Income (SSI) government benefits, and Medicaid benefits.
✔	Set aside money for the dependent in a special needs trust. This trust could take the form of an irrevocable life insurance trust (ILIT), or an irrevocable secular trust, with special needs provisions.
✔	Establish and fund a Section 529A ABLE (Achieving a Better Life Experience) account for the benefit of the individual with special needs.
✔	Remove all assets that are in excess of $2,000 (the federal maximum to qualify for benefits) from individual ownership in the name of the dependent with special needs.
✔	Notify other family members and friends of the existence of any third party special needs trust, and reiterate the importance that any funds intended for the individual with special needs be directed to the trust and not to the individual, so as to preserve eligibility for government benefits.

Special Needs Trusts

Trusts are a general tool that are beneficial in many financial planning situations. Many trust benefits, such as asset protection and control, are appropriate considerations for the family of an individual with special needs. A special needs trust is a specific type of trust that is used to provide benefits to persons or beneficiaries with special needs. Typically, these trusts are established to ensure that benefits available from federal and state agencies are preserved and maintained. Federal benefits include available funds and healthcare, such as provided by Social Security disability, Medicaid, and the SSI (Supplemental Security Income) program through Social Security. Many of these programs will not pay benefits if the person has even limited resources. For example, to qualify for SSI, an individual cannot have more than $2,000 in assets and a couple cannot have more than $3,000.

While special needs trusts are used to improve the quality of life and to provide additional resources to the person with special needs without interfering with available governmental resources, there are several types of special needs trusts that should be considered. While there are more than three, the more common special trusts are discussed here and include the Third Party Special Needs Trust, the self settled type trust that is established and exempt under 42 U.S.C. Sec. 1396p(d)(4)(A), and what is referred to as a pooled trust.

> ### ☷ *Key Concepts*
>
> 1. Explain the benefits for special needs trusts.
>
> 2. Identify and explain the three types of special needs trusts.
>
> 3. Identify the key elements to a letter of intent.

Third Party (Family) Special Needs Trust (SNT)

A **third party SNT** is sometimes referred to as a family trust because the trust is a receptacle for funds from a parent, guardian, or other family member. The assets of these trusts, if properly structured, are not counted or considered for purposes of available federal or state benefits for the beneficiary. These trusts make it possible to receive federal, state, and local funds.

These trusts can be funded by a parent or guardian during their life or at their death and are sometimes funded with the proceeds from a life insurance policy. The funds are contributed to a trust by the grantor or settlor for the benefit of the person with the special needs (beneficiary). The assets were never the property of, or owned by, the beneficiary and are therefore not counted as assets for purposes of federal or state benefits.

The trust provisions must be established so as to not provide food, shelter, or any asset that could be converted into food or shelter, such as cash. It may provide for other benefits, such as medical treatment, therapy, education, travel, computer equipment, or other opportunities allowing the individual with special needs to pursue new and enjoyable experiences. These types of benefits can improve the lifestyle of the beneficiary and not interfere with or reduce governmental benefits.

For example, on the website for Social Security, under SSI, it states that "Money paid directly by someone to provide you with items other than food and shelter does not reduce your SSI benefits. (Items that are not "food or shelter" include medical care, telephone bills, education, entertainment, etc.)."

Assets exceeding $2,000 owned by or distributed to a person with a disability may jeopardize federal government benefits. A common way to structure assets either during life or at death that are intended to provide benefits for a dependent with a disability is through the use of a special needs trust.

A special needs trust, created to hold contributed or inherited assets, or its trustee, is the legal owner of the trust property. The dependent with special needs is not the owner of these trust assets, but rather the beneficiary of such a trust. Special needs trusts are irrevocable. However, an irrevocable life insurance trust with a second-to-die life insurance policy insuring parents of a dependent with special needs may satisfy this need. Also, a revocable living trust (inter vivos) may also satisfy this need as it will become irrevocable upon the death of the grantor (parent). In any case, the special needs trust may provide benefits for education, transportation, insurance, rehabilitation, and other life enhancing benefits. The trustee needs to have discretion over the distribution and management of income and assets, but should be explicitly prevented by trust provisions from any action that would jeopardize eligibility for government benefits. The remainder beneficiaries can be other children, grandchildren, or charities.

Exhibit 17.3 | Third Party (Family) Special Needs Trust

Advocate/Guardian
Provides advice to trustee to improve quality of life of dependent with special needs

Trustee
(Independent Party/ Could be a Sibling)

Property Transferred
To Trust by Grantor, or Others (Usually Parent)

TRUST

Remainder Beneficiaries (Examples)
- Other siblings of dependent with special needs
- Grandchildren of grantor
- Charity

Provisions
Trustee has discretion but cannot distribute monies for purposes that would adversely affect government benefits

Income Beneficiary
(Dependent with Special Needs) (for life)

It is a good idea for the grantor of such a trust (generally the parent) to name an advocate (the advocate could be the guardian) for the dependent (beneficiary). The advocate is usually someone close to the dependent who understands both the grantor's wishes and the beneficiary's needs. The advocate works closely with the trustee in determining appropriate distributions that will maintain or improve the quality of life for the beneficiary without jeopardizing government benefits.

The grantor of a special needs trust can write a set of instructions to the advocate and to the trustee. This set of instructions frequently takes the form of a "letter of intent." While not legally enforceable, much like a side letter to a will, the letter of intent expresses the wishes of the grantor. Assuming that the guardian, advocate, and trustee are carefully selected, these wishes are likely to be followed.

Special Needs Trusts Under 42 U.S.C. Sec. 1396p(d)(4)(A)

Special needs trusts under 42 U.S.C. Sec. 1396p(d)(4)(A), which are considered to be self-settled in nature, are typically established by the individual with special needs (for trusts established on or after December 13, 2016), their parent, grandparent, legal guardian, or by a court, and will avoid disqualification of Medicaid and SSI benefits. This law was effective with Omnibus Budget and Reconciliation Act of 1993, was updated by the 21st Century Cures Act of 2016, and permits individuals with special needs or disabilities to establish a trust on their behalf or to direct that settlement proceeds from a personal injury case be protected in a trust for their benefit and still qualify for benefits under Medicaid and SSI. Their statutory language for this section is:

A trust containing the assets of an individual under age 65 who is disabled ... and which is established for the benefit of such individual by the individual, a parent, grandparent, legal guardian of the individual, or a court if the State will receive all amounts remaining in the trust upon the death of such individual up to an amount equal to the total medical assistance paid on behalf of the individual under a State Medicaid plan under this subchapter.

The funds can be contributed to the trust and they can still qualify, but the assets remaining at the death of the beneficiary must be paid to the State to the extent funds and assistance from the State have been paid to or for the beneficiary. These trusts may also be referred to as payback trusts or self-settled trusts.

It should be obvious that it would be better if the trust were not self-settled. However, in some cases, a beneficiary may receive an award from a litigation settlement or from proceeds from a life insurance policy or from an inheritance. If a financial planner were involved, the last two should be able to be paid into a third party trust. However, these funds, which are the property of the beneficiary, can be contributed to a trust as described above.

Pooled Trust (42 U.S.C. Sec. 1396p(d)(4)(C))

The other exception that resulted from the Omnibus Budget and Reconciliation Act of 1993 is a **pooled trust** that is managed by a nonprofit association. While each beneficiary will have their own account, the assets will generally be pooled and managed together for investment purposes. This type of trust can be funded by a parent, grandparent, legal guardian of the individual, or even by the beneficiary. These accounts must be established solely for the benefit of individuals who are disabled. To the extent that amounts remaining in the beneficiary's account upon the death of the beneficiary are not retained by the trust, the trust pays to the State, from such remaining amounts in the account, an amount equal to the total amount of medical assistance paid on behalf of the beneficiary under the State Medicaid plan. In other words, the assets remaining at the death of the beneficiary will either go to the nonprofit association or to the State.

Achieving a Better Life Experience (ABLE) Accounts

The Tax Increase Prevention Act of 2014 (TIPA) allows states to establish **"Achieving a Better Life Experience" (ABLE) accounts** to assist persons with disabilities. ABLE accounts operate similarly to state-sponsored Section 529 Qualified Tuition Plans in that contributions made to the plan are made with after-tax dollars, earnings grow tax-deferred, distributions are tax-free if used to pay for qualified expenses (disability-related expenses for ABLE accounts), and the earnings portion of nonqualified distributions are subject to tax plus a 10 percent penalty.

Contributions to an ABLE account can be made by anyone (no phaseout limits). Unlike QTPs, each disabled beneficiary is permitted only one ABLE account, and the maximum contribution to the account is equal to the annual gift tax exclusion ($15,000 in 2021) per year for each beneficiary. New rules enacted under the Tax Cuts and Jobs Act for the years 2018-2025 allow rollovers from 529 plans to 529A ABLE accounts as long as the beneficiary is the same, or is a family member of the original beneficiary. When funds are rolled over from a Sec. 529 plan to a 529A ABLE account, the amount rolled over is treated as an annual contribution, subject to the $15,000 maximum.

The Tax Cuts and Jobs Act of 2017 allows for certain additional contributions above the $15,000 limit, and for a saver's credit, in tax years 2018-2025. The ABLE account's designated beneficiary can contribute an additional amount up to the lesser of (a) the Federal poverty level for a one-person household, or (b) the individual's gross compensation (as an employee, and for whom no contribution has been made to a defined contribution, 401(k), 403(b), or 457, plan) for the year. The designated beneficiary can also claim the saver's credit (under Section 25B of the tax code) for contributions to the ABLE account. This non-refundable credit is in an amount that is up to $2,000 per year.

The beneficiary of the ABLE account must be entitled to benefits under Social Security disability (SSDI) or Supplemental Security Income (SSI), or must file a disability certification (under penalty of perjury) that the individual has obtained a signed physician's diagnosis for a disability[1] that occurred before the age of 26, and that the diagnosis will be retained and provided to the ABLE program administrator or IRS upon request.

Qualified disability-related expenses include education, housing (including mortgage payments, property insurance required by the mortgage holder, real estate taxes, rent, heating fuel, gas, electricity, water, sewer, and garbage removal), transportation, assistive technology and personal support services, employment training and support, legal fees, health care expenses, financial management and administrative services, basic living expenses, and expenses for oversight and monitoring, among other expenses.[2] Final Treasury Regulations issued in 2020 clarify that qualified disability expenses include basic living expenses and are not limited to items for which there is a medical necessity or which solely benefit a disabled individual, and that they include expenses used to maintain or improve the beneficiary's health, independence, or quality of life. Distributions are tax-free when used to pay for qualified disability-related expenses during the year in which the distribution occurred. A grace period is permitted under which expenses paid within 60 days of the end of the year in which a distribution occurred may be counted as expenses paid during the prior year (the year of the distribution). However, the same expenses cannot also be counted in the year actually paid. Expenses incurred during a time when the beneficiary is not disabled do not qualify.

The ABLE account balance, contributions to the account, and distributions from the account are NOT counted in determining eligibility for any federal means-tested program; however, if the account balance exceeds $100,000, SSI payments will be suspended until the balance falls below $100,000.

Only one ABLE account may be established for each eligible individual. The account may be established by the eligible individual, or by certain other individuals. To reduce the risk of impermissible establishment of multiple ABLE accounts for a single beneficiary, Treasury Regulations provide a hierarchy of individuals who are permitted to establish an ABLE account on behalf of the beneficiary or

---

1. The definition of disability is based on a medically determinable physical or mental impairment that results in marked and severe functional limitations and that can be expected to result in death or that has lasted or can be expected to last at least 12 months, or blindness. Sec. 529A(e)(2)(A)
2. https://secure.ssa.gov/apps10/poms.nsf/lnx/0501130740

exercise signatory authority over the beneficiary's ABLE account. This hierarchy consists of (in the order presented):

- an individual selected by the eligible individual,
- the eligible individual's agent under a power of attorney, conservator, or legal guardian,
- the spouse of the eligible individual,
- a parent of the eligible individual,
- a sibling of the eligible individual,
- a grandparent of the eligible individual, or
- a representative payee appointed by the SSA.

The individual establishing the account may self-certify, under penalty of perjury, that he or she is authorized to establish the account and that no other person of higher priority is willing and able to establish an account for the benefit of the eligible individual. An eligible individual with legal capacity is permitted to replace the individual with signatory authority over the account and to name a successor signatory.[1]

Individuals setting up ABLE accounts are permitted to choose among any of the states' programs, thus allowing for the opportunity to utilize the program that best meets their needs regarding details such as investment options and fees. Investment selections in ABLE accounts can be changed twice per year.[2]

If the beneficiary recovers to the extent of no longer being eligible for an ABLE account, the funds may remain in the ABLE account and the account will retain its status as an ABLE account in case the beneficiary again becomes eligible in the future. However, during the time in which the beneficiary is no longer eligible, no additional contributions may be made to the account and any distributions made will be taxed as non-qualified distributions.

Letter of Intent

The **letter of intent** is a "life plan" document. It describes the family of the individual with special needs and the individual with special needs wishes for the future once the initial caregiver is no longer able to provide care. It should include pertinent information about the history of the dependent with special needs, their medical needs, living arrangement preferences, and hobbies, as well as a list of contact persons (doctor, lawyer, accountant, guardians, etc).

---

1. Treas. Reg. §1.529A-2.
2. Transfers from investment accounts to money market accounts to facilitate distributions do not count as changes to investment selection, nor do changes under an automatic rebalancing strategy to maintain an established asset allocation.

Exhibit 17.4 | Sample Letter of Intent

This sample letter provides a brief idea of some of what should be covered in a letter of intent. An actual letter would contain far more details than what is indicated here.

To Whom It May Concern:
Re: Our daughter, Lori X

1. **Contact the following people if anything should happen to us:** *Names, addresses, mail and e-mail addresses of other children, extended family, case manager, and a close family friend.*

2. **Current situation and family life:** Lori is a thirteen-year-old with autism who lives with her brother and parents. At home, she enjoys reading, playing computer games, cooking, and helping with chores. She enjoys family outings such as hiking, swimming, visiting friends, and going to restaurants and movies. At least once a week, she goes out with her support worker *(name and contact info)* to outings in the community such as swimming and basketball at the YMCA. She is a happy, engaging, and highly verbal child who enjoys the chance to socialize. In addition, she loves animals and spending time with her family cat.

3. **Education:** Lori is included in a regular class at James Madison Middle School with one-to-one support. Her strengths are reading, memory, and music. Since she is unable to print by hand, she uses a laptop computer. When class lessons are too complicated, her assistant allows her to access related computer games and programs instead. In the future, she could attend (with support) a high school that offers vocational opportunities such as cooking or animal care. Alternatively, she could attend a self-contained class at the high school level with students who have high functioning autism or a mild intellectual disability.

4. **Future Residence:** Lori would like to someday share an apartment with a roommate. She will likely need a support worker to check in with her daily (or less frequently) to help with activities of daily living, banking, or general support. Lori's name is already on a waiting list for the Supported Independent Living Apartment Program, offered through *Name of Agency.* Contact our case manager *(name and contact)* for details. Alternatively, she could move in with her brother, who plans on having a basement apartment for Lori in his home.

5. **Employment:** Lori has a keen interest in animals and cooking, and is skilled with computers. She would probably enjoy working or volunteering at an animal shelter, a pet store, or in the food service industry. Perhaps she could also find work requiring some computer expertise.

6. **Medical Care:** Lori has no medical challenges. She is seen for a yearly check up by Dr. Smith *(contact information),* who is familiar with Lori's strengths and challenges. In addition, she sees an eye doctor *(name and contact information)* and dentist *(name and contact information)* with special needs expertise. Lori is not allergic to any medications. However, in the past, she has experienced adverse side effects from the following medications, which should be avoided in the future: *(list drugs and adverse reactions).*

7. **Behavior Management:** Lori occasionally pinches and gets teary when she is anxious. The best strategy is to provide her with a written schedule or calendar of what will be happening in the day. Also, she has been seen by a behavior therapist at the *Name of Clinic (contact info).* They have agreed to consult on any future behavioral issues that may arise.

8. **Social:** Lori participates in several community programs, including YMCA sports for kids *(day, time, location),* a community cooking class *(day, time, location),* and therapeutic horseback riding *(day, time, location).* She also greatly enjoys visiting our close family friends *(name and contact info)* at least once per week.

9. **Religious/Spiritual Life:** Most Sundays, Lori attends services with us at *(Name) Church.* In addition, she occasionally attends youth group social programs for pre-teens.

10. **Guardian and Trustee:** Guardians and trustees have been assigned in our wills, which were last updated on *(insert date) and* are on file with *(attorney name, contact info).*

Both parents' signatures.

A detailed and comprehensive letter of intent will generally serve the dependent with special needs better than one that is brief or less comprehensive. A whole notebook of information, pictures, and documents about the dependent with special needs can provide assistance to the many persons who may be involved in providing care to the dependent with special needs. Sensitive information such as Social Security numbers, account numbers, and account access should be encrypted / redacted or otherwise made secure.

Exhibit 17.5 | Letter of Intent - Sample Contents (Not Exhaustive)

- **Contacts** - including advocates, siblings, other family members, trustee, and/or case worker, including names, addresses, email addresses, phone numbers.
- **Dependent Description** - including likes, dislikes, current living arrangement, relationships with others, etc.
- **Medical History** - including primary doctor, specialists, medications, medications to be avoided,
- **Education** - including current education level, any ongoing education, copies of diplomas, plans and aspirations for the future.
- **Employment** - including any past and current jobs and any future job interests and abilities.
- **Religion** - including any services or programs usually attended.
- **Future Residential Possibilities** - including contacts, facilities, etc.
- **Social** - including any interests, programs, extra curricular activities.
- **Behavior** - including any behavioral issues that may need special care or attention.
- **Tax Information** - including any tax returns with Social Security numbers redacted.

PLANNING FOR DIVORCE

Financial planners regularly assist clients post-divorce. However, they can also be valuable resources for those who are planning for, or are in the middle of, a divorce. Divorce can be both emotionally and economically devastating for all parties involved. From a financial standpoint, it is more expensive to maintain two households than one. Divorced persons are likely to encounter concurrent increases in expenses and decreases in income, and ultimately, the spouse with lower income is likely to have a substantial reduction in lifestyle. Clients who previously never had the need to live on a budget may suddenly be required to do so.

Key Concepts

1. Identify the recommendations for couples that are going through a divorce.

2. Identify the common mistakes that are made in a divorce.

3. List the recommendations for a terminally ill planning situation.

Property settlements, child support, and alimony are major factors in divorce and are generally financial in nature. Often, the financial data that divorcing couples have is incomplete and/or unreliable. It is not uncommon that one or both parties are unaware of retirement benefits, asset values, projected cash flows, and/or tax basis of assets, just to mention a few of the common issues.

Divorce Planning in Relation to Major Financial Planning Areas

A look at each of the financial planning areas will reveal some unique concerns for divorcing spouses:

1. **Fundamentals:** In planning for the fundamental areas of financial planning, the planner will advise clients to carefully consider the distribution of assets. Each spouse getting an equal value doesn't necessarily mean both end up in the same financial condition. The types of assets received by each party must be evaluated. Planning for fundamentals will also focus on cash flow, particularly after-tax cash flow. Division of investment assets may also significantly affect cash flow. Careful negotiation will be required to protect the lifestyle of the divorcing client.

   Where minor children are involved, divorcing clients will also need to address how long child support payments will continue - will payments continue just to age 18 or through college? Clients will also need to determine whether either or both parents will be responsible for the cost of private elementary and secondary schools and college, and how these expenses and any other child-related expenses will be split.

2. **Insurance and Risk Management:** Addressing the insurance needs of a divorcing client will be another important function of the financial planner. If the client is to receive alimony or child support payments, a decision must be made as to whether there should be a life insurance policy to protect those alimony or child support payments that the client will rely upon. If it is determined that a policy is needed, additional decisions must be made regarding who should own the policy and who will pay the premiums. These decisions may affect after-tax cash flow since the income tax treatment may differ depending upon how the policy ownership is structured.

   Another insurance issue that is likely to arise in divorce is the need for one party to obtain a new medical insurance policy. If medical insurance was provided as a family benefit by one spouse's employer, the ex-spouse will no longer meet the definition of a dependent spouse under that policy. COBRA (Consolidated Omnibus Budget Reconciliation Act) coverage may be available for a limited period of time, typically 36 months for a divorced spouse, but will require the ex-spouse to pay the full premium amount, up to 102 percent. This additional expense may have a significant impact on cash flow, or it may mean that medical insurance is not affordable.

   In the divorce discussion, the parties will also need to address which parent is responsible for maintaining health insurance for children and how any coinsurance or co-pay amounts are to be split between the parents, including coinsurance and co-pays for vision and dental care. The Affordable Care Act requires insurers to make dependent coverage available until the age of 26, relieving many concerns regarding medical care coverage for adult children still in college, but a discussion regarding who will pay for medical expenses remains relevant.

3. **Investments:** Planning for divorcing clients will also require that investment risk tolerance and capacity be re-evaluated. It is possible that risk tolerance will decline due to the increased dependence on investment assets and on the income they produce, as well as due to less disposable income being available to make up for lost value. The decision on how investment assets are to be divided should also factor in the tax impact of each investment.

4. **Income Taxation:** Clients who are about to be divorced will have a number of income tax related issues to address, including:

   - How income is to be shared, including alimony and child support. For income tax purposes, alimony is not tax deductible to the payer and is not taxable income to the receiver if the divorce is executed after December 31, 2018. For divorces prior to January 1, 2019, alimony is deductible by the payer and taxable to the receiver. In order to be considered alimony, the payments must be in cash (or like cash), must be paid under a divorce or separate mainte-nance agreement, must not be for the support of minor children, and must end at the death of the receiver. Child support payments are not tax deductible to the payer and are not taxable income to the receiver.

   - The additional roles of life insurance in a divorce must be considered for their income tax con-sequences. As mentioned previously, it may make sense for alimony or child support pay-ments to be protected from the loss that could occur in the event of the death of the payer. The income tax consequences can vary depending upon whether the parties use a new or existing life insurance policy and depending upon the persons who are owner, payer, and beneficiary.

   - The income tax consequences of custody of the child(ren) is another important discussion point for divorce negotiations. The right to claim a child as a dependent on the income tax return is generally allocated to the custodial parent (the parent with whom the child spent the most number of nights during the year). If the decree or agreement was entered into after 2008, a noncustodial parent can claim the child as a dependent only where the custodial par-ent signs a Form 8332 to release a claim to the exemption, and the noncustodial parent must attach the form to his or her return. If the decree or agreement was entered into prior to 2009, the noncustodial parent may be able to attach certain pages from the decree rather than Form 8332. The decision on the dependency exemption has become even more import-ant since the enactment of child tax credits and education credits because the availability of these credits generally falls on the return of the parent claiming the child as a dependent.

5. **Retirement Planning:** Divorce will also have a substantial impact on retirement planning for both parties. It is likely that the division of retirement assets and increased cost of providing separate households will require adjustments to the retirement plans of both ex-spouses. It could create a need to delay retirement to a later date, to continue working part-time in retirement, or to accept a different lifestyle than expected for the retirement years.

   Determining a fair and equitable division of pension plan and other retirement assets will be of utmost importance. **A Qualified Domestic Relations Order (QDRO)** is an order made under state law that tells the administrator or trustee of a qualified retirement plan how much to pay out to the nonowner-spouse pursuant to a divorce. Without a QDRO, a withdrawal by an owner-spouse from a qualified plan to pay a property settlement can trigger income and penalty taxes, even though the owner does not actually receive the proceeds. A properly written QDRO ensures that a qualified plan can be divided as part of the property settlement in a divorce, without any negative tax consequences to either spouse. Some retirement plans, however, may not accept certain QDROs. For example, a plan may not provide for a payout before retirement age, so a QDRO specifying immediate payment will not be given effect. In such cases, the plan documents will govern any payout in a divorce. In cases where a rollover is immediately available, the financial planner will need to evaluate whether retirement assets should be rolled to a new account or left with the current institution.

A discussion regarding Social Security benefits will also be important for divorcing spouses. In some cases, it may be recommended that the divorce be delayed so the marriage lasts the 10 years required for spousal benefits from Social Security for divorced spouses. A divorced spouse should also understand that Social Security spousal benefits will be forfeited if they remarry, unless the later marriage ends in less than ten years (by death, divorce, or annulment). There is an exception for survivor benefits being paid to a divorced spouse who remarries after age 60.

6. **Estate Planning:** A planner should also advise divorcing clients to review their estate plans. Changes may include naming a guardian for minor children, drafting a new will, adding a power of attorney where one did not exist before, or changing the power of attorney. In addition, titles to assets (house, car, joint accounts, etc.) may need to be changed, and careful consideration should be given to the choice of new property titles. A wife who plans to resume use of her maiden name will also encounter the task of changing her name on all property, as well as with the Social Security Administration and state Department of Motor Vehicles, among others. Joint credit cards should be closed and new accounts opened in individual names.

In the brief discussion provided here, it should be clear that a planner must address numerous issues in divorce planning. It is inevitable that the planner will work with a team of professionals including the client's attorney and CPA.

Financial Planning Recommendations for Divorcing Couples

The client or planner should gather, compare, verify, prepare, analyze, estimate, and project!
- Gather data to get a clear and complete understanding of the current and projected financial situation.
- Properly compile current investment and banking statements, organizing, and valuing all assets (e.g., businesses).
- Clearly analyze all liabilities. Determine if there are joint obligations that cannot be severed. For each liability, determine the monthly obligation, term of indebtedness, value of the corresponding asset, interest rate, and any other applicable information.
- Make a projection of future income needs of the client.
- Prepare both a current and projected Statement of Financial Position and Income Statement complete with explanatory footnotes.
- Gather five years of past federal and state income tax returns. A detailed analysis of the information in the tax returns along with bank statements and investment statements will help to reduce the risk of overlooked or hidden assets.
- Collect any monthly, quarterly, or annual financial statements of an owned business plus five years of business income tax returns. In addition, if the business has any debt, or has ever had any debt, financial statements provided to any such lender will yield useful information, as will financial statements and loan applications for any personal credit (e.g., mortgages, auto loans, credit cards) that has been obtained by either party within the last five years.
- Analyze post divorce insurance needs.
- Analyze post divorce emergency fund requirements.
- Analyze post divorce retirement and education cash flow needs.
- Be sure to know the tax basis of each asset as well as the fair market value.
- Estimate any post divorce job training costs.
- Consider the built-in tax cost associated with assets in the property settlement.

All of this information, once collected, or prepared, should be thoroughly reviewed by a competent party to get a clear and complete picture of the current financial situation of the couple. Cash flow and ongoing access to credit are important, as both parties may be required to pay legal retainers and at least one party may find it necessary to establish a new household.

Common Mistakes in Divorce

Some of the most common financial planning mistakes that divorcing couples make are:

- Failure to adequately establish individual credit prior to the divorce.
- Failure to differentiate between separate property, gifted or inherited property, and property acquired during the marriage.
- Failure to discover hidden assets.
- Failure to completely resolve joint obligations by the time of the divorce, thus causing credit problems, especially where the party assigned the obligation is unreliable or irresponsible. This situation can have serious credit implications.
- Failure to make good choices regarding the property settlement of pension plans and other qualified plans where each spouse has a federal property right.
- Failure to be clear on the tax basis of particular assets and thus tax implications of assets divided by agreement.
- Failure to provide a complete and contractually binding agreement regarding college education support for children beyond age 18.
- Failure to change beneficiary designations on insurance contracts and retirement plans, including qualified plans, IRAs, SEPs, and SIMPLEs.
- Failure to insure any support agreement from the risk of death, disability, or inability to pay of the payer. For example, if the husband is to provide child support to age 18 and college support to age 22, and he dies prematurely, did the spouse own a life insurance policy on his life that would replace the support income? What about the disability of an ex-spouse or just plain laziness? What about bankruptcy of an ex-spouse? Could a spouse bankrupt against assigned joint obligations, thus transferring the obligation for them back to the other spouse, and causing a financial catastrophe for the non-bankrupt spouse?
- Failure to follow through, prior to the financial settlement, on paperwork to change the titling of assets and to account for assets to be transferred in the divorce property settlement.
- Failure to know the Social Security benefits of a spouse married for 10 or more years to a covered worker.

Even after proper planning and after avoiding common mistakes, it is important for spouses to prepare and maintain a budget so as to avoid financial troubles. There may be additional expenses setting up a new household and it is easy to spend more than the amount budgeted.

PLANNING FOR TERMINAL ILLNESS

At birth, we have an approximate life expectancy of about 78 years. This means that for any given birth day, half of those persons born on that date are expected to live less than, and half are expected to live longer than, 78 years. The sad reality is that of the half who die before age 78, some die each year and the number of cumulative deaths usually forms a graph that is an upward sloping exponential function.

It is common that when people are in their 50s, 60s, and 70s, they begin to develop a comprehensive estate plan answering such questions as to whom, and how, assets will pass? Other questions to be answered are: (1) What are my thoughts on funeral and burial arrangements? (2) How will I provide for myself in the interim and for those I love after I pass? (3) Who will I empower to make my health care decisions? (4) What arrangements do I want with regard to the artificial sustainment of my life? (5) What do I want my legacy to be to my family, friends, community, or the world?

If people do not plan for those eventualities, usually the state of residence legislates the answers. The legislature passes these kinds of laws because many people fail to plan for their succession.

For a client diagnosed with a terminal illness, the above questions are relevant but the remaining time to begin to finalize a plan is compressed. In addition to dealing with the medical and emotional issues associated with being diagnosed as terminal, the client will frequently want to "get their financial house in order." A return to step 1 in the planning process will be necessary to adjust goals and time horizons and to review the beneficiary designations to ensure all prior implementation recommendations have been completed.

Preparing for Care

Many terminal illnesses will result in the eventual need for significant assistance with medical and custodial care. The terminally ill individual and family will need to assess whether care will be provided at home or in an institution, who will provide the care, and what levels and types of care are desired.

The Family Medical Leave Act allows eligible employees to take unpaid, job-protected leave for certain family and medical reasons. While on leave, the employee can continue group health insurance coverage as if he or she were not on leave. Eligible employees are entitled to 12 weeks of unpaid leave for the birth of a child, adoption of a child, to care for a family member (spouse, child, or parent) who has a serious health condition, or for a serious health condition that makes the employee unable to perform his or her essential job functions. Twenty-six weeks of leave is available during any 12-month period for the employee to provide care for a covered military service member who is a member of the employee's family (spouse, child, parent).

A few states have enacted paid FMLA laws, and a growing number are considering such laws. As of July 2020, eight states (CA, CT, MA, NJ, NY, OR, RI, and WA) and Washington D.C. offer some paid FMLA benefits.

The Tax Cuts and Jobs Act of 2017 created a business tax credit for employers who pay compensation to employees who are on family and medical leave. Employers who pay wages equal to at least 50 percent of the employee's normal wages to qualified employees who are on FMLA can claim a business credit equal to 12.5 percent of the wages paid during the period in which the employee is on FMLA. This tax benefit may provide encouragement for employers to provide at least partial continuing salary payments to employees who are caring for terminally ill family members, easing some of the financial strain on the family. Under the TCJA, this tax credit was available for tax years beginning after December 31, 2017 and before January 1, 2020. The Taxpayer Certainty and Disaster Tax Relief Act of 2019 extended the credit through December 31, 2020, and the Taxpayer Certainty and Disaster Tax Relief Act of 2020 further extended the credit through December 31, 2025.

The terminally ill individual must also consider the types of care that are desired. Most states now recognize a form of Advance Medical Directive (AMD) called Five Wishes, which is a medical proxy document designed with a focus on aging with dignity and providing peace of mind when difficult decisions must be made. Five Wishes addresses "the personal, emotional, and spiritual needs of a person, not just the medical ones." The five wishes that are communicated in the document are:

- Wish 1- The person I want to make health care decisions for me when I can't make them for myself.
- Wish 2 - My wish for the kind of medical treatment I want or don't want.
- Wish 3 - My wish for how comfortable I want to be.
- Wish 4 - My wish for how I want people to treat me.
- Wish 5 - My wish for what I want my loved ones to know.

Financial Planning Recommendations for Terminal Illness Planning

- Prepare or update personal financial statements.
- Prepare up-to-date estate documents (will, durable power of attorney for healthcare, advance medical directives, and do not resuscitate orders.
- Review all property titling arrangements to make sure they are as desired.
- Review all named beneficiaries of life insurance, qualified plans, other tax advantaged plans (IRAs, SEPs, SIMPLEs).
- Review all funeral and burial arrangements, including selection of location, minister, eulogizer, music, flower, determination of announcement in paper, etc.
- Evaluate the impact on cash flow and survivor needs of accelerated death benefits (a provision in a life insurance policy allowing a terminally ill insured access to death benefits during their lifetime) or viatical settlements (the sale of a life insurance policy on a terminally or chronically ill insured to a licensed viatical settlement company) as a means to increase cash flow for medical, quality of life, or other needs during the terminally ill individual's remaining lifetime.
- Consider home health care and Hospice services.
- Identify Social Security benefits to survivors.
- Inform the executor of accounts, account access, online accounts, and passwords, in accordance with the state's Fiduciary Access to Digital Assets laws.
- Consider organ donation.
- Consider income, estate, and gift tax consequences.

> ### ✍ Quick Quiz 17.3
>
> 1. There are few steps that need to be undertaken with a client who is going through a divorce.
>   a. True
>   b. False
>
> 2. One of the common mistakes made in a divorce is to not identify the types of property, such as separate or inherited property.
>   a. True
>   b. False
>
> 3. In addition to the recommendations for a terminally ill person, the financial planner should consider the emotional issues.
>   a. True
>   b. False
>
> False, True, True.

The above recommendations are certainly sound, but the person with the terminal illness, the family, and caregivers must also deal with the emotional issues. In some cases, the relationship may change or the person with the terminal illness may be in denial. The emotional issues will certainly impact the success of the financial objectives.

PLANNING FOR NON-TRADITIONAL HOUSEHOLDS

While many financial planners have clients who are married with children, the percentage of the population that is getting married in the United States is declining and the age at which individuals get married is increasing. The chart below depicts the percent of young adults who are married versus living with a partner from 1969 - 2019.

Exhibit 17.6 | Living Arrangements Among Young Adults Ages 25-34 (Percent)

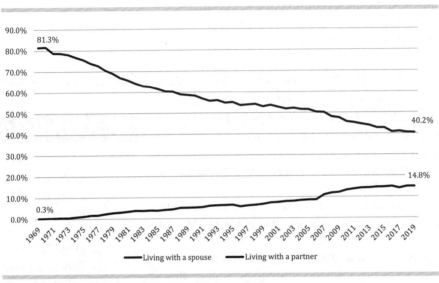

Source: U.S. Census Bureau.

As the chart indicates, the percent of younger people that are married is going down. In addition, the number of non-traditional households is on the rise.

The so-called "**non-traditional household**" is a broad phrase that may include any household other than the traditional husband, wife, and children. It could be heterosexual or homosexual couples living together with or without children. The adults may or may not be romantically involved, but may wish to include each other and their respective descendants in their estate plan.

There are many federal and state laws that provide a surviving spouse of a married couple with certain rights. Examples include Social Security survivor benefits, rights under the state intestacy laws, rights to decide funeral and burial arrangements, tax filing choices, and the unlimited marital deduction to name a few.

> ### ⠿ *Key Concepts*
>
> 1. Explain what is meant by non-traditional household.
>
> 2. Explain how the Defense of Marriage Act and, subsequently, United States v. Windsor impact federal law with respect to the definition of marriage.
>
> 3. Identify the four ways property passes to heirs or legatees.

In general, there are few, if any, laws which govern property division, support payments, or other rights for non-married couples. Unmarried couples must take great care to avoid intestacy laws that do not provide for non-married partners. Also, unmarried couples should carefully consider and prepare wills, durable powers of attorney for health care, and advance medical directives. Frequently, legal difficulties arise regarding funeral and burial wishes for deceased partners.

Civil Unions and Registered Partners

A civil union is a separate legal status conveying to the partners most of, if not all, the rights available to married couples under state (but not federal) law. Many states that previously offered civil unions have eliminated this form of legal status in favor of same-sex marriage; however, a few states continue to allow for civil unions or domestic partnerships and rights and responsibilities vary among jurisdictions.

California's Domestic Partner Rights and Responsibilities Act of 2003 expanded previous rights to include almost all rights and responsibilities of spouses under state law. These rights include hospital visitation, a right to be appointed a conservator and make medical decisions, inheritance rights, joint responsibilities for debts, and the right to seek financial support from each other upon the dissolution of the relationship for "registered" domestic partners. These persons can even file the state income tax return as married filing jointly or separately.

The **Defense of Marriage Act (DOMA)** was signed into law on September 21, 1996 and was "to define and protect the institution of marriage." Under Section 7, Definition of 'marriage' and 'spouse' the law states, "In determining the meaning of any Act of Congress, or of any ruling, regulation, or interpretation of the various administrative bureaus and agencies of the United States, the word 'marriage' means only a legal union between one man and one woman as husband and wife, and the word 'spouse' refers only to a person of the opposite sex who is a husband or a wife." Since the Internal Revenue Code is an act of Congress, the definitions of marriage and spouse are largely dictated by the definition of marriage under federal law. However, in the 2013 landmark case, United States v. Windsor, the Supreme Court effectively declared DOMA as unconstitutional. The result of this ruling is that there is no longer a distinction for federal purposes between marriages of heterosexuals and marriages of homosexuals. Thus, if two people are married, regardless of sexual orientation, they are treated as married under federal law, including laws under the Internal Revenue Code.

The important point here is that the financial planning client in a non-traditional relationship must understand the state law of the state in which they reside, as well as Federal law.

Planning for Non-Traditional Families in Relation to Major Financial Planning Areas

As with other special circumstances, a look at each of the financial planning areas will be necessary for non-traditional families:

1. **Fundamentals:** When addressing financial planning fundamentals for non-traditional families, the planner may find that in some cases accounts have been combined and in other cases a decision has been made to keep finances separate. In many cases a Domestic Partnership Agreement or Cohabitation Agreement should be recommended for clients. These agreements require the partners to specify how household expenses will be shared, to identify how real and personal property is owned, to establish who is responsible for maintenance and repairs to the home, and to declare whether gifts or inheritances that are made to one partner will be considered joint or separate.

2. **Insurance and Risk Management:** The availability to an unmarried domestic partner of medical insurance benefits offered by the employer of one of the partners will vary from state-to-state and employer-to-employer. If coverage is available, the cost of coverage will very likely be taxable income at the federal level (unless the partner qualifies as a dependent for tax purposes). For life insurance purposes, an insurable interest will generally exist when there is a sharing of economic resources between the domestic partners, enabling one partner to purchase a life insurance policy on the life of the other partner. The purchase of life insurance may be a particularly high priority in light of the fact that the partner will not qualify for any survivor benefits from Social Security upon the death of the other partner.

3. **Investments:** Like other assets, investments may be titled in just one name or in joint names. Unlike a married couple, there will be no unlimited marital deduction for gifts, so titling property jointly should be considered with due regard to the gift tax consequences. Bank and brokerage accounts titled jointly will generally not result in a gift to the other joint party until one partner withdraws more than his or her contribution, but real estate investments that are titled jointly may result in an immediate gift. To avoid having brokerage assets pass through probate at the death of a partner, a Transfer on Death (TOD) beneficiary designation may be used. The beneficiary of a TOD account has no rights to the brokerage account assets during the owner's lifetime, only at death.

4. **Income Taxation:** Unmarried couples will not be able to file their taxes using the more favorable Married Filing Jointly (MFJ) tax status on their federal tax return. For unmarried couples, it is possible, but unlikely, that one partner could claim the other as a dependent on their federal income tax return. Claiming an unrelated person as a dependent requires that the dependent live with the taxpayer, and that two tests be met: (1) the support test, and (2) the income test. The support test requires the taxpayer to provide more than 50 percent of the support of the dependent, and the income test requires that the dependent have income below a set amount ($4,300 in 2021).

5. **Retirement Planning:** It is usually recommended that unmarried couples plan for retirement separately since they will generally have no rights to retirement plan assets if the relationship ends. In addition, unmarried couples will not be entitled to collect benefits based on their partner's Social Security.

6. **Estate Planning:** For estate planning purposes, there will be no unlimited marital deduction available for federal estate or gift taxes for unmarried couples, nor will they be able to split gifts (designate gifts as being made 1/2 by each partner) to third parties as married couples are permitted to do. Since state intestacy laws typically only allow blood relatives to inherit a decedent's estate, a valid will should be in place to ensure that assets will pass to the intended partner. If there is discord among family members regarding the relationship and a will contest might be expected, it is best to avoid passing assets to the partner through the will. Instead, other will substitutes, such as titling property as joint with rights of survivorship or revocable trusts (discussed below), should be used in the estate plan. Since the law tends to favor blood relatives for making medical decisions as well, incapacity planning documents such durable powers of attorney for health care or health care proxies should be in place to name the partner as the agent to make medical decisions, if it is desired that the partner should be the one to make those choices.

Property Transfers at Death

In general, all property owned by a decedent passes to the heirs or legatees in one of four alternative ways:

1. by state contract law (e.g., life insurance, annuities, TODs, PODs),
2. by state titling law where there is a survivorship feature (e.g., JTWROS, TE),
3. by state trust law, or
4. by state probate or succession law including both testate and intestate successions.

Forms of testamentary transfers such as beneficiary designations on contracts (life insurance, annuities, qualified plans, IRAs, SEPs, SIMPLEs,) Pay on Death bank accounts (PODs), and transfer on death investments accounts (TODs), may be used as a will substitute. Other will substitutes include real property titling joint tenancy with rights of survivorship (JTWROS) and revocable trusts that become irrevocable at the death of the grantor. These will substitutes used to pass assets are much more difficult arrangements to challenge than a will in probate court.

Wills are presented in the probate court and are frequently problematic for unmarried couples as they may get challenged by the decedent's relatives. However, it may be advantageous to have a will that, while not passing assets, does confer powers such as the power to name an executor, to appoint a guardian for children, and for the making of gifts of personal property by virtue of a side letter.

It is also a wise idea to even restate beneficiary designations and titling with survivorship rights in the will even though the asset is passing out of probate so as to provide additional evidence of the decedent's wishes for the probate court.

Generally, for non-married persons wishing to provide for the surviving partners, it is preferred to avoid probate due to the public nature and openness of the process. Whether assets will be passed by contract, titling, or trust will depend on the concerns and reservations the party with the assets has toward the surviving partner. In general, "if you don't trust 'em, trust 'em," (i.e. create a trust to hold assets).

> ### ✍ Quick Quiz 17.4
>
> 1. Traditional marriage has been on the rise over the last decade.
>   a. True
>   b. False
>
> 2. Both heterosexual and homosexual marriages receive the same treatment under federal law.
>   a. True
>   b. False
>
> 3. All property must pass through probate.
>   a. True
>   b. False
>
> ───────────────
> False, True, False.

PLANNING FOR JOB LOSS OR JOB CHANGE

Financial planners regularly suggest that clients have an emergency fund of three to six times their nondiscretionary monthly cash flows. However, this rule of thumb is potentially misguided even though it may be the average of all averages. The reality is there are a variety of risks that might require the use of an emergency fund that includes, but are not limited to, job loss.

In a poor labor market, it will take longer on average to find a replacement job than for a similar job in a vibrant labor market. Some workers are highly specialized and do not have adaptable skill sets to generalized employment, so it may take those workers much longer than six months to find a replacement job, especially in a poor labor market.

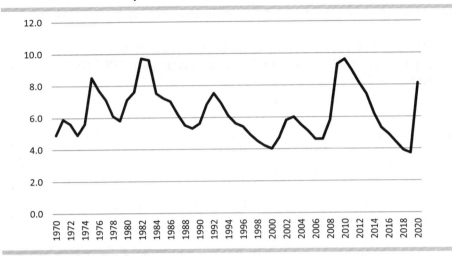

Exhibit 17.7 | Unemployment Rates from 1970 - 2020

Questions to ask include:
- Is the market for the client's type of job a national market or a local market?
- Is the client willing to relocate?
- How long does the client think it would take to replace his job if lost? (Clients are more likely to have a better idea about how long it would take to replace a lost job in the client's field than the planner.)

Once these factors are considered, a new emergency fund ratio should be established for this client (e.g., it could be 1-2 months for a tenured faculty member and it could be 18 months for a specialized position at a local market). Note that the effects of the 2020 COVID-19 pandemic, which resulted in millions of workers being suddenly and unpredictably displaced with little opportunity to seek alternative employment, should be expected to have a lasting psychological impact on those workers and their families. The result is likely to manifest as a decreased risk tolerance toward the risk of job loss, leading to a desire for higher emergency fund ratios, at least in the near-term.

> **Key Concepts**
>
> 1. Explain the general rule of thumb regarding the amount of money necessary for an emergency fund.
>
> 2. Explain the recommendations for a windfall recipient.

Cash Flows

Job loss that is unplanned can cause significant cash flow consequences, including no income, no savings, and continued nondiscretionary expenses. There cannot be enough emphasis on cash flow planning including the use of debt, sale of assets, cutting expenses, and taking funds from retirement accounts if absolutely necessary.

Age as a Factor

Age is a significant factor in finding work. During 2011, those unemployed over age 55 took, on average, 52.2 weeks to find work and 10 percent of those age 55 and older simply quit looking for work.[1] This is twice as long as the average 30 year old required to replace a job. Keep in mind that the replacement job may or may not, and often does not, offer the same salary and benefits as the job that was lost.

When job loss happens, it may be an ideal time to try self-employment or a second career in an area of interest or return to school to retool. Each of these options also has cash flow implications that must be considered.

Those workers age 62 or older may consider beginning Social Security retirement benefits to supplement their income, although the monthly benefit will be permanently reduced if benefits begin prior to full retirement age. Surviving spouses (including divorced spouses), however, may begin collecting survivor benefits as early age 60 while allowing their own benefit to continue to accrue until full retirement age or beyond.

Health Insurance

Health insurance becomes a major issue for the unemployed. COBRA, if available, will provide benefits from 18 months to 36 months, but the premiums are expensive. It is very likely that the former employer was paying part of the insurance premiums. With COBRA, the individual is responsible for 100 percent of the premiums and may even be charged an administrative premium. An unemployed client may want to consider a high deductible plan to provide health benefits. Clients should request that the former employer keep the client on health insurance for a transition period.

Financial Planning Advice

The financial planner should recommend that the client who has just lost a job should immediately start looking for work. Recent skills and recent contracts are critical to finding a replacement job. The planner should recommend that the client try competitors of the former employer.

The client should be advised to immediately file for unemployment benefits and for any employer severance if possible. The planner should also recommend that the client network with people in the same field and also make it clear to friends and family that the client is looking for a new job. Unemployment compensation programs do provide some protection for workers who lose a job, but programs vary by state and are designed to provide only modest income replacement. Eligibility for benefits requires attachment to the labor force throughout a base period, typically the 52 weeks prior to the time of unemployment. Also, to be eligible, the worker must be physically and mentally capable of working and available to go to work in suitable employment. Disqualification for benefits may occur if the individual voluntarily leaves a job without good cause, is discharged for misconduct, is involved in a labor dispute, refuses to accept suitable work,

> ### ☑ *Quick Quiz 17.5*
>
> 1. Clients only need savings equal to 3 to 6 months of income as an emergency fund.
>   a. True
>   b. False
>
> 2. A windfall recipient, in addition to often being ecstatic, has a lot of work to do to help ensure that the unexpected wealth is not squandered.
>   a. True
>   b. False
>
> _____
>
> False, True.

___

1. U.S. Labor Department (December 2011).

or receives disqualifying income such as dismissal wages or pension benefits. Benefits are usually subject to a one-week non-retroactive waiting period and usually continue for only up to 26 weeks. Benefit amounts are based on past earnings, but they are subject to a rather modest maximum, such as $350 or $400 per week (although some states are as low as $235, and some states are as high as $600 or more). During the COVID-19 pandemic of 2020, benefits were temporarily increased above the normal state maximums via supplements from the federal government, states were given the option to offer benefits to independent contractors and others who are typically not eligible for benefits, and states were permitted to extend benefits for an expanded period of time. Expansive measures such as these are occasionally offered during periods of widespread unemployment, but are not predictable or guaranteed and should not be assumed to be available when planning for future potential periods of unemployment.

During the period of unemployment, a client may want to reassess their career objectives but the key to planning when job loss occurs is very precise budgeting and managing of cash flows. From a portfolio perspective, it may make sense to evaluate the portfolio to determine the amount of liquid assets that are available to the client to use in the event of an extended period of unemployment. It might make more sense to make small adjustments in the portfolio sooner rather than when there is little or no alternative.

PLANNING FOR A FINANCIAL WINDFALL

A financial **windfall** is often treated by the recipient as quite different than earned money. Windfalls can include lottery winnings, an unexpected inheritance, stock options, IPOs, sometimes marrying someone with money, or the sale of a business. Once someone has sudden wealth, especially if the information about that wealth is public information, there will be scores of people willing to give the recipient suggestions. Most of these are likely to be bad, or at least suspect advice.

Financial planners who assist clients with new found or sudden wealth do not just provide financial advice and education, but provide assistance to the client in the transition from one set of economic circumstances to another. Planners should keep in mind that the windfall recipient is often under great emotional stress for a wide variety of reasons, most likely caused by the uncertain future as to what to do.

The curious fact is that there is story after story of lottery winners subsequently going broke. Why? The answer may lie in the fact that before the windfall they had a support, advice, and money knowledge system consistent with their then economic situation and lifestyle. The realization is that people who have always been wealthy have experience with wealth and also with the management of spending, using debt, investing, and wealth transfer. Many of those who experience a sudden financial windfall do not have such experiences.

Exhibit 17.8 | Did You Know?

44%	Percent of lottery winners who spent 100% of their winnings within 5 years.
24%	Percent of lottery winners who bought property in a foreign country.
32%	Percent of lottery winners who have gained weight.
48%	Percent of lottery winners who are still in their same career job after winning.
45%	Percent of lottery winners who started a new business.
68%	Percent of lottery winners who continue to play the lottery weekly.

www.statisticbrain.com, "Lottery Winner Statistics," Statistics were compiled from 34 national lottery winners. Average age of 46.

The worst course of action for a windfall recipient to do after receiving a windfall is to spend freely in an attempt to immediately change to an unsustainable lifestyle. One of the best things they could do is to do nothing. They should take the time to carefully consider goals of debt payoff, funding education, and funding and planning for retirement. The client should proceed very slowly and should seek expert financial advice and get many opinions. They should use as a guide "the first principle of financial planning is to protect the principal!"

Planning for Financial Windfalls in Relation to Major Financial Planning Areas

Financial planning clients in receipt of sudden wealth must also review each of the major planning areas:

1. *Fundamentals:* In some cases, the client may be offered the alternatives of taking a lump-sum payment or an annuity. The financial planner may be called upon to evaluate the relative merits of these alternatives. The comparison will require a time-value-of-money calculation of the present value of the annuity based on an appropriate discount rate. These calculations are discussed in chapter 7. In addition to calculating the present value of the annuity, the client will need to consider his or her ability to handle large sums of money. The client will need the assistance of the financial planner to invest the funds wisely and to avoid irrational exuberance.

2. *Insurance and Risk Management:* Lawsuits tend to follow money, making the windfall recipient a potential target for high-stakes liability lawsuits. When the financial windfall is public information, the client should re-evaluate his umbrella liability insurance to ensure coverage for larger potential claims. Other types of existing insurance policies should also be reviewed, but proceed with caution before deeming life or disability insurance as no longer necessary since a reversal of wealth could result in the need for these policies, which may be difficult to replace.

3. *Investments:* As with other financial planning clients, actual investments will depend upon many factors such as current economic conditions and the client's risk tolerance, time horizon, age, and goals. As discussed previously, advice regarding where and how to invest will be plentiful, but not always in the client's best interest. A clearly defined Investment Policy Statement (IPS) will provide guidance in determining suitable investments.

4. *Income Taxation:* A monetary windfall may originate from a number of sources, and the taxation of each can be very different. Lottery winnings are taxed as ordinary income. Structured settlements for personal injury, wrongful death, and workers' compensation payments for sickness or injury are tax free; however, payments received as a result of punitive damages or workers' compensation to replace lost wages are taxable. Amounts received as a gift are income tax free. A bequest received in three or fewer installments is typically not taxable, but if it is paid in more than three installments, it may be partially or fully taxable as income. Inherited IRAs and qualified retirement plans are taxable income to the beneficiary when distributed.

5. *Retirement Planning:* Retirement planning for clients who receive large monetary windfalls may shift from a focus on accumulating enough that they don't run out of money, to a focus on efficient distributions. The planner will need to consider which accounts make the most sense for lifetime distributions and which for passing assets to heirs efficiently.

6. *Estate Planning:* A client may find himself or herself unexpectedly in a whole new transfer tax (i.e., gift and estate taxes) situation due to a monetary windfall. Additional planning will be required to efficiently transfer assets to the next generation by gift during lifetime or through the estate at death. Trusts may be utilized to provide professional management of assets as well as to provide for asset protection or spendthrift protection. Clients who win the lottery, which is a

highly publicized windfall, are likely to receive numerous requests for gifts, loans, and charitable contributions. These clients may feel that they have an obligation to help support family and charities, and will seek advice on how to do so appropriately. Many will find it helpful to earmark a specific dollar amount of their annual budget to gifts and charitable contributions, and then each year select the most worthy among the various requests.

Financial Planning Recommendations for a Financial Windfall Recipient

- Get educated - learn about investments, your risk tolerance, etc.
- Take time (18-36 months) to decide what to do, "protect the principal."
- Find at least one competent CPA, financial adviser, and legal adviser (be efficient with their time, particularly those that charge by the hour).
- Do not quit your job.
- Do not invest in a new business.
- Do not invest in illiquid assets.
- Do not give others discretion over your money.
- Do not forget the tax consequences, if any.
- Do not incur debt or sign personal guarantees, for anyone.

DISCUSSION QUESTIONS

SOLUTIONS to the discussion questions can be found exclusively within the chapter. Once you have completed an initial reading of the chapter, go back and highlight the answers to these questions.

1. List six special circumstances outside a normal financial planning engagement.

2. How prevalent are dependents with special needs?

3. What are some of the important concerns of a parent or guardian regarding a dependent with special needs?

4. Where can parents or guardians obtain information about benefits for dependents with special needs?

5. What are some of the tasks that should be completed by a caregiver of a dependent with special needs?

6. What are the three types of special needs trusts?

7. Describe a third party special needs trust.

8. What are some of the requirements for a special needs trust under 42 U.S.C. Sec. 1396p(d)(4)(A)?

9. List several topics that might be included in a letter of intent.

10. List the recommendations for divorcing couples.

11. What are some of the common mistakes that are made in a divorce?

12. What are the recommendations for someone with a terminal illness?

13. What are the trends regarding married status in the United States?

14. Why is it important to understand federal and state law regarding the definition of marriage?

15. What are the four ways property can transfer at death?

16. How many months of income is the recommended amount to be accumulated as an emergency fund?

17. What are the general recommendations for someone who has a financial windfall, such as winning the lottery or received a substantial inheritance?

MULTIPLE-CHOICE PROBLEMS

A sample of multiple choice problems is provided below. Additional multiple choice problems are available at money-education.com by accessing the Student Practice Portal.

1. Which of the following is not an example of a special needs situation?
    a. Planning for Candice, who has a daughter who is autistic.
    b. Planning for the Smith family with three boys ages 2, 3 and 4.
    c. Planning for Sam and Pat, who live together but are not married.
    d. Planning for Joe the plumber, who just won the Powerball jackpot for $823 million.

2. Trusts are a general tool that are beneficial in many financial planning situations. Many trust benefits, such as asset protection and control, are appropriate considerations for a family with an individual with special needs. Which of the following is not generally associated with planning for an individual with special needs?
    a. Family trust or third party trust.
    b. A trust under 42 U.S.C. Sec. 1396p(d)(4)(A).
    c. A pooled trust.
    d. A special general advocate trust.

3. The statement, "Zayn is a very pleasant young man who is interested in animals and is generally skilled with computers" might be found in what document?
    a. Family trust or third party trust.
    b. A will.
    c. A letter of intent.
    d. A dossier.

4. Divorce is a very emotional time for those who are going through it and assistance from a financial adviser is generally helpful. Which of the following are common mistakes that are made by those going through divorce?
    a. Failure to obtain individual credit.
    b. Failure to establish the tax basis of assets that are separated.
    c. Failure to change beneficiary designations on retirement plans.
    d. All of the above are common mistakes.

5. Some studies have suggested that up to 70% of lottery winners lose their winnings within as short as a seven-year period. What are some of the reasons that might cause this or cause others who have come into a windfall to lose it?
    a. Some will invest in businesses without requisite knowledge or experience.
    b. Some will purchase assets that have high maintenance costs combined with other lavish spending.
    c. Some will fail to obtain professional advice on managing the money.
    d. All of the above.

> **Additional multiple choice problems are available at money-education.com by accessing the Student Practice Portal. Access requires registration of the title using the unique code at the front of the book.**

QUICK QUIZ EXPLANATIONS

Quick Quiz 17.1
1. True.
2. True.
3. False. A financial planner should be aware of financial issues, but also other issues, such as the emotional issues.
4. False. Generally, to qualify for federal benefits, a person should not have more than about $2,000. Additional funds for the benefit of the individual with special needs may be accumulated in a Special Needs Trust or ABLE account.

Quick Quiz 17.2
1. True.
2. True.
3. True.

Quick Quiz 17.3
1. False. There are a lot of documents that must be reviewed for a person going through a divorce and there are a lot of task that must be completed.
2. True.
3. True.

Quick Quiz 17.4
1. False. Traditional marriage has been decreasing not increasing over the last decade.
2. True.
3. False. Property may pass through probate or by way of law or contracts.

Quick Quiz 17.5
1. False. They may need more or less depending on their individual situation.
2. True.

18

DAVID AND AMY RUDOLPH CASE & CASE ANALYSIS PART 2

1. Describe an initial meeting and summarize data and draw conclusions for the lifecycle approach.
2. Prepare a comprehensive engagement letter.
3. Gather internal and external data and prepare financial statements.
4. Create the pie chart approach.
5. Prepare financial statement analysis using a ratio analysis approach.
6. Prepare each of the ratios and compare them to the benchmark.
7. Prepare the two-step, three panel, metrics approach with schedules.
8. Prepare the cash flow approach, the tax analysis approach, the strategic approach, and the present value of all goals approach.
9. Identify opportunities and challenges related to a client's cash inflows and outflows and make recommendations to assist the client in meeting their current needs and long-term financial goals.*
10. Make a presentation to the client using current and projected financial statements and ratios.
11. Prepare a closing engagement letter that includes the responsibility for implementation and monitoring.

Ties to CFP Certification Learning Objectives

INTRODUCTION

January 1, 20X3

The Rudolphs have returned to continue their financial planning engagement one year later with additional objectives to achieve in the current year. They have accomplished many of their financial planning objectives since their last meeting with their financial planner. Given that the Rudolphs are established clients, it is not necessary for the planner to use all of the financial planning approaches (including the complete life cycle approach, two-step/three-panel approach, and strategic approach) in order to arrive at current recommendations.

DAVID & AMY RUDOLPH CASE - INTERNAL DATA

The Family

David Rudolph (age 52, born on December 4th) is the owner of an office furniture company, DR Office Furniture Inc., (DRI) and is married to Amy Rudolph (age 36, born on February 14th) who is a self-employed real estate broker. David's salary is $283,250. The clients' net worth is approximately $3.9 million; of which $2.75 million consists of the value of his business, DRI, as per a recent valuation.

This marriage is both David and Amy's second marriage. David has a 31-year-old son, Trevor, from his first marriage to Joyce. Trevor is married and has one child, Trevor Jr. (age 3). Trevor is experiencing financial difficulty because he lost his job in the recent economic downturn and has been unsuccessful in his employment search. Trevor Jr. is now living with David and Amy because Trevor is constantly traveling seeking employment. David and Amy have become very close to Trevor Jr., who they have discovered is extremely intelligent. David and Amy are so taken with Trevor Jr. that they want to explore fully funding his college education, given their affection for him and his high potential for academic success.

Amy has a child from her former marriage, Madelyn (age 15, born on March 31st), who still resides with Amy's former husband, George (age 36, born on October 23rd), who is her legal guardian. Madelyn has become quiet the spender as she progresses into her teenage years, much to the concern of David and Amy. Madelyn has obtained her learner's permit to drive and will be licensed to drive when she becomes age 16.

David and Amy have one child of their own, Danny (age 2). Danny has been recently diagnosed as autistic. David and Amy are concerned for Danny's future and also that he may be permanently dependent upon them or other caretakers.

Amy was divorced from George three years ago and they continue to have a very contentious relationship. Amy is self-employed as a realtor and has Schedule C net income of $150,000 per year before self-employment tax or any deduction for any qualified or tax advantaged retirement plan.

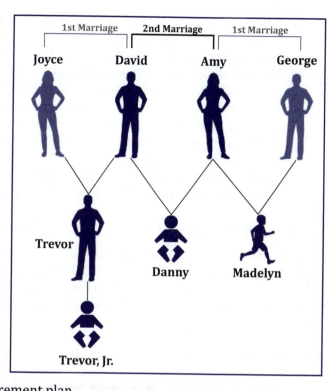

Personal and Financial Objectives (Achieved Within the Last Year)

1. The Rudolphs' risk management portfolio is now appropriate (see Insurance - with the exception of long-term care insurance).
2. The Rudolphs refinanced their lake house.
3. The Rudolphs paid off their boat loan.
4. The Rudolphs paid credit cards down to $5,000.
5. The Rudolphs had an attorney prepare basic estate planning documents (durable power of attorneys for healthcare, advance medical directives, and wills).

Personal and Financial Objectives (Current)

1. The Rudolphs want to determine the amount of money to fully fund Trevor Jr.'s college education today using a 529 Savings Plan. The Rudolphs realize that as grandparents to Trevor Jr., they can reclaim amounts in the education savings plan should they need the funds in the future. They are planning for Madelyn's education, but not Danny's education. They have changed the beneficiary to Madelyn on the 529 Savings Plan originally established for Danny, and combined the two accounts.
2. David has decided to immediately sell 32.7273 percent of his 75 percent interest in DRI for $900,000 cash with a put option to sell the remainder of his interest in 10 years for $1,850,000 increased by three percent per year. This will leave David with a controlling interest of 50.46 percent (75 x 0.67273). David and Amy have just recently inherited a piece of artwork that they will sell to fund the taxes owed on the current sale of DRI stock.

3. David still has a goal to retire at age 62. Capital needs analysis is required (annuity model and capital preservation model) to know how much funding is needed. Any funding deficit of David's retirement needs will create the need for current annual year-end funding.
4. The Rudolphs want recommendations to revise their estate planning to avoid probate and to provide for Madelyn and Danny in the event of David and Amy's death.
5. The Rudolphs want to consider the advantages and disadvantages of each possible entity form that Amy might use for her business. They were audited last year and the CPA and IRS agent told them that tax returns with Schedule C income get audited more than tax returns with income from flow-through entities.
6. The Rudolphs want a full review of their investment portfolio.
7. David and Amy want to consider purchasing long-term care insurance.

Updated Summary of Initial Data Collected - Life Cycle Approach

Using the approaches learned in Chapter 3, the financial planner will initially prepare the life cycle characteristics approach. This approach seeks to efficiently establish which phase or phases of the life cycle the client is in and to then deduce from that assessment the likely client goals and risks. The life cycle approach, while easy and efficient, lacks sufficient detail to permit the financial planner to prepare a complete financial plan.

Based on recent client communications, the information collected is as follows:

Updated Summary of Data Collected - Life Cycle Approach	
Ages	• David (age 52) • Amy (age 36)
Marital Status	• Married (MFJ income tax filing status)
Children & Grandchildren	• Trevor (age 31) - From David's previous marriage, with one child Trevor Jr. (age 3) - Trevor is unemployed • Madelyn (age 15) - From Amy's previous marriage; lives with George (former husband) - learner's permit to drive; spending issue • Danny - Child of David and Amy (age 2) - Special Needs
Net Worth	• Approximately $3.8 million (dependent on DRI valuation)
Income	• Amy $150,000 self-employed (Schedule C) - proprietorship • David owner of DRI / employee salary $283,250
Self-Employed	• Amy is self-employed and has no employees • David is the owner / employee of a C corporation (DRI) with 31 employees

The financial planner has chosen to update the summary of data collected, but preliminary conclusions are not necessary for an established client.

EXTERNAL DATA

Economic Information

- The Rudolphs expect salary increases of 2.5 percent annually in keeping with inflation.
- Inflation is expected to average 2.5 percent annually for the foreseeable future.
- Education inflation is expected to be five percent annually.
- Real GDP has been 2.75 percent and is expected to continue to be 2.75 percent for the next several years.
- It is expected that the S&P 500 will return approximately nine percent this year and annually for the foreseeable future.
- T-bills are considered the appropriate proxy for the risk-free rate of return and are currently earning 3.5 percent.
- The Rudolphs expect that Trevor Jr. and Madelyn will spend $20,000 a year in today's dollars for four years of college education beginning at age 18. They expect to earn 8 percent annually in the 529 Savings Plan that they plan to implement for Trevor Jr.
- The Rudolphs have the same risk tolerance (as reflected in Part 1) and want to use 8 percent as their expected portfolio rate of return.

Bank Lending Rates

- 15-year mortgage is 4.75 percent.
- 30-year mortgage is 5.0 percent.
- Any closing costs associated with refinance are an additional three percent of the amount mortgaged.
- Secured personal loan is 8.0 percent.
- Credit card rates are 18 percent.

Exhibit 18.1 | Economic Outlook - Investments

	Return	Standard Deviation
Small Company Stocks	12%	18%
Large Company Stocks (Actively Managed)	10%	16%
S&P 500	9%	14%
Corporate Bonds	6%	5%
Long-term Treasury Bonds	6%	4%
T-bills	3.5%	2%

The internal data on the Rudolphs are all updated for the client's current circumstances and include:

- Insurance information (life, health, long-term disability, long-term care, property and liability, automobile, and boat)
- Financial statements (balance sheets for 1/1/20X2 and 1/1/20X3 and projected income statement for 20X3)
- Information related to investment assets
- Information related to personal use assets
- Other financial profile data, including income tax, savings, retirement, and estate information

Insurance Information

Life Insurance

	Policy 1	Policy 2	Policy 3
Insured	David Rudolph	David Rudolph	Amy Rudolph
Face Amount	$2,500,000	2 x Salary = $566,500	$250,000
Type	Term Policy 30 Year Level Term	Group Term - Employer Provided	Term Policy Ten Year Level Term
Cash Value	$0	$0	$0
Annual Premium	$10,000	$700	$500
Beneficiary	Amy/Contingent Beneficiary is Danny	Amy/Contingent Beneficiary is Danny	Madelyn/Contingent Beneficiary is David
Owner	David Rudolph	David Rudolph	Amy Rudolph

Health Insurance

David currently has an indemnity group health and major medical hospitalization plan through his company. Amy, David, Danny, and Madelyn are currently covered by his health insurance plan. DRI pays the entire premium for the health insurance policy. Madelyn is covered under both David and George's health insurance plans. David's plan has the following characteristics:

- $500 per individual deductible
- $1,000 total family deductible
- 80% coinsurance clause for major medical
- $3,000 annual family maximum out-of-pocket limit

Long-Term Disability Insurance

Disability Policies	David's Policy	Amy's Policy
Type	Own Occupation	Own Occupation
Insured	David	Amy
Guaranteed Renewable	Yes	Yes ·
Benefit	60% of Gross Pay	60% of Gross Pay
Premium Paid By	Employer	Amy
Residual Benefits Clause	Yes	Yes
Elimination Period	90 Days	90 Days
Annual Premium	$2,000	$2,000

Long-Term Care Insurance

Neither David nor Amy have long-term care insurance, but want to consider it now.

Property and Liability Insurance

Homeowners Insurance

	Personal Residence	Lake House
Type	HO3 with endorsements	HO3 with endorsements
Dwelling	$800,000	$450,000
Other Structures	$80,000	$45,000
Personal Property	$400,000	$100,000
Personal Liability	$100,000	$100,000
Medical Payments	$10,000	$10,000
Deductible	$2,000	$2,000
Co-Insurance %	80 / 20	80 / 20
Annual Premium	$3,000	$3,800

There is no flood insurance on the personal residence or the lake house.

Note that the HO3 policies were endorsed, the coverage was reduced for the personal residence, increased for the lake house, and deductibles were raised on both policies in the last year.

Auto Insurance

	Auto #1 David's Car	Auto # 2 Amy's Car
Type	PAP	PAP
Liability (Bodily Injury)	$100,000/$300,000/$50,000	$100,000/$300,000/$50,000
Medical Payments	$10,000	$10,000
Uninsured Motorist	$100,000/$300,000	$100,000/$300,000
Collision Deductible	$2,000	$2,000
Comprehensive Deductible	$2,000	$2,000
Annual Premium	$750	$1,000

Boat Insurance

Boat	
Type	Personal Boat
Personal Property	$70,000
Personal Liability	$100,000/$300,000/$50,000
Deductible	$2,000
Annual Premium	$1,000

Liability Insurance

The Rudolphs own a personal liability insurance policy (PLUP) with $3 million of coverage at an annual cost of $1,350.

Exhibit 18.2 | Summary of Risk Management Data

	Coverage	Benchmark	Comments / Recommendations
Life Insurance			
Policy 1 - David	$2,500,000	$2,750,000	Adequate coverage Ownership issue for estate tax Beneficiary Changed
Policy 2 - David	$566,500		Group Term - adequate Changed beneficiary
Policy 3 - Amy	$250,000	$1,500,000	Depends on risk tolerance and priorities Changed owner Consider trust for Madelyn
Health Insurance	Yes	Adequate	Adequate coverage DRI provided
Disability Insurance			
David	60% Gross Pay / Guaranteed Renewable	60 - 70%	Adequate coverage DRI provided - Taxable
Amy	60% Gross Pay / Guaranteed Renewable	60 - 70%	Added disability insurance adequate
Long-Term Care Insurance	None	36-60 months of savings	Currently considering
Property & Liability Insurance			
Personal Residence	$800,000	≤ FMV	Reduced coverage to FMV* Endorsed HO3
Lake House	$450,000	≤ FMV	Raised coverage to FMV* Endorsed HO3
Automobile # 1 and # 2	100 / 300	100 / 300	Adequate coverage Raised deductibles
Boat	100 / 300	≤ FMV	Purchased adequate coverage
Liability Insurance	$3 million	$1 - 4 million	Purchased adequate coverage

*Assumes the replacement cost of the dwelling is equal to the fair market value of the property

Financial Statements

Balance sheets (Statement of Financial Position) for the year beginning (1/1/20X2) and year end (12/31/20X2) are presented. In addition, an income statement (Statement of Income and Expenses) is presented the year ending 12/31/20X2 as adjusted and projected for next year (20X3). A reconciliation of the decline in net worth from 1/1/20X2 to 1/1/20X3 is provided.

Exhibit 18.3 | Financial Statements: Statement of Financial Position (Previous Year)

Statement of Financial Position
David and Amy Rudolph
Balance Sheet as of 1/1/20X2

Assets[1]			Liabilities and Net Worth		
Current Assets			**Current Liabilities[2]**		
JT Cash & Checking	$25,000		W Credit Cards	$15,000	
JT Money Market	$270,000		**Total Current Liabilities**		$15,000
Total Current Assets		$295,000			
Investment Assets			**Long-Term Liabilities[2]**		
H DR Office Furniture, Inc[3]	$3,325,000		JT Principal Residence	$1,169,619	
H Brokerage Account 1	$500,000		H Lake House	$148,038	
H Education Accounts[4](529)	$46,000		H Boat	$70,276	
H 401(k) Plan	$50,000		**Total Long-Term Liabilities**		$1,387,933
W Traditional IRA	$15,000				
W Roth IRA	$20,000				
Total Investment Assets		$3,956,000	**Total Liabilities**		$1,402,933
Personal Use Assets					
JT Principal Residence	$800,000				
H Lake House	$450,000				
JT Furniture, Clothing	$100,000		**Total Net Worth**		$4,313,067
H Car # 1	$25,000				
W Car # 2	$35,000				
H Boat	$55,000				
Total Personal Use Assets		$1,465,000			
Total Assets		$5,716,000	**Total Liabilities & Net Worth**		$5,716,000

1. Assets are stated at fair market value.
2. Liabilities are stated at principal only as of January 1, 20X2 before January 20X2 payments.
3. This value represents David's 75% interest and the value is based on his estimate.
4. Section 529 Savings Plans for Madelyn (current balance $25,760) and Danny (current balance $20,240). David currently saves $3,000 per year into each of these accounts ($6,000 total). See portfolio.

Title Designations:
H = Husband (Sole Owner)
W = Wife (Sole Owner)
JT = Joint Tenancy with Survivorship Rights

Exhibit 18.4 | Financial Statements: Statement of Financial Position (Current Year)

Statement of Financial Position David and Amy Rudolph Balance Sheet as of 12/31/20X2 (and 1/1/20X3)					
Assets[1]			**Liabilities and Net Worth**		
Current Assets			**Current Liabilities**[2]		
JT	Cash & Checking	$20,000	W Credit Cards	$5,000	
JT	Money Market	$170,000	**Total Current Liabilities**		$5,000
Total Current Assets		$190,000			
Investment Assets			**Long-Term Liabilities**[2]		
H	DR Office Furniture, Inc[3]	$2,750,000	JT Principal Residence	$1,153,009	
H	Brokerage Account 1	$600,000	H Lake House	$145,335	
H	Education Account 1[4](529)	$50,000	H Boat	$0	
H	David's 401(k) Plan	$65,076	**Total Long-Term Liabilities**		$1,298,344
W	Traditional IRA	$12,000			
W	Roth IRA	$16,280			
W	Amy 401(k) Plan	$33,000			
Total Investment Assets		$3,526,356	**Total Liabilities**		$1,303,344
Personal Use Assets					
JT	Principal Residence	$800,000			
H	Lake House	$450,000			
JT	Furniture, Clothing	$100,000	**Total Net Worth**		$3,878,012
H	Car # 1	$25,000			
W	Car # 2	$35,000			
H	Boat	$55,000			
Total Personal Use Assets		$1,465,000			
Total Assets		$5,181,356	**Total Liabilities & Net Worth**		$5,181,356

1. Assets are stated at fair market value.
2. Liabilities are stated at principal only as of January 1, 20X3 before January 20X3 payments.
3. This value represents David's 75% interest and the value is based on a professional appraisal of $3,666,667 for the entire company.
4. This is for Madelyn. David currently saves $6,000 per year into this account (see portfolio).

Title Designations:

H = Husband (Sole Owner)
W = Wife (Sole Owner)
JT = Joint Tenancy with Survivorship Rights

Exhibit 18.5 | Financial Statements: Income Statement
(Adjusted for Recommendations Made in 20X2 and Expected for 20X3)

Statement of Income and Expenses
David and Amy Rudolph
Statement of Income and Expenses
Expected (Approximate) For This Year (20X3)

			Totals
Cash Inflows			
David's Salary	$283,250		
Amy's Salary	$150,000		
Total Cash Inflows			$433,250
Cash Outflows			
Savings			
Money Market	$0		
401(k) Plan David	$23,000		
401(k) Plan Amy	$17,500		
Education (529 Plan)	$6,000		
Total Savings			$46,500
Taxes			
Federal Income Taxes Withheld	$63,800		
State Income Taxes Withheld	$16,417		
David's Social Security Taxes*	$13,710		
Amy's Social Security Taxes & Estimated Payments*	$21,195		
Property Tax Principal Residence	$4,000	ND	
Property Tax Vacation Home	$4,000	ND	
Total Taxes			$123,122
Debt Payments (Principal & Interest)			
Principal Residence	$86,335	ND	
Lake House	$14,232	ND	
Boat	$0		
Credit Cards	$10,000	ND	
Total Debt Payments			$110,567
Living Expenses			
Utilities Principal Residence	$5,000	ND	
Lake House Expenses (net of rental income of $5,000)	$15,000	ND	
Gasoline for Autos	$5,000	ND	
Lawn Service	$2,000	ND	
Entertainment	$15,000		
Vacations	$25,000		
Church Donations	$10,000	ND	
Clothing	$18,000	ND	
Auto Maintenance	$2,000	ND	
Satellite TV	$1,800	ND	
Food	$8,000	ND	
Miscellaneous	$10,000	ND	
Total Living Expenses			$116,800
Insurance Payments			
HO Insurance Principal Residence	$3,000	ND	
HO Insurance Lake House	$3,800	ND	
Boat Insurance	$1,000	ND	
Auto Insurance	$1,750	ND	
Disability Insurance Amy	$2,000	ND	
PLUP	$1,350	ND	
Life Insurance #1	$10,000	ND	
Life Insurance #3	$500	ND	
Total Insurance Payments			$23,400
Total Cash Outflows			$420,389
Net Discretionary Cash Flows			$12,861

* Social Security taxes are calculated using 2021 rates.   ND = Non-discretionary cash flow

Change in Net Worth - Reconciliation (From 1/20X2 to 1/20X3)

Change in Net Worth	
$4,313,067	Before Recommendations
$3,878,012	After Recommendations
($435,055)	Net Reduction (decline)
Reconciliation	
($575,000)	DRI Valuation Decline Adjustment
($105,000)	Cash and Cash Equivalents Adjustment
$145,356	Other Investments Increases
$99,589	Change in Liabilities Reduction
($435,055)	Reconciled Decline in Net Worth

Investment Assets

General Information

- The Rudolphs have an overall required rate of return of eight percent on their overall portfolio and eight percent for the 529 Savings Plan for Trevor Jr.
- They have a moderate risk tolerance.
- David expects to be able to sell his interest in DRI to partially fund his retirement.
- Their emergency fund is primarily invested in a taxable money market account earning 0.75 percent annually.

DR Office Furniture, Inc. (DRI)

David started working for DR Office Furniture, Inc. over 20 years ago when he inherited the business from his father. The fair market value of DRI at the time of David's inheritance was $1 million (and the tax law at that time created a basis for David that was equal to the fair market value at the date of his father's death). Today, it is one of the largest office furniture companies in the southeast.

David previously sold 25 percent of the equity in his company to his top employees and value of the business is expected to grow at three percent each year. Paul Carter, Brian Conner, and Sally Walker (the top employees) have agreed to buy the business in 10 years. David insists that this sale will provide an adequate capital balance upon which to retire. DR Office Furniture, Inc. has traditionally offered employees health insurance, group term life insurance, a 401(k) plan with a Roth component, and an integrated profit sharing plan. The profit sharing plan requires age 21 and one year of service for participation.

Originally, when attempting to value his business, David's accountant advised him to use a multiple of revenue approach. David's accountant suggested using a multiple of 2.5 times revenue to value the business. David had estimated the value of the business based on revenues for 20X1 for his initial valuation. An expert appraiser was recently hired and the company was valued at $3,666,667. David's interest is 75 percent. The Rudolphs' balance sheet has been updated accordingly.

Brokerage Account 1

Immediately after his meeting with the financial planner last year, David decided to sell all of his mutual funds and invest the proceeds into four stocks. The brokerage account 1 consists of the stocks indicated below. Any interest and dividends earned on investment are reflected in the account balance and are not counted or separately stated in the income statement. The investment portfolio is illustrated at the beginning of the year and at the end of the year.

Exhibit 18.6 | Investment Portfolio (Brokerage Account 1) - Stocks as of 1/1/20X2

									Stocks		
Name	Shares	Cost per Share	FMV per Share	Beta	P/E Ratio	Div. Yield	Annual Div.	Standard Deviation	Expected Return	Total FMV
A	500	$50	$35	0.79	5	2.4%	$0.84*	0.12	8%	$17,500
B	1,000	$80	$99	0.97	15	3.2%*	$3.17	0.14	10%	$99,000
C	500	$100	$10	1.5	9	0.1%	$0	0.16	9%	$5,000
D	7,570	$10	$50	1.2	22	0.4%	$0.20	0.19	12.3%	$378,500
									Totals	$500,000

* The dividend is expected to grow at 6% per year.

Exhibit 18.7 | Investment Portfolio (Brokerage Account 1) - Stocks as of 1/1/20X3

									Stocks		
Name	Shares	Cost per Share	FMV per Share	Beta	P/E Ratio	Div. Yield	Annual Div.	Standard Deviation	Expected Return	Total FMV
A	500	$50	$46	0.79	5	2.4%	$0.84*	0.12	8%	$23,000
B	1,000	$80	$117.70	0.97	15	3.2%*	$3.17	0.14	10%	$117,700
C	500	$100	$10.20	1.5	9	0.1%	$0	0.16	9%	$5,100
D	7,570	$10	$60	1.2	22	0.4%	$0.20	0.19	12.3%	$454,200
									Totals	$600,000

* The dividend is expected to grow at 6% per year.

Education Account 1 (529 Plan)

The contributions to this account are invested in a diversified portfolio of mutual funds based on the age of the beneficiary. David selected an overall investment strategy that resulted in "moderate risk" investments. This savings account is for Madelyn and any remaining funds will be used for Trevor, Jr. by changing the beneficiary on the account to Trevor, Jr. when Madelyn finishes college.

DRI 401(k) Plan with Roth Account Option

After his financial planning meeting last year, David reallocated 100 percent of this account from cash to a balanced mutual fund consisting of 50 percent equities and 50 percent fixed income investments. His expected return of eight percent is equal to the required rate of return. David made his first contribution to this account in 20X1.

Traditional IRA

The Traditional IRA is invested in a series of zero coupon bonds. The investment returns in this account over the past six years have been:

Year	Returns
1	6.50%
2	4.75%
3	- 3.25%
4	- 2.5%
5	5.25%
6	9.09%

David is uncertain what his compound rate of return has been and whether these bonds are appropriate for his goals.

Roth IRA

The Roth IRA is currently invested in a tax-free municipal bond mutual fund, earning 1.75 percent per year. The income is reinvested and not reflected on the income statement.

Amy's 401(k) Plan

Amy has 60 percent of her contributions invested in an equity index mutual fund and 40 percent of her contributions invested in a corporate bond mutual fund.

Personal Use Assets

Personal Residence

The Rudolphs purchased their personal residence for $1,500,000 three years ago (they have made exactly 36 payments as of January 1, 20X3). Their mortgage payment is $7,195 per month. They borrowed $1,200,000 over 30 years at six percent. They were considering refinancing the house but decided not to refinance when the appraised value came in at only $800,000 due to market conditions. They pay their homeowners insurance premiums and property taxes separately from their mortgage. The Rudolphs requested a reassessment of their property taxes, which lowered to $4,000 annually.

Lake House

The lake house was formerly David's personal residence prior to moving to the current primary residence. He purchased the lake house for $250,000, by putting down 20 percent and borrowing the rest at seven percent for 30 years. His payment was $15,967 per year. He refinanced in 20X2 at 4.75 percent for 15 years. The total amount refinanced was $152,479.14, with payments of $1,186.03 per month, and he has made exactly 12 payments as of January 1, 20X3. The lake house is rented for 14 days per year to one of David's key customers for $5,000. The $5,000 is used against expenses and is included in the income statement. The property taxes are $4,000 a year and homeowners insurance is $3,800 per year. Both taxes and insurance are paid separately.

Boat

The Rudolphs purchased their boat for $125,000 five years ago. It is a 54' Hatterus with twin inboard motors. Their boat payment was $1,267 per month. They borrowed $100,000 over 10 years at nine percent on a signature loan to finance the purchase of the boat. The Rudolphs have paid off this loan and have also purchased a boat insurance policy at a cost of $1,000 per year.

Other Financial Profile Information

Income Tax Information

The Rudolphs are in the higher marginal income tax brackets for federal income tax purposes and their state income tax rate is four percent. Capital gains are taxed at a maximum of 20 percent at the federal level and four percent at the state level.

David's Social Security Tax Withholding*		
HI	($283,250-$142,800) x 0.0145 =	$2,036.53
Social Security Retirement and HI	$142,800 x 0.0765 =	$10,924.20
	$83,250 x 0.009 =	$749.25
	Total	$13,709.98

Also see Self-Employment Tax Analysis

Savings and Retirement Information[1]

David has a safe harbor 401(k) plan through his company (DRI). He defers a total of $23,000 each year, including a catch-up contribution. David has not elected Roth contributions, therefore, his contributions are made pretax. His company matches dollar for dollar on the first three percent of salary and then $0.50 on the dollar on the next two percent of salary to a maximum contribution of four percent of his covered compensation and subject to the plan's maximum compensation limit.[2] David also has an integrated profit sharing plan through his company (DRI). The company adds the amount necessary to the profit sharing plan to have a total contribution of $57,500, including David's $23,000 deferral (with catch-up) and the company match. Amy is self-employed and is currently contributing $17,500 to a 401(k) retirement plan on a pre-tax basis.

The Rudolphs define adequate retirement income as 80 percent of pre-retirement income. They both plan to live until age 95 after retiring at David's age 62.

David recently received a notice from Social Security that his full normal age retirement benefit in today's dollars would be $2,200 per month. Normal age retirement for David is 67, so he will receive 70 percent of those benefits at age 62. For capital needs analysis, they want the financial planner to consider David's age only and ignore the age disparity between the spouses.

Estate Information

The Rudolphs have wills, durable power of attorneys for healthcare, and advance medical directives. However, they have serious concerns about avoiding probate and providing for both Madelyn and Danny.

---

1. Note: David could have contributed a higher amount but chose to only contribute a total of $23,000.
2. The DRI 401(k) plan limits plan compensation to a maximum of $245,000 for matching and profit sharing contributions.

FINANCIAL STATEMENT ANALYSIS - RATIO ANALYSIS APPROACH

Introduction

As discussed in Chapter 3, the financial statement analysis - ratio analysis approach utilizes ratios to gain insight into the client's financial situation. The approach assesses:

1. the client's ability to pay short-term obligations and fund an emergency,
2. the client's ability to manage debt,
3. whether the client is committed financially to all of his goals,
4. the progress of the client in achieving the goal of financial security based on the client's age and income, and
5. how well the investment assets have performed to benchmarks.

The ratios should be compared to appropriate benchmarks to provide a more meaningful analysis.

Exhibit 18.8 | Ratio Analysis Ratio Analysis

Liquidity Ratios Based on 20X3 Financial Statements				
Ratio	**Formula**		**Comment**	**Benchmark**
Emergency Fund Ratio*	Cash & Cash Equivalents / Monthly Non-Discretionary Cash Flows	$\frac{\$190,000}{\$18,231} = 10.4$	Very Strong	3 - 6:1
Current Ratio	Cash & Cash Equivalents / Current Liabilities	$\frac{\$190,000}{\$5,000} = 38:1$	Very Strong	0.5:1

Monthly non-discretionary cash flows are $18,231 as indicated on the Statement of Income and Expenses - ND ($218,767 ÷ 12).

Debt Ratios Based on 20X3 Financial Statements				
Housing Ratio 1 (HR 1) (Includes both homes.)	Housing Costs / Gross Pay	$\frac{\$115,367}{\$433,250} = 26.6\%$	Okay	$\leq 28\%$
Housing Ratio 2 (HR 2) (Includes both homes.)	Housing Costs + Other Debt Payments / Gross Pay	$\frac{\$125,367}{\$433,250} = 28.9\%$	Good	$\leq 36\%$
Debt-to-Total Assets	Total Debt / Total Assets	$\frac{\$1,303,344}{\$5,181,356} = 25.15\%$	Very Strong	Age Dependent
Net Worth-to-Total Assets	Net Worth / Total Assets	$\frac{\$3,878,012}{\$5,181,356} = 74.84\%$	Very Strong	Age Dependent

Ratios for Financial Security Goals Based on 20X3 Financial Statements				
Savings Rate (Overall)	Savings + Employer Match / Gross Pay	$\frac{\$81,000}{\$433,250} = 18.7\%$	Very Strong	Goal Driven At Least 10-13%
Savings Rate (Retirement)	Employee Contributions + Employer Contributions / Gross Pay	$\frac{\$75,000}{\$433,250} = 17.31\%$	Very Strong	10 - 13%
Investment Assets-to-Gross Pay (Does not include education savings.)	Investment Assets + Cash & Cash Equivalents / Gross Pay	$\frac{\$3,476,356 + \$190,000}{\$433,250} = 8.5:1$	Very Strong	Approx. 4:1 at Age 50

Performance Ratios Based on 20X2 and 20X3 Financial Statements				
Return on Investments =	$\dfrac{I_1 - (I_0 + Savings)}{I_0}$	= -12.8% (See calculation below)	Very Poor	8-10%
Return on Assets =	$\dfrac{A_1 - (A_0 + Savings)}{A_0}$	= -10.7% (See calculation below)	Very Poor**	2-4%
Return on Net Worth =	$\dfrac{NW_1 - (NW_0 + Savings)}{NW_0}$	= -11.9% (See calculation below)	Very Poor**	The higher the better. This ratio is likely to become smaller as the client's net worth increases.

** The substantial change in the value of DRI because of the expert appraisal has resulted in a
negative return on total assets and a negative return on net worth.

Performance Ratios Calculations***	
Return on Investments = (Excludes cash and cash equivalents)	$\dfrac{\$3,526,356 - (\$3,956,000 + \$46,500 + \$34,500)}{\$3,956,000} = -12.9\%$
Return on Assets =	$\dfrac{\$5,181,356 - (\$5,716,000 + \$46,500 + \$34,500)}{\$5,716,000} = -10.8\%$
Return on Net Worth =	$\dfrac{\$3,878,012 - (\$4,313,067 + \$46,500 + \$34,500)}{\$4,313,067} = -11.9\%$

*** $34,500 of savings is derived from the employer match of 4% of $245,000 (compensation limit for the DRI Plan) which equals $9,800 plus $24,700 from the profit sharing plan. (See Chapter 10, Schedule C Part 2.)

Observations

The short-term liquidity and ability to pay ratios are excellent. The housing and debt ratios are good. The Rudolphs' savings rate is excellent (18.7 percent) as is the investment assets-to-gross pay ratio (8.5:1) for his age.

Once again, the issue is the credibility of the valuation of DRI. David says it grows in value at an annual rate of three percent. This valuation should be documented by net after-tax cash flows growing year over year by at least three percent.

The investment performance ratios are very poor, but are heavily skewed because of the change in the balance sheet value of DRI and the decline in the value of the principal residence. The performance ratios need to be compared to market returns for the year. However, investment returns are best measured over a longer time period (five years) and then compared to market benchmarks.

The performance ratios suggest the financial planner should take a much closer look at the investment portfolios and the valuation of DRI.

Liquidity and Debt Ratios 1/1/20X3 - Schedule A

	Actual	Metric	Comments
Emergency Fund	10.4 x	3 - 6 month	More than adequate.
Housing Ratio:			
1 - Combined	26.6%	≤ 28%	These are high at age 51 / 35 but do not exceed the metric
2 - Combined	28.9%	≤ 36%	
Evaluation of Debt			On personal residence there continues to be a loan-to-value issue.

Observations

The Rudolphs' emergency fund is substantial at 10.4 times monthly non-discretionary cash flows. The housing ratios are within the metric limits.

Informational Inputs		
Non-Discretionary Cash Flows*	$18,230.58 per month $218,767 annually	Income Statement
Cash and Cash Equivalents	$190,000	Balance Sheet
Principal Residence (PR)**	P&I & T&I = $93,335	Income Statement
Lake House (LH)***	P&I & T&I = $22,032	Income Statement
Other Debt Payments (Boat)	$5,000	Income Statement
Credit Card Payments	$433,250	Income Statement
Gross Pay	$18,230.58 per month $218,767 annually	Income Statement

*Monthly non-discretionary cash flows are $18,230 as indicated on the Statement of Income and Expenses - ND ($218,767 ÷ 12).
**$86,335 + $4,000 + $3,000 = $93,335
***$14,232 + $4,000 + $3,800 = $22,032

Long-Term Savings and Investments - Schedule B

To achieve financial security (retirement) requires persistent savings of 10 to 13 percent of gross pay and investment assets appropriate for the age of the client and the client's gross pay. Many clients have multiple goals such as retirement, education funding, lump-sum expenditures, and legacy aspirations. The more goals a client has, the greater the need for an increased savings rate.

Schedule B - Part 1

	Actual	Metric	Comments
Retirement Security Goal			
Overall Savings Rate	18.7%	At least 10% - 13% of gross pay	Excellent
Retirement Savings Rate	17.3%	10% - 13% of gross pay	The total savings rate is consistent with the retirement goal.
Investment Assets as % of Gross Pay (Excludes education savings)	8.5 x	8 x	They currently exceed the necessary investment assets for retirement (for their age). Education assets are excluded. Valuation of DRI remains critical.
Educational Funding	$6,000 per year	$6,000 per year	Adequate
Lump-Sum Goals	None	None	Okay
Estate Planning	Documents	Documents	Estate planning issues remain: (1) avoid probate, and (2) provide for minors.

Schedule B - Part 2

David			
	401(k) Plan (EE) Deferral	$23,000	(including Over 50 Catch-Up)
	ER Match	$9,800	
	Profit Sharing (ER)	$24,700	
	David Total	**$57,500**	(See Retirement Information)
	Education	$6,000	
Amy	401(k) Plan (EE) Deferral	$17,500	
	Combined Total	**$81,000**	

$$\text{New Savings Rate:} \quad \frac{\$81,000}{\$433,250} = 18.7\% \quad \text{Excellent}$$

Observations

The Rudolphs have an excellent savings rate of 18.7 percent [($75,000 + $6,000) ÷ $433,250)] overall and have investment assets equal to 8.5 x their gross pay which, using David's age, the benchmark or metric is 8 x. The only problem is the ownership of the business. DRI makes up 78 percent of the investment assets. There is a serious issue regarding valuation and concern over whether the employees will be willing and able to buy the business in ten years at David's retirement. This issue is central to the overall plan and alternatives need to be addressed.

IMMEDIATE AND LONG-TERM OBJECTIVES AND ANALYSIS

Personal and Financial Objectives (Current)

1. The Rudolphs want to determine the amount of money to fully fund Trevor Jr.'s college education today using a 529 Savings Plan. The Rudolphs realize that as grandparents to Trevor Jr., they can reclaim amounts in the education savings plan should they need the funds in the future.
2. David has decided to currently sell 32.7273 percent of his 75 percent interest in DRI for $900,000 cash with a put option to sell the remainder of his interest in 10 years for $1,850,000 increased by three percent per year. David and Amy have recently inherited a piece of artwork that they will sell to fund the taxes owed on the current sale of DRI stock. The artwork is not listed on the balance sheet.
3. David still has a goal to retire at age 62. Capital needs analysis is required (annuity model, capital preservation model, and purchasing power preservation model) to know how much funding is needed. Any funding deficit of David's retirement needs will create the need for current annual year-end funding.
4. The Rudolphs want recommendations to revise their estate planning to avoid probate and to provide for Madelyn and Danny in the event of David and Amy's demise.
5. The Rudolphs want to consider the advantages and disadvantages of each possible entity form that Amy might use for her business. They were audited last year and the CPA and IRS agent told them that Schedule C income tax returns get audited more than other entity forms.
6. The Rudolphs want a full review of their investment portfolio.
7. David and Amy want to consider purchasing long-term care insurance.
8. The Rudolphs plan to name a special needs trust for Danny as the contingent beneficiary of Life Insurance Policy 1. Amy's will, if she survives David, will also provide for funding the special needs trust for Danny.

Objective 1: Education Funding - 529 Savings Plan 2 for Trevor Jr.

- Objective: The Rudolphs want to determine the amount of money to fully fund Trevor Jr.'s college education today using a 529 Savings Plan.
- The planner needs to provide an analysis of the funding option required for the 529 Savings Plan for Trevor Jr.

Risk Tolerance:

- The Rudolphs have a moderate risk tolerance but expect to earn eight percent in this particular investment account.

Trevor 529 Savings Plan Funding

Informational Inputs	
Present Value of Education in Today's Dollars	$20,000
Expected Education Inflation Rate	5%
Expected Years of College Education	4 years
Beginning Year of College Education (age 18)	15 years from now
Investment Portfolio Expected Return	8%

Calculation Method: Traditional Method - in real dollars

Step 1: Determine the present value of the cost of four years of college education at age 18 using real dollars with the $20,000 payment being made at the beginning of each year of Trevor Jr.'s college.

10BII Keystrokes	12C Keystrokes
[ORANGE] [BEG/END]	[g] [BEG]
4 [N]	4 [n]
1.08 [÷] 1.05 – 1 x 100 = [I/YR]	1.08 [ENTER] 1.05 [÷] 1 [-] 100 [x] [i]
20,000 [PMT]$_{AD}$	20,000 [PMT]$_{AD}$
0 [FV]	0 [FV]
[PV]	[PV]
Answer: <76,727.97>	Answer: <76,727.97>

Step 2: Determine the present value today (at Trevor Jr.'s age 3) using real dollars, of the lump-sum amount needed to deposit now to fully fund Trevor Jr.'s education.

10BII Keystrokes	12C Keystrokes
15 [N]	15 [n]
1.08 [÷] 1.05 – 1 x 100 = [I/YR]	1.08 [ENTER] 1.05 [÷] 1 [-] 100 [x] [i]
0 [PMT]	0 [PMT]
76,727.97 [FV]	76,727.97 [FV]
[PV]	[PV]
Answer: <50,284.81>	Answer: <50,284.81>

Given the funding requirement of $50,284.81 today to fully fund Trevor Jr.'s college education, David and Amy could each contribute half ($25,142.41) to the 529 Plan. The $25,142.41 contribution each is well below the annual gift exclusion limit for 529 Savings Plans when front loading is elected (front loading allows the donor treat the gift as if it were made ratably over a five year period for gift tax purposes).

Objective 2: Sale of DRI

- Objective: David has decided to currently sell 32.7273 percent of his 75 percent interest in DRI for $900,000 cash with a put option to sell the remainder of his interest in 10 years for $1,850,000 increased by three percent per year. David and Amy have inherited a piece of artwork that they will sell to fund the taxes owed on the current sale of DRI stock.
- The planner needs to provide an analysis of the impact of the sale of DRI.

If David sells 32.7273 percent of his current 75 percent interest in DRI to other executives for $900,000 cash, then he can retain $1,850,000 of stock representing 50.4545 percent ownership (a controlling interest). Then David can receive a put option to put 50.4545 percent of DRI at $1,850,000 (at his age 62) plus a three percent inflationary increase per year.

Tax Implications of the Sale of DRI Stock

Amount of Sale	$900,000	
Less Basis in Stock	$245,454	24.54% of whole (32.7273% of 75% interest)
Gain	**$654,546**	from sale of DRI (subject to capital gains taxation)
Estimated Federal Capital Gains Tax (20%)*	$130,909	($654,546 x 0.20)
Estimated State Capital Gains Tax (4%)	$26,182	($654,546 x 0.04)
Tax on Sale	**$157,091**	

The 3.8% surtax is not included and the total gain is assumed to be taxed at the top rate of 20% for simplicity reasons.

Artwork (Payment of Taxes)

David and Amy inherited a piece of art from Amy's Uncle, George Freeman, who recently died. While the client appreciates being thought of by Uncle George, the artwork is not particularly aesthetically pleasing to them. The fair market value was $160,000 at Uncle George's death. Due to the step-up in basis on inherited property, Amy's tax basis is $160,000. Therefore, considering their funding goals, Amy and David have agreed to immediately sell the art to pay the capital gains taxes on the sale of DRI. There will be no gain on the sale of the art.

Objective 3: Retirement Capital Needs Analysis

- Objective: David still has a goal to retire at age 62. Capital needs analysis is required (annuity model, capital preservation model, and purchasing power preservation model) to know how much funding is needed.
- Objective: Any funding deficit of David's retirement needs will create the need for current annual year-end funding.
- The planner needs to provide an analysis of David's capital needs analysis for retirement funding along with an analysis of any additional required funding.

- His latest estimate for Social Security benefits is $2,200 per month in today's dollars at normal age retirement of 67. He will retire at 62, and therefore, receive 70 percent of the full benefit from Social Security.

Retirement Needs Analysis:

David and Amy Current Income	$433,250	
80% Wage Replacement	0.80	
Subtotal	**$346,600**	(See Retirement Chapter for calculation)
Less: Social Security	$18,480	($2,200 x 12) x 0.70
Total	**$328,120**	First year retirement income in today's dollars.

When calculating David's retirement needs analysis, inflation of 2.5 percent is used as well as the required investment rate of return of 8 percent.

Step 1: Calculate the future value of $328,120 in 10 years (David's age 52 to his age 62) using the inflation rate.

10BII Keystrokes	*12C Keystrokes*
10 [N] 2.5 (inflation) [I/YR] 0 [PMT] 328,120 [PV] [FV] **Answer: <420,021.34>**	10 [n] 2.5 (inflation) [i] 0 [PMT] 328,120 [PV] [FV] **Answer: <420,021.34>**

Step 2: Calculate the amount needed at retirement, based on the annual income need of $420,021.34 being withdrawn for 33 periods (62 - 95), using the two alternative methods of capital needs analysis.

Annuity Model to Capital Needs Analysis

10BII Keystrokes	*12C Keystrokes*
[ORANGE] [BEG/END] 33 [N] 1.08 [÷] 1.025 – 1 x 100 = [I/YR] 420,021.34 [PMT]$_{AD}$ 0 [FV] [PV] **Answer: <6,777,966.85>**	[g] [BEG] 33 [n] 1.08 [ENTER] 1.025 [÷] 1 [-] 100 [x] [i] 420,021.34 [PMT]$_{AD}$ 0 [FV] [PV] **Answer: <6,777,966.85>**

Capital Preservation Model to Capital Need Analysis

10BII Keystrokes	12C Keystrokes
33 [N] 8 [I/YR] 0 [PMT] 6,777,966.85 [FV] [PV] **Answer: <534,706.55>**	33 [n] 8 [i] 0 [PMT] 6,777,966.85 [FV] [PV] **Answer: <534,706.55>**

This model adds $534,706.55 to capital needs of $6,777,966.85 for a total of $7,312,673.40.

Exhibit 18.9 | Summary of Capital Needs Models

	Annuity Model	Capital Preservation Model
Capital Needed at Retirement (age 62)	$6,777,966.85	$7,312,673.40

An evaluation of whether the Rudolphs have or will have sufficient money to fund their retirement needs is required. The Rudolphs are subject to single-asset risk (DRI). Therefore, the financial planner considers the current sale of a portion of DRI stock to fund retirement in the analysis.

Retirement Assets Available Today (considering sale of DRI stock)

Cash and Cash Equivalents	$123,704
Brokerage Account #1	$600,000
Brokerage Account #2	$900,000 from sale of DRI
David 401(k) Plan	$65,076
IRA	$12,000
Roth IRA	$16,280
Amy 401(k) Plan	$33,000
	$1,750,060

Given the $1,750,000 in assets available today to invest for retirement funding, the following calculations are made to assess the adequacy of current retirement funding.

Calculate the future value of $1,750,000 invested today plus the ongoing annual retirement savings ($81,000) at the client's required rate of return (8%) until David's age 62.

10BII Keystrokes	12C Keystrokes
10 [N] 8 [I/YR] 81,000 [PMT]$_{OA}$ 1,750,000 [PV] [FV]$_{@62}$ **Answer: <4,951,530.31>**	10 [n] 8 [i] 81,000 [PMT]$_{OA}$ 1,750,000 [PV] [FV]$_{@62}$ **Answer: <4,951,530.31>**

At age 62, David will have $4,951,530 saved for retirement funding, plus his 50.4545% ownership in DRI. The expected value of his ownership in DRI at age 62 is as follows:

10BII Keystrokes	12C Keystrokes
10 [N] 3 [I/YR] 0 [PMT] 1,850,000 [PV] [FV]$_{@62}$ **Answer: <2,486,245.30>**	10 [n] 3 [i] 0 [PMT] 1,850,000 [PV] [FV]$_{@62}$ **Answer: <2,486,245.30>**

Retirement Funds Available at David's Age 62

Value at David's Age 62 of Current Funding	$4,951,530	
Value at David's Age 62 of DRI Stock	$2,486,245	50.4545% ownership interest
	$7,437,775	

Observations

Based on the previous capital needs analysis, the $7,437,775 in retirement funding exceeds the annuity model requirement ($6,777,967) and the capital preservation model requirement ($7,312,673).

Current Income Utilization Compared to Wage Replacement in Today's Dollars

Client's current income	$433,250	
Less: Social Security (includes self employment)	($34,905)	($21,195 + $13,710)
Savings, not including employer match	($46,500)	
Lake house loan will be paid off	($14,232)	
Result is close to 80% wage replacement ratio	$337,613	*

* This is very close to their estimated needs of $346,600.

Objective 4: Estate Planning
- Objective: The client wants recommendations to revise their estate planning to avoid probate and to provide for Madelyn and Danny in the event of David and Amy's death.
- The planner needs to recommend the establishment of trusts to avoid probate and provide for Madelyn and Danny.

Life Insurance Policy 1 should be transferred to a Life Insurance Trust (LIT#1) for the benefit of income to Amy for her life and the remainder to Danny. The initial trustee is Amy, but successor trustees need to be named to ultimately provide a lifetime of care for Danny. This trust could have provisions that it will only pay for expenses that are not paid by a federal or state agency to create a special needs trust. Another benefit of this trust is that it will avoid probate. When the Rudolphs gain a better perspective on the extent of Danny's long-term needs, they may consider replacing Life Insurance Policy 1 (term policy) with a permanent policy or combination of term and permanent.

Life Insurance Policy 2 should name as its beneficiary Life Insurance Trust #1 (LIT#1). It will avoid probate and will be managed during Amy's life by Amy.

Life Insurance Policy 3 should be transferred to Life Insurance Trust #2 with David as both Trustee and income beneficiary and Madelyn having the remainder interest upon David's death. Provisions can be made to accumulate earnings until such time as Madelyn is financially mature (for example, she receives 25 percent at age 35 and 25 percent at age 45 and the balance at age 55).

The professional costs of creating the two trusts will be approximately $3,000 and will be paid from their current income statement on a non-recurring basis.

Objective 5: Business Entity Change for Amy's Sole Proprietorship
- Objective: The client wants to consider the advantages and disadvantages of each possible entity form that Amy might use for her business. They were audited last year and the CPA and IRS agent told them that Schedule C income tax returns get audited more than other entity forms.
- The planner needs to analyze business entity forms to establish a recommendation of business type for Amy.

Amy is a sole proprietor with Schedule C income. She wants to explore other business entity options to avoid future IRS audits (due to Schedule C income risk for audit) and to obtain personal liability protection. Amy is seeking a form of business entity where the cost of formation and maintenance of the organization is not excessive.

Partnerships
Being a sole proprietor, Amy would need a partner in order to form her business as a partnership. David could become a minimal ownership partner (1%) in order to form the entity, which has medium to high costs of formation dependent upon the type of partnership. However, the general, limited, and limited liability partnerships would not give Amy the personal liability protection she seeks. Amy has not indicated interest in transferring assets to younger family members, therefore the family limited partnership is not being considered.

Limited Liability Companies (LLC)

An LLC is a viable option for Amy's business. Typically, single member / owner LLCs are disregarded as an entity for federal income tax purposes and she would in that case still be filing her income under Schedule C. However, she may elect to have the LLC taxed as an S corporation or a C corporation, avoiding Schedule C income. She could also consider bringing David in as a member of the entity, in which case she could file as a partnership, S corporation, or C corporation for federal income tax purposes, each of which will avoid Schedule C income. The cost of formation of an LLC can be high, but the benefit of protection from personal liability may be worth making the transition from sole proprietorship. It would be important for Amy to maintain the entity separately to keep her liability protection.

Corporations

C corporations are state chartered legal entities formed by one or more individuals and owned by corporate shareholder(s). The cost of formation can be high, but liability is limited to shareholder investment as long as the entity follows corporate formalities and is maintained as a separate entity from the shareholder(s) / owner(s). A C corporation is taxed separately from shareholders (double taxation issue), unless S corporation status is elected. The owner/employee's compensation is not considered to be self-employment income, which fulfills Amy's requirement to avoid Schedule C income.

S corporations are state chartered legal entities (same formation as C corporations). The cost of formation can be high. An S corporation is limited to 100 shareholders with one class of stock.[3] To obtain the income tax benefit of being an S corporation, the C corporation files an "S" election with the IRS. The "S" election avoids the double taxation issue of a C corporation and allows the income of the S corporation to be passed through to shareholders. As with a C corporation, corporate formalities must be followed to maintain the corporation as a separate entity from the shareholder(s) / owner(s) in order to limit liability. The S corporation entity is a viable option for Amy's needs.

Recommendation

An LLC or S corporation is likely the best options for Amy's business needs. Both forms of entity can avoid Schedule C income and offer the personal liability protection she desires. Amy can seek the services of an attorney to make her final decision as to entity form and for the creation of the entity itself.

Objective 6: Investment Analysis

- Objective: The clients want a full review of their investment portfolio.
- The planner needs to provide an analysis of the clients' entire investment portfolio including:
  1. Brokerage Accounts 1 and 2
  2. Education Funding Accounts
  3. David's 401(k) plan
  4. Traditional IRA
  5. Roth IRA
  6. Amy's 401(k) plan

---

3. IRC Section 1361.

Investment Portfolio of Stock (Brokerage Account 1)

The Rudolphs' investment policy statement is as follows:

Rudolphs Investment Policy Statement As of January 1, 20X3	
Retirement Goals	• Generate adequate retirement capital • Retire debt free
Education Goals	• Provide for Trevor Jr. and Madelyn's education
Return Requirements	• They require an 8% return on their overall portfolio • They require a 8% return on their education portfolio
Risk Tolerance	• They have a moderate risk tolerance
Time Horizon	• Retirement for David is 10 years away • Retirement for Amy is 10 years away • Education for Trevor Jr. is 15 years away • Education for Madelyn is 3 years away
Constraints	• They still have liquidity issues with a majority of their net worth being in a small business that they are planning to sell and then use the proceeds for retirement. The value of this business will increase at least by 3% per year based on the current sale arrangement. • They have a very short time horizon to fund Madelyn's education, which is only three years away.

Investment Portfolio Analysis

The Rudolphs' investments are compared to their investment policy statement for an analysis of their progress towards accomplishing their goals.

Overall Investment Growth

The Rudolphs' investment assets declined by 12.8 percent from $3,956,000 (20X2) to $3,526,356 (20X3) which is net of savings contributions and is also due to the revaluing of DRI (a decline of 17.3%).

This decline in the portfolio value is not an immediate concern as the restated value is still sufficient to meet their retirement goals and given their current savings rate of 18 percent. Since the Rudolphs have an overall required rate of return of eight percent and the remaining value of DRI is $1,850,000 ($2,750,000 - $900,000) with growth at three percent (or more) per year, the financial planner must revisit the Rudolphs' asset allocation and expected return for their overall portfolio.

	Expected Return	Amount Invested	Weighting	Weighted Expected Return
DRI	3.00%	$1,850,000	53.2%	1.6%
Brokerage Account 1	11.66%	$600,000	17.3%	2.0%
Brokerage Account 2	8.00%	$900,000	25.9%	2.1%
David's 401(k) Plan	8.20%	$65,076	1.9%	0.2%
Traditional IRA	3.20%	$12,000	0.3%	0.0%
Roth IRA	1.75%	$16,280	0.5%	0.0%
Amy 401(k) Plan	8.20%	$33,000	0.9%	0.1%
Total		$3,476,356		5.9%

*Excluding the education accounts.

Note: The expected return for each investment is calculated in the subsequent sections. The portfolio expected return is 5.9 percent, which is below the Rudolphs' overall required rate of return of eight percent.

DRI Stock

One of the major investment concerns last year was the liquidity and valuation of DRI stock. The liquidity risk has partially been addressed, since David has decided to sell 32.7273 percent of DRI stock for $900,000. The most recent valuation of DRI stock resulted in restating the business value to $2,750,000 from $3,325,000. The valuation concerns from last year have been appropriately addressed by the new valuation.

David has also "locked in" his price on DRI stock by using a put option as part of the buy/sell agreement. As the owner of the put option, David has the right to sell his remaining interest in DRI stock in 10 years, at $1,850,000 with an annual growth rate of three percent (or more). Assuming the value of DRI stock increases by three percent over the next 10 years, the value of David's interest in DRI stock will be $2,486,245:

N	=	10
i	=	3
PV	=	<$1,850,000>
PMT	=	0
FV	=	?
Answer	=	$2,486,245.30

Although David's interest in DRI has decreased, 47 percent ($1,850,000 ÷ $3,880,921) of his net worth is still invested in DRI stock, which is extremely high.[4] The put option helps to reduce the Rudolphs' risk of losing a substantial amount of their net worth if the value of DRI declines.

---

4. From revised Statement of Financial Position.

Another issue to consider is the financial ability of DRI key employees to fund the remaining purchase of David's stock in 10 years. If the key employees are unable to fund the purchase, it may delay David's retirement goal. David may have to find a different buyer or the sale price may be different than the current agreement under the put option.

Recommendation

A thorough review of the buy/sell agreement is required to evaluate the riskiness and likelihood of David's key employees' ability to purchase the business in 10 years if the value grows at three percent or more each year.

Brokerage Account 1 ($600,000 Stock Portfolio)

Although the financial planner was surprised to learn that David sold his mutual fund portfolio and invested in stocks, an evaluation of the riskiness, expected return, and impact on the Rudolphs' overall asset allocation is required.

The expected return of his stock portfolio is:

Name	Expected Return	Amount Invested	Weighting	Expected Return for the Portfolio
A	8%	$23,000	($23,000 ÷ $600,000) = 0.0383	0.0031
B	10%	$117,700	($117,700 ÷ $600,000) = 0.1962	0.0196
C	9%	$5,100	($5,100 ÷ $600,000) = 0.0085	0.0008
D	12.3%	$454,200	($454,200 ÷ $600,000) = 0.7570	0.0931
				0.1166 or 11.66%

The expected return of 11.66 percent for this portfolio is appropriate given the Rudolphs' required rate of return of eight percent.

Based on the information provided by the Rudolphs for their stock portfolio, there is an issue with the risk return relationship between two of their stocks.

Name	Standard Deviation	Expected Return
A	0.12	8%
B	0.14	10%
C	0.16	9%
D	0.19	12.3%

Stock B has a standard deviation of 14 percent and an expected return of 10 percent and Stock C has a standard deviation of 16 percent and an expected return of nine percent. Stock C is considered "inefficient" because it provides less return and is more risky than Stock B.

It is likely that after reviewing the buy / sell agreement, the planner may decide to recommend that David allocate this portfolio to well diversified stock and bond mutual funds.

Recommendations

- David should keep the stock portfolio until a more thorough analysis of his buy/sell arrangement with his key employees is completed.
- A determination of the standard deviation of the portfolio using financial software to make sure the portfolio is appropriate given their moderate risk tolerance is required.
- The Rudolphs should sell Stock C and invest in a stock that has a more appropriate risk/return relationship.
- The stock portfolio is not well diversified, as 75.7 percent of the portfolio is invested in Stock D. Since the client is going to keep the stock portfolio in the short term, the Rudolphs should sell at least 50 percent to 75 percent of Stock D and allocate it across industries not currently represented in their portfolio. Generally, a stock portfolio of 15 stocks is considered relatively diversified, so the Rudolphs should purchase 10 to 12 more stocks. More information is required on the current stocks to evaluate which industries are currently represented and not represented in the portfolio.
- The Rudolphs should also sell about 50 percent of Stock B and allocate the proceeds equally to each new stock purchased.

Brokerage Account 2 ($900,000 Proceeds from DRI Sale)

Prior to the sale of 32.7273 percent of DRI, the Rudolphs' asset allocation was:

Equities in Portfolio
• DRI: $2,750,000
• Brokerage Account 1: $600,000
• David's 401(k) Plan – balanced fund: $32,538 ($65,076 total with ½ in equities and ½ in bonds)
• Amy's 401(k) Plan: $19,800 ($33,000 x 60% in a stock index fund)
Total Equities = $3,402,338
Bonds in Portfolio
• David's 401(k) Plan – balanced fund: $32,538 ($65,076 total with ½ in equities and ½ in bonds)
• Traditional IRA: $12,000
• Roth IRA: $16,280
• Amy's 401(k) Plan: $13,200 ($33,000 x 40% in a corporate bond fund)
Total Bonds = $74,018
Allocation is 97.9% Equities / 2.1% Bonds

David should invest the $900,000 proceeds into balanced mutual funds, which have an equal weighting of both equity and fixed income investments.

Their new asset allocation will be:

Equities in Portfolio
• DRI: $2,750,000 - $900,000 = $1,850,000
• Brokerage Account 1: $600,000
• Brokerage Account 2: $450,000 ($900,000 in balanced mutual fund with ½ in equities and ½ in bonds)
• David's 401(k) Plan – balanced fund: $32,538 ($65,076 total with ½ in equities and ½ in bonds)
• Amy's 401(k) Plan: $19,800 ($33,000 x 60% in a stock index fund)
Total Equities = $2,952,338
Bonds in Portfolio
• Brokerage Account 2: $450,000 ($900,000 in balanced mutual fund ½ equities and ½ bonds)
• David's 401(k) Plan – balanced fund: $32,538 ($65,076 total with ½ in equities and ½ in bonds)
• Traditional IRA: $12,000
• Roth IRA: $16,280
• Amy's 401(k) Plan: $13,200 ($33,000 x 40% in a corporate bond fund)
Total Bonds = $524,018
Allocation is 84.9% Equities / 15.1% Bonds

The asset allocation is heavily weighted to equities, which is due to the client's investment in his company (DRI) stock. This is not uncommon for entrepreneurs and presents challenges for the planner to overcome. An analysis of the buy/sell agreement is needed to make an evaluation regarding the likelihood and financial ability of the key employees to fulfill the agreement. Once the buy/sell agreement has been evaluated, the planner may recommend the allocation of Brokerage Account #1 to a mutual fund or bond portfolio.

Assume that a balanced mutual fund invests 50 percent in stocks that match the performance of the market (S&P 500) of nine percent and 50 percent of the portfolio will match the performance of corporate bonds of seven percent. The expected return for the balanced mutual fund below is eight percent, which is appropriate given the client's required rate of return of eight percent on their overall portfolio.

S&P 500	50% x 9%	Expected Return =	4.5%
Corporate Bond Fund	50% x 7%	Expected Return =	3.5%
	4.5% + 3.5%	**Total Expected Return =**	**8.0%**

Recommendation:
• Invest the $900,000 proceeds in a balanced mutual fund (50/50 equities and fixed income) with an overall expected rate of return of eight percent.

Education Account

The 529 Savings Plan balance for Madelyn (and Danny) was $46,000 as of 1/1/20X2 and was $50,000 the following year (1/1/20X3), but the Rudolphs contributed $6,000 to the fund during 20X2. Therefore the account declined 4.3 percent for the year.

With a 529 Savings Plan, the investment options may be limited based on the age of the children and their time horizon until they enter college. Some 529 Savings Plans have the option of aggressive allocation or moderate allocation based on the child's age. In the Rudolphs' case, there is not enough information to determine the riskiness of the investments held. However, since some 529 Savings Plans become more conservative as the beneficiary approaches 18, it is likely that the Rudolphs' education investments are appropriate. The client and planner agree to investigate.

The Rudolphs are considering establishing a 529 Savings Plan for Trevor Jr. given their affection for him and his high potential for academic success. When this account is established it will be Education Account #2 and likely be invested appropriately based on the age of Trevor, Jr., and time until he attends college.

401(k) Plan with Roth Account Option

One year ago, this account was invested 100 percent in cash. Since that time, David has reallocated the account to a balanced mutual fund, which provides an equal weighting investment in equities and bonds. Since his expected return of eight percent is expected to equal his required rate of return, no further recommendations are needed at this time.

Traditional IRA

This portfolio continues to be invested in a series of zero coupon bonds. Amy's compounded rate of return on the bond investments in the Traditional IRA is 3.2 percent:

$$GM = \sqrt[6]{(1.065)(1.0475)(0.9675)(0.975)(1.0525)(1.0909)} - 1 \times 100$$

$$GM = \sqrt[6]{1.2083} - 1 \times 100$$

$$GM = 1.0320 - 1 \times 100 = 3.2\%$$

Although the 3.2 percent return is less than the Rudolphs' overall required rate of return, zero coupon bond investments are appropriate in this account, because zero coupon bonds in a traditional IRA avoid the phantom income tax issue. Amy still needs to provide information on the actual investments in this portfolio so the bonds can be evaluated on their riskiness and expected returns.

Recommendation
- Provide a detailed list of the securities held in this account.

Roth IRA

During the last meeting with the Rudolphs, the financial planner recommended that Amy change the Roth IRA investment into a higher growth investment, rather than tax-free municipal bonds. Amy and David have been focused on negotiating the terms of selling DRI and have not reallocated the investments in Amy's Roth IRA. Currently, the planner is still recommending that Amy sell the Municipal bonds and invest in higher growth investments, like a balanced mutual fund. This account balance is small and the planner is not immediately concerned about the asset allocation implications of changing into a balanced mutual fund.

If Amy reallocates this portfolio into a balanced mutual fund, her expected return would be eight percent, whereas if she continues to leave the account invested in Municipal bonds, her expected return is 1.75 percent.

Recommendation
- Reallocate the Municipal bond investments into a balanced mutual fund.

Amy's 401(k) Plan

Amy's current allocation for her 401(k) plan contributions is 60 percent in an equity index mutual fund and 40 percent in a corporate bond mutual fund. Her allocation seems appropriate given her retirement time horizon of 30+ years.

Index Fund	60% x 9%	Expected Return = 5.4%
Corporate Bond Fund	40% x 7%	Expected Return = 2.8%
	5.4% + 2.8%	Total Expected Return = 8.2%

The expected rate of return of 8.2 percent is appropriate given their required rate of return of eight percent on their overall portfolio.

Recommendation
- None at this time.

Objective 7: Long-Term Care Insurance
- Objective: David and Amy want to consider purchasing long-term care insurance.
- The planner needs to provide an analysis of long-term care options and costs.

The client has indicated they will consider this objective during the next six months.

Tax Analysis

Federal Tax Analysis
(using 2021 brackets)

Tax Analysis	Amount
	Amount
Amy's Schedule C	$150,000
David's Salary	$283,250
401(k) Deferrals - David	($23,000)
401(k) Deferrals - Amy	($17,500)
Total Income	$392,750
Adjustments:	
Less 1/2 SE Tax	($10,597)
AGI	$382,153
Less Personal Exemptions	0
Less Itemized Deductions	($65,000)
Less QBI Deduction	$0
Taxable Income	$317,153
Income Tax (2021 MFJ bracket)	$64,159
Less Child Tax Credit	$0
Self Employment Tax	$21,194
Total	$85,353
Withholding & Est. Payments	$84,995
Refund (Due to IRS)	($358)

Self-Employment Tax

Self Employment Income	$150,000
Times 92.35%	$138,525 A
Max Social Security Wage Base (2021)	$ 142,800.00
Less Wages For Employment	$0
Net	$142,800 B
Smaller of A or B	$138,525
OASDI (amount above times 12.4%)	$17,177.10
A times 2.9%	$4,017.23
Total	$21,194.33
1/2 SE Tax	$10,597.16

Itemized Deductions

	2021
Real property taxes	$8,000.00
Mortgage interest (limited to $750,000 of mortgage debt)	$45,000.00
Income taxes for State (limit for real proprty tax + state tax is $10,000)	$2,000.00
Church	$10,000.00
Itemized Deductions	$65,000.00

Conclusion: The Rudolphs' federal tax is calcualted using 2021 numbers. Their tax may increase depending on what happens to future tax rates. However, there is not much of a difference between what is withheld / estimated and what they owe the IRS. Therefore, the difference is ignored in all other analyses.

Note: For simplicity purposes, we have not included the Medicare surtax of 0.9% or the capital gains from the sale of DRI stock, and assumed the QBI deduction was fully phased out. We did reduce the child tax credit as a result of the capital gains increasing AGI above the phaseout threshold. We assumed the mortgage on the primary residence was after 12-15-17 (limiting the deduction for mortgage interest to $750,000 of debt).

The tax analysis reveals that the Rudolphs' tax withholding is appropriate. They are neither substantially under withheld nor substantially over withheld. Any refund or amount due after completing an actual tax return will be inconsequential and is not considered in this analysis.

Implementation

The Rudolphs have decided to implement the following recommendations:
1. 529 Savings Plan for Trevor Jr.
2. David selling 32.7273 percent of his 75 percent interest in DRI for $900,000 cash with a put option to sell the remainder of his interest in 10 years for $1,850,000 increased by 3 percent per year. David and Amy will use the proceeds from the sale of the inherited piece of artwork to fund the taxes owed on the current sale of DRI stock.
3. David will use savings and the sale of DRI stock to implement the retirement funding goal. At this time, the Rudolphs have decided to fund any deficit of David's retirement needs with either a modification in retirement withdrawals (decrease in amount) or a delay in retirement.
4. David and Amy have decided to have the trusts created to avoid probate and provide for Madelyn and Danny.

5. Amy has decided to change her business entity form from sole proprietor to either an LLC or S corporation to avoid the higher risk of an IRS audit as a Schedule C filer and for personal liability protection. She will seek the services of an attorney to implement this recommendation.
6. David has agreed to sell 75 percent of stock D and 50 percent of Stock B. He will purchase 10 more stocks across multiple industries, allocating an equal amount to each new stock (Brokerage Account 1).
7. David has agreed to invest the $900,000 proceeds from DRI (Brokerage Account 2) into balanced mutual funds.
8. Amy has agreed to reallocate her Roth IRA into a balanced mutual fund.

THE CASH FLOW APPROACH

The cash flow approach adjusts the cash flows on the income statement as projected after implementing all of the financial planner's recommendations. The approach starts with the discretionary cash flows at the bottom of the income statement and accounts for the recommendations in the order of priority by charging the cost of the expense against the discretionary cash flows regardless of any negative cash flow impact. The cash flow approach is discussed in detail in Chapter 3. The analysis is prepared carefully to differentiate between recurring cash flows and non-recurring cash flows.

Cash Flow Approach with Recommendations

Rudolph Cash Flow Approach with Implementation of 1/2/20X3 Recommendations			
	Income Statement Recurring Impact	Balance Statement Non-Recurring Impact	Comments/Explanations
Beginning Cash Flow (Income Statement)	$12,861		
Recommendations:			
Risk Management:	None	None	
• Life Insurance -Change Owner to Trusts	0	0	
Debt Management:	None	None	
Education Funding		($50,284.81) $50,284.81	From Money Market Fund 529 #2 for Trevor Jr.*
Retirement Savings:			
• DRI - Sell 32.7273 percent		($900,000) $900,000	Reduction in value of DRI Creates Brokerage Account #2
• Receive and Sell Art		$160,000	Listed as Asset
Tax on Sale of DRI		($157,091)	Listed as Liability
Estate Planning:			
• Create ILIT Trusts	($3,000)		Legal Costs of $3,000
TOTALS	**$9,861**	**$2,909**	

( ) indicates a negative impact on cash flow and + indicates a positive impact on cash flow.
* The 529 Plan will be funded from the money market account.

RESTATED FINANCIAL STATEMENTS

The revised Balance Sheet is presented for 1/2/20X3, as if all of the recommendations have been implemented. Other than the long-term care issue, the Rudolphs are in excellent position from a financial planning perspective. The Rudolphs' financial planner and attorney will want to monitor any legislation regarding estate tax that may affect their client.

Exhibit 18.10 | Financial Statements: Statement of Financial Position
(End of Year-Revised after Implementation of Recommendations)

Statement of Financial Position (With Adjustments for Recommendations) David and Amy Rudolph Balance Sheet as of 1/2/20X3					
Assets[1]			**Liabilities and Net Worth**		
Current Assets			**Current Liabilities[2]**		
JT	Cash & Checking	$20,000	JT	Taxes-Sale of DRI	$157,091
JT	Money Market	$119,715	W	Credit Cards	$5,000
JT	Cash from Art (inherited)[6]	$160,000	**Total Current Liabilities**		**$162,091**
Total Current Assets		**$299,715**			
Investment Assets			**Long-Term Liabilities[2]**		
H	DR Office Furniture, Inc[3]	$1,850,000	JT	Principal Residence[5]	$1,153,009
H	Brokerage Account #1	$600,000	H	Lake House[5]	$145,335
H	Brokerage Account #2[3]	$900,000	H	Boat[5]	$0
H	Education Account #1[4] (529)	$50,000	**Total Long-Term Liabilities**		**$1,298,344**
JT	Education Account #2 (529)	$50,285			
H	David's 401(k) Plan	$65,076			
W	Traditional IRA	$12,000			
W	Roth IRA	$16,280			
W	Amy 401(k) Plan	$33,000			
Total Investment Assets		**$3,576,641**	**Total Liabilities**		**$1,460,435**
Personal Use Assets					
JT	Principal Residence	$800,000			
H	Lake House	$450,000			
JT	Furniture, Clothing	$100,000	**Total Net Worth**		**$3,880,921**
H	Car # 1	$25,000			
W	Car # 2	$35,000			
H	Boat	$55,000			
Total Personal Use Assets		**$1,465,000**			
Total Assets		**$5,341,356**	**Total Liabilities & Net Worth**		**$5,341,356**

1. Assets are stated at fair market value.
2. Liabilities are stated at principal only as of January 1, 20X3 before January payments.
3. This is David's remaining 50.4545% interest after selling stock in DRI to other executives. Brokerage account #2 has the $900,000 from the sale of DRI.
4. This is for Madelyn. David currently saves $6,000 per year into this account (see portfolio).
5. Current portion of long-term liabilities is $17,635 and $7,490, respectively. Paid off boat 1/2/20X2.
6. David and Amy inherited artwork from her Uncle George and subsequently sold the artwork.

Sold DRI Stock and funded Brokerage Account #2	$900,000
Sold Money Market and funded 529 Plan for Trevor Jr.	$50,285
Inherited Artwork and Sold It	$160,000
Tax Liability on Sale of DRI	$157,091

SUMMARY

When the Rudolphs returned to the financial planner this year for additional services they had the following strengths and weaknesses:

Strengths

1. Income of $433,250 annually.
2. Savings rate of 18.7%.
3. Net Worth of approximately $4 million.
4. Investment assets of approximately $3.5 million.
5. Adequate life insurance coverage on David.
6. Adequate health insurance coverage.
7. Adequate disability insurance coverage on David and Amy.
8. Adequate homeowners insurance coverage on the principal residence and the lake house.
9. Adequate automobile insurance coverage.
10. Excellent financial ratios, except investment performance ratios.
11. Improved net discretionary cash flows ($12,861).
12. Adequate insurance coverage on the boat.
13. Adequate coverage under their personal liability umbrella policy.
14. Some estate planning documents prepared.
15. Reduced property taxes on their principal residence.

Weaknesses (and Responses)

1. Questionable life insurance coverage on Amy. *(Remains unresolved.)*
2. No long-term care insurance coverage on David or Amy. *(Remains unresolved.)*
3. Poor investment returns. *(Repositioned investments; should perform as expected.)*
4. Need additional estate planning to avoid probate and provide for minors. *(Corrected.)*
5. Negative equity on the client's principal residence. *(Unresolved due to market.)*
6. The debt rates of the lake house is too high. *(Resolved.)*
7. DRI. *(Sold portion of client interest and now has put option.)*
8. Amy's business remains as a sole proprietorship. *(Proper entity recommended; client will implement this year.)*
9. Need to set up a special needs trust for Danny.

Recommendations - Implemented

The financial planner solved the client's weaknesses as follows:

- The 529 Savings Plan funding amount for Trevor Jr. has been calculated and funded.
- The Rudolphs' capital needs (annuity method and capital preservation method) for retirement funding has been calculated and is adequate.
- Any deficit in retirement capital needs has been determined with recommendations for solving any potential shortage. Calculated, but the Rudolphs think it is unnecessary.
- The Rudolphs have implemented two ILITs for estate planning (to avoid probate and provide for Madelyn and Danny).
- The financial planner is continuing to work on the investment returns and is encouraging the clients to consider long-term care policies for both David and Amy.
- The ongoing valuation of DRI remains critical to the plan.

Unmet Goals

The goal to be debt free at David's age 62 (retirement) is questionable given the mortgage on the principal residence.

Expected investment returns remain an issue that will require periodic monitoring and reevaluation.

APPENDIX

A

GLOSSARY

A

Above-the-Line Deductions – Deductions for adjusted gross income, also known as adjustments to income.

Accuracy-Related Penalty – A penalty of 20 percent of the underpayment amount imposed on taxpayers who file incorrect tax returns in certain situations.

Achieving a Better Life Experience (ABLE) Account – A tax-advantaged savings account established to assist persons with disabilities.

Active Listening – Requires the listener's undivided attention. Active listening involves concentration on what the speaker is saying. The listener must put aside irrelevant thoughts.

Adjusted Gross Income – Gross income less above-the-line deductions.

Affect Heuristic – Deals with judging something, whether it is good or bad.

Aggregate Demand Curve – A graphical representation of the quantity of goods and services consumers are willing to buy at any given price level.

Aggregate Supply Curve – A graphical representation between quantity supplied and price.

Aggressive Growth Funds – Typically invest in small cap stocks, where price appreciation is the primary objective.

Alpha – The difference between the actual return generated by the fund relative to the expected return give the level of riskiness of the fund, as measured by beta.

Always Bar List – CFP Board's list of unacceptable conduct that will always bar an individual from becoming certified.

American Opportunity Tax Credit (AOTC) – The AOTC provides a tax credit of up to $2,500 (2021) per student for the first four years of qualified education expenses for postsecondary education.

Amortization Schedule – Illustrates the repayment of debt over time. Each debt payment consists of both interest expense and principal repayment.

Anchoring – Attaching or anchoring one's thoughts to a reference point even though there may be no logical relevance or is not pertinent to the issue in question. Anchoring is also known as conservatism or belief perseverance.

Ancillary Probate – Concurrent second probate process conduced in a non-domiciliary state in which the decedent owns property.

Annual Exclusion – An exclusion from gift taxes for present interest transfers less than or equal to $15,000 (in 2021) per year per donee.

Annuity – A recurring cash flow, of an equal amount that occurs at periodic (but regular) intervals.

Annuity Due – Occurs when the timing of the first payment is at the beginning of the first period. The period may be the beginning of a month, quarter, or year.

Annuity Due Payment from a Lump-Sum Deposit – The payment that can be generated at the beginning of each period, based on a lump-sum amount deposited today.

Annuity Method – Determines how much a client needs to fund their retirement based on the assumption that the person will die exactly at the assumed life expectancy with a retirement account balance of zero.

Anonymous Case Histories – Summary of the relevant events in certain cases of misconduct, accompanied by an explanation of any discipline penalty, action by CFP Board, and other information.

Arithmetic or Average Return – The sum of all returns divided by the number of periods.

Articles of Incorporation – The charter document for a corporation that must be filed with the Secretary of State in the state of organization.

Articles of Organization – The charter document of an LLC that must be filed with the Secretary of State in the state of organization.

Asset Accumulation Phase – This phase is usually from the early 20s to mid 50s when additional cash flow for investing is low and the debt-to-net worth ratio is high.

Asset Allocation – The dividing of a portfolio into various asset classes.

ssets – A balance sheet category that represents ıything of economic value that can ultimately be ʰnverted to cash.

ttorney-in-Fact – Agent or power holder of a power ʰattorney.

vailability Heuristic – When a decision maker relies ʰpon knowledge that is readily available in his or her ıemory, the cognitive heuristic known as "availability" ʰinvoked.

B

Balance Sheet – A statement of financial position that ʰepresents the accounting for items the client "owns" ʰassets) and items that are "owed" (liabilities). The ʰalance sheet provides a snapshot of the client's assets, ʰiabilities, and net worth as of a stated date.

Balanced Funds – Typically invest in both fixed ʰncome securities and equity securities.

BAPCPA of 2005 – Amends the Truth in Lending Act in ʰarious respects, including requiring certain creditors ʰo disclose on the front of billing statements a ʰinimum monthly payment warning for consumers.

Basis – Represents the total capital or after-tax income ʰused by a taxpayer to purchase an investment.

Behavioral Finance – Contains much of the scientific framework and lessons learned from Traditional Finance, amends some of it with basic assumptions based on normal, more human-like behavior, and supplements other aspects of it with notions from psychology and sociology.

Below-the-Line Deductions – Deductions from adjusted gross income, including itemized or standard deductions, and the qualified business income deduction.

Beneficiary – The person(s) entitled to receive the death benefit of a life insurance policy at the insured's death. Also, the person(s) who hold(s) the beneficial title to a trust's assets.

Beta – A measure of systematic risk and provides the correlation of the volatility of a portfolio as compared to the market benchmark.

Bonds – A debt issuance where the bond issuer makes a promise to make periodic coupon payments

(interest) and repayment of the par value (principal) at maturity.

Business Cycle – Measures economic activity over time. The business cycle is characterized by expansion, peak, contraction or recession, and trough.

Business Risk – The inherent risk of doing business in a particular industry.

C

Call Risk – The risk that a bond will be retired early by the issuing company.

Calls – Gives the holder the right to buy the underlying security at a certain price by a certain date.

Candidate for CFP® Certification – Individuals who have completed a CFP Board registered education program may present themselves as a "Candidate for CFP® certification" for a period of up to five years following completion of the education program while fulfilling the remaining exam and experience requirements.

Capital Asset Pricing Model (CAPM) – Informs investors about a reasonable required return for shareholders when investing in individual stocks, but the model is easily applied to mutual funds. The required return is based on risk-free rates of interest, expected market returns, and the level of systematic risk of the fund or portfolio.

Capitalization of Earnings Model – A capital needs analysis method based on producing a perpetual stream of income.

Capital Market Line (CML) – The macro aspect of the Capital Asset Pricing Model (CAPM). It specifies the relationship between risk and return in all possible portfolios.

Capital Preservation Model (CP) – A capital needs analysis method that assumes that at the client's life expectancy, the client has exactly the same account balance as he did at the beginning of retirement.

Capitalization of Earnings Method – A method that preserves the capital and initially uses a numerator of gross income and denominator of riskless rate of return to determine life insurance needs. It can be further adjusted to account for taxes, personal consumption, and inflation.

CARD Act of 2009 – Prevents credit card companies (and banks) from charging hidden fees and extraordinary interest rates as well as promoting easy to understand statements.

Cash and Cash Equivalents – A balance sheet category that represents assets that are highly liquid, which means they are either cash or can be converted to cash (within the next 12 months) with little to no price concession from the principal amount invested.

Cash Flow Approach – This approach takes an income statement approach to recommendations. It uses the three-panel approach and uses a pro forma approach (as if) "to purchase" the recommendations thus driving down the discretionary cash flow. Next, positive cash flows or the sale of assets are identified to finance the recommendations which were purchased.

Cash Flow Statement – Explains how cash and cash equivalents were used or generated between two balance sheets.

Ceiling – A maximum limit on the amount that may be deductible. Expenses are only deductible up to the ceiling amount.

Certificant – An individual who is currently certified by the CFP Board.

Certified Financial Planner Board of Standards, Inc. ("CFP Board") – Board that maintains professional standards necessary for competency and ethics in the financial planning profession for those professionals who have been granted the right to use their designation.

CFP Board Counsel - Has the authority to investigate and file a complaint against a Respondent for alleged violations of the *Code and Standards* or the *Pathway to CFP® Certification Agreement*. The term includes CFP Board staff operating at the direction of CFP Board Counsel.

Chapter 11 Bankruptcy – Known as "reorganization bankruptcy" for corporations, sole proprietorships, and partnerships.

Chapter 13 Bankruptcy – Also known as a "wage earners plan," is for individuals or self-employed workers that want to keep their assets and payoff a portion of their debts over time.

Chapter 7 Bankruptcy – For individuals or businesses to use for protection from creditors under federal and state bankruptcy laws.

Checking the Box – When an eligible entity chooses to be taxed as either a corporation or a partnership.

Client – Any person, including a natural person, business organization, or legal entity, to whom the CFP® professional provides or agrees to provide Professional Services pursuant to an Engagement.

Closed Questions – Seeks a response that is very specific and commonly involves an answer that can be accomplished with a single word or two. Closed questions lead with is, are, do, did, could, would, have, or "is it not true that..."

Closed-end Investment Companies – A type of investment company that trades on stock market exchanges. Closed-end funds do not generally issue additional shares after their initial offering.

Code of Ethics – Organized into six overriding principles that provide a framework for the ethical and professional standards and ideals for CFP® professionals.

Coefficient of Determination (R-Squared) – A measure of how much return is a result of the correlation to the market or what percentage of a security's return is a result of the market.

Cognitive-Behavioral Paradigm (Cognitive-Behavior School of Thought) – Humans are beings are subject to the same learning principles that were established in animal research. The basic principles of classical and operant conditioning are assumed to account for an individuals' behavior and understandings throughout their lives.

College Savings Plans (529 Savings Plans) – A plan that allows for college saving on a tax-deferred basis with attendance at any eligible education institution. Distributions from a College Savings Plan are federal and state income tax-free, as long as they are used to pay for qualified education expenses.

Commission – Compensation generated from a transaction involving a product or service and received by an agent or broker, usually calculated as a percentage on the amount of the transaction. This includes 12b-1 fees, trailing commissions, surrender charges and contingent deferred sales charges.

Commission and Fee – If a CFP® professional or any related party receives both fees and sales-related compensation for providing professional activities, the CFP® professional's compensation is described as "Commission and Fee."

Community Property – A civil law originating statutory regime under which married individuals own an equal undivided interest in all property accumulated during their marriage. Property acquired before the marriage and property received by gift or inheritance during the marriage retains its status as separate property.

Competence – Requires attaining and maintaining an adequate level of knowledge and skill, and application of that knowledge and skill in providing services to clients.

Complements – Products that are consumed jointly.

Composure – A client's ability to remain calm and focused when under pressure.

Confidentiality – Ensuring that information is accessible only to those authorized to have access.

Confirmation Bias – A commonly used and popular phrase is that "you do not get a second chance at a first impression." People tend to filter information and focus on information supporting their opinions.

Conflict of Interest – (a) When a CFP® professional's interests (including the interests of the CFP® Professional's Firm) are adverse to the CFP® professional's duties to a Client, or (b) When a CFP® professional has duties to one Client that are adverse to another Client.

Conservation (Risk Management) Phase – This phase is from late 20s to early 70s, where cash flow, assets, and net worth have increased and debt has decreased somewhat. In addition, risk management of events like unemployment, disability due to illness or accident, and untimely death become a priority.

Constant Growth Dividend Discount Model – Values a company's stock by discounting the future stream of cash flows or dividends.

Consumer Price Index (CPI) – Measures the overall price levels for a basket of goods and services consumers purchase.

Corporate Bonds – Bonds issued by firms to raise capital to fund ongoing operations, retire debt, fund capital projects or acquisitions.

Corporations – Chartered legal entities formed by one or more individuals by meeting state statutory requirements necessary for the formation of a corporation.

Correlation Coefficient – Measures the movement of one security relative to that of another security.

Cost Basis – Initial basis an investor acquires in an asset by using capital to purchase the investment.

Country Risk – The risk of political and economic stability or instability of a country that a company faces when doing business in a particular country.

Covariance – The measure of two securities when combined and their interactive risk (relative risk).

Coverdell Education Savings Account (ESA) – A tax deferred trust or custodial account established to pay for qualified higher education or qualified elementary / secondary school expenses.

Current Ratio – Measures how many times the client can satisfy their short-term liabilities with current assets (cash and cash equivalents).

Cyclical Unemployment – Occurs when there is an overall downturn in business activity and fewer goods are being produced causing a decrease in the demand for labor.

D

Debt – The lending of funds in return for periodic interest payments and the repayment of the principal debt obligation.

Debt Management – The analysis of debt because clients can have too much debt, debt that has high interest rates, and debt that is generally not well managed. The analysis of debt includes calculating housing ratios 1 and 2 and comparing those to well established benchmarks (metrics) of 28% / 36%. In addition, the financial planner will evaluate the quality and the cost of each client's individual debt.

Debt Ratios – Measure how well the client is managing their overall debt structure.

Debt-to-Total Assets Ratio – Indicates what percentage of assets is being provided by creditors. The lower this ratio the better, as it indicates that the assets owned have a low amount of debt owed.

Deductions – Items that are subtracted from gross income, either below- or above-the-line, in order to arrive at taxable income.

Default (under CFP Board's Procedural Rules) - A Respondent is in default if he or she fails to acknowledge receipt of a Notice of Investigation within the required time limit, fails to file an answer to a complaint within the required time limit, fails to provide proof of compliance with an interim suspension order within the required time limit, or fails to pay the hearing fees assessed by CFP Board. A Default may result in an administrative order of suspension or revocation (or an administrative temporary or permanent bar for candidates for CFP® certification).

Default Risk – The risk that a company may not be able to make interest or principal payments under a debt obligation.

Defense of Marriage Act (DOMA) – Signed into law on September 21, 1996 and was "to define and protect the institution of marriage." Under Section 7, Definition of 'marriage' and 'spouse' the law states, "In determining the meaning of any Act of Congress, or of any ruling, regulation, or interpretation of the various administrative bureaus and agencies of the United States, the word 'marriage' means only a legal union between one man and one woman as husband and wife, and the word 'spouse' refers only to a person of the opposite sex who is a husband or a wife." However, in the 2013 landmark case, United States v. Windsor, the Supreme Court effectively declared DOMA as unconstitutional. The result of this ruling is that there is no longer a distinction for federal purposes between marriages of heterosexuals and marriages of homosexuals.

Deflation – A decrease in the overall price levels of goods and services.

Demand – Represents the quantity consumers are willing to purchase of a good or service, at a particular price.

Dependent – A person who is a qualifying child or qualifying relative of the taxpayer.

Dependent with Special Needs – Could be an infant, adolescent, or adult. The dependent could have a wide range of challenges from very mild physical, emotional, or psychological, to a situation where around the clock care is required.

Derivatives – Financial securities that derive their value from some underlying asset.

Developmental Paradigm ("Developmental" School of Thought) – Believes that human development occurs in stages over time. Relationships that are formed early in life become a template for establishing relationships in adulthood. As to emotions, the Developmental Paradigm assumes that all humans develop and progress in a predictable sequence.

Diligence – Requires the provision of services in a reasonably prompt and thorough manner, including the proper planning for, and supervision of, the rendering of professional services.

Disability Insurance – Insurance that provides replacement income to the insured while the insured is unable to work because of sickness (illness) or injury (accident).

Disciplinary and Ethics Commission (DEC) – Composed of CFP® professionals and members of the public; has the authority to issue a final order imposing discipline in the form of a sanction.

Disciplinary Rules – Prior to June 2020, the Disciplinary Rules provided detailed procedures followed by CFP Board in enforcing the *Standards of Professional Conduct*. Replaced by the Procedural Rules in June 2020.

Discount Rate – The interest rate that the Federal Reserve charges financial institutions for short-term loans.

Discretionary Cash Flows – Expenses which can be avoided in the event of loss of income.

Disinflation – A slowdown in the rate of inflation or a slowdown in the general price increase of goods and services.

Disposition Effect – The cognitive bias is "faulty framing" where normal investors do not mark their stocks to market prices. Investors create mental accounts when they purchase stocks and continue to mark their value to purchase prices even after market prices have changed. The normal investor does not consider the stock a loser until the stock is sold.

Distribution (Gifting) Phase – This phase is from the late 40s to end of life and occurs when the individual has high additional cash flow, low debt, and high net worth.

Do Not Resuscitate (DNR) – Documents declare the principal's wish to avoid having cardiopulmonary resuscitation (CPR) performed in the event their heart stops beating.

Doctrine of Constructive Receipt – A cash method taxpayer must report income when it is credited to the taxpayer's account or when it is made available without restriction.

Doctrine of the Fruit and the Tree – Income earned by one taxpayer cannot be assigned to another taxpayer. It is designed to prevent taxpayers from assigning income to a family member in a lower income tax bracket while retaining the asset that produces the income.

Donee – The person who receives the gift.

Donor – The person who gives the gift.

Due Care – Engaging in conduct that a reasonable and prudent individual would exercise under the same or similar circumstances.

Durable Power of Attorney for Health Care – A written document enabling one individual, the principal, to designate another person(s) to act as his "attorney-in-fact." A durable power of attorney survives the incapacity and/or disability of the principal.

E

Economic Benefit Doctrine – States that if a taxpayer receives an economic benefit as income, the value of that benefit will be subject to tax.

Economic Indicators – Describes the current and future economy and business cycle. The three economic indicators are: Index of Leading Economic Indicators, Index of Lagging Economic Indicators, and Index of Coincident Economic Indicators.

Education Funding Needs Analysis – Determination of the lump sum or annual savings required to pay for college.

Effective Annual Rate – An investment's annual rate of return when compounding occurs more than once per year.

Effective Transfer – A transfer of a person's assets to the person or charitable institution intended by that person.

Efficient Frontier – Compares various portfolios based on their risk-return relationship. An efficient portfolio provides the highest amount of return for any given level of risk.

Efficient Transfer – A transfer in which costs of the transfer are minimized consistent with the greatest assurance of effectiveness.

Emergency Fund Ratio – Measures how many months of non-discretionary expenses the client has in the form of cash and cash equivalents or current assets.

Employer-Provided Education Assistance Program - A program established by an employer to reimburse employees for education expenses. The education expenses may or may not be directly related to the employee's current job duties; it depends on the employer's policy.

Engagement – An oral or written agreement, arrangement, or understanding.

Engagement Letter – A legal agreement between a professional organization and a client that defines their business relationship.

Equal Credit Opportunity Act – Prohibits discrimination, when evaluating a decision to grant consumer credit.

Equilibrium Price – Represents the price at which the quantity demanded equals the quantity supplied.

Equity – Represents ownership in a business or property.

Equity Mutual Funds – Typically invest in equity securities.

ERISA (Employee Retirement Income Security Act)- Designed to protect employee retirement savings accounts from creditors and from plan sponsors.

Estate Planning – The process of accumulation, management, conservation, and transfer of wealth considering legal, tax, and personal objectives.

Estate Tax – Imposed on the decedent's right to transfer property to his heirs when a citizen or resident of the United States dies.

Excess Reserves – Represents the amount of cash or deposits with the Federal Reserve in excess of the minimum amount required.

Exchange Rate Risk – The risk that international investments and domestic companies that import or export goods are subject to changes in relationship to the price of a dollar, relative to foreign currencies.

Exchange Traded Funds (ETF's) – A form of an investment company that invests in securities that are included in a particular index.

Exclusions – Income items that are specifically exempted from income tax.

Executive Risk – The risk of moral character of the executives running the company. The extent to which executives break laws, regulations, or ethical standards that may negatively impact a company.

Expected Return – The rate of return expected for an asset or investment portfolio.

Expenses – An income statement category. Expenses represent those items that are paid regularly by the client during the time period being presented. Examples of expenses include mortgage principal and interest, utilities, taxes, insurance, telephone, water, cable or satellite, internet, and cell phone.

External Data – The external data, also known as the external environment includes the current economic, legal, political, sociological, tax, and technology environments. Examples of external data are the current interest rates, status of the housing, job, insurance and investment markets, the local cost of living, and the expected inflation rate.

Extrinsic Motivation – An outside reward (you expect to get something in return) or avoidance of punishment.

F

Failure to File Penalty – A five percent penalty of the unpaid tax balance for each month or part thereof that a tax return is late.

Failure to Pay Penalty – A penalty of 0.5 percent per month or part thereof that a taxpayer fails to pay tax that is owed.

Fair Credit Billing Act – Requires timely, written verification to a consumer disputing a billing error.

Fair Credit Reporting Act – Protects consumer's information collected by the major credit bureaus (Equifax, TransUnion, and Experian).

Fair Debt Collection Practices Act – Prevents third-party debt collectors from using deceptive or abusive methods to collect debts.

Fair Market Value – The price a willing buyer and willing seller would agree to when both have reasonable knowledge of the facts of the transaction and neither is under any compulsion to buy or sell.

Fair Packaging and Labeling Act (FPLA) – Helps consumers compare the value of products and to prevent unfair or deceptive packaging and labeling of many household items.

Family Limited Partnership – A special type of limited partnership created under state law with the primary purpose of transferring assets to younger generations using annual exclusions and valuation discounts for minority interests and lack of marketability.

Federal Deposit Insurance Corporation (FDIC) – Formed in 1933, as a result of the bank failures that occurred in the 1920's and 1930's. The three goals of the FDIC are to insure deposits, manage receiverships, and supervise financial institutions.

Federal Funds Rate – The bank to bank lending rate.

Federal Pell Grant – Need-based financial aid for students who have not earned an undergraduate degree or a professional degree. A Pell Grant does not have to be repaid. Pell Grants are awarded based on financial need.

Federal Perkins Loan – A program for undergraduate and graduate students with exceptional financial need. The Perkins Loan is a low interest rate loan (5%), which was offered through a university's financial aid office. The university serves as the lender and the federal government provides the funds. No new Perkins loans are available after September 30, 2017.

Federal Supplemental Educational Opportunity Grant (FSEOG) – A grant awarded to students with exceptional financial need. Pell Grant recipients with the lowest EFC are considered first for a FSEOG.

Federal Trade Commission (FTC) – Works for the consumer to prevent fraudulent, deceptive, and unfair business practices in the marketplace and to provide information to help consumers identify, prevent, and avoid them.

Federal Work-Study (FWS) – Jobs on campus or off campus for undergraduate or graduate students to help students pay for their education expenses. To be eligible students must have financial need.

Fee-Only – All of the certificant's and firm's compensation comes exclusively from the clients in the form of fixed, flat, hourly, percentage or performance-based fees, and the certificant and certificant's firm do not receive any form of sales-related compensation.

Fee Simple Ownership – The complete ownership of property with all the rights associated with outright ownership.

Fellowships – Paid to students for work, such as teaching while studying for a Master's degree or conducting research while working towards a Doctorate of Philosophy degree (Ph.D.). Fellowships can last anywhere from a few weeks to a few years, depending on the depth and level of work involved.

Fiduciary – At all times when providing financial advice to a client, a CFP® professional must act in the best interest of the client. Includes the duty of loyalty, duty of care, and duty to follow client instructions.

Financial Dependence – Reliance on unearned income from another person to the extent that it creates anxiety around the fear of being cut off from that income.

Financial Enabling – Occurs when one individual provides financial assistance that keeps others dependent.

Financial Enmeshment – Occurs when parents involve children in adult financial decisions and conflicts at a time when the child is not yet emotionally and cognitively prepared to cope with such decisions and conflicts.

Financial Exploitation – The fraudulent or otherwise illegal, unauthorized, or improper act or process of an individual, including a caregiver or fiduciary, that uses the resources of an older individual for monetary or personal benefit, profit, or gain, or that results in depriving an older individual of rightful access to, or use of, benefits, resources, belongings, or assets.

Financial Industry Regulatory Authority (FINRA) – A self-regulatory organization for all security firms doing business in the United States.

Financial Infidelity – The act of engaging in significant financial transactions without the knowledge and support of a spouse or partner.

Financial Needs Method – A method that evaluates the income replacement and lump-sum needs of survivors in the event of an income producer's untimely death.

Financial Plan – A written document that generally sets out a list of recommendations to achieve a set of goals and objectives based on an understanding of a client's current financial and personal situation.

Financial Planning – Defined by CFP Board as a collaborative process that helps maximize a Client's potential for meeting life goals through Financial Advice that integrates relevant elements of the Client's personal and financial circumstances.

Financial Risk – The amount of leverage the company is using in its capital structure. Leverage is a measure of the amount of debt a company uses to capitalize the business.

Financial Statement Analysis – The process of calculating financial ratios and comparing the actual ratios to industry established benchmarks.

Financial Statement and Ratio Analysis Approach – The ratio analysis provides an opportunity to assess the client's strengths, weaknesses, and deficiencies when the client's ratios are compared to benchmark metrics. The ratio approach usually follows the pie chart approach and provides the planner with the actual ratios with which to compare the benchmarks in the metrics approach.

Financial Therapy – A process informed by both therapeutic and financial competencies that helps people think, feel, communicate, and behave differently with money to improve overall well-being through evidence-based practices and interventions.

Financial Well-Being – A state of being wherein a person can fully meet current and ongoing financial obligations, can feel secure in their financial future, and is able to make choices that allow them to enjoy life.

Fiscal Policy – Represents the government's position on whether to expand or contract the economy. Congress uses taxes and government spending to implement its fiscal policy.

Fitness Standards – Ensure specific character and fitness standards as to an individual's conduct before certification.

Fixed Expenses – Those expenses that are due and payable regardless of whether income is available to cover the cost. There is less discretion over fixed expenses in the short term. Examples of fixed expenses include mortgage payment, car payment, boat payment, student loan payment, property taxes, and insurance premiums.

Fixed Income or Bond Funds – Typically invest in bonds of various maturities.

Floor – A minimum amount that must be exceeded before expenses may be deductible. Only the total expenses above the floor amount may be deducted.

Framing (or the framing effect) – A cognitive bias under which the manner in which something is framed impacts how the context is evaluated or interpreted even though the same facts have been provided.

Free Application for Federal Student Aid (FAFSA) – A form used to determine a student's eligibility for all types of financial aid, including grants, work-study, and loans. The FAFSA is used to determine the Expected Family Contribution amount (EFC, prior to 2023; Student Aid Index (SAI) beginning in 2023).

Frictional Unemployment – Occurs when people are voluntarily unemployed because they are seeking other job opportunities.

Full Employment – The rate of employment that exists when there is efficiency in the labor market.

Future Value – The value at some point in the future of a present amount or amounts after earning a rate of return for a period of time.

Future Value of an Annuity Due – The future value of equal periodic deposits, made at the beginning of the period.

Future Value of an Ordinary Annuity – The value of equal periodic payments or deposits, at some point in the future. The future value of an ordinary annuity assumes that deposits are made at the end of a period or end of a year.

Futures Contract – A commitment to deliver an amount of a certain item at a specified date at an agreed upon price.

G

Gambler's Fallacy – One of the incorrect assumptions from the world of probabilities; in the realm of probabilities, misconceptions can lead to faulty predictions as to occurrences of events.

GDP Deflator – Measures the current price of goods and services (nominal GDP) relative to a base year (real GDP).

General Obligation Bonds – Bonds backed by the taxing authority that issued the bonds. The bonds are repaid through taxes that are collected by the municipality.

General Partnership – A joint business venture among two or more persons/entities to conduct business as co-owners in which all owners have unlimited liability with regard to the debts and obligations of the partnership.

Geometric Return – A time-weighted compounded rate of return.

Gift – A voluntary transfer, without full consideration, of property from one person (a donor) to another person (a donee) or entity.

Gift Tax – An excise tax on the right to transfer assets gratuitously to another person during life.

Global Funds – Not only invest in foreign securities and markets, but also in U.S. domestic securities.

Government or Regulation Risk – The potential risk that a country may pass a law or regulation that negatively impacts a particular industry.

Graduate PLUS Loans – Loans for student's seeking graduate and professional degrees. A Graduate PLUS Loan is based on the student's credit history and is not based on financial need.

Grantor – The person who creates and initially funds a trust. The grantor is also known as the settlor or creator.

Grants – Money provided to students for postsecondary education that does not require repayment.

Gross Domestic Product (GDP) – Represents the total final output of a country, by its citizens and foreigners in the country, over a period of time.

Gross Income – All income from whatever source derived unless it is specifically excluded by some provision of the Internal Revenue Code.

Gross National Product (GNP) – Measures the total final output by the citizens of a country, whether produced domestically or in a foreign country. GNP does not include the output of foreigners in a country.

Growth and Income Funds – Invest in both equities and fixed income securities. However, a much larger percentage of the fund is allocated to equities.

Growth Mutual Funds – Typically invest in large and mid cap stocks, where price appreciation is the primary objective.

H

Hazard – A condition that creates or increases the likelihood of a loss occurring.

Head of Household Filing Status – A filing status that provides a basic standard deduction and tax bracket sizes that are less favorable to the taxpayer than those for the surviving spouse status, but more favorable than those for the single filing status.

Hearing Panel – When a formal complaint is filed by CFP Board Counsel, a hearing takes place before a panel of at least three individuals. A majority of the Hearing Panel must be CFP® professionals, and a majority must be DEC members.

Heir – A person who inherits under state law.

Herding – This cognitive bias is explained just by looking at the word. People tend to follow the masses or the "herd."

Hindsight Bias – Another potential bias for an investor. Hindsight is looking back after the fact is known.

Holding Period – The period for which a taxpayer owns an asset.

Holding Period Return – Represents the total return for an investment portfolio over the period of time the portfolio was held by an investor.

Holographic Will – Handwritten will.

Homeowners Insurance Coverage – A package policy covering dwelling, dwelling extensions (garage), personal property, loss of use, medical payments for others, and liability.

Horizontal Analysis – Lists each financial statement item as a percentage of a base year and creates a trend over time.

Housing Ratio 1 (HR1) – This ratio, established by the banking industry, reflects the proportion of gross pay on an annual or monthly basis that is devoted to housing (principal, interest, taxes, and insurance). It does not include utilities, lawn care, maintenance, etc. The benchmark for HR 1 is less than or equal to 28 percent.

Housing Ratio 2 (HR2) – Also referred to as HR 1 plus all other debt. This ratio was established by the banking industry to determine if the total amount of debt is appropriate for a given level of income. If housing ratio 2 is met, the borrower will likely qualify for a conventional loan. The benchmark for HR 2 should be less than or equal to 36 percent of gross pay on a monthly or annual basis.

Human Communications – Comprised of fundamental elements. Societal groups use a system of signs in their communication process. A sign could be a word, object, gesture, tone, quality, image, substance or other reference according to a code of shared meaning among those who use that sign for communication purposes.

Human Life Value (HLV) Method – A method that uses projected future earnings after taxes and individual consumption to determine the family's share of earnings (FSE) as the basis for measuring life insurance needs.

Humanistic Paradigm (The "Humanistic" School of Thought) – Dominated by theorists whose models have their origins from a shared philosophical approach. For a client to grow, the relationship requires a transparent and genuine counselor. The adviser needs a philosophical stance that humankind is basically good and that people have the inherent capability of self-direction and growth under the right set of circumstances.

I

Income – For tax purposes, is broadly defined, and means the gross amount of money and the fair market value of property, services, or other accretion to wealth received, but it does not include borrowed money or a return of invested dollars.

Income Funds – Typically invest in corporate and government bonds.

Index Fund – Purchases a basket of stocks to match or replicate the performance of a particular market index.

Inflation – Represents an increase in the price of a basket of goods and services representing the economy as a whole over a period of time.

Inflation Adjusted Rate of Return – The nominal rate of return adjusted for inflation. The real (after inflation) rate of return equals $[(1+Rn) \div (1 + i) - 1] \times 100$, where Rn is the nominal return and i is the inflation rate.

Information Ratio – Measures the excess return above a benchmark, such as the S&P 500, per unit of risk.

Intangible Personal Property – Property that cannot physically be touched such as stocks, bonds, patents, and copyrights.

Integrity – Demands honesty and candor which must not be subordinated to personal gain and advantage.

Interest Rate – The price that a consumer pays to borrow funds or that an investor earns on funds invested.

Interest Rate Risk – The risk that changes in interest rates will inversely impact both equities (stocks) and fixed income securities (bonds).

Interim Suspension – If a CFP® professional's conduct poses an immediate threat to the public, and the gravity of the conduct significantly impinges upon the stature and reputation of the marks, an interim suspension order may be issued, and become effective immediately, suspending the CFP® professional's right to use the marks while the investigation takes place.

Internal Data – The client's internal data has both quantitative and qualitative elements. Some quantitative data includes family specifics, insurance, banking, investment, tax, retirement, and estate planning information. Some qualitative data includes the client's values, attitudes, expectations, goals, needs, and priorities.

Internal Rate of Return (IRR) – A compounded annual rate of return. IRR allows for the comparison of projects or investments with differing costs and cash flows. The rate that equates the PV of a series of cash flows to an initial investment.

International Funds – Invest in securities and firms that are outside of the U.S. domestic market.

Intrinsic Motivation - Intrinsic motivation comes from within and is often associated with satisfaction and enjoyment.

Intrinsic Value – The underlying value of a security, when considering future cash flows and the riskiness of the security.

Investing – The process where capital resources are allocated and committed by investors with the expectation of earning a future positive economic return.

Investment Advisers Act of 1940 – Requires investment advisers to register with their state or the SEC.

Investment Assets – A balance sheet category that includes appreciating assets or those assets being held to accomplish one or more financial goals.

Investment Assets-to-Gross Pay Ratio – Measures progress towards a client's retirement goal, based on the client's age and income.

Investment Companies – Financial services companies that sell shares to the public and use the proceeds to buy portfolios of securities. Mutual funds are one type of investment company where investors buy shares in a fund and own a pro rata portion of the investment portfolio, entitling them to a share of capital gains, interest and dividend income.

Investment Company Act of 1940 – Set standards to regulate investment companies such as open-end and closed-end funds, and unit investment trusts.

Investment Planning Process – Comprised of steps the financial planner and client follow to build an investment portfolio designed to accomplish the client's investment goals.

Investment Policy Statement – A written document that specifically identifies an investor's investment goals and the strategies and parameters that will be employed to reach the goals.

J

Jensen's Alpha – An absolute risk adjusted performance measurement.

Joining - In the mental health field, joining refers to making a connection with the client and establishing a trusting relationship.

Joint Tenancy with Right of Survivorship (JTWROS) Typically how spouses own joint property. Joint tenancy is an interest in property held by two or more related or unrelated persons called joint tenants. Each person holds an undivided, equal interest in the whole property. A right of survivorship is normally implied with this form of ownership, and at the death of the first joint tenant, the decedent's interest transfers to the other joint tenants outside of the probate process according to state titling law.

K

Keogh Plan – A qualified plan for a self-employed person. An important distinction of Keogh plans is the reduced contribution that can be made on behalf of the self-employed individual.

L

Legatee – A person named in a will.

Leptokurtic – A distribution that appears to be normal but has more area under the two tails than a normal distribution (i.e., fat tails).

Letter of Admonition – A publishable written reproach of the CFP® professional's behavior (a form of discipline under the pre-2020 Disciplinary Rules).

Letter of Intent – A "life plan" document that describes the family of the dependent with special needs and the dependent's wishes for the future once the initial caregiver is no longer able to provide care. It should include pertinent information about the history of the dependent with special needs, their medical needs, living arrangement preferences, and hobbies, as well as a list of contact persons (doctor, lawyer, accountant, guardians, etc).

Liabilities – A balance sheet category that represents client financial obligations that are owed to creditors.

Liability Risk – A risk that may cause financial loss (injury to another for which the client is determined to be financially responsible).

Life Cycle Approach – This approach provides the planner with a brief overview of the client's financial profile which permits the planner to have a relatively focused conversation with the client. It is used very early in the engagement.

Life Insurance – At its most basic is income replacement insurance via the death benefit paid upon the death of the insured.

Lifetime Learning Credit – Provides a tax credit of up to $2,000 (2021) per family for an unlimited number of years of qualified education expenses. The qualified education expenses must be related to a postsecondary degree program or to acquire or improve job skills.

Limited Liability Company – Separate legal entity formed by one or more individuals by meeting state statutory requirements necessary for the formation of an LLC that may be taxed as a sole proprietorship, partnership, or corporation.

Limited Liability Partnership – A hybrid entity generally comprised of licensed professionals that provides partial liability protection to its members and may be taxed as either a corporation or partnership.

Limited Partnerships – Associations of two or more persons as co-owners to carry on a business for profit except that one or more of the partners have limited participation in the management of the venture and thus limited risk exposure.

Liquidity Ratios – These ratios measure the ability to meet short-term obligations.

Living Will / Advance Medical Directive – Legal document expressing an individual's last wishes regarding life sustaining treatment.

Long-Term Liabilities – Financial obligations owed that are due beyond the next 12 months. Long-term liabilities are usually the result of major financial purchases and resulting obligations that are being paid off over multiple years (house, vacation, boat, student loan).

Loss Frequency – The expected number of losses that will occur within a given period of time.

Loss Severity – The potential size or financial damage of a loss.

M

Macroeconomics – The study of large economic factors that impact the entire economy such as gross domestic product (GDP), unemployment, and inflation.

Managing Partner – A partner named to have responsibilities for specific tasks or for day-to-day operations.

Marginal Tax Rate – The highest tax bracket in which a taxpayer's income falls. It is the rate that will apply to the next dollar of income earned.

Market Portfolio – Represents 100 percent risky assets.

Market Risk – The risk that in the short term, the daily fluctuations of the market tend to bring all securities in the same direction.

Married Filing Jointly Filing Status – A filing status that allows married couples to combine their gross incomes and deductions.

Married Filing Separately Filing Status – A filing status used when married couples do not choose to file a joint return.

Metrics Approach – This approach uses quantitative benchmarks for a measurement of where a client's financial profile should be. When combined with the two-step/three-panel approach, metrics help establish objectives that are measurable compared to ratio analysis.

Microeconomics – The study of factors that impact small or individual economies, such as supply and demand for a product.

Modern Portfolio Theory – A set of principles, ideas, and theoretical models developed to help investors make efficient and informed portfolio decisions.

Monetary Policy – Represents the intended influence on the money supply and interest rates by the central bank of a country.

Money Market Mutual Funds – Invests in short-term government securities, certificates of deposit, commercial paper and bankers acceptances.

Monte Carlo Analysis – A mathematical simulation to determine the probability of success of a given plan. Monte Carlo analysis is useful for financial planners to help measure the probability of assumptions being true or false.

Moral Hazard – A character flaw or level of dishonesty an individual possesses that causes or increases the chance for a loss.

Morale Hazard – Indifference to losses based on the existence of insurance.

Mortgages – A form of long-term debt, secured by a lien on real estate, such as a home.

Motivational Interviewing (MI) - A communication technique the focus of which is on guiding the client to express the desire and reason a change is needed (their motivation for change), to discover their ability to change, and to commit to making the change.

Multicultural Psychology - An extension of general psychology that recognizes that multiple aspects of identity influence a person's worldview, including race, ethnicity, language, sexual orientation, gender, age, disability, class status, education, religious or spiritual orientation, and other cultural dimensions, and that both universal and culture-specific phenomena should be taken into consideration when psychologists are helping clients, training students, advocating for social change and justice, and conducting research.

Municipal Bonds – Bonds issued to fund projects and spending for state or local governments. The three primary types of municipal bonds are general obligation bonds, revenue bonds, and private activity bonds.

N

Named-Perils Policy – A policy that provides protection against losses caused by the perils that are specifically listed as covered in the policy.

Natural Rate of Unemployment – The lowest unemployment rate where labor and product markets are in balance. At the natural rate of unemployment both price and wage inflation are stable.

Net Discretionary Cash Flow – Represents the amount of cash flow available after all savings, expenses, and taxes have been paid.

Net Present Value (NPV) – Measures the excess or shortfall of cash flows based on the discounted present value of the future cash flows, less the initial cost or investment. NPV uses the investor's required rate of return for similar projects as the discount rate.

Net Worth – A balance sheet category that represents the amount of total equity (assets - liabilities = net worth) a client has accumulated.

Net Worth-to-Total Assets Ratio – The compliment of the debt-to-assets ratio. These two should add up to one. This provides the planner with the percentage of total assets owned or paid for by the client.

Nominal GDP - Measures the value of goods and services in current prices.

Nominal Interest Rates - The actual rate of return earned on an investment without adjustment for inflation.

Non-discretionary Cash Flows - Mostly fixed expenses which are required to be met monthly or annually regardless of loss of income.

Nonrefundable Tax Credits – Tax credits that can reduce the tax on taxable income to zero, but cannot generate a tax refund.

Non-traditional Household – A broad phrase that may include any household other than the traditional husband, wife, and children. It could be heterosexual or homosexual couples living together with or without children. The adults may or may not be romantically involved, but may wish to include each other and their respective descendants in their estate plan.

Nonverbal Behaviors – Nonverbal cues, or body language, can communicate feelings and attitudes from the client to the financial adviser and are mainly provided from the body and the voice. Body position and body movement are important, while voice tone and voice pitch are also telling.

Normal Distribution – Describes how returns are dispersed around the average return.

Nudge - Choice architecture that alters people's behavior in a predictable way without forbidding any options or significantly changing their economic incentives. To be a nudge the intervention must be easy and cheap to avoid.

Nuncupative Will – Oral will consisting of dying declarations.

O

Open Market Operations – The process by which the Federal Reserve will buy or sell U.S. Treasury securities such as T-bills, notes, and bonds.

Open Questions – Result in a person answering with a lengthy response that usually begin with words such as how, what, when, where, who and why.

Open-end Investment Company – Also referred to as a mutual fund, is an investment company where investors purchase their shares from and sell them back to the mutual fund itself.

Open-Perils Policies – Policies that are called "all-risks" policies, because they cover all risks of loss (perils) that are not specifically excluded from the contract.

Operating Agreement – A written agreement similar to corporate bylaws that specify the rules and regulations for the operation of an LLC.

Opportunity Cost – Represents the value of the best alternative that is foregone.

Options – Includes both calls and puts.

Ordinary Annuity – Occurs when the timing of the first payment is at the end of a period. The period may be, for example, the end of a month or the end of a year.

Ordinary Annuity Payment from a Lump-Sum Deposit – The payment that can be generated at the end of each period, based on a lump-sum amount deposited today.

OSHA (Occupational Safety and Health Administration) – Created by Congress under the Occupational Safety and Health Act of 1970 to promote safe and healthy working conditions for workers by providing training, outreach, education, and assistance.

Overconfidence Bias – Usually concerns an investor that listens mostly to himself or herself, overconfident investors mostly rely on their skills and capabilities to do their own homework or make their own decisions.

Overreaction – A common emotion towards the receipt of news or information.

P

Passive Listening – Described as listening in the normal or usual conversation or conversational setting to which most people are accustomed at seminars, in class, at social gatherings, or at sermons.

Performance Ratios – These ratios determine the adequacy of returns on investments.

Perils – The proximate or actual cause of a loss, such as fire, liability, or accidental death.

Personal Automobile Policy (PAP) – A package policy that protects against loss due to damage to the owned automobile, damage to the property of others, and bodily injury to the insured, family members, and others.

Personal Financial Planning – The process of formulating, implementing, and monitoring financial decisions integrated into a plan that guides an individual or a family to achieve their financial goals.

Personal Liability Umbrella Policy (PLUP) – A policy usually sold in millions of dollars of coverage (e.g. $1M, $3M, $5M) and provides excess liability coverage and legal defense for liability claims that may arise and that exceed the limits of the underlying homeowners and automobile policies.

Personal Risk – A risk that may cause the loss of income (untimely death, disability, health issues), or alternatively cause an increase in the cost of living (disability, health issues).

Personal Risk Management – A systematic process for identifying, evaluating, and managing pure risk exposures faced by an individual.

Personal Use Assets – A balance sheet category that includes those assets that help to maintain the client's lifestyle.

Phase-Out – A gradual reduction of a tax credit or deduction as income rises. Used as a means to limit certain tax benefits to the middle class by eliminating them for high income taxpayers.

Physical Hazard – A tangible condition or circumstance that increases the probability of a peril occurring and/or the severity of damages that result from a peril.

Pie Chart Approach – This approach is a visual presentation of how the client allocates financial resources. It provides a broad perspective on the client's financial status and it is generally used after the collection of internal data and the preparation of financial statements.

Piercing the Veil – Occurs when a court disregards the status of the entity that gives the owners limited liability because the owners failed to maintain a clear and consistent identity for the entity.

PLUS Loans – Loans for parents to borrow to help pay for a dependent's undergraduate education expenses. PLUS Loans are not based on financial need, but require that the parent does not have any adverse credit history.

Points – One point is equal to one percent of the loan amount, often associated with a mortgage. Points are prepaid interest, usually paid at closing, in exchange for a lower interest rate on the loan.

Pooled Trust – An exception that resulted from the Omnibus Budget and Reconciliation Act of 1993; managed by a nonprofit association. While each beneficiary will have their own account, the assets will generally be pooled and managed together.

Positive Psychology – The scientific study of the strengths that enable individuals and communities to thrive. The field is founded on the belief that people want to lead meaningful and fulfilling lives, to cultivate what is best within themselves, and to enhance their experiences of love, work, and play.

Power of Appointment – A power to appoint the assets of one person to another and may be either general or limited.

Power of Attorney – Legal document that authorizes an agent to act on a principal's behalf.

Practice Standards – The Practice Standards set forth the Financial Planning Process. A CFP® professional must comply with the Practice Standards when providing Financial Planning, or Financial Advice that Requires Financial Planning, or when he Client has a reasonable basis to believe the CFP® professional will provide or has provided Financial Planning.

Pre-2019 Standards of Professional Conduct – Prior to October 2019, CFP Board's Standards of Professional Conduct were comprised of three categories: 1) the Code of Ethics, 2) the Rules of Conduct, and 3) the Financial Planning Practice Standards.

Prepaid Tuition Plan – A plan that will allow a parent to purchase college credits today and use those credits when the child attends college.

Present Value – The value today of one or more future cash payments discounted at an interest rate.

Present Value of a Future Amount – The current value today of a future amount. The future amount is discounted over time using a discount rate (an interest rate that reflects the individual's risk or opportunity cost that could be earned on a similar project or investment) to arrive at the present value.

Present Value of an Annuity Due – The timing of the first payment is at the beginning of a time period (today) representing today's value of that even cash flow stream. On a timeline, the first payment occurs at time period zero (now).

Present Value of an Ordinary Annuity – Today's value of an even cash flow stream received or paid over time. The present value of an ordinary annuity assumes that the first annuity payment is made at the end of a period.

Present Value of Goals Approach – This approach considers each short-term, intermediate-term, and long-term goal, determines their respective present value, then sums all of these together and treats the sum as an obligation (liability) that is then reduced by current resources of investment assets and cash and cash equivalents.

Presumptive Bar List – CFP Board's list of conduct that is presumed to be unacceptable and will bar an individual from becoming certified unless that individual files a Petition for Fitness Determination request.

Price Earnings (P/E) Approach – Valuing equity securities is an earnings-based valuation model that places a premium on the amount investors are willing to pay for each dollar of earnings.

Principal – The grantor of a power of attorney.

Private Activity Bonds – Bonds issued to finance a joint project between the private sector and a municipality. Private activity bonds are often issued to fund the building of professional sports stadiums.

Private Censure – An unpublished written reproach mailed by the Commission to a censured respondent.

Probate Process – The legal proceeding that serves to prove the validity of existing wills, supervise the orderly distribution of decedent's assets to the heirs, and protect creditors by insuring that valid debts of the estate are paid.

Procedural Rules – Provide detailed procedures followed by CFP Board in enforcing the *Code of Ethics* and *Standards of Conduct*, effective June 2020.

Process of Financial Planning – The process of financial planning includes: (1) understanding the client's personal and financial circumstances, (2) identifying and selecting goals, (3) analyzing the client's current course of action and potential alternative courses of action, (4) developing the financial planning recommendations, (5) presenting the financial planning recommendations, (6) implementing the financial planning recommendations, and (7) monitoring progress and updating.

Producer Price Index (PPI) – Measures the inflation rate for raw materials used in manufacturing.

Professionalism – Requires behaving with dignity, courtesy, and respect to clients, fellow professionals, and others in business-related activities.

Professionals Eligible for Reinstatement (PER) – Formally referred to as registrants, an individual who, though not currently certified, has been certified by CFP Board in the past and has an entitlement to potentially use the CFP® marks. This includes individuals who have relinquished their certification and who are eligible for reinstatement without being required to pass the current CFP® certification examination.

Property Risk – A risk that may cause the loss of property (automobile, home, or other asset).

Prospect Theory – Provides that people value gains and losses differently and will base their decisions on perceived gains rather than perceived losses.

Public Censure – A written reproach published in a press release and on CFP Board's website.

Purchasing Power Preservation Model (PPP) – A capital needs analysis method that assumes that at a client's life expectancy, the client will have a capital balance with purchasing power equal to the purchasing power at the beginning of retirement.

Purchasing Power Risk – The risk that inflation will cause prices to increase and a dollar today will not be able to purchase the same amount of goods and services tomorrow.

Pure Annuity Concept – The basic capital needs analysis approach which assumes a lump sum balance at retirement will provide income for a set period of time (based on the estimated life expectancy) and at the end of that time frame the account balance will be zero.

Pure Risk – A risk for which there is a possibility of loss, but no possibility of gain. The possibility of a home being damaged or destroyed by a fire is an example of a pure risk. Most pure risks are insurable.

Puts – Gives the holder the right to sell the underlying security at a certain price by a certain date.

Q

Qualified Business Income (QBI) – The net amount of income, gain, deductions, and losses with respect to a pass-through trade or business, which is used in determining the below-the-line deduction of 20% of QBI.

Qualified Domestic Relations Order (QDRO) – An order made under state law that tells the administrator or trustee of a qualified retirement plan how much to pay out to the non-owner-spouse pursuant to a divorce.

Qualified Business Income Deduction – A new below-the-line deduction created by the Tax Cuts and Jobs Act. The deduction is generally 20% of the qualified income from a pass-through business entity and is available regardless of whether the standard deduction or itemized deductions are selected by the taxpayer.

Qualified Tuition Plans (Savings Plans) – A plan that allows families to save for education expenses on a tax-deferred basis. Section 529 of the Internal Revenue Code authorized states and educational institutions to adopt qualified tuition plans. The two types of qualified tuition plans are prepaid tuition and college savings plans.

R

Ratio Analysis – The process of calculating key financial ratios for a client, comparing those metrics to industry benchmarks and then making an evaluation regarding any deficiencies.

Ratios for Financial Security Goals – These ratios assess the progress that the client is making toward achieving long-term financial security goals.

Real Estate Investment Trusts (REITs) – A type of mutual fund that pools investor contributions to purchase real estate or make construction or mortgage loans.

Real GDP – Measures the value of goods and services at a base year price.

Real Property – Property that is land and buildings attached to the land.

Realization Event – Generally occurs when an asset has been sold or exchanged. Gains on capital assets are subject to tax only when there has been both a realization event and a recognition event.

Recency Bias – Occurs when too much weight is given to recent observations or stimuli versus long-term historical trends. This may cause a client to erroneously believe that recent trends are likely to repeat themselves over the long term.

Recognition Event - Occurs when a realized gain is included on a taxpayer's income tax return. All realized gains are generally recognized unless a provision in the Code provides otherwise.

Reflective Listening – Occurs when the receiver devotes reflective attention to both the content being said and the feelings that are being expressed.

Refundable Tax Credits – Tax credits that can be used not only to reduce or eliminate the current year's tax, but also to generate a tax refund.

Regulation Best Interest (or Regulation BI) – Established a best interest duty of care for broker-dealers when making a recommendation of any securities transaction or investment strategy involving securities to a retail customer.

Regulation Full Disclosure (or Regulation FD) – Requires companies to disclose all material information simultaneously to both the investment community and individual investors.

Reinvestment Rate Risk – The risk that an investor will not be able to reinvest income received from current investments at the same rate of return as the current investment return.

Remaining Work Life Expectancy (RWLE) – The work period that remains at a given point in time before retirement.

Reserve Requirement – The Federal Reserve requires that banks maintain a certain percentage of their deposits on hand, in the form of cash.

Residence Domiciliary – An individual's legal state of residence.

Respondent – Any person who has agreed to CFP Board's Terms and Conditions of Certification and Trademark License (CFP® professionals) or Pathway to CFP® Certification Agreement (candidates for CFP® certification).

Retirement Funding (Capital Needs Analysis) – The process of calculating the amount of investment capital needed at retirement to maintain the pre-retirement lifestyle and mitigate the impact of inflation during the retirement years.

Retirement Life Expectancy (RLE) – The time period beginning at retirement and extending until death; the RLE is the period of retirement that must be funded.

Retirement Needs Analysis – The process of determining how much money a person needs to accumulate to be financially independent during retirement.

Return on Assets (ROA) Ratio – This ratio measures total asset returns. This ratio must be used cautiously when the client is adding assets that are leveraged with debt.

Return on Investments (ROI) Ratio – A critical performance ratio, as it measures the compounded rate of return on a client's investments.

Return on Net Worth (RONW) Ratio – This ratio further refines the performance set of ratios to calculate the rate of return on net worth.

Revenue Bonds – Bonds issued to raise capital to fund a particular revenue-generating project. The revenue generated by the project will be used to repay the bond issuance.

Reverse Mortgage – A technique that permits homeowners to use their home equity while still living in the home.

Revocation – Permanent revocation of a CFP® professional's right to use the marks.

Risk – The uncertainty associated with investment returns. It is the possibility that actual returns will be different from what is expected.

Risk Adjusted Performance Measures – Sharpe, Treynor and Jensen's Alpha, which can be used to measure the performance of any type of investment including stocks, bonds and mutual funds.

Risk Avoidance – Avoiding an activity so that a financial loss cannot be incurred.

Risk Management Recommendations – Recommendations usually are related to the insurance portfolio because perils (the cause of a loss) are event driven (e.g., untimely death) or unpredictable, and can occur at any time.

Risk Premium – The increase in return an investor should be compensated to take on the risk of a market portfolio versus investing in a risk-free asset.

Risk Reduction – Implementing activities that will result in the reduction of the frequency and/or severity of losses.

Risk Retention – The state of being exposed to a risk and personally retaining the potential for loss.

Risk Tolerance Questionnaire – Evaluates a client's willingness to take risk by addressing risk issues.

Risk Transfer – Transferring or shifting the risk of loss through means such as insurance or a warranty.

S

S Corporation – A corporation formed under state law that elects to be taxed under Subchapter S of the Internal Revenue Code.

Sales-Related Compensation – More than a de minimis economic benefit, including any bonus or portion of compensation, resulting from a Client purchasing or selling Financial Assets, from a Client holding Financial Assets for purposes other than receiving Financial Advice, or from the referral of a Client to any person or entity other than the CFP® Professional's Firm. Sales-Related Compensation includes, for example, commissions, trailing commissions, 12b-1 fees, spreads, transaction fees, revenue sharing, referral or solicitor fees, or similar consideration.

Sarbanes-Oxley Act of 2002 – The legislation established new or enhanced standards for all U.S. public company boards, management, and public accounting firms.

Savings and Investing Management – Management that may result in recommendations that require both an increase in savings and an increase in the emergency fund. The savings rate (savings and reinvestment of dividends, interest, and capital gains, plus an employer match/gross pay) should equal 10 - 13 percent if the client only has one goal, that being financial security. If the client and family have multiple goals including retirement, college education, and lump-sum goals (e.g., new house or second home) the savings rate must be increased.

Savings Contributions – An income statement category. Examples of savings contributions include 401(k) plan, 403(b) plan, IRA (traditional or Roth), education savings, and any other type of savings account.

Savings Rate – A rate calculated by taking gross savings in dollars (including employee elective deferrals into 401(k), 403(b), and 457 plans plus any employer match), and any other savings divided by gross pay.

Scholarships – A grant of financial assistance made available to students to assist with the payment of education-related expenses. Scholarships are available for academic or athletic achievement. Scholarships can be provided to undergraduate or graduate students.

Sector Fund – Restricts investments to a particular segment of the market. For example, technology, healthcare, telecommunications, financial, and pharmaceutical.

Securities Act of 1933 – Requires that any new security be registered with the Securities and Exchange Commission (SEC) by filing a registration statement with the SEC.

Securities Exchange Act of 1934 – Created the Securities and Exchange Commission (SEC) and provides the SEC with the authority to regulate the secondary market.

Securities Investor Protection Corporation (SIPC) – Formed in 1970 as a statutorily created nonprofit membership corporation funded by its member securities broker-dealers, with the goal of returning cash and securities to investors in the event a brokerage firm becomes insolvent.

Security Market Line (SML) – The relationship between risk and return as defined by the CAPM (when graphically plotted).

Self-Efficacy - Belief in one's own ability to be successful at a given task or in a particular situation.

Semivariance – Measures the possibility of returns below the average. Therefore, semivariance is a measure of downside risk.

Sensitivity Analysis – A tool used to understand the range of outcomes for each variable in a retirement plan. It rotates each variable toward the undesirable side of the risk to determine the impact of a small change in that variable on an overall plan.

Serial Payments – Payments that are adjusted upward periodically throughout the payment period at a constant rate, in order to adjust for inflation's impact.

Sharpe Ratio – A relative risk adjusted performance indicator, meaning the ratio by itself does not provide any insight. A Sharpe ratio for one fund needs to be compared to the Sharpe ratio for another fund to take on meaning.

Short-Term Liabilities – Represent those obligations that are "current" in nature or due within the next 12 months ($\leq$ 12 months).

Side Instruction Letter – Also known as a personal instruction letter, details the testator's wishes regarding the disposition of tangible possessions (household goods), the disposition of the decedent's body, and funeral arrangements. A side instruction letter is not legally binding, but generally followed.

Similarity Heuristic – Used when a decision or judgment is made when a similar situation occurs.

Single Filing Status – A filing status used by an unmarried taxpayer who does not qualify as a surviving spouse or head of household.

Small, Mid, and Large Cap Funds – May have an objective regarding the size of a firm's market capitalization.

Social Consciousness - An awareness of and sense of responsibility for problems or injustices that exit within society.

Socialization - The process by which individuals acquire social skills, beliefs, values, and behaviors necessary to function effectively in society or in a particular group.

Socially Responsible Funds – Restrict their investments to firms that are good corporate citizens and do not operate in industries such as alcohol, gambling, or tobacco.

Sole Ownership – The complete ownership of property by one individual who possesses the property fee simple, meaning all ownership rights associated with the property, including the right to use, sell, gift, alienate, convey, or bequeath the property.

Sole Proprietorship – A business venture owned and operated by a single individual.

Solution-focused therapy (SFT) – A future-focused and goal-directed approach to therapy

Special Needs Trusts Under 42 U.S.C. Sec. 1396p(d)(4)(A) – Considered to be self-settled in nature, are typically established by the individual with special needs, their parent, grandparent, legal guardian or by a court and will avoid disqualification of Medicaid and SSI benefits.

Specified Service Trade or Business (SSTB) – A trade or business involving performance of services in the fields of health, law, accounting, actuarial services, consulting, performing arts, athletics, financial services, investing, investment management, trading or dealing in securities, and any trade or business where the principal asset of the business is the reputation or skill of one or more of its owners. SSTBs are permitted only limited use of the QBI deduction.

Spendthrift Clause – A clause in a trust document which does not allow the beneficiary to anticipate distributions from the trust, assign, pledge, hypothecate, or otherwise promise to give distributions from the trust to anyone. If such a promise is made, it is void and may not be enforced against the trust.

Stafford Loans – Student loans administered by the U.S. Department of Education.

Standard Deduction – A standard amount that is specified by Congress and includes inflation adjustments. Taxpayers may deduct the greater of the standard deduction or allowable itemized deductions.

Standard Deviation – Measures the total risk (variability) of an investment.

Standards of Conduct – Establish expected high standards and also describe the level of professionalism required. The Standards are broken into six Sections: (A) Duties owed to clients, (B) Financial planning and application of the Practice Standards, (C) Practice Standards for the financial planning process, (D) Duties owed to firms and subordinates, (E) Duties owed to CFP Board, and (F) Prohibition on circumvention.

Statement of Income and Expenses – A financial statement that represents all income earned or expected to be earned by the client, less all expenses incurred or expected to be incurred during the time period being covered.

Statement of Net Worth – Explains changes in net worth between two balance sheets by reporting financial transactions that are not reported on the income statement or other financial statements.

Statutory Will – A will meeting state statutes generally drawn up by an attorney and signed in the presence of witnesses.

Strategic Approach – This approach uses a mission, goal, and objective approach considering the internal and external environment and may be used with other approaches.

Structural Unemployment – Occurs when there is inequality between the supply and demand for workers.

Substitutes – Products that serve a similar purpose.

Suitability – Having a reasonable basis to believe that a recommended transaction or investment strategy is appropriate for a client, after considering the client's age, other investments, financial situation and needs, tax status, investment objectives, investment experience, investment time horizon, liquidity needs, risk tolerance and other relevant issues. See FINRA Rule 2111.

Superannuation – The risk of outliving available savings.

Supply – Represents the quantity firms are willing to produce and sell of a good or service, at a particular price.

Surviving Spouse Filing Status – A filing status for a surviving spouse with a dependent child that affords the same basic standard deduction and tax rates as the married filing jointly status.

Suspension – Temporary suspension of a CFP® professional's right to use the marks for a term of up to five years for those individuals the Commission deems susceptible to rehabilitation.

Systematic Risk – Represents the risk that is inherent in the "system" and cannot be eliminated through diversification. The system represents U.S. market risk.

T

Tangible Personal Property – Property that is not realty and has physical substance.

Tax Credit – An amount that reduces the calculated tax liability of the taxpayer.

Taxable Income – Determined by subtracting allowable deductions from income.

Teacher Education Assistance for College and Higher Education (TEACH) Grant – A grant that provides up to $4,000 per year for students who intend to teach in a public or private elementary, middle, or high school that serves a community of low-income families.

Tenancy by the Entirety – Similar to property owned JTWROS between spouses because property ownership is automatically transferred to the surviving spouse upon death.

Tenancy in Common – An interest in property held by two or more related or unrelated persons. Each owner is referred to as a tenant in common. Tenancy in common is the most common type of joint ownership between nonspouses.

Testator – Writer of a will.

Third Party SNT – sometimes referred to as a family trust because the trust is a receptacle for funds from a parent, guardian or other family member. The assets of these trusts, if properly structured, are not counted or considered for purposes of available federal or state benefits for the beneficiary, thus making possible federal, state, and local funds.

Time Value of Money (TVM) – A mathematical concept that determines the value of money, over a period of time, at a given rate of interest.

Traditional Finance (Modern Portfolio Theory) – Also described in the literature as Modern Portfolio Theory though some of the concepts of the theory are not necessarily modern and have been subject to much debate and change over recent decades. Traditional finance is premised on four basic premises: (1) Investors are Rational; (2) Markets are Efficient; (3) The Mean-Variance Portfolio Theory Governs; and (4) Returns are Determined by Risk (Beta).

Treynor Ratio – A relative risk adjusted performance indicator. A Treynor ratio for one fund requires comparison to the Treynor ratio for another fund.

Trust – A structure that vests legal title (the legal interest) to assets in one party, the trustee, who manages those assets for the benefit of the beneficiaries (who hold the equitable title) of the trust.

Trustee – The individual or entity responsible for managing the trust assets and carrying out the directions of the grantor that are formally expressed in the trust instrument.

Truth in Lending Act – Protects consumers so that they fully understand the terms of a loan.

Two-step / Three-panel Approach – A step-by-step approach where the client's actual financial situation is compared against benchmark criteria. It stresses the management of risk, seeks to avoid financial dependence, and promotes savings and investing to achieve financial independence.

U

U.S. Government Bonds – Bonds issued by the U.S. government to finance the national debt and to fund deficit spending. The three primary types of bonds issued by the U.S. government are Treasury Bills, Treasury Notes, and Treasury Bonds.

U.S. Government Series EE (issued after 1989) and Series I Bonds – Bonds that can be redeemed to pay for qualified education expenses and the interest earned on the bonds is excluded from taxable income. For purposes of excluding interest income using U.S. Government savings bonds, qualified education expenses include tuition and fees, but do not include room and board.

U.S. Personal Savings Rate – The average saving amount in the U.S. Calculated as personal savings as a percentage of disposable personal income.

Unemployed – Refers to those individuals 16 years of age and older who are not working and are making an effort to seek employment.

Unemployment Benefits – Designed to provide an unemployed worker with income for a period of time. The worker must be unemployed and also actively seeking work.

Uneven Cash Flow – An investment or project that has periodic cash flows that are not the same dollar amount or that are a combination of inflows and outflows.

Uniform Gift to Minors Act (UGMA) – Allows minors to own cash or securities. The UGMA/UTMA accounts are governed by state law that requires the custodian of the account, usually a parent or grandparent, to manage the account for the benefit of the minor child.

Uniform Transfer to Minors Act (UTMA) – Allows minors to own cash, securities, and real estate. The UGMA/UTMA accounts are governed by state law that requires the custodian of the account, usually a parent or grandparent, to manage the account for the benefit of the minor child.

Unit Investment Trust (UIT) – An investment company that passively manages a portfolio of either bonds or stocks, known as a bond or equity UIT.

Unsystematic Risk – Represents the risk that can be diversified away, by combining multiple stocks, from multiple industries, into one portfolio.

Utility – The benefit firms and consumers receive when allocating or spending financial resources.

V

Value Funds – Typically invest in securities that are deemed to be out of favor or extremely under-valued. They generally have a lower PE ratio than growth funds.

Variable Expenses – Those expenses that can be dispensed with and are more discretionary over the short term. Examples of variable expenses include entertainment expenses, vacation expenses, travel expenses, and charitable contributions.

Vertical Analysis – Lists each line item on the income statement as a percentage of total income and presents each line item on the balance sheet as a percentage of total assets. The restated percentage is known as a common size income statement or balance sheet.

W

Wage Replacement Ratio (WRR) – An estimate of the percent of income needed at retirement compared to earnings prior to retirement.

Warrant – A long-term option that gives the holder the right to buy a certain number of shares of stocks in a particular company by a certain date.

Weighted Average Return – Based on the dollar amount or percentage of a portfolio invested in each asset. Investments with a larger allocation or weighting will contribute more to the overall return of the portfolio.

Will – A legal document that provides the testator, or will maker, the opportunity to control the distribution of property, appoint an executor and avoid the state's intestacy law distribution scheme.

Windfall – Often treated by the recipient as quite different than earned money. Windfalls can include lottery winnings, an unexpected inheritance, stock options, IPOs, sometimes marrying into money, or the sale of a business.

Work Life Expectancy (WLE) – The period of time a person is expected to be in the work force, generally 30-40 years.

Workers' Compensation – Designed to protect employees when injured at work. It will provide income replacement if the employee is unable to work. It will also provide medical expense coverage if the employee is injured while at work and it can provide a death benefit to an employee's beneficiary.

Z

Zero-Coupon Bonds – Bonds sold at a deep discount to par value and do not pay periodic interest payments. Instead, the bonds increase in value each year, so that at maturity the bonds are worth their par value.

Zero Growth Dividend Model – Values a security based on the stock's capitalized amount of the annual dividends.

APPENDIX

B

INDEX

J